£14·00

THE
ENCYCLOPAEDIA
OF
EXECUTIONS

THE
ENCYCLOPAEDIA
OF
EXECUTIONS

JOHN J. EDDLESTON

JOHN BLAKE

Published by John Blake Publishing Ltd, 3 Bramber Court,
2 Bramber Road, London W14 9PB, England

First published in hardback in 2002

ISBN 1 903402 23 9

British Library Cataloguing-in-Publication Data: A catalogue record
for this book is available from the British Library.

Design by ENVY

Printed and bound in Great Britain by Clays Ltd

1 3 5 7 9 10 8 6 4 2

Papers used by John Blake Publishing Ltd are natural, recyclable products
made from wood grown in sustainable forests. The manufacturing processes
conform to the environmental regulations of the country of origin.

ACKNOWLEDGEMENTS

My deepest gratitude must go to Yvonne Berger. She assisted me with the research, working on around half of the cases in this book. She also proofread every single entry and her criticisms have only ever improved the final work.

I must also thank the ever-helpful staff of the Public Record Office at Kew. In all my visits there I have found them efficient, friendly and eager to assist. I find it a pleasure to work there and this book would not have been possible without their assistance.

To a lesser extent, I must also thank the staff of the British Newspaper Library at Colindale. Though the system there seems archaic to say the least, they have produced hundreds of newspapers for me over the years and occasionally the production staff have endeavoured to supply papers in less than one hour. Sometimes they have even been the right papers.

Finally I would like to thank my publisher for having the courage to produce such a long and detailed work without seeking to dilute the information.

INTRODUCTION

I first developed an interest in this book many years ago.
A chance remark from someone asking if there was a definitive
list of the executed led me to start a research project that lasted
more than three years and ended in this work, which runs to
more than half a million words.

Wherever possible I have used primary sources, chiefly the
assizes documents held in the Public Record Office at Kew. In many
cases, however, such documents have either simply not been kept or
were destroyed by enemy action during the war. Only in such cases
have I referred to secondary sources such as newspapers, but then
I have used at least two such papers, often more, to double-check
names, dates and places. This will perhaps explain why, in a very few
cases, I have been unable to find the names of the barristers, or the
age of a victim. I trust that these few gaps will not detract from
the wealth of information these pages hold.

The book covers every single judicial execution carried out in
England, Wales, Scotland, Northern Ireland, the Isle of Man and the
Channel Islands in the twentieth century, a total of 865 executions.
I have also included, for the sake of completeness, a list of
executions by prison, some important statistics and a day-by-day
diary showing events throughout the year.

The story behind each of those 865 executions lies within these
pages, as do the tales of the victims, who number over 1,000. Read the
stories of the killers and their victims, the spies and the treacherous
and remember that every story is true, every event really happened
and every one of those lives was lost.

JOHN J. EDDLESTON
SUSSEX, 2002

CONTENTS

"And May The Lord Have Mercy On Your Soul..."

THE ENCYCLOPAEDIA OF THE EXECUTED

LOUISA MASSET, WHO was half-French and half-English, lived at 29 Bethune Road, Stoke Newington, London, with her married sister, Leonie Cadisch and Leonie's husband, Richard.

Employed as a day-governess and piano teacher, Louisa had left her child, Manfred, with a foster-mother, Miss Helen Gentle, at 210 Clyde Road, Tottenham, for a fee of 37/- per month, visiting him every Wednesday and taking him for trips to the park. This state of affairs had existed since the child was a very small baby.

Next door to Louisa lived 19-year-old Eudor Lucas, a Frenchman, and soon he and Louisa had become close friends. The relationship developed and before long, a weekend away in Brighton was suggested, by Louisa. There had never been any suggestion, from either party, that the liaison would develop beyond the casual and it seemed that Louisa was simply well ahead of her time in that she saw nothing wrong in seeing Eudor without committing herself to marriage. It was an attitude she would come to regret, once it had become public.

On October 13th, 1899, Louisa wrote to Miss Gentle and informed her that Manfred's father wanted the child returned to him, in France. Louisa had agreed to this request and therefore wanted Manfred delivered to her so that she could take him across on the ferry. Arrangements were made and exactly two weeks later, on Friday, October 27th, Louisa met Helen outside the Birdcage, a public house on Stamford Hill, and took possession of the child.

At 1.45pm that same afternoon, mother and child were together at London Bridge railway station. The boy appeared to be distressed and Louisa was seen taking him into the buffet in order to buy him a cake. They remained there until about 3.00pm when they left together. A witness, Ellen Rees, would later say that Louisa was back at London Bridge station at about 6.00pm, and that then she was alone.

At about the same time that Louisa was supposedly returning to London Bridge, Mary Teahan and her friend, Margaret Biggs, entered the ladies waiting room on platform

NAME Louisa Josephine Jemima Masset	
AGE AT EXECUTION 33	
DATE OF EXECUTION Tuesday, 9th January, 1900	
PLACE OF EXECUTION Newgate	
HANGMAN James Billington	
ASSISTANT William Billington	
DATE OF TRIAL 13th December – 18th December, 1899	
LOCATION OF TRIAL Old Bailey	
PRESIDING JUDGE Mister Justice Bruce	
PROSECUTION COUNSEL Charles Mathews, Richard D. Muir	
DEFENCE COUNSEL Lord Coleridge, Arthur Hutton	
NUMBER OF VICTIMS 1	

VICTIMS DETAILS
NAME ELIZABETH Manfred Louis Masset
AGE 3
DATE OF MURDER Friday, 27th October, 1899
PLACE OF MURDER Dalston Junction Station, London
METHOD OF KILLING Battered/Asphyxiated
RELATIONSHIP TO KILLER Son

1900

three of Dalston Junction station. There she discovered the body of Manfred Masset, naked except for a black shawl. It appeared that he had been battered with a brick, which still lay near the body, and then suffocated. Louisa meanwhile had caught the train to Brighton, where she enjoyed a weekend of love with Eudor.

On Monday, October 30th, Helen Gentle received a letter from Louisa saying that Manfred had missed her terribly but was now in France and sent her his love. The newspapers though had been full of the discovery of the dead child and feeling that the description matched that of Manfred, Helen Gentle had already been to the mortuary and formally identified the body. The letter was handed over to the police.

At about the same time that Helen was making that identification, a bundle of child's clothes had been found in a waiting room at Brighton station, and Miss Gentle later identified these as belonging to Manfred. Furthermore, the parcel was wrapped in a piece of paper that had been torn from a larger piece found at Helen Gentle's house.

9

The tears on both pieces were shown to match exactly. Finally, as if all this were not enough, the shawl used to wrap the poor child's body was identified by a draper as similar to one he had sold to Louisa Masset on October 24th, and the brick found near the body could have come from a rockery in the garden of 29 Bethune Road.

On her return to London, on the Monday, Louisa went about her normal routine, even attending one of her pupils that evening. On her journey home, after the lesson was over, she saw newspaper headlines referring to the murder of her son and would later claim that this was the first she knew of the matter. She went immediately to Streatham Road, Croydon and the house of George Richard Symes, her brother-in-law. She told him what had happened and then waited there for the police to arrive.

At her trial, Louisa's defence was that she had decided to place her son in the care of a Mrs Browning, who had just started up a children's home. Apparently Louisa had first encountered Mrs Browning and her assistant on one of her Wednesday trips to the park. Having met up a few times, Mrs Browning had told her of the new school and offered to take Manfred as a pupil. Louisa, concerned about Manfred's education, had finally agreed.

On Friday October 27th, Louisa had met these two ladies at London Bridge station where she had handed over Manfred, a parcel of clothes given to her by Helen Gentle, and the sum of £12 which was to cover the boy's education for one year. If Manfred had been murdered, she insisted, then it must have been these two ladies who did it. Louisa, however, had no receipt for the money and the address of the children's home, in Chelsea, was of course fictitious.

Louisa claimed that she was already in Brighton when she was supposedly seen again at London Bridge station. She argued that this witness must simply have been mistaken. Louisa said she had arrived in Brighton, enjoyed a meal at Mutton's restaurant on the sea-front and then gone on to her hotel. The evidence, though, was too telling and Louisa Masset was adjudged to be guilty and sentenced to death.

There was to be no reprieve, even when the manager of Mutton's, and one of his waiters came forward and said that they believed they could positively identify Louisa as a woman who did indeed have a meal in the establishment at the time in question.

It has been said that Louisa admitted her guilt before she became the first person to die on the gallows this century. In fact, she merely said that the sentence was just. This could also be the statement of a mother who felt she had not done her best for a son she loved dearly.

A DA CHARD-WILLIAMS had a nice little business. She would help out women who could not care for their babies by offering to take them, for a fee. She would then find homes for those children, passing them on with another fee. It was a trade known as baby-farming, but Ada knew a way to make it even more lucrative.

Florence Jones was a young, unmarried mother who could not look after her daughter, Selina. She read with interest the advertisement in her local newspaper, which offered to adopt a child, and wrote off to the advertiser, Mrs Hewetson, at the address in Hammersmith.

What Florence could not know was that this address was a newsagents where Mister Chard-Williams picked up the mail, at a cost of one penny per item. In due course, a reply was sent off to Miss Jones, terms were agreed and on August 31st, 1899, Florence met Ada who was, of course, masquerading as Mrs Hewetson.

The meeting took place at Charing Cross station and Florence was shown a house in Hammersmith where workmen were busy. She was told that this was where her child would be taken care of, once the alterations were complete. Florence noted down the address as she still owed Mrs Hewetson £2 of the £5 fee they had agreed on. Florence finally handed over her daughter, some clothes, and the sum of £3.

When Florence Jones made the trip back to Hammersmith, in order to pay the £2, there was no trace of her child or Mrs Hewetson. Florence reported this to the police and an investigation began.

The police visited the newsagents shop and determined that Mrs Hewetson was in reality Mrs Chard-Williams, but found that the home address she had given was false. For some time, the investigation got nowhere and then, on September 27th, the body of a baby was washed up on the banks of the Thames, in Battersea. The child was identified as Selina Jones.

Eventually the Chard-Williamses were traced to an address in Grove Road, Barnes, but they had moved from that address in October. However, the police officers on the case were soon contacted by Ada herself, much to their surprise. She had seen

NAME	Ada Chard-Williams
AGE AT EXECUTION	24
DATE OF EXECUTION	Tuesday, 6th March, 1900
PLACE OF EXECUTION	Newgate
HANGMAN	James Billington
ASSISTANT	Not Known
DATE OF TRIAL	16th February – 17th February, 1900
LOCATION OF TRIAL	Old Bailey
PRESIDING JUDGE	Mister Justice Ridley
PROSECUTION COUNSEL	Charles Mathews, Mister Bodkin
DEFENCE COUNSEL	Ernest E. Wild, F. MacMahon Mahon
NUMBER OF VICTIMS	1 (Probably more)

VICTIMS DETAILS	
NAME	Selina Ellen Jones
AGE	21 months
DATE OF MURDER	circa Saturday, 23rd September, 1899
PLACE OF MURDER	Grove Road, Barnes, London
METHOD OF KILLING	Battered/Strangled
RELATIONSHIP TO KILLER	None

newspaper reports of the child's death and on December 5th, 1899, wrote to the C.I.D. and confirmed that she had been operating as a baby farmer, but denied any involvement in murder. She added that Selina had been passed on to a Mrs Smith of Croydon. Ada was nevertheless traced, arrested and charged, along with her husband, with the murder of Selina Jones.

Perhaps the most damning piece of evidence at the trial was the method of disposal of the body. Little Selina had been tied up in a parcel and the string had been knotted in a rather peculiar fashion. Other parcels, containing clothing, were found at Ada's home and many of these had been tied in the same manner.

Ada Chard-Williams was found guilty of murder. Her husband, William, received a not guilty verdict, though the jury did state that they believed he was an accessory after the fact, a charge that was not pursued.

Although Ada was charged with just one murder, other children's bodies had been found in the Thames and all had been wrapped in parcels tied up with string that had been knotted in a rather unusual way.

HENRY SMITH WAS killed because of a debt of one shilling.

Sweetshop owner Henry had a yard and stable at the back of his shop, where he would let people keep their horses and carts, for the sum of 6d per week. One of those who took advantage of this arrangement was Smith's next door neighbour, a hawker named Henry Grove.

By February 24th, 1900, however, Grove had not paid his rent for two weeks and Smith had told him that he would not be allowed to use the yard again, until he had paid the shilling he owed. Late that night Grove, returning home the worse for drink, ignored the order and attempted to use the yard anyway.

Smith came out of his shop and tried to prevent Grove entering, whereupon an argument started. At one stage Grove said he would kill Smith and Mrs Smith, who had witnessed this, told her husband to let Grove do as he wished, in order to avoid trouble. Henry Smith returned to his shop, but Grove was not prepared to let the matter rest. He followed Smith inside and struck him twice with his fists.

For a time it seemed as if that would be the end of the matter but Grove now went back into the yard, picked up a couple of rusty scythes, and took them back to his own garden. A few minutes later he returned to Smith's yard with one of these scythes. Finding Henry there, Grove proceeded to batter him to the ground with the handle and the flat of the blade. When Mrs Smith tried to intervene, she too was hit, but her cries caused neighbours to call in the police and Groves was arrested.

Henry Smith was very badly injured. His right arm and leg were fractured. His left leg was broken, as was one of his ribs, and he had received two severe blows to the back of his head. So poor was his condition that a magistrate called at the hospital to take a statement from him, in the presence of Henry Grove.

Smith managed to hang on to life for another few weeks but finally died from his injuries on March 20th, 1900. The assault charge now became one of murder.

NAME	Henry Grove
AGE AT EXECUTION	26
DATE OF EXECUTION	Tuesday, 22nd May, 1900
PLACE OF EXECUTION	Newgate
HANGMAN	James Billington
ASSISTANT	Not Known
DATE OF TRIAL	3rd May, 1900
LOCATION OF TRIAL	Old Bailey
PRESIDING JUDGE	Mister Justice Lawrance
PROSECUTION COUNSEL	Mister Bodkin, Guy Stephenson
DEFENCE COUNSEL	Mister Warburton
NUMBER OF VICTIMS	1

VICTIMS DETAILS	
NAME	Henry Smith (Died Tuesday, 20th March)
AGE	34
DATE OF MURDER	Saturday, 24th February, 1900
PLACE OF MURDER	Enfield, London
METHOD OF KILLING	Battered
RELATIONSHIP TO KILLER	None

At his trial, Grove's defence was that Smith had struck the first blow and that he had defended himself. He also denied using the scythe, or indeed any other weapon, and claimed that all the blows had been with his bare fists. This was refuted by the statement Smith had made before he died and from the evidence of Mrs Smith.

The jury were out for an hour before returning a guilty verdict, adding a strong recommendation to mercy. It did nothing to save Grove, who became the first man hanged in the twentieth century.

ALFRED HIGHFIELD AND Edith Poole seemed such a devoted couple. They had been seeing each other for six years and had set a provisional wedding date for August, 1900.

On Easter Monday, the young couple argued and Edith now refused to have anything more to do with Alfred. In later statements, Alfred would blame Edith for losing him his job as a labourer at the Westminster Brewery Company, but in the early stages at least, Alfred appeared to blame himself for the break-up and wrote to Edith apologising. It was no use. She did not want to have anything more to do with him.

Edith's family were still on good terms with Alfred and on May 13th, her brother invited Alfred to tea. Edith was there and it may be that there was a plan to manoeuvre them together. During that meeting, Alfred asked Edith if they could see each other again but Edith was firm in her resolve that the relationship was over. It was a quiet and subdued Alfred who later went out with the family, for a walk.

Alfred and Edith strolled behind the rest of the group, talking quietly to each other. As the party ambled down Great Queen Street, near Lincoln's Inn Fields, they heard a cry and turning around, saw Alfred kneeling over the prostrate figure of Edith. Running back, Edith's brother pulled Alfred off his sister and saw to his horror that her throat had been cut. She was rushed to hospital where she died, nine days after the attack. Alfred now faced a charge of murder.

At the trial, Alfred's defence was one of manslaughter. He claimed that he had asked Edith to start seeing him again. When she had refused, he had taken out the razor he carried with him, in order to take his own life. Edith had struggled with him and he argued that he must have accidentally cut her throat. This scenario did not appear to agree with the statements Alfred had made immediately after the attack, though. When told how badly injured Edith was, Alfred said: "I know what I have done. I don't care if I die for it."

At first, the jury were unable to agree on a verdict. After 90 minutes of deliberation they returned to court to inform the judge that eleven had voted one way, with the twelfth person in opposition. Sent back to their chamber by the judge, the 12 finally agreed that Alfred was guilty of murder, but added a recommendation to mercy on account of the excitement he was in at the time, his youth, and his previous good character.

Alfred Highfield did not escape the noose though, and was hanged exactly eight weeks after his sweetheart had died.

NAME	Alfred Highfield
AGE AT EXECUTION	22
DATE OF EXECUTION	Tuesday, 17th July, 1900
PLACE OF EXECUTION	Newgate
HANGMAN	James Billington
ASSISTANT	Not known
DATE OF TRIAL	27th June, 1900
LOCATION OF TRIAL	Old Bailey
PRESIDING JUDGE	Mister Justice Ridley
PROSECUTION COUNSEL	Horace Avory, Mister Bodkin
DEFENCE COUNSEL	Charles Mathews, Mister Randolph, Mister Perrott
NUMBER OF VICTIMS	1

VICTIMS DETAILS	
NAME	Edith Margaret Poole (Died Tuesday, 22nd May)
AGE	19
DATE OF MURDER	Sunday, 13th May, 1900
PLACE OF MURDER	Great Queen Street, London
METHOD OF KILLING	Cut throat
RELATIONSHIP TO KILLER	Girlfriend

CATHERINE WAS THE second wife of William Irwin and before they parted, in May 1899, they had had four children, the last being born in February of that year.

The parting had been amicable enough and the couple still saw each other quite frequently. As William was not working, Catherine would help him out with money whenever she could. However, William became jealous of a male friend named Sexton who seemed to be spending rather too much time with Catherine, although Sexton would later deny that any impropriety had taken place.

There is little doubt that this jealousy was an important factor in the break-up of Catherine and William's relationship. It was Sexton who visited her in hospital when she was confined with her last child and it was Sexton who found rooms for her when she left William. Indeed, on June 20th, Sexton was with Catherine until 11.30pm and William was fully aware of that, as he had been watching outside her home.

On the night of June 21st, 1900, William again tried to borrow money from Catherine, but she had said she had none. Angry words were exchanged and William was heard to say that she had just driven the last nail into her coffin.

The following morning, at 8.00am, Catherine was leaving home for her job as a draper's assistant at Messrs. Peter Robinson's of Oxford Street, when she was accosted by her husband. William demanded to speak to her, even though she was in the company of a fellow worker, Emily Wright. Catherine pulled away, saying she had to get to work and at that point William plunged a knife into her breast.

Catherine was rushed to hospital and William was arrested and charged with attempted murder. Later that same day, Catherine died, from a pierced right lung, at the Middlesex Hospital. Before dying she had made a deposition, outlining what had happened to her. In that statement she said that William had asked to speak to her and upon being told that she was on her way to work, he had replied "Take that, then", and had stabbed her.

NAME	William James Irwin
AGE AT EXECUTION	61
DATE OF EXECUTION	Tuesday, 14th August, 1900
PLACE OF EXECUTION	Newgate
HANGMAN	James Billington
ASSISTANT	Not known
DATE OF TRIAL	27th July, 1900
LOCATION OF TRIAL	Old Bailey
PRESIDING JUDGE	Mister Justice Bigham
PROSECUTION COUNSEL	Horace Avory, Mister Bodkin
DEFENCE COUNSEL	
NUMBER OF VICTIMS	1

VICTIMS DETAILS

NAME	Catherine Amelia Irwin
AGE	35
DATE OF MURDER	Friday, 22nd June, 1900
PLACE OF MURDER	Great Titchfield Street, London
METHOD OF KILLING	Stabbed
RELATIONSHIP TO KILLER	Wife

William's defence at the Old Bailey was that he had inflicted the fatal wound in a moment of passion. It was true that he had been jealous of the relationship he believed existed between Sexton and Catherine. When William had been in work, Sexton had been in the habit of visiting Catherine during the day and had carried on seeing her after the marriage had failed. Under these circumstances, William held that he could only be guilty of manslaughter.

The jury, though, found him guilty as charged, but added a recommendation to mercy. It was to no avail. William James Irwin was hanged on August 14th.

CHARLES BENJAMIN BACKHOUSE and his younger brother, Frederick, both miners, lived at 75 Piccadilly, Swinton, near Rotherham. It was an address well known to the police, especially the local constable, John William Kew.

The Backhouse family had a reputation for violence. On July 5th, 1900, a summons had been served on Frederick for an assault upon his brother's wife. That summons had been served by Kew and was due to be answered on July 9th.

Two days before, on July 7th, the brothers vanished and so, on the 9th, Frederick did not bother to turn up at court. As a result, he had been fined 40/- in his absence, or sentenced to serve one month's imprisonment.

All this seemed to have little effect on the Backhouse brothers. Just five days after the summons had been served, Charles bought a revolver and nine cartridges and the two brothers were seen using the weapon to threaten people in the town. Naturally this matter was reported to the police and it was Kew who went along to investigate.

As Kew arrived at Piccadilly, the brothers were just leaving. The officer stopped them and said that he was entitled to search them. He then put his hands out, as if to begin that search. Immediately Charles Backhouse took a step backwards, drew the gun and shot Kew in the stomach. Even though he was badly wounded, Kew managed to grab Charles and pulled his hands, one of which still held the gun, behind his back. Frederick ran forward, seized the gun and shouting, "Here's another for you", fired again at Kew, hitting him in the right hip.

As the brothers ran off, Kew fell to the ground and was then helped to his own house which was close by, where he managed to reveal who had shot him. He died the following day, the postmortem showing that the wound inflicted by Charles had been the fatal shot. When they were arrested, Frederick admitted that they had shot Kew, claiming that they were drunk at the time.

At the trial, the jury sought to return a verdict of guilty of murder in the case of Charles, and guilty of aiding and abetting in the commission of the offence, in the case of

NAME	Charles Benjamin Backhouse
AGE AT EXECUTION	23
DATE OF EXECUTION	Thursday, 16th August, 1900
PLACE OF EXECUTION	Leeds
HANGMAN	James Billington
ASSISTANT	William Billington
DATE OF TRIAL	27th July, 1900
LOCATION OF TRIAL	Leeds
PRESIDING JUDGE	Mister Justice Ridley
PROSECUTION COUNSEL	Harold Thomas, Mister Edmondson
DEFENCE COUNSEL	Mister Mitchell-Innes
NUMBER OF VICTIMS	1

VICTIMS DETAILS	
NAME	P.C. John William Kew (Died Wednesday, 11th July)
AGE	Not known
DATE OF MURDER	Tuesday, 10th July, 1900
PLACE OF MURDER	Outside 75 Piccadilly, Swinton
METHOD OF KILLING	Shot
RELATIONSHIP TO KILLER	None

Frederick. The judge explained that this amounted to a verdict of guilty of murder for both brothers, to which the foreman of the jury then said that they wished to recommend Frederick to mercy on account of his age. Both men were sentenced to death.

On August 14th, two days before he was due to die, Frederick Lawder Backhouse was reprieved, being sentenced instead to life imprisonment. There was no such mercy for his brother, who was hanged alongside Thomas Mellor, the first double hanging of the new century.

ALTHOUGH THOMAS MELLOR killed both his daughters, he was found not guilty of the murder of Annie, but only because no evidence was offered on that charge after he had been found guilty of the murder of Ada.

The Beecroft girls were Mellor's illegitimate daughters, their mother, Ada Beecroft, having been committed to the Menston Asylum, where she died in November 1899. Some time before Ada's death, Mellor had moved in with another woman, named Priscilla Redshaw, but this entire group were evicted from their lodgings at 6 Fourth Court, on May 4th, 1900.

On May 5th, Mellor went to visit his brother, Arthur. Thomas, Priscilla and the two girls were by now living in very squalid conditions and he wanted to ask Arthur if he would allow them all move into his home. Arthur replied that there was simply not enough room. Arthur's wife was concerned about what would happen now and asked Thomas what he would do with the children, especially as he had also been unsuccessful in getting them admitted to the workhouse. Thomas was heard to reply: "The water is big enough to hold them and me and all."

At about 9.30pm on May 11th, Thomas Mellor took his daughters out, telling Priscilla that they would be back at about ten the following morning.

At 11.00pm that same night, a man was seen walking along the pathway of the Leeds/Liverpool canal. He had with him two small girls. Later still, at 11.30pm, the same man was seen in a local restaurant, where he spent the night. He no longer had the girls with him and he would be later identified as Thomas Mellor.

The bodies of the two girls were found early on the morning of May 12th, by a gentleman named William Wilson. Mellor was arrested and confessed to putting the girls into the canal. He went on to claim, though, that he had had no intention of drowning them. His defence was that as he was about to get onto the canal pathway, he passed two men and thought that if he put the girls into a shallow part of the water, their cries would attract these men, who would then offer

NAME	Thomas Mellor
AGE AT EXECUTION	29
DATE OF EXECUTION	Thursday, 16th August, 1900
PLACE OF EXECUTION	Leeds
HANGMAN	James Billington
ASSISTANT	William Billington
DATE OF TRIAL	28th July, 1900
LOCATION OF TRIAL	Leeds
PRESIDING JUDGE	Mister Justice Ridley
PROSECUTION COUNSEL	Harold Thomas, Mister Edmondson
DEFENCE COUNSEL	Horace Marshall
NUMBER OF VICTIMS	2

VICTIMS DETAILS

NAME	Ada Beecroft, Annie Beecroft
AGE	6, 4
DATE OF MURDER	Saturday, 11th May, 1900
PLACE OF MURDER	Canal at Glebe Road, Holbeck, Leeds
METHOD OF KILLING	Both drowned
RELATIONSHIP TO KILLER	Both daughters

assistance and thereby the girls would be taken into care. The judge, quite rightly, pointed out that if this was indeed Mellor's intention, it would surely have made more sense for him to abandon the girls on the street, where they would have eventually have been found.

The jury returned a verdict of guilty but with a strong recommendation to mercy, on the rather astonishing grounds of the prisoner's kindness to his children.

WILLIAM LACEY, A native of Jamaica, became the first black man to be hanged in the twentieth century.

William had met his wife Pauline through another negro, Augustus O'Connor, who was married to one of Pauline's sisters, Mary Ann. At that time, Pauline was living at 38 Hoo Street in Port Tennant, near Swansea. The couple fell in love and married on Easter Tuesday, 1900, at Swansea register office. Shortly afterwards they moved to Pontypridd.

The relationship between them was a stormy one from the beginning and was not helped by William's jealousy. He had, on occasion, even refused to go to work at the Great Western Colliery, because he felt Pauline would be seeing other men whilst he was out.

Pauline tried to make the marriage work but eventually she felt compelled to write to her father, telling him what was going on. He replied on July 4th, offering Pauline a place at his home. This drove William into a fresh rage and he threatened Pauline that he would "do for her" if she left, drawing his hand across his throat to make his meaning clear.

The following day, Thursday the 5th, another row took place. William had not been to work any day that week, even though Pauline had prepared his lunch for him each day. On the Friday, William again refused to go to work and another furious argument took place. Finally a scream was heard and when the landlady checked on the couple, she found Pauline lying dead. A bloodstained razor lay close to the body and William was nowhere to be seen.

In due course, William walked in to the local police station. He confessed to killing Pauline because she had told him that when he got home from work, she would be missing.

At the magistrate's court though, Lacey gave a different story. William now said that his wife had chosen to die and had asked him to cut her throat. According to him, she had lain on the floor, the razor under her arm, and begged him to kill her. He had refused and tried to get the razor off her. In the ensuing struggle, she had cut her own throat but was not dead and asked William to finish the job off, which he did.

NAME	William Augustus Lacey
AGE AT EXECUTION	29
DATE OF EXECUTION	Tuesday, 21st August, 1900
PLACE OF EXECUTION	Cardiff
HANGMAN	James Billington
ASSISTANT	William Billington
DATE OF TRIAL	2nd August, 1900
LOCATION OF TRIAL	Swansea
PRESIDING JUDGE	Mister Justice Grantham
PROSECUTION COUNSEL	S.T. Evans, R.E. Vaughan Williams
DEFENCE COUNSEL	W. Bowen Rowlands, A.C. Thomas
NUMBER OF VICTIMS	1

VICTIMS DETAILS

NAME	Pauline Lacey
AGE	19
DATE OF MURDER	Friday, 6th July, 1900
PLACE OF MURDER	21 Barry Terrace, Pontypridd
METHOD OF KILLING	Cut throat
RELATIONSHIP TO KILLER	Wife

The story changed again when William was tried at Swansea. This time he said that he had taken no part whatsoever in Pauline's death, which was a straightforward case of suicide. She had killed herself because she believed William had been intimate with her sister. William explained his previous stories by saying that he must have been excited at the police station and at the magistrate's court and had not known what he was saying.

The jury chose not to believe any of Lacey's stories and after a short deliberation, returned a verdict of guilty.

THE ENCYCLOPAEDIA OF EXECUTIONS

CHARLES BLEWITT'S WAS certainly an intriguing case. The trial details quoted above refer to the second time he had faced the charge of murder. His first trial, also at Leeds, took place before Mister Justice Ridley, on July 30th, 1900, when the jury were unable to reach a verdict.

The story seemed to be a simple one. Mary Ann Blewitt had last been seen alive on the evening of June 8th. The next day, Charles left Leeds and for some days, his house remained locked, and the blinds drawn.

On the 17th of that same month, the landlord, Thomas Armitage, together with Charles's parents, forced the door of the house, to see if any trace of the family could be found. In the living room they found Mary Ann. She was sitting in a rocking-chair, a shawl covering her head and when that shawl was removed, they were horrified to see that her throat had been cut. There were also wounds on her arms and hands.

Charles Blewitt, a tanner by trade, was the obvious suspect. He had been out of work for some nine weeks before the death of Mary Ann and perhaps financial pressures had put a strain on his relationship with her. He had vanished soon after his wife had last been seen alive, and investigations showed that Mary had been dead for at least a week when she was discovered.

Charles was now in Halifax, using the name of Oliver Jackson. One day a workmate showed him a newspaper report of his wife's death. He seemed to be totally unconcerned at the news. The prosecution at his subsequent trial would make much of this attitude. Surely if he had been innocent of any crime, he would have become disturbed upon discovering that his wife had died?

It was July 3rd when Blewitt was captured. He claimed to know nothing of the death of Mary Ann, his defence being that she must have committed suicide. He stated that he had merely gone away for a few days to find work and fully intended to return home, once he had been successful in his aims.

The suggestion of suicide, however, did not quite ring true. Blood had been found on a pair of boots in the house and it was shown that these boots belonged to Charles. Doctor

NAME	Charles Oliver Blewitt
AGE AT EXECUTION	33
DATE OF EXECUTION	Tuesday, 28th August, 1900
PLACE OF EXECUTION	Leeds
HANGMAN	James Billington
ASSISTANT	William Billington
DATE OF TRIAL	6th August – 7th August, 1900
LOCATION OF TRIAL	Leeds
PRESIDING JUDGE	Mister Justice Bruce
PROSECUTION COUNSEL	Mister Banks, F. Brent Grotrian
DEFENCE COUNSEL	W.J. Waugh, C. Felix Palmer
NUMBER OF VICTIMS	1

VICTIMS DETAILS	
NAME	Mary Ann Blewitt
AGE	33
DATE OF MURDER	circa Friday, 8th June, 1900
PLACE OF MURDER	7 Star Fold, Beeston, Leeds
METHOD OF KILLING	Cut throat
RELATIONSHIP TO KILLER	Wife

George Heald, the police surgeon who examined the body, said that there were what appeared to be defence wounds on the body and no razor or knife had been found anywhere near Mary Ann, suggesting that she would have had to have cut her own throat and then put the weapon away.

The prosecution, though, could show no realistic motive for the murder and those doubts led to the first jury being unable to agree on their verdict. The second jury had no such problems.

THERE CANNOT BE any more foolish place to commit a murder than right outside a police station, but that is precisely what John Charles Parr did.

Parr and Sarah Willett had been engaged but in the summer of 1900, she had ended the relationship. She had discovered that Parr had been in prison for theft. He had also lied about his occupation, telling her that he was a French Polisher when in fact he was not even in regular employment. Sarah found these lies impossible to accept.

On August 25th, Parr was in a pub with three women friends. He drew a small revolver and said that it was his intention to kill Sarah and himself. To emphasise that his intentions were serious, he then fired the gun into the street shouting: "Instead of hearing of a marriage, you will hear of a burial." Surprisingly, this matter was not reported to the police.

On August 27th, Sarah Willett went with two girlfriends to the Forester's Music Hall in London's East End. Parr knew of this arrangement and turned up as well, asking Sarah to buy him a drink. When she refused, Parr simply picked up her glass and drained it. It was obvious to the three women that Parr was looking for trouble and so, wishing to avoid a confrontation, Sarah and her friends; Emily Samson and Kate Burgess, left the music hall. Parr decided to follow them.

As the three girls walked down Bethnal Green Road, Parr stopped them again and demanded to know if Sarah would take him back. She refused, replying: "I don't want you. All I want is an honest, hard-working fellow – not one who robs others." She then pulled away and threatened to walk into the police station opposite to where they were now standing. Parr told Sarah to go ahead and she turned to do so, whereupon he drew out the revolver and shot her in the head. When a police officer ran out he found Parr with the gun still in his hand, shouting, "I have done it. I have done it."

When he was taken into the station for questioning, Parr exclaimed: "It is all her own fault, and she deserves it." Sarah was also taken into the police station in order to receive treatment, but died minutes later.

NAME	John Charles Parr
AGE AT EXECUTION	19
DATE OF EXECUTION	Tuesday, 2nd October, 1900
PLACE OF EXECUTION	Newgate
HANGMAN	James Billington
ASSISTANT	Not known
DATE OF TRIAL	13th September, 1900
LOCATION OF TRIAL	Old Bailey
PRESIDING JUDGE	Mister Justice Bucknill
PROSECUTION COUNSEL	Horace Avory, Richard D. Muir, Guy Stephenson
DEFENCE COUNSEL	Mister Biron
NUMBER OF VICTIMS	1

VICTIMS DETAILS	
NAME	Sarah Willett
AGE	19
DATE OF MURDER	Monday, 27th August, 1900
PLACE OF MURDER	Near Bethnal Green Road Police Station, London
METHOD OF KILLING	Shot
RELATIONSHIP TO KILLER	Girlfriend

At his trial, Parr tried to rely on a defence of insanity. Mister Biron referred to a history of madness within Parr's family and the fact that the prisoner himself had received a severe blow to the head, years ago, in an accident in a gymnasium. He further contended that the revolver, which was little more than a toy, had gone off by accident.

The jury were not swayed, returning a guilty verdict, but they did add a recommendation to mercy on account of Parr's youth.

WILLIAM BURRETT MARRIED Ada in July 1900, and thereafter lived off her earnings as a prostitute. It was not a state of affairs that Ada relished and she begged her husband to find work so that she could give up the profession she had been forced to follow. The pleas fell on deaf ears.

In mid July, the Burretts took a room in Alexander Street, Plaistow, but the arguments over William's reluctance to find work continued. On the morning of Saturday, August 25th, Mrs Fitzpatrick, the landlady of the house, heard the front door slam. At about the same time, a young boy selling newspapers in the street, looked in at the open door of the same house and saw what he took to be a bundle of rags at the foot of a flight of stairs. The bundle turned out to be the body of Ada Burrett. She had been stabbed a number of times. The same boy reported that he had then seen a man leave the house and that he had a large knife sticking out of one of his pockets.

Ada was not dead. She was taken to hospital, where she made a statement outlining the attack her husband had made. She had been stabbed nine times in all, the crucial wound being one in her abdomen. She died in the hospital at 8.30pm that evening.

At the subsequent inquest, the doctor who had been called to the scene of the crime, Doctor James Parker, confessed that he had not attended to the unfortunate woman until the police had arrived as he wanted them to see exactly what state she was in!

Once the police had arrived, this so-called medical man did dress some of Ada's wounds and had her taken to hospital. Had this doctor shown a more caring attitude, it is possible that William Burrett might well have eventually faced a much lesser charge.

Burrett was tried at the Old Bailey, where the dying deposition of his wife was read out. She stated: "I was quarrelling with my husband; I told him he would have to go to work. He has not done any work since I was married. He took a big knife and stabbed me all over.... He then ran away. It was about twenty past seven in the morning."

Other witnesses were called who testified that they had heard William make repeated

NAME William Burrett
AGE AT EXECUTION 35
DATE OF EXECUTION Wednesday, 3rd October, 1900
PLACE OF EXECUTION Chelmsford
HANGMAN James Billington
ASSISTANT Not known
DATE OF TRIAL 14th September, 1900
LOCATION OF TRIAL Old Bailey
PRESIDING JUDGE Mister Justice Bucknill
PROSECUTION COUNSEL Horace Avory, Mister Bodkin
DEFENCE COUNSEL Arthur Hutton
NUMBER OF VICTIMS 1

VICTIMS DETAILS
NAME Ada Gubb Burrett
AGE 21
DATE OF MURDER Saturday, 25th August, 1900
PLACE OF MURDER Alexandra Street, Plaistow, London
METHOD OF KILLING Stabbed
RELATIONSHIP TO KILLER Wife

threats to his wife. For his part, William's defence was that as he had killed his wife in the heat of an argument, he was guilty only of manslaughter.

The jury did not agree and found William guilty of murder. At his execution, it was recorded that Burrett had been given a drop of over nine feet.

UNTIL THE BEGINNING of September 1900, Joseph Holden had lived in the workhouse at Bury. In due course he moved in with one of his married daughters, who lived in Nuttall Street, and repaid her kindness by killing her son, John.

Late on the night of Wednesday, September 5th, Holden walked in to his local police station and confessed that he had drowned John Dawes in a quarry, at Limefield. Holden went on to describe how he had first thrown the boy on to some rocks and then had grabbed him by the neck and breeches and thrown him into the quarry. He had then gone down into the quarry himself and thrown the child into the water. The body was later discovered, in six feet of water, exactly where Holden had said it would be. Medical reports would show that the child had still been alive when he was put into the water and that death had been caused by drowning.

Police investigations showed that Holden had also attacked another of his grandsons, George Eldred of Ingham Street, on August 21st, whilst Holden was still living in the workhouse. He had taken this child to a different quarry, at Birtles, and told him to cut some tobacco. Whilst the boy was engaged in this task, Holden had picked up a large stone and thrown it at the child's head. He would later say that this had been an accident, and that he had thrown the stone and hit the child by mistake. It may well have been this incident that caused Holden's daughter to invite him to live with her in the hope that a more stable family life would make her father more content.

At his trial, Joseph Holden, looking far older that his 57 years, pleaded guilty to the charge of murder. The defence was one of insanity and the jury had first to determine if Holden was in a fit medical condition to plead.

After due consideration, Holden was found to be fit to plead and again said that he was guilty. After being sentenced to death, Holden left the dock showing no concern for his fate. Later, in prison awaiting his execution, Holden would express remorse for what he had done, but no real motive for the crime could be suggested.

On December 11th, seven days after

NAME	Joseph Holden
AGE AT EXECUTION	57
DATE OF EXECUTION	Tuesday, 4th December, 1900
PLACE OF EXECUTION	Manchester
HANGMAN	James Billington
ASSISTANT	William Warbrick
DATE OF TRIAL	13th November, 1900
LOCATION OF TRIAL	Manchester
PRESIDING JUDGE	Mister Justice Darling
PROSECUTION COUNSEL	Mister McKeand, Mister Pope
DEFENCE COUNSEL	Mister Gibbon
NUMBER OF VICTIMS	1

VICTIMS DETAILS	
NAME	John Dawes
AGE	8
DATE OF MURDER	Wednesday, 5th September, 1900
PLACE OF MURDER	Limefield, Bury, Lancashire
METHOD OF KILLING	Drowned
RELATIONSHIP TO KILLER	Grandson

Holden had been hanged, a question was asked in the House of Commons, by Mister Harwood, the Member for Bolton. He sought confirmation that all had been done to inquire into the sanity of Joseph Holden. Mister Ritchie, for the Home Department, replied that two eminent gentlemen, experts in the field, had made a full investigation and he had decided, on their findings, not to interfere with the due course of the law.

JOHN BOWES, A bricklayer by trade, chose not to work, preferring instead to live off the earnings of his wife and 21-year-old daughter. He drank heavily and often mistreated his family. The drink seemed to increase his feelings of jealousy and he would often accuse his wife of having affairs with other men.

Isabella, though, was not the kind of woman to have affairs. She was a respectable woman who worked hard, scrimping a living by picking coal off the beach and selling it, for which, if she was lucky, she would earn five or six shillings per day. She tried her best to put up with her husband's accusations and violence but even she reached the end of her tether on August 21st, 1900.

On that day Bowes, drunk yet again, had attacked his wife, torn up some of his daughter's clothes, and threatened to kill both of them. They left him the same day and went to live with Isabella's uncle. Bowes swore that he would get even with Isabella and his daughter for what he saw as their desertion.

On September 8th, Bowes saw his wife on the beach, looking for the coal that paid her living. He stormed up to her and after a brief argument, picked up a heavy piece of wood that lay close by and struck her on the head. Isabella fell to the ground unconscious but Bowes struck her about the head another three or four times. His anger finally satiated, Bowes realised what he had done, knelt down and cradled his wife's head in his arms and even tried to wash some of the blood off her face. He was found, still in this position, by a policeman, whom he told of the argument, saying that he had only hit Isabella with his fists. Bowes later confessed that he had in fact used the piece of wood, describing it himself as one he would not have used to fell a bullock with. Still alive, Isabella was taken to hospital but never recovered consciousness. She died a few hours later.

Bowes readily admitted his guilt and seemed genuinely remorseful for what he had done. He said that he had loved Isabella and would die happily for killing her. He paid that penalty on December 12th.

NAME	John Bowes
AGE AT EXECUTION	50
DATE OF EXECUTION	Wednesday, 12th December, 1900
PLACE OF EXECUTION	Durham
HANGMAN	James Billington
ASSISTANT	William Billington
DATE OF TRIAL	24th November, 1900
LOCATION OF TRIAL	Durham
PRESIDING JUDGE	Mister Justice Grantham
PROSECUTION COUNSEL	Mister Luck, Mister Meek
DEFENCE COUNSEL	Edward Shortt
NUMBER OF VICTIMS	1

VICTIMS DETAILS	
NAME ELIZABETH	Isabella Bowes
AGE	Not Known
DATE OF MURDER	Saturday, 8th September, 1900
PLACE OF MURDER	Seaham Harbour, Near Sunderland
METHOD OF KILLING	Battered
RELATIONSHIP TO KILLER	Wife

JAMES BERGIN WAS engaged to Margaret Morrison and they were due to be married at Christmastime, 1898. Unfortunately, Bergin lost his job and the wedding had to be postponed. A new date was set but, as Bergin was a Catholic and Margaret a Protestant, her family managed to have the wedding cancelled again and eventually in having it called off.

Bergin returned to his family in Ireland where he stayed until July 1900. He then returned to Liverpool and went to see the Morrisons. Margaret's mother refused to admit him to the house and said that her daughter wished to have nothing more to do with him. Bergin's reply was: "I'll take her life and no other man shall have her."

Two days later, Bergin returned to the Morrison house, was admitted and offered tea. Mrs Morrison allowed Bergin and Margaret to talk alone whilst she waited with Janet, her other daughter, in the kitchen. A curious event then occurred.

Hearing a commotion, Mrs Morrison went to investigate. She found Bergin, with his trousers torn and holding a broken bottle that had contained carbolic acid, which had burned his leg. Perhaps even more surprisingly, Margaret was holding a razor in her hand.

On October 20th, Bergin again called on Margaret, but was told that she was not at home. Bergin claimed to have heard her voice and added: "Remember Mrs Morrison, she is your daughter, and if any other man walks out with her, I will take her life."

On October 27th, Mrs Morrison and Margaret were in Stanley Road, Bootle, when they met Bergin. He accompanied them to Liverpool, where they all met up with Margaret's father. Bergin announced that he wished to take Margaret to the Haymarket Theatre and, surprisingly, her parents gave their consent.

At 11.00pm, Margaret and Bergin were walking together down Bankhall Street. A man and a boy who were walking a few yards behind them suddenly heard a loud noise and saw a bright flash of light. Margaret fell to the pavement and Bergin crouched down beside her. Another flash was seen, close to her head.

NAME	James Joseph Bergin
AGE AT EXECUTION	28
DATE OF EXECUTION	Thursday, 27th December, 1900
PLACE OF EXECUTION	Liverpool
HANGMAN	James Billington
ASSISTANT	Thomas Billington
DATE OF TRIAL	4th December, 1900
LOCATION OF TRIAL	Liverpool
PRESIDING JUDGE	Mister Justice Darling
PROSECUTION COUNSEL	L. Sanderson, Leslie Scott
DEFENCE COUNSEL	Rigby Swift
NUMBER OF VICTIMS	1

VICTIMS DETAILS

NAME ELIZABETH	Margaret Morrison (Died Monday, 29th October)
AGE	28
DATE OF MURDER	Saturday, 27th October, 1900
PLACE OF MURDER	Bankhall Street, Liverpool
METHOD OF KILLING	Shot
RELATIONSHIP TO KILLER	Girlfriend

Bergin had shot Margaret twice. The witnesses ran after Bergin, but he escaped. Margaret was taken to hospital, where she died two days later. Bergin had meanwhile gone to the house of a friend of his, Mrs Coleman, and it was there that he was arrested on October 28th.

At the trial, evidence was called to show that three members of Bergin's family had been certified insane. The judge pointed out that at one stage, Bergin had told Mrs Morrison that he would kill Margaret and do 20 years for it. This meant that he was aware of the consequences of his actions and so a defence of insanity must fail.

The jury returned the expected verdict but with a recommendation to mercy. Nevertheless, Bergin was hanged the day after Boxing Day.

WILLIAM WOODS WALKED into the police station at Bushmills at 6.40am on September 26th and announced to duty officer, Constable Henry Sharpe, that he had just killed a woman. To emphasise that he was telling the truth he then pointed to blood on his trousers and added, "We were both drunk."

It was Sergeant Walker who went to the address given by Woods and there found the body of Bridget McGivern, lying on her bed. Her head had almost been severed from her shoulders.

The small, one-roomed cottage at Eagry was actually the home to Bridget and her two children, 14-year-old Charles and two-year-old John, her husband having died some years before. The alarm had in fact already been raised locally by Charles who had found his mother's body when he had risen from his bed that morning. Interviewed by the police, Charles reported that Woods had visited them the previous night, carrying a bottle of whisky. He had drunk much of this but had also tried to force some upon Bridget, who had refused.

There were two beds in the cottage and in due course the two boys had climbed into one with their mother whilst Woods threw himself down upon the other. The next morning, Charles found his mother gone but the fire lit. Only later did he notice Bridget lying on the bed with a man's scarf around her throat. When he went over to rouse her, Charles also saw that there was a great deal of blood about and ran to the neighbours for help.

There was evidence that the crime was premeditated. Alexander Black, the assistant at Mrs Taggart's, the general store at Bushmills, reported that Woods had called in on September 25th and purchased a new razor, saying it was for a man in the country. This last comment was perhaps given because Woods himself had a full beard and moustache. That razor was now missing and would remain so until November 17th, when a young girl, Ellen Elliott, found it whilst playing in a derelict house, close to the police station.

Woods, though, denied that the crime was premeditated, saying instead that he had committed it in a fit of homicidal mania. The jury took just 30 minutes to decide that he had

NAME William Woods
AGE AT EXECUTION 58
DATE OF EXECUTION Friday, 11th January, 1901
PLACE OF EXECUTION Belfast
HANGMAN Thomas Scott
ASSISTANT Not known
DATE OF TRIAL 9th December, 1900
LOCATION OF TRIAL Belfast
PRESIDING JUDGE Mister Justice Madden
PROSECUTION COUNSEL Mister O'Shaughnessy, George Hill Smith
DEFENCE COUNSEL Thomas Harrison
NUMBER OF VICTIMS 1

VICTIMS DETAILS
NAME Bridget McGivern
AGE circa 40
DATE OF MURDER Wednesday, 26th September, 1900
PLACE OF MURDER Eagry, Bushmills, County Antrim
METHOD OF KILLING Cut throat
RELATIONSHIP TO KILLER Girlfriend

planned the crime in cold blood and knew full well what he was doing. Sentenced to death Woods remarked "Oh, it's not so bad as a bad marriage."

In fact, this was the second time Woods had been on trial for his life. In 1890 he had killed another of his paramours, Mary Irwin, in Claudy, having cut her throat and then mutilated her body with a scythe. On that occasion his defence of provocation had succeeded and having been found guilty of manslaughter, he had been sentenced to 12 years, being released in 1899.

CONSTABLE JOHN BENSTED found it hard to believe his eyes. Lucy Smith lay on her back in the kitchen at 23 Venour Road, her head almost hacked from her body. On the floor were two bloodstained knives, and sitting on a chair was the man who admitted that he had killed her.

Samson Silas Salmon had lived with Lucy, his cousin, and her husband, Samuel, since the beginning of 1899. He had paid them 13/- a week for his lodgings, a sum that was easy for him to find from his wages as a labourer at the local chemical works.

Even after Salmon lost that job, the Smiths allowed him to stay on, although he could no longer afford to pay them. Salmon, though, took to drink and his personality changed.

On December 10th, 1900, Salmon struck Lucy, Samuel, and a neighbour, Mister Baker. He was also brandishing a knife and after a struggle, Samuel Smith, aided by his neighbour, managed to evict Salmon from the house. Later that same day, Salmon returned, climbed a rear wall of the house and announced that he intended to sleep in the cellar. Still showing rather too much tolerance, Samuel said that Salmon could return to his room, on condition that he remained quiet. Salmon agreed and even suggested that Smith could lock him in the room if he wished.

The following day, December 11th, Salmon was again very argumentative. He threatened to kill the Smiths, or their daughter, but later apologised again and left the house saying that it was his intention to look for work away from London. For a time, peace reigned.

On December 15th, Samuel Smith returned home from work at 8.00am and upon opening his front door, found Salmon waiting in the hallway. Smith immediately demanded to know what Salmon was doing there but all Salmon did was to ask him to fetch a policeman. Upon investigating further, Samuel discovered his wife's body in the kitchen and that is where Constable Bensted came into the picture.

At his trial, Salmon admitted that he had once more climbed over the rear wall of number 23, and hidden himself in the yard. Eventually Lucy came into the yard to throw

NAME	Samson Silas Salmon
AGE AT EXECUTION	32
DATE OF EXECUTION	Tuesday, 19th February, 1901
PLACE OF EXECUTION	Newgate
HANGMAN	James Billington
ASSISTANT	Not known
DATE OF TRIAL	28th January – 29th January, 1901
LOCATION OF TRIAL	Old Bailey
PRESIDING JUDGE	Mister Justice Wills
PROSECUTION COUNSEL	Charles Mathews, Richard D. Muir, Guy Stephenson
DEFENCE COUNSEL	Mister Biron
NUMBER OF VICTIMS	1

VICTIMS DETAILS	
NAME	Lucy Smith
AGE	32
DATE OF MURDER	Saturday, 15th December, 1900
PLACE OF MURDER	23 Venour Road, Bow
METHOD OF KILLING	Cut throat
RELATIONSHIP TO KILLER	Cousin

away some ashes from the fire. As she returned to the kitchen, Salmon followed her in and after an argument, hit her and then slashed her throat. He claimed to have been drunk at the time, but he had shown no evidence of being under the influence when he was arrested.

When Salmon had first been seen by Constable Bensted, the officer had asked if indeed it was he who had murdered his cousin. Salmon had answered: "I did it and I will swing for it." On that score at least, Samson Silas Salmon was correct.

RHODA KING TOOK her seat in an empty third-class carriage of the 11.20 morning train from Southampton to London. She was going to visit her son's sick wife, in Battersea.

When the train reached Eastleigh, the door opened and a rather well-dressed young man, George Parker, got into the compartment and sat in the opposite corner, with his back to the engine.

At Winchester, a third person entered the compartment. William Pearson, a farmer of 1 Christchurch Road, Winchester, was heading up to London on business. He placed his newspaper on his lap and allowed the rhythm of the train to lull him to sleep.

As the train left Wimbledon, Mrs King was looking out of the window when suddenly she heard a loud report and turning, saw that William Pearson had been shot in the head. The other occupant of the carriage was now busily rifling through his pockets.

Upon seeing that Rhoda King was looking at him, the young man told her to be quiet or she would get the same. Whether or not she would have obeyed was irrelevant, for as soon as he had spoken, Parker proceeded to shoot Mrs King, hitting her just below the left eye.

As the train pulled into Vauxhall station, Parker opened the door and jumped down onto the platform and ran off. Mrs King, recovering her composure, followed Parker and shouted: "Stop that man!"

Immediately a number of porters and passengers gave chase and ran after Parker, towards Vauxhall Bridge. Eventually a police officer on point-duty joined in the chase and seeing that his avenue of escape was blocked, Parker turned into the gasworks where he was cornered and taken prisoner.

At Parker's trial, Rhoda King was the star witness. Although she had managed to make a full recovery, her cheek was still blackened from the close brush she had had with death.

The story Mrs King told was that Parker had also demanded money from her but her testimony also claimed that after she had given him a shilling, Parker had offered her a sovereign from the dead man's pockets.

Parker told a slightly different story. He had spent the previous night with his girlfriend, a married woman named Elizabeth

NAME	George Henry Parker
AGE AT EXECUTION	23
DATE OF EXECUTION	Tuesday, 19th March, 1901
PLACE OF EXECUTION	Wandsworth
HANGMAN	James Billington
ASSISTANT	William Billington
DATE OF TRIAL	2nd March, 1901
LOCATION OF TRIAL	Old Bailey
PRESIDING JUDGE	Mister Justice Phillimore
PROSECUTION COUNSEL	Richard D. Muir, Arthur Gill, Mister Leycester
DEFENCE COUNSEL	Perceval Clarke
NUMBER OF VICTIMS	1

VICTIMS DETAILS	
NAME	William Pearson
AGE	43
DATE OF MURDER	Thursday, 17th January, 1901
PLACE OF MURDER	On the railway, near Surbiton
METHOD OF KILLING	Shot
RELATIONSHIP TO KILLER	None

Rowland, in Southampton. On the morning of the shooting, he had told Elizabeth that he was going to London to try to find work whilst she returned to Portsmouth, where she lived. They had then travelled as far as Eastleigh together.

The weapon had been purchased in Southampton, with the purpose of killing Elizabeth and then himself. Parker however had changed his mind and had robbed and killed Pearson on impulse. He said he had never demanded money from Rhoda King.

IN THE EARLY hours of September 23rd, 1900, the body of a young woman was found on Yarmouth beach. She had been strangled and the mohair bootlace the assailant had used was knotted tightly around her neck. There were also indications of sexual interference, but the woman had not been raped.

News of the murder spread rapidly, causing Mrs Rudrum, who rented out rooms from her address in the Rows, to come forward. She told the police that on September 15th, a woman calling herself Hood, and her small child, had booked into her establishment.

On the night of Saturday, September 22nd, this woman had put her child to bed and gone out to meet someone. She had never returned. Mrs Rudrum was then shown the body from the beach and identified the dead woman as Mrs Hood. She went on to point out that a watch and chain were missing from the body, thus indicating that the motive might well have been robbery.

Further inquiries led to other sightings of Mrs Hood. She had been seen outside the Town Hall, possibly waiting for someone to arrive. Later that same evening she had been seen in the company of a man in a local public house and finally, two witnesses came forward who said that they might have witnessed the murder itself.

This young courting couple had spent some time on the beach, close to where the body would be found. They saw a woman and a man together but assumed that they were simply lovers like themselves, even when they heard the woman cry out for mercy.

The piece of evidence that actually shifted the police investigation was given again by Mrs Rudrum. She recalled that one day, Mrs Hood had received a letter that had had a Woolwich postmark. Could it be that the dead woman came from that area? Another clue was a laundry mark found on some of the victim's clothing – 599. Investigations moved to London.

In due course, a laundry manager at Bexley Heath came forward and identified the mark. She informed the officers investigating the

NAME	Herbert John Bennett
AGE AT EXECUTION	22
DATE OF EXECUTION	Thursday, 21st March, 1901
PLACE OF EXECUTION	Norwich
HANGMAN	James Billington
ASSISTANT	Thomas Billington
DATE OF TRIAL	25th February – 2nd March, 1901
LOCATION OF TRIAL	Old Bailey
PRESIDING JUDGE	Lord Chief Justice, Lord Alverstone
PROSECUTION COUNSEL	Mister Gill, A.H. Puyner, Richard D. Muir
DEFENCE COUNSEL	Edward Marshall-Hall, G. Thorn Drury, Mister Forrest Fulton
NUMBER OF VICTIMS	1

VICTIMS DETAILS	
NAME	Mary Jane Bennett
AGE	24
DATE OF MURDER	Saturday, 22nd September, 1900
PLACE OF MURDER	Great Yarmouth beach
METHOD OF KILLING	Strangled
RELATIONSHIP TO KILLER	Wife

case that the real identity of Mrs Hood was Mary Jane Bennett.

Mary Bennett was a married woman. She had wed Herbert Bennett, who had turned out to be a great disappointment and, as a result, was now separated from him. Herbert had made such great promises when they married but it soon transpired that he would never really amount to much. He had also started to beat her, especially after their child had been born. Then, after an abortive trip to South Africa, which lasted just six days, Mary had decided that enough was enough and the separation had taken place. Mary had stayed in Bexley Heath, whilst Herbert moved to Woolwich to be closer to his work at the Arsenal.

Further inquiries showed that Herbert Bennett had a new woman in his life – Alice Meadows. Earlier that year, Bennett had taken Alice to Yarmouth, where they had stayed at the Crown and Anchor Hotel. Police checks with the staff of that hotel showed that they remembered Bennett and readily identified him as a man who had once again stayed at their establishment, this time on the night of the murder. Apparently he had only come in a few minutes before midnight and had appeared breathless.

It was now time to interview Bennett. When spoken to by the police, he denied ever having been to Yarmouth in his life. That was obviously a lie. The police had already spoken to Alice Meadows and she had confirmed that they had stayed, in separate rooms, at the Crown and Anchor.

Bennett went on to explain that on the night of his wife's death, he had been out with two workmates. They in turn were interviewed and though they did confirm that they had been out drinking with Bennett, both said that it was not until one week after the murder. Bennett was arrested and charged.

At first glance, the case against Bennett seemed to be an open and shut one. In addition to the identification given by the staff of the Crown and Anchor, and that given by William Dorking, the landlord of the inn where Mary had been seen with a man, there was perhaps the most damning piece of evidence of all. When Bennett's rooms were searched, a watch and chain were found and these were identified as the ones Mrs Bennett had been wearing on the night she was killed. As if all this were not enough, Bennett was identified as a man seen on Yarmouth station, early on the Sunday morning, waiting for a train to London.

Bennett still denied having anything to do with his wife's murder. He admitted that she had asked him if she could have a holiday and he had suggested and even paid for a trip to Yarmouth, but insisted that that was as far as it went.

The trial was due to be heard at Norwich, but such was the publicity that Bennett's lawyers successfully argued that their client could not possibly receive a fair trial in that city. The case was moved to London.

The case proved to be much more involved than it had at first appeared. Witnesses were called to show that Mary Jane had two watches and two chains. A photograph taken of Mary on Yarmouth beach a week or so before her death was enlarged to show that there was some doubt as to whether the chain

she wore was the same as that found in Bennett's rooms.

Another witness was a newsagent named O'Driscoll. He stated that four days after the murder, a man had come into his shop and asked for a paper containing a report of the Yarmouth murder. O'Driscoll noted that the man had mohair laces in his boots, but that one was missing. He swore that this man was not Bennett.

The defence also called Sholto Douglas, a manufacturer of fancy goods, who swore that he had met Bennett at Lee Green in South London, on the evening of the murder. This meant that Bennett could not possibly have been in Yarmouth at the time, killing his wife.

Nevertheless, after a somewhat protracted trial, Bennett was found guilty, the death sentence being carried out on March 21st, 1901. It has been said that he did not die instantly, and struggled on the end of the rope for a couple of minutes. What is certain is that when the customary black flag was hoisted to signify that the execution had been carried out, the flag pole broke and this was taken by many as a sign that an innocent man had been hanged.

There was one final twist to the story of Herbert Bennett. On July 12th, 1912, the body of Dora Gray was found on Yarmouth beach, not far from where Mary Jane had been discovered. Dora had been strangled with a bootlace too, and that crime was never solved.

JOSEPH SHUFFLEBOTHAM HAD married Elizabeth, his second wife, on December 28th, 1899. He already had five children from his previous marriage and Elizabeth, also marrying for the second time, had four of her own. From the very beginning, the relationship was a tempestuous one, especially perhaps since all nine children were still living at home.

On March 21st, 1900, Joseph was found guilty of assaulting his wife and for that offence, was fined 40/-. Less than two weeks later, on April 4th, she was granted a formal separation order but chose to stay with Joseph and give him one more chance. Things did not improve.

On October 1st, a second summons for assault was taken out by Elizabeth. This time Joseph failed to answer the summons and so a warrant was put out for his arrest. In the meantime, he had gone to Yorkshire to find work as a collier, so the warrant lay on file until he could be traced. Whilst Joseph was away, Elizabeth gave birth to his child. They now had ten children to look after.

Joseph returned to his wife in November and on the 24th of that month, the arrest warrant was executed. This time the fine was 20/-. Just over a week later, on December 3rd, Elizabeth finally reached the end of her patience, left her husband and returned to her mother's house. Joseph tried repeatedly to get her back.

On December 28th, Joseph again went to his mother-in-law's house and demanded to speak to his wife. When his request was not granted, he broke down the front door and in the struggle that followed, slashed his wife's throat. Joseph then ran out of the house and later tried to kill himself by cutting his own throat. All this occurred on what had been their first wedding anniversary.

When interviewed by the police, Shufflebotham said that he had been attacked in the house and had only sought to defend himself. He had knocked on the door of his mother-in-law's house and, getting no reply, had put his weight against it. The door must have been open because Joseph stumbled in, only to be attacked by his wife and struck a number of times. He had then reached out and

NAME	Joseph Arthur Shufflebotham
AGE AT EXECUTION	38
DATE OF EXECUTION	Tuesday, 2nd April, 1901
PLACE OF EXECUTION	Stafford
HANGMAN	James Billington
ASSISTANT	William Billington
DATE OF TRIAL	15th March, 1901
LOCATION OF TRIAL	Stafford
PRESIDING JUDGE	Mister Justice Phillimore
PROSECUTION COUNSEL	Reginald C.E. Plumptre, R.E.C. Kettle
DEFENCE COUNSEL	B.C. Brough
NUMBER OF VICTIMS	1

VICTIMS DETAILS	
NAME	Elizabeth Shufflebotham
AGE	Not known
DATE OF MURDER	Friday, 28th December, 1900
PLACE OF MURDER	Biddulph Moor
METHOD OF KILLING	Cut throat
RELATIONSHIP TO KILLER	Wife

picked up a knife, which he had used in the heat of the moment. The story was not believed, especially since it was known that Shufflebotham had many times threatened to kill his wife if she did not return to him.

Before his execution, Shufflebotham made a full confession to the prison chaplain, adding that he had used a razor to inflict the fatal wound.

1901

IN 1900, THE Liverpool-based ship the Lorton, had a busy year. Under the direction of her captain, James McMurty, she sailed from Hamburg to Portland, Oregan, on April 1st.

From Portland she sailed in turn to Durban in South Africa, then on to Newcastle, in New South Wales, before setting off for Caleta Buena, in South America. On those journeys, the Lorton picked up two new crew members: Victor Baileff in Durban, and an Italian, Valeri Giovanni, in New South Wales.

Giovanni was the only Italian on the crew and for some reason Baileff did not get on with him and enjoyed teasing him. Whilst much of this teasing was probably very innocuous, Giovanni would later say that Baileff also threatened him and on one occasion, tried to throw him from the rigging of the ship.

Whatever really passed between the two men, things came to a head when the ship docked in Caleta Buena. Here Baileff and Giovanni took part in a fist fight, with Giovanni coming off second best. He determined to get his revenge the first chance he could.

On December 7th, 1900, the ship set sail for Falmouth, with a cargo of nitrates. Things seemed to settle down for a few weeks but on February 8th, Giovanni went to the captain and complained about the teasing he was still getting from Baileff and some of the other crew members. The captain promised to intervene if the problem continued, but since Giovanni never returned to him, no further action was taken.

One week later, on February 15th, both Giovanni and Baileff were at work, washing down the decks, at 5.30am. One hour later, at 6.30am, Baileff was sent below to repair a sail, whilst Giovanni was told to clean out one of the lifeboats. Now, at last, Giovanni saw his chance.

Going down to the galley, Giovanni asked for a drink of water and whilst the cook had his back turned, the Italian stole a knife. He then sneaked off, towards the point where Baileff was working.

The first intimation that anything was amiss came when the Second Mate, Garnett, heard a cry. Going below decks to investigate,

NAME	Valeri Giovanni
AGE AT EXECUTION	31
DATE OF EXECUTION	Tuesday, 9th July, 1901
PLACE OF EXECUTION	Bodmin
HANGMAN	James Billington
ASSISTANT	William Billington
DATE OF TRIAL	17th June, 1901
LOCATION OF TRIAL	Bodmin
PRESIDING JUDGE	Mister Justice Wills
PROSECUTION COUNSEL	Mister Fraser Macleod, J.R. Randolph
DEFENCE COUNSEL	W.T. Lawrance
NUMBER OF VICTIMS	1

VICTIMS DETAILS	
NAME	Victor Baileff
AGE	Not known
DATE OF MURDER	Friday, 15th February, 1901
PLACE OF MURDER	On board the Lorton heading for Falmouth
METHOD OF KILLING	Stabbed
RELATIONSHIP TO KILLER	None

Garnett found Baileff bent backwards with Giovanni's arm around his throat. Garnett saw Giovanni raise the knife he had taken and plunge it into Baileff's heart. It was but one wound of eight, and Baileff died immediately.

When the ship finally docked at Falmouth, Giovanni was taken into custody and at his subsequent trial, pleaded guilty, though on the advice of his counsel, he subsequently withdrew that plea and entered one of not guilty. The facts though were indisputable and the verdict a foregone conclusion.

In July 1901, Valeri Giovanni faced the hangman and became the first man to die on the scaffold of Bodmin jail for 19 years.

IN JANUARY 1900, Charles Watkins married Letitia Harriett Hamilton, for whom this was a second marriage – she already had a daughter from her first. Within five weeks they had parted, due to his fondness for drink, and she had returned to live at her brother's house, in Gravesend. Soon afterwards, Watkins had turned up at the house and created such a disturbance that the police had to be called.

In due course, a deed of separation was drawn up, but Charles soon slipped into arrears with his payments until finally he received a summons to appear at court on April 2nd, 1901. After the hearing, Charles argued with Letitia's brother, Frederick Hamilton, and threats were made. They were certainly not idle threats either as, the next day, Charles Watkins bought a revolver and 50 cartridges from Blanch and Sons in Gracechurch Street.

Watkins was living in rooms at Mrs Gertrude Bevan's house at 13 Rebecca Terrace, Rotherhithe, and early on the morning of Good Friday, April 5th, she heard a loud report from Watkins's room. Rushing up to investigate she found the room full of smoke and the unmistakable aroma of gunpowder. Charles explained that he had been testing his new revolver and had accidentally discharged it. Mrs Bevan seemed content to accept this story.

That same day, Watkins travelled to Gravesend where he met a man named Taylor, who was engaged to Letitia's daughter. After a brief and quite friendly talk, the two men parted company but Taylor, aware that threats had been made and thinking that Watkins might be in Gravesend to cause trouble, walked over to the Hamilton house to warn them that Watkins was in town.

It was just after two in the afternoon when Watkins appeared in front of Frederick Hamilton's house in Old Road West. Hamilton saw his brother-in-law, threw open the window and demanded to know what he wanted. Words were exchanged and then, suddenly, shots rang out. A commercial traveller, Frederick Charles Wells, who was passing at the time, saw Watkins fire three times at the figure leaning out of the window.

NAME	Charles Richard Thomas Watkins
AGE AT EXECUTION	54
DATE OF EXECUTION	Tuesday, 30th July, 1901
PLACE OF EXECUTION	Maidstone
HANGMAN	James Billington
ASSISTANT	William Billington
DATE OF TRIAL	12th July, 1901
LOCATION OF TRIAL	Maidstone
PRESIDING JUDGE	Mister Justice Mathew
PROSECUTION COUNSEL	Morton Smith, Mister Hohler
DEFENCE COUNSEL	Percival Hughes
NUMBER OF VICTIMS	1

VICTIMS DETAILS	
NAME	Frederick William Acland Hamilton
AGE	46
DATE OF MURDER	Friday, 5th April, 1901
PLACE OF MURDER	138 Old Road West, Gravesend
METHOD OF KILLING	Shot
RELATIONSHIP TO KILLER	Brother-in-law

Frederick Hamilton, hit in a lung, staggered back into his room and died. Charles Watkins did not attempt to avoid arrest for the murder he had just committed. He walked across to the other side of the road, calmly lit a cigarette and waited for the police.

At his trial, Watkins's defence was that Hamilton had constantly provoked him. It was pointed out that Watkins made no threats when he spoke to Taylor and that therefore Hamilton must have said something which caused him to lose his temper. The fact remained, though, that Watkins had bought a gun, tested it, and had taken it with him to Gravesend. The jury had no problem in returning a guilty verdict.

MISTER EDWARDS WAS in bed when a cry woke him. Checking the time he saw that it was 1.45am. He crossed to the window and looked down into Dalberg Road. At first he saw nothing but then a young woman appeared from around the corner of Jelf Road. She was followed by a man who took out a razor and drew it across her throat. Mister Edwards ran out to offer the woman assistance, but by the time he reached her, the assailant had fled.

Half an hour later, at 2.15am, Ernest Peachey, who ran a coffee stall at the corner of Acre Lane, saw Ernest Wickham approaching. Ordering a coffee, Wickham tried to light a cigarette but could not manage it. Looking closer, Peachey saw that the reason for this was that Wickham's hands were covered in blood, making the cigarette too damp. When Peachey asked him what had happened, Wickham replied that he had been fighting.

By the time the police arrived in Dalberg Road, the unfortunate woman, Amy Russell, had died. Investigations showed that she had been walking out with one Ernest Wickham who lived at 40 Santley Street, Brixton.

A trail of blood led the police to the coffee stall and Mister Peachey who confirmed that he had recently served Wickham, whose hands were heavily blood stained. It now became a matter of urgency to interview Wickham and upon rousing him from his bed, at 4.00am that same morning, it was noted that his hands were still covered in dried blood. A search of his rooms revealed bloodstained boots and clothing, and a razor, which when opened, still dripped with the crimson liquid.

It was a simple matter to piece together what had happened. The pair were known to have entered the Raglan Beerhouse on Cornwall Road, at around midnight on June 26th. Amy seemed to be distressed. Apparently she had been arguing with the man with her, a man the landlord identified as Wickham. Indeed, the landlord had asked Amy what the matter was, and she had asked him in turn if life was really worth living. Wickham replied for her: "If life is not worth living, then you will die tonight."

Ernest Wickham showed no fear at his

NAME	Ernest Walter Wickham
AGE AT EXECUTION	30
DATE OF EXECUTION	Tuesday, 13th August, 1901
PLACE OF EXECUTION	Wandsworth
HANGMAN	James Billington
ASSISTANT	William Billington
DATE OF TRIAL	23rd July, 1901
LOCATION OF TRIAL	Old Bailey
PRESIDING JUDGE	Mister Justice Wills
PROSECUTION COUNSEL	Charles Mathews, Mister Bodkin
DEFENCE COUNSEL	Clarke Hall, Mister Frampton
NUMBER OF VICTIMS	1

VICTIMS DETAILS	
NAME	Amy Eugenie Russell
AGE	35
DATE OF MURDER	Thursday, 27th June, 1901
PLACE OF MURDER	Dalberg Road, Brixton, London
METHOD OF KILLING	Cut throat
RELATIONSHIP TO KILLER	Girlfriend

trial. When asked to say whether he was guilty or not guilty, Wickham replied: "Anything you like." His defence counsel entered a plea of not guilty on Wickham's behalf.

Wickham's defence was that he was drunk at the time of the attack and had no intention of killing Amy. The jury were out for a matter of minutes before saying that he was guilty. Asked if he had anything to say before sentence was passed, Ernest Wickham said nothing and struggled to leave the dock before the death sentence was completed. To the end he showed no interest in what was going on.

FOR SOME TIME there had been bad blood between John Joyce and the young Nugent boys. This had reached a climax on June 7th, 1901, when Joyce had been charged with assault on one of the Nugents, and now, even though he had been discharged, he wanted revenge.

Mrs Emma Moore lived in a small court off Price Street in Birmingham. She knew Joyce well and also knew of the arguments between him and the Nugents who lived opposite to her. So, when she saw Joyce, early on the morning of June 10th, carrying a knife, and waiting near the Nugent's house, she knew there was going to be trouble.

Mrs Moore saw Joyce go to an empty house in the court and when she confronted him and asked him what he was up to, Joyce simply said he must have gone to the wrong house and left the area. At 8.00pm, Joyce was back. Mrs Moore saw him hammering on the Nugents' front door. As it was opened, by John Nugent, Joyce rushed in shouting: "I mean to do for some of you tonight." Mrs Moore, not wanting to miss any of the action, followed Joyce into the house and later described what she had seen.

On getting into the house, Joyce had picked up a lighted lamp, which he then threw at John Nugent. The lamp broke in pieces at Nugent's feet and went out. At that, Mrs Nugent, seeing that Joyce was carrying a knife down his sleeve, felt that it was time the police were called. She asked John to fetch an officer, whilst she held Joyce pinned to the wall. As Nugent ran out of the house to do as he had been asked, Joyce struggled free and went after him, followed yet again by the ever-present Mrs Moore.

It was over in seconds. As Joyce overtook Nugent, he grabbed him, spun him around and stabbed him forcefully in the chest. Nugent staggered back a few paces and then fell slowly to the ground. The old man died on his way to the infirmary.

The trial of John Joyce was almost a formality. Evidence of the feud between him and the Nugents was given, followed by the eye-witness descriptions of Mrs Nugent and of course, the omnipresent Mrs Moore, who related all she had seen and heard on the day

NAME	John Joyce
AGE AT EXECUTION	36
DATE OF EXECUTION	Tuesday, 20th August, 1901
PLACE OF EXECUTION	Birmingham
HANGMAN	James Billington
ASSISTANT	William Billington
DATE OF TRIAL	31st July, 1901
LOCATION OF TRIAL	Birmingham
PRESIDING JUDGE	Mister Justice Phillimore
PROSECUTION COUNSEL	Etherington Smith, J.W.P. Mosley
DEFENCE COUNSEL	S.G. Dorset, Norris Foster
NUMBER OF VICTIMS	1

VICTIMS DETAILS

NAME	John Nugent
AGE	61
DATE OF MURDER	Monday, 10th June, 1901
PLACE OF MURDER	Price Street, Birmingham
METHOD OF KILLING	Stabbed
RELATIONSHIP TO KILLER	None

of the murder. Although there could be only one verdict, the jury did nevertheless add a recommendation of mercy, no doubt feeling that Joyce had been provoked by the family in the past.

On August 20th, John Joyce, an ex-soldier, was hanged at Winson Green prison, Birmingham. Finally the feud was at an end.

MARCEL FOUGERON, A Frenchman who spoke little English, had been in London for some two months. Down on his luck and thrown out of his lodgings in Whitfield Street, he decided to visit a jeweller's shop, in Lower Charles Street. Hermann Jung had run the shop for many years and, as a member of the Swiss Benevolent Society it was well known that he was willing to help foreigners in need of employment.

Mrs Jung saw Fougeron come into the shop and heard him talking, quite amicably, in French. She then went downstairs to get on with her own work and, for the next three hours or so, went about her business whilst the two men chatted upstairs.

At 3.40pm, Mrs Jung heard some kind of struggle in the shop. Going to investigate, she found her husband lying on the floor, a knife protruding from his neck, and Fougeron rushing out of the door. Bravely, she gave chase. Constable Troughton saw the commotion and ran after Fougeron, blowing his whistle as he turned into Rydon Crescent. A second officer, Constable Bevan, now joined in and Fougeron was captured and taken back to the shop.

When they reached the shop, Mrs Jung immediately identified Fougeron as the man who had attacked her husband. Hermann Jung had by now died from his injuries. It was apparently a case of cold-blooded murder.

At his subsequent trial, the prosecution contended that this was a simple case of attempted robbery. Fougeron had sought financial aid from Jung and then had struggled with the old man whilst trying to rob him, finally stabbing him. The defence, though, was startling.

Marcel Fougeron claimed that Hermann Jung was an anarchist. Fougeron stated that after the two of them had met a number of times, Jung had suggested that Fougeron assassinate, or attack Mister Chamberlain, the Colonial Secretary, whom Jung held to be responsible for the poor treatment of the Boers. Fougeron had refused to do the deed, whereupon Jung had blocked his way out of the shop and demanded repayment of all the money he had given to Fougeron over the past few weeks, which he estimated to be around £5.

NAME	Marcel Fougeron
AGE AT EXECUTION	23
DATE OF EXECUTION	Tuesday, 19th November, 1901
PLACE OF EXECUTION	Newgate
HANGMAN	James Billington
ASSISTANT	Henry Pierrepoint
DATE OF TRIAL	28th October – 29th October, 1901
LOCATION OF TRIAL	Old Bailey
PRESIDING JUDGE	Mister Justice Bigham
PROSECUTION COUNSEL	Charles Mathews, Mister Bodkin
DEFENCE COUNSEL	Bernard O'Connor, F. Danford Thomas
NUMBER OF VICTIMS	1

VICTIMS DETAILS	
NAME	Hermann Francis Jung
AGE	64
DATE OF MURDER	Tuesday, 3rd September, 1901
PLACE OF MURDER	4 Lower Charles Street, Clerkenwell, London
METHOD OF KILLING	Stabbed
RELATIONSHIP TO KILLER	None

When Fougeron said he was unable to repay the money, a struggle had broken out, during which Jung had thrown a piece of iron at Fougeron, narrowly missing his head. In self-defence, Fougeron had then stabbed Jung and tried to make his escape.

The piece of iron referred to, when found, was covered in a thick layer of dust, implying that it had not been touched for some time. The defence failed and Marcel Fougeron was sentenced to death. He was taken from court protesting to the end that he was a hero and that Britain should thank him for what he had done.

THE MCKENNAS HAD seemed a devoted couple, but when Patrick lost his job, things changed. In order to make ends meet, they had taken in lodgers – Mr and Mrs Palmer – and it wasn't long before Patrick convinced himself that his wife was sleeping with Mr Palmer.

Patrick took to drinking heavily, one of his favourite haunts being the Derby Hotel, which was run by James Billington, the hangman. The heavy drinking only served to increase McKenna's volatility. Things did not improve when Patrick found himself a job. A joiner by trade, he was only able to find labouring work.

Even with the lodgers, and Patrick's new job, Anna McKenna was still short of money, especially as Patrick often took days off work whenever he felt like it. One such day was Monday, September 30th.

Anna visited the pawnbrokers to get some cash and when she returned, Patrick asked to see the money and demanded that she give him two pence. When she refused, another argument broke out. So violent were Patrick's words that Anna ran off and hid in her daughter-in-law's house nearby. Patrick went looking for her but was told that she was not there.

At 5.00pm, Patrick returned and this time saw Anna through the kitchen window. He forced his way in and the argument began again.

Emma McKenna, the daughter-in-law, had been cutting up some meat and the knife she had been using lay on the table. Patrick picked it up and threatened to cut Anna's throat. Not showing any fear, Anna dared him to use the weapon and finally, Patrick lunged out and stabbed her in the throat. She died very soon afterwards, in the arms of William Billington, the son of James, who had been called to offer aid.

When the police arrived, McKenna was found in his own house, hiding underneath the stairs. He still had the knife in his hand but was so drunk that he was not charged with murder until the following day when he had sobered up.

It was obviously a crime of passion. McKenna was full of remorse and even the judge at the trial told the jury that he would be

NAME	Patrick McKenna
AGE AT EXECUTION	53
DATE OF EXECUTION	Tuesday, 3rd December, 1901
PLACE OF EXECUTION	Manchester
HANGMAN	James Billington
ASSISTANT	Henry Pierrepoint
DATE OF TRIAL	13th November, 1901
LOCATION OF TRIAL	Manchester
PRESIDING JUDGE	Mister Justice Bucknill
PROSECUTION COUNSEL	Mister Sutton, Mister Pope
DEFENCE COUNSEL	Mister Gibbons
NUMBER OF VICTIMS	1

VICTIMS DETAILS	
NAME	Anna McKenna
AGE	Not known
DATE OF MURDER	Monday, 30th September, 1901
PLACE OF MURDER	Bolton, Lancashire
METHOD OF KILLING	Cut throat
RELATIONSHIP TO KILLER	Wife

delighted if they could find evidence to reduce the charge to manslaughter, telling them that they had to be sure there was malice aforethought in Patrick's actions in order to return a verdict of guilty of murder. That was indeed the verdict and despite a petition signed by over 30,000 people, McKenna was hanged by James Billington, the publican he knew so well.

Billington, who was very ill at the time, was deeply affected by McKenna, who was crying as the hangman and his assistant entered the condemned cell. Henry Pierrepoint was later to reveal that as he stood on the trap, McKenna's last words were: "Oh Lord, help me!" It was James Billington's last execution. He died just ten days later.

THE MILLERS HAD a complicated family relationship. John Miller was the son of Mary Ferguson by her first husband, who had since died. She had subsequently married Joseph Ferguson who was therefore John's step-father. The other Miller, John Robert, was a nephew of John Miller and the entire family worked in the amusement industry, travelling from fair to fair. For some time the Millers had been in dispute with Joseph Ferguson over some property owned by Mary. They wanted what they felt was theirs and if they had to use violence to get it, then that was fine by them.

On September 20th, 1901, the Millers entered a shop in North Shields and bought a long-bladed knife. The younger man paid, saying that he was about to go to sea as a cook. Later that same day, the two men knocked on the door of the Ferguson house.

A young boy, Robert Stevenson Oliver, would say later that it was the younger Miller who knocked at the door. Eventually it was opened by Joseph Ferguson whereupon the Millers rushed in. A scuffle took place, which ended when Ferguson fell dead, having been stabbed six times about the head and face. As Mary came downstairs to see what was going on, she was met by John Robert Miller, the knife in his hand, boasting that he had just killed her husband.

Another witness, Isabella Mason, said she saw both men in a back lane after the killing. The elder Miller, referring to Ferguson, was heard to say that he had been stabbed in "… four or five places." Mrs Mason then heard the younger man complain that the other had given him drink and enticed him to do the deed.

Both men were arrested and put on trial for murder. The elder Miller denied any involvement and said that he had tried to stop it, whilst the younger said that he was drunk at the time, and repeated that his uncle had enticed him into being involved. He added that he had been kicked in the head by a horse when he was a boy and had suffered headaches ever since. He claimed he must have been insane at the time of the killing.

Neither of their explanations were accepted and both men were sentenced to

NAME	John Miller; John Robert Miller
AGE AT EXECUTION	67; 31
DATE OF EXECUTION	Saturday, 7th December, 1901
PLACE OF EXECUTION	Newcastle
HANGMAN	William Billington
ASSISTANT	John Billington, John Ellis
DATE OF TRIAL	15th November, 1901
LOCATION OF TRIAL	Newcastle
PRESIDING JUDGE	Mister Justice Grantham
PROSECUTION COUNSEL	J.E. Joel, E. Meynell
DEFENCE COUNSEL	Mister Mitchell-Innes, Horace Marshall
NUMBER OF VICTIMS	1

VICTIMS DETAILS

NAME	John Ferguson
AGE	circa 60
DATE OF MURDER	Friday, 20th September, 1901
PLACE OF MURDER	55 Hudleston Street, Cullercoats, Northumberland
METHOD OF KILLING	Stabbed
RELATIONSHIP TO KILLER	Step-father; none

death. Once the day of the execution grew near, John Robert Miller lost all his bravado and became hysterical in his cell. In order to avoid any further distress for him, the authorities staggered the executions, so that the younger man would not be unnerved by the sight of his uncle on the scaffold. The elder man was hanged at 8.00am with his nephew following him an hour and a half later. It was John Ellis's first execution.

JOHN THOMPSON HAD once lived with Mary Lieutand, even though she was married to another man, but the relationship had faltered and they had split up, she going to live with a friend, Mrs Ivy Dawson. Thompson found it impossible to accept that it was all over and harangued Mary, asking her to return to him.

Thompson was an engine fitter and earned good money. However, in July 1901, he stole some metal files and was fined £1. Although this was not a great sum the conviction preyed upon his mind and he began to behave irrationally.

Thompson moved around the area, looking for work in different places, and it was not until early September that he returned to Gateshead and once again began pestering Mary to come back to him. Still she would not be moved. On September 16th, Thompson bought himself a revolver.

As Mary and Mrs Dawson arrived home on the 17th, they were dismayed to see Thompson waiting. He grabbed Mary's arm and asked her again to return to him. She pulled away and said that she wanted nothing more to do with him. For good measure Mrs Dawson added her own request for him to stop bothering Mary. The two ladies then walked on to Mrs Dawson's house, but Thompson forced his way in, drawing out his gun as he did so. A shot was fired and Mary was hit below the shoulder blade. She was not seriously injured but Mrs Dawson shouted that she should run for her life.

Mary pushed past Thompson and ran across the road, where she managed to gain access to number 122. Once again she tried to close the door but Thompson had followed her and managed to force his foot into the doorway. Mary could not close the door, but Thompson could not force it open either. However, he did manage to get his arm through the gap and pointing the gun in Mary's general direction, fired twice more. One of the bullets hit Mary in the arm, causing another fairly slight wound but the other struck her in the head and she collapsed. Immediately Thompson was overcome with remorse and cradled the dying Mary in his arms. Her last words were to tell him that she still loved him. When the police arrived, Thompson offered no

NAME John George Thompson
AGE AT EXECUTION 38
DATE OF EXECUTION Tuesday, 10th December, 1901
PLACE OF EXECUTION Durham
HANGMAN William Billington
ASSISTANT Thomas Billington
DATE OF TRIAL 23rd November, 1901
LOCATION OF TRIAL Durham
PRESIDING JUDGE Mister Justice Grantham
PROSECUTION COUNSEL Mister Luck, Mister Simey
DEFENCE COUNSEL Edward Shortt
NUMBER OF VICTIMS 1

VICTIMS DETAILS
NAME Maggie Ann Lieutand
AGE 33
DATE OF MURDER Tuesday, 17th September, 1901
PLACE OF MURDER 122 Milling Street, Gateshead
METHOD OF KILLING Shot
RELATIONSHIP TO KILLER Girlfriend

resistance. He meekly handed over the gun and admitted that he was responsible.

At the trial, Thompson again readily admitted his guilt, his defence being one of temporary insanity. Medical evidence was called on his behalf but this was contradicted by Doctor Steele, the medical superintendent of the Durham County Asylum, who said he found no evidence of insanity. The plea having failed, John George Thompson was found guilty and sentenced to death.

THE STORY OF Alick Claydon, a shoe finisher, is one of terrible brutality.

Alick had always been fond of a drink and that had led his wife, Louisa, to seek a separation in 1899. Later the couple were reconciled but Alick still had a major drink problem.

In early July, 1901, Alick had been away from home, on an extended drinking spree, but on the evening of Saturday, July 6th, he met his wife at a public house. They had a few drinks together and left for home. It would later be said that Alick was definitely sober.

At about 1.00am, Louisa's daughter was woken by a light in her room and the sounds of someone moving about. Upon checking to see what the noise was she found Alick, her step-father, walking about outside her room. She asked him what the problem was, to which he replied that he was just going downstairs to get some food and that she should just go back to sleep. He omitted to mention was that he had just murdered her mother.

Some time before 1.00am, Claydon had woken and gone down into his shoe shop where he picked out a large, heavy file. Returning to his bedroom he battered his wife to death and for good measure stabbed her repeatedly, one blow piercing her heart. It was at this time that his step-daughter heard him moving about. After talking to her, Alick went back downstairs, cooked himself some eggs, went back to bed and crawled in, next to his wife's corpse.

Three hours later, at 4.00am, Claydon woke again. He put his hand upon his wife's body and found that she was cold to the touch. He then got up and went for a long walk. His wife would be discovered at 10.00am, by her daughter, who immediately called in the police. The murder weapon still lay on top of the bedclothes.

Claydon had, however, already been arrested. Found wandering aimlessly in Moulton, some four miles away, he had been approached by a constable who thought he might be in need of assistance. When spoken to, Claydon admitted that he had just killed his wife.

The defence at Claydon's trial argued that the killing had been one of provocation. The

NAME	Alexander (Alick) Claydon
AGE AT EXECUTION	43
DATE OF EXECUTION	Friday, 13th December, 1901
PLACE OF EXECUTION	Northampton
HANGMAN	William Billington
ASSISTANT	Not known
DATE OF TRIAL	21st November, 1901
LOCATION OF TRIAL	Northampton
PRESIDING JUDGE	Mister Justice Bigham
PROSECUTION COUNSEL	Mister Lacey Smith, H. Russell
DEFENCE COUNSEL	W. Ryland, D. Atkins
NUMBER OF VICTIMS	1

VICTIMS DETAILS	
NAME	Louisa Claydon
AGE	Not known
DATE OF MURDER	Sunday, 7th July, 1901
PLACE OF MURDER	
METHOD OF KILLING	Battered/Stabbed
RELATIONSHIP TO KILLER	Wife

couple had rowed and he had battered her in the heat of the moment. It was also suggested that Claydon was not responsible for his actions. He had once attempted suicide, there was a history of insanity in his family and Claydon was known to suffer from fits. None of these arguments swayed the jury.

Claydon was sentenced to death, but now it was the State's turn to show that it too could be brutal. Claydon was originally due to hang on Thursday, December 12th, but his execution was temporarily delayed, prolonging his agonies, due to a Royal visit to the town of Northampton.

O N FEBRUARY 21ST, 1901, John Harrison bigamously married Alice Wright, despite the fact that she was already a married woman. Thereafter, she earned a living for them both by prostituting herself around the streets of Ormskirk, in Lancashire

On July 26th the couple decided to move on and walked to Skelmersdale, where they were seen the following morning, having a drink together in the Engine Inn on Liverpool Road. They did have some sort of argument there, but still left together, heading towards Bickerstaffe.

At the top end of Bickerstaffe Moss lay Rose Cottage. A few hundred yards past this was Rose Farm and at 10.00am, Alice Wright called and asked the farmer, Peter Marsh, if he owned the cottage down the lane. When he said that he did, Alice asked if she could rent it. Mister Marsh accompanied Alice back to the cottage where he saw John Harrison waiting for them. Terms were agreed and the couple moved in to their new, unfurnished home.

At 1.20pm, 15-year-old Rachael Coxhead passed Rose Cottage and noticed that it had a smashed window. Thinking that someone might have broken in, she went to investigate and looking in saw a woman's body on the floor. She assumed it was a drunk who had decided to use the empty cottage as a place to sleep it off.

At 9.00pm, a distressed Harrison called at Rose Farm and informed Peter Marsh that he had just found his wife dead. Marsh told him to inform the police at Skelmersdale, which Harrison did, but only after calling in at a number of public houses along the way. By the time officers arrived at the cottage, it was midnight. Although Alice had been strangled, a pool of blood lay around the body, as her hand had also been cut. It was noted that there was blood on Harrison's shirt sleeve and on the strength of that, he was arrested.

Harrison's story was that he had left the cottage at about 2.00pm and walked to St Helen's where he had called in at the Prince of Wales Inn and met up with a bookmaker named Harry Dingwall. When this story was checked, Dingwall confirmed that he had been in the pub that day, but denied having met Harrison. Added to that, there was Rachael Coxhead's evidence that she had

NAME	John Harrison
AGE AT EXECUTION	31
DATE OF EXECUTION	Tuesday, 24th December, 1901
PLACE OF EXECUTION	Liverpool
HANGMAN	William Billington
ASSISTANT	John Billington
DATE OF TRIAL	2nd December, 1901
LOCATION OF TRIAL	Liverpool
PRESIDING JUDGE	Mister Justice Bucknill
PROSECUTION COUNSEL	Mister Foard, Blackwood Wright
DEFENCE COUNSEL	F.A. Greer, Mister Morris
NUMBER OF VICTIMS	1

VICTIMS DETAILS	
NAME	Alice Ann Wright
AGE	Not known
DATE OF MURDER	Saturday, 27th July, 1901
PLACE OF MURDER	Rose Cottage, Bickerstaffe
METHOD OF KILLING	Strangled
RELATIONSHIP TO KILLER	Girlfriend/bigamous wife

been to the cottage at 1.20pm, some 40 minutes before Harrison claimed he had left it.

The only motive that could be suggested was one of an argument between the couple which had ended with Harrison strangling Alice. Evidence was also given that Harrison was mentally unstable. At a previous address he had been known to fire his revolver inside the darkened rooms and had slept in the cemetery, on top of his mother's grave. Despite this he was adjudged to be sane and sentenced to death.

1902

FRANCES O'ROURKE WAS a good girl. Her father was a tailor and whenever he asked her to run an errand she would happily skip off and do as she was told.

On the last day of 1901, Frances left home at about 2.00pm and arrived at Mister Jenkinson's shop about an hour later. After waiting around for some time, she picked up a parcel for her father and left to go home at around 3.50pm.

At just after 4.30pm, Frances was seen by a young girl named Muggeridge, getting into a four-wheel, horse-drawn van, just down from the Cross Keys Inn on the road between Tonbridge and Tunbridge Wells. Other witnesses would see the van pass them and would note that a young girl was sitting on the front seat, next to a man. At 5.30pm, the same van was seen being driven at a furious pace from the direction of Vauxhall Pond, towards Tonbridge.

When Frances did not return to her home in Southborough, a search was launched, but no trace of the child could be found. It was not until the following morning that a labourer on his way to work passed Vauxhall Pond and noticed a body in the water.

Frances was almost naked and there was evidence that an attempt had been made to rape her before she had been stabbed behind one ear. The knife was entangled in her matted hair and her clothes were found piled up in a field nearby. The search began for the van.

A woman named Hollanby had seen the van and knew who usually drove it. So it was that the police went to speak to Harold Apted, who lived in Tonbridge and drove a dark-coloured van from which he delivered the coal and wood his father sold.

Investigations showed that there was fresh blood on Apted's shirt and jacket and the knife was identified as one belonging to a man named Hawkins who admitted that he had lent it to Apted. Finally, the van was found to show signs of a recent scrubbing which had still not removed all traces of blood in the back.

Apted's story was a weak one. He claimed to have lost the knife some months beforehand. He denied being in some of the

NAME	Harold Amos Apted
AGE AT EXECUTION	20
DATE OF EXECUTION	Tuesday, 18th March, 1902
PLACE OF EXECUTION	Maidstone
HANGMAN	William Billington
ASSISTANT	John Billington
DATE OF TRIAL	25th February – 26th February, 1902
LOCATION OF TRIAL	Maidstone
PRESIDING JUDGE	Mister Justice Wright
PROSECUTION COUNSEL	C.F. Gill, Theobald Mathew
DEFENCE COUNSEL	G.F. Hohler, C.M. Pitman
NUMBER OF VICTIMS	1

VICTIMS DETAILS	
NAME	Frances Eliza O'Rourke
AGE	7
DATE OF MURDER	Tuesday, 31st December, 1901
PLACE OF MURDER	Southborough, Near Tonbridge, Kent
METHOD OF KILLING	Stabbed
RELATIONSHIP TO KILLER	None

places he had been seen on the day of the murder, though he did admit to being near Vauxhall Pond.

It took the jury less than an hour to return their verdict, recommending Apted to mercy on account of his youth. There was one final twist to the story.

On the very day that Apted was hanged at Maidstone, Alexander Moore, who lived at Prospect Road, Southborough, was charged with sending threatening letters to the parents of the murdered girl. In those missives he said he would kill them and their entire families.

RICHARD WIGLEY, A married man, had been seeing Mary Bowen for some years. When they met, he was a slaughterman at Berrington, whilst she worked as a barmaid at the Lion Inn, Westbury. Once they started seeing each other, Mary left her job and took employment at another public house, near Berrington, so they could spend more time together.

After some years together, Mary suddenly ended the relationship and went back to her old job at the Lion Inn. Richard took to visiting Mary as often as he could but she told him not to hold out any hope that they could get back together, adding that it would be better if he didn't see her any more. She also told the other staff at the Lion that if he called for her again, they were to say she was not available.

Richard was an even-tempered man, except when he had been drinking at which times he became violent. In late November, he received some unexpected money and spent it on a major drinking binge, in Shrewsbury. After a few days of this he determined to see Mary again, but before he went to Westbury, he sharpened one of his butcher's knives.

On Saturday, November 30th, Richard rose early and left for Westbury, arriving there before 10.00am. He was wearing his butcher's apron and carrying two knives in a leather pouch. Once inside the Lion he asked for and received a beer. He drank it quietly but upon asking for another, was told by Mary that he had had enough. He asked her to trust him and once again requested another beer, but Mary would not change her mind. She turned her back on him and walked briskly away.

What Mary did not know was that Wigley had followed her. In a passageway he caught up with her, put his left arm around her neck and with his right, pulled a knife from his apron pouch and drew the blade across her throat, causing an enormous gash. She died almost immediately.

When questioned by the police, and again at his trial, Richard Wigley said that he had killed Mary for love and that if he could not have her, no one else would. A letter was found in his possession in which he stated his intentions and said he was ready to die for what he had to do.

NAME	Richard Wigley
AGE AT EXECUTION	34
DATE OF EXECUTION	Tuesday, 18th March, 1902
PLACE OF EXECUTION	Shrewsbury
HANGMAN	Henry Pierrepoint
ASSISTANT	John Ellis
DATE OF TRIAL	27th February, 1902
LOCATION OF TRIAL	Shrewsbury
PRESIDING JUDGE	Mister Justice Phillimore
PROSECUTION COUNSEL	R.H. Amphlett, L.R. Wilkinson
DEFENCE COUNSEL	S.R.C. Bosanquet
NUMBER OF VICTIMS	1

VICTIMS DETAILS	
NAME	Mary Ellen Bowen
AGE	28
DATE OF MURDER	Saturday, 30th November, 1901
PLACE OF MURDER	The Lion Inn, Westbury, Shropshire
METHOD OF KILLING	Cut throat
RELATIONSHIP TO KILLER	Girlfriend

Evidence was called as to Wigley's sanity. His mother had been admitted to the Salop County Lunatic Asylum and it was argued that Wigley had killed Mary as a result of a sudden fit of insanity, brought on by a combination of jealousy and drink. Despite this, the jury held him to be fully responsible for his actions.

On more than one occasion, Wigley had said that he was ready to swing for what he had done. The law saw that he did.

SARAH HEBDEN WORKED as an agent for the Royal Liver Friendly Society and each week would collect premiums from her friends and neighbours, to the tune of around £5. From this she would earn £2 commission, passing the rest on to the Society. In addition to this money, she was also in the habit of keeping something between £5 and £10 in a tea caddy in her front bedroom.

Sarah was a creature of habit. Every Monday, Tuesday and Wednesday, she would rise at 7.00am. On Thursdays though, the day she paid her premiums to her employer, she would get up at 6.30am, take care of business and then visit friends in either Elloughton or Leeds. On November 28th, 1901, she had arranged to visit Elloughton, but she never arrived.

On the same day, a young girl named Jackson called on Sarah but received no reply to her knocking. This was so unusual that the girl went next door instead, where Margaret Bonar, Sarah's sister lived. Knowing her sister's habits, Mrs Bonar became most concerned and contacted the office of the Royal Liver to see if they had heard from Sarah. When they told her that Sarah had not made her usual Thursday payment, Mrs Bonar knew that something was terribly wrong.

Margaret saw that there was a window open at the rear of Sarah's house and her young daughter, Florence, managed to get through this. It was Florence who found the battered body of Sarah Hebden near the foot of the stairs. The insurance money was missing and the tea caddy, broken open and emptied of its contents, was discovered underneath Sarah's bed.

Police inquiries soon centred upon Margaret Bonar's illegitimate son, Arthur Richardson. He already had a police record, having robbed another aunt for which he received a prison sentence of six months. In fact, he had only been released on November 20th, eight days previously.

Police officers spoke to William Wright Shelton, who was Richardson's landlord, and he confirmed that at 5.30am on the morning of the murder, Richardson had complained that he had no money. However, at 7.30am that same day, William Isaac Fenton had met up with Richardson, who was jangling money in his pocket. Later still, Richardson ordered a new suit of clothes and an overcoat for himself.

The final piece of evidence was a gold watch found on Richardson when he was picked up. This had belonged to Sarah Hebden and though Richardson protested his innocence to the end, he was found guilty of murder after his trial at York.

Before his execution, Richardson left a full written confession to the murder of his aunt. He then took the short walk to the execution chamber and became the first man to be hanged at Hull in 124 years. It was just eight days after his 30th birthday.

NAME	Arthur Richardson
AGE AT EXECUTION	30
DATE OF EXECUTION	Tuesday, 25th March, 1902
PLACE OF EXECUTION	Hull
HANGMAN	William Billington
ASSISTANT	John Billington
DATE OF TRIAL	6th March, 1902
LOCATION OF TRIAL	York
PRESIDING JUDGE	Mister Justice Lawrance
PROSECUTION COUNSEL	T. Milvain M.P., H.S. Cautley M.P.
DEFENCE COUNSEL	Mister Kershaw
NUMBER OF VICTIMS	1

VICTIMS DETAILS	
NAME	Sarah Hebden
AGE	62
DATE OF MURDER	Thursday, 28th November, 1901
PLACE OF MURDER	97 Hodgson Street, Hull
METHOD OF KILLING	Battered
RELATIONSHIP TO KILLER	Aunt

WHEN THE PAMPHILON family moved in to 73 Second Avenue, they got on well with their new neighbours, including Charles Robert Earl, a retired baker, who lived a few doors away from them. Then, in the Spring of 1901, for some reason unknown to them, the situation changed.

In July of that year, Earl caused a disturbance outside number 73, whereupon Mister Pamphilon went outside and after a brief scuffle, knocked Earl to the ground. Earl repaid this by returning later and smashing the windows. The police were called, Earl was arrested and later fined in court.

The Pamphilons had a lodger, Mrs Hibberd, and soon after the court case, Earl met her in the street and told her that he had not yet finished with the Pamphilons. She suggested that he let the matter drop but Earl swore that he would have his revenge, no matter what the consequences. He was certainly to prove true to his words.

On the afternoon of March 6th, 1902, Earl purchased a revolver and cartridges, which he had to be shown how to use. That evening, he decided that he would sort out this feud once and for all.

Earl knew that Mrs Pamphilon worked in Kensington High Street, but when he went there to see her, was told that she had gone home early. The Pamphilons were entertaining friends when they heard the doorbell ring. Margaret Pamphilon went to the door and was immediately accosted by Earl who demanded to know if her husband was in. Before she could even reply, three shots rang out and Mrs Hibberd heard Earl shout: "Take that!" By the time the rest of the occupants of the house reached the front door, Earl had run off and Margaret Pamphilon lay dead, with two bullet wounds in her arm and one in her forehead.

When he was arrested, Earl admitted the shooting, saying: "All right, I'll go quietly. I was just going to give myself up. It is for Mrs Pamphilon. I hope I shot her." He subsequently explained that he believed the Pamphilons were responsible for his wife leaving him. There was no foundation for that belief.

Tried at the Old Bailey, Earl's defence was

NAME	Charles Robert Earl
AGE AT EXECUTION	56
DATE OF EXECUTION	Tuesday, 29th April, 1902
PLACE OF EXECUTION	Wandsworth
HANGMAN	William Billington
ASSISTANT	Henry Pierrepoint
DATE OF TRIAL	11th April – 14th April, 1902
LOCATION OF TRIAL	Old Bailey
PRESIDING JUDGE	Mister Justice Grantham
PROSECUTION COUNSEL	Mister Biron, Mister Graham-Campbell
DEFENCE COUNSEL	Lister Drummond
NUMBER OF VICTIMS	1

VICTIMS DETAILS	
NAME	Margaret Pamphilon
AGE	Not known
DATE OF MURDER	Thursday, 6th March, 1902
PLACE OF MURDER	73 Second Avenue, Mortlake, London
METHOD OF KILLING	Shot
RELATIONSHIP TO KILLER	None

one of insanity, suggesting that at the time of the shooting, he was not responsible for his actions. The fact that he had first gone to Mrs Pamphilon's place of work indicated that he was fully aware of what he was doing though. In fact, the jury did not even bother to leave the box before returning their guilty verdict.

When asked if he had anything to say, Earl replied: "I shot the woman because she was twenty times worse than a common harlot and her husband knows it, and he is a bigger liar than her. I am guilty my Lord."

THE NAME TOTTENHAM is synonymous with football and it was that which brought a group of boys on to the marshes on January 26th, 1902. After a kick-about, the ball went into a ditch and when the lads went to retrieve it, they found the body of a young woman.

She was identified as Charlotte Cheeseman and from the look of the surrounding area, she had accompanied someone to the spot, been attacked, and then her body pushed down into the ditch. There were many wounds consistent with Charlotte having been kicked repeatedly. She had also been stabbed by some tool, such as a sharp chisel.

Once Charlotte's family were traced, the police discovered that she had been seeing an ex-soldier, George Woolfe. They had often been seen quarrelling and Woolfe had been violent towards Charlotte a few weeks before. Other witnesses said that they had heard Woolfe say that he intended to "get shot" of her.

Investigations showed that on the night of the murder, Woolfe and Charlotte had been together in the Rosemary Branch, a pub where both were known to the landlord, Gilbert Dent. Later that night they were in the Park Hotel, where Charlotte was slightly the worse for drink and Woolfe, for some reason, was looking very angry.

The police, though, could find no trace of Woolfe. He was no longer at his rooms at 20 Eagle Wharf Road, Hoxton. Friends of his were interviewed and it became clear that at midnight on January 25th, he had met up with three men in yet another public house. Woolfe had argued with one of them, a gentleman named Sapsford, who had struck Woolfe. That would prove to be important later.

The last time Woolfe had been seen was on the day following the murder when he had called at Charlotte's house and asked her mother if Charlotte had come home.

The police decided to see if their man had re-enlisted. No one named Woolfe had, but a man named Slater had just joined the Surrey Militia and was stationed at St George's Barracks. When interviewed, Slater turned out to be George Woolfe, and was arrested on February 6th.

At his trial, Woolfe admitted being with Charlotte on the night that she died but said

NAME George Woolfe	
AGE AT EXECUTION 21	
DATE OF EXECUTION Tuesday, 6th May, 1902	
PLACE OF EXECUTION Newgate	
HANGMAN William Billington	
ASSISTANT John Billington	
DATE OF TRIAL 14th April – 16th April, 1902	
LOCATION OF TRIAL Old Bailey	
PRESIDING JUDGE Mister Justice Grantham	
PROSECUTION COUNSEL Richard D. Muir, Mister Bodkin	
DEFENCE COUNSEL Arthur Hutton, E.W. Fordham	
NUMBER OF VICTIMS 1	

VICTIM'S DETAILS
NAME Charlotte Cheeseman
AGE 22
DATE OF MURDER Saturday, 25th January, 1902
PLACE OF MURDER Tottenham Marshes, London
METHOD OF KILLING Battered/Stabbed
RELATIONSHIP TO KILLER Girlfriend

that they had parted at around 7.30pm. Witnesses were then called from both public houses to show this was a lie. There was also evidence that Woolfe had been badly scratched when he had called at Charlotte's house on the 26th. Woolfe said he had been injured in the fight with Sapsford, but he in turn gave evidence that no blood had been drawn. The jury took less than an hour to return their guilty verdict.

On May 6th, 1902, George Woolfe stepped into history as the last man to be executed at Newgate.

THOMAS AND ELIZABETH Marsland married on November 23rd, 1901, and almost from the first, he mistreated her.

Their first lodgings were with Hannah Lowe at 40 Edge Lane Hollow, Royton, but they were thrown out when Hannah objected to the way Thomas treated his wife. On at least three occasions, Hannah had seen Thomas strike his wife and she was not about to countenance such behaviour.

The Marslands tried to make a fresh start, but by February 1902, Elizabeth had left Thomas and moved to 1 Horsedge Fold, Oldham. Elizabeth decided to build a new life for herself and worked very hard at her job as a char at the offices of James William Kelly, in Union Street.

On Sunday, March 30th, Elizabeth returned to Hannah Lowe's and stayed with her for a few days over that Easter weekend. In fact, Elizabeth did not leave Hannah's home until Friday, April 4th, when she went directly to work at around 9.30am.

Elizabeth's next-door neighbour in Horsedge Fold was James Kelly, her employer, and he saw Elizabeth talking to her estranged husband near the Greaves Arms, in Yorkshire Street. It was by now around 10.10am. At 1.45pm that day, Thomas Marsland entered a shop in the town centre and bought himself a new razor for one shilling. He was served by Harry Forester.

Elizabeth Marsland returned home at 6.15pm. As she passed Kelly's house she was noticed by Elizabeth Jane Kelly, and the two women had a brief conversation. Ten minutes later, Elizabeth Kelly saw her neighbour at her front door, putting on her apron.

It was exactly 7.30pm when Elizabeth Kelly heard screaming from next door. Although this went on for two or three minutes, she did not see fit to investigate, even when, 15 minutes afterwards, she saw Thomas locking the door and walking off down the street.

Constable Michael Conway was on duty near the Mumps railway bridge when Marsland approached him, at around 8.20pm, and announced that he had come to give himself up for murdering his wife. He explained that he had gone to his wife's house

NAME	Thomas Marsland
AGE AT EXECUTION	21
DATE OF EXECUTION	Tuesday, 20th May, 1902
PLACE OF EXECUTION	Liverpool
HANGMAN	William Billington
ASSISTANT	John Billington
DATE OF TRIAL	2nd May, 1902
LOCATION OF TRIAL	Liverpool
PRESIDING JUDGE	Mister Justice Walton
PROSECUTION COUNSEL	J.T. Foard, A.H. Maxwell
DEFENCE COUNSEL	Mister Harrison
NUMBER OF VICTIMS	1

VICTIMS DETAILS	
NAME	Elizabeth Marsland
AGE	23
DATE OF MURDER	Friday, 4th April, 1902
PLACE OF MURDER	1 Horsedge Fold, Oldham
METHOD OF KILLING	Battered/cut throat
RELATIONSHIP TO KILLER	Wife

and waited for her to come home. They had quarrelled and he had battered her before cutting her throat.

Marsland, it seems, was determined to hang himself. An identity parade was organised so that Harry Forester could pick out the man he had sold the new razor to. Forester walked down the line but failed to pick out Marsland, whereupon the prisoner stepped forward and cried: "That is the man. I bought a razor from him and paid a shilling for it."

SAMUEL MIDDLETON LIKED a drink, but the drink didn't like him. Once under the influence he became quarrelsome and violent and had often been heard arguing with his long-suffering wife, Hannah, who was described by those who knew her as a sober and industrious woman. Many times he had even threatened to kill her.

The evening of Saturday, May 10th, started out like so many others had. Samuel had much too much to drink, returned home and argued yet again with Hannah. The neighbours would later report that they heard raised voices and the sounds of furniture being turned over. Then, suddenly, it all went very quiet.

At 3.00am the following day, the house occupied by the Middletons was seen to be on fire. The fire brigade were called but the conflagration was such that both the Middleton cottage and the one next door, were burned to the ground. Upon checking through the debris, once the fire had died down, officers found a charred female body. Naturally they wished to know what had happened to Samuel, the only other occupant of the house.

Later that same day, Samuel was discovered, wandering aimlessly on the road leading to the nearby town of Droitwich. He was asked where he was going and replied: "Anywhere. I have killed my wife and they'll soon catch me." When formally interviewed by the police, two days later, Samuel admitted that he had battered his wife with a poker, after a furious row, during which she had scratched and bitten him. He went on to show a mark on his cheek as proof that this were true.

At this point in the argument, Samuel had tried to leave the house but Hannah had leapt upon him and he had no choice but to strike her with the nearest weapon to hand, which just happened to be the poker. Realising that Hannah was dead he now set fire to the house, in order to cover up what he had done.

Middleton's defence was one of provocation. The argument was fierce and Hannah had forced him to strike her in the heat of the moment and whilst he was under the influence of drink. This meant that he was incapable of forming the intention to kill and the crime was not one of murder, but manslaughter.

The jury however were convinced of Samuel's guilt and returned that verdict after just a few minutes' deliberation. As Samuel would receive the death sentence for that crime, the law decided that there was little purpose in pursuing the other charge, that of arson.

NAME	Samuel Middleton
AGE AT EXECUTION	46
DATE OF EXECUTION	Tuesday, 15th July, 1902
PLACE OF EXECUTION	Worcester
HANGMAN	William Billington
ASSISTANT	Not known
DATE OF TRIAL	25th June, 1902
LOCATION OF TRIAL	Worcester
PRESIDING JUDGE	Mister Justice Wright
PROSECUTION COUNSEL	R.H. Amphlett, H.G. Farrant
DEFENCE COUNSEL	E.G.M. Carmichael
NUMBER OF VICTIMS	1

VICTIMS DETAILS	
NAME	Hannah Middleton
AGE	Not known
DATE OF MURDER	Saturday, 10th May, 1902
PLACE OF MURDER	Foxlydiate, near Redditch
METHOD OF KILLING	Battered
RELATIONSHIP TO KILLER	Wife

IN THIS BOOK there are many stories of drunken men killing their partners who were usually sober. In the case of William Churcher and Sophia Hepworth, the roles were reversed in that it was the woman who had the drink problem.

Sophia Hepworth was a married woman but she had lived with Churcher for 13 years. She was very fond of a drink and was often seen to be under the influence. On the night of her death she was so drunk that she ran down the street where she lived and ended up in the river, watched by a crowd of her neighbours.

It was by now 11.00pm and Churcher was arriving home from work. He managed to fish Sophia out of the river and took her home, much to the bemusement of the onlookers. Once they were alone, Churcher began to remonstrate with his partner about how she had embarrassed him. The discussion over Sophia's drinking habits soon became a full-blown argument during which Churcher picked up a knife and stabbed Sophia in the throat, shoulder, arms and hands. In the morning he left the house and the neighbours reported what they had seen and heard to the police.

When the police forced an entry to the house, on April 12th, they found the dead woman sitting in a chair, covered in blood and with her head wrapped in a towel. In all she had been stabbed 33 times, but it was the two deep wounds in her throat that had caused her death.

When he was arrested, Churcher admitted killing Sophia but claimed at his trial that she had thrown a lamp and two vases at him and had then attacked him with a knife. They had struggled and he had taken out his own knife and used it to defend himself. However, the judge pointed out that Churcher had stayed in the house with the dead woman, had not reported the attack at the time and had made no mention of provocation until the case came to trial. There was also the matter of the number of wounds. Whilst one or two might have fitted in with a plea of provocation, 33 was stretching things too far. Finally, some of the neighbours testified that they had heard Sophia begging for Churcher not to hurt her. This did not fit in with his

NAME William Churcher	
AGE AT EXECUTION 35	
DATE OF EXECUTION Tuesday, 22nd July, 1902	
PLACE OF EXECUTION Winchester	
HANGMAN William Billington	
ASSISTANT John Billington	
DATE OF TRIAL 2nd July, 1902	
LOCATION OF TRIAL Winchester	
PRESIDING JUDGE Mister Justice Bigham	
PROSECUTION COUNSEL Mister Evans Austin, E.B. Charles	
DEFENCE COUNSEL Mister Bentinck	
NUMBER OF VICTIMS 1	

VICTIMS DETAILS
NAME Sophia Jane Hepworth
AGE 30
DATE OF MURDER Thursday, 10th April, 1902
PLACE OF MURDER Clarence Buildings, Alverstone, Gosport
METHOD OF KILLING Stabbed
RELATIONSHIP TO KILLER Girlfriend

story, in which he was the innocent party, fighting for his own life.

After a short deliberation, the jury returned a guilty verdict, but with a strong recommendation to mercy on the grounds of the extreme provocation Churcher had received at the hands of the dead woman. The judge said that he would forward this to the proper quarter but added that he personally saw no reason for a reprieve.

The learned judge was correct in his assumption and Churcher was hanged on July 22nd.

NANCY PRICE WAS a married woman but her husband, Joseph, was much older than her and extremely deaf. He ran a fish and chip shop near Chesterfield and whilst he was busy, his wife sought other interests in their home town of Sutton-cum-Duckmanton.

For some years Nancy had been involved with John Bedford, an unmarried labourer. Bedford was much closer to her own age but nevertheless jealous of the fact that she was married.

On June 25th, 1902, Joseph Price was again in his shop whilst his wife was out with Bedford. The lovers visited the White Hart public house at Calow where they were seen by Alice Round who was asked by Nancy to come to her home in order to pick up a skirt. After Alice had been at Nancy's house for a short time, Bedford turned up. The three were then there together for a few minutes until Alice said she had to get home. Nancy offered to walk with her part of the way.

The following morning, Bedford was again at the White Hart, but he was alone. After having a drink, he spotted a friend of his, Frederick Wagstaffe, whereupon Bedford shouted across to him: "I've done it, I've killed her." In order to stress that he was telling the truth, Bedford then pointed to bloodstains on his trousers and boots and brandished the key to Price's house.

Wagstaffe did not believe what he had been told but Bedford was determined to convince him. He offered to take Wagstaffe round to Price's house and show him the body. Wagstaffe agreed to accompany him back but asked that another man, Robert Davison, be allowed to come with them. The three men then walked round to Price's house.

The body of Nancy Price was lying on the sofa. She had obviously been mending one of her stockings when she had been attacked. In her left hand was the stocking and still clutched in the fingers of her right hand was the darning needle she had been using. Once again Bedford admitted that it was he who had killed her and then showed the two shocked onlookers the poker he had used. Then, before the three men left the room, Bedford took hold of Nancy's hand and said:

NAME	John Bedford
AGE AT EXECUTION	41
DATE OF EXECUTION	Wednesday, 30th July, 1902
PLACE OF EXECUTION	Derby
HANGMAN	William Billington
ASSISTANT	Henry Pierrepoint
DATE OF TRIAL	11th July, 1902
LOCATION OF TRIAL	Derby
PRESIDING JUDGE	Mister Justice Lawrance
PROSECUTION COUNSEL	Mister Appleton, Mister Lawrance
DEFENCE COUNSEL	B. Stephen Foster
NUMBER OF VICTIMS	1

VICTIMS DETAILS	
NAME	Nancy Price
AGE	48
DATE OF MURDER	Wednesday, 25th June, 1902
PLACE OF MURDER	Parker's Lane, Sutton-cum-Duckmanton, Derbyshire
METHOD OF KILLING	Battered
RELATIONSHIP TO KILLER	Girlfriend

"God bless thee. I love thee, but thou hast not been true."

Back in the White Hart, one of the witnesses contacted the police and Bedford was arrested. He was quite content to return to the cottage and tell the same story to the police, again pointing out the poker. The only thing he added was that he felt he should have done it three years before.

Not surprisingly, it took the jury just a few minutes to confirm the guilty verdict and John Bedford, the killer who drew attention to his crime, was sentenced to death.

WILLIAM LANE HAD spent 12 years as a policeman in Bradford. Having left the force, he first worked on the railways but afterwards became an inquiry agent. A lot of William's work was connected with marital infidelity and one of his early clients was John William Dyson, who believed that his wife, Elizabeth, was having an affair. Whether Elizabeth was involved in a relationship or not at that time was somewhat irrelevant, as she was very soon involved in one with Lane.

John Dyson divorced his wife, who then started to use the name Elizabeth Gordon, even though her maiden name had been Murgatroyd. William Lane in turn left his family and he and Elizabeth began living together, though Lane often returned to his wife's house and occasionally even took Elizabeth there to stay. Lane's wife seemed to tolerate this until Lane mentioned that he wanted to turn her out and move Elizabeth in. At this suggestion, Lane's sons took the part of their mother. On one occasion both Lane and his sons used knives to settle an argument, with Lane coming off worse. Eventually Lane and Elizabeth left his wife's home and began travelling around the Black Country.

William Lane and Elizabeth Dyson were rather fond of drink and on the day of Elizabeth's death, they had visited a number of public houses. Lane was singing and playing the piano and Elizabeth seemed to be without a care in the world. That night though, things changed drastically.

The couple were seen on the road between Dudley and Rowley, just before midnight. Then people in the neighbourhood heard terrible screams. They rushed to see what the trouble was and found Lane kneeling by the prostrate body of Elizabeth. He had a knife in one hand and Elizabeth's throat had been slashed.

Once arrested, Lane made no attempt to deny that he was responsible, but claimed that it had been part of a suicide pact. The idea had been Elizabeth's and it was she who produced the knife, handed it to Lane, and asked him to cut her throat. After some hesitation, Lane did the deed but the wound was not deep enough so he cut her

NAME	William Lane
AGE AT EXECUTION	47
DATE OF EXECUTION	Tuesday, 12th August, 1902
PLACE OF EXECUTION	Stafford
HANGMAN	William Billington
ASSISTANT	John Billington
DATE OF TRIAL	22nd July, 1902
LOCATION OF TRIAL	Stafford
PRESIDING JUDGE	Mister Justice Walton
PROSECUTION COUNSEL	C.F. Vachell, H. Staveley Hill
DEFENCE COUNSEL	R. Feetham
NUMBER OF VICTIMS	1

VICTIMS DETAILS	
NAME	Elizabeth Dyson
AGE	67
DATE OF MURDER	Thursday, 26th June, 1902
PLACE OF MURDER	Tividale, Staffordshire
METHOD OF KILLING	Cut throat
RELATIONSHIP TO KILLER	Girlfriend

a second time at which point he lost his courage and found that he could not turn the blade upon himself.

At his trial, Lane pleaded guilty but had his case put back by the judge whilst he reconsidered his position. Coming back into court, he now entered a plea of not guilty, relying on a defence of insanity.

The judge described it as a very sad case but in his summing up pointed out that a verdict of manslaughter was impossible unless the jury were sure that Lane was insane at the time of the killing. The jury took just a few minutes to show that they had not been convinced and Lane was sentenced to hang.

SOMETIMES FATE WARNS us of things. One such warning was given to Miriam Jane Tye.

Miriam owned a house in Barmore Street, Battersea, and rented out rooms to working men. One lodger was George William Hibbs, a labourer who, by June 1902, had lived at Barmore Street for about two and a half years.

Hibbs had a reputation for being a surly individual and was also known to have something of a temper. On June 1st, he demonstrated this by attempting to stab Miriam. They had argued, and Hibbs happened to be holding a shoemaker's knife with which he lunged at her. The blade passed through some of her clothing but luckily missed her flesh. Hibbs apologised and his apology was accepted by Mrs Tye. It seems she had chosen to ignore the warning signs, possibly because there were indications of a romance between the two.

On June 28th, at about 11.00am, Hibbs asked Miriam if she had a clean shirt for him. She refused to give him one, saying that he would only pawn it and use the money to buy drink. Hibbs walked away and brooded on what she had said.

Later that same day, another lodger heard screams coming from Miriam's room. Rushing to investigate he found his landlady lying on the floor, bleeding badly from a wound in her stomach. Near the body lay a bloodstained shoemaker's knife and Hibbs was standing to one side.

Miriam was still alive and managed to gasp out that Hibbs had stabbed her. He remained silent and walked out of the room. The doctor and the police were sent for and Miriam Tye was rushed to hospital.

George Hibbs was in the kitchen. When he was questioned by the police he claimed to know nothing of the attack. He was nevertheless taken in and charged with attempted murder. On June 30th, Mrs Tye died from her wounds and the charge against Hibbs was changed to one of murder.

The trial defence was that Hibbs was guilty only of manslaughter as he had no intention to kill. It was a simple case of an argument getting out of hand and Mrs Tye had been accidentally killed in the heat of the moment.

NAME	George William Hibbs
AGE AT EXECUTION	40
DATE OF EXECUTION	Wednesday, 13th August, 1902
PLACE OF EXECUTION	Wandsworth
HANGMAN	William Billington
ASSISTANT	Henry Pierrepoint
DATE OF TRIAL	24th July, 1902
LOCATION OF TRIAL	Old Bailey
PRESIDING JUDGE	Mister Justice Lawrance
PROSECUTION COUNSEL	Richard D. Muir, Mister Biron, R.B. Murphy
DEFENCE COUNSEL	Arthur Hutton
NUMBER OF VICTIMS	1

VICTIMS DETAILS	
NAME	Miriam Jane Tye (Died Monday, 30th June)
AGE	57
DATE OF MURDER	Saturday, 28th June, 1902
PLACE OF MURDER	Barmore Street, Battersea, London
METHOD OF KILLING	Stabbed
RELATIONSHIP TO KILLER	None

The prosecution though called evidence of the earlier attack. The jury duly rejected the manslaughter plea after deliberating for about an hour, though they did add a strong recommendation to mercy.

For his part, Hibbs still claimed to have no recollection of the crime and said as much before the judge passed the sentence of death. However, just before his execution, Hibbs confessed by saying: "I should like this to be known. I stabbed Miriam because I loved her dearly. It was through jealousy. Of course, I had been drinking...." And with that, Hibbs walked to the gallows.

HENRY GROVES, KNOWN to his friends as 'Soldier', was murdered because of five shillings. In late July, 1902, that sum of money had been taken from John MacDonald whilst he was asleep, at the Salvation Army Shelter, in Middlesex Street, and he blamed Groves for taking it. On August 21st, MacDonald was seen sharpening a knife and announced that he was going to: "... kill Groves over that dollar I lost." It was a threat he would carry out exactly one week later.

On August 28th, MacDonald saw Groves in a crockery shop in Old Castle Street. MacDonald entered the shop and an argument broke out between the two men. After a few minutes of quarrelling, Groves left the shop and began walking up Old Castle Street, followed by a rather irate MacDonald.

Groves turned into Wentworth Street and it was there, at the gateway to the school, at the top end of that street, that MacDonald caught up with Groves, pulled him around and hit him. Groves, although he was much the older of the two, immediately hit MacDonald back, knocking him to the ground. So bad was the scene that a gentleman named Samuel Dodds had to intervene, separating the antagonists no fewer than three times. MacDonald had had enough. Chasing after Groves one more time, Dodds noticed that MacDonald was drawing a knife from his pocket. Dodds tried to intervene yet again, but this time he was just too late. MacDonald caught Groves, spun him around and stabbed him in the front of the neck.

Dodds bravely leapt on top of MacDonald and held him until the police arrived. Groves meanwhile managed to stagger a distance of some 50 yards before he fell dead. The knife had severed an artery and penetrated his windpipe.

At the Old Bailey, MacDonald tried to say that he had been so drunk that he had no memory of what had happened and had no intention of killing Groves. This was countered, of course, by his threat of August 21st, and the fact that some 45 minutes before the stabbing, he had shown Dodds the murder weapon and intimated that he intended to stick it into Groves. Finally, evidence was given that at the police station, MacDonald

NAME	John MacDonald
AGE AT EXECUTION	24
DATE OF EXECUTION	Tuesday, 30th September, 1902
PLACE OF EXECUTION	Pentonville
HANGMAN	William Billington
ASSISTANT	John Billington, Henry Pierrepoint
DATE OF TRIAL	11th September, 1902
LOCATION OF TRIAL	Old Bailey
PRESIDING JUDGE	Mister Justice Walton
PROSECUTION COUNSEL	Charles Mathews, Travers Humphreys
DEFENCE COUNSEL	Mister Purcell
NUMBER OF VICTIMS	1

VICTIMS DETAILS	
NAME	Henry Groves
AGE	Not known
DATE OF MURDER	Thursday, 28th August, 1902
PLACE OF MURDER	Wentworth Street, Spitalfields, London
METHOD OF KILLING	Stabbed
RELATIONSHIP TO KILLER	None

had pointed to the knife and said: "That is the knife I did it with and I did it intentionally."

On September 30th, 1902, John MacDonald earned his place in history when he became the first man to die on the gallows at Pentonville.

HENRY WILLIAMS'S STORY is one of the saddest in this book. It truly is a tale of a man destroying the thing he loves.

By the year 1900, Henry Williams had been seeing Ellen Andrews, a widow, for some seven years. Although they were not married, Ellen had given birth to Henry's child, a girl, Margaret Anne, whom Henry absolutely worshipped. That same year, Henry went to fight in the Boer War and was to stay away until July 1902. By the time he returned, his beloved daughter was five years old.

In an ideal world, Henry would have resumed his relationship with Ellen. The problem was that Henry believed Ellen had been enjoying an affair with a sailor. Ellen denied that anything improper had taken place but Henry was not to be convinced. He determined to hurt Ellen as much as she had hurt him. At the same time, there was another factor playing on Henry's mind. If he left his daughter with her unfaithful mother, perhaps she would grow up in the same mould and break some other man's heart. How could he pay back Ellen and yet protect his daughter from such a future?

In September 1902, Ellen and her daughter were staying at Worthing in Sussex, and on Wednesday the 10th, Henry went down to see them. Once again he accused Ellen of infidelity and ended with the comment that he wouldn't hurt her, but that he would break her heart. That same day he returned to London, with his daughter.

That same evening, a saddened Henry took a drink in the Lord Palmerston public house on King's Road. Whilst there he spoke to a friend about Margaret and his feelings. He asked how could he allow her to call him 'Daddy' and then said that he had killed her. At first he wasn't believed but later, when the police came into the pub and arrested him, everyone knew that what he had said was true.

Henry had put his daughter to bed, laying a doll by her side. With tears in his eyes he had told her that they were going to play a game. He gently covered her eyes with a handkerchief and then cut her throat. He was seen leaving the house shortly afterwards. After he had left, his room was searched and

NAME	Henry Williams
AGE AT EXECUTION	31
DATE OF EXECUTION	Tuesday, 11th November, 1902
PLACE OF EXECUTION	Pentonville
HANGMAN	William Billington
ASSISTANT	Henry Pierrepoint
DATE OF TRIAL	23rd October, 1902
LOCATION OF TRIAL	Old Bailey
PRESIDING JUDGE	Mister Justice Jelf
PROSECUTION COUNSEL	Richard D. Muir, Mister Biron
DEFENCE COUNSEL	Percival Hughes, Mister Ganz
NUMBER OF VICTIMS	1

VICTIMS DETAILS	
NAME	Margaret Anne Andrew
AGE	5
DATE OF MURDER	Wednesday 10th September 1902
PLACE OF MURDER	Waterford Rd, Fulham
METHOD OF KILLING	Cut throat
RELATIONSHIP TO KILLER	Daughter

the body of the little girl discovered, draped with a union flag.

The defence at Henry's trial tried to argue that he had been insane at the time of the murder but although Ellen received much abuse from the crowds outside the court, Henry was found guilty. Returning their verdict, the jury said that they wished to add a strong recommendation to mercy. It did not save Henry Williams and under the circumstances, he was probably glad that it did not.

PATRICK LEGGETT HAD been in trouble with the police since 1883 when he was only 11 years old and over the next few years was birched on more than one occasion, sent to a reformatory and finally to prison.

One of the families who suffered at least some of Leggett's violence was that of his long-suffering wife, Sarah Jane. He suspected her of going with other men and his jealousy and threats had finally led to her leaving Leggett and going to stay with her brother, William Blakeley, and his family at 93 Wylie's Back Land.

There were just a few houses in the row and at number 96 lived Sarah Jane's cousin, Christina Giffen, known by the nickname of Teezy. On November 20th, Sarah and Christina went into Partick, taking Christina's baby with them. By the time they arrived back at number 93, it was around 6.00pm and as the women entered the front door, it was Sarah Jane who was carrying the baby in her arms.

"Christ Teezy, take the bairn," cried Sarah and even as she handed the child over, a figure stepped from behind the doorway and a heavy blow landed on the side of Christina's head. She fell to the floor unconscious and when she woke, a few minutes later, she found the room filled with her neighbours, whilst Doctor Macauley was tending to the prostrate figure of Sarah Jane.

In those few minutes, Patrick Leggett had stepped forward and plunged a knife into his wife's back. It had been Sarah's screams that had brought neighbours such as Mrs Douglas, who lived at 100 Wylie's Back Land and Elizabeth White, who was from number 104. They had seen Leggett stab his wife and then run from the house. Other neighbours, such as Elizabeth Harkness from number 97, would later testify that she had heard Leggett threaten his wife weeks before.

Patrick Leggett had escaped and run down to the river Clyde where he had thrown himself in. Whether this was a genuine suicide attempt or not is debatable, for he soon began to cry out for help. It was Donald McCallum, the ferryman at Linthouse, who fished him out.

At his trial, Leggett's defence was one of insanity. To counter this, the prosecution called, in addition to those already mentioned, John Bratton a friend of Leggett's who had been drinking with him just before he attacked Sarah Jane. Leggett had showed him a knife and said that he was going home to "rip up" his wife. Further evidence was given by Professor Hugh Galt and Doctor James Devon, both of whom had examined Leggett and found no trace of insanity.

In the event the jury took just five minutes to decide that Leggett was sane and guilty as charged.

NAME	Patrick Leggett
AGE AT EXECUTION	30
DATE OF EXECUTION	Wednesday, 12th November, 1902
PLACE OF EXECUTION	Duke Street, Glasgow
HANGMAN	William Billington
ASSISTANT	Not known
DATE OF TRIAL	22nd October, 1902
LOCATION OF TRIAL	Glasgow
PRESIDING JUDGE	Lord Justice Traynor
PROSECUTION COUNSEL	T.C. Guy, A.V. Lee
DEFENCE COUNSEL	D.P. Fleming
NUMBER OF VICTIMS	1

VICTIMS DETAILS	
NAME	Sarah Jane Leggett
AGE	27
DATE OF MURDER	Saturday, 13th September, 1902
PLACE OF MURDER	93 Wylie's Back Land, Whiteinch, Glasgow
METHOD OF KILLING	Stabbed
RELATIONSHIP TO KILLER	Wife

THE CATALOGUE OF injuries perpetrated by Harry Mack on Esther Bedford, was appalling. The couple had lived together since June and to begin with they seemed to be comfortable. Then, in August 1902, the violence began.

On Saturday August 2nd, Mrs Haigh, the landlady, heard noises coming from the bedroom. Upon going to see what the trouble was, she found Mack dragging Esther about the room by her hair. He also hit her in the face and kicked her.

Less than a week later, on August 8th, Mack complained to Mrs Haigh that all Esther had given him for his dinner was potatoes. He then went into the kitchen where Esther was, struck her in the face and kicked her again.

On August 9th, Esther was asleep. Mack told a fellow lodger that he would wake her and proceeded to do so by kicking her. Later that night, Mack hit her in the face with a shovel.

On Monday August 11th, Mrs Haigh heard screams coming from Mack's room and there she found Esther on the bed, her face a mass of scalded tissue. Mack had thrown a kettle of boiling water at her and then stormed out. He returned at 9.00pm, kicked Esther and then hit her in the face so that her blisters burst. He then went back out, returned at midnight and kicked Esther in the stomach.

Esther was in great pain overnight and early the following morning, the doctor and the police were called. Esther was taken to hospital and Mack taken into custody. Esther's bladder had been ruptured and it was plain that she was not going to survive. On August 14th, her deposition was taken, in which she denied that Mack had ever kicked her! She added that the scalding incident was an accident and blamed herself for all her injuries. She died the following day.

At Henry Mack's trial, evidence was given by Doctor Monteith, and others, that there was not the extensive bruising they would have expected to find if the catalogue of assaults was true. The defence held, therefore, that the descriptions of the attacks had been exaggerated.

The judge was fair in his summing up, informing the jury that they must be

NAME	Henry McWiggins (Harry Mack)
AGE AT EXECUTION	29
DATE OF EXECUTION	Tuesday, 2nd December, 1902
PLACE OF EXECUTION	Manchester
HANGMAN	William Billington
ASSISTANT	Henry Pierrepoint
DATE OF TRIAL	14th November – 15th November, 1902
LOCATION OF TRIAL	Manchester
PRESIDING JUDGE	Mister Justice Jelf
PROSECUTION COUNSEL	Mister Sutton, Mister Pope
DEFENCE COUNSEL	Gilbert Jordan
NUMBER OF VICTIMS	1

VICTIMS DETAILS	
NAME	Esther Elizabeth Bedford (Died Friday, 15th August)
AGE	32
DATE OF MURDER	Tuesday, 12th August, 1902
PLACE OF MURDER	22 Hopwood Street, Oldham
METHOD OF KILLING	Battered
RELATIONSHIP TO KILLER	Girlfriend

satisfied that there was a great deal of violence if they were to return a verdict of guilty. Failing that, they would have to acquit the prisoner as the verdict must be murder, or nothing. It took the jury just 20 minutes to decide that it was murder.

On the morning of his execution, the condemned man admitted that Harry Mack was not his proper name. At the time, the real name was not revealed but prison records show that Henry or Harry Mack was Henry McWiggins.

WILLIAM CHAMBERS MARRIED Emily Oakley in 1892, but the marriage was not a happy one. Emily put up with William's ill-treatment for almost 10 years before she finally left him. They did get back together for a short time, but finally split in early September 1902, when Emily returned to live at her mother's house in Eversholt.

To underline the fact that the marriage was over, Emily took legal advice and discussed taking out a separation order. On September 22nd, Chambers heard from his wife's solicitor, pointing out that he had to make his wife an allowance or an order for maintenance would be taken out. Chambers replied that he would not pay her one penny.

At 7.00pm on September 23rd, Emily Chambers, her mother Mary Oakley and her married sister, Mrs Hazell, together with her daughter, were sitting in Mrs Oakley's front room. Suddenly Chambers burst in through the back door, carrying a double-barrelled shotgun. Without speaking he brought the gun to bear on Mary Oakley and shot her through the neck. The shot shattered her spinal cord, killing her instantly. Turning, he aimed the weapon at his wife, and fired the second barrel at her. Emily was hit in the lower face and neck. She was dead within a few minutes.

Chambers now had to reload and Mrs Hazell took this opportunity to flee from the room, taking her daughter with her. Thinking that Chambers might be right behind her, she spent some moments holding shut the door to the room where her mother and sister lay. Then, when she felt sure that it was safe, Mrs Hazell ran out of the house.

William Chambers had achieved what he had set out to do and was not interested in pursuing his sister-in-law. Leaving by the back door he escaped across some allotments where he stopped, turned the gun upon himself and fired into his face. The shot blew away part of his jaw but did not even render him unconscious, let alone kill him. Dropping the gun, he staggered off to the nearest public house where he managed to mumble that he wanted a brandy. The wounds were obvious to all and the landlord, feeling that the police might well wish to talk to this man, took

NAME	William Chambers
AGE AT EXECUTION	47
DATE OF EXECUTION	Thursday, 4th December, 1902
PLACE OF EXECUTION	Bedford
HANGMAN	William Billington
ASSISTANT	Thomas Henry Scott
DATE OF TRIAL	14th November, 1902
LOCATION OF TRIAL	Bedford
PRESIDING JUDGE	Lord Chief Justice, Lord Alverstone
PROSECUTION COUNSEL	C. Lacey-Smith, G.A. Bonner
DEFENCE COUNSEL	Charles Stimson
NUMBER OF VICTIMS	2

VICTIMS DETAILS	
NAME	Emily Chambers, Mary Oakley
AGE	Not known
DATE OF MURDER	Tuesday, 23rd September, 1902
PLACE OF MURDER	Eversholt, near Woburn
METHOD OF KILLING	Shot; shot
RELATIONSHIP TO KILLER	Wife; mother-in-law

Chambers into his back room where he kept him talking until the authorities arrived.

Mrs Hazell was the prime witness at the trial of William Chambers. He claimed to have no memory of the events and the defence cited this as evidence of his insanity. Found guilty, the law made sure that William Chambers had recovered sufficiently from his injuries before he kept an appointment in the execution cell at Bedford.

FOR CLOSE ON 15 years, Thomas Barrow and Emily Coates, had lived together as man and wife at 17 Red Lion Street, Wapping, even though she was also his stepdaughter. Towards the end of that time, the arguments between the two became more and more frequent and when Barrow began using physical violence towards Emily, she decided it was time to move out. Had Emily simply left Barrow, the matter might have been left to rest but she chose instead to serve him with a warrant for assaulting her. This was presented to Barrow on Thursday, October 16th, and had to be answered by Saturday 18th.

On the Friday, Barrow went around to Emily's lodgings and demanded to see her. When she refused to talk to him, and the door was slammed in his face, Barrow crouched down and shouted through the letterbox that she would hear something more of him before noon the following day. It was a threat that Barrow was to make good with devastating effect.

The following morning, as Emily set off for work, a figure ran up behind her – it was Barrow. Once he reached Emily he drew out a knife and stabbed her five times. One wound penetrated her heart and Emily died instantly. When he was arrested, Barrow would only say: "This will end it all; now all I want is a rope round my neck."

At the subsequent trial, Doctor Scott, the medical officer of Brixton prison where Barrow had been held, gave evidence that Barrow had complained to him of suffering from pains in the head. He had suffered from sunstroke whilst he had been serving in the navy and had once attempted suicide by charcoal suffocation. Barrow claimed therefore that he was temporarily irresponsible at the time of the killing and so could not be guilty of murder. The jury did not even bother to leave the box before making it clear that they disagreed.

NAME Thomas Fairclough Barrow
AGE AT EXECUTION 49
DATE OF EXECUTION Tuesday, 9th December, 1902
PLACE OF EXECUTION Pentonville
HANGMAN William Billington
ASSISTANT John Billington
DATE OF TRIAL 19th November, 1902
LOCATION OF TRIAL Old Bailey
PRESIDING JUDGE Mister Justice Bigham
PROSECUTION COUNSEL Richard D. Muir, Arthur Gill
DEFENCE COUNSEL Mister Biron
NUMBER OF VICTIMS 1

VICTIMS DETAILS
NAME Emily Coates
AGE 32
DATE OF MURDER Saturday, 18th October, 1902
PLACE OF MURDER Glamis Road, Shadwell
METHOD OF KILLING Stabbed
RELATIONSHIP TO KILLER Stepdaughter/girlfriend

JEREMIAH CALLAGHAN AND Hannah Shea had lived together for a number of years and had four children. Callaghan led a precarious life, seldom working and as a result, lived in a lodging house in Tredegar, whilst Hannah and the children stayed at the workhouse. They still met up regularly but the separation was telling on Callaghan, who had come to believe that his wife was seeing other men.

On October 4th, Hannah and the children left the workhouse to walk to Tredegar in order to meet up with Callaghan who was now working as a labourer for a stone mason. Upon her arrival she sent her son, also named Jeremiah, to tell his father that they would all meet when he had finished work. Whilst she was waiting, Hannah visited one or two public houses.

When they did finally meet, Callaghan accused Hannah of drinking, a claim which she denied. He did not believe her and threw her to the ground. They later patched up their differences and Callaghan met up with Hannah at yet another public house where several pints of beer were consumed.

At 6.00pm, Callaghan, Hannah and the children left Tredegar to walk back to the workhouse. By this time, Callaghan was very much the worse for drink and on a steep path that leads out of Tredegar, he fell down twice. Hannah stayed with him as the children walked on and eventually, with some difficulty, they approached the workhouse.

At this point, Jane Hannam, a friend of Hannah's, greeted the party. As they talked, Callaghan, without any warning, leapt forward, pushed Hannah against a wall pulled a knife from his pocket, and drew the blade across her throat. Hannah managed to break away from him and run back down the hill a little way where she collapsed and died. Callaghan showed no interest in what was happening, going into the workhouse where he was seen smoking a pipe and dancing in the courtyard.

At his trial, Callaghan's defence was that he did not know what he was doing at the time and must have been suffering from delirium tremens. It was said that his condition could be described as 'mixed drunk' where one

NAME	Jeremiah Callaghan
AGE AT EXECUTION	42
DATE OF EXECUTION	Friday, 12th December, 1902
PLACE OF EXECUTION	Usk
HANGMAN	William Billington
ASSISTANT	John Billington
DATE OF TRIAL	22nd November, 1902
LOCATION OF TRIAL	Monmouth
PRESIDING JUDGE	Mister John Forbes K.C.
PROSECUTION COUNSEL	J.R.V. Marchant, St John G. Micklethwait
DEFENCE COUNSEL	Harold Hardy
NUMBER OF VICTIMS	1

VICTIMS DETAILS	
NAME	Hannah Shea
AGE	38
DATE OF MURDER	Saturday, 4th October, 1902
PLACE OF MURDER	Near Bedwelty Workhouse, Tredegar
METHOD OF KILLING	Cut throat
RELATIONSHIP TO KILLER	Girlfriend

moment he would be fully aware of what was going on about him and the next would be totally oblivious. Callaghan himself chose to make a statement in which he said his first memory was when he woke up in prison.

To counter this, Doctor Boulton from Cardiff jail was called. He had known Callaghan since 1887, and argued that he had always been of sound mind and so fully aware of what he was doing. The jury chose to agree with Doctor Boulton's testimony.

1902

SAMUEL AND ISABELLA Walton had been married for nine years and had one child, a daughter. They had in fact parted very soon after the wedding had taken place but after some discussion, had decided to try again to make the relationship work. Unfortunately, this second attempt would also end in failure.

On August 23rd, 1902, after an argument, Samuel turned his wife and young child out onto the streets, late at night. The only place Isabella could think of going was to her mother's house, which she duly did. Here she thought long and hard about her relationship with her husband and finally took the decision to end the marriage once and for all. She took legal advice and chose to take out a separation order on the grounds of Samuel's persistent cruelty.

It was on September 4th that Isabella was granted custody of her child and a maintenance order of 10/- a week against Samuel. The first payment was due to be made one week later, on September 11th. Samuel did not react kindly to this state of affairs.

On September 9th, Samuel sold all his furniture and left home. The following day, the day before the first payment should have been made, Samuel purchased a revolver and a box of cartridges. Leaving friends in no doubt as to his intentions, he showed them the gun and said: "I have my first ten shillings to pay tomorrow and I will likely pay it with this."

Thursday, September 11th came and Samuel turned up at his mother-in-law's house. When the door was opened to him, by Mrs Young, he said he had come to pay the first 10/- and would require a receipt for it. As Mrs Young was going upstairs to fetch some writing paper, Samuel drew out his revolver and shot her. She died instantly.

Entering the house, Samuel then found his wife and child and shot them both. Isabella managed to escape from the house but she had been hit three times and would die from her injuries on September 18th. Meanwhile, Samuel went upstairs, cut his own throat and lay on a bed, cradling his dying child. It was in this position that he was found by the police, the child dying later that same day.

NAME	Samuel Thomas Walton
AGE AT EXECUTION	31
DATE OF EXECUTION	Tuesday, 16th December, 1902
PLACE OF EXECUTION	Durham
HANGMAN	William Billington
ASSISTANT	John Billington
DATE OF TRIAL	24th November, 1902
LOCATION OF TRIAL	Durham
PRESIDING JUDGE	Mister Justice Channell
PROSECUTION COUNSEL	Hans Hamilton, Mitchell Innes
DEFENCE COUNSEL	F.L. Mortimer
NUMBER OF VICTIMS	3

VICTIMS' DETAILS

NAME	Isabella Walton (Died Thursday, 18th September)
AGE	49
DATE OF MURDER	Thursday, 11th September, 1902
PLACE OF MURDER	Middleton Moor, Spennymoor
METHOD OF KILLING	Shot
RELATIONSHIP TO KILLER	Wife

NAME	Nora Walton; Mrs Young
AGE	10 months; 58
DATE OF MURDER	Thursday, 11th September, 1902
PLACE OF MURDER	Middleton Moor, Spennymoor
METHOD OF KILLING	Shot; shot
RELATIONSHIP TO KILLER	Daughter; mother-in-law

Samuel was rushed to hospital where his life was saved, but only for him to be eventually sentenced to death for the triple killing.

MARY STEWART HAD enjoyed her time at her uncle's house but it was now time, at 7.30pm, to make her way home. Luckily, her own home was only about 10 minutes away if she went by the footpath across the fields and it was not felt therefore that she needed an escort, even if she was only seven years of age.

Mary took her time walking home and at some time before eight, whilst she was still on the pathway, a man was seen to catch up with her, talk to her briefly and then take her by the hand. The two then walked off together, still moving in the direction of Mary's home. Unfortunately, Mary never did make it home that night and a search was organised. It was not until Monday, August 18th, that her body was discovered about 150 yards off the footpath, in a brickyard. The child had been cut, raped and then strangled. Investigations soon showed that there was a certain amount of circumstantial evidence against a labourer named Thomas Nicholson.

It was known that Nicholson was in the neighbourhood of the pathway at around 8.00pm on the night of the murder. He was not actually identified as the man who had been seen with Mary but he had been seen in the general vicinity, so could well have been the man who spoke to the child. It was also shown that he had been drinking that night and was undoubtedly rather inebriated. Finally, he had been seen, standing at the door of his house, fully dressed, at 3.00am on the morning after the murder, looking rather nervous and worried.

Nicholson was asked to account for his movements after 6.00pm on August 16th. He said that he had been drinking in the Mason's Arms and had only left at closing time. When this alibi was checked, it was found that he had indeed been in the pub, but a number of other patrons swore that he had left at around 6.30pm. The police now checked Nicholson's home and found the trousers he had been wearing at the time in question. There were bloodstains on these and also on Nicholson's shirt and coat. Finally, a pocket knife was found and this too was bloodstained. With that, Nicholson was charged with the murder of Mary Stewart. He made no reply when

NAME	Thomas Nicholson
AGE AT EXECUTION	24
DATE OF EXECUTION	Tuesday, 16th December, 1902
PLACE OF EXECUTION	Durham
HANGMAN	William Billington
ASSISTANT	John Billington
DATE OF TRIAL	26th November, 1902
LOCATION OF TRIAL	Durham
PRESIDING JUDGE	Mister Justice Channell
PROSECUTION COUNSEL	J.E. Joel, Mister Simey
DEFENCE COUNSEL	Mister Mitchell Innes
NUMBER OF VICTIMS	1

VICTIMS DETAILS	
NAME	Mary Ina Stewart
AGE	7
DATE OF MURDER	Saturday, 16th August, 1902
PLACE OF MURDER	Bill Quay, near Newcastle-upon-Tyne
METHOD OF KILLING	Strangled
RELATIONSHIP TO KILLER	None

charged, merely hanging his head down upon his chest.

The jury at Nicholson's trial believed that the evidence, circumstantial though it was, was enough to convince them that Nicholson had indeed been the man who met up with Mary on that pathway and who then took her into the brickyard where he violated and then murdered her. They had no trouble in returning a guilty verdict.

WILLIAM AND ELIZABETH Brown seemed like an ordinary, average couple. Married for 22 years, they had had their arguments, but these had always been resolved.

On the night of Elizabeth's death, the Browns were seen in two public houses in Mortlake. There seemed to be no problems in the first but in the second pub they were heard arguing. Nevertheless, they returned home together and it seemed that one more marital tiff had been glossed over.

The following morning, William Brown went to a neighbour's house and announced that his wife was dead. Upon investigating, the neighbour discovered Elizabeth's body at the foot of the stairs. She had suffered a terrible beating. The police were called and William was arrested and charged with murder. Brown first claimed that he was innocent and that Elizabeth had fallen down the stairs but later he made a statement admitting that he had killed his wife.

At his trial, Brown withdrew his confession and said that he could not recall ever making such a statement. His story now was that his wife must have been attacked outside the house. She had then managed to drag herself home and was most probably trying to get upstairs to seek his assistance when she succumbed to her injuries. The story was proved to be a tissue of lies.

One of the prosecution witnesses was a small boy named Cox. He had been playing in the street when the Browns returned home from the pub and very soon afterwards, he had heard a woman's voice cry: "Murder!" Cox walked to the window of the Brown's residence and looked in whereupon he saw William repeatedly kicking his wife in the head and body. Cox then ran to a neighbour's house to summon help. The neighbour did return with Cox and tried to gain entrance to the house but then heard a voice, which may have been Elizabeth's, saying that she didn't want to see anyone. No further attempts to gain entry were made.

Medical evidence was then called to catalogue the injuries that Elizabeth had received. Her face, head and body were masses of bruises. Her breastbone was

NAME	William Brown
AGE AT EXECUTION	42
DATE OF EXECUTION	Tuesday, 16th December, 1902
PLACE OF EXECUTION	Wandsworth
HANGMAN	Henry Pierrepoint
ASSISTANT	John Ellis
DATE OF TRIAL	26th November, 1902
LOCATION OF TRIAL	Old Bailey
PRESIDING JUDGE	Mister Justice Bigham
PROSECUTION COUNSEL	Mister Biron, R.B. Murphy
DEFENCE COUNSEL	Percival Hughes, Paul Methven
NUMBER OF VICTIMS	1

VICTIMS DETAILS	
NAME	Elizabeth Brown
AGE	Not known
DATE OF MURDER	November, 1902
PLACE OF MURDER	Mortlake
METHOD OF KILLING	Battered
RELATIONSHIP TO KILLER	Wife

broken in two separate places and 14 ribs were also shattered. In the opinion of the doctors, it was impossible for Elizabeth to have been attacked outside as they felt she could not have moved after being attacked in such a fashion.

William Brown entered the witness box and denied that he had murdered his wife. He still held to the story that she must have been attacked outside and added that if he had confessed to the police, he must have done so in the excitement of the moment.

The jury took just an hour to decide that Brown was guilty. Asked if he had anything to say, he repeated that he was innocent of the charge.

WILLIAM JAMES BOLTON was a married man, though that didn't stop him paying attention to Jane Allen. They became lovers and although Mrs Bolton then left her husband, she was not prepared to simply let the matter rest.

On October 18th, Bolton arrived at Jane's house at about 11.00pm, only to be told that she thought it would be better if he didn't call there any more. His wife had been around and had made a scene. Nevertheless, Bolton was allowed to stay the night. At approximately 11.30pm, Bolton and Jane went upstairs to bed and Bolton asked the lodger, Mrs Butterick, if she would give him a call at 6.50am.

Mrs Butterick slept beyond 6.50am and when she did wake, at 8.30am, it was to the sound of Jane Allen repeating the phrase: "Oh Bill, don't." Mrs Butterick ran upstairs where she found Jane lying on the bed, bleeding from a number of stab wounds. William Bolton was also bleeding from his throat and held a knife in his right hand. Mrs Butterick ran off to fetch the police.

About half and hour later, two police constables, Burton and Shaw, entered the house. As they did, they were met by Bolton coming down the stairs. Constable Burton asked Bolton what he had done and Bolton replied that he did not know. Jane's body was discovered upstairs and Bolton taken to hospital. There he announced to Constable Shaw that he had no idea what had made him do it. By Monday, October 20th, Bolton had recovered enough to be charged with murder.

At his trial, Bolton came up with a new variation on his defence. In the first place, Doctor Lamb gave evidence that there were three wounds on Jane's body and that these could not possibly have been self-inflicted. This meant that Bolton could not deny stabbing her, but was it a case of murder? Bolton said that the first he knew of the crime was waking up to the sound of a woman's voice saying: "Oh Bill, are you mad? What are you doing?" It was only then that he saw that he had stabbed Jane, obviously whilst he had been asleep. When he realised what he had done he had tried to cut his own throat but she had stopped him.

NAME	William James Bolton
AGE AT EXECUTION	44
DATE OF EXECUTION	Tuesday, 23rd December, 1902
PLACE OF EXECUTION	Hull
HANGMAN	William Billington
ASSISTANT	John Billington
DATE OF TRIAL	2nd December, 1902
LOCATION OF TRIAL	York
PRESIDING JUDGE	Mister Justice Channell
PROSECUTION COUNSEL	H.T. Kemp, Brent Grotrian
DEFENCE COUNSEL	F.L. Mortimer
NUMBER OF VICTIMS	1

VICTIMS DETAILS	
NAME	Jane Elizabeth Allen
AGE	Not known
DATE OF MURDER	Saturday, 18th October, 1902
PLACE OF MURDER	10 Andrew Marvel Terrace, Hull
METHOD OF KILLING	Stabbed
RELATIONSHIP TO KILLER	Girlfriend

Mister Mortimer, the defence barrister, tried to persuade the jury that if Bolton had killed in his sleep then he could have had no intention to kill and therefore was only guilty of manslaughter. In his summing up, the learned judge said that in his opinion, manslaughter was not an option and that Bolton was guilty of murder, or nothing. Given those two choices, the jury did not even bother to leave the box before deciding that Bolton was guilty of murder and he was hanged two days before Christmas.

GEORGE PLACE, a miner, seemed to have fallen on his feet. In addition to finding some fine lodgings with Eliza Chetwynd, he had started to court her daughter, also named Eliza, and she had responded. One thing led to another and after about a year of lodging with the Chetwynds, George and the younger Eliza were living together as man and wife and she found herself pregnant.

When the child, a boy, was born on August 13th, his mother thought that it might be prudent, in order to safeguard her position, to take out a bastardy order against George. To this, George took great exception. He stormed out of the house on August 21st, and did not return for two days. Eliza, it seems, had made the right decision.

On August 23rd, George announced quite openly, in a public house, that he was going to pay out all three of the Chetwynds, and to emphasise the point, brandished a revolver he had recently purchased.

In the early hours of the following morning, Place went to the room where Eliza, her mother, and the child were sleeping, and calmly shot all three of them. The elder Eliza and the still unnamed child died instantly, but the younger Eliza lived for a couple of hours. Joseph Chetwynd, Eliza's brother, heard the three shots and then saw Place come from the bedroom and simply say: "They're all done. It's all over."

Another brother, Jesse, then came running out of his room whereupon Place calmly stretched out the hand which still held the revolver and asked him to put a bullet into him. Jesse reached out to take the weapon but Place then drew back his hand and decided to hold on to the gun until the police arrived.

Place said that it had been his intention to commit suicide after he had killed the Chetwynds, but had changed his mind afterwards. No doubt after killing three members of the family, Place might well have thought that Jesse Chetwynd could have carried out his request.

Place's defence was one of insanity. He had, after all, been kind to Eliza and the bastardy order must have unhinged his mind. However, prison doctors were called to refute this and Place was found guilty of murder.

NAME	George Place
AGE AT EXECUTION	28
DATE OF EXECUTION	Thursday, 30th December, 1902
PLACE OF EXECUTION	Warwick
HANGMAN	Henry Pierrepoint
ASSISTANT	John Ellis
DATE OF TRIAL	8th December, 1902
LOCATION OF TRIAL	Warwick
PRESIDING JUDGE	Lord Chief Justice, Lord Alverstone
PROSECUTION COUNSEL	Mister Pritchett, C.F. Lloyd
DEFENCE COUNSEL	Horace Rowlands
NUMBER OF VICTIMS	3

VICTIMS DETAILS

NAME	Eliza Chetwynd; Eliza Chetwynd
AGE	60; 20
DATE OF MURDER	Sunday, 24th August, 1902
PLACE OF MURDER	Baddesley Ensor
METHOD OF KILLING	Shot; shot
RELATIONSHIP TO KILLER	None; girlfriend

NAME	Unnamed Child
AGE	11 days
DATE OF MURDER	Sunday, 24th August, 1902
PLACE OF MURDER	Baddesley Ensor
METHOD OF KILLING	Shot
RELATIONSHIP TO KILLER	Son

1902

FOR SOME TIME, Amelia Sach had run a home for unmarried mothers in East Finchley. There, for a fee, she would attend the young women when they gave birth and would later help to find a suitable foster home for the infant. Sometimes though it was rather difficult to find a good home and it was then that her partner, Annie Walters from Islington, proved to be useful.

Annie Walters was older than Amelia. Rather simple minded, she had a tried-and-tested method of dealing with unwanted children. She would administer a few drops of chlorodyne, a morphine-based drug, and in due course the babies would die from asphyxia. On the occasions that this method did not result in death, Annie would help things along by smothering the child.

In August 1903, a Miss Galley gave birth to a boy at Sach's establishment. Sach told the new mother that she had a home for the child and would require a fee of £30, a considerable sum in 1903.

The police had for some time been suspicious of the activities of the two women and so, on November 18th, when Walters was seen to leave her lodgings with a small bundle, she was followed. She was trailed to South Kensington where she was stopped at the District Railway Station. When the bundle was examined it was found to contain the dead body of Miss Galley's child. The medical examination showed that asphyxia was the cause of death. There was a bruise on the back of the boy's head, suggesting that death may have been caused by extreme pressure over the face.

Walter's story was that she had been asked to take the child to Kensington where she would be met by a potential foster mother. The child had proved difficult and so she had administered two drops of chlorodyne. She had not known that the child was dead until she was stopped by the police.

For her part, Amelia Sach denied that she had ever given children to Walters. When her home was searched, however, over 300 articles of baby clothing were found, suggesting that there may have been many more victims. In all, perhaps 20 deaths could be put at the door of Walters and Sach.

NAME	Amelia Sach; Annie Walters
AGE AT EXECUTION	29; 54
DATE OF EXECUTION	Tuesday, 3rd February, 1903
PLACE OF EXECUTION	Holloway; Holloway
HANGMAN	William Billington
ASSISTANT	Henry Pierrepoint
DATE OF TRIAL	15th January – 16th January, 1903
LOCATION OF TRIAL	Old Bailey
PRESIDING JUDGE	Mister Justice Darling
PROSECUTION COUNSEL	Charles Mathews, Mister Bodkin
DEFENCE COUNSEL	Mister Leycester, Guy Stephenson
NUMBER OF VICTIMS	1 (possibly as many as 20)

VICTIMS DETAILS	
NAME	Galley (A male infant)
AGE	3 months
DATE OF MURDER	circa Tuesday, 18th November, 1902
PLACE OF MURDER	Islington
METHOD OF KILLING	Poisoned/asphyxiated
RELATIONSHIP TO KILLER	None; none

The only hope for the two women could have been that they might have escaped with a verdict of manslaughter. However, in his summing up, the judge stated that the verdict had to be one of murder, or nothing at all. The jury took 40 minutes to decide that it was indeed murder. Before sentence was passed, both women again reaffirmed their innocence. On February 3rd, Annie Walters and Amelia Sach became the first women to be executed at Holloway.

WILLIAM HUGHES HAD been a soldier serving in India, but had returned to England in 1890. Two years later he married Jane Hannah Williams, his first cousin, and for a time at least they were very happy together, she bearing him three children, two boys and a girl.

In 1901, one of the children died and things changed between William and his wife. Soon afterwards William left his family, causing Jane to apply to the Parish Council for relief, which was granted on December 31st, 1901. In due course, Jane was accused of misconduct by the council officials and the relief was suspended. Jane was not too concerned, though, as she had taken work as a housekeeper for Thomas Maddocks, a widower who had five children of his own. Things were not going so well for William, however. In August 1902 he was sentenced to three months' imprisonment for deserting his family, not being released until November 6th.

A few days after he got out of jail, William bumped into his wife, who asked him what he intended to do about supporting his children. William replied that they were now in the workhouse and as far as he was concerned, they could stay there. Shortly after this, on November 10th, William borrowed a shotgun and two cartridges from his brother-in-law and travelled to Maddocks's house. He intended to kill his wife and Maddocks, whom he believed was having an affair with her.

Thomas Maddocks junior, aged 11, slept in the same room as Jane, as indeed did all the children. When a knock came to the door, she assumed it was Thomas's father and so asked the boy to open the door. She was surprised to find that the visitor was her estranged husband, so she pulled a skirt over her night-dress and went downstairs to talk to him. William demanded to know where Maddocks was and having been told that he was at work, pulled the trigger and fired both barrels into his wife.

At 3.25am the following morning, William Hughes gave himself up to Constable Thomas Pryce Rees. When the police went to the scene of the crime, they found that the shots had been fired from such close range that

NAME	William Hughes
AGE AT EXECUTION	42
DATE OF EXECUTION	Tuesday, 17th February, 1903
PLACE OF EXECUTION	Ruthin
HANGMAN	William Billington
ASSISTANT	John Billington
DATE OF TRIAL	29th January, 1903
LOCATION OF TRIAL	Ruthin
PRESIDING JUDGE	Mister Justice Bruce
PROSECUTION COUNSEL	D.A.V. Colt Williams, Trevor F. Lloyd
DEFENCE COUNSEL	E. Jones Griffiths M.P., E. Owen Roberts
NUMBER OF VICTIMS	1

VICTIMS DETAILS	
NAME	Jane Hannah Hughes
AGE	32
DATE OF MURDER	Monday, 10th November, 1902
PLACE OF MURDER	Old Rhosrobin, Wrexham
METHOD OF KILLING	Shot
RELATIONSHIP TO KILLER	Wife

Jane's clothing had caught fire and her body was slightly charred.

Tried at Ruthin and sentenced to death, William's last request was for a photograph of himself and his family looking happy. The request was granted.

JOHN WILLIAM DARBY ran a grocery from 22 Wyndham Road, Camberwell and had advertised the business for sale. He was therefore more than pleased when a young man named Edgar Edwards called on him and said he was interested in purchasing it.

The time came when the prospective buyer wished to see the books. John Darby started to get the various financial items together whilst his wife, carrying their infant daughter in her arms, showed Mister Edwards upstairs to the living quarters. Once he was alone with the young woman, Edwards took a large sash weight from a rolled-up newspaper and battered her to death. When Mister Darby arrived with the shop accounts, he too was bludgeoned to death. Finally, the crying child was strangled into silence. In the space of a few minutes, Edgar Edwards had murdered three people.

There was little doubt that the crime had been premeditated. In late November, Edwards had told an ex-girlfriend, Sarah Summers, that he was negotiating to buy a small business. A couple of days later he had called on another friend, a gentleman named Goodwin, and asked him if he and his wife would like to run a shop for him.

They agreed terms and Mister Goodwin even bought a sash weight for Edwards, which the latter said he would need to wedge open a door at the shop.

On the day of the murders, Edwards had asked Mrs Goodwin to pawn his umbrella for him. For this Edwards received just 1/6d and this was probably all the money he had on him when he visited the Darbys. Yet later that same day he was to show a receipt for £30 which he claimed was part payment on the shop, given to him by John Darby.

The Darbys had certainly been alive at some time on December 1st. A baker named Newby had delivered bread at 8.45am and another tradesman, Whittingham, had seen John Darby at 11.00am. This, in fact, was the last time that any of the Darby family were seen by anyone other than their killer.

Edwards had arranged to meet the Goodwins at the corner of Wyndham Road at 11.30am. In fact, at that precise time he was busy hiding the three bodies in an upstairs

NAME	Edgar Owen (Edwards)
AGE AT EXECUTION	44
DATE OF EXECUTION	Tuesday, 3rd March, 1903
PLACE OF EXECUTION	Wandsworth
HANGMAN	William Billington
ASSISTANT	Henry Pierrepoint
DATE OF TRIAL	12th February – 13th February, 1903
LOCATION OF TRIAL	Old Bailey
PRESIDING JUDGE	Mister Justice Wright
PROSECUTION COUNSEL	Richard D. Muir, Arthur Gill
DEFENCE COUNSEL	Percival Hughes, Paul Methven
NUMBER OF VICTIMS	3

VICTIMS DETAILS

NAME	John William Darby; Beatrice Darby; Ethel Darby
AGE	Not known; 25; 10 weeks
DATE OF MURDER	Monday, 1st December, 1902
PLACE OF MURDER	22 Wyndham Road, Camberwell, London
METHOD OF KILLING	Battered; battered; strangled
RELATIONSHIP TO KILLER	None; none; none

room, which he then locked. This made him a little late for his meeting with the Goodwins and Edwards only turned up a few minutes after noon. The three then all went to the shop at number 22, which Edwards opened with a key. He showed the Goodwins around but told them they would have to stay out of the one locked room as that was where some of the Darby's furniture and belongings were being stored until they could be collected. Later that same day, Edwards began pawning some of the Darby's belongings, including a gold watch and chain, for which he received £7.

Edwards remained in the shop with the Goodwins until December 10th. In the meantime, though, this cold-blooded killer was putting other plans into action. On December 3rd, Edwards saw an estate agent and gave a couple of false references, one of which was in the name of William Darby. Using these, Edwards took a lease on 89 Church Road, Leyton. On the same day, Mrs Baldwin, Beatrice's sister called at the shop. Edwards told her that the family were staying with friends and would be back at any time. She chose not to wait.

On December 5th, Edwards hired a pony and trap and began moving furniture from Wyndham Road to Church Road. He was also seen moving some sacks, and a trunk. Finally, on December 10th, all the items Edwards wanted had been moved and he left Wyndham Road, never to return. Six days after this a neighbour in Church Road, Sophia Frear, saw Edwards digging a large hole in the garden of number 89. By the following morning the hole had been filled in and the soil levelled off. Edwards had, it seemed, gotten away with three murders and gained quite a few pounds from his venture. It had all been so very easy. Surely it would be just as easy if he repeated the exercise a second time?

On December 23rd, John Garland, another grocer who also had a business for sale, was invited to Church Road to discuss terms. After some discussion, Garland turned to leave and was immediately struck from behind by means of a heavy sash weight. A number of blows rained down on John Garland but somehow he managed to escape and raise the alarm. Edgar Edwards was arrested for assault.

The first thing that puzzled the police was the discovery of not one but two sash weights, both stained with blood. One had obviously been used on John Garland, but what about the other? Had Edwards used the same weight on Garland as he had on the Darbys, he might conceivably have escaped a murder charge.

The police searched the premises at Church Road and found a number of pawn tickets in various names, including that of Darby. Soon they were interviewing Mrs Baldwin, who told them of her visit to her brother-in-law's shop on December 3rd and the man she found there. It was only a matter of time before news of the mysterious hole in the garden was mentioned and upon digging down, officers found the dismembered bodies of John William Darby and his family.

Until now, Edwards had demonstrated that was a cool and calculating individual but after his arrest, he attempted to show he was insane. At his trial he refused to plead, telling the clerk of the court that he had no business in asking him such a question. Eventually a not guilty plea was entered but Edwards seemed to treat the entire proceedings as one huge joke, often bursting into laughter.

Only one defence witness was called, an uncle who revealed that the prisoner's real name was Edgar Owen and stating that there were a number of instances of insanity in the family. He added that Edgar had claimed to have fallen from some scaffolding some years before and had sustained a severe head injury as a result. There was also an attempt to show that the very ferocity of the crime tended to demonstrate insanity.

After the guilty verdict was announced Edwards again burst into laughter. Asked if he had anything to say he replied: "No, get on with it, as quick as you like" and as the dread words of the death sentence were spoken, Edwards observed that it was just like being on the stage.

Edwards was apparently a well-behaved prisoner but his last words, spoken to the prison chaplain, were reported to be: "I've been looking forward to this."

SAMUEL SMITH, A native of Devon and a sailor by trade, had first met Lucy Lingard when he used to call at her home at 3 Taylor's Terrace, Hope Street, to have his meals with her and her husband John. A friendship developed between Samuel and Lucy until finally she left her husband and, taking her four children with her, moved in with Samuel at Fourth Terrace. Samuel, of course, spent long periods away at sea, but when he did return, the idyllic life Lucy might have expected did not materialise, for Samuel Smith had a very short temper.

On November 18th, Samuel returned home and that evening spent time in the local pub, with Lucy. They left early, taking a quart of beer home with them, but upon getting into their house, Samuel, without warning, struck out, blackening Lucy's eye. She immediately went to bed, thinking perhaps that it would be better if she simply stayed out of his way. Not long after this, two neighbours, Mrs Martin and Mrs Summerfield, paid a visit and Lucy took this opportunity to go back downstairs. The three women had a long talk, during which Lucy explained how she had received her black eye. This in turn caused the two visitors to chastise Samuel for his behaviour. He apologised and explained that he had just lost his temper.

It was just after 11.00pm when the two neighbours left, but a few minutes later a child's scream rang out. Lily Ward, another neighbour, ran across to Samuel's house and found him standing over Lucy's body. The poor woman had been stabbed 11 times and showed extensive injuries on her arms where she had tried to defend herself from the onslaught.

Put on trial for murder, Samuel tried to put the blame on drink but was found guilty and sentenced to death. In prison awaiting execution, he made a full confession to the chaplain, explaining that it had been a deliberate act. Samuel admitted that he had first stabbed Lucy a number of times and had then thrown the knife into the fireplace.

Lucy, though was not dead. She was writhing on the floor, apparently in agony when, far from offering her assistance, he returned to the fireplace, retrieved the knife

NAME	Samuel Henry Smith
AGE AT EXECUTION	45
DATE OF EXECUTION	Tuesday, 10th March, 1903
PLACE OF EXECUTION	Lincoln
HANGMAN	William Billington
ASSISTANT	John Billington
DATE OF TRIAL	20th February, 1903
LOCATION OF TRIAL	Lincoln
PRESIDING JUDGE	Mister Justice Kennedy
PROSECUTION COUNSEL	Mister Etherington Smith, Mister Lawrance
DEFENCE COUNSEL	Mister Binner
NUMBER OF VICTIMS	1

VICTIMS DETAILS	
NAME	Lucy Margaret Lingard
AGE	33
DATE OF MURDER	Tuesday, 18th November, 1902
PLACE OF MURDER	4 Fourth Terrace, Hope Street, Grimsby
METHOD OF KILLING	Stabbed
RELATIONSHIP TO KILLER	Girlfriend

and attacked her again. To his credit, Samuel also stated that no blame whatsoever attached itself to Lucy. Having made his peace with God, Samuel Smith then took his last walk into the execution chamber.

AT 12.30PM ON October 22nd, 1903, Maud Marsh died at the Crown, Islington. Doctor Stoker, who had attended, refused to issue a death certificate. He had attended another woman who had died displaying identical symptoms. The doctor was convinced that he had witnessed a case of poisoning and decided on a postmortem.

Doctor Stoker was looking for arsenic but only found minute traces of the drug. He therefore sent tissue samples to two of his colleagues who found the arsenic present had been nothing more than impurities in another poison. That other substance was shown to be tartar emetic, an antimony-based poison. A total of 20.12 grains of tartar emetic were found in Maud's remains. Three days after Maud's death, George Chapman was arrested for murder, under his real name of Severiano Antoniovitch Klosowski.

Klosowski had certainly led a chequered life. Born in Poland, he had arrived in England in 1888, and taken employment as a hairdresser's assistant in a shop underneath the White Hart pub at 89 Whitechapel High Street. In 1889, he married Lucy Baderski of Walthamstow and the couple soon had a son. Lucy was rather dismayed when, within a few weeks of the wedding, another woman appeared, having travelled from Poland. She had two young children in tow and claimed to be married to Klosowski. She was sent packing and in 1891, Klosowski, Lucy and their son emigrated to America, where sadly the boy died. Lucy returned to England soon after, to be joined by her husband two weeks later. On May 12th, she gave birth to a daughter. The following year she decided she had finally had enough of her husband's womanising ways and left, taking her daughter with her.

At the end of 1893, Klosowski met up with a woman named Annie Chapman. They lived together until December 1894, during which time Klosowski took to using her name and thereafter became known as George Chapman.

Once the relationship with Annie had ~~ended~~, Chapman needed to find new lodgings. ~~...~~ took a room with John Ward, one of his ~~custo~~mers. One of John Ward's other lodgers

NAME	George Chapman (Severin Klosowski)
AGE AT EXECUTION	37
DATE OF EXECUTION	Tuesday, 7th April, 1903
PLACE OF EXECUTION	Wandsworth
HANGMAN	William Billington
ASSISTANT	Henry Pierrepoint
DATE OF TRIAL	16th March – 19th March, 1903
LOCATION OF TRIAL	Old Bailey
PRESIDING JUDGE	Mister Justice Grantham
PROSECUTION COUNSEL	Mister Sutton, Charles Mathews, Mister Bodkin
DEFENCE COUNSEL	George Elliott, Arthur Hutton, V. Lyons
NUMBER OF VICTIMS	3

VICTIMS DETAILS

NAME	Isabella Mary Spink; Elizabeth Taylor; Maud Eliza Marsh
AGE	19; not known; not known
DATE OF MURDER	Saturday 25th December, 1897; Wednesday, 13th February, 1901; Wednesday, 22nd October, 1902
PLACE OF MURDER	Prince of Wales Pub, Bartholomew Square, Finsbury; Monument Pub, Union St, Islington; Crown Pub, High Street, Islington
METHOD OF KILLING	Poisoned (by antimony)
RELATIONSHIP TO KILLER	Girlfriend; girlfriend; girlfriend

was Isabella Spink who had recently been deserted by her husband, Shadrach. George and Isabella grew close and at one stage, John Ward's wife complained to her husband that she had seen Chapman and Isabella kissing. Chapman pointed out that there was no impropriety as they would soon be married.

In March 1896, Chapman and Isabella moved to Hastings where he opened another shop. It was a great success. Chapman would provide shaves whilst Isabella played the piano for the customer's enjoyment.

Although Chapman found it easy to start up a relationship, he appeared to find it impossible to end one. Whatever the truth of the matter, he may well have already grown tired of Isabella during their stay in Hastings because on April 3rd, 1897, Chapman bought an ounce of tartar emetic from Davidson's chemists. A fatal dose was around 15 grains. The ounce was equivalent to over 400 grains.

In September 1897, Chapman and Isabella returned to London, where he took the lease on the Prince of Wales pub in Bartholomew Square. It was there, on Christmas Day, that Isabella died after a period of illness. The cause of death was given as Phthisis, a consumptive disease.

At Easter, 1898, Chapman decided he needed a new barmaid. The woman who successfully applied for the position was Elizabeth Taylor, known to her friends as Bessie. It was not long before the couple were lovers. There may well have been some gossip over how fast the pair had taken up with each other after Isabella's death, for the new lovers spent a year running The Grapes public house in Bishop's Stortford before returning to London in 1899.

On March 23rd, 1899, Chapman and Bessie moved to the Monument pub in Union Street. It was there, on February 13th, 1901, that Bessie died, again after a period of illness. She had been attended by Doctor Stoker, who gave the cause of her death as intestinal obstruction.

In August of that same year, Maud Marsh advertised for employment and having been interviewed by Chapman, became the next barmaid. George wasted little time. In September they visited her mother and announced that they wished to marry.

In June 1902, Chapman moved to the Crown. The lease on the Monument was just about up when a fire broke out. Chapman and Maud were not there at the time and the cause of the fire was difficult to determine. The insurance company suspected arson and refused to pay compensation. Chapman simply moved down the road and took over the Crown.

No sooner had Chapman moved in than his weakness for an attractive barmaid manifested itself again. Florence Rayner worked behind the bar and Chapman fell for her, asking her to go to America with him. She refused and the following month, left his employment. Chapman had now tired of Maud. It was time for her to go.

The scenario was so very familiar. Maud fell ill and was fussed over by her attentive lover. She did not improve, though, and by the time her sister, Mrs Morris, paid a visit, Maud's condition was very poor indeed.

On Mrs Morris's insistence, Maud was taken into Guy's Hospital where she stayed from July 28th until August 20th. Over that period, Maud slowly recovered but, on her return to the Crown, she fell ill again, dying on October 22nd.

Once Chapman had been arrested, the police began to look into the deaths of Isabella and Bessie. Both bodies were exhumed; Bessie's on November 22nd and Isabella's on December 9th. Both were found to be remarkably well preserved, and the subsequent postmortems showed 3.83 grains of tartar emetic in Isabella and 29.12 grains in Bessie. On December 31st, Chapman was charged with two more murders.

The trial lasted four days. No witnesses were called for the defence, Chapman's counsel instead relying on the fact that there was no apparent motive for the deaths of the three women and that there was no evidence to show that it was Chapman who had administered poison. The jury, though, took just 10 minutes to return a guilty verdict.

Chapman had to be supported by two prison officers as he was taken down to the cells. On April 7th, 1903, he had to be supported again whilst he stood over the trap at Wandsworth.

It has been suggested that Chapman was Jack the Ripper. The only 'evidence' is the fact that Chapman was in Whitechapel in 1888 and that he had once been a barber-surgeon, but it is unlikely that someone who butchered prostitutes would later turn to poison.

A SOLDIER HAS to have a very good reason for staying in bed after reveille has sounded. When Harry Short of the Royal Field Artillery remained in bed on the morning of February 17th he had the best possible excuse: he had been shot dead, a bullet having entered his skull through his chin and smashing on into his brain.

One of the first suspects in the killing was Bombadier William George Hudson. On January 27th, Short had made a complaint against Hudson, as a result of which the latter was court-martialled. Fortunately for him he was acquitted on February 5th, but thereafter a sour atmosphere existed between the two men and Hudson seemed to bear a grudge against his former friend, threatening that he would get even somehow.

Soldiers are known for being fond of a tipple and when Hudson and two friends returned to barracks on the night of February 16th, Hudson for one was very much the worse for drink. He was being rather obstreperous and shouted that he wanted to get Short who had been moved to another room after the court-martial. With some difficulty the two friends managed to undress Hudson and get him into bed. However, shortly afterwards, Hudson was seen going into his storage box and bringing something out. When a comrade asked him what he was doing, Hudson replied that he was just getting his supper.

The next morning, Short was found dead in his bed. Three men now came forward to say that they had been woken in the early hours by a loud report but had seen nothing in the darkness and had simply gone back to sleep. The sound had been timed at about 12.20am.

One of the first steps was to examine all the guns in the barracks. One carbine, although it had been cleaned, bore unmistakable traces of cordite in the barrel, showing that it had recently been fired. This same gun had been reported missing from a soldier's rack on the morning of the murder but subsequently found in a room near to where Short's body lay, a room in which ̵on, and others, slept.

̵re was no direct evidence pointing to ̵n beyond the acrimony that had existed

NAME	William George Hudson
AGE AT EXECUTION	26
DATE OF EXECUTION	Tuesday, 12th May, 1903
PLACE OF EXECUTION	Manchester
HANGMAN	William Billington
ASSISTANT	Henry Pierrepoint
DATE OF TRIAL	24th April, 1903
LOCATION OF TRIAL	Manchester
PRESIDING JUDGE	Mister Justice Lawrance
PROSECUTION COUNSEL	Mister Sutton, R. Smith
DEFENCE COUNSEL	Gilbert Jordan
NUMBER OF VICTIMS	1

VICTIMS DETAILS	
NAME	Harry Short
AGE	Not known
DATE OF MURDER	Tuesday, 17th February, 1903
PLACE OF MURDER	Fulwood Barracks, near Preston
METHOD OF KILLING	Shot
RELATIONSHIP TO KILLER	None

between him and Short and the fact that he had been heard saying that he had: "... done for Short." It was also revealed that Hudson had been seen cleaning the murder weapon on the morning after the murder.

It was still enough for the jury though, who found Hudson guilty but added a recommendation to mercy on account of his youth.

ON DECEMBER 28TH 1902, the S.S. Brunswick anchored off Cajueira Tutoia, a small island off the coast of Brazil, in order to pick up a cargo of cotton and hides. Whilst the ship was being loaded, the Chief Officer, William Thomas Watson, noticed a ship's boat with the name Veronica painted on its side. A signal was made from the boat and the upshot was that five men asked permission to come aboard the Brunswick.

The five men were certainly a mixed bunch. Three of them – Gustav Rau, Otto Monsson and Henry Flohr – were German. The fourth, Willem Schmidt, was Dutch and the fifth, Moses Thomas, was an American negro. Rau seemed to be the spokesman and he told a very sorry story indeed.

According to Rau the Veronica had sailed from Ship Island in the gulf of Mexico, bound for Montevideo with a cargo of lumber. They had sailed on October 11th with a crew of 12 and almost from the first, misfortune had dogged their steps.

On October 25th, a Swede, Gustav Johansen, had died at sea. About a month afterwards, on November 23rd, Alexander MacLeod had fallen from the topsail and been killed. Finally, on December 20th, fire had been discovered in the Captain's cabin and the remainder of the crew had abandoned ship in two boats. They had no idea what had happened to the other boat, which they had very soon become separated from.

At first Rau's story was accepted but over the next few days, as the Brunswick sailed for Europe, certain discrepancies were revealed. Rau was noticed to be wearing a pair of the Captain's socks and was also in possession of his suit and yet surely these would have been in the Captain's cabin when the fire broke out. Also it became apparent that Thomas seemed to be frightened of the others. He asked if he could be berthed apart from them, a request that was granted.

On January 12th, 1903, land was sighted. At this point Thomas approached the Captain of the Brunswick and told him a different story. He said that the rest of the crew of the Veronica had been murdered by the other four men. On arrival at Liverpool the other four survivors were arrested and taken in for

NAME	Gustav Rau (August Mailahn); Willem Schmidt (Dirk Herlaar)
AGE AT EXECUTION	28; 30
DATE OF EXECUTION	Tuesday, 2nd June, 1903
PLACE OF EXECUTION	Liverpool
HANGMAN	William Billington
ASSISTANT	John Billington
DATE OF TRIAL	12th May – 14th May, 1903
LOCATION OF TRIAL	Liverpool
PRESIDING JUDGE	Mister Justice Lawrance
PROSECUTION COUNSEL	A.A. Tobin, E. Smith
DEFENCE COUNSEL	A.H. Maxwell, W.H. Aggs
NUMBER OF VICTIMS	7

VICTIMS DETAILS

NAME	Alexander MacLeod; Julius Herrson; Patrick Durran
AGES	Not known
DATE OF MURDER	circa Monday, 8th December, 1902
PLACE OF MURDER	On board the Veronica at sea
METHOD OF KILLING	Battered/drowned; battered/drowned; battered/drowned
RELATIONSHIP TO KILLER	None; none; none

NAME	Fred Abrahamson; Captain Alexander Shaw
AGES	Not known
DATE OF MURDER	circa Szunday, 14th December, 1902
PLACE OF MURDER	On board the Veronica at sea
METHOD OF KILLING	Shot/battered; shot
RELATIONSHIP TO KILLER	None; none

NAME	Gustav Johansen; Alexander Bravo
AGES	Not known
DATE OF MURDER	circa Wednesday, 17th December, 1902; circa Friday, 19th December, 1902
PLACE OF MURDER	On board the Veronica at sea
METHOD OF KILLING	Shot; possibly shot/drowned
RELATIONSHIP TO KILLER	None; none

questioning. At first, all four stuck to the same story: Moses Thomas, the ship's cook had led a mutiny and it was he who had killed the crew of the Veronica. They had merely obeyed his instructions in order to save

1903

themselves. Thomas, of course, told a different story and it was his that seemed to have the ring of truth about it. The authorities could not accept that one man, Thomas, had subdued the rest who had lived in terror of him. In due course, Henry Flohr changed his story too and now the truth of what Thomas had said was revealed.

It transpired that Macleod, the first mate and a rough Canadian sailor, ruled his crew with a rod of iron. For some time he had crossed swords with Schmidt and one night he struck him and knocked him down. Schmidt and Rau then sounded out the other members of the crew and, armed with the only two revolvers on the ship, decided to mutiny.

MacLeod was the first to be attacked. Battered with iron belaying pins, he was subsequently locked up in part of the ship's hold. At the same time Herrson and Durran were also battered whilst Captain Shaw and Fred Abrahamson were shot.

Over the next few days, these five members of crew were again battered and finally thrown overboard to drown, or were simply shot and their corpses thrown into the sea. With five men dead, there was now no turning back.

On the 17th of December, Gustav Johansen was also shot and thrown overboard, leaving just six survivors on the ship. By this time, only three men, Rau, Schmidt and Monsson, had taken any active part in these killings and it was decided that the two others should now play a part in order to drag them into the conspiracy.

On December 19th, Alexander Bravo accidentally allowed a sail to hit Schmidt. Immediately Schmidt decided that he had to die and that Thomas and Flohr should do the killing. They were told to batter and stab Bravo and then throw his body overboard. The two men stalked Bravo, as instructed, but only made gestures as if they were attacking him. Bravo took his chance and dived into the sea where he was shot at, and possibly hit, by Schmidt. It was then decided to set fire to the ~~nica~~ in order to make the story of ~~...~~unes at sea seem realistic.

~~...~~ result of the evidence of Thomas and

Flohr, the other three survivors were now charged with seven counts of murder, piracy and conspiracy. The trial lasted three days with a new juror having to be sworn in on the third day to replace one member who had fallen ill. All three defendants, Rau, Schmidt and Monsson, were found guilty of the murder of Captain Shaw, the one charge that had been proceeded with, and sentenced to death. In the case of Otto Monsson, the jury added a recommendation to mercy on account of his youth and previous good behaviour.

Eventually he was reprieved but Rau and Schmidt, who had committed what was a largely stupid and purposeless crime, were hanged together at Walton jail.

CHARLES HOWELL WAS a soldier in the Suffolk Regiment, stationed in Colchester, and for some time he had been seeing Maud Luen, a local girl.

Monday June 1st, was Whit Monday and on that day Howell had again been out with Maud. At 9.00pm, as Howell was walking Maud home, she was heard to say: "No, I will not go there. It's no use." They parted soon afterwards and Howell returned to his barracks. Later, when talking to one of his comrades, Howell referred to Maud in very unkind terms, adding for good measure that she would not be alive in the morning.

At 9.40pm, Maud Luen was talking to a friend of hers, a Mrs Tredger, in a lane close to the barracks. After they had been talking for a few minutes, Howell came up to them and asked Maud if she would forgive him. Maud replied that she would, but only if he would go away and leave her alone. Playfully Howell put his arm around Maud's shoulders and asked her for a kiss. Before she could reply to this request, it was noticed that Howell was holding something in his right hand. Within seconds he had raised what turned out to be his service razor and slashed Maud's throat, in full view of Mrs Tredger. So deep and vicious was the wound that Maud died almost immediately.

At the same moment a sergeant from the Regiment came cycling past on his way back to the barracks. Being quickly appraised of the situation, he arrested Howell and took him along to the guard room. Here Howell readily admitted what he had done and said that if Maud wasn't dead, she ought to be. Later he was handed over to the civil police and formally charged with murder.

The defence put forward was one of insanity. Howell's mother was called and testified that relations of hers had been admitted to asylums. She added that her son had spent some time in South Africa and had not been the same since his return. He would often be found crying like a child, for no apparent reason. This testimony, added to the fact that no real motive could be suggested, pointed to the fact the Howell was insane at the time of the attack.

In summing up, Mister Justice Wright

NAME	Charles Howell
AGE AT EXECUTION	30
DATE OF EXECUTION	Tuesday, 7th July, 1903
PLACE OF EXECUTION	Chelmsford
HANGMAN	William Billington
ASSISTANT	John Ellis
DATE OF TRIAL	19th June, 1903
LOCATION OF TRIAL	Chelmsford
PRESIDING JUDGE	Mister Justice Wright
PROSECUTION COUNSEL	C.E. Jones, Graham Campbell
DEFENCE COUNSEL	Mister Jelf
NUMBER OF VICTIMS	1

VICTIMS DETAILS	
NAME	Maud Luen
AGE	19
DATE OF MURDER	Monday, 1st June, 1903
PLACE OF MURDER	Colchester
METHOD OF KILLING	Cut throat
RELATIONSHIP TO KILLER	Girlfriend

pointed out that the jury had to satisfy themselves that Howell knew what he was doing before he could be convicted of murder. He added that in his opinion there was no evidence of insanity and that it would be up to the Home Secretary to take advice on this matter, if a sentence of death was subsequently passed.

The guilty verdict was returned but a recommendation was added that the prisoner's state of mind should be inquired into. Nevertheless, the Home Secretary of the day saw no reason to commute the sentence.

SAMUEL DOUGAL HAD a way with women. By the time he met Camille Holland, Dougal had already been married three times, with his first two wives dying in somewhat unusual circumstances.

He had married his first wife in 1869, and after 16 years of marriage she suddenly became ill and died in agony. He remarried within a couple of months but in October 1885, his second wife also died after suddenly becoming ill. Both of these wives were buried in Canada, where Dougal lived for 10 years. Sarah White became his third wife in 1892, marrying Dougal in Dublin, on August 7th. Back in England Dougal soon found himself in trouble for forgery and ended up being sentenced to 12 months' imprisonment, with hard labour. He was released in December 1896. Sarah left him not long afterwards and Dougal decided to move to London.

By 1898, Camille Holland had settled down in a boarding house at 37 Elgin Crescent, Bayswater. Previously she had lived in Liverpool and Kilburn, where she had stayed with her aunt, Sarah Holland. More importantly perhaps, Camille had over £6.000 in cash and a large quantity of property. In the autumn of that year, she first met Samuel Dougal and like so many others before her, she fell for his charm. Camille was by now 54 years of age and she was no doubt flattered by the attentions of Dougal. The couple spent a weekend together in Southend and very soon afterwards, in December 1898, they rented a furnished house together, at Hassocks, near Brighton.

In January 1899, the couple purchased Coldhams Farm near Clavering in Essex. They moved first to Saffron Walden whilst the contracts were completed and finally moved into the farm, which Dougal renamed Moat House Farm, on April 27th, 1899.

On May 9th, a servant girl named Florence Havis was taken on by Camille. She began work on May 13th, but on the very next day, Dougal made a pass at her and tried to kiss her. The situation worsened on May 16th when Dougal tried to gain entry to Florence's room at night. Florence screamed and was rescued by Camille who, for safety's sake, took to sleeping with Florence in another room.

NAME	Samuel Herbert Dougal
AGE AT EXECUTION	57
DATE OF EXECUTION	Tuesday, 14th July, 1903
PLACE OF EXECUTION	Chelmsford
HANGMAN	William Billington
ASSISTANT	John Billington
DATE OF TRIAL	22nd June – 23rd June, 1903
LOCATION OF TRIAL	Chelmsford
PRESIDING JUDGE	Mister Justice Wright
PROSECUTION COUNSEL	Mister Gill, W.J. Grubbs, Graham Campbell
DEFENCE COUNSEL	George Elliott, Basil Watson, J.P. Valetta
NUMBER OF VICTIMS	1 (possibly more)

VICTIMS DETAILS

NAME	Camille Cecile Holland
AGE	55
DATE OF MURDER	Friday, 19th May, 1899
PLACE OF MURDER	Moat House Farm, Clavering, Essex
METHOD OF KILLING	Shot
RELATIONSHIP TO KILLER	Girlfriend

At 6.30pm on May 19th, Camille was seen, by Florence, going out with Dougal. He returned home alone two hours later and told Florence that Camille had gone off to London, even though she had been carrying no luggage with her. He added that she would probably return later that night. He continued this masquerade later, even going so far as to meet the London train but of course, Camille did not return. On the following day, Dougal said that he had heard from Camille, who had now gone off on holiday. That same day, Florence's mother, having been told by her daughter of the various events at the farm, arrived to take Florence home with her. That evening Dougal's legal wife, Sarah, joined him at the farm.

Camille Holland was never seen again but her bank account still remained active. Cheques were drawn in favour of Dougal on a regular basis. All her shares were sold and all the household bills were paid. In the meantime, Dougal busied himself with the filling in of an old drainage ditch on the farm.

Over the next couple of years many hundreds of pounds were appropriated by Dougal. At the same time he entertained a number of young women at the farm. His wife put up with this until January 1902, when she left. Dougal sued for divorce, getting his decree on August 1st.

Camille Holland's disappearance was the talk of the area and it was natural that the gossip should eventually come to the ears of the police. The authorities began to investigate and in early 1903, they finally had their breakthrough.

A cheque, dated April 28th 1902, ostensibly signed by Camille, was examined and her nephew, Ernest, swore that the signature was a forgery. Dougal, suspicious when the police had interviewed him a few days earlier, had already vanished, having first withdrawn a further £605 from Camille's account.

On March 18th, 1903, a man entered the Bank of England in London and handed over £140 in ten pound notes to the cashier, asking for them to be changed for notes of a smaller denomination. The cashier saw that the serial numbers on the notes matched those that had been circulated by the police as having been drawn by Samuel Dougal. The police were contacted whilst an attempt was made to delay the customer. The ruse was successful and the man, who of course turned out to be Dougal, was arrested, though he did try to escape on the way to the police station.

As a holding measure Dougal was charged with the forgery of the April 28th cheque and the police began a thorough search of Moat House Farm. The filling in of the drainage ditch was recalled and it was there, on April 27th 1903, that a badly decomposed body was discovered. The body was identified as Camille's by means of the tattered clothing and examination showed that she had been shot in the head. The bullet that caused her death was found inside the skull and it was shown too that this could have been fired from a revolver that Dougal possessed.

Dougal was found guilty of murder after a two-day trial. Whilst awaiting execution he wrote to the Home Secretary, admitting that he had shot Camille, but said that it had been an accident. This last attempt to avoid the hangman failed but the Dougal case still had drama to come.

The prison chaplain, Reverend J.W. Blakemore, who attended the execution, delayed the proceedings for some minutes. He stood before the hooded figure of Dougal on the trap and demanded to know if he was guilty or not guilty. Dougal did not reply. Again the chaplain demanded to know if he had murdered Camille Holland or not and finally, from beneath the hood, Dougal was heard to say: "Guilty." The lever was then pulled and Dougal was launched into eternity.

1903

IT HAD BEEN a pleasant and successful evening for Thomas Porter and his fellow poacher, Thomas Preston, and now it was time for them to return home to Sileby. They entered the village together and to their horror, saw the local police officer, Constable William Wilkinson.

Wilkinson was standing just outside the churchyard, talking to a man named Middleton, and at that time, poaching was probably the farthest thing from his mind. It was just coming up to 10.30pm and he was having a friendly conversation when suddenly a number of shots rang out and Wilkinson fell dead.

Porter and Preston were recognised immediately and were seen making for Porter's house. The police were called and the premises surrounded. From 1.00am until around 7.00am, officers were held at bay by the two men, Porter appearing in an open window and threatening to shoot anyone who came close enough.

After six hours of siege, the two poachers decided that there could be no realistic way out of this situation and gave themselves up. Both men were then charged with the murder of Constable Wilkinson. The two men were tried together and had slightly different defences, though both claimed that they were drunk at the time and so not responsible for their actions.

Porter for his part admitted that he had fired the fatal shot but claimed that he had just wanted to scare the policeman away and had not intended to hit him. His defence was therefore one of accidental killing. Preston agreed that Porter had done the shooting but added that at that particular time he had become separated from his partner and so had no idea what he was about to do. He therefore bore no responsibility for the crime. The jury did not agree and determined that both men were equally guilty of murder. Both were then sentenced to death.

Porter and Preston were hanged together at Leicester on July 21st. On the scaffold, Porter was the first to speak, saying in a loud voice… "I am innocent." Almost immediately the same words were echoed by Preston.

NAME	Thomas Porter; Thomas Preston
AGE AT EXECUTION	29; 24
DATE OF EXECUTION	Tuesday, 21st July, 1903
PLACE OF EXECUTION	Leicester
HANGMAN	William Billington
ASSISTANT	John Billington
DATE OF TRIAL	29th June – 30th June, 1903
LOCATION OF TRIAL	Leicester
PRESIDING JUDGE	Mister Justice Ridley
PROSECUTION COUNSEL	Mister Disney, Peter Grain
DEFENCE COUNSEL	Mister Blaiklock, Mister McCurdy
NUMBER OF VICTIMS	1

VICTIMS DETAILS	
NAME	William Ariel Wilkinson
AGE	32
DATE OF MURDER	Monday, 25th May, 1903
PLACE OF MURDER	Outside the churchyard, Sileby
METHOD OF KILLING	Shot
RELATIONSHIP TO KILLER	None; none

LEONARD PACHETT HAD married his wife Sarah in February, 1900. From the very outset there were constant arguments and in due course, at the beginning of 1903, the couple separated. A brief attempt was made to rekindle the relationship and in March 1903, they spent a week together in Shirebrook. When, at the end of that single week, Sarah left Leonard for the last time, he was heard to say that he would kill her if her ever caught up with her again. After this final separation, Sarah took employment as a housekeeper to Mister King, in Lincoln. She had worked for that gentleman before and he was more than happy to take her back again. Meanwhile, Leonard was working as a bricklayer, at Gainsborough.

On May 23rd, Pachett went to visit Lincoln where he spoke to a neighbour of Mister King and again made threats against his wife. He did actually see Sarah for a few hours on that day, before returning to Gainsborough.

May 26th saw Pachett purchasing a new collar and tie from a shop owned by Mrs Morley. To that woman he remarked that he was planning to do something he had never done before and that she would soon read about him in the newspapers. Then, later that afternoon, he again went to Lincoln and was seen talking to Sarah by Mister King. He later would testify that the couple left his house at about 6.15pm, ostensibly so she could see Leonard off on his train back to Gainsborough. Some 45 minutes later, Pachett and his wife were seen talking by a gate in Boultham Lane. Three days later, on Friday the 29th, Sarah's body was found in the field alongside the gate where she had last been seen. She had been manually strangled.

Pachett's defence was that at the time of his wife's murder, he had been back at Gainsborough. He claimed that his wife had seen him to the Great Northern Station, at Lincoln, and he had caught the 8.05pm train.

Witnesses were called in his defence but none could swear that they had seen Pachett back in Gainsborough at a time consistent with him having caught the 8.05. Further, two men were called who had seen a man fitting Pachett's description close to a pond in Boultham Lane, a little after 8.00pm. Finally, a

NAME	Leonard Pachett
AGE AT EXECUTION	26
DATE OF EXECUTION	Tuesday, 28th July, 1903
PLACE OF EXECUTION	Lincoln
HANGMAN	William Billington
ASSISTANT	John Billington
DATE OF TRIAL	6th July, 1903
LOCATION OF TRIAL	Lincoln
PRESIDING JUDGE	Mister Justice Ridley
PROSECUTION COUNSEL	Mister Appleton, Mister White
DEFENCE COUNSEL	T.H. Walker
NUMBER OF VICTIMS	1

VICTIMS DETAILS	
NAME	Sarah Ann Pachett
AGE	Not known
DATE OF MURDER	Tuesday, 26th May, 1903
PLACE OF MURDER	Boultham, Lincoln
METHOD OF KILLING	Strangled
RELATIONSHIP TO KILLER	Wife

fellow lodger testified that upon Pachett returning to his house he mentioned that he had just committed a murder.

Pachett had been heard threatening his wife, had been seen with her close to where her body was discovered, had lied about his movements and had told a roommate that he had killed someone, three days before the body was found. It was enough for the jury to decide, after a very short deliberation, that Pachett was guilty as charged.

ON MAY 7TH, 1903, the police called at 12 Alexandra Road, Thames Ditton. Getting no answer to their knocking, the door was forced. Very shortly, in the front bedroom, the body of a woman was discovered. This was Caroline Tuffen and she had been battered to death.

The story behind the murder was a most interesting one. Caroline had been married to William Joseph Tuffen. They had first lived in Wimbledon, then at Kingston and finally had taken the house at Alexandra Road on March 2nd, 1903. Later that month Mary Stone, who had until very recently been in service, moved into the house with William and his wife.

At about 10.30pm on April 23rd, Tuffen and his wife were seen walking to a local pub. They were heard to be arguing as they strolled along together.

On April 29th, a visitor to the house saw that only Mary Stone and William Tuffen were at home. Mary was sitting on William's knee and the pair appeared to be very familiar with each other.

On May 5th, it was the turn of Caroline's brother to visit the house. He asked after his sister and being far from satisfied with the answer he received, reported the matter to the police. It was this report that resulted in the visit on May 7th.

It was estimated that the woman had been dead for about 14 days, which was consistent with the date she last been seen alive: April 23rd. William and Mary Stone had by now vanished, most probably having left on the evening of May 6th. During the previous two weeks they must have lived with the dead and decomposing body of Caroline in the house.

An immediate search was launched for Tuffen and Mary Stone, who were soon spotted at Norbiton railway station and arrested. When Mary was questioned she claimed to know nothing whatsoever about the death of Caroline. Tuffen had apparently told her that his wife had gone away. Nevertheless the couple were both charged with murder and being an accessory after the fact.

When the trial opened, there began a series of deliberations over which charge

NAME	William Joseph Tuffen
AGE AT EXECUTION	23
DATE OF EXECUTION	Tuesday, 11th August, 1903
PLACE OF EXECUTION	Wandsworth
HANGMAN	Henry Pierrepoint
ASSISTANT	John Ellis
DATE OF TRIAL	22nd July, 1903
LOCATION OF TRIAL	Guildford
PRESIDING JUDGE	Mister Justice Darling
PROSECUTION COUNSEL	H.F. Dickens, Ernest M. Pollock
DEFENCE COUNSEL	Henry Lynn
NUMBER OF VICTIMS	1

VICTIMS DETAILS	
NAME	Caroline Tuffen
AGE	21
DATE OF MURDER	circa Thursday, 23rd April, 1903
PLACE OF MURDER	12 Alexandra Road, Thames Ditton
METHOD OF KILLING	Battered
RELATIONSHIP TO KILLER	Wife

should be proceeded with. Counsel for the defence insisted that only one charge should be preferred but after due discussion, Mister Justice Darling decided that both charges should stand. Both prisoners pleaded not guilty.

In many ways, the arguments over the charge had been largely irrelevant. When the jury returned, they had found Tuffen guilty of murder and Stone guilty of being an accessory after the fact. At this point the judge stated that such a verdict meant that Stone too was guilty of murder. Sentence of death was then passed on both prisoners.

In due course, Mary Stone received a reprieve but on August 11th, William Tuffen was hanged at Wandsworth.

ONE OF THE problems with being a barmaid is that just occasionally, certain male customers might become a little too insistent on monopolising your time. Most barmaids are quite used to giving a gentle let down, but some are more brutal in their attitude. One such was Martha Jane Hardwick, and her inability to deal with a persistent customer cost her her life.

Martha lived with her sister, Jane Starkey, who was the landlady of the Lord Nelson pub. In return for her board and lodgings, Martha would help out in the bar, especially at the busier times. She was a popular worker, but with one man she was perhaps a little too popular.

Charles Slowe was constantly asking Martha to go out with him and he became such a nuisance to her that Martha took to avoiding him whenever she could. If she saw Slowe come into one of the bars, she would go to serve in the other and in time, Slowe came to resent this and was heard to threaten Martha with violence. Of course, this only served to make the situation even worse as now Martha took even greater pains to avoid Slowe.

On the night of Wednesday, September 23rd, Slowe was again in the Lord Nelson and Martha again walked out of the bar as he came in. At about 10.00pm Slowe left and no doubt Martha thought that she had managed to avoid him for yet another night. She could not have been more wrong. Just as the pub was closing, shortly after midnight, Martha was standing in one of the doorways watching the last of the customers off the premises. She did not see Slowe come up behind her and the next thing people knew, Slowe seemed to be hitting Martha in her side and shouting: "I've got you now."

It took a few fatal seconds for the witnesses to realise that Slowe held a knife in his hand and that Martha had been repeatedly stabbed. As she sank to the floor, Slowe ran out of the pub to be rapidly followed by Jane Starkey. Slowe tried his best to escape but Jane managed to shout for help and a passer-by named Peeling chased Slowe and eventually captured him.

There could be no doubt that Slowe had

NAME	Charles Jeremiah Slowe
AGE AT EXECUTION	28
DATE OF EXECUTION	Tuesday, 10th November, 1903
PLACE OF EXECUTION	Pentonville
HANGMAN	William Billington
ASSISTANT	John Billington
DATE OF TRIAL	21st October, 1903
LOCATION OF TRIAL	Old Bailey
PRESIDING JUDGE	Mister Justice Bigham
PROSECUTION COUNSEL	Arthur Gill, R.B. Murphy
DEFENCE COUNSEL	Harold Morris
NUMBER OF VICTIMS	1

VICTIMS DETAILS	
NAME	Martha Jane Hardwick
AGE	20
DATE OF MURDER	Thursday, 24th September, 1903
PLACE OF MURDER	Lord Nelson public house, Whitechapel Road, London
METHOD OF KILLING	Stabbed
RELATIONSHIP TO KILLER	None

killed Martha but his defence tried to blame it on a fit of uncontrollable jealousy caused by the provocation he had endured from Martha. Although it was suggested that the offence was unpremeditated, it was noted that Slowe had returned to the pub a couple of hours after first leaving and the jury were convinced of his guilt.

Asked if he had anything to say before sentence of death was passed, Slowe looked directly at the judge and said in a loud voice: "I shall meet it without fear."

1903

NO ONE WAS quite sure why the engagement between Edward Palmer and his girlfriend, Esther Swinford, had been called off. For Esther, it was a simple matter of Edward not being trustworthy. She had given him money, which he had said he would save up so they could buy furniture for their home, but she had subsequently discovered that he had spent it on other things, most probably drink.

As far as Edward was concerned the relationship had been ended by him because he had discovered some mysterious secret about Esther's past. Whatever the truth, the marriage did not take place, even though the banns had been read.

Once the wedding had been cancelled, a change came over Edward Palmer. He moved away from Swindon and took to carrying a revolver with him. This so alarmed his brother that at one stage he forcibly took it from him. Unfortunately, the weapon was later returned to Edward.

Esther worked as a barmaid at the Ship Inn, in Swindon. In early September Edward, who had previously worked as a gardener, was successful in obtaining employment at the Great Western Railway works and so moved back to the railway town of Swindon. On September 18th, he took the opportunity to visit Esther.

Palmer knew that it was a quiet time of day at the Ship. In fact, at the time he called at the pub, it was totally empty except for Esther herself, who was behind the bar. She may have been a little surprised to see her ex-fiancé, but he seemed calm enough when he asked for a bottle of beer, so she served him.

The landlord and landlady of the pub were in their rooms at the back when they suddenly heard a very loud report. They both rushed into the bar and were shocked to find Esther lying on the floor and Palmer standing over her, the gun still in his hand. Esther died a few minutes later. When the police arrived, Palmer offered them no resistance. As a matter of routine the prisoner was searched and in one of his pockets, the police discovered a photograph of Esther on the back of which Palmer had written: "The curse of my life."

NAME	Edward Richard Palmer
AGE AT EXECUTION	24
DATE OF EXECUTION	Tuesday, 17th November, 1903
PLACE OF EXECUTION	Devizes
HANGMAN	William Billington
ASSISTANT	John Billington
DATE OF TRIAL	28th October, 1903
LOCATION OF TRIAL	Devizes
PRESIDING JUDGE	Mister Justice Wills
PROSECUTION COUNSEL	J.A. Foote, Mister Seton
DEFENCE COUNSEL	Thornton Lawes
NUMBER OF VICTIMS	1

VICTIMS DETAILS	
NAME	Esther Swinford
AGE	19
DATE OF MURDER	Friday, 18th September, 1903
PLACE OF MURDER	Ship Inn, Swindon
METHOD OF KILLING	Shot
RELATIONSHIP TO KILLER	Ex-girlfriend

Palmer's story was that the gun had gone off accidentally. He admitted that he had carried a loaded revolver when he went to see Esther but claimed that he just wished to frighten her. She had refused to speak to him and he took out the gun to scare her into at least having a conversation with him. As he was pointing the weapon in her direction, it went off and Esther was hit.

The jury did not agree with this plea of manslaughter and felt that the crime had been one of deliberate murder.

BERNARD WHITE WAS a private in the 2nd Battalion Essex Regiment. In 1901, he dated Maud Garrett for six weeks but then he was posted to South Africa. By the time he returned to England, Maud was engaged to another man, Private Jones of the R.A.M.C.

On May 21st, 1903, Jones was in hospital at Warley and Maud went to visit him. Whilst there she saw a face she recognised: Bernard White. White was with two friends, but they made a discreet exit. They would testify that the two appeared to be on affectionate terms and later White told them he had arranged to meet Maud the next night.

May 22nd saw White and the same two friends out drinking. The three left at 9.15pm to return to barracks and on the way, met Maud who was waiting, as arranged.

White knew that he would not be able to spend much time with Maud, but there was a way around this. He would report back to camp and then would sneak back out.

The men who shared a tent with White disagreed about the exact time he left camp again. The best estimate was some time between 10.00pm and 10.15pm. They all agreed, though, that he carried a cane.

A number of witnesses reported hearing noises that night. Captain FitzGerald, whose quarters faced the spot where Maud's body would be found, heard screams between 10.00pm and 10.30pm.

A gamekeeper also heard screams but he put the time at 10.45pm. Finally, Colour-Sergeant Henry Roberts, returning to camp, heard groans at some time before 10.30pm. This same sergeant passed a man in civilian clothes 50 yards from where Maud lay.

At 11.00pm, White returned to his tent. The time was easy to fix, as he stepped on one of his friends and woke him.

At about 5.00am on May 23rd, a labourer on his way to work saw a pool of blood on the road and followed it to a hollow where Maud lay. She had been battered to death and marks around her mouth and body appeared to have been made by a cane.

News of the murder spread rapidly. White was questioned but denied seeing Maud after he had gone back out of camp. At 10.15am, though, White went to his sergeant and

NAME	Bernard White
AGE AT EXECUTION	21
DATE OF EXECUTION	Tuesday, 1st December, 1903
PLACE OF EXECUTION	Chelmsford
HANGMAN	William Billington
ASSISTANT	Henry Pierrepoint
DATE OF TRIAL	12th November – 13th November, 1903
LOCATION OF TRIAL	Chelmsford
PRESIDING JUDGE	Mister Justice Lawrance
PROSECUTION COUNSEL	Mister Gill, Graham Campbell
DEFENCE COUNSEL	Forrest Fulton
NUMBER OF VICTIMS	1

VICTIMS DETAILS	
NAME	Maud Garrett
AGE	20
DATE OF MURDER	Friday, 22nd May, 1903
PLACE OF MURDER	Little Warley, Brentwood
METHOD OF KILLING	Battered
RELATIONSHIP TO KILLER	Ex-girlfriend

reported that he did know someone who fitted the description of the murdered girl. He was arrested and handed over to the civilian authorities.

Bernard White denied murder. He admitted knowing Maud but claimed that once outside the camp he had found no sign of her and had eventually returned to his tent. However, the police scientists had found blood on White's boots, socks, trousers, rings and cane. White said that this had come from an old cut.

White's fate was sealed, but one question about the case remains. Why did the civilian seen by Colour-Sergeant Roberts never come forward?

ELIZA RANGE WAS the wife of a labourer on the Lancashire and Yorkshire Railway and had been married for 17 years. She was rather too fond of drink though, and this led to friction between her and her husband, William. Eventually Eliza left her husband but after a separation of 15 years, she returned to him, taking with her a son, Arthur, who by coincidence was 15 years old.

Eliza and her husband might have agreed to live together again, but not as man and wife. Each was free to seek other relationships and Eliza found her solace in the company of Charles Whittaker. Whilst Mister Range went off to work on the railway, Whittaker would visit Eliza at her home and this is exactly what he did on August 8th, 1903. At half-past ten that morning, as Arthur Range enjoyed his breakfast, Eliza and Charles Whittaker were drinking beer in the kitchen.

Arthur saw his mother pour Whittaker a drink and then announce that she needed to have a wash. As she walked into the scullery, Arthur saw Whittaker rise from his chair and follow her, a knife in his hand. Whittaker then pushed Eliza into a corner so that she would be blocked from Arthur's view but the blood-curdling scream that followed left the child in no doubt as to what was taking place inside that scullery.

As Arthur rushed to help his mother, Whittaker dashed out of the back door. Eliza lay on the scullery floor, having been stabbed four times and was beyond all help. By the time Arthur managed to fetch the police and a doctor, his mother was already dead, the fatal blow having been one deep wound in her neck.

It was not until the following day, August 9th, that Charles Whittaker walked into the police station and announced: "I'm the man that committed that murder yesterday and I've come to give myself up." Then, as if to apologise for the delay, Whittaker went on to explain: "I would have come sooner only I wanted a drink."

In his statement Whittaker said that he had discovered that Eliza was being unfaithful to him. He had demanded that she give up the other man, but she had refused so he stabbed her. That confession was enough to put a noose around Charles Whittaker's neck.

NAME	Charles Wood Whittaker
AGE AT EXECUTION	43
DATE OF EXECUTION	Wednesday, 2nd December, 1903
PLACE OF EXECUTION	Manchester
HANGMAN	John Billington
ASSISTANT	John Ellis
DATE OF TRIAL	13th November, 1903
LOCATION OF TRIAL	Manchester
PRESIDING JUDGE	Mister Justice Ridley
PROSECUTION COUNSEL	Ambrose Jones, Mister Pope
DEFENCE COUNSEL	J.B. Sandbach
NUMBER OF VICTIMS	1

VICTIMS DETAILS	
NAME	Eliza Range
AGE	Not known
DATE OF MURDER	Saturday, 8th August, 1903
PLACE OF MURDER	99 Husband Street, Collyhurst
METHOD OF KILLING	Stabbed
RELATIONSHIP TO KILLER	Girlfriend

ALTHOUGH ELLEN NEWMAN was a married woman, she left her husband in June 1902, and went to live with James Duffy at Windsor Terrace, Grangetown. This new relationship was rather volatile, culminating in November 1902, when Duffy slashed Ellen's throat and then his own. Luckily both Ellen and Duffy recovered from the injuries he had inflicted. Ellen moved to Back Durham Street, whilst Duffy received a prison sentence of one month's hard labour for what he had done. When Duffy came out of jail Ellen, somewhat surprisingly perhaps, took him back to live with her.

In addition to his violent streak, Duffy was also extremely lazy. He saw no reason to work when he could live off the money Ellen made as a prostitute. What did it matter if she slept with other men, as long as he could live a life of indolence? Even so, money was tight and Duffy, rather than thinking his lack of industry was the cause, put the blame squarely on Ellen's shoulders. This led to more violence and the vicious circle of poverty, violence and more poverty, was complete.

Saturday September 5th, 1903, saw Mrs Hope, the lodger, arriving at Back Durham Street at around 11.15pm. Duffy was asleep in the chair, suffering from the aftereffects of too much drink, but woke as Mrs Hope entered the room. After a brief discussion about where he had left his money, Duffy struck his 15-year-old son, at which point Mrs Hope intervened and told him to leave the boy alone. Duffy said he was going up to bed, whereupon Ellen Newman walked out of the house, announcing that she would no longer "… live with a pig like him." Duffy went after her, apologised, and managed to persuade Ellen to return. The household finally settled down for the night.

At 1.45am on September 6th, Duffy rose, dressed and walked down to the Central Police Station. Here he announced that he wished to give himself up for murder. He then handed over the key to his home and when the police checked on his story, they found the body of Ellen Newman sprawled across the bed.

Duffy's claim was that he had killed Ellen in self-defence. He said he had gone to bed

NAME	James Duffy
AGE AT EXECUTION	46
DATE OF EXECUTION	Tuesday, 8th December, 1903
PLACE OF EXECUTION	Durham
HANGMAN	William Billington
ASSISTANT	John Billington
DATE OF TRIAL	21st November, 1903
LOCATION OF TRIAL	Durham
Presiding Judge	Mister Justice Grantham
PROSECUTION COUNSEL	Hans Hamilton, Mister Marshall
DEFENCE COUNSEL	Mister Chadman
NUMBER OF VICTIMS	1

VICTIMS DETAILS	
NAME	Ellen Newman
AGE	Not known
DATE OF MURDER	Sunday, 6th September, 1903
PLACE OF MURDER	4 Back Durham Street, Sunderland
METHOD OF KILLING	Strangled
RELATIONSHIP TO KILLER	Girlfriend

and once again the argument had started up. Ellen had a very quick temper and at one stage, she had picked up a lamp and made as if to throw it at Duffy. He had then grabbed her around the throat and before he knew it, she was dead. In support of his comments about Ellen's temper, her sister was called to give evidence and she admitted that once, Ellen had attacked her with a knife.

None of this affected the final verdict, though, and on December 8th, James Duffy kept an appointment with the Billington brothers at Durham jail.

THE STORY OF William Haywood would be difficult to accept as a work of fiction.

William had been married to Jane for many years and was still working, labouring in the Pokehouse Wood quarry, which lay alongside the river Lugg. The couple lived together at Yarpole and were regular customers at the Mortimer's Cross Inn, which was about a mile from where William worked.

On the night of July 10th, William slept in the quarry so he could get an early start. Nevertheless, he did find time to call at the Mortimer's Cross at 7.00am on the 11th, where he consumed one pint and purchased another, along with a bottle of whisky, to take to the quarry.

At 8.00am, Jane Haywood was seen taking William's breakfast up to him. Five hours later, at 1.00pm, William Haywood was back at the Mortimer's Cross. He had another drink and mentioned that he had thrown a stone at his wife's head, hit her, and found that he couldn't stop the bleeding. He added: "If she is dead when I get back, I'll bury her in the brook."

William was next seen at 8.45pm. He was on his way to the inn again, but he was pushing a wheelbarrow on which lay the body of his wife. The police were called and William calmly told them that his wife had met with an accident. As he was telling his story, the officers suggested that it might be an idea to remove the body from the wheelbarrow, as it appeared unseemly. William obligingly tipped Jane out and then lay down, next to her body.

When the police went to the quarry, they found the bottles that William had taken up with him. Both had been drained dry. There were also a number of bloodstained stones and sticks. Haywood was charged with murder.

The trial was no less remarkable than the crime. The defence being one of inanity, evidence was given by Doctor Cuthbert Stanislas Morrison of the Hereford City and County Lunatic Asylum. He classified Haywood as: "… an imbecile of the higher grade." He went on to say that Haywood was mentally unstable and that the effects of the alcohol had led to a sudden explosive impulse to kill when he had received some slight provocation from Jane. In short, Haywood was undoubtedly insane at the time of the attack.

The summing up was itself amazing. Mister Justice Bigham stated that the jurors ought not to trouble their minds with nice questions raised by medical men. He went on to say that lunatics should not escape punishment simply because they were lunatics. He appeared to be agreeing that Haywood was insane, but directing the jury to find him guilty anyway!

The jury were out for just a few minutes before returning the desired verdict of guilty. On December 15th, Haywood, who was undoubtedly mad, was hanged at Hereford.

NAME	William Haywood
AGE AT EXECUTION	61
DATE OF EXECUTION	Tuesday, 15th December, 1903
PLACE OF EXECUTION	Hereford
HANGMAN	Henry Pierrepoint
ASSISTANT	John Ellis
DATE OF TRIAL	28th November, 1903
LOCATION OF TRIAL	Oxford
PRESIDING JUDGE	Mister Justice Bigham
PROSECUTION COUNSEL	Stamford HUTTON, REGINALD Coventry
DEFENCE COUNSEL	S.R.C. Bosanquet
NUMBER OF VICTIMS	1

VICTIMS DETAILS	
NAME	Jane Haywood
AGE	Not known
DATE OF MURDER	Saturday, 11th July, 1903
PLACE OF MURDER	Pokehouse Wood Quarry, Leominster
METHOD OF KILLING	Battered
RELATIONSHIP TO KILLER	Wife

ESTHER ATKINS WAS a prostitute and when she found what she believed were three clients at once, she wasn't about to turn down the chance of making a few extra shillings. She wasn't to know was that the men were thinking only of robbery.

Mister Carter, the cab driver who picked up the four passengers, noted that two of the men were wearing uniforms of the Scots Fusiliers. The other one was not in uniform, but he did make their intentions clear. He said that they believed she had £10 or £12 and they meant to have it. There was little Carter could do but drop them at the Red Church at around 11.30pm.

At 2.00am on October 7th, William Smith was approached by Thomas Cowdrey, who said he had been walking by a churchyard when he heard a cry of: "Murder!" Cowdrey said he had seen two soldiers attacking a woman whereupon Smith told Cowdrey to go to the military police. From there he was referred to the civil police. Shortly after that he took officers to the spot where the assault had taken place and there the police found Esther Atkins.

Esther was almost naked and covered by a mass of bruises and wounds. Cowdrey refused to go anywhere near the body, which was to prove significant later when blood was found on his clothing.

The first step was to try to trace the two soldiers whom Cowdrey said he had seen. The regiment was put on parade. Cowdrey checked every face but identified none. Meanwhile, two soldiers – William Brown and John Dunbar – had been confined to barracks. When Brown suddenly produced a pair of women's shoes, suspicion fell upon him.

A second identity parade was organised on October 8th, and this time Cowdrey picked out Brown. Soon afterwards another soldier, John Robinson, reported that Brown and Dunbar had returned to barracks at 12.15am on the night of the murder and Brown had asked him for a towel so he could wipe blood off his hands. Brown was arrested and attention now turned to Dunbar. When questioned by Major Woods, Dunbar confessed that he and Brown had broken out of barracks, after 9.30pm on October 6th.

NAMES	William Brown; Thomas Cowdrey
AGE AT EXECUTION	27; 36
DATE OF EXECUTION	Wednesday, 16th December, 1903
PLACE OF EXECUTION	Winchester
HANGMAN	William Billington
ASSISTANT	John Billington
DATE OF TRIAL	24th November – 27th November, 1903
LOCATION OF TRIAL	Winchester
PRESIDING JUDGE	Mister Justice Wills
PROSECUTION COUNSEL	C. Mathews, Mister Simon
DEFENCE COUNSEL	H.P. St Gerrans, Mister Charles, Mister Spranger
NUMBER OF VICTIMS	1

VICTIMS DETAILS	
NAME	Esther Atkins
AGE	Not known
DATE OF MURDER	Tuesday, 6th October, 1903
PLACE OF MURDER	Long Valley, Aldershot
METHOD OF KILLING	Battered
RELATIONSHIP TO KILLER	None; none

They had been to the Crimea pub, where they met up with Cowdrey and Esther. As a result, Dunbar was arrested on October 9th. One week later, Cowdrey too was arrested.

The trial lasted four days with each man blaming the others. In due course, Brown and Cowdrey were found guilty whilst Dunbar was found not guilty.

On the morning of their execution, Brown said: "Before I leave this world, I wish to say that I helped to do it." Cowdrey then added. "Give me five minutes to tell the truth. God help my innocence. I'm going to Heaven. Brown did it, he has said so."

THE ENCYCLOPAEDIA OF EXECUTIONS

1903

GEORGE BREWSTER RAN a farm at Scampton Grange, where two of his servants were Charles Ashton and Annie Marshall. Charles was a general labourer and Annie a domestic servant.

September 20th was a Sunday and Annie liked to attend church on the Sabbath. At 5.30pm, she left the farm to walk to Rillington church, about three miles away. She said she would be back by 9.00pm.

Annie did not return and at 9.30pm, Mister Brewster heard two shots, followed by a scream. When Ashton returned, at about 10.30pm, Brewster mentioned these shots and asked Ashton if he had heard them. Ashton said he had.

By September 21st, Annie had still not returned and Brewster again spoke to Ashton. Charles said he had seen Annie the previous day, standing near the gate that led to the village green, but he could add nothing more.

The next day, Ashton was carting up some corn when he went up to the men working in the same field and said he had just found Annie's hat. The hat was wet and yet, when Charles pointed out where he had found it, the ground around it was perfectly dry. He then made an amazing observation.

Ashton went on to explain how the hat must have got wet. He surmised that someone had killed Annie, carried her to a place known as Black Bridge, and had there thrown her body into the river. He went on to mention the shots heard on Sunday and persuaded the men to accompany him to the river to search for Annie.

When the group reached the river it was Ashton who spotted something floating in the water. The bundle turned out to be Annie's body. She had been shot twice in the head and there were other marks of violence upon her. After hearing the story of how the body had been discovered, the police arrested Ashton and charged him with murder.

After some time in custody, Ashton gave the police a key to a box that contained the clothing he had worn on the night of Annie's death. This clothing was found to be covered in blood. A revolver was also found, as was a purse which was shown to have

NAME	Charles William Ashton
AGE AT EXECUTION	19
DATE OF EXECUTION	Tuesday, 22nd December, 1903
PLACE OF EXECUTION	Hull
HANGMAN	William Billington
ASSISTANT	John Billington
DATE OF TRIAL	1st December, 1903
LOCATION OF TRIAL	York
PRESIDING JUDGE	Mister Justice Grantham
PROSECUTION COUNSEL	T. Milvain, F. Brent Grotrien
DEFENCE COUNSEL	R.H. Vernon Wragge
NUMBER OF VICTIMS	1

VICTIMS DETAILS	
NAME	Annie Marshall
AGE	16
DATE OF MURDER	Sunday, 20th September, 1903
PLACE OF MURDER	Scampton, Near Malton
METHOD OF KILLING	Battered/shot
RELATIONSHIP TO KILLER	None

belonged to Annie. Faced with all this evidence, Ashton confessed.

No motive could be suggested for the crime. The fact remained, though, that Ashton had purchased the revolver on the day before the murder and he had of course been carrying it with him when he met up with Annie.

There was a suggestion that Ashton attempted to seduce Annie and when she resisted, he shot her. The judge explained that the apparent absence of motive was no excuse for the crime. The jury found Ashton guilty, though he was recommended to mercy on account of his youth.

86

THE SWANNS TOOK in lodgers and one of these was John Gallagher. John was younger than Emily but he found her attractive and in due course the couple became lovers. When William discovered the truth, he turned Gallagher into the street. This did little to cool the ardour of the lovers.

On June 5th, 1903, Gallagher was in the house when Emily and William took to arguing. Gallagher, naturally, took the part of his lover, threatened Swann and told him what would happen if he harmed Emily.

The following day, Gallagher met Emily at the house of a mutual friend, Mrs Ward, where they all had a few drinks. Eventually the time came for Emily to return home. Soon afterwards Emily returned, sporting a bruised and rapidly blackening eye. "See what our Bill has done," she exclaimed and immediately Gallagher was on his feet threatening to give William Swann a taste of his own medicine. Emily was heard to mutter: "I hope he kills him" and the two then returned to her house.

Once John and Emily were inside, the sounds of a struggle were heard, above which Emily was shouting: "Give it to him Johnnie, punch him to death." After five minutes of this, John and Emily returned to Mrs Ward's, where Gallagher helped himself to another drink and boasted that he had broken four of Swann's ribs. He then threatened to break some more and, as if to keep his promise, returned to Swann's house. Once again the sounds of a struggle could be heard.

Later that same day, Emily Swann returned again to Mrs Ward's house and said she had found her husband dead. Gallagher, realising what he had done, vanished from the scene but was arrested at Middlesborough on August 4th.

John Gallagher and Emily Swann were both charged with murder. No defence was offered for Gallagher beyond the fact that he had been drinking and had only decided to attack Swann once he had seen what had been done to Emily. Emily's defence was that she had not enticed Gallagher to action.

In his summing up, Mister Justice Darling spent some time outlining that one who incited another to kill was just as guilty of the crime. If, therefore, the jury came to believe that Emily had incited Gallagher, she was guilty as charged.

Gallagher and Swann were both found guilty of murder and sentenced to death. On the morning of December 29th, the pair were stood next to each other on the gallows. Emily saw her lover already positioned as she took her place. "Good morning John," she was heard to say. Gallagher replied: "Good morning, love." Then, with a final: "Goodbye, God bless you" from Emily, the two lovers were hanged.

NAMES	John Gallagher; Emily Swann
AGES AT EXECUTION	30; 42
DATE OF EXECUTION	Tuesday, 29th December, 1903
PLACE OF EXECUTION	Leeds
HANGMAN	William Billington
ASSISTANT	John Ellis
DATE OF TRIAL	9th December, 1903
LOCATION OF TRIAL	Leeds
PRESIDING JUDGE	Mister Justice Darling
PROSECUTION COUNSEL	Tindal Atkinson, W.J. Waugh
DEFENCE COUNSEL	Mister Mitchell Innes, Harold Newell
NUMBER OF VICTIMS	1

VICTIMS DETAILS

NAME	William Swan
AGE	Not known
DATE OF MURDER	Saturday, 6th June 1903
PLACE OF MURDER	George Square, Wombwell, Barnsley
METHOD OF KILLING	Battered
RELATIONSHIP TO KILLER	None; husband

1903

HENRY STARR'S RELATIONSHIP with his wife was an on-and-off affair. The couple were married in the spring of 1903, and for the first few months, seemed to be very happy, living with Mary's mother. There must have been some friction in the household though, because soon Henry took to drinking heavily and eventually left his wife.

By this time Mary was pregnant and gave birth in August, whereupon Henry asked her if she would come to live with him. Mary agreed to give the relationship another chance.

In early November, Mary returned again to her mother. She looked half-starved and told of how she had been mistreated by Henry. A few days later, on the 16th of that month, Mary received a letter from Henry, asking if she would return to him but pointing out that if she said no, it was his intention to seek for custody of their child. Mary consulted a solicitor and took out a maintenance order for 6/- a week against Henry. For good measure, she also obtained a separation order and a custody order for the child. Henry was not pleased.

The following day, November 24th, there was a knock on the door of the house where Mary was living. Her mother heard her go downstairs and a few moments later, heard her daughter shout: "Murder, mother." Mary's mother ran downstairs and was horrified to find her lying on the hearth rug with Starr standing over her, hacking at her with a bloodstained knife.

Mary's mother grabbed at Starr, causing him to drop the weapon. Rushing quickly to the kitchen, Starr returned with another knife and proceeded to attack Mary's mother, also striking her with some heavy object. The poor woman believed that she had breathed her last, but then Starr abruptly stopped his frenzied attack upon her.

By the time the police arrived, Henry Starr had vanished. A search revealed a number of public houses in which he had been seen and finally he was run to ground in one of them. He still had blood on his hands and clothing and investigations showed that Starr had been seen wandering the streets of Blackpool on the night before the attack, murmuring to himself that he would "... do it."

NAME	Henry Bertram Starr
AGE AT EXECUTION	31
DATE OF EXECUTION	Tuesday, 29th December, 1903
PLACE OF EXECUTION	Liverpool
HANGMAN	John Billington
ASSISTANT	Henry Pierrepoint
DATE OF TRIAL	7th December, 1903
LOCATION OF TRIAL	Liverpool
PRESIDING JUDGE	Mister Justice Ridley
PROSECUTION COUNSEL	Blackwood Wright, Walter Russell
DEFENCE COUNSEL	Mister Madden
NUMBER OF VICTIMS	1

VICTIMS DETAILS	
NAME	Mary Hannah Starr
AGE	Not known
DATE OF MURDER	Tuesday, 24th November, 1903
PLACE OF MURDER	Lord Street, Blackpool
METHOD OF KILLING	Stabbed
RELATIONSHIP TO KILLER	Wife

Starr's defence was that he had been suffering from delirium tremens. A friend who shared a room with Starr testified that he had indeed been suffering from delirium on the Saturday evening, but medical evidence was called to show that this attack would not have lasted until Tuesday, the day of the murder. The jury returned their verdict without even leaving the courtroom.

This had not been the first time Starr had been on trial for his life. On April 29th, 1896 he had been tried at Manchester for the murder of Eleanor Coulthard at Clitheroe. On that occasion he had been found not guilty.

ROSE MCCANN'S HUSBAND worked in America and sent her money regularly for her and their 11-year-old son, Francis. She kept the house and could often be seen walking into the town of Trillick to do her shopping. On Friday, November 20th. Rose left home, carrying her basket, at 4.00pm.

By late evening, Rose had not returned so Francis set out to look for her. Finding no signs he returned home and spoke to a neighbour, Mr Kilfeather. They both then set out but again no trace of Rose could be found. Mr Kilfeather roused other neighbours and a full-scale search was organised.

Eventually, blood was discovered near a gate. In the field onto which the gate opened, the searching party found Rose McCann's basket, then her shawl and finally, her body. She had been raped and battered to death.

Witnesses gave details of Rose's movements. Hugh McCaughey, the 12-year-old son of another neighbour, said he had seen Rose just after she left home. They walked into Trillick together and, after visiting three shops, had set out for home at 5.00pm. They had parted at the top of the lane which led to Rose's house, some time before 5.30pm.

James Irvine was a farm labourer and he was working in a field close to where Rose's body was found. At 5.30pm he had heard a woman laughing and this was followed almost immediately by a shout.

One of the shops Rose had visited was owned by Margaret Brady and she said that at the same time that Rose had been there she had also seen two men. One of these was Hugh Brennan whilst the other was Joseph Moran, a traveller who worked on the fairs.

Investigations showed that Moran had been behaving strangely. At around 7.00pm on the night of the murder he had visited the house of Mickey McLaughlin, his cousin. Moran went to bed and now, a full day later, had still not risen. Further, he had been showing off a brand new knife but when he was visited by a friend who asked to borrow it, Moran said he didn't own one.

The police appeared at the house on Saturday, November 21st. Moran was still in bed and when Sergeant Laidley searched him,

NAME	Joseph Moran
AGE AT EXECUTION	26
DATE OF EXECUTION	Tuesday, 5th January, 1904
PLACE OF EXECUTION	Londonderry
HANGMAN	William Billington
ASSISTANT	Not known
DATE OF TRIAL	2nd December – 3rd December, 1903
LOCATION OF TRIAL	Belfast
PRESIDING JUDGE	Lord Justice Baron
PROSECUTION COUNSEL	F.H. Campbell, Dennis Henry, J.R. Patchell
DEFENCE COUNSEL	T. Patton
NUMBER OF VICTIMS	1

VICTIMS DETAILS	
NAME	Rose Ann McCann
AGE	circa 38
DATE OF MURDER	Thursday, 20th November, 1902
PLACE OF MURDER	Trillick, Near Badesy, County Tyrone
METHOD OF KILLING	Battered/cut throat
RELATIONSHIP TO KILLER	None

the knife was found in his jacket pocket. The blade was twisted and tests carried out by Professor Barklie in Belfast showed extensive bloodstaining around the handle.

Moran faced three trials. The first began on March 11th, at Omagh, before Lord Justice O'Brien but the jury were unable to reach a verdict. The second trial, also at Omagh, before Mister Justice Gibson, began on July 9th and again the jury failed to agree. At the third trial, however, the jury took just one hour and 20 minutes to find Moran guilty.

SIDNEY SMITH LOVED Alice Woodman. For some months, Smith courted her, but unfortunately, Alice's parents did not approve of Sidney. He decided that the time had come for an ultimatum. On September 9th, 1903, he wrote to Alice saying that unless she came to live with him, their relationship was over.

Alice did not hesitate. The very next day, she moved into his lodgings at 2 St George's Avenue, Cheltenham. One week later they moved to a new address at Bubb's Cottages, in York Street, and on October 25th, Alice went to the Registry Office to see about announcing the banns. It was then that things began to go wrong.

Sidney lost his job and within a short time, his financial problems became very severe. At the beginning of November, he mentioned to his sister-in-law that he couldn't get married now because he couldn't afford it. Soon afterwards, he was heard announcing that he couldn't cope with things any longer and was thinking of putting a rope around his neck. Then came the final straw. Sidney was given notice to quit the house in York Street. He was told that he had to be out by December 14th, at the latest. On December 5th, Sidney bought himself a new razor.

At 9.30pm on December 13th, Sidney and Alice were at the house of a friend, Frances Eliza Dix. They seemed friendly and Sidney appeared happier than he had for weeks. He had come to a decision, and announced that he was going to Worcester to look for work.

The last sighting of Sidney and Alice together was made by a policeman, Constable Charles William Poulton, who saw them at 1.00am on December 14th. The couple were slightly the worse for drink and were heading home. As they passed Poulton, Sidney shouted "Good night policeman", and walked on.

Harriett Skinner lived next door to Alice, at number 2. She knocked at Alice's door early on the morning of the 14th, but received no reply. When she returned that afternoon and again got no response to her calls, she went for help and an entry was forced. Alice was already dead and Sidney, a wound in his throat, lay seriously ill close by. The police and a doctor were called. As the officers waited for the medical aid to arrive,

NAME	Sidney George Smith
AGE AT EXECUTION	23
DATE OF EXECUTION	Wednesday, 9th March, 1904
PLACE OF EXECUTION	Gloucester
HANGMAN	William Billington
ASSISTANT	John Billington
DATE OF TRIAL	15th February, 1904
LOCATION OF TRIAL	Gloucester
PRESIDING JUDGE	Mister Justice Ridley
PROSECUTION COUNSEL	Mister Mirehouse, Reginald Coventry
DEFENCE COUNSEL	Stamford Hutton
NUMBER OF VICTIMS	1

VICTIMS DETAILS	
NAME	Alice Woodman
AGE	21
DATE OF MURDER	Monday, 14th December, 1903
PLACE OF MURDER	1 Bubb's Cottages, York Street, Cheltenham
METHOD OF KILLING	Cut throat
RELATIONSHIP TO KILLER	Girlfriend

they asked Sidney what had happened. He could not speak, but when a piece of paper and a pencil were pushed into his hand, he wrote down: "I kild [sic] her." When asked what time this had happened, he scribbled: "Three o'clock."

There could be no doubt that Sidney had killed Alice Woodman and then went on to attempt suicide. At his trial, the jury took just five minutes to reach their verdict and as the sentence of death was intoned, tears were streaming down Smith's face.

ON SUNDAY, DECEMBER 27th, 1903, 12-year-old Elizabeth Mary Lynas went to church with some of her friends. After the service they all walked home together, Elizabeth finally saying goodbye at the corner of Bennison Street, where she lived.

In fact, Elizabeth never arrived home that night and in due course, her worried parents contacted the police and reported her as missing. A search was organised and in a short time, the child's body was found, in some woods near the Workhouse. She had been tied hand and foot and her throat had been cut. There were other signs of violence on the body but she had not been sexually assaulted. The search widened now to see if any clues could be found. This led to the discovery of extensive bloodstains in the yard of number 9, Bennison Street, just a few doors away from Elizabeth's home at number 17. Also found nearby was the tam-o'-shanter hat that Elizabeth had been wearing. It seemed clear that the poor girl had been killed in this yard and then dumped where she was found. Number nine was now thoroughly searched and a bloodstained razor was found on a kitchen shelf. Later a towel, also heavily bloodstained, was discovered and this confirmed police suspicions that the killer lived in this house.

Three people lived at number 9; James Henry Clarkson, his sister, and his father. It was soon shown that two of those people could satisfactorily account for their movements and so inquiries now centred on James.

James claimed that he had gone to the Applegarth public house at 7.55pm, not returning until 8.20pm. This would have been after the time that Elizabeth was murdered and would mean that James could not be the killer, providing his alibi stood firm. However, though he was well known in the area, no one could be found who remembered seeing him in the pub at the time he gave. Taken in for questioning, James's clothing was examined as a matter of routine and when it was found to be bloodstained, he was formally charged with murder.

Throughout his trial, James Clarkson maintained his innocence, though evidence

NAME	James Henry Clarkson
AGE AT EXECUTION	19
DATE OF EXECUTION	Tuesday, 29th March, 1904
PLACE OF EXECUTION	Leeds
HANGMAN	William Billington
ASSISTANT	Henry Pierrepoint
DATE OF TRIAL	8th March, 1904
LOCATION OF TRIAL	York
PRESIDING JUDGE	Mister Justice Lawrance
PROSECUTION COUNSEL	T.W. Milvain, H.B. Grotrian
DEFENCE COUNSEL	Edward Shortt
NUMBER OF VICTIMS	1

VICTIMS DETAILS	
NAME	Elizabeth Mary Lynas
AGE	12
DATE OF MURDER	Sunday, 27th December, 1903
PLACE OF MURDER	Yard at 9, Bennison Street, Guisborough, Cleveland
METHOD OF KILLING	Cut throat
RELATIONSHIP TO KILLER	None

was given that whilst he had been held in prison, he had been heard to cry aloud: "What made me do it?"

His father, Samuel, gave evidence that James had once fainted at the sight of a wound and had also collapsed on another occasion when hearing the description of an accident. Could such an apparently delicate person have cold-bloodedly slashed a child's throat? After a deliberation of just half an hour, the jury chose to believe that James Henry Clarkson had indeed carried out such an act, and found him guilty of murder. He was hanged just two days before his 20th birthday.

HENRY JONES AND Mary Gilbert cohabited together in Back West Street, Hanley, Staffordshire. The landlord there was James Johnson and under the same roof had lived a third lodger, a woman who died of bronchitis in mid-January. From that time onwards, Henry came to believe that there was something going on between Mary and James.

There were many arguments between Henry and Mary over this supposed relationship until finally, James gave Henry notice to leave his house. Over the next few days, Henry's jealousy grew to such a stage that on January 28th, he said to Police Sergeant Turner that James and Mary would not last long. In the case of Mary Gilbert, that was a prediction that would prove devastatingly accurate.

On that same night of January 28th, James Johnson went off to work as usual, leaving Mary alone with her three children. Henry returned home at 9.00pm, perfectly sober, and began yet another quarrel. The argument was a brief one and by the time they retired for the night, Mary and Henry appeared to be on friendly enough terms once more.

No disturbance was heard during the night. It was 4.00am when Charles, Mary's eldest child, rose and went to her room to see if it was time for him to light the fire, a task he did each morning. Henry told Charles that it was much too early and the boy returned to his bed. Two hours later, Charles went back to his mother's room and this time was told, again by Henry, to run and fetch a policeman. Charles went downstairs and at that moment, James Johnson returned from work. After being told by Charles of Henry's request, James noticed a piece of paper on the mantelpiece. It was a note, written by Henry, and read: "I have killed her through J. Johnson." The police were called and it was discovered that Mary was dead and Henry had cut his own throat, His wounds were dressed and he later made a full recovery in hospital. Upon his discharge, he was arrested and charged with murder.

Henry Jones readily admitted his guilt, his only regret being that he had not managed to kill himself as well. He explained how he had

NAME	Henry Jones
AGE AT EXECUTION	50
DATE OF EXECUTION	Tuesday, 29th March, 1904
PLACE OF EXECUTION	Stafford
HANGMAN	John Billington
ASSISTANT	John Ellis
DATE OF TRIAL	12th March, 1904
LOCATION OF TRIAL	Stafford
PRESIDING JUDGE	Mister Justice Kennedy
PROSECUTION COUNSEL	Mister Farrant, Mister Davidson
DEFENCE COUNSEL	Mister Plumptre
NUMBER OF VICTIMS	1

VICTIMS DETAILS	
NAME	Mary Elizabeth Gilbert
AGE	48
DATE OF MURDER	Friday, 29th January, 1904
PLACE OF MURDER	4 Back West Street, Hanley
METHOD OF KILLING	Battered/cut throat
RELATIONSHIP TO KILLER	Girlfriend

hit Mary over the head with a hammer and then cut her throat. Since there was no sign of any disturbance in the room it appeared that poor Mary had been asleep at the time she was attacked.

After hearing his confession, the jury took less than four minutes to return their guilty verdict and Jones was sentenced to death.

MARTHA ELIZA SIMPSON earned her living as a prostitute and the man who lived with her, Charles Dyer, was fully aware of this fact.

On Wednesday, February 3rd, 1904, Dyer asked Martha to pawn some items for him. Martha walked to the pawnbrokers with her close friend, Margaret Moran, and managed to obtain the princely sum of 1/-, which she duly handed over to Dyer. He then went out for a drink with Arthur Hockley, one of the two men who lodged with Margaret Moran.

Whilst Dyer enjoyed his drink, Martha met a client whom she took back to Margaret's, where she performed the usual services required of one who followed her profession. Dyer met her there later and the two of them left together some time before midnight. By 12.15am, Dyer was back at Margaret's house where he announced: "Oh Meg, I have done it. Save her if you can." Margaret managed to get Dyer to clarify his statement and he went on to claim that he had killed Martha because she had been with another man.

Margaret Moran and her two lodgers, Hockley and John Moran, who was no relation to Margaret, walked together to Dyer's house where they found Martha sitting in an armchair. There were no signs of a struggle and what looked like a peaceful scene was only spoiled by the fact that Martha was covered in blood, a vicious wound across her throat.

Charles Samuel Dyer, also known as Charlie Hammond, was hanged at Birmingham on April 5th. His execution was the first at that establishment for which the raising of the black flag and the tolling of the chapel bell were dispensed with.

NAME	Charles Samuel Dyer (Charlie Hammond)
AGE AT EXECUTION	25
DATE OF EXECUTION	Tuesday, 5th April, 1904
PLACE OF EXECUTION	Birmingham
HANGMAN	William Billington
ASSISTANT	John Billington
DATE OF TRIAL	17th March, 1904
LOCATION OF TRIAL	Birmingham
PRESIDING JUDGE	Mister Justice Wills
PROSECUTION COUNSEL	J.J. Parfitt, J.W.P. Mosley
DEFENCE COUNSEL	S.G. Dorsett, Norris Foster
NUMBER OF VICTIMS	1

VICTIMS DETAILS	
NAME	Martha Eliza Simpson
AGE	21
DATE OF MURDER	Thursday, 4th February, 1904
PLACE OF MURDER	2 Back 21, Inge Street, Birmingham
METHOD OF KILLING	Cut throat
RELATIONSHIP TO KILLER	Girlfriend

1904

WILLIAM KIRWAN MANAGED to commit murder in front of what is arguably the best possible witness: a policeman!

Kirwan, a sailor, was married to Mary Pike's sister. An insanely jealous man, he became convinced that his wife was using their home for immoral purposes and sleeping around with other men.

On February 26th, 1904, Kirwan's wife had chosen to visit her sister at her home in Great Newton Street, Liverpool. A short time later, William himself turned up. In the house at that time were his wife, Mary Pike, two children and a lodger named Russell. Upon the door being opened to him, Kirwan rushed into the house and again made accusations of infidelity against his wife, saying that this had taken place at her sister's house. She of course denied that any impropriety had taken place and this was duly confirmed by her sister, Mary Pike. Kirwan, far from satisfied, then drew a revolver out of his pocket and fired four times – twice at Mary and twice at his wife. Kirwan's wife was hit, but she was not badly wounded.

Hearing all this racket, the lodger, Russell, rushed downstairs from his room and bravely assisted the two ladies and the children out of the parlour, into the passageway outside and finally down into the cellar. Whilst all this was happening, Kirwan was busily reloading his revolver.

Seeing that his quarry had, at least temporarily, escaped his clutches, Kirwan now walked out into the street and discharged a bullet into the air. Mister Russell had by now managed to open a window in the cellar and shouted for someone to fetch a policeman. Kirwan did not seem the least concerned at this and calmly stood opposite the house, waiting for the officers to arrive. After a very short interval, the police did indeed arrive and promptly arrested William Kirwan. Unfortunately, Mary Pike chose this precise moment to rush out of her house and volunteer the somewhat superfluous observation that Kirwan was the man who had attacked them. Kirwan saw his opportunity, struggled free of the police officer who was holding him, drew out his revolver again and fired at a distance of two

NAME	William Kirwan
AGE AT EXECUTION	39
DATE OF EXECUTION	Tuesday, 31st May, 1904
PLACE OF EXECUTION	Liverpool
HANGMAN	William Billington
ASSISTANT	Henry Pierrepoint
DATE OF TRIAL	9th May, 1904
LOCATION OF TRIAL	Liverpool
PRESIDING JUDGE	Mister Justice Bucknill
PROSECUTION COUNSEL	A. Hyslop Maxwell, Robert S. Segar
DEFENCE COUNSEL	Mister Madden
NUMBER OF VICTIMS	1

VICTIMS DETAILS	
NAME	Mary Pike
AGE	Not known
DATE OF MURDER	Friday, 26th February, 1904
PLACE OF MURDER	Great Newton Street, Liverpool
METHOD OF KILLING	Shot
RELATIONSHIP TO KILLER	Sister-in-law

yards. Mary Pike fell wounded, at which point the revolver was finally taken from Kirwan.

Kirwan admitted that he intended to kill both Mary and his wife and was charged with attempted murder. His only regret seemed to be that he had not succeeded in this plan.

A few days after the shooting, Mary Pike died in hospital and the charge became one of wilful murder. At the subsequent trial, the returning of a guilty verdict was little more than a formality.

KWOK TIM LOY owned 22a Frederick Street, and rented out rooms to fellow Chinese. One of his lodgers was Ping Lun and one of Ping's closest friends was John Go Hing, who lived at 384 New Chester Road, Rock Ferry.

At 8.30pm on March 20th, 1904, Go Hing was at Frederick Street, playing a form of dominoes. There were a large number of spectators, many of whom were gambling on the outcome.

Some 40 minutes later, at 9.10pm, Ping Lun entered the room. He watched a couple of games and then said he wished to place a bet. Go Hing turned to Lun and explained that he would not accept as he refused to gamble with a friend. Ping insisted, but Go Hing would not be moved. Ping watched with dismay as the game was played and he realised that the bet would have been a winner.

He demanded to be paid. John Go Hing repeated that the bet had not been accepted. Ping Lun stormed out of the room, returning a couple of minutes later and demanding again that he be paid.

By now, Go Hing had moved from the table and was standing with his back to the fireplace. For a third time he refused to pay, whereupon a revolver was drawn and two shots fired. One missed completely but the other bullet struck Go Hing in the stomach. As Ping Lun made good his escape, two more shots were fired.

There were a number of witnesses and all made much the same statement. Moy Chung, Ah Chee, Yeung Lai, Moy Lee, Ah Wah, Jim Sing and Kwok Kim Loy all said that they had heard the argument and seen Ping Lun shoot his friend. The revolver was found in a passageway outside the house and Lun was arrested that same night when he returned to Frederick Street. When the injured man died, Lun was charged with murder.

Lun's story was that Go Hing had borrowed £3 from him before Christmas 1903, and had only paid £1 back. When in addition to this long-standing debt, Go Hing had refused to pay out the bet, Lun had snapped, gone upstairs for his gun and shot him.

Sentenced to death, Ping Lun was executed

NAME	Ping Lun
AGE AT EXECUTION	43
DATE OF EXECUTION	Tuesday, 31st May, 1904
PLACE OF EXECUTION	Liverpool
HANGMAN	William Billington
ASSISTANT	Henry Pierrepoint
DATE OF TRIAL	10th May, 1904
LOCATION OF TRIAL	Liverpool
PRESIDING JUDGE	Mister Justice Bucknill
PROSECUTION COUNSEL	John Mansfield, F.E. Smith
DEFENCE COUNSEL	Mr Madden, Mr Hurst
NUMBER OF VICTIMS	1

VICTIMS DETAILS	
NAME	John Go Hing (Died Wednesday, 23rd March)
AGE	29
DATE OF MURDER	Sunday, 20th March, 1904
PLACE OF MURDER	22a Frederick Street, Liverpool
METHOD OF KILLING	Shot
RELATIONSHIP TO KILLER	None

alongside William Kirwan on May 31st. It has been said that as the executioner and his assistant walked into the cell, the unfeeling Billington said, "Come on Ping Pong", to which the Chinaman took exception.

There is also the matter of the hanged man's correct name. Many books have given his name as Pong Lun. The original trial depositions all refer to him as Ping Lun, as does his own statement, and I hold that a man should know how to spell his own name!

JOHN SULLIVAN, A Durham-born seaman, and Dennis Lowthian, a cabin boy, both served on board the Waiwera, which set sail from London for New Zealand on January 6th, 1904. From the early stages a close friendship existed between Sullivan and Lowthian and this soon developed into intimacy. Sullivan, though, was insanely jealous.

Lowthian may well have felt stifled by this close attention. What is plain is that by the time the ship had reached the Cape of Good Hope, the friendship had cooled. Sullivan made it plain that he wanted things to continue; Lowthian made it equally plain that he couldn't care less.

On March 28th, Sullivan cracked. After his latest attempt to get closer to Lowthian had failed, Sullivan hit him in the mouth and even went so far as to touch a knife against Lowthian's flesh, though he didn't cut him. For that, Sullivan served seven days' imprisonment on the ship.

Once Sullivan was free, the once-warm friendship degenerated into constant arguments. On May 8th, Sullivan picked up a chopper and remarked that it would be a good thing to use to do away with someone. Eight days later, a similar chopper was seen underneath Sullivan's mattress.

The last threat was issued on the evening of May 18th. Sullivan walked up to Lowthian and shouted: "I will break your neck. I cannot stand this much longer and there will be a murder on this ship before morning." Later that evening, at about 9.00pm, Lowthian was talking to a crewman by the name of Fisher. Whilst they talked, Fisher saw Sullivan approach, lift an axe and bring it crashing down on Lowthian's head.

The ship's doctor was called but it was clear that Lowthian would not recover. Even as the doctor examined him, the young man gave a shudder and died. Sullivan was arrested and when spoken to later by the captain, said that a letter in his pocket would reveal all. The letter was long and rambling and ended with the phrase: "I shall cut his head off and take it overboard with me."

Back in England, Sullivan's defence was one of unsound mind. He had formerly served in the navy and it was said that since that time he had suffered from heart disease, melancholia and defective teeth, though what relevance the latter could have had was debatable.

Found guilty, two of the jurymen said that they wished to recommend Sullivan to mercy on the grounds that he had been provoked. Asked if he had anything to say before sentence was passed, Sullivan replied: "I consider that the judge summed up the case as if he had a personal grudge against me, and he also went to sleep while my lawyer was pleading for my life."

NAME	John Sullivan
AGE AT EXECUTION	40
DATE OF EXECUTION	Tuesday, 12th July, 1904
PLACE OF EXECUTION	Pentonville
HANGMAN	William Billington
ASSISTANT	John Billington
DATE OF TRIAL	23rd June, 1904
LOCATION OF TRIAL	Old Bailey
Presiding Judge	Mister Justice Grantham
PROSECUTION COUNSEL	Richard D. Muir, Mister Leycester
DEFENCE COUNSEL	Arthur Hutton
NUMBER OF VICTIMS	1

VICTIMS DETAILS	
NAME	Dennis Lowthian
AGE	17
DATE OF MURDER	Wednesday, 18th May, 1904
PLACE OF MURDER	On board the Waiwera at sea
METHOD OF KILLING	Battered
RELATIONSHIP TO KILLER	None

LIFE SEEMED TO hold no joys for Samuel Rowledge. Although he had been engaged for almost a year to Alice Foster, he was out of work and this fact depressed him considerably.

On March 15th, at about noon, Rowledge went to visit his sister-in-law, Elizabeth. Her husband, Alfred Rowledge, had suggested that he might be able to assist Samuel in his search for employment. In the course of his conversation with Elizabeth, Samuel suggested that it might be best for everyone if he shot Alice and himself. Little credence was given to this threat. Surely it was just the murmurings of someone who was down on his luck…

At 4.00pm that afternoon, Samuel Rowledge visited a pawnshop and redeemed a revolver he had left there some time before. He then headed off to his mother's house. At some time after 7.00pm, Alfred Rowledge also visited his mother's house and there he found his brother Samuel and Alice Foster, talking in the kitchen. It should be noted that at this time, although Alfred had spoken to his wife, she had not mentioned Samuel's earlier threat, so he had no idea what thoughts might be in his brother's mind.

When he saw his brother, Alfred remonstrated with him and asked why he had not done the job he had found for him. Alice became annoyed at this, because Samuel had told her that he had been working that afternoon. She accused him of being lazy and of lying to her. It was the straw that broke Samuel Rowledge's back. Samuel calmly walked out of the room without saying a word. When he returned a minute or so later, he had a revolver in his hand. Again he did not speak as he moved closer to Alice and Alfred. Then, when he was no more than three feet away, he fired once, hitting Alice. Alfred did not intend waiting around to see what would happen next. He ran out into the garden and as he did, heard two more shots being fired. Samuel, meanwhile, calmly sat down and waited for the police to arrive.

There could be no argument that Samuel had killed Alice. The only question was whether it could be classed as manslaughter

NAME	Samuel Rowledge
AGE AT EXECUTION	37
DATE OF EXECUTION	Wednesday, 13th July, 1904
PLACE OF EXECUTION	Northampton
HANGMAN	William Billington
ASSISTANT	Henry Pierrepoint
DATE OF TRIAL	22nd June, 1904
LOCATION OF TRIAL	Northampton
PRESIDING JUDGE	Mister Justice Bray
PROSECUTION COUNSEL	W.A. Metcalfe, Harold Russell
DEFENCE COUNSEL	Mister Stimson
NUMBER OF VICTIMS	1

VICTIMS DETAILS	
NAME	Alice Foster
AGE	32
DATE OF MURDER	Tuesday, 15th March, 1904
PLACE OF MURDER	Northampton
METHOD OF KILLING	Shot
RELATIONSHIP TO KILLER	Girlfriend

or not. The defence pointed out that Samuel had said that he intended to kill Alice and himself. Had he carried out that threat completely, the verdict at the inquest would probably have been that he killed Alice and himself whilst suffering from temporary insanity. The fact that he had not actually killed himself after all did not, in their opinion, mean that Rowledge was sane.

In the event, the prosecution case carried the day and Rowledge was executed at Northampton in July.

AGNES ALLEN HAD a daughter, Margaret, from a marriage that had, unfortunately, failed. Since that time she had lived with a man named Bulloch who had fathered another daughter, Susan, upon her. But that relationship too had now broken up and Agnes had taken up with a third man, Thomas Gunning, who was a brute of a man, especially when he was in drink.

On Friday, April 22nd, Gunning came home from work at 6.00pm. An argument broke out with Agnes, following which Gunning went out drinking. When he returned, at 10.30pm, he demanded that Agnes sew some buttons on a shirt for him but she refused, saying that it was too late. This only served to make Gunning angry and he swore that he would "swing for her" one day.

The next day, Gunning arrived home at 1.30pm, with a friend, Joseph Doyle, in tow. Both men were obviously drunk but this did not stop them going out again later, to visit more pubs. Gunning finally returned home, alone, at 10.30pm, half an hour after Agnes had retired for the night.

Immediately Gunning demanded that Agnes get out of bed and make him some soup. When she refused, he dragged her out of bed by the hair, threw her to the floor and kicked her hard in the left side of her head. Margaret Allen, who had witnessed this, ran from the house to fetch a policeman but, unable to find one, returned to the house and asked her mother to come away with her. Agnes did not reply, so Margaret ran from the house, taking her half-sister Susan with her, and stayed with a friend.

The house at 42 Green Street was actually owned by Mr Douglas Tracey and at some time between 1.00am and 2.00am on April 23rd he was woken by Thomas Gunning roaring that he was in the dark. Douglas went into Gunning's room and lit the lamp and there, by the flickering light, saw the naked body of Agnes Allen lying on the floor. There was a good deal of blood on her face and around her body and it was quite obvious that she was dead. Gunning, seeing what he had done, began to cry and sob. Later, after the police were called, a number of bloodstained items including a shovel, a brick, a hammer

NAME	Thomas Gunning
AGE AT EXECUTION	48
DATE OF EXECUTION	Tuesday, 26th July, 1904
PLACE OF EXECUTION	Duke Street, Glasgow
HANGMAN	William Billington
ASSISTANT	John Billington
DATE OF TRIAL	5th July, 1904
Location of Trial	Glasgow
PRESIDING JUDGE	Lord Justice Traynor
PROSECUTION COUNSEL	A. Orr Deas
DEFENCE COUNSEL	Christopher Johnston
NUMBER OF VICTIMS	1

VICTIMS DETAILS

NAME	Agnes Allen
AGE	Not known
DATE OF MURDER	Saturday, 23rd April, 1904
PLACE OF MURDER	42 Green Street, Bridgeton, Glasgow
METHOD OF KILLING	Battered
RELATIONSHIP TO KILLER	Girlfriend

and a pair of tongs were removed from the house. Gunning had used all of them on Agnes Allen.

The trial was little more than a formality, with the jury only taking 15 minutes to decide that Gunning was guilty, though they did add a recommendation to mercy. Gunning broke down completely as the sentence of death was passed and had to be assisted from the dock.

GEORGE BREEZE, A miner, and football player for Seaham White Star, had a good friend in a fellow miner named Chisholm. So when, on June 11th, George had an argument with his father and mentioned that he would be better off living elsewhere, Chisholm offered George a place in his home. Unfortunately, Breeze then fell in love with Chisholm's wife, Margaret.

The matter might have ended there, but Margaret was not happy with her husband and she began to feel for George as he felt for her. Mister Chisholm was not blind to what was going on and the entire triangle led to three people being rather unhappy with their lot, especially since George slept on a sofa in the same room where the Chisholms occupied the double bed.

On Wednesday, July 6th, Margaret got her husband's breakfast ready and saw him off to work at 4.20am. George was still sleeping on the sofa when Chisholm left and when he did rise, Margaret told him that she had had words with her husband. She seemed to be very unhappy and George, knowing that the woman he loved so dearly was sleeping each night with another man, was equally distraught. Margaret finished by saying that she wished she was dead.

George calmly asked Margaret is she would like him to kill her. She replied that she didn't care, adding that she did not think he had the heart to do it. George then proved her wrong by placing his hands around her throat and strangling her. He then left the house, leaving Margaret's young child standing by its mother's body. By now it was 8.30am and very soon a neighbour would call and discover what had happened.

George Breeze though had no thought of escape. On the table near the body was a full written confession, which ended by saying that he had gone to give himself up to the police. This Breeze did, walking into Durham police station and admitting to the murder. He had already written out a second confession which he handed over. This confession was a heart-breaking document, outlining the depth of his love for the woman he had killed.

So eager was George Breeze to be condemned to death that before his trial could start, a report had to be submitted, confirming that he was fit to plead. When the case came to court, Breeze pleaded guilty and refused to be defended.

Asked if he had anything to say before the death sentence was passed, Breeze replied that he was not sorry for what he had done and was quite ready to die. After the sentence was intoned, Breeze thanked the judge and added that he hoped there would be no reprieve. His only wish now was to join the woman he loved.

NAME	George Breeze
AGE AT EXECUTION	21
DATE OF EXECUTION	Tuesday, 2nd August, 1904
PLACE OF EXECUTION	Durham
HANGMAN	William Billington
ASSISTANT	John Ellis
DATE OF TRIAL	16th July, 1904
LOCATION OF TRIAL	Durham
PRESIDING JUDGE	Mister Justice Grantham
PROSECUTION COUNSEL	Hans Hamilton, Coutts Trotter
DEFENCE COUNSEL	Mister Ball
NUMBER OF VICTIMS	1

VICTIMS DETAILS	
NAME	Margaret Jane Chisholm
AGE	20
DATE OF MURDER	Wednesday, 6th July, 1904
PLACE OF MURDER	9 Back South Railway Street, Seaham
METHOD OF KILLING	Strangled
RELATIONSHIP TO KILLER	Girlfriend

1904

PEOPLE OFTEN ASK a policeman for directions and so, when John Thomas Kay stopped a constable in the street and asked him the way to the police station, there seemed nothing unusual in the request. The officer was heading that way and kindly offered to accompany the gentleman there. On the way, Kay told him something that turned an apparently routine request into something much more.

"I might as well tell you, it's murder I think. I've killed the woman I live with. I did it with a hatchet." Kay went on to say that he had hit the woman at least three or four times – he was not sure exactly how many. The officer, after listening intently to the story, made sure that Kay reached his destination and then reported the conversation to his superiors.

When Kay's house was entered, the police found that an attack had indeed taken place, but the victim, Jane Hirst, was still alive though deeply unconscious. She had a number of wounds in her scalp and although medical assistance was summoned, Jane died soon after the doctor had arrived. Now it most certainly was a case of murder.

Inquiries showed that Jane Hirst was a married woman who had separated from her husband, due in no small part to her fondness for drink. She had been living with Kay since September 1903 and since he too was a heavy drinker, the relationship was volatile to say the least.

On April 5th for instance, the couple had argued fiercely and Kay had thrown her out of the house, refusing to let her back in until the following day. Not surprisingly, part of Kay's defence was that he was under the influence of drink at the time of the attack on Jane. He said that he had been drinking constantly for some weeks beforehand, as had Jane herself. He also claimed that he had discovered that Jane had been unfaithful to him and that this had preyed upon his mind. In fact, he had attempted suicide because of this knowledge and all this evidence, when taken together, was a clear indication that his mind was unhinged at the time. He was therefore not aware of what he was doing and was only guilty of manslaughter.

Like so many other such pleas, this

NAME	John Thomas Kay
AGE AT EXECUTION	52
DATE OF EXECUTION	Tuesday, 16th August, 1904
PLACE OF EXECUTION	Leeds
HANGMAN	John Billington
ASSISTANT	Henry Pierrepoint
DATE OF TRIAL	29th July, 1904
LOCATION OF TRIAL	Leeds
PRESIDING JUDGE	Mister Justice Channell
PROSECUTION COUNSEL	Harold Thomas, Mister Ball
DEFENCE COUNSEL	Mister Mitchell-Innes
NUMBER OF VICTIMS	1

VICTIMS DETAILS	
NAME	Jane Hirst
AGE	28
DATE OF MURDER	Tuesday, 10th May, 1904
PLACE OF MURDER	224 Sheffield Road, Ickles, Rotherham
METHOD OF KILLING	Battered
RELATIONSHIP TO KILLER	Girlfriend

defence failed. Kay was adjudged to be guilty of murder and sentenced to death.

SAMUEL HOLDEN, A market porter, had lived with Susan Humphries for three years at various addresses throughout the city of Birmingham. Now they were living in a furnished room in Coventry Street, a rather poor area in 1904. It was something of a comedown for a man with a distinguished war record. Holden had served in the Boer War, where he was wounded, and had been awarded the South African Medal, with four clasps.

Possibly because of the circumstances they both found themselves in, Samuel and Susan were heavy drinkers and the drink caused them to argue. Their rows were a regular event and the neighbours were well aware of the tensions that existed between the couple.

On July 2nd, 1904, Eliza Jane Walton, who lived in a house opposite to Holden, heard a cry. She looked across in time to see Holden stab Susan two or three times. He then ran into the street shouting: "Fetch a doctor, I've killed her." The doctor and the police were called but Susan died on the way to hospital.

Holden's defence was one of provocation. He maintained that he had stabbed Susan in the heat of the moment at the end of a long and furious row. In his summing up, the judge referred to Holden's war record, remarking that whilst his previous life entitled him to every consideration, the case must be tried on its merits alone. The jury were to consider only the evidence, not what may have happened before. After 20 minutes' deliberation, the jury returned and announced that Holden was guilty of murder.

On the morning of his execution, Samuel Holden faced his death like a soldier. It was said that he walked firmly to the scaffold, smoking an expensive cigar.

NAME	Samuel Holden
AGE AT EXECUTION	43
DATE OF EXECUTION	Tuesday, 16th August, 1904
PLACE OF EXECUTION	Birmingham
HANGMAN	William Billington
ASSISTANT	John Ellis
DATE OF TRIAL	29th July, 1904
LOCATION OF TRIAL	Birmingham
PRESIDING JUDGE	Lord Chief Justice, Lord Alverstone
PROSECUTION COUNSEL	Mister Disney, Reginald Coventry
DEFENCE COUNSEL	S.G. Dorsett, Norris Foster
NUMBER OF VICTIMS	1

VICTIMS DETAILS	
NAME	Susan Humphries
AGE	Not known
DATE OF MURDER	Saturday, 2nd July, 1904
PLACE OF MURDER	2 Back 109 Coventry Street, Birmingham
METHOD OF KILLING	Stabbed
RELATIONSHIP TO KILLER	Girlfriend

1904

1904

AT 6.30AM, THE errand boy arrived at Miss Farmer's newsagents shop. He was surprised to find the shop open and no sign of his employer.

By 7.30am there was still no sign of Miss Farmer. Shortly afterwards another boy came in and was told about her non-appearance. He in turn passed this on to his employer, who contacted the police.

When a policeman entered the shop he spotted a set of false teeth and a boot lying close to the counter. Walking into the back he saw a pair of spectacles on the stairs. Finally, entering Miss Farmer's bedroom he found her lying face-down on the bed, her hands tied behind her and a towel around her mouth. There was a faint pulse but by the time Doctor Grant arrived, she was dead.

The bedroom was in a state of disarray and jewellery was missing. Death had probably been accidental, the towel being forced too far into Miss Farmer's mouth, but as this had been done in the furtherance of a crime, it was murder nonetheless.

An appeal for witnesses brought results. Richard Barnes, a painter, said that late on October 11th, he had seen two men standing on Commercial Road, close by the shop. One of those men was Charles Wade.

The following morning, at about 6.00am, as Barnes was enjoying a drink in a coffee house, he saw the same two men crossing the road, walking in the direction of the shop.

Another witness named Rae described two men whom he had seen coming out of the shop at 6.20am on the morning of the murder. The descriptions fitted Charles Wade and his half-brother, Conrad Donovan, whose real name was Joseph Potter. Both men had records for robbery and were arrested on October 16th. Barnes and Rae attended identity parades at Brixton prison and picked out Wade and Donovan.

The missing property was not found in either of the prisoners' homes. Mister Rae volunteered that he had seen pictures of the men before he had come forward and two other witnesses failed to pick out either man in the line-up. There certainly seemed to be an element of doubt but even so, the jury took just 10 minutes to decide that both were

NAMES	Joseph Potter (Conrad Donovan); Charles Wade
AGES AT EXECUTION	35; 22
DATE OF EXECUTION	Tuesday, 13th December, 1904
PLACE OF EXECUTION	Pentonville
HANGMAN	William Billington
ASSISTANT	Henry Pierrepoint
DATE OF TRIAL	18th November – 21st November, 1904
LOCATION OF TRIAL	Old Bailey
PRESIDING JUDGE	Mister Justice Grantham
PROSECUTION COUNSEL	Charles Mathews, Arthur Gill
DEFENCE COUNSEL	Perceval Hughes, Paul Methven, Gathorne Hardy
NUMBER OF VICTIMS	1

VICTIMS DETAILS	
NAME	Matilda Emily Farmer
AGE	65
DATE OF MURDER	Wednesday, 12th October, 1904
PLACE OF MURDER	478 Commercial Road, Stepney, London
METHOD OF KILLING	Asphyxiated
RELATIONSHIP TO KILLERS	None; none

guilty. As the death sentence was passed, both loudly protested their innocence.

On December 5th, eight days before the two were to hang, workmen repairing the murder house found the missing jewellery under the floorboards This only served to indicate that the thieves had not escaped with as much as the police had originally thought.

Shortly before the appointed hour, Conrad Donovan made a simple statement to the prison chaplain: "No murder was intended." With those four words, he had confirmed that the sentence was the correct one.

TO THE SOUTH of the ancient walls of York lies Alma Terrace. In 1904 this was where John Dalby lived and where, on July 29th of that year, he received his last ever visitor.

Edmund Hall had travelled from Leeds to see his father-in-law. He was seen going to the door of the old man's house, knocking, and being admitted. Very soon after, neighbours heard the sounds of a struggle from next door, followed by a groan.

Two of the neighbours, Mister Liddall and Mister Jagger, went to investigate. Getting no answer at the front door, they walked around to the rear of the house. They knocked again and almost immediately the door was opened by John Dalby, who half-staggered and half-fell into their arms. He was bleeding profusely from a severe wound in his neck and tried to say something, but was unable to utter a word.

Jagger shouted, "Get a doctor" and at the sound of his voice, Hall appeared from inside the house, announced that he would go for a doctor, leapt over the wall at the back of the house and vanished into the street. A doctor was eventually summoned by the two men with Dalby, but the victim died in hospital later that same day.

Hall was known to the witnesses, so the police knew exactly who they were looking for. Knowing that he came from Leeds, it was a simple deduction to work out that he had probably travelled to York by train. The police waited at the station and later that night, Hall was arrested as he sat on his train, waiting for it to pull out. He looked totally unconcerned and was busily smoking a rather large cigar.

Taken to the police station, Hall was found to be wearing a gold watch and chain identified as belonging to John Dalby. Furthermore, a bar of the chain was missing and this was found in Dalby's front room where he had been attacked. Still attached to it was the spade guinea that always adorned it.

Hall had been in the army and had served in India. In court it was revealed that he had been discharged in 1879, suffering from melancholia, which in turn had been induced by sunstroke. Back in England he had then

NAME	Edmund Hall
AGE AT EXECUTION	49
DATE OF EXECUTION	Tuesday, 20th December, 1904
PLACE OF EXECUTION	Leeds
HANGMAN	John Billington
ASSISTANT	Henry Pierrepoint
DATE OF TRIAL	1st December, 1904
LOCATION OF TRIAL	York
PRESIDING JUDGE	Mister Justice Darling
PROSECUTION COUNSEL	Mister Grotrian, Mister Wilberforce
DEFENCE COUNSEL	G.F.L. Mortimer
NUMBER OF VICTIMS	1

VICTIMS DETAILS	
NAME	John Dalby
AGE	78
DATE OF MURDER	Friday, 29th July, 1904
PLACE OF MURDER	Alma Terrace, York
METHOD OF KILLING	Cut throat
RELATIONSHIP TO KILLER	Father-in-law

been injured in a lift accident and this too had affected his mind. The medical officer of Wakefield prison, Doctor Clark, testified that he had examined Hall and in his opinion, the smallest cause could lead him to violence. The jury however chose to put greater importance on testimony that Hall had unsuccessfully tried to purchase a revolver on July 28th, the day before Dalby was killed. This implied that the crime was premeditated and that Hall had been fully aware of what he was doing.

AT 11.45PM ON Saturday, September 10th, 1904, Mary Jones retired to her bed at the Bridgend Hotel, Ystrad. Mary was the wife of the landlord, John Emlyn Jones, but he stayed downstairs with some of the staff, clearing up. It was not until 2.00am on the Sunday morning that a weary Mr Jones finally climbed into bed beside his wife.

As Jones retired, the room was still reasonably well lit. The gas lamp was on and a nightlight burned on the dressing table. So, when a noise disturbed Mary at 3.30am she was able to see the room clearly and could not help but notice that there was a man's face peering at her through the brass frame at the foot of the bed.

The intruder was crouching. Mary jumped up in bed, calling for her husband, but before John Jones could come to her aid the intruder was upon her and struck her very hard with some heavy object. The blow landed on the left side of Mary's head and immediately blood flowed from a deep wound in her temple.

By this time, John had leapt out of bed and as he moved to grapple with the intruder, the stranger moved towards him and met him halfway. A fierce struggle began with the man raining repeated blows onto Jones with the object, which Mary could now see was wrapped in brown paper.

It soon became clear that John Jones was getting the worst of the tussle. Bravely, Mary went to her husband's aid and managed to pull the man by the arm. At the same time, she somehow managed to open the bedroom door and the two men now tumbled out onto the landing outside the bedroom.

There were various members of staff living on the premises and one of these was John Henry Carpenter, the cellarman. Mary shouted up to the attic where he slept, calling "Jack! Jack!" Carpenter, by now woken by the racket from downstairs, shouted back that he was coming and Mary called back "Come down quick, there is someone here murdering us."

Even before Carpenter could pull on his trousers, though, the struggle was over. The intruder had fled, leaving John Jones clutching the banister for support. It was

NAME	Eric Lange (Eugene Lorenz)
AGE AT EXECUTION	30
DATE OF EXECUTION	Wednesday, 21st December, 1904
PLACE OF EXECUTION	Cardiff
HANGMAN	William Billington
ASSISTANT	John Ellis
DATE OF TRIAL	28th November, 1904
LOCATION OF TRIAL	Swansea
PRESIDING JUDGE	Mister Justice Bray
PROSECUTION COUNSEL	W.D. Benson, Ivor Bowen
DEFENCE COUNSEL	Morgan Morgan
NUMBER OF VICTIMS	1

VICTIMS DETAILS

NAME	John Emlyn Jones
AGE	37
DATE OF MURDER	Sunday, 11th September, 1904
PLACE OF MURDER	Bridge Inn, Pentre, Ystrad, Rhondda
METHOD OF KILLING	Battered/Stabbed
RELATIONSHIP TO KILLER	None

clear that he was badly injured. The stricken man was lifted onto his bed and then Mary went up to the room occupied by Katie Richards, her niece, and asked her to run for the doctor. In the event, both Katie and John Carpenter went to fetch Dr Thomas, who lived 300 yards away.

It was 3.45am when Dr William Evans Thomas arrived, only to find that his patient was already dead, having been stabbed as well as battered. Five minutes later, Inspector John Williams arrived and made a careful inspection of the premises. The intruder had affected his entrance by climbing up a ladder that had been placed against the pub wall, reaching up to the window of a lavatory some 13 feet from the ground. Downstairs, the cash register in the bar was partly open but the intruder had decided to see if he could find anything of value upstairs for a pair of men's brown shoes were found at the foot of the stairs. The killer, whoever he was, had run off without collecting his shoes.

Inside the bedroom, on the floor at the left side of the bed, Inspector Williams found an old rasp wrapped in brown paper and tied tightly with cord. This was the weapon that had been described by Mrs Jones and since the paper bore a number of spots of blood, it was obviously the cosh used to attack her and her husband.

The killer, whoever he was, would certainly be a conspicuous individual and easy enough to spot. Almost certainly bloodstained, he had also been without a cap and had worn no shoes. These details were quickly passed to all the police stations in the area and it was this report that led Constable David John Woods to go to Rhondda Road, where the railway line from Pentre ran.

Constable Woods took up his position at 4.30am and it was a full hour later that he saw someone walking along the line, coming from the direction of Pentre. As the man drew level with his hiding place, Woods jumped out and identified himself as a police officer. Shining his lantern upon the man, Woods saw that there was a patch of what looked like blood on the man's right cheek and a fresh scratch on his nose. His trousers were torn at the knee and blood seeped through from a wound on his leg. The man wore no cap and, even more significantly, no boots either. He was immediately arrested. He identified himself as Eric Lange, a Russian seaman born at Riga.

It was not long before some interesting facts were discovered about Eric Lange. Walter Burbidge, who had been a drayman at the Bridge Inn, identified Lange as being none other than Eugene Lorenz, who had actually worked at the inn for a previous landlord, Mister Gould. Sure enough, when records were checked, it was shown that a man named Lorenz had worked at the inn from July 19th to August 24th, 1901.

The barmaid at the time had been Florence Morgan. She remembered Lorenz and realised now that Lange was the same man. She went on to say that Lange had been a in the bar a number of times over the past week and now at last she knew why his face seemed so familiar to her.

At his trial, Lange's defence was that he simply was not the killer of John Jones. He admitted that he had gone to the inn, with an accomplice named 'Harry' with the intention of stealing the day's takings. He and Harry had gained access through the toilet window and having found nothing of value downstairs,

Lange decided to see if there was anything worth taking upstairs. Removing his shoes, Lange went into the bedroom and when Mrs Jones woke, he struck her with the file that he had taken along to use as a jemmy. He agreed that he had been the man grappling with John Jones but claimed that he had won the fight and was making good his escape when Jones leapt on him from behind. The next thing he knew, Jones had been stabbed by Harry.

The prosecution suggested that Harry was a complete fiction and that Lange had committed the crime alone. The jury agreed and Lange, alias Eugene Lorenz, was sentenced to death.

At 8.00am on the morning of Wednesday, December 21st, 1904, Lorenz, was hanged as a crowd estimated at 600 strong waited outside the prison gates. Lange had made one last request. As the executioners entered the condemned cell, he asked that his hands be pinioned in front of him, rather than behind, but since this was contrary to prison regulations, the request was refused.

1904

NO ONE COULD understand it. John Flanagan had simply vanished from the face of the earth.

Flanagan, who sold eggs at the local market in Clones, had last been seen on April 16th, 1903, when he left the market in the company of a local butcher named Joseph Fee. That had been at 12.30pm and Flanagan had told Patrick Moran, who helped him in the market, that he would only be gone 10 minutes. Two and a half hours later, Fee had returned to the market alone and when asked about Flanagan, was happy to say that they had transacted some business, enjoyed a glass of port wine to celebrate and then parted company.

Naturally the police spoke to Fee, especially after James Nicholl who ran the local grocer's and hardware shop reported that Fee had called in his shop at some time between 1.00pm and 3.00pm, held up a spade and, leaving the shop shouted, "Charge me with this." Still, no trace of the missing man could be found, nor of the £80 or so he would have had on his person when he vanished.

Over the next few months, people noticed that Fee had started to spend more freely. He now bought a better class of animal to slaughter and sell in his shop. But still there was nothing concrete to link him to Flanagan's disappearance. Nothing, that is, until the Town Sergeant complained to Fee about a pile of manure behind his slaughterhouse in Fermanagh Street. It was growing in size and somewhat of a nuisance and so Fee was ordered to move it, or failing that, reduce it in size. Fee said that he would comply and paid two local men McCoy and Farmer, to move it for him, but he did ask them to leave a couple of barrowloads at the bottom.

The two men started to work on December 16th 1903, and after some time, one of them noticed a boot. He pulled at it and when it finally yielded he found to his horror that part of a human foot had come away inside the boot. The rotting body of John Flanagan had finally been found. He had been battered to death and there was also a slit in his throat.

Arrested for the crime, Fee faced three trials. The first, in Monaghan, lasted from

NAME	Joseph Fee
AGE AT EXECUTION	23
DATE OF EXECUTION	Thursday, 22nd December, 1904
PLACE OF EXECUTION	Armagh
HANGMAN	Henry Pierrepoint
ASSISTANT	Not known
DATE OF TRIAL	8th December – 10th December, 1904
LOCATION OF TRIAL	Belfast
PRESIDING JUDGE	Mister Justice Wright
PROSECUTION COUNSEL	T. O'Shaughnessy
DEFENCE COUNSEL	Hill Smith
NUMBER OF VICTIMS	1

VICTIMS DETAILS	
NAME	John Flanagan
AGE	Not known
DATE OF MURDER	16th April, 1903
PLACE OF MURDER	Clones, County Monaghan
METHOD OF KILLING	Battered/cut throat
RELATIONSHIP TO KILLER	None

March 3rd to March 5th, 1904, before Mister Justice Kenny. The jury were unable to agree. The same thing happened in July when Fee faced his second trial, also at Monaghan, before Mister Justice Johnson, the proceedings lasting from the 5th to the 8th of that month. At his third trial, the jury took just one hour to finally decide that Fee was guilty as charged.

ARTHUR JEFFRIES WAS one of a gang of poachers who operated around the Rotherham area. Another member of the gang, and perhaps Arthur's closest friend, was Samuel Barker. In October 1904, a disagreement broke out between Jeffries and the rest of the gang. When the other men chose to go poaching without him, Jeffries resented it greatly. He had issued threats against the other gang members and added that he would 'do' for one of them.

It was 11.45pm on November 12th, 1904. Four of the poachers – Barker, Broadhead, Morris and Strutt – were walking home together when they were passed by the running figure of Arthur Jeffries. The group were not concerned. They knew that Jeffries lived just ahead of them and assumed that he was merely in a hurry to be home. This was confirmed a few minutes later as the group reached an alleyway that led to Jeffries's home. There was Arthur, standing with his wife at the end of the alley. The four friends were walking past Jeffries when Barker said: "Good night, Arthur." Instead of taking the friendly greeting, Jeffries answered: "Good night to you, you bugger." Barker laughed at the comment and added: "Bugger you too, Arthur."

It was a harmless enough remark but Jeffries immediately grabbed Barker and hit him. A fight started and the two men entered the darkness of the alleyway. Within a very short time, both men had tumbled to the far end of the alley and then Barker fell to the ground, a stab wound in his side that would later be measured as eight and a half inches deep. He was carried to a friend's house but died within minutes. When Jeffries was arrested he expressed genuine remorse over what he had done. He could not believe that Barker was dead. The police searched the area carefully by the light of the following day, but the murder weapon was never discovered.

In court, Jeffries claimed that the fatal blow had been struck in the heat of the moment, during a fight, and that therefore his crime was one of manslaughter. His defence counsel pointed out that no one had actually seen the fatal blow struck or even if it had

NAME	Arthur Jeffries
AGE AT EXECUTION	44
DATE OF EXECUTION	Thursday, 29th December, 1904
PLACE OF EXECUTION	Leeds
HANGMAN	John Billington
ASSISTANT	Henry Pierrepoint
DATE OF TRIAL	8th December, 1904
LOCATION OF TRIAL	Leeds
PRESIDING JUDGE	Mister Justice Grantham
PROSECUTION COUNSEL	T.R.D. Wright, Mister Hall
DEFENCE COUNSEL	Mister Coutts-Trotter
NUMBER OF VICTIMS	1

VICTIMS DETAILS	
NAME	Samuel Barker
AGE	Not known
DATE OF MURDER	Saturday, 12th November, 1904
PLACE OF MURDER	Alley in Rotherham
METHOD OF KILLING	Stabbed
RELATIONSHIP TO KILLER	None

been Jeffries who first produced the weapon. In his summing up, though, the judge – a country squire and himself no lover of poachers – said that the only possible verdict was murder if Jeffries had struck the blow which killed Barker.

After half an hour of deliberation the jury returned a guilty verdict but added a recommendation to mercy. It did nothing to save Jeffries's life. On the morning of his execution, he walked firmly to the gallows. His last words were: "Lord, receive my spirit."

EDWARD HARRISON WAS a violent man. In September 1904, not for the first time, he assaulted his wife and she decided to take some positive action against him. Taking legal advice, Mrs Harrison had her husband summonsed for assault for which he was given a choice of a 20/- fine, or 10 days' imprisonment. Since he was unable to pay, Edward Harrison went to jail. Elizabeth Jane Rickus, Harrison's married daughter, knew that unless some more permanent solution could be found, her father would go on assaulting her mother. Surely it would be better if alternative accommodation could be found so that when Harrison was released, he would be unable to find his wife.

Upon his release, it seemed as if Harrison was at last getting his life into some sort of order. He obtained employment as a potman at a public house in Deptford, and shortly afterwards called on his daughter and her husband and asked them if they knew where his wife was.

Elizabeth said she did not know where her mother was. At that, Harrison, in a rather melodramatic manner, sank to his knees and cried: "If I don't know soon where she is, there will be murder here." Having made this outburst, he then stood and went quietly on his way.

On January 26th, whilst speaking to his brother-in-law, Harrison again made threats towards his daughter. Later that same morning, the body of Elizabeth Rickus was discovered in her kitchen, lying in a pool of blood. Her throat had been cut so deeply that her head was almost severed from her body.

Harrison was arrested that same evening, at his place of employment. Without being prompted he said that he knew what the police had come for and observed that he would probably swing for what he had done. At the police station he even remarked that he was pleased with himself.

At his trial, Harrison attempted to rely on a plea of self-defence. He said that he had gone back to see his daughter and ask again for the whereabouts of his wife. According to Harrison, they had begun to argue and at one stage, she had picked up a knife and rushed at her father. He had moved to defend himself

NAME	Edward Harrison
AGE AT EXECUTION	62
DATE OF EXECUTION	Tuesday, 28th February, 1905
PLACE OF EXECUTION	Wandsworth
HANGMAN	John Billington
ASSISTANT	Henry Pierrepoint
DATE OF TRIAL	10th February, 1905
LOCATION OF TRIAL	Old Bailey
PRESIDING JUDGE	Mister Justice Darling
PROSECUTION COUNSEL	Arthur Gill, Graham Campbell
DEFENCE COUNSEL	R.B. Murphy
NUMBER OF VICTIMS	1

VICTIMS DETAILS	
NAME	Elizabeth Jane Rickus
AGE	30
DATE OF MURDER	Thursday, 26th January, 1905
PLACE OF MURDER	Deptford, London
METHOD OF KILLING	Cut throat
RELATIONSHIP TO KILLER	Daughter

from this onslaught and they had grappled for the weapon, eventually falling onto the floor. Harrison said that it must have been during that struggle that Elizabeth's throat was accidentally slashed.

Had this story been accepted, then the charge would have been reduced to one of manslaughter. However, the scenario did not agree with the facts. Harrison had been heard to issue threats to kill his daughter and at the police station he had expressed pleasure in his efforts. Finding him guilty the jury nevertheless added a strong recommendation to mercy on the grounds that Harrison had been provoked by his family.

Hanged at Wandsworth, Harrison's last words on the drop were: "I did it!"

IF EVER A union of babysitters and childminders were to be formed, there is little chance that John Hutchinson would ever appear in its Hall of Fame.

Hutchinson, a labourer, lodged with Mister Matthews and his wife, a young working couple who had a five-year-old son, Albert. At about 5.00pm on January 31st, 1905, circumstances dictated that Albert was left alone with Hutchinson for a short period of time. What should have been a simple child-minding exercise soon turned into something much more sinister. Shortly after 5.00pm, Hutchinson was walking the streets of Nottingham, looking for a policeman. When he finally found one, he went up to the officer and told him that he had just committed a murder. The policeman then accompanied Hutchinson back to the Matthews's residence.

Albert Matthews was most certainly dead. If the cutting of the child's throat had not achieved this aim, then the actual decapitation would have. The body had been horribly mutilated and the severed head lay under the sofa in the living room.

Hutchinson's story was fairly straight-forward. He had been looking after Albert when the child struck him with a poker. Whilst remonstrating with the boy might possibly have been a reasonable course of action, Hutchinson had taken matters rather too far and butchered him with a sharp knife.

The only defence possible was one of insanity. Witnesses were brought forward who said that a number of Hutchinson's relatives had committed suicide. Hutchinson himself had had two severe head injuries during his life – one when he was a child and another in 1896, when he was 20 years old. From that time onwards he had been subject to epileptic fits and it was therefore held that when he had killed Albert he was suffering from an epileptic maniacal seizure, so could not be held responsible for his actions.

Doctor Powell, the superintendent of the Nottinghamshire County Asylum, was then called. He had observed the prisoner carefully and in his opinion, there was no evidence of any form of insanity. That testimony carried the day. Hutchinson was found guilty and sentenced to death.

NAME	John Hutchinson
AGE AT EXECUTION	29
DATE OF EXECUTION	Wednesday, 29th March, 1905
PLACE OF EXECUTION	Nottingham
HANGMAN	John Billington
ASSISTANT	Henry Pierrepoint
DATE OF TRIAL	9th March, 1905
LOCATION OF TRIAL	Nottingham
PRESIDING JUDGE	Mister Justice Phillimore
PROSECUTION COUNSEL	Mister Magee
DEFENCE COUNSEL	Nowroji Tarachand
NUMBER OF VICTIMS	1

VICTIMS DETAILS	
NAME	Albert Matthews
AGE	5
DATE OF MURDER	Tuesday, 31st January, 1905
PLACE OF MURDER	Narrow Marsh, Nottingham
METHOD OF KILLING	Cut throat
RELATIONSHIP TO KILLER	None

ALTHOUGH ALFRED BRIDGEMAN'S engagement had been broken off during Christmas 1904, he still remained on excellent terms with his girlfriend and often spent time at her home, in Compton Street. Unfortunately, the same warm relationship did not exist between Bridgeman and the woman who would have become his mother-in-law, Catherina Balhard. On Friday, March 3rd, 1905, Bridgeman went around to Mrs Balhard's house and created a disturbance. She put this down to his intemperate drinking habits and no further action was taken.

On the Saturday, Bridgeman was drinking rather heavily again but this time he was with his girlfriend, in a public house close to where she lived. They left the pub together and walked to her house.

The next sighting of Bridgeman was made by Mrs Shadbolt, who was a lodger living with Mrs Balhard. She saw Bridgeman leaving his girlfriend's room and go back downstairs. She heard his footsteps returning back upstairs shortly afterwards and then heard the noise of an argument coming from Catherina's room, followed by a terrible scream.

Mrs Shadbolt left her room in time to see Bridgeman run from the house. Upon investigation, Catherina Balhard was found to be dead, her throat cut with savage ferocity. Bravely Mrs Shadbolt ran after Bridgeman but lost him in the maze of streets.

When Bridgeman was arrested on Monday, March 6th, in Hunter Street, he still had in his possession the bloodstained razor that he had used to kill Catherina. Furthermore, Bridgeman confessed that he had argued with Mrs Balhard because he heard that she had been saying bad things about him, and added that he was " ... ready to swing for it when the time comes." The case against him seemed to be very strong indeed.

Once again the combined defence of drink and insanity was used. Bridgeman claimed that he had no idea what he had done, due to being heavily under the influence of drink at the time. He then called evidence that whilst he had been in South Africa some years before, a large piece of iron had fallen onto his head in a blockhouse and ever since he had been troubled with headaches and blackouts.

NAME	Alfred Bridgeman
AGE AT EXECUTION	22
DATE OF EXECUTION	Wednesday, 26th April, 1905
PLACE OF EXECUTION	Pentonville
HANGMAN	John Billington
ASSISTANT	Henry Pierrepoint
DATE OF TRIAL	5th April, 1905
LOCATION OF TRIAL	Old Bailey
PRESIDING JUDGE	Mister Justice Jelf
PROSECUTION COUNSEL	Charles Mathews, Arthur Gill
DEFENCE COUNSEL	Mister Curtis Bennett
NUMBER OF VICTIMS	1

VICTIMS DETAILS	
NAME	Catherina Balhard
AGE	48
DATE OF MURDER	Saturday, 4th March, 1905
PLACE OF MURDER	Compton Street, St Pancras, London
METHOD OF KILLING	Cut throat
RELATIONSHIP TO KILLER	None

None of this impressed the jury, who took just a few minutes to return their guilty verdict.

WHEN WILLIAM JONES arrived for work on the morning of March 27th, 1905, he was surprised to find the paint store still locked. Jones summoned help from Mister Chapman, who actually owned the building at 34 High Street, and Jones finally managed to gain entry through a rear window.

Thomas Farrow lay dead in the back parlour, brutally beaten to death. His wife Ann lay upstairs in bed. She too had been battered, though she was still alive; she would lose her fight for life four days later.

The motive was robbery; a cash box had been forced open and a clear, bloody fingerprint was found on one side of that box. In 1905, fingerprinting was a young science but the police knew that if they found a match, they would find their killer.

Meanwhile, a number of witnesses came forward. Ellen Stanton had seen two men running down Deptford High Street at about 7.15am and the description she gave matched that given by Henry Littlefield, who said that he had seen the Stratton brothers, on the morning of the murder. They had been behaving strangely and Alfred had apparently been hiding something under his coat.

The Strattons had vanished from their usual haunts but the police traced Hannah Mary Cromerty, Alfred's mistress, who lived at 23 Brookmill Road, Deptford. She told the police how Alfred had left the house in the early hours on March 27th and when he returned, had warned her to say that he had been at home all night. Hannah went on to say that he smelled strongly of paraffin, which the shop sold, had painted his boots and had given away the trousers he had been wearing.

When Albert's landlady was interviewed, she said she had once seen a pair of silk stockings that had been cut down to form masks, underneath Albert's bed. Those masks had been found at the shop.

In due course, Alfred was picked up in a public house on April 3rd, and Albert traced to an address in Stepney the following day. Both men were fingerprinted and it was seen that the print found on the metal cash box matched the right thumb of Alfred Stratton.

At the trial, the fingerprint evidence proved crucial. Even so, the judge was more than fair

NAMES	Alfred Stratton; Albert Ernest Stratton
AGES AT EXECUTION	22; 20
DATE OF EXECUTION	Tuesday, 23rd May, 1905
PLACE OF EXECUTION	Wandsworth
HANGMAN	John Billington
ASSISTANTS	Henry Pierrepoint, John Ellis
DATE OF TRIAL	5th May – 6th May, 1905
LOCATION OF TRIAL	Old Bailey
PRESIDING JUDGE	Mister Justice Channell
PROSECUTION COUNSEL	Richard D. Muir
DEFENCE COUNSEL	H.G. Rooth, Curtis Bennett
NUMBER OF VICTIMS	2

VICTIMS DETAILS	
NAMES	Thomas Farrow; Ann Farrow (Died Friday, 31st March)
AGES	69; 65
DATE OF MURDER	Monday, 27th March, 1905
PLACE OF MURDER	34 High Street, Deptford, London
METHODS OF KILLING	Battered; battered
RELATIONSHIP TO KILLERS	None; none

in his summing up, saying that he did not think the jury should convict on this evidence alone. Nevertheless, the jury did return guilty verdicts. It was the first murder trial in Britain in which fingerprint evidence played a part.

The Stratton brothers were executed on May 23rd. Some books have claimed that they were hanged by the Billington brothers, but this is not the case. John Billington officiated, but he was assisted by Henry Pierrepoint and John Ellis.

1905

ALFRED JOHN HEAL fell for the girl next door. He lived at number 83 Westmacott Street, and the focus of his attentions, Ellen Goodspeed, lived at number 81. By April 1905, a wedding date had been fixed for Easter Monday. Unfortunately for the two lovers, fate then took a hand and in late March, Heal lost his job. The wedding had to be postponed.

Before Ellen had started seeing Heal, she had spent some time walking out with another man, Wyndham Homes, and since he still lived in the vicinity, both Ellen and Heal saw him regularly. If they ventured into the local pub, Homes was there. If they walked down the street together, Homes was about and in time this began to prey upon Heal's mind. He managed to convince himself that Homes and Ellen had been much more than friends and that she must have sacrificed her virginity to him.

These suspicions caused arguments until things finally came to a head on the night of April 27th. Heal had gone out some time after 8.00pm, leaving Ellen Goodspeed with his father, William Heal, his mother, also called Ellen, and his sister, yet another Ellen, who preferred to be known as Nellie. Heal did not return until after 9.00pm.

The first to leave this group was William, who retired to his bed at 9.30pm, to be followed by his wife 30 minutes later. This left Heal in the kitchen with Ellen and his sister. Nellie finally went up to bed at 10.30pm.

At 11.30pm, the entire household was woken by a terrible screaming. Ellen Goodspeed ran into Mr and Mrs Heal's bedroom, blood pouring from a wound in her throat. Alfred Heal was downstairs, and all he would say was: "Mother, she has not been true to me."

Ellen was rushed to hospital where she started to make a good recovery. Meanwhile, Alfred languished in jail, charged with attempted murder. He seemed contrite and wrote to Ellen apologising for what he had done. However, in that same letter he again referred to his belief that Ellen could not come to him untouched by other men.

In hospital the area around Ellen's wound suddenly began to show signs of inflammation. A fever developed and quickly

NAME	Alfred John Heal
AGE AT EXECUTION	22
DATE OF EXECUTION	Tuesday, 20th June, 1905
PLACE OF EXECUTION	Wandsworth
HANGMAN	John Billington
ASSISTANT	John Ellis
DATE OF TRIAL	31st May, 1905
LOCATION OF TRIAL	Old Bailey
PRESIDING JUDGE	Mister Justice Grantham
PROSECUTION COUNSEL	Charles Mathews, Mister Bodkin, Guy Stephenson
DEFENCE COUNSEL	Travers Humphreys, W.H. Thorne
NUMBER OF VICTIMS	1

VICTIMS DETAILS	
NAME	Ellen maria Goodspeed (Died Sunday, 7th May)
AGE	24
DATE OF MURDER	Thursday, 27th April, 1905
PLACE OF MURDER	81 Westmacott Street, Camberwell
METHOD OF KILLING	Cut throat
RELATIONSHIP TO KILLER	Girlfriend

grew worse. On May 7th, Ellen died and Heal was charged with murder.

The postmortem revealed that Ellen would not have lived long anyway. She was suffering from a kidney disease and this would have claimed her life within 10 years. The direct cause of death was given as inflammation of the brain, caused by poison from the wound Heal had inflicted.

Tried and sentenced to death, perhaps the hardest thing for Alfred Heal to bear was the knowledge that his suspicions had all been groundless. That same postmortem confirmed that Ellen Goodspeed was still a virgin.

IN MAY 1905, five Algerians began lodging at the same house in Kent. The five were: Daka Belkacem, Mezrou Mohamed, Ferat Mohamed Ben Ali, and two brothers, Frank Salem and Hadjou Idder. They earned a living by travelling around the area, selling various goods.

On June 13th, Ben Ali, Idder and Belkacem moved to Ashford, whilst Salem moved to lodgings in Robertsbridge. Then, on June 16th, some of the group travelled on to Tenterden. Various witnesses claimed to have seen at least three of the Algerians around the town that evening. Ben Ali and Idder were certainly together and evidence would later be given to suggest that Salem was also in the area, though he would deny this. What is indisputable, though, is that Salem was not at his lodgings that evening, as he claimed.

On the morning of June 17th, the body of Hadjou Idder was discovered near St Michael's Church. He had been beaten about the head by means of a large stick, and his throat had been cut. Other signs nearby appeared to show three separate sets of tracks and therefore indicated that perhaps three persons had spent the previous night there. The police felt sure that they were looking for two assailants.

The remaining four compatriots were arrested and all were charged with murder. Mezrou was soon discharged by the magistrates as they felt he had no case to answer. Soon afterwards Daka Belkacem also had the charges against him dismissed, leaving Ben Ali and Salem, the victim's brother, facing the capital charge. It was then that Ben Ali took a course of action that was to save Salem's life. Ben Ali made a full confession, stating categorically that he was alone with Idder and that Salem was nowhere in the area when his brother had died.

Ben Ali claimed that the two had travelled from Ashford on June 16th, and after selling some items, had looked for somewhere to sleep. Idder had suggested the field and though Ben Ali was not very happy, he did lie down and managed to get to sleep.

At 1.00am, Ben Ali stated, he woke to find that he was being sexually assaulted by Idder. Immediately he drew his knife and slashed

NAME	Ferat Mohamed Ben Ali
AGE AT EXECUTION	19
DATE OF EXECUTION	Tuesday, 1st August, 1905
PLACE OF EXECUTION	Maidstone
HANGMAN	Henry Pierrepoint
ASSISTANT	John Ellis
DATE OF TRIAL	13th July, 1905
LOCATION OF TRIAL	Maidstone
PRESIDING JUDGE	Mister Justice Bray
PROSECUTION COUNSEL	Mister Boxall, G.F. Hohler
DEFENCE COUNSEL	Mister Waterlow
NUMBER OF VICTIMS	1

VICTIMS DETAILS	
NAME	Hadjou Idder
AGE	40
DATE OF MURDER	Saturday, 17th June, 1905
PLACE OF MURDER	Field near St Michael's Church, Tenterden, Kent
METHOD OF KILLING	Battered/cut throat
RELATIONSHIP TO KILLER	None

Idder's throat. He then picked up a large stick and battered Idder about the head. In fact, the postmortem had indicated that the beating was probably inflicted first, but Ben Ali's story did seem convincing.

The magistrate's court felt that it was still better to return a verdict of murder against both Ben Ali and Salem and both were committed for trial but, at Maidstone, Ben Ali's confession carried the day and Salem was acquitted.

One question remains. Whose feet made that third set of prints near the body of Hadjou Idder?

THERE WERE A few people living with the Storeys: the lodger, William Hancocks, his wife and two young children and another lodger, a widow named Wyley.

Hancocks had three children but the oldest, a daughter named Mary Elizabeth, was in service elsewhere in Birkenhead, though she often returned to spend time with her family. One such occasion was on March 23rd, 1905.

Just after Mary had arrived, her mother had to go out. Mary went up to her parents' room with her father and the other two children. She had not been in the bedroom for long when a scream for help reverberated around the house.

Mrs Storey and Mrs Wyley ran to see what the problem was, just as Mrs Hancocks returned home. In Hancocks's room they found Mary and her father lying across the bed. He had his hands around her throat and Mary managed to gasp that she was choking.

Hancocks leapt to his feet and picked up a knife, saying that he would kill his wife. At this the three women ran into Mrs Wyley's room, to be followed by Mary seconds later. Hancocks tried to force his way in, but the door was locked. For a while this stalemate was maintained and then all went quiet.

In due course, the four came out. Mrs Hancocks said she had to go out again but said that her daughter would be alright now, especially as the other two women would remain.

After a few minutes, Hancocks reappeared and told Mary to go and take care of the children. At first she refused, but Hancocks seemed to be quiet and reasonable so finally she acquiesced.

Soon another piercing cry came from upstairs. Once more the two ladies ran to investigate. On the stairs they were met by Hancocks who pushed past them and ran into the street. Meanwhile Mary staggered out of her parents' room and collapsed. She had stab wounds in her head, arms and hands. Rushed to hospital, she died four days later. In the meantime, Hancocks had gone down to the River Mersey and thrown himself in. He was rescued and taken into custody.

At his trial, Hancocks's defence was that the wounds had been caused accidentally,

NAME	William Alfred Hancocks
AGE AT EXECUTION	**35**
DATE OF EXECUTION	Wednesday, 9th August, 1905
PLACE OF EXECUTION	Knutsford
HANGMAN	John Billington
ASSISTANT	Henry Pierrepoint
DATE OF TRIAL	20th July, 1905
LOCATION OF TRIAL	Chester
PRESIDING JUDGE	Mister Justice Channell
PROSECUTION COUNSEL	B. Francis-Williams, Mister Colt-Williams
DEFENCE COUNSEL	R.M. Montgomery
NUMBER OF VICTIMS	1

VICTIMS DETAILS	
NAME	Mary Elizabeth Hancocks (Died Sunday, 26th March)
AGE	15
DATE OF MURDER	Thursday, 23rd March, 1905
PLACE OF MURDER	The Old Priory, Birkenhead
METHOD OF KILLING	Stabbed
RELATIONSHIP TO KILLER	Daughter

during a struggle. He said he had not intended to kill, so the crime was one of manslaughter. The jury did not agree and found him guilty.

In the case of William Hancocks, the hangman had a problem as the condemned man only had one arm. The ever resourceful Henry Pierrepoint came up with a solution and invented a special strap that fastened Hancocks's arm behind his back.

After the execution had been carried out, prison officers found two letters in Hancocks's cell. It transpired that he was a bigamist and had left a letter for each of his wives.

THE TIN TRUNK was certainly well secured. It was padlocked, strapped and sealed with red wax. The first step for the police on the morning of April 13th, 1905, was to force open the lock.

When the lid was lifted, they found a layer of wooden planks, tightly ribbed together. The planks had been sealed with glue and Boric acid, making the trunk airtight. Once they had been breached, the next layer was a quilt and a tablecloth. And underneath those were the bodies of a woman and two small boys.

The police had been acting on information from Ellen Gregory, who was the mother of the woman in the trunk and the grandmother of the two children: Beatrice Devereux and her twin boys, Laurence and Evelyn. Officers set about tracing the whereabouts of Beatrice's husband, Arthur.

Beatrice and Arthur had first met at Hastings in 1895, and had married in London on November 2nd, 1898. The following year, on August 24th, Stanley, was born and the family moved from to Stroud. Four years later, in 1903, the twins were born, on April 5th.

Arthur Devereux was a chemist and in 1904 he became manager of a shop at Kilburn. However, on January 2nd, 1905, Devereux was given his notice because the shop had become unsuccessful.

Arthur was now out of work, with a wife and three young sons to support. Shortly before, the family had moved to a new block of flats in Milton Avenue, and since this was cheaper than their previous address, that at least saved him some money.

On January 28th, 1905, Mrs Gregory had been out shopping with her daughter. When they parted, Beatrice appeared to be in good spirits. That would prove to be an important piece of testimony, because according to what Arthur would later tell police, Beatrice left her mother, went home and killed the twins and herself.

That weekend Devereux began the disposal of the bodies. On January 30th, the milkman called and was told that Mrs Devereux and the babies had gone away. At about the same time, Arthur bought a sheet of zinc to seal up the trunk. After trying for three days, he gave up and used wooden planks

NAME	Arthur Devereux
AGE AT EXECUTION	Not known
DATE OF EXECUTION	Tuesday, 15th August, 1905
PLACE OF EXECUTION	Pentonville
HANGMAN	Henry Pierrepoint
ASSISTANT	John Ellis
DATE OF TRIAL	26th July – 29th July, 1905
LOCATION OF TRIAL	Old Bailey
PRESIDING JUDGE	Mister Justice Ridley
PROSECUTION COUNSEL	Charles Mathews, Mister Bodkin
DEFENCE COUNSEL	George Elliott, Arthur Hutton, Cecil Fitch
NUMBER OF VICTIMS	3

VICTIMS DETAILS

NAMES	Beatrice Devereux; Laurence Rowland Devereux; Evelyn Lancelot Devereux
AGES	25; 2; 2
DATE OF MURDER	Saturday, 28th January, 1905
PLACE OF MURDER	60 Milton Avenue, Harlesden
METHOD OF KILLING	Asphyxiation (by morphine)
RELATIONSHIP TO KILLER	Wife; son; son

instead. Then, at the beginning of February he took lodgings in Harrow Road.

George Willoughby and Harold Allingham worked as removal men for Mister Bannister. On February 7th, they moved four boxes from Milton Avenue to Harrow Road. The fifth, a large and rather heavy tin trunk, was put into storage at the company's warehouse in Kensal Rise.

One week later, on February 14th, Mrs Gregory called on her daughter. She was shocked to find that the family had moved, so made inquiries and discovered that a van had called and moved some boxes. The name of the company was passed on and this led Mrs Gregory to discover the trunk.

Meanwhile, Arthur had found a new position, working for a chemist named Bird, at Coventry. He was traced and arrested and on the return trip to London, confessed that he had concealed the bodies, but denied having anything to do with their deaths.

Devereux's story was that on January 28th, he had returned home and found the house smelling strongly of chloroform. Checking upstairs he alleged that he had found his wife and twin sons dead in bed. He stated that it was clear that Beatrice had killed the children and then taken her own life. Devereux said that he then put Stanley to bed, telling him to be quiet, and then set about putting the bodies into the trunk.

There were a number of important points that indicated Devereux might have been lying. He had lost his job and evidence was given that he had apparently never been as close to the twins as he had to Stanley. Perhaps the most damning evidence was a letter he had written to Mister Bird when applying for the Coventry job. This letter, penned on January 13th, described Arthur as a widower with one child, and was held to show that the killings were premeditated.

Devereux countered this by denying that he was closer to Stanley. As for the note, he had written for other jobs, also describing himself as a widower. He knew that many employers would automatically turn down a man with a family. His intention was to get the job, move to Coventry with Stanley and have his wife and the twins move in with her mother until he could find them a place where they could be together.

Evidence was called to show that Devereux had come from an unstable family. This was not an attempt to prove a plea of insanity but to demonstrate that if Devereux's thinking processes were not as lucid as the average man's, then he could well have panicked and decided that concealment was best.

Perhaps the best evidence for the defence was the background of Beatrice herself. In July 1903, her brother, Sidney, had disappeared, his clothing being found on Plymouth Hoe. He had, presumably, drowned himself. Mrs Gregory herself admitted under oath that her daughter had suffered from depression when Arthur lost his job. Finally, there was the testimony of Mrs Harries.

Mrs Harries had known Beatrice for many years. She testified that in 1899, Beatrice had called on her. She was very depressed at that time and intimated that she was considering suicide. Furthermore, she went on to add that

if she did kill herself, she would take Stanley with her rather than leave him to the mercies of the world. Unfortunately for Arthur Devereux, the prosecution showed that Mrs Harries had herself been confined to asylums on several occasions between 1899 and 1905, thus removing much of her credibility.

In his summing up, the judge said that he saw no motive for Beatrice Devereux to commit suicide. This is astonishing. If Arthur was guilty of murder, then his motive was his financial concerns. Surely if Beatrice had killed herself, the same motive would apply? If she had no motive for killing herself, then by the same token, Arthur had no motive to kill her!

Some writers have claimed that Devereux had administered the morphine dissolved in the chloroform, as a cough medicine. Unfortunately they ignore the medical evidence given, which showed that there was no indication whatsoever of chloroform having been taken by any of the deceased.

The jury took just 10 minutes to decide that Arthur was guilty and he was condemned to hang. On the morning of his execution, just before he left the condemned cell, he said: "I have nothing to add to what I have already said." He was making one last protestation of his innocence.

THE KILLING OF Rebecca Tattersall was a murder just waiting to happen.

Rebecca and her husband, Thomas, lived together with their four children, in Wakefield. They quarrelled often and of late, these quarrels had become, if anything, more frequent and much more violent. So much so that Rebecca had appealed to her brother for protection and when that had little effect, had reported the matter to the police. The authorities, having looked into the matter, were so concerned that they placed the house under the special supervision of the police, who made regular visits to ensure that all was well.

Despite these precautions, in mid-June 1905, Tattersall made yet another violent assault on his wife, during which he tried to strangle her. At the end of that same month he assaulted her yet again and, although the words must have been largely superfluous, threatened to kill Rebecca.

In the early hours of Monday, July 3rd, Rebecca's 10-year-old daughter heard some strange gurgling noises coming from her parents' bedroom. Thinking that her mother might be ill, she decided to investigate. The child got out of bed and walking down the corridor, encountered her father walking downstairs. Before she could ask what the matter was, Tattersall said quietly: "If you scream, I will murder you." The frightened girl made no noise as her father left the house.

The reason for this threat soon became apparent. When she checked her mother, the child found that Rebecca Tattersall's throat had been cut and her head had been smashed in with a hatchet. The police were called at once.

Tattersall was soon apprehended and at his trial, claimed that he was not responsible for his actions. He had suffered from severe attacks of influenza and had once tried to commit suicide. He had also been drinking heavily on the night of his wife's death and this had not helped matters.

Neither helped Thomas George Tattersall, who was found guilty and sentenced to death. He was executed at Leeds just a day more than six weeks after he had murdered his long-suffering wife. A plasterer by trade, one of Tattersall's last contracts before his death had been working on the execution chamber at Wakefield prison.

NAME	Thomas George Tattersall
AGE AT EXECUTION	31
DATE OF EXECUTION	Tuesday, 15th August, 1905
PLACE OF EXECUTION	Leeds
HANGMAN	John Billington
ASSISTANT	William Warbrick
DATE OF TRIAL	29th July, 1905
LOCATION OF TRIAL	Leeds
PRESIDING JUDGE	Mister Justice Jelf
PROSECUTION COUNSEL	Mister Longstaffe, Mister Ball
DEFENCE COUNSEL	Mister Mellor
NUMBER OF VICTIMS	1

VICTIMS DETAILS

NAME	Rebecca Tattersall
AGE	Not known
DATE OF MURDER	Monday, 3rd July, 1905
PLACE OF MURDER	Wakefield
METHOD OF KILLING	Cutthroat/Battered
RELATIONSHIP TO KILLER	Wife

1905

GEORGE WILLIAM BUTLER was the third man in the life of Mary Allen. She had already been married twice but for the past three years had been living with Butler in Marylebone, his wife in all but name.

George Melhuish was Mary Allen's son by her first marriage. In the early summer of 1905, George went to stay with his mother and from the very first, there was an atmosphere of tension between him and her new lover.

At the end of July the antipathy between the two men finally spilled over into violence. They fought and Butler came off much the worst, his jaw being injured so badly that he needed hospital treatment. Even on his release from the hospital Butler was still in great pain, which did little to improve his mood, or his feelings towards George Melhuish.

On September 17th, Butler argued with Mary Allen. Later that same day he was speaking to a neighbour and referred to Mary in a derogatory fashion, pointing out that she was not his wife. He claimed that she and her son had conspired against him and had deliberately broken his jaw. He ended by saying that one day he would "do for the two of them".

A week later, On September 24th, Butler was visited by his own son and a great quantity of beer was consumed. His jaw was still giving him trouble and he was forced to drink the beer through a small tube. He told his son what had happened and again threatened both Mary and George, saying that when he was better he was going to buy a revolver and blow out their brains. He finished with: "You must not be surprised if I am charged with murder." His son believed it was the beer talking and did not take the threats seriously.

On the morning of Monday, September 25th, Mary Allen was heard calling for help. When George ran into her room he discovered that Butler had stabbed her four times. The police were summoned and all Butler would say was that her son had broken his jaw. Mary Allen died two days later.

Butler's defence was that he did not know what he was doing, due to the effects of the large amount of alcohol he had consumed.

NAME	George William Butler
AGE AT EXECUTION	50
DATE OF EXECUTION	Tuesday, 7th November, 1905
PLACE OF EXECUTION	Pentonville
HANGMAN	Henry Pierrepoint
ASSISTANT	John Ellis
DATE OF TRIAL	19th October, 1905
LOCATION OF TRIAL	Old Bailey
PRESIDING JUDGE	Mister Justice Jelf
PROSECUTION COUNSEL	Charles Mathews, Mister Bodkin
DEFENCE COUNSEL	Mister Huntly-Jenkins
NUMBER OF VICTIMS	1

VICTIMS DETAILS	
NAME	Mary Allen (Died Wednesday, 27th September)
AGE	Not known
DATE OF MURDER	Monday, 25th September, 1905
PLACE OF MURDER	Union Street, Marylebone, London
METHOD OF KILLING	Stabbed
RELATIONSHIP TO KILLER	Girlfriend

Evidence was also called to show the difficulties he had faced ever since George Melhuish had moved into his house. However, Butler had been heard to issue threats on a number of occasions and it appeared that he had considered murder before he had actually done the deed. Found guilty, Butler was hanged at Pentonville on November 7th.

PASHA LIFFEY WAS a native of Basutoland and had served as a carrier with the British Army during the Boer War. After hostilities were over, Liffey had come to Britain, where he obtained employment as a boxer in a fairground booth. In July 1905, the fair he worked for visited Larkhall and Pasha Liffey became well known in the area.

Mary Welsh left her home in Dykehead Rows, Larkhall, to visit the shops, just after 9.00pm on Friday, August 11th. Her husband, Henry, had asked Mary to fetch him some rum and she was happy to oblige. One hour before this, at 8.00pm, James Bryce, the landlord of the London Hotel, had been forced to evict a customer from his public bar as he was beginning to annoy the regulars. That customer was Pasha Liffey.

James McGhie and his son were returning from Larkhall when they passed a couple lying on the ground. It seemed to be a man and a woman having sex and James passed a comment about this not being the kind of behaviour one should see. The man shouted back: "Walk on and mind your own business." A few minutes later a miner, James Carberry, approached the same spot but this time the man leapt to his feet and ran off towards Dykehead Rows. Carberry recognised the dark man as Pasha Liffey and, when he went to see why the woman hadn't moved, Carberry saw to his horror that there was blood on her face and she appeared to be dead. He gave chase, but lost Liffey close to the head of the Summerlee Pit. Returning to the woman, Carberry now saw that it was none other than Mary Welsh and that her throat had been cut with a small penknife, which lay close to the body.

Pasha Liffey now broke into the offices at the pit head, discarded some of his own bloodstained clothing and stole some clothes that belonged to some of the mine officials. The following morning he calmly returned to the scene of his crime and asked one of the villagers for directions to Hamilton and Glasgow. He was then seen to set off along the road to Hamilton and it was on the way that Sergeant Stewart caught up with him and arrested him.

At his trial, witnesses were called to show

NAME	Pasha Liffey
AGE AT EXECUTION	20
DATE OF EXECUTION	Tuesday, 14th November, 1905
PLACE OF EXECUTION	Duke Street, Glasgow
HANGMAN	Henry Pierrepoint
ASSISTANT	Not known
DATE OF TRIAL	24th October, 1905
LOCATION OF TRIAL	Glasgow
PRESIDING JUDGE	Lord Justice Adam
PROSECUTION COUNSEL	A. Orr Deas
DEFENCE COUNSEL	A.J. Laing
NUMBER OF VICTIMS	1

VICTIMS DETAILS	
NAME	Mary Jane Welsh
AGE	63
DATE OF MURDER	Friday, 11th August, 1905
PLACE OF MURDER	Larkhall, Lanarkshire
METHOD OF KILLING	Cut throat
RELATIONSHIP TO KILLER	None

that Liffey had been drinking heavily on the day of the murder and the suggestion was that he was so befuddled with drink that he had not known what he was doing, and that therefore this should be a case of manslaughter. At one stage his barrister even asked that consideration also be given for his nationality, as he obviously had practically savage instincts!

The jury, however, took just 35 minutes to decide, by a majority verdict, that Pasha was guilty but still added a recommendation to mercy.

WILLIAM YARNOLD HAD been in the army for 28 years and had served in India for 10 of those. More recently he had seen action in South Africa and it was whilst he was serving in the Boer War that his wife, Annie, decided to leave him and live with another man, George Miles.

When William returned to England his wife did return, but they stayed together for no more than a week before she moved back in with Miles. William was far from pleased.

Annie and William met, by accident, a couple of times in the Hope and Anchor Inn on Newport Street. The first of these occasions was on September 30th and the second, less than a week later, on October 4th. On neither occasion did they have a kind word for each other, but on the day of the second meeting, after Annie had returned home, William decided to follow.

It was 4.30pm when William Yarnold arrived at the house. Annie was brushing her window ledge and talking to a neighbour, Mrs Staite. She saw William approaching and demanded to know what he wanted. William muttered, "Nothing much" and, as Annie turned her back on him, drew out a long-bladed knife and plunged it into her back. Annie was very badly injured but then something occurred that had nothing to do with William, but could certainly have contributed to Annie's death.

Frank Thomas was the landlord of the York House Inn. He heard a scream and ran out to see what the problem was. He found Annie lying injured, the knife still embedded in her back. For some reason, Thomas determined that the knife should be removed and proceeded to do so. He would later testify that it took all his strength to take the knife out and that Annie immediately began to bleed profusely. One cannot help but wonder that if he had left well alone, William Yarnold might not have faced a charge of murder.

Yarnold was arrested at 8.00pm, in Droitwich Street. Annie was by now in hospital and the following day gave a dying deposition. She said that the reason the marriage had floundered in the first place was because William used to beat her and at one stage he had refused to work, preferring

NAME	William Yarnold
AGE AT EXECUTION	48
DATE OF EXECUTION	Tuesday, 5th December, 1905
PLACE OF EXECUTION	Worcester
HANGMAN	Henry Pierrepoint
ASSISTANT	John Ellis
DATE OF TRIAL	18th November, 1905
LOCATION OF TRIAL	Worcester
PRESIDING JUDGE	Mister Justice Kennedy
PROSECUTION COUNSEL	M. Farrant, Reginald Coventry
DEFENCE COUNSEL	Mister Hardy
NUMBER OF VICTIMS	1

VICTIMS DETAILS

NAME	Annie Yarnold
AGE	42
DATE OF MURDER	Wednesday, 4th October, 1905
PLACE OF MURDER	The Moors, Worcester
METHOD OF KILLING	Stabbed
RELATIONSHIP TO KILLER	Wife

instead to force her into prostitution and live off her earnings. She died a few days after the attack.

It took the jury just 10 minutes to decide that Yarnold was guilty of murder, though they did recommend him to mercy on account of Annie's cohabitation with another man. Despite that, and a local petition that attracted 6,000 signatures, the sentence was upheld.

On December 5th, 1905, William Yarnold became the first man to die on the gallows at Worcester since March 22nd, 1805.

WILLIAM HARRIS OWNED the lodging house at 94 Newgate Street, Newcastle upon Tyne, and two of his tenants were Henry Perkins and Patrick Durkin.

On the evening of July 13th, Durkin entered the house much the worse for drink. Very soon afterwards, at around 7.30pm, he was followed in by Perkins, who was in much the same state. By this time, Durkin had fallen asleep in the kitchen. The charwoman, Annie Jackson, thought that Perkins might disturb his fellow lodger, so asked him to be quiet. Perkins nodded and then helped himself to a seat whilst Annie carried on with her work.

It was not long before Annie Jackson noticed that Perkins had something in his hand and asked him what it was. He replied that it was a newspaper, but then he walked over to where Durkin was sleeping, put his knee upon the man's chest and drew back what Annie now saw was a knife. Bravely, Annie pulled Perkins away from Durkin before the knife could make contact and then announced that she was going to fetch William Harris. Even as she was on her way out of the room, Annie heard a cry and knew that the knife had now found its mark.

William Harris managed to bandage the wound in Durkin's throat, but the poor man was to die from blood poisoning six days later, in the Infirmary. Meanwhile, on the day of the attack, Police Constable Walter Wood had seen Perkins in the city centre. He was arrested and later charged with murder.

Perkins tried to claim that he felt Durkin was about to attack him and had struck out only in self-defence. Other lodgers were called and they confirmed that there had been bad feeling between the two men for some time. They also mentioned that Perkins had tried to stab Durkin some time before, only being prevented from doing so by being forcibly restrained.

It appears that the bad blood between the two men started when Perkins had said that he had a fortune of £4,000 and Durkin had called him a liar. It was such a trifling matter, but it cost the lives of two men.

NAME	Henry Perkins
AGE AT EXECUTION	40
DATE OF EXECUTION	Wednesday, 6th December, 1905
PLACE OF EXECUTION	Newcastle
HANGMAN	Henry Pierrepoint
ASSISTANT	John Ellis
DATE OF TRIAL	16th November, 1905
LOCATION OF TRIAL	Newcastle
PRESIDING JUDGE	Mister Justice Darling
PROSECUTION COUNSEL	J.E. Joel, E. Meynell
DEFENCE COUNSEL	Mister Hedley
NUMBER OF VICTIMS	1

VICTIMS DETAILS	
NAME	Patrick Durkin (Died Wednesday, 19th July)
AGE	Not known
DATE OF MURDER	Thursday, 13th July, 1905
PLACE OF MURDER	94 Newgate Street, Newcastle
METHOD OF KILLING	Stabbed
RELATIONSHIP TO KILLER	None

1905

SAMUEL CURTIS HAD lived with Alice Clover since 1890 and the two had earned their living by selling rags, bones and scrap. Samuel, though, did not treat Alice as she would wish and, in November 1904, she finally left him without letting him know where she was going. Over the next few weeks, many of Samuel's friends heard him describing in detail what he would do to Alice if he ever caught up with her. In fact, Samuel began to tour the county, looking for the woman he felt had wronged him. Slowly the weeks turned into months and still Samuel had no luck in finding Alice.

On July 21st, 1905, after some nine months of searching, Samuel discovered that Alice was living in Wrotham. As if spending all that time searching was not enough in itself to make him angry, Samuel also found that Alice was now living with another man. It was time to settle some old scores.

The following day, July 22nd, Samuel visited a local shop and purchased a sharp new knife. He then found Alice, who was in a public house, and deliberately picked an argument with her. Alice got up and walked out of the pub, only to be followed by Samuel who, the knife in his hand, struck Alice two heavy blows in the throat. She fell dead and Samuel was taken into custody.

Samuel's defence was one of provocation. There was no way he could deny being responsible for Alice's death, but if his plea was accepted, the charge might be reduced to one of manslaughter. The verdict, when it came, was guilty but with a strong recommendation to mercy on account of Alice being unfaithful.

The Home Office felt that there was no justification for what Curtis had done, though, and the sentence was carried out in December.

NAME	Samuel Curtis
AGE AT EXECUTION	60
DATE OF EXECUTION	Wednesday, 20th December, 1905
PLACE OF EXECUTION	Maidstone
HANGMAN	Henry Pierrepoint
ASSISTANT	William Fry
DATE OF TRIAL	1st December, 1905
LOCATION OF TRIAL	Maidstone
PRESIDING JUDGE	Mister Justice Grantham
PROSECUTION COUNSEL	Theobald Mathew, Mister Pitman
DEFENCE COUNSEL	Mister Weigall
NUMBER OF VICTIMS	1

VICTIMS DETAILS	
NAME	Alice Clover
AGE	34
DATE OF MURDER	Saturday, 22nd July, 1905
PLACE OF MURDER	Outside the Post Boys public house, Wrotham
METHOD OF KILLING	Stabbed/cut throat
RELATIONSHIP TO KILLER	Girlfriend

FREDERICK EDGE BELIEVED that life had passed him by. Sometime during the morning of September 28th, 1905, he paid a visit to his sister, Elizabeth Tittley, and gave her a parcel, telling her that it contained most of his clothes for his younger brother, Arthur. As he left he looked sadly into her eyes and said: "I have no mother. I have no father. I have no home. I have no money. I have nothing." He kissed her and added that she might never see him again.

Elizabeth might have been forgiven for thinking that Frederick was contemplating suicide, but he had something even more drastic in mind. Leaving Elizabeth's house, Frederick returned to his lodgings at 40 Wilson Street, a house owned by Frank and Rose Evans.

The Evanses had three children: Lizzie, who was 12, 10-year-old Emma and a five-month-old baby named Francis Walter. Edge had lived with the family for five weeks, but was now in arrears with his rent. That morning Rose had told Edge that they couldn't subsidise him and he would have to leave. Edge had packed his few belongings, but having given Rose a fish he had purchased, was been told that he could return to have lunch with the family. Edge ate his last meal in the Evans household at 2.00pm.

Rose had her household chores to do and she left Edge in the kitchen whilst she went upstairs to clean the rooms. At the time, Francis was asleep on a settee downstairs. After a few minutes, Rose thought she heard a noise downstairs, followed by the sound of the front door being slammed shut. Worried that Francis might have been disturbed by the noise, Rose went downstairs to check on him and found that the child's throat had been cut so deeply that his head had almost been severed from his body.

At 2.35pm, Frederick Edge walked into the police station and announced to Constable William Connolly that he wished to surrender himself for the murder of a child at Wilson Street. He then handed over a bloodstained razor.

Edge claimed that he had killed the child for spite. He made a full written confession in which he claimed that he had been having a

NAME	Frederick William Edge
AGE AT EXECUTION	23
DATE OF EXECUTION	Wednesday, 27th December, 1905
PLACE OF EXECUTION	Stafford
HANGMAN	Henry Pierrepoint
ASSISTANT	John Ellis
DATE OF TRIAL	8th December, 1905
LOCATION OF TRIAL	Stafford
PRESIDING JUDGE	Mister Justice Kennedy
PROSECUTION COUNSEL	Mister Farrant, Mister Bosanquet
DEFENCE COUNSEL	H. Staveley-Hill M.P.
NUMBER OF VICTIMS	1

VICTIMS DETAILS	
NAME	Francis Walter Evans
AGE	Five months
DATE OF MURDER	Thursday, 28th September, 1905
PLACE OF MURDER	40 Wilson Street, Newcastle-under-Lyme
METHOD OF KILLING	Cut throat
RELATIONSHIP TO KILLER	None

sexual relationship with Rose Edge and she had of late refused him her favours. This was yet another attempt on Edge's part to get back at the Evans family – there was no truth to the story.

Edge went on to say that ideally he would have liked to have killed Rose herself but unfortunately the opportunity to do so had not presented itself, so he had attacked Francis instead. With such a detailed confession, there could only be one outcome. Edge was executed on December 27th. Finally the life that he hated so much was at an end.

1905

GEORGE SMITH COULD not have been described as the best husband in the world. He had not worked for some considerable time, preferring instead to live off the income his wife brought in. Martha was in domestic service and by all accounts a hard-working employee.

In June 1905, Martha went to work for Harold Shelton, in Burley Road, Leeds. The job did not last long, but that was no fault of Martha's. One day, when Mister Shelton came home, he found Martha hiding in the kitchen. Her face was bruised and Shelton finally managed to get her to reveal that her husband had been around. They had argued and he had beaten her.

When George Smith next called at Mister Shelton's home he was given a lecture by Shelton and told in no uncertain terms not to call again. Contrite at first, Smith returned the next day and demanded that his wife leave the house immediately. After various arguments and threats, Martha reluctantly complied.

At first, Martha returned to her mother's house in Wakefield but soon afterwards she found another position, this time with Mr and Mrs Glendenning, and their daughter, at Ilkley.

On September 12th, Miss Glendenning arrived home at 6.30pm to find the back door locked. She called out for Martha, but there was no reply. Eventually, Miss Glendenning gained entry through the cellar kitchen, where she fell over the body of Martha Smith.

Martha had been stabbed over 40 times, but the wound that had proved fatal was the gash in her throat. Poor Martha had bled to death and pools of blood on the kitchen floor showed that this is where the attack had taken place. The police sought to interview only one man: George Smith.

Smith was arrested in Wakefield two days after the murder. Questioned about his wife's death he described the events in a matter-of-fact way. He had gone to speak to his wife and found her in the kitchen. Martha had told him that their marriage was over. She had then pushed him away to emphasise the point, whereupon Smith had struggled with her. There was a penknife in his hand and Smith insisted that he had just jabbed at Martha repeatedly. He claimed to have no

NAME	George Smith
AGE AT EXECUTION	50
DATE OF EXECUTION	Thursday, 28th December, 1905
PLACE OF EXECUTION	Leeds
HANGMAN	Henry Pierrepoint
ASSISTANT	John Ellis
DATE OF TRIAL	7th December, 1905
LOCATION OF TRIAL	Leeds
PRESIDING JUDGE	Mister Justice Jelf
PROSECUTION COUNSEL	Harold Thomas, R.A. Shepherd
DEFENCE COUNSEL	E.H. Chapman
NUMBER OF VICTIMS	1

VICTIMS DETAILS	
NAME	Martha Smith
AGE	Not known
DATE OF MURDER	Tuesday, 12th September, 1905
PLACE OF MURDER	The Kells, Riddings Road, Ilkley
METHOD OF KILLING	Cut throat/stabbed
RELATIONSHIP TO KILLER	Wife

recollection of cutting his wife's throat.

The trial was a formality, but witnesses were called to trace Smith's movements on the day of the murder. His landlady, Mrs Storey, testified that he had left home at 9.45am, smartly dressed, having told her that he was going to look for work in Halifax. When he had gone, she noticed that a knife was missing.

This evidence, along with Smith's own story, was more than enough to convict him and the jury took less than 15 minutes to return their verdict. There were cheers of approval from the public gallery.

IN 1903, JOHN SILK was discharged from the army, having served his country well in India and South Africa. Returning to Chesterfield, Silk took up residence with his mother, Mary Fallon. Mary was a cripple and only got about with difficulty on a pair of crutches. She was treated well by her son, except when he had had too much to drink. On those occasions, Silk could be extremely violent towards her.

On August 5th, 1905, Silk was seen near his home. He was very drunk and swore that there would be a murder done that night. He then went home and started an argument with his mother. She had asked him to fetch her a half-bottle of whisky but he had refused. After telling her what he thought, Silk went back out and had even more to drink.

Silk finally returned home at 11.15pm. By then the lodger, Thomas Meakin, had also returned home. He would later testify that Silk was very argumentative. He picked yet another row with his mother, this time about a lamp in the room being in the wrong position. When Mary went to move the lamp, Silk hit her with his open hand. She staggered, the lamp fell, overturned and went out, plunging the room into darkness.

Meakin had had enough. Getting to his feet he said he was going to fetch a policeman. As he left the house he heard the smashing of glass and when he returned soon afterwards, Meakin found the door bolted against him. Unable to gain access he was forced to spend the night outside, having failed to find a policeman.

On the morning of August 6th, a newsvendor, Henry Dye, called at Mary Fallon's home. He found that the door was now unlocked and there, lying on the floor, was Mary. Around the body was the leg of a broken chair and a broken crutch. Both had been used to batter Mary about the head.

When the police arrived they entered the house and found John Silk upstairs, asleep in his bed. He was arrested and taken to the police station where he was charged with his mother's murder. A subsequent postmortem on Mary showed that she had been brutally battered. There were many bruises on her body and four of her ribs were broken.

NAME	John Silk
AGE AT EXECUTION	30
DATE OF EXECUTION	Friday, 29th December, 1905
PLACE OF EXECUTION	Derby
HANGMAN	Henry Pierrepoint
ASSISTANT	John Ellis
DATE OF TRIAL	5th December, 1905
LOCATION OF TRIAL	Derby
PRESIDING JUDGE	Mister Justice Bucknill
PROSECUTION COUNSEL	J.H. Etherington Smith, Mister Magee
DEFENCE COUNSEL	Dominic Daly
NUMBER OF VICTIMS	1

VICTIMS DETAILS	
NAME	Mary Fallon
AGE	51
DATE OF MURDER	Saturday, 5th August, 1905
PLACE OF MURDER	3 Spa Lane, Chesterfield
METHOD OF KILLING	Battered
RELATIONSHIP TO KILLER	Mother

Silk's defence was that he was drunk and was not conscious of what he was doing at the time of the attack. It did nothing to save him from the scaffold.

MRS GARRITY GAVE her daughter Kate a bottle and jug and asked her to pop out and buy some beer and whisky. She handed over a 2/- piece to cover the cost and at 8.10pm, Kate went off to the shop. Kate's route would have taken her past the corner of Greenfield Lane and Moss Hey Street, where there was an entry that led to some wasteland. Mrs Garrity waited and when Kate did not return, a search was organised. No trace of her daughter could be found.

The following morning, Mr Garrity went to his work at the stable down an entry that led down from Greenfield Lane. He noticed that there were some sacks missing from the yard, looked around for them and found them in a corner of the entry. He noticed that they were covering something and, on closer inspection, made the shocking discovery that it was the body of his daughter. The jug and bottle lay close by her body. They were empty, which meant that Kate had never made it to the shop. The 2/- piece was missing.

Several witnesses stated that they had seen Jack Griffiths outside the entry at about 8.20pm. Another said that she had seen a man pulling a girl into the alleyway.

Griffiths knew the murdered girl. At one stage he had been her boyfriend, but on December 8th they had argued and he had hit her and threatened her. She took him to court and Griffiths was bound over to keep the peace.

Investigations revealed that Griffiths had been drinking in a pub on Greenfield Lane on the night of Kate's death and witnesses said that they had seen him leave at about 8.00pm. He had now been put in the right place, at the right time.

A series of clog marks had been found in the alley. These led to a wall, which presumably the assailant had climbed because on the other side of that wall were two very clear prints where the man had landed on the ground. It was noted that a piece of the iron on the right clog was missing and when Griffiths was interviewed, it was discovered that his right clog was missing a piece of iron.

In the yard beyond the wall, some blue powder was found and Griffiths's right clog

NAME	John (Jack) Griffiths
AGE AT EXECUTION	19
DATE OF EXECUTION	Tuesday, 27th February, 1906
PLACE OF EXECUTION	Manchester
HANGMAN	Henry Pierrepoint
ASSISTANT	John Ellis
DATE OF TRIAL	5th February – 6th February, 1906
LOCATION OF TRIAL	Manchester
PRESIDING JUDGE	Mister Justice Grantham
PROSECUTION COUNSEL	Mister Langdon, Mister Rhodes
DEFENCE COUNSEL	Mister Shawcross
NUMBER OF VICTIMS	1

VICTIMS DETAILS	
NAME	Catherine (Kate) Garrity
AGE	17
DATE OF MURDER	Tuesday, 19th December, 1905
PLACE OF MURDER	Shaw, Near Oldham
METHOD OF KILLING	Strangled
RELATIONSHIP TO KILLER	Ex-girlfriend

still had some blue powder adhering to it. Finally, blood stains were found on Griffiths's right cuff, right sleeve and inside his jacket pocket. All this evidence was more than enough to convict Griffiths. The case though had one final, curious twist.

Before the execution, Kate Garrity's mother received an anonymous letter postmarked Ashford, in Kent. Signed only S.H.B., the letter contained a full confession to the murder of Kate!

THERE WERE TWO men in the life of Sarah Ann McConnell: her husband James, whom she had left in September, 1905, and Harry Walters, the man she subsequently lived with.

Harry and Sarah had moved in to a furnished room at 12 Court, Allen Street, some time in October 1905. On December 23rd, there were three callers at Sarah's room.

The first was Margaret Revill, a fish hawker. According to Revill, Walters was at home and his manner was most belligerent. Margaret gave evidence that before she left, Walters threatened to kill Sarah as soon as they were alone.

The next caller was Jane Elizabeth Drakard, the landlady, who came to collect her rent. It was 5.40pm and Sarah lay almost naked on the hearth rug, her legs wide apart and a great deal of blood issuing from her. Jane Drakard ran for her assistant, Emily Bradshaw and together they returned to the scene and threw a black skirt over the body, before going for help.

Very soon afterwards, the final visitor appeared: 11-year-old Margaret Osborne. Sarah owed Margaret's mother a few pence and Margaret had been sent to collect it. She saw Harry Walters kneeling by Sarah's side, calling her name and trying to revive her.

Some five minutes after Margaret's visit, Harry Walters knocked at the door of another neighbour, Anne Austwick. He told Anne that his wife seemed to be dead and asked her if she would attend to her whilst he went for a policeman. Within a couple of minutes, Harry had found Constable Frank Winfield.

The murderer of Sarah McConnell had behaved in a terribly savage manner. Police found a bloodstained ginger beer bottle and a long-handled broom at the house. Forensic tests showed that the bottle had first been roughly inserted into Sarah's vagina, followed later by the broom handle, which had been thrust in to a depth of over 20 inches. Sarah had been impaled to such an extent that the top of the broom handle had injured her neck and the lower half of her body was awash with blood.

Harry Walters denied any knowledge of the murder. He denied uttering any threats whilst

NAME	Harold (Harry) Walters
AGE AT EXECUTION	39
DATE OF EXECUTION	Tuesday, 10th April, 1906
PLACE OF EXECUTION	Wakefield
HANGMAN	Henry Pierrepoint
ASSISTANT	Thomas Pierrepoint
DATE OF TRIAL	23rd March, 1906
LOCATION OF TRIAL	Leeds
PRESIDING JUDGE	Mister Justice Walton
PROSECUTION COUNSEL	J. Strachan, C.F. Lowenthal
DEFENCE COUNSEL	H.T. Waddy, Mister Coutts Trotter
NUMBER OF VICTIMS	1

VICTIMS DETAILS	
NAME	Sarah Ann McConnell
AGE	43
DATE OF MURDER	Saturday, 23rd December, 1905
PLACE OF MURDER	12 Court, 7 House, Allen Street, Sheffield
METHOD OF KILLING	Battered
RELATIONSHIP TO KILLER	Girlfriend

Margaret Revill was in the house and claimed that he had gone to a number of local pubs and had a few drinks, not returning home until 5.30pm, when he found the body.

At his trial, Harry persisted in his claim of knowing nothing of the murder. When the prosecution called evidence to show that there were extensive bloodstains on his clothing, he explained them away by saying that he must have picked up some blood when he tried to see if he could help.

Found guilty and sentenced to death. Harry Walters was executed at Wakefield on April 10th, 1906.

EDWARD GLYNN HAD known Jane Gamble for two years and they had been living together as man and wife for some time. On February 11th, though, Glynn told Jane's mother that they were no longer together.

The problem it seemed was that Jane had found herself another man, named Henry Gibson, and Glynn was well aware of this fact. On February 16th, he followed Jane to the house of a friend of hers, Emily Day, and here threatened to cut Jane's throat if he caught her with Gibson. Just 12 days later, on February 28th, similar threats were made, again in front of witnesses.

Things finally came to a head on the night of March 3rd, 1906. Glynn was seen loitering in Canal Street, brandishing a knife and muttering that he would "do her in". This was at 10.30pm and just half an hour later, at 11.00pm, Jane and Henry Gibson walked down that same street on their way back from a public house.

Suddenly, Jane Gamble fell forward. Gibson turned and saw that Glynn was stabbing Jane repeatedly. Satisfied that his work was done, Glynn ran off, to be chased by Gibson and a man named Richard Dixon, who had also witnessed the attack.

Meanwhile, Constable Aubrey had discovered Jane lying injured and heard her whisper Glynn's name and address.

Constable Aubrey went to Glynn's address and waited until he appeared, at 2.40am. Glynn denied that he was the assailant, claiming that he had been at Bulwell in various public houses at the time that the crime was committed. Nevertheless, he was arrested and charged with the attack.

Jane died a day and a half later. So severe had been the knife blows that the blade was still embedded in her neck. The charge was now one of murder. Glynn's alibi collapsed when no one could be found who had seen him in any pub in Bulwell and after a deliberation of 15 minutes, the jury returned a guilty verdict.

Before his execution, Edward Glynn made a full confession to the murder, in front of his solicitor and three prison warders.

NAME	Edward Glynn
AGE AT EXECUTION	26
DATE OF EXECUTION	Tuesday, 7th August, 1906
PLACE OF EXECUTION	Nottingham
HANGMAN	Henry Pierrepoint
ASSISTANT	William Willis
DATE OF TRIAL	17th July, 1906
LOCATION OF TRIAL	Nottingham
PRESIDING JUDGE	Mister Justice Walton
PROSECUTION COUNSEL	W. Ryland Adkins M.P., B.S.S. Foster
DEFENCE COUNSEL	B. Campion
NUMBER OF VICTIMS	1

VICTIMS DETAILS

NAME	Jane (Jenny) Gamble (Died Sunday, 4th March)
AGE	22
DATE OF MURDER	Saturday, 3rd March, 1906
PLACE OF MURDER	Canal Street, Nottingham
METHOD OF KILLING	Stabbed
RELATIONSHIP TO KILLER	Ex-girlfriend

ELIZABETH BALDWIN HAD lived with Thomas Mouncer, on and off, for some time and now they were lodging with Mrs Pattison in Olive Street, Middlesborough. There was however a problem. Mouncer was jealous of a mutual friend named Cram and had told Elizabeth in no uncertain terms what he would do if he ever caught her with Cram.

On May 12th, Thomas, Elizabeth and Cram were all out for a drink together and at one stage, Cram announced that Elizabeth was "the best woman in the world". Mouncer objected to what he thought was over friendliness, but no argument developed and when Elizabeth and Mouncer left together at around 11.00pm, they appeared to be friendly enough.

At 12.30am, Mrs Pattison was disturbed by noises coming from the room Mouncer shared with Elizabeth. She went along to listen outside their door and heard Elizabeth's voice saying, "Oh, Tom, don't." Mrs Pattison knocked gently on the door and asked if everything was all right. Mouncer's voice came in reply and he assured her that all was well. Mrs Pattison returned to her own bedroom and though she did hear some gurgling noises soon afterwards, she did not return to Mouncer's room.

At 6.30am on May 13th, Thomas Mouncer walked up to a police sergeant on duty in Corporation Street and confessed that he had murdered Elizabeth. He then handed over his key to the sergeant and was taken to the police station. Elizabeth's body was later found, fully clothed, on top of the bed.

At his trial, Mouncer tried to convince the jury that the killing was accidental. He stated that he and Elizabeth had been out drinking and upon their return, she had started to abuse him. The argument had developed and finally, Elizabeth had rushed at him with a knife. In the struggle that followed, Mouncer managed to take the knife from Elizabeth, without injury to himself and then threw her onto the bed. Mouncer said that she did not move and that he believed she had fallen asleep. It was only the following morning when he awoke and saw that she had not moved, that he realised she was dead.

This highly unlikely story did nothing to sway the jury.

NAME	Thomas Acomb Mouncer
AGE AT EXECUTION	25
DATE OF EXECUTION	Thursday, 9th August, 1906
PLACE OF EXECUTION	Wakefield
HANGMAN	Henry Pierrepoint
ASSISTANT	Thomas Pierrepoint
DATE OF TRIAL	21st July, 1906
LOCATION OF TRIAL	York
PRESIDING JUDGE	Mister Justice Grantham
PROSECUTION COUNSEL	A.W. Bairstow, J.O. Andrews
DEFENCE COUNSEL	Edward Shortt
NUMBER OF VICTIMS	1

VICTIMS DETAILS	
NAME	Elizabeth Baldwin
AGE	31
DATE OF MURDER	Sunday, 13th May, 1906
PLACE OF MURDER	Olive Street, Middlesborough
METHOD OF KILLING	Strangled
RELATIONSHIP TO KILLER	Girlfriend

SOPHIA LOVELL HAD been going out with Frederick Reynolds for some 18 months, but Sophia's mother did not approve. Mrs Lovell was convinced that Frederick's jealousy would lead Sophia into trouble and when the old lady died, in August 1906, her last request of her daughter was that she give up this unsuitable man.

Sophia already had her own doubts about Frederick, and so did not find the promise to her mother too difficult to keep. Shortly after Mrs Lovell died, Sophia told him that the relationship was over. For a full month, Frederick was not too worried about the break-up. He might well have thought that given time, Sophia would come to her senses and the affair would be back on, but then she met Henry Lambourne.

On September 8th, Sophia was out with a group of girlfriends when a pleasant young man introduced himself. Henry Lambourne was good looking and there was an instant attraction between him and Sophia. He politely asked if he might see her again the following day and Sophia readily agreed. They met on September 9th and to his delight, made arrangements for the evening of Monday, September 10th.

At 9.30pm on September 10th, Henry and Sophia were enjoying an innocent stroll down Willow Walk when they noticed that they were being followed. Sophia recognised Reynolds and suggested that they ignore him, but Reynolds was looking for a showdown. As the young couple turned their backs on Reynolds, he came quickly up to Sophia and hit her on the back of the head. She turned to face her assailant, whereupon Reynolds hit out twice more. Sophia fell to the ground and instantly Reynolds was upon her, drawing a knife from his pocket. Lambourne did his best to pull him off but with a cry of "I have sworn to do it, and I am doing it", Reynolds slashed Sophia's throat.

Henry Lambourne screamed out for assistance and two men, Thomas Jones and William Fisher, rushed out of the Alcot Arms. It was too late for poor Sophia, however: she was already dead. Reynolds meanwhile had made good his escape but at 10.15pm, he gave himself up to the police

NAME	Frederick Reynolds
AGE AT EXECUTION	23
DATE OF EXECUTION	Tuesday, 13th November, 1906
PLACE OF EXECUTION	Wandsworth
HANGMAN	Henry Pierrepoint
ASSISTANT	John Ellis
DATE OF TRIAL	25th October, 1906
LOCATION OF TRIAL	Old Bailey
PRESIDING JUDGE	Mister Justice Lawrence
PROSECUTION COUNSEL	Mister Bodkin, Charles Mathews
DEFENCE COUNSEL	None
NUMBER OF VICTIMS	1

VICTIMS DETAILS	
NAME	Sophie Lovell
AGE	18
DATE OF MURDER	Monday, 10th September, 1906
PLACE OF MURDER	Willow Walk, Bermondsey, London
METHOD OF KILLING	Cut throat
RELATIONSHIP TO KILLER	Ex-girlfriend

and made a full confession.

At the trial, Reynolds pleaded guilty and refused to take legal advice. The judge, Mr Justice Lawrence, ordered a brief adjournment whilst Reynolds considered his position but on his return to court, the only concession he would make was to say that he had meant to say that he was guilty of the crime but had not intended to go as far as he did. The judge directed that under those circumstances, a 'not guilty' plea should be entered.

Reynolds still refused the offer of legal counsel, however, and after the evidence had been heard, the jury took just two minutes to find him guilty of wilful murder.

IT WAS AN innocent enough question. A neighbour asked Edward Hartigan why he hadn't gone to work. The reply he got was filled with threats. "How can I work without grub? " spat Edward. He went on to refer to his wife, implying that it was her fault that he had not had enough to eat. "I will make her remember; she will not leave me without grub again; I will disable her for life." This little speech was made on Tuesday, August 7th and not long afterwards, Hartigan was to prove that he was, at least, a man of his word.

Both Edward Hartigan and his wife Catherine were known to be fond of a drink. After making the outburst quoted above, Edward went off to have a few drinks. He returned home at 6.30pm.

On entering the house, Hartigan was met by his daughter, Nellie and asked her if her mother was in, and whether the beds had been made. The girl went upstairs to check and returned to inform her father that Catherine was asleep on her bed, whilst his remained unmade. She added as an afterthought that he shouldn't bother to wake her.

Edward flew into a rage and stormed upstairs. He dragged Catherine off the bed and began to beat her. His daughter ran to a neighbour's house for help. A neighbour duly attended and found Edward, who was wearing heavy clogs at the time, kicking Catherine in her side. The situation was calmed down and, unfortunately as it turned out, Hartigan was left alone again with Catherine.

Sometime later, the same neighbour noticed Hartigan standing in the street. Thinking that this would be a good opportunity to sort things out, the neighbour went up to Hartigan and asked him why he couldn't live in peace with his wife. "It's too late," replied Hartigan, "I've done it." It transpired that 'it' referred to the murder of his wife.

Hartigan had now admitted what he had done to a neighbour. There was little point in concealing the crime from the authorities, so, shortly afterwards, Hartigan walked into his local police station and admitted his crime again. Catherine Hartigan was still

NAME	Edward Hartigan
AGE AT EXECUTION	58
DATE OF EXECUTION	Tuesday, 27th November, 1906
PLACE OF EXECUTION	Knutsford
HANGMAN	Henry Pierrepoint
ASSISTANT	William Willis
DATE OF TRIAL	6th November, 1906
LOCATION OF TRIAL	Chester
PRESIDING JUDGE	Mister Justice Walton
PROSECUTION COUNSEL	Ellis J Griffith M.P., Ambrose Jones
DEFENCE COUNSEL	T.E. Morris
NUMBER OF VICTIMS	1

VICTIMS DETAILS	
NAME	Catherine Hartigan
AGE	45
DATE OF MURDER	Tuesday, 7th August, 1906
PLACE OF MURDER	Stockport
METHOD OF KILLING	Battered
RELATIONSHIP TO KILLER	Wife

alive, but she died very soon afterwards. Her skull had been smashed in by means of a coal hammer and there were 18 separate wounds on her head.

When Hartigan came to trial, he claimed that he had been greatly provoked by his wife and had attacked her in a sudden frenzy. He had not meant to kill her. Found guilty, he made a full confession before he faced the executioner.

ALBERT WATSON AND his wife, Emma, ran a small poultry farm and market garden near Basildon. The farm had no running water and the only source of this life-giving fluid was a small pond some 300 yards away. This pond had been dug by a farmer who lived nearby. Mister Buckham, who ran Sawyer's Farm, had come to an agreement with the Watsons and had informed them that they could take water as and when they needed it. This agreement though, was not looked upon favourably by Buckham's two sons, Robert Charles and Richard.

At 5.30am on August 23rd, 1906, three shots were heard echoing through the fields around Honeypot Lane. The first two shots were fired in quick succession, the third following about a minute later. Less than five hours later, a rather breathless Richard Buckham ran to Mr Stevens who lived nearby and told him that he had just discovered the bodies of Albert and Emma Watson in the pond in Honeypot Lane.

Stevens contacted the police and went to investigate Richard Buckham's claims. True enough, both victims had been shot. Albert Watson had one large wound in his back, his wife had wounds on her neck, chest and arm and it appeared that she had been shot twice. After examining the scene, the police surmised that Albert and Emma had both been shot, Albert dying almost immediately from his gaping wound. Emma had perhaps been groaning on the ground when her attacker reloaded, walked slowly forward and shot her again at a much shorter range.

Both the Buckham brothers, along with other neighbours, helped the police to search the area for a murder weapon. It did not escape the officers, though, that Robert was looking somewhat agitated. Questioned as to his movements, Robert admitted that he knew more about the crime than he had first suggested.

Robert's story was that he and Richard had come across the Watsons taking water from the pond. Richard had warned them off, whereupon Albert Watson told him exactly what he could do with himself. Richard raised the double-barrelled shotgun he was carrying and shot both the Watsons. After he had finished off Emma, he took the keys from Albert's pocket, went to his farm and stole a watch and a small amount of cash.

Richard admitted that he had carried out the shooting. He said he had fired in the heat of passion and had never meant to kill the Watsons. Both brothers were arrested and charged with murder.

The story was repeated at the trial and 17-year-old Robert, who would have been too young to hang in any case, was acquitted. Richard Buckham was not so fortunate.

NAME	Richard Buckham
AGE AT EXECUTION	20
DATE OF EXECUTION	Tuesday, 4th December, 1906
PLACE OF EXECUTION	Chelmsford
HANGMAN	Henry Pierrepoint
ASSISTANT	No assistant named
DATE OF TRIAL	14th November, 1906
LOCATION OF TRIAL	Chelmsford
PRESIDING JUDGE	Mister Justice Lawrence
PROSECUTION COUNSEL	J. Harvey Murphy, D.R. Chalmers Hunt
DEFENCE COUNSEL	Ronald Walker
NUMBER OF VICTIMS	2

VICTIMS DETAILS	
NAMES	Albert Watson; Emma Watson
AGES	47; 50
DATE OF MURDER	Thursday, 23rd August, 1906
PLACE OF MURDER	Honeypot Lane, Basildon, Essex
METHOD OF KILLING	Shot; shot
RELATIONSHIP TO KILLER	None; none

WALTER MARSH HAD led a distinguished military life. By the early part of the century, he had served 17 years in the army and had fought at the battle of Omdurman. In 1901, he had married Eliza Gascoyne, but had left soon afterwards to fight in the Boer War. Marsh finally left the army in 1903, and he and Eliza took a public house at Sheffield. Unfortunately this did not succeed and in due course, they moved to Chesterfield. By 1906, Marsh was working as a rent collector and agent for his landlord, Edward Silcock.

The marriage was no longer a happy one and Marsh frequently assaulted Eliza. On June 7th, Eliza tried to take out a summons for cruelty, but this was not granted, as there was not enough corroboration of her evidence. Eliza had by now moved out of the marital home and gone to live with her father at 20 Shipley Street, but soon afterwards she was persuaded by Walter to return home.

The truce between Walter and Eliza was a temporary one. On July 4th, Edward Silcock called at Goyt Terrace to see Marsh and pick up some papers he needed. Walter was not at home, so Edward only stayed a few minutes. Before he left though he gave Eliza a shilling to buy some beer for his tenants. When Walter arrived home and heard the story, he chose instead to believe that Eliza had entertained Silcock in some other way and that the shilling was for sexual services. When Walter took those suspicions to Edward Silcock, he was instantly dismissed from his job.

Two days later, on July 9th, Eliza asked Walter for a half sovereign, which he gave to her. She then said she was going to lie down for half an hour. It was just after 5.00pm when Walter Marsh appeared in the doorway of his house and announced to his neighbours: "I've done it this time." As he spoke he was wiping the blood off a razor, and then invited the stunned witnesses to call for the police.

At his trial, Marsh tried to put forward that the killing had been a case of self-defence. He claimed that he had taken out the razor to shave himself and that whilst he was doing so, told Eliza that he had been trying to find another house. She did not reply and, angry that he was being ignored, he then told her

NAME	Walter Marsh
AGE AT EXECUTION	39
DATE OF EXECUTION	Thursday, 27th December, 1906
PLACE OF EXECUTION	Derby
HANGMAN	Thomas Pierrepoint
ASSISTANT	John Ellis
DATE OF TRIAL	5th December, 1906
LOCATION OF TRIAL	Derby
PRESIDING JUDGE	Mister Justice Ridley
PROSECUTION COUNSEL	W. Ryland Adkins M.P., Mister Tangye
DEFENCE COUNSEL	Mister Hole
NUMBER OF VICTIMS	1

VICTIMS DETAILS	
NAME	Eliza Marsh
AGE	22
DATE OF MURDER	Monday, 9th July, 1906
PLACE OF MURDER	6 Goyt Terrace, Brampton
METHOD OF KILLING	Cut throat
RELATIONSHIP TO KILLER	Wife

that she was fit for nothing except for lying in bed, drinking beer and reading cheap novels. Eliza then threw an ornament at Walter before attacking him with a window roller. All he did, Walter insisted, was defend himself with the razor he was holding.

Found guilty after a deliberation of 20 minutes, Walter Marsh refused to allow a petition for his reprieve to be organised, saying that life-long imprisonment held more fear for him than death.

IN 1900, JANE Harrison was running the White Hart Inn with her husband, Edward. Unfortunately, very soon afterwards, he was admitted to the Hatton Mental Asylum.

One of the customers at the White Hart was John Davis and it seems that there was much more between John and Jane than had been imagined for when, soon afterwards, Jane moved to Great Lister Street, Davis's wife paid her a visit and an argument followed over the relationship. Over the next few years, Jane Harrison and her sons moved first to John Street and then finally, to Tower Place. Davis meanwhile had moved to Garstang near Liverpool, where he found employment, but he still travelled back to Aston on a regular basis, and paid visits to Jane.

On October 27th, 1906, Jane ran into an old friend, Charles Hunter. She invited him home with her and after talking for some time, Jane said she would go for some beer. When she hadn't returned after some considerable time, Hunter went looking for her and found her arguing with Davis. Concerned for her safety, Hunter intervened and Davis ran off. A few days later Davis mentioned that he had seen Jane with her 'protector' and made it plain that he believed he had been replaced in Jane's affections.

November 17th saw Edwin Harrison, Jane's son, go to work as normal. Some time later, at 10.00am, a neighbour, Ada McLaughlin, saw Davis go into Jane's house. Some 20 minutes after that, a terrible scream rang through the air and Mrs McLaughlin rushed into her yard to see Jane Harrison, her throat cut, begging for help.

Davis left the house and tried to make good his escape but Mrs McLaughlin's cries of "Stop him! Murder! He's cut a woman's throat!" caused a crowd to gather and Davis was held. Jane was rushed to hospital, where she died an hour later.

Davis came up with a story that suggested Jane Harrison had cut her own throat. He claimed that they had chatted and then he had decided to have a shave. Jane complained that she had a terrible headache and as he took out the razor she snatched it from him and cut her throat. It was true that there was no blood on Davis's clothing, and it was just about

NAME	John Davis
AGE AT EXECUTION	53
DATE OF EXECUTION	Tuesday, 1st January, 1907
PLACE OF EXECUTION	Warwick
HANGMAN	John Ellis
ASSISTANT	William Willis
DATE OF TRIAL	10th December, 1906
LOCATION OF TRIAL	Birmingham
PRESIDING JUDGE	Mister Justice Ridley
PROSECUTION COUNSEL	J.J. Parfitt, Mister Cave
DEFENCE COUNSEL	Richard A. Willes
NUMBER OF VICTIMS	1

VICTIMS DETAILS	
NAME	Jane Harrison
AGE	47
DATE OF MURDER	Saturday, 17th November, 1906
PLACE OF MURDER	17 Tower Place, Aston
METHOD OF KILLING	Cut throat
RELATIONSHIP TO KILLER	Girlfriend

possible that the wound could have been self-inflicted, but other points counted heavily against Davis. Jane had been blacking her fire grate. Her hands were covered in blacklead and yet there was none on the razor.

Davis was found guilty and, on New Year's Day, the killer who suggested that throat cutting was a cure for a headache was hanged at Warwick.

DAVID LANGWELL AND Percy Page were enjoying their holiday. Until July 19th, that is, when they were walking near St Saviour's Rectory and found the body of a man in a field. There were signs of a struggle and there was a good deal of blood on the body and on a large, heavy stone that lay nearby.

The body had no identification upon it but the man's socks did have the initials 'F.C.' on them. This, together with information on two silver watch chains found on the body, led to Victor Jules Goute coming forward to identify the dead man as Pierre Le Guen, a man who used to be one of his tenants.

Le Guen was a farm worker and a married man though he was separated from his wife, Marie Francoise, who was now cohabiting with another man. She was now called in to make a formal identification, as was her brother, Thomas Connan.

Though Pierre's body had been found on July 19th, he had lain in the field for around two days. He had last been seen alive by Francois Poucain at around 10.30pm on July 17th but in addition to this, Joseph Mesmeur, who had been milking cows close to where the body would be found, recalled hearing a low groan at 5.15am on July 18th.

Police inquiries soon began to point towards a possible motive for the murder. Marie Vigne ran a restaurant in the town and said that Pierre had eaten there on Friday, July 13th. Though he had paid for his meal with a £1 note, Pierre also had several sovereigns in a purse. That purse, along with Pierre's watch, had not been found.

One of the silver chains was broken and it was surmised that this had been the one that held the watch. The other was now taken to jeweller's shops and identified as one sold to Thomas Connan. Further inquiries showed that Connan had owed money to Pierre.

In due course, Connan was arrested and claimed that his sister, Marie Le Guen, had put him up to murder. Marie said it was all her brother's doing, whilst Connan claimed that Marie had lured her estranged husband to the field, made love with him and then they had both attacked Pierre when he fell asleep. It is likely that there was more truth to Connan's

NAME	Thomas Connan
AGE AT EXECUTION	29
DATE OF EXECUTION	Tuesday, 19th February, 1907
PLACE OF EXECUTION	St Helier, Jersey
HANGMAN	Henry Pierrepoint
ASSISTANT	Not known
DATE OF TRIAL	7th January – 9th January, 1907
LOCATION OF TRIAL	St Helier
PRESIDING JUDGE	Bailiff Mister Venables-Vernon
PROSECUTION COUNSEL	H.E. Le Vidit Durell
DEFENCE COUNSEL	C.S. Le Gros
NUMBER OF VICTIMS	1

VICTIMS DETAILS	
NAME	Pierre Le Guen
AGE	35
DATE OF MURDER	Wednesday, 18th July, 1906
PLACE OF MURDER	St Saviour, Jersey
METHOD OF KILLING	Battered
RELATIONSHIP TO KILLER	Brother-in-law

story, since blood was found on Marie's clothes and boots.

In the event, the jury took two hours to find Connan guilty of murder and Marie Le Guen guilty of complicity, for which she received 20 years. On February 19th, Thomas Connan became the first man to be hanged on the island since Joseph Philip Le Brun, who was executed on August 11th, 1875 for the murder of his sister.

EDMUND CLARKE WAS a peaceable man. A Sunday school teacher, happily married to Ethel for five years, they had three children and lived with her father, Joseph Jones. All went well until Jones got into some financial difficulties and had to give over his interest in the house to his son-in-law. Now he lived with them and it was a change of circumstance he hated.

For some months this state of affairs continued and there were constant arguments about money. Things grew worse and soon accusation and counter accusation were made. For his part, Jones complained to the police that Clarke had assaulted him and when it seemed that they were not prepared to take any action, Jones was heard to threaten Clarke and say that if he ever found him asleep on the sofa, he would take the opportunity to kill him.

On December 1st, 1906, Edmund Clarke returned home from work at around 8.00pm. Shortly after giving him his evening meal, Ethel Clarke took two of the children out. When she left, her husband had finished his food and was having a quiet doze on the sofa.

Ethel returned one hour later and found her husband in the same position, but now he had blood flowing from a wound in his head. The doctor and the police were called but by the time they arrived, Edmund was dead. It was then noted that in addition to a number of blows on the head, Edmund had also had his throat cut. A search of the premises revealed a bloodstained poker and two razors. Joseph Jones was arrested.

At his trial, Jones admitted killing Edmund but claimed that he had done so in self-defence. His story was that after his daughter had gone out, Edmund had started abusing him and had finally attacked him. Jones was forced to pick up a poker to defend himself and then, using the razors, had cut Edmund whilst he was still semi-conscious.

It was a simple matter for the prosecution to show that there were no signs of a struggle in the house and that it was highly unlikely that Jones would have inflicted the injuries Edmund had received in the situation he described. They held that Jones had struck Edmund with the poker whilst he slumbered

NAME	Joseph Jones
AGE AT EXECUTION	60
DATE OF EXECUTION	Tuesday, 26th March, 1907
PLACE OF EXECUTION	Stafford
HANGMAN	Henry Pierrepoint
ASSISTANT	William Willis
DATE OF TRIAL	7th March, 1907
LOCATION OF TRIAL	Stafford
PRESIDING JUDGE	Mister Justice Walton
PROSECUTION COUNSEL	F. Fitzgerald, F.W. Sherwood
DEFENCE COUNSEL	R.J. Lawrence
NUMBER OF VICTIMS	1

VICTIMS DETAILS	
NAME	Edmund Clarke
AGE	28
DATE OF MURDER	Saturday, 1st December, 1906
PLACE OF MURDER	Quarry Bank, Stafford
METHOD OF KILLING	Battered/cut throat
RELATIONSHIP TO KILLER	Son-in-law

on the sofa and then had taken the razors and cut the helpless man's throat.

That was the version the jury believed and Joseph Jones was duly found guilty of murder, although the verdict also carried a recommendation to mercy.

THE MURDER OF Fanny Moore was one of the most inhuman acts in this book.

Fanny lived with her husband and two of her six children; Edwin aged 33, and Bertie, aged 11. Her husband was a cab driver and was often out in the evenings. This was the case on the night of Saturday, March 2nd, 1907. Fanny was alone with Bertie when Edwin arrived home.

Edwin had consumed a few drinks but according to his brother, he was not drunk. Sitting himself down, Edwin waited for his mother to bring out his supper but when it arrived, it was not to his liking. He threw the plate onto the floor, stood up and stamped on it, breaking it into pieces. Not satisfied with this, he then proceeded to follow his mother around the room, motioning as if to strike her.

Fanny Moore was just a little too quick for Edwin who, exasperated at not being able to catch her, picked up a paraffin lamp and threw it at Fanny. The lamp missed but it shattered into many pieces as it hit the floor. More importantly, the wick remained alight.

Edwin Moore finally caught up with his mother and, seeing the lighted wick, reached out for a newspaper. Edwin then lit the newspaper and holding on tightly to his mother's arm, put the newspaper to her blouse. As the blouse burst into flames, Edwin was heard to shout "I will kill the lot of you if I can get at you."

By now, Fanny Moore was well alight. She managed to struggle free and made her way into the kitchen, screaming loudly. A neighbour heard those blood-curdling cries and rushed in to offer assistance. By this time, Edwin began to realise what he had done and tried to put out the flames himself. It was no use. Fanny Moore was too badly burned. She died within a few minutes.

When interviewed by the police and again at his trial, Edwin Moore consistently denied having anything to do with his mother's death. According to Edwin, he had been out in the yard when he heard a loud explosion from inside the house. When he went to investigate he found his mother and the room itself covered in flames, which he had tried to douse.

The defence tried to make much of

NAME	Edwin James Moore
AGE AT EXECUTION	33
DATE OF EXECUTION	Tuesday, 2nd April, 1907
PLACE OF EXECUTION	Warwick
HANGMAN	John Ellis
ASSISTANT	William Willis
DATE OF TRIAL	11th March, 1907
LOCATION OF TRIAL	Birmingham
PRESIDING JUDGE	Mister Justice Phillimore
PROSECUTION COUNSEL	J.J. Parfitt, B. Stephen Foster
DEFENCE COUNSEL	Bernard Marshall
NUMBER OF VICTIMS	1

VICTIMS DETAILS	
NAME	Fanny Adelaide Moore
AGE	52
DATE OF MURDER	Saturday, 2nd March, 1907
PLACE OF MURDER	Leamington
METHOD OF KILLING	Burned
RELATIONSHIP TO KILLER	Mother

discrepancies in the story of Bertie Moore, the only witness to these terrible events. By the time the neighbour had rushed in, all that could be seen was Edwin trying to beat out the flames and this was consistent with the story he told. The jury, however, gave credence to Bertie, making allowances for the natural shock that an 11-year-old child would undergo after seeing his mother die in such a manner.

WILLIAM SLACK WAS a painter. On March 18th, 1907, he was busy working in Avondale Road, Chesterfield, when a woman, Lucy Wilson went up to him and engaged him in conversation.

The conversation between William and Lucy did not last long and William went back to his painting. However, at 5.00pm, they met up again, this time opposite the workhouse in Highfield Road. This time, after talking for a few minutes, William reached into his pocket, took out a recently sharpened hatchet and struck Lucy a number of blows about the head. William then calmly walked away, pushing the pram containing Lucy's baby.

The attack had been witnessed by a number of people, including a postman, James Gordon Bennett and a coachman, Thomas Wright. They rushed to Lucy's aid, but she was beyond all help, so they ran off to fetch the police. William Slack was arrested in nearby Newbold Road, still pushing the pram in front of him.

Slack's story was that he had attacked Lucy because she would not leave him alone. A few weeks beforehand, Slack's wife had left him and this may have been due to his claim that he had been having an affair with Lucy. He went on to say that he had now broken off the relationship, but Lucy had persisted in following him around. He had told her to leave him alone or he would kill her. When she had ignored his threat, he had carried it out.

This was well within character for William Edward Slack. Once before, in 1899, his wife had left him and he had reported the matter to the police. For one reason or another, Slack convinced himself that the police in general, and one officer in particular – Constable Hudson – knew where she was but had refused to let him know. As a result, in March of that year he had attacked Hudson with two knives, seriously injuring him. For that offence, Slack had received a sentence of seven years.

At the trial, the jury did not even bother to leave the box before returning the guilty verdict. Asked if he had anything to say, Slack told the judge where he could stick the black cap and then took a hair from his head, blew

NAME	William Edward Slack
AGE AT EXECUTION	47
DATE OF EXECUTION	Tuesday, 16th July, 1907
PLACE OF EXECUTION	Derby
HANGMAN	Henry Pierrepoint
ASSISTANT	John Ellis
DATE OF TRIAL	25th June, 1907
LOCATION OF TRIAL	Derby
PRESIDING JUDGE	Mister Justice Coleridge
PROSECUTION COUNSEL	W. Ryland Adkins, Mister McCardie
DEFENCE COUNSEL	Harold Wright
NUMBER OF VICTIMS	1

VICTIMS DETAILS	
NAME	Lucy Wilson
AGE	40
DATE OF MURDER	Monday, 18th March, 1907
PLACE OF MURDER	Highfield Road, Chesterfield
METHOD OF KILLING	Battered
RELATIONSHIP TO KILLER	None

it away and shouted: "That's what I care for you." As the sentence was pronounced, Slack turned his back on the judge and had to be physically turned around by two warders.

The bravado was maintained to the end. At the execution Slack persisted in muttering loudly as the priest intoned his prayers.

ARTHUR CHARLTON HAD split from his wife, Lilian, in 1894 and since the beginning of 1906, she had lived with an unemployed, half-caste sailor named Charles Paterson. Lilian had taken with her the three children from her marriage and so her sons, Joseph and George, and daughter, Tellie, also lived with her and Paterson.

Charles Paterson had rather a short fuse and easily lost his temper. Most of his anger seemed to be directed at Lilian and she often became the victim of physical violence. Several times she went to the police to complain, often taking her son with her to back up her stories and at the end of the first week of June, Lilian also went to the Magistrate's Court to take out a warrant for Charles's arrest. Unfortunately, she had no money to pay for the warrant and the Magistrates refused to give her a free one. Lilian returned to Charles's ill treatment.

At 1.15pm on June 29th, Charles returned home, whereupon Lilian asked him for some money. Charles said he had none to give her and after an argument, he went upstairs, changed his clothes and went out for the rest of the afternoon. He returned just after 6.30pm and the argument started up afresh. Realising she wasn't getting very far, Lilian finally stormed off upstairs, to be followed a few minutes later by Paterson.

Lilian's son, George, had been cleaning his boots and saw Paterson follow his mother upstairs. When he heard a scream very soon afterwards, George dashed upstairs to offer assistance. In fact, he ran so quickly that he broke two of the uprights on the stair banister. George found the bathroom door locked shut, and so immediately kicked it open. Paterson, standing close by the bath, smiled broadly at George who saw that his mother lay on the floor, her throat slashed.

George ran back down stairs and went to Joseph Henry Hutchinson's shop, just down the road, to try to get some help. Henry said he would go into the house to see if he could assist Lilian whilst George brought the police. When he got into number 86, Henry Hutchinson could see that Lilian was beyond all help. Paterson meanwhile was standing in his yard and when he saw Henry, he readily

NAME	Charles Paterson
AGE AT EXECUTION	37
DATE OF EXECUTION	Wednesday, 7th August, 1907
PLACE OF EXECUTION	Liverpool
HANGMAN	Henry Pierrepoint
ASSISTANT	Thomas Pierrepoint
DATE OF TRIAL	16th July, 1907
LOCATION OF TRIAL	Liverpool
PRESIDING JUDGE	Mister Justice Channell
PROSECUTION COUNSEL	Mister Ewart
DEFENCE COUNSEL	None
NUMBER OF VICTIMS	1

VICTIMS DETAILS	
NAME	Lilian Jane Charlton
AGE	39
DATE OF MURDER	Saturday, 29th June, 1907
PLACE OF MURDER	86 Crondall Street, Moss Side, Manchester
METHOD OF KILLING	Cut throat
RELATIONSHIP TO KILLER	Girlfriend

told him what he had done. He seemed to be very nonchalant about what had just happened, and after relating his story, blaming the killing on his temper, Paterson calmly asked Henry if he had any tobacco he could let him have.

When the police arrived, Paterson also confessed his guilt to them. With such admissions, and testimony from Lilian's children that Paterson had often threatened to kill her, the verdict was a foregone conclusion.

ALTHOUGH THERE WAS much circumstantial evidence linking Richard Brinkley with the murder of two people and the attempted murder of two others, the only hard evidence came from a man who may well have lied.

Brinkley had become close to an elderly lady named Johanna Maria Louisa Blume. She had already told both her daughter and her granddaughter that she did not intend to leave them any property in her will and, it seemed, had drawn up a will in favour of Richard Brinkley instead. However, the prosecution at his subsequent trial would argue that the will was a forgery and that in an attempt to cover his tracks, Brinkley had tried to kill Reginald Clifford Parker, one of the witnesses.

According to Parker, on the night of April 20th, 1907, Brinkley called on him at his lodgings at 32 Churchill Road, Croydon, ostensibly to talk about a guard dog that Parker was obtaining for him. Brinkley brought with him a bottle of stout, which he opened, taking a drink himself and offering some to Parker, who accepted. Brinkley then asked for a glass of water, and when Parker left to fetch it, was left alone with the now-opened bottle.

When Parker returned, the two men left together, and after they had gone, the owner of the house, Parker's ex-landlord, Richard Beck, arrived home along with his wife Elizabeth and daughters Daisy and Hilda.

Hilda Beck went straight to bed, thus avoiding the drama that was about to follow. In due course, Richard Beck saw the opened bottle of stout and helped himself to a drink. He also gave some to his wife, Elizabeth and his daughter Daisy. By now, the bottle contained prussic acid and both Richard and Elizabeth died. Daisy was very ill, but eventually made a full recovery.

The case against Brinkley was a strong one. According to Parker, Brinkley had asked him to draw up a form of will at the end of 1906. In December of that year, Brinkley had also asked him to sign a piece of paper that he said related to an outing. Parker, rather naively perhaps, signed this without looking at it and the suggestion was that this is how Brinkley got Parker's signature on the Blume will.

NAME	Richard Clifford Brinkley
AGE AT EXECUTION	53
DATE OF EXECUTION	Tuesday, 13th August, 1907
PLACE OF EXECUTION	Wandsworth
HANGMAN	Henry Pierrepoint
ASSISTANT	John Ellis
DATE OF TRIAL	22nd July – 25th July, 1907
LOCATION OF TRIAL	Guildford
PRESIDING JUDGE	Mister Justice Bigham
PROSECUTION COUNSEL	Richard D. Muir, Haber Hart
DEFENCE COUNSEL	Mister Frampton
NUMBER OF VICTIMS	2

VICTIMS DETAILS	
NAMES	Richard Beck; Elizabeth Beck
AGES	55; 57
DATE OF MURDER	Saturday, 20th April, 1907
PLACE OF MURDER	32 Churchill Road, Croydon
METHOD OF KILLING	Poisoned (by prussic acid)
RELATIONSHIP TO KILLER	None; none

Once Mrs Blume died, her relatives decided to contest the will presented by Brinkley. Since the signature of Parker had been obtained by false pretences, the deception would become apparent just as soon as the lawyers spoke to Parker. If Parker were dead, though, then the deception might be maintained.

The plan was then for Brinkley to poison Parker. It was shown that Brinkley had been given prussic acid on two occasions, and had the opportunity to obtain more. William Vale treated animals and had known Brinkley for many years. In June 1906, Brinkley called on Vale and asked for some prussic acid, which he would use to poison a dog. He was given 60 drops. A few days later he returned and said he had spilled the original supply, at which he was given another 60 drops. More significantly, Brinkley saw the cupboard in which the poison was kept – and he was aware that the cupboard was kept unlocked at all times!

A handwriting expert, Mister Gurnin, gave evidence that in his opinion, the signature of

Mrs Blume on the will, did not appear to be the same as that on other documents and receipts.

Inspector Dew at work on Chelsea railway station said that he saw Brinkley, whom he knew well, on the station at about 6.00pm on the night of April 20th. There was a train to Clapham Junction at 6.15pm and a connection from there would have got him to Croydon at about 7.20pm. Finally, Jack Holden, a boy employed at a beer store, said that he had sold some stout to Richard Brinkley on that Saturday night.

When the apparently cast-iron case was examined though, it was not as strong as it first appeared. To begin with, Brinkley held that the Blume will was a genuine document and that Parker had witnessed it voluntarily. Furthermore, Brinkley said he had offered Parker £100 for his trouble, to be paid after the old woman had died and he had come into his inheritance. Parker, of course, denied this and yet his wife, from whom he was now separated for perhaps the fourth or fifth time, said that Parker had told her that he was due £100 for a document he had witnessed.

John Holden had identified Brinkley but two other customers in the shop at the time remembered nothing of Brinkley coming in and asking for a bottle of stout. Inspector Dew had seen Brinkley on Chelsea station and it had been assumed that this is how Brinkley had travelled from his lodgings at 4 Maxwell Road, Fulham, to the Beck residence at Croydon, but when the records were examined, no one had purchased a ticket from Chelsea to Croydon that night and Brinkley denied visiting Parker at all on the night of the murder.

It must also be noted that if Brinkley's intention was to poison Parker, he went about it in a very clumsy way indeed. This man who had demonstrated such creativity in the matter of the forged will, poisoned a bottle of stout that he then left on the kitchen table whilst he walked out with his intended victim! It would surely have been simplicity itself for him to have cajoled Parker into taking one more drink before they went out.

Perhaps the single most telling piece of evidence against Brinkley was the comment he made when he was arrested. To the police officer taking him into custody, Brinkley said, "If anyone says I bought beer, they have got to prove it." At this stage, no one had mentioned the fact that the poison had been given in a bottle of stout.

The jury thought that the evidence was enough to convict Brinkley, who was hanged on August 13th, 1907. One wonders, though, just how much of Parker's testimony had been the truth.

As A BABY FARMER, Rhoda Willis, who also used the name Mrs Leslie James, could not be described as successful.

Rhoda's story really began on October 26th, 1906, when David Evans's wife left him. David saw a newspaper advertisement offering a housekeeper's services and, finding it difficult to manage by himself, replied. A lady signing herself Leslie James replied to Mr Evans and after interviewing her, he took her on from January 28th, 1907, at his home at 55 George Street, Pontypool.

Mrs James was a most persuasive woman and mentioned to David that she knew a way to make some extra money. They could advertise in the local newspaper, saying they were a married couple and offer to adopt a newborn baby, for a financial consideration. At first David Evans wanted nothing to do with the idea, but eventually he demurred and the notice appeared, in the Evening Express, giving a box number for replies.

There were a few replies for Rhoda, alias Leslie, to consider. One letter came from Lydia English of Llanishen, a married lady whose unmarried sister, Maud Treasure, was in a certain delicate condition, with the child being due some time around the end of May. Lydia English did meet Mrs James, who informed her that she would consider taking the child for a sum of £6 to begin with, and another £2 to follow later when arrangements had proved to be satisfactory. Mrs English promised to contact Mrs James when the child was born.

In the meantime, another reply had come from Emily Stroud, whose child was born on March 20th, 1907. For Rhoda this was a much more interesting proposition, as she would not have to wait until May. Letters were exchanged, meetings took place, and on April 10th, Rhoda, still using the name Leslie James, went to Abertillery to pick up the baby.

Rhoda Willis kept the baby with her, at David Evans's house, until May 7th. On that day she left, telling Mr Evans that she was taking the baby to a friend's house, from where it would be adopted. In fact, Rhoda had already arranged to take in another child and as she could not cope with two, the first one had to be disposed of. Rhoda took the child to

NAME	Rhoda Willis (Leslie James)
AGE AT EXECUTION	44
DATE OF EXECUTION	Wednesday, 14th August, 1907
PLACE OF EXECUTION	Cardiff
HANGMAN	Henry Pierrepoint
ASSISTANT	Thomas Pierrepoint
DATE OF TRIAL	23rd July – 24th July, 1907
LOCATION OF TRIAL	Swansea
PRESIDING JUDGE	Mister Commissioner Shee
PROSECUTION COUNSEL	Sir David Brynmor Jones M.P., Mister Lleufer Thomas
DEFENCE COUNSEL	Ivor Bowen
NUMBER OF VICTIMS	1

VICTIMS DETAILS	
NAME	Female Child (surnamed Treasure)
AGE	1 day
DATE OF MURDER	Tuesday, 4th June, 1907
PLACE OF MURDER	On a train between Llanishen and Cardiff
METHOD OF KILLING	Asphyxiated
RELATIONSHIP TO KILLER	None

the Salvation Army Home in Charles Street, Cardiff, where it was dumped on the doorstep with a badly misspelt note claiming it had been left by its mother who could not cope. The child was not discovered for some time and by the time it was found, it was suffering badly from exposure. It was taken in and cared for, but died on May 15th, 1907.

On the day after the first child had been dumped, Rhoda was picking up the second. A Mr Rees had replied to the advertisement. He was married and his wife had given birth to a daughter on May 5th, but now he had obtained a new position, which necessitated them moving abroad. For one reason or another they could not take the child with them and he was looking for a good home for it. Rhoda picked the child up on May 8th. On the same day she called at a lodging house at 132 Portmanmoor Road, where she spoke to the landlady, Hannah Wilson and asked if she was interesting in adopting the baby girl. Mrs Wilson said she might consider it and Rhoda decided to move in that same day.

This situation remained until June 4th when Mr Rees wrote to Rhoda saying that his new job had fallen through and his wife was pining for her daughter. The following day, Rhoda returned the baby to Mr and Mrs Rees. Still, there was no need for concern for on June 3rd, Maud Treasure had given birth to a girl. Lydia English sent a telegram to Rhoda, and arrangements were made for her to pick up the child.

On the same day that Mr Rees picked up his daughter, Rhoda Willis collected Maud Treasure's child, together with some clothing and £6 in gold. That afternoon she travelled back to her lodgings in Portmanmoor Road.

Hannah Wilson would subsequently report that Rhoda went out later that day and came home drunk. Mrs Wilson helped put her lodger to bed and heard nothing more from her until the following morning. Then, a loud thud alerted Mrs Wilson that something had fallen upstairs. Going up to investigate she found Rhoda lying on the floor, having presumably fallen out of bed. As Hannah Wilson assisted Rhoda, she noticed a bundle close by the bed. Closer inspection revealed that it was the body of a newly born girl.

The police were called and Rhoda Willis was arrested. Medical examination showed that the child had been suffocated and Rhoda was charged with the murder. She denied the charge. Rhoda claimed that when she had picked the baby up, she had noticed spittle coming from its mouth. She thought it might be ill, but Lydia English reassured her and wrapped the child up for the journey to Cardiff. Rhoda caught the train, but upon getting home, found that the baby was dead. She denied being responsible for its death.

At the trial, a handwriting expert gave evidence that the note left with the Stroud baby at the Salvation Army Hostel, had probably been written by Rhoda. The fact that she could so callously leave a newborn child in the cold, probably contributing to its subsequent death, weighed heavily against her and a verdict of guilty was returned.

On August 14th, 1907, Rhoda Willis, prisoner number 135, was executed at Cardiff. It was her 44th birthday.

1907

ON JULY 16TH, 1907, Unity Butler, the only child of William Butler and his wife, returned to school at 1.30pm, after having her lunch at home.

It seemed to be a day like any other. William Butler returned home at 5.30pm and saw his lodger, William Austin, busily cleaning his boots. There was no sign of Unity, but her father simply assumed she had gone out with her mother.

At 6.00pm, Austin left the house, only to return a few minutes later to collect his bicycle. He then left again, never to return to Cranbourne Terrace.

It was almost 11.00pm when Mrs Butler returned home and immediately Unity was missed. A search was organised and very soon Unity was found. Her partially clothed and strangled body lay underneath the bed in William Austin's room. A neighbour, Ludwig Poegell, had heard screams coming from the Butler house at around 4.30pm and this seemed to fix the time of the attack. A search was launched for the missing lodger.

Austin was not seen again until 9.30pm when a friend, Walter West, saw him on his bicycle. Austin seemed to be upset and when West asked him what the problem was, he replied that he had committed a crime and was going to drown himself. The police were contacted and in due course, Austin was arrested and taken to the police station. Here a letter was found on him, addressed to Unity's parents, apologising for what he had done.

Austin's explanation was that Unity had been 'fast'. He claimed that she had often spent time on the bed in his room and on this particular day she had sneered at him and called him names. He had lost his temper, grabbed her and strangled her with a piece of rope.

His own confession was enough to convict Austin, despite his accusations against Unity.

NAME William George Thomas Charles Austin (William Saunders)	
AGE AT EXECUTION 31	
DATE OF EXECUTION Tuesday, 5th November, 1907	
PLACE OF EXECUTION Reading	
HANGMAN Henry Pierrepoint	
ASSISTANT Thomas Pierrepoint	
DATE OF TRIAL 14th October, 1907	
LOCATION OF TRIAL Reading	
PRESIDING JUDGE Mister Justice Jelf	
PROSECUTION COUNSEL F.C. MacKarness M.P., Hugh Sturges	
DEFENCE COUNSEL Mister Hardy	
NUMBER OF VICTIMS 1	

VICTIMS DETAILS
NAME Unity Annie Butler
AGE 13
DATE OF MURDER Tuesday, 16th July, 1907
PLACE OF MURDER 5 Cranbourne Terrace, Clewer, Windsor
METHOD OF KILLING Strangled
RELATIONSHIP TO KILLER None

THE RELATIONSHIP BETWEEN William Duddles and his landlords, the Gear family were, to say the least, strange. William Gear and his wife, Catherine, had a grandchild living with them, a lodger named Robert Stebbings, and also Duddles, a long-term lodger, who had even lived with them at a previous address and moved with them when they came to Sutton Marsh. The trouble was that Duddles and Catherine did not really get on, were frequently heard arguing and Duddles had been known to call her a whore.

The last occasion this particular epithet was used against Catherine, was on October 7th, 1907 when the argument between the two became so heated that William Gear intervened and struck Duddles. Though Duddles did try to fight back, William Gear got the better of him and the episode seemed to be at an end.

The following day, Tuesday, Duddles went to work, returning around noon and being given his dinner. Once he had finished, he announced that he was going to buy some beer and duly returned, after an hour or so, with a full gallon. Since there was plenty of alcohol to go round, the neighbour, Edwin Hocking, together with his lodger – named Towson – were invited in and the whole party sat down to drink. The atmosphere was friendly enough and when, in due course, the last dregs had been drained, William Gear said he would go to get more. Taking his granddaughter with him, Gear left at around 4.00pm.

Whilst Gear was visiting the Ship Inn at Gedney, Towson and Hocking decided to return to their own house and have tea. They left Duddles with Catherine Gear but when they returned, 15 minutes later, there was no sign of Duddles and Catherine lay on the floor of her cottage, a bloodstained hammer nearby. Catherine was barely alive and quickly Hocking went to fetch Doctor James Moore.

On the way, Hocking encountered William Gear on his way home and told him what had happened. Close by, Duddles had met Robert Stebbings and whilst they were talking, William Gear was seen in the distance. Stebbings would later remark that Duddles

NAME	William Duddles
AGE AT EXECUTION	47
DATE OF EXECUTION	Wednesday, 20th November, 1907
PLACE OF EXECUTION	Lincoln
HANGMAN	Henry Pierrepoint
ASSISTANT	Thomas Pierrepoint
DATE OF TRIAL	1st November, 1907
LOCATION OF TRIAL	Lincoln
PRESIDING JUDGE	Mister Commissioner Atkinson
PROSECUTION COUNSEL	R.D. Adkins M.P., Mister Lawrance
DEFENCE COUNSEL	C.E. Dyer
NUMBER OF VICTIMS	1

VICTIMS DETAILS	
NAME	Catherine Gear
AGE	36
DATE OF MURDER	Tuesday, 8th October, 1907
PLACE OF MURDER	Sutton Marsh, Lincolnshire
METHOD OF KILLING	Battered
RELATIONSHIP TO KILLER	None

had behaved very strangely and took a different path, so that he could avoid Gear.

Meanwhile, Police Sergeant Charles Taylor had arrived at the cottage and, having heard the story, decided to see if Duddles had returned to the Ship Inn. Taylor arrived there at 6.20pm, to find Duddles leaning against a fence. He was very drunk, was sporting a blackening eye and had blood on his hands. He was marched back to the cottage and at about the same time he arrived with Sergeant Taylor, Catherine Gear died from her injuries.

Tried and found guilty, William Duddles was executed at Lincoln in November, 1907, the first there for four years.

MARGARET LEYSHORE HAD eaten her lunch and was on her way back to school. As she passed 7 Bridgend Road, something caught her eye and she looked into the house. What she saw caused her to beckon her young sister, Rebecca, and together the two girls gazed through the window.

The house was occupied by 70-year-old Rachel Stills and her two sons, George and John. As Margaret and Rebecca looked through the window, they could see Mrs Stills lying on the floor, on her back, with one of her sons, George, kneeling over her. George had his back to the window, so he couldn't have known that he was being watched.

No doubt frightened after what she had seen, Rebecca Leyshore walked across to the other side of the road. It was then that George Stills opened the front door. His hands were covered in blood and he said something in Welsh, which neither Rebecca nor Margaret understood. Ten minutes later, Stills reappeared but now he was dragging his mother's body after him. Having dumped the unmoving woman on the pavement, he lifted her dress and threw it over her head, went back inside and slammed the door.

Sarah Pryor, a neighbour, moved forward, together with another neighbour, Mrs Evans, when they saw Rachel Stills being dragged outside. Stills had certainly noticed them, for he warned them off before he went back inside. Mrs Evans knocked on the front door whilst Sarah Pryor pulled Rachel's skirts back down.

Rachel Stills bore extensive lacerations and bruises and subsequent medical examination would show that she had been beaten and kicked to death. When the police gained access to the house they found George wiping blood from his hands on an old piece of cloth. His brother John was just putting on his boots but George looked up at the police and exclaimed: "I am the one you want." The clothes of both men were checked, of course, and although no bloodstains were found on any of John's clothes, extensive stains were found on George's.

The defence was again one of drink. Thomas Jones, who had known George for 16 years, had seen him leaving the pub at

NAME	George (Notty) Stills
AGE AT EXECUTION	30
DATE OF EXECUTION	Friday, 13th December, 1907
PLACE OF EXECUTION	Cardiff
HANGMAN	Henry Pierrepoint
ASSISTANT	Thomas Pierrepoint
DATE OF TRIAL	21st November, 1907
LOCATION OF TRIAL	Cardiff
PRESIDING JUDGE	Mister Justice Sutton
PROSECUTION COUNSEL	J. Lloyd Morgan M.P., A.C. Lawrence
DEFENCE COUNSEL	B. Francis Williams
NUMBER OF VICTIMS	1

VICTIMS DETAILS	
NAME	Rachel Hannah Stills
AGE	70
DATE OF MURDER	Tuesday, 10th September, 1907
PLACE OF MURDER	7 Bridgend Road, Pontycymmer
METHOD OF KILLING	Battered
RELATIONSHIP TO KILLER	Mother

12.50pm and testified that at the time, he appeared to be drunk. Margaret Anne Stone was also called, and said she had seen Rachel Stills at 11.30am on the day she had died. She was quite sober, but did sport some bruises on her face. It was plain that George had a temper when drunk and had beaten his mother before.

For his part, George admitted hitting his mother but claimed he had only given her one blow before taking her outside. Having heard details of the injuries though, the jury had no hesitation in finding George Stills guilty of murder.

JANE MCGILLIVRAY WAS growing rather concerned about the strange smell emanating from the flat below hers. So bad did it become that she ended up by calling in the police and finally, on Saturday, September 29th, Constable George Mackie Robertson came along to investigate.

Constable Robertson knew that the occupant of the flat below Mrs McGillivray was John Barclay Smith, who had lived in the village of Lhanbryde for some years and was well known in the area. Before entering the flat, through a window, Constable Robertson checked with some of the other neighbours and discovered that Smith had last been seen on the morning of the 24th, by Alexander Cobban. That had been at around 6.00am and Smith had been with a stranger. Cobban, unfortunately, had not seen this man's face and could offer no description of him.

Upon gaining entrance to the kitchen, Constable Robertson found the body of John Smith, lying on a bed. He was lying on his back, undressed but partially covered by bedding and there was a great deal of blood about. As for the weapon that had been used, Robertson noticed a roadman's hammer close to the fireplace and this too was heavily bloodstained. Someone had battered Smith to death and the object of the crime appeared to be robbery. Smith's waistcoat lay on the bed with a watch pocket uppermost but there was no watch to be found.

Other people besides Alexander Cobban had seen Smith with a stranger on the morning of the 24th and slowly a description was put together. This matched another description, that of a deserter from the Highland Light Infantry, based at the Fort George Barracks. The police were now looking for a man named Joseph Rutherford. Further investigation, though, suggested that Rutherford was just an alias and that the man's real name was Joseph Hume.

Hume was finally picked up, in Stirling, on October 24th. He gave details of his movements, saying that on the morning of September 25th he had travelled to Edinburgh. Jewellers and pawnbrokers were now checked in that city and this led to James Miller, a pawnbroker, coming forward to say

NAME	Joseph Hume (Rutherford)
AGE AT EXECUTION	25
DATE OF EXECUTION	Thursday, 5th March, 1908
PLACE OF EXECUTION	Inverness
HANGMAN	Henry Pierrepoint
ASSISTANT	None
DATE OF TRIAL	6th February – 7th February, 1908
LOCATION OF TRIAL	Aberdeen
PRESIDING JUDGE	Lord Justice Mackenzie
PROSECUTION COUNSEL	A.M. Anderson
DEFENCE COUNSEL	Alexander Moncrieff, J.D. Dallas
NUMBER OF VICTIMS	1

VICTIMS DETAILS	
NAME	John Barclay Smith
AGE	Not known
DATE OF MURDER	circa Tuesday, 24th September, 1907
PLACE OF MURDER	Lhanbryde, Elgin
METHOD OF KILLING	Battered
RELATIONSHIP TO KILLER	None

he had pawned a watch from Hume. That watch matched the description of the one stolen from John Barclay Smith.

Tried for murder, Hume denied that he had played any part in the crime but he was found guilty despite the fact that no blood was found on any of his clothing. He went to the gallows without ever confessing to the crime.

IN THE WEEKS up to the end of October, 1907, there had been a number of thefts at the Co-Operative premises in Windy Nook and the management had decided to do something about it. A rota was drawn up and volunteers stayed in the store at night, hoping to catch the thief red-handed.

On the night of October 31st, four employees stayed in the butchery department: John Patterson, George Ather, John Joseph Cowell and Christopher Carr. The lights were turned down and a device was linked to the lamp so that it could be turned up quickly.

At some time after 4.00am, a noise was heard. A figure came into the room and Cowell pulled on the string he held, turning up the lamp to reveal a masked man, dressed in dark clothes. The four colleagues leapt upon the intruder and a violent struggle followed.

The man fought hard, even after Carr battered him with a butcher's wooden stool, and Ather struck him on the legs with a hammer. It was then that Cowell cried out that the man had a gun. A shot rang out and Patterson fell dead, a bullet in his brain. A second shot and Carr fell, wounded in the leg. The other two backed off and the burglar made good his escape.

In his haste to escape, the killer had left behind items of disguise, a skeleton key and a long hazel stick. He had escaped through a side window and had stood on a barrel beneath that window. The barrel contained lard and a clear footprint lay in the fat. There were other footprints outside and impressions of these were taken by the police.

The police were looking for a man who had been injured in the affray and it was for that reason that Joseph William Noble came to their attention. He was arrested at his place of work, the Park Lane branch of the North Eastern Railway, at Gateshead, and found to be covered in bruises. He claimed that he had fallen in the yard whilst carrying a pile of iron, but the wounds were more consistent with a beating.

Whilst Noble was in custody, his house was searched. A jemmy and other burglar's tools were discovered, along with a number of hazel sticks that matched the one left

NAME	Joseph William Noble
AGE AT EXECUTION	48
DATE OF EXECUTION	Tuesday, 24th March, 1908
PLACE OF EXECUTION	Durham
HANGMAN	Henry Pierrepoint
ASSISTANT	Thomas Pierrepoint
DATE OF TRIAL	2nd March – 3rd March, 1908
LOCATION OF TRIAL	Durham
PRESIDING JUDGE	Mister Justice Channell
PROSECUTION COUNSEL	J. Scott-Fox, Bruce Williamson, Walter Hedley
DEFENCE COUNSEL	Edward Shortt, Morgan Griffiths-Jones
NUMBER OF VICTIMS	1

VICTIMS DETAILS	
NAME	John Patterson
AGE	33
DATE OF MURDER	Friday, 1st November, 1907
PLACE OF MURDER	Co-Operative Store, Windy Nook
METHOD OF KILLING	Shot
RELATIONSHIP TO KILLER	None

behind. No gun was found, but a bag of cartridges was discovered of the same type as those removed from Patterson and Carr. Finally, Noble's shoes fitted the footprints at the scene of the crime.

Noble's defence was that it was a case of mistaken identity, as he had been nowhere near Windy Nook at the time in question. The circumstantial evidence against him was enough for the jury, though, and he was found guilty. He was hanged at the same time as Robert Lawman.

ROBERT LAWMAN, A miner, had been separated from his wife for some time and had been living with Amelia Bell Wood for more than three years.

Amelia took new lodgings on Thursday, January 30th, 1908, at 1 Hyde Park Street, Gateshead, where the landlady was Mrs Elizabeth Senior. The following day, Lawman moved in with Amelia after introducing himself to Mrs Senior.

The next day, February 1st, Lawman and Amelia asked Mrs Senior if she would fetch them some beer and whisky, for which they gave her the money. Mrs Senior did as she was asked and after handing over the drink, began to prepare breakfast. It was whilst she was busying herself with this task that Mrs Senior heard a low moan from her lodger's bedroom. Thinking that one of them might be ill, she knocked on the door and called out to them. Not only was there no reply, but when she tried the door, it was locked. Still, people deserved their privacy and so, thinking no more about it, Mrs Senior went back to making breakfast.

Not many minutes had passed before Mrs Senior heard another noise from her lodger's room. This time it could not be ignored, because it was a loud, blood-curdling scream. Once again Mrs Senior knocked on the door and once again she had no answer and found the room to be locked. She wasted no more time, ran out into the street and returned with a couple of burly policemen.

When the door was forced, Amelia Bell Wood was found lying dead in a pool of blood, her throat gashed hideously. Lawman too had a cut throat and was bending over Amelia's body. He was rushed to Gateshead Hospital, where prompt medical attention saved his life.

Interviewed by the police, Lawman would only say: "I have killed her; I loved her, and I will swing for her." He later explained that their relationship was in difficulties and it had been suggested that they part. He had decided that he could not live without her and so would kill her and himself.

Lawman's story so affected the trial judge, Mister Justice Channell, that the learned gentleman had tears in his eyes as he passed the death sentence after Lawman had been

NAME	Robert Lawman
AGE AT EXECUTION	35
DATE OF EXECUTION	Tuesday, 24th March, 1908
PLACE OF EXECUTION	Durham
HANGMAN	Henry Pierrepoint
ASSISTANT	Thomas Pierrepoint
DATE OF TRIAL	28th February, 1908
LOCATION OF TRIAL	Durham
PRESIDING JUDGE	Mister Justice Channell
PROSECUTION COUNSEL	C.F. Lowenthal, H.S. Mundahl
DEFENCE COUNSEL	Morgan Griffiths-Jones
NUMBER OF VICTIMS	1

VICTIMS DETAILS	
NAME	Amelia Bell Wood
AGE	24
DATE OF MURDER	Saturday, 1st February, 1908
PLACE OF MURDER	1 Hyde Park Street, Gateshead
METHOD OF KILLING	Cut throat
RELATIONSHIP TO KILLER	Girlfriend

found guilty of murder. After hearing the terrible words, Lawman stood to attention, saluted the judge and in a firm and loud voice cried out: "I thank you, my Lord."

THE MARRIAGE OF John and Charlotte Ramsbottom was not a very long-lived one. They became man and wife on October 1st, 1907. She gave birth to their child on December 12th and less than two months later, on February 4th, 1908, she had moved out of their house at Lees Street, Manchester and returned to her mother, Elizabeth Ann Mac Craw, who was licensee of the Prince of Wales pub.

The cause of the split was John's incessant drinking and Charlotte's belief that he was having an affair. John tried to patch things up, going to the pub on February 8th, to ask Charlotte to return to him. When she refused, John was granted permission to move into the pub, from where he travelled to work each day.

Things were fine until February 17th when John left work at midday, did not return to the beerhouse that night; neither did he go to work again the following day. When he finally turned up on the 19th, he was dismissed. Meanwhile, John had obtained a gun licence and on the 20th, he purchased a gun and some cartridges.

The next day, February 21st, the inhabitants of the Prince of Wales heard arguing, followed by the sound of a shot. Charlotte's brother, James MacCraw, and her mother, rushed into the room to find that Charlotte had been shot. The baby had slept thorough the attack on Charlotte and she, despite her wound, grabbed the child and rushed from the room.

John, though, continued firing. The next shot hit a water pipe, but the next two hit James MacCraw and the second of these, striking him in the stomach, killed him. Wearing only his shirt, John Ramsbottom ran from the house to his mother's house at 98 Lees Street, where he was arrested.

John's defence was one of insanity. His mother gave evidence that her brother and an uncle had died in asylums and that John had often behaved strangely, walking on his toes and muttering to himself. None of this convinced the jury and John was sentenced to death.

NAME	John Ramsbottom
AGE AT EXECUTION	34
DATE OF EXECUTION	Tuesday, 12th May, 1908
PLACE OF EXECUTION	Manchester
HANGMAN	Henry Pierrepoint
ASSISTANT	Not known
DATE OF TRIAL	23rd April, 1908
LOCATION OF TRIAL	Manchester
PRESIDING JUDGE	Mister Justice Coleridge
PROSECUTION COUNSEL	Spencer Hogg, Mister Bigham
DEFENCE COUNSEL	Mister Merriman
NUMBER OF VICTIMS	1

VICTIMS DETAILS	
NAME	James MacCraw
AGE	22
DATE OF MURDER	Friday, 21st February, 1908
PLACE OF MURDER	Prince of Wales public house, 45 Abbey Hey Lane, Gorton, Manchester
METHOD OF KILLING	Shot
RELATIONSHIP TO KILLER	Brother-in-law

FRED BALLINGTON HAD a drink problem. Ever since he had lost his job as a butcher in Glossop, he had taken to consoling himself in various public houses and eventually Ann, his wife, had had enough. In early May, 1908, with the help of her son, she threw Fred out of the house, forcing him to take lodgings in Hulme. Fred had tried his best to get back with Ann, but she was immovable.

On May 25th, Fred followed Ann to London Road station, where they argued yet again. When the train for Glossop pulled in, Ann got into a carriage but Fred still followed her and got in beside her. There were other people in the carriage and Fred asked to talk to her in private but she was not to be moved. Eventually he knew he was beaten and asked Ann for some money so that he might go to Blackpool and hopefully find himself a job. She reached into her purse and took out some coins, which she gave to Fred. He counted the money; 18 pence was all he seemed to be worth.

Fred turned to leave the carriage and said, "I'll say goodbye then." He turned back and kissed her but she was not pleased by the gesture. Fred saw the look on her face, turned again towards the carriage door and said "Now it is goodbye, and goodbye for ever."

Determined on having the last word, Ann called him a scamp. It was at that point, in front of the witnesses, that Fred Ballington stepped forward and stabbed his wife in the throat. Immediately he turned the knife upon himself and cut his own throat. Ann died later in the Royal Infirmary, but Fred recovered from his wound.

Subsequently charged with murder and attempted suicide, Fred looked shocked at what the police officer was telling him. He had not yet been told that Ann was dead and now that he knew, he said quietly, "Murder! Is she dead? The sooner they hang me the better, then I shall follow her and be with her."

The trial was little more than a formality but so moved was the judge by the sad story he had heard, that – as with Justice Channell in the case of Robert Lawman – it is said he had tears in his eyes as he pronounced the sentence of death.

NAME	Frederick Ballington
AGE AT EXECUTION	41
DATE OF EXECUTION	Tuesday, 28th July, 1908
PLACE OF EXECUTION	Manchester
HANGMAN	Henry Pierrepoint
ASSISTANT	William Willis
DATE OF TRIAL	7th July, 1908
LOCATION OF TRIAL	Manchester
PRESIDING JUDGE	Mister Justice Bucknill
PROSECUTION COUNSEL	Spencer Hogg, Mister Rathbone
DEFENCE COUNSEL	Gilbert Jordan
NUMBER OF VICTIMS	1

VICTIMS DETAILS	
NAME	Ellen Ann Ballington
AGE	43
DATE OF MURDER	Monday, 25th May, 1908
PLACE OF MURDER	London Road Station, Manchester
METHOD OF KILLING	Stabbed
RELATIONSHIP TO KILLER	Wife

1908

THOMAS AND GERTRUDE Siddle had been married for three and a half years, but had not lived happily together. Thomas seldom worked and failed to provide for his family and in March, 1908, Gertrude left him and obtained a separation order. She then went to live with a Mrs Brown, taking the two children with her. Thomas did not appreciate Gertrude's actions and on one occasion was heard to say to Mrs Brown that his wife would never live with another man. Soon afterwards, Gertrude moved to Mrs Felcey's house in Tyne Street, Hull.

On Tuesday, June 9th, Thomas went to visit his wife to ask once again if she would return to him. During the conversation, Thomas noticed that Gertrude was wearing a new ring upon her finger. In fact, the ring had been given to Gertrude by Mrs Felcey, as Gertrude had been forced to pawn her own ring so that she could provide food for the children. Thomas, though, assumed that the ring had been given to Gertrude by another man.

When Thomas asked about the ring, he did not believe Gertrude's explanation and after a brief argument, said it was time he left. As he walked to the door, Thomas had the youngest child in his arms. He turned, said goodbye and moved to shake hands with his wife. As she held out her own hand, he moved suddenly, drew a razor from his pocket and slashed Gertrude's throat.

Gertrude managed to run out of the house and reached a chemists shop run by Mr Suddaby. He dressed the wound and Gertrude was rushed to the infirmary, but died soon after being admitted. Whilst all this was happening, Thomas calmly sat down and waited for the police to arrive.

In his defence, Thomas claimed that the crime was not premeditated. He said that whilst they were arguing and as he approached the front door, he put his hand into his pocket and felt the razor there. He took it from his pocket just to scare Gertrude but said that at that moment he must have lost his head and did not realise what was happening until he saw blood on his hands.

Another line of defence was that Thomas had been drinking heavily for some weeks prior to the crime. In court, a letter was produced from the prison doctor, Mr Horton, revealing that on reception, Siddle was suffering from chronic alcoholism but had now recovered. Mr Horton did not appear in court and this fact was commented upon by Mister Justice Grantham who said that it was lamentable that he had not been called in a case of such gravity.

NAME Thomas Siddle
AGE AT EXECUTION 29
DATE OF EXECUTION Tuesday, 4th August, 1908
PLACE OF EXECUTION Hull
HANGMAN Henry Pierrepoint
ASSISTANT John Ellis
DATE OF TRIAL 14th July, 1908
LOCATION OF TRIAL York
PRESIDING JUDGE Mister Justice Grantham
PROSECUTION COUNSEL Bruce Williamson, Horace Marshall
DEFENCE COUNSEL Mister Rowan-Hamilton
NUMBER OF VICTIMS 1

VICTIMS DETAILS
NAME Gertrude Siddle
AGE 22
DATE OF MURDER Tuesday, 9th June, 1908
PLACE OF MURDER Tyne Street, Hull
METHOD OF KILLING Cut throat
RELATIONSHIP TO KILLER Wife

IN JUNE 1905, Matthew Dodds married a very eligible widow. Mary was a woman of property with six houses in the village of Hamsterley. The marriage, though, was not a happy one. It was somewhat surprising, therefore, when in February 1907, Mary Jane made out a will leaving everything to her husband.

On August 22nd, 1907, Mary Jane had suffered enough. If leaving Dodds all her property had not changed his attitude, perhaps a new will would. Accordingly she drew up a document in which the bequest to her husband was reduced to £40. The new will certainly preyed on Dodds's mind, for in January 1908, he copied out the old one. Mary Jane agreed to sign it and once more everything would go to him in the event of her death. That event was now much closer than Mary Jane knew.

On February 20th, the neighbours heard screaming from the Dodds' residence and, when Dodds spoke to them later, it was to tell them that his wife was dead from a terrible accident. He had found her, badly burned, lying on the fire in the living room.

The inquest did not concur with Dodds's claim that the death of his wife was an accident. It did not, however, say that he had killed her. The verdict was an open one and on February 23rd, 1908, Mary Jane was laid to rest in the local churchyard.

Open verdict or not, the police thought there was more to this case than appeared at first. On the day of the funeral, officers chose to question Dodds more closely. He was arrested on suspicion of murder, Mary Jane's body was exhumed and a postmortem was carried out. The medical officer determined that before she had been burned, Mary Jane had been strangled – a fact that should have been rather easy to spot when the body was first discovered. The shawl Mary Jane had been wearing was wound so tightly around her throat that the woman who was laying the body out had to cut into the neck to release it!

Dodds was now charged with murder. At his trial, the defence was that Mary's death was accidental. She had fallen over a fender into the fire and in falling had twisted and tightened the shawl around her neck.

NAME	Matthew James Dodds
AGE AT EXECUTION	44
DATE OF EXECUTION	Wednesday, 5th August, 1908
PLACE OF EXECUTION	Durham
HANGMAN	Henry Pierrepoint
ASSISTANT	Thomas Pierrepoint
DATE OF TRIAL	1st July, 1908
LOCATION OF TRIAL	Durham
PRESIDING JUDGE	Mister Justice Grantham
PROSECUTION COUNSEL	C.F. Lowenthal, H.S. Mundahl
DEFENCE COUNSEL	Edward Shortt, S. Fleming
NUMBER OF VICTIMS	1

VICTIMS DETAILS	
NAME	Mary Jane Dodds
AGE	50
DATE OF MURDER	Thursday, 20th February, 1908
PLACE OF MURDER	Hamsterley
METHOD OF KILLING	Strangled
RELATIONSHIP TO KILLER	Wife

Nevertheless, a guilty verdict was returned.

The new Criminal Appeal Act was now in force. Matthew Dodds was now to have the distinction of being the first man to appeal under the new Act. Unfortunately for him, he was not the first to succeed.

The Appeal court reviewed the evidence carefully. The strangulation and the fact that metal stays from Mary Jane's corsets were found under the fire grate weighed heavily against the condemned man, as this would have meant she would have had to have sat upon the fire, accidentally! The appeal was dismissed and the death sentence confirmed.

1908

SINCE SHE HAD been 16 years of age, Jane Withers had been beyond the control of her long-suffering parents. Most of the time since she had lived away from home, often with men, and things were no different by 1908.

In mid-January of that year, Jane visited her parents, David and Elizabeth Withers, and showed them some bruises given to her by her latest boyfriend, Edward Johnstone. He was actually in prison now but Jane added that he would be out soon and she was very frightened of him. Nevertheless, she still went back to the lodgings she shared with Johnstone, at the house of Frank and Mary Christie in Collyford.

By the summer, Edward Johnstone was out of prison and back to his usual ways. On the night of June 6th he drank heavily and was no doubt feeling the effects of that when he woke on the morning of the 7th.

That morning, Mary Christie gave Jane a glass of whisky and sugar and asked her if she would help with the housework. Jane did not reply but drew her finger across her throat and gestured with her head towards Johnstone, implying that he was in something of a fragile mood and that she should be careful how she behaved. Nevertheless, Jane did help Mary and some hours later, they were in the kitchen together when Johnstone came in.

Without a word, Johnstone put his arm around Jane's neck. At first it looked like some harmless game but then Mary Christie saw blood spurting from a wound and Jane fell to the floor. Johnstone then ran out of the house, dropping a razor to the floor as he went.

Frank Christie ran to Jane's aid. He crouched down and cradled her head in his arms. Jane was unable to speak, made a low gurgling noise and then died in his arms. Meanwhile, some men who had heard Mary Christie's pleas for help had run after Johnstone. He was finally captured in a nearby wood by James Smith, John Watson and Adam Thommeny. When told that he had killed Jane, Johnstone merely replied, "Thank God."

The trial was little more than a formality,

NAME	Edward Johnstone
AGE AT EXECUTION	32
DATE OF EXECUTION	Wednesday, 19th August, 1908
PLACE OF EXECUTION	Perth
HANGMAN	John Ellis
ASSISTANT	William Willis
DATE OF TRIAL	23rd June, 1908
LOCATION OF TRIAL	Perth
PRESIDING JUDGE	Lord Justice Ardwall
PROSECUTION COUNSEL	William Thomson, Oswald Dykes
DEFENCE COUNSEL	James Macdonald
NUMBER OF VICTIMS	1

VICTIMS DETAILS	
NAME	Jane Wallace (Withers)
AGE	25
DATE OF MURDER	Sunday, 7th June, 1908
PLACE OF MURDER	Collyford, Fife
METHOD OF KILLING	Cut throat
RELATIONSHIP TO KILLER	Girlfriend

but nevertheless the jury still added a strong recommendation to mercy.

THERE HAD BEEN a time when the farm at Tirkeeran had been jointly owned by two brothers, John and William Berryman, but when William married a local farm girl, Jean Turner, in 1906, John had sold his half so that now William owed it all. John still worked there but now that he was only an employee he began to grow jealous and morose, and there were often arguments between the brothers about this new arrangement.

On March 18th, John Wallace, the owner of a neighbouring farm, was working in one of his fields when John Berryman ran up to him and, in something of a state, blurted out that he had found his brother and sister-in-law dead on the kitchen floor. John Wallace went with Berryman back to the farmhouse and saw the two bodies, lying in a pool of blood. He then ran to fetch the police.

The police investigation showed that the couple had been attacked during their midday meal. It appeared that William had been attacked whilst still engrossed in his meal, as his mouth still contained partly chewed food. Jean had probably been attacked immediately afterwards, as her arms bore defence wounds. Both had been alive when the police first arrived but had died without ever regaining consciousness.

That same afternoon, Albert Moore noticed something sticking out of a pile of manure not far from the scene of the murder. Upon checking, Moore saw that it was the handle of a hammer and when this was examined it was found to have hair and blood adhering to it. This in turn implicated John Berryman, who had reported seeing a stranger leaving the farm, carrying a parcel, whilst he was washing his hands prior to going in for his own meal. No one else had seen any stranger and what reason would such a man have had for taking the murder weapon away with him and then hiding it so close by?

The funeral of the two victims took place on March 20th and on the same day, John Berryman was arrested. By now, Nancy Doherty had come forward and she had told the police that she was passing the farm on the day of the murder. She had seen John Berryman running from the farm when Jane

NAME	John Berryman
AGE AT EXECUTION	53
DATE OF EXECUTION	Thursday, 20th August, 1908
PLACE OF EXECUTION	Londonderry
HANGMAN	Henry Pierrepoint
ASSISTANT	Not known
DATE OF TRIAL	20th July – 22nd July, 1908
LOCATION OF TRIAL	Londonderry
PRESIDING JUDGE	Mister Justice Gibson
PROSECUTION COUNSEL	Richard R. Cherry, J.W. Bird, Thomas H. Maxwell
DEFENCE COUNSEL	Denis S. Henry, J.R. Patchell
NUMBER OF VICTIMS	2

VICTIMS DETAILS

NAMES	William Berryman; Jean Berryman
AGES	55; 33
DATE OF MURDER	Wednesday, 18th March, 1908
PLACE OF MURDER	Tirkeeran, Near Garvagh, County Derry
METHOD OF KILLING	Battered; Battered
RELATIONSHIP TO KILLER	Brother; sister-in-law

came out and cried, "John, come back, he's dying." Berryman had then rushed back to the farm as Jane shouted, "Murder, murder...."

At John Berryman's trial it became clear that the final straw had been an argument about timber. William had made a deal to purchase some and John had objected about the price. At this William had pointed out to his brother that he no longer had any say in the working of the farm. That argument had led to three people losing their lives.

ONE THING COULD be said with certainty about James Phipps: he was an easy man to identify. As a child he had lost an eye when another boy threw a stone at him. Since that time he had worn a glass eye and a white bandage.

At 7.30pm on October 12th, 1908, Phipps was noticed by several children who were playing close to Wharton church. After studying them for a few moments, Phipps called out "Who will go for some cigarettes for me?" Elizabeth Warburton stepped forward and said that she would fetch them. Phipps gave her the money and awaited the child's return. In due course, Elizabeth came back, handed over the cigarettes and watched as Phipps took one from the packet and began to smoke it.

Once he had finished his smoke, Phipps again interrupted the children's game and asked Elizabeth if she could direct him to the house of a man named Hulse. Elizabeth said she could and the two were seen walking off together, across an open field.

The evening grew late and Elizabeth's parents were becoming concerned. It was not like their daughter to stay out so late. They went to investigate, found the other children and heard the story of what had taken place. Then, along with a group of neighbours who had offered to help, Mister and Mrs Warburton set off across the fields in the direction Elizabeth had been seen walking.

As the party walked, they saw a man, who turned out to be James Phipps, walking towards them. He was identified as the man who had gone off with Elizabeth, but he was now alone. When they reached Phipps, Mister Warburton asked him where Elizabeth was. "I won't tell you," replied Phipps who then continued on his way. Stunned into disbelief for a few moments, the party of searchers saw Phipps break into a quick walk and then, as he reached the road, a run. They gave chase. A passing cyclist saw the hue and cry and managed to stop Phipps. Luckily for Phipps, the man then spotted a constable and handed the fugitive over, before the crowd could catch up with him.

Phipps made no attempt to hide what he had done. He said some girls had thrown

NAME	James Phipps
AGE AT EXECUTION	21
DATE OF EXECUTION	Thursday, 12th November, 1908
PLACE OF EXECUTION	Knutsford
HANGMAN	Henry Pierrepoint
ASSISTANT	Thomas Pierrepoint
DATE OF TRIAL	23rd October, 1908
LOCATION OF TRIAL	Chester
PRESIDING JUDGE	Mister Justice Lawrance
PROSECUTION COUNSEL	Ellis J. Griffith, Mister Montgomery
DEFENCE COUNSEL	Walter B. Yates
NUMBER OF VICTIMS	1

VICTIMS DETAILS	
NAME	Elizabeth Warburton
AGE	10
DATE OF MURDER	Monday, 12th October, 1908
PLACE OF MURDER	Wharton, Near Winsford
METHOD OF KILLING	Strangled
RELATIONSHIP TO KILLER	None

stones at him, he had caught one of them and wrung her neck for her. He had then thrown the body into a water-filled ditch. When the police checked, they found Elizabeth's body exactly where Phipps had said it would be.

The defence was one of insanity. Phipps's mother and father were both called to give evidence that their son had been depressed since losing his job as a painter in May of that year. He had twice tried to kill himself: once by drowning and once by cutting his throat. Unfortunately for James Phipps, the jury were not impressed.

CHARLES WILSON MADE his living by travelling the country, selling umbrellas. On Thursday, October 8th, 1908, he left his cottage in Feltwell, Norfolk and set out on his latest sales trip. He told his wife that he would be home on Sunday.

At about 1.00pm on October 11th, after a successful trip, Charles Wilson climbed into his pony-driven cart and set out for Feltwell and home.

In the village itself, at some time between 2.00pm and 3.00pm, a 14-year-old boy named Banham, was playing in the fields. He looked across towards the cottage where the Wilson family lived and though it was some 700 yards away, saw a man who had a dog with him, go up to the house and walk in. It may be argued that at that distance it was impossible for Banham to recognise the features of the man, but he claimed that he could recognise the clothing. He knew that the man he had seen was James Nicholls.

After a few minutes, Nicholls came back out, dragging a woman into the road. A cry for help was heard and the woman was dragged back into the house. Later as Banham saw Nicholls leave the house and walk off in one direction, he noticed that Mister Wilson was approaching in his cart, from the other.

Charles Wilson had noticed as he passed Feltwell church, that it was 3.30pm, and later estimated that he got to his home slightly after 4.00pm. The door was locked, but eventually he managed to force an entry and found the body of his wife lying on the floor. The doctor would later put the time of death at around 3.20pm. She had been battered to death with an axe.

Nicholls, meanwhile, had walked to Maggee's Farm, arriving there at 4.00pm. Here he met two people he knew and told them that Charles Wilson had just murdered his wife. Significantly, news of the murder had not been broadcast yet, but Nicholls already knew that Mrs Wilson had been killed.

Police inquiries turned up a Mister Southgate who recalled seeing James Nicholls walking towards the Wilson house at about 2.20pm. He had a dog with him and this piece of news confirmed the story told by Banham.

NAME	James Nicholls
AGE AT EXECUTION	35
DATE OF EXECUTION	Wednesday, 2nd December, 1908
PLACE OF EXECUTION	Norwich
HANGMAN	Henry Pierrepoint
ASSISTANT	Thomas Pierrepoint
DATE OF TRIAL	27th October, 1908
LOCATION OF TRIAL	Norwich
PRESIDING JUDGE	Mister Justice Grantham
PROSECUTION COUNSEL	Theobald Mathew, G.H.B. Kenrisk
DEFENCE COUNSEL	Gerald Dodgson, E.A. Bracey
NUMBER OF VICTIMS	1

VICTIMS DETAILS	
NAME	Susan Wilson
AGE	70
DATE OF MURDER	Sunday, 11th October, 1908
PLACE OF MURDER	Feltwell, Norfolk
METHOD OF KILLING	Battered
RELATIONSHIP TO KILLER	None

Shortly afterwards, Nicholls was arrested in the pub.

Nicholls's defence was that he had walked past the cottage and heard the sounds of arguing. He had then assumed that Wilson was killing his wife and this was why he had told that story at Maggee's Farm. Much was made of the fact that the only real witness was the 14-year-old Banham who could not be exactly sure where he was standing when he claimed to have seen Nicholls entering the farm.

After a deliberation of just 15 minutes, Nicholls was found guilty of murder, a decision upheld at the Appeal court on November 13th.

ISAAC POLLARD WAS passing the offices of Fieldhouse and Jowett, at Swaine Street, when a red-faced man came out and stood in the doorway.

Pollard asked him what the matter was and the man replied that they were 'having a bit of bother' in the office. He then went back inside. Three minutes later, he was back and when Pollard asked how he had fared, he said that everything was all right now.

Seven hours later, Pollard heard of a terrible murder that had taken place in the office. He gave the police an excellent description of the man and this, together with information from other witnesses, enabled the police to put a name to him.

Until the previous December, John William Ellwood had worked for Fieldhouse and Jowetts but had left after a disagreement. He knew the routine of the offices intimately and was aware that Wilkinson, the company cashier, paid a visit to the office each Friday, sometimes with large quantities of cash.

Thomas Wilkinson's injuries had been inflicted by a poker that was found on the office floor. Since there was no fire in the office, the poker must have been brought by the killer, and Samuel Ellis, who ran a shop just down the road from the murder site, gave evidence that he had sold a poker to Ellwood.

The office boy said that Wilkinson had given him a letter, on the morning of the murder, which he had delivered to Ellwood. A secretary testified that a telephone call had been received at 11.00am and someone had made an appointment to see Wilkinson at 2.00pm. Finally, the landlord of the Fountain Brewery, again close to the offices, said that Ellwood had been in his pub between 1.30pm and 1.45pm. Ellwood was arrested on the day after the murder and the last piece of evidence came from his clothing, on which a large number of bloodstains were discovered.

Ellwood tried to explain all the evidence away. The bloodstains had been deposited on his clothing when a small boy had fallen over in the yard and suffered a nose bleed. He called his brother-in-law, who lived with Ellwood, to confirm that this story was true. Moreover, he maintained, the letter he had received from Wilkinson was in connection

NAME	John William Ellwood
AGE AT EXECUTION	44
DATE OF EXECUTION	Thursday, 3rd December, 1908
PLACE OF EXECUTION	Leeds
HANGMAN	Henry Pierrepoint
ASSISTANT	Thomas Pierrepoint
DATE OF TRIAL	10th November – 11th November, 1908
LOCATION OF TRIAL	Leeds
PRESIDING JUDGE	Mister Justice Pickford
PROSECUTION COUNSEL	C.F. Lowenthal, Frank Newboult
DEFENCE COUNSEL	Charles Mellor, J.J. Wright, Godfrey Ellis
NUMBER OF VICTIMS	1

VICTIMS DETAILS	
NAME	Thomas Wilkinson
AGE	56
DATE OF MURDER	Friday, 31st July, 1908
PLACE OF MURDER	18 Swaine Street, Bradford
METHOD OF KILLING	Battered
RELATIONSHIP TO KILLER	None

with a new position Ellwood was seeking. Wilkinson had offered to help but, unfortunately, Ellwood had since destroyed the letter.

Finally Ellwood called his wife, Ada, who testified that he had been at home from 2.00pm until 2.20pm. If that was true, he could not be the murderer, as the crime was committed at about 2.00pm. Ellwood's wife also confirmed the contents of the letter.

It was a question of which witnesses the jury chose to believe and after an absence of an hour, they made it clear that they preferred the prosecution's version of events.

WHEN MARGARET BOULDRY left her husband she took her baby with her and found lodgings in the house of a Mister Wraight, at Saltwood, near Hythe in Kent. William knew where they were and visited them from time to time. On the evening of October 10th, Margaret was alone with her child when her husband called to see her. She let him in and they talked for a while but pretty soon an argument broke out between them.

The argument grew to be quite heated and at that moment, Mister Wraight arrived home. Concerned for the safety of his lodger, he sought to separate the couple and calm the situation down. His intervention only caused Bouldry to turn his attention to him and the two men then began an argument of their own. In due course, Bouldry struck Wraight, knocking him to the floor.

As Mister Wraight tried to haul himself back to an upright position, he saw Bouldry turn and move towards his wife. Margaret ran out into the hallway, rapidly pursued by her husband, who as he left, took something from his pocket. Wraight got to his feet and followed them out.

There was no sign of anyone in the hallway, but sounds of a violent row were heard coming from the kitchen. Upon his arrival in the kitchen, Wraight saw that Margaret and William were now struggling with each other and that William was holding a knife. Wraight tried to pull William away but he couldn't manage it. The only hope was to fetch a policeman.

When Wraight returned, all was quiet. There was no sign of William Bouldry but there, lying on the kitchen floor in a pool of blood, was Margaret, her throat cut, her crying baby still clutched tightly in her arms. Margaret was still alive but died from her wounds some 20 minutes later.

When he was arrested at Hythe, Bouldry admitted attacking his wife but said that cutting her throat was an accident. He had not meant to hurt her. He was found guilty of murder but with a recommendation to mercy.

NAME	William Bouldry
AGE AT EXECUTION	41
DATE OF EXECUTION	Tuesday, 8th December, 1908
PLACE OF EXECUTION	Maidstone
HANGMAN	Henry Pierrepoint
ASSISTANT	William Willis
DATE OF TRIAL	20th November, 1908
LOCATION OF TRIAL	Maidstone
PRESIDING JUDGE	Mister Justice Ridley
PROSECUTION COUNSEL	Mister Lawless, W.R. Briggs
DEFENCE COUNSEL	Mister Harbord
NUMBER OF VICTIMS	1

1908

VICTIMS DETAILS

NAME	Margaret Bouldry
AGE	Not known
DATE OF MURDER	Saturday, 10th October, 1908
PLACE OF MURDER	Saltwood, Near Hythe
METHOD OF KILLING	Cut throat
RELATIONSHIP TO KILLER	Wife

1908

FOR SIX YEARS a feud had simmered between Harry Parker, Thomas Tompkins and his employer, Mr Mead. It had been in 1902 that Mead had issued a summons against Parker for assault and ever since that successful prosecution, Parker had borne a grudge.

It was on August 26th, 1908, that Parker went to the bakery owned by Mead, with a view to picking some kind of argument with him and Tompkins. Parker arrived at 5.00am and did indeed gain his argument, with Thomas Tompkins. At the height of that discussion, Parker reached out and seized an oak bar, which happened to be studded with nails. Only one blow was struck, but a single nail penetrated Tompkins skull and he died soon afterwards.

When first interviewed by police, Parker said that he had not gone to the bakery with the intention of hurting anyone and the killing was accidental but soon afterwards, his own publicity got to Parker and a sense of bravado came over him. He sought to give the crime greater impact and now claimed that the killing was intentional. At one stage he announced: "It was a bad job I did not do them both in and make a clean job of it."

Parker's defence counsel tried to save the situation by pointing out that his client had not gone to the bakery armed with any weapon and that a single blow only had been given, but Parker's own words counted heavily against him and the guilty verdict was returned.

NAME	Harry Taylor Parker
AGE AT EXECUTION	32
DATE OF EXECUTION	Tuesday, 15th December, 1908
PLACE OF EXECUTION	Warwick
HANGMAN	Henry Pierrepoint
ASSISTANT	John Ellis
DATE OF TRIAL	26th November, 1908
LOCATION OF TRIAL	Birmingham
PRESIDING JUDGE	Mister Justice Sutton
PROSECUTION COUNSEL	Ryland Adkins, B.S. Foster
DEFENCE COUNSEL	P.E. Sandlands
NUMBER OF VICTIMS	1

VICTIMS DETAILS	
NAME	Thomas Tompkins
AGE	61
DATE OF MURDER	Wednesday, 26th August, 1908
PLACE OF MURDER	Stoney Stainton Road, Coventry
METHOD OF KILLING	Battered
RELATIONSHIP TO KILLER	None

PATRICK COLLINS, A miner, was a lodger in the Lawrence household. In addition to Collins and Mr and Mrs Lawrence, the house also held 19-year-old Annie Lawrence, her brother, William, and yet another lodger, John Donovan.

After living with the Lawrence family for a short time, Collins and Annie began to walk out together. In early August, 1908, Annie ended that relationship and found herself another young man. Patrick Collins tried his best to rekindle the friendship, but Annie was not to be moved.

On August 17th, 1908, Annie rose at 5.00am to make breakfast for her brother and both lodgers. All three were miners and though the brother and Donovan did come down for breakfast, they passed on the message that Collins was staying in bed and did not intend going to work that day. They had their meal and left for work.

Annie's mother had also remained in bed but at 7.00am her rest was disturbed by a scream from downstairs. She rose quickly, went downstairs and tried the kitchen door. It was locked from the inside. After some struggling, Mrs Lawrence managed to force the kitchen door open. Inside she found her daughter lying in a pool of blood, Collins standing over her and two knives lying next to the body. After a few seconds, Collins pushed past Mrs Lawrence and ran out of the house.

The police did not need to organise a search for the killer of Annie Lawrence. In due course he walked into the station and gave himself up. Collins told the police that he had intended going to work that morning but after some thought had decided that first he wanted to see how Annie reacted towards him. He told her brother that he was staying at home, intending to get Annie on her own when the others had left the house, he went down into the kitchen and asked Annie for a kiss. If she had responded, he would then have gone to work, content in the knowledge that she had feelings for him after all. Annie, though, refused his advances and ran around a table, saying that she would shout for her mother if he did not leave her alone. They struggled, he lifted a knife and stabbed her.

Whilst a single stab wound might have

NAME	Patrick (Noah Percy) Collins
AGE AT EXECUTION	24
DATE OF EXECUTION	Wednesday, 30th December, 1908
PLACE OF EXECUTION	Cardiff
HANGMAN	Henry Pierrepoint
ASSISTANT	John Ellis
DATE OF TRIAL	11th December, 1908
LOCATION OF TRIAL	Swansea
PRESIDING JUDGE	Mister Justice Bucknill
PROSECUTION COUNSEL	J. Ellis Griffith, Clement Edwards
DEFENCE COUNSEL	Ivor Bowen
NUMBER OF VICTIMS	1

VICTIMS DETAILS	
NAME	Annie Dorothy Lawrence
AGE	19
DATE OF MURDER	Monday, 17th August, 1908
PLACE OF MURDER	5 Aberfawr Terrace, Abertridwr, Near Caerphilly
METHOD OF KILLING	Stabbed
RELATIONSHIP TO KILLER	Ex-girlfriend

tended to confirm Collins's story, Annie had in fact been stabbed seven times. Attempts were also made to show that Collins came from a family of weak intellect, but neither approach saved him from the gallows.

1909

AT A FEW MINUTES to noon on November 7th, 1908, a normal busy Saturday in Shaftesbury Avenue turned into a scene of utter pandemonium.

Benjamin Goodkin, who had just been into the offices of Cartnell and Schlitte, bankers and foreign money changers, to ask directions, had discovered that he was heading in the wrong direction and had turned to retrace his steps, when all hell broke loose.

A piece of metal was thrown through the banker's window, from inside the office, shattering the glass. People stopped and turned to see what the problem was and were shocked to see two men grappling on the floor. The taller of the two seemed to be coming off worst, for the smaller man was stabbing him repeatedly with a dagger.

Eventually the assailant managed to get to his feet and run off. George Thomas Carter, a cabman, stepped in front and tried to stop him. His reward was a lunge of the knife and a deep wound in his left hand. Next, a policeman, Constable Albert Allan Howe moved to apprehend the man but he received a stab in the shoulder. At this point a number of other men leapt upon the man and managed to subdue him until Constable Howe had recovered enough to take him into custody.

Later identified as John Esmond Murphy, alias James McDonald, the attacker was later charged with the murder of Frederick Schlitte and with wounding Carter and Howe.

It was a sorry story that was eventually told in court. Schlitte had managed to make a statement before he had died and in this he explained that at about noon he had looked up to see Murphy standing before him in the banking hall, a gun levelled at his chest. Without speaking, Murphy had fired the gun once, the bullet burying itself in Schlitte's flesh. Schlitte had thrown himself upon Murphy, knocking the gun from his hand and they had fallen to the floor whereupon Murphy had drawn a knife and stabbed Schlitte repeatedly. He in return had managed to throw something through the window hoping to attract attention. The rest of the story was filled in by the two wounded men,

NAME John Esmond Murphy (James McDonald)
AGE AT EXECUTION 21
DATE OF EXECUTION Wednesday, 6th January, 1909
PLACE OF EXECUTION Pentonville
HANGMAN Henry Pierrepoint
ASSISTANT William Willis
DATE OF TRIAL 14th December – 15th December, 1908
LOCATION OF TRIAL Old Bailey
PRESIDING JUDGE Mister Justice Pickford
PROSECUTION COUNSEL Mister Bodkin, Mister Graham-Campbell
DEFENCE COUNSEL George Jones, Buddle Atkinson
NUMBER OF VICTIMS 1

VICTIMS DETAILS
NAME Frederick George Wilhelm Maria Julius Schlitte (Died Monday, 9th November)
AGE 47
DATE OF MURDER Saturday, 7th November, 1908
PLACE OF MURDER Offices of Cartnell and Schlitte, 84 Shaftesbury Avenue, London
METHOD OF KILLING Shot/stabbed
RELATIONSHIP TO KILLER None

along with Martin Lister and George Walter Armitt, two more cab drivers.

For his part, Murphy claimed to have no memory of the attack. Witnesses were called who gave him an excellent character but they added that he had spent much of the last three months practising his shooting at a range in Oxenden Street, Haymarket. Suggestions were made that he was epileptic and had suffered some sort of seizure when he went into the offices in Shaftesbury Avenue.

None of this saved Murphy from the gallows. Found guilty of murder he was executed in January.

JEREMIAH O'CONNOR HAD lodged with the Donnelly family for three years and had caused them no problems, apart from occasionally taking too much drink. The weekend of December 12th and 13th, 1908, was one of those occasions and O'Connor had drunk so much that he couldn't go to work on the Monday. A coal miner by trade, O'Connor spent the day recovering from his excesses, but the way he felt did nothing to excuse his actions of that night.

At 8.45pm, neighbours saw O'Connor walking down a lane with 10-year-old Mary Donnelly. Neither of them were to return home that evening. The police were informed and a search of the area launched the following day.

It did not take the authorities long to find O'Connor, who had been living rough in a local woods. He claimed to know nothing of the disappearance of little Mary, but was held whilst further inquiries were made. The following day, the body of Mary Donnelly was discovered. Its location was along the lane where O'Connor was seen walking with her and he was now charged with murder.

O'Connor claimed that he had only gone for a walk with the murdered child, when they had been approached by a stranger, an Irish navvy, who had taken Mary away with him. O'Connor had tried to intervene and save the child but the navvy had drawn a knife and wounded him. He showed a number of wounds which he claimed proved that his story was true.

At his trial though, medical opinion was that the wounds on O'Connor were self-inflicted. It was enough for the jury to convict him of wilful murder.

NAME	Jeremiah O'Connor
AGE AT EXECUTION	52
DATE OF EXECUTION	Tuesday, 23rd February, 1909
PLACE OF EXECUTION	Durham
HANGMAN	Henry Pierrepoint
ASSISTANT	William Willis
DATE OF TRIAL	1st February, 1909
LOCATION OF TRIAL	Durham
PRESIDING JUDGE	Mister Justice A.T. Lawrence
PROSECUTION COUNSEL	C.F. Lowenthal, H.S. Mundahl
DEFENCE COUNSEL	Kevin H. Marshall
NUMBER OF VICTIMS	1

VICTIMS DETAILS	
NAME	Mary Donnelly
AGE	10
DATE OF MURDER	Monday, 14th December, 1908
PLACE OF MURDER	West Stanley
METHOD OF KILLING	Stabbed
RELATIONSHIP TO KILLER	None

1960

SOME TIME BEFORE 10.00am on Christmas Eve, 1908, the residents of Great Albion Street, Halifax realised that something was dreadfully wrong at number 20, where Ernest Hutchinson lived with Hannah Whiteley and her five-year-old daughter, Eveline.

The little girl could be seen at an upstairs window, crying bitterly, but even more tellingly, a trickle of blood had begun to issue from beneath the front door. It was determined that an entry should be forced and it was Thomas Greevy, who lived opposite, who managed to climb in through a window. He found Hannah dead in a pool of blood behind the front door, and Hutchinson on the stairs, a wound in his throat.

The police determined that Hannah had been stabbed several times in the neck and breast. Hutchinson had apparently cut his own throat with a razor, but no major arteries had been severed and he recovered in hospital.

Interviewed by the police, Hutchinson said that he had first met Hannah in 1907, and they had started living together in April, 1908. On November 17th, 1908, Hutchinson had struck Hannah because he heard her letting someone out of the house. He suspected it was another man. He had been summonsed for using obscene language on this occasion. He went on to say that they had had many arguments, mainly caused by her fondness for drink.

On the day of Hannah's death, Hutchinson had been drinking until 11.00pm, having spent some time with a group of carol singers. Getting home soon afterwards he saw Hannah letting a man out of the house. Finding money on a plant stand, Hutchinson put two and two together and accused Hannah of sleeping with the man for money. An argument broke out, during which Hannah grabbed a razor and lashed out at him, cutting his throat. He happened to have a knife in his hand at the time and struck out with it.

The jury at Hutchinson's trial were out for just 15 minutes before returning a verdict of guilty but with a strong recommendation to mercy on account of Hutchinson's youth. A petition was also organised and this collected 8,500 signatures. Nevertheless, on March 2nd,

NAME	Ernest Hutchinson
AGE AT EXECUTION	24
DATE OF EXECUTION	Tuesday, 2nd March, 1909
PLACE OF EXECUTION	Wakefield
HANGMAN	Henry Pierrepoint
ASSISTANT	Thomas Pierrepoint
DATE OF TRIAL	12th February, 1909
LOCATION OF TRIAL	Leeds
PRESIDING JUDGE	Mister Justice Coleridge
PROSECUTION COUNSEL	Bruce Williamson, A.J. Robinson
DEFENCE COUNSEL	Mister Fleming
NUMBER OF VICTIMS	1

VICTIMS DETAILS	
NAME	Hannah Maria Whiteley
AGE	29
DATE OF MURDER	Thursday, 24th December, 1908
PLACE OF MURDER	20 Great Albion Street, Halifax
METHOD OF KILLING	Stabbed
RELATIONSHIP TO KILLER	Girlfriend

1909, Ernest Hutchinson was hanged at Wakefield, by the Pierrepoint brothers.

FOR CLARA HOWELL, the evening of November 27th, 1908, began as quite a pleasant one. With Thomas Mead, her partner of the past seven years, Clara visited the house a friend named Robinson. Other people were there too and it was not until 11.00pm that she and Thomas made their way home to Crook's Yard.

At about midnight, two police constables on duty close to Crook's Yard, heard the sound of a disturbance coming from inside one of the houses. It was an obvious domestic dispute but such was the noise coming from the house that the officers felt it was their duty to knock on the door and ask the occupants to be quiet. For a time at least, Thomas Mead did as he had been asked.

One hour later, the next-door neighbour, Sarah Whittaker, was disturbed by the noise of yet another argument. This time the policemen had moved on so there was no one to stop the racket, which went on until 3.00am. Finally it fell silent and Mrs Whittaker was able to get back to sleep.

Later that day, Thomas Mead was seen to leave the house, locking the door behind him. He did not return that evening. That night, Mead went back to Robinson's house and asked him if he could stay the night there. Permission was granted but by now, Mead had told no less than four people that he had killed Clara Howell.

On the Sunday, an entrance was forced in the house in Crook's Yard and the body of Clara Howell was discovered. She had been battered with a broom handle but the blow that actually killed her was a fist to the stomach, which ruptured an intestine.

The trial of Thomas Mead raised an interesting point of law. The defence argued that Mead's mind was unhinged by drink and therefore, as he did not know what he was doing, he was guilty of manslaughter and not murder.

Mister Justice Coleridge, in his summing-up, said that the jury must return a verdict of murder or, if they were convinced that Mead was incapable of forming the intention to kill, then they must return a verdict of manslaughter. The defence held that this phraseology implied that Mead must be

NAME	Thomas Mead
AGE AT EXECUTION	33
DATE OF EXECUTION	Friday, 12th March, 1909
PLACE OF EXECUTION	Leeds
HANGMAN	Henry Pierrepoint
ASSISTANT	John Ellis
DATE OF TRIAL	10th February, 1909
LOCATION OF TRIAL	Leeds
PRESIDING JUDGE	Mister Justice Coleridge
PROSECUTION COUNSEL	H.T. Waddy, Bruce Williamson
DEFENCE COUNSEL	J. Willoughby Jardine
NUMBER OF VICTIMS	1

VICTIMS DETAILS	
NAME	Clara Howell
AGE	36
DATE OF MURDER	Saturday, 28th November, 1908
PLACE OF MURDER	Crook's Yard, Well Street, Off West Street, Leeds
METHOD OF KILLING	Battered
RELATIONSHIP TO KILLER	Girlfriend

totally mad from drink, in order to avoid the death sentence. The case went to appeal.

The appeal was heard before Mister Justice Darling, Mister Justice Walton and Mister Justice Pickford, on February 23rd. The judges carefully considered the wording used at the trial and felt that they did not give any such presumption to the jury. Mister Justice Coleridge had expressly explained that Mead had not entered a defence of insanity. These words countered any implication that Mead had to be insane from drink.

The appeal failed and Thomas Mead was hanged at Leeds on March 12th, 1909.

EDMUND ELLIOTT HAD been seeing Clara Jane Hannaford for over 18 months, even though she was still not quite 16 years of age. In due course, Clara's parents decided that since Elliott did not seem to be interested in holding down a steady job, they couldn't approve of him seeing Clara. In the summer of 1908, Clara's father, George Henry Hannaford, forbade his daughter from seeing Elliott again.

Clara's uncle was serving in the Royal Navy and it was through him that a young seaman named William Johnstone Lilley, was introduced to the Hannaford family and called on Emily at her parent's house, at 2 Henry Street, Plymouth. Clara's parents approved of Lilley and gave permission for him to take their daughter to the Theatre Royal, on the evening of November 17th.

William Lilley picked Clara up at 6.40pm, and arranged to meet up with Mr and Mrs Hannaford at the Athenaeum Hotel after the show. Whilst walking to the hotel, a young man came up to Clara and whispered something to her. Clara spent a few minutes in conversation with the man but all Lilley heard was the last sentence when the man said: "If you come up the lane, I'll prove it." Lilley would later identify the speaker as being Elliott.

At 10.40pm, Lilley and Clara met George and Fanny Hannaford in the hotel, as arranged. Lilley had a drink, but within minutes, Clara had said she was going home and left him with her parents. She returned after six or seven minutes, a gaping wound in her throat, and died on the way to the hospital.

There were a number of witnesses to what had happened in those intervening minutes. John Tremlett heard a scream at about 10.45pm and saw Elliott with his arm around Clara's throat. He later traced a trail of blood back to the rear of number 25, Queen Lane. Mary Secombe saw Elliott stop Clara when she was halfway down Queen Lane. Elliott struck Clara and knocked her hat off and then, to her horror, Mary saw him slash her throat. In the confusion that followed, Elliott made good his escape.

Edmund Elliott had no intention of running. He returned to his home at 46 Well

NAME	Edmund Walter Elliott
AGE AT EXECUTION	19
DATE OF EXECUTION	Tuesday, 30th March, 1909
PLACE OF EXECUTION	Exeter
HANGMAN	John Ellis
ASSISTANT	Thomas Hyscott
DATE OF TRIAL	11th March, 1909
LOCATION OF TRIAL	Exeter
PRESIDING JUDGE	Mister Justice Ridley
PROSECUTION COUNSEL	John O'Connor M.P., Raymond Asquith
DEFENCE COUNSEL	W.T. Lawrance
NUMBER OF VICTIMS	1

VICTIMS DETAILS	
NAME	Clara Jane Hannaford
AGE	15
DATE OF MURDER	Tuesday, 17th November, 1908
PLACE OF MURDER	Queen Lane, Plymouth
METHOD OF KILLING	Cut throat
RELATIONSHIP TO KILLER	Ex-Girlfriend

Street, changed his clothes and then took a walk to the Central Police Station where he asked: "Are you looking for Ted Elliott?" He was arrested and when told he would be charged with murder, asked: "Is she dead?"

The trial took place at Exeter and there could be little doubt as to the verdict. Found guilty after an absence of 15 minutes, Elliott was recommended to mercy on account of his youth but at the end of March, 1909, Elliott became the first man to be hanged at Exeter prison in the twentieth century.

AMY YAP SING had been ill for eight weeks, with peritonitis, and had been confined to bed at 13 Dickinson Street, Liverpool. She received quite a few visitors, many being Chinese people from the lodging house she ran, but the two who came most often were Yun Yap, and See Lee.

On December 3rd, 1908, both Yun Yap and See Lee visited Amy at the same time. They had a few drinks together whilst they stayed with Amy and when they left, they were on the best of terms.

On December 4th, around 9.00pm, Yun Yap visited. He gave Amy an apple and stood at the foot of her bed, talking to her. He had only been there a couple of minutes when See Lee entered the room. Not a word passed between the two men before a shot rang out and Yun Yap fell across the foot of Amy's bed, a bullet in his side. See Lee turned on his heel and walked out, again without saying a word.

Details of the crime were circulated to all forces around Liverpool. Around 10.00pm, on Saturday, December 5th, Constable William Miller of the railway police, saw a Chinese male on Platform 1 of Lime Street station. Miller interviewed the man, who said he was going to Glasgow, before visiting friends in Cardiff and then moving on to Hong Kong.

The next train for Glasgow was due to leave at 12.45am on Sunday. At 12.30am, Miller saw the man he was keeping an eye on head for the booking office. Once again he went to interview him but this time he noticed that the man was carrying a Sailor's Discharge Book that had the name See Lee stamped upon it. Miller called for assistance and See Lee was arrested.

At the hospital, Yun Yap gave a statement in which he said he had no idea why he had been shot by a man he believed to be his friend. He would die from his injuries on December 7th, making the charge one of murder.

For his part, See Lee claimed that Yun Yap had been jealous of his closeness to Amy and when he had entered her bedroom, Yun Yap had pulled out a gun and pointed it at him. There had been a struggle and See Lee managed to wrestle the gun from Yun Yap's hand. He then fired because he feared for his own life.

NAME	See Lee
AGE AT EXECUTION	38
DATE OF EXECUTION	Tuesday, 30th March, 1909
PLACE OF EXECUTION	Liverpool
HANGMAN	Henry Pierrepoint
ASSISTANT	Thomas Pierrepoint
DATE OF TRIAL	12th March, 1909
LOCATION OF TRIAL	Liverpool
PRESIDING JUDGE	Lord Chief Justice, Lord Alverstone
PROSECUTION COUNSEL	H.R. Rathbone, G.C. Rees
DEFENCE COUNSEL	Lindon Riley
NUMBER OF VICTIMS	1

VICTIMS DETAILS	
NAME	Yun Yap (Died Monday, 7th December)
AGE	40
DATE OF MURDER	Friday, 4th December, 1908
PLACE OF MURDER	13 Dickinson Street, Off Upper Frederick Street, Liverpool
METHOD OF KILLING	Shot
RELATIONSHIP TO KILLER	None

See Lee's story did not agree with the evidence of Amy Yap Sing, however, and the jury, believing that it had been See Lee who had been jealous, returned the only verdict they could.

1909

JOSEPH JONES HAD been married for 20 years, and for most of that time the marriage had been happy. This changed on November 7th, 1908, when Jones hit Charlotte, who promptly packed her bags and moved back to her mother's. She then took out a summons for assault and Jones was fined 20/-, on November 11th. The following day Charlotte and her mother returned to the marital home when they thought Jones would be out. Unfortunately, Joseph Edwin Jones was at home after all.

At 3.30pm, Mrs Jones entered the house by the back door. A few minutes later, a shot was heard and Joseph appeared at the front, bleeding from a throat wound. He said his wife attacked him with a razor. She had then gone upstairs, to the bedroom, and shot herself. There were however, a few points of concern about the incident.

In the first place, Jones had attempted to purchase a revolver from a pawnshop on November 9th. Secondly, Jones had told two women that he was expecting his wife to call. Finally, the doctor said the victim's wound could not have been self-inflicted. The jury chose to believe that Jones had planned the whole thing and found him guilty.

The defence were not prepared to let the matter rest. The pawnbroker was questioned again and it transpired that it was another man, Edward Bailey, who had attempted to buy a revolver. Mrs Jones and her mother had already visited the house on November 11th and Charlotte had had ample time to find the gun and load it, ready for use. The gun had been in Jones's possession for some years and the doctors were shown to have no experience of gunshot wounds.

At the appeal, in front of the Lord Chief Justice, Mrs Fanny Jones testified that on the morning of November 11th, she had heard Joseph Jones ask his wife to come home. She had replied that she wouldn't. This indicated that Jones could not have been expecting her.

A firearms expert, Edward John Churchill, said that in his opinion the gun had been fired from between three and six inches and the wound could have been self-inflicted.

The decision came on March 26th. It was only possible to allow the appeal under

NAME	Joseph Edwin Jones
AGE AT EXECUTION	39
DATE OF EXECUTION	Tuesday, 13th April, 1909
PLACE OF EXECUTION	Stafford
HANGMAN	Henry Pierrepoint
ASSISTANT	John Ellis
DATE OF TRIAL	5th March, 1909
LOCATION OF TRIAL	Stafford
PRESIDING JUDGE	Mister Justice Channell
PROSECUTION COUNSEL	Mister Mackarness M.P., Mister Sherwood, S.R.C Bosanquet
DEFENCE COUNSEL	R.J. Lawrence
NUMBER OF VICTIMS	1

VICTIMS DETAILS	
NAME	Charlotte Jones
AGE	38
DATE OF MURDER	Thursday, 12th November, 1908
PLACE OF MURDER	1 Pugh's Buildings, Merridale Street, Wolverhampton
METHOD OF KILLING	Shot
RELATIONSHIP TO KILLER	Wife

section 4, in that the verdict could only be set aside on the grounds that it was unreasonable or could not be supported according to the evidence, or that there had been a miscarriage of justice. The Lord Chief Justice could see no motive for Mrs Jones attempting to kill her husband and asked why, if she had wished to, she had not used the revolver that she supposedly later used to kill herself.

ON THE NIGHT of December 23rd, 1908, four people walked from Merthyr Tydfil to some old disused coke ovens at Ynysfach. William Joseph Foy had been seeing Mary Ann Rees, a prostitute with the rather unattractive nickname of 'Sloppy', for some time. The other couple were John Bassett and Mary Ann Graney.

After arriving at Ynysfach, the four settled down but then Mary Ann Rees made a comment and stormed off into the night. Foy did not explain to the others what had upset her, but said he would find her and bring her back. He then walked off in the same direction and was gone for about 15 minutes.

When Foy returned he was alone and explained with a laugh that Mary Ann would not be returning as he had just thrown her down the shaft of a disused blast furnace. On the advice of the others, Foy then walked back into Merthyr and gave himself up to the police.

Foy reached the High Street, where he found Sergeant Charles Hunter and Constable Richard Henry Lewis, to whom he said: "I want you to lock me up." Hunter asked what for and Foy answered: "Murder. I have thrown Sloppy down a hole in the old works." The reason he gave was that she had told him that she was going to inform the authorities that he had been living off her earnings as a prostitute.

The body of Mary Ann Rees was found at the bottom of a 39-foot deep shaft and Foy was charged with murder. At his trial, his defence was that the killing had been accidental. Foy explained that he had caught up with Mary Ann and asked her to come back. When she refused, he had tried to pull her back. She managed to struggle free and in doing so, fell backwards down the shaft. He claimed that he had made his statement to the police in the excitement of the moment.

The story, though, did not agree with the evidence. In the first place, Foy had been laughing when he had told Bassett and Graney what had happened and had said nothing to them about it being an accident. Furthermore, had Mary Ann fallen accidentally then surely she would have screamed as she plunged into the darkness?

NAME	William Joseph Foy
AGE AT EXECUTION	25
DATE OF EXECUTION	Saturday, 8th May, 1909
PLACE OF EXECUTION	Swansea
HANGMAN	Henry Pierrepoint
ASSISTANT	John Ellis
DATE OF TRIAL	31st March, 1909
LOCATION OF TRIAL	Cardiff
PRESIDING JUDGE	Mister Justice Bray
PROSECUTION COUNSEL	W. Llewellyn Williams M.P., Elidyr B. Herbert
DEFENCE COUNSEL	Ivor Bowen
NUMBER OF VICTIMS	1

VICTIMS DETAILS	
NAME	Mary Ann Rees
AGE	33
DATE OF MURDER	Thursday, 24th December, 1908
PLACE OF MURDER	Ynysfach, Merthyr Tydfil
METHOD OF KILLING	Battered
RELATIONSHIP TO KILLER	Girlfriend

Perhaps she had not made a noise because she had been unable to do so. Foy was found guilty and sentenced to death.

The case went to the Court of Appeal, where the judges agreed that the circumstances dictated that it was either a case of murder or accident. In his opinion, the evidence meant that the only verdict a jury could reach was one of murder, and the sentence was upheld.

William Joseph Foy had one final flourish. On the morning of his execution he walked to the scaffold wearing a fern in his buttonhole and smoking a cigarette.

IT WAS A simple plan. Emily Allen, who had lived with Morris Reuben for two and a half years, and Ellen Stevens, would look out for a man who looked like he might have a few shillings on him. He would be allowed to buy them a few drinks and then they would go to Rupert Street where Morris and his brother Marks, would persuade him to part with the rest of his cash and any property that they might take a shine to.

William Sproull was the second engineer on the Dorset and on the evening of March 16th he, and his shipmate Charles McEachran, went along to the Three Nuns Hotel, where they had a few drinks. At about 11.00pm, two women came over to talk to them: Emily Allen and Ellen Stevens. After some discussion the two men agreed to accompany them back to Rupert Street.

As Sproull and McEachran were about to leave the house, two men suddenly appeared and attacked them. McEachran was hit over the head and rendered unconscious, but Sproull put up more of a fight. The struggle spilled out into the street and then Marks Reuben settled it by using his knife, driving it to the hilt into the body of Sproull.

When McEachran came round he found himself leaning against a building in a side street, a police inspector standing over him. The body of Sproull still lay in Rupert Street and a trail of blood led the police straight to the door of number 3.

Inside the murder house, police found Ellen Brooks in bed, insensible from drink. Morris Reuben was just dressing and admitted that he had robbed Sproull. He said that the two sailors had started the fight and that he and his brother had intervened to protect the ladies. The police arrested and charged all four.

Once the case came to trial, no evidence was offered against either Emily Allen or Ellen Stevens and they were therefore found not guilty. The trial against the two brothers then proceeded, with Allen now giving evidence for the prosecution. With her testimony before them, the jury took just 10 minutes to return the guilty verdicts.

Both men struggled in the dock before being taken down and Morris was heard to

NAMES	Morris Reuben; Marks Reuben
AGE AT EXECUTION	23; 22
DATE OF EXECUTION	Thursday, 20th May, 1909
PLACE OF EXECUTION	Pentonville
HANGMAN	Henry Pierrepoint
ASSISTANT	Thomas Pierrepoint
DATE OF TRIAL	22nd April – 23rd April, 1909
LOCATION OF TRIAL	Old Bailey
PRESIDING JUDGE	Mister Justice Jelf
PROSECUTION COUNSEL	Richard D. Muir, Travers Humphreys, Huntly Jenkins
DEFENCE COUNSEL	Daniel Wardle, David White
NUMBER OF VICTIMS	1

VICTIMS DETAILS	
NAME	William Sproull
AGE	36
DATE OF MURDER	Tuesday, 16th March, 1909
PLACE OF MURDER	3 Rupert Street, Whitechapel, London
METHOD OF KILLING	Stabbed
RELATIONSHIP TO KILLERS	None; none

exclaim "Why is there no recommendation?"

At the subsequent appeal, an attempt was made to at least save Morris from the gallows. He had not struck the fatal blow and the defence argued that for that reason he should have the murder verdict reduced to one of manslaughter. The judges pointed out that the Reuben brothers had a common design in robbing Sproull and that therefore they were equally guilty of murder and the appeals were rejected.

On 21st May, 1909, the Pierrepoint brothers executed the Reuben brothers.

SOME MURDERERS KILL in the heat of passion or in a moment of temper, others seem to be deliberate, cruel and without feelings. Such a killer was John Edmunds.

Cecilia Harris was a widow who lived on a lonely farm near Abersychan, in Wales. At 5.00pm on February 20th, 1909, Cecilia was alone in the farmhouse when she spotted a figure on the mountain nearby.

Approximately half an hour later, Cecilia went outside to dispose of a bucket of ashes from the fireplace, when she saw that the same man, who she knew as John Edmunds, was now in her garden and he was carrying a gun. Rather than showing fear as might be expected, Cecilia ordered him off her property. She watched as he moved away, sat down and lit himself a cigarette. Not satisfied that he had gone far enough, Cecilia again ordered Edmunds away, whereupon he lifted the gun and pointed it in her direction. Thinking that it might be better not to take any further chances, Cecilia went back inside and locked the door.

As Cecilia Harris watched from an upstairs window, Edmunds approached the farmhouse again and, finding the door locked, broke a window in order to gain entry. Cecilia managed to dash back downstairs and hurried out of the house, intending to go for help. Edmunds simply pointed the gun and fired, the bullet hitting Cecilia in the mouth, causing her to collapse near the garden gate.

Showing no mercy whatsoever, Edmunds slowly walked to where Cecilia lay, lay down near her, lifted her clothes and raped her. When he had finished, Cecilia tried to calm him down by asking if her face was badly cut. Edmunds remarked that she looked a hell of a mess and offered to bandage her wounds. He then assisted her back to the farmhouse's kitchen.

Having been shot and raped, Cecilia wanted only to get Edmunds out of her house. She told him that if he would leave her alone, she would give him what money was in the house. Edmunds agreed, and took 5/6d, all the money Cecilia had, along with her watch. It was then that he saw the large knife on the kitchen table.

Grasping her hair, Edmunds pulled back

NAME	John (Jack) Edmunds
AGE AT EXECUTION	24
DATE OF EXECUTION	Saturday, 3rd July, 1909
PLACE OF EXECUTION	Usk
HANGMAN	Henry Pierrepoint
ASSISTANT	John Ellis
DATE OF TRIAL	7th June, 1909
LOCATION OF TRIAL	Monmouth
PRESIDING JUDGE	Mister Justice Ridley
PROSECUTION COUNSEL	Mister Cranstoun, A.J. David
DEFENCE COUNSEL	S.R.C. Bosanquet
NUMBER OF VICTIMS	1

VICTIMS DETAILS	
NAME	Cecilia Harris (Died Wednesday, 5th May)
AGE	59
DATE OF MURDER	Saturday, 20th February, 1909
PLACE OF MURDER	Garnwen Farm, Abersychan, near Pontypool
METHOD OF KILLING	Shot/cut throat
RELATIONSHIP TO KILLER	None

Cecilia's head and cut her throat. Not content with the hideous wound he had inflicted, he then proceeded to bang her head repeatedly on the floor, so that the blood would flow faster from her. Then Edmunds picked up the knife again and made to inflict a second wound. Despite her terrible injuries, Cecilia managed to gasp out a plea for her life and asked Edmunds to think of his mother. At last the cold and evil Edmunds released his victim and left her there to die.

Cecilia was a determined woman, and managed to stagger out of the house. A neighbour's child, Kathleen Evans was just turning into the gate to visit, when she saw Cecilia, her face covered in blood. The child ran away in terror.

Losing blood all the way, Cecilia Harris walked three-quarters of a mile before she found help. Finally, reaching the farm of William Rees, Cecilia was assisted inside. It was at Rees's house, in front of his wife, Polly, that Cecilia wrote a poignant note, still preserved in the files at the Records Office in London. The pencilled scrap of paper reads:

"Jack Edmunds shot me and cut my throat he got my money." The writing is very shaky and spots of blood can still be seen on the paper.

John Edmunds apparently felt little or no guilt over what he had done. That same evening he visited Mrs Phelps's greengrocer shop in the High Street, where he purchased oranges. He paid with the 5/- piece which formed part of the cash he had stolen from Cecilia Harris. The following morning he was arrested at his mother's house and claimed to know nothing about the attack.

Edmunds said he had been nowhere near the farm on the day of the attack. Despite his protestations, there were five witnesses who swore they had seen him in the vicinity: William Henry Annetts, Joseph Jones, Albert Trumper, Percy Evans and William Rees, to whose farm Cecilia had managed to stagger. In addition to their evidence, forensic tests showed that hairs and fibres found on Cecilia's clothing matched those found on his and there were fresh semen and blood stains on his clothing.

For some time it seemed as if despite what she had been through, Cecilia Harris would live. It was not until May 5th that she finally died. A postmortem revealed that she had also suffered from heart trouble and bronchitis.

Put on trial for murder and found guilty, Edmunds appealed on the grounds that Cecilia Harris's death had been due to her illnesses and not his attack. It was quite rightly dismissed.

On July 3rd, 1909, exactly 19 weeks after the attack on Cecilia, her brutal killer paid the price for his crime. Few people mourned his passing.

MICHAEL BROWN HAD started working for the firm of G. and J. Johnson, linen manufacturers, as an office boy. However, by the age of 16 he had already moved up the corporate ladder to the extent that one of his duties was now to go to the bank every Friday, to cash the wages cheque.

Friday, February 16th was no different from any other Friday in this respect, and Michael visited the bank at Buckhaven, where he cashed a cheque for £85, receiving £25 in single notes, £20 in half sovereigns and £40 in silver. He then set out by tram for East Wemyss, where he was seen by the conductor, sitting next to a man aged somewhere in his twenties. They alighted from the tram at the same stop and were seen walking down School Wynd. Alice Warrender, who lived in School Wynd saw Michael and the young man walking down towards the factory. At that time she put them at around 40 yards from the public lavatory.

Michael, though, did not return to the factory with the wages. At 12.10pm a schoolboy went into those same public lavatories on School Wynd but immediately rushed out, screaming. Inside he had discovered the battered body of a young man. A passing chimney sweep ran across to see what the problem was. The body lay on the floor of the cubicle, his face covered in blood and a dirty white handkerchief tied around his throat. The boy's cap had been pushed firmly into his mouth, in all probability to stifle his cries.

At 12.50pm William Johnson, one of the partners in G. and J. Johnson, heard that the body of a young man had been found in the lavatory. It was he who positively identified the body as that of Michael Brown. There was no sign of the £85 the boy should have been carrying.

The police immediately suspected that the crime had been carried out by a local man. It was surmised that he had escaped down a side street after leaving the toilet, as he had not been seen on the busy main road. This meant that he must have known his way around the village and so must be local. The tram conductor and Alice Warrender came forward to issue

NAME	Alexander Edmundstone
AGE AT EXECUTION	23
DATE OF EXECUTION	Friday, 16th July, 1909
PLACE OF EXECUTION	Perth
HANGMAN	John Ellis
ASSISTANT	(William Willis)
DATE OF TRIAL	8th June – 9th June, 1909
LOCATION OF TRIAL	Perth
PRESIDING JUDGE	Lord Justice Guthrie
PROSECUTION COUNSEL	A.M. Anderson, James Smith Clark
DEFENCE COUNSEL	Mister Christie, Napier Armit
NUMBER OF VICTIMS	1

VICTIMS DETAILS	
NAME	Michael Swinton Brown
AGE	16
DATE OF MURDER	Friday, 16th February, 1909
PLACE OF MURDER	Public Lavatory in School Wynd, East Wemyss, Fife
METHOD OF KILLING	Battered
RELATIONSHIP TO KILLER	None

descriptions of the man they had seen close to Michael and this fitted a young unemployed miner, Alexander Edmundstone. Furthermore, when Edmundstone's home was visited it was found that he was not at home. His mother said he had left at 10.30am, to find work on the boats.

As inquiries continued it was determined that Edmundstone had purchased a new suit and overcoat that afternoon and had paid with £1 notes, which the bank were able to say had been given out to Michael Brown. Furthermore, he had told the draper's assistant that he intended going to Perth.

After tracing Edmundstone to the St John's Temperance Hotel in Perth, the police found that he had moved on to Glasgow, where bloodstained clothing was found at Mrs Brice's, the landlady of the house he had stayed at. After that, however, the trail went cold.

On March 22nd, Jack Atherton, a hawker, visited the police station in Manchester to obtain a licence to operate in the city. He was told to return the next day but as he turned to leave he spotted a wanted poster. The description of the man, wanted for a murder in East Wemyss, seemed to be very close to that of another lodger at the house he was staying at in Brunswick Street.

The next day, Atherton returned to the police station with his landlady's son, Sam Bridgewood. They both looked carefully at the poster and agreed that it did seem to bear an uncanny resemblance to Albert Edwards, who was staying at the house. Edwards was, after all, a Scot and he did seem to be rather generous with money. The two men took their suspicions to Sam's mother and it was she who called in the police.

Detective Inspector Riding called at the house in Brunswick Street on March 24th. Albert Edwards was interviewed and admitted being Alexander Edmundstone. He also admitted to killing Michael Brown, but claimed he had not known what he was doing at the time.

At his trial, Edmundstone relied on a defence of insanity, saying that he was not responsible for his actions on February 16th. It did nothing to sway the jury.

John Ellis officiated at Edmundstone's execution and should have been assisted by William Willis. On the appointed day, however, Willis fell ill and Ellis carried out the sentence alone.

THE ENCYCLOPAEDIA OF EXECUTIONS

JAMES RICHARDS SPENT a good deal of time working away from home and so saw relatively little of his wife, Hester. On one of the occasions he returned home, in September 1907, he found a man living in his house. Hester introduced this man as Frederick Evans, her cousin, and James accepted him into his home.

In fact, Fred Evans was actually Walter Davies and he was no relation to Hester. Whilst James was away, Walter and Hester would live as man and wife and in due course, they ran off together, living at various addresses in Leeds and Ilkley. By the end of 1908, though, Hester was back with her husband who, somewhat remarkably, still allowed Davies into his home as a lodger, along with another man named Muswell.

On the morning of March 30th, 1909, James Richards left for work at 6.00am. At 8.30am, Muswell also went out, leaving Hester alone with Davies. It was 11.00pm before James returned to find the battered body of his wife upstairs. There was no sign of Davies.

Walter Davies was not arrested until April 17th, in Blyth. He was charged with murder and vehemently denied that he was guilty. According to Davies, he had left the house soon after Muswell and had visited the post office. Later he had bought some whisky before returning to the house at some time before 10.00am. He found Hester's body, knew he would be blamed and decided to make a run for it.

At his trial, it was stated that bloodstains had been found on Davies's clothing. This, along with evidence that he had made threats to Hester as to what would happen to her if she ever returned to her husband, were enough to convict him of murder.

The appeal was heard on June 24th. Davies sought to call as a witness the wife of the policeman who had finally arrested him. He claimed that the blood on his clothing was his own and had been deposited when he had suffered a nose bleed after his arrest. The policeman had denied this had happened and Davies wished to call his wife who had seen the nose bleed occur. Permission was refused and the appeal was dismissed.

NAME Walter Davis (Fred Evans)
AGE AT EXECUTION 37
DATE OF EXECUTION Friday, 9th July, 1909
PLACE OF EXECUTION Wakefield
HANGMAN Henry Pierrepoint
ASSISTANT Thomas Pierrepoint
DATE OF TRIAL 11th June, 1909
LOCATION OF TRIAL York
PRESIDING JUDGE Mister Justice Bucknill
PROSECUTION COUNSEL C.F. Lowenthal, Walter Healey
DEFENCE COUNSEL G.F. Mortimer, Milton Barber
NUMBER OF VICTIMS 1

VICTIMS DETAILS
NAME Hester Harriet Richards
AGE 51
DATE OF MURDER Tuesday, 30th March, 1909
PLACE OF MURDER 19 Farrer Street, Middlesborough
METHOD OF KILLING Battered
RELATIONSHIP TO KILLER Girlfriend

WILLIAM HAMPTON WAS a native of St Erth, but had spent a number of years working as a miner in America. He returned to England in November, 1907 and again settled down in Cornwall.

It was not long before Hampton became friendly with a local girl, Emily Tredrea, who lived with her parents in the end house of a terrace known as Vicarage Row. The only adult in the house was actually Emily's mother, Grace. Her father, like Hampton a miner, was working in South Africa and spent long periods away from home.

The friendship between William Hampton and Emily Tredrea blossomed. They became engaged in early 1908, and shortly afterwards, he moved into the family house as a lodger. All went well until May, 1909.

On Saturday, May 1st, Emily dropped a bombshell by announcing to William that she did not care for him anymore, and in fact she had grown to hate him. The following evening, Mrs Tredrea had to go out, to visit Hampton's grandmother, who had a bad leg. William took the opportunity to talk to Emily about what she had said the day before, but she would only confirm that she wanted nothing more to do with him. Suddenly William rushed at Emily, placed his hands around her throat and throttled the life out of her. Their argument had been overheard by Emily's brother, William, aged nine, who crept part of the way downstairs and actually witnessed Hampton's attack on Emily, and the placing of her lifeless body in a chair.

William Tredrea tried to leave the house and run for his mother. At first, Hampton stopped him but later allowed him out. As William Tredrea ran off in one direction, Hampton was jumping over a fence at the side of the house and heading off over the fields.

Hampton knew that it was useless trying to escape, but his one thought was that if he gave himself up to the authorities in St Erth, local abhorrence of his crime might well lead to a risk of personal injury. He therefore walked across to Hayle, and surrendered himself there. William Tredrea was an excellent witness for the prosecution and Hampton's only hope was a defence of provocation. His counsel pointed out that the

NAME	William Hampton
AGE AT EXECUTION	23
DATE OF EXECUTION	Tuesday, 20th July, 1909
PLACE OF EXECUTION	Bodmin
HANGMAN	Henry Pierrepoint
ASSISTANT	Thomas Pierrepoint
DATE OF TRIAL	24th June, 1909
LOCATION OF TRIAL	Bodmin
PRESIDING JUDGE	Mister Justice Phillimore
PROSECUTION COUNSEL	Raymond Asquith, Stafford Howard
DEFENCE COUNSEL	R.G. Seton
NUMBER OF VICTIMS	1

VICTIMS DETAILS	
NAME	Emily Barnes Trewarthen Tredrea
AGE	16
DATE OF MURDER	Sunday, 2nd May, 1909
PLACE OF MURDER	Vicarage Row, St Erth, Near Penzance
METHOD OF KILLING	Strangled
RELATIONSHIP TO KILLER	Girlfriend

crime had taken place in the kitchen, where there were many knives, but that Hampton had used his bare hands. This indicated that there was no premeditation and that therefore the offence was manslaughter and not murder. The jury were out for just 15 minutes before making it plain that they did not agree.

SOME KILLERS SEEM determined to attract attention to themselves. One such was Mark Shawcross.

Emily Ramsbottom was a married woman. Separated from her husband, she had been living with Shawcross on and off for about four years. They had argued in the past but in May 1909, after yet another argument, she left him and refused to return.

On May 13th, Emily's body was found in a field. She had been manually strangled and a handkerchief tied around her throat and fastened with a reef knot. Shawcross, with whom she was known to keep company, had vanished.

The police soon turned up witnesses who said that they had seen Shawcross walking with Emily on the night before her body was found. Newspaper reports were published and it was soon well known that Mark Shawcross was the man the police wished to interview.

On May 15th, the police received an unsigned letter. It was a confession to the murder of Emily Ramsbottom. The writer stated, "I killed her with my bare hands and as quickly as possible. She was almost dead when I tied the handkerchief round her neck." The writing was that of Mark Shawcross.

Another letter was sent by Shawcross to Thomas Horsfield, the foreman of a works where he had once been employed. This one was signed and accused the man of being a slave driver. It went on: "There will be very little of you this time next week. I might as well die for two as well as one, so you can expect a visit." Again, it was tantamount to a confession to the murder of Emily.

On May 20th, Mark Shawcross returned to his lodgings and was immediately arrested and charged with murder. He denied the charge, saying that he had left Emily, alive and well, at 11.00pm on May 12th, and had then walked to Todmorden where he intended looking for work. He admitted writing the letters but said that he had constructed the one to the police from newspaper reports. He had had nothing to do with Emily's death.

Found guilty and sentenced to death, Shawcross appealed against the verdict. The defence claimed that the confessions were

NAME	Mark Shawcross
AGE AT EXECUTION	30
DATE OF EXECUTION	Tuesday, 3rd August, 1909
PLACE OF EXECUTION	Manchester
HANGMAN	Henry Pierrepoint
ASSISTANT	Thomas Pierrepoint
DATE OF TRIAL	6th July, 1909
LOCATION OF TRIAL	Manchester
PRESIDING JUDGE	Mister Justice Hamilton
PROSECUTION COUNSEL	John Mansfield, Phillip Walton
DEFENCE COUNSEL	Mister Bigham
NUMBER OF VICTIMS	1

VICTIMS DETAILS	
NAME	Emily Ramsbottom
AGE	27
DATE OF MURDER	Wednesday, 12th May, 1909
PLACE OF MURDER	Footpath near Pink Bank Lane, Gorton, Manchester
METHOD OF KILLING	Strangled
RELATIONSHIP TO KILLER	Girlfriend

long and rambling and obviously the work of an unsound mind. The appeal was dismissed, however, because there was other evidence, such as the sighting of the couple close to the spot where he body was subsequently found.

Shawcross said that he had only written his 'confession' to the police because he was worn out and sick of life. He wanted to put the blame on himself and to die. He succeeded in both his aims.

1909

IT WAS QUITE a good night in fish merchant Benjamin Vandersluis's shop, on Waterloo Road, London. He was busy serving customers when at about 11.25pm, a Norwegian sailor, Julius Wammer came in with three women, one of whom he recognised as Cissie Archer.

Cissie went over to a display of crabs and began looking through them, selecting which ones she might like when, without warning, Wammer drew out a revolver and shot her. Screaming, Cissie ran out of the shop, across Waterloo Road and collapsed and died at the corner of Stamford Street. Wammer, meanwhile aimed his gun at another of the women who had come into the shop with him. He fired, missed her and struck Benjamin Vandersluis in the hand. Aiming at the woman one final time, Wammer again pulled the trigger, but the gun jammed. It was at this moment that John Lush and a friend named Leverton jumped onto Wammer and beat him to the floor.

Wammer told the police that he had not wished to hurt Benjamin Vandersluis. It had only been his intention to kill the two women. On the previous Friday, July 2nd, Wammer had been out with Cissie and the other woman and when he got back to the Trafalgar Hotel in York Road, where he was staying, he noticed that he was missing a gold chain. He believed that the two women had stolen the chain from him, but rather than taking the somewhat obvious approach of asking them about it, he had determined to kill them both.

Wammer's defence was that since he had returned to England from his last voyage he had been drinking constantly and this had affected his mind to such an extent that he was incapable of forming the intention to kill. However, he had brooded on the matter of the missing chain since July 2nd and had obviously formed some sort of plan to get revenge. He was found guilty and sentenced to hang.

NAME	Julius Wammer
AGE AT EXECUTION	43
DATE OF EXECUTION	Tuesday, 10th August, 1909
PLACE OF EXECUTION	Wandsworth
HANGMAN	Henry Pierrepoint
ASSISTANT	William Willis
DATE OF TRIAL	21st July, 1909
LOCATION OF TRIAL	Old Bailey
PRESIDING JUDGE	Lord Chief Justice, Lord Alverstone
PROSECUTION COUNSEL	Richard D. Muir, Mister Graham-Campbell
DEFENCE COUNSEL	Mister Fordham
NUMBER OF VICTIMS	1

VICTIMS DETAILS	
NAME	Cissie Archer
AGE	24
DATE OF MURDER	Wednesday, 7th July, 1909
PLACE OF MURDER	Waterloo Road, London
METHOD OF KILLING	Shot
RELATIONSHIP TO KILLER	None

THE CONCERT AT the Imperial Institute had been enjoyed by all the distinguished guests and now, as the audience moved to leave, Sir William Hutt Curzon-Wylie, the Aide-de-Camp to the Secretary of State for India, stood at the entrance, talking to a young, slightly built Indian. Suddenly the young man raised his hand and fired five shots at Sir William's head. Four of those shots hit their target and Sir William was dead before he hit the floor.

The man nearest to the shooting, Doctor Lalcaca, moved forward to apprehend the killer. The Indian now turned the gun on Lalcaca and fired two bullets into him; the doctor would die later from his wounds. Meanwhile, the killer turned the gun to his own head and pulled the trigger. There was a hollow click, but the gun failed to fire and the man was overpowered and taken into custody.

The assassin identified himself as Madar Lal Dhingra, who had been in England since November 1906, studying engineering at University College, London, and living in lodgings at Ledbury Road, Bayswater. He believed that his country, India, should be freed from the yoke of British rule and had chosen to carry out a political assassination.

There could be no doubt that the crime had been planned. In January 1909, Madar had obtained a licence for a revolver. Then he had purchased an eight-shot Colt automatic and later obtained a Belgian six-shot revolver.

In March, Madar wrote to Miss Beck, the secretary of the National Indian Association. He knew that Sir William was the Honorary Treasurer so it was clear that he had already determined who his target was to be. In June Madar received an invitation from Miss Beck to attend a concert to be given on July 1st. He knew that Sir William would be there.

On July 1st, Madar left his lodgings at 8.45pm, arriving at the Institute at 9.00pm. Sir William and his wife arrived at about 10.30pm and Madar made his move just half an hour later.

At his trial, Madar refused to be represented, saying that he did not recognise the court. As far as Sir William was concerned, he had committed no crime. He

NAME	Madar Lal Dhingra
AGE AT EXECUTION	25
DATE OF EXECUTION	Tuesday, 17th August, 1909
PLACE OF EXECUTION	Pentonville
HANGMAN	Henry Pierrepoint
ASSISTANT	Thomas Pierrepoint
DATE OF TRIAL	23rd July, 1909
LOCATION OF TRIAL	Old Bailey
PRESIDING JUDGE	Lord Chief Justice, Lord Alverstone
PROSECUTION COUNSEL	Mister Bodkin
DEFENCE COUNSEL	None
NUMBER OF VICTIMS	2

VICTIMS DETAILS	
NAMES	Sir William Hutt Curzon-Wylie; Doctor Cawas Lalcaca
AGES	61; 48
DATE OF MURDER	Thursday, 1st July, 1909
PLACE OF MURDER	Imperial Institute, South Kensington, London
METHOD OF KILLING	Shot; shot
RELATIONSHIP TO KILLER	None; none

had merely assassinated an enemy. The additional death of Doctor Lalcaca had been an accident.

Madar asked that a statement be read out. Among other things it referred to England as being responsible for the deaths of millions of his countrymen. As far as Madar was concerned, the English were an occupying force .

The jury did not even bother to leave the box before giving their guilty verdict. When asked if he had anything to say before the sentence was passed, Madar reiterated that he did not recognise the court. Sentenced to death, he thanked the judge and said he was proud to lay down his life for his country.

IN 1900, RICHARD Justin's wife died, leaving him with two young sons. Some years later he met Margaret Ellen Thompson, who had a small daughter of her own. The couple began walking out together and in 1908 they married and moved into new lodgings at 84 Lepper Street. There was, however, one problem. Margaret's daughter Annie, now Justin's step-daughter, was illegitimate and Justin couldn't stand that. He hated the child and began to beat her systematically.

Richard Justin worked as a labourer for the Belfast Corporation in Alexandra Park whilst Margaret toiled each day in the Whitehouse Mill. Each day Annie would be placed in the care of Margaret's ex-landlady, Bridget McWilliams, who lived in nearby Hardinge Street. It was the only respite little Annie ever knew.

Annie Loughlins was a neighbour of Justin's and, at 9.00am on March 12th, Justin came to her and said that Annie had fallen out of bed. Annie went to number 84 to see what she could do but by the time the doctor arrived it was too late. Little Annie was already dead and, from the marks upon her body, the police came to believe that someone had given her a severe beating.

The inquest on the dead child opened on March 15th and a number of witnesses came forward to show that it had been Richard Justin who had beaten his step-daughter. For example, Margaret Craig, who had once lodged in the same house, came forward to say that she had seen Justin drag the child into the yard and begin punching her. Bridget McWilliams testified that she had seen new bruises on the child's body each day and when she asked Annie who had done this, the girl replied "Da."

Annie Thomson was Margaret's sister and she had stayed with the family over the previous Christmas and New Year. She reported that every night she had seen Justin strip the little girl naked and then beat her with a bamboo cane so that she wouldn't go too near the fire. All of these women now reported the abuse Annie had endured, but none had done anything about it at the time.

As a result of this testimony, Justin was

NAME	Richard Justin
AGE AT EXECUTION	31
DATE OF EXECUTION	Thursday, 19th August, 1909
PLACE OF EXECUTION	Belfast
HANGMAN	Henry Pierrepoint
ASSISTANT	Not known
DATE OF TRIAL	22nd July, 1909
LOCATION OF TRIAL	Belfast
PRESIDING JUDGE	Mister Justice Wright
PROSECUTION COUNSEL	R.R. Cherry M.P., George Hill Smith
DEFENCE COUNSEL	Thomas Campbell
NUMBER OF VICTIMS	1

VICTIMS DETAILS	
NAME	Annie Thompson
AGE	4
DATE OF MURDER	Friday, 12th March, 1909
PLACE OF MURDER	84 Lepper Street, Belfast
METHOD OF KILLING	Battered
RELATIONSHIP TO KILLER	Step-daughter

arrested and charged with murder. At his trial, the judge explained that if the child had died from systematic beatings then this was a case of murder. However, he did not rule out manslaughter and left the matter entirely up to the jury.

It took the jury 45 minutes to decide that Justin was guilty of murder. They may well have been swayed in part by a report that upon searching Annie's room the police had found not only the bamboo cane that Annie Thomson referred to, but also an iron bar and a piece of wood, which had also been used to torture the little girl.

JOHN FREEMAN LODGED with his brother, Robert James Freeman, and Robert's wife, Florence and all three got on very well, except when one or more of them was drunk. On August 28th, 1909, all three were the worse for drink and the events of that night were to cost the lives of two people.

John and Robert had been drinking in the Myton Tavern and were both rather inebriated by the time they left. On the way home, the two brothers argued, Robert having accused John of having an affair with Florence. The argument continued as the two men arrived home, to find Florence also drunk.

Robert was never sure what happened next. All he knew was that suddenly he had a wound above his eye, which needed hospital treatment, and his wife was lying dead, having been stabbed in the throat.

Other people had a clearer idea of what had occurred. William Gibson and Patrick Geraghty were passing the house when they heard screams. Looking in through the window, they saw John holding Florence against his body, with her back against his chest. To their horror, Gibson and Geraghty saw that he was just drawing a knife out of her neck. Florence ran out, into Gerachty's arms, whilst Gibson ran for the police.

A neighbour, Mary Elizabeth Clark, said that she had heard Robert Freeman shout at his wife: "You have been with him again." Florence called him a liar and then the two men began to fight. Very soon afterwards, Mary heard Florence scream and saw her run out into the street.

Meanwhile, the two Freeman brothers were oblivious to what had happened and had started fighting again. As Police Sergeant Boyes arrived, Robert Freeman was holding his brother down and John was taken into custody.

At John Freeman's trial, the judge showed the extent of the gap that existed between the various strata of society at the time, by describing the area of the murder as a slum populated by lower working-class men whose main nourishment was alcohol. Not surprisingly, Freeman was found guilty and condemned to death.

Before the sentence was carried out,

NAME	John Freeman
AGE AT EXECUTION	46
DATE OF EXECUTION	Tuesday, 7th December, 1909
PLACE OF EXECUTION	Hull
HANGMAN	Henry Pierrepoint
ASSISTANT	John Ellis
DATE OF TRIAL	19th November, 1909
LOCATION OF TRIAL	York
PRESIDING JUDGE	Mister Justice Bucknill
PROSECUTION COUNSEL	C.F. Lowenthal, Mister Headley
DEFENCE COUNSEL	Mister Hoare
NUMBER OF VICTIMS	1

VICTIMS DETAILS	
NAME	Florence Lily Freeman
AGE	30
DATE OF MURDER	Saturday, 28th August, 1909
PLACE OF MURDER	4 Kingston Place, Porter Street, Hull
METHOD OF KILLING	Stabbed
RELATIONSHIP TO KILLER	Sister-in-law

Robert said he had forgiven his brother. That was something John had wanted to hear and he announced that he could now die a happy man.

ABEL ATHERTON LODGED with the Patrick family at Chopwell, near Gateshead. Things were fine until Atherton began to take more than a passing interest in the Patrick's 15-year-old daughter, Frances. He was then asked to leave. As he left the house, Abel was heard to threaten his ex-hosts.

On August 11th, 1909, Atherton returned to the Patrick's house and accused Mr Patrick of sexually abusing his own daughter. This was why they had wanted him out of the house, he argued, not because of any improper conduct between him and the girl. This was all nonsense, of course, and when Atherton saw that his words alone were having no real effect, he left the house, returned later with a shotgun and brandished it towards Mrs Patrick and her daughter.

Elizabeth ran forward and began to grapple with Atherton. A shot rang out, but fortunately it hurt no one. Almost immediately a second shot was fired and this hit Mrs Elizabeth Patrick in her side. She was killed instantly.

The sight of what he had done deeply affected Atherton, who gave himself up after he had failed to cut his own throat. His only regret seemed to be that he had not finished himself off afterwards. He maintained that the shooting was an accident and that he had not intended to hurt anyone, but was still charged with wilful murder.

Throughout the trial, Atherton maintained that he was not guilty of murder. He had not intended to hurt anyone, insisted that he had never pointed the gun directly at Elizabeth Patrick or anyone else and that he had not pulled the trigger. The gun had gone off accidentally as they struggled and as there was no intent to kill, he was guilty only of manslaughter.

The jury did not agree and Atherton was sentenced to death.

Right up to the moment of his execution, Atherton maintained that he was not guilty of murder. Standing on the drop, waiting for Henry Pierrepoint to pull the lever, Atherton said in a loud, firm voice, "Yer hangin' an innocent man." They were the last words that he was ever to utter.

NAME	Abel Atherton
AGE AT EXECUTION	29
DATE OF EXECUTION	Wednesday, 8th December, 1909
PLACE OF EXECUTION	Durham
HANGMAN	Henry Pierrepoint
ASSISTANT	William Willis
DATE OF TRIAL	10th November – 11th November, 1909
LOCATION OF TRIAL	Durham
PRESIDING JUDGE	Mister Justice Walton
PROSECUTION COUNSEL	C.F. Lowenthal, A.J. Lawrie
DEFENCE COUNSEL	Morgan Griffiths-Jones
NUMBER OF VICTIMS	1

VICTIMS DETAILS	
NAME	Elizabeth Ann Patrick
AGE	33
DATE OF MURDER	Wednesday, 11th August, 1909
PLACE OF MURDER	20 Thames Street, Chopwell, Near Gateshead
METHOD OF KILLING	Shot
RELATIONSHIP TO KILLER	None

SAMUEL ATHERLEY AND Matilda
Lambert had lived together on and off for
seven years and though they were not
married, she had borne him three children:
John, Annie and Samuel. During those seven
years, she had left him four times and on each
occasion had gone to live with her married
sister. At the beginning of May 1909, Samuel
and Matilda were back together and had
moved to Robinson's Yard, in Arnold.

The problem was that Samuel was an
insanely jealous man. He believed that John
Watson, the husband of Matilda's sister,
Sarah, was the father of Annie, the middle
child, and this caused a good deal of friction
between them.

On July 8th, there was a violent quarrel
between Samuel and Matilda. Another quarrel
took place on July 9th, and Matilda was heard
to say that Samuel would have to leave and
find somewhere else to live. A third argument
was heard soon afterwards, by Atherley's
long-suffering neighbours.

Early on the morning of July 10th, Thomas
Marriott, one of those neighbours, was
walking past Atherley's house when he saw
Samuel at a broken window, beckoning to
him. Marriott went to investigate and saw that
Atherley was trying to staunch a wound in his
throat, and gesturing upstairs. Marriott there
found the bodies of Matilda and the three
children. All had their throats cut and the two
youngest children had also been battered with
a hammer.

On the way to the hospital, Atherley told
constables Lowe and Lomas that he had killed
his family at 3.00am. This confession was
enough to convict Atherley of murder and he
was sentenced to hang after the jury had
deliberated for just 10 minutes.

The night before his execution, Atherley
wrote to his brother Henry, saying that he was
innocent of murder as he had not known what
he was doing at the time he committed the
crime. The next morning, he was hanged by
Henry Pierrepoint.

NAME	Samuel Atherley
AGE AT EXECUTION	30
DATE OF EXECUTION	Tuesday, 14th December, 1909
PLACE OF EXECUTION	Nottingham
HANGMAN	Henry Pierrepoint
ASSISTANT	Thomas Pierrepoint
DATE OF TRIAL	12th November, 1909
LOCATION OF TRIAL	Nottingham
PRESIDING JUDGE	Mister Justice Pickford
PROSECUTION COUNSEL	Ryland Adkins, Mister Blaiklock
DEFENCE COUNSEL	Mister Hadfield
NUMBER OF VICTIMS	4

VICTIMS' DETAILS	
NAMES	Matilda Lambert; John Lambert
AGES	27; 8
DATE OF MURDER	Saturday, 10th July, 1909
PLACE OF MURDER	Robinson's Yard, Arnold, Near Nottingham
METHOD OF KILLING	Cut throat; cut throat
RELATIONSHIP TO KILLER	Girlfriend; son
NAMES	Annie Lambert; Samuel Lambert
AGES	5; 2
DATE OF MURDER	Saturday, 10th July, 1909
PLACE OF MURDER	Robinson's Yard, Arnold, Near Nottingham
METHOD OF KILLING	Cut throat/battered; cut throat/battered
RELATIONSHIP TO KILLER	Daughter; son

GWEN ELLEN JONES had been married to Morris Jones, but they had separated and she had taken the two children with her. In due course she moved in with William Murphy, whom she stayed with for more than five years.

Work was scarce in Wales at this time and eventually Murphy decided to go to Yorkshire to seek employment. It was whilst he was away that Gwen began living with Robert Jones, at 51 Baker Street, Holyhead.

Murphy returned to Holyhead a few weeks before Christmas and on Wednesday, December 8th, he called at Gwen's father's house, looking for Gwen. John Parry, Gwen's father, explained that he had not seen his daughter but Murphy had his suspicions and voiced these by saying that if he saw her with another man, he would kill her.

Murphy soon discovered where Gwen was and he determined to carry out his threat just as soon as possible. He visited Robert Jones's house a couple of times and was once even invited in and given breakfast, but none of this changed Murphy's mind about what he had to do.

William Murphy arranged to meet Gwen at 7.00pm on Christmas night but she failed to appear. Murphy then went for a drink and it was near the pub that he saw Gwen in the company of Elizabeth Jones. Gwen explained that she had turned up at the agreed meeting point but Murphy hadn't been there. Still, she was here now and, at around 8.30pm, the two walked off together, across the fields near the town.

Gwen had been drinking and staggered a little as she walked, falling against Murphy a number of times. As they strolled, she told him that she was leaving Holyhead for Bethesda but offered to have sex with him one last time before she went. What happened next is told in detail in Murphy's subsequent statement to the police. It makes horrific reading.

After having sex, Murphy started to make love to Gwen for a second time. She had a type of ruff around her neck and he gently placed his fingers underneath this, asking her why she did not remove it. Gwen replied that it was hooked on and rather difficult to take

NAME	William Murphy
AGE AT EXECUTION	49
DATE OF EXECUTION	Tuesday, 15th February, 1910
PLACE OF EXECUTION	Caernarfon
HANGMAN	Henry Pierrepoint
ASSISTANT	William Willis
DATE OF TRIAL	26th January, 1910
LOCATION OF TRIAL	Beaumaris
PRESIDING JUDGE	Mister Justice Pickford
PROSECUTION COUNSEL	J. Ellis Griffiths M.P., Trevor F. Lloyd
DEFENCE COUNSEL	Austin Jones
NUMBER OF VICTIMS	1

VICTIMS DETAILS	
NAME	Gwen Ellen Jones
AGE	36
DATE OF MURDER	Saturday, 25th December, 1909
PLACE OF MURDER	Field near Waltham Avenue, Holyhead
METHOD OF KILLING	Strangled/cut throat
RELATIONSHIP TO KILLER	Girlfriend

off. It was at that moment that Murphy began his attack.

Tightening his grip, Murphy began strangling Gwen. She struggled quite a bit but eventually his strength proved too much for her and she collapsed onto the ground. Releasing his grip, Murphy now took a knife from his pocket and cut Gwen's throat, forcing his fingers into the wound and pulling it open. Finally, after pulling her head backwards to open the wound even more, he pushed the body into a drainage ditch where he held it face down under the water until he was absolutely sure that she was dead. Murphy them walked back to the pub and ordered another pint. It was now 9.25pm.

It was in the pub that Murphy saw an old friend, John Jones, and confessed to him that he had just murdered Gwen. When Jones refused to believe him, Murphy took him to the murder site and showed him the body. Jones ran off to find a policeman and ran into Police Sergeant Henry Roberts near the Market Place. As Jones was blurting out his story, Murphy walked up and calmly

185

announced: "Are you looking for me? Well, here I am."

Having made a full confession to the crime, Murphy's only defence could be one of insanity, but even the terrible details of what he had done could not persuade the jury that he had not known exactly what he was doing. As a result, in February 1910, William Murphy became the only man to be executed at Caernarfon in the last century.

ALTHOUGH HE WAS only three years old, John Collins liked nothing better than to walk to the end of his street each day, and meet his mother as she came home from working at the local cotton mill. On December 28th, 1909, when Mrs Collins reached her street, she was surprised to find that John wasn't there. Carrying on home she found that John had set out as usual. A quick search was arranged but when no sign of the boy could be found, the police were called.

In no time at all, the police had discovered what had happened to John. This was not due to superb detection methods, but rather to the fact that a young man named Joseph Wren had walked up to a police sergeant in Victoria Street, and confessed to murder.

Joseph Wren's story was indeed true. When two constables went along to the spot he had indicated, they found the body of the infant. An attempt had been made to strangle him and when this had failed, his throat had been cut with a blunt knife that lay nearby.

There was little local sympathy for what was a cold-blooded murder but when Joseph Wren's story is examined, it will be seen that he too had known the cruelties of life. Discharged from the Royal Navy in 1907, due to defective eyesight, Wren had been unable to find regular work since. He had a girlfriend, named Calvert, and she had given birth to Wren's daughter, but he could not afford to marry her and the desperate straits he found himself in came to a head on December 28th.

On that day, at approximately 5.00pm, Wren met his brother in Yorkshire Street. Wren said that he had not eaten for three days and added that he wanted to return to prison, for five or six years, even if it meant committing murder. They parted at 5.30pm and Wren then went on to pick up John Collins and take him to the slag heap ,where he murdered him.

At the trial, Wren denied telling his brother that he intended to commit murder and tried to put forward a defence of insanity. The jury were not moved and took less than an hour to return their guilty verdict.

An attempt was made to launch a petition for the reprieve of Wren, especially as he was held to be a victim of unemployment and

NAME	Joseph Wren
AGE AT EXECUTION	23
DATE OF EXECUTION	Tuesday, 22nd February, 1910
PLACE OF EXECUTION	Manchester
HANGMAN	Henry Pierrepoint
ASSISTANT	John Ellis
DATE OF TRIAL	4th February, 1910
LOCATION OF TRIAL	Manchester
PRESIDING JUDGE	Mister Commissioner Avory
PROSECUTION COUNSEL	Gordon Hewart
DEFENCE COUNSEL	Mister Sandbach
NUMBER OF VICTIMS	1

VICTIMS DETAILS	
NAME	John Collins
AGE	3
DATE OF MURDER	Tuesday, 28th December, 1909
PLACE OF MURDER	Slag heap, near Queen's Park pit, Burnley
METHOD OF KILLING	Strangled/cut throat
RELATIONSHIP TO KILLER	None

poverty, but it attracted less than 2,000 signatures. The final sadness was the realisation that John Collins had simply been in the wrong place, at the wrong time. From his prison cell, Wren wrote that he had intended to kill his own daughter but as she was not available, he took the first child he found.

1910

WHEN GEORGE HENRY Perry left the army in 1908, he found it very difficult to find a job. His girlfriend's parents, the Covells, were kind enough to allow him to live with them, until he got on his feet.

The problems started when Mr Covell began to realise that Perry wasn't exactly being conscientious in his search for work. In the two years to 1910, Perry, a window cleaner by trade, worked just nine weeks. Soon even the long-suffering Mr Covell had had enough and on January 9th, 1910, Perry was told that he would have to find somewhere else to live.

On the morning of Monday, January 10th, Perry left the Covells' house as he had been instructed. Later that same day though, he returned and asked to see Annie Covell, his girlfriend. Mrs Covell saw nothing wrong with this and let Perry back into the house.

Perry had not been with Alice very long when Mrs Covell heard a terrible scream. Rushing to investigate, Mrs Covell found Alice lying on the floor with Perry kneeling on top of her. He appeared to be hitting Alice in the side and then suddenly, to her horror, Mrs Covell realised that Perry held a large bread knife in his hand. She rushed out to find a policeman. Whilst she was gone, Perry finished the job off by cutting Alice's throat.

As the policeman arrived, Perry was just leaving the house. Far from resisting arrest in any way, Perry simply told the policeman what he had done and went along quietly to the police station.

Perry first appeared in court on February 9th and in answer to the charge, pleaded guilty. The judge, Mister Justice Coleridge, suggested that Perry talk to his counsel before submitting such a plea and put the case back a couple of days. When the case resumed on February 11th, Perry pleaded not guilty but once the evidence had been heard, the jury took just a few minutes to return the verdict Perry himself had requested two days before.

On March 1st, George Henry Perry became the first of three men to die at Pentonville in 1910.

NAME	George Henry Perry
AGE AT EXECUTION	27
DATE OF EXECUTION	Tuesday, 1st March, 1910
PLACE OF EXECUTION	Pentonville
HANGMAN	Henry Pierrepoint
ASSISTANT	William Willis
DATE OF TRIAL	11th February, 1910
LOCATION OF TRIAL	Old Bailey
PRESIDING JUDGE	Mister Justice Coleridge
PROSECUTION COUNSEL	Richard D. Muir, H.D. Roome
DEFENCE COUNSEL	Curtis Bennett
NUMBER OF VICTIMS	1

VICTIMS DETAILS	
NAME	Annie Covell
AGE	27
DATE OF MURDER	Monday, 10th January, 1910
PLACE OF MURDER	Ealing, London
METHOD OF KILLING	Stabbed/cut throat
RELATIONSHIP TO KILLER	Girlfriend

THE THOMAS FAMILY were known to have a good sum of money hidden away in their cottage. It was common knowledge, and it cost them their lives.

On the morning of Friday, November 12th, the bodies of Charles Thomas and his wife were discovered by a neighbour. A hammer had been used to batter them beyond recognition, but there was no shortage of clues by which the killer could be traced.

The thief had gained entry through a window that he had broken, protecting himself by the use of a child's garment. This was traced to Mrs West, who lived in another cottage close by. Furthermore, the front door key to the murder cottage, was found on the window sill of Mrs West's house. The police did not think for one moment that Mrs West had committed this crime. However, the killer might be someone who not only knew about the Thomas's money, but also had a grudge against Mrs West.

When questioned, the only name Mrs West could suggest was William Butler. He had once lodged at her house but they had parted on bad terms when he had shown too much affection for her 15-year-old daughter, Florence. The parting was so acrimonious that a summons had to be issued against Butler, who had threatened that he would ruin Mrs West.

The police, meanwhile, had completed their search at Tank cottage and now knew that the man who had broken into the house had not found what he was looking for. A cash box containing over £150 was discovered and, as far as could be ascertained, the murderer had only escaped with about £3, which included five florins, paid to Mister Thomas by an agent from a benefit society.

When Butler, whose real name was Thomas Clements, was interviewed, it was determined that on the day before the murder, he had had no money, but on the day afterwards, he had spent about £3, of which 10/- was in florins. He explained that he had obtained this money from Mrs Solomon Andrews. The lady denied all knowledge. Butler was arrested and charged.

The lies continued. Butler said that he had gone to bed at 6.40pm on November 11th and

NAME	Thomas Clements (William Butler)
AGE AT EXECUTION	62
DATE OF EXECUTION	Thursday, 24th March, 1910
PLACE OF EXECUTION	Usk
HANGMAN	Henry Pierrepoint
ASSISTANT	John Ellis
DATE OF TRIAL	23rd February – 24th February, 1910
LOCATION OF TRIAL	Monmouth
PRESIDING JUDGE	Mister Justice Grantham
PROSECUTION COUNSEL	Mister Cranstoun, St John G. Micklethwait
DEFENCE COUNSEL	Mister Sherwood
NUMBER OF VICTIMS	2

VICTIMS DETAILS	
NAMES	Charles Thomas; Mary Thomas
AGES	82; 72
DATE OF MURDER	Thursday, 11th November, 1909
PLACE OF MURDER	Tank Cottage, Bassaleg, near Newport
METHOD OF KILLING	Battered; battered
RELATIONSHIP TO KILLER	None; none

remained there until 6.40am the following morning. This was easily disproved when a friend of his, William Williams, came forward and said that Butler was at his house between 9.00pm and 9.30pm. Finally, forensic tests showed that there were spots of blood on Butler's trousers and jacket, in areas that would be likely to be affected during the course of battering the Thomases in their bed.

Thomas Clements, alias William Butler, had tried to steal a hidden cache of money, put the blame on someone he had a grudge against, and get away with murder. He failed on all three fronts.

MISTER MILLS HAD enjoyed his first day in his new job. Now it was time to lock up and John Healey, the carpenter and stage hand, was showing him around.

As they went down into the pit, Mills hung back. For that reason he did not see the figure, hiding under one of the seats, leap out and plunge a knife into Healey.

Charles Gray, the hall keeper, heard Healey call out for him: "Help me, Charlie, he's stabbed me." Gray went to fetch a glass of water and on the way, saw a face he recognised, near the stage door. It was Thomas William Jesshope, a fireman who had recently been sacked. "Have you done anything to Jack?" enquired Gray. "Yes," replied Jesshope, pulling a knife from his pocket, "and this is the knife I've done it with."

Thomas Jesshope had been employed for a year at the Empire, but had often turned up the worse for drink. On Friday March 25th, 1910, Jesshope was on duty at 7.00pm. At 9.00pm he was seen by William Nutt, the stage manager, and warned because he appeared to be tipsy. By 10.20pm, Jesshope was totally drunk and incapable. Nutt reported the matter to Percy Ford, the manager.

The following day, at 8.00pm, Ford saw Jesshope who was again drunk. This time Jesshope was sacked. For some reason, he chose to blame his dismissal not on Nutt or Ford , but on John Healey. Jesshope began to actively plot revenge.

Jesshope was not seen again until 11.00am the following morning. He was waiting outside the stage door when Charles Gray turned up for work. Jesshope asked him where Healey was and was told that he was inside, cleaning the stage, Jesshope said that he would wait for him one evening instead.

After killing Healey, Jesshope made no attempt to escape. He wandered outside and was seen by a friend of his, named Ware. Ware knew of Jesshope's dismissal and asked him if he had managed to find another position. Jesshope calmly replied "No, I shan't do any more work. I have just given Jack six inches of steel."

Police Sergeant Curtis was the officer responsible for cautioning Jesshope, who, looking down at the body, said "You have

NAME	Thomas William Jesshope
AGE AT EXECUTION	32
DATE OF EXECUTION	Wednesday, 25th May, 1910
PLACE OF EXECUTION	Wandsworth
HANGMAN	Henry Pierrepoint
ASSISTANT	William Willis
DATE OF TRIAL	29th April, 1910
LOCATION OF TRIAL	Old Bailey
PRESIDING JUDGE	Mister Justice Lawrence
PROSECUTION COUNSEL	Mister Bodkin, Travers Humphreys, Roland Oliver
DEFENCE COUNSEL	Temple Martin
NUMBER OF VICTIMS	1

VICTIMS DETAILS	
NAME	John Healey
AGE	43
DATE OF MURDER	Monday, 28th March, 1910
PLACE OF MURDER	Empire Music Hall, Coldharbour Lane, Camberwell, London
METHOD OF KILLING	Stabbed
RELATIONSHIP TO KILLER	None

got what you asked for. You got me the sack last week."

The only defence could be one of insanity. Evidence was given that there was a history of epilepsy in the family and that nine or ten years previously, Jesshope had suffered from a fit and needed to be placed in a padded room.

At the subsequent appeal, further evidence was given as to Jesshope's mental state, but the judge rejected this, stating that it was for the Home Secretary to deal with any question of insanity now that sentence had been passed. The Home Secretary chose not to interfere.

JAMES HENRY HANCOCK, a native of Sheffield, moved from that city, to Cambridge, in 1894. Not long afterwards he met Eliza Marshall of Water Street, Chesterton and in 1896, he moved in with her.

There were many quarrels between the two, and some of these grew so violent that Eliza was forced to seek protection from her brother, Alfred Doggett. There was an obviously strained relationship between Hancock and Doggett and the fact that both were hawkers of coke and business rivals as well, only served to exacerbate the situation.

On Friday March 4th, 1910, Hancock was meant to travel to Cottenham, to sell coke. There was yet another argument between Hancock and Eliza and in a fit of pique, Hancock went across to the stable and unharnessed the horse. Eliza went to fetch her brother who re-harnessed the horse and then proceeded to drive into Cottenham, with Eliza, and service the customers that Hancock should have had.

When Doggett and Eliza returned at 5.00pm, Hancock was sitting in the front room of Eliza's house. What happened next differs according to whether one believes Hancock or Eliza.

According to Eliza, Hancock asked her if she would have a cup of tea. She refused and added that Hancock should be ashamed of himself for the way he had behaved. He then pushed past her and went to the stable. When Eliza followed a few moments later, she saw Hancock attack Doggett and stab him.

Hancock's story was that when Eliza came back into the house, he asked her if Doggett was in the stable. When she answered 'yes' he took a knife out of the drawer to use it to clean some wurzels for the horse. When he entered the stable, Doggett swore at him and then attacked him and when they fell in the ensuing struggle, Hancock argued, Doggett must have landed on the knife.

After the event, Hancock spoke freely. To one witness he said he was sorry that he had killed Doggett, adding that he had meant to kill Eliza. To another he said he had killed the wrong one. In the police station he said, "I don't care. I shall get three weeks before I get my neck stretched. He went out with my

NAME	James Henry Hancock
AGE AT EXECUTION	55
DATE OF EXECUTION	Tuesday, 14th June, 1910
PLACE OF EXECUTION	Cambridge
HANGMAN	Henry Pierrepoint
ASSISTANT	Not known
DATE OF TRIAL	28th May, 1910
LOCATION OF TRIAL	Cambridge
PRESIDING JUDGE	Mister Justice Phillimore
PROSECUTION COUNSEL	Theobald Mathew, W.R. Briggs, D.H. Prynne
DEFENCE COUNSEL	Grafton D. Pryor, G.A. Wootten
NUMBER OF VICTIMS	1

VICTIMS DETAILS	
NAME	Alfred Doggett
AGE	59
DATE OF MURDER	Friday, 4th March, 1910
PLACE OF MURDER	Water Street, Chesterton
METHOD OF KILLING	Stabbed
RELATIONSHIP TO KILLER	None

horse and van, and I won't allow anyone to go out with that." Finally, at 2.00am the following morning, Hancock observed "When they got back old Liza started swearing and he started shouting. I soon stopped him and I should soon have stopped her if she hadn't just at the time got out of the way."

The final nail came at the trial. Hancock was left-handed. Medical evidence was given that if he had held the knife in his left hand, and in a struggle had fallen underneath Doggett, it would have been impossible to inflict the wound found on the dead man.

THE ROOTS FOR the murder of Thomas Henderson lay in the year 1903. It was then that Thomas Craig became acquainted with Annie Finn. They fell in love but almost immediately Craig was sentenced to seven years in prison. Annie promised to wait for him, and to write.

For some years, Annie remained true to her promise, but then, in September 1909, she met Thomas Henderson and fell in love again. The letters to Craig grew less frequent and then stopped.

On July 4th, 1909, Craig wrote a long letter to Annie, which contained the following lines: "You have only to die once. I am not afraid to die and face death…. Your happiness will be a short one. I will forgive you if you are still Annie F., but if you are not – well, it's God help you." Seven months later, on February 5th, 1910, Annie Finn married Thomas Henderson.

On the afternoon of Saturday, March 26th, Mary Jane Henderson, Thomas's mother, answered a knock at her front door. The young man standing there introduced himself as an old friend of Annie's and asked where she was living now. Mary Jane offered to take the visitor, Thomas Craig, around to their home.

When they reached the house, Thomas Henderson was standing on a chair, knocking a nail in the wall. Annie answered the door. It had been seven years since she had seen Craig and now she greeted him: "You're Tommy Craig, aren't you?"

"And you're Annie Finn."

"No, I'm Mrs Henderson now."

Craig was invited in and immediately asked Annie why she had not remained faithful to him. When she answered that she had preferred her husband to him, Craig drew out a revolver and began firing. Thomas Henderson was shot dead. Annie was hit twice. Craig ran out of the house and managed to avoid capture in the maze of streets.

A major manhunt was launched, but no trace of Craig could be found. Nevertheless, police were alerted all over the region and in due course, received information that Dilston Hall and Rafferton Farm had been broken into and that a man had been seen sleeping in a

NAME	Thomas Craig (Crake)
AGE AT EXECUTION	24
DATE OF EXECUTION	Tuesday, 12th July, 1910
PLACE OF EXECUTION	Durham
HANGMAN	Henry Pierrepoint
ASSISTANT	William Willis
DATE OF TRIAL	25th June, 1910
LOCATION OF TRIAL	Durham
PRESIDING JUDGE	Mister Justice Grantham
PROSECUTION COUNSEL	Bruce Williamson, Willoughby Jardine
DEFENCE COUNSEL	Morgan Griffiths-Jones
NUMBER OF VICTIMS	1

VICTIMS DETAILS	
NAME	Thomas William Henderson
AGE	22
DATE OF MURDER	Saturday, 26th March, 1910
PLACE OF MURDER	Carters Yard, 60 Oakwell Gate, Gateshead
METHOD OF KILLING	Shot
RELATIONSHIP TO KILLER	None

hayloft at Dilston Cottage Farm. When police surrounded the barn on April 16th, Thomas Craig gave himself up without a struggle.

His defence was that the killing was unintentional. He had only meant to wing Henderson and moreover, he maintained, there was the provocation he had suffered when he had lost the woman he loved.

Found guilty but with a recommendation to mercy, Thomas Craig was hanged at Durham in July, 1910.

FREDERICK FOREMAN AND Elizabeth Ely were both workers in the fields on the farms around Grays, in Essex. They had known each other for some time and lived together in an old, disused railway carriage in a field at East Hall, Wennington.

On the evening of Monday, May 16th, 1910, screams were heard from the field where Foreman and Ely lived. The following morning, Foreman reported that he had found the body of his girlfriend by the side of a footpath which went across the field.

Foreman's story was that he and Elizabeth had argued on the Monday night and that she had decided to leave him. That was the last he saw of her until he found her body. He said he knew nothing about her murder and could be of no more assistance.

Medical and police examinations showed that Elizabeth had actually died from exposure. She had been severely beaten; there were five very severe cuts about her head and her right leg had been broken. There were also three separate patches of bloodstains around the field indicating that the attack had been a prolonged one involving someone dragging the woman about and beating her repeatedly.

The first concrete piece of evidence linking Foreman with the murder came when it was discovered that he had told some fellow workers that his wife was dead, before he had actually discovered her body. He was taken in for questioning, the railway carriage searched and Foreman's clothing examined. There were a number of bloodstains on Foreman's clothes and boots as a result of which, he was charged with murder.

At the trial it was shown that on the night of her death, Elizabeth Ely had been seen in various public houses, with Foreman. They had been heard quarrelling and it appeared that Foreman believed that Elizabeth had been with another man. The prosecution held that the argument had boiled over once the couple were in the field approaching the railway carriage. Foreman had struck Elizabeth, kicked her and then struck her a number of times with a heavy willow stick. The jury agreed and returned a guilty verdict.

NAME	Frederick Foreman
AGE AT EXECUTION	45
DATE OF EXECUTION	Thursday, 14th July, 1910
PLACE OF EXECUTION	Chelmsford
HANGMAN	Henry Pierrepoint
ASSISTANT	John Ellis
DATE OF TRIAL	15th June, 1910
LOCATION OF TRIAL	Chelmsford
PRESIDING JUDGE	Mister Justice Phillimore
PROSECUTION COUNSEL	Curtis Bennett, Mister Crawford
DEFENCE COUNSEL	G.F. Emery
NUMBER OF VICTIMS	1

VICTIMS DETAILS	
NAME	Elizabeth Ely
AGE	35
DATE OF MURDER	Monday, 16th May, 1910
PLACE OF MURDER	East Hall, Wennington, near Grays
METHOD OF KILLING	Battered
RELATIONSHIP TO KILLER	Girlfriend

JOHN RAPER COULSON and his wife did not live happily and on May 23rd, 1910, she had a summons served upon him at his place of work, alleging assault. That night the neighbours heard the sounds of quarrelling coming from the Coulson house. It was a sound they were used to and no one made any attempt to interfere.

At 6.00am on May 24th, a neighbour called on Jane Coulson. They had a brief conversation and at that time, Jane was certainly alive and well. By 8.45am, John Coulson was calling at a pawnbrokers where he pledged his wife's wedding ring. Some 15 minutes later, another neighbour, Mrs Fieldhouse, called at Jane's house, but this time there was no reply.

At 11.00am, Coulson was at work, where he showed some of his workmates the summons he had received. It was noted that on the back, someone, presumably Coulson himself, had written that he had murdered his wife and child. That same day he wrote to his sister, repeating that claim, and that night, in a public house, he showed a group of his friends the summons with the message on the back.

All these events led suspicious acquaintances to contact the police and that night, constables Gill and Walker called at Coulson's house to ask after his wife. Coulson told the officers that his wife had gone away and, apparently satisfied, they left soon afterwards.

At 11.00pm, however, Constable Walker returned and found the house locked up and in darkness. Thinking that there might be something in this matter after all, he gained entrance to the house and found the bodies of Jane and Thomas Coulson. Jane was lying on the bedroom floor, the child was on the bed and nearby lay a bloodstained carving knife.

Soon afterwards, John Coulson returned, his clothes soaking wet. He claimed he had tried to drown himself, but had failed. He was immediately arrested and charged with two murders.

At his subsequent trial, the jury did not even bother to leave the box before returning their verdict. He was hanged at Leeds on the same day that John Alexander Dickman was executed at Newcastle.

NAME	John Raper Coulson
AGE AT EXECUTION	32
DATE OF EXECUTION	Tuesday, 9th August, 1910
PLACE OF EXECUTION	Leeds
HANGMAN	Thomas Pierrepoint
ASSISTANT	William Warbrick
DATE OF TRIAL	21st July, 1910
LOCATION OF TRIAL	Leeds
PRESIDING JUDGE	Mister Justice Coleridge
PROSECUTION COUNSEL	Mister Waddy, Coutts Trotter
DEFENCE COUNSEL	Mister Mockett
NUMBER OF VICTIMS	2

VICTIMS DETAILS	
NAME	Jane Ellen Coulson; Thomas Coulson
AGE	29; 5
DATE OF MURDER	Tuesday, 24th May, 1910
PLACE OF MURDER	4 Springfield Place, Dudley Hill, Bradford
METHOD OF KILLING	Cut throat/cut throat
RELATIONSHIP TO KILLER	Wife; son

JOHN INNES NISBET had worked as a cashier for the Stobswood Colliery for 28 years. Part of his duties involved a fortnightly trip to pay the wages. On Friday March 18th, 1910, John Nisbet drew £370-9s-6d, in cash, then caught the 10.27am, train from Newcastle Central to Alnmouth.

Nisbet's wife, Cicely Elizabeth, always walked down to Heaton station on the days her husband went to collect the wages. When the train pulled in, she would exchange a few words with him. March 18th was no different. Cicely had a brief conversation with John, during which she noticed that there was another man in his third-class compartment. She only had a momentary glimpse of this passenger, and only in profile.

At Stannington station, two men sitting in the next carriage – Percival Harding Hall and John William Spink – got off and nodded to Nisbet. They also noticed that there was a man in the same carriage.

Nisbet should have left the train at the next station, Widdrington, but did not do so. At the next stop, Morpeth, John Alexander Dickman did alight. He had only bought a ticket as far as Stannington and had to pay a small excess fare. The train then moved on, to Alnmouth.

As the train was being prepared for the return journey, Thomas Charlton, a foreman porter, noticed streams of blood issuing from beneath a seat. When he investigated, he discovered the body of John Nisbet. He had been shot five times in the head. The money bag was missing.

The first puzzle for the authorities was to establish how many men they were looking for. The postmortem showed that the bullets in Nisbet's head were of two different calibres, implying two guns and two assailants.

Once the crime details were published, there was no apparent shortage of witnesses. Spink and Hall came forward. Hall said that he had seen two men getting into the carriage next to his. One of those men was Nisbet, whom he knew very well. He gave a description of the other man. Spink gave a similar story.

Charles Raven, a commercial traveller, who also knew Nisbet well, said that he had

NAME	John Alexander Dickman
AGE AT EXECUTION	45
DATE OF EXECUTION	Tuesday, 9th August, 1910
PLACE OF EXECUTION	Newcastle
HANGMAN	John Ellis
ASSISTANT	William Willis
DATE OF TRIAL	4th July – 6th July, 1910
LOCATION OF TRIAL	Newcastle
PRESIDING JUDGE	Mister Justice Coleridge
PROSECUTION COUNSEL	E. Tindal Atkinson, C.F. Lowenthal
DEFENCE COUNSEL	Mister Mitchell-Innes, Lord William Percy
NUMBER OF VICTIMS	1

VICTIMS DETAILS	
NAME	John Innes Nisbet
AGE	44
DATE OF MURDER	Friday, 18th March, 1910
PLACE OF MURDER	Train from Newcastle to Alnmouth
METHOD OF KILLING	Shot
RELATIONSHIP TO KILLER	None

seen Nisbet with a man at Central station, though he added that he did not see either getting onto the train.

An artist, William Hepple also came forward. He had seen John Alexander Dickman with another man, on Central station. The description of the murder victim fitted the man he had seen. It was Hepple who first gave Dickman's name to the police.

When Dickman was arrested, he had £17-10/- in his possession. No gun was found and no money that could be traced back to the colliery wages.

Dickman was placed in an identity parade, where he was picked out by both Spink and Hall as being the man in the carriage with Nisbet. Finally, when Mrs Dickman attended court, she fainted, saying that she had recognised the profile of Dickman as the same as that borne by the man in the carriage with her husband.

As if all this testimony were not damning enough, forensic tests showed traces of mammalian blood on one of a pair of gloves found in Dickman's possession and there

195

were small bloodstains and much larger paraffin stains on a coat Dickman wore. The paraffin could well have been used to remove larger traces of blood.

John Dickman's story was a simple one. He admitted that he had spoken to Nisbet, whom he knew, at Central station. He had boarded the same train but had travelled in a different carriage. Dickman said that he had been travelling to Stannington to visit William Hogg, the manager of the Dovecot Colliery, on mining business. He had fallen asleep and missed his stop, not waking until Morpeth where he paid an excess fare and began walking towards Stannington. On the way he had fallen ill and had a lie down for half an hour, then he returned to Morpeth, arriving at 1.20pm, from where, 20 minutes later he caught the train back to Newcastle.

This story was, at least in part, backed up by William Sanderson, a spirit merchant, who saw Dickman in Morpeth at 1.30pm on March 18th. He swore that Dickman did not appear to be distressed in any way.

On June 9th, the missing money bag was found down an air-shaft at the Hepscott Colliery, near Stannington. There was no sign of the wages it had contained.

Dickman's trial lasted for three days and after a deliberation lasting two and a half hours, the jury decided that he was guilty. However, let us examine some of the evidence more closely.

The prosecution held that Nisbet had been murdered, by Dickman, somewhere between Stannington, where he was last seen alive, and Morpeth, where Dickman left the train. According to the prosecution, Dickman would then have walked to Hepscott Colliery where he hid the money bag after removing its contents. This, of course, was all supposition unless it could be backed up by witnesses. And the witnesses were, at the very least, unreliable.

First let us consider the evidence of Hepple and Raven. Both testified to seeing Dickman talking to Nisbet at Central station. Dickman, of course, never denied that fact, so their evidence only serves to confirm what he had already said.

Hall and Spink identified Dickman as the man they had seen in the carriage with Nisbet. What is not widely known is that the police assisted them in this identification. When Hall and Spink were waiting to attend the parade, they were invited to take a look through a window. The room they looked into was the one in which Dickman sat. They claimed they could see very little, so the same officer took them to a door through which they both had a clear view of the back of Dickman. They saw his clothing and his hair and would have had little problem in picking him out at the parade.

Moreover, Mrs Nisbet had known Dickman for 18 years! It is true that she only knew him by sight and had never spoken to him, but nevertheless, why did she not recognise him immediately if Dickman was indeed the man in the carriage with her husband?

Lastly, there was the matter of the paraffin used on Dickman's coat. Dickman's wife agreed that she had used paraffin to remove oil stains from his coat. She was not called to give evidence, however.

Such was the feeling of unease at the case against Dickman that the Home Secretary referred the matter to the Court of Appeal, the first time he had used these powers. Even with the new evidence over the identification parade, the appeal was rejected on the grounds that it was felt there was sufficient other evidence.

Dickman was hanged at Newcastle on August 9th, 1910. Perhaps the last words should be left to Dickman himself. When sentenced to death by Mister Justice Coleridge, he replied: "I declare to all men I am innocent."

THE MARRIAGE OF THOMAS and Louisa Ann Rawcliffe was happy enough, except when Thomas drank too much. At such times he had been known to threaten his wife, but for the rest of the time he was a good husband and father to their three children.

On September 6th, Thomas Turney, Louisa's brother, called at her house to see her. Thomas Rawcliffe answered the door and said that his wife was not available. She had gone out to the shop to buy some tea and sugar. Turney was satisfied with the explanation and left. In fact, by that time, Louisa Ann Rawcliffe was already dead.

At 6.15am on September 7th, Thomas Rawcliffe stood outside his house and shouted to Police Constable Thomas Wilkinson: "Come and see what I have done." When Wilkinson went over, Rawcliffe told him that he had strangled his wife at 7.00pm the previous night. Constable Wilkinson went upstairs to the bedroom where he found the body of Louisa Rawcliffe lying on the bed. The youngest child was sleeping in the same bed and the two other children were asleep in the room.

Rawcliffe's story was that Louisa had been ill of late and this had preyed upon her mind to such an extent, that they had agreed on a suicide pact. Rawcliffe then strangled his wife and drank down some poison. This story, though, did not explain why Rawcliffe was still alive and carried little weight with the jury.

Perhaps more significant was the testimony of Rawcliffe's mother, Ann. She gave evidence that at the age of three, Rawcliffe had fallen from a bedroom window and suffered head injuries. In fact, he had remained unconscious for six or seven weeks and had never been the same since. This certainly affected at least one of the jury members, for when they returned to court after some two hours' deliberation, the foreman had to announce that whilst 11 of them were agreed, the 12th was not.

The judge asked the single juryman to identify himself and it transpired that this gentleman required clarification about the legal definition of insanity. Once this matter had been discussed, the jury retired again and soon returned a verdict of guilty, but with a recommendation to mercy because of Rawcliffe's accident as a child.

Despite the testimony of his mother and doctor, and the jury's recommendation, Rawcliffe did not escape the hangman. On November 15th, 1910, he became the first man to be executed at Lancaster for 23 years.

NAME	Thomas Rawcliffe
AGE AT EXECUTION	31
DATE OF EXECUTION	Tuesday, 15th November, 1910
PLACE OF EXECUTION	Lancaster
HANGMAN	John Ellis
ASSISTANT	Thomas Pierrepoint
DATE OF TRIAL	27th October, 1910
LOCATION OF TRIAL	Lancaster
PRESIDING JUDGE	Mister Justice Avory
PROSECUTION COUNSEL	H.R. Rathbone, Mister Kennedy
DEFENCE COUNSEL	Mister McKeever
NUMBER OF VICTIMS	1

VICTIMS DETAILS	
NAME	Louisa Ann Rawcliffe
AGE	27
DATE OF MURDER	Tuesday, 6th September, 1910
PLACE OF MURDER	1 Tyler's Yard, Cheapside, Lancaster
METHOD OF KILLING	Strangled
RELATIONSHIP TO KILLER	Wife

FROM THE BEGINNING, Henry Thompson was violent towards his wife, Mary.

On July 18th, 1910, the warring couple became tenants of 18 York Road and the following day, sublet some rooms to a married couple, Martin and Catherine Reynolds. On the night of Friday, July 30th, Henry and Mary went out at 9.00pm. They returned at 9.45pm and shortly afterwards, Catherine Reynolds went out to do some shopping. The following Monday was a Bank Holiday and all the shops would be shut, so she had to get some food in. Later, at around 11.30pm, Catherine and Martin Reynolds, had supper before retiring at midnight.

Catherine woke during the small hours to find Mary Thompson in her bedroom begging to be hidden. Soon afterwards, Henry Thompson came in to ask Catherine if she had seen his wife. Catherine said she hadn't, but Henry saw Mary crouching down between the bed and the wall, kicked her, lifted her up and carried her out.

For the rest of the night, Catherine slept fitfully. At one stage she thought she heard Mary cry: "Harry, don't choke me." and later heard something apparently being dragged across the floor.

The next day, there was no sign of Mary. Henry said that Mary was fine but had decided to have an easy day in bed as it was her birthday.

Mary McCumsky was a friend of Mary Thompson and she called at 10.00pm and asked to see Mrs Thompson. Henry would not allow her to go upstairs, however, and at one stage hit her in the chest when she tried to defy him.

By now, Catherine had become very worried about Mary and later, finally managed to gain entry to the bedroom. Henry was in bed, fast asleep, his wife laying next to him. Tentatively Catherine touched Mary's bare leg and noticed that it was very cold.

Fearing the worst, she ran to a neighbour's house for help and Frances Blower came back with her. She pulled back the covering from Mary's face, revealing that she was dead.

When the police arrived, Henry was still asleep. Arrested and taken to the police station, he claimed that he had nothing to do with her death. His statement was: "I don't know anything about this. The bloody thing was lying like a stuffed dummy in the bed beside me."

At his trial, Henry insisted that Mary had come home very drunk and must have died from some sort of fit. When he woke up on Sunday, he found her dead in bed but took no action in case people thought he was responsible. This story, though, did not explain the fact that Mary had been strangled.

NAME	Henry Thompson
AGE AT EXECUTION	54
DATE OF EXECUTION	Tuesday, 22nd November, 1910
PLACE OF EXECUTION	Liverpool
HANGMAN	John Ellis
ASSISTANT	William Willis
DATE OF TRIAL	4th November, 1910
LOCATION OF TRIAL	Liverpool
PRESIDING JUDGE	Mister Justice Avory
PROSECUTION COUNSEL	H.R. Rathbone, Mister Croshaw
DEFENCE COUNSEL	Mister Singleton
NUMBER OF VICTIMS	1

VICTIMS DETAILS	
NAME	Mary Thompson
AGE	circa 48
DATE OF MURDER	Sunday, 31st July, 1910
PLACE OF MURDER	18 York Street, Liverpool
METHOD OF KILLING	Strangled
RELATIONSHIP TO KILLER	Wife

IF PEOPLE IN Britain are asked to name a famous murder case, the chances are that many would mention Crippen.

Crippen was born in Coldwater, Michigan, in 1862. He met his second wife, Belle Elmore, in 1893, in New York and they were married in Jersey City. After various moves around America, Crippen came over to London, alone, in April, 1900. At the time he was a representative for Munyon's Remedies, a firm who made homeopathic medicines, and also involved himself in a dental practice in New Oxford Street. It was not until August that Belle came over to join him.

Belle Elmore was the stage name of Cora Turner, but even that was not Belle's real name. She had been born Kunigunde Mackamotzki, the child of a Russian-Polish father and a German mother. Belle had ambitions and dreamt of becoming an opera singer. Her new husband paid for her training but unfortunately, she did not in fact have much talent. Still set on a career on the stage, Belle turned to music hall. She didn't have a great deal of success there either, but she did make some friends in the business and also became Treasurer of the Music Hall Ladies Guild, in London.

Crippen and his wife lived in various addresses in London until September 1905, when they rented number 39 Hilldrop Crescent, Holloway. Prior to this, in November 1903, Crippen had returned to America on business, not getting back to England until June, 1904. It was whilst he was away that Belle became close to Bruce Miller, an American music-hall artist.

Belle had always had a temper. She was always finding fault with her husband and though they maintained a veneer of contentment, the relationship between them was always thereafter under a strain. One of the reasons they rented Hilldrop Crescent was so that they could have separate bedrooms. According to Crippen, sexual relations between him and his wife ceased around 1907.

Crippen, though, had his consolations. He had fallen in love with Ethel Le Neve, a typist who worked for him and in 1907, she became his mistress. This situation existed for three

NAME	Hawley Harvey Crippen
AGE AT EXECUTION	48
DATE OF EXECUTION	Wednesday, 23rd November, 1910
PLACE OF EXECUTION	Pentonville
HANGMAN	John Ellis
ASSISTANT	William Willis
DATE OF TRIAL	18th October – 22nd October, 1910
LOCATION OF TRIAL	Old Bailey
PRESIDING JUDGE	Lord Chief Justice, Lord Alverstone
PROSECUTION COUNSEL	Richard D. Muir, Travers Humphreys, S. Ingleby Oddie
DEFENCE COUNSEL	A.A. Tobin, Huntley Jenkins, H.D. Roome
NUMBER OF VICTIMS	1

VICTIMS DETAILS	
NAME	Cora Turner (Belle Elmore)
AGE	34
DATE OF MURDER	circa Tuesday, 1st February, 1910
PLACE OF MURDER	39 Hilldrop Crescent, Holloway, London
METHOD OF KILLING	Poisoned (by hyoscine)
RELATIONSHIP TO KILLER	Wife

years, with Belle constantly threatening to leave Crippen.

Paul and Clara Martinetti were close friends of the Crippens. On the evening of January 31st, 1910, they were invited for dinner at Hilldrop Crescent. They left at about 1.00am on February 1st. As they bade farewell to Belle, they could not have known that it was the last time she would ever be seen alive.

According to Crippen, after the Martinettis had left, an argument broke out between him and Belle. During the evening, Paul had needed to use the lavatory and Crippen had not gone upstairs with him to show him where it was. Belle saw this as the height of bad manners and determined that she would leave Crippen once and for all.

What is certain, is that Crippen told Belle's friends that she had gone to America, later saying that she had fallen ill and subsequently that she had died. They, however, noticed that Ethel was wearing Belle's jewellery and by the end of February she had moved in with Crippen. The friends took their suspicions to the police.

On July 8th, Chief Inspector Walter Dew, went to Hilldrop Crescent, where he found Ethel Le Neve. Ethel told him that Crippen was at his place of work and took the officer to see him there. Crippen offered to show Dew over the house, which he duly did, and in due course, told him a different story.

Crippen admitted that his wife was not dead. She had left him for another man, most probably Bruce Miller. Dew may well have thought this story believable, but he told Crippen that he was still not satisfied and that he had better ensure that Belle turned up. Crippen said that he would place an advertisement in the newspaper asking Belle to contact him.

On the following day, July 9th, Crippen shaved off his moustache and with Ethel disguised as a boy, made for the continent. In Brussels, they purchased tickets for Canada, joining the S.S. Montrose at Antwerp. Back in London, Dew had returned to Hilldrop Crescent and was surprised to find that Crippen and Le Neve had vanished. He searched the house again and noticed some loose bricks in the cellar. Underneath he found the fleshy remains of a human body; headless, limbless and boneless. The hunt for Crippen was on.

Crippen and Le Neve were travelling as father and son, but such was their affection for each other that they constantly held hands. Moreover, Ethel's disguise was poor, the trousers being ripped and held together with safety pins. Captain Kendall had his suspicions and telegraphed a message to Scotland Yard. Dew determined to intercept him. Boarding the S.S. Laurentic, a faster vessel, Dew set out to give chase.

On Sunday, July 31st, Dew and two Canadian officers boarded the Montrose as it sailed up the St Lawrence. All three were disguised as pilots and Crippen seemed puzzled as to why so many were needed. All became clear when he was arrested. After three weeks, Dew returned to England with his prisoners. It was decided that Crippen would be tried for murder and that later Ethel

Le Neve would face her charge of being an accessory. Crippen's trial began on October 18th, his defence being that the body in the cellar was not Belle.

The prosecution first tried to prove that the body was Belle's by demonstrating that one piece of flesh showed a scar. It was known that Belle had a scar on her lower abdomen. They then attempted to show that the cause of death was hyoscine poisoning. It was known that Crippen had bought five grains of the poison on January 17th, 1910, and experts testified that traces of the poison had been found in the remains, consistent with the victim having ingested about half a grain.

Doubt was thrown on much of this evidence, but more damning was the fact that some of the remains were found wrapped in the remains of a pyjama jacket. Crippen denied that the jacket was his, but it had a tag put in by the manufacturers, Jones Brothers Limited. A representative was called from the firm who testified that this particular cloth and pattern were not used until late 1908. This indicated that the remains must have been put in the cellar after 1908 and were therefore consistent with them being Belle's.

The jury took just under half an hour to return their guilty verdict and Crippen was sentenced to death. Ethel was tried on October 25th and found not guilty. Crippen's last wish was that a photograph of Ethel and her letters be buried with him. The request was granted.

MRS WHITE NEEDED to speak to old Mrs Wilson, who ran the second-hand clothes shop at 22 High Street. When she first went at 7.00pm, there was a bicycle parked against the shop window. Mrs White didn't want to discuss her business in front of other people, so she went away. At 8.00pm, Mrs White returned, but she still didn't get to speak to Mrs Wilson. This time though it wasn't because Mrs Wilson had a customer – it was because she was dead.

The body lay on the floor in the sitting room at the back of the shop. At first it looked as if she might have been strangled, but it turned out that Isabella Wilson had been struck, bound and gagged and had suffocated because of a cushion forced into her mouth.

The motive had been robbery. Mrs Wilson had a habit of wrapping her coins, mainly sovereigns, in pieces of paper, which she would then stuff into her purse. When her purse was found, it was empty but lying close by was a piece of paper which bore the distinct impression of 19 coins, 17 large and two slightly smaller. That number would later prove to be highly significant.

Shopkeepers in the area were interviewed and it soon became clear that a man had been seen loitering around the shop at about 1.00pm. Furthermore, this man had once lodged next door to Isabella Wilson's shop, so he could be named. It was William Broome. This was further confirmed when George Dollar came forward and said he had seen Broome in the High Street at some time between noon and 3.00pm.

Broome was now living in London and when he was interviewed he denied having been in Slough at all on the day of the murder. The police noticed, though, that he had two parallel scratches on one cheek. Suspicions arose that these might be defence scratches caused by the old woman, even though Broome explained that he had got the scratches in a fight in Camden Town on Saturday, July 16th. The police cautioned Broome and searched his rooms, soon finding 19 sovereigns and two half sovereigns, hidden in a box. Broome was then arrested.

For the time being, Broome stuck to his original story. On the day of the murder, he

NAME	William Broome (Brooks)
AGE AT EXECUTION	26
DATE OF EXECUTION	Thursday, 24th November, 1910
PLACE OF EXECUTION	Reading
HANGMAN	John Ellis
ASSISTANT	William Willis
DATE OF TRIAL	14th October – 15th October, 1910
LOCATION OF TRIAL	Aylesbury
PRESIDING JUDGE	Mister Justice Bucknill
PROSECUTION COUNSEL	Ryland Adkins M.P., B.S. Foster
DEFENCE COUNSEL	Mister Poyserby
NUMBER OF VICTIMS	1

VICTIMS DETAILS	
NAME	Isabella Wilson
AGE	70
DATE OF MURDER	Friday, 15th July, 1910
PLACE OF MURDER	22 High Street, Slough
METHOD OF KILLING	Asphyxiated
RELATIONSHIP TO KILLER	None

had been inn the area around Scotland Yard, looking for work, from 10.20am until about 1.00pm. He had then gone to the Trafalgar pub in St Martin's Lane, where he had some bread and cheese for lunch. From there he went home to 146 Albany Street and read a newspaper for one and a half hours before going out again for some tea.

Dogged police work turned up two chemists whom Broome had visited on the day of the murder. A chemist at Paddington station reported that Broome had called in at some time before 3.00pm asking for some lotion or preparation that would remove some scratches from his face. At 5.00pm, he was seen in another establishment in Oxford Street, where he made a purchase of lotion and cotton wool. To be on the safe side, the police talked again to the witnesses who had reported seeing Broome in Slough on July 15th. All said that he had no scratches on his face at that time. Finally, Anna Lextus, the wife of Charles Lextus, who owned the house in which Broome lodged, said that she had seen Broome at about 5.00pm on July 15th and remarked upon the scratches on his face. Broome had laughingly said that people might think he had been robbing someone for their money.

Faced with this evidence, Broome now told a new story. He had caught a train from Paddington to Windsor, intending to call at the Headquarters of the Yeomanry, for whom he was a reservist. The building was closed, so he went to Slough, where he arrived at some time between noon and 1.00pm. He stayed there for a while and returned to London by 10.00pm. This timetable did not, of course, agree with the evidence of the chemists or his landlady.

Broome was found guilty of murder and sentenced to death, but there were nevertheless some interesting unanswered questions about the case.

The piece of paper found near the body contained 17 large and distinct impressions on which were found traces of gold. It was held that these impressions were of 17 gold sovereigns. There were also two smaller, slightly less distinct impressions, making up 19 in all, and these it was assumed had held half sovereigns. Throughout the trial and the subsequent appeal it was stressed that this number agreed with what had been found in Broome's possession. Yet 19 sovereigns and two halves, a total of 21 coins had been found in Broome's lodgings.

It was held that Broome had no money before the crime was committed, but his girlfriend, Ellen Bunce testified that Broome had money on the day before the murder. On Thursday the 14th, Broome had taken her out and paid for both her tea and her supper.

The final piece of evidence was a postcard sent by Broome to a friend. This card was postmarked as being sent from Edgware Road in London at 3.15pm on the day of the murder. Whilst there is no guarantee that Broome posted the card himself and that the time disagreed with his movements as outlined in the second story, we have already seen that this story did not fit in with the times given by the chemists and Broome's landlady.

It is likely that Broome murdered Isabella Wilson for her money, but there are many questions about the case that still remain unresolved.

NOAH WOOLF WALKED into the police station at Upper Holloway Road and, producing a bloodstained knife, politely said that he wished to give himself up for the murder of Andrew Simon. He then, equally politely, offered to take the police back to the Home for Aged Hebrew Christians, were he would show them the body. The police went to the Home, to discover that nobody there knew anything of the crime up to that point.

Until relatively recently, Woolf had also lived at the Home. He was somewhat argumentative and so subsequently was not popular with the other residents, and many of them complained to the matron, Amelia Young, and the Reverend Michael Machim who ran a mission attached to the Home.

At the end of June, Reverend Machim called a meeting at the Home and it was then that Andrew Simon went to see him. He explained that he had come to the Home to live out his days in peace and objected most strongly to the atheistic utterances constantly made by Woolf. The man was obviously not a believer in the prophecies of the Bible and was not fit to be in the Home. It was determined that Woolf had to go.

On July 4th, Woolf left the Home. He was given 10/- and a grant of money every week for three months. He blamed Simon for his eviction and determined to have the matter out with him.

On October 27th, Woolf called at the Home and was seen talking to Simon in the street outside. By now of course, Woolf's grant from Reverend Machim had stopped. The matter remained unresolved and Woolf decided to return the next day.

Amelia Young said that she had seen Woolf arrive at about 10.30am on October 28th. She saw him go up to Simon's room, leaving at approximately 11.00am. The next sighting of Woolf was at the police station when he confessed to murder.

Woolf said he had gone to see Simon to ask him to withdraw the accusations he had made. Woolf believed that if Simon did so, he might be readmitted into the Home. Simon refused to withdraw anything and so Woolf had stabbed him a number of times. Then, as the body lay on the floor, Woolf had stabbed

NAME	Noah Woolf
AGE AT EXECUTION	58
DATE OF EXECUTION	Wednesday, 21st December, 1910
PLACE OF EXECUTION	Pentonville
HANGMAN	John Ellis
ASSISTANT	William Willis
DATE OF TRIAL	18th November, 1910
LOCATION OF TRIAL	Old Bailey
PRESIDING JUDGE	Mister Justice Darling
PROSECUTION COUNSEL	Mister Bodkin, Mister Leycester, H.D. Roome
DEFENCE COUNSEL	Mister Lawrie
NUMBER OF VICTIMS	1

VICTIMS DETAILS	
NAME	Andrew Simon
AGE	67
DATE OF MURDER	Friday, 28th October, 1910
PLACE OF MURDER	The Home for Aged Hebrew Christians, Upper Holloway, London
METHOD OF KILLING	Stabbed
RELATIONSHIP TO KILLER	None

him three or four more times, to be sure that he was dead. In all, there were eight major stab wounds on Simon's body, as well as a number of minor cuts.

There could be no verdict other than guilty of murder. Before his execution, Woolf wrote on a slate in his cell: "Thank one and all for their great kindness to me, while in your charge. I pray God's will be done. The Lord receive my spirit – Noah Woolf." They were hardly the utterances of an atheist!

MARY JENKINS AND Henry Ison had lived together for the past 13 years. On Saturday, July 23rd, 1910, Henry, Mary and two women friends of theirs, were drinking together in The Yorkshire Hussar Inn from where they left to go to Ison's house at around 5.00pm.

By 6.30pm, Henry and Mary were both drunk and he insisted that the other two should leave. There were no more developments until around 8.20pm when Mary was seen rushing out of the house by a neighbour, Amy Northrop. Amy saw Ison pull Mary back by her hair and kick her on the thigh as he dragged her back inside. Frederick Wadsworth, another neighbour, was disturbed by the noises coming from next door. The sounds of arguing culminated in a loud thud.

Later that evening, Ison called on Mrs Elizabeth Bradshaw, Mary's sister, and told her that she should go to Mary as they had had a few words. Mary's sister found her lying unconscious by the fireplace, a poker nearby. The police had already arrived, having been called by the neighbours, and Ison told them that he had given her a sovereign, and she had returned saying that she had lost it. He had then hit her to teach her a lesson.

Ison subsequently changed his story and claimed that he had found Mary lying on the hearthrug. At the trial, Mister Mellor for the defence pointed out that no blood had been found on the poker, though four human hairs had been discovered adhering to it, but it was said that it was unlikely that Mary's injuries could have been caused by a fall downstairs. Ison was found guilty, but with a strong recommendation to mercy.

Before sentence was passed, Ison was asked if he had anything to say. He exclaimed: "I think it is a very unjust sentence. I am innocent. I am not guilty of murder."

NAME	Henry Ison
AGE AT EXECUTION	45
DATE OF EXECUTION	Thursday, 29th December, 1910
PLACE OF EXECUTION	Leeds
HANGMAN	Thomas Pierrepoint
ASSISTANT	William Willis
DATE OF TRIAL	24th November, 1910
LOCATION OF TRIAL	Leeds
PRESIDING JUDGE	Mister Justice Hamilton
PROSECUTION COUNSEL	Edward Shortt, J. Willoughby Jardine
DEFENCE COUNSEL	Charles Mellor
NUMBER OF VICTIMS	1

VICTIMS DETAILS

NAME	Mary Jenkin (Mary Letitia Whittaker) (Died Sunday, 24th July)
AGE	43
DATE OF MURDER	Saturday, 23rd July, 1910
PLACE OF MURDER	47 Boynton Street, Leeds
METHOD OF KILLING	Battered
RELATIONSHIP TO KILLER	Girlfriend

ADA ROKER HAD known George Newton for three years and they had been engaged for six months.

At the beginning of December, 1910, George and Ada were alone in the sitting room at 10 Biggerstaff Road. When Annie Roker, Ada's mother, came in, she noticed that her daughter was bleeding from the mouth. She asked what had gone on, but neither of them would say.

Prior to Christmas, George called a number of times to see Ada and all appeared to be well between them, until the evening of December 24th. It was clear that George was in a mood and when Ada said she intended to iron George's handkerchief for him, he replied that he "might as bloody well go home". This was overheard by Eliza Roker, the wife of Charles, Ada's brother. Ada managed to calm George down and Eliza left them alone. When she returned, she found Ada with a very red face.

At 7.00pm that evening, Elizabeth, Ada's sister, returned home, only to be met on the stairs by George who pushed past her. Elizabeth was so disturbed by his appearance that she exclaimed: "Oh George, what have you done?" George ran out into the street and vanished.

Elizabeth heard a noise coming from the kitchen and opening the door, she discovered Ada, lying on the floor in a pool of blood. Her throat had been cut and her arms fastened to her body by means of a strap, buckled around her body just above the elbows.

Elizabeth ran for her mother, who was at her florist's stall in Devons Road, Bow. The two ladies returned home whilst Ada's brother, Charles, went to look for Newton. Charles's first port of call was Newton's house at 42 Lett Road, where he lodged with his married sister and her husband, Henry Allan. Henry said that Newton was not at home and Charles went on his way. In fact, Henry had lied to protect his brother-in-law and Newton was in the house.

Newton had gone to his sister's house immediately after the murder, told Henry all that had happened, and shown him the razor he had used. Soon after Charles Roker had left, there came another knock on Henry's

NAME	George Newton
AGE AT EXECUTION	19
DATE OF EXECUTION	Tuesday, 31st January, 1911
PLACE OF EXECUTION	Chelmsford
HANGMAN	John Ellis
ASSISTANT	William Conduit
DATE OF TRIAL	13th January, 1911
LOCATION OF TRIAL	Old Bailey
PRESIDING JUDGE	Mister Justice Grantham
PROSECUTION COUNSEL	F.G. Frayling
DEFENCE COUNSEL	Mister Grantham
NUMBER OF VICTIMS	1

VICTIMS DETAILS	
NAME	Ada Roker
AGE	21
DATE OF MURDER	Saturday, 24th December, 1910
PLACE OF MURDER	10 Biggerstaff Road, Stratford, London
METHOD OF KILLING	Cut throat
RELATIONSHIP TO KILLER	Girlfriend

door. This time it was Constable Sidney Mills. Newton came downstairs and gave himself into custody.

An attempt was made to claim that George was insane at the time of the attack. A medical report from S.R. Dyer, the Medical Officer of Brixton prison where Newton had been held, confirmed that George had a sister in an asylum and that 30 years before, an aunt had also been confined, but Dyer held that apart from a quick temper, Newton was normal.

In due course, the jury became convinced that it was anger and jealousy that had led Newton to kill Ada.

FOR MANY YEARS, Thomas Seymour had been at sea, finally being discharged with a good report. In 1907, he married his first cousin, Mary, who had recently come in to a legacy of £80.

There were those who suggested that the only reason Thomas married was so that he could get his hands on that money. What is certain is that there were a number of arguments between the two, and most of these were over the fact that Mary kept a tight control over her cash.

By 1911 though, most if not all of the money had been frittered away and whatever affection there had ever been between Thomas and Mary had also long since evaporated. It was on Saturday, March 11th, of that year that a relative, Elizabeth Jones, called to see how Mary was keeping. Thomas opened the door to Elizabeth but it was clear that he did not want her inside the house. Somehow though, possibly because her weight was against the door, Elizabeth gained entry and immediately noticed, in the corner of the room, the body of Mary Seymour.

Mary had been brutally battered to death by means of a stonemason's hammer, her skull being shattered in the process. To dry up the blood, Thomas, had thrown a shovelful of hot ashes onto Mary's head and seemed totally indifferent to the crime he had committed. He pulled on his coat, said he was going to give himself up to the police and then walked to Ronson Street, where he found a constable and admitted he had killed his wife.

Throughout the various hearings that subsequently took place, Thomas Seymour showed no concern for his fate. At the magistrate's court he freely admitted his guilt and demanded that they deal with the matter there and then instead of wasting his time sending it to a higher court. The course of the law had to be followed though, and Seymour was committed for trial at the next Liverpool Assizes.

In fact, Thomas appeared before Mister Justice Avory three times. When first asked how he wished to plead, Seymour answered "Guilty", in a firm voice. The judge then sent him back to the cells to give him time to consider his plea and when Seymour

NAME	Thomas Seymour (McKillican)
AGE AT EXECUTION	65
DATE OF EXECUTION	Tuesday, 9th May, 1911
PLACE OF EXECUTION	Liverpool
HANGMAN	John Ellis
ASSISTANT	Thomas Pierrepoint
DATE OF TRIAL	19th April, 1911
LOCATION OF TRIAL	Liverpool
PRESIDING JUDGE	Mister Justice Avory
PROSECUTION COUNSEL	Not known
DEFENCE COUNSEL	Mister Kenyon
NUMBER OF VICTIMS	1

VICTIMS DETAILS	
NAME	Mary Seymour
AGE	69
DATE OF MURDER	Friday, 10th March, 1911
PLACE OF MURDER	3 Breckfield Place, Everton, Liverpool
METHOD OF KILLING	Battered
RELATIONSHIP TO KILLER	Wife

returned, he again insisted on pleading guilty. He was now handed over to Mister Kenyon, whom the judge asked to take on his defence and again given time to reconsider. On the third appearance, once more Seymour, by now growing weary with the entire proceedings, insisted that he was guilty of killing Mary.

His only sign of interest had occurred when he had been charged in his real name of Thomas McKillican, and had insisted that his name was Seymour. There only remained the task of passing the sentence of death and on May 9th, the killer who seemed to want to hang, finally got his wish.

IN AUGUST 1910, Elizabeth Kempster's husband died, leaving her alone with her six-year-old son. Fortunately for Elizabeth, she soon found someone else who seemed to care for her and just before Christmas she moved in with Michael Collins.

At first they were very happy together. The situation changed on March 19th, 1911. For some reason, Elizabeth became aloof. Collins tried to find out what was bothering her, but she would say nothing. At 8.00pm that evening they went out for a drink together and when Collins again asked Elizabeth what was on her mind she would only say that she wished he would go.

The following day, Monday the 20th, Elizabeth would not even speak to Collins and this state of affairs continued into Tuesday. Collins was now becoming very worried indeed and insisted that Elizabeth confide in him. Her only reply was that she still wanted him to leave and that she would face the trouble she was in by herself. Things did not improve during the rest of that week.

On Saturday, March 25th, Collins purchased a new razor from Morris Koseleepsky's stall in Whitechapel. Earlier that day he had spent some time with his friend and neighbour, George Crease. Collins seemed to be very depressed and told Crease that he had had yet another argument with Elizabeth. He ended the conversation by saying that he thought it would be best if he did away with Elizabeth and himself.

At 6.00pm, Crease was with James Rowley when Collins came up to them. His hands were covered in blood and he confessed to them that he had just killed Elizabeth. Some 45 minutes later, Collins walked into Leman Street police station and repeated the story to the officer on the desk.

At his trial at the Old Bailey, Collins explained that after a week of worrying about Elizabeth, he had asked her to make a final decision on whether they were to live together or apart. After a few moments' thought, Elizabeth had said "Apart". With a cry of "Nothing shall part us but death," Collins had taken up a hammer and struck Elizabeth in the face. She fell to the floor, whereupon Collins took up his newly purchased razor and cut her throat.

With such a confession, there could really be only one verdict and it was one that Collins welcomed, saying that he wanted no mercy whatsoever.

NAME	Michael Collins
AGE AT EXECUTION	26
DATE OF EXECUTION	Wednesday, 24th May, 1911
PLACE OF EXECUTION	Pentonville
HANGMAN	John Ellis
ASSISTANT	Thomas Pierrepoint
DATE OF TRIAL	28th April, 1911
LOCATION OF TRIAL	Old Bailey
PRESIDING JUDGE	Mister Justice Grantham
PROSECUTION COUNSEL	Mister Graham-Campbell, Mister Oddie, Harold Murphy
DEFENCE COUNSEL	W.W. Grantham
NUMBER OF VICTIMS	1

VICTIMS DETAILS	
NAME	Elizabeth Anne Kempster
AGE	29
DATE OF MURDER	Saturday, 25th March, 1911
PLACE OF MURDER	Number 42, A-Block, Peabody Buildings, Glasshouse Street, London
METHOD OF KILLING	Battered/cut throat
RELATIONSHIP TO KILLER	Girlfriend

0590

SARAH CHILVERS HAD been married twice and had one son, James Hawes, who lived with her and the third man in her life, Arthur Garrod, at Garrett's Buildings, in Ipswich. For most of the time, the couple seemed to be happy enough, but Garrod was a somewhat jealous man.

At 7.00pm on Sunday, February 5th, Sarah gave her son 6d, which allowed him and Arthur to go down to the Red Lion public house for a drink or two. They were seen in that establishment, and left together at around 7.20pm.

James noticed that Arthur appeared to be rather subdued and when they reached home, he explained why. Arthur told James that he had seen Sarah drinking whisky with another man whose name was Payne. James thought nothing more of this accusation and soon retired to his bed.

James had been upstairs for perhaps an hour when he heard a groaning noise from downstairs. Going to investigate, he found the room in great confusion, with furniture scattered about the place. Furthermore, his mother and Arthur Garrod both lay on the floor with their throats cut. Sarah was beyond help but the groaning James had heard came from Arthur, who was still very much alive. James ran for assistance and found Constable Painter, who entered the house and asked Arthur if he had done this thing. Arthur replied: "I have done it. She is as dead as a rat, and I wish I were dead too."

In fact, two weapons had been used on Sarah Chilvers. Her forehead bore two deep wounds inflicted by a chopper that lay on the floor and bore traces of blood and human hair. The fatal wound had been inflicted by a penknife that Arthur still had in his hand when Constable painter came upon the scene.

At his trial, Arthur explained that he had argued with Sarah over her drinking with Payne. At the height of that row, Sarah had begun screaming "Murder!" and Arthur suddenly thought that he might as well "do both of us in". He had reached out and picked up the chopper that he used to strike Sarah, then, when she was lying on the floor, he took out his knife and cut her throat. Arthur claimed that he had not intended killing or

NAME	Arthur Garrod
AGE AT EXECUTION	49
DATE OF EXECUTION	Tuesday, 20th June, 1911
PLACE OF EXECUTION	Ipswich
HANGMAN	John Ellis
ASSISTANT	Not known
DATE OF TRIAL	1st June, 1911
LOCATION OF TRIAL	Ipswich
PRESIDING JUDGE	Mister Justice Avory
PROSECUTION COUNSEL	Beaumont Morice, A.S. Carr
DEFENCE COUNSEL	Rowley Ellison
NUMBER OF VICTIMS	1

VICTIMS DETAILS	
NAME	Sarah Chilvers
AGE	45
DATE OF MURDER	Sunday, 5th February, 1911
PLACE OF MURDER	4 Garrett's Buildings, Ipswich
METHOD OF KILLING	Battered/cut throat
RELATIONSHIP TO KILLER	Girlfriend

even hurting Sarah until she began threatening him and screaming.

The jury considered their verdict for half an hour and then found Arthur Garrod guilty but added a recommendation to mercy on account of the great provocation he had received. It was to have no effect. Arthur was hanged at Ipswich two days before the Coronation of George V and Queen Mary.

1900

ANN HARRIS LIVED alone in her small cottage in Walcote. When she made no appearance on the morning of January 25th, 1911, her neighbours forced an entry and were horrified to find the body of the old lady, lying on the floor.

The house had been ransacked and amongst the items missing were some jewellery and a gold watch. The neighbours then recalled a tramp they had seen the day before. He had been seen trying the door of the cottage next door to Ann's.

William Palmer was a fish hawker and he was identified as having been in the area on January 24th. He had been dressed in little more than rags and it may have been he who had tried the cottage door. Further checks showed that Palmer had been seen at Lutterworth station at 6.10pm on January 25th. He had purchased a ticket to London and paid for it with a handful of silver 3d pieces and Ann Harris was known to collect these.

It was not until January 28th that Palmer was arrested in Folkestone. He denied any involvement in the murder. Palmer's story was that he had been in Lutterworth and, on the afternoon of January 24th had found a handkerchief containing a quantity of money, by the roadside.

Using this, Palmer went to Lutterworth station and bought a ticket to London. However, he chose to break his journey at Rugby, where he visited two pubs and sent a telegram to friends in Manchester. From Rugby, he travelled to London, where he purchased a ticket for Folkestone.

The only real evidence against Palmer was the fact that he had a large number of 3d coins. The police found 43 such coins in Ann Harris's house. If Palmer had stolen some, why had he not stolen them all?

On June 3rd, the landlord of a pub in Rugby was cleaning the cisterns in the toilets when he found some jewellery and a gold watch. This property was identified as belonging to Ann Harris. And Palmer had already said that he had been in Rugby.

The entire trial turned on how long that watch had been in the cistern. For Palmer to have placed it there, it would have had to be

NAME	William Henry Palmer
AGE AT EXECUTION	50
DATE OF EXECUTION	Wednesday, 19th July, 1911
PLACE OF EXECUTION	Leicester
HANGMAN	John Ellis
ASSISTANT	George Brown
DATE OF TRIAL	12th June – 13th June, 1911
LOCATION OF TRIAL	Leicester
PRESIDING JUDGE	Mister Justice Pickford
PROSECUTION COUNSEL	Ryland Adkins, Drysdale Woodcock
DEFENCE COUNSEL	Mister Campion
NUMBER OF VICTIMS	1

VICTIMS DETAILS

NAME	Ann Harris
AGE	72
DATE OF MURDER	Tuesday, 24th January, 1911
PLACE OF MURDER	Walcote, near Lutterworth
METHOD OF KILLING	Strangled
RELATIONSHIP TO KILLER	None

for some five months and evidence was given that it had been immersed for about that time. The defence countered this with the evidence of a jeweller who testified that in his opinion it had been there two or three days. Nevertheless, a guilty verdict was returned.

At the appeal, even the judges admitted that there was no direct evidence as to the commission of the offence, but still the verdict was upheld.

As the executioner prepared Palmer for his fate, he shouted "Are you going to let these fellows murder me?" and fought all the way to the scaffold.

ALICE BREWSTER HAD decided that this was to be her last voyage. She had been a stewardess on the China, as well as on other ships, for long enough. When the ship docked in London, she would look forward to a long and well-deserved retirement.

The China was sailing from Australia to London, making various stops along the way. On June 7th, 1911, she docked at Colombo in Ceylon, (now Sri Lanka), where she stayed for one day. On the evening of June 8th, she set sail for the next port of call: Aden. It was whilst the ship was between those two ports that Alice Brewster was murdered.

At 5.30am on June 11th, Francisco Godhino called Annie Crutchley, another stewardess. This was part of his daily duties. Godhino, a bath attendant, was responsible for making sure that the senior members of staff were awake, ready to start their daily duties. After calling Miss Crutchley, Godhino asked where Miss Brewster was sleeping and was told that she was in the cabin opposite. As Godhino went to wake Miss Brewster, Annie Crutchley ran a bath for herself. Whilst the bath was still filling, a frightened Godhino returned and again knocked on Annie Crutchley's door. He told her that something had happened to Miss Brewster and asked her to come quickly.

The body of Alice Brewster lay on her cabin floor, covered by the mattress from her bed. When the mattress was lifted, it was clear that Alice had been battered to death. Miss Crutchley also noticed that the cabin porthole was open and the mattress was damp where the sea had washed in. She thought this was surprising. It had been somewhat stormy lately and most sensible people kept their cabin portholes well and truly bolted shut.

The Captain of the ship launched an immediate inquiry and it soon became apparent that the prime suspect was none other than Francisco Godhino himself.

Miss Brewster had been Godhino's immediate superior and had often found fault with his work. Fellow workers described Miss Brewster as hard working but rather changeable and her occasionally stern approach did not sit well with Godhino. On June 7th for instance, a menu card had

NAME	Francisco Carlos Godhino (Reuben Almeida)
AGE AT EXECUTION	40
DATE OF EXECUTION	Tuesday, 17th October, 1911
PLACE OF EXECUTION	Pentonville
HANGMAN	John Ellis
ASSISTANT	William Conduit, Albert Lumb
DATE OF TRIAL	6th September – 7th September, 1911
LOCATION OF TRIAL	Old Bailey
PRESIDING JUDGE	Mister Justice Avory
PROSECUTION COUNSEL	Richard D. Muir, Travers Humphreys
DEFENCE COUNSEL	H.D. Roome
NUMBER OF VICTIMS	1

VICTIMS DETAILS	
NAME	Alice Emily Brewster
AGE	54
DATE OF MURDER	Sunday, 11th June, 1911
PLACE OF MURDER	Onboard P & O Liner China, at sea
METHOD OF KILLING	Battered
RELATIONSHIP TO KILLER	None

been found in one of the cabins. On the back was written a number of accusations about Alice Brewster and a male member of the crew. Although she laughed these comments off, it was suggested that the handwriting bore more than a passing resemblance to that of Godhino.

Godhino was asked to account for his movements on the night of the murder. He explained that it had been a very hot night and because of that he had not slept in his quarters, preferring instead to sleep in the open on the fore hatch. After trying to get to sleep for some time, he felt thirsty and went to fetch himself a glass of water. On the way to the bathroom he passed the security officer on duty – that would be at around 11.30pm, perhaps midnight. He then returned to the fore hatch, where he managed to get to sleep. Waking at five he woke Miss Crutchley and then went to Miss Brewster's cabin. He saw the bed on the floor and when he lifted up one corner, saw her foot and a great deal of blood. He then went for help.

There were three major problems with

Godhino's story. Firstly, the security man did recall seeing him, but said that it was closer to 3.00am. Secondly, Godhino could not produce his port key and such an instrument was mooted as the probable murder weapon. It was later discovered in a bathroom that Godhino had access to, in a sink, with water still running over it. And finally, Godhino had changed his trousers at 7.30am on the morning the body was discovered. Those trousers were found soaking in a tub, but there were still clear signs of bloodstains on them. Godhino was told he should consider himself under arrest.

When the ship finally docked in England, Godhino was taken into police custody. Before his first court appearance, he made an amazing statement to Detective Sergeant Mitchell, in whose custody he was. In his broken English, Godhino mumbled, "If I say my fault, will they pardon me? Is King George here? If I say my fault and ask pardon, perhaps he relieve me. It was both our faults. We fighting."

At the Old Bailey, in September, Godhino appeared before Mister Justice Avory. One of the first debates was over whether the statement Godhino had made to Mitchell was admissible. After some argument, the judge ruled that it was. The defence then tried to discredit it by suggesting to Mitchell that he had not in fact written down the exact words. Tested at one point by Mister Roome to write down and then repeat a version that he uttered, Sergeant Mitchell did not do very well.

The prosecution, though, were able to show that Godhino had made some sort of utterance that implicated himself and a guilty verdict was returned.

The appeal relied on the view that the statement had, after all, been inadmissible. The Appeal Court judges ruled that it was relatively unimportant, as there was other evidence linking Godhino to the crime. He had been seen in the area, had lied about his movements, could not produce his port key and had bloodstains on his trousers. The appeal was rejected and Godhino's sentence upheld.

MARY JANE HILL'S marriage was a short one. The ceremony tying her to her new husband took place on July 16th, 1911. Nine days later, she was dead.

Shortly after the wedding, Edward Hill and his wife took rooms on the top floor of a house at 22 Caledonia Street, London. During the move to Caledonia Street, Mary Hill noticed that 22/- she had borrowed from her mother-in-law was missing. The only person who could have taken it was Edward, but he denied all knowledge of the lost money. From then on Mary did not trust Edward.

Two days after the move, a friend of Mary's, Mrs Miller, called. She noticed that the floor of the living room was covered in flock. The newlyweds had argued and Edward had cut open the bed and thrown its contents around the room. Edward went out on a drinking spree that night. At 2.00am on July 25th, Mrs Barton, the landlady, saw Mary Hill letting him in.

At 8.00am a fellow lodger, Mrs Dodge, paid a visit to Mary Hill. Edward was lying on the bed, apparently asleep. Two hours later, at 10.00am, Mary Hill went to see Mrs Barton and asked her to hold some money for her. She had lost money once to Edward; she wasn't about to take another chance.

Mary Hill returned to her room and very soon afterwards, Mrs Barton heard someone running up and down the stairs. Looking out of the window she was in time to see Edward leaving. Some time in the next hour, a fire was discovered in the top floor front room. It was soon put out, but it was no help to Mary Hill. She lay on the floor, her face covered with two pillows and a linen bandage knotted tightly around her neck. A paraffin lamp had been placed underneath the bed, in an attempt to set it on fire and burn the house down.

Hill was arrested in a pub close to his mother's house in St George's Road, Southwark. He denied all knowledge of the crime, claiming that he had been at his mother's house but statements taken from some of the other customers in the pub showed that Hill was in there drinking at the time.

The trial was really a case of which witnesses the jury chose to believe. In the end, Mrs Barton won the day and Hill was found guilty. Only then was it revealed that he had received a prison sentence in 1903 for setting fire to a house.

On the morning of his execution, Hill scribbled a last message on a slate. When this was read it was seen that he had thanked the Governor, doctors and officers of Pentonville prison for their kindness during his stay in the condemned cell.

NAME	Edward Hill
AGE AT EXECUTION	41
DATE OF EXECUTION	Tuesday, 17th October, 1911
PLACE OF EXECUTION	Pentonville
HANGMAN	John Ellis
ASSISTANTS	William Conduit, Albert Lumb
DATE OF TRIAL	11th September – 12th September, 1911
LOCATION OF TRIAL	Old Bailey
PRESIDING JUDGE	Mister Justice Avory
PROSECUTION COUNSEL	Mister Bodkin, Mister Graham-Campbell
DEFENCE COUNSEL	A.C. Fox-Davies, Mister Purcell
NUMBER OF VICTIMS	1

VICTIMS DETAILS	
NAME	Mary Jane Hill
AGE	circa 45
DATE OF MURDER	Tuesday, 25th July, 1911
PLACE OF MURDER	22 Caledonia Street, King's Cross, London
METHOD OF KILLING	Strangled/asphyxiated
RELATIONSHIP TO KILLER	Wife

HARRIETT ECKHARDT LIKED men and men liked her. Ahead of her time, Harriett was a hedonist and this led directly to her death.

Harriett married, for the second time, in 1907. Her second husband, Ernest Eckhardt, worked on board a ship that regularly travelled between London and Goole, so he was seldom at home. Harriett saw her opportunity and took a lover: Frederick Henry Thomas.

Ernest soon discovered that Harriett had started seeing another man. In April 1911, Ernest told his wife that if Thomas called again whilst he was away, she was not to admit him to the house. Harriett agreed but broke the promise just as soon as she could. Obviously, Ernest had to try a different approach. Unfortunately, the approach he chose was totally disastrous.

Ernest had a friend named Bruno Koch, who lived at the German Sailors Home in Limehouse. On Wednesday August 16th, 1911, Ernest Eckhardt invited Koch to spend the evening with him and his wife, an invitation which Koch accepted. At 6.00pm when Ernest reported back to his ship, he made the mistake of leaving Koch with his wife. Indeed, Ernest encouraged Koch to take Harriett to the Elephant and Castle theatre that same evening.

Perhaps Ernest felt that he could trust Koch to keep Harriett company without anything more developing between them. If that was the case, then he was very badly mistaken. Koch was invited to stay the night and spent it sharing Harriett Eckhardt's bed. He also stayed on Thursday and Friday. Harriett had found herself a new diversion whilst her husband was away, but if she was to spend her time with Koch, she had to prevent Thomas from paying his usual visit. With that in mind, Harriett sent a letter to Thomas, telling him that her husband had not gone away after all. She then settled down to enjoy her latest conquest.

Thomas, though, suspected the truth. He had known Harriett for some time and was fully aware of her appetites. He determined to see if his suspicions were well founded.

At some time between 1.00am and 2.00am

NAME	Frederick Henry Thomas
AGE AT EXECUTION	38
DATE OF EXECUTION	Wednesday, 15th November, 1911
PLACE OF EXECUTION	Wandsworth
HANGMAN	John Ellis
ASSISTANT	Thomas Pierrepoint
DATE OF TRIAL	16th October, 1911
LOCATION OF TRIAL	Old Bailey
PRESIDING JUDGE	Mister Justice Scrutton
PROSECUTION COUNSEL	Mister Bodkin, Mister Leycester, Percival Clarke
DEFENCE COUNSEL	Mister St. John Hutchinson
NUMBER OF VICTIMS	1

VICTIMS DETAILS

NAME	Harriett Ann Eckhardt
AGE	circa 32
DATE OF MURDER	Saturday, 19th August, 1911
PLACE OF MURDER	Rothbury Terrace, Azof Street, Greenwich
METHOD OF KILLING	Cut throat
RELATIONSHIP TO KILLER	Girlfriend

on Saturday, August 19th, Harriett and Koch were disturbed by a knock on the front door. Both got out of bed and went downstairs to investigate. Koch went into the kitchen to hide, and Harriett opened the door.

Koch would later report that he heard a man's voice. He thought that Ernest Eckhardt might have returned and felt that he might not be very pleased when he discovered how his trusted friend had been entertaining his wife. Fearful that he might be attacked, Bruno Koch waited quietly. He heard the man run upstairs and investigate various rooms, then he heard him come back downstairs and leave the house. If Koch now expected Harriett to come for him and take him back to her bed, he was disappointed. There was no sound in the house, so Koch simply waited.

At some time after 7.00am, Koch finally decided that he had waited long enough. Leaving the kitchen, he was horrified to discover Harriett's body at the foot of the stairs. Her throat had been cut and near the body lay a postcard on which a message was written referring to him and Mrs Eckhardt and adding that the writer hoped they had all had a good evening.

The first suspect was, rather naturally, Ernest Eckhardt but it was soon shown that at the time of the murder of his wife, he had been on board ship somewhere between Goole and London. When interviewed though, Ernest was able to give the police the name of Frederick Henry Thomas.

When Thomas was interviewed, he made no attempt to hide his guilt. He calmly told the police to go round to his house where they would find a full confession on his mantelpiece. True enough, when the police visited his home, at 245 Brunswick Road, Poplar, where Thomas lived with his own wife and children, they found two documents exactly where Thomas had indicated.

The first of these two papers was a letter sent by Harriett to Thomas, explaining that he couldn't visit her as Ernest had not gone away. The other was a long confession detailing exactly how Thomas had killed Harriett. The confession was dated August 19th and began, "I must admit I have murdered the woman I love. I have done it because I knew Bruno Koch was there." It went on to describe how the crime had been committed: "As I came out of the room door I made one slash at her throat with the razor and I think I must have cut her head half off."

Arrested and charged with murder, Thomas was put into a police cell, where he removed a razor from his boot and slashed his own throat. Found in time, he was rushed to hospital where his wound was attended to.

Thomas's defence was one of compulsive insanity at the time of the murder. The defence failed but there was one moment of pure farce as the man fought for his life. In the middle of the trial, one of the jurymen announced that he had been rendered deaf by a bad head cold. As a result he had not heard what had been said in court and did not even know what the charge was! He was dismissed and a replacement juryman sworn in.

When the verdict was finally announced, the judge in his summing-up took the opportunity to state that this case should be a warning to all men against unbridled lust and jealousy. For Harriett Eckhardt and Frederick Thomas, the warning had come too late.

MICHAEL FAGAN AND his wife, Annie, lodged with Mary Ellen Kennedy, who had a little girl, Lucy, aged two and a half. The two women got on quite well and sometimes went out shopping together. One such occasion was Saturday, September 9th. Annie and Mary Ellen went out at about 5.45pm, leaving Lucy with Michael. He promised that he would look after her whilst they were away.

Whilst they were out, the two women split up and it was Annie Fagan who arrived back at Arlington Street first. When Mary Ellen herself arrived home, at 7.10pm, she was met by a graven-faced Annie, who told her there was something wrong.

Little Lucy was upstairs on her mother's bed. She was unconscious and there were signs that she had been badly beaten. The poor girl had a blackening eye and cuts on her face. The doctor was called and Lucy was rushed to hospital. Michael Fagan was nowhere to be seen.

Annie and Mary Ellen were both standing at the front door when Fagan finally made an appearance. Immediately Annie demanded to know what had happened. Fagan replied that he had done nothing and when Annie pressed him on the point, saying that Lucy was in the hospital, he threatened to put her in the same place. The police were now contacted and when Police Sergeant Herbert Johnson arrived, he found Fagan upstairs, lying on his bed, sobbing and crying.

Taken to the police station, Fagan admitted that he had struck Lucy with his belt. His phrase was: "I never did nothing to the child – I just smacked its arse, that's all." That 'smacking', though, was so severe that Lucy had sustained substantial injuries through her clothing. It was suggested that not only had Fagan used his belt, but that he had also kicked the child. He denied this vehemently, even when Lucy died, just before midnight on September 11th, and he was charged with her murder.

Even though Michael Fagan had been drinking before he was left alone with Lucy Kennedy, there could be no excuse for what he had done. Mister Justice Avory had no hesitation in sentencing him to death and

NAME	Michael Fagan
AGE AT EXECUTION	27
DATE OF EXECUTION	Wednesday, 6th December, 1911
PLACE OF EXECUTION	Liverpool
HANGMAN	John Ellis
ASSISTANT	George Brown
DATE OF TRIAL	8th November, 1911
LOCATION OF TRIAL	Liverpool
PRESIDING JUDGE	Mister Justice Avory
PROSECUTION COUNSEL	Gordon Hewart
DEFENCE COUNSEL	Mister Madden
NUMBER OF VICTIMS	1

VICTIMS DETAILS

NAME	Lucy Kennedy (Died Monday, 11th September)
AGE	2
DATE OF MURDER	Saturday, 9th September, 1911
PLACE OF MURDER	128 Arlington Street, Liverpool
METHOD OF KILLING	Battered
RELATIONSHIP TO KILLER	None

Fagan became the first of eight men to die on the gallows in December 1911.

EDITH GRIFFITHS HAD known Walter Martyn for about a year. He worked as a barman at the Black Bull Inn on Rochdale Road, Heywood and in early September, 1911, he moved in with Edith and her stepmother, Elizabeth Griffiths, at 113 Adelaide Street.

Some two years before all this, Edith had been engaged to a man named Openshaw and though that relationship had ended, there was a child, a girl, now 15 months old and this fact was always at the back of Martyn's mind.

On September 28th, 1911, Elizabeth Griffiths arrived home from work at 7.30pm. Half an hour later, Martyn went out with Edith. Elizabeth would never see Edith alive again.

Witnesses later helped to piece together what had happened. James Fitton who had known Martyn for six years, saw him with a girl, walking towards Hooley Bridge at around 8.30pm. Less than two hours later, at 10.15pm, Martyn was seen, alone, in the Brown Cow Hotel by James Gordon.

By 10.40pm, Martyn was back at the Black Bull, where he was served with a rum and seen by the landlord, Richard Ramsbottom. Martyn told Ramsbottom that his girl was dead and that he had seen her with another man in Crimble Woods. He finished his rum, went outside and approached Constable Arthur Taylor.

Martyn told Constable Taylor that he had seen a man and a woman behaving in an indecent manner in the woods. He then went on to say he had been attacked by a group of youths who had thrown stones at him and now wished to make a complaint. Taylor took Martyn to the police station in order to sort the matter out.

Martyn had not been in the station for very long when his employer, Richard Ramsbottom, came in to relate what Martyn had said to him about his girlfriend being dead. Martyn now said that he had gone for a walk with Edith and she had asked him for some sweets. He had given her a penny but whilst he waited outside, she managed to give him the slip. He went looking for her and found her with another man in the woods. There had been an argument between the two men. The other man finally ran away and

NAME	Walter Martyn
AGE AT EXECUTION	22
DATE OF EXECUTION	Tuesday, 12th December, 1911
PLACE OF EXECUTION	Manchester
HANGMAN	John Ellis
ASSISTANT	George Brown
DATE OF TRIAL	21st November, 1911
LOCATION OF TRIAL	Manchester
PRESIDING JUDGE	Mister Justice Avory
PROSECUTION COUNSEL	Roe Rycroft, Mister Kennedy
DEFENCE COUNSEL	Mister Openshaw
NUMBER OF VICTIMS	1

VICTIMS DETAILS	
NAME	Edith Griffiths
AGE	25
DATE OF MURDER	Thursday, 28th September, 1911
PLACE OF MURDER	Crimble Woods, Heywood
METHOD OF KILLING	Strangled
RELATIONSHIP TO KILLER	Girlfriend

Martyn had then killed Edith in a fit of temper.

Finally, after much questioning, the final version came out. After getting to the woods, Martyn had mentioned that he was thinking of leaving his job. Edith said that she would break off their relationship and find another man. Martyn had lost his temper, pushed her back against a tree and strangled her with a handkerchief.

Martyn was tried, found guilty and sentenced to death, but there was one final sad twist before he was executed. Martyn's father was not a strong man and upon hearing that his son was held for murder, collapsed and died on October 2nd, 1911.

THE MARRIAGE OF John and Rosetta Tarkenter could hardly be said to be a perfect one. There had been constant rows due to John's fondness for drink, and these had led to him leaving the house from time to time, once for a period of nine years. In August 1910, John Tarkenter left his wife for the fourth time and would not return until some time in June 1911.

This time it looked as if things might be different. When John returned in June, he wasn't drinking and started behaving quite reasonably towards Rosetta and their grown-up son, George, who lived with them in Hilton Street. Then, at the beginning of July, John started drinking again and the arguments started afresh.

Tuesday July 18th began like so many other days. John Tarkenter went into his son's bedroom just after 5.00am, in order to wake him for work. Whilst George got himself ready, he heard his parents talking in their bedroom and would later remark that they sounded quite friendly. At 5.20am, George left for work.

When George returned home at 5.40pm, he was surprised to find the door locked. Opening it with his key, he found no fire in the grate and no food prepared for him. He called up to his mother, but received no reply. Going upstairs to check, George found his mother lying in bed underneath a pile of blankets. Her throat had been cut and she was dead. Of his father John, there was no sign.

When George went next door to number 4 Hilton Street, in order to get some assistance, William Cuddey recalled that he had heard three screams from Rosetta at around 6.00am. He had heard so many arguments between John Tarkenter and his wife, though, that he thought no more about it. Later, he saw John near the Bulls Head Hotel and the two went on a pub crawl.

The police were called but Tarkenter was already in custody. Having been drinking throughout the day, officers had heard that he was causing a disturbance in Hilton Street. At around 4.00pm, Constable Charles Kerslake had called on Tarkenter and warned him as to his behaviour. Tarkenter had invited the constable upstairs, saying

NAME	John Edward Tarkenter
AGE AT EXECUTION	41
DATE OF EXECUTION	Tuesday, 12th December, 1911
PLACE OF EXECUTION	Manchester
HANGMAN	John Ellis
ASSISTANT	George Brown
DATE OF TRIAL	22nd November, 1911
LOCATION OF TRIAL	Manchester
PRESIDING JUDGE	Mister Justice Avory
PROSECUTION COUNSEL	Gordon Hewart, Mister Kennedy
DEFENCE COUNSEL	Mister McLeary
NUMBER OF VICTIMS	1

VICTIMS DETAILS	
NAME	Rosetta Tarkenter
AGE	43
DATE OF MURDER	Tuesday, 18th July, 1911
PLACE OF MURDER	2 Hilton Street, Royston, Oldham
METHOD OF KILLING	Cut throat
RELATIONSHIP TO KILLER	Wife

that he would see something interesting, but Kerslake had declined. Had he done as he was asked, the murder would have been discovered hours before.

After the visit from Kerslake, Tarkenter had gone out drinking again and had finally been arrested in St. Mary's Gate, where he told Sergeant Thomas Taylor that he had murdered his wife.

At his trial, Tarkenter pleaded not guilty. He admitted killing Rosetta, but claimed that she had provoked him during an argument and that he was therefore guilty only of manslaughter. The jury were not convinced and Tarkenter was sentenced to death. He was hanged alongside Walter Martyn, at Manchester.

AT 1.30AM ON July 13th, 1911, Mrs Ann Ace answered a knock at the front door of her home, Frogmore Cottage, Knelston. The caller was her married daughter, Margaret Phillips, who announced that she had left her husband Henry, bringing three of their four children with her, the fourth being left with a neighbour. This was not the first time Margaret had left her husband in the 13 years they had been married. Henry was a violent man, and having hit her the previous night, Margaret had decided that she had stood all she could.

On July 22nd, Henry Phillips was served with a summons for persistent cruelty, and was told to appear in court at Penmaer on August 8th.

Margaret stayed with her mother and sister, also named Ann Ace, until July 24th, when she rented two rooms at the house of Albert Davies. He also lived in Frogmore Lane, so Margaret would still be able to visit her family.

Ann Ace's house had no running water, necessitating a rather long walk to a well half a mile away. At 6.40am on July 26th, the younger Ann visited that well with two large cans and on her way home, met her sister, Margaret. The two women had a brief conversation before Ann said she had better be getting back. She had not gone very far when she heard Margaret shout: "Oh Harry! Harry!"

Ann ran the short distance to her mother's house and shouted for help. The elder Ann, together with her lodger, Thomas Casement, dashed into Frogmore Lane, in time to see Henry Phillips attacking his wife. Margaret managed to stand, her throat bleeding profusely, but soon collapsed into her sister's arms. Casement saw Henry run off across the fields and gave chase but had to give up when Henry threatened to kill him too. He would later report that Henry also shouted: "Is the bugger dead?"

Henry Phillips did not run far. At eight-thirty he walked into the "Welcome to Town Inn", run by John Thomas. Henry enjoyed a pint before buying four bottles to take away and asking John to step outside whilst he told him something. John Thomas did so and was

NAME	Henry Phillips
AGE AT EXECUTION	44
DATE OF EXECUTION	Thursday, 14th December, 1911
PLACE OF EXECUTION	Swansea
HANGMAN	John Ellis
ASSISTANT	William Willis
DATE OF TRIAL	10th November, 1911
LOCATION OF TRIAL	Cardiff
PRESIDING JUDGE	Mister Justice Channell
PROSECUTION COUNSEL	Clement Edwards, Mister Beasley
DEFENCE COUNSEL	T.R. Jenkins
NUMBER OF VICTIMS	1

VICTIMS DETAILS	
NAME	Margaret Phillips
AGE	39
DATE OF MURDER	Wednesday, 26th July, 1911
PLACE OF MURDER	Frogmore Lane, Knelston, Reynoldstone, Gower
METHOD OF KILLING	Cut throat
RELATIONSHIP TO KILLER	Wife

informed by Henry that he had just killed his wife. Thomas thought Phillips was joking.

Meanwhile, a search of the area had been organised. After some hours, a police constable noted a track through a field of corn and, walking slowly down it, discovered Henry Phillips, having finished his bottles of beer, sleeping peacefully!

Having been seen by Margaret's sister, and Thomas Casement, in the act of attacking his wife and having confessed his guilt to John Thomas, there could be little doubt as to the final verdict. Found guilty of wilful murder, Henry Phillips was executed at Swansea.

JOSEPH FLETCHER HAD a drink problem and his wife Caroline had often been seen sporting bruises and black eyes.

The Fletchers had five children living with them at 76 Bostock Street, Liverpool: Catherine Ann, the oldest at 17, John aged 15, Francis 10, William six years old and 15-month-old Albert. Caroline had been heard to remark to her sister, Mary Slatterly, that if it wasn't for the kids, she would leave.

On Saturday, September 2nd, 1911, Joseph Fletcher came home from work at 12.30pm. Catherine, his daughter, was sent to the shops and returned with a pint of beer and some cheese for his dinner. Joseph only accepted the beer. By 6.00pm, when Catherine came back from the pawnbrokers, Joseph was already out, drinking.

At 9.30pm, Caroline sent her daughter to fetch Joseph. Joseph said he would return when he had finished his pint, but 10 minutes later Caroline sent her son John on the same errand. This time neither returned and after 10 minutes, Catherine was sent again. Finally, Joseph returned home. He was drunk, but still sent Catherine to get another pint.

Joseph settled down to enjoy a smoke and, having filled his pipe, asked John to give him a light. John handed his father a lighted paper, but Joseph had wanted a match and knocked the paper from his son's hand. Caroline could see that Joseph was in one of his moods and said she was going to bed. Joseph said he was going back out and as soon as he was out, Caroline locked the door behind him. It was a bad mistake.

Joseph Fletcher had heard the door being locked and demanded to be let back in. Once inside he rushed straight to the parlour where Caroline had locked herself in, smashed down the door and grabbed his wife by the throat. He punched her and started to choke her. Caroline had been holding the baby and Catherine took the child from her. Her hands free now, Caroline managed to escape into the kitchen.

Joseph followed his wife and forced her into a rocking chair. Taking up a second chair, Joseph battered his wife, at one stage forcing a chair leg into her mouth and putting his strength behind it.

NAME	Joseph Fletcher
AGE AT EXECUTION	40
DATE OF EXECUTION	Friday, 15th December, 1911
PLACE OF EXECUTION	Liverpool
HANGMAN	John Ellis
ASSISTANT	George Brown
DATE OF TRIAL	11th November 1911
LOCATION OF TRIAL	Liverpool
PRESIDING JUDGE	Mister Justice Avory
PROSECUTION COUNSEL	Mister Ryecroft
DEFENCE COUNSEL	Mister Rees
NUMBER OF VICTIMS	1

VICTIMS DETAILS

NAME	Caroline Fletcher
AGE	38
DATE OF MURDER	Saturday, 2nd September, 1911
PLACE OF MURDER	76 Bostock Street, Liverpool
METHOD OF KILLING	Battered
RELATIONSHIP TO KILLER	Wife

Catherine and John had rushed out into the street and found a constable. Joseph Fletcher meanwhile had left the house and, knowing full well what he had done, found another officer, Constable James Rawson, whom he told that his wife had fallen downstairs. The officer accompanied him back to Bostock Street where he arrested Fletcher.

An attempt was made to excuse Fletcher's actions by reason of drink, but like so many other cases, it was not held to be a reason for the behaviour he had exhibited and Fletcher was sentenced to death.

0900

WHEN SHE WAS just three weeks old, Mary Elizabeth Speller had been adopted by Mary Laura Cripps. Now, in July 1911, after having three children by a man named Austen, Mary Speller was living with the woman she thought of as her mother, at 73 Lime Kiln Street, Dover. Also living there was Mary Speller's boyfriend, George William Parker and the owner of the house, Florence Penny.

Life was far from perfect for George and Mary, and this situation was not helped by their lack of money and his temper. In early July, George had kicked one of the children out of bed, where it had been found by Mary Cripps. This was typical of George's behaviour when he did not get his way.

On the morning of Saturday, July 22nd, George Parker was heard complaining to Mary Speller and saying: "I suppose we shall have to go without a Sunday dinner, as we did last Sunday." This was perhaps a sign that George was not in the best of moods.

These signs were further reinforced that afternoon when George was in his bedroom and called Mary Speller up to see him. She went up as he had asked and 45 minutes later, called her mother. When Mary Cripps arrived at the door, George said he did not want her in his room and she was forced to go back downstairs.

Just five minutes later, Mary Cripps heard the sound of smashing glass and a cry of: "Mother! Mother!" Rushing upstairs, Mary Cripps found her adoptive daughter with her throat cut. Mary Speller still had her baby in her arms as she ran downstairs and out into the street. Here George Scott, who had been passing by and had seen Mary leaning out of the window, tried to help her. Meanwhile, George Parker was upstairs, showing Mary Cripps the razor he had used.

Florence Penny had also heard the breaking glass and the screams and now she came out and saw Mary outside with George Scott. Florence took the baby from Mary, who now collapsed to the floor and died soon afterwards. Parker decided it was time to make good his escape. He pushed past the small knot of people around Mary's body and ran off up the street. Immediately George

NAME	George William Parker
AGE AT EXECUTION	26
DATE OF EXECUTION	Tuesday, 19th December, 1911
PLACE OF EXECUTION	Maidstone
HANGMAN	John Ellis
ASSISTANT	Albert Lumb
DATE OF TRIAL	28th November, 1911
LOCATION OF TRIAL	Maidstone
PRESIDING JUDGE	Mister Justice Scrutton
PROSECUTION COUNSEL	A.S.C. Carr
DEFENCE COUNSEL	Lawrence E. Jones
NUMBER OF VICTIMS	1

VICTIMS DETAILS	
NAME	Mary Elizabeth Speller
AGE	26
DATE OF MURDER	Saturday, 22nd July, 1911
PLACE OF MURDER	73 Lime Kiln Street, Dover
METHOD OF KILLING	Cut throat
RELATIONSHIP TO KILLER	Girlfriend

Scott gave chase and, catching up with Parker, struck him a blow that stopped him in his tracks. He then held Parker until the police arrived.

At Parker's trial it became clear that July 22nd had been a particularly bad day for him. He was two weeks in arrears with his rent and that same morning, Mrs Penny had told him that she thought it was best if he sought alternative accommodation. The jury thought this no excuse for what had happened later and took just 15 minutes to find Parker guilty of murder.

O N JULY 15TH, 1911, Charles Coleman was released from St Albans prison, having served a sentence for mutilating a dog. This was but the latest in a series of prison sentences he had served, including one for attempted murder, but by his second day of freedom, Coleman was again being interviewed by the police, this time for a senseless and brutal murder.

At one stage, Coleman had lived close to Rose Gurney and her daughter Eleanor, so, when he accidentally met up with Rose on his release, they travelled back to Rickmansworth together and enjoyed a quiet drink at the Swan. It was then 9.40pm and they were seen together by Mary Ann Peek who said that they seemed to be very friendly towards each other.

At 9.50pm, Charles and Rose were seen by Harry Ginger, the nightwatchman at a local brewery. The couple were walking towards a stile close to the park and Harry would also say that they appeared friendly. It was near that same stile that Rose's body was discovered the following morning.

When Charles was interviewed, human bloodstains were found on his clothing but a knife found in his possession showed no traces of blood. He admitted that he had been with Rose but said he had left her at the stile when she met two other men, one of whom was named George.

Charles could not satisfactorily explain the blood on his clothing and since that suit had been issued to him by the prison on his release, and had not been stained when issued, the blood must have been acquired in the short time he had been a free man.

Although the evidence was purely circumstantial, Coleman was charged with murder. He claimed to have no knowledge of the crime but his defence counsel sought to prove that there was a history of insanity in the family. Doctor Charles Parker said that in his opinion, Coleman had not been mentally responsible since he had attempted to cut his landlady's throat in 1897. It was also shown that he had made several suicide attempts, including one whilst in police custody for an earlier offence.

Despite the lack of any real evidence linking him with the crime, Coleman was found guilty and sentenced to death. He made no confession before he was executed, saying only: "If I did it, I did it, but I don't remember anything about it."

NAME	Charles Coleman
AGE AT EXECUTION	36
DATE OF EXECUTION	Thursday, 21st December, 1911
PLACE OF EXECUTION	St Albans
HANGMAN	John Ellis
ASSISTANT	William Willis
DATE OF TRIAL	21st November, 1911
LOCATION OF TRIAL	Hertford
PRESIDING JUDGE	Mister Justice Lawrance
PROSECUTION COUNSEL	Theobald Mathew, Holford Knight
DEFENCE COUNSEL	A. Taylor
NUMBER OF VICTIMS	1

VICTIMS DETAILS	
NAME	Rose Anna Gurney
AGE	49
DATE OF MURDER	Saturday, 15th July, 1911
PLACE OF MURDER	Rickmansworth Park
METHOD OF KILLING	Stabbed
RELATIONSHIP TO KILLER	None

FOR 50 YEARS, George Loake had worked on the railway and had been promoted to a driver of express trains. In 1903, George, a widower with nine children, married a divorcee, Elizabeth Newitt, who already had two of her own. This large family lived in a rented house at 110 Portland Street, Walsall and were very happy together.

In the summer of 1909, George was shunting a train at the Bescot sidings when the engine struck the buffers at speed. Loake was badly injured, receiving a very severe blow to the head. Even though he had a massive swelling, the medical 'expert' called to deal with him said no treatment was needed and George was sent home to recover. Two hours later Loake was in such acute pain, that he threw himself into the canal. Rescued by his neighbours, Loake eventually recovered, but his employers appeared to be no more caring than the doctor had been. They blamed George for the accident and suspended him.

Slowly George grew better but his family noticed that his personality had changed. Ever since the accident he had become very short tempered. His language became obscene and he took to drinking heavily. And once he was drunk, his personality grew even worse.

In March 1911, George left his engine whilst he went to buy more drink. This time his understanding employers dismissed him. This meant that not only did George lose his income, but he lost all the rights he had to a pension that had accumulated over 50 years of excellent service.

With little or no money coming into the house, and so many mouths to feed, it became impossible to make ends meet. The rent fell into arrears and in June, 1911, Loake and his family were evicted from Portland Street. Elizabeth had no choice but to leave George, take her own two children with her, and move in with George and Jane Dolloway who lived in The Butts, Walsall.

On August Monday, George Loake went to see his wife and begged her to return to him. When she refused, an argument broke out, the entire episode being witnessed by 11-year-old Thomas Dolloway. Thomas saw Elizabeth

NAME	George Loake
AGE AT EXECUTION	64
DATE OF EXECUTION	Thursday, 28th December, 1911
PLACE OF EXECUTION	Stafford
HANGMAN	Thomas Pierrepoint
ASSISTANT	William Willis
DATE OF TRIAL	20th November, 1911
LOCATION OF TRIAL	Stafford
PRESIDING JUDGE	Mister Justice Pickford
PROSECUTION COUNSEL	Doctor Hazell, Mister Brice
DEFENCE COUNSEL	R.J. Lawrence
NUMBER OF VICTIMS	1

VICTIMS DETAILS	
NAME	Elizabeth Loake
AGE	46
DATE OF MURDER	Monday, 28th August, 1911
PLACE OF MURDER	8a The Butts, Off Warwick Street, Walsall
METHOD OF KILLING	Stabbed
RELATIONSHIP TO KILLER	Wife

turn to leave the room and George leap upon her, throw his arm around her throat and stab her repeatedly in the face and neck.

George Loake walked outside, to be followed by his wife, who managed to stagger out into the road. As George raised the knife to his own throat, a passing policeman, Constable Woolley, struck him on the hand with his truncheon, causing him to drop the weapon.

The defence of insanity failed. Despite all the evidence of his terrible accident, his head injury and his consequent change of personality, George Loake was judged to be perfectly sane and responsible for his actions.

SOLOMON AND ANNIE Milstein ran a restaurant at number 62 Hanbury Street but when, in November 1911, business began to drop off, Solomon came up with the idea of turning the basement into an illegal gambling den. His wife did not approve, but she decided to let Solomon have his way.

From the first, the cellar proved to be very popular with the local clientele. Solomon, in partnership with Joe Goldstein, a professional boxer, and another man, would operate a number of friendly games, but the real money spinner was faro. For this, the trio would charge 3d for each deal of the cards and every so often this would be divided equally between the three partners, after a sum of 5/- had been paid to Milstein for the rent of the room.

Trade built up very rapidly and soon another sideline was introduced. If a customer ran a little short of money, Solomon Milstein would be more than happy to provide loans against the deposit of a little personal property. So for instance, on December 24th, 1911, Lazarus Rickman gave Solomon a silver watch and chain, for which he obtained a sovereign, which he promptly lost at faro!

Throughout all this time though, Annie had been asking Solomon to stop the gambling aspect of the operation. She didn't object to people using the cellar to meet and play cards but she couldn't countenance the risking of money and after repeated discussions with her husband, he finally came around to her way of thinking. So it was that on December 26th, Solomon approached Joe Goldstein, explained the situation and said that he did not want any more games of faro in the basement. Goldstein said he understood and went down into the cellar to tell the players that tonight would be the last night when they could play cards for money.

At some time after 11.00pm, Goldstein decided that he wanted to leave. As it was the last night that there would be any money to divide up, the pot of three pences was counted and split between the three partners. Each man received some 4/6d and Solomon Milstein got his share in assorted copper coins.

At about the same time as this share out was being made, another unlucky gambler, Hermann Leferron, borrowed £2-10s from

NAME	Myer Abramovitch
AGE AT EXECUTION	28
DATE OF EXECUTION	Wednesday, 6th March, 1912
PLACE OF EXECUTION	Pentonville
HANGMAN	John Ellis
ASSISTANT	Albert Lumb
DATE OF TRIAL	7th February – 8th February, 1912
LOCATION OF TRIAL	Old Bailey
PRESIDING JUDGE	Mister Justice Ridley
PROSECUTION COUNSEL	Mister Bodkin, Mister Graham-Campbell
DEFENCE COUNSEL	Mister Elkin
NUMBER OF VICTIMS	2

VICTIMS DETAILS	
NAMES	Solomon Milstein; Annie Milstein
AGES	35; 37
DATE OF MURDER	Wednesday, 27th December, 1911
PLACE OF MURDER	62 Hanbury Street, Spitalfields, London
METHOD OF KILLING	Battered; battered
RELATIONSHIP TO KILLER	None; none

Solomon and gave him a silver watch, gold chain and a silver match box as security. Leferron stayed until 12.45am on December 27th, by which time he too had been cleaned out. He left with four other men and as far as he was concerned, they were the last group to leave. Solomon Milstein then locked up the place for the night.

Marks Verbloot lived at 62a Hanbury Street, which was the flat above the restaurant. At about 2.30am, he heard loud groaning. At first he thought it might have come from the old woman who lived in the flat above him, but after the noise had gone on for over half an hour, Marks also began to smell burning rags. He opened the window and saw a warm glow coming from the restaurant downstairs. The place appeared to be on fire! Marks summoned the police and went downstairs to investigate.

The restaurant door was wide open but the inner door that led to the Milsteins' rooms was firmly locked. The door was forced and it was seen that the bed in the room was on fire. Water was thrown over this and soon the flames were put out. It was too late for the Milsteins, though. They lay next to each other in bed. Both had been battered to death and whoever had killed them had then put hot fire irons into the bed, after dousing it with paraffin.

The first thing the police had to do was to trace all the card players of the previous night. In due course most were traced and interviewed, but one man, who had been seen by some of the others, did not come forward. The police were now looking for Myer Abramovitch.

Myer was a costermonger who sold fruit in a local market. He had also hawked fruit around the restaurant and the downstairs gambling den and although people were not sure if he had ever gambled or not, one or two suggested that he might have lost heavily at faro. What was more interesting was that Lazarus Rockmann said that he had seen Myer wearing a silk neckerchief on the night of the murder. Just such a neckerchief had been found in the restaurant.

On December 28th, at just before 1.00am, Henry Seychur, another of the card players who had already spoken to the police, stood at the corner of Leman Street and Commercial Road, when he saw Myer Abramovitch at a coffee stall nearby. Seychur knew that the police had not yet spoken to Myer, so Seychur went up to him and asked him why he had not been to see the police as yet. Myer made no reply, but when Seychur said he would walk with him to the police station, Myer fell in beside him.

At the police station, the silk neckerchief was shown to Myer. Without being prompted, Myer immediately said: "That is mine; I done it because I lost all my money on gambling." When Myer was searched, the two watches that had been given as security against loans by Rickman and Leferron were found in his pocket. It also became apparent that Myer was wearing two suits of clothes. Over his own, he wore a bloodstained suit that was identified as having belonged to Solomon Milstein.

The trial was a mere formality and when the sentence of death was pronounced, Myer Abramovitch broke down and wept. There was an attempt, both at the trial and the subsequent appeal, to show that Myer was insane. He was even known in the area as 'Myer the Fool' and 'Myer the Insane' but none of this saved him from the hangman's noose.

This, of course, was not the first time Hanbury Street had seen violent death. In 1888, on the opposite side of the road at number 29, Jack the Ripper had claimed Annie Chapman as one of his victims.

IN 1908, HILDA Shawcross married John Williams. For a time, they lived together at 7 Brighton Street, Seacombe, but then they began living apart and Hilda entered service at 9 Victoria Mount, Oxton, Birkenhead. John and Hilda still saw each other frequently. Sometimes she would visit him at Seacombe and on other occasions, he would visit her at her place of employment. On December 10th, 1911, Hilda decided it was her turn to visit John.

The couple seemed to be friendly enough during the visit and at one stage went for a long walk together whilst his landlady, Mrs Wright, prepared tea for them. When John and Hilda returned, Mrs Wright noted that John appeared to have been drinking, but they had their tea and at 9.30pm, Hilda felt it was time that she returned home.

John said he would see Hilda home and at around 10.00pm they were seen together getting off a bus at Charing Cross, Birkenhead. Less than half an hour later, at 10.20pm, John Williams was arrested in Oxton Road. Obviously drunk and waving around a bottle of whisky, he was shouting to all who could hear: "I have done my wife. I have committed a murder." Five minutes after this, Mr Ryecroft was taking a short cut through a narrow passageway called Price's Lane, when he found the body of Hilda Williams.

John Williams was so drunk that he could not be charged with murder that night. The police noted that he spent much of the night singing songs and hymns in his cell and charged him once he had sobered up.

Once again the defence was one of insanity. Evidence was given that Williams suffered from hallucinations and had attempted suicide three times but it took the jury only 15 minutes to decide that he had been fully aware of what he was doing and was therefore guilty of wilful murder.

NAME	John Williams
AGE AT EXECUTION	38
DATE OF EXECUTION	Tuesday, 19th March, 1912
PLACE OF EXECUTION	Knutsford
HANGMAN	John Ellis
ASSISTANT	Albert Lumb
DATE OF TRIAL	28th February, 1912
LOCATION OF TRIAL	Chester
PRESIDING JUDGE	Mister Justice Coleridge
PROSECUTION COUNSEL	T. Artemus Jones, R. Sutton
DEFENCE COUNSEL	T.H. Parry
NUMBER OF VICTIMS	1

VICTIMS DETAILS	
NAME	Hilda Mary Josephine Williams
AGE	39
DATE OF MURDER	Sunday, 10th December, 1911
PLACE OF MURDER	Price's Lane, Birkenhead
METHOD OF KILLING	Cut throat
RELATIONSHIP TO KILLER	Wife

WHEN FRANK ERNEST Vonderache called at 63 Tollington Park to see his cousin Eliza Barrow, he was dumbfounded to hear that she was dead and buried. Frank demanded to see the owner of the house where Eliza had lodged, Frederick Henry Seddon, but was told that Mister Seddon was not available. Determined to find out exactly what had happened, Frank continued to call, and on the third occasion, finally managed to see Mister Seddon.

Frank was informed that Miss Barrow had died on September 14th and been buried on September 16th. What was perhaps even more of a shock was the discovery that all of Eliza Barrow's property now belonged to Frederick Seddon.

Eliza Barrow had been a woman of fairly substantial means. In addition to a large number of shares, she had also owned a public house, the Buck's Head and the barber shop next door. All this had apparently been signed over to Seddon in return for a yearly annuity. Now that Miss Barrow was dead, the annuity ceased to exist and Frederick Seddon had made a rather good investment. Frank Vonderache thought there might be more to this arrangement than at first met the eye, so he took his suspicions to the police.

Initial investigations showed that Eliza Barrow had first gone to live with the Seddons in late July 1910 and had agreed to pay Frederick Seddon 12/- a week for a number of rooms. Seddon was the district superintendent for the London and Manchester Assurance Company and was quite used to dealing with financial matters. According to Seddon, in March 1911, Miss Barrow had approached him about a number of her financial concerns and as a result of their discussions, Seddon agreed to an arrangement whereby Miss Barrow signed over the Buck's Head at Camden Town and the barber shop adjoining it, to him. In return he offered her £1 per week, for life.

This, though, was not the first time such a discussion had taken place. In October 1910, a block of India Stock had been transferred to Seddon in return for an annuity of £2-2s per week. When this stock was subsequently sold by Seddon, it realised £1,520 for him.

NAME	FREDERICK Henry Seddon
AGE AT EXECUTION	40
DATE OF EXECUTION	Thursday, 18th April, 1912
PLACE OF EXECUTION	Pentonville
HANGMAN	John Ellis
ASSISTANT	Thomas Pierrepoint
DATE OF TRIAL	4th March – 14th March, 1912
LOCATION OF TRIAL	Old Bailey
PRESIDING JUDGE	Mister Justice Bucknill
PROSECUTION COUNSEL	Richard D. Muir, S.A.T. Rowlatt, Travers Humphreys
DEFENCE COUNSEL	Edward Marshall Hall, Wellesley Orr, R. Dunstan
NUMBER OF VICTIMS	1

VICTIMS DETAILS	
NAME	Eliza Mary Barrow
AGE	50
DATE OF MURDER	Thursday, 14th September, 1911
PLACE OF MURDER	63 Tollington Park, Islington
METHOD OF KILLING	Poisoned (by arsenic)
RELATIONSHIP TO KILLER	None

With this money he purchased seven properties in Mile End, which brought him in some £200 per year.

In the summer of 1911, Seddon had acquired all Miss Barrow's property, which was now costing him some £3 a week. Obviously, the longer Miss Barrow lived, the more it would cost him. The corollary to this was that the sooner she died, the more profit Seddon would make from the deals.

Miss Barrow had first fallen ill on September 1st, 1911. The doctor was called and he attended a number of times before she died on September 14th. The cause of death was given as acute enteritis but now the police were convinced that Miss Barrow's death had proved to be much too convenient for Frederick Seddon.

On November 15th, 1911, Eliza Barrow's body was exhumed. Bernard Spilsbury performed the postmortem and determined that there were no signs of any disease that could account for Eliza Barrow's death. Further tests showed that the remains held more than two grains of arsenic and now, at last, the true cause of death had been determined. On December 4th, Seddon was arrested at his home and charged with the murder of Eliza Barrow.

There were perhaps four people in the Seddon household who could have administered poison to Miss Barrow. Two of these – the maid and Seddon's daughter – could be eliminated as they never prepared Miss Barrow's food. The other two – Seddon and his wife, Margaret Ann – did have the opportunity and in due course, on January 15th, 1912, Mrs Seddon was also arrested and faced the same charge as her husband.

A great deal of evidence was called against Frederick Seddon and his wife. It was shown that there had been arsenical fly papers in the house and these were the kind that had to be soaked in water. Mrs Seddon admitted that these had been scattered around Miss Barrow's room, at the old lady's request, and that just before Miss Barrow had died, these had all been placed in one large bowl, close to where Miss Barrow slept, implying perhaps that she might have drunk this liquid accidentally.

When the evidence had all been given, the jury were out for an hour before returning a not guilty verdict against Margaret Seddon and a guilty one against Frederick. In passing sentence, the judge, Mister Justice Bucknill, acknowledged that both he and the condemned man belonged to the same brotherhood – freemasonry. But however much the learned judge may have regretted it, he nevertheless passed the sentence of death by hanging.

There was, however, one other person who could have administered the poison. And that was Eliza Barrow herself.

Medical evidence had been given that the fatal dose of arsenic was most probably given in one large quantity some two to three days before Eliza Barrow died. However, before she was buried, Frederick Seddon asked the undertaker to cut off a lock of Miss Barrow's hair. When this was tested, it was shown to contain arsenic and normally this is an indication of the taking of arsenic over a considerable time. It may well have been that

Seddon himself was administering the poison over a long period, but if he had planned the crime, negotiated the appropriation of Miss Barrow's property so carefully and thought things through so well, why had he also not had the intelligence to destroy the evidence by having Miss Barrow cremated?

What is certainly true is that before he was executed on April 18th, 1912, Frederick Seddon wrote one last letter to his sister, and in that letter, he still maintained that he was an innocent man.

IT WAS A short-lived affair. Arthur Birkett had been walking out with fellow mill worker Alice Beetham for just five weeks when she ended the relationship on May 16th, 1912. Within a week, she was dead, murdered by the man who loved and wanted her so much.

Other workers knew all about the way Arthur felt about Alice, so they saw no cause for alarm when he approached her in the weft room at the Jubilee Mill. He said something to her and she appeared to ignore him and walk away. Arthur bounded after her, threw his arm around her and pulled her head back. People laughed at the antics of the two lovebirds, thinking that he was trying to steal a kiss from a reluctant and shy maiden, but the laughter died in their throats as they saw the deep red blood spurt from Alice's neck.

Even before the dumbstruck witnesses could move, Arthur had turned the razor upon himself and inflicted two severe cuts in his own neck. He fell by Alice's side and at last people were galvanised into action.

Alice was barely alive and would die before she could be taken to hospital. Arthur's wounds, though not much less severe, did not prove fatal and he was placed onto a cart in preparation for his removal to the infirmary. Those who had seen what had happened crowded around and someone asked him why he had done this terrible thing. Though pale and weak, Arthur managed to mumble that she had thrown him over and he wanted no other woman but her.

The first policeman on the scene was Constable Walter Eddleston. There were many witnesses and all told much the same story. At the trial, which took place in July, Susie Tattersall, Edith Rimmer, John Edward Dewhurst, Edward Partington and others all stated that Arthur had killed the woman he adored. There could be no doubt as to the jury's verdict and after sentence of death was pronounced, Arthur Birkett had to be carried back to the cells.

Although the death of Alice Beetham had been a cruel and unnecessary one, there was much public sympathy for the broken-hearted man who had taken her life. A petition was organised for Arthur's reprieve and it

NAME	Arthur Birkett
AGE AT EXECUTION	22
DATE OF EXECUTION	Tuesday, 23rd July, 1912
PLACE OF EXECUTION	Manchester
HANGMAN	John Ellis
ASSISTANT	Albert Lumb
DATE OF TRIAL	5th July, 1912
LOCATION OF TRIAL	Manchester
PRESIDING JUDGE	Mister Justice Bucknill
PROSECUTION COUNSEL	Gordon Hewart, A.R. Kennedy
DEFENCE COUNSEL	H. Lindon Riley
NUMBER OF VICTIMS	1

VICTIMS DETAILS	
NAME	Alice Beetham
AGE	18
DATE OF MURDER	Monday, 20th May, 1912
PLACE OF MURDER	Jubilee Mill, Gate Street, Blackburn
METHOD OF KILLING	Cut throat
RELATIONSHIP TO KILLER	Ex-girlfriend

gathered over 60,000 signatures in just four days. Even the dead girl's mother signed, and later visited Birkett in Strangeways prison, to show that she had forgiven him. Birkett's own mother even went so far as to write directly to Queen Mary, asking her to intercede, but all she received in reply was a standard letter informing her that the request had been forwarded to the Home Office.

Unfortunately for Arthur Birkett, all these efforts came to nothing and he faced the hangman on July 23rd, 1912. He was within four days of his 23rd birthday.

ROSE PHILP HAD been married to her husband, Sargent, for 11 years and had borne him six children, five of whom were still alive, their ages ranging from nine years to seven months. They were content until Sargent lost his right eye in an accident at work. Employees had little or no legal protection in these unenlightened days and Sargent was dismissed.

Rose put up with the financial loss for some time, but eventually she had had enough and in June, 1912, she took the youngest child and moved in with her sister, Alice Hawkins, at 31 Morby Road, London.

On July 8th, a separation order was taken out by Rose. After the hearing, Sargent made a desperate attempt to get his wife to return to him but she would only reply: "What is the use when you have no home?" Exactly one week later, Sargent turned up at Alice Hawkins's house and left the other four children with his wife.

Things quietened down until July 25th, when Sargent again turned up at Alice's house in Morby Road. In addition to the two sisters, their mother, Mrs Keighley, also lived in the house and it was she who had to tell Sargent that his wife was not in, and put up with his verbal abuse and threats. His parting shot was that he would rather swing than pay money under the separation order.

The following day, at 11.30am, Sargent was back at Morby Road. This time Rose was at home and Sargent excitedly told her that he had obtained a new job and was due to start work on Monday. Once again he asked her to come back to him, but once again, Rose said she would only do so when he had a house for them. That was the final straw. Sargent drew a knife and attacked Rose.

Rose, though wounded, managed to run down the steps of number 31 and gained entrance to Mary Hollis's house at number 29. Unfortunately, her escape was only to be a temporary one. Sargent had followed her and it was in the kitchen of Mary's house that Sargent cut Rose's throat.

Rose's screams attracted a great deal of attention. As Sargent turned the knife upon himself and moved as if to cut his own throat, two more neighbours, Thomas John

NAME	Sargent Philp
AGE AT EXECUTION	33
DATE OF EXECUTION	Tuesday, 1st October, 1912
PLACE OF EXECUTION	Wandsworth
HANGMAN	John Ellis
ASSISTANT	Thomas Pierrepoint
DATE OF TRIAL	12th September, 1912
LOCATION OF TRIAL	Old Bailey
PRESIDING JUDGE	Mister Justice Lush
PROSECUTION COUNSEL	Mister Bodkin, Travers Humphreys
DEFENCE COUNSEL	Curtis Bennett
NUMBER OF VICTIMS	1

VICTIMS DETAILS	
NAME	Rose Philp
AGE	35
DATE OF MURDER	Friday 26th July, 1912
PLACE OF MURDER	31 Morby Road, Old Kent Road, London
METHOD OF KILLING	Cut throat
RELATIONSHIP TO KILLER	Wife

Langridge from number 40 and John Reeves from number 29, threw themselves upon him and tore the weapon from his grasp. As they grappled with Sargent, Rose's mother walked down the street and seeing her, Sargent shouted: "I told you what I would do, and I have done it."

The trial was a short affair. With so many witnesses, Sargent's only hope was to try to plead that he was insane and not responsible for his actions. He failed in that attempt.

MINNIE MORRIS ENJOYED life and did not see any reason why she should tie herself to one man. A Londoner, she was in Norfolk for the fruit picking, as was William Tucker, another Londoner. Minnie and William saw each other two or three times a week but Minnie was also seeing a local man, Robert Galloway, and he felt that she should be faithful to him.

A sign of things to come occurred one day at the Black Bear Inn. Minnie was enjoying a drink with Tucker when Galloway came in and asked her to go out with him. His advances were repelled and Galloway threatened both Minnie and Tucker before he stormed out.

On July 16th, 1912, Galloway and Minnie were again in the Black Bear, leaving together at 2.00pm, when they were seen walking off towards Lynn, by George Pilmby, the son of the licensee.

Some time between 2.00pm and 3.00pm, Bertie Robert Ash was cycling down Burrett Lane when he saw a man and a woman lying together by the side of the road. The man was on top of the woman and appeared to have one hand on either her mouth or her breast. Ash was not one to pry, and cycled on his way. Around 15 minutes later, Ash was cycling back the other way. The woman was now alone and with a cap draped over her face. Thinking she was asleep, Ash cycled home.

Meanwhile, Galloway had visited the Bell public house and then moved on to the Black Bear again. Here he wrote his name on a slip of paper and handed it over to Francis Pilmby, saying somewhat mysteriously that it might be useful to him in the future. Later he did the same with an envelope, giving it to a man named Thomas Peake and telling him that it might be worth £3 soon and that he would see him at the Assizes. He then walked to Wisbech, where he went up to police Sergeant Jacobs and confessed that he had strangled a woman on the Lynn road.

At his trial, Galloway claimed that the motive was one of jealousy but said he had no recollection of the crime, due to being drunk at the time. However, he had

NAME	Robert Galloway
AGE AT EXECUTION	27
DATE OF EXECUTION	Tuesday, 5th November, 1912
PLACE OF EXECUTION	Norwich
HANGMAN	Thomas Pierrepoint
ASSISTANT	George Brown
DATE OF TRIAL	19th October, 1912
LOCATION OF TRIAL	Norwich
PRESIDING JUDGE	Mister Justice Darling
PROSECUTION COUNSEL	F.T. Henle, J.I. Macpherson
DEFENCE COUNSEL	H. Lancaster
NUMBER OF VICTIMS	1

VICTIMS DETAILS	
NAME	Minnie Morris
AGE	21
DATE OF MURDER	Tuesday, 16th July, 1912
PLACE OF MURDER	Burrett Lane, Walsoken
METHOD OF KILLING	Strangled
RELATIONSHIP TO KILLER	Girlfriend

previously made a full statement to the police detailing exactly how he had committed the crime. It took the jury five minutes to decide that Galloway was guilty as charged.

GILBERT SMITH HAD served his country well in the Boer War, and other campaigns. He had been awarded medals and when he was discharged in November, 1906, his conduct had been noted as good. The following year, he married Rosabella and although they were to have no children, they seemed happy enough to begin with.

By late May, 1912, the couple had drifted apart to such an extent that Rosabella felt constrained to leave her husband and move in with her neighbours, Mr and Mrs Brown. Of course, the newly separated couple saw each other from time to time, but little passed between them.

Saturday July 20th was the day of the Dursley Fete and it was in the refreshment tent that Gilbert and Rosabella were seen in conversation together. They must not have been happy words they exchanged, for later, Rosabella would report that Gilbert had threatened her life.

Rosabella must have taken the threats seriously, for the following morning, as she headed off alone to visit the workhouse, she saw Gilbert waiting at the end of the lane. Although it was only 7.30am, Rosabella returned to her lodgings and asked Harold Brown to accompany her at least part of the way. The two left together and walked towards Smith.

As they came level with Gilbert, he looked up at Harold Brown and told him that he could not allow Rosabella to pass. Her heart no doubt thumping in her chest, fearful of what her husband might do, Rosabella bravely walked on, not daring to look back in case Gilbert Smith was coming up behind.

Rosabella had gone some 30 yards and perhaps had begun to relax a little when suddenly Gilbert threw his arm around her neck, drew out a razor and cut his wife's throat. Harold Brown struck Gilbert as hard as he could but he could see that it was too late for poor Rosabella. As Brown ran off to fetch help, Gilbert Smith calmly walked away.

Harold Brown was not away for very long but when he did return, the first thing he heard was a low groan which seemed to come from a clump of trees. Gingerly walking over to investigate, Brown found Gilbert

NAME	Gilbert Oswald Smith
AGE AT EXECUTION	35
DATE OF EXECUTION	Tuesday, 26th November, 1912
PLACE OF EXECUTION	Gloucester
HANGMAN	Thomas Pierrepoint
ASSISTANT	Albert Lumb
DATE OF TRIAL	28th October, 1912
LOCATION OF TRIAL	Gloucester
PRESIDING JUDGE	Mister Justice Ridley
PROSECUTION COUNSEL	Mister Sturges, Mister Montefiore Brice
DEFENCE COUNSEL	H. McKenna
NUMBER OF VICTIMS	1

VICTIMS DETAILS	
NAME	Rosabella Smith
AGE	30
DATE OF MURDER	Sunday, 21st July, 1912
PLACE OF MURDER	Rockstowes, Dursley
METHOD OF KILLING	Cut throat
RELATIONSHIP TO KILLER	Wife

Smith, his throat badly cut. He would later recover in the infirmary.

Smith could hardly deny his guilt, though he did try to blame Rosabella's sister for coming between him and his wife and an attempt was made to show that he suffered from epilepsy which had been made worse when he had once served in the heat of India.

Found guilty and sentenced according to law, Gilbert Smith had the distinction of being the first man to die on Gloucester prison's new indoor gallows.

ETHEL KING AND her friend, Mrs Walford, were walking down Abbey Lane in West Ham, London, on the evening of September 12th, 1912. As they reached one of the more secluded parts of the lane, they passed what they assumed was a courting couple. It was only when they had gone some way past the young lovers, that a blood-curdling scream rang out.

Ethel King and her friend turned and gazed back towards the couple they had passed but moments before. The girl was now lying on the ground and the man was in the process of falling. Something shiny fell by his side and to their horror the man crawled slowly forward, a gaping wound in his throat, until he managed to drag himself close to the woman and put his arm around her waist.

The young woman, Clara Carter, was dead, her throat gashed. The man, William Beal, was rushed to hospital where he began slowly to recover from his wounds. It was there that he was interviewed by the police on October 2nd, 1912.

Beal's story was that Clara, his girlfriend, had attacked him. He related that they had been walking together when he suddenly felt something sharp sticking in his leg. It was later to transpire that this was where Beal kept his cut-throat razor and he maintained that Clara had removed this from his pocket, slashed his throat and then cut her own. He went on to say that she had tried to kill him twice before – once with a ginger beer bottle and once with a hat pin. On this occasion he remembered falling to the ground and then nothing more until he woke up in hospital.

The problem for Beal was that the evidence of Edith King and Mrs Walford did not confirm his story. When they looked around, the woman was already on the ground and Beal was just collapsing. Surely if she had attacked him, he would have fallen first. There was also the fact that they said they had seen the razor fall from his side, not Clara's. Beal was arrested and charged with murder.

Both counsel at the trial used the same explanation for what had happened. The prosecution claimed that Beal was jealous of Clara and had therefore killed her. The

NAME	William Charles Adolphus Beal
AGE AT EXECUTION	20
DATE OF EXECUTION	Tuesday, 10th December, 1912
PLACE OF EXECUTION	Chelmsford
HANGMAN	John Ellis
ASSISTANT	Not known
DATE OF TRIAL	11th November, 1912
LOCATION OF TRIAL	Old Bailey
PRESIDING JUDGE	Mister Justice Phillimore
PROSECUTION COUNSEL	Mister Bodkin, Cecil Whiteley
DEFENCE COUNSEL	Lister Drummond
NUMBER OF VICTIMS	1

VICTIMS DETAILS	
NAME	Clara Elizabeth Carter
AGE	17
DATE OF MURDER	Thursday, 12th September, 1912
PLACE OF MURDER	Abbey Lane, Stratford, West Ham
METHOD OF KILLING	Cut throat
RELATIONSHIP TO KILLER	Girlfriend

defence agreed that jealousy was the motive but they held that it was Clara who was jealous of Beal and so it was she who had attacked him.

In addition to the testimony of Edith King and her friend, Doctor Montgomery Paton also gave evidence. In his opinion, it was highly improbable that the wounds on Clara's throat were self-inflicted, whereas those on Beal's probably were. The defence collapsed and after an absence of about an hour, the jury found Beal guilty but with a strong recommendation to mercy because of his youth.

ALFRED LAWRENCE HAD lodged with Emily Hubbard and her husband for 11 years. It was a pleasant arrangement for Lawrence, a sailor, because he was also Mrs Hubbard's lover.

On May 25th, 1912, Lawrence went back to sea. Soon afterwards, he noticed a rather embarrassing problem and when he went to see the ship's doctor, was horrified to find that he was suffering from syphilis. At the end of July, Lawrence came home from sea and, returning to his lodgings, made it his business to talk to Emily about what the doctor had said. Emily went to see her own doctor on August 1st.

Eleven days later, the next bombshell hit Alfred Lawrence when a letter arrived from his employers, the Union Castle Steamship Company, terminating his employment as he was medically unfit. Three days later, Emily Hubbard visited her doctor again and discovered that she also had syphilis.

On August 19th, Lawrence arrived home at lunchtime and asked Emily's daughter, 12-year-old Charlotte, to fetch him a bottle of beer. This she did and was rewarded with a halfpenny. In the meantime, Emily had told a neighbour, Fanny Potter, that she was going upstairs for a lie down.

Speaking quietly to Charlotte, Lawrence told her to go outside and play. Charlotte was happy to oblige but after being outside for a few minutes she heard the sound of breaking glass.

Looking up, Charlotte saw that Lawrence had broken the bedroom window by thrusting his hand through it. As she gazed wide-eyed at this scene, Lawrence called out: "Come and see what I have done to your mother!"

In fact, Lawrence had battered Emily with a coal hammer and then cut her throat five times. Then, going to his own room, he had slashed his own throat before shoving his arm through the window. Prompt medical attention saved his life but Emily was beyond all help.

A police search of the house revealed a note written by Lawrence: "I have done this for a woman's honour. If you want any information ask her husband." At the hospital, Lawrence expanded on this by stating that he

NAME	Alfred John Lawrence
AGE AT EXECUTION	32
DATE OF EXECUTION	Wednesday, 18th December, 1912
PLACE OF EXECUTION	Maidstone
HANGMAN	John Ellis
ASSISTANT	William Willis
DATE OF TRIAL	27th November, 1912
LOCATION OF TRIAL	Maidstone
PRESIDING JUDGE	Mister Justice Channell
PROSECUTION COUNSEL	Theobald Mathew, Mister Shaw
DEFENCE COUNSEL	Mister Thesiger
NUMBER OF VICTIMS	1

VICTIMS DETAILS	
NAME	Emily Violet Hubbard
AGE	47
DATE OF MURDER	Monday, 19th August, 1912
PLACE OF MURDER	Portland Place, Dover
METHOD OF KILLING	Cut throat/battered
RELATIONSHIP TO KILLER	Girlfriend

had found Emily with the other lodger and he had killed her because she would not seek treatment for the disease she had given him. Her husband knew all about the problem and he had told her not to go to the hospital, so as far as Lawrence was concerned it was all her husband's fault.

At his trial, Lawrence claimed to have no knowledge of the crime or of writing the note. An attempt was made to suggest that since syphilis could cause madness, it was possible that he had been insane at the time through some kind of fit, even though he appeared to be perfectly lucid now.

The jury took 15 minutes to reject that defence.

ON APRIL 9TH, 1912, William Galbraith married Mary Kirby and the happy couple went to live with Mary's parents, Elizabeth and William Kirby, at 39 North Ormesby Road, Middlesborough. They seemed to be totally devoted to each other and in July, when William suggested that they should live with his mother instead, Mary readily agreed.

That same month, William and Mary moved to Duncan Street, Stockton where they remained together until August 3rd. On that day, possibly due to a disagreement between Mary and her mother-in-law, Mary returned to Middlesborough.

The split made William very unhappy and he entreated a neighbour, Elizabeth Hepponstall, to beg Mary to return to him. By now though, William was out of work and Mary declined his offer. This affected William so much that he made up his mind that if he could not have his wife, he would kill her.

On August 12th, William visited his wife at Middlesborough and was granted permission to stay there. The couple were very friendly towards each other that first day but on Tuesday, the 13th, they quarrelled yet again about her refusal to return to him.

That night, before they retired for the night, William asked his mother-in-law, Elizabeth, to call him very early the next morning, as he wished to return to Stockton.

Elizabeth Kirby called William at 4.45am on August 14th, but she heard no reply. She tried again soon afterwards and once again there was no reply. Elizabeth assumed that William must have risen even earlier and already gone and so returned to her own bed. It was 6.00am before she heard her daughter shout for her and rushed to see what the problem was. The door was locked but William opened it and Elizabeth noticed that his hands were dripping in blood. William pushed past his mother-in-law, and left the house.

William made no attempt to escape. He walked straight to the nearest police station and gave himself up to Constable William Robinson. All he would say was that he blamed his own mother for the break-up between him and his wife.

NAME	William Wallace Galbraith
AGE AT EXECUTION	27
DATE OF EXECUTION	Friday, 20th December, 1912
PLACE OF EXECUTION	Wakefield
HANGMAN	Thomas Pierrepoint
ASSISTANT	William Willis
DATE OF TRIAL	20th November, 1912
LOCATION OF TRIAL	York
PRESIDING JUDGE	Mister Justice Pickford
PROSECUTION COUNSEL	C.F. Lowenthal, A.H. Marshall M.P.
DEFENCE COUNSEL	Rowan Hamilton
NUMBER OF VICTIMS	1

VICTIMS DETAILS	
NAME	Mary May Galbraith
AGE	20
DATE OF MURDER	Wednesday, 14th August, 1912
PLACE OF MURDER	39 North Ormesby Road, Middlesborough
METHOD OF KILLING	Cut throat
RELATIONSHIP TO KILLER	Wife

There could be little doubt that the crime was premeditated. At the trial, John Bevis Laidler gave evidence that on the night before the killing of Mary, Galbraith had been with him and others in the Brunswick Hotel, Stockton. At one stage, Galbraith had bought him a drink adding that it would be the last John would ever have with him and he would read astounding headlines in the newspapers in the days to come. About that at least, Galbraith was certainly correct.

THE ENCYCLOPAEDIA OF EXECUTIONS

AT ABOUT 6.30PM on Friday, September 6th, 1912, Edward Gifford, the local gamekeeper was making his way home through the lower reaches of Buckland Hill Wood at Wadhurst when he heard a scream.

Heading up the hill, Gifford saw two people lying on the grass. He demanded that they come out and tell him what was going on. The man came out immediately but the other figure, whom Gifford took to be a woman, remained where she was.

Gifford recognised the man as a local, though he did not know his name. He gave no real explanation as to what he and the woman were doing and Gifford decided to speak to the woman and ask her what had caused her to scream. As he went deeper into the woods, the man walked off and then Gifford saw why. The 'woman' was a 10-year-old girl and she had been murdered.

At this point, two other local men came into the wood and Gifford sent one of them for the police. When the constable arrived, Gifford was able to give a good description of the man he had seen. The description fitted Albert Rumens.

The girl was identified as Mabel Ann Maryan who had celebrated her 10th birthday just five days before. Her mother, Sarah, told police that Mabel Ann had gone out looking for blackberries and close by her body was found a small can with a few scant berries inside. Further investigations revealed that Rumens had been seen entering the woods with the girl. William Chapman, also 10 years old, had been speaking to Mabel when Rumens had come up and started speaking to her. At 8.00pm, Rumens had even been to the murdered girl's house, next door but one to his own, and told the girl's mother that he had been in the woods with her.

At 8.30pm, Rumens was seen at the local pub by John Manktelow, where he announced that people were saying he had killed Mabel. He was arrested there moments later and picked out from six others by Gifford as the man he had seen in the woods.

There could be little defence for what Rumens had done and he was soon

NAME	Albert Rumens
AGE AT EXECUTION	44
DATE OF EXECUTION	Tuesday, 7th January, 1913
PLACE OF EXECUTION	Lewes
HANGMAN	John Ellis
ASSISTANT	Henry Pierrepoint
DATE OF TRIAL	16th December, 1912
LOCATION OF TRIAL	Lewes
PRESIDING JUDGE	Mister Justice Channell
PROSECUTION COUNSEL	C.F. Gill, Theobold Mathews
DEFENCE COUNSEL	Sutherland Graeme
NUMBER OF VICTIMS	1

VICTIMS DETAILS

NAME	Mabel Ann Maryan
AGE	10
DATE OF MURDER	Friday, 6th September, 1912
PLACE OF MURDER	Buckland Hill Wood, Wadhurst
METHOD OF KILLING	Asphyxiated
RELATIONSHIP TO KILLER	None

sentenced to death. On January 7th, 1913, Rumens became the first man to be executed at Lewes since 1892.

THE HORSE-DRAWN CARRIAGE called for Countess Sztaray and she was pleased to see that it was David Potter, a cabbie she knew well. The horse stepped out but before they had gone very far, Potter asked the Countess who the man was on the balcony over the veranda. The Countess was horrified. There was only one possible explanation: a burglar. Potter was instructed to turn the cab round and head back to 6 South Cliff Avenue, so that the police could be called.

Inspector Arthur Walls was on the scene within minutes. He saw the head and shoulders of a man, just where Potter had said he was, and called for him to come down and identify himself. The reply was a shot that hit Walls above his heart. A second shot rang out and Inspector Walls was dead. The assassin ran off into the surrounding streets and escaped. The only clue was a hat that he had lost in the excitement.

An immediate police cordon was thrown around the town. The station was watched and officers had instructions to look for anyone behaving suspiciously. The break-through came on the very next day.

George Mackay, using the name John Williams, was in Eastbourne with his girlfriend, Florence Seymour. They had originally lodged at Bolton Road but on the day of the murder had moved to 4 Tideswell Road where they had registered as Mr and Mrs Sinclair, using yet another false name. On November 10th, a hurried telegram was sent off to John's brother, who headed south from London, meeting a friend, Edgar Power, on the way.

Power realised what was going on and asked John Williams straight out if he had committed the murder. He, of course, denied the fact, but Florence had already seen Williams break up a revolver and bury it on the beach. The 'Williams' brothers headed off to London whilst Power and Florence saw them off on the train.

Police officers thought that it was worth following Power and his lady friend and were soon puzzled to see them scrabbling about on the beach, apparently searching for something. They were taken in for questioning and revealed what they thought

NAME	George Mackay (John Williams)
AGE AT EXECUTION	29
DATE OF EXECUTION	Wednesday, 29th January, 1913
PLACE OF EXECUTION	Lewes
HANGMAN	John Ellis
ASSISTANT	William Willis
DATE OF TRIAL	12th December – 14th December, 1912
LOCATION OF TRIAL	Lewes
PRESIDING JUDGE	Mister Justice Channell
PROSECUTION COUNSEL	Sir Frederick Lowe M.P., Cecil Whiteley
DEFENCE COUNSEL	Patrick Hastings, C.F. Baker
NUMBER OF VICTIMS	1

VICTIMS DETAILS	
NAME	Arthur Walls
AGE	44
DATE OF MURDER	Wednesday, 9th October, 1912
PLACE OF MURDER	6 South Cliff Avenue, Eastbourne
METHOD OF KILLING	Shot
RELATIONSHIP TO KILLER	None

John Williams might have done. Late that night, police officers returned to the beach and after much searching, found the murder weapon. Colleagues in London picked up John Williams the following day.

Williams did not have very much of a defence. He asked the police if they really believed he would have the effrontery to catch a train from Eastbourne, when the station was full of plain-clothes officers, if he had killed Inspector Walls. The police, of course, believed that this was exactly what he had done and once he had been linked to the weapon, there was little chance of him escaping his fate.

AS CHARLES MATTHEWS drove his two passengers towards Fenchurch Street station, he suddenly heard three loud reports and a scream from the woman in the back. Thinking that he had had a burst tyre, Matthews pulled into the kerb. Almost immediately the cab door opened and the woman fell into his arms, shouting that she had been shot.

As Matthews and a couple of passers-by tendered assistance, two more shots rang out. The male passenger had just shot himself in the right temple.

The woman, Florence Alice Bernadette Silles, a music-hall artiste who went by the stage name of Flo Dudley, had married in March 1906, her husband dying in April 1907. Florence had then become an actress and when she met Edward Hopwood in May 1912, he made it clear that he did not approve of her career.

Hopwood, the male passenger in the taxi cab, ran his own company, Commerce Limited. He claimed that he had plenty of money, was a single man and would support Florence. In fact, he was married with three children and was in severe financial difficulties.

On September 13th, 1912, Florence's sister, Annie Bland, of 65 Balfour Road, Ilford, received a letter addressed to Hopwood. He had used her address for mail, but this was from a solicitor. She opened the envelope and read with dismay that Hopwood had been bouncing cheques. Four days later, when faced with this revelation, he stuttered that it was all a misunderstanding and blamed his company secretary, John Travers Hosgood.

On September 26th, Hopwood purchased a gun in Brighton. Two days later, he shot Florence, and himself, in the back of Charles Matthews's taxi cab.

At Hopwood's trial, the events of September 28th were reconstructed. At 10.20pm, Hopwood and Florence had met in the Holborn Viaduct Hotel. Nothing of their conversation was known except that the waiter, George Alfred Warren heard Hopwood say that he "had done it for the best".

Leaving the hotel, Hopwood hailed a cab and asked the driver, Matthews, to take them

NAME	Edward Hopwood
AGE AT EXECUTION	45
DATE OF EXECUTION	Wednesday, 29th January, 1913
PLACE OF EXECUTION	Pentonville
HANGMAN	Thomas Pierrepoint
ASSISTANT	Albert Lumb
DATE OF TRIAL	9th December – 11th December, 1912
LOCATION OF TRIAL	Old Bailey
PRESIDING JUDGE	Mister Justice Avory
PROSECUTION COUNSEL	Richard D. Muir, Percival Clarke
DEFENCE COUNSEL	Defended himself
NUMBER OF VICTIMS	1

VICTIMS DETAILS

NAME	Florence Alice Bernadette Silles (Flo Dudley)
AGE	34
DATE OF MURDER	Saturday, 28th September, 1912
PLACE OF MURDER	In a taxi-cab, Fenchurch Street, London
METHOD OF KILLING	Shot
RELATIONSHIP TO KILLER	Girlfriend

to Fenchurch Street. As they approached the station, the shots were heard and Florence Silles lost her life.

Hopwood did not deny killing Florence but said that it had been an accident. He stated that, in the back of the cab, he had asked her if they were to part. When she said that she thought it best, he drew the gun from his pocket and tried to shoot himself. Florence grabbed at the weapon, whereupon it went off accidentally and a bullet struck her in the head. Whilst medical opinion agreed that Florence's head wound was consistent with such a story, the fatal wound had been one in one of Florence's lungs. Hopwood explained that by saying that as he gripped the gun in panic, it continued to fire.

The jury were not convinced.

0903

ANNIE WENTWORTH WAS working at Cotton Hall House for the second time. Her first period of employment had ended in December 1907, but she had returned in August 1912. During that time, Annie had become friendly with another servant, Edith Alice Armstrong, and one of the things she told Edith about was her boyfriend, Eric James Sedgewick.

Annie had first met Eric in January, 1908. He had served in the army and received a good discharge. Annie, though, had seen another side to his character.

Eric had something of a temper. In October 1912, he had come down from London to see Annie, having first sent her a telegram telling her where to meet him. Annie couldn't leave the house, so was unable to make the appointment. Hours later, Sedgewick turned up at Cotton Hall House in a temper.

During November, something happened that caused Annie to break off the relationship. Eric travelled to Eton on November 10th and had gone out with Annie at 8.00pm. Later Annie seemed to be very subdued. Eric travelled back to London and the following morning, Annie told Edith that he had said something "… which will worry me until my grave".

Although Annie did not tell Edith what this terrible secret was, it can be deduced from the correspondence between them, held in the files at the Public Record Office. Annie, it seems, had 'surrendered herself' to Eric. On the evening of November 10th, Eric had confessed that he had been unfaithful to her. Annie wrote to Eric telling him that all was over between them. She never wanted to see him again.

Eric tried his best to explain. He wrote to her on November 19th, saying that he loved her dearly. She replied on November 23rd, repeating what she had said before.

Eric travelled to Eton on November 24th, arriving at 3.50pm. Edith answered the door to him and went to tell Annie that he had arrived. Annie begged Edith to go downstairs with her. Edith did as she asked but later left them alone in the servant's hall.

Edith busied herself in the kitchen. At one stage she went into the hall to fetch

NAME	Eric James Sedgewick
AGE AT EXECUTION	29
DATE OF EXECUTION	Tuesday, 4th February, 1913
PLACE OF EXECUTION	Reading
HANGMAN	John Ellis
ASSISTANT	George Brown
DATE OF TRIAL	15th January, 1913
LOCATION OF TRIAL	Aylesbury
PRESIDING JUDGE	Mister Justice Bankes
PROSECUTION COUNSEL	Sir Ryland Adkins M.P., Drysdale Woodcock
DEFENCE COUNSEL	Bernard Campion
NUMBER OF VICTIMS	1

VICTIMS DETAILS	
NAME	Annie Wentworth Davis
AGE	22
DATE OF MURDER	Sunday, 24th November, 1912
PLACE OF MURDER	Cotton Hall House, Eton Wick Road, Eton
METHOD OF KILLING	Stabbed
RELATIONSHIP TO KILLER	Girlfriend

something but for the most, she kept well away. Then, finally, Edith walked back into the hall and saw Annie, slumped in a chair, with blood pouring from a wound. Sedgewick was standing over her, trying to revive her and repeating: " She's not dead. She's not dead." Annie had been stabbed in the left breast. Eric was taken out of the way and was heard to cry; "For God's sake, can't somebody stop the bleeding?"

Found guilty of the murder of the woman he loved, Eric Sedgewick was hanged on February 4th, 1913. It was 11 years to the day since his discharge from the army.

ALTHOUGH GEORGE CUNLIFFE lived in Plymouth, he was in fact a native of Wigan. He had served in the Royal Navy and had taken his discharge in July, 1912. At about the same time, he got involved with a young lady named Kitty Butler and soon they began living together.

To begin with, things were fine between George and Kitty, but soon a gulf began to open between them and when George was arrested on Saturday November 2nd, and charged with being drunk and disorderly, Kitty refused to pay his fine with the result that he was sent to prison for five days. He, perhaps naturally, was absolutely furious.

Whilst he was serving his short sentence, Cunliffe complained to one of the prison guards about the treatment he had received at the hands of the woman he lived with. At first his only intention seemed to be revenge, but in due course, Cunliffe calmed down and finally decided that when he was released, he would go back home to Wigan.

George Cunliffe was released from jail on the morning of November 8th and arrived back home, at King Street, at about 11.00am. Kitty was entertaining one of her friends, Susan Gill and she heard George ask Kitty for some money. Kitty's immediate reply was to tell George that if he wanted money, he had better work for it and should go down to the docks, where he might find a job. In an instant, George was upon her, his hands gripping Kitty around the throat. Susan Gill ran for help but whilst she was away, George Cunliffe locked the door, took his razor and cut Kitty's throat. He then turned the razor upon himself, just as the police were arriving.

Once George recovered from his wounds, he was placed on trial before Mister Justice Coleridge, the main witness being Susan Gill. Found guilty of murder, Cunliffe was executed at Exeter on February 25th, 1913.

NAME	George Cunliffe
AGE AT EXECUTION	28
DATE OF EXECUTION	Tuesday, 25th February, 1913
PLACE OF EXECUTION	Exeter
HANGMAN	John Ellis
ASSISTANT	George Brown
DATE OF TRIAL	3rd February 1913
LOCATION OF TRIAL	Exeter
PRESIDING JUDGE	Mister Justice Coleridge
PROSECUTION COUNSEL	S.H. Emanuel, Mister McDonald
DEFENCE COUNSEL	R. Scoble Armstrong
NUMBER OF VICTIMS	1

VICTIMS DETAILS	
NAME	Kate (Kitty) Butler
AGE	26
DATE OF MURDER	Friday, 8th November, 1912
PLACE OF MURDER	72 King Street, Plymouth
METHOD OF KILLING	Cut throat
RELATIONSHIP TO KILLER	Girlfriend

0903

ON THE NIGHT of January 27th, 1913, Frederick Thomas Fry was on his way home. He walked down Lynmouth Road, Bristol, and turned into Mina Road. It was then that he saw the body of Ada James.

Ada's throat had been cut, but she was still conscious and spoke feebly to Fry, trying to tell him what had happened and gesturing towards a footpath at the end of the street. A few minutes later, at 9.35pm, Constable Parfitt came upon the scene and whilst they waited for the ambulance to arrive, Parfitt gave Ada some paper and a pencil. She wrote a brief note stating that she had been attacked by Edward Henry Palmer.

At about the same time that Ada was writing her note, Palmer was knocking on the door of a closed chemists shop at the junction of Warwick Road and Stapleton Road. The assistant, George Dodman, let Palmer in and served him with 2d worth of laudanum.

By 4.30am on January 28th, Palmer was knocking on the door of his uncle, Albert Blackmore, at 22 Bean Street. Palmer begged for water, saying that he had taken poison and later was arrested by Constable William Crook. When Palmer was searched, a letter was found, addressed to his mother. In part it read: "Forgive me and my dear girl for our trouble. It is all over now for ever. I cannot stand the disgrace any more."

Palmer readily admitted that he had killed Ada, but denied that it was murder. He explained that he had been unable to find work in Bristol and since he had once before worked in Canada, had announced to Ada his intention to return there. At the time they were on a pathway on Narroways Hill and hearing that he was leaving her, Ada took off the ring he had given her, threw it in his face and said that once he had gone, she would work on the streets again, as she had done before. Palmer asked Ada if she was serious and when she confirmed that she was, he attacked her and killed her.

Unfortunately for Palmer, evidence was called to show that on February 26th, he had tried to redeem a revolver he had pledged to a pawnbrokers. Since he did not have enough money for the ticket, he bought a razor instead, the same razor he would use on Ada

NAME	Edward Henry Palmer
AGE AT EXECUTION	23
DATE OF EXECUTION	Wednesday, 19th March, 1913
PLACE OF EXECUTION	Bristol
HANGMAN	Thomas Pierrepoint
ASSISTANT	George Brown
DATE OF TRIAL	19th February, 1913
LOCATION OF TRIAL	Bristol
PRESIDING JUDGE	Lord Justice Coleridge
PROSECUTION COUNSEL	S.H. Emmanuel, G.R. McDonald
DEFENCE COUNSEL	J.G. Trapnell
NUMBER OF VICTIMS	1

VICTIMS DETAILS	
NAME	Ada Louisa James (Died Tuesday, 28th January)
AGE	21
DATE OF MURDER	Monday, 27th January, 1913
PLACE OF MURDER	Narroways Hill Footpath, near Mina Road, Bristol
METHOD OF KILLING	Cut throat
RELATIONSHIP TO KILLER	Girlfriend

the following night. This implied that the crime was premeditated and was enough for the jury to find Palmer guilty of wilful murder.

THE CASE OF Walter Sykes was, to say the least, a very curious one.

On the evening of Friday, November 15th, 1912, a number of children had attended a singing class, in Kimberworth. When the class had finished, all the children returned home, except for two. Later, the bodies of the two cousins, Amy Collinson and Frances Nicholson were found in a field, with their throats cut. The eldest girl had also been raped.

It was natural that the police should talk to the rest of the children to ascertain if any of them had seen anyone talking to the two dead girls, after the rehearsal. One girl said that the previous week she had seen a man talking to Amy. She identified that man as Walter Sykes.

When he was interviewed, on December 29th, Sykes made a full confession to the double murder, using the most obscene language imaginable. He later made a more formal, written confession in which he said he had murdered the girls by means of a penknife but he had been drunk at the time. Subsequently, he withdrew both confessions and said he had had nothing to do with the deaths.

There was also a small amount of circumstantial evidence against Sykes. There were marks found near the scene of the crime that indicated the killer had worn corduroy trousers. Sykes had been wearing such a pair when he left work on the day of the murder and these had subsequently been thrown away onto Hemsworth Green, from where they were later recovered by the police. Sykes had also worn boots with protectors on them and other marks found near the bodies could have been made by such boots.

In custody awaiting trial, Sykes said that if the police would talk to his employer, Mister Gedney, he would be cleared of the charges against him. Gedney was interviewed, but was unable to account for Sykes's movements on November 15th, thus causing Sykes's alibi to collapse.

At the trial itself, the judge suggested that apart from the confession, there was no case against Sykes, who was, nevertheless, found guilty and condemned to death. At the appeal, it was claimed that the conviction was unsafe

NAME	Walter William Sykes
AGE AT EXECUTION	24
DATE OF EXECUTION	Wednesday, 23rd April, 1913
PLACE OF EXECUTION	Wakefield
HANGMAN	Thomas Pierrepoint
ASSISTANT	Albert Lumb
DATE OF TRIAL	10th March, 1913
LOCATION OF TRIAL	Leeds
PRESIDING JUDGE	Mister Commissioner Foote
PROSECUTION COUNSEL	C.F. Lowenthal, Willoughby Jardine
DEFENCE COUNSEL	L.G. Hoare
NUMBER OF VICTIMS	2

VICTIMS DETAILS	
NAME	Amy Collinson; Frances Alice Nicholson
AGE	10; 7
DATE OF MURDER	Friday, 15th November, 1912
PLACE OF MURDER	Abdy's Farm, Kimberworth
METHOD OF KILLING	Cut throat; cut throat
RELATIONSHIP TO KILLER	None; none

because it relied solely on the confession. It was held, though, that a man may be convicted on his own confession, even if he subsequently withdrew it, providing that the evidence points to the possibility that he could have committed the crime. In this case, the scant circumstantial evidence did back up Sykes's confessions and the verdict was allowed to stand.

0303

HAD IT NOT been for a couple of false teeth, William Walter Burton might well have got away with murder.

Winifred Mitchell was employed as a cook at Manor Farm, and had worked there since early in 1912. Mister Good, who owned the farm, also employed William Burton as a groom and gardener. Slowly the two servants grew closer together until William decided that the time was right to consummate the relationship.

Without doubt, Winifred resisted the blandishments of Burton for some considerable time. Letters were later found which made it quite plain that she had refused to succumb on more than one occasion and Burton had said that this meant she did not really love him after all. He persisted and eventually, some time in early 1913, Winifred surrendered her virginity to William Burton.

It is not known what happened exactly over the next few weeks, but one day in early March, Winifred went to Burton and told him that she believed she was pregnant. She had been sick repeatedly and surely that was one of the first signs? In more normal circumstances, perhaps Burton would have done the gentlemanly thing and offered to marry Winifred but there was one slight problem with that scenario: Burton was already married.

There were some discussions about Winifred and Burton running away together, but in reality he had no intention of leaving his wife. He had to find some other way to get Winifred and the unborn child out of his life and it seemed to him that a more permanent solution was called for.

On Monday, March 31st, Winifred left the farm at 3.00pm. Winifred Bailey, a fellow servant, saw Winifred cycling off towards the plantation woods. Earlier that afternoon, Burton had asked Leonard Mitcham if he could borrow his father's gun to shoot some rabbits in the wood. The two men went out shooting, finally parting at some time after 2.30pm. By 4.00pm, Burton was back at his duties and Winifred, it seemed, had vanished off the face of the earth.

In the past, Winifred had often said that one day she might go to live in London, or

NAME	William Walter Burton
AGE AT EXECUTION	29
DATE OF EXECUTION	Tuesday, 24th June, 1913
PLACE OF EXECUTION	Dorchester
HANGMAN	Thomas Pierrepoint
ASSISTANT	George Brown
DATE OF TRIAL	3rd June – 4th June, 1913
LOCATION OF TRIAL	Dorchester
PRESIDING JUDGE	Mister Justice Ridley
PROSECUTION COUNSEL	J. Alderson Foote, S.H. Emanuel
DEFENCE COUNSEL	J.G. Trapnell
NUMBER OF VICTIMS	1

VICTIMS DETAILS	
NAME	Winifred Mary Mitchell
AGE	23
DATE OF MURDER	Monday, 31st March, 1913
PLACE OF MURDER	Gussage St Michael, Dorset
METHOD OF KILLING	Shot
RELATIONSHIP TO KILLER	Girlfriend

even Canada, so there were no immediate searches for her. It was not even regarded as suspicious when later that night, Burton was seen riding her bicycle to her mother's house.

In due course, Burton called on Rose Mary Mitchell, Winifred's mother and asked her if she had received any news of her daughter. It was merely an attempt to keep up the pretence that he had no idea where she was and when Mrs Mitchell said she was now becoming concerned and thought it best to report the matter to the police, Burton agreed with her. The case had now become one of a missing person and gossip in the village became more pronounced.

On April 6th, George Gillingham was walking through the woods when he saw something white in the undergrowth. Looking closer he noticed that it was a partial denture with a couple of false teeth. George picked them up and put them in his pocket. Some time later, on April 30th, he handed them over to the police. Once the police had gone to the woods and been shown exactly where the teeth had been found, the story of their discovery filtered down to a group of small boys who recalled that this was very close to the spot where they had seen a large hole dug into the soil on the afternoon of Sunday, March 30th. They took their story to the police, who now mounted a full-scale search of the area.

The area where the boys had seen the hole was by now carefully camouflaged with a large bush, but the police poked around the area with long sticks. On May 2nd, one officer suddenly shouted that his stick had come up with some human hair attached to it. The soil around the spot was removed and there, lying face down, was the body of Winifred. She had been shot in the head.

It seemed that Winifred had met someone in the woods, by arrangement, and that this man had shot her close to where the false teeth had been discovered. Her body had then been dragged to the already prepared grave and buried, the area being covered with the flourishing bush, which served to hide the spot from prying eyes. It seemed as though there was only one man who could have had both opportunity and motive. William Burton was arrested.

From the moment of his arrest, the evidence piled up against Burton. He had been seen in the woods both before and after the disappearance of Winifred. Once the body had been found, Burton had tried to get Leonard Mitcham to lie about the times he had borrowed his father's gun. Frederick White said that he had seen Burton riding a woman's bicycle on the day Winifred disappeared. He had asked Burton about it and he had replied that it was Winnie's bike and he was taking it to her mother's. He added that Winnie had decided to go to Canada, a story that was now known to be false. Finally, Arthur Bush, who had been at school with Burton and was a lifelong friend, testified that Burton had admitted that he had made love to Winifred and now feared that she was pregnant.

Found guilty of murder, Burton made a full confession to the vicar of Gussage before the execution. The final irony, though, was that medical examination of Winifred's body had shown that although she was not a virgin, she was also not pregnant.

0903

THE RELATIONSHIP BETWEEN Henry Longden and Alice More, had become rather strained. They had been living together for some time, but lately he had constantly been finding fault with all she did. For Alice, the final straw came on March 16th, 1913, when Longden came home from work and complained that Alice had not lit the fire. The following day, she packed her bags and moved into fresh lodgings.

Had this merely been the story of an affair ending, we may well have never heard any more of Henry Longden, but, as far as Henry was concerned, Alice was involved with another man.

Alice worked for an organisation named the East and West Society of China, whose aim was to stimulate trade between England and the Far East. In the course of her work, Alice had met a gentleman named Silva, who ran a business supplying crockery. Henry Longden now convinced himself that there were much more than mere business contacts between Alice and Mr Silva.

On April 9th, Longden saw Alice with Mr Silva and went up to them to sort matters out. At one stage, he turned to Silva and accused him of having induced Alice to leave his home. Silva denied all knowledge of this and when this was confirmed by Alice herself, Longden turned to her and threatened that soon he would deal with her. On that score, Longden was to waste no time at all.

The next day, at 2.00pm, Alice was seen staggering down Taviton Street, a gaping wound in her throat. Walking behind her was the determined figure of Henry Longden, no doubt checking that he had done enough damage to ensure that Alice would not recover. Once he was satisfied, Longden turned a butcher's knife upon himself and slashed his own throat.

Whilst Alice did not survive her wounds, prompt medical attention managed to save Longden's life. Charged with murder, he appeared at the Old Bailey in June. His defence counsel made a brave attempt to save him, claiming that the crime was not premeditated and that he had suffered extreme provocation. The jury, although they

NAME	Henry Longden
AGE AT EXECUTION	52
DATE OF EXECUTION	Tuesday, 8th July, 1913
PLACE OF EXECUTION	Pentonville
HANGMAN	John Ellis
ASSISTANT	William Willis
DATE OF TRIAL	2nd June, 1913
LOCATION OF TRIAL	Old Bailey
PRESIDING JUDGE	Mister Justice Rowlatt
PROSECUTION COUNSEL	Mister Bodkin, E.C.P. Boyd
DEFENCE COUNSEL	T.C.P. Gibbons
NUMBER OF VICTIMS	1

VICTIMS DETAILS	
NAME	Alice Catlow More
AGE	27
DATE OF MURDER	Thursday, 10th April, 1913
PLACE OF MURDER	Taviton Street, Gordon Square, London
METHOD OF KILLING	Cut throat
RELATIONSHIP TO KILLER	Girlfriend

added a strong recommendation to mercy, returned a guilty verdict and Longden was sentenced to death.

THOMAS FLETCHER AND Lilian Wharton had set the date for their wedding and were due to be married on March 26th, 1913. It was then that Lilian's mother decided she had to intervene.

On the day before the wedding was to take place, Mrs Wharton took Thomas to one side and suggested that he postpone the ceremony as he was unable to provide a home for himself and his wife. Thomas was taken aback and suggested at one stage that perhaps they could still get married and then Lilian would live at home until he found them a house. Mrs Wharton was not to be moved, and the wedding was cancelled.

For some days, Thomas brooded over what had happened. He visited the public house where Lilian lived, a few times, but the more he spoke to Lilian, the more he realised that she was now thinking the same way as her mother and there was no sign of a new wedding date being set. It was then that Thomas took a fateful decision and visited a pawnbroker's at Dudley, where he purchased a gun.

At 10.00am on April 1st, 1913, Thomas Fletcher again visited the Fountain Inn, where he was served with two glasses of brandy by Lilian's mother. Then, when Mrs Wharton left the public bar to attend to some chore in the yard, leaving Thomas and Lilian alone, he made his move.

Mrs Wharton heard a shot ring out and as she turned, saw Lilian staggering towards her crying, "Tom has shot me." Lilian turned and walked out into the street, where she collapsed, as Mrs Wharton followed her, passing the still form of Thomas Fletcher lying on the bar room floor. It transpired that Lilian had been shot in the abdomen; she would die a week later. Thomas had shot himself in the face, and would lose an eye.

Put on trial for murder, the prosecution alleged that Thomas Fletcher had gone to the public house with the deliberate intention of killing Lilian and himself and was therefore guilty of murder. Fletcher, a patch over his right eye, contended that he had bought the gun for the sole purpose of killing himself. When he had been left alone with Lilian, he drew the gun and made to shoot himself. She

rushed forward and tried to pull the gun from his grasp and it must have gone off accidentally. He saw her move away from him and took the opportunity to shoot himself. He did not know until later that Lilian had been hit and had had no intention of shooting her, let alone killing her.

The jury were not convinced and Fletcher was sentenced to death.

NAME	Thomas Fletcher
AGE AT EXECUTION	28
DATE OF EXECUTION	Wednesday, 9th July, 1913
PLACE OF EXECUTION	Worcester
HANGMAN	John Ellis
ASSISTANT	Thomas Pierrepoint
DATE OF TRIAL	7th June, 1913
LOCATION OF TRIAL	Worcester
PRESIDING JUDGE	Mister Justice Bray
PROSECUTION COUNSEL	Mister Cranstoun, M. Bryce
DEFENCE COUNSEL	Reginald Coventry
NUMBER OF VICTIMS	1

VICTIMS DETAILS	
NAME	Lilian Wharton (Died Tuesday, 8th April)
AGE	21
DATE OF MURDER	Tuesday, 1st April, 1913
PLACE OF MURDER	Fountain Inn, Albion Street, Brades
METHOD OF KILLING	Shot
RELATIONSHIP TO KILLER	Girlfriend

0590

A N EVICTION NOTICE can be traumatic at the best of times, but the one served on John Vickers Amos ended up costing four lives, including his own.

Amos was the tenant of the Sun Inn at Bedlington, the licensee being a Mister James Woodirons. On April 15th, 1913, Mister Woodirons chose to make a call on his tenant and was not pleased at what he saw. The condition of the stock was not to Mister Woodirons's satisfaction and after some discussion with Amos, it was decided that he should be given one week's money in lieu of notice, and told to quit the public house immediately.

John Amos told Mister Woodirons in no uncertain terms that he had no intention of leaving, so when the licensee returned later in the day with the new tenants, Richard and Sarah Grice, he felt it prudent to take along Police Constable George Mussell.

Mister Woodirons, both Grices and George Mussell entered the Sun Inn and prepared to take over from John Amos. As extra back-up, Mister Woodirons had also taken along two of his employees, Mister Craigs and Mister Learmont, and whilst the police constable and Sarah Grice stayed upstairs, the rest began checking the stock in the cellar.

A shot suddenly rang out and Sarah Grice fell down the cellar steps. She had been shot in the head. John Amos had taken a Winchester gun from behind the bar and now pointed this at the police officer. Whilst Mussell was talking to Amos, the people in the cellar saw their opportunity and ran upstairs and out of the pub. As they did so, another shot rang out and Constable Mussell fell dead, shot in the neck.

One of the first police officers on the scene was Sergeant Andrew Barton. He walked calmly into the pub to talk to Amos, but he too was shot dead.

Quite a crowd had by now gathered outside the Sun Inn and Amos appeared at the doorway, with the gun, and challenged any of them to approach. At one stage he lit a cigarette and shouted that he wanted Woodiron, the owner, so that he could kill him. After half an hour of this stalemate,

NAME	John Vickers Amos
AGE AT EXECUTION	35
DATE OF EXECUTION	Tuesday, 22nd July, 1913
PLACE OF EXECUTION	Newcastle
HANGMAN	Thomas Pierrepoint
ASSISTANT	William Willis
DATE OF TRIAL	2nd July – 3rd July, 1913
LOCATION OF TRIAL	Newcastle
PRESIDING JUDGE	Mister Commissioner Harrison
PROSECUTION COUNSEL	Bruce Williamson, Willoughby Jardine
DEFENCE COUNSEL	W.J. Waugh, Leon Freedman
NUMBER OF VICTIMS	3

VICTIMS DETAILS	
NAME	Andrew Barton; George Bertram Mussell
AGE	40; 30
DATE OF MURDER	Tuesday, 15th April, 1913
PLACE OF MURDER	Sun Inn, Bedlington
METHOD OF KILLING	Shot; shot
RELATIONSHIP TO KILLER	None; none
NAME	Sarah Ellen Grice
AGE	33
DATE OF MURDER	Tuesday, 15th April, 1913
PLACE OF MURDER	Sun Inn, Bedlington
METHOD OF KILLING	Shot
RELATIONSHIP TO KILLER	None

Amos suddenly turned and made off over some fields, followed by police officers and some of the braver, or perhaps more foolhardy, civilians.

For three hours, the surrounding country-side was searched without success. Then, in a field a quarter of a mile from the scene of the three murders, footprints were seen going towards a large culvert, under Church Lane. The police called forward one of the local miners, Joseph Potter, who had his gun with him, and asked him to fire a shot into the drain. For a time nothing happened but then the police asked the miner to fire a second shot close to the culvert. This time, a figure came out of the drain. It was Amos, and he had been wounded in the head by the first shot. His gun was later recovered from inside the drain.

The only defence possible was one of insanity. Amos had once been a miner himself and evidence was called to show that in June 1912 he had been injured in an underground explosion that had killed two men. The very next month, he was involved in a second explosion that had killed eight men and as a result of these two experiences his health had suffered badly. He had trouble sleeping and his nerves were bad. He claimed to have no memory of the shooting or of hiding in the culvert later on.

The jury were not convinced. When it was shown that between Mister Woodirons giving Amos notice to quit and his return with the Grices, John Amos had sent his son, George, to buy a box of cartridges, it was plain that he had planned to use the gun to keep Woodiron and the rest at bay. They held that he was fully aware of what he was doing and returned a verdict of guilty of murder.

1903

THERE WERE SIGNS that the relationship between Frank Greening and Elizabeth Hearne was not all it should be. Perhaps the clearest of those signs manifested itself when Frank set fire to her.

March 20th saw Elizabeth visiting her friend, Edith Mumford, at 21 Ashley Street, Birmingham. After being there for a short time, Greening turned up. Shortly afterwards, Edith was called away by her mother and as she returned to the room, saw Greening leaving the house. In the room where Elizabeth had been left, Edith found the lamp smashed and Elizabeth's clothing on fire. Edith threw water over her friend, but Elizabeth still required medical treatment.

Just over two weeks later, Edith Mumford visited the Queen's Head pub, with her stepfather, Frederick West. She had not been there long when Elizabeth came in with Annie West, Edith's mother. Frank Greening was also with them but left when Frederick did.

A curious incident followed. Frederick West returned to the Queen's Head, bearing a postcard on which was written a pencilled message from Greening, threatening Elizabeth. After reading the card, Elizabeth and Edith left the pub, returning to Edith's house at 5 Back 115 Bissell Street.

Ida Ann Bolding also shared the house with Edith. At about 2.50pm, Frank Greening came in and an argument over a house key followed. At one point, Elizabeth remarked that she was "… not frightened of that shooter either". Greening smiled, drew out a revolver and fired three shots in Elizabeth's direction. Then Greening turned the gun onto Edith, and fired once at her.

Elizabeth Hearne had been hit in the stomach, thigh and shoulder. Edith had not been injured and would provide valuable testimony against Greening, as would Ida Bolding.

In fact, Greening had run to the house of Alfred and Clara Garrattley, a couple of friends who lived at 85 Lower Essex Street. At first he told them that Liz had met with an accident but then said that she was dead and he had shot her.

At 9.20pm, Detective Constable Henry Jones saw Greening in Claybrook Street and

NAME	Frank Greening
AGE AT EXECUTION	34
DATE OF EXECUTION	Wednesday, 13th August, 1913
PLACE OF EXECUTION	Birmingham
HANGMAN	Thomas Pierrepoint
ASSISTANT	George Brown
DATE OF TRIAL	14th July, 1913
LOCATION OF TRIAL	Birmingham
PRESIDING JUDGE	Mister Justice Atkin
PROSECUTION COUNSEL	Sir Ryland Adkins M.P., Mister Costello
DEFENCE COUNSEL	Richard A. Willes
NUMBER OF VICTIMS	1

VICTIMS DETAILS	
NAME	Elizabeth Ellen Hearne (Davies) (Died Monday, 7th April)
AGE	27
DATE OF MURDER	Sunday, 6th April, 1913
PLACE OF MURDER	5 Back 115 Bissell Street, Birmingham
METHOD OF KILLING	Shot
RELATIONSHIP TO KILLER	Girlfriend

ordered him to stand still. Greening was seen to reach underneath his coat and, knowing full well that he might be drawing out his gun, Henry Jones stood firm and shouted that he too might be armed. In fact Greening had already disposed of the revolver and was unarmed.

At his trial for murder, the testimony of the eye witnesses sealed Greening's fate, even though Elizabeth's own brother, George Pitt, gave evidence that his sister had a very sharp tongue.

THE ENCYCLOPAEDIA OF EXECUTIONS

JAMES RYDER WAS a drunkard who mistreated his wife, Elizabeth. By 1913, so bad had things become that on one of James's trips away, Elizabeth's sons, James and Jack, took the opportunity to move in secretly so that they could protect their mother.

On May 8th, James Ryder senior returned home, but seeing his two sons there, decided to leave. He returned the following day in order to pick up some things and, after some discussion, decided that he would stay.

Five days later, on May 13th, a postcard arrived for Elizabeth, bearing a cryptic message: it began "Dear L" and ended "Yours P." Ryder became suspicious and accused Elizabeth of having an affair. Elizabeth admitted that she was 'L' for Liz, but claimed that 'P' was Aunt Polly. This did not satisfy Ryder, because the woman who had allegedly sent the card was named Mary Martha Thomasson.

The following day, the arguments over the postcard continued. Soon after the row started, Jack returned to the house, followed at 11.45pm by Elizabeth's son, James. The sleeping arrangements at the Ryder household were somewhat unconventional. Elizabeth slept on a bed in the kitchen while the three men all slept in the one bedroom upstairs. The family retired for the night.

The next day, May 15th, both Elizabeth's sons were up by 5.00am and left for work soon afterwards. James returned at 11.45pm and, finding no sign of his mother, decided to check upstairs. Elizabeth's body lay on his bed, her throat cut.

Elizabeth's husband was arrested and confessed to killing his wife. When police inquiries pieced together his movements of the night of Elizabeth's death, they discovered that Ryder had been drinking in the Cricketers Inn. By 9.50pm he was so drunk that the landlord, Frederick George Hodder, refused to serve him and a fellow customer, George Smyth, gave evidence that Ryder had confessed to him that he had killed Elizabeth. Smyth believed it was merely the ramblings of a drunken man.

Once he had sobered up, Ryder withdrew his confession and claimed that he knew nothing about the crime. He persisted in

NAME	James Ryder
AGE AT EXECUTION	47
DATE OF EXECUTION	Wednesday, 13th August, 1913
PLACE OF EXECUTION	Manchester
HANGMAN	John Ellis
ASSISTANT	Not known
DATE OF TRIAL	5th July, 1913
LOCATION OF TRIAL	Manchester
PRESIDING JUDGE	Mister Justice Bailhache
PROSECUTION COUNSEL	Mister Henriques, Mister Oliver
DEFENCE COUNSEL	Mister Merriman
NUMBER OF VICTIMS	1

VICTIMS DETAILS

NAME	Ann Elizabeth Ryder
AGE	46
DATE OF MURDER	Thursday, 15th May, 1913
PLACE OF MURDER	32 Briscoe Street, Ardwick, Manchester
METHOD OF KILLING	Cut throat
RELATIONSHIP TO KILLER	Wife

this at his trial and produced evidence that discounted the bloodstains found on his clothing.

Hugh Welsh was also very drunk on the night of May 15th, 1913, and at one stage he had met Ryder. They argued and it ended when Ryder lashed out and struck Welsh in the face. Welsh required hospital treatment for his injuries and was taken there by Isaac Farrington, who had witnessed the altercation.

The only real evidence against Ryder was his own confession, now withdrawn, and the fact that he had been jealous over the matter of the postcard. The jury still felt that this was enough and James Ryder was sentenced to death.

0903

JULIAN BIROS, A Spaniard, earned his living by doing odd jobs on board the various ships that docked at Cardiff. He did not have a fixed home as such and often slept at the Crown Fuel Works, as did large numbers of transient workmen who had no base in Cardiff.

One of those workers was John McGill. On March 22nd, 1913, he met up with Hugh McLaren, who lived at 58 Adam Street. McLaren asked McGill if he had seen Biros, though he referred to him as "that dago" and promised to "cut his throat from lug to lug" when he ran into him. McHugh gave no reason for his ire.

That evening, Biros slept at the Fuel Works, as did Patrick McGuirk. They both rose at 7.00am the following morning and walked down to the Roath basin to watch the S.S. Dee docking. Biros perhaps thought that he might be able to pick up some casual work but if he did, it would be a hope he would be unable to test.

At 8.00am, James Walsh saw McGuirk and Biros and joined them in conversation. He had been there some 20 minutes when they noticed McLaren approaching.

McLaren greeted the three men with a jaunty, "Don't you know this is Easter Sunday boys? We'll make some tea." So saying, he took a packet of tea out of his pocket and immediately Biros recognised it as belonging to him. Biros demanded that McLaren hand over his tea, but McLaren's reply was to draw out a knife and plunge it into Biros's left side. The attack had been witnessed not only by McGuirk and Walsh, but also by Alphonso Burke who was on board the S.S. Dee. Whilst Walsh tried to help Biros, McGuirk ran for the police. Biros died that afternoon in the hospital.

The police knew where McLaren lived and just as they approached his house from one end of Adam Street, McLaren appeared from the other. He offered no resistance and after being cautioned announced, "I got nothing to say. I could kill a dozen dagos like that. They could not touch me for it."

McLaren's defence was that he was not responsible for Biros's death, the true cause being the medical attention he had received.

NAME	Hugh McLaren
AGE AT EXECUTION	29
DATE OF EXECUTION	Thursday, 14th August, 1913
PLACE OF EXECUTION	Cardiff
HANGMAN	John Ellis
ASSISTANT	William Willis
DATE OF TRIAL	18th July, 1913
LOCATION OF TRIAL	Swansea
PRESIDING JUDGE	Mister Justice Coleridge
PROSECUTION COUNSEL	Ivor Bowen, Clem Edwards M.P.
DEFENCE COUNSEL	Ernest Evans
NUMBER OF VICTIMS	1

VICTIMS DETAILS	
NAME	Julian Biros
AGE	22
DATE OF MURDER	Sunday, 23rd March, 1913
PLACE OF MURDER	Quayside, Roath Basin, Cardiff
METHOD OF KILLING	Stabbed
RELATIONSHIP TO KILLER	None

That defence was rejected and McLaren, a man who killed purely for racist motives, was condemned to death.

O N JUNE 5TH, 1913, Thomas Duncan, a ploughman, and a friend of his, James Thomson, were walking past Hopetoun Quarry when something caught Thomas's eye. There, in the weed, floated the bodies of two small boys, apparently tied together with rope. The two friends managed to pull the tragic bundle towards the shore using a branch snapped from a nearby tree but as the bodies floated towards them the rope holding them together broke and only one body was recovered at that time.

Thomas took the news of his find to his father, Peter, and he advised Thomas to fetch the police without delay. The authorities were called and in due course, both bodies were retrieved. It was clear that the children had been in the water for some time, but the cold water had preserved the bodies quite well. Further, only two children in the entire area had been missing for some time: the two sons of a widower, Patrick Higgins.

Constable James Adamson and Constable Galbraith soon brought Higgins in for questioning. His two sons had last been seen towards the end of 1911 and various witnesses had heard different tales from Higgins as to why his sons were no longer around. To some he said that he had found them a good home in Edinburgh. Others had heard that they had been taken to Canada. One neighbour had even been told that they had drowned in an accident. It was these stories which had kept friends and family from contacting the police earlier. They had simply believed what Patrick Higgins had told them. In fact, it now seemed obvious that Higgins had killed both his sons to save himself the cost of their upkeep.

Put on trial for murder, Higgins relied on a defence of insanity. He claimed that he had been discharged from the army after having fits. He was examined by Professor Harvey Littlejohn and Doctor Cross both of whom said they could find no trace of epilepsy in the prisoner but another practitioner, Doctor Martin, said that he believed Higgins to be feeble minded, with a very poor short-term memory.

The final decision was down to the jury who found Higgins guilty as charged.

NAME	Patrick Higgins
AGE AT EXECUTION	38
DATE OF EXECUTION	Thursday, 2nd October, 1913
PLACE OF EXECUTION	Edinburgh
HANGMAN	John Ellis
ASSISTANT	William Willis
DATE OF TRIAL	10th September – 11th September, 1913
LOCATION OF TRIAL	Edinburgh
PRESIDING JUDGE	Lord Justice Johnston
PROSECUTION COUNSEL	Mister Ure, William Mitchell
DEFENCE COUNSEL	Mister Kemp
NUMBER OF VICTIMS	2

VICTIMS DETAILS	
NAMES	William Higgins; John Higgins
AGES	6; 4
DATE OF MURDER	circa Wednesday, 25th October, 1911
PLACE OF MURDER	Hopetoun Quarry, Abercorn, West Lothian
METHOD OF KILLING	Drowned; drowned
RELATIONSHIP TO KILLER	Son; son

Surprisingly, as the judge passed the sentence of death, he did not wear the customary black cap.

FREDERICK SEEKINGS HAD been living with Martha Beeby for some time and for the most part, they seemed to get on well enough. Things changed though on July 28th, a day noted for the annual Feast of Brampton.

The Feast, a type of village fair, took place all day and although Frederick was working as usual, he managed to get to the Bell Inn by 8.00pm, where he enjoyed a few drinks. Later, Martha came in to the same hostelry and they stayed together until closing time. By then, Seekings was rather drunk and Tom Stocker, the landlord, was so concerned about Seekings not being able to turn up the following day and finish some labouring work he had started, that he chose to accompany them part of the way home.

On the way, there occurred a curious incident when Martha fell, or more likely was pushed, into a drainage ditch. Tom Stocker helped her out and, after making sure she was all right, returned to the Feast. It was now about 10.30pm.

At around 11.00pm, Ernest Favell left the Feast in the company of Edward Abraham. As they got home they found Mrs Favell waiting for her husband and she reported that she had heard some strange noises in the darkness. Ernest went for his cycle lamp and then he and Edward went to investigate. They found Seekings standing by Martha's body. Her throat had been cut.

Seekings was taken into custody and claimed that Martha had cut her own throat. He told the police that Martha had taken a knife off him and turned it upon herself. At his trial, though, medical opinion was that the wound could not possibly have been self-inflicted and it was shown that when arrested, the knife was found in Seekings's jacket pocket.

For his part, Seekings continued to claim that he had no memory of attacking Martha. At one stage he confessed that he was very drunk, saying: "I was the worse for drink or I would not have done such a thing, if I did do it."

The jury took 15 minutes to decide that Seekings had done the deed, had also been aware of what he was doing and was therefore guilty of murder.

NAME	Frederick Seekings
AGE AT EXECUTION	39
DATE OF EXECUTION	Tuesday, 4th November, 1913
PLACE OF EXECUTION	Cambridge
HANGMAN	Thomas Pierrepoint
ASSISTANT	Not known
DATE OF TRIAL	15th October, 1913
LOCATION OF TRIAL	Cambridge
PRESIDING JUDGE	Mister Justice Bray
PROSECUTION COUNSEL	Beaumont Monie, T. Shaw
DEFENCE COUNSEL	Grafton Pryor
NUMBER OF VICTIMS	1

VICTIMS DETAILS	
NAME	Martha Jane Beeby
AGE	45
DATE OF MURDER	Monday, 28th July, 1913
PLACE OF MURDER	Brampton, Huntingdonshire
METHOD OF KILLING	Cut throat
RELATIONSHIP TO KILLER	Girlfriend

MATILDA PENNY WAS separated from her husband, and her two sons had chosen to live with different parents. George stayed with his mother in their cottage on Pollard's Moor, whilst Augustus, known to everyone as 'Gus', had gone to live with his father in Portsmouth.

In the summer of 1913, Matilda had come into some money and when Gus heard of this, he decided he would pay his mother a visit and try to get some of it for himself. It seems though that in this Gus was unsuccessful because he was seen drinking heavily in the local public house.

Gus's brother, George, worked behind the bar and would later report that Gus had been hitting the whisky bottle rather hard. He actually bought some to take back to his mother, perhaps hoping that this bribe might well soften her heart and open up her purse strings. Again it seems Gus was not successful, because that same evening he took a shotgun and shattered his mother's head with a single shot whilst she lay in bed. The body was found by George when he returned from working in the pub. George ran off to fetch the local policeman, Constable Joyce. Of Gus, there was no sign.

The following morning a search of the surrounding area was organised but it appeared that Gus had avoided the best efforts of the police to locate him. Then, an 11-year-old boy named Evelyn Light revealed that he had seen Gus climb out of a well and run towards a hedge in a nearby field. Sure enough, when officers checked, they found Gus sitting underneath the hedge. He was arrested and charged with the murder of his mother.

Augustus Penny claimed that he had not known that the gun was loaded and had only intended to frighten his mother. Nevertheless, he pleaded guilty at his trial and was sentenced to death.

On a cold November morning, Augustus John Penny was hanged at Winchester prison. Local legend is that the murder weapon subsequently passed into the hands of Mister Evelyn Light who used it for years to come, for shooting rabbits!

NAME	Augustus John Penny
AGE AT EXECUTION	30
DATE OF EXECUTION	Wednesday, 26th November, 1913
PLACE OF EXECUTION	Winchester
HANGMAN	John Ellis
ASSISTANT	Albert Lumb
DATE OF TRIAL	8th November, 1913
LOCATION OF TRIAL	Winchester
PRESIDING JUDGE	Mister Justice Low
PROSECUTION COUNSEL	G.W. Ricketts, E. Duke
DEFENCE COUNSEL	Blake Rodgers
NUMBER OF VICTIMS	1

VICTIMS DETAILS	
NAME	Matilda Penny
AGE	57
DATE OF MURDER	Monday, 23rd June, 1913
PLACE OF MURDER	Pollard's Moor, Copyhorne, near Totton
METHOD OF KILLING	Shot
RELATIONSHIP TO KILLER	Mother

0903

IN JULY, 1913, Mr Bradforth, the tenant of the top floor rooms at number 12 Saratoga Road, Clapton, complained to his landlord about an offensive smell that seemed to be drifting up from the flat below. The landlord called in Joseph Lidden, who inspected the drains and found nothing wrong. Investigating further in the now vacant ground floor flat, Lidden lifted a floorboard and from the recess beneath, pulled out the decomposing body of a child. As if that in itself were not enough, he could plainly see a second body.

In fact, there were three bodies buried in the flat and it was not too difficult to determine who they were. Some six weeks before the discovery, Frederick Albert Robertson had moved into the flat with his wife, Lily, and three children. Soon afterwards, on June 24th, Lily had been admitted to hospital, where she still remained. Frederick, had left the flat on July 12th.

Investigations revealed that when Lily had been admitted to hospital, the children had been taken care of by a family friend. They had then returned to their father, who tried to get them taken into care. On June 28th, Robertson visited the Salvation Army to see if they had room for three children. Here he saw Mary Legge, who said that they did not have the space, but on the same day, Robertson told a fellow tenant, Phoebe Isabella Smith, that the children had been accepted.

Robertson was finally arrested in City Road, London. His description had been circulated and since Robertson had a wooden leg, he was relatively easy to spot. When arrested, he initially claimed that he had abandoned the children by the workhouse at Homerton, but this failed to explain how the bodies had found their way back to his rooms.

At the trial, evidence was called to show that Robertson had found himself a new lady friend, named Gertrude Flude and it was suggested that he needed to get rid of his children in order to start a new life. Found guilty of murder, the appeal was heard soon afterwards and this time Robertson tried to suggest that the three children had all died from natural causes. Once again he was not believed and the sentence of death was upheld.

NAME	Frederick Albert Robertson
AGE AT EXECUTION	26
DATE OF EXECUTION	Thursday, 27th November, 1913
PLACE OF EXECUTION	Pentonville
HANGMAN	John Ellis
ASSISTANT	William Willis
DATE OF TRIAL	22nd October – 24th October, 1913
LOCATION OF TRIAL	Old Bailey
PRESIDING JUDGE	Mister Justice Lush
PROSECUTION COUNSEL	Mister Bodkin, Percival Clarke, Mister Gattie
DEFENCE COUNSEL	E.J. Purchase, Arthur Bryan
NUMBER OF VICTIMS	3

VICTIMS DETAILS

NAMES	Nellie Kathleen Robertson; Frederick Ernest Robertson
AGES	2; 2
DATE OF MURDER	circa Saturday, 28th June, 1913
PLACE OF MURDER	12 Saratoga Road, Clapton, London
METHOD OF KILLING	Probably asphyxiated
RELATIONSHIP TO KILLER	Daughter; son
NAME	Beatrice Maud Robertson
AGE	10 months
DATE OF MURDER	circa Saturday, 28th June, 1913
PLACE OF MURDER	12 Saratoga Road, Clapton, London
METHOD OF KILLING	Probably asphyxiated
RELATIONSHIP TO KILLER	Daughter

DANIEL BARDSLEY WAS a bookseller and stationer who ran his business from premises in Yorkshire Street, Oldham. His routine was well known to all his employees and ex-employees. One of those ex-employees was Edward Hilton, a young man of 17.

On July 26th, 1913, Mister Bardsley was left alone in the shop at 10.15pm, when he heard a knock on the back door. Upon asking who it was, Edward Hilton identified himself and said he had come to buy something. Daniel Bardsley opened the door; his battered body was found the following morning. The weapon used on him had been a heavy Indian club.

It was not long before Edward Hilton came to the attention of the investigating officers and he readily admitted robbery, but said that he was not guilty of murder. His story was that he and a stranger had decided to steal from Mister Bardsley. Once the shop door had been opened, the stranger had pushed past Hilton and smashed Bardsley over the head with the club. Soon this 'stranger' was identified as Ernest Edward Kelly, who admitted that the Indian club was his property.

The story that Kelly told was somewhat different. He agreed that robbery had been the intention and that he had taken along the club to persuade Mister Bardsley to co-operate. Kelly had swung the club at Bardsley, missing him. He then dropped the club to the floor whereupon it was picked up by Hilton who struck Bardsley twice. When faced with this story, Hilton denied hitting Bardsley and added that after Kelly had struck, he had run upstairs to fetch some water for the injured man.

Both men were found guilty of murder and sentenced to death, but on December 16th, Hilton's sentence was commuted to one of life imprisonment. Evidence had been called to show that he had been mentally defective from childhood and at the time of the crime, he had been under the age of 18.

The people of Oldham were incensed. A crowd gathered outside Oldham Town Hall, demanding that Kelly too should be reprieved. The Mayoress wrote a personal message to

NAME	Ernest Edward Kelly
AGE AT EXECUTION	20
DATE OF EXECUTION	Wednesday, 17th December, 1913
PLACE OF EXECUTION	Manchester
HANGMAN	John Ellis
ASSISTANT	Not known
DATE OF TRIAL	24th November, 1913
LOCATION OF TRIAL	Manchester
PRESIDING JUDGE	Mister Justice Avory
PROSECUTION COUNSEL	Gordon Hewart, Mister Henriques
DEFENCE COUNSEL	Mister Ryecroft
NUMBER OF VICTIMS	1

VICTIMS DETAILS	
NAME	Daniel Wright Bardsley
AGE	54
DATE OF MURDER	Saturday, 26th July, 1913
PLACE OF MURDER	Yorkshire Street, Oldham
METHOD OF KILLING	Battered
RELATIONSHIP TO KILLER	None

the Queen and there were deputations to the Home Secretary. All felt that if anything, the more guilty of the two had been reprieved.

On the morning of the execution, a large crowd walked the seven or so miles to Strangeways prison and although a large police presence kept them away from the prison gates, they made their feelings plain.

In his last letter to his parents, written just before his execution, Kelly maintained his innocence, saying again that Hilton had struck the fatal blows.

0903

GEORGE FREDERICK LAW had lodged with the Cotterill family for more than two and a half years, but on Sunday, October 19th, 1913, he was told that he would have to find somewhere else as the family needed the house for themselves. Law did not take this well.

That same afternoon, Law was talking to Mr Peace, the man engaged to Edith Cotterill, one of the daughters of the house. Law intimated to Peace that if James Cotterill did not change his mind, it would be the worse for him and his family.

James Cotterill did not withdraw the notice to quit, though. Indeed, on the Monday, he repeated it. Law replied that he would not leave unless he was forcibly carried out. He then made further threats and Cotterill took these so seriously that he hid the three razors he possessed.

The fears over Law's behaviour seemed to be well founded. Just after midnight, Law was walking around the house, searching for something. James asked him what he was looking for and Law replied that he was trying to find a cigarette but at 2.00am he was up and about again and now he asked James where the razors were. Naturally, James Cotterill chose not to divulge that information.

At 6.00am on October 21st, Law left the house. James Cotterill presumed Law had gone to work as normal and soon afterwards, he and his daughter, Edith also left for work. James's wife, Annie remained in bed as she wasn't feeling too well. Two hours later, at 8.00am, Law was back at the house and was seen at the back door, by a neighbour. Strange sounds were heard coming from the house after he had gone inside but the next sighting of Law was in a nearby public house where he said he felt faint and treated himself to a brandy and soda.

It was the evening before James Cotterill arrived home. Finding the doors all locked and gaining no reply to his constant knocking, he managed to gain entry through a window. Annie was still in bed but she was quite dead. She had been strangled and there were also some deep cuts on her head.

Law was arrested just after midnight at his sister's house in Nottinghamshire and almost

NAME	George Frederick Law
AGE AT EXECUTION	34
DATE OF EXECUTION	Wednesday, 31st December, 1913
PLACE OF EXECUTION	Wakefield
HANGMAN	Thomas Pierrepoint
ASSISTANT	Albert Lumb
DATE OF TRIAL	2nd December, 1913
LOCATION OF TRIAL	Leeds
PRESIDING JUDGE	Mister Justice Darling
PROSECUTION COUNSEL	V.M. Coutts Trotter, G. Marsden
DEFENCE COUNSEL	L. Hoare
NUMBER OF VICTIMS	1

VICTIMS DETAILS	
NAME	Annie Cotterill
AGE	Not known
DATE OF MURDER	Tuesday, 21st October, 1913
PLACE OF MURDER	Sheffield
METHOD OF KILLING	Strangled
RELATIONSHIP TO KILLER	None

immediately began to behave somewhat strangely. From prison, he wrote to James Cotterill, the letter implying that it was Edith who had been killed and regretting that he could not think who the culprit was.

Whether this was a genuine sign of the state of Law's mind or a ploy to suggest madness, it failed to save him from the gallows. The jury took 30 minutes to decide his fate.

WHEN CHRISTINA BRADFIELD did not return to her lodgings on the night of December 10th, 1913, her landlady, Miss Holden, was not perturbed. Quite often Christina, who was manageress of her brother's tarpaulin company, would visit his house and stay the night.

The following day, when Christina didn't turn up for work, though, her brother made some inquiries. Miss Venables, the office typist, said she had left the warehouse at 6.40pm the previous evening. At that time, Miss Bradfield was alone with two of the employees – George Ball and Samuel Eltoft.

Ball had worked there since 1910 but Eltoft, the younger man, had only joined in 1912. Both men were employed as packers and when Mr Bradfield spoke to them, they were able to shed no light on the whereabouts of his sister. Furthermore, Ball claimed that Miss Bradfield had given him the keys and it was he who had opened up that morning. Mr Bradfield thought this unlikely. His sister had never been known to entrust the keys to anyone else, certainly not a simple packer, who this morning was sporting some fresh scratches on his face.

Later that same day, December 11th, Francis Robinson noticed that a bundle was obstructing a lock gate on the Leeds and Liverpool canal. Francis managed to pull the bundle out onto the bank and then noticed two human feet protruding from one end.

The sacking contained the trussed-up body of a woman, who had been battered to death. Robinson also discovered a broken umbrella that had the initial 'C.C.B.' on a silver mount. A medallion found with the body had the three wise monkeys as a motif and this was identified by Mister Bradfield as belonging to his sister. Christina Bradfield had been found.

It now became imperative to interview the two men who had been seen with her on the Wednesday evening. In the small hours of Friday morning, Samuel Eltoft was picked up at his lodgings, but when police called for Ball, at his lodgings in Boundary Lane, his landlord, John Kennedy, informed them that he was not at home.

The crime and the search for Ball were

NAME	George Ball (Sumner)
AGE AT EXECUTION	22
DATE OF EXECUTION	Thursday, 26th February, 1914
PLACE OF EXECUTION	Liverpool
HANGMAN	John Ellis
ASSISTANT	William Willis
DATE OF TRIAL	2nd February – 5th February, 1914
LOCATION OF TRIAL	Liverpool
PRESIDING JUDGE	Mister Justice Atkin
PROSECUTION COUNSEL	Gordon Hewart, W.J. Lias
DEFENCE COUNSEL	A.A. Tobin, J.E. Singleton
NUMBER OF VICTIMS	1

VICTIMS DETAILS

NAME	Christina Catherine Bradfield
AGE	40
DATE OF MURDER	Wednesday, 10th December, 1913
PLACE OF MURDER	86 Old Hall Street, Liverpool
METHOD OF KILLING	Battered
RELATIONSHIP TO KILLER	None

publicised all over Liverpool. It was then that Walter Eaves came forward. Eaves said that on December 10th, at about 7.30pm, he had been in Old Hall Street, waiting for his girlfriend. Suddenly a shutter fell from one of the windows of Bradfield's warehouse, and struck him on the head. He was not hurt, but his hat was damaged. Almost immediately, a young man, whom he subsequently identified as Eltoft, came out to fix the shutter and Eaves complained to him over what had occurred. Eltoft went back inside only for another man to come out, offer his apologies and give Eaves 2/-, to cover the damage. Shortly afterwards, the two men re-appeared from inside the yard, pushing a cart on which was a large bundle of sacking, and headed off towards the canal. Though he could not have known it at the time, Eaves had just witnessed the disposal of a body.

The search for Ball was widespread. His picture was flashed onto cinema screens in the town and his description was published in newspapers across the country. There were sightings in many places but all petered out to nothing. George Ball seemed to have vanished off the face of the earth.

On Saturday, December 20th, an old school friend of Ball's spotted a man who seemed to be rather familiar. The more he looked, the more convinced he became that this man was none other than Ball. The witness followed the man to a public house on St James Street and then on to a lodging house, after which he contacted the police. Later that night, the man was interviewed and subsequently identified as George Ball. He was arrested on his birthday.

Ball had disguised himself well. He wore a pink shade over his right eye and spectacles as an added touch. His distinctive bushy eyebrows had been clipped back and he had given his name as King. All the time the police had been scouring Liverpool for Ball, he had been walking the main streets, visiting pubs and living openly.

In addition to the testimony of Miss Venables and Walter Eaves, there were other damning pieces of evidence against Ball and Eltoft. Miss Bradfield's watch had been found on Ball when he was arrested. John Kennedy, Ball's landlord, testified that on the night of the murder, Ball had arrived home at 9.00pm, two hours later than usual. On the Thursday though, he had come home at 7.00pm, changed his clothes and rushed back out without even having a bite to eat. There was also the fact that Ball suddenly appeared to have come into money. On the morning of the murder, Kennedy had let Ball borrow 3d. Yet just a few hours later, Ball was able to give Eaves 2/-, apparently from his own money.

Ball seemed unperturbed by all this accumulated evidence. Waking up on the first morning in the police cells, his only concern was to discover how Everton had fared the previous day.

Both men had different defences at their trial. Eltoft claimed that he had been outside the warehouse when Miss Bradfield died. Ball had asked him to wait for a few minutes and then had appeared with the cart on which the bundle of sacking lay. Ball then asked him to help him dispose of the bundle in the canal, adding that it was only rubbish from the factory. Eltoft did as he was asked and was unaware of

what he had thrown into the dark waters.

Ball told a much stranger story. He and Eltoft had been alone with Miss Bradfield when a stranger had burst in, brandishing a revolver, intent on stealing the money kept on the premises. During the robbery the man hit Miss Bradfield once or twice and when he fled with the takings, Ball discovered that he had a dead body on his hands. In panic he decided to dispose of it, with Eltoft's assistance. He accounted for his possession of Miss Bradfield's watch by saying that it had fallen out of the bag she kept it in when the assailant fled. He had simply picked it up in case it should be found by someone else.

Unfortunately for Ball, his story did not fit the known facts. Christina Bradfield had been battered to death by means of a large number of blows, not the one or two that he referred to. There was also the fact that bloodstains had been found on Ball's clothing, though none had been found on Eltoft's.

Ball was found guilty of murder. Eltoft was found not guilty of murder but guilty of being an accessory after the fact, for which he received four years' imprisonment.

Before he was executed, Ball cleared his conscience and made a full confession to the Bishop of Liverpool.

FIVE PEOPLE LIVED at the house at 9 Middle Cross Street, Wolverhampton. In addition to Martha Hodgkins, there was also her son, Francis James Hodgkins, her nephew, Arthur Higgins, and the lodger, Josiah Davies. In August 1913, Davies became unemployed and from then on, money was always a problem as far as he was concerned.

For some time, it had been Davies's practice to take a cup of tea up to Martha each morning. Finally, Francis asked him to stop doing this as it disturbed his mother's rest, but the important point to note is that it was only Davies who ever engaged in this habit.

On the morning of November 4th, at 5.30am, Arthur Higgins and Francis Hodgkins were surprised to find Davies up and about as they got ready for work. He had made the fire up and prepared breakfast for them, something he hadn't done since he lost his job, but they simply accepted this change in behaviour and went off to their respective jobs.

At number 10, next door to the Hodgkins, lived Ann Doughty and her husband. Ann's bedroom was next to Martha's and at 7.00am, she distinctly heard a woman's voice cry 'murder!' She thought the shout came from outside and even checked by looking out of the window but when she saw nothing, she went back to bed.

At 8.30am, Ann rose and started her household duties. Four hours later she decided to visit her next-door neighbour, but when she got there, she saw no sign of Martha and eventually went upstairs to see if she could find her. Martha Hodgkins lay in her bed, a silk tied tightly around her throat. Under the bed lay a half-empty, cold cup of tea.

The motive for the crime appeared to be one of robbery. Martha was never without cash, but her purse was now empty. It seemed clear that someone had brought her a cup of tea and then killed her for her money. The question was, who had committed the murder?

Both Arthur Higgins and Francis Hodgkins denied taking the tea up to Martha and this pointed to Davies being the culprit. When it was discovered that Davies, who had last had any money when he drew his unemployment pay of 2/4d on October 10th, had been

NAME	Josiah Davies
AGE AT EXECUTION	58
DATE OF EXECUTION	Tuesday, 10th March, 1914
PLACE OF EXECUTION	Stafford
HANGMAN	John Ellis
ASSISTANT	George Brown
DATE OF TRIAL	18th February, 1914
LOCATION OF TRIAL	Stafford
PRESIDING JUDGE	Mister Justice Lush
PROSECUTION COUNSEL	J. Cranstoun
DEFENCE COUNSEL	R.J. Lawrence
NUMBER OF VICTIMS	1

VICTIMS DETAILS	
NAME	Martha Hodgkins
AGE	54
DATE OF MURDER	Tuesday, 4th November, 1913
PLACE OF MURDER	9 Middle Cross Street, Wolverhampton
METHOD OF KILLING	Strangled
RELATIONSHIP TO KILLER	None

spending money in various public houses around the town, he was arrested and charged with murder.

The evidence against Davies was purely circumstantial, but whilst being held in prison awaiting trial, he confessed his guilt to a warder and the prison doctor.

In February 1914, that guilt was confirmed by a jury and Davies was hanged at Stafford in March. It was to be the last execution at that prison and one John Ellis, the hangman, would well remember. It was noted after the execution that the rope had grazed Davies's skin, and Ellis received an official reprimand.

JAMES HONEYANDS, A naval stoker, lodged with Mrs Perry and became friendly with her daughter, Amelia Bradfield, even though Amelia was a married woman, her husband also being in the navy and serving on H.M.S. Monmouth. When Honeyands discovered that Amelia's husband was returning home on leave, he found the news difficult to accept.

On the night of October 18th, 1913, Amelia spent some time in the Courtney Arms pub in Plymouth. Honeyands came in, saw Amelia and began an argument with her. Eventually he stormed out, only to encounter Amelia's mother, Mrs Perry, outside. Within a few seconds, Amelia had followed him out and a fresh argument began, involving all three protagonists.

As the row reached its peak, James Honeyands drew out a revolver and fired three times in Amelia's direction. One of the bullets missed but the other two found their mark. As Amelia fell to the pavement, Honeyands turned the gun upon himself but it failed to fire. He then made to run off, but a postal worker named Harvey, who had seen all that had happened, gave chase, bravely threw Honeyands to the ground and held him until the police arrived.

Amelia Bradfield was rushed to hospital, where she died several days after the incident. It was reported that at one stage, her violent coughing had expelled a bullet from her lungs! Whether that was true or not, when Amelia finally passed away, Honeyands was charged with murder.

The trial took place at Exeter in February. Although evidence was given that there was insanity in Honeyands's family, he was still found guilty, but with a strong recommendation to mercy.

NAME	James Honeyands
AGE AT EXECUTION	21
DATE OF EXECUTION	Thursday, 12th March, 1914
PLACE OF EXECUTION	Exeter
HANGMAN	John Ellis
ASSISTANT	George Brown
DATE OF TRIAL	3rd February, 1914
LOCATION OF TRIAL	Exeter
PRESIDING JUDGE	Mister Commissioner Harrison
PROSECUTION COUNSEL	R.E. Dummett, W.A. Jowitt
DEFENCE COUNSEL	J.G. Trapnell
NUMBER OF VICTIMS	1

VICTIMS DETAILS	
NAME	Amelia Bradfield (Died Tuesday, 27th October)
AGE	18
DATE OF MURDER	Saturday, 18th October, 1913
PLACE OF MURDER	Outside the Courtney Arms public house, Courtney Street, Plymouth
METHOD OF KILLING	Shot
RELATIONSHIP TO KILLER	None/girlfriend

ELIZABETH BURDEN WAS involved with two men: Robert Upton, whom she had known for two years, and Charles Gribben, whom she had been involved with for 18 months. This volatile situation became even worse though when, on December 10th, 1913, she told both men that she was ending her relationships with them and intended to marry a third man, named Jack Bloy.

Robert Upton did not take this news well and threatened Elizabeth, saying that she would get neither Charlie nor Jack Bloy for he would 'do' for the pair of them. He was to carry out at least part of this threat within the month.

Both Upton and Gribben drank heavily and on the night of December 20th, Gribben arrived home, at the room they shared, and fell into a drunken sleep in his armchair. Joseph Upton, Robert's 14-year-old son, was also present and some time later, he saw his father arrive. He too was much the worse for drink and at 11.00pm, sent Joseph to buy some meat. Joseph returned soon afterwards and went to bed. At 3.30am on December 21st, Joseph saw his father take a razor, kneel on Gribben's chest and try to cut his throat. Joseph prevented this attack but some time later, when Robert made a second attempt, Joseph was not quick enough for him.

Charles Gribben was still alive and Joseph ran for help to another man who lived in the same house, James Evans. It was Evans who bound Gribben's throat and then went for medical help and the police. Meanwhile, Gribben managed to weakly raise an arm and point towards Upton, indicating that he was the guilty party. Upton immediately took the razor out for a second time and slashed his own throat. The police duly arrived and overpowered Upton, whereupon both men were taken to the hospital. Upton survived but Gribben died from his wounds, making the charge one of murder.

The trial was brief. Elizabeth Bloy, as she now was, having married a couple of weeks before the murder, said she had seen Gribben that day at her father's house. He appeared to be the worse for drink but was also jolly enough. Once again the defence were trying to lay the blame for the crime on alcohol, but it failed to save Upton.

NAME	Robert Upton
AGE AT EXECUTION	50
DATE OF EXECUTION	Tuesday, 24th March, 1914
PLACE OF EXECUTION	Durham
HANGMAN	John Ellis
ASSISTANT	William Willis
DATE OF TRIAL	5th March, 1914
LOCATION OF TRIAL	Durham
PRESIDING JUDGE	Mister Justice Ridley
PROSECUTION COUNSEL	Bruce Williamson, Mister Armitage
DEFENCE COUNSEL	Hugh O'Neill
NUMBER OF VICTIMS	1

VICTIMS DETAILS	
NAME	Charles Gribben
AGE	64
DATE OF MURDER	Sunday, 21st December, 1913
PLACE OF MURDER	42 Stanley Street, Jarrow
METHOD OF KILLING	Cut throat
RELATIONSHIP TO KILLER	None

EDGAR BINDON FELL in love with the girl next door, Maud Mulholland, but her parents did not approve of him and eventually, at their request, she gave him up. Soon afterwards she started a new romance, with Bernard Campion, but this too was broken off. In late October, though, Maud renewed her relationship with Bernard and this was to lead to her death.

At 10.30pm on November 4th, 1913, Bindon called at Maud's house, 80 Theobald Road. He was brandishing a gun, which Maud's father courageously took off him, noting later that the gun was fully loaded. Bindon was allowed to see Maud but she told him that she wanted nothing more to do with him. The following day, Bindon bought himself a new revolver, from a gentleman named Robert Bevan.

On November 9th, Bernard Campion visited Maud at her home and at 6.00pm, they went out for a walk together. They returned just before 10.00pm, Maud then offering to walk with him to the tram stop. The last time Bernard saw Maud, she was heading home, along Church Road.

Fifteen-year-old Randolph Howe was in his bedroom when, at 10.50pm, he heard what sounded like a shot. Looking out of his window, into the lane that ran at the back of Eton Place, he saw a woman running, followed by a man who was firing a gun at her.

John Hoskins and Henry John Griffiths were in Cowbridge Road. They saw Maud run out of a narrow lane and fall to the ground. As they looked on, Bindon appeared and fired again into Maud's body whilst she lay on the pavement. In all, Maud had received five wounds, two of which were held to be exit wounds. The fatal shot had penetrated her heart.

Bindon made no attempt to avoid capture and at the police station he stated: "It is alright. I have had my revenge and will die with a good heart." The case against Bindon was cast iron but it still took the jury an hour to reach their verdict, finally finding him guilty but with a strong recommendation to mercy.

Later, Mister W.E. Wentworth, the foreman of the jury was interviewed by the press and explained away the delay. The jury, he said,

NAME	Edgar Lewis George Bindon
AGE AT EXECUTION	19
DATE OF EXECUTION	Wednesday, 25th March, 1914
PLACE OF EXECUTION	Cardiff
HANGMAN	John Ellis
ASSISTANT	William Willis
DATE OF TRIAL	6th March, 1914
LOCATION OF TRIAL	Cardiff
PRESIDING JUDGE	Mister Justice Rowlatt
PROSECUTION COUNSEL	W. Llewelyn Williams M.P., Wilfred Lewis
DEFENCE COUNSEL	Ivor Bowen, Hugh Jones
NUMBER OF VICTIMS	1

VICTIMS DETAILS	
NAME	Maud Mulholland
AGE	20
DATE OF MURDER	Sunday, 9th November, 1913
PLACE OF MURDER	Cowbridge Road, Cardiff
METHOD OF KILLING	Shot
RELATIONSHIP TO KILLER	Girlfriend

had immediately decided that Bindon was guilty. The time was taken up in deciding on the recommendation. Seven had wanted a simple guilty verdict, two had wanted a recommendation to mercy and three had wanted to add the word 'strong'. Eventually, the minority ruled the day.

WHEN JOSEPH SPOONER and his wife, Catherine, separated in December, 1913, she took her six children and moved in with her married sister, Margaret, at 62 Oliver Street, Liverpool. Joseph took lodgings for himself just around the corner, at 3 Upper Parliament Street, so he could still see his family.

With so many children to worry about, money was obviously a concern for Catherine and so, in January 1914, she summonsed her husband for maintenance and was awarded a sum of 12/- a week. Joseph soon fell in arrears and by the end of February, he had only paid Catherine 6/- in total. This could not continue unchecked for long and on Thursday, February 26th, Catherine took out a second summons, this time for arrears of maintenance.

At 9.00am on that same morning, Joseph Spooner called on his sister-in-law and asked if he could see his wife. He was informed that Catherine wasn't at home. Joseph waited in the street and was seen, by Mary Elizabeth Dutton from number 64, talking to his wife on the corner of Oliver Street and Upper Parliament Street at 9.35am.

Meanwhile, Joseph Spooner's youngest daughter, Elizabeth Alice, was playing in her aunt's house at 71 Oliver Street. Very soon after speaking to his wife, Spooner called at number 71 and was allowed to see Elizabeth. At 11.10am, Spooner was seen with Elizabeth, again by the observant Mary Dutton.

Isabella Exon ran a sweet shop at 251 Upper Parliament Street and at 11.30am, Spooner and his daughter came into her shop, where he purchased some sweets. The two went off together, hand in hand.

Mary Dutton's nine-year-old daughter, Grace Ann, knew Elizabeth Spooner well and had called for her, earlier that day. Grace saw Elizabeth with her father, some time after 11.00am, before going back into her own house at number 64. At 11.50am, Grace went into the back yard of her house and was horrified to find the body of little Elizabeth Spooner.

Although Elizabeth was bleeding badly from her throat, she was still conscious, though she could not speak. Near her body lay

NAME	Joseph Spooner
AGE AT EXECUTION	42
DATE OF EXECUTION	Thursday, 14th May, 1914
PLACE OF EXECUTION	Liverpool
HANGMAN	William Willis
ASSISTANT	Thomas Pierrepoint
DATE OF TRIAL	22nd April, 1914
LOCATION OF TRIAL	Liverpool
PRESIDING JUDGE	Mister Justice Bray
PROSECUTION COUNSEL	Greaves Lord, Robert Segar
DEFENCE COUNSEL	Mister Madden
NUMBER OF VICTIMS	1

VICTIMS DETAILS	
NAME	Elizabeth Alice Spooner (Died Friday, 27th February)
AGE	3
DATE OF MURDER	Thursday, 26th February, 1914
PLACE OF MURDER	Rear of 64 Oliver Street, Liverpool
METHOD OF KILLING	Cut throat
RELATIONSHIP TO KILLER	Daughter

an envelope containing the sweets her father had purchased for her. Joseph Spooner was arrested, just around the corner, at 2.20pm.

The defence was one of insanity. Spooner made a statement in which he said he had no idea what had made him do this terrible thing, and evidence was given that when he and his wife had temporarily split up six years ago, he had tried to commit suicide, indicating that he had a weak mind.

None of this saved Spooner, who was sentenced to death. He was executed at Liverpool on May 14th. That gallows had last been used to execute George Ball, and he had died on the same day that Spooner had attacked his daughter.

0904

WALTER WHITE WAS very much in love with Frances Hunter and marriage had been discussed. With such plans, it made sense for Walter to meet some of Frances's family and he was pleased when it was arranged that they should visit her brother, who lived at Gilfach, Glamorgan.

The meeting was marred by one incident: the landlady, Mrs Blewitt, flatly refused Frances entry to her house. Walter asked what the problem was, but the lady would give no intimation. Instead she took Walter's address and said she would write to him.

When Mrs Blewitt did write, the letter contained little beyond a request that Walter should return and visit her alone if he wanted to know more. This he did and was devastated to be told that Frances had once lived with another man as his wife.

Walter was of the old-fashioned school, and to him it was important that his wife should be untouched. There was also the fact that Frances had never mentioned any of this to him. She had deceived him.

Walter returned home to Swindon, and wrote a number of letters. He wrote to his mother, and to Frances's father, and in both letters he said his life had been ruined by his sweetheart and that he was about to meet his Maker. The letters finished, Walter set out for the Goddard Arms Hotel, where Frances was a maid.

Walter arrived at the hotel at just about 6.00pm and the two lovers were seen going out into the yard. A few minutes later the manager heard three shots. Running out to the yard he found Frances lying dead in the coal house and White standing over her, the revolver still in his hand. He turned to the manager and coolly asked him to contact the police.

When the police arrived, White offered no resistance. He told them what he had learned from Mrs Blewitt and of the letters he had written. He then went on to tell them what had happened when he had met up with Frances.

The couple had gone into the yard to talk. White had told her what Mrs Blewitt had said and asked Frances if it was true. Tearfully, Frances admitted that it was. White then told

NAME	Walter James White
AGE AT EXECUTION	22
DATE OF EXECUTION	Tuesday, 16th June, 1914
PLACE OF EXECUTION	Winchester
HANGMAN	John Ellis
ASSISTANT	Thomas Pierrepoint
DATE OF TRIAL	28th May, 1914
LOCATION OF TRIAL	Winchester
PRESIDING JUDGE	Mister Justice Ridley
PROSECUTION COUNSEL	Rayner Goddard, Mister Mathias
DEFENCE COUNSEL	Mister Trapnell
NUMBER OF VICTIMS	1

VICTIMS DETAILS	
NAME	Frances Priscilla Hunter
AGE	24
DATE OF MURDER	Wednesday, 29th April, 1914
PLACE OF MURDER	Goddard Arms Hotel, Swindon
METHOD OF KILLING	Shot
RELATIONSHIP TO KILLER	Girlfriend

Frances that she would never deceive anyone ever again, as he was going to kill her. Far from running in fear, Frances simply gazed up at him and said: "For God's sake, do it then." She then kissed him goodbye and White drew his revolver and shot her.

The defence claimed that the circumstances of the crime clearly showed that White was not responsible for his actions. He had prepared carefully for the crime, though, and stated his intentions in two letters. For that reason a verdict of guilty was returned and on June 16th, 1914, Walter James White became the second victim of Mrs Blewitt's revelations.

DONALD PALMER WAS most disturbed by the sounds coming from the carriage next to his on the 7.25pm London Bridge to Brighton train.

The train had not long left Horley when Palmer had heard a number of screams. He leaned out of the window and tried to see what was going on. To his horror, he saw a woman on the floor of the carriage and a man standing over her, holding a large knife. Palmer pulled the communication cord and as the train was by now very close to Three Bridges, the driver pulled in at that station.

Immediately the assailant leapt from his third-class compartment and tried to make his escape. A guard blocked his way and the man then tried to get into another compartment, possibly in the hope of escaping through the other side. Rail officials and passengers leapt upon the man and threw him to the floor. So violent were his struggles that he had to be bound with ropes and left writhing on the ground until the police arrived. The reason for his attempted escape was all too apparent. In the carriage he had vacated lay the body of a young woman, her throat cut from ear to ear. She had also been stabbed.

The woman was Ada Stone, a married lady who was now separated from her husband. The new love in her life was the man who had just slashed her throat – Herbert Brooker, who had recently been discharged from the navy.

Brooker and Stone had been keeping company since the previous Christmas and marriage had been discussed. The existing husband would have to be traced first, though, and Brooker said he would place advertisements in order to see if he could be found. This was not enough for Ada, who had often complained that she did not see enough of Brooker. This in turn led to a number of arguments.

Brooker readily admitted that he had killed Ada Stone. He said that they had both been drinking quite a bit. Once again Ada had started to argue with him whilst they were on the train, at which point Brooker drew a knife that he carried down by the side of his leg, and silenced Ada forever.

There could be little doubt that the crime

NAME	Herbert Brooker
AGE AT EXECUTION	32
DATE OF EXECUTION	Tuesday, 28th July, 1914
PLACE OF EXECUTION	Lewes
HANGMAN	John Ellis
ASSISTANT	Thomas Pierrepoint
DATE OF TRIAL	7th July, 1914
LOCATION OF TRIAL	Lewes
PRESIDING JUDGE	Mister Justice Darling
PROSECUTION COUNSEL	Rowland Harker, St John Hutchinson
DEFENCE COUNSEL	Barrington Ward, Stormouth Darling
NUMBER OF VICTIMS	1

VICTIMS DETAILS	
NAME	Ada Stone
AGE	29
DATE OF MURDER	Saturday, 25th April, 1914
PLACE OF MURDER	Near Three Bridges Railway Station, West Sussex
METHOD OF KILLING	Cut throat/stabbed
RELATIONSHIP TO KILLER	Girlfriend

was murder. Brooker confessed that he had been carrying the knife for a week and hid it so that Ada should not see it. He was found guilty but with a recommendation to mercy on account of his previous good character and his service in the navy. The judge, however, pointed out Brooker's previous conduct was irrelevant. He had been tried on the facts of this case and found guilty. Accordingly, there was only one possible sentence.

0904

PERCY CLIFFORD MARRIED his wife, Maud, in 1911. There were immediate problems with the marriage, especially since Percy refused to do any work and Maud had been forced to go onto the streets in order to earn money to keep them. She finally left him in October 1913 and they lived at separate addresses in their native London.

In due course, Percy persuaded Maud to meet up with him and discuss their problems and to do this, on Saturday, April 4th, 1914, they travelled down to Brighton and took a room at the lodging house owned by Mary and Thomas Upton, in North Road.

The first few days passed uneventfully until, on April 7th, a Tuesday, Mary took up the morning tea, at 8.00am. At that time Maud was certainly alive and well for it was she who shouted her thanks from within the room.

At around noon, Mary Upton heard two reports, which she assumed to be a car tyre bursting outside, but when by 3.00pm she had still seen no sign of her two guests, she went back up to their room and knocked. Receiving no reply, Mary opened the door and entered the Clifford's bedroom. The couple were both in bed, but the amount of blood she saw caused Mary to call her husband Tom and he in turn, contacted the police.

Both the Cliffords had been shot in the head. A Doctor Maguire attended the scene, examined Maud, who was dead, and said that her wound could not possibly have been self-inflicted. Percy, who was still alive, was rushed to the hospital, where he remained unconscious for eight days. Later, when he had been charged with murder and was put on trial for his life, Percy still carried the bullet in his head. To attempt to remove it would have been far too dangerous.

The trial at Lewes lasted just a few hours. There could be no doubt that it had been Percy's hand that fired the fatal shot and the only debate could be whether it was murder or if the crime could possibly be reduced to manslaughter. When evidence was given that Percy had been heard, before Christmas, stating that he intended to shoot his wife and himself, it became clear that the crime had been premeditated and the jury

NAME	Percy Evelyn Clifford
AGE AT EXECUTION	32
DATE OF EXECUTION	Tuesday, 11th August, 1914
PLACE OF EXECUTION	Lewes
HANGMAN	John Ellis
ASSISTANT	Not known
DATE OF TRIAL	8th July, 1914
LOCATION OF TRIAL	Lewes
PRESIDING JUDGE	Mister Justice Darling
PROSECUTION COUNSEL	Barrington Ward, Miles Hansell
DEFENCE COUNSEL	Stormouth Darling
NUMBER OF VICTIMS	1

VICTIMS DETAILS	
NAME	Maud Clifford
AGE	24
DATE OF MURDER	Tuesday, 7th April, 1914
PLACE OF MURDER	57 North Road, Brighton
METHOD OF KILLING	Shot
RELATIONSHIP TO KILLER	Wife

took only 25 minutes to decide that Percy was guilty of murder.

The appeal was dismissed on July 27th, and Percy Clifford became the 10th man ever to be executed at Lewes prison.

CHARLES FREMBD AND his wife Louisa ran a small grocery business in Harrow Road. By August 1914, they had been married some 15 months; Louisa was Charles's second wife. It was not a happy marriage, however, and the couple were constantly having arguments.

Dorothy Woolmore had been a domestic servant for the Frembds since October 1913, and lived with them on the premises. On the night of August 27th, Dorothy went to bed at about 11.00pm, leaving Charles and his wife downstairs. It was some 20 minutes later that Louisa retired for the night, to be followed at 11.50pm by Charles. Dorothy was later to report that she heard no noises in the night.

Dorothy woke at 8.20am the following morning and her first thought was to get downstairs as quickly as possible. Normally Louisa called her at 7.30am and when Dorothy saw that Louisa herself was not up and about, she became worried that she might have fallen ill. Going upstairs again, Dorothy knocked on the bedroom door but, getting no reply, went back downstairs and busied herself with her duties.

Some time later, there had still been no sign of Louisa or Charles, so Dorothy went back up to their bedroom and knocked again. This time, though, she was not content to just walk away and having received no answer, Dorothy pushed open the unlocked door. Louisa lay on the bed, her face covered in blood. Charles was lying next to her and was also bleeding from a stab wound. Dorothy ran for help.

Charles Frembd recovered from his injuries, only to be charged with the murder of his wife. Charles's story was that after they had gone to bed, Louisa started again with her constant nagging. By 2.00am he could take no more and had cut her throat, later stabbing himself.

Frembd's defence was one of insanity. Evidence was given by Doctor Sidney Dyer, the Medical Officer of Brixton prison, that Frembd did indeed show signs of senile mental decay but unfortunately for Frembd, Dyer also stated that he was fit to plead and stand trial.

Executed at Chelmsford, Charles Frembd

NAME	Charles Frembd
AGE AT EXECUTION	71
DATE OF EXECUTION	Wednesday, 4th November, 1914
PLACE OF EXECUTION	Chelmsford
HANGMAN	John Ellis
ASSISTANT	Not known
DATE OF TRIAL	15th October 1914
LOCATION OF TRIAL	Old Bailey
PRESIDING JUDGE	Mister Justice Rowlatt
PROSECUTION COUNSEL	Mister Bodkin
DEFENCE COUNSEL	Mister Moran
NUMBER OF VICTIMS	1

VICTIMS DETAILS	
NAME	Louisa Frembd
AGE	52
DATE OF MURDER	Friday, 28th August, 1914
PLACE OF MURDER	44 Harrow Road, Leytonstone, London
METHOD OF KILLING	Cut throat
RELATIONSHIP TO KILLER	Wife

became the oldest person in this book to suffer death by hanging.

AS SOON AS hostilities broke out between Britain and Germany in 1914, Carl Lody, a patriotic officer in the German Naval Reserve, offered his services to his country, as a spy. The offer was accepted but in these early days of the conflict, there was little training in the finer points of espionage. Lody was simply supplied with a stolen American passport in the name of Charles Inglis, and sent to Britain with no training in codes or the use and manufacture of secret inks.

Lody spoke excellent English, with an American accent, so initially, his cover proved to be adequate. He started off travelling to Edinburgh to determine details of the fleet stationed in the Firth of Forth and from there sent a telegram to a German agent in Stockholm. It was this telegram, spotted by the wartime censors, which put the authorities on to Lody.

Not knowing that he was now under surveillance, Lody now spent two weeks cycling around Rosyth, before moving on to London to look at the air defences around the capital. From there he returned to Edinburgh, then to Liverpool and on to Dublin. It was in Ireland, on October 2nd, whilst on his way to the naval base at Queenstown, that Lody was finally picked up.

The trial took place at the Guildhall at the end of October and Lody was sentenced to death. Moved to the Tower, he spent his last night writing to his mother and even found the time to pen a note thanking the 3rd Battalion of the Grenadier Guards for their respect and courtesy during his time there.

On the morning of his execution, Lody turned to the Assistant Provost Marshal and said: "I suppose you will not shake hands with a spy?" Impressed by his courage, the reply was: "No, but I will shake hands with a brave man." Lody then became the first man to be shot at the Tower during World War One.

NAME	Carl Hans Lody
AGE AT EXECUTION	Not known
DATE OF EXECUTION	Friday, 6th November, 1914
PLACE OF EXECUTION	The Tower of London
DATE OF TRIAL	October, 1914
LOCATION OF TRIAL	The Guildhall, Westminster
PRESIDING JUDGE	Not known
NUMBER OF VICTIMS	Shot for spying

SARAH ANN, THE wife of John Francis Eayres, had been married once before. Her first husband, John Weldon, had died in 1905, leaving her with three children – two boys and a girl. Some six years after this, she had married Eayres and the two had settled down in School Place, Peterborough.

William Rodgers lived next door to the Eayres, at number 2 School Place, and at around 5.30pm on August 22nd, 1914, he heard quarrelling from number 4. This arguing continued for about half an hour and at one stage spilled out into the street where the two protagonists were seen by Harry George Marsters who lived at 11 School Place. He would later report that he saw John Eayres and his wife fighting on the pavement.

Things eventually went quiet and at 7.00pm, William Rodgers went out briefly, into his back yard. At that time, John Eayres was in his own yard, gazing through the living-room window. Rodgers said nothing to his neighbour, and 40 minutes later, walked into the town centre.

Some time that evening, both John and Sarah must have also walked into Peterborough. He was seen in Broad Street at 8.00pm by Thomas Smith Hawksworth, who saw him again before 9.30pm. The two men had a brief conversation before Sarah appeared. Hawksworth watched as John and Sarah walked off home together.

By 9.40pm, William Rodgers arrived home and was met by his rather distressed wife. She had heard groaning from the yard next door and asked her husband to investigate. Rodgers did so and found John Eayres on the ground, covered in blood. The police were called and they found the body of Sarah in the outside toilet.

It seemed obvious that John had cut Sarah's throat before cutting his own. He was rushed to hospital, where he made a full recovery and was soon able to face a charge of wilful murder. Eayres himself, though, could offer no help. In his statement, he claimed that he remembered Sarah throwing a cup or basin at him, which hit him on the side of his nose, but he had no memory of anything that had happened afterwards.

This loss of memory did not save Eayres

NAME	John Francis Eayres
AGE AT EXECUTION	59
DATE OF EXECUTION	Tuesday, 10th November, 1914
PLACE OF EXECUTION	Northampton
HANGMAN	John Ellis
ASSISTANT	William Willis
DATE OF TRIAL	20th October, 1914
LOCATION OF TRIAL	Northampton
PRESIDING JUDGE	Mister Justice Avory
PROSECUTION COUNSEL	C.E. Dyer, Drysdale Woodcock
DEFENCE COUNSEL	Bernard Campion
NUMBER OF VICTIMS	1

VICTIMS DETAILS	
NAME	Sarah Ann Eayres
AGE	53
DATE OF MURDER	Saturday, 22nd August, 1914
PLACE OF MURDER	4 School Place, Albert Place, Peterborough
METHOD OF KILLING	Cut throat
RELATIONSHIP TO KILLER	Wife

from the noose. Hanged in November, it was the 100th execution that John Ellis had taken part in.

HENRY QUARTLEY LIVED at Porlock with his unmarried sister, Emily Ann Quartley. Their neighbours, in Parson Street, were Henry and Fanny Pugsley, and for a time they were all on good terms. Then, in late 1913, for some unknown reason, the situation changed.

In November 1913, Henry Quartley went to the Pugsleys' house and abused the pair of them. For good measure he also threatened to blow out Henry Pugsley's brains and as a result, the Pugsleys took out a summons against Quartley, for using abusive language to them. That summons was dismissed, but relationships were strained from then on and in May 1914, the Pugsleys issued a second summons, claiming that Quartley had used insulting expressions whilst walking past their house.

On the evening of June 3rd, 1914, Henry Pugsley and his wife returned home and after stabling his pony, the couple walked past Quartley's house and up to their own. On the way they passed Alice Middleton who was talking to a friend, Mrs Chapman. Henry Quartley was in his garden at this time and he abruptly rushed out behind the Pugsleys and, drawing a shotgun, fired at them.

Henry Pugsley was hit in the back and had to be helped into his house, where he died within half an hour. Alice Middleton had also been hit, but she eventually recovered from her wounds. Quartley, meanwhile, had run back into his own house, where he quickly dashed upstairs, followed almost immediately by Constable Greedy. Another shot was heard. Quartley had tried to kill himself, but the shot had only grazed his face. Before he could fire again he was disarmed and taken into custody by officer Greedy.

Taken to the police station, a note was found in Quartley's pocket. It read: "I got no grievance against no one else only those two Pugsleys. They were the most dangerous crew I ever knew and have only got to thank themselves, as they started it."

Quartley's trial lasted just 12 minutes. Pleading guilty, he said he saw no reason going over the whole thing again and refused to even talk to Mister Duckworth who had been given the job of defending him. He said

NAME	Henry Quartley
AGE AT EXECUTION	55
DATE OF EXECUTION	Tuesday, 10th November, 1914
PLACE OF EXECUTION	Shepton Mallet
HANGMAN	Thomas Pierrepoint
ASSISTANT	None
DATE OF TRIAL	20th October, 1914
LOCATION OF TRIAL	Taunton
PRESIDING JUDGE	Mister Justice Atkin
PROSECUTION COUNSEL	Mister Vachell
DEFENCE COUNSEL	Mister Duckworth
NUMBER OF VICTIMS	1

VICTIMS DETAILS	
NAME	Henry Pugsley
AGE	59
DATE OF MURDER	Wednesday, 3rd June, 1914
PLACE OF MURDER	Parson Street, Porlock
METHOD OF KILLING	Shot
RELATIONSHIP TO KILLER	None

again that he had killed Pugsley and was not afraid to die. He was then sentenced to death.

A RNOLD WARREN WAS a married man, living apart from his wife, Ethel Mary Warren, and his son, two-year-old James. Whilst Arnold lodged at 98 Leamington Street, Ethel and the child lived at 2 Cromwell Cottages, Dannett Street and, since Ethel worked, it was her usual practice to have Arnold's mother, Mary Elizabeth Warren, take care of James during the day, at her house at 48 Gaul Street. Because Ethel was rather pushed for time, it was 11-year-old Edith Kate Skidmore who would call for James each day, take him to his grandmother's, and then take him back home.

Arnold and Ethel had been married for eight years, but she had left him due to his heavy gambling. The last straw had come on May 22nd when, during an argument about his fondness for horses, he struck out and hit her. Ethel walked out, issued a summons against Arnold on May 27th and received an award of 10/- a week.

None of this brought Arnold to his senses. At around 1.55pm, on July 10th, Ethel bumped into her husband at the clock tower at Humberstone Gate. He told her he had quit his job and was now gambling more than ever. He went on to say that he had drawn all his money out and had put it on one horse. He threatened to finish himself off if the horse lost and produced a blue bottle of poison to emphasise the point.

At 5.30pm that same day, Edith Skidmore took James from his grandmother's house. Her usual routine was to take the boy for a walk before returning him to his mother. Today she took him to the Fosse Road Recreation Ground.

It was here that Edith noticed Arnold, lying down on the grass. They chatted and then Arnold gave her a note to take to Mary, saying he would look after his son. Edith ran off, arriving back at Gaul Street some time after 6.30pm. The note was a request to borrow a saw, but when Edith returned, there was no sign of either Arnold or James.

Stanley Frederick Hackney and Alice Bray were taking a stroll at 8.10pm when they saw what they thought was a courting couple. As they walked nearer, Stanley saw that it was in fact a man and a child and that the child was

NAME	Arnold Warren
AGE AT EXECUTION	32
DATE OF EXECUTION	Thursday, 12th November, 1914
PLACE OF EXECUTION	Leicester
HANGMAN	John Ellis
ASSISTANT	William Willis
DATE OF TRIAL	23rd October, 1914
LOCATION OF TRIAL	Leicester
PRESIDING JUDGE	Mister Justice Avory
PROSECUTION COUNSEL	G.A. McCurdy, L.W.J. Costello
DEFENCE COUNSEL	H.W. Disney
NUMBER OF VICTIMS	1

VICTIMS DETAILS	
NAME	James Warren
AGE	2
DATE OF MURDER	Friday, 10th July, 1914
PLACE OF MURDER	Fosse Road Recreation Ground, Leicester
METHOD OF KILLING	Cut throat
RELATIONSHIP TO KILLER	Son

covered in blood. They discovered James, his throat cut, and Arnold, semi-conscious having taken a draught of laudanum.

Arnold Warren recovered in hospital and made a statement admitting his guilt. He had made a bet on a horse at Haydock and when this lost, he went to the recreation ground knowing that Edith usually walked through here. His intention had been to kill the boy and himself.

Warren was sentenced to death. Ironically, the name of the horse that lost and tipped him over the edge was 'Early Hope'.

0904

GEORGE ANDERSON AND his wife had been married for two years and lived with his step-daughter, Harriett Whybrow and Harriett's husband, Joseph. When George's wife died, on June 8th, 1914, he stayed on in the house at 213 High Street.

By the end of June, Anderson's relations with Harriett were more than friendly. On June 27th, Emma Whitbread, the next-door neighbour, saw Harriett sitting on George's lap, after Joseph had gone to work. Once Joseph returned and found out about this, he argued with Anderson. Later that same day, when the argument began afresh, Anderson picked up a chopper and tried to strike at Joseph.

Bravely, Harriett intervened and managed to get the chopper off Anderson. The police were called and after they had calmed things down, Joseph Whybrow demanded that they put Anderson out of the house. That night Anderson was forced to sleep in an outhouse.

On Monday, the 29th of June, Anderson apologised, but Joseph still refused to allow him back inside. Once he had gone to work though, Harriett did let Anderson in and once again she was seen sitting on his lap. The same sort of thing happened on Tuesday. Joseph went to work at 8.30am and by 10.00am, Anderson was inside the house with Harriett.

By 1.00pm, the sounds of a quarrel were emerging from the Whybrow house. At 1.30pm, there was another argument and by 3.00pm, Harriett visited Emma for a short time. Once she returned, a third argument broke out, but by the time Emma Whitbread saw Harriett leave at 3.30pm, things had gone quiet. All Emma heard after that was Anderson sharpening something and the sound of him muttering, "This will do nicely."

Anderson left the house soon afterwards and some time later, ran into Harriett near the Cross at Waltham. Nearby, Philip Henry Rodwell was selling bananas from a stall and he saw Anderson arguing with Harriett. He also saw Anderson suddenly produce a knife from inside his coat and slash Harriett's throat. Anderson then walked to the nearest pub, where he was arrested by Constable Walter Darlington.

NAME	George Anderson
AGE AT EXECUTION	59
DATE OF EXECUTION	Wednesday, 23rd December, 1914
PLACE OF EXECUTION	St Albans
HANGMAN	John Ellis
ASSISTANT	George Brown
DATE OF TRIAL	21st November, 1914
LOCATION OF TRIAL	Hertford
PRESIDING JUDGE	Mister Justice Lawrence
PROSECUTION COUNSEL	C.E. Jones, Mister Wylie
DEFENCE COUNSEL	Mister Bernard
NUMBER OF VICTIMS	1

VICTIMS DETAILS	
NAME	Harriett Ann Whybrow
AGE	31
DATE OF MURDER	Tuesday, 30th June, 1914
PLACE OF MURDER	213 High Street, Waltham Cross
METHOD OF KILLING	Cut throat
RELATIONSHIP TO KILLER	Step-daughter

Anderson came up with a rather implausible explanation for his actions. He claimed that he had met up with Harriett and that they had visited a few pubs together. As they walked, Harriett was annoying him by constantly nudging him as he was trying to cut himself a plug of tobacco with his knife. He stated that at one stage he had thrown his arm out to shrug her off and that this is when he must have cut her throat, accidentally. He denied having sharpened the knife earlier in the day and claimed he had gone to the pub unaware that Harriett had been injured.

It took the jury 17 minutes to dismiss this unlikely story and on December 23rd, Anderson became only the second man this century to be hanged at St Albans.

TOWARDS THE END of February 1915, a letter was intercepted at the Postal Censor's Office, addressed to F.R. Lybecq at Post Box 447, Rotterdam. The address was a contact for spies and so the letter was ironed to see if it held any messages. Immediately another letter, written in German, was revealed.

The sender's address was 54 Howard Street and it purported to come from a company named W. Dorst and Co. Checks revealed that the sender was in fact Carl Frederick Muller, who lodged at 38 Guildford Street, London, with Mary Elizabeth Tansley. Muller was arrested at that address on February 25th and a postcard found in his possession incriminated a second man, John Hahn, a British subject, born in Battersea on February 28th, 1887. He too was arrested.

Because Hahn was British, he was entitled to be tried before a jury in a civil court, which meant that Muller would too. The two were brought up at the Old Bailey, in June.

Hahn was sorry for what he had done and, pleading guilty, threw himself onto the mercy of the court. Both men were found guilty but it was held that Muller had been the instigator. As a result, whilst Muller received the death sentence, Hahn escaped with seven years' imprisonment.

NAME	Carl Frederick Muller
AGE AT EXECUTION	58
DATE OF EXECUTION	Wednesday, 23rd June, 1915
PLACE OF EXECUTION	The Tower of London
DATE OF TRIAL	2nd June – 4th June, 1915
LOCATION OF TRIAL	Old Bailey
PRESIDING JUDGE	Lord Chief Justice, Sir Rufus Isaacs, Justice Avory and Justice Lush
PROSECUTION COUNSEL	Mister Bodkin, G.A. Branson, Edward Boyd
DEFENCE COUNSEL	Curtis Bennett, Eustace Fulton
NUMBER OF VICTIMS	Shot for spying

1915

0905

IN APRIL 1915, a letter was sent from the Hotel Bristol, in Copenhagen, to Franz Kulbe, in Holland. Kulbe was a name used by Kaptain Von Prieger of the German Admiralty. It was reasonable to assume that someone at that hotel was in the pay of the German High Command.

The writer was found to be Robert Rosenthal. He had already spent a good deal of time in England and had sent a number of telegrams. When these were examined in detail, it was found that they contained a code that gave outlines of English ship movements at Edinburgh, Portsmouth and Hull.

It was only a matter of time before Rosenthal came back to England and in due course, he was arrested at Newcastle, trying to make his way to Bergen. At first he denied everything, but when faced with the evidence of his telegrams and the letter from the Hotel Bristol, he leapt to his feet, clicked his heels together and announced that he was a spy.

Whilst held in custody awaiting trial, Rosenthal wrote to Lord Kitchener, apologising for what he had done and claiming to have knowledge of an American official in Berlin who was spying for Germany. He eventually named Melton Feder, who was in charge of the American Relief Commission, but none of this saved Rosenthal from his fate.

Tried in July, Rosenthal became the only World War One spy to suffer death by hanging.

NAME	Robert Rosenthal
AGE AT EXECUTION	22
DATE OF EXECUTION	Thursday, 15th July, 1915
PLACE OF EXECUTION	Wandsworth
HANGMAN	Thomas Pierrepoint
ASSISTANT	Robert Baxter
DATE OF TRIAL	6th July, 1915
LOCATION OF TRIAL	The Guildhall, Westminster
NUMBER OF VICTIMS	Hanged for spying

IN MAY, 1915, British intelligence discovered that information had been forwarded from Southampton, detailing the positions of ships. A search of all telegrams sent from that port soon determined that on May 26th, one had been sent to Dierks and Co, in The Hague.

The telegram was an order for cigars, but the brand names did not make sense and it was held that it was probably a coded message. The telegram had been signed with the name Janssen.

Janssen had reported to the police at Hull on May 13th, and said that he was staying at the York Hotel, Anlaby Road. On May 20th, he had moved to Corys Hotel at 7 Spring Street, London and then on to the Crown Hotel, in Southampton. Meanwhile, checks revealed that other telegrams had been sent to The Hague. These had come from Edinburgh and had been signed Dierk, of the Roseberry Hotel, 99 Leith Street. Dierk turned out to be Willem Roos, who was now in London. On May 29th, Janssen was arrested in Southampton and four days later, Roos was picked up.

Immediately, the two men began to incriminate themselves. Janssen denied knowing Roos but Roos said he knew Janssen well! The evidence was strong enough to convict both and they were shot together in July.

NAMES Haicke Marinus Petrius Janssen; Willem Johannes Roos

AGES AT EXECUTION 29; 33

DATE OF EXECUTION Friday, 30th July, 1915

PLACE OF EXECUTION The Tower of London

DATE OF TRIAL 16th July – 17th July, 1915

LOCATION OF TRIAL The Guildhall, Westminster

NUMBER OF VICTIMS Shot for spying

1905

THE SCREAMS FROM the Marriott household attracted a neighbour, who found Nellie Marriott lying in a pool of blood. Her husband Walter was leaning over her, begging her to speak to him. But Nellie's throat bore a terrible wound and it was obvious that she was dying. The police were called and whilst he was waiting for them, Walter sat with his head in his hands and muttered: "What have I done to my lass?"

What Walter had done was to plunge a knife into Nellie's neck so that seven and a half inches of blade went down into her chest. There seemed to be no way the wound could have been self-inflicted so the question was, had Walter murdered her or was it an accident?

Walter Marriott claimed that he and Nellie had argued and during the fracas, she had threatened to throw a bottle at him. He claimed that she had then picked up a bread knife and made to use it. He had grappled with her and during that struggle, Nellie had been stabbed accidentally.

At Walter's trial, medical evidence suggested that it was most unlikely that the wound could have been inflicted in this way. As a result, a guilty verdict was returned and Walter was sentenced to death.

NAME	Walter Marriott
AGE AT EXECUTION	24
DATE OF EXECUTION	Tuesday, 10th August, 1915
PLACE OF EXECUTION	Wakefield
HANGMAN	Thomas Pierrepoint
ASSISTANT	William Willis
DATE OF TRIAL	19th July, 1915
LOCATION OF TRIAL	Leeds
PRESIDING JUDGE	Mister Justice Rowlatt
PROSECUTION COUNSEL	Tindal Atkinson, Bruce Williamson
DEFENCE COUNSEL	C. Mellor
NUMBER OF VICTIMS	1

VICTIMS DETAILS	
NAME	Nellie Marriott
AGE	23
DATE OF MURDER	Saturday, 5th June, 1915
PLACE OF MURDER	12 Wortley Street, Barnsley
METHOD OF KILLING	Stabbed
RELATIONSHIP TO KILLER	Wife

AT SOME TIME DURING the early afternoon of Sunday, May 16th, 1915, Nora Barrett was seen, at her front door, by one of her neighbours. Soon afterwards, at around 1.30pm, the man she lived with, Frank Steele, was seen locking the door before hurrying away. For the rest of that day, the blinds at 31 Nelson Street, remained down and there was no sign of Nora.

By 1.45pm that same day, Steele was in the centre of Gateshead, where he bumped into an old friend and workmate, William Johnson. Steele looked to be very excited and somewhat the worse for drink and when Johnson asked him what the matter was, Steele replied that he had just murdered Nora. Johnson did not believe what his friend had said, and put his ramblings down to drink.

Going from his meeting with Johnson to his mother's house, Steele again confessed that he had murdered Nora, but again he was not believed. Somewhat reluctantly, Steele returned home to Nelson Street.

The next day, Monday May 17th, Steele again visited his mother and again confessed to having killed Nora. This time he appeared to be sober and rational and so his mother contacted the police. When they arrived, Steele again confessed to murder and handed over his front door key. When officers paid a visit to Nelson Street, they found Nora lying on the bed, her throat cut. She had been dead at least 24 hours.

Steele admitted that there was no motive for the crime. He and Nora had lived together for over three months and had been happy enough during that time. His only explanation was that he had had so much to drink that he had not known what he was doing. His defence counsel, Mister Rowan Hamilton, tried to suggest that under the circumstances, it was clear that Steele had not been able to form the intention to kill and was therefore not guilty of murder, asking instead for a verdict of manslaughter.

Once again, though, drink was held to be no excuse for the taking of a human life and a verdict of wilful murder was returned.

NAME	Frank Steele
AGE AT EXECUTION	28
DATE OF EXECUTION	Wednesday, 11th August, 1915
PLACE OF EXECUTION	Durham
HANGMAN	John Ellis
ASSISTANT	Not known
DATE OF TRIAL	6th July, 1915
LOCATION OF TRIAL	Durham
PRESIDING JUDGE	Mister Justice Ridley
PROSECUTION COUNSEL	J. Scott Fox, C.F. Lowenthal
DEFENCE COUNSEL	S.O. Rowan Hamilton
NUMBER OF VICTIMS	1

VICTIMS DETAILS	
NAME	Nora (Nana) Barrett
AGE	21
DATE OF MURDER	Sunday, 16th May, 1915
PLACE OF MURDER	31 Nelson Street, Gateshead
METHOD OF KILLING	Cut throat
RELATIONSHIP TO KILLER	Girlfriend

1905

ALMOST FROM THE time he was born, in Bethnal Green in 1872, George Joseph Smith led a life of deceit, dishonesty and criminality.

By the age of 10 he had been in trouble so many times that he was sent to a reformatory in Gravesend. He remained there until he was 16, but it did nothing to change him. He received two prison sentences: one of seven days for a minor theft and one of six months for stealing a bicycle. Released in 1891, he went into the army, where he stayed for three years.

The discipline of the army also had little effect on Smith. In July 1896 he was sentenced to a year in prison, for larceny and receiving. He served this particular sentence under the false name of George Baker.

Upon his release, Smith moved to Leicester where, using another false name, Oliver Love, he opened a baker's shop at 20 Russell Square. He had not, however, turned over a new leaf, as he opened the shop with £115 that a woman had stolen on his behalf.

Smith had always had a way with women. He found it easy to persuade them to do what he wished and when he married Caroline Beatrice Thornhill, on January 17th, 1898, it may have seemed that he had at last settled down. Nothing could have been further from the truth.

The bride's family had boycotted the ceremony, as they thoroughly disapproved of Smith, who was still masquerading as Mr Love. Pressure from the family soon caused Caroline to leave Smith and live instead with a cousin in Nottingham. Smith soon followed her and persuaded her to return to him. In quick succession they lived in London, Brighton, Hove and Hastings where he wrote false references for Caroline, enabling her to obtain posts as a domestic servant. At his bidding she then stole from those employers, until she was arrested in 1899 and given a prison sentence. Her husband meanwhile had left her and run off to London, where he married his landlady. She was later abandoned like so many others.

Caroline was released from prison in 1900 and was visiting London when she saw a face she knew she would never forget. There,

NAME	George Joseph Smith
AGE AT EXECUTION	43
DATE OF EXECUTION	Friday, 13th August, 1915
PLACE OF EXECUTION	Maidstone
HANGMAN	John Ellis
ASSISTANT	Thomas Pierrepoint
DATE OF TRIAL	22nd June – 1st July, 1915
LOCATION OF TRIAL	Old Bailey
PRESIDING JUDGE	Mister Justice Scrutton
PROSECUTION COUNSEL	Archibald Bodkin, Travers Humphreys
DEFENCE COUNSEL	Edward Marshall Hall, Montague Shearman
NUMBER OF VICTIMS	3

VICTIMS DETAILS

NAMES	Beatrice Constance Annie Mundy; Alice Burnham
AGES	33; 25
DATES OF MURDER	Saturday, 13th July, 1912; Friday, 12th December, 1913
PLACE OF MURDER	80 High Street, Herne Bay; 16 Regents Road, Blackpool
METHOD OF KILLING	Drowning; drowning
RELATIONSHIP TO KILLER	Bigamous wife; bigamous wife
NAME	Margaret Elizabeth Lofty
AGE	38
DATE OF MURDER	Friday, 18th December, 1914
PLACE OF MURDER	14 Bismarck Road, Highgate, London
METHOD OF KILLING	Drowning
RELATIONSHIP TO KILLER	Bigamous wife

walking down Oxford Street, was Oliver Love, the man who had caused her to be sent to jail. She found a policeman and reported her husband to him. The upshot was that on January 9th, 1901, Smith was sentenced to two years for receiving stolen goods.

When he was freed, in October 1903, Smith settled down to the life he would lead for the rest of his criminal career. Becoming a dealer in second-hand goods, he would travel the country extensively in search of them, preying on the occasional gullible woman as he went.

In 1908 he was back in Brighton. There he

met Florence Wilson, a widow, who lived just down the coast in Worthing. The very next day he asked her to marry him and she agreed. They then took a trip to London where Smith persuaded Mrs Wilson to draw her savings out of the Post Office and give it to him for safe keeping. On July 3rd, 1908, Smith and the money vanished from her life forever. He then moved to Bristol where he opened a second-hand furniture shop.

It was in Bristol that Smith met his next wife, Edith Pegler. They married on July 30th, 1908, she then joining him on his travels through Bedford, Luton, Croydon, London and Southend.

In October 1909 he married yet again, in Southampton. This time the bride was Sarah Freeman and she knew Smith as George Rose. Once again the conquest was taken to London and after relieving Miss Freeman of £300, he deserted her at the National Gallery.

At this stage, Smith developed an interest in buying property. After all, he had to put his money somewhere and bricks and mortar seemed as good an investment as any. He went to Southend where he bought 22 Glenmore Street, then returned to Bristol where he bought 86 Ashley Down Road. Smith was quite enjoying a life of persuading young ladies to part with their favours and their money, but in 1910, all that was to change.

In the summer of 1910, Smith was at Clifton where he met Bessie Mundy. He soon discovered that she had a bank balance of £2,500, a very considerable sum in 1910. After a whirlwind romance, he married her at Weymouth on August 26th, using the name Henry Williams. He then set about removing the money from her bank account.

Unfortunately for Smith though, there was a problem. Bessie's money had come from her late father and was protected in a trust. She couldn't get at it and neither therefore could he. All Bessie had was a monthly income of £8 and Smith, considering this was beneath his efforts, left Bessie after just a few weeks of marriage. He left her a letter implying that she had given him venereal disease, and returned to Bristol and Edith Pegler.

In March 1912, Smith's travels took him to

Weston-Super-Mare and here he happened to bump into Bessie, who was there on holiday. He did his best to explain and apologise for leaving her and as a result, Bessie forgave him and took him back. In May of that year they moved together to Herne Bay, where they rented a house at 80 High Street.

Smith was nothing if not adaptable. He knew that Bessie's trust was unbreakable, but he also discovered that if Bessie died, and left a will, naming him as beneficiary, then he would inherit the entire sum. Just six days later, on July 8th, 1912, the couple made wills in favour of each other.

On July 9th, Smith bought a nice new tin bath. The price was £2 but he haggled and got 2/6d discount. The bath was delivered to 80 High Street that afternoon.

Smith certainly moved quickly once he had decided on a course of action. On July 10th he took Bessie to see Doctor French and told him that she had had a fit. The doctor could find nothing wrong with Bessie but he did prescribe a mild sedative. Two days later the same doctor was called out to attend Bessie at her home. Again he could find nothing wrong with her, but her husband did seem to be concerned, so he returned later in the day.

On July 13th, the doctor was again called to 80 High Street, but this time Bessie was dead. Smith sent French a note asking him to attend and when he got there he found Bessie naked in the bath with her head below the soapy water. The doctor lifted the body from the water and tried to revive her, but it was too late. The inquest on July 15th gave a verdict of Death by Misadventure and poor Bessie was buried on July 16th. By July 18th, Smith had sold most of their furniture and returned the tin bath to the ironmongers. He had, after all, no further use for it.

Bessie's relatives had their suspicions and tried to contest the will, but it was to no avail. In September, Smith received the sum of £2,500 and returned to Edith in Bristol. Deciding to put the money to work, he then bought seven houses in the town and opened several bank accounts, in varying names. He had made quite a decent amount from Bessie and it had all been so easy. Smith decided that this could well be the way to go from now on.

In October 1913, Smith met Alice Burnham at Southsea. Once again he swept the unfortunate woman off her feet, proposed to her and was accepted. They married on November 4th, in Portsmouth and for once, Smith used his real name. The day before, Alice's life had been insured for £500.

On December 10th, 1913, Smith and his latest bride, went to Blackpool for a holiday. Smith first tried to book into Susannah Marsden's guest house at 25 Adelaide Street, but when she told him that there was no bath available, he moved on to Margaret Crossley's establishment at 16 Regent's Road.

As soon as they had unpacked, Smith took Alice to see Doctor George Billing at 121 Church Street South. Apparently Mrs Smith had a nasty headache but when the doctor examined her, he could find nothing wrong with her. Nevertheless he prescribed some tablets and a powder to clear her bowels.

On the evening of December 12th, Smith and his bride went for a walk and before they left, Smith asked the landlady's daughter to run a bath for his wife, for when she returned. They got back just after 8.00pm and Mrs Smith went straight up to take her bath. At 8.15pm Smith appeared in the kitchen where the Crossley family were taking tea. He had two eggs in his hand, which he said were for breakfast the following morning. The bathroom was partly above the kitchen and at this point Mrs Crossley observed water coming through the ceiling. Smith rushed upstairs and then returned shouting "Fetch the doctor! My wife cannot speak to me." Upon entering the bathroom, Alice was seen to be under the water. All attempts to revive her failed and she was buried on December 15th.

In September 1914, Smith, using the name Charles Oliver James, married Alice Reavil at Woolwich in London. She was a poor domestic servant when Smith met her and by the time he deserted her on September 23rd, she was poorer still by £78 and some furniture.

In December of that same year, Smith met the lady who would become his last wife and victim. On December 17th, and using the name John Lloyd, he married Margaret Lofty at Bath. He already knew that her life was insured for £700 and Smith determined that this amount would be his as soon as possible. The couple moved into rooms at 14 Bismarck Road, Highgate, in London.

The usual scenario was repeated. Margaret was taken to see Doctor Bates, who was told that she had a bad headache. The poor woman seemed too scared to speak whilst the doctor examined her. Smith then visited a solicitor with his new wife, where she made a will leaving everything to him. That evening, at 8.00pm, Louisa Blatch, the landlady heard a noise from the bathroom. Shortly afterwards, Smith was heard, in the front parlour, playing 'Nearer My God to Thee' on the harmonium. Just a few minutes later, he went upstairs and announced that he had found his wife dead in the bath.

Margaret Lofty was buried on December 21st, which meant that Smith could return to Bristol and Edith, in time for Christmas. This time though, he had if anything moved too quickly.

When she died, Margaret had been a bride for just two days and this made front-page news. An article appeared in the News of the World, which was seen by both Joseph Crossley, the husband of the Blackpool landlady, and Alice Burnham's father. Both thought that the circumstances were too close to what had already happened and both went to the police.

Smith, meanwhile, must have thought that he had got away with murder once again. On January 4th, 1915, he visited his solicitor, Mister Davies, of 60 Uxbridge Road, and asked him to prove Margaret's will as soon as possible. When he returned there on February 1st to see how things were progressing, Smith was arrested for bigamy.

The police, of course, were just using the bigamy charge to hold Smith whilst they made further investigations. The bodies of the three dead wives were exhumed and on March 23rd, Smith was charged with the murders of Bessie Mundy, Alice Burnham and Margaret Lofty.

The trial, was in many ways a fiasco. Smith interrupted constantly, hurling insults at witnesses. Mrs Crossley was described as a lunatic and Detective Inspector Arthur Neil, who had led the investigation, was told he was a scoundrel. Told to be quiet by his counsel, Smith banged his fist on the dock and shouted "I don't care what you say" and at one point, during the judge's summing-up, he shouted, "I am not a murderer, though I may be a bit peculiar."

One of the most important pieces of evidence came from Bernard Spilsbury, the pathologist. The baths that Smith used to kill his wives in were the old type, with a high, sloping back. Spilsbury first showed that someone falling asleep or even having a fit or an attack in such a bath, could not slide down into the water and drown. Then, in an ante-room near the court, he demonstrated how Smith probably committed the murders. Using a volunteer nurse, Spilsbury lifted up her knees with his left hand whilst simultaneously pressing down on her head with his right. The poor woman was instantly rendered unconscious and had to be revived!

It took the jury just over 20 minutes to determine that Smith was guilty of the murder of Bessie Mundy, the only one he had been indicted with. Smith was visibly shocked. During his last days in the condemned cell, Smith frequently wept and was clearly in terror of what was going to happen. His last words were, "I am innocent " before he was hanged on August 13th.

The following day, Smith's first, and only legal wife, Caroline Thornhill, married Tom Davies a soldier in the Royal Engineers.

1905

THOMAS WARNER AND his wife had a number of lodgers in their house at 70 Mina Road, Walworth. The most recent arrival was George Marshall, who had been there for about a year.

George had been introduced to Thomas Warner by another of the lodgers, Alice Anderson, and it seemed that there was some sort of understanding between George and Alice, for she used to prepare his meals and keep his room tidy for him. For his part, this led George to believe that Alice was his and his alone.

On the night of Saturday, July 3rd, 1915, Thomas Warner visited the Duke of York pub in Bagshot Street. Marshall was a barman there and it was he who served Warner, asking him if he had seen Alice. Warner replied that he hadn't.

Thomas Warner retired for the night at 10.20pm, but he was still awake at 11.00pm and heard Marshall coming in. Ten minutes later, Warner was disturbed by Marshall shouting: "Mister Warner, I want you up here a minute."

Warner pushed his feet into his slippers and made his way to Marshall's room. There were a couple of depressions in the bedding and just as Marshall asked Warner if he thought someone had been lying on the bed, Alice Anderson came into the room. Marshall believed that whilst he had been at work, Alice had been entertaining another man in his room. Further, Marshall suspected it was an insurance agent named Slade. Thomas Warner did not wish to get involved and retired again to his bed.

Another 10 minutes passed, before Thomas Warner and his wife were disturbed again, this time by a loud thumping noise. Warner went to investigate but this time it was no argument that he could ignore. There at the foot of the stairs lay the body of Alice Anderson, her throat cut from ear to ear.

By the time Constable Frederick Butler arrived, it was 12.05am. Butler called Marshall downstairs and he came without resistance, remarking: "I ain't half give her a gash. I meant to do it, the wicked cow. I'll give her make this place a knocking shop."

Marshall continued to talk at the police

NAME	George Marshall
AGE AT EXECUTION	45
DATE OF EXECUTION	Tuesday, 17th August, 1915
PLACE OF EXECUTION	Wandsworth
HANGMAN	John Ellis
ASSISTANT	George Brown
DATE OF TRIAL	20th July, 1915
LOCATION OF TRIAL	Old Bailey
PRESIDING JUDGE	Mister Justice Avory
PROSECUTION COUNSEL	Mister Bodkin
DEFENCE COUNSEL	Mister Wardle
NUMBER OF VICTIMS	1

VICTIMS DETAILS	
NAME	Alice Anderson
AGE	45
DATE OF MURDER	Saturday, 3rd July, 1915
PLACE OF MURDER	70 Mina Road, Walworth, London
METHOD OF KILLING	Cut throat
RELATIONSHIP TO KILLER	Girlfriend

station. His motive was jealousy, pure and simple. He believed she was his girl but had been seeing other men, especially Slade.

Pleading provocation, Marshall's defence was greatly damaged when it was shown that Alice had been lying on her bed when she had been attacked. She had then managed to stagger to the top of the stairs before collapsing. This scenario showed that Marshall had deliberately cut Alice whilst she was relaxing and so could not claim that it had been in the heat of an argument.

O N MARCH 16TH, 1915, the British authorities received information that there was a spy active in England. The report gave his name as Ernest Melin of 23 Upper Park Road, Hampstead.

It was not until April 15th that some hard evidence was discovered. On that date a letter arrived, containing a payment of £50, from Schwedersky and Company of Rotterdam. The name and address were already known through Trebitsch Lincoln, a traitor, whose son would face the hangman for murder in March, 1926.

It was this same type of diligence that led to a second agent in June, 1915. Two postcards had been sent to H. Flores, Binnenweg 127, Rotterdam and these led police to Augusto Roggen, who was operating from Edinburgh. Roggen was arrested on June 10th and four days later, a letter from Melin was intercepted that contained information written in invisible ink.

Both men were tried at the Guildhall in August. Whilst there was a good deal of evidence against Melin, there was very little of substance against Roggen. Nevertheless, both men were found guilty and sentenced to be shot.

NAMES	Ernest Waldemar Melin; Augusto Alfredo Roggen
AGES AT EXECUTION	49; 34
DATES OF EXECUTIONS	Friday, 10th September, 1915; Friday, 17th September, 1915
PLACE OF EXECUTION	The Tower of London
DATES OF TRIALS	20th August – 21st August, 1915; 20th August, 1915
LOCATION OF TRIAL	The Guildhall, Westminster
NUMBER OF VICTIMS	Shot for spying

1905

ON JUNE 4TH, 1915, a telegram was sent from Rotterdam to Fernando Buschman of 36a Harrington Road, South Kensington, London. The message read: "Please return immediately for personal discussion with Flores have other business this side in view. Paid to Brazilian Legation your account May 26th twenty five pounds." The telegram was signed "Dierks and Co."

Both the names Flores and Dierks were known as contacts used by German spies and so an instruction was given for the arrest of Buschman. He was picked up the next day.

Buschman claimed that he was a partner in the firm of Marcelino Bello and Co, a general merchants and importers of Las Palmas, but it was shown that he was in fact a Brazilian, of German extraction, married to the daughter of a large soap manufacturer in Dresden. He had been sent to England to report on aviation matters.

Possibly the strongest piece of evidence against Buschman was a booklet, detailing his movements. All of these were verified by other documentation, except for certain visits to Southampton, Portsmouth and London. The authorities were suspicious as to why these three journeys, out of a list of many others, should be false entries. Surely these had been trips on which Buschman had been working for his German masters?

There was one other matter. Buschman had landed in this country on April 15th, 1915, but his current passport was only issued on April 22nd. The old one could not be found and it was held that this had been destroyed because it contained stamps that would have proved Buschman had travelled within German territory.

On October 18th, Buschman was removed to the Tower where he was shot the following morning.

NAME	Fernando Buschman
AGE AT EXECUTION	25
DATE OF EXECUTION	Tuesday, 19th October, 1915
PLACE OF EXECUTION	The Tower of London
DATE OF TRIAL	29th September – 30th September, 1915
LOCATION OF TRIAL	The Guildhall, Westminster
NUMBER OF VICTIMS	Shot for spying

THE LETTER SENT to Dierks and Co., 166 Loosduinsche Kade, The Hague, seemed to be innocent enough until treated by heat, when it revealed details of ships and defences at Ramsgate, written in German.

The message had been sent from a Reginald Rowland of the Ivanhoe Hotel, in Bloomsbury, London. When Mr Rowland was arrested, on June 4th, it transpired that he had been using other names, but claimed that he wished to be known as George T. Breeckow. Further inquiries revealed that he had an accomplice, Lizzie Wertheim, who had been obtaining information for Breeckow in the Edinburgh and Inverness area. She was arrested on June 9th.

Lizzie, despite her Germanic name, was a British citizen which entitled her and Breeckow to be tried before a civil court. They faced a jury at the Old Bailey, in September.

The jury were out for 11 minutes before deciding that both were guilty of espionage, but it was held that Lizzie had been controlled by Breeckow. So it was that whilst he received a death sentence, she was given 10 years.

NAME	George T. Breeckow (George T. Parker) (Reginald Rowland)
AGE AT EXECUTION	33
DATE OF EXECUTION	Tuesday, 26th October, 1915
PLACE OF EXECUTION	The Tower of London
DATE OF TRIAL	14th September – 20th September, 1915
LOCATION OF TRIAL	Old Bailey
PRESIDING JUDGE	Messrs Justice Bray, Sankey, and Low
PROSECUTION COUNSEL	Travers Humphreys, Richard D. Muir
DEFENCE COUNSEL	Eustace Fulton
NUMBER OF VICTIMS	Shot for spying

0905

THE AUTHORITIES HAD noticed that a number of telegraphic money orders had gone to the same individual, Irving Guy Ries, of the Hotel Cecil, in London. These had all come from N.M. Cleton of Rotterdam. Discrete inquiries were made.

It was shown that Ries had been travelling widely throughout Britain. Since he had landed at Liverpool on July 4th, he had spent time in Newcastle, Glasgow, and Edinburgh, before travelling to London, arriving there on July 28th. On his documents, Ries claimed to be a traveller in grain and horse fodder and it was noticed that whilst he had visited various suppliers, he had not followed up his original enquiries, nor had he placed any orders.

On August 8th it was discovered that Ries had travelled to England from the United States, and that his passport was a forgery. The next day he booked a first-class passage to Copenhagen from Newcastle and, the day after that, he was arrested.

On August 11th, a message was intercepted from the German Headquarters at Wesel, to their consulate at Rotterdam, giving them authority to pay sums of money to Ries.

Convicted of espionage and sentenced to be shot, Ries would only reveal that he was German and that Ries was not his real name. He claimed that he came from a good family who would be shamed by what had happened to him.

NAME	Irving Guy Ries
AGE AT EXECUTION	55
DATE OF EXECUTION	Wednesday, 27th October, 1915
PLACE OF EXECUTION	The Tower of London
DATE OF TRIAL	4th October – 5th October, 1915
LOCATION OF TRIAL	The Guildhall, Westminster
NUMBER OF VICTIMS	Shot for spying

CONSTABLE WILLIAM CLARK was on duty in Church Street, Leighton Buzzard, when he saw William Benjamin Reeve stagger out of Plantation Street, covered in blood. Clark took Reeve to his father's house at 84 Church Street and from there, walked to Reeve's house at 8 Plantation Road. There he found the body of Harriett Reeve in an armchair, the bottom of her face blown away. Nearby, Clark found a shotgun, both barrels of which had been fired, and a bloodstained razor.

It was a fairly simple matter to piece together the events of that day. William Reeve had done no regular work for some time. This state of a affairs caused many rows between himself and his wife Harriet. These disputes often became violent when he had been drinking. At 8.45am, Reeve had met up with Thomas Major who was returning a dog he had found to its owner, the landlord of the White Hart. Reeve accompanied Major and they were given a couple of free pints for their trouble. Later, the two men visited various other pubs, before parting at 3.00pm.

Reeve carried on drinking, though, and at 4.00pm was seen in the Stag Inn, Church Street. He spent most of his time there playing dominoes and did not leave until 6.00pm. On the way home he stopped to talk to a neighbour and arrived back at number 8, at 6.30pm.

Just before this, Harriett had arrived home from work. When William came in he was drunk and very argumentative and so Harriett, no doubt to keep him out of his father's way, gave her 16-year-old son, also named William Benjamin, and his friend, George Hemmings, money to go to the pictures.

Soon after the boys had left, Harriett's next-door neighbour, Martha Barns, heard quarrelling, followed by a short silence and two shots. Later, she and others saw Reeve stagger past towards Church Street and his encounter with Constable Clark.

Reeve had fired both barrels into Harriett, killing her instantly. His own wound had been self-inflicted by the razor found nearby. It was later said that only the prompt attention given to him by Constable Clark saved his life and allowed him to face a charge of murder.

NAME	William Benjamin Reeve
AGE AT EXECUTION	42
DATE OF EXECUTION	Tuesday, 16th November, 1915
PLACE OF EXECUTION	Bedford
HANGMAN	John Ellis
ASSISTANT	None
DATE OF TRIAL	19th October, 1915
LOCATION OF TRIAL	Bedford
PRESIDING JUDGE	Mister Justice Shearman
PROSECUTION COUNSEL	J.S. Pritchett, L.W.J. Costello
DEFENCE COUNSEL	William N. Burkett
NUMBER OF VICTIMS	1

VICTIMS DETAILS	
NAME	Harriett Reeve
AGE	40
DATE OF MURDER	Monday, 5th July, 1915
PLACE OF MURDER	8 Plantation Road, Leighton Buzzard
METHOD OF KILLING	Shot
RELATIONSHIP TO KILLER	Wife

At the trial, Reeve's defence was that the gun had gone off accidentally. When he had first met Thomas Major, Reeve had mentioned that he had left his gun at home, fully loaded and Major had said he should be careful in case one of the children got hold of it and hurt someone. Reeve was now saying that he was about to unload it when it had gone off, killing Harriett.

The story was, at best, unlikely, and did nothing to convince the jury, who found Reeve guilty of murder.

IN JUNE, 1915 the Postal Censor's Office discovered a letter dated the 29th of that month, addressed to M. Goedhardt, 147 Van Blankenburgstraat, The Hague. As a matter of routine, the letter was ironed and the heat produced brought up a message that had been written in invisible ink. A bulletin was then issued for workers to watch out for any future correspondence to this same address.

The next message was a postcard, addressed to Mr Niendecker and this too bore a secret message. It purported to come from someone who called himself 'Lopez'. One week later, another letter was sent, this time signed 'Belmonte' and giving a return address at 28 Greek Street, London. Upon checking this address, officials discovered no one who might have sent the letter.

The breakthrough came on August 27th when another letter asked for an advance of £50. This time the return address was 1 Margaret Street, Oxford Circus, and the note contained no secret writing. The investigators assumed that such an open message probably gave the correct address and discrete inquiries into the occupants of 1 Margaret Street, were made.

The landlady there was Mrs Emma Waack and she had two foreign lodgers who had not registered with the authorities as they should have. When further checks were made, it was found that the writing of one of them, Albert Meyer, matched that on the letters.

Meyer lived with his wife and both were now arrested, though Catherine Rebecca Meyer was later released without charge. It transpired that Meyer's father owned the Hotel Bristol, in Copenhagen, an address that would be mentioned in other spy cases.

The evidence was enough to convict Meyer, a Dutchman born in Constantinople, of espionage. He was transferred to the Tower on November 26th and shot there the next morning.

NAME	Albert Meyer
AGE AT EXECUTION	23
DATE OF EXECUTION	Saturday, 27th November, 1915
PLACE OF EXECUTION	The Tower of London
DATE OF TRIAL	5th November – 6th November, 1915
LOCATION OF TRIAL	The Guildhall, Westminster
NUMBER OF VICTIMS	Shot for spying

JOHN THORNLEY AND Frances Johnson had been going out together for two and a half years and had now, finally, made a formal commitment by becoming engaged. Soon afterwards though, they had an argument. Frances broke off the engagement and returned John's ring to him. This upset John very deeply and he was heard by a number of people to state that if he could not have Frances, no one would.

On the night of September 18th, Frances's parents were away from home. Rather than leave their daughter alone, they allowed her to invite a friend, May Warren, to stay with her for the night. Before retiring for the night, the two girls went to the theatre, where they were seen by Thornley, who was also there. Frances and May went back to her house, finally going to bed at midnight.

At 3.00am, May was woken by the sound of someone getting in through the kitchen window. She lay in bed, petrified, as footsteps were heard on the stairs and in the half-light cast by a street lamp she made out the figure of John Thornley.

May heard Frances ask who was there and then shout for help. There followed some gurgling noises and then May saw Thornley make good his escape. So frightened was she that it was some time before she could pluck up the courage to investigate. She found Frances dead in her bed, a gaping wound in her throat and defence cuts on her arms. Near her body was a note that read: "Dear Ma and Pa. I told you I would kill or cure Frances. I have done it. I hope you will forgive me for breaking God's law."

After committing the crime, Thornley tried to drown himself in the canal, but in this he failed. He was arrested two days later and denied all knowledge of the murder, despite the note he had written and left at the scene of the crime. At his trial, he tried to put forward a defence of insanity but medical evidence was given that he was perfectly sane. He was hanged at the same time as Young Hill.

NAME	John James Thornley
AGE AT EXECUTION	26
DATE OF EXECUTION	Wednesday, 1st December, 1915
PLACE OF EXECUTION	Liverpool
HANGMAN	John Ellis
ASSISTANT	George Brown
DATE OF TRIAL	27th October, 1915
LOCATION OF TRIAL	Chester
PRESIDING JUDGE	Mister Justice Coleridge
PROSECUTION COUNSEL	Ralph Bankes, R.O. Roberts
DEFENCE COUNSEL	Trevor Lloyd
NUMBER OF VICTIMS	1

VICTIMS DETAILS	
NAME	Frances Johnson
AGE	24
DATE OF MURDER	Sunday, 19th September, 1915
PLACE OF MURDER	Devonport Street, Macclesfield
METHOD OF KILLING	Cut throat
RELATIONSHIP TO KILLER	Girlfriend

1905

0905

ON JULY 6TH, 1915, James Crawford joined the crew of the S.S. Antillian at New Orleans in the United States. The Antillian carried a general cargo, but also a consignment of mules. These animals required a number of men to administer to their needs, and this was the job Crawford took on, along with Young Hill, and others.

On July 25th, the Antillian docked at Avonmouth, where the mules were unloaded before she sailed on for Liverpool, where she arrived the following day, Monday, July 26th. That night, at around 7.30pm, John Andrew Moore was on duty on the bridge whilst the ship was at anchor, when he saw a most unusual sight.

James Crawford was running, apparently in terror, along the saloon deck, from the direction of the forecastle. Even more unusually, there was a gaping wound in Crawford's throat and as Moore ran down to investigate, the young man collapsed into his arms.

When Moore went into the forecastle to see what had happened, he found Young Hill, a razor in his hand, holding a group of other muleteers at bay and threatening to kill the first man who approached him. Deciding that he needed something to even things up a little, Moore reported the matter to the Captain and the Chief Officer, who both appeared in the forecastle, armed with revolvers. Faced with these superior odds, Hill lay down his razor and allowed himself to be taken prisoner.

By the time the police had arrived, Crawford was dead and Hill was facing a charge of wilful murder. When interviewed, it transpired that Crawford had been killed over a bucket of water!

On one of the bunks was a seaman named Crockett, who had been lying ill for a number of days. According to witnesses Leslie Rucker, Louis Keys and Lorenzo Sullivan, Crockett had asked for water and Hill had offered him some dirty water from a bucket. Crawford had taken exception to this and remonstrated with Hill, at which point Hill grabbed his head, forced it back, and drew a razor across his throat.

Hill agreed that the argument had been over water but he claimed that he had told

NAME	Young Hill
AGE AT EXECUTION	28
DATE OF EXECUTION	Wednesday, 1st December, 1915
PLACE OF EXECUTION	Liverpool
HANGMAN	John Ellis
ASSISTANT	George Brown
DATE OF TRIAL	29th October, 1915
LOCATION OF TRIAL	Liverpool
PRESIDING JUDGE	Mister Justice Ridley
PROSECUTION COUNSEL	A.H. Maxwell, Mister Segar
DEFENCE COUNSEL	Mister Griffiths
NUMBER OF VICTIMS	1

VICTIMS DETAILS	
NAME	James Crawford
AGE	25
DATE OF MURDER	Monday, 26th July, 1915
PLACE OF MURDER	On board S.S. Antillian, docked at Liverpool
METHOD OF KILLING	Cut throat
RELATIONSHIP TO KILLER	None

Crawford that he only wished to help the sick man and was sure the water was clean. Crawford had come at him, attacked him and pulled something from his pocket. Thinking that this was a knife, Hill had defended himself by drawing the razor he had in his pocket and using it on his assailant. In simple terms, Hill was claiming that the crime was self-defence.

The testimony of the three witnesses named carried more weight than Hill's words, and he was found guilty of murder.

ALICE KAYE WAS pregnant and whilst her husband, Ernest, was away in the army, her aunt, Mrs Donkersley, was staying with her each night.

It was 8.30pm when Mrs Donkersley arrived on the evening of November 6th, but she could get no reply to her repeated knocking. The house was in darkness, so Mrs Donkersley went next door and asked if she could wait until Alice returned home. Throughout the evening, she made further attempts to gain entry to Alice's house and by midnight, when there was still no signs of life, she asked the neighbour if she could stay with her for the night.

The next morning Mrs Donkersley tried again to obtain entry to her niece's house. There was still no reply, so she asked a man named Oldfield, who happened to be passing, to force an entry. Alice's body was found on the kitchen floor. Her throat had been cut.

The police could find no clues to the attacker and newspaper reports carried this information to the public at large. Then, on Monday, November 8th, Harry Thompson approached a police officer in Ramsden Street, and confessed that he was the killer they were looking for.

Thompson said that he had been involved with Alice for two years but had only recently found out that she was a married woman. He had met her husband but Alice had told him that he was her brother and Thompson had believed her. The relationship between Thompson and Alice was confirmed when his lodgings were searched and letters were found from her. In one of these, dated November 5th, arrangements had been made for a meeting on the 6th, the day of the murder and this also seemed to confirm Thompson's story.

At the police court, Harry Thompson again admitted that he had killed Alice, saying that they had argued over his discovery that she was married. He had slashed out at her in a temper and did not know she was dead until he read about it in the newspaper. On the strength of that confession, Thompson was committed for trial.

What should have been a straightforward case became much more complex when

NAME	Harry Thompson
AGE AT EXECUTION	55
DATE OF EXECUTION	Wednesday, 22nd December, 1915
PLACE OF EXECUTION	Wakefield
HANGMAN	Thomas Pierrepoint
ASSISTANT	Edward Taylor
DATE OF TRIAL	29th November, 1915
LOCATION OF TRIAL	Leeds
PRESIDING JUDGE	Mister Justice Sankey
PROSECUTION COUNSEL	R.J. Thompson Tebbs
DEFENCE COUNSEL	Rowan Hamilton
NUMBER OF VICTIMS	1

VICTIMS DETAILS	
NAME	Alice Kaye
AGE	27
DATE OF MURDER	Saturday, 6th November, 1915
PLACE OF MURDER	27 Burycroft, Honley, near Huddersfield
METHOD OF KILLING	Cut throat
RELATIONSHIP TO KILLER	Girlfriend

Thompson withdrew his confession. He now claimed that he had visited Alice on the day of the murder and stayed with her until some time between 5.00pm and 6.00pm. She was alive and well when he left her and explained his confession by saying he was unbalanced by reading that the woman he loved had been murdered.

It took the jury half an hour to decide that the first version of events had been the truth and that Thompson was guilty of murder. He was hanged on December 22nd, despite the fact that the only thing linking him to the crime was his own confession and that the jury had recommended him to mercy.

ON JANUARY 4TH, 1899, John McCartney married Bridget Wyles. The fact that he was a married man did not stop him from going through with a second ceremony, using the name Harry MacDonald, when he wed Charlotte Kent.

By June, 1915, 'Harry MacDonald' was a private in the East Yorkshire Regiment and he and Charlotte, using the forenames Hilda Bertha, took lodgings with Eliza Rogers, at Brass Castle Hill. Charlotte lived there on a permanent basis and McCartney visited whenever he could get leave. For some time they were happy together, but them McCartney became convinced that Charlotte was seeing other men and a number of arguments broke out.

On August 1st, the latest argument became somewhat violent. McCartney grabbed Charlotte by the throat and proceeded to drag her down a passageway. Eliza saw this, managed to stop the attack and demanded that McCartney leave the house. He was allowed to visit Charlotte after that, but further arguments and rows only served to confirm that Eliza had made the right decision in forbidding McCartney from staying overnight again.

On September 9th, Eliza asked Charlotte to visit a fish shop she also owned, in order to fix a blind for her. Eliza was afraid to go alone, and took Eliza's daughter-in-law, Mrs Waddington, with her. The two women were followed to the shop by McCartney and then followed back to Charlotte's lodgings.

At 7.00pm that same evening, McCartney announced to Charlotte that he had a pass and therefore could stay with her that night. Eliza Rogers refused him permission to stay, so McCartney then asked Charlotte to go away with him. She refused but, anxious to defuse the situation, told him that if he went back to his camp, she might go away with him the next day. Then, in front of Eliza, McCartney took out a razor and cut Charlotte's throat. He then turned the blade upon himself and cut his own throat.

At his trial, it took the jury 10 minutes to decide that McCartney was guilty of murder. As the verdict was announced, McCartney cried: "Oh! No, no. I was mad when I did it."

NAME	John William McCartney (Harry MacDonald)
AGE AT EXECUTION	40
DATE OF EXECUTION	Wednesday, 29th December, 1915
PLACE OF EXECUTION	Wakefield
HANGMAN	Thomas Pierrepoint
ASSISTANT	Robert Baxter
DATE OF TRIAL	24th November, 1915
LOCATION OF TRIAL	York
PRESIDING JUDGE	Mister Justice Atkin
PROSECUTION COUNSEL	H. Neild, H.C. Tobbs
DEFENCE COUNSEL	C. Paley Scott
NUMBER OF VICTIMS	1

VICTIMS DETAILS	
NAME	Charlotte Kent (Hilda Bertha MacDonald)
AGE	29
DATE OF MURDER	Thursday, 9th September, 1915
PLACE OF MURDER	30 Brass Castle Hill, Pocklington, near York
METHOD OF KILLING	Cut throat
RELATIONSHIP TO KILLER	Bigamous wife

CLARA THOMAS, WHO preferred to use the name Elsie Godard, was a married woman who had not lived with her husband for some time. She had shared a house with Lee Kun, a Chinese man, in Pennyfields at Poplar, but that relationship too appeared to be on the rocks and Clara had moved in with a friend of hers, Harriet Wheaton. This was only a few doors away from where Lee lived.

On October 16th, 1915, Clara and Harriet were sitting in her front room when Lee came into the house and asked Clara if he could speak to her. Lee then grabbed Clara by the arm and led her outside into the back yard. Almost immediately, Harriet Wheaton heard the sounds of a struggle taking place and upon going out, saw that Lee had drawn out a large knife and was stabbing Clara repeatedly.

Bravely, Harriet used a broom handle to beat him off. When Lee turned on her and advanced towards her with the knife, plucky Harriet kept him at bay until her screams could summon help. Kun was arrested and taken into custody.

Kun's story was that Clara had stolen some money from him and refused to pay it back. He had gone into the yard to remonstrate with her about this and she had suddenly produced a knife and attempted to stab herself. Lee had tried to stop her and in the struggle that ensued, Clara was stabbed. The story did not hold water and Lee Kun was found guilty and sentenced to death.

Perhaps more important was Kun's appeal. The defence counsel argued that the evidence had not been translated for Kun, who spoke poor English, and that therefore, even though he had been represented, he was not able to fully understand the proceedings and had not had a fair trial.

One example that served to illustrate this problem was the post-verdict speech of the judge. Mister Justice Darling had not asked the accused if he had anything to say before sentence of death was passed. Upon hearing the verdict, he had merely sentenced Kun to death. He realised his mistake, recalled Kun to the dock, and only then asked him if he had anything to say!

The appeal was rejected. It was held that all the evidence had been translated for Kun

NAME	Lee Kun
AGE AT EXECUTION	27
DATE OF EXECUTION	Saturday, 1st January, 1916
PLACE OF EXECUTION	Pentonville
HANGMAN	John Ellis
ASSISTANT	Not known
DATE OF TRIAL	17th November 1915
LOCATION OF TRIAL	Old Bailey
PRESIDING JUDGE	Mister Justice Darling
PROSECUTION COUNSEL	Not known
DEFENCE COUNSEL	Not known
NUMBER OF VICTIMS	1

VICTIMS DETAILS

NAME	Clara Thomas (Elsie Godard)
AGE	Not known
DATE OF MURDER	Saturday, 16th October, 1915
PLACE OF MURDER	Pennyfields, Poplar, London
METHOD OF KILLING	Stabbed
RELATIONSHIP TO KILLER	Ex-girlfriend

at the police court and the evidence at the trial at the Old Bailey had not differed from that. He was, therefore, aware of what was going on. It was held that in future, it would be safer and wiser if the evidence were translated in the case of a foreigner whose grasp of English was poor.

Kun had managed to gain himself a few extra weeks of life. His execution had originally been fixed for December 7th, 1915, but the appeal meant that it was now postponed until January 1st.

SARAH WOODALL HAD been separated from her husband William for four years. In due course she became involved with Frederick Holmes and they began living together.

Holmes was a jealous man. In early November, 1915, Sarah was with one of her friends, Maud Baker, when they ran into George Wake. George had known Sarah for eight years and they all a few drinks together. George asked Sarah to meet him again later that same day and she agreed. After having another drink or two, they returned to her rooms at 64 Higher Ardwick. Frederick Holmes was there and he took objection to Sarah bringing another man home. Holmes threatened to murder the pair of them and flew at Wake in a rage.

Sarah screamed: "Police! Murder!" at the top of her voice. Holmes ran out in a panic, leaving Sarah and George Wake to spend the night together. The following morning, George noticed that he had blood on his collar, from the fracas.

On November 22nd, Sarah and Frederick Holmes moved to new lodgings at 13 Clifford Street. The house was owned by John and Ellen Weller who lived a few doors away at number nine. Ellen made all the arrangements with Sarah and never saw the man who had moved in with her.

On December 8th, the rent was due on Sarah's rooms and Ellen Weller called to collect it. She received no reply to her knocking and determined to return the following day to try again.

Elizabeth and Alfred Thompson also lived in rooms at number 13 and had been there for five years, Alfred acting as caretaker. They had seen the man who lived with Sarah and had noticed him leaving the house at 11.30am on December 8th. Elizabeth saw him lock the door after he had left.

That night, at 10.15pm, Holmes saw Sarah Metcalfe in Bridge Street. She was an old flame and had actually lived with Holmes for two years. Holmes told her that he had a new job to go to in Ripon and had to leave the following day. He asked her if she would put him up that night. Sarah said yes and they slept together at 3 Willow Street.

NAME	Frederick Holmes
AGE AT EXECUTION	44
DATE OF EXECUTION	Wednesday, 8th March, 1916
PLACE OF EXECUTION	Manchester
HANGMAN	John Ellis
ASSISTANT	Edward Taylor
DATE OF TRIAL	18th February, 1916
LOCATION OF TRIAL	Manchester
PRESIDING JUDGE	Mister Justice Bailhache
PROSECUTION COUNSEL	Lindon Riley, Mister Oliver
DEFENCE COUNSEL	F. Brocklehurst
NUMBER OF VICTIMS	1

VICTIMS DETAILS	
NAME	Sarah Woodall
AGE	38
DATE OF MURDER	Wednesday, 8th December, 1915
PLACE OF MURDER	13 Clifford Street, Manchester
METHOD OF KILLING	Cut throat
RELATIONSHIP TO KILLER	Girlfriend

Ellen Weller returned to collect the rent on the morning of December 9th. Again there was no reply but this time she had had the foresight to bring a duplicate key. Ellen let herself in and discovered the body of Sarah Woodall lying on the bed. Frederick Holmes was arrested the same night, in Copeland Street. He readily confessed to killing Sarah asking only that the words: "With Malice Aforethought" be removed from his charge sheet.

There remained one unanswered question. When the police searched the murder room, they found two bloodstained men's collars beneath Sarah's bed. One of those bore the name 'Wake'. Why had Sarah taken such a worthless item from her old lodgings?

IN THE CASE of Reginald Haslam, the Appeal Court suggested that had he been married to his victim, he might well have escaped with his life. Wives it seems, were more expendable!

At 5.10pm on December 23rd, 1915, Haslam walked into the Central Police Station at Burnley and said he had just murdered a woman. He appeared to be drunk and handed over a key, saying that he lived at 6 Ellis Street.

Constables Bridge and Washbrook were sent to Haslam's home, where they found Isabella Conway on the sofa. She was covered with a shawl and a piece of green ribbon had been tied very tightly around her neck.

Haslam said that he had been living with Isabella until the previous Monday, December 20th, when they had had a major row and he had gone back to his mother's. He had decided to go back to her, on December 22nd.

Haslam arrived at Ellis Street at 11.30pm but after knocking, found that Isabella would not admit him. Looking through the letterbox, he saw a pair of uniformed legs and realised that Isabella had company.

The soldier was William Ashton, who was married to Haslam's sister. They had their own marital problems and Ashton had heard that his wife had been 'playing around'. After some minutes, Ashton left, leaving Haslam and Isabella together.

An argument followed. Haslam demanded to know why Ashton had been there. Isabella replied that she would have whom she liked in her house, that she had slept with Ashton and that if Haslam had not returned, Ashton would have been staying that night.

Haslam rose at 11.00am the following morning. Isabella had a headache and asked Haslam to bring her up a pot of tea. The argument of the previous night was then renewed and Isabella confessed to sleeping with a string of men. Finally, Haslam reached out and grabbed Isabella by the throat, throttling her into unconsciousness. He then undid her blouse to check if her heart was still beating. When he found that it was, he took some green ribbon and tied it around her throat. He then left the house and went to his mother's at 3 Pitt Street.

NAME	Reginald Haslam
AGE AT EXECUTION	25
DATE OF EXECUTION	Wednesday, 29th March, 1916
PLACE OF EXECUTION	Manchester
HANGMAN	John Ellis
ASSISTANT	Edward Taylor
DATE OF TRIAL	18th February, 1916
LOCATION OF TRIAL	Manchester
PRESIDING JUDGE	Mister Justice Bailhache
PROSECUTION COUNSEL	Mister Proctor
DEFENCE COUNSEL	Mister Sandbach
NUMBER OF VICTIMS	1

VICTIMS DETAILS	
NAME	Isabella Holmes Conway
AGE	35
DATE OF MURDER	Thursday, 23rd December, 1915
PLACE OF MURDER	6 Ellis Street, Burnley
METHOD OF KILLING	Strangled
RELATIONSHIP TO KILLER	Girlfriend

That afternoon, Haslam went on a pub crawl, meeting an old friend, Frank Cunningham. Haslam bought a drink for Frank and said: "This will be the last you ever have with me." He then told Frank that he had murdered 'Bell', then walked to the police station and gave himself up.

Tried at Manchester, found guilty and sentenced to death, but with a strong recommendation to mercy, Haslam appealed on the grounds that he had been provoked. The appeal was heard on March 13th, 1916 when the Lord Chief Justice announced that had Haslam and Isabella been married, the provocation might well have reduced the charge. Haslam was only living with Isabella and therefore the appeal was rejected.

EARLY IN JUNE, 1915, a standard search of telegrams sent to addresses abroad revealed a batch of five curious messages sent from 59 Union Street, Glasgow, to August Brochner, at number 11 Toldbodgade, Christiania.

The messages were all signed either Ludovico Hurwitz, or Ludovico Hurwitz y Zender and after due consideration, the authorities contacted Glasgow police and asked them to arrest Zender. Upon arrival at Union Street though, they discovered that Zender had already left the country, sailing for Bergen on the Haakon VII, on May 28th. As a result, Zender's description and details were circulated to all ports and points of entry, on the off chance that he might return to this country.

On July 2nd, 1915, Zender did indeed return and was promptly arrested at Newcastle-upon-Tyne, and charged with spying. For his part, Zender claimed that he was there to purchase canned fish for a company in Peru, the country of his birth.

After a two-day trial in March 1916, Zender was sentenced to death. He was the last spy to be shot during the period of the First World War.

NAME	Ludovico Hurwitz y Zender
AGE AT EXECUTION	37
DATE OF EXECUTION	Tuesday, 11th April, 1916
PLACE OF EXECUTION	The Tower of London
DATE OF TRIAL	20th March – 22nd March, 1916
LOCATION OF TRIAL	Caxton Hall, Westminster
NUMBER OF VICTIMS	Shot for spying

UNTIL THE OUTBREAK of the Great War in 1914, Roger David Casement was something of a hero to the British people. A member of the British Consular Service, he had exposed scandals in Africa and South America for which, in 1911, he was awarded a knighthood.

At about the same time, Casement retired from the consular service and took up the cause of Irish Nationalism. It should be remembered that at this point, Eire was still a part of the United Kingdom and Casement was still a British subject and, although he argued for Irish independence, Casement still kept his British citizenship.

The war with Germany broke out in August 1914. Two months later, on October 15th, Casement left Ireland and went to Germany. It was his behaviour in that country that would lead to the later charges against him.

For 18 months, Casement stayed in Berlin, trying to persuade the German government to support an Irish rebellion against British rule. Further, he toured various prisoner of war camps trying to convince Irish prisoners to enlist in a brigade he was forming in order to fight on the German side. It was rumoured that those who did not agree, which was the vast majority, were treated more harshly by their German captors.

In 1916, the German authorities had agreed to assist the Irish rebels by sending them a shipment of arms to use in a planned rising on Easter Sunday. In fact, most of these weapons were useless and obsolete ones captured from the Russians on the Eastern front and so Casement sent a message to his comrades in Ireland, warning them not to use the guns. The British authorities intercepted this message and used it to trace the shipment, which was seized. Shortly afterwards, on April 20th, 1916, Casement landed in Tralee Bay from a German submarine. He was captured within hours and taken to the Tower of London, pending his trial.

The government held that Casement was a British subject who had conspired with His Majesty's enemies in a time of war. This was an act of treason and Casement was subsequently charged and tried at the Old Bailey.

NAME	Roger David Casement
AGE AT EXECUTION	52
DATE OF EXECUTION	Thursday, 3rd August, 1916
PLACE OF EXECUTION	Pentonville
HANGMAN	John Ellis
ASSISTANT	Robert Baxter
DATE OF TRIAL	26th June – 29th June, 1916
LOCATION OF TRIAL	Old Bailey
PRESIDING JUDGE	Lord Chief Justice Sir Rufus Isaacs, Mister Justice Horridge, and Mister Justice Avory
PROSECUTION COUNSEL	Sir Frederick Smith, Sir George Cave
DEFENCE COUNSEL	A.M. Sullivan, Artemus Jones, Professor J. Morgan
NUMBER OF VICTIMS	Hanged for treason

The press of the day did much to whip up public opinion and the government certainly did their part to help. Found guilty and sentenced to death, Casement was subsequently stripped of his knighthood. There were a few attempts to have the condemned man treated with some sympathy but the government countered this by allowing extracts from Casement's diaries to be published. These revealed him to be a homosexual and ended what little support he might have had.

When the notice of execution was posted outside Pentonville prison, the assembled crowds cheered. Only in Ireland was Roger Casement respected as a hero who had fought for the independence of his homeland.

Casement's last request was that his body be sent back to Ireland for burial. The request was denied and he was buried within the prison precincts, as were all condemned men. It was not until February 1965, on the orders of Harold Wilson, the prime minister of the day, that Casement's body was exhumed and returned to Ireland where it was buried in Glasnevin Cemetery, Dublin. Finally, Roger Casement's last wish had been granted.

060

FLORENCE BEATRICE BUTLER was a married woman, though she had been separated from her husband, Thomas George Butler, for more than five years. She and her nine-year-old daughter, Nellie, now lived with Florence's mother, Frances Julia Griffiths in Bath Terrace. The family also had a lodger who had been there for 10 months and by coincidence, his surname too was Butler, though he was no relation.

William Allen Butler was attracted towards his landlady's daughter and in February 1916, he started walking out with Florence. A month later, in March, Florence found she was pregnant by him. Frances knew of Florence's condition and made no move to interfere.

By May 19th though, Florence had told her mother that William had started beating her, and showed Frances bruises on her legs and body. So it was that at 3.30pm on May 20th, Frances told William Butler that he would have to leave her house just as soon as he had somewhere else to go.

At 6.40pm that evening, Florence made to go out and William demanded to know where she was going. Florence told him that it was none of his business and left the house without further comment. Ten minutes later, William also went out. Florence returned at 9.30pm and William followed her in at 10.00pm.

By 10.15pm, Frances Griffiths decided it was time to make the beds in order that the family could retire for the night. Downstairs she left William, Florence, Nellie and a neighbour, Elizabeth Rice. Frances had not been upstairs for very long when she heard Nellie screaming.

The only witness to what had happened was little Nellie Butler. She reported that as soon as Frances had gone upstairs, Mrs Rice had returned home. Almost immediately William Butler had drawn out a penknife, gone over to Florence and plunged the blade into her heart. Without uttering a word, William then walked out of the house.

At 11.05pm, William walked into Ladywood police station and gave himself up for murder. He blamed the fact that Florence had been pregnant and said he had been jealous of

a male friend of hers, Mr Ireland. A letter found on him was addressed to his mother: "Dear Mother. We like one another but it is better to part sooner or later as I am sick of my life."

Found guilty of murder, the man who was sick of his life lost it at Birmingham in August 1916.

NAME	William Allen Butler
AGE AT EXECUTION	39
DATE OF EXECUTION	Wednesday, 16th August, 1916
PLACE OF EXECUTION	Birmingham
HANGMAN	John Ellis
ASSISTANT	Edward Taylor
DATE OF TRIAL	12th July, 1916
LOCATION OF TRIAL	Birmingham
PRESIDING JUDGE	Mister Justice Avory
PROSECUTION COUNSEL	H.M. Giveen, Reginald Coventry
DEFENCE COUNSEL	Doctor W. Dawson Sadler
NUMBER OF VICTIMS	1

VICTIMS DETAILS	
NAME	Florence Beatrice Butler
AGE	29
DATE OF MURDER	Saturday, 20th May, 1916
PLACE OF MURDER	2 Bath Terrace, Chequers Walk, Birmingham
METHOD OF KILLING	Stabbed
RELATIONSHIP TO KILLER	None

DANIEL SULLIVAN HAD married Catherine, a widow with two children at the time, in 1909. Almost from the first day, Daniel was extremely cruel towards his new bride and beat her without mercy. Catherine's sister, Hannah Grant, suggested that she leave Daniel, but for one reason or another, most probably for the sake of the children, Catherine endured the situation and stayed.

At 7.30pm on July 8th, 1916, Catherine was seen by her son, Frederick John Colbert, who said that she was alive and well. At that time, Daniel was not in the house and when Frederick went out, Catherine and her daughter Bridget were left at home.

Frederick returned at 9.30pm and found that not only had Daniel returned, but he was kicking Catherine, who lay screaming on the floor. Frederick ran to his aunt's house, but Hannah Grant was out. He then ran for a neighbour, Mrs Woods, but she was in bed asleep. Frederick went back home to find that Daniel was still kicking Catherine. Although Frederick tried to stop the attack, he failed, so he ran for the police instead.

By the time constables Thomas Davies and James Bevan reached the house, Sullivan was sitting downstairs with the baby on his lap. Catherine lay badly injured on the floor and Davies, with the assistance of yet another neighbour, Mary Ann Ryan, helped to get Catherine upstairs to bed. Meanwhile, Bevan was arresting Sullivan on a charge of inflicting grievous bodily harm. Catherine died from her injuries at 3.00am the following morning, and the charge was amended to one of murder.

One of the most valuable witnesses was Bridget Ann Colbert, Catherine's nine-year-old daughter. Catherine had gone to bed, taking the baby with her, after having her evening meal and when Sullivan returned shortly afterwards and demanded to know where she was, he was not pleased with the answer. "There will be a corpse leaving this room tonight," he cried before going to the bedroom and punching Catherine in the face.

Sullivan struck his wife several times and dragged her from the bed with the comment: "Get up and get my supper." Catherine was then kicked towards the kitchen door, at

NAME	Daniel Sullivan
AGE AT EXECUTION	38
DATE OF EXECUTION	Wednesday, 6th September, 1916
PLACE OF EXECUTION	Swansea
HANGMAN	John Ellis
ASSISTANT	George Brown
DATE OF TRIAL	22nd July, 1916
LOCATION OF TRIAL	Swansea
PRESIDING JUDGE	Mister Justice Ridley
PROSECUTION COUNSEL	J.A. Lovat Fraser
DEFENCE COUNSEL	St. John Francis Williams
NUMBER OF VICTIMS	1

VICTIMS DETAILS	
NAME	Catherine Sullivan (Died Sunday, 9th July)
AGE	35
DATE OF MURDER	Saturday, 8th July, 1916
PLACE OF MURDER	20 Cwm-Canol Street, Dowlais, Merthyr Tydfil
METHOD OF KILLING	Battered
RELATIONSHIP TO KILLER	Wife

which point Bridget's brother, Frederick, came in and witnessed the rest of the attack.

When arrested, Sullivan had been very drunk, but had claimed that it was his wife who had the drink problem. The neighbour, Mary Ryan, was able to show that this was a lie, though. She had visited Catherine between 6.00pm and 7.00pm and testified that she had been perfectly sober at the time.

Daniel Sullivan was found guilty of murder and on September 6th, this cruel brute of a man received his punishment at Swansea jail.

IN DECEMBER 1915, late one night, a stranger called at the house of Mr and Mrs Gregory, in Alexandra Road, Plymouth. He explained that he was Frederick Brooks, a private in the Worcester Regiment, and he had just attended a funeral. He had been delayed and now could not get back to Tregantle. Could they put him up for the night?

The Gregorys agreed to put Brooks up and did so again in March 1916, when he paid a second visit. On June 14th, Brooks stayed for a third time, leaving the following morning at 10.00am. Just four days later, Brooks paid his fourth and final visit to Plymouth, but this time he did not call at Mr Gregory's house.

On that Monday, 12-year-old Alice Gregory had gone to school as usual. During the morning, Brooks called at the school, which was also in Alexandra Road, and informed the head teacher that he carried a message from Alice's mother saying that she had her permission to leave school and direct him to a place near Mutley Plain, where he had some business to attend to. Alice's schoolmistress, Alice Peek, interviewed the child and finding that Brooks was indeed known to her and her family, she allowed Alice to leave the school.

It was 4.30pm before Brooks approached Constable Wyatt in Bedford Street, Plymouth and explained that he wished to give himself up for killing a girl. Taken into custody, Brooks then directed officers to a field at Efford where the strangled body of Alice Gregory was discovered. She had not been sexually assaulted.

Like so many other killers in this book, Brooks tried to put forward a defence of insanity. His brother, Joseph, gave evidence at the trial stating that Frederick suffered from fits. During these attacks he would become extremely violent and afterwards would have no recollection of what he had done. The jury were not impressed and took 35 minutes to return their verdict.

NAME	Frederick Brooks
AGE AT EXECUTION	28
DATE OF EXECUTION	Tuesday, 12th December, 1916
PLACE OF EXECUTION	Exeter
HANGMAN	John Ellis
ASSISTANT	William Willis
DATE OF TRIAL	3rd November, 1916
LOCATION OF TRIAL	Exeter
PRESIDING JUDGE	Mister Justice Rowlatt
PROSECUTION COUNSEL	Radcliffe Cousins
DEFENCE COUNSEL	F.J. Tucker
NUMBER OF VICTIMS	1

VICTIMS DETAILS	
NAME	Alice Clara Gregory
AGE	12
DATE OF MURDER	Monday, 19th June, 1916
PLACE OF MURDER	Efford, Plymouth
METHOD OF KILLING	Strangled
RELATIONSHIP TO KILLER	None

IN EARLY 1914, Caroline McGhee separated from her husband, Michael, and went to live with her mother. However, prior to Christmas, 1915, she went to live with James Howarth Hargreaves.

On August 8th, 1916, Caroline spent the afternoon drinking with a friend of hers, Lily Armitage. At 5.30pm, the two women met Hargreaves in the Nelson Tavern, where they drank together until 6.45pm when Hargreaves returned home. Soon afterwards, Lily and Caroline returned to Lily's home, but by 7.00pm they were back out, this time to the Commercial Hotel where they were joined by two soldiers, William Sumner and Edward Uttley.

After a solid day's drinking, Caroline, Lily and the two soldiers, went back to Hargreaves's house, taking a bottle of whisky with them. Lily Armitage and one of the soldiers, William Sumner, left together at 11.30pm. At midnight, Edward Uttley left. Hargreaves showed him to the door and warmly shook his hand.

For the past seven weeks, Hargreaves's sister, Savinah Caroline Hindley, had been living with him. On August 8th, she went to bed at 9.15pm and said she was not disturbed at all during the night. She rose at 6.20am the following morning and noticed that there were four empty glasses downstairs.

Her brother was already up, but he was behaving most strangely and at one stage said that he wished he were dead. Savinah then went to her brother's bedroom where she collected her shawl. At that time, Savinah saw nothing to arose her suspicions.

That afternoon, at 2.25pm, Hargreaves walked up to Constable Robert Wilson, who was on duty in Katherine Street. Hargreaves seemed to be very agitated and cried out: "Oh Bob, what must I do, I've murdered a woman at our house." He then handed over his key.

Caroline McGhee lay in Hargreaves's bed. She was wearing only her underwear and had a massive wound to the back of her head. A bloodstained poker was found on the floor. The body was examined by Doctor Donald Gordon Falconer at 3.10pm and he said that Caroline had been dead around 12 hours.

Hargreaves made a full confession saying

NAME	James Howarth Hargreaves
AGE AT EXECUTION	54
DATE OF EXECUTION	Tuesday, 19th December, 1916
PLACE OF EXECUTION	Manchester
HANGMAN	John Ellis
ASSISTANT	William Willis
DATE OF TRIAL	28th November, 1916
LOCATION OF TRIAL	Manchester
PRESIDING JUDGE	Mister Justice Avory
PROSECUTION COUNSEL	Doctor Atkinson, Lindon Riley
DEFENCE COUNSEL	J.B. Sandbach
NUMBER OF VICTIMS	1

VICTIMS DETAILS	
NAME	Caroline McGhee
AGE	36
DATE OF MURDER	Wednesday, 9th August, 1916
PLACE OF MURDER	9 Orange Street, Ashton-under-Lyne
METHOD OF KILLING	Battered
RELATIONSHIP TO KILLER	Girlfriend

that Caroline had been very drunk. They had finished off the whisky between them and then an argument had broken out. Caroline had thrown the empty bottle at Hargreaves, hitting him the face and he had then picked up the poker and battered her.

There remain two unanswered questions about the case, however. If the whisky bottle hitting him was the cause of Hargreaves killing Caroline, why were there no signs of injury on him? Secondly, if Caroline was already dead in bed at 3.00am, why did Savinah see no signs of the crime when she entered that same room after 6.00am?

FOR 17 YEARS, Joseph Deans had made his living as a gold miner in South Africa. In 1913, he returned to Sunderland and in July 1915, he started seeing Catherine Convery, a widow of Devonshire Street.

From the beginning, Deans was a possessive and jealous man and more than once he had been heard to issue threats against Catherine. In October 1916, he tried to purchase a revolver, but as he didn't have a licence, he was turned away. One night soon afterwards, he had with him an axe and a razor and stated that the axe was for Catherine and the razor for himself. On October 6th, he bought himself a hatchet, remarking at the time that he was going to use it to kill his woman with. Unfortunately, he was not taken seriously.

On the night of October 7th, Deans was seen in the Grey Horse public house. As he left the pub he was heard muttering, "I will do it tonight."

When, later that same night, Catherine staggered into the same public house, blood streaming from a wound in her head, crying, "He has murdered me this time!" the threats were at last taken seriously. It was too late now, though, and Catherine died six days later, her health no doubt not helped by the fact that she had had to walk to the hospital.

Joseph Deans had attempted to kill himself, by cutting his throat, but in that he failed. Charged with murder he replied: "It is all that woman. She has had hundreds of pounds from me, and wants to toss me over now." Tried at Durham, it took the jury only five minutes to find Deans guilty and asked if he had anything to say before sentence of death was passed, Deans replied: "I killed the woman and I am pleased I killed her."

NAME	Joseph Deans
AGE AT EXECUTION	44
DATE OF EXECUTION	Wednesday, 20th December, 1916
PLACE OF EXECUTION	Durham
HANGMAN	John Ellis
ASSISTANT	George Brown
DATE OF TRIAL	15th November, 1916
LOCATION OF TRIAL	Durham
PRESIDING JUDGE	Mister Justice Low
PROSECUTION COUNSEL	Mister Cautley M.P.
DEFENCE COUNSEL	W.W. Cambier
NUMBER OF VICTIMS	1

VICTIMS DETAILS

NAME	Catherine Convery (Died Friday, 13th October)
AGE	48
DATE OF MURDER	Saturday, 7th October, 1916
PLACE OF MURDER	Monkwearmouth, Sunderland
METHOD OF KILLING	Battered
RELATIONSHIP TO KILLER	Girlfriend

COMPANY SERGEANT-MAJORS are not noted for their popularity and such was certainly the case with Henry Lynch of the Welsh Fusiliers. A number of the men under his command would admit that they disliked him, but perhaps none had feelings as intense as those of Thomas Clinton.

In November 1916, Lynch had placed Clinton in the guard room for a minor offence and this only served to make the feelings between the two men even more acute. Over the next few months, It was said that Clinton had often been heard making derogatory comments against Lynch, and on one occasion is supposed to have remarked: "He's a swine and it's a wonder he has not been laid out before."

It was January 13th, 1917 when Clinton took a rifle from the guard room, held it in the 'on guard' position and marched into the room where Lynch was busily writing, to ask why he hadn't yet received his midday meal. Opening the door, Clinton announced: "Now then, Sergeant-Major." At that, the gun went off and Henry Lynch rose, staggered towards the door crying: "I'm dead. I'm dead." He then collapsed to the floor.

Clinton's defence was that the shooting was accidental. As he had held the gun towards Lynch, it had simply gone off. A lance corporal had witnessed the shooting and described the events outlined. His testimony indicated that the firing of the gun could have been interpreted as accidental but Clinton's apparent hatred of his sergeant-major and his previous comments weighed heavily against him. The testimony of Captain Webb, who described Lynch as a diligent officer with almost 22 years' service in the army, and detailed the fact that he had been wounded in the war, also did not help Clinton's case.

The final nail in Clinton's coffin came from the trial judge, Mister Justice Shearman. In his summing-up he stated, astoundingly, that there could be no verdict of manslaughter. The jury must either find Clinton guilty of murder, or acquit him. With their hands thus tied, the jury had little choice but to return a guilty verdict after 20 minutes' deliberation.

NAME	Thomas Clinton
AGE AT EXECUTION	28
DATE OF EXECUTION	Wednesday, 21st March, 1917
PLACE OF EXECUTION	Manchester
HANGMAN	John Ellis
ASSISTANT	Not known
DATE OF TRIAL	15th February, 1917
LOCATION OF TRIAL	Manchester
PRESIDING JUDGE	Mister Justice Shearman
PROSECUTION COUNSEL	A.H. Maxwell, Lindon Riley
DEFENCE COUNSEL	Gilbert Jordan
NUMBER OF VICTIMS	1

VICTIMS DETAILS	
NAME	Henry Lynch
AGE	39
DATE OF MURDER	Saturday, 13th January, 1917
PLACE OF MURDER	Camp of the Welsh Fusiliers, Barrow
METHOD OF KILLING	Shot
RELATIONSHIP TO KILLER	None

Sentenced to death, Thomas Clinton, was executed at Manchester on March 21st. One cannot help but wonder if the ends of justice had really been served.

A T SOME TIME after 1.00pm on February 15th, 1917, Lily Tindale, the 13-year-old daughter of the bailiff of Constitution Hill Farm, was seen entering the stack yard of the farm. Soon afterwards, John William Thompson, a shepherd who had worked and lodged at the farm since May, 1916, was also seen entering the stack yard. Soon afterwards, he disappeared from the premises.

When Lily did not return to the house, her parents became somewhat concerned and began looking for her. Her father recalled that she had been in the yard earlier, so began his search there. It was he who found her body. Lily lay covered in straw. Her throat had been cut and her clothing had been disarranged.

Tests would later show that Lily had not been raped, though that might well have been the intention of her assailant. An interesting clue had been discovered, though. On Lily's body lay a plug of tobacco. The police were already looking for Thompson, but when it was discovered that at noon that day, he had been at the Molescroft Inn, about half a mile away, where he had purchased some tobacco, the search became even more intensive.

It would be 6.00pm before Thompson was picked up, at Beverley. When he was found, his clothing was heavily bloodstained, as were his hands, his pipe and a clasp knife found in his pocket. To account for all this gore, Thompson explained that he had been bleeding a sheep, but when tests showed that all the blood was of human origin, the case against him was complete.

Tried at York in March, Thompson was found guilty and executed 18 days later. It was less than six weeks since the murder of Lily Tindale had taken place.

NAME	John William Thompson
AGE AT EXECUTION	43
DATE OF EXECUTION	Tuesday, 27th March, 1917
PLACE OF EXECUTION	Leeds
HANGMAN	Thomas Pierrepoint
ASSISTANT	William Willis
DATE OF TRIAL	9th March, 1917
LOCATION OF TRIAL	York
PRESIDING JUDGE	Mister Justice McCardie
PROSECUTION COUNSEL	Edward Shortt M.P., C.F. Lowenthal
DEFENCE COUNSEL	C. Paley Scott
NUMBER OF VICTIMS	1

VICTIMS DETAILS	
NAME	Lily Tindale
AGE	13
DATE OF MURDER	Thursday, 15th February, 1917
PLACE OF MURDER	Constitution Hill Farm, Molescroft, near Beverley
METHOD OF KILLING	Cut throat
RELATIONSHIP TO KILLER	None

IT WAS EASY to determine the time of death in the case of Lieutenant William Watterton. His body lay in a trench, battered to death by means of a lavatory brush and a heavy jagged stone, and in the struggle for his life, Watterton had fallen and broken his watch. It had stopped at almost exactly nine o'clock.

Lieutenant Watterton had a daughter, and she had recently become enamoured of a young sergeant in the R.A.M.C., named Leo O'Donnell. On the night of Monday, January 1st, 1917, O'Donnell had called on Watterton to ask him for permission to marry his daughter. The lady, meanwhile, had gone out with a friend of hers. She would later testify that she left her father alone in the house with O'Donnell, who had with him a trimmed-down lavatory brush.

When Miss Watterton returned at 9.15pm, there was no one about. At 11.30pm, O'Donnell called and told her that shortly after she had left, her father had remembered an appointment. Watterton had dressed and left at about 8.10pm. As he did so, O'Donnell mentioned the lavatory brush and observed that her father appeared to have taken it.

The police asked O'Donnell to account for his movements. He replied that he had gone to the mess at 8.15pm, then on to the Headquarters office building to do some work before going to a social. He gave the names of several friends who had spoken to him but when they were asked to confirm this, every one denied having seen O'Donnell there.

Sergeant James Wood was in the mess from 7.00pm until 9.00pm. He remarked that the room was quiet and that if O'Donnell had come in, he would have seen him. O'Donnell was arrested and charged.

Whilst being held at Winchester prison, O'Donnell tried to get a fellow prisoner to get someone to say he had been in Winchester on the night of the murder. If such a man could be found, O'Donnell would pay him £500. He also wrote to Miss Watterton and asked her to say that they were together at the time of the killing.

The defence was that O'Donnell had not committed the crime. And to account for himself, O'Donnell proceeded to tell a

NAME	Leo George O'Donnell
AGE AT EXECUTION	26
DATE OF EXECUTION	Thursday, 29th March, 1917
PLACE OF EXECUTION	Winchester
HANGMAN	John Ellis
ASSISTANT	Robert Baxter
DATE OF TRIAL	9th February – 10th February, 1917
LOCATION OF TRIAL	Winchester
PRESIDING JUDGE	Mister Justice Darling
PROSECUTION COUNSEL	Clavell Salter
DEFENCE COUNSEL	H. du Parcq
NUMBER OF VICTIMS	1

VICTIMS DETAILS	
NAME	William F. Watterton
AGE	48
DATE OF MURDER	Monday, 1st January, 1917
PLACE OF MURDER	Aldershot
METHOD OF KILLING	Battered
RELATIONSHIP TO KILLER	None

fantastic story of blackmail. According to O'Donnell, about a month before Christmas, Watterton had confided to him that a man had appeared and claimed to be Watterton's son, Watterton having admitted to an affair with a Spanish girl whilst in Gibraltar. The young man was blackmailing Watterton and it was he who had killed Watterton on the night of January 1st.

The jury treated all these stories with the contempt they deserved, and found O'Donnell guilty.

0308

GEORGE FORTT RAN a lodging house for Greek sailors and seamen at Bute Road, Cardiff. His 19-year-old daughter, Winifred, lived with him and in 1917, she became very friendly with one of the lodgers, Alec Bakerlis.

What should have been a pleasant relationship was marred by the fact that Bakerlis was insanely jealous. Every time Winifred as much as spoke to another lodger, he threw a temper tantrum and demanded that she should not behave in such a fashion. Eventually, things became so bad that George Fortt told Bakerlis he would have to find new lodgings.

In due course, Bakerlis moved to a house run by George Antonio, in Wharf Street and Winifred, realising that things were unlikely to improve, decided to finally break off all contact with him. In December, Winifred gave some letters and a ring, to Rhonda Heard, a friend, and asked her to return them to Bakerlis. When Rhonda approached Bakerlis and tried to hand the items over, he refused to take them, saying he would only accept them from Winifred's own hand.

It was Christmas night and Winifred and Rhonda were standing near the Bute Street Bridge, close to her father's lodging house, when Bakerlis approached them and asked for the letters and the ring. Winifred was wearing the ring at the time, so removed it and handed it over, adding that she would go home for the letters if he would wait a minute. That, it seems, was a signal for Bakerlis to throw one of his tantrums.

Immediately Bakerlis lashed out and knocked Winifred to the ground. Then, taking out a knife, he began stabbing her repeatedly. In addition to Rhonda Heard, there were other witnesses to this frenzied attack. Jane Redguist was nearby, heard the screams and saw Bakerlis stab Winifred at least twice more before he ran off. Two young boys, William Gale and Thomas Powell, saw Bakerlis running away and Police Constable Arthur Moss, on duty near the Bute Street station, saw Bakerlis running towards him, the bloody knife still in his hand.

Moss stopped Bakerlis, who readily admitted what he had done. Winifred was still alive but she died from blood poisoning

NAME	Alec Bakerlis
AGE AT EXECUTION	24
DATE OF EXECUTION	Tuesday, 10th April, 1917
PLACE OF EXECUTION	Cardiff
HANGMAN	John Ellis
ASSISTANT	Edward Taylor
DATE OF TRIAL	6th March, 1917
LOCATION OF TRIAL	Cardiff
PRESIDING JUDGE	Mister Justice Bailhache
PROSECUTION COUNSEL	W. Llewelyn Williams M.P., J.A.Lovat-Fraser
DEFENCE COUNSEL	Marlay Samson
NUMBER OF VICTIMS	1

VICTIMS DETAILS	
NAME	Winifred Ellen Fortt (Died Thursday, 28th December)
AGE	19
DATE OF MURDER	Monday, 25th December, 1916
PLACE OF MURDER	Bute Street, Cardiff
METHOD OF KILLING	Stabbed
RELATIONSHIP TO KILLER	Girlfriend

on December 28th, making the charge one of murder.

The trial took place at Cardiff in March and the jury took a mere 10 minutes to find Bakerlis guilty.

WALTER HENRY RHODES was enjoying a quiet drink in the Sussex Stores public house. It was almost closing time and as he finished his pint, Rhodes noticed a young Canadian soldier leaving the pub, in the company of an attractive young woman. He also noticed that they were rapidly followed by two men.

Almost immediately there came from outside the sound of breaking glass and the noise of some kind of fight. Rhodes and some of the other customers went outside to see what was going on. The Canadian soldier lay in the road, dying from a stab wound. The girl was bending over him, trying to cradle him in her arms. Of the two men who had followed them out of the pub, there was now no sign.

In due course, the police arrested two men: William James Robinson and John Henry Gray. Evidence was given by Maggie Harding, the woman who had been with Alfred Williams, the murdered Canadian, that the two men had simply walked up to them and one, Robinson, had picked a fight during which he drew a knife and plunged it into Williams. Rhodes also testified that Robinson and Gray were the two men he had seen follow Williams and Miss Harding out of the pub. This destroyed the defence put forward by Robinson and Gray that it was a case of mistaken identity and that they were nowhere near the pub when the attack took place. Robinson was found guilty of murder and sentenced to death. Gray received three years for manslaughter.

It was whilst Robinson was in prison awaiting execution that he wrote a remarkable letter to Miss Harding. In that letter he began by saying that he was guilty of the crime and was satisfied with his sentence. Maggie Harding destroyed the letter, but the significance of its contents had been noted and the prison warder who had read it in the course of his duties forwarded it on to the Home Office, where it was copied. It was this written confession, surprisingly, that formed the basis of Robinson's appeal!

The letter had gone on to say that on the day before Williams's death, Robinson had been in another pub where he had argued with some Canadian soldiers. When he saw

NAME	William James Robinson
AGE AT EXECUTION	26
DATE OF EXECUTION	Tuesday, 17th April, 1917
PLACE OF EXECUTION	Pentonville
HANGMAN	John Ellis
ASSISTANT	Robert Baxter
DATE OF TRIAL	5th March – 7th March, 1917
LOCATION OF TRIAL	Old Bailey
PRESIDING JUDGE	Lord Justice Coleridge
PROSECUTION COUNSEL	Richard D. Muir
DEFENCE COUNSEL	Not known
NUMBER OF VICTIMS	1

VICTIMS DETAILS	
NAME	Alfred Williams
AGE	35
DATE OF MURDER	Sunday, 26th November, 1916
PLACE OF MURDER	Sussex Stores Pub, Upper St Martins Lane, London
METHOD OF KILLING	Stabbed
RELATIONSHIP TO KILLER	None

Williams, he mistook him for one of the men he had argued with and attacked him on the spur of the moment. The defence held that since there was clearly no intention to kill, Robinson should not hang for murder.

This somewhat interesting concept did not persuade the appeal court judges and the sentence of death was upheld.

ROBERT GADSBY HAD been a widower since February 1916, but he soon found another love in the shape of Julia Johnson, who was separated from her husband Thomas.

At 9.20am on February 28th, 1917, Robert returned to the house in Park Place, Bell Lane, that he shared with his daughter Mathilda and her husband, Benjamin Hart.

Robert handed his watch over to Mathilda, washed his hands and then walked to the police station, where he admitted that he had cut Julia's throat.

Robert went on to say that he had been around to Julia's house that morning and they had argued. She had sworn at him and ordered him out of her house. He in turn accused her of going with other men and at the height of the row, he took out his penknife, held on to Julia with one hand, and cut her throat with the other. When it came to giving evidence at the inquest though, Robert Gadsby told a somewhat different story.

Robert now claimed that he had his knife open in his hand as he was cutting himself a twist of tobacco when Julia leapt upon him with a knife and cut his neck. In the struggle that followed, he cut her throat, the whole thing being over in less than five minutes.

At the trial, which took place at Leeds on March 19th, Robert elaborated on this second story. When he had said goodnight to Julia on the night of Sunday, February 25th, he had noticed a man waiting for her. When he entered her house on the day of her death, Julia thought there would be an argument over this other man, but Robert told her that he had only come for the ring he had given her and $4 of the $8-15s she owed him.

At this point, Julia had become tearful and reminded Robert that he had once said they would never part. So saying, she threw her arms around his neck and when he brusquely removed them, Julia grabbed a kitchen knife and attacked him. As he had suggested before, he was cutting himself some tobacco at the time and as he fought her off, he must have cut her accidentally.

The story did not convince the jury, who came to the conclusion that Robert had deliberately murdered Julia.

NAME	Robert Gadsby
AGE AT EXECUTION	65
DATE OF EXECUTION	Wednesday, 18th April, 1917
PLACE OF EXECUTION	Leeds
HANGMAN	Thomas Pierrepoint
ASSISTANT	Robert Baxter
DATE OF TRIAL	19th March, 1917
LOCATION OF TRIAL	Leeds
PRESIDING JUDGE	Mister Justice McCardie
PROSECUTION COUNSEL	W. Valentine Ball
DEFENCE COUNSEL	Mister Gingall
NUMBER OF VICTIMS	1

VICTIMS DETAILS

NAME	Julia Ann Johnson
AGE	54
DATE OF MURDER	Wednesday, 28th February, 1917
PLACE OF MURDER	3 Thrift Crescent, Waterloo Lane, Bramley
METHOD OF KILLING	Cut throat
RELATIONSHIP TO KILLER	Girlfriend

IN 1916, THOMAS McGuiness was in Aberdeen and it was there that he met an attractive waitress. The two grew friendly until, in March, Thomas announced that he was going to move to Dundee. His new girlfriend decided to accompany him.

Once the couple began living together, Thomas McGuiness began to show a different side to his personality. He now began to mistreat his paramour and her young son, Alexander. After some months, Mrs Imlach took her child and moved to Edinburgh. In due course, McGuiness too went to Edinburgh and for some reason, Mrs Imlach decided to give McGuniness another chance and they made a new start, this time in Glasgow, where they lodged in Baltic Street.

McGuiness hadn't changed, though. He again began to mistreat little Alexander, sometimes putting lighted cigarettes to his flesh and on one occasion throwing him downstairs. When the couple moved again, this time to Springfield Road, the torture grew even worse.

Another move, this time to Blackburn Street in Govan, did not make matters any better. In fact, things came to a head in March 1917 when, in addition to continuing his mistreatment of the boy, McGuiness only opted to give the child's mother a mere 3/- to keep the house in food.

On March 8th, at 10.00am, Alexander's mother went out to try to put some food on the table. At that time, the little boy was asleep in bed, but when she returned, 15 minutes later, McGuiness was holding Alexander on his knee. The child's eyes were closed, his upper lip was swollen, his face was blue on one side and he was gasping for breath. McGuiness would only say "Alick has taken a fit."

The child was rushed to a neighbour's house whilst McGuiness said he would go and fetch the doctor. Instead he left the house and did not return, possibly because the neighbour had mentioned that the police should be called in. A search was now launched for McGuiness. He was arrested later the same day, at Springburn, by Detective Inspector Storrar.

Young Alexander was later to die of his

NAME	Thomas McGuiness
AGE AT EXECUTION	25
DATE OF EXECUTION	Wednesday, 16th May, 1917
PLACE OF EXECUTION	Duke Street, Glasgow
HANGMAN	John Ellis
ASSISTANT	Not known
DATE OF TRIAL	24th April – 25th April, 1917
LOCATION OF TRIAL	Glasgow
PRESIDING JUDGE	Lord Justice Johnston
PROSECUTION COUNSEL	George Morton
DEFENCE COUNSEL	John Wilson, J.R. Gibb
NUMBER OF VICTIMS	1

VICTIMS DETAILS	
NAME	Alexander Imlach
AGE	5
DATE OF MURDER	Thursday, 8th March, 1917
PLACE OF MURDER	101 Blackburn Street, Govan, Glasgow
METHOD OF KILLING	Battered
RELATIONSHIP TO KILLER	None

injuries. Put on trial for murder, an attempt was made to show that McGuiness had mental problems. His mother said that he had been subject to fits as a child, whilst his sister said that he had always behaved in a strange way. As if to emphasise this, McGuiness twitched whilst he was standing in the dock, wobbled on his feet and looked as if he was about to faint. He was taken down to the cells, where he received medical attention.

In the event, none of this did anything to save McGuiness, who was found guilty by a majority verdict.

THERE WERE FOUR people living in the semi-detached house at number 16 Central Park Avenue. In addition to William Hodgson and his wife, Margaret, whom he had married in September, 1910, there were also the two children – three-year-old Margaret, who had a birthday due on April 27th, and one year-old Cyril.

By all accounts, the Hodgsons were a happy couple. Margaret stayed at home to look after the children and William worked as a buyer in the silk department at Robb Brothers, a drapers. This apparent domestic bliss was to be changed on April 16th.

At 7.00am, the milkman, Thomas Robinson, delivered as he usually did, knowing that he would return that afternoon in order to collect the empty bottles. Around 40 minutes later, Eleanor Law, the neighbour at number 14, which was the house attached to number 16, reported hearing little Margaret's voice saying, "Don't do that", followed by footsteps in the yard. Later an attempt would be made to put a rather sinister interpretation on this occurrence, but it should be stressed that Mrs Law saw no reason for concern in the tone of that request from the child who lived next door.

William Hodgson said he left for work at 8.30am, as he always did. There was subsequently some disagreement over the actual time of his departure. A neighbour who lived opposite, Eliza Godfrey Ward Westmore, would report that she heard a door bang at 9.00am and upon looking out of her window, saw William on his doorstep. He was carrying a small parcel and Mrs Westmore watched him as he walked down the street.

Under normal circumstances, a note was kept of the time employees arrived for work at Messrs Robb Brothers, but occasionally the member of staff responsible for time-keeping was not as diligent as she should have been and some days no records were kept. This, unfortunately for Hodgson, was one of those days and his exact time of arrival was not noted. All that could be said with certainty was that he normally started work sometime between 8.57am and 9.23am. Since no mention was made of Hodgson being late, we can only assume that he was at work by 9.23am that morning.

Thomas Robinson, the milkman, returned at 3.30pm, but could not get a reply to his knocking. Nothing else aroused the suspicions of people in Central Park Avenue until around 6.00pm when Eleanor Law, tired of hearing baby Cyril crying, decided to go next door to see if anything was the matter. Perhaps the child was ill and Margaret needed some help.

Eleanor knocked on the glass panel in the front door. There was no reply. Going around to the back, Eleanor saw that the vestibule door was unlocked. She opened it, went in and entered the kitchen.

The room was full of blood and on the floor lay two battered bodies, that of Margaret senior and her daughter. Nearby lay a bloodstained axe. Eleanor had seen enough. She ran out and sought the help of William Samuel Wells, who happened to be passing at the time.

NAME	William Thomas Hodgson
AGE AT EXECUTION	34
DATE OF EXECUTION	Thursday, 16th August, 1917
PLACE OF EXECUTION	Liverpool
HANGMAN	John Ellis
ASSISTANT	Edward Taylor
DATE OF TRIAL	11th July – 13th July, 1917
LOCATION OF TRIAL	Chester
PRESIDING JUDGE	Mister Justice Avory
PROSECUTION COUNSEL	Ellis Griffiths M.P., Trevor Lloyd
DEFENCE COUNSEL	Lindon Riley, Ralph Sutton
NUMBER OF VICTIMS	2

VICTIMS DETAILS	
NAMES	Margaret Alderson Hodgson; Margaret Hodgson
AGES	37; 3
DATE OF MURDER	Monday, 16th April, 1917
PLACE OF MURDER	16 Central Park Avenue, Wallasey, Liverpool
METHODS OF KILLING	Battered; battered
RELATIONSHIPS TO KILLER	Wife; daughter

1917

Wells timed his entrance to the house at 6.07pm. He entered the kitchen and saw, in addition to the scene of carnage, an empty moneybox and purse on the table. He then went upstairs, found baby Cyril, who was unharmed, and took him out of the house. It appeared that the baby had remained alone for some time. He was very hungry and his nappy was soaking wet. He was also still wearing his nightgown from the previous evening.

At about the same time that the police were beginning their investigation of the murder scene, William Hodgson was entering the Charing Cross Hotel, where he often went after work for a quick drink or two with William Marshall Wilson, a workmate. Today was no different, and after the drinks, the two men started to walk home. At Wheatland Lane, they parted, Hodgson remarking that he had to get home as he was going to babysit that evening whilst his wife took his daughter to the pictures.

As soon as he arrived home, Hodgson knew something was wrong. For a start, the house was crawling with police, who would not tell him what had happened. At one stage he stood just inside the kitchen, but the bodies had by now been moved so Hodgson did not see his wife and child. Taken to the police station, Hodgson was finally told what had happened and was then charged with the double murder. He denied the charge.

All the evidence against Hodgson was purely circumstantial. His clothes and boots were taken for forensic examination and whilst some blood was found on his clothing, he explained this by saying he had cut himself shaving some days before. More telling perhaps was the fact that only one small spot of blood was found on his boots. If he had wielded the flat end of an axe on his wife and child, surely his boots would have displayed more bloodstains. After all, there were many splashed on the walls and furniture.

Doctor Thomas Napier, who examined the bodies at 6.45pm, put the time of death at some eight to 10 hours beforehand. This put the time of the attack at 8.45am at the earliest. Even by Eliza Westmore's evidence, that gave Hodgson only 15 minutes to kill two people,

clean himself up a little, fake a robbery and then leave for work at 9.00am. According to his own statement of course, he had already left the house, at 8.30am.

The police did discover what seemed to be a motive. Hodgson had been having an affair with a young waitress named Helena Llewellyn, and she was now pregnant. Helena did not know that Hodgson was a married man and her parents had been pressing him to marry their daughter.

Hodgson was put on trial for murder, found guilty and sentenced to death. There remains, though, one awkward, unanswered question about the case.

In part of Hodgson's statement he referred to the fact that a man had called a few days before his wife was killed. This man had offered to do the garden and Margaret had told him to call back when her husband was at home. She went on to say that he should not call after 8.30am or before 7.00pm, thus telling him precisely when she was alone with the children.

The police had found a spade in the back garden and the soil had been recently turned over. They never determined with any certainty who had done that digging.

ON JUNE 20TH, 1917, whilst the Great War was still taking lives by the thousands each day, a group of British sailors was taking a well-earned leave in the city of Newcastle. Amongst those sailors was a cluster of friends: McDonald, Grant, Alfred Birling, Alfred Gough and Henry Hollyer.

At 6.00pm, the group came into the centre of the city and found themselves finally at the Mechanic's Arms pub. Here they met up with two ladies, Isabella Caroline Smith and Sarah Shearer and somewhat later, they were also joined by Ruby Wright and Margaret Brown, who preferred to be called Muriel.

The night progressed and as closing time came, the sailors were invited to accompany the ladies back to Ruby's home in West Street, where further drink would be made available. The knot of people had been in West Street for about an hour when two men arrived: William Cavanagh and James Innes.

William Cavanagh was seeing Ruby on a regular basis and so having all these sailors in her house did not put him in the best of moods. Things degenerated even further just after midnight when some of the women present started jeering at Cavanagh because he was not in the services and therefore not serving his country in her time of need.

The dispute became a full-scale fight. Innes knocked McDonald to the ground outside in the street and then went back inside to give assistance to Cavanagh. He, meanwhile, had struck Hollyer in the face, causing him to collapse to the floor. Then, as the fight continued all around, Cavanagh drew out a knife as Alfred Gough made a move towards him. Gough was stabbed in the jaw and then Cavanagh stabbed Hollyer in the small of his back.

Alfred Gough made a full recovery but Hollyer died in hospital on June 25th. Police inquiries were made and on the strength of the sailors' evidence, Cavanagh, Innes and Ruby Wright were all charged with murder.

As the trial opened the prosecution stated that they would offer no evidence against Ruby. She was formally found not guilty and discharged, leaving the two men to face the capital charge.

Indeed, Ruby gave evidence on their

NAME	William Cavanagh (William James Thompson)
AGE AT EXECUTION	29
DATE OF EXECUTION	Tuesday, 18th December, 1917
PLACE OF EXECUTION	Newcastle
HANGMAN	Thomas Pierrepoint
ASSISTANT	Robert Baxter
DATE OF TRIAL	12th November, 1917
LOCATION OF TRIAL	Newcastle
PRESIDING JUDGE	Mister Justice Salter
PROSECUTION COUNSEL	Edward Shortt M.P., E. Meynell
DEFENCE COUNSEL	Charles Mellor
NUMBER OF VICTIMS	1

VICTIMS DETAILS

NAME	Henry Arthur Hollyer (Died, Monday, 25th June)
AGE	27
DATE OF MURDER	Thursday, 21st June, 1917
PLACE OF MURDER	1 West Street, Newcastle
METHOD OF KILLING	Stabbed
RELATIONSHIP TO KILLER	None

behalf, stating that the sailors had brought four bottles of whisky back to the house and that Hollyer had struck the first blow. Both these statements were hotly denied by Gough and the other sailors. Eventually the jury returned their verdicts. James Innes was found not guilty but Cavanagh, who was also known as William James Thompson, was guilty. Sentenced to death, he lost his appeal on December 3rd and was executed 15 days later.

A LTHOUGH HE WAS only 13 years old, Henry Cox had been forced to grow beyond his years. His parents, Thomas and Elizabeth argued incessantly. Thomas did his best to promote peace and protect his eight-year-old brother, Benjamin, but nothing he did prevented his father and mother from attacking each other.

There were some attempts at organising a normal family life. Thursday, August 9th, 1917 for instance, saw the entire family collecting sticks for the fire, but even then, Henry's parents were at each other from dawn until dusk.

August 10th seemed to pass without incident, for once, but this was more than made up on the following day. At 2.30am on August 11th, Henry Cox was woken by his mother screaming. Henry heard his father shout: "What do you want to tell so many lies of me for?" and was in time to see him strike Elizabeth. The entire family slept in the one bedroom, so Henry comforted his brother, lit the lamp and saw that his mother had been injured. Noticing her eldest son awake, Elizabeth asked Henry if he would fetch her some water so that she could bathe her head. Henry, a dutiful son, did as he was asked.

Just as Henry was about to leave the bedroom, he heard his mother scream again, turned and was in time to see his father standing close by Elizabeth and something flashing close by her neck. At that point the light went out but Henry knew what must have happened. "Has he cut your throat," gasped Henry? "Yes," answered his mother. Henry lit the lamp again and saw that his mother was lying on the floor. Henry Cox, sitting up on the bed, had also cut his own throat but he demanded that Henry return to his bed. No doubt in fear of his life, Henry did as he was told.

At 7.20am, Henry Cox was woken by his father, who asked him to run to a neighbour and raise the alarm. In fact, Henry ran to his aunt's, Mary Ward's house at 30 Old Street, Ludlow, and told her what had happened. She called for the police and returned to Cox's house, together with Constable Charles Morris. Elizabeth Cox had by then been dead for some time, but Henry was still on the bed,

NAME	Thomas Cox
AGE AT EXECUTION	59
DATE OF EXECUTION	Wednesday, 19th December, 1917
PLACE OF EXECUTION	Shrewsbury
HANGMAN	John Ellis
ASSISTANT	William Willis
DATE OF TRIAL	8th November, 1917
LOCATION OF TRIAL	Shrewsbury
PRESIDING JUDGE	Mister Justice Atkin
PROSECUTION COUNSEL	D. Cotes-Preedy
DEFENCE COUNSEL	Alexander Graham
NUMBER OF VICTIMS	1

VICTIMS DETAILS	
NAME	Elizabeth Cox
AGE	49
DATE OF MURDER	Saturday, 11th August, 1917
PLACE OF MURDER	37 Upper Galdeford, Ludlow
METHOD OF KILLING	Cut throat
RELATIONSHIP TO KILLER	Wife

weak from loss of blood. All he could gasp was that he had no idea why he had done it.

Tried at Shrewsbury, Cox attempted to say that he must have been insane at the time of the attack. The defence mentioned that Cox had once before attempted to commit suicide, but this had no bearing on the state of his mind on August 11th and his pleas were rejected.

HAD IT NOT been for an old watch and a mackintosh, Arthur de Stamir would probably have got away with murder.

On the night of November 12th, 1917, the Tighe family retired for the night at 11.30pm. Captain Tighe suffered from asthma, so he slept in a different room to his wife.

The following morning, at 7.30am, as the maid was passing Captain Tighe's room, she heard groaning. Going in, she discovered that Tighe had been battered with a poker. He was rushed to hospital but died there on November 17th.

A window at the back, on the ground floor, was slightly open and the murder weapon had been taken from a set in the dining room. The only things missing were an old oxidised metal watch and a mackintosh. The police believed that Tighe had disturbed the thief and that the only reason the mackintosh had been taken was to cover bloodstains.

On Tuesday December 11th, a pawnbroker contacted the police to say that a man had been trying to sell items that might be stolen. The pawnbroker had asked the man to call back. The police staked out the premises and waited.

Later the same day, the man returned, carrying over £200 worth of silver plate from a house in Streatham. He was arrested and identified as Arthur de Stamir, whose real surname was Stamrowsky.

When de Stamir's rooms were searched, amongst other items found was an old oxidised watch and a mackintosh. De Stamir was charged with murder.

The defence was fanciful. Arthur claimed that on November 7th he had met an Australian soldier who gave his name as Reginald Fisher. Soon, de Stamir was agreeing to go on a robbery with Fisher. Winkfield Lodge was chosen as the target.

The two men entered and after searching the lower rooms, Fisher took a poker to force open any drawers or locks. They went upstairs and entered Tighe's room. Tighe woke up and moved his hand along the pillow, whereupon Fisher brought the poker down on Tighe's head. They only had time to steal the watch but Fisher took a mackintosh to cover his tunic.

NAME	Arthur Harold Victor Stamrowsky (de Stamir)
AGE AT EXECUTION	26
DATE OF EXECUTION	Tuesday, 12th February, 1918
PLACE OF EXECUTION	Wandsworth
HANGMAN	John Ellis
ASSISTANT	George Brown
DATE OF TRIAL	10th January, 1918
LOCATION OF TRIAL	Old Bailey
PRESIDING JUDGE	Mister Justice Darling
PROSECUTION COUNSEL	Travers Humphreys, Percival Clarke
DEFENCE COUNSEL	J.A.C. Keeves
NUMBER OF VICTIMS	1

VICTIMS DETAILS	
NAME	Edward Kenrick Bunbury Tighe (Died Saturday, 17th November)
AGE	55
DATE OF MURDER	Monday, 12th November, 1917
PLACE OF MURDER	Winkfield Lodge, Park Side, Wimbledon, London
METHOD OF KILLING	Battered
RELATIONSHIP TO KILLER	None

Arthur said that he met Fisher two days later. They agreed that they should not see each other again. Fisher, though, was short of money so de Stamir agreed to buy the mackintosh from him, for which he gave 10/-.

If Fisher really existed then de Stamir had been with him when Fisher killed Tighe and so de Stamir would be equally guilty of murder. If Fisher did not exist, then de Stamir had committed the offence alone. Either way he was guilty.

Arthur de Stamir was hanged in February, but if he had had the sense to throw away an old watch and a mackintosh, he might well have escaped with a prison term.

O N NOVEMBER 8TH, 1917, John
Mackinlay, a soldier in the Canadian
army, met up with Oliver Imlay, at the
Y.M.C.A., in Waterloo Road. They had a few
drinks in a pub, where they fell into
conversation with an Australian soldier. The
three men left together and, close to Waterloo
Bridge, the Australian said he had seen
someone he knew and pointed out another
Aussie soldier, who was with a man and two
women. The entire group chatted for a while
and then the girls left.

The Canadians revealed where they were
staying, but the second Australian told them
he could show them somewhere better. They
walked down an alley off Blackfriars Road
and suddenly Mackinlay heard a soft thud. He
turned to see Imlay fall to the ground.
MacKinlay was also attacked and rendered
unconscious. Imlay died three days later, from
a fractured skull.

Ernest Edward Sharp was an absentee
from the Australian army and when he was
picked up on November 23rd, he said that he
wished to make a statement. Sharp said that
he had gone absent in September. In October
he met up with two other men: Thomas
Vincent Maguire and Joseph Jones.

On the night of November 8th, Sharp had
met Jones and Maguire on Waterloo Bridge.
They were with two girls, Hetty O'Connor and
Emily Birmingham, and two Canadian
soldiers. Not long afterwards, the girls left and
Jones told the Canadians about a place they
could stay. Once they reached Blackfriars
Road, Jones pulled Sharp to one side and
battered Imlay with a truncheon. Jones then
rifled through his pockets. Meanwhile,
Maguire had attacked the other Canadian,
MacKinlay. All three men were arrested.

On the first day of the trial it was
announced that Sharp would give evidence
for the prosecution, so no evidence would be
offered against him on the charge of murder.
He pleaded guilty to robbery, for which he
received seven years.

Maguire's defence was that it had been
Jones who struck the blows. Jones said that
there had been a fight between Sharp and one
of the Canadians. When he intervened, he was
struck and simply fought back.

NAME	Joseph Jones
AGE AT EXECUTION	26
DATE OF EXECUTION	Thursday, 21st February, 1918
PLACE OF EXECUTION	Wandsworth
HANGMAN	John Ellis
ASSISTANT	William Willis
DATE OF TRIAL	14th January – 15th January, 1918
LOCATION OF TRIAL	Old Bailey
PRESIDING JUDGE	Mister Justice Darling
PROSECUTION COUNSEL	Archibald Bodkin, Cecil Whiteley
DEFENCE COUNSEL	Arthur Bryan, Reginald Holt
NUMBER OF VICTIMS	1

VICTIMS DETAILS	
NAME	Oliver Gilbert Imlay (Died Sunday, 11th November)
AGE	24
DATE OF MURDER	Thursday, 8th November, 1917
PLACE OF MURDER	Valentine Place, Blackfriars Road, London
METHOD OF KILLING	Battered
RELATIONSHIP TO KILLER	None

Sharp's testimony was crucial. As a result,
both men were found guilty of robbery with
violence, but Jones alone was found guilty of
murder. Maguire received 10 years; Jones got
10 years for the robbery and a death sentence
for the murder.

It may appear nonsensical to give a man a
death sentence and 10 years but an appeal
might have overturned the death sentence,
leaving Jones with a term of imprisonment.

Jones did indeed appeal. His defence
considered that since he had been convicted
on the evidence of accomplices who had
received prison sentences, the verdict was not
safe. The appeal court judges disagreed,

ON NOVEMBER 2ND, 1917, Thomas Geoffrey Henry left his home at 17, Regent Square, Bloomsbury, at 8.30am. As he passed the railings, which protected the gardens in the centre, he noticed a parcel.

Thomas reached through the railings and grasped the parcel. It was too heavy to lift from this awkward angle, so he climbed over and retrieved it. Inside, he found the sparsely dressed torso of a woman. Off to one side was another parcel, which contained two severed legs.

The remains were examined by the pathologist Bernard Spilsbury, who said that death had been caused by some injury that had drained the body of blood. Since there were no marks on the body that could account for this, he surmised that some sort of injury to the head or throat had occurred.

Part of the wrapping had been three strips of white fabric that had stamped upon them "Argentine La Plata, cold storage." Such fabric was used to wrap meat and since the body had been dissected with some degree of skill, the possibility was that the killer was a butcher. There was also a red cotton laundry mark "11 II". The final clue was a piece of brown paper that had been wrapped up with the torso. On this was scribbled the mis-spelt message "Blodie Belgium". Was the woman of Belgian extraction and had been murdered by someone who had German sympathies? After all, the Great War was still raging.

The first breakthrough came from the laundry mark. This was recognised and traced to a French lady, Emilienne Gerard of 50 Munster Square, near Regent's Park. The police went to that address and found that it was owned by the lady who lived next door at number 48.

Mary Elizabeth Rouse had rented number 50 to Paul and Emilienne Gerard on April 3rd, 1916. The husband had joined the French army in July, 1916 and though he had been home a number of times, he was now fighting in the trenches. Mary Rouse did have another key, though, and so the police were able to gain access.

A number of interesting things were discovered at Munster Square. There were bloodstains in the bedroom but Spilsbury said

NAME	Louis Marie Joseph Voisin
AGE AT EXECUTION	50
DATE OF EXECUTION	Saturday, 2nd March, 1918
PLACE OF EXECUTION	Pentonville
HANGMAN	John Ellis
ASSISTANT	Edward Taylor
DATE OF TRIAL	16th January – 18th January, 1918
LOCATION OF TRIAL	Old Bailey
PRESIDING JUDGE	Mister Justice Darling
PROSECUTION COUNSEL	Richard D. Muir, Percival Clarke
DEFENCE COUNSEL	L. Morgan May
NUMBER OF VICTIMS	1

VICTIMS DETAILS	
NAME	Emilienne Gerard
AGE	31
DATE OF MURDER	Wednesday, 31st October, 1917
PLACE OF MURDER	101 Charlotte Street, London
METHOD OF KILLING	Battered (possibly asphyxiated)
RELATIONSHIP TO KILLER	None (possible girlfriend)

that the murder was not committed there. It was more likely that the murderer had called here to pick up some linen in which to wrap the body parts.

Even more interesting was an I.O.U., lying on the table. It was for £50, dated August 15th and due to mature on November 15th. Signed Louis Voisin, it gave an address: 101 Charlotte Street, London. Another talk with Mary Rouse revealed the fact that Emilienne had been a housekeeper for Voisin and that he was a butcher.

Emilienne Gerard had last been seen alive on the evening of October 31st, 1917, the night of a Zeppelin raid. It was now time to determine the movements of Louis Voisin on that same night.

When interviewed, Voisin remembered the raid but said he had not left his rooms that evening. This was confirmed by the woman he lived with, Berthe Roche, who was also known as Berthe Martin. When other tenants of the house were questioned, though, it was revealed that Roche had been seen washing blood out of one of Voisin's shirts on the morning of November 1st.

Voisin was now asked to account for his movements on the morning the remains had been dumped. There had been a heavy shower of rain before 6.15am and since the parcels were not soaked, it was held that they must have been deposited in the square sometime between 6.15am and 8.30am, when they were discovered. Voisin said he had been working at Smithfield until just before 7.45pm but two of his workmates said that he had left the market at 6.30pm, giving him ample time to dump the parcels.

The police now had enough to justify an examination of the basement flat where Voisin lived. A large number of bloodstains were found in the doorway that led to the yard and Spilsbury determined that this was most probably where the murder took place. The next piece of evidence came on Saturday, November 3rd when a search of the cellar at Voisin's address revealed a sawdust-filled barrel in which lay Emilienne's head and hands. Finally, when Voisin was given a piece of paper and asked to write "Bloody Belgium", he made the same spelling mistake as had been seen on the note. On November 6th, Louis Voisin and Berthe Roche were both charged with murder.

It was difficult to determine exactly how Emilienne had met her death. Now that the head had been found Spilsbury determined that she had suffered a large number of blows, but none of these had been inflicted with any degree of violence. Had Voisin been the killer, his strength should have meant he was able to finish Emilienne off without much trouble.

Perhaps it was Berthe, a much weaker individual, who had dealt those blows. At least there was no doubt as to why the hands had been removed along with the head. Emilienne had a disfigurement on one hand, caused by a scald she had suffered some years before.

On January 2nd, 1918, at the police court hearing, Voisin declared that Berthe Roche was innocent of any involvement. He further added that the murder had taken place at Munster Square, even though this was in direct conflict with the evidence. Even with this statement, Voisin was not taking all the blame upon himself, for he declared that he too was innocent.

At the Old Bailey he said that at about 11.00am, on the morning of November 1st, he had gone to Emilienne's flat and received no answer to his knocking. Since he had his own key, he let himself in and discovered that she had been murdered. The floor and carpet were full of blood and her head and hands had been left wrapped up on the kitchen table. Someone had killed her and was trying to frame him for the death. In a state of panic, he took the remains and hid them in his cellar. He was, therefore, not guilty of murder.

By the second day of the trial, it was clear that there was not enough evidence to convict Berthe Roche of murder. The judge directed the jury to find her not guilty but a second charge, of being an accessory after the fact, would be held over until the next sessions. The following day, it took the jury 15 minutes to return a guilty verdict on Voisin.

Voisin's execution was originally set for February 26th but was postponed on the orders of the Home Secretary until the case against Berthe Roche had been heard. She was convicted of being an accessory and received a sentence of seven years. She did not serve the full term, dying whilst in custody on March 22nd, 1919.

AT 11.00PM ON November 27th, 1917, Verney Hasser, an Australian soldier, went to his sergeant of the guard and reported that Joseph Durkin, the man who shared his hut, had shot himself.

The camp was a training centre for the use of the Bren gun and both Durkin and Hasser were instructors in the weapon. It was known that they had recently argued over a local woman, but it was other factors that led the sergeant to deduce that this was a case of murder, not suicide.

To begin with, the murder weapon lay by the side of the dead man. A single shot had passed through his cheek, come out by his right ear and passed on through the blanket and kit bag he was using as a pillow and on through the end wall of the hut.

The first odd thing about the case was that the cartridge had been removed from the gun. The only way this could have occurred was by pulling back the bolt. It was obvious that Durkin could not have done this once he had been shot and since Verney was the only other occupant of the hut, he must have removed the cartridge and put the gun back in the dead man's hand. Hasser tried to argue that this was a normal reaction for a soldier, but it did not explain why the gun had been put back where he found it.

There was also the fact that Durkin had rather short arms and it would have been impossible for him to hold the rifle in the required position for him to pull the trigger himself. The fact that there was no singeing around the entry wound in Durkin's cheek also implied that the muzzle had been held about five inches away from his flesh, again more suggestive of murder than suicide.

Hasser claimed that he had retired for the night at 9.40pm and had not stirred again until he heard the shot an hour later. Corporal Milne, who slept in the hut where the ammunition was kept, reported that this was a lie, as he had seen Hasser enter the hut after he had supposedly been in bed. There was also the fact that Hasser's bed had not been slept in and he was wearing full uniform. Surely someone reporting that a comrade had shot himself would not bother to dress fully before seeking help.

NAME	Verney Hasser
AGE AT EXECUTION	30
DATE OF EXECUTION	Tuesday, 5th March, 1918
PLACE OF EXECUTION	Shepton Mallet
HANGMAN	John Ellis
ASSISTANT	William Willis
DATE OF TRIAL	15th January – 16th January, 1918
LOCATION OF TRIAL	Devizes
PRESIDING JUDGE	Mister Justice Avory
PROSECUTION COUNSEL	J.A. Foote, T.H. Parr
DEFENCE COUNSEL	S.H. Emanuel
NUMBER OF VICTIMS	1

VICTIMS DETAILS	
NAME	Joseph Harold Durkin
AGE	24
DATE OF MURDER	Tuesday, 27th November, 1917
PLACE OF MURDER	Sutton Veney Camp
METHOD OF KILLING	Shot
RELATIONSHIP TO KILLER	None

There was more than enough evidence to charge Hasser with murder and after a two-day trial, the jury took 90 minutes to decide that he was guilty.

AT 9.00PM ON January 13th, 1918, Mary Casey, the wife of Samuel, who owned the Shaftesbury Hotel in Birmingham, was on duty at reception when a couple came in and asked for a room.

Louis Van De Kerkhove was a Belgian who had escaped from that country when the Germans invaded in 1914. With him was his long-time lover, another Belgian named Clemence Verelst. It was Louis who signed the register, as Clemence was illiterate, and together the two went up to room 10.

At 9.55pm, a cry of "Murder!" was heard from room 10 by two chambermaids, Pauline Hyman and Sarah Rosenthal. They spoke to the bootboy, James Kilkenny, who was 14 years old, and he went to knock on the door to see what the problem was. The door was opened by Louis, who was wearing only a shirt and who announced, "I have done it now" and threw down a bloodstained knife. At that moment, Clemence crawled out of the door, gasping, "God help me, I'm dying." She had been stabbed a number of times. Kilkenny ran to fetch the police and to call for an ambulance.

Constable Frederick Goodman was the first officer on the scene and he accompanied both Louis and Clemence in the ambulance, dropping Louis off at the police station, which was along the way.

Van De Kerkhove could not deny that he had stabbed Clemence and when she died two days later, he was charged with her murder. In his defence, he told a story implying that he had been sorely provoked. He claimed that he had first met Clemence at a tea shop in London and that after meeting a few times, they had become lovers and started living together, moving first to Staines and then to Birmingham.

Almost from the first, Clemence had treated Louis badly. She had stolen his money, been with other men and when he had threatened to leave her, had once stabbed him in the arm. They had parted a couple of times and when they did get back together, Clemence had started her old tricks all over again.

On the day Clemence was attacked, she had met Louis at the White Horse public house from where they left together to go to the hotel.

NAME	Louis Van De Kerkhove
AGE AT EXECUTION	32
DATE OF EXECUTION	Tuesday, 9th April, 1918
PLACE OF EXECUTION	Birmingham
HANGMAN	John Ellis
ASSISTANT	George Brown
DATE OF TRIAL	18th March, 1918
LOCATION OF TRIAL	Birmingham
PRESIDING JUDGE	Mister Justice Lawrence
PROSECUTION COUNSEL	T. Hollis Walker, Sir Ryland Adkins M.P.
DEFENCE COUNSEL	Richard A. Willes
NUMBER OF VICTIMS	1

VICTIMS DETAILS	
NAME	Clemence Verelst (Died Tuesday, 15th January)
AGE	35
DATE OF MURDER	Sunday, 13th January, 1918
PLACE OF MURDER	Room 10, Shaftesbury Hotel, Station Street, Birmingham
METHOD OF KILLING	Stabbed
RELATIONSHIP TO KILLER	Girlfriend

She was able to make a statement after she had been stabbed in which she said Louis had accused her of living with another man and had attacked her in a fit of jealousy.

In the event, the jury preferred to believe that Louis had attacked Clemence out of jealousy and took his story of being provoked with a pinch of salt.

Louis Van De Kerkhove. This picture is taken from his identity card.

WHEN RUTH MOORE first separated from her husband, she lived alone at Church Lane, Outwood, but soon she found a new man and in due course, John Walsh moved in with her. The relationship was a very volatile one and the couple were constantly arguing.

In December 1916, Ruth and John moved to Calder Terrace, taking his brother, Martin, with them. There were just as many rows and eventually Martin said he had had enough and in June 1917, he moved out, leaving Ruth and John alone.

Things now became so bad that Ruth ordered Walsh out of the house. This particular request was overheard by Ruth's neighbour, Mrs Lockwood. Walsh did indeed leave, for a period of two weeks, but in July, he returned to the house and was allowed to stay. There were more arguments though and once again, Walsh was ordered to leave.

On July 11th, Walsh knocked on the door of Mrs Lockwood's house and asked to speak to her husband. He was not in at the time, so Walsh then asked for a cigarette, adding: "I have done it. I have done her in." Mrs Lockwood then persuaded Walsh to give himself up to the police and once he had gone, two other neighbours forced an entry to Ruth's house and found her dead.

At the police station, Walsh explained that he had gained entry to the house at around 5.00am and finding Ruth asleep in bed had taken the opportunity to strangle her. He added: "I can only say that I am guilty, but it is through sickness. I am upset and I am willing to swing. That is all I have to say."

At Walsh's trial, the defence attempted to suggest that there should be a verdict of manslaughter. Doctor Taylor gave evidence that Ruth had a bad heart and it would have taken very little pressure to kill her. Walsh now claimed that he had only grabbed her by the throat to waken her and had not intended to kill her.

The jury only took a few minutes to consider the medical evidence and Walsh's earlier confession before deciding that he was guilty of murder. Passing sentence, Mister Justice Darling remarked that it was a cruel and treacherous murder and that Walsh should hold out no hope for a reprieve.

NAME	John William Walsh
AGE AT EXECUTION	35
DATE OF EXECUTION	Tuesday, 17th December, 1918
PLACE OF EXECUTION	Leeds
HANGMAN	Thomas Pierrepoint
ASSISTANT	William Willis
DATE OF TRIAL	30th November, 1918
LOCATION OF TRIAL	Leeds
PRESIDING JUDGE	Mister Justice Darling
PROSECUTION COUNSEL	H.L. Tebbs
DEFENCE COUNSEL	Charles Mellor
NUMBER OF VICTIMS	1

VICTIMS DETAILS	
NAME	Ruth Elizabeth Moore
AGE	42
DATE OF MURDER	Thursday, 11th July, 1918
PLACE OF MURDER	Calder Terrace, Bottomboat, near Wakefield
METHOD OF KILLING	Strangled
RELATIONSHIP TO KILLER	Girlfriend

MARY ELLEN ROONEY had not had a great deal of luck with the men in her life. Married twice, with four children from her first marriage, she had also been widowed twice, her second husband being killed in France in July 1918. After that tragedy, Mary Ellen returned to her mother's home at 17 Elm Grove, Liverpool and was courted by her dead husband's older brother, William Rooney, who lived in the same street at number 4.

The time came when William asked Mary Ellen to marry him. She refused, but William did not take that with good grace. Instead he threatened Mary Ellen with a knife and she grew so frightened of his behaviour that for a time she moved to the south of England. In due course she returned and that would prove to be the worst decision of her life.

When Mary Ellen returned to Liverpool, she found that her mother had a soldier, named Champion, staying with her while he was on leave. This only served to make Rooney jealous, especially when he discovered that Champion had taken Mary Ellen out. On one occasion when Rooney saw the couple in the street, he shook his fist at them and shouted threats. It would not be long before those threats turned into action.

It was just after 3.00pm on November 2nd, 1918, when Mary Ellen went into a shop at Paddington, to purchase some eggs. Rooney followed Mary Ellen into the shop and immediately attacked her with a butcher's boning knife. He then dragged her outside and stabbed her twice more in the street before Dinah Jacks, the shop proprietor's daughter, called her father, who managed to knock Rooney to the ground. It was too late for Mary Ellen, who died from her injuries later that afternoon.

Rooney's defence counsel tried to put forward a plea of insanity. Rooney was described as coming from 'tainted stock': his father, two brothers and a sister had all been in an asylum and on the day of the murder, Rooney had earlier had a drink with Mary Ellen. They had appeared to be friendly and yet just a few hours later, he killed her in a frenzied attack.

There was even a suggestion that there had been a supernatural event which had unhinged Rooney's mind. When arrested he told the police that he had seen something the previous night, and again on the morning of the killing and it may well be that he had felt he had seen his dead brother's spirit.

None of this convinced the jury that Rooney was insane and he was executed at Manchester in December.

NAME	William Rooney
AGE AT EXECUTION	51
DATE OF EXECUTION	Tuesday, 17th December, 1918
PLACE OF EXECUTION	Manchester
HANGMAN	John Ellis
ASSISTANT	Not known
DATE OF TRIAL	25th November, 1918
LOCATION OF TRIAL	Manchester
PRESIDING JUDGE	Mister Justice Lush
PROSECUTION COUNSEL	E.G. Hemmerde
DEFENCE COUNSEL	Mister Sandbach
NUMBER OF VICTIMS	1

VICTIMS DETAILS	
NAME	Mary Ellen Rooney
AGE	30
DATE OF MURDER	Saturday, 2nd November, 1918
PLACE OF MURDER	Paddington, Liverpool
METHOD OF KILLING	Stabbed
RELATIONSHIP TO KILLER	Sister-in-law

ANNIE MAYNE HAD very healthy sexual appetites and would no doubt have felt very much at home in the Swinging 1960s. Unfortunately for her, she had these appetites whilst the Great War was still in full flight and society simply did not approve.

Annie had married Charles Mayne but when he came home one day and found her making love to his employer, Ben Benson, he walked out saying that Benson was welcome to her. So it was that Annie moved in with Ben who in 1916, joined the army and was posted to France.

Those healthy appetites were still there, though, and as Ben fought for his country, Annie took a string of lovers. However, she was always careful and kept them well out of sight when Ben returned home on leave. All went well until August 26th, 1918, when Ben came home unexpectedly.

The house was empty, so Ben settled down to wait for Annie to return. When she did, she was in the company of a young soldier and both of them had had rather too much to drink. Not noticing that Benson was home, Annie and the soldier headed off towards the bedroom, to be followed in due course by a rather angry Benson.

When Benson pushed open the bedroom door, he was dismayed to find his Annie making love to the young soldier, whom he then proceeded to chase down the street. Returning to the house he confronted Annie and a heated argument followed after which Annie slept in the master bedroom whilst Ben took the couch.

The following morning, Annie received two letters. Ben demanded to see them, suspecting that they were from lovers, but Annie refused to hand them over. The row of the previous night erupted with renewed fervour and reached a peak when Benson hit Annie and threatened to kill her. Annie staggered back, wiped the blood from her lips and laughingly told Benson that he could do what he liked, as she had spent all his money and intended to go on seeing other men whilst he was away. At that, Benson grabbed a razor laying by the kitchen sink and slashed her throat. Annie died in hospital shortly afterwards and Benson was arrested and charged with murder.

The only defence could be one of provocation but Benson was still found guilty of murder and sentenced to hang. He was the first of three soldiers to die on the Leeds gallows in the space of two days.

NAME	Benjamin Hindle Benson
AGE AT EXECUTION	41
DATE OF EXECUTION	Tuesday, 7th January, 1919
PLACE OF EXECUTION	Leeds
HANGMAN	Thomas Pierrepoint
ASSISTANT	Robert Baxter
DATE OF TRIAL	2nd December, 1918
LOCATION OF TRIAL	Leeds
PRESIDING JUDGE	Mister Justice Avory
PROSECUTION COUNSEL	H.T. Kemp, Herbert Smith
DEFENCE COUNSEL	Charles Mellor
NUMBER OF VICTIMS	1

VICTIMS DETAILS	
NAME	Annie Mayne
AGE	29
DATE OF MURDER	Tuesday, 27th August, 1918
PLACE OF MURDER	Hunslet
METHOD OF KILLING	Cut throat
RELATIONSHIP TO KILLER	Girlfriend

PRIVATE PERCY BARRETT and Lance Corporal George Cardwell were both absent without leave from an army camp near London. They had travelled north together and were now staying with Annie Pratt, Cardwell's married sister, at Ackworth Moor.

Both men explained their presence by saying that they were discharged, wounded soldiers and on the strength of this story, had obtained work at nearby Hemsworth Colliery. For leisure, the two were fond of travelling into Pontefract.

Rhoda Walker ran a watchmakers and jewellers shop in Town End, Pontefract and she had a lodger, Gertrude Lawn, who worked at a local bank. On August 16th, 1918, Gertrude returned home for lunch and left for work again at 1.55pm. At 2.55pm, Rhoda was seen dressing her shop window by Thomas Edward Driver.

At 3.55pm, Alice Poppleton, the postmistress, called in with some letters. Five minutes later, at around 4.00pm, Mary Horbury, who was in the street outside the shop, noticed that the window had been disturbed and a hand from inside the shop was removing rings and other items. At the same time, Kathleen Bensted saw a soldier standing outside the shop as if he was keeping watch. She also noticed that he was wearing six wounded stripes on his arm. When Gertrude Lawn returned home again, at 4.20pm, she found the battered body of Rhoda Walker, lying in a pool of blood.

Cardwell and Barrett returned to Ackworth and from there caught the train to Halifax where they spent some time with Martha, Cardwell's mother, who lived at 72 Oldfield Yard, Foundry Street. Unaware of what they had done, Martha took some items of jewellery from her son and his friend produced and pawn them. Cardwell and Barrett then went down to London.

The pawned items gave the police a trail to investigate and in due course, Cardwell was arrested at 8.15pm on August 20th, in Walworth. Barrett was arrested at 9.50pm on the same night. When searched, both men were found to be in possession of rings, watches, brooches and other items that could be traced back to Rhoda's shop.

NAMES	George Walter Cardwell; Percy George Barrett
AGES AT EXECUTION	22; 20
DATE OF EXECUTION	Wednesday, 8th January, 1919
PLACE OF EXECUTION	Leeds
HANGMAN	Thomas Pierrepoint
ASSISTANT	Robert Baxter
DATE OF TRIAL	3rd December, 1918
LOCATION OF TRIAL	Leeds
PRESIDING JUDGE	Mister Justice Avory
PROSECUTION COUNSEL	Charles Mellor, G.F.L. Mortimer
DEFENCE COUNSEL	R.A. Bateman F.J.O. Coddington
NUMBER OF VICTIMS	1

VICTIMS DETAILS	
NAME	Rhoda Walker (Died Saturday, 17th August)
AGE	62
DATE OF MURDER	Friday, 16th August, 1918
PLACE OF MURDER	Town End, Pontefract
METHOD OF KILLING	Battered
RELATIONSHIP TO KILLERS	None; none

Charged with murder, each man now tried to blame the other. Barrett claimed that when he entered the shop, the old woman had already been attacked. He had never touched her and had had no idea that Cardwell had intended using violence.

Cardwell, who had joined the army from Borstal at the age of 17, served in the Great War, been wounded five times and gassed once, said he had sent Barrett into the shop to buy a watch-key. Only when he saw a bloodstained hand rifling through the window did he realise what had happened.

In the event, the jury chose to believe that both men were guilty. They went to their deaths together, still protesting their innocence to the end.

ADA EDGE WAS enjoying a quiet cycle ride through the English countryside near Newbury. But as she pedalled down Love Lane, at Shaw-cum-Donnington, she saw a man stagger towards her, his face covered in blood.

The man, Joseph Rose was certainly distinctive. Not only did he have a gaping wound in his throat, but he had a shock of white hair and the pink eyes of an albino. Rose seemed to want Ada to come with him towards a nearby hedge.

At that moment, two gentlemen, one of whom was Frederick Schelling, a Swiss baker, approached. Finally Rose managed to make the men understand what he was trying to tell them, and checking where he had indicated, Schelling and his companion found the bodies of Sarah Rose and her daughter, Isabella.

Once Rose had recovered the power of speech, he managed to explained that although Sarah was his first cousin, they were also lovers and that Isabella was their child. This family lived with Sarah's parents in tents at Enbourne and on the day of the murders, the three of them had left for Newbury.

Rose went on to say that they stopped to have a bite to eat in Love Lane when a man, known to his wife, whom she called Harry, had appeared and attacked them. The police did not believe the story and despite the fact that they launched a full-scale search for the murder weapon, and found none, Joseph Rose was charged with murder.

There were a number of pieces of evidence to consider. First there was the testimony of John Rose, Sarah's father. He said that Joseph and his daughter had lived together for 18 months and were on friendly terms when they left Enbourne.

Conflicting evidence was given by Daisy Black, who knew Sarah by sight. She reported that she had seen Sarah on the morning of the 28th, at about 11.30am, with a man with white hair and pink eyes. They had been arguing and at one stage, the man, whom she identified as Joseph Rose, struck Sarah in the face. The defence countered this by saying that no signs of bruising had been found on Sarah's face.

Joseph did not give evidence at the trial. The jury considered the matter carefully and

NAME	Joseph Rose
AGE AT EXECUTION	25
DATE OF EXECUTION	Wednesday, 19th February, 1919
PLACE OF EXECUTION	Oxford
HANGMAN	John Ellis
ASSISTANT	Edward Taylor
DATE OF TRIAL	16th January, 1919
LOCATION OF TRIAL	Reading
PRESIDING JUDGE	Mister Justice Rowlatt
PROSECUTION COUNSEL	Mister Lort-Williams M.P.
DEFENCE COUNSEL	Reginald Coventry
NUMBER OF VICTIMS	2

VICTIMS DETAILS	
NAME	Sarah Rose; Isabella Rose
AGE	19; five months
DATE OF MURDER	Monday, 28th October, 1918
PLACE OF MURDER	Love Lane, Shaw-cum-Donnington, near Newbury
METHOD OF KILLING	Cut throat; cut throat
RELATIONSHIPS TO KILLER	Cousin/girlfriend; daughter

finally decided that Rose was the killer, not the mysterious and unidentified Harry.

On February 19th, Joseph Rose became the first man in 27 years to be hanged at Oxford. If he was indeed guilty of the murder of his lover and child, there remain two unanswered questions. What was his motive and what happened to the knife he used?

HENRY BECKETT, WHO also called himself Henry Perry, was a soldier in the Army Veterinary Corps and was about to be demobbed. Needing somewhere to stay, he was introduced to the Cornish family by his sister, Mrs Bird.

Beckett's family tree was extremely complex but it seemed that Alice Cornish was a step-aunt of Beckett's. Whatever the true situation, Beckett was received warmly by the Cornish family and accepted into their home. Beckett even found the time to become friendly with a local widow named Mrs Sparks, and there was talk of an engagement between the two.

After five weeks, Beckett had an argument with Alice Cornish and as a result, he was asked to leave. Beckett did as he was asked and stayed for a couple of nights with Mrs Sparks.

On April 28th, 1919, Beckett left Mrs Sparks's house at 10.00am. He had some beer and then went for a walk, with no particular destination in mind. At 1.30pm he found himself passing the Cornish residence.

Alice Cornish was the only person home. She saw Beckett, called him in and another argument developed between them. Beckett picked up a poker and battered Alice over the head. Still alive, she was carried to the shed at the bottom of the back garden where she was struck again, this time with a pick axe. Beckett, seeing that she was still not dead, went back to the kitchen and, taking a large carving fork to the shed, stabbed Alice Cornish in the throat. He then cut off one of her fingers in order to steal a ring she had been wearing.

The next person to come home was Marie, who had just finished school. As she turned away from Beckett he struck her on the head a number of times with a hammer. He then threw her body down the cellar steps.

Shortly afterwards, 15-year-old Alice arrived home. She was battered with the same hammer that had been used on her sister. Then, whilst she lay on the floor, Beckett struck her in the throat with an axe. He then carried her to the top of the cellar steps.

In due course, Walter Cornish arrived home from work. He was not pleased to see

NAME	Henry Perry (Beckett)
AGE AT EXECUTION	36
DATE OF EXECUTION	Thursday, 10th July, 1919
PLACE OF EXECUTION	Pentonville
HANGMAN	John Ellis
ASSISTANT	William Willis
DATE OF TRIAL	27th May, 1919
LOCATION OF TRIAL	Old Bailey
PRESIDING JUDGE	Mister Justice Darling
PROSECUTION COUNSEL	Percival Clarke, Adrian Clark
DEFENCE COUNSEL	Mister Fox-Davies
NUMBER OF VICTIMS	4

VICTIMS DETAILS

NAMES	Walter Cornish; Alice Cornish (Died Wednesday April 30th)
AGE	48; 43
DATE OF MURDER	Monday, 28th April, 1919
PLACE OF MURDER	13 Stukeley Road, Forest Gate, London
METHODS OF KILLING	Battered; battered/stabbed
RELATIONSHIPS TO KILLER	None; step-aunt

NAMES	Alice Cornish; Marie Cornish
AGES	15; 6
DATE OF MURDER	Monday, 28th April, 1919
PLACE OF MURDER	13 Stukeley Road, Forest Gate, London
METHODS OF KILLING	Battered; battered
RELATIONSHIPS TO KILLER	None; none

Beckett there and demanded to know where his wife and family were. Beckett said that they had all gone to the station to meet him and Walter Cornish seemed to accept this. Still having strong words with Beckett, he decided to cook himself some food. As Walter was preparing a rasher of bacon, Beckett struck him over the head with an axe.

Walter Cornish proved to be a tougher prospect than his family had been. He managed to struggle with Beckett, who had to strike again and again. At one stage, as Cornish put up his hand to ward off a blow from the axe, his finger was cut off. Cornish managed to get outside, where his screams for help were heard by Charles Henry

Amey, his next-door neighbour. Beckett ran off, his clothes, hands and face heavily bloodstained, whilst Walter Cornish was taken to the hospital.

Before he died two days later, Walter Cornish was able to tell the police all about the attack on him by Beckett. The police knew exactly who they were looking for.

On May 2nd, William James Green, who also happened to be a special constable, was serving a woman in his shop on Barking Road, East Ham, when he saw a strangely dressed man walk past. The man wore trousers much too long for him and when Green took a closer look, he became convinced that the man was Beckett. He followed the man until they passed a police station. Green summoned help and the man, who was indeed Henry Beckett was apprehended. The ring he had cut from Alice Cornish was still in his possession.

The four members of the Cornish family were buried in Woodgrange Cemetery, Manor Park, on May 6th. Exactly three weeks later, the trial of Beckett took place at the Old Bailey.

Beckett did not deny killing the Cornish family, but claimed that he was not responsible for his actions. He stated that he had been captured by the Turks during the war, and tortured. In that same campaign he had been wounded in the head by shrapnel, and blown up by high explosives. Ever since he had suffered from terrible dreams and had heard voices commanding him to do things. A battery of medical opinion was called to support these claims.

Sir Robert Armstrong-Jones, superintendent of the Claybury Asylum, said he believed Beckett to be insane. A Doctor Stoddart said that he was mentally deficient and Doctor Norman testified that Beckett was not capable of judging between right and wrong. Despite all this evidence, the jury took a mere 10 minutes to find Beckett guilty of murder.

It was now that Beckett's history could be revealed. He had lived a life of crime and in all he had 17 different convictions and had served three terms of imprisonment, the last ending in November 1916 after five years.

That history came to an end on July 10th, 1919 when Beckett was executed for four brutal murders.

JOHN CROSSLAND MARRIED Ellen, in 1903. Their first child, Selina, was born soon afterwards and three other children were to follow in due course. In 1914, when war broke out, Crossland fought at Mons, where he was wounded in the leg.

The end of the war also saw the end of the marriage. In that same year, John left home, leaving Ellen with her four children: Selina, Joseph now aged 13, 10-year-old Evelyn and nine-year-old Harold. She took out a maintenance order against John, who fell behind with his payments and served a two-month prison sentence for arrears, starting in January 1919.

Soon after coming out of jail, in March, a reconciliation took place. However, it was not long before the arguments broke out again. Crossland had heard that whilst he had been inside, his wife had been living with a man named Billy Kitchen. There was actually no truth in this, but it created such friction that on Friday, May 2nd, Ellen contacted the police and asked them to throw John out of the house. Since the separation order was still in force, the police did so.

Crossland still believed the stories about Kitchen and saw no reason why he should be bound by maintenance. On May 7th, he served Ellen with a summons to show why the order should not be revoked. Before the matter could be decided, he had already taken the law into his own hands.

As Selina Crossland left for work on the morning of Thursday, May 8th, she was surprised to find her father waiting outside. He asked Selina to leave the door open as he needed to collect some papers.

Joseph slept in the same room as his mother. He saw his father, in his bare feet, walk over to where Ellen lay sleeping. Joseph raised his head, but his father whispered that everything was all right. Shortly afterwards, John Crossland left the house and in due course, Joseph went downstairs and made up the fire. Only later did he find it impossible to rouse his mother and, having run next door to Mrs Lomax for assistance, discovered that Ellen had in fact been battered to death.

At 11.30am, John walked into the police station and gave himself up. He agreed with

NAME	John Crossland
AGE AT EXECUTION	34
DATE OF EXECUTION	Tuesday, 22nd July, 1919
PLACE OF EXECUTION	Liverpool
HANGMAN	John Ellis
ASSISTANT	Robert Baxter
DATE OF TRIAL	3rd July, 1919
LOCATION OF TRIAL	Liverpool
PRESIDING JUDGE	Mister Justice Salter
PROSECUTION COUNSEL	Mister Merriman, Cecil Whitley
DEFENCE COUNSEL	Mister Madden
NUMBER OF VICTIMS	1

VICTIMS DETAILS	
NAME	Ellen Crossland
AGE	35
DATE OF MURDER	Thursday, 8th May, 1919
PLACE OF MURDER	22 Prince Albert Street, Blackburn
METHOD OF KILLING	Battered
RELATIONSHIP TO KILLER	Wife

much of Joseph's story but added that he had approached Ellen and asked her about the papers he needed. She said she had burned them and in the row that followed, she fell back and hit her head. He agreed that his feet had been bare but he had no laces and had simply taken his shoes off for comfort.

The jury had to decide if Crossland had deliberately murdered his wife, or if she had died as a result of an accident. Joseph Crossland had reported no sounds of argument so they felt that murder was the more likely explanation.

6090

JOHN AND MINNIE Foster had been married for 15 years and had a total of six children. During all that time, though, John had been a heavy drinker and had been known to be rather violent towards his long-suffering wife.

On the night of Tuesday, 10th June, 1919, the couple were seen out together, taking a leisurely walk. They seemed friendly enough, perhaps because for once at least, John was sober. Unfortunately for Minnie, things were about to change rather drastically.

At 6.45am the following morning, neighbours heard the sounds of a terrible argument coming from the Fosters' home. After some minutes, the row was terminated by a loud scream and it seemed likely that John had done something awful to his wife. So, when a few minutes later, John Foster ran out of his house and tried to escape, a woman who lived nearby pluckily stopped him in his tracks and held him until the police could be summoned.

When the police entered the house, the neighbour's worst fears were confirmed. Minnie lay on the bed, her youngest child still clutched in her arms, unhurt. Minnie's throat had been cut and there were defence wounds on her left wrist and right forearm. There were obvious signs of a struggle and a bloodstained razor, the point of which had been broken off, lay on the mantelpiece.

Foster said that he had killed his wife because she had led an immoral life. Investigations showed that there was no truth in this statement and that Minnie had been a hard-working, industrious and faithful wife.

At the trial, the defence tried to claim that Foster was insane when he killed his wife. Evidence was called to show that three of his maternal uncles had committed suicide – two by hanging and one by drowning – and this was held to point to there being some hereditary imbalance in his mind.

The jury did not agree and John Foster was hanged at Pentonville, 50 days after he had murdered his wife.

NAME	Thomas Foster
AGE AT EXECUTION	46
DATE OF EXECUTION	Thursday, 31st July, 1919
PLACE OF EXECUTION	Pentonville
HANGMAN	John Ellis
ASSISTANT	Edward Taylor
DATE OF TRIAL	25th June, 1919
LOCATION OF TRIAL	Old Bailey
PRESIDING JUDGE	Mister Justice Avory
PROSECUTION COUNSEL	Richard D. Muir, Percival Clarke
DEFENCE COUNSEL	E.J. Purchase
NUMBER OF VICTIMS	1

VICTIMS DETAILS	
NAME	Minnie Foster
AGE	33
DATE OF MURDER	Wednesday, 11th June, 1919
PLACE OF MURDER	Stainsbury Street, Bethnal Green
METHOD OF KILLING	Cut throat
RELATIONSHIP TO KILLER	Wife

THE CRIME COMMITTED by Henry Thomas Gaskin has led to him being compared with Jack the Ripper. The comparison is not unjustified.

Gaskin had served in the Great War and whilst he was away, his wife became involved with another soldier, eventually becoming pregnant. By the time Gaskin returned to Hednesford, his wife had gone to live with her mother but Gaskin wanted to sort matters out with her once and for all.

On February 19th, Gaskin met up with a friend of his, Thomas Saunders. They had a few drinks at the Anglesey Arms and then Gaskin gave his friend a note to take to Elizabeth. The note read: "Meet me round the pool at once – important."

At 2.00pm, Gaskin and his wife met up on the Rugeley Road. They were seen arguing by Thomas Henry Borton, who also saw Gaskin walk away in one direction, into a small wood on Hednesford Hill, and his wife head off in the opposite direction.

When Elizabeth did not return home that evening, her mother, Emily Talbot, raised the alarm. The following morning a search was organised, but no trace of the missing woman could be found. Gaskin was spoken to as a matter of routine, but denied having seen Elizabeth.

On Friday, February 21st, Gaskin was spoken to again and held on suspicion whilst the search for Elizabeth continued. Two days later, on the 23rd, Gaskin asked to speak to Inspector Woolley, who was in charge of the investigation.

To Woolley's surprise, Gaskin offered to show him where the Elizabeth's body was hidden. He took the officer to the gas works in Victoria Street and pointed out a tank of water surrounding the gasometer. There, in a narrow culvert, the headless body of Elizabeth Gaskin was discovered.

The wounds on Elizabeth's body were horrific. The entire front of the body had been ripped open. One leg was almost severed and a piece of gas piping had been thrust down the neck, through the body, skewering Elizabeth. Gaskin calmly explained that this had been to weigh the body down. He went on to describe how they had met up in the woods where he

NAME	Henry Thomas Gaskin
AGE AT EXECUTION	27
DATE OF EXECUTION	Friday, 8th August, 1919
PLACE OF EXECUTION	Birmingham
HANGMAN	John Ellis
ASSISTANT	William Willis
DATE OF TRIAL	4th July, 1919
LOCATION OF TRIAL	Stafford
PRESIDING JUDGE	Mister Justice Roche
PROSECUTION COUNSEL	C.E. Vachall, Granville Ram
DEFENCE COUNSEL	Graham Milward
NUMBER OF VICTIMS	1

VICTIMS DETAILS	
NAME	Elizabeth Gaskin
AGE	23
DATE OF MURDER	Wednesday, 19th February, 1919
PLACE OF MURDER	Woods on Hednesford Hill
METHOD OF KILLING	Strangled/battered
RELATIONSHIP TO KILLER	Wife

had choked her. Later he had returned to the body and started to dismember it, at one stage pushing the headless torso along in a wheelbarrow but giving up this idea when he saw he was leaving tracks in the snow.

At his trial, Gaskin put forward a defence of insanity. Whilst the crime was undoubtedly terrible, the jury held that Gaskin had been fully aware of what he was doing and returned a guilty verdict.

Gaskin was executed in August, 1919. His name outlived him though. Today, the wood in which he brutally murdered his wife is known as Gaskin's Wood.

WHEN HENRY BALL walked into the police station at 2.00am on July 29th, and announced that he had found a dead body in one of his bedrooms, he was, not unnaturally, detained whilst further inquiries were made.

Ball was certainly telling the truth about the body. Lucy Nightingale had been lodging with Ball for two weeks and though he claimed she was his housekeeper, it became clear that Lucy was working as a prostitute with the connivance of her landlord.

The story Ball told was a curious one. His wife was an inmate of the Colney Hatch asylum and on the day of the murder he had been to visit her. Before he left he had enjoyed a drink in the Blackstock pub, where he had been with two men, Harold Horatio Morgan and Frank George Warren. Ball went on to say that Morgan had spent the previous night with Lucy and had said that he and Warren were about to visit her again.

Ball said he had returned home at 9.30pm, and fallen asleep in a chair downstairs. Waking in the early hours of the morning, he had called out for Lucy and, receiving no answer, had gone upstairs. He had found her, tied and trussed having been strangled to death.

Morgan and Warren were soon picked up. The two had been shipmates until recently, when they had skipped from their vessel, taking with them a quantity of whisky and cigarettes from the stores. They had very different stories to tell.

Warren lived with Olive Parton, in Harringay, and he reported that Morgan had called at his house, told him that a woman had done him out of 20/- and added that he meant to have his revenge. At Morgan's request, Warren had accompanied him to the house at Prah Road, but it had been Morgan who had killed the woman.

Morgan however, said that he and Warren had gone to the house and Lucy had suggested that they stay the night. She wanted Warren to sleep with her whilst Morgan shared a room with Ball. Morgan had no objections and settled down for the night. Not long afterwards, the sound of a scream disturbed him, to be followed by Warren

NAME	Frank George Warren (Burke)
AGE AT EXECUTION	41
DATE OF EXECUTION	Tuesday, 7th October, 1919
PLACE OF EXECUTION	Pentonville
HANGMAN	John Ellis
ASSISTANT	George Brown
DATE OF TRIAL	17th September – 18th September, 1919
LOCATION OF TRIAL	Old Bailey
PRESIDING JUDGE	Mister Justice Darling
PROSECUTION COUNSEL	Travers Humphreys, Cecil Whiteley
DEFENCE COUNSEL	G.I. Hardy
NUMBER OF VICTIMS	1

VICTIMS DETAILS	
NAME	Lucy Nightingale
AGE	26
DATE OF MURDER	Monday, 28th July, 1919
PLACE OF MURDER	13 Prah Road, Finsbury Park, London
METHOD OF KILLING	Strangled
RELATIONSHIP TO KILLER	None

rushing downstairs. They returned to Harringay and Morgan spent the night on Warren's floor.

The police charged all three. Ball was charged with being an accessory, Morgan and Warren were charged with murder. Before the matter came to court, the charges against Ball were dropped.

At the trial it became clear that Warren's story bore little relation to the truth. When he had returned home on the night of Lucy's death, he had given Olive Parton three rings and these had belonged to Lucy Nightingale. On the second day, the jury retired and in due course, found Warren guilty and Morgan not guilty.

MARY DOYLE WAS a married woman, but her husband John was away, serving in the Army. In due course, Mary found herself another beau in the form of James Adams who lived at 4 Cedar Place and the two began living at his home. Unfortunately, the new relationship soon ran into trouble.

In late July, 1919, John Doyle came back home to Glasgow and found that his wife wished to return to him. He agreed and on August 1st, Mary told her lover, James Adams, that she wanted to go back to her husband and try to start all over again. James did not take the news well.

That afternoon, Mary visited her sister, Grace Scott, who lived with her husband Charles Nicol Scott and their two young daughters at 29a Cameron Street. After the two sisters had caught up on each other's news, Grace asked Mary if she would mind the children that night whilst she and Charles went to the pictures. Mary readily agreed.

By the early evening, Mary Doyle was alone with her two nieces, the eldest of which was Annie Scott. Then, the neighbourhood was disturbed by blood-curdling screams coming from number 29a.

The neighbours rushed in, only to find Mary Doyle lying in a corner of the kitchen between the scullery and the fireplace, a massive gash in her throat. Of the assailant there was no sign, but Annie Scott managed to say that it had been James Adams, who had entered the house, thrown his arm around Mary's neck and then blood had gushed from the terrible wound.

A search was launched for Adams but in the early hours of August 2nd he walked into the Central Police Station and gave himself up. He would only utter two words: "Murdered her..."

At his trial, Adams tried to claim that it had all been a terrible accident. He had become very depressed when he discovered that Mary intended going back to her husband and had decided to take his own life. Arriving at Cameron Street he took out the razor to take his own life but Mary had caught him by the arm and in a fit of

NAME	James Adams
AGE AT EXECUTION	32
DATE OF EXECUTION	Tuesday, 11th November, 1919
PLACE OF EXECUTION	Duke Street, Glasgow
HANGMAN	John Ellis
ASSISTANT	Not known
DATE OF TRIAL	21st October, 1919
LOCATION OF TRIAL	Glasgow
PRESIDING JUDGE	Lord Justice Salvesen
PROSECUTION COUNSEL	D.P. Fleming
DEFENCE COUNSEL	C.H. Brown, W.D. Patrick
NUMBER OF VICTIMS	1

VICTIMS DETAILS	
NAME	Mary Doyle (Kane)
AGE	29
DATE OF MURDER	Friday, 1st August, 1919
PLACE OF MURDER	29a Cameron Street, Glasgow
METHOD OF KILLING	Cut throat
RELATIONSHIP TO KILLER	Girlfriend

excitement, he had cut her throat. The jury found the story impossible to believe and Adams was duly sentenced to hang.

He was executed on the first anniversary of the Armistice.

0909

REBECCA JANE QUINN was an unmarried woman with a young child when she met Ernest Bernard Scott and they started seeing each other. The new romance did not last very long though, for within three weeks, Rebecca was dead.

Rebecca was employed as a housekeeper and at 9.45am on August 11th, Scott visited the house of Margaret Davison and asked her to take a message to Rebecca telling her that her child had been scalded. In fact, the child was uninjured and this was merely a ploy to get Rebecca to return home. Margaret, of course, did not know this, and so did as she was asked. A few minutes later, both women set off together for Rebecca's mother's house, where the child was supposedly being taken care of.

They had not gone very far when Scott met up with them and all three walked on together, Scott between the two women. A few minutes passed and then Scott took out a razor and cut Rebecca's throat. As Margaret Davison screamed for help, Scott ran off towards Bebside.

Later that day, Scott gave himself up to the police saying: "Take me. I've killed a woman." Later he admitted that he had borrowed the razor that morning from a barman, Frederick Thomas Robson, with the sole intention of using it to kill Rebecca.

Scott declined to have any legal assistance at his trial, saying that he was guilty of taking Rebecca's life but not of murdering her. He explained that the reason for his actions were that she had given him up and had spent the previous night in the company of another man. The trial lasted just over an hour and the jury reached their verdict without leaving the box.

On November 26th, Scott was hanged at Newcastle at 8.00am. Seventy-five minutes later he was followed to the gallows by Ambrose Quinn.

NAME	Ernest Bernard Scott
AGE AT EXECUTION	28
DATE OF EXECUTION	Wednesday, 26th November, 1919
PLACE OF EXECUTION	Newcastle
HANGMAN	John Ellis
ASSISTANT	Edward Taylor
DATE OF TRIAL	5th November, 1919
LOCATION OF TRIAL	Newcastle
PRESIDING JUDGE	Mister Justice Lawrence
PROSECUTION COUNSEL	J.A. Compston, W. Valentine Ball
DEFENCE COUNSEL	None
NUMBER OF VICTIMS	1

VICTIMS DETAILS	
NAME	Rebecca Jane Quinn
AGE	25
DATE OF MURDER	Monday, 11th August, 1919
PLACE OF MURDER	New Delaval Colliery, near Blyth
METHOD OF KILLING	Cut throat
RELATIONSHIP TO KILLER	Girlfriend

AMBROSE QUINN WAS a mechanic in the R.A.F., and in 1919, he became convinced that whilst he had been in the service, his wife had been unfaithful to him.

The Quinns had married in August 1914 and they began married life living with Elizabeth's father, Thomas Ridley, at 63 Hawes Street. Quinn enlisted in 1917, and served his country well over the next couple of years. The trouble began in June 1919, when Quinn was granted three months' leave. Almost immediately he began objecting to his wife's way of life, saying that she spent too much time at the cinema.

Things came to a head on July 19th, when Elizabeth said she wanted to go to a street dance, which formed part of the peace celebrations. Once again Scott objected and an argument broke out that developed into blows. Later that day, Scott also discovered that Elizabeth had been to a dance on Whit Monday, June 9th, before he came home on leave. Two men, one of whom, Joseph Shepherd, Scott knew, had seen Elizabeth home and now Scott became convinced that this mysterious other man was more than a friend to Elizabeth.

Scott met up with Shepherd and demanded to know who this other man was, but it was not until August 3rd, that he finally found out. Two days later, Scott walked out of Hawes Street and went to live with his mother. Three days after that, Scott complained to the police that Elizabeth was not fit to look after their children.

On the night of August 9th, Scott was out drinking with a group of friends. He only had three halves before he left at 10.15pm. Very soon he happened to run into Elizabeth, close to her father's house, and he cut her throat. Immediately Quinn ran to the nearest police station and gave himself up, saying that he had no intention of killing her.

The trial lasted just one day and Ambrose Quinn was found guilty, but with a strong recommendation to mercy.

NAME	Ambrose Quinn
AGE AT EXECUTION	28
DATE OF EXECUTION	Wednesday, 26th November, 1919
PLACE OF EXECUTION	Newcastle
HANGMAN	John Ellis
ASSISTANT	Robert Baxter
DATE OF TRIAL	6th November, 1919
LOCATION OF TRIAL	Newcastle
PRESIDING JUDGE	Mister Justice Lawrence
PROSECUTION COUNSEL	W.J. Waugh, H.S. Mundahl
DEFENCE COUNSEL	Walter Hedley
NUMBER OF VICTIMS	1

VICTIMS DETAILS	
NAME	Elizabeth Ann Quinn
AGE	25
DATE OF MURDER	Saturday, 9th August, 1919
PLACE OF MURDER	Hawes Street, Scotswood Road, Newcastle-upon-Tyne
METHOD OF KILLING	Cut throat
RELATIONSHIP TO KILLER	Wife

WHEN HENRY WILSON, a young lad, entered the park at Warley, just outside Birmingham on June 27th, 1919, his mind was no doubt full of happy thoughts. He enjoyed himself playing amongst the trees and then suddenly he saw it: the horribly mutilated body of a man. All thoughts of play vanished and Wilson went to fetch the police.

The body was lying on its back, a large heavy log placed over the face. When this was removed it was seen that there were a number of deep puncture wounds behind each ear and the lower jaw had been fractured. The genital area had also been mutilated, but at least the police were able to determine who the man was. The body was that of a Chinese male and only one such gentleman had recently been reported missing. They were looking at the body of Zee Ming Wu.

Zee was a lodger at a boarding house in Coleshill Street, Birmingham. The house was occupied by a large number of Chinese and another of these, Li Ding Jig, had reported that Zee was missing when he had failed to turn up for work on June 24th and had then failed to return to the boarding house at night.

On that same day, June 24th, a man purporting to be Zee had entered a post office in London an attempted to draw the entire balance of Zee's account, some £240. The clerk had been suspicious and tried to detain the man, but he had escaped. It looked now to be a simple case of murder for gain.

The man who had tried to draw the cash had been Djang Djing Sung, who lodged with a gentleman named Arthur Grosvenor, in Pershore Road, Birmingham. Having failed to draw the cash in London, he now returned to Birmingham but went back to London on July 4th, staying with a friend of his named Kuo Doung Dsou, in Aldine Street, Shepherd's Bush. Over the next couple of weeks, Sung travelled back and forth between Birmingham and Dsou's house in London, intending to wait for the right time to make another attempt to draw the money out of Zee's account.

On July 25th, whilst on one of those visits to London, Sung argued with Dsou and tried to kill him. Arrested by the police for that assault, Zee's bank book was found in his possession and Sung was charged with murder.

NAME	Djang Djing Sung
AGE AT EXECUTION	33
DATE OF EXECUTION	Wednesday, 3rd December, 1919
PLACE OF EXECUTION	Worcester
HANGMAN	John Ellis
ASSISTANT	Edward Taylor
DATE OF TRIAL	22nd October, 1919
LOCATION OF TRIAL	Worcester
PRESIDING JUDGE	Mister Justice Rowlatt
PROSECUTION COUNSEL	A. Powell, A.E.N. Jordan
DEFENCE COUNSEL	Reginald Coventry
NUMBER OF VICTIMS	1

VICTIMS DETAILS	
NAME	Zee Ming Wu
AGE	Not known
DATE OF MURDER	Monday, 23rd June, 1919
PLACE OF MURDER	Warley Woods, near Birmingham
METHOD OF KILLING	Battered
RELATIONSHIP TO KILLER	None

Sung's defence was that the killer was Li Ding Jig. He claimed that Jig had killed Zee, stolen his bank book and ordered Sung to go to London to draw out the money. In fear of his life, Sung had obeyed. The jury did not accept Sung's story and returned a guilty verdict. Even as the sentence was passed, Sung was heard to shout out that it was Jig who had committed the murder.

1920

MARGARET BALL'S FIRST husband, Joseph, had been killed in France in 1915, fighting for his country. At Christmastime that same year though, Margaret married again, this time to Alfred Hird, whose real name was Lewis Massey.

There were problems with the relationship from the very start. Lewis believed that Margaret was too fond of drink and she in turn complained about his cruelty to her. Indeed, in 1919, Margaret obtained a separation order that included maintenance to the value of 25/- a week, on the grounds of that cruelty.

Lewis tried to patch things up. On November 1st, he begged Margaret to take him back but she refused. Two days later, on Monday, November 3rd, Margaret issued another summons against Lewis, this time for issuing threats against her. Still Lewis would not give up. On Tuesday he saw Margaret again and once more asked her to take him back. She refused and said that if he did not leave her alone, she would go back to the police.

On November 5th, Lewis returned to his lodgings in Hunslet Road and told his fellow lodgers that he had murdered his wife. From there he went to the house of his married sister, at Otley Road and it was here that he was arrested. Margaret Hird was indeed dead, having been battered to death with a hatchet. The end of the attack was witnessed by Margaret's 10-year-old daughter, Emily.

According to Lewis, he had gone to see Margaret and found her with her sister, Elizabeth Hackney. Both women were drunk and he and Margaret had argued, during the course of which she had seized a poker and struck him on the head. There was a mark on Lewis's head and this could well have been the truth, but he then seized a nearby hatchet and used it to kill Margaret. When arrested, Lewis had remarked: "Is she dead? I am very pleased. I meant to do her in."

It was perhaps that single statement which counted so heavily against Lewis Massey, for he was found guilty of murder and sentenced to death, even though medical testimony had described him as

NAME	Lewis Massey (Alfred Hird)
AGE AT EXECUTION	29
DATE OF EXECUTION	Tuesday, 6th January, 1920
PLACE OF EXECUTION	Leeds
HANGMAN	Thomas Pierrepoint
ASSISTANT	William Willis
DATE OF TRIAL	3rd December, 1919
LOCATION OF TRIAL	Leeds
PRESIDING JUDGE	Mister Justice Coleridge
PROSECUTION COUNSEL	W.J. Waugh, A.S. Matthews
DEFENCE COUNSEL	J.R. MacDonald
NUMBER OF VICTIMS	1

VICTIMS DETAILS	
NAME	Margaret Hird (Died Wednesday, 5th November)
AGE	35
DATE OF MURDER	Tuesday, 4th November, 1919
PLACE OF MURDER	8 Alfred Terrace, Camp Road, Leeds
METHOD OF KILLING	Battered
RELATIONSHIP TO KILLER	Wife

being of rather low intelligence. On January 6th, 1920, he was one of three men to die on the gallows.

HYMAN PERDOVITCH COULD by no stretch of the imagination be hailed as a pioneer of industrial relations. When he found that he had a grievance with his boss, he murdered him in front of witnesses.

Perdovitch was a machinist at Wilkes' factory in Salford and had long complained that the foreman, Solomon Franks, placed all the heaviest work on his team. The complaints fell on deaf ears though and relations between Franks and Perdovitch deteriorated steadily. August 12th, for instance, saw a discussion between the two men, which showed the animosity they felt. Franks had given a particular job to Perdovitch and when he asked him when it would be ready, Perdovitch replied that Franks could have it when it suited him and not before.

The fateful day was August 15th. At around 8.45am, Franks passed Perdovitch's machine. No words were exchanged between them, but Perdovitch followed him and seemed to be whispering something to Franks. Suddenly, two blows were struck at the back of Franks' neck and with a loud groan, Franks fell to the ground. Only later would other workmen realise that Perdovitch had been holding a knife and two deep wounds had been inflicted on the foreman.

There were quite a few witnesses as the workroom was crowded at the time. Nathan Lewis worked the machine next to Perdovitch's and he saw the whole thing. Morris Shere had seen Franks fall and saw the blood gushing from the wounds. Nathan Nelson missed the actual attack but he saw the body on the floor and heard Lewis ask Perdovitch what he had done. Nelson also heard the reply: "It's alright, I've finished him. He deserved it, the bastard."

Franks died before he could reach hospital but the police did not have to hunt for the killer. At 9.00am, Hyman Perdovitch had walked into Chapel Street Police Station where he told Constable Samuel Marsh that he had just injured a man at Wilkes'. Then, to emphasise that he was serious, he handed over the bloodied knife he had used.

Perdovitch claimed at his trial that he had not intended to kill Franks, only to harm him.

NAME	Hyman Perdovitch
AGE AT EXECUTION	39
DATE OF EXECUTION	Tuesday, 6th January, 1920
PLACE OF EXECUTION	Manchester
HANGMAN	John Ellis
ASSISTANT	Robert Baxter, Edward Taylor
DATE OF TRIAL	5th December, 1919
LOCATION OF TRIAL	Manchester
PRESIDING JUDGE	Mister Justice McCardie
PROSECUTION COUNSEL	B.S. Wingate Saul, Gilbert Jordan
DEFENCE COUNSEL	Mister Lustgarten
NUMBER OF VICTIMS	1

VICTIMS DETAILS	
NAME	Soloman Franks
AGE	49
DATE OF MURDER	Friday, 15th August, 1919
PLACE OF MURDER	Wilkes Brothers Factory, Booth Street, Salford
METHOD OF KILLING	Stabbed
RELATIONSHIP TO KILLER	None

Leaving aside the fact that he would still have been held to be guilty of murder had his intention only been to inflict serious harm, there was also the testimony of 16-year-old Rebecca Reuben to consider.

Perdovitch lodged with the Reuben family at 10 Elsworth Street, and on the day before the killing, Perdovitch had given her 2/6d, saying that he was going on his holidays to Strangeways! This seemed to indicate a certain premeditation and the jury had no hesitation in returning a guilty verdict.

Hyman Perdovitch was hanged at Strangeways alongside David Caplan.

LILY WATERMAN, AGED 13, had gone to visit her married sister, Freda Caplan, at the small milliner's shop she ran from her home at 141 West Derby Road. Lily, though, could not get an answer, even on her second visit, and when she reported this to her mother and brother, they became very concerned.

Myer Waterman, Freda's brother, went to West Derby Road. He too received no answer, but spotted an unlatched kitchen window and managed to gain entry.

The first person Myer found, was David Caplan himself, who lay on the floor with his throat cut. Upstairs, Freda and Herman lay on her bed, their heads battered in. The youngest child, Maurice, lay in his cot. His head too had been smashed in. The weapon was a bloodstained iron, which lay nearby.

All four members of the Caplan family were rushed to hospital. Herman and Maurice were found to be dead on arrival and Freda died the following day. Only David Caplan was stabilised but he remained in hospital until October 31st.

The Caplans had been married for nine years but the marriage had never been a happy one. On September 9th, 1920, Freda had moved out of the house and gone to live at her mother's. Freda's sister, Miriam Waterman, had moved in to look after the children and Freda returned each day to run her business. Nine days later, on September 18th, Caplan had been convicted of assaulting his wife and was heard to swear that he would have his revenge.

Miriam remained at West Derby Road until October 3rd. Five days later Freda was granted a separation order.

Meanwhile, in the hospital, Caplan was beginning to talk. On October 22nd he commented to Constable Martin Kennedy, that if he had killed his children, he deserved all he got.

On October 27th, it was Constable John Ward's turn to be on watch and Caplan asked him if Freda was dead. The Constable said nothing but Caplan added that he must have been off his head. Four days later he was discharged from hospital, arrested and charged with murder.

NAME	David Caplan
AGE AT EXECUTION	42
DATE OF EXECUTION	Tuesday, 6th January, 1920
PLACE OF EXECUTION	Manchester
HANGMAN	John Ellis
ASSISTANT	Robert Baxter, Edward Taylor
DATE OF TRIAL	2nd December, 1919
LOCATION OF TRIAL	Manchester
PRESIDING JUDGE	Mister Justice McCardie
PROSECUTION COUNSEL	Mister Merriman, Douglas Stuart
DEFENCE COUNSEL	Mister Madden
NUMBER OF VICTIMS	3

VICTIMS DETAILS

NAMES	Freda Caplan (Died Wednesday 15th October); Herman Caplan
AGES	33; 6
DATE OF MURDER	Tuesday, 14th October, 1919
PLACE OF MURDER	141 West Derby Road, Liverpool
METHOD OF KILLING	Battered; battered
RELATIONSHIPS TO KILLER	Wife; son

NAME	Maurice Caplan
AGE	3
DATE OF MURDER	Tuesday, 14th October, 1919
PLACE OF MURDER	141 West Derby Road, Liverpool
METHOD OF KILLING	Battered
RELATIONSHIP TO KILLER	Son

Caplan claimed that he must have been insane at the time of the attack, but at his trial, that defence failed and he was sentenced to death.

ANNIE COULBECK LIVED alone near the Horse Market, in Caistor, but there was a man in her life, William Wright, and by October, 1919, she was pregnant by him.

William was seen going into Annie's house on the afternoon of October 28th, but later that same day, when he went into the Talbot public house, he was alone, and behaving rather strangely.

At one stage, Annie came up in the conversation and William was heard to say: "Murder – black cap – three weeks – hanged by the neck – finished." He left the pub just before 10.00pm and again went to Annie's house.

The next day, a neighbour, concerned that Annie had not been seen, found her door open and discovered her body. She had been strangled with a scarf and it was not long before William Wright was picked up for questioning. He immediately made a full admission to the crime of murder.

According to William's statement to the police, upon returning to Annie's house the previous night, he had asked her about a brooch she was wearing. Annie told him that it had belonged to her mother but William had never seen it before and jumped to the conclusion that it had been given to Annie by another man. When she denied this, William had simply reached out and strangled her and then, once Annie was dead, he had calmly put out the lamp and gone home.

An attempt was made to show that William was insane at the time of the crime. Evidence was given that his mother had been in an asylum in 1919, his sister was suffering from a form of religious mania and one of his uncles had died in the Lincoln County Asylum. Whilst that may well have shown a tendency towards William being somewhat unstable, his behaviour in the Talbot, before Annie had been killed, showed that he was thinking of murder at that time. This in turn suggested that the killing was premeditated and implied that William Wright was fully aware of his actions.

Found guilty of murder and sentenced to death, William had been wrong about just

NAME	William Wright
AGE AT EXECUTION	39
DATE OF EXECUTION	Wednesday, 10th March, 1920
PLACE OF EXECUTION	Lincoln
HANGMAN	Thomas Pierrepoint
ASSISTANT	William Willis
DATE OF TRIAL	2nd February, 1920
LOCATION OF TRIAL	Lincoln
PRESIDING JUDGE	Mister Justice Horridge
PROSECUTION COUNSEL	Mister Cracroft
DEFENCE COUNSEL	Mister Emery
NUMBER OF VICTIMS	1

VICTIMS DETAILS	
NAME	Annie Coulbeck
AGE	34
DATE OF MURDER	Tuesday, 28th October, 1919
PLACE OF MURDER	Pigeon Spring, Horse Market, Caistor
METHOD OF KILLING	Strangled
RELATIONSHIP TO KILLER	Girlfriend

one point when he made his cryptic speech in the Talbot. After being sentenced, it was almost five weeks before he was hanged, not three!

MARY DIXON WAS a widow with no family of her own. For two years, on and off, she had lived with William Hall but in September 1920, she left him to work as a night woman at a lodging house in Grey Street, Sunderland.

William did not take the parting easily and on November 5th, told his sister that he was going to see Mary the following day, at around 6.00pm, with the intention of bringing her back with him. On the 6th, at the time he had stated, William called at the lodging house and after speaking to Mary for a short time, she put on her hat and went out with him. That night, William's sister heard them talking in their room at 10.00pm. The voices were not raised and there were no sounds that could be described as an argument.

When William's sister found his blinds drawn the next day, she at first thought nothing of it, but when there was still no signs of life later that day, she contacted the police and an entry was forced. William lay on his bed, a gaping wound in his throat. Mary's throat had also been cut but whereas William was still alive, Mary was quite dead.

Once he had recovered, Hall was charged with murder. On the advice of his counsel, he pleaded guilty under provocation. He explained that he had asked Mary to stay the night but when she had told him that she intended returning to the lodging house, he was provoked into killing her. Witnesses were called who said they had seen the couple in the Tynemouth Castle pub that evening and they had appeared to be on friendly terms. The prosecution though called witnesses who had heard Hall threaten Mary before and a neighbour, Mrs Hedley, reported that he had told her he intended to meet Mary that night and then drew his finger across his throat as if implying what he was going to do.

Found guilty and asked if he had anything to say before the death sentence was pronounced, Hall replied: "If there was nothing gained in what I did, I can stand under God and say there was nothing lost, for she was a dead wrong woman." He then stood erect whilst the sentence was read out and after thanking the judge, was escorted to the cells below.

NAME	William Hall
AGE AT EXECUTION	66
DATE OF EXECUTION	Tuesday, 23rd March, 1920
PLACE OF EXECUTION	Durham
HANGMAN	John Ellis
ASSISTANT	Robert Baxter
DATE OF TRIAL	4th March, 1920
LOCATION OF TRIAL	Durham
PRESIDING JUDGE	Mister Justice Bailhache
PROSECUTION COUNSEL	Mister Mortimer, Rowan Hamilton
DEFENCE COUNSEL	C. Paley Scott
NUMBER OF VICTIMS	1

VICTIMS DETAILS	
NAME	Mary Ann Dixon
AGE	51
DATE OF MURDER	Thursday, 6th November, 1919
PLACE OF MURDER	34 Moorgate Street, Sunderland
METHOD OF KILLING	Cut throat
RELATIONSHIP TO KILLER	Girlfriend

LIEUTENANT FREDERICK ROTHWELL Holt, of the 4th Loyal North Lancashire Regiment, had had a difficult war. Invalided out suffering from amnesia and depression, he had first gone to Malaya, to recuperate, but returned to England in 1918.

Kathleen Breaks, known as Kitty, was a married woman but that didn't stop her falling in love with the handsome army officer. Besides, her marriage had failed almost as soon as it had taken place and she had lived apart from her husband from soon after the wedding day itself. Holt returned Kitty's feelings and the couple became very close. Holt lived comfortably enough on his inherited income of £500 a year.

The year 1919 was their second year together and now, in October, at Holt's suggestion, Kitty insured her life for £5,000 and made a will in favour of her partner. Holt had previously tried to take out a policy on Kitty's life with his ex-employers, the Atlas Insurance Company, but they refused to accept the proposal until he and Kitty were actually married.

Kitty had a habit of going for walks on stormy and rough nights. She revelled in the elements and said they helped to clear her thoughts. It was that kind of night on December 23rd, 1919 and Kitty decided on a walk on the sands at Lytham St Annes.

Early the following morning, her body was found on the dunes. She had been shot three times, though at first, the investigating officers believed she had been stabbed.

A clear line of footprints led from the body, through the dunes and the police made a search for clues along this line. They soon found Kitty's hat and umbrella and a pair of man's bloodstained gloves. A few days later, on December 28th, four children playing close to the murder spot found a Webley revolver that had four cartridges fired and two still in their chambers. Tests would show that the Webley was the murder weapon and that both it and the gloves belonged to Frederick Holt. Further tests would show that the footprints matched exactly with impressions made by a pair of Holt's shoes. Holt was arrested but apparently failed to understand what the police could possibly want with him.

NAME	Frederick Rothwell Holt
AGE AT EXECUTION	32
DATE OF EXECUTION	Tuesday, 13th April, 1920
PLACE OF EXECUTION	Manchester
HANGMAN	John Ellis
ASSISTANT	William Willis
DATE OF TRIAL	23rd February – 27th February, 1920
LOCATION OF TRIAL	Manchester
PRESIDING JUDGE	Mister Justice Greer
PROSECUTION COUNSEL	Sir Gordon Hewart, Mister Merriman, Mister Jordan
DEFENCE COUNSEL	Edward Marshall Hall, Mister Wingate-Saul, Mister McKeaver
NUMBER OF VICTIMS	1

VICTIMS DETAILS	
NAME	Kathleen Harriet Elsie Breaks
AGE	26
DATE OF MURDER	Tuesday, 23rd December, 1919
PLACE OF MURDER	Beach at Lytham St Annes, near Blackpool
METHOD OF KILLING	Shot
RELATIONSHIP TO KILLER	Girlfriend

As the trial opened in Manchester, the defence barrister, Sir Edward Marshall Hall, endeavoured to show that Holt was unfit to plead and a jury was sworn in expressly to decide on Holt's sanity. Holt had a persecution mania and seemed to have some very strange ideas. He believed that the police had sent dogs and germ-laden flies to his cell to hurt him. The jury, however, decided that he was sane and a second jury was then sworn in to hear the charge of murder.

The prosecution held that the motive for murder was the insurance policy of £5,000 and the will leaving that money to Holt in the event of Kitty's death. They carefully traced Holt's movements on the day of her murder. It was shown that the couple had travelled by train together from Bradford, where Kitty lived at Ryecroft Farm, Dudley Hill. Holt had left the train at Ansdell whilst Kitty went on to Blackpool. Kitty had later changed for dinner at the Palatine Hotel, leaving at about 9.00pm for her last walk on the sands. Holt had been seen by John Garlick, a tram conductor, getting onto his car at Lake Road at about

7.30pm. Garlick knew Holt but he would probably have remembered the occasion anyway. Holt was the only passenger on top of the open car whilst it was pouring with rain!

Holt, though, did appear to have an alibi. His entire family – father, stepmother and sister – swore that on the night of the murder, after coming in and out of the house a few times, Holt finally arrived home at 10.10pm, had his supper and then went to bed. If the timetable the Holt family gave were believed, then Frederick Holt could not possibly have killed Kitty Breaks.

Holt seemed to be oblivious to everything that was going on around him in court. Most of the time he spent just staring into space and at one stage, when Marshall Hall was reading out some of the love letters Holt had sent to Kitty, in an endeavour to prove that he loved her too much to kill her for financial gain, Holt was seen reading a newspaper that he was holding upside down!

Holt was found guilty and sentenced to death, greeting that sentence with a shrug of his shoulders. Taken down to the cells he said to Major FitzClarance, the prison governor, "Well that's over. I hope my tea won't be late." The execution was set for March 16th, but postponed when notice of appeal was submitted.

Holt's appeal was granted the distinction of being heard with additional evidence. This was that Holt had contracted syphilis in Malaya and that this may have affected his mind. The Home Secretary even ordered a medical enquiry to look into the state of Holt's mind, especially since it was known that both a grandfather and a cousin had been declared insane.

All these avenues failed and Holt was finally hanged at Strangeways prison on April 13th, 1920.

G LADYS MAY IBRAHIM was married to Ahmed and they had two children, two-year-old May and Aysha, eight months. On December 12th, Ahmed left Cardiff, for business in London. At that time his wife and children were alive and well.

Gladys was certainly alive at 10.00pm on December 13th, for at that time she was seen by her next-door neighbour, Alice Ali, who went into Gladys's house and talked with her for a time. The baby too was fine that evening, sleeping in its pram in the kitchen.

The following day, at around 12.20pm, Alice Ali found the front door of number 52 unlocked and upon entering, found the bodies of Gladys and her daughter. Alice ran off to fetch the police and returned shortly afterwards with Inspector Adams. Both victims had had their throats cut and Gladys had been raped, after death. The other daughter was alive in a bedroom upstairs.

There were immediately a number of clues for the police to work on. There had been an old fashioned gramophone in the house, the type with a large horn, but now this had vanished and only a few broken fragments of the horn could be found. The house had been ransacked but nothing else of value appeared to have been taken. In fact, something new had been left behind. Amongst the debris of the house, police found a suitcase. Inside was an empty razor case and some letters addressed to Tom Caler.

The gramophone and letters soon led police to call on Caler, a fireman on the S.S. Fountains Abbey, which was docked in Cardiff. Pridu Rahn, the night watchman on duty at the docks, told police that he had seen Caler returning at around 2.00am, carrying a gramophone, and some sort of parcel, wrapped up in a coat. Upon being approached, Caler had thrown the parcel into the water. Pridu noticed that the gramophone had had no horn.

When interviewed, Caler claimed that he had been aboard the ship from 10.00pm onwards. This was countered by the evidence of one of his shipmates, Said Mohamed, who said that Caler had gone ashore at 3.00pm on December 13th, and had not returned until around 2.00am on December 14th. At that

NAME	Thomas Caler
AGE AT EXECUTION	23
DATE OF EXECUTION	Wednesday, 14th April, 1920
PLACE OF EXECUTION	Cardiff
HANGMAN	John Ellis
ASSISTANT	William Willis
DATE OF TRIAL	15th – 16th March, 1920
LOCATION OF TRIAL	Cardiff
PRESIDING JUDGE	Mister Justice Salter
PROSECUTION COUNSEL	Marlay Samson, H.O.C. Beasley
DEFENCE COUNSEL	T.W. Langman
NUMBER OF VICTIMS	2

VICTIMS DETAILS	
NAME	Gladys May Ibrahim; Aysha Emily Ibrahim
AGE	22; eight months
DATE OF MURDER	Sunday, 14th December, 1919
PLACE OF MURDER	52 Christina Street, Cardiff
METHOD OF KILLING	Cut throat; cut throat
RELATIONSHIP TO KILLER	None; none

time, Caler had a gramophone with him and some broken records.

Finally there was the evidence of Hamed Fellah who said he had seen Caler leaving 52 Christina Street, at around 8.00pm on December 13th. At 11.00pm, Fellah saw Caler again. They had a brief conversation and when Fellah left him, Caler was heading back towards Christina Street.

Had Caler been having an affair with Gladys, or had he simply murdered her after talking his way into her house? This never became clear at the trial, but the evidence linking Caler with the crime was strong enough for the jury to decide that he was guilty of the double murder.

A LTHOUGH MILES MCHUGH was a married man, with a wife back in Chorley, he was living and working in Yorkshire, and engaged in a long-lasting affair with Edith Swainston.

McHugh had told Edith he was a single man, and she believed him. Their relationship deepened and in March 1919, she gave birth to his child. Things seemed to be fine between them, until just before Christmas.

Before she had known McHugh, Edith had been walking out with Herbert Holman. He had been out of Middlesborough for some time, but on December 23rd, he returned, renewed his acquaintance with Edith and offered to marry her if she would give up McHugh. Edith must have mentioned this to McHugh, for the next day, December 24th, they were seen arguing in a passageway close to Thomas Frederick Piper's house. The argument ended with McHugh grabbing Edith around the throat and starting to throttle her. Piper, who was Edith's brother-in-law, had to pull them apart.

On January 24th, 1920, Edith visited McHugh at his lodgings and they were seen leaving together. McHugh would later claim that they finally parted, at Edith's house, at around 5.00pm and McHugh was seen in the area at that time by Mary Ann Potter.

At 6.00pm, Edith's body was discovered by 19-year-old Frank Cox. Her throat had been cut and in the opinion of a doctor called to the scene, the injury could not have been self-inflicted. Three hours later, McHugh was picked up by the police. At that time, he denied even knowing Edith Swainston.

The police noticed that there was blood on McHugh's hands. At first he said he had cut himself on a plate but then confessed that he had been there when Edith died, and had cut himself at that time.

According to McHugh's story, the events with Holman had led him to decide to return home to Chorley and he had told Edith about this on the afternoon of the 24th. She had become depressed and had drawn out a razor, which she made to draw across her throat. He tried his best to stop her and as he grabbed at the weapon, she cut his hand badly.

The medical evidence showed that

NAME	Miles McHugh
AGE AT EXECUTION	32
DATE OF EXECUTION	Friday, 16th April, 1920
PLACE OF EXECUTION	Leeds
HANGMAN	Thomas Pierrepoint
ASSISTANT	Edward Taylor
DATE OF TRIAL	9th March, 1920
LOCATION OF TRIAL	York
PRESIDING JUDGE	Mister Justice Bailhache
PROSECUTION COUNSEL	W.J. Waugh, G. Chapman
DEFENCE COUNSEL	J. Robert Macdonald
NUMBER OF VICTIMS	1

VICTIMS DETAILS	
NAME	Edith Annie Swainston
AGE	24
DATE OF MURDER	Saturday, 24th January, 1920
PLACE OF MURDER	Passage parallel to Church Street, Middlesborough
METHOD OF KILLING	Cut throat
RELATIONSHIP TO KILLER	Girlfriend

McHugh's story was untrue and he was convicted of murder after the jury had deliberated for less than 20 minutes. Later, McHugh was being escorted across the yard, back to the prison vehicle, when a group of his friends were heard to shout: "Good night Miley. God knows you are innocent."

The appeal failed on March 30th and McHugh was executed just over two weeks later.

THOMAS WILSON HAD been demobbed from the army in November, 1919, whereupon he returned to his wife, Annie. The relationship had been under strain for some time though and shortly afterwards, the couple parted. Annie obtained a separation order and settled down to a life away from Thomas.

On January 16th, 1920, Thomas called around to see Annie at her home in Kirkstall. Annie was with three of her daughters, including one who was just two years old.

From the moment he arrived, it was plain that Thomas was looking for an argument. He began by asking for a receipt for the money he had paid to Annie for maintenance, but the way he asked was tantamount to an invitation to quarrel. When Thomas went on to ask Annie about a man he believed she was friendly with, Annie told him to mind his own business.

Thomas now leapt onto his estranged wife, taking a knife from the kitchen table as he did so. One of his daughters tried to pull him off, without success. She even took a framed picture down from the wall and struck her father over the head as hard as she possibly could. This only served to get Thomas to turn his attention to her and his other two daughters.

Seeing that they were now in danger, the girls ran upstairs and locked themselves into one of the bedrooms, whilst Thomas hammered on the door, trying to gain entry. Not wishing to wait around in the room, the three daughters managed to escape through the window and ran off to find a policeman. Once he realised that they had escaped, Thomas Wilson went back downstairs to attend to his wife once more.

When a police officer arrived at the house, he found that the doors and windows were all locked. Smashing a window, the officer climbed into the house, only to be attacked by Wilson, who was brandishing a knife. Not one to accept any nonsense, the officer simply hit Wilson over the head with his truncheon, thus removing the threat.

The house was searched and there, underneath the bed, was Annie Wilson. Her

NAME	Thomas Hargreaves Wilson
AGE AT EXECUTION	45
DATE OF EXECUTION	Thursday, 6th May, 1920
PLACE OF EXECUTION	Leeds
HANGMAN	Thomas Pierrepoint
ASSISTANT	Robert Baxter
DATE OF TRIAL	18th March, 1920
LOCATION OF TRIAL	Leeds
PRESIDING JUDGE	Mister Justice Roche
PROSECUTION COUNSEL	R. Watson
DEFENCE COUNSEL	Mister Macdonald
NUMBER OF VICTIMS	1

VICTIMS DETAILS	
NAME	Annie Maria Wilson
AGE	46
DATE OF MURDER	Friday, 16th January, 1920
PLACE OF MURDER	14 Evanston Row, Kirkstall, Leeds
METHOD OF KILLING	Cut throat
RELATIONSHIP TO	Wife

throat had been cut and she died a few minutes later, from her injuries.

Wilson, like so many others before him, tried to claim that he was not responsible for his actions at the time he killed his wife. The jury at his trial felt that he was.

1920

WHEN BERT SALISBURY first met Alice Pearson, she was a married woman, serving as a nurse in the First World War and he was a soldier suffering from shrapnel wounds. When the war was over and both returned to England, Alice left her husband, Mark William Pearson, telling him that she had fallen in love with someone else.

The couple moved to Southport where they rented rooms. Bert found it impossible to find a job and so they were forced to live on Alice's savings, which amounted to some £700.

On the evening of March 21st, 1920, at 7.30pm, Salisbury walked alone into the Blundell Arms public house, at Formby, and ordered a drink. He stayed there for the rest of the night, at one stage arguing with the barman, Richard Mawdsley, because of the way he looked at him. It was then that a fellow customer, John Clayton, noticed that Salisbury had a revolver in his pocket.

At closing time, Salisbury left the pub and, due to his unsteady gait, was taken along to the local police station where he was arrested for being drunk and disorderly. When he was searched, the police found the revolver and confiscated it. Salisbury was then put into the cells and left to sober up.

At 7.00am the following morning, Sergeant King went along to see if Salisbury was alright. To his astonishment, Salisbury said that he had killed his wife the previous night. He told King that she was lying on the river bank and told him exactly where to find the body. When the police went along to check, they found Alice Pearson. She had been shot four times. When King returned to tell Salisbury that he had found Alice, Salisbury asked if she was dead. When told that she was, he added "Thank God for that."

Salisbury's story was that he and Alice had agreed to live on her money. Then, when there was nothing left they would both die. He would kill her and then himself. On the night of March 21st, Salisbury and Alice were down to their last £3 and it was time to bring the agreement into force.

When the trial opened, Salisbury was asked how he wished to plead, and answered in a firm voice "Guilty." The judge refused to

NAME	Herbert Edward Rawson Salisbury
AGE AT EXECUTION	35
DATE OF EXECUTION	Tuesday, 11th May, 1920
PLACE OF EXECUTION	Liverpool
HANGMAN	John Ellis
ASSISTANT	Robert Baxter
DATE OF TRIAL	22nd April, 1920
LOCATION OF TRIAL	Liverpool
PRESIDING JUDGE	Mister Justice McCardie
PROSECUTION COUNSEL	A.J. Ashton, O.F.G. Stanley
DEFENCE COUNSEL	Mister Madden
NUMBER OF VICTIMS	1

VICTIMS DETAILS	
NAME	Alice Pearson
AGE	39
DATE OF MURDER	Sunday, 21st March, 1920
PLACE OF MURDER	Embankment of River Alt, at Formby
METHOD OF KILLING	Shot
RELATIONSHIP TO KILLER	Girlfriend

accept the plea and entered one of Not Guilty. Once the evidence had been heard, he further directed that the only possible verdicts could be guilty of murder or guilty but insane. After a few minutes deliberation, the jury chose the former and Salisbury was sentenced to death.

By Salisbury's own request, no appeal was submitted. He told his solicitor that he wished to die. On May 11th, Bert Salisbury's wish was granted and the second part of the death agreement between him and Alice Pearson was finally enacted.

AT 2.40PM ON February 14th, 1920, William Whittington, a grocer, took a 6d piece from little Ivy Woolfenden and changed it for pennies for her. She was pleased because, as she gleefully announced: "A penny of this is mine."

Less than an hour later, at 3.30pm, Elizabeth Roberts, aged 10, was playing with her friend Doris Woolfenden, Ivy's sister, when Elizabeth's uncle, William Waddington called out to her. Waddington asked Elizabeth to fetch Ivy as he wanted her to run an errand. At first, Ivy didn't want to go, but when Waddington called her, she ran to him and was seen to go into Waddington's house at 192 Edge Lane Road.

Not long afterwards, Waddington left his house, locked the door and gave Elizabeth Roberts the key. When Elizabeth asked him what had happened to Ivy, he said he did not know and then walked off down the street.

At 4.15pm, Waddington's sister, Emma Roberts, who was Elizabeth's mother, saw Waddington walking towards Henshaw Street. He seemed excited and his face was very red. He explained that he was going for a walk. Thinking nothing more of it, Emma returned home.

Not long afterwards, Waddington's mother arrived home and, finding the door locked, went to her daughter Emma's for the key. She then, along with her other daughter, Mary, returned home to number 192.

As soon as the door was opened, it was obvious that something was wrong. Little Ivy was found in the cellar, lying face down, her lower body uncovered. She had been severely battered and was barely alive. Rushing back to Emma's, Mrs Waddington enlisted the help of a postman, John McHugh, who went to number 192 and gently carried the broken body of Ivy Woolfenden upstairs. In the cellar, McHugh noticed a bloodstained coal hammer, a rag, also bloodstained and saddest of all, the one penny coin that Ivy had been so proud of.

A crowd gathered outside the house and one of them, Travis Marsh, was sent to fetch the police. An ambulance was also called but as Ivy was being carried to it, she died. It was now 4.55pm.

A massive search was launched for William

NAME	William Waddington
AGE AT EXECUTION	35
DATE OF EXECUTION	Tuesday, 11th May, 1920
PLACE OF EXECUTION	Liverpool
HANGMAN	John Ellis
ASSISTANT	Robert Baxter
DATE OF TRIAL	21st April, 1920
LOCATION OF TRIAL	Liverpool
PRESIDING JUDGE	Mister Justice McCardie
PROSECUTION COUNSEL	A.J. Ashton, O.F.G. Stanley
DEFENCE COUNSEL	Milner Helme
NUMBER OF VICTIMS	1

VICTIMS DETAILS	
NAME	Ivy Woolfenden
AGE	7
DATE OF MURDER	Saturday, 14th February, 1920
PLACE OF MURDER	192 Edge Lane Road, Oldham
METHOD OF KILLING	Battered
RELATIONSHIP TO KILLER	None

Waddington and he was eventually found on Rochdale Road, in Todmorden. He claimed to know nothing of the crime and said that he had spent the day walking from Leeds to Todmorden. This was plainly untrue as he had been seen in Oldham by his niece, his sister and others. When his clothing was checked, bloodstains were discovered and there were scratches on his hands and arms.

The evidence was overwhelming and Waddington received a sentence of death. He was hanged with Herbert Salisbury at Liverpool.

O N THE EARLY evening of February 3rd, Thomas Senior and his brother Henry enjoyed a few games of draughts after their evening meal at their home, 50 Robson Street, Glasgow. Later, at around 6.45pm, Henry got himself ready to go out for the evening, saying he was meeting his young lady. At one stage he went to a small money box and took out £10 in cash. Henry's mother remonstrated with him and said he shouldn't carry so much money with him. Henry took his mother's advice, put most of the cash back and when he finally left the house, had just about £2 on him.

Henry Senior did not return home that night and the next day, when his brother read that a body had been found in Queen's Park, he noted that the description matched that of Henry. Thomas went to the police and later that day made a positive identification of the dead man. Henry Senior had been brutally battered to death, and the money, his shoes and his overcoat taken from him.

There had been a number of muggings in Glasgow lately and the victims had managed to piece together a basic description of the two men who were responsible. At this time, these attacks had not been linked to the murder of Henry Senior but soon witnesses were coming forward to give descriptions that matched those of the muggers.

A taxi driver came forward to say that he had given a ride to two men, one of whom had a pair of shoes in his jacket pocket and had bloodstained hands.

Andrew Graham and Alexander John Smith both told the police that they had seen two men washing blood from their hands in the lavatory at Queen's Park. Finally, a tram-car conductor, John McIntosh, said that he had seen two men on his car, at 10.15pm. They got on at Queen's Park and travelled to Union Street.

Three days after that attack, on February 6th, a report came in from the police at Glasgow Central Station. Two men fitting the descriptions of the wanted men, along with two women, had boarded the Belfast boat train. By now the police had managed to put names to the two men: Albert Fraser and James Rollins and the two women they had

NAME Albert James Fraser; James Rollins
AGES 24; 22
DATE OF EXECUTION 26th May, 1920
PLACE OF EXECUTION Duke Street, Glasgow
HANGMAN John Ellis
ASSISTANT William Willis
DATE OF TRIAL Glasgow
PRESIDING JUDGE Lord Justice Sands
PROSECUTION COUNCEL John L. Wark, Albert Russell
DEFENCE COUNCEL George Morton, Archibald Crawford, Robert Gibson
NUMBER OF VICTIMS 1

VICTIMS DETAILS
NAME Henry Senior
AGE 35
DATE OF MURDER Tuesday, 3rd February, 1920
PLACE OF MURDER Queen's Park, Glasgow
METHOD OF KILLING Battered
RELATIONSHIP TO KILLERS None; none

been friendly with were Helen White and Elizabeth Stewart.

Detective Superintendent Keith travelled over to Belfast and with the help of local officers, began touring the rougher parts of that city. It wasn't long before he saw Fraser and Rollins, arrested them and took them to the police station for questioning. Both men denied being involved in the attack upon Senior but bloodstains were found on the cuff of Fraser's jacket and, more importantly perhaps, a slip of paper in one of Rollins's pockets gave an address where police found Helen and Elizabeth. Both readily agreed to turn King's Evidence and all four were then escorted back to Glasgow.

The trial opened on May 4th with the most valuable witness being Helen White. She described how Fraser had told her to pick up a man so they could rob him. Apparently Henry Senior's lady friend had not turned up at the appointed meeting place and Helen fell into conversation with him instead.

They walked along Hope Street, Argyll Street and to Glassford Street where they boarded a tram, followed by Rollins and Fraser all the way. At Queen's Park, Helen and

Henry alighted and walked until they found a gap in a fence which they passed through before sitting on the grass. After a minute or so Rollins came through the fence and demanded to know what they were doing there. Henry replied that he was "... out with my girl" and then the attack upon him began.

It was Rollins who grabbed Henry from behind, almost choking him to death in the process. Then Fraser, using a dummy revolver, battered the helpless man until he fell unconscious to the floor. Throughout the attack Helen begged them to stop but they ignored her. After robbing Henry of the few shillings he carried, his coat and his shoes, they bundled his body into some bushes and caught a tram back to their lodgings. Later, Helen was instructed to pawn the overcoat, which she did, for 17/-.

With the testimony of the two women, the jury were left in little doubt as to the guilt of the two defendants and took a mere 20 minutes to decide that they were guilty of murder.

Three other charges were left on file against both men: that they had attacked and robbed Malcolm Morrison at 321 Argyle Street on January 23rd, attacked and robbed George McLachlan in Overnewton on January 30th and finally, that they had attacked and robbed James Dempsey at Glasgow Cross on February 2nd.

SARAH JANE HOWARD, who had once worked on the Ipswich trams, had a three-year-old son, but her prospective new employer did not seem to mind. William John Kittle, of 133 Camden Road, had advertised for a housekeeper and Sarah seemed to be presentable enough, so in September 1919, she began her duties.

In January 1920, Kittle noticed that Sarah was pregnant again. They had a long conversation at the end of which Mr Kittle reluctantly concluded that Sarah would have to seek alternative accommodation before the child was born in March. It was from then on that Sarah took to leaving the house each evening around 7.00pm and returning some time between 9.00pm and 9.30pm. Kittle assumed that she was seeing her young man.

On February 6th, Sarah went out as usual but failed to return. Not only did William Kittle notify the police, but he began investigating on his own and his questions led to the name Frederick Storey.

Storey was also employed by the tram company, as a driver, and on February 7th, Kittle confronted him and asked him about Sarah. Storey admitted that he knew her, but claimed not to have seen her since the previous Sunday. Shortly afterwards, her body was found, close to a railway line, alongside some allotments. She had been battered to death. This brought Storey into the frame, for he had use of one of the allotments.

Police investigations revealed a number of people who had seen Sarah on the night she had died. Albert Edward Woodley had seen her boarding his tramcar at St. Peter's Church, just after 8.00pm and saw her alight at Black Bridge 10 minutes later. Shortly afterwards he saw Storey, walking towards where Sarah had last been seen. Woodley saw Storey again, just before 9.10pm, in Wherstead Road, walking towards the town centre.

This last timing was confirmed by Constable William Snell, who knew Storey. They had met up in Wherstead Road at 9.15pm, and chatted for 10 minutes, finally parting at 9.25pm.

On the strength of rumours suggesting that Storey was the father of Sarah's child, a

NAME	Frederick William Storey
AGE AT EXECUTION	42
DATE OF EXECUTION	Wednesday, 16th June, 1920
PLACE OF EXECUTION	Ipswich
HANGMAN	John Ellis
ASSISTANT	Not known
DATE OF TRIAL	28th May – 29th May, 1920
LOCATION OF TRIAL	Bury St Edmunds
PRESIDING JUDGE	Mister Justice Darling
PROSECUTION COUNSEL	C.F. Gill, Travers Humphreys, Sefton Cohen
DEFENCE COUNSEL	A.S. Leighton
NUMBER OF VICTIMS	1

VICTIMS DETAILS	
NAME	Sarah Jane Howard
AGE	27
DATE OF MURDER	Friday, 6th February, 1920
PLACE OF MURDER	Maiden Hall Allotments, near Ipswich
METHOD OF KILLING	Battered
RELATIONSHIP TO KILLER	Girlfriend/none

search of his house was made. A bloodstained hammer was discovered, along with items of his clothing, also stained with blood. There were also a large number of scraps of newspaper, stained with blood, which looked as if they had been used to wipe someone's hands. Storey was asked about these and claimed that he had cut himself shaving and that he also suffered from bad nose bleeds. His daughter, 21-year-old Myra Priscilla Storey, confirmed that she had seen him cut his face and his wife confirmed the nose bleeds but Storey was arrested and charged with murder all the same.

The trial lasted two days and at the end of the evidence, the jury took only 15 minutes to find Storey guilty.

WILLIAM ALDRED TRIED his very best to get a relationship with Ida Prescott off the ground, but she was having none of it.

Aldred had known Ida, a widow, for more than a year and although they were on friendly terms, he wanted it to develop into something more. He asked her repeatedly to walk out with him, but Ida always said no.

On February 14th, 1920, St. Valentine's Day, a day for romance and love, Aldred asked Ida once again if she would go out with him. Once again she refused.

The following day, the same scenario was repeated. Again Ida was immovable. Then, on February 16th, William Aldred thought he would have one last try. Calling at Ida's home in Clifton, Aldred asked the question Ida had heard so many times before. When she refused, as he expected her to, they argued about it before he went away but said he would return for supper, as he had done many times in the past.

When Aldred came back, Ida was in the kitchen with her daughter, Irene. Another argument broke out between Ida and Aldred over her refusal of his advances and when she walked out of the room, into the back kitchen, Aldred followed her. After a few seconds, Ida reappeared, her hands held to her neck. William Aldred had cut her throat.

The defence was one of insanity. Counsel showed that from 1893 to 1903, Aldred had been declared unfit for work due to his suffering from locomotor ataxia, a wasting disease associated with the degeneration of nerve fibres. In 1915, his wife had died and he had taken to drinking heavily. It was the effects of his drinking that led him being admitted, in 1916, to the imbecile ward of the Barton Institution. Released after a short period, he was re-admitted in August of that year, for a few more weeks.

Witnesses were called who described Aldred as being 'peculiar' in his manner. For two months before the murder, he had not gone to bed, preferring instead to spend his nights sitting upright in a chair.

Despite all this evidence, the prison doctor testified that in his opinion, Aldred was perfectly sane when he cut Ida's throat, and it was his words that swung the day.

NAME	William Thomas Aldred
AGE AT EXECUTION	54
DATE OF EXECUTION	Tuesday, 22nd June, 1920
PLACE OF EXECUTION	Manchester
HANGMAN	John Ellis
ASSISTANT	Not known
DATE OF TRIAL	13th May, 1920
LOCATION OF TRIAL	Manchester
PRESIDING JUDGE	Mister Justice McCardie
PROSECUTION COUNSEL	Mister Merriman, Mister Derbyshire
DEFENCE COUNSEL	Jessel Ryecroft
NUMBER OF VICTIMS	1

VICTIMS DETAILS	
NAME	Ida Prescott
AGE	44
DATE OF MURDER	Monday, 16th February, 1920
PLACE OF MURDER	90 Manchester Road, Clifton, Manchester
METHOD OF KILLING	Cut throat
RELATIONSHIP TO KILLER	None

1920

ARTHUR GOSLETT NEVER denied that he had killed his wife, and yet the reason he said he had done so was never believed.

On Sunday May 2nd, the body of a woman was found floating in the River Brent near some allotments near Brentmead Place, Golder's Green. Nearby, close to the bottom end of Weston Avenue, there were clear signs of some sort of struggle having taken place and the smears of blood on the grass indicated that the woman had been attacked here, dragged to the water and thrown in. A postmortem would show that she had still been alive when she was put into the water and that the direct cause of death was drowning.

The woman was soon identified as Evelyn Goslett of Golder's Green Road. She had been married twice, her first husband having died some years before. She had given birth to three children by her first husband and one by her second, Arthur Goslett.

The police went around to the dead woman's house and soon pieced together Evelyn's movements of the night before. At 8.00pm, Mrs Goslett had eaten supper with her two lodgers: Marjorie Orell and Daisy Holt. Soon afterwards, Evelyn went out, never to be seen alive again by the two ladies.

At 9.40pm, Evelyn's eldest son, Jules Mear, came home and told the ladies that the front door had been wide open. Fearful that there might be an intruder, the house was searched from top to bottom, but no one was found. The lodgers both reported that they had heard someone come in shortly before, go upstairs and walk around in Mr and Mrs Goslett's bedroom, but had thought nothing more about it.

At some time after 10.30pm, Mr Goslett returned home and came into the dining room. Marjorie Orell's husband, George, came in shortly before 11.00pm and half an hour later, the two women went to bed leaving Mr Orell and Arthur Goslett together.

On the following morning, the maid, Constance Hanrahan came in to attend to her duties at 7.50am. As she entered the kitchen she was somewhat surprised to see Mr Goslett making himself a cup of tea. He said he had a bad head and added that his wife had

NAME	Arthur Andrew Clement Goslett (Godrey)
AGE AT EXECUTION	44
DATE OF EXECUTION	Tuesday, 27th July, 1920
PLACE OF EXECUTION	Pentonville
HANGMAN	John Ellis
ASSISTANT	Edward Taylor
DATE OF TRIAL	21st June – 22nd June, 1920
LOCATION OF TRIAL	Old Bailey
PRESIDING JUDGE	Mister Justice Shearman
PROSECUTION COUNSEL	Sir Richard D. Muir, Eustace Fulton
DEFENCE COUNSEL	Curtis Bennett, E.J. Purchase
NUMBER OF VICTIMS	1

VICTIMS DETAILS

NAME	Evelyn Goslett
AGE	43
DATE OF MURDER	Saturday, 1st May, 1920
PLACE OF MURDER	Weston Avenue, Golder's Green
METHOD OF KILLING	Battered/drowned
RELATIONSHIP TO KILLER	Wife

not come home. The maid passed this information on to the rest of the household so by the time the occupants of the house assembled for breakfast, it was common knowledge. Arthur Goslett calmed matters down a little by asking Jules to go round to his grandmother's house, to see if Evelyn had gone there for any reason. Jules did so, but he was already aware that his mother had arranged to meet Arthur near Brent Bridge on the evening of May 1st. When the police called around later to say that his mother's body had been found in the river, Jules passed his story on to the police and when interviewed, Arthur Goslett admitted that he had killed his wife.

Goslett said that at 7.00am on May 1st, he had asked his wife to meet him that evening at 9.15pm, at the Prince Albert pub. He wanted her to look at a house he was thinking of buying, and she agreed to meet him.

That evening, as Goslett approached the pub, he saw his wife, took her arm and asked her to come along with him. They walked on to the river bank and when he reached a secluded spot, he took a tyre lever out of his pocket and hit her on the back of the head. After three or four blows, Evelyn fell to the ground. Goslett bent down, kissed her hand and apologised for what he had done. Then, lifting her gently, he placed her in the river and returned home.

What was even more astonishing, was Goslett's reason for committing this brutal crime. The reason he gave was that Daisy Holt had forced him to do it. He even said that on returning home after killing Evelyn, he spent the night in bed with Daisy. Daisy denied the entire story.

Goslett maintained this story at his trial. Two marriage certificates were produced. One, dated June 12th, 1914, showed that Arthur Goslett had married Evelyn Mear, the dead woman. The other, dated February 7th, 1919, showed that using the name Arthur Godfrey, he had married Daisy Ellen Holt.

Daisy, it seems, was pregnant at the time and in July 1919 she went into a nursing home where she gave birth to a child. Shortly afterwards, the man she knew as Godfrey told her that his real name was Goslett and that he was already married. He had a solution, though. Daisy would pretend to be the widow of his brother who had been killed in the war. That way she would be welcomed in his house and could stay on as a lodger. Rather reluctantly, Daisy agreed to this subterfuge

According to Goslett, after this state of affairs had lasted for some weeks, Daisy began to put pressure on him to do away with his wife. She threatened to expose him as a bigamist if he did not do as she asked, and finally, he had succumbed to her blandishments and carried out the dreadful deed.

Daisy's story was rather different. She had indeed been 'married' to Goslett and had born him a child, which was now in a nursing home. However, shortly after coming to live in the Goslett household, she had taken a job at a fruiterer's, run by a Mrs Hyams. A customer there recognised her as Daisy Holt and exposed her to Mrs Goslett.

Evelyn Goslett was quite nice about the whole matter and simply said that she would try to arrange somewhere else for Daisy to live with the child. It was quite natural for her not to want a woman her husband had slept with to live under her roof, but Goslett had intimated that if Daisy went, he would take some drastic action of his own. That was why he had murdered his wife.

Daisy went on to deny spending the night of May 1st in Goslett's bed, though she did admit, under cross examination that she had slept with him at least once since she had come to live under his roof.

For Arthur Goslett there could be no escape from the noose, but if the jury believed his story, then Daisy could have been charged as well. In the event, they chose to believe what Daisy had said, especially as no corroborative evidence could be found to show that she was lying.

Goslett was hanged at Pentonville in July 1920. Daisy Holt was never charged with any offence.

1920

JAMES AND ADA Ellor married at St. Mark's church, Bredbury, on July 7th, 1907. Ada had already buried one husband and when the Great War came along, she might have thought that it might happen all over again. James joined the Cheshire Regiment in 1914 and later, having been transferred to the Shropshire Light Infantry, was gassed and then wounded.

In March 1918, Ada was pregnant. The news was rather spoiled for her, however, when a letter arrived from James. Dated March 30th, the letter said that he had fallen in love with another woman and she too was pregnant. To Ada's surprise, a few days later she received another letter telling her to ignore the earlier one. James claimed that he had not written that first letter and begged Ada to burn it. Ada said she had but kept it, thinking that she may need it later.

There were other problems too. James was a heavy drinker and was often brutal towards Ada. She stood this as long as she could but on March 25th, 1920, she left him, moved to 8 Travis Street, and took out a summons against him for persistent cruelty.

The next day, James ran into Harry Forbes, Ada's son by her first marriage. James asked Harry where Ada was but Harry refused to divulge the address. James then handed over 10s-9d, which he said was Ada's share of his army pension. Lulled by this display of kindness, Harry told James that Ada was lodging at Maria Sayer's house, in Travis Street.

When James Ellor called on his wife, at around 10.30am on March 27th, Harry Forbes was there. He thought Ellor looked contrite and later reported that he was actually on his knees, begging Ada to return to him. By 3.30pm, though, James Ellor was approaching Constable Evan Hughes, in Market Street, to tell him that he had just murdered his wife.

On the way to the station, Ellor demonstrated that he cared little for what he had done. He stopped at a sweet stall and bought 2d worth of mint drops, and informed the stallholder, George Key: "I've done a murder."

Ellor claimed that he did not know what he was doing at the time of the murder. He said

NAME	James Ellor
AGE AT EXECUTION	35
DATE OF EXECUTION	Wednesday, 11th August, 1920
PLACE OF EXECUTION	Liverpool
HANGMAN	John Ellis
ASSISTANT	Edward Taylor
DATE OF TRIAL	6th July – 8th July, 1920
LOCATION OF TRIAL	Chester
PRESIDING JUDGE	Lord Justice Coleridge
PROSECUTION COUNSEL	Ralph Sutton
DEFENCE COUNSEL	W.N. Stable
NUMBER OF VICTIMS	1

VICTIMS DETAILS	
NAME	Ada Ellor
AGE	42
DATE OF MURDER	Saturday, 27th March, 1920
PLACE OF MURDER	8 Travis Street, Hyde
METHOD OF KILLING	Battered
RELATIONSHIP TO KILLER	Wife

that he and Ada had argued and at one stage she had told him to go and put his head on the railway line. He lost all control, picked up a hammer and battered her to death.

Ellor referred to his war record and claimed that the gas poisoning still affected him. He heard voices and did not know what he was doing. Unfortunately for Ellor, he spoke about all this to a fellow prisoner whilst on remand at Manchester. This man, Joseph Kearon, testified that Ellor was faking and had been fully aware of his actions.

After due consideration, the jury were convinced that Ellor was not insane and he was sentenced to hang.

AT 5.30PM ON Saturday, September 25th, 1920, Mrs Reed, who lived at Five Ash Road, in Northfleet, heard someone tapping at her front window. Going to investigate, she opened the door and Harriet Lever staggered into her home and fell into her arms. It was then that Mrs Reed noticed that Harriet's throat had been cut.

About 15 minutes before this, Harriet's husband, George Lever, had walked up to police Sergeant Holt who was on duty in Prince's Road, handed him a bloodstained razor and admitted that he had murdered his wife near the tramway depot in Perry Street.

When the story of George Lever was told, it proved to be a serious indictment of the caring attitude of the authorities in this country. George had been in the army for 20 years, had risen to the rank of sergeant major, and had served his country well, being finally discharged due to a nervous debility. The powers that be then decreed that as he had not completed 21 years, he was not entitled to a pension! As a result of this scandalous decision, George and his wife were forced to live in abject poverty and were finally put out of their rooms.

Harriet had been married before and she now went to live with her sister-in-law, Mrs Nisbet. George remained homeless until, on the day he killed his wife, he called at her lodgings and told her that he had managed to find a room for her and the children. This was merely a ruse so that he could get her alone and cut her throat. The crime was said to be motiveless as they had been quite happy together but when one examines the circumstances, the true motive appeared to be one of sheer desperation with the way of life George and Harriet had come down to.

Having ruined George Lever's life, the State now prepared to take it. The trial took place in November, with the appeal being dismissed soon afterwards. No reprieve was forthcoming and George was hanged on January 7th, 1921. Such was the way that Britain treated someone who had served her for 20 years.

NAME George Edwin Freeman Quinton Lever
AGE AT EXECUTION 51
DATE OF EXECUTION Friday, 7th January, 1921
PLACE OF EXECUTION Maidstone
HANGMAN Thomas Pierrepoint
ASSISTANT Robert Baxter
DATE OF TRIAL 29th November, 1920
LOCATION OF TRIAL Maidstone
PRESIDING JUDGE Mister Justice Avory
PROSECUTION COUNSEL Harold Morris, Walter Briggs
DEFENCE COUNSEL Mister Rollo
NUMBER OF VICTIMS 1

VICTIMS DETAILS
NAME Harriett Lever
AGE 35
DATE OF MURDER Saturday, 25th September, 1920
PLACE OF MURDER Perry Street, Northfleet
METHOD OF KILLING Cut throat
RELATIONSHIP TO KILLER Wife

1920

ON AUGUST 20TH, 1920, 13-year-old William Weller was playing on the Crumbles beach at Eastbourne. Running along the shingle, he tripped over an obstruction and fell over. He had fallen over a human foot. There was a body buried on the beach.

Police were soon able to identify the body as that of Irene Munro. She had been on holiday, having arrived on Monday the 16th, and was staying at the house of Ada Wynniatt at 393 Seaside, a thoroughfare that ran parallel to the promenade.

Irene had been battered to death. Some of her front teeth were missing and there were puncture wounds on her mouth, forehead and left ear. Something had been used to strike her about the face and head but the blow that killed her was inflicted by a heavy, bloodstained stone found nearby, which had been lifted high and dropped onto her head. Although Irene's skirt had been folded back as high as her hips, she had not been raped but her handbag was missing.

It proved easy to reconstruct the movements of the murdered girl. She had last been seen alive on Thursday at 3.00pm, when she told her landlady that she intended visiting Hampden park. Frederick Charles Rogers, a painter who was decorating 393 Seaside, said that he saw Irene head off in the direction of the park. She returned after a few minutes saying that it was chilly and picked up a heavier coat.

At about the same time, a bus conductor, George Blackshaw, saw two men get off his bus at the Archery Tavern. As the bus pulled away he noticed an attractive young girl walk towards these two men and greet them. He would later testify that the girl was Irene Munro.

The next sighting of Irene was around 4.00pm, when she was seen walking past 393 Seaside, in the company of two men. The descriptions fitted the two men who had alighted from the bus at the Archery Tavern.

Shortly afterwards, William Putland and his friend, Frederick Wells, saw the same threesome walking down to the Crumbles. Putland and Wells were at a loose end with

NAMES	Jack Alfred Field; William Thomas Gray
AGES AT EXECUTION	19; 29
DATE OF EXECUTION	Friday, 4th February, 1921
PLACE OF EXECUTION	Wandsworth
HANGMAN	Thomas Pierrepoint
ASSISTANT	Robert Baxter, William Willis
DATE OF TRIAL	13th December – 17th December, 1920
LOCATION OF TRIAL	Lewes
PRESIDING JUDGE	Mister Justice Avory
PROSECUTION COUNSEL	C.F. Gill, Sir Henry Curtis Bennett, Cecil Whiteley
DEFENCE COUNSEL	Edward Marshall-Hall, James Cassels, John Flowers, C.P. Robinson
NUMBER OF VICTIMS	1

VICTIMS DETAILS	
NAME	Irene Violet Munro
AGE	17
DATE OF MURDER	Thursday, 19th August, 1920
PLACE OF MURDER	Crumbles Beach, Eastbourne
METHOD OF KILLING	Battered
RELATIONSHIP TO KILLERS	None; none

nothing better to do so, they followed the group for some time.

The final sighting was made by some navvies working on the beach. They saw the two men with the girl, playing with a kitten. Eventually one of the men put the kitten in the hut with the navvies and asked them to look after it. The three then walked off towards the spot where Irene's body would subsequently be found.

Perhaps the best witness was William Putland, who identified one of the men as William Gray, who lived at Longstone Road, Eastbourne. Putland did not know the other man but investigations showed that the description given fitted a known companion of Gray's, Jack Field who also lived locally. The two men were finally arrested on September 5th. Both had in fact been picked up earlier and released. Now the police were certain that they had the right men.

The two had the same alibi. Field said that on the day of the murder he had left home at 2.00pm, and gone to Gray's home. The two of them then walked along the coast to Pevensey Bay where they visited the castle. After some time spent relaxing, a woman they both knew, Hilda Baxter, passed by and they spoke to her. This Miss Baxter then walked back to Eastbourne with them where they arrived at about 5.10pm. The two men then spent the evening together at the Hippodrome and in a public house where they spoke to some friends before going home at about 10.45pm.

The alibi was quite detailed but unfortunately for Field and Gray, when Miss Baxter was interviewed, she denied ever having met them at Pevensey Castle and certainly did not see them on the day of the murder. To this, Field replied that he must have been mistaken but that the rest of the story was true.

There were witnesses, though, who could fill in part of the timetable. Dorothy Ducker, a local barmaid at the Albermarle pub, said that they were both in her pub from 1.00pm until 1.30pm, when they left together. Around 15 minutes later they returned, staying this time until about 2.30pm. They returned for the final time at 6.45pm when she remarked that Gray looked rather dirty and dishevelled and had wet boots. Gray had said that Field had been larking about and pushed him into some water.

The trial began on December 13th, 1920. Field went into the witness box but Gray did not. At one stage on December 15th, Field grew tired of the proceedings and went to sleep, but he was awake on the final day, when both men were found guilty.

At the appeal, both men gave evidence and told different stories. Field agreed that they had met Irene and gone for a walk. The evidence of the witnesses was all true. They had picked up the kitten and handed it to the navvies but after that, Gray made it plain that he wanted to be left alone with Irene. Field took the hint and went for a walk to Pevensey Castle.

On the way back he saw Gray walking towards him and when he asked what had happened, Gray confessed that he had argued with Irene and she had gone home. Once the reports of the discovery of Irene's body

appeared, Gray confessed that he had killed her. Field decided to stand by his friend.

Gray claimed to know nothing whatsoever of the murder. He testified that after being condemned to death, he and Field were at Lewes station, waiting to be taken to Wandsworth. The two men had a conversation in which Field admitted the truth. After the two men had separated at the Hippodrome, Field was walking home when Irene approached him and asked him the way to the Artillery. He walked with her and on the Crumbles said something which she did not like. She slapped his face and he struck her a number of times. Realising she was dead, he buried the body.

Gray's story was shown to be worthless. To begin with, his story did not fit the known timetable or the evidence of the eye witnesses. Further, two prison guards, Robert William O'Callaghan and Henry Jackson, testified that they were present in the waiting room and that no conversation had taken place.

Field's story was plausible, but if it had been true why would he have not said so long before and saved himself from a death sentence? The judges thought it more likely that both men were spinning tales in an attempt to avoid the rope.

1920

WHEN GEORGE ARTHUR Bailey placed an advertisement asking for young girls who were looking for employment to contact him, the police took an interest and kept watch. They saw several attractive ladies go to visit him, but it seemed that there was no cause for concern.

Bailey claimed that he had invented a new notation for musical scores. He wished to train ladies to teach the system and give it wider publicity. This did not explain, though, why he only wanted the most attractive women.

When for instance Gladys Millicent Edwards replied, Bailey wrote back complaining that she had not stated her appearance. He went on to say that he only wanted "smart, exceptionally attractive persons of height, preferably full build."

On the 29th of September, 1920, there were three ladies at Bailey's home, Barn Cottage: Lillian Victoria Rose Marks, Gladys Edwards and a Miss Field. After they had finished work, Bailey asked Miss Marks if she would return that evening. She agreed.

On the 30th of September, Miss Field and Miss Edwards returned and noticed that Lillian Marks was absent. Bailey said that she had gone out. Once the day's work was finished, it was Miss Edwards's turn to be asked back, but when she returned at 8.00pm, the house was in darkness.

By October 2nd, Lillian Marks had made a complaint against Bailey. She had finished work very late on September 29th, and Bailey had induced her to stay the night. During the night he had come into her bedroom and tried to force himself upon her.

When officers went to Barn Cottage to investigate, they found much more than a case of assault. Lying on a bed upstairs was the body of Kate Bailey, a pink fluid oozing from her mouth. A postmortem showed that she had been pregnant and had been poisoned.

When Bailey was arrested, he claimed that his wife had committed suicide. He was waiting for Miss Marks to arrive back and his wife was seen to drink down an egg cup of prussic acid. Just then Miss Marks arrived and he had been forced to hide the body upstairs. He admitted that he had gone into Miss

NAME	George Arthur Bailey
AGE AT EXECUTION	22
DATE OF EXECUTION	Wednesday, 2nd March, 1921
PLACE OF EXECUTION	Oxford
HANGMAN	John Ellis
ASSISTANT	Edward Taylor
DATE OF TRIAL	13th January – 17th January, 1921
LOCATION OF TRIAL	Aylesbury
PRESIDING JUDGE	Mister Justice McCardie
PROSECUTION COUNSEL	Hugo Young, R.O. Sullivan
DEFENCE COUNSEL	Sinclair Johnson
NUMBER OF VICTIMS	1

VICTIMS DETAILS	
NAME	Kate Lilian Bailey
AGE	22
DATE OF MURDER	Wednesday, 29th September, 1920
PLACE OF MURDER	Barn Cottage, Little Marlow
METHOD OF KILLING	Poisoned (by prussic acid)
RELATIONSHIP TO KILLER	Wife

Marks's bedroom but insisted that he had done so just to make sure that she wasn't wandering around.

To his brother-in-law, James William Jennings, Bailey had told a different story. Bailey had told him that his wife had gone into Wycombe Hospital for a premature birth and had subsequently died. As for the poisons, Bailey claimed that he was hoping to set up in practice as an amateur vet, as a sideline.

At the trial that condemned him to death, and which held female jury members for the first time, perhaps the cruellest testimony of all for George Bailey was that given by an expert on music who testified that his new system of notation was absolutely worthless.

FREDERICK QUARMBY KILLED out of jealousy. But was he a sane man and should he have hanged?

For two years, Quarmby had known Christine Smith and had enjoyed a loving relationship with her. She, though, was fond of entertaining other men and on more than one occasion, her activities had come to the attention of the police. Indeed, her home may well have been used as a brothel.

There were signs that Quarmby was building up to some sort of action. He told a previous landlady of his, Lilian Mary Porter, that Christine had been a rotter to him, but that he had a gun and was going to shoot her. In fact Quarmby did not own a gun, but in the week beginning November 29th, 1920, a man fitting his description purchased a knife at a Blackpool shop. He was remembered because he insisted on having both edges sharpened.

By December 1920, Quarmby was lodging with Mrs Horsfall at Charnley Road, Blackpool. On the third of that month, he was seen going out, by his landlady, at 5.15pm. He met up with Christine and, at 8.15pm, they were seen in a public house, enjoying a drink.

Christine had a lodger named Bigland and at 9.30pm that night, he heard screams coming from Christine's rooms. He found the door locked and heard groaning noises coming from within. He demanded that the door be opened but a male voice from within refused. Bigland ran off to fetch the police.

Before officers arrived, Mrs Bramhall, the next-door neighbour, who had also heard the screams, had gone out into her yard. She saw Quarmby appear and seeing her, he calmly announced: "I have murdered Mrs Smith."

What seemed to be a straightforward case of murder assumed greater import at Quarmby's trial. A great deal of comment was made on the subject of his sanity. In the first place, the defence held that sharpening the knife on both sides was hardly the sign of a sane mind. When this was dismissed, they brought in Doctor Wilkinson of Liverpool who had hypnotised Quarmby and taken him back to the time of the murder. He testified that Quarmby showed definite signs of mental instability and had killed in a moment of impulsive insanity.

NAME	Frederick Quarmby
AGE AT EXECUTION	47
DATE OF EXECUTION	Friday, 6th May, 1921
PLACE OF EXECUTION	Manchester
HANGMAN	John Ellis
ASSISTANT	Not known
DATE OF TRIAL	24th February – 25th February, 1921
LOCATION OF TRIAL	Manchester
PRESIDING JUDGE	Mister Justice Acton
PROSECUTION COUNSEL	F.R. Merriman, J.H. Thorpe
DEFENCE COUNSEL	W. Madden, E. Rowson
NUMBER OF VICTIMS	1

VICTIMS DETAILS	
NAME	Christine Ann Alexandra Smith
AGE	31
DATE OF MURDER	Friday, 3rd December, 1920
PLACE OF MURDER	Pendlehurst, Ripon Road, Blackpool
METHOD OF KILLING	Cut throat
RELATIONSHIP TO KILLER	Girlfriend

None of this swayed the jury of nine men and three women and they deliberated for only 15 minutes. Quarmby lost his appeal, which was again based largely on the evidence produced under hypnosis, and was hanged at Manchester in May.

Whilst he had been in prison awaiting execution, Quarmby had sent a letter to the Chief Constable, wishing him and his family a Merry Christmas!

THE RELATIONSHIP BETWEEN Olive Jackson and Thomas Wilson, was a very strange one. When arrested for her murder, Wilson would claim that jealousy of Henry Roskell had been the cause, but Olive was only his landlady and was actually living with another man, George Joseph William Duff.

Olive had been living with Duff, at 89 Newby Street, for 12 years. She was a widow with two sons and a daughter. Thomas Wilson, a sailor, had lodged with Duff and Olive for five years and for some reason, thought that there was a special relationship between Olive and himself.

Christmas saw a number of parties at Newby Street and at one of these a man named Henry Roskell decided that he wanted to kiss all the girls under the mistletoe. Wilson objected to Roskell's behaviour, especially with Olive, and from that moment on a jealous fire burned within him.

On April 9th, Wilson was enjoying a drink with Olive in McMaster's pub on Walton Road. At 9.15pm, Duff came in and joined them and a few minutes later, they were joined by Caroline Lawson, an old friend of Olive's. They sat together until 10.00pm when Caroline invited them all back to her house for a few more drinks. Olive said she would go, but Wilson said he would go home with Duff.

Wilson did not remain at Newby Street for long. Walking to Caroline Lawson's house, he found that there were quite a few people there. He was invited in but asked if 'Harry' was there. When told that he was, Wilson refused to go in and managed to persuade Olive to return home with him. The two were seen walking off towards her house.

Although it was gone 11.30pm when they reached Newby Street, there were still plenty of people about. Alfred Appleton was returning home and noticed the couple outside the gate to number 89. He saw Wilson draw out a revolver and fire four or five shots into Olive. Appleton shouted: "Stop that man!" as Wilson ran off.

Constable Frank Bowman gave chase, but lost Wilson in the winding streets, so it was not until 11.45am the following morning that Wilson was picked up at Lime Street Station.

NAME	Thomas Wilson
AGE AT EXECUTION	43
DATE OF EXECUTION	Tuesday, 24th May, 1921
PLACE OF EXECUTION	Manchester
HANGMAN	John Ellis
ASSISTANT	Not known
DATE OF TRIAL	2nd May, 1921
LOCATION OF TRIAL	Manchester
PRESIDING JUDGE	Mister Justice Acton
PROSECUTION COUNSEL	A.J. Ashton, Mister Powell
DEFENCE COUNSEL	W. Madden
NUMBER OF VICTIMS	1

VICTIMS DETAILS	
NAME	Olive Jackson
AGE	43
DATE OF MURDER	Saturday, 9th April, 1921
PLACE OF MURDER	Newby Street, Walton, Liverpool
METHOD OF KILLING	Shot
RELATIONSHIP TO KILLER	None

Wilson made another run for it but was cornered in the Lord Nelson pub. It transpired that he had spent the night in the Commercial Hotel where he had registered using the name G. Smith.

Wilson made no attempt to deny murder. He related that he had returned home for his gun and then gone to find Olive. On the way home they had argued and she had said that he had no right to make demands on her. She was with Duff and if something happened to him, she would look for another man as fine as he, not a worm like Wilson. That was the final insult and Wilson had then drawn his gun and fired.

0360

DORIS APPLETON WORKED in a seamen's boarding house in Cardiff and this is where she first met a coloured marine fireman named Lester Hamilton. The two started seeing each other, even though Doris was only 17.

On the evening of February 12th, 1921, at 7.00pm, Doris and her mother were enjoying a quiet drink in the Universal Hotel. Lester was with them and remained behind afterwards when Doris left, with her mother. The two walked a short distance together and finally parted at Cathay's Bridge. It was the last time Doris's mother would see her daughter alive.

At 8.30pm, Lester turned up at Doris's house. He had a friend with him and sought to take him inside. According to the later testimony of Doris's sister, Edna, Doris did not like the look of the stranger and refused him admission. Lester countered this by asking where she had been. Doris did not answer but Edna shouted that she had been with her.

Once again Lester tried to get his friend inside the house but Doris was firm and shouted: "Don't invite that kind of man into my mother's house." Lester took offence at this slight, drew out a gun and shot Doris dead. He then walked out of the house, and after travelling a short distance, shot himself in the head.

Although Lester Hamilton's wound was a serious one, he made a full recovery and was put on trial for his life. The defence claimed that Lester had gone to the house and found Doris with a Japanese sailor. When he confronted her about this, she made derogatory remarks about his colour and the judge informed the jury that if they felt that there was sufficient provocation, the verdict could be one of guilty of manslaughter.

In the event, after an absence of almost an hour, the jury felt that there could only be one verdict and Lester Hamilton was sentenced to death.

NAME	Lester Augustus Hamilton
AGE AT EXECUTION	25
DATE OF EXECUTION	Tuesday, 16th August, 1921
PLACE OF EXECUTION	Cardiff
HANGMAN	John Ellis
ASSISTANT	William Willis
DATE OF TRIAL	25th July, 1921
LOCATION OF TRIAL	Swansea
PRESIDING JUDGE	Mister Justice Salter
PROSECUTION COUNSEL	Sir J. Ellis Griffith, Wilfred Lewis
DEFENCE COUNSEL	T.W. Langman
NUMBER OF VICTIMS	1

VICTIMS DETAILS	
NAME	Doris Appleton
AGE	17
DATE OF MURDER	Saturday, 12th February, 1921
PLACE OF MURDER	57 Cwmdare Street, Cardiff
METHOD OF KILLING	Shot
RELATIONSHIP TO KILLER	Girlfriend

EDWARD AND ELIZABETH O'Connor had eight children and when his persistent cruelty towards Elizabeth caused her to leave him, he had problems keeping up with the maintenance payments. So it was that on July 25th, 1921, Elizabeth issued a summons against Edward for wilful neglect. For Edward, this was the last straw.

Each day from July 25th to July 30th, Edward called at his old home in order to pick up some of his belongings, but when he called on the 30th, he struck Elizabeth before he left.

With such a large family to take care of, space was at a premium and occasionally, Elizabeth would spend the night at her mother's house, 4 Sash Street. This is what she did on the night of Saturday, July 30th, taking her eldest daughter, Maggie, and the baby with her. The other six children were left at number 7, in the care of 12-year-old Ellen.

Ellen slept in the back bedroom, in the same bed as nine-year-old Edward and 11-year-old Elizabeth. In the other room, seven-year-old Mary and five-year-old Thomas shared one bed, whilst three-year-old Bernard had a bed to himself.

At around 4.00am on July 31st, Ellen was woken by the sound of footsteps on the stairs and saw the familiar figure of her father in the doorway. He asked where his wife and eldest daughter were and was told that they were "… at Granny's". At that point, Bernard began to cry. Ellen ran to her brother's bed and tried to comfort him, only to be followed by her father who drew out a razor and, without a word, cut the throats of Thomas and Mary.

Ellen was terrified, but for some reason, O'Connor left her and Bernard alone. Instead he returned to the back bedroom, where he cut the throats of Elizabeth and Edward. He then walked out of the house.

Constable Harry Sedgley was on duty in Gaol Square at 5.00am when O'Connor approached him, saying: "Come on, I will find you a job." He then handed over two bloodstained razors and added: "I have done three or four of the kids in with these."

In fact, although three children needed urgent medical attention, only Thomas was dead. When charged with murder, O'Connor showed no remorse, saying only that he had

NAME	Edward O'Connor
AGE AT EXECUTION	43
DATE OF EXECUTION	Thursday, 22nd December, 1921
PLACE OF EXECUTION	Birmingham
HANGMAN	John Ellis
ASSISTANT	Robert Wilson
DATE OF TRIAL	16th November, 1921
LOCATION OF TRIAL	Stafford
PRESIDING JUDGE	Mister Justice Roche
PROSECUTION COUNSEL	Sir Park Goff
DEFENCE COUNSEL	Mister Bostock Hill
NUMBER OF VICTIMS	1

VICTIMS DETAILS	
NAME	Thomas O'Connor
AGE	5
DATE OF MURDER	Sunday, July 31st, 1921
PLACE OF MURDER	7 Sash Street, Stafford
METHOD OF KILLING	Cut throat
RELATIONSHIP TO KILLER	Son

intended to kill his wife, because she had taken him to court.

O'Connor did not deny killing Thomas but did deny that it had been a wilful act. He claimed that he had not intended to kill or even injure any of the children and something had snapped inside him when he found his wife absent from the house.

Nevertheless, the jury held that he was responsible for his actions.

ELIZABETH BENJAMIN HELPED run a credit draper's business from 62 Dumbarton Road, Glasgow. It was her habit to collect the payments each Monday.

On those Mondays, Elizabeth usually returned home at some time between 4.00pm and 5.00pm. When, on October 31st, she had still not arrived back by the early evening, her brother Maxwell and sister Esther made some enquiries. Later that same night Elizabeth's disappearance was reported to the police.

The police began by retracing Elizabeth Benjamin's round. She had been seen by Elizabeth Graham, to whom Miss Benjamin mentioned that she had changed £2 worth of silver. She also said that she had yet to visit Helen Harkness, another customer. This was at around 3.45pm.

Some of the houses around George Street, where the Harkness family lived, shared a common washhouse where the women did their laundry. Margaret Baird needed to use the washhouse on Tuesday, November 1st, and took the key from Helen, who had last used it. Then, as Margaret busied herself, she happened to glance out of the window and saw what looked like a woman's body on the green. Closer inspection showed that the body's hands had been tied with a rope and a coat strap tied tightly around her mouth.

That same day, Maxwell Benjamin called on one of his customers, a Mrs Tolland, who said it was the talk of the district that a woman's body had been found. Benjamin went back to the police and was taken by them to view the body. He identified it as his sister.

It was Margaret Baird who, on November 5th, spotted a trail of blood leading up to the Harknesses' flat. Further police investigation led John Harkness, William's brother, to say that he had been at his mother-in-law's house on the night of October 31st when Helen had come to say that William needed to see him. When the two brothers spoke, William admitted to him that he had hit a woman on the head with a hammer and added that he and Helen now needed help to carry the body to the Clyde, or the canal, and dump it. John then viewed the body, in the washhouse, but would only help carry it as

NAME	William Harkness
AGE AT EXECUTION	31
DATE OF EXECUTION	Tuesday, 21st February, 1922
PLACE OF EXECUTION	Glasgow, Duke Street
HANGMAN	John Ellis
ASSISTANT	Robert Baxter
DATE OF TRIAL	30th January – 31st January, 1922
LOCATION OF TRIAL	Glasgow
PRESIDING JUDGE	Lord Justice Hunter
PROSECUTION COUNSEL	A.M. MacRobert, R.C. McFarlane
DEFENCE COUNSEL	William Mitchell, J.C.M. Guy
NUMBER OF VICTIMS	1

VICTIMS DETAILS	
NAME	Elizabeth Benjamin
AGE	14
DATE OF MURDER	Monday, 31st October, 1921
PLACE OF MURDER	67 George Street, Whiteinch, Glasgow
METHOD OF KILLING	Battered/asphyxiated
RELATIONSHIP TO KILLER	None

far as the green. On the strength of this evidence, both William and Helen Harkness were charged with murder.

At the trial, evidence was given that the blow to her head would not have killed Elizabeth. The cause of her death had been suffocation, a handkerchief having been forced into her mouth. That the attack had taken place in number 67 was beyond doubt as bloodstains had been found there.

Both defendants were found guilty and sentenced to death. However, on February 18th, Helen's sentence was commuted to one of life imprisonment. For William, there was no such escape.

1922

JAMES WILLIAMSON AND his wife, Mary, had five children and lived at Easington. He was a war veteran who had been wounded in both legs in Salonica and as a result, walked with a distinct limp.

In 1922, relations between Mary and James became somewhat strained and in December of that year she took the children with her and moved to her parents' house in Houghton-le-Spring. On the 17th, Mary went further and obtained a separation order at Castle Eden police court, claiming that James had ill-treated her. She was awarded 30/- a week maintenance.

James Williamson bitterly resented the separation order and maintenance award and was heard to remark to his 14-year-old daughter that the next time he laid hands on her mother, he would make sure that she never saw her face again.

Williamson visited his wife on December 29th, 1921, and was invited to stay over the New Year period. The couple appeared to be friendly enough and a reconciliation was held to be likely. The festive season passed and James returned home. He came back to Houghton-le-Spring on January 6th, 1922, and was again allowed to stay the night. He slept on a mat by the fire and his wife and children shared a 'shake-down' bed in the same room.

The following morning, Mary checked the post and finding that the payment due from James had not arrived, an argument broke out. James insisted he had sent the payment on time but Mary refused to believe him. At the height of the row, and after Mary's parents had left the house, James leapt to his feet and cut Mary's throat, in front of two of the children. They ran out to fetch the neighbours and when help arrived, they found James kneeling over his wife, sawing away at her throat. In fact, Mary's head was almost severed from her body.

Once again the defence was one of insanity, but the jury were only out five minutes before returning with a guilty verdict. After the sentence had been passed, James saluted the judge and said: "I thank you sir."

Perhaps the saddest part of this entire case was that the final argument which led to Mary Williamson's death and her husband's execution, had been totally unnecessary. The missing payment had simply been delayed in the post. It arrived two days after Mary was killed.

NAME	James Hutton Williamson
AGE AT EXECUTION	37
DATE OF EXECUTION	Tuesday, 21st March, 1922
PLACE OF EXECUTION	Durham
HANGMAN	Thomas Pierrepoint
ASSISTANT	William Willis
DATE OF TRIAL	1st March, 1922
LOCATION OF TRIAL	Durham
PRESIDING JUDGE	Mister Justice Bray
PROSECUTION COUNSEL	Mister Mitchell-Innes
DEFENCE COUNSEL	C. Paley Scott
NUMBER OF VICTIMS	1

VICTIMS DETAILS	
NAME	Mary Williamson
AGE	38
DATE OF MURDER	Saturday, 7th January, 1922
PLACE OF MURDER	Houghton-le-Spring
METHOD OF KILLING	Cut throat
RELATIONSHIP TO KILLER	Wife

WHEN DAVID THOMAS returned home from work at about 5.30pm on Wednesday, October 26th, 1921, he was surprised to find the doors all locked. He called out to his wife, Margaret, but there was no reply. Eventually, Mr Thomas was forced to find a ladder and gain entrance through a bedroom window that had been left open. Going downstairs to the kitchen, David Thomas finally discovered why Margaret had ignored his shouts. His wife lay on the floor, her head battered in.

The police had an idea of the approximate time of death. Mr and Mrs Thomas had eaten breakfast together at about 6.20am and he had left for work soon afterwards. The breakfast things were still on the table and since Margaret had been a fastidious housekeeper, she must have been murdered soon afterwards.

The police also had a suspect. Earlier in the week, a tramp, or gentleman of the road, had called and been given some bread and cheese. The morning of the murder, the same man had called at a neighbour's house and asked for a drink of water. The tramp was eventually found, on November 17th, and taken in for questioning. He was identified as William Sullivan.

One of the first pieces of incriminating evidence against Sullivan was a pair of serge trousers he had tried to sell. These trousers were identified by Mr Thomas as belonging to him. This indicated that Sullivan had been in the house and stolen them. It put him at the scene of the crime and as a result, Sullivan was charged with murder.

At the trial, Sullivan's defence was that he had simply not committed the crime and had been with another man named Stuart at the time it was committed. Indeed, the defence tried to paint a scenario in which the killer was none other than Mr Thomas himself. The alibi was not backed up by Stuart, though, and this counted heavily against Sullivan. After two and a half hours of deliberation, the jury decided that it was more likely that Sullivan was the killer and he was found guilty. Asked if he had anything to say, Sullivan would only repeat: "I am not guilty, and have always said so."

NAME	William Sullivan
AGE AT EXECUTION	41
DATE OF EXECUTION	Thursday, 23rd March, 1922
PLACE OF EXECUTION	Usk
HANGMAN	John Ellis
ASSISTANT	Thomas Phillips
DATE OF TRIAL	7th February – 8th February, 1922
LOCATION OF TRIAL	Monmouth
PRESIDING JUDGE	Mister Justice Darling
PROSECUTION COUNSEL	Arthur Powell, Lort Williams M.P.
DEFENCE COUNSEL	S.R.C. Bosanquet
NUMBER OF VICTIMS	1

VICTIMS DETAILS	
NAME	Margaret Thomas
AGE	48
DATE OF MURDER	Wednesday, 26th October, 1921
PLACE OF MURDER	Lapstone Cottage, Pen-groes-oped, near Pontypool
METHOD OF KILLING	Battered
RELATIONSHIP TO KILLER	None

An appeal having failed, Sullivan was executed at Usk prison on March 23rd, 1922.

He was the fourth man to be executed there this century, and the last. Just eight days later, the prison was closed down.

1922.

EDWARD BLACK WAS in severe financial trouble. An insurance agent, his customers were pressing him for the delivery of policies. Unfortunately, the policies did not exist and Black had pocketed the money. If only he could collect on his wife's life, he might be able to get out of this mess.

On October 21st, 1921, Annie Black fell ill with severe stomach pains. It may well have been a genuine illness ,which put an idea into Black's head. What is certain is that on October 29th, someone signed the poisons register, in the name of E.E. Black, at the local branch of Timothy White's chemist. The signature was for two ounces of arsenic.

Annie grew steadily worse and the doctor failed to understand why. Indeed, Annie often complained that her medicine burned like pepper, but only when it was administered by her husband.

On November 8th, Black vanished, leaving his wife in the hands of her daughter, Marion Ivy Nicholls, and her neighbours. Cases were coming to court and Black knew that whatever happened now, he would be unable to meet his responsibilities.

Three days later, on November 11th, Annie Black died. A postmortem revealed the presence of arsenic in her body. On November 15th, a warrant was issued for Black on charges of obtaining money under false pretences but that would merely be a holding charge.

For some days, the search for Black continued. He had been a native of Burnley and it was felt that he might return there, but no trace of him was seen until a letter arrived at the shop of a local tradesman in Tregonissey. The letter stated that Black was not responsible for Annie's death. It was postmarked Southport.

Descriptions and photographs of Black had been published in newspapers and one was seen by the landlady of Cashin's Temperance Hotel in Bell Street, Liverpool. The guest calling himself Stevens bore a striking resemblance to the wanted man.

On November 21st, the police knocked on Mister Stevens's door. A voice inside asked who it was and when the police identified themselves, the same voice asked them to

NAME	Edward Ernest Black
AGE AT EXECUTION	36
DATE OF EXECUTION	Friday, 24th March, 1922
PLACE OF EXECUTION	Exeter
HANGMAN	John Ellis
ASSISTANT	Seth Mills
DATE OF TRIAL	1st February – 2nd February, 1922
LOCATION OF TRIAL	Bodmin
PRESIDING JUDGE	Mister Justice Rowlatt
PROSECUTION COUNSEL	Holman Gregory, Mister Murphy
DEFENCE COUNSEL	Mister Pratt
NUMBER OF VICTIMS	1

VICTIMS DETAILS	
NAME	Annie Black
AGE	50
DATE OF MURDER	Friday, 11th November, 1921
PLACE OF MURDER	Tregonissey, Cornwall
METHOD OF KILLING	Poisoned (by arsenic)
RELATIONSHIP TO KILLER	Wife

wait. The police broke the door down. Edward Black was sitting on the bed, his hands to his throat, blood issuing from between his fingers. Black was overpowered and taken to hospital.

At his trial, Black denied everything. He had not purchased poison; he had not murdered his wife; he had not cheated his customers. A more accurate insight into his character was painted by his stepdaughter, 16-year-old, Marion Nicholls. She testified that Black had forced himself upon her from the age of 15 onwards.

After an absence of 40 minutes, Edward Ernest Black was found guilty as charged and sentenced to death.

ON THE MORNING of January 1st, 1922, a gentleman named Thomas Gore noticed a dog pawing furiously at a patch of ground on an allotment. Curiosity roused, Mr Gore returned the following morning and decided to dig down to see what had so excited the animal. Two feet down he found something he had not bargained for: the fully clothed body of a young woman.

A quick check of missing people led police to the name Maud Atkin. She had last been seen alive on November 21st and two lodgers she had known identified the clothing as hers. The police were now most interested in talking to Maud's husband, Percy James Atkin, who had himself been missing since Christmas Eve.

The Atkin family had lived at 25 Francis Street, Derby, with their two children. The youngest of these, a baby girl, was soon traced to Percy Atkin's mother, but the other child, a boy named Leslie, had also last been seen with his father. The more police investigated, the more tangled the affairs of Percy James Atkin seemed to become.

Percy and Maud had been married for some time but the marriage had faltered of late and Maud had taken to spending most of her time living with her parents at the other side of Derby. Percy, though, was known to have other interests. He had become friendly with another girl, Margaret Milton, and eventually he had proposed to her, omitting to mention that he was already married.

On November 10th, 1921, just four days before the wedding was to take place, a neighbour, Mrs Keys, told Margaret that her

NAME	Percy James Atkin
AGE AT EXECUTION	29
DATE OF EXECUTION	Friday, 7th April, 1922
PLACE OF EXECUTION	Nottingham
HANGMAN	John Ellis
ASSISTANT	Robert Baxter
DATE OF TRIAL	16th – 17th February, 1922
LOCATION OF TRIAL	Derby
PRESIDING JUDGE	Mister Justice Horridge
PROSECUTION COUNSEL	Sir W. Ryland Adkins
DEFENCE COUNSEL	Sir Henry Maddocks
NUMBER OF VICTIMS	1

VICTIMS DETAILS	
NAME	Maud Atkin
AGE	27
DATE OF MURDER	Monday, 21st November, 1921
PLACE OF MURDER	Chaddesden, near Derby
METHOD OF KILLING	Asphyxiated (buried alive)
RELATIONSHIP TO KILLER	Wife

future husband was a married man. Until then, Percy had always maintained that he was single, but he now confessed that he had been married but his wife had died in March. Satisfied with what Percy said, Margaret allowed the wedding to go ahead on November 14th.

Percy had told his new bride that his old one was dead. He now set about making the fiction into fact. On November 14th, Percy Atkin told the lodgers that he and Maud were looking for a new home on the other side of the town. A few days later he said he had found a place and on November 21st, he and Maud moved out the last of their belongings.

That evening, Percy was seen walking down the lane that led to the allotments at about 11.00pm. He was with a woman whom the witness,

The body of Maud Atkin lying in the grave Percy dug on his Derbyshire allotment.

Henry Belderstone, could not identify. Six weeks later, Maud's body would be found close to the same spot.

On December 12th, more trouble found its way to Percy's door. A relative of Maud's, concerned that she had not been heard from for a couple of weeks, visited Margaret at her home. Again the subject of the first Mrs Atkin was raised and when Percy came home, he was once more faced with an irate wife who demanded to know if he had been married or not. Percy finally confessed to her that he had been married when the wedding had taken place between him and Margaret. He had argued with his wife and she had left him. He had no idea where she was now.

Percy Atkin was picked up by the police, at New Malden, on January 3rd, 1922. Leslie, his son was with him, alive and well. When asked what he knew about the death of his wife, Percy Atkin told a most unlikely story.

Atkin said that on November 20th, he had confessed his bigamy to Maud. At first she had threatened him with the police but after much talking she had calmed down and said instead that she wanted nothing more to do with him and intended moving to her parents' house permanently. She said she would catch the last train the following day and he said he would see her off.

On the night of November 21st, the couple were walking down the lane, close by the allotments, when Maud suddenly removed her wedding ring, threw it onto the ground and stormed off into the darkness. Percy spent some minutes looking for the ring and then went after his wife. Suddenly he stumbled over something, looked down and saw to his horror that it was the body of Maud. She had stumbled and fallen onto some large stones. Terrified of what would be thought, Atkin recalled that he had recently dug a large hole on his allotment, in which he intended to plant an apple tree. Instead, he placed Maud into the hole and covered her up. Therefore, he maintained, he was not guilty of murder although he did hide the body.

The story simply did not hold water. Doctor Stone, who examined Maud's body, testified that her death could not possibly have been caused in the way Percy

had described. The cause of death was asphyxiation. It was not possible to determine whether Maud had been strangled or smothered and she was probably alive when placed into her grave.

The medical evidence carried the day and on April 7th, 1922, Percy James Atkin faced the hangman. His own death was probably much more humane than the one he had inflicted on his poor wife Maud.

FREDERICK ALEXANDER KEELING, a married man, had lived apart from his wife for some time and had subsequently been with a succession of other women. By November 1921, Keeling was living with a woman named Haines and in the same lodging house lived Emily Agnes Dewberry.

Keeling had chosen to supplement his income by a little adroit fraud and had managed to obtain a four-pound pension he was not entitled to. This information came to the ears of Emily Dewberry and, being an honest woman, she reported the matter to a pensions officer.

An investigation indicated that there was some substance to Emily's claim and a warrant was issued against Keeling. Both he, and Emily as a witness, were due to appear in court on November 24th.

On the due date, neither Emily nor Keeling appeared and police officers were sent to their home to determine the reason. Receiving no reply, the door to Emily's room was forced. She was found, dead, and close to her body was a hammer upon which were the initials F.K. A warrant was issued for the arrest of Frederick Alexander Keeling.

It was not until December 9th that Keeling was traced and arrested. The authorities knew about Haines and watched her until she met Keeling in a public house. When questioned, he denied all knowledge of the murder and claimed that Emily must have been killed by a stranger. In support of his story, his girlfriend testified that Keeling had only been out of her sight for a few minutes during the entire day of the murder. He had simply not had the time to commit the murder.

At the trial though, the police testified that in addition to Keeling's hammer being the murder weapon, blood had been found on his clothing. This, together with the obvious motive of revenge, were enough for the jury to convict Keeling of murder.

NAME	Frederick Alexander Keeling
AGE AT EXECUTION	54
DATE OF EXECUTION	Tuesday, 11th April, 1922
PLACE OF EXECUTION	Pentonville
HANGMAN	John Ellis
ASSISTANT	Seth Mills
DATE OF TRIAL	6th March – 7th March, 1922
LOCATION OF TRIAL	Old Bailey
PRESIDING JUDGE	Mister Justice Darling
PROSECUTION COUNSEL	Percival Clarke, H.D. Roome, W. Bentley Purchase
DEFENCE COUNSEL	Thorn Drury, A.C. Fox-Davies
NUMBER OF VICTIMS	1

VICTIMS DETAILS	
NAME	Emily Agnes Dewberry
AGE	46
DATE OF MURDER	Thursday, 24th November, 1921
PLACE OF MURDER	St Georges Road, Tottenham, London
METHOD OF KILLING	Battered
RELATIONSHIP TO KILLER	None

1922

MARGARET EVANS HAD known Edmund Tonbridge for a few years and in that time, she had borne him one child out of wedlock and was now pregnant by him again. Surely now he would do the decent thing and marry her?

The first child had been born in November 1920 and for a considerable time, Tonbridge had paid Margaret 15/- a week as his part of the responsibility. This arrangement continued until August 1921 when the child was adopted by a family named Wignall. Now Margaret was with child once more and it looked as if the whole thing would start up all over again.

Margaret mentioned marriage on more than one occasion and on January 14th, 1922, she met Edmund at Clapton Station to discuss the matter again. They met some time before 7.00pm that evening and went for a walk along the banks of the River Lea. In his pocket, Tonbridge had the solution to all his problems: a bottle of potassium cyanide.

A policeman standing on the bridge, saw the young couple walking towards him. Whilst they were still some way off he saw them embrace and sway gently together. Not wishing to pry on what seemed to be a loving moment, the officer averted his eyes. He heard the splash of something falling in the water, though could not make out what it was, but when the man walked past him, alone, the officer stopped him and asked what had happened to the woman.

The young man denied that he had been with a woman and at this blatant lie, the officer took him back to where he had stood with the woman. There, in the water, was the woman's body. The man, who had now identified himself as Edmund Tonbridge, was taken into custody.

Tonbridge's story was that they had gone for a walk to discuss marriage. Margaret had told him that she was pregnant and claimed that he was the father. However, he had in his pocket a letter from one George Andrews, which showed that it was he who was the father of this child, and indeed the first one that Tonbridge had paid out so much money for. Faced with this evidence, Margaret had reached into Tonbridge's pocket and taken

NAME	Edmund Hugh Tonbridge
AGE AT EXECUTION	38
DATE OF EXECUTION	Tuesday, 18th April, 1922
PLACE OF EXECUTION	Pentonville
HANGMAN	John Ellis
ASSISTANT	Robert Baxter
DATE OF TRIAL	5th March, 1922
LOCATION OF TRIAL	Old Bailey
PRESIDING JUDGE	Mister Justice Darling
PROSECUTION COUNSEL	Travers Humphreys, Eustace Fulton
DEFENCE COUNSEL	E.J. Purchase
NUMBER OF VICTIMS	1

VICTIMS DETAILS	
NAME	Margaret Evans
AGE	25
DATE OF MURDER	Saturday, 14th January, 1922
PLACE OF MURDER	Towpath of River Lea, Spring Hill, Clapton, London
METHOD OF KILLING	Poisoned (by prussic acid)
RELATIONSHIP TO KILLER	Girlfriend

out a bottle of prussic acid he was carrying, for photographic purposes. She drank down the deadly liquid and then fell backwards into the river.

The story was soon shown to be false. The letter from Andrews was a forgery that Tonbridge had written himself and Margaret's body showed signs of bruising around the face, which might have been caused by a blow from a fist.

The trial only lasted one day and Tonbridge, branded a cold, calculating and brutal murderer, was sentenced to death.

THE HOUSE AT 11 Brandiforth Street, Bamber Bridge, was filled with people. In addition to the householder, Hiram Thompson, and his wife, Ellen, there was also their 17-year-old unmarried daughter, also named Ellen, a son, John and their married daughter, Priscilla Warbrick and her husband, Thomas.

Hiram and his wife did not live happily. He was a heavy drinker and there were many arguments over the amount of money he frittered away on alcohol. Most of those developed into physical assaults on the long-suffering Ellen and since Hiram was usually drunk three or four times a week, life was far from perfect.

April 25th, 1922 began as so many other days had in the Thompson household. The children busied themselves preparing for work. Priscilla left the house at 7.00am and daughter Ellen left half an hour later. Soon Hiram and his wife were left alone.

The morning was relatively uneventful. When Ellen and her sister, Priscilla, returned for lunch, their mother was her usual self and Hiram, was nowhere to be seen. By 1.00pm, both daughters had returned to work. leaving their mother at her household chores.

The first person home that evening was Ellen Thompson. She arrived at Brandiforth Street at 5.45pm, to find her mother lying dead in the kitchen. Again there was no sign of Hiram. By the time Priscilla got back, Sergeant Thomas O'Toole was in attendance. A talk to a neighbour, Elizabeth Darwen, who lived a couple of doors down, at number 15, revealed that Ellen had last been seen alive at around 3.30pm.

Investigations showed that Hiram had been in the Hospital Inn, just after noon, where he had consumed four pints, leaving at 1.45pm. The next sighting was in another pub, the McKenzie's Arms, in Station Road. Hiram had gone into there at 6.20pm, had one pint and left.

Sergeant O'Toole continued his search and found Hiram Thompson talking to one of his oldest friends, Henry Wilson, who was working in his front garden. According to Wilson, Hiram had engaged him in casual chat and then mentioned that he had just killed his wife.

NAME	Hiram Thompson
AGE AT EXECUTION	52
DATE OF EXECUTION	Tuesday, 30th May, 1922
PLACE OF EXECUTION	Manchester
HANGMAN	John Ellis
ASSISTANT	William Willis
DATE OF TRIAL	13th May, 1922
LOCATION OF TRIAL	Manchester
PRESIDING JUDGE	Mister Justice Branson
PROSECUTION COUNSEL	Edward Wooll, Mister Leslie
DEFENCE COUNSEL	Mister Blackledge
NUMBER OF VICTIMS	1

VICTIMS DETAILS

NAME	Ellen Thompson
AGE	49
DATE OF MURDER	Tuesday, 25th April, 1922
PLACE OF MURDER	11 Brandiforth Street, Bamber Bridge, near Preston
METHOD OF KILLING	Cut throat/battered
RELATIONSHIP TO KILLER	Wife

At the police station, when charged, Thompson replied: "Who said it was me that cut her throat?" The evidence though, told a different story. Hiram Thompson's clothing was heavily bloodstained. Forensic tests showed that Ellen's throat had been cut whilst she was standing and blood had spurted all over the room. She had then been battered, most probably with an iron heater, which was bloodstained and matted with hair. Traces of those same hairs were also found on Hiram Thompson's clothing.

This evidence, together with Thompson's confession to Henry Wilson and his history of violence towards his wife, made the verdict of murder a foregone conclusion.

HERBERT ROWSE ARMSTRONG was the epitome of the English gentleman. Although only five feet three inches tall, he wore spats and sported a magnificent walrus moustache.

He had qualified as a solicitor in Liverpool in 1895 and served in the Boer War with the First Lancashire Royal Fusiliers. Married to Katherine Mary Friend in 1907, they moved to Hay-on-Wye and he became become a junior partner in the firm of Cheese and Armstrong. When Mister Cheese and his wife both died, within a day of each other in April, 1914, Armstrong took over the practice.

In August 1914, Armstrong enlisted in the Royal Engineers. He never served abroad but was promoted to the rank of major. In 1915, he was based near Bournemouth and there it was that he first met Mrs Marion Gale, who would play a part in his later life. By the end of the war, Armstrong and Katherine had been married for seven years, had three children and were living in 'Mayfield', a large house near Hay where the lawns seemed to suffer from a veritable plague of dandelions.

In May 1920, Armstrong was demobbed and in the following month, Katherine Armstrong made a new will leaving all her property to her husband. This will superseded an earlier will dated 1917, in which Katherine had made provision for her children and only left a bequest of £50 per annum to her husband. The second will was almost certainly a forgery.

At about the same time, Katherine began to fall ill. She had always been something of a hypochondriac and obsessive about her health, but now her illnesses seemed to be genuine.

On August 4th, 1920, Herbert purchased three tins of powdered weedkiller to deal with his dandelions. Shortly afterwards, Katherine Armstrong began to suffer from delusions and on August 22nd, she was admitted to the Barnwood House Hospital for Mental Disorders, in Gloucester.

On January 14th, 1921, Armstrong contacted the hospital and asked if his wife could return home. She seemed to be much better and all the delusions had ended. He omitted to point out that three days before, he

NAME	Herbert Rowse Armstrong
AGE AT EXECUTION	53
DATE OF EXECUTION	Wednesday, 31st May, 1922
PLACE OF EXECUTION	Gloucester
HANGMAN	John Ellis
ASSISTANT	Edward Taylor
DATE OF TRIAL	April 3rd – April 13th, 1922
LOCATION OF TRIAL	Hereford
PRESIDING JUDGE	Mister Justice Darling
PROSECUTION COUNSEL	Ernest Pollock
DEFENCE COUNSEL	Henry Curtis Bennett
NUMBER OF VICTIMS	1 (possibly 2)

VICTIMS DETAILS	
NAME	Katharine Mary Armstrong
AGE	48
DATE OF MURDER	Tuesday, 22nd February, 1921
PLACE OF MURDER	Hay-on-Wye
METHOD OF KILLING	Poisoned (by arsenic)
RELATIONSHIP TO KILLER	Wife

had purchased a quarter of a pound of arsenic from John Davies, the chemist in Hay.

Katherine Armstrong was released from the hospital on January 22nd and the next day, her considerate husband engaged a nurse, Muriel Kinsey, to take care of her. Muriel was not to last long, however, as she said that she could not cope with her patient after Katherine had threatened to kill herself. Four days later, on January 27th, a full-time nurse, Eva Allen, was employed.

Over the next few weeks, Katherine was struck by repeated attacks of vomiting and muscular spasms. Her health grew worse until finally, on February 22nd, two weeks after her 48th birthday, she died. The cause was given as "heart disease arising from nephritis and gastritis". She was buried on February 25th.

Herbert Armstrong was not exactly devastated by his wife's death. He went on a month-long holiday and on his return, asked Mrs Gale to marry him. She turned him down. Armstrong returned to his legal practice.

Hay boasted another firm of solicitors, led by Oswald Martin. For some time he had been in dispute with Armstrong over the sale of an estate and now Martin was putting pressure on Armstrong for completion, especially since Armstrong held a £500 deposit from Martin's client.

On September 20th, 1921, Martin was surprised to receive delivery of a box of Fuller's chocolates. His wife, Constance Martin, sampled one of the chocolates but since neither of them had a particularly sweet tooth, the gift was put away, until a dinner party on October 8th.

Oswald Martin had invited his two brothers, and their wives and after they had dined, the chocolates were brought out. Only Dorothy, Gilbert Martin's wife, had any and the following day she was violently ill, much to the embarrassment of her hostess, who thought some of her cooking might have been to blame.

Oswald Martin had waited long enough for completion of the estate deal and had now formally stated that his client wished to withdraw and required the return of his deposit. Armstrong suggested that they discuss the matter over tea and invited Martin to Mayfield on October 26th. Martin duly appeared and took tea. At one stage, Armstrong offered Martin a scone, with the phrase "Excuse my fingers...." Upon returning home, Oswald Martin fell violently ill and was laid up in bed for five days.

At last the pieces began to fall together. Martin had been taken ill after dining with Armstrong. Dorothy Martin had been sick after having a chocolate mysteriously sent through the post.

A Doctor Hincks, who was in attendance, decided to send samples of Martin's urine and vomit for analysis, along with the box of chocolates. They were sent to the Clinical Research Association in London, where it was found that the urine and vomit contained arsenic, as did two of the chocolates in the box. The police were called in.

Armstrong was a highly respected solicitor, so the police investigation had to proceed slowly and in secret. During that time, the unfortunate Oswald Martin had to fend off many new invitations from Armstrong to attend tea or dinner. It was not until December 31st that he could relax.

On that day, Armstrong was interviewed at his offices in Broad Street, and arrested on a charge of attempting to murder Mister Martin. He was searched and in one of his pockets was a small package containing one-twentieth of an ounce of arsenic. There were also a few ounces of arsenic in one of his desk drawers.

The attempted murder charge was but a holding charge. On January 2nd, 1922, Katherine Armstrong's body was exhumed. It contained 3.5 grains of arsenic. On January 19th, Herbert Rowse Armstrong was charged with murder.

The trial was to last for ten days. The prosecution suggested that Katherine Armstrong had been murdered for gain but the defence pointed out that Armstrong had used very little of the money he had received after her death.

More telling was the small packet of arsenic found on Armstrong when he was arrested. Armstrong claimed that he had taken an ounce and divided it into 20 small packets, one for each of 20 dandelions. The judge found this hard to credit and pressed Armstrong on the point. Armstrong could not explain why he had not simply made up one large batch and dealt with all the dandelions at the same time.

Armstrong was found guilty of murder and after a failed appeal, was executed at Gloucester on May 31st, 1922. But it's possible that he may have been involved in another death. In October 1921, an estate agent named William Davies died suddenly. He too had been in dispute with Armstrong.

1922

ON THE MORNING of Tuesday, March 14th, 1922, the chambermaid of the Spencer Hotel knocked on the door of room 14. Receiving no reply, she entered and saw, still lying in bed, Lady Alice White, her face and the pillow covered in blood.

Lady White had been battered so severely that part of her brain protruded through her skull. Though she was still alive, she was much too ill to be moved, and received medical treatment in her bedroom. She died early the following morning.

The police felt that Lady White had been attacked by a burglar. The fact that nothing had been taken indicated that the thief had been disturbed. The first step was to interview all the staff and one, a pantry boy named Henry Jacoby, reported he had heard whispering in the small hours of March 14th.

Jacoby had mentioned this to the night porter, Platt, and they searched the premises but found nothing. Jacoby then went back to his bedroom, and knew nothing more until Lady White was discovered.

Inquiries on staff histories led to some interesting information on the co-operative pantry boy. Before coming to work at the hotel, three weeks before, Jacoby had lived in lodgings from which some money had been reported missing. He was arrested on that charge and questioned more closely on the murder of Lady White. It was not long before Henry Jacoby was admitting something more serious than theft.

Jacoby's story began after his search with Platt. Going back to his bedroom, Jacoby had taken a hammer and gone upstairs to see if he could find any cash. The second door, that to room 14, opened when he turned the handle.

Jacoby switched on his torch at which point Lady White woke. She gave a cry at seeing an intruder and Jacoby struck her with the hammer. He then went back downstairs, washed the hammer and went to bed.

At his trial, Jacoby pleaded not guilty and told a different story. This time, after returning to his room he had gone back upstairs, armed with the hammer. Seeing a room door slightly open, Jacoby went in to investigate and saw a figure. He lashed out and only then did he see that he had struck Lady White.

NAME	Henry Julius Jacoby
AGE AT EXECUTION	18
DATE OF EXECUTION	Wednesday, 7th June, 1922
PLACE OF EXECUTION	Pentonville
HANGMAN	John Ellis
ASSISTANT	Thomas Phillips
DATE OF TRIAL	28th April, 1922
LOCATION OF TRIAL	Old Bailey
PRESIDING JUDGE	Mister Justice McCardie
PROSECUTION COUNSEL	Percival Clarke, H.D. Roome, W. Bentley Purchase
DEFENCE COUNSEL	Lucian Fior
NUMBER OF VICTIMS	1

VICTIMS DETAILS	
NAME	Alice White (Died Wednesday, 15th March)
AGE	65
DATE OF MURDER	Tuesday, 14th March, 1922
PLACE OF MURDER	Room 14, Spencer Hotel, Portman Street, London
METHOD OF KILLING	Battered
RELATIONSHIP TO KILLER	None

The jury went out to consider their verdict and after a short time, came back to ask if they could return a verdict of manslaughter if they were convinced that Jacoby had not intended to kill. The judge pointed out that even if he had intended to inflict grievous harm, there could be no verdict of manslaughter. As a result, the verdict was guilty, but with a strong recommendation to mercy.

IT WAS A peaceful June day in Eaton Place as Sir Henry Wilson arrived home. As he moved towards his front door, two men stopped forward, drew revolvers and began firing. A number of shots were fired and Sir Henry received six wounds, the two fatal ones being chest wounds from opposite sides.

There were witnesses to the murder. A group of men were working in the street and a couple of police constables were in the area. A chase began and it was then that the two killers saw a taxi cab and tried to hail it. The driver was about to open the door when he heard cries of: "Stop them!" Believing that there might have been a robbery he slammed the door shut, turned his cab around and began following the men.

Over the next few minutes, the two tried desperately to escape, shooting three more men: Constable Marsh, Constable Sayer and Alexander Clarke, until eventually they were overpowered and taken into custody. They identified themselves as James Connelly and John O'Brien.

It soon transpired that these names were false and the men who had killed Sir Henry were actually Joseph O'Sullivan and Reginald Dunne. Both had served in the British Army in the First World War, and both men had been badly wounded in France. Indeed, O'Sullivan had lost his right leg below the knee. At the time of their arrests, Dunne was training to be a teacher and O'Sullivan was working at the Ministry of Labour but both were espousers of the Irish Republican cause and Sir Henry Wilson, who had been a military adviser to the Ulster government, was a prime target as far as they were concerned.

The trial opened at the Old Bailey on July 18th and was to last just three hours. Both men refused to plead to the charge of murder but both admitted shooting Sir Henry. After the case for the prosecution had been put forward, Dunne expressed a desire to read a statement in his defence. This was considered by the judge, though he eventually refused to allow it as it was nothing more than a propaganda statement for the Republicans. At this, both O'Sullivan and Dunne withdrew instructions from their counsel and no defence was put forward.

NAMES	Joseph O'Sullivan; Reginald Dunne
AGES AT EXECUTION	25; 24
DATE OF EXECUTION	Thursday, 10th August, 1922
PLACE OF EXECUTION	Wandsworth
HANGMAN	John Ellis
ASSISTANT	Edward Taylor, Seth Mills
DATE OF TRIAL	18th July, 1922
LOCATION OF TRIAL	Old Bailey
PRESIDING JUDGE	Mister Justice Shearman
PROSECUTION COUNSEL	Sir Ernest Pollock, Eustace Fulton, Travers Humphreys, Mister Giveen
DEFENCE COUNSEL	Artemus Jones, Jeremiah McVeagh
NUMBER OF VICTIMS	1

VICTIMS DETAILS	
NAME	Field Marshall Sir Henry Wilson
AGE	58
DATE OF MURDER	Thursday, 22nd June, 1922
PLACE OF MURDER	Outside 36 Eaton Place, London
METHOD OF KILLING	Shot
RELATIONSHIP TO KILLERS	None; none

There could only be one verdict and after sentence of death was pronounced, O'Sullivan announced to Mister Justice Shearman: "You may kill my body, my Lord, but my spirit you will never kill."

1922

THERE WAS SOMETHING of an atmosphere at the Pheasant Inn in Bilston. To begin with, the man who kept the house, Elijah Pountney, had a drink problem. He could satisfy his cravings for drink whenever he wished and he did so to excess.

Another factor was the presence of a lodger, Edmund McCann, who had lived there for some six months. Elijah felt that his wife, Alice, paid too much attention to McCann and became convinced that there was something going on.

At first, Elijah tried to adopt a legal pathway. On March 3rd, at 10.00pm, Elijah sent for the police and asked them to turn McCann out. Elijah went on to complain to the police that his wife was encouraging McCann's attentions and added that if this continued, Elijah would be sure to kill her.

Elijah and Alice had a son who lived with them. John Edward Pountney was in the kitchen, early on the afternoon of April 16th. His mother was peeling potatoes when Elijah entered, walked over to Alice and muttered something to her. At once Alice pulled back and cried out: "What, in front of my son?" Elijah walked out of the kitchen, only to return a few minutes later with Joseph Henry Norton, a friend.

Norton had been drinking in the bar since 12.30pm and Alice told him that Elijah had accused her of being pregnant with McCann's child. Elijah replied by pushing Norton forward, towards Alice, telling him to kiss her as it might be the last chance he ever got. Norton was angered by this remark and remonstrated with Elijah.

Once more Elijah briefly left the kitchen only to return and put his arm gently around his wife. Then there was a sudden, rapid movement and Alice staggered, blood pouring from a wound in her throat. Elijah calmly left the pub.

In fact, Elijah Pountney walked down to the canal and threw himself in. He was seen in the water by 15-year-old William Doughty, who called two policemen. Together they pulled Elijah from the water, whereupon Sergeant George Cartwright came upon the scene and arranged for Pountney to be taken to the station.

NAME	Elijah Pountney
AGE AT EXECUTION	48
DATE OF EXECUTION	Friday, 11th August, 1922
PLACE OF EXECUTION	Birmingham
HANGMAN	John Ellis
ASSISTANT	Robert Baxter
DATE OF TRIAL	7th July, 1922
LOCATION OF TRIAL	Stafford
PRESIDING JUDGE	Mister Justice Shearman
PROSECUTION COUNSEL	Graham Milward, F.T. Vachell
DEFENCE COUNSEL	A.J. Long
NUMBER OF VICTIMS	1

VICTIMS DETAILS	
NAME	Alice Gertrude Pountney
AGE	47
DATE OF MURDER	Sunday, 16th April, 1922
PLACE OF MURDER	The Pheasant Inn, Broad Street, Bilston
METHOD OF KILLING	Cut throat
RELATIONSHIP TO KILLER	Wife

Pountney's story was that he had heard Alice and McCann planning to run away together. She had deliberately favoured McCann, giving him oysters whilst he had to make do with bacon.

In one thing at least, Pountney had been wrong. Medical examination showed that Alice had not been pregnant at the time of her death.

At his trial, the defence tried to show that drink, coupled with his concerns over Alice and McCann, had unhinged Elijah Pountney's mind. Unfortunately, this was greatly weakened by the fact that Elijah had issued threats against Alice.

AT 6.00PM ON May 30th, 1922, Robert Fullerton gave his daughter, Maggie, 2d to buy some sweets for herself. The little girl skipped out of the house at 48 Little York Street. When she had not returned by 7.00pm, the Fullertons called in the police but despite an extensive search, no trace of Maggie could be found.

Two witnesses were found who pieced together something of the child's disappearance. Annie Aldis, another child, said that a man had tried to get her to go away with him. Later that evening she had seen the same man talking to Maggie. Annie was able to give a brief description.

A more detailed description of the same man was given by a farmer, Mr Kirkwood, who said he had seen a man carrying a child fitting Maggie's description. They had been heading across the fields at Cave Hill at around 9.00pm. Half an hour later, Kirkwood had seen them again. This time they were hand in hand but the little girl was crying.

Despite a three-day search of the area around Maggie's home and the entire Cave Hill area, nothing was found until the afternoon of Saturday, June 3rd. It was 2.00pm on that day when Samuel Armstrong, a gamekeeper, noticed something hidden under a cover of leaves. Closer inspection revealed the naked body of a small girl. She was identified as Maggie Fullerton and a medical examination confirmed that she had been raped.

The police had already noted that the description of the man seen with Maggie on the day she had vanished fitted a man already in custody on a charge of stealing clothing from his lodgings in Henry Street, which crossed Little York Street. When this man, Simon McGeown, was placed into a parade, both Annie Addis and Mr Kirkwood made positive identifications. McGeown was charged with murder.

At his trial, McGeown's defence was that there was insufficient evidence to prove that he was the man seen with Maggie. The jury took 45 minutes to decide that he was, and he was sentenced to death.

Only now could it be revealed that McGeown had a chequered history. He had

NAME	Simon McGeown
AGE AT EXECUTION	38
DATE OF EXECUTION	Thursday, 17th August, 1922
PLACE OF EXECUTION	Belfast
HANGMAN	John Ellis
ASSISTANT	William Willis
DATE OF TRIAL	22nd July, 1922
LOCATION OF TRIAL	Belfast
PRESIDING JUDGE	Lord Justice Andrews
PROSECUTION COUNSEL	John McGonigal, G. Hill Smith
DEFENCE COUNSEL	G.B. Hanna M.P.
NUMBER OF VICTIMS	1

VICTIMS DETAILS	
NAME	Margaret (Maggie) Fullerton
AGE	7
DATE OF MURDER	Tuesday, 30th May, 1922
PLACE OF MURDER	Cave Hill, Belfast
METHOD OF KILLING	Battered/strangled
RELATIONSHIP TO KILLER	None

always wanted to join the Army which he did at age 14. When he was 18 he was posted to India, where he contracted malaria. He made a full recovery but a change in his behaviour was noted. Some 18 months later he was discharged after a court-martial but when the Great War broke out, McGeown re-enlisted and served in France for three years during which he was wounded, gassed twice and finally invalided out. Then, during the period 1918 to 1922, he had six convictions for petty crime and served a total of 30 months in prison.

A man who had once served his country well thus ended his life at the end of a rope.

ON DECEMBER 20TH, 1921, an advertisement appeared in The Morning Post. Irene Wilkins, the unmarried daughter of a London solicitor, was seeking a post as a school cook. The advertisement gave a few basic details and her home address: 21 Thirlmere Road, Streatham.

The following day, Irene received a telegram, inviting her to catch the 4.30 train to Bournemouth where a car would meet her at the station. She sent a telegram of confirmation and packed her bag for the journey. She arrived at Bournemouth at 7.03 and so was unaware that her own telegram had been returned – address unknown.

Also travelling to Bournemouth on that train had been an engineer, Frank Humphris. He had noticed Irene and saw her again as she got into a grey-green car, driven by a chauffeur in uniform.

The following morning, Charles Nicklen was out walking when he reached Fifteen Acre Meadow at Boscombe. He noticed a bundle in the field. It turned out to be the body of Irene Wilkins. Irene was lying on her back with her dress pulled up. Her head showed that she had been battered with a blunt instrument and had also been punched in the face. Later examinations would show that she had not been raped. There were tyre tracks near the body.

The police soon discovered that the tracks had been made by Dunlop Magnum tyres. A report was published in the local newspapers and one of the people who read it was Frank Humphris. He immediately came forward and reported details of the car he had seen. All cars and chauffeurs in the district were questioned, including Thomas Henry Allaway.

Allaway was the driver for a businessman, Mr Sutton. He drove a Mercedes car fitted with three Dunlop Magnums and one Michelin tyre, but the Michelin was on the wrong wheel if the tracks in the field were to be matched. They asked Allaway if he had changed any of the tyres recently. He said he had not. Further, Mister Sutton was happy to point out that there was only one key to the garage and he had it in his possession. The car had not been taken out after 6.00pm on the night of the murder, so Allaway's alibi that he

NAME	Thomas Henry Allaway
AGE AT EXECUTION	36
DATE OF EXECUTION	Saturday, 19th August, 1922
PLACE OF EXECUTION	Winchester
HANGMAN	John Ellis
ASSISTANT	Edward Taylor
DATE OF TRIAL	3rd July – 7th July, 1922
LOCATION OF TRIAL	Winchester
PRESIDING JUDGE	Mister Justice Avory
PROSECUTION COUNSEL	T.W. Inskip
DEFENCE COUNSEL	Mister Fox Davies
NUMBER OF VICTIMS	1

VICTIMS DETAILS	
NAME	Irene May Wilkins
AGE	31
DATE OF MURDER	Wednesday, 21st December, 1921
PLACE OF MURDER	Boscombe, Bournemouth
METHOD OF KILLING	Battered
RELATIONSHIP TO KILLER	None

had been drinking in a local pub was not checked.

Two weeks after the murder, Frank Humphris saw again the car he had seen Irene getting in to. Aware of its significance now, he took down the registration number, LK 7405, and passed it on to the police. Unbelievably, the police failed to follow up his report. If they had done so, their enquiries would have taken them back to Allaway.

A month later, the young female clerk who had taken down the details of the telegram sent to Irene Wilkins, was transferred to the Boscombe Post Office. Soon afterwards she heard a voice she recognised. It was the same person who had sent the telegram.

Aware that the police wanted to interview the man, she told a fellow clerk of her suspicions, but by the time they could get to the door, the man had gone.

A few weeks passed and then the female clerk heard the voice again. This time she was a little quicker and managed to see the man standing near a grey-green car. She took its number and reported it to the police – but amazingly, they failed to follow up this lead too.

Only days later, the chauffeur was seen again by the clerk. This time she told one of her fellow workers, who followed the man to an address in Portman Mews. It was the address of Mr and Mrs Sutton. This was reported, and yet again, the police took no action.

In April 1922, Allaway left the employ of Mr Sutton but chose to take his employer's chequebook with him and fled to Reading. Finally, the police began to look at the accumulated evidence they had, and decided it was time they interviewed Allaway.

When Thomas Allaway was arrested in Reading, a number of betting slips were found in his pocket and the handwriting on these matched that on the telegram form that had been sent to Irene Wilkins. The tyres on Mister Sutton's Mercedes were examined again. It was noted that the Michelin was well worn and upon looking at the spare, the police discovered that it was an almost new Dunlop Magnum. Soon a witness was found who gave evidence that he had seen Allaway changing the tyre, after the murder had taken place.

There still remained Mister Sutton's evidence that the car had not been taken out after 6.00pm on the night of the murder. A search of Allaway's old room revealed a garage key. Allaway had copied the key and so had been able to take the car out whenever he chose. The alibi had collapsed.

Thomas Allaway was found guilty of murder and confessed that guilt to the prison governor before he kept his appointment with the hangman.

1922

ON MAY 20TH, 1922, William James Yeldham married Elsie Florence. Within a few days, both would be charged with murder.

Yeldham lived in some outbuildings at a farm near Ilford. Unemployed, he had little money and lived in squalor but he still had an eye for the ladies and that eye had fallen upon Elsie. Unfortunately, another eye had also fallen on Elsie – that of George Stanley Grimshaw, and although he was almost three times Elsie's age, and already married, she did not exactly push him away. The situation served only to make Yeldham more jealous and when, on May 17th, Yeldham saw Elsie and George walking into the woods together, he determined to follow them.

What happened next is subject to much conjecture. According to Yeldham, he saw George put his arm around Elsie's waist and something snapped inside him. He walked up behind George and after a brief fight, Yeldham pulled out a spanner he just happened to have on him, and battered Grimshaw to death. Another version of events, though, had Yeldham and Elsie conspiring to lure George to the woods, where he was murdered.

There could be no doubt that Yeldham was the killer of George Grimshaw. On May 22nd, Yeldham sold George's watch and when the couple were picked up, Elsie admitted that she had stolen £15 from George's body after Yeldham had killed him. Both were charged with murder.

Yeldham's story was that when he first met Elsie, she was a prostitute. He hated the way that she made her living and determined to change her way of life. The problem was that he had no money. He stole a bicycle and sold it. For that offence he served six months in prison and by the time he came out, he discovered that Grimshaw was paying rather too much attention to the woman he wanted. The rest of his story was the jealous boyfriend scenario outlined above but he denied that there had been any conspiracy or plan. It was a crime committed on the spur of the moment and the two had only decided to rob Grimshaw after he was dead.

For her part, Elsie said that she much preferred Yeldham to Grimshaw but on the

NAME	William James Yeldham
AGE AT EXECUTION	23
DATE OF EXECUTION	Tuesday, 5th September, 1922
PLACE OF EXECUTION	Pentonville
HANGMAN	John Ellis
ASSISTANT	William Willis
DATE OF TRIAL	17th July – 19th July, 1922
LOCATION OF TRIAL	Old Bailey
PRESIDING JUDGE	Mister Justice Shearman
PROSECUTION COUNSEL	Percival Clarke
DEFENCE COUNSEL	Mister Lucy
NUMBER OF VICTIMS	1

VICTIMS DETAILS	
NAME	George Stanley Grimshaw
AGE	54
DATE OF MURDER	Wednesday, 17th May, 1922
PLACE OF MURDER	Higham's Park, Chingford
METHOD OF KILLING	Battered
RELATIONSHIP TO KILLER	None

day of the killing, she and Yeldham had argued so she went off to see George instead. Suddenly Yeldham appeared from nowhere and struck George from behind. Once she saw that Grimshaw was dead, she stole the money he had on him. The jury were not convinced and found both William and Elsie guilty of murder. Mister Justice Shearman sentenced them both to death.

Two weeks before she was due to die, Elsie's sentence was commuted to one of life imprisonment. For Yeldham there was no such mercy shown.

ROSE HANNAH ROBINSON had married for the second time. Her husband, George Robinson, was a kind man who took good care of Rose, her son and her daughter, Frances Pacey. Frances had a young man in her life and by coincidence, his name was also George Robinson.

Frances and young George Robinson had been seeing each other for about a year but, at least as far as Frances was concerned, it was never a meaningful relationship. On April 9th, Rose overheard her daughter telling George that it was over between them. She also heard George threaten to kill himself.

For some months, nothing more was heard from George Robinson and Frances probably thought that this chapter of her life had closed for ever. Tuesday September 5th was to prove her wrong.

On that day, Rose Robinson got out of bed at 6.00am to prepare breakfast for her son, who left the house at 6.30am. Just over an hour later, Rose too went out, leaving Frances in bed. Mary Turner lived next door to Rose Robinson, and at 7.45am she heard a scream from that house. Very soon afterwards, Frances staggered into Mary's house, still wearing her night-gown, blood pouring from a wound in her throat. Mary called the doctor and accompanied Frances to hospital, sending her daughter to fetch Rose. Frances was semi-conscious by the time she reached the hospital; she died from her wounds that same afternoon without regaining consciousness or making any statement.

Meanwhile, another drama was unfolding at George Robinson's house. George lived with his mother, Mary, and his sister, Mary Ann. At 8.00am on this fateful day, Mary Ann saw her brother come into the house and rush upstairs. He looked wild and his shirt was covered in blood. Mary Ann followed him upstairs and found George in bed, with a wound in his throat. Concerned, she called out the doctor and he sent George off to the same hospital that Frances had been admitted to. A bloodstained razor and case were found in George's jacket pocket. Mary Ann gave this razor to Police Constable Richard Burnell. It was jagged and broken. Frances' throat bore a

NAME	George Robinson
AGE AT EXECUTION	27
DATE OF EXECUTION	Wednesday, 13th December, 1922
PLACE OF EXECUTION	Lincoln
HANGMAN	Thomas Pierrepoint
ASSISTANT	Robert Baxter
DATE OF TRIAL	30th October, 1922
LOCATION OF TRIAL	Lincoln
PRESIDING JUDGE	Mister Justice Lush
PROSECUTION COUNSEL	Leslie Marks, C.E. Loseby
DEFENCE COUNSEL	A.M. Lyons
NUMBER OF VICTIMS	1

VICTIMS DETAILS	
NAME	Frances Florence Pacey
AGE	18
DATE OF MURDER	Tuesday, 5th September, 1922
PLACE OF MURDER	Dorrington
METHOD OF KILLING	Cut throat
RELATIONSHIP TO KILLER	Girlfriend

1922

jagged wound in which a piece of metal had been found.

The final piece of evidence linking George Robinson to the crime was a grey-coloured flat cap. Such a cap was found in Frances' bedroom and since it belonged to no-one in the house, must have been dropped by her attacker. This cap was shown to Mary Ann Robinson and identified as belonging to her brother. George Robinson was now charged with murder.

Robinson had waited for five months to claim the life of Frances Pacey. The law took another three to claim his.

1922

THE SMALL CROWD gathered in the front room of the White Horse Hotel at 9.30pm., on September 23rd, 1922, were all happy. In just two days' time, the landlady, Edith, would marry for the second time. Her intended husband was James Owen Kitchener and already the couple had received presents, which Edith was showing off.

With Edith were two of her married daughters, Ivy Prentice and Gertrude D'Arcy and also Evelyn Kitchener, one of James's daughters. In fact, this would be the second wedding in a very short period, as Ivy had married three days before, on September 20th.

As the group gazed at the gifts, a figure appeared in the doorway, a double-barrelled shotgun in his hand. Slowly the gun was raised and a shot rang out. Edith turned and saw Frank Fowler, a man she knew well, aiming the gun at her. Until that moment, there had been a candle burning in the room but the blast of the gun had extinguished it. Light still drifted in from outside, though, and Edith could see clearly enough to throw herself at Fowler and grapple with him.

Once more the gun went off but this time the shot passed through a window. The noise attracted some customers from the bar and they managed to overpower Fowler.

It was only then that Gertrude shouted: "Bring a light. Ivy is shot!"

In fact, Ivy Prentice was already dead, a large wound above her left breast. Her killer, as he was pinned to the floor, shouted: "I have had my bloody revenge."

Fowler had known Ivy since she was a child and there was no suggestion that there had been any kind of intimacy between them. Yet he was extremely jealous of her relationship with her husband, Robert.

Back in March, Fowler had walked up to Prentice in the bar of the White Horse and hissed at him. Later that same evening, Fowler returned, removed his hat and made the cryptic comment: "How is that for a bloody haircut?" Prentice looked puzzled but all Fowler would add was: "I will have my own back on you one day, you bugger."

There were other mysteries too. When arrested, Fowler shouted: "Teasdale knows

NAME	Frank Fowler
AGE AT EXECUTION	35
DATE OF EXECUTION	Wednesday, 13th December, 1922
PLACE OF EXECUTION	Lincoln
HANGMAN	Thomas Pierrepoint
ASSISTANT	Robert Baxter
DATE OF TRIAL	31st October, 1922
LOCATION OF TRIAL	Lincoln
PRESIDING JUDGE	Mister Justice Lush
PROSECUTION COUNSEL	Richard O'Sullivan, Mister Sanderson
DEFENCE COUNSEL	Mister Lyon
NUMBER OF VICTIMS	1

VICTIMS DETAILS	
NAME	Ivy Dora Prentice
AGE	18
DATE OF MURDER	Saturday, 23rd September, 1922
PLACE OF MURDER	The White Horse Hotel, Market Deeping
METHOD OF KILLING	Shot
RELATIONSHIP TO KILLER	None

something about this." Arthur Teasdale was an ex-customer of the White Horse but when he was interviewed, he said he knew nothing and could not explain what Fowler meant.

No-one could explain what real or imagined slight had caused Frank Fowler to seek revenge on Robert Prentice by killing his wife, but neither lack of motive nor strange behaviour was held to reduce the crime to one of manslaughter.

These tragic events did nothing to alter the wedding plans of Ivy Prentice's mother. Just two days after the murder, Edith married the new man in her life.

ROSILLA BARTON HAD been married once, but her husband died in 1916. She was still an attractive woman and it was only two years before she was married again, this time to William Rider. This second ceremony took place in February, 1918 and the couple went to live at 2 Elborrow Street, Rugby.

Unfortunately, soon Rider began to beat his new wife. In all, Rosilla left him four times over the next few years, each time returning home to her mother, Rachael Freeman, who lived in Harbury. Each time Rider persuaded her to return, promising that he would change.

This continued until early 1921, when Rachael Freeman discovered that her son-in-law already had a wife and had therefore married her daughter bigamously. Without hesitation, Rachael sent another of her daughters, 15-year-old Winifred Harriet Freeman, to tell Rosilla.

Rider managed to persuade Rosilla that he had been misunderstood. Whatever had existed between him and his wife was long dead, he insisted. The upshot was that not only did Rosilla stay with him, but Winifred also moved into the house.

The inevitable happened and by August, Winifred was pregnant. Rachael wasted no time in going to Rugby and bringing Winifred home with her. Before she left she told Rosilla what had happened, but again Rider made promises and the couple stayed together.

On August 25th, Rider and Rosilla went to Harbury, where they stayed with her married sister. The very next day, Rider and Winifred disappeared, presumably having run away together.

Nothing was heard from the couple until September 6th when Winifred reappeared. That same evening, Rachael heard that Rider had been seen in the area and, as a precaution, made sure that all the doors and windows were securely locked.

Next morning, Rachael's son went to work and after seeing to his breakfast, Rachael returned to the bed she shared with Rosilla and another daughter, 13-year-old Minnie. At 7.50am, Rachael was awoken by a cry from Rosilla: "Oh Bill, don't!" Opening her eyes, Rachael saw Rider standing at the

NAME	William Rider
AGE AT EXECUTION	40
DATE OF EXECUTION	Tuesday, 19th December, 1922
PLACE OF EXECUTION	Birmingham
HANGMAN	John Ellis
ASSISTANT	William Willis
DATE OF TRIAL	17th November, 1922
LOCATION OF TRIAL	Warwick
PRESIDING JUDGE	Mister Justice Lush
PROSECUTION COUNSEL	Richard O'Sullivan, Mister Bartholemew
DEFENCE COUNSEL	Harold Eaden
NUMBER OF VICTIMS	1

VICTIMS DETAILS	
NAME	Rosilla Patience Barton
AGE	24
DATE OF MURDER	Thursday, 7th September, 1922
PLACE OF MURDER	Harbury, Warwickshire
METHOD OF KILLING	Shot
RELATIONSHIP TO KILLER	Bigamous wife

foot of the bed, carrying a sixteen-bore shotgun, which he pointed at Rosilla and fired. She died immediately from a massive wound in the head.

At his trial, Rider claimed it was an accidental shooting, but the evidence was against him. In addition to his threats and the ill-treatment of Rosilla, Rider could offer no explanation as to why he had entered the bedroom, in his bare feet, carrying a gun.

1923

JOHN OAKES WAS the tenant of a house in Higher Cambridge Street, which he shared with two couples – Winifred Drinkwater and her husband, Peter, and George Edisbury and the woman he called his wife, Annie Grimshaw.

Annie was a married woman but had been separated from her husband for some time. She had been living with George since 1916, and both George and Annie were rather fond of drink. Winifred Drinkwater did not approve of the life George and Annie led and often taunted them about it, claiming occasionally that Annie was a prostitute and that George was living off her earnings.

Things were no different on the afternoon of July 29th, 1922. After imbibing freely of drink, George and Annie returned home and were preparing a meal for themselves in the kitchen. Once again Winifred passed derogatory comments about Annie's way of life. At that time though, George did not rise to the bait.

That evening both couples went out. Winifred and her husband went to do their shopping but George and Annie were out drinking again. By the time Winifred returned alone, George and Annie were already home and both were very much the worse for drink by now.

After going out to look for her husband, Winifred once more made her way back to the house in Higher Cambridge Street. By now it was 10.10pm and after spending a few minutes talking to John Oakes at the front door, George Edisbury appeared and angrily reproached Winifred for her earlier comments. He denied that Annie was a prostitute and ended by saying: "You have wanted me out of here some time, but I will see you cut first." He then produced a razor and slashed Winifred's throat. At that moment, Winifred's husband, Peter, returned home and Winifred breathed her last whilst he held her in his arms.

George meanwhile had run off into the night, finally arriving at his brother's house in Moss Side. From there George travelled to his sister's house at Rusholme where he confessed to killing Winifred. He was so drunk that his sister didn't believe him and

NAME	George Frederick Edisbury
AGE AT EXECUTION	44
DATE OF EXECUTION	Wednesday, 3rd January, 1923
PLACE OF EXECUTION	Manchester
HANGMAN	John Ellis
ASSISTANT	Not known
DATE OF TRIAL	27th November, 1922
LOCATION OF TRIAL	Manchester
PRESIDING JUDGE	Mister Justice Acton
PROSECUTION COUNSEL	Mister Crosthwaite
DEFENCE COUNSEL	Milner Helme
NUMBER OF VICTIMS	1

VICTIMS DETAILS	
NAME	Winifred Drinkwater
AGE	50
DATE OF MURDER	Saturday, 29th July, 1922
PLACE OF MURDER	64 Higher Cambridge Street, Chorlton-on-Medlock
METHOD OF KILLING	Cut throat
RELATIONSHIP TO KILLER	None

allowed him to spend the night at her home. It was there that George was arrested the following morning.

At his trial, George claimed that he had no memory of the events of July 29th as he had been drinking all day. He claimed that he and Annie had been on good terms with Winifred and also said that he had no recollection of telling his sister that he had cut a woman's throat. His counsel claimed that there was no premeditation and that the crime should be one of manslaughter, due to the provocation he had endured and the effects of the alcohol he had consumed. The jury rejected that defence and George Edisbury was found guilty of murder.

LILY SIDDALL HAD been working in a laundry since February 1922 and she felt that she knew her employer, Sing Lee, quite well. She knew how he would behave in certain circumstances and so when she was told a story that seemed to be completely out of character, her suspicions were roused.

On Sunday, September 10th, when Lily went to open up the shop as usual, she was surprised to find that Sing Lee did not come in at his usual time. The previous evening, when Lily had left the laundry, only Sing and one of his employees, Lee Doon were left on the premises. Lily sought out Doon and asked him if he knew anything about Sing's disappearance. Doon smiled and informed her that Sing had gone back to China. To Lily, this was highly unlikely, but for that day at least, said nothing more about the matter.

Lily was a resourceful lady and rather than just take her suspicions to the police, she decided to do some checking up of her own. She knew that Sing had relatives and friends in Liverpool, so Lily went to see them and ask if they knew anything about Sing going back to China. Not only was it news to them, but almost without exception, they said it was highly unlikely.

Returning to the shop, Lily had her worst suspicions confirmed when she found Doon digging a large hole in the cellar. Waiting no longer, Lily went to the police.

When police arrived at the laundry, the hole Lily had mentioned, had vanished. In its place was a large pile of coal and coke. The fuel was moved and the police started to dig. There, some two feet below ground level, they found a trunk and when the trunk was opened the bloody and battered body of Sing Lee was discovered. Lee Doon was arrested and charged.

Doon admitted killing Sing, but said it had been an accident. He had found Sing taking morphine and pointed out to him how stupid and dangerous the practice was. An argument followed and when this developed into a fight, Doon hit Sing in self-defence. To his horror he found that he had killed him and in a panic, decided to hide the body and tell people that Sing had gone back to China.

The postmortem findings did not agree

NAME	Lee Doon (Leong Lun)
AGE AT EXECUTION	27
DATE OF EXECUTION	Friday, 5th January, 1923
PLACE OF EXECUTION	Leeds
HANGMAN	Thomas Pierrepoint
ASSISTANT	Thomas Phillips
DATE OF TRIAL	2nd December, 1922
LOCATION OF TRIAL	Leeds
PRESIDING JUDGE	Mister Justice Greer
PROSECUTION COUNSEL	Mister Waugh
DEFENCE COUNSEL	W.P. Donald
NUMBER OF VICTIMS	1

VICTIMS DETAILS	
NAME	Sing Lee
AGE	34
DATE OF MURDER	Saturday, 9th September, 1922
PLACE OF MURDER	231 Crookes, Sheffield
METHOD OF KILLING	Battered/strangled
RELATIONSHIP TO KILLER	None

with Doon's story. Sing had been hit many times and had also been strangled. The prosecution painted what was to the jury a more believable picture: Doon had killed Sing with the intention of stealing from him.

Found guilty, Doon was executed at Armley jail on January 5th, 1923. His case had received little publicity, being overshadowed by the much more newsworthy Thompson and Bywaters affair.

1923

IN JULY 1920, the Thompsons, Percy and Edith, moved into 41 Kensington Gardens, Ilford. They did not have a happy marriage. He was a rather dull and serious man and she was the kind of young, vivacious woman who loved the idea of being in love. The catalyst to their lives was to arrive in June 1921.

Frederick Bywaters was a friend of Edith's younger brothers and sisters. He worked as a ship's steward and had just returned from a four-month voyage to Australia when he was invited to join Avis Graydon, Edith's sister, and the Thompsons, on holiday on the Isle of Wight. The attraction between him and Edith was instant and at some stage during that first week, probably on June 14th, 1921, they kissed for the first time.

Frederick Bywaters was a personable young man and it was not just Edith Thompson who warmed to his charm. Percy liked him so much that he invited Frederick to lodge with them, in Ilford, after the holiday was over. Slowly, irrevocably, Edith and Frederick grew closer together and it is likely that at some stage over the next month, they became lovers.

On Monday August 1st, Edith and Percy had an argument which ended in physical violence. Bywaters intervened and stopped Percy hitting his wife. Later, Percy and Edith discussed a separation and when Bywaters asked Percy if he would grant his wife a divorce, he refused and told Bywaters to leave his house.

Bywaters went back to sea a number of times and whilst he was away, Edith wrote him regular letters. Long and often rambling they show a woman who was deeply in love and very unhappy with her lot. She discussed suicide and enclosed clippings relating to murder trials current at the time. She intimated that she had tried to kill her husband but it seems highly probable that these were just the outpourings of a sad and frustrated soul.

Frederick Bywaters returned from what was to be his last sea voyage on Saturday September 23rd, 1922. Over the next week or so he met Edith a number of times. They had lunches together, went for walks and met in cafes for tea.

NAMES	Edith Jessie Thompson; Frederick Edward Bywaters
AGES AT EXECUTION	30; 21
DATE OF EXECUTION	Tuesday, 9th January, 1923
PLACES OF EXECUTION	Holloway; Pentonville
HANGMEN	John Ellis; William Willis
ASSISTANTS	Robert Baxter, Seth Mills, Thomas Phillips
DATE OF TRIAL	6th December – 11th December, 1923
LOCATION OF TRIAL	Old Bailey
PRESIDING JUDGE	Mister Justice Shearman
PROSECUTION COUNSEL	Sir Thomas Inskip, Travers Humphreys, Roland Oliver
DEFENCE COUNSEL	Sir Henry Curtis Bennett, Cecil Whiteley, Walter Frampton, Huntley Jenkins, Ivan Snell, Myles Elliott
NUMBER OF VICTIMS	1

VICTIMS DETAILS

NAME	Percy Thompson
AGE	34
DATE OF MURDER	Wednesday, 4th October, 1922
PLACE OF MURDER	Junction of Belgrave Road and Kensington Gardens, Ilford, London
METHOD OF KILLING	Stabbed
RELATIONSHIP TO KILLERS	Husband; none

On October 3rd, 1922, they had lunch together yet again, in Cheapside, parted company and then met again later in the day. They finally separated at about 5.30pm. Bywaters had been aware for some time that this same evening, Edith and her husband were going to the Criterion theatre. That evening, Freddy visited Edith's sister, Avis, where he stayed until 11.00pm.

At midnight, Percy and Edith arrived at Ilford station after their evening out, and began walking together up Belgrave Road. At the intersection with Kensington Gardens, a man wearing an overcoat came up behind them, pushed Edith out of the way, and began to argue with Percy. There was a struggle, a knife was brandished and Percy Thompson fell to the pavement. He had been stabbed a number of times, most of the wounds being very superficial, but one in the neck had severed his carotid artery. Edith shouted for help and asked a gentleman who came to her aid to fetch a doctor. It was no use, Percy died within minutes.

The assailant ran off down Seymour Gardens, where he disposed of the murder weapon down a drain. Edith had recognised the overcoat the assailant was wearing and knew that Frederick Bywaters was the man who had killed her husband. The police soon determined that Edith and Frederick had been having a relationship and that therefore he had a motive for killing Percy. As a result, Frederick Bywaters was arrested on October 4th. Edith Thompson was arrested the same night.

To begin with both made statements saying they knew nothing of the murder but the following morning, at the police station, when Edith caught a glimpse of Bywaters, all her strength went and she said "Oh God! Why did he do it? I didn't want him to do it. I must tell the truth." She went on to confirm that she had recognised Bywaters as the man who attacked her husband and both were then charged with murder. A week later, her letters to Bywaters were found on board his ship.

At the subsequent trial, it was held that Frederick Bywaters had murdered Percy Thompson, at the instigation of Edith, thus making her equally guilty of murder. Bywaters denied throughout that she had incited him but passages from the letters read out in court damned her in the eyes of the jury. Guilty verdicts were returned against both defendants. Even then Bywaters denied that Edith had had anything to do with the death of her husband.

The lovers were both hanged on the morning of January 9th, 1923. It has been said that Edith had to be half-carried, half-dragged to the execution chamber and that after she had been launched into eternity it was found that she had haemorrhaged badly, possibly indicating that she might have been pregnant. Some sources have denied this, but it is true that at every subsequent execution of a woman, the condemned was made to change into a pair of canvas briefs on the morning the sentence was carried out.

Whilst Frederick Bywaters was undoubtedly guilty of murder, there is no evidence that Edith Thompson knew of his intention, or condoned what he did. It might well be argued that Edith Thompson was hanged for adultery as much as she was for murder.

1923

LILY JOHNSTON LIVED with her mother, Mary, in a cottage in Cookstown. In another cottage nearby lived her aunt, Martha Johnston.

Each working day Lily would set off from home at around 7.30am, to walk the short distance to Gunning's Mill. On that journey to work she would have to pass a spot known locally as Kidds Bridge.

On November 2nd, 1922, Lily left for work at 7.35am. At a few minutes to 8.00am, her aunt, Martha, left to walk into Cookstown. As Martha passed over Kidds Bridge she looked into a field to see a man assaulting a woman.

The bareheaded man, whom she did not recognise, pushed the woman onto the ground and then began kicking her. Martha heard the poor woman call out "God save me". Martha hurried on until she came upon two workmen.

One of these workmen, Patrick Devlin, dashed to Kidds Bridge and saw the end of the attack. The man in the field was still kicking the woman and, seeing Devlin, made for the road. As he left, the assailant passed within a few feet of Devlin, who saw that it was a man he had known for 10 years – William Rooney.

That identification was confirmed by Samuel Nelson who cycled past at the same time. Neither Devlin nor Nelson made any attempt to minister to the woman who had been on the receiving end of the brutal attack.

Eventually, the body of the woman was found and identified as Lily Johnston. Rooney was not found until some time between 7.00pm and 8.00pm on November 3rd, when he called at the house of Philip Cavanagh and complained of being hungry. Cavanagh offered him food and a cup of tea but then detained Rooney until the police arrived. Rooney denied any involvement in the crime.

The night before the murder, Rooney had been in custody. Arrested for being drunk by Constable John Harron, Rooney had managed to escape at around 6.00am. His cap had been left behind at the police station, meaning that he would have been bareheaded at the time of the attack.

At the trial, much was made of the fact that Martha Johnston had not recognised Rooney as the man in the field, even though she had

NAME	William Rooney
AGE AT EXECUTION	40
DATE OF EXECUTION	Thursday, 8th February, 1923
PLACE OF EXECUTION	Londonderry
HANGMAN	William Willis
ASSISTANT	Two assistants, not named
DATE OF TRIAL	5th January – 8th January, 1923
LOCATION OF TRIAL	Belfast
PRESIDING JUDGE	Lord Justice Moore
PROSECUTION COUNSEL	James Williamson, T.H. Maxwell
DEFENCE COUNSEL	George B. Hanna
NUMBER OF VICTIMS	1

VICTIMS DETAILS	
NAME	Lily Johnston
AGE	21
DATE OF MURDER	Thursday, 2nd November, 1922
PLACE OF MURDER	Lewis's Field, Kidds Bridge, Cookstown, County Tyrone
METHOD OF KILLING	Battered
RELATIONSHIP TO KILLER	None

known him for many years. Countering this was the testimony of Devlin and Nelson and that of another witness, Ruby Hunter, who had seen Rooney near a stream at 1.30pm, apparently wiping his boots with a damp cloth. Allied to this was the fact that human blood was found on Rooney's drawers, vest, shirt and coat. The jury took 25 minutes to determine that the prisoner was guilty.

Asked if he had anything to say Rooney exclaimed "All I have to say is that I am innocent of the charge. It is perjury that has been sworn against me."

EMMA PERRY WAS the wife of Edwin, whose brother George had lodged with them at 3 Spencer Street, Burslem, since July 1922.

On Boxing Day, Edwin and Emma visited the Staff of Life public house at lunch time and had a drink with Hamlet Richardson and his wife. They returned home with the Richardsons, to find George, who was very drunk indeed, already there. They all shared some beer and the Richardsons left at 1.30pm.

By 3.00pm, Edwin had decided that he needed to take a nap so went upstairs to his bed, leaving George and Emma in the kitchen. Edwin slept for an hour and a half, rising at 4.30pm. Going back downstairs, Edwin noticed his wife was still sitting in the chair in the kitchen and he assumed that she too had fallen asleep. It was then that he noticed blood down the front of her dress and saw that Emma's throat had been cut.

George was nowhere to be seen, so Edwin called next door where he told Mary Ellen Shaw to go into the house. Mary found Emma and called in her husband who brought some cotton wool and tried to stop the bleeding.

George Morris was a boatman for the Mersey Weaver Company and at 5.00pm was on board the boat Ribble. Suddenly he heard a splash and upon investigating, found a man, George Perry, floating in the water. George fished Perry out by means of a boat hook and then took him to his brother's house at 93 Reid Street. When they arrived, Perry remarked that he could swim and so should have tied a brick around his neck. In due course he confessed to killing Emma Perry and the police were called.

When interviewed by Constable John Hallam, Perry said: "Jack, I have cut her throat. She has been on at me all week. I did not know what I had done until it was done." He was then arrested and charged.

Perry's defence was that he did not know what he was doing because he was so drunk. There was also a suggestion that he was predisposed towards insanity and often behaved strangely. Nevertheless, Perry was found guilty and hanged at Manchester.

NAME	George Perry
AGE AT EXECUTION	50
DATE OF EXECUTION	Wednesday, 28th March, 1923
PLACE OF EXECUTION	Manchester
HANGMAN	John Ellis
ASSISTANT	Not known
DATE OF TRIAL	22nd February, 1923
LOCATION OF TRIAL	Stafford
PRESIDING JUDGE	Mister Justice Shearman
PROSECUTION COUNSEL	Geoffrey Lawrence
DEFENCE COUNSEL	Kenneth Wood
NUMBER OF VICTIMS	1

VICTIMS DETAILS	
NAME	Emma Perry
AGE	48
DATE OF MURDER	Tuesday, 26th December, 1922
PLACE OF MURDER	3 Spencer Street, Burslem
METHOD OF KILLING	Cut throat
RELATIONSHIP TO KILLER	Sister-in-law

1923

1923

WHEN DANIEL CASSIDY and his wife separated, she returned to her native Dublin.

However, over the festive period at the end of 1922, Mrs Cassidy returned to Sunderland to attend a New Year's party to be held on the first day of 1923. She arrived back in Sunderland on December 14th.

The party was at the house of one of Mrs Cassidy's married daughters, Agnes Hodgson, and the entire family were invited, with one exception. Although Daniel lived at number 38, opposite the scene of the party, with yet another daughter, Mrs Quinn, he was not invited and as he saw the party progress, he began to seethe with resentment.

As the celebrations were in full swing, at around 6.00pm, the door burst open and in walked Daniel, carrying a gun. He managed to fire five shots before he was overpowered by one of the guests, James Coggin. Cassidy's wife and the daughter he had been living with, were both seriously wounded, but Bernard Quinn, Daniel's son-in-law, who had been happily playing the melodeon at the time, was hit fatally, one bullet penetrating his heart.

Daniel Cassidy claimed that he had gone across the street with the intention of upsetting the party but had not wished to shoot anyone, let alone kill them. He blamed his wife for turning his family against him and simply wanted to get his own back by spoiling her fun. Once he had seen that people had been hurt, it had been his intention to turn the gun upon himself but he was wrestled to the ground before he could achieve this.

Cassidy's defence tried to suggest that he was insane at the time of the shooting and therefore should escape the death penalty. It was stated in court that in 1914, Cassidy had spent some time in a mental home. The prosecution, however, showed that this was only for a period of ten days and that Cassidy had only been under observation. At no stage had it ever been suggested that he was not as sane as the next man. In addition, he had issued threats on December 31st when he had gone across to Agnes's house to borrow 6d. Agnes said she didn't have it but would get it from her mother, to which Cassidy replied: "It doesn't matter. Tell that – she is looking for

NAME	Daniel Cassidy
AGE AT EXECUTION	60
DATE OF EXECUTION	Tuesday, 3rd April, 1923
PLACE OF EXECUTION	Durham
HANGMAN	Thomas Pierrepoint
ASSISTANT	Not known
DATE OF TRIAL	23rd February, 1923
LOCATION OF TRIAL	Durham
PRESIDING JUDGE	Mister Justice Roche
PROSECUTION COUNSEL	Walter Hedley, Doctor R.F. Burnand
DEFENCE COUNSEL	Doctor J. Charlesworth
NUMBER OF VICTIMS	1

VICTIMS DETAILS	
NAME	Bernard Quinn
AGE	30
DATE OF MURDER	Monday, 1st January, 1923
PLACE OF MURDER	1 Woodbine Street, Hendon, Sunderland
METHOD OF KILLING	Shot
RELATIONSHIP TO KILLER	Son-in-law

trouble." As a result of all this the jury had no hesitation in returning a verdict of guilty.

AT 11.10PM on Monday, February 6th, 1923, taxi-driver Herbert Richard Golding picked up a young couple in Leicester Square. On instructions he then drove them to Watford and upon arrival was immediately told to drive instead to Templewood Avenue, Hampstead, where apparently the young lady worked. They arrived there at about 1.30am.

All the houses were in darkness and the young man instructed Golding to take them back to Leicester Square. As they neared Swiss Cottage he heard a slight scream but thought nothing more of it.

The cab pulled into Leicester Square but now the man asked Golding if he would drive to the nearest police station. No doubt cursing quietly to himself, Golding did as he was asked and turned off towards Vine Street.

Upon arrival at the police station, the young man leapt out and rushed in to talk to the officer on duty. Golding noticed that his hands were heavily bloodstained and that the young lady had not moved.

Inside the police station, the man identified himself as Bernard Pomroy, confessed that he had just murdered his girlfriend, and that her body and the knife he had used were on the back seat of the cab waiting outside.

At the trial, Pomroy refused all entreaties from the judge and said he did not wish to be legally represented. The story of Pomroy and the dead girl, Alice May Cheshire, was nevertheless revealed.

The two had known each other for three years and had recently become engaged. Alice May had a sister, an attractive girl named Mabel, and one day she dropped a bombshell on her father, Esau Cheshire, by telling him that she was pregnant. The second bombshell came when she told him that the father was Bernard Pomroy, her sister's fiancé.

Esau Cheshire had a long talk with Pomroy, who finally said that he would go to see Alice on the Monday night. Esau tried to persuade him to stay with them, as Alice was due to come home anyway on the Tuesday, but Pomroy was determined to see her earlier. He contacted Alice and invited her to the theatre.

On the Monday night, the last night of Alice's life, Pomroy called for her at

NAME	Bernard Pomroy
AGE AT EXECUTION	25
DATE OF EXECUTION	Thursday, 5th April, 1923
PLACE OF EXECUTION	Pentonville
HANGMAN	John Ellis
ASSISTANT	Edward Taylor
DATE OF TRIAL	1st March, 1923
LOCATION OF TRIAL	Old Bailey
PRESIDING JUDGE	Mister Justice Horridge
PROSECUTION COUNSEL	Percival Clarke, Eustace Fulton
DEFENCE COUNSEL	None
NUMBER OF VICTIMS	1

VICTIMS DETAILS	
NAME	Alice May Cheshire
AGE	21
DATE OF MURDER	Tuesday, 6th February, 1923
PLACE OF MURDER	In a taxi cab, near Swiss Cottage, London
METHOD OF KILLING	Cut throat
RELATIONSHIP TO KILLER	Girlfriend

Templewood Avenue. One of Alice's workmates, Gladys Payne, a fellow servant, testified that as the two were leaving, Pomroy had shouted to her: "Why not say goodbye properly, in case she does not come back again?" Gladys thought it was merely a bad joke.

His refusal to defend himself or offer any explanation meant that the trial was a mere formality. Bernard Pomroy was hanged at Pentonville just 58 days after he had murdered Alice.

WHEN JOHN WHITE returned home at 7.00pm on December 18th, 1922, he was horrified to find his sister, Margaret, lying dead in the drawing room. The room had been ransacked and a small amount of cash stolen.

Margaret White had last been seen alive at 9.15am when the postman had called. At 4.30pm, a girl selling eggs had received no reply when she came to the door, so Miss White was probably dead by then. There were no signs of a forced entry, so Margaret must have admitted her killer.

The police found a card giving the name Fred Wood and advertising his services as an upholsterer. Finally, a newly upholstered chair was found, together with scraps of felt from the repair. The card gave an address but when it was checked it was discovered that Wood had moved on, without leaving a forwarding address, on the day of the murder. A detailed description was published and on December 23rd, Wood walked in to the police station at Lincoln.

Wood said that he had travelled around since Miss White's death and the first he had known of it was when he read a newspaper article. She had been alive and well when he left and he had only come in to clear his name.

A few days before December 18th, Wood had called on Miss White and repaired an ottoman. When he returned, on the 18th, she asked him if he would show her how to fix a chair. He spent an hour with her, for which she paid him, and he then caught the 11.30am bus to Stockport from where he boarded a train for Leeds.

Passengers were traced. Many testified that Wood was on the Stockport bus, but on the 12.30pm, not the 11.30am. Moreover, before the 18th, Wood had been borrowing money but suddenly he could now afford the 6/- fare to Leeds. He was arrested and charged.

At the inquest, a curious incident occurred. Wood had handed in a sealed statement which he said was not to be opened until after the inquest. It was decided to ignore his instructions. To shouts and banging from Wood, the statement was read out. It gave Wood's version of events.

After showing Miss White how to fix the

NAME	Frederick Wood (Ronald Lee) (George Wood)
AGE AT EXECUTION	29
DATE OF EXECUTION	Tuesday, 10th April, 1923
PLACE OF EXECUTION	Liverpool
HANGMAN	John Ellis
ASSISTANT	Thomas Phillips
DATE OF TRIAL	28th February – 2nd March, 1923
LOCATION OF TRIAL	Chester
PRESIDING JUDGE	Mister Justice Swift
PROSECUTION COUNSEL	Sir Ellis J. Griffiths, Austin Jones
DEFENCE COUNSEL	Goodman Roberts
NUMBER OF VICTIMS	1

VICTIMS DETAILS	
NAME	Margaret Gilchrist White
AGE	50
DATE OF MURDER	Monday, 18th December, 1922
PLACE OF MURDER	'Invermay', 96 Acre Lane, Cheadle Hulme
METHOD OF KILLING	Strangled
RELATIONSHIP TO KILLER	None

chair, she had gone upstairs for the money. Wood heard a crash and a groan and upon going to see what the matter was, found Miss White in a fit, with her hands clasped tightly around her own throat.

Wood tried to pull her hands away but did not have the strength due to an injury that rendered one arm very weak. He panicked, stole money in order to make his escape, and fled. In short, Margaret White had strangled herself!

The jury felt this impossible to contemplate and returned a guilty verdict.

IN 1915, RICHARD Tillett began living with a married woman, Wilhelmina Grierson and in 1918, they adopted a one-year-old child. However, the house in Bridge Street, where Wilhelmina and Richard lived, was squalid and known to be a place where methylated spirit drinkers congregated.

On March 12th, Richard, an engineman, went to work at 9.50pm. Ten minutes later, a middle-aged man knocked at the front door of the Bridge Street house. The door was opened by Michael Reilly, an 18-year-old who often ran errands for Mrs Grierson. Michael let in the visitor but Wilhelmina asked him to leave. Not only did he refuse but he asked Michael to run and fetch him some matches. When Michael returned he stayed for another hour and when he left, the visitor was still there.

At 1.00am, the next morning, Wilhelmina called on her next-door neighbour, Mrs McLeod and told her that a man in her house would not leave. Mrs McLeod went back to number 25 with Wilhelmina and recognised the visitor as a man she had asked to leave on previous occasions, John Henry Savage. This time he refused to budge. It was clear that Mrs McLeod would need to use more persuasion but she wasn't properly dressed and went home first to put some more clothes on. As she left number 25, Mrs McLeod heard the door slam shut.

By now it was 1.30am and almost as soon as Mrs McLeod arrived back at her own home she heard a terrible scream from number 25. Returning with her 17-year-old daughter, Mrs McLeod tried to get inside Wilhelmina's house but failed. Suddenly the door was thrown open and Savage stepped outside. Bravely Mrs McLeod grabbed him and demanded to know what he had done. All Savage did was flourish a razor before he ran off. Inside the house, Wilhelmina was discovered with her throat cut.

A description of the wanted man was circulated and at 6.15am, he was seen coming out of Cables Wynd into Great Junction Street. Arrested, it was noticed that his hands were heavily bloodstained and that he smelt strongly of methylated spirits.

Savage's defence relied on a plea of insanity. In court, Richard Tillett said that

NAME	John Henry Savage
AGE AT EXECUTION	50
DATE OF EXECUTION	Monday, 11th June, 1923
PLACE OF EXECUTION	Edinburgh, Calton
HANGMAN	John Ellis
ASSISTANT	William Willis
DATE OF TRIAL	21st May, 1923
LOCATION OF TRIAL	Edinburgh
PRESIDING JUDGE	Lord Justice Alness
PROSECUTION COUNSEL	William Watson, Mister Fenton, J.M. Hunter
DEFENCE COUNSEL	Mister Wilson, M.L. Walker
NUMBER OF VICTIMS	1

VICTIMS DETAILS	
NAME	Wilhelmina Nicolson (Grierson)
AGE	42
DATE OF MURDER	Wednesday, 14th March, 1923
PLACE OF MURDER	25 Bridge Street, Leith
METHOD OF KILLING	Cut throat
RELATIONSHIP TO KILLER	None

Savage had been to the house several times and had once asked if he could live there. He seemed disappointed when permission was refused.

Mrs McLeod spoke of the trouble she had had with Savage on the morning of March 14th and on previous occasions. Finally, a warden at the lodging house where Savage had slept said that he knew him as someone who continually drank meths and it was wise to avoid him when he was drunk.

It was clear that Savage had severe drink problems and that this had been largely responsible for the crime but nevertheless, it did not save him from the gallows.

ROWLAND DUCK HAD served in the army in the Great War, where he had been blown up by a shell. Ever since that time he had suffered from epilepsy, nervousness and emotional stress, but none of this served to save him from the gallows.

Rowland lived with his wife and three children in Cambria Street, Fulham and in order to eke out the family finances, they took in a lodger, Nellie Pearce. Nellie earned her living as a prostitute and one of her clients turned out to be none other than her landlord, Rowland Duck. Unfortunately for Rowland, Nellie gave him venereal disease and this knowledge made the highly nervous Rowland even more uncontrollable.

On May 2nd, Rowland came home drunk and told his wife that Nellie would have to leave the house. The next morning he went into Nellie's bedroom and whilst she was still asleep, drew a knife across her throat. He then wrapped the body in a blanket and shoved it under the bed. His work finished, Duck then walked to the nearest police station and told the officer exactly what he had done.

At the trial, there was no attempt to deny that Rowland Duck was the killer of Nellie Pearce. But was he responsible for his actions? His mother, Charlotte, gave evidence that ever since he had been injured in the war, even a very small amount of drink would send him 'funny' and often she would have to hold him until he calmed down. Medical evidence from Doctor Eric Coplans showed that Duck was very nervous and showed clear signs of suffering from epilepsy.

Other medical evidence was given that whilst suffering a seizure, Duck could well commit acts and then later not be aware that he had done them and Duck's own testimony seemed to bear this out. He claimed that as he was wrapping the body in the blanket, he noticed that Nellie's throat was cut and wondered if he had done it. After half an hour's deliberation, the jury still found him guilty.

An appeal was lodged and once again an attempt was made to show that Duck could have killed without knowing what he was doing and so was at worst guilty only of manslaughter. The appeal was rejected because Duck had confessed at the police station. There he had made a full statement outlining exactly what he had done and why. At the trial though, he claimed to have no recollection of the crime whatsoever. In the eyes of the judges, this was not consistent. The sentence was upheld.

NAME	Rowland Duck
AGE AT EXECUTION	25
DATE OF EXECUTION	Wednesday, 4th July, 1923
PLACE OF EXECUTION	Pentonville
HANGMAN	John Ellis
ASSISTANT	Robert Wilson
DATE OF TRIAL	31st May, 1923
LOCATION OF TRIAL	Old Bailey
PRESIDING JUDGE	Mister Justice Swift
PROSECUTION COUNSEL	Sir Richard D. Muir, Roland Oliver
DEFENCE COUNSEL	J.C. Lockwood
NUMBER OF VICTIMS	1

VICTIMS DETAILS	
NAME	Nellie Pearce
AGE	18
DATE OF MURDER	Thursday, 3rd May, 1923
PLACE OF MURDER	Cambria Street, Fulham, London
METHOD OF KILLING	Cut throat
RELATIONSHIP TO KILLER	None

A T 11.00AM ON May 25th, 1923, William Griffiths was drinking in the Eagle Inn, where he was seen by his friend and workmate, Henry Wood. Griffiths stayed until around 2.00pm at which point he had consumed so much that the landlord, James Underhill, refused to serve him with any more drink.

From the Eagle, Griffiths and Henry Wood walked to the auction yards where they worked, arriving there just before 3.00pm. Griffiths was by now very drunk and rather irritable, threatening at one stage to throw a hammer at Wood. By 6.00pm, once the pubs had opened again, Griffiths was back at the Eagle where he stayed for an hour. At 10.00pm, closing time, Griffiths was back at the Eagle, expecting to be served.

Emma Hibbs lived next door to Catherine Hughes and she retired for the night at 10.00pm. Not long afterwards, she heard Griffiths return home and an argument between him and his mother over the amount he spent on drink. After a few minutes of this, Emma heard several loud screams, followed by a groaning, and finally a knock on her front door.

When Emma opened her door she was greeted by William Griffiths, who said he had killed his mother. Emma sent one of her children for the doctor and told William to take himself off to the police station.

It was 11.05pm when William Griffiths approached Constable Frank Thomas Roberts, who was on duty near the Royal Oak. Again he confessed to having killed his mother and Roberts noticed that Griffiths was bleeding from a slight wound on his left temple.

At the station, Griffiths explained that he had argued with his mother and she had struck him with an enamel jug. When the murder scene was examined, the jug was found and there were no signs of blood upon it. However, a candlestick was found, and this was bloodstained. In his drunken condition it may well be that Griffiths had mistaken the weapon his mother had used.

Catherine Hughes had tried to defend herself from her son's murderous attack. In an attempt to ward off the blows from the razor,

NAME	William Griffiths
AGE AT EXECUTION	57
DATE OF EXECUTION	Tuesday, 24th July, 1923
PLACE OF EXECUTION	Shrewsbury
HANGMAN	John Ellis
ASSISTANT	Seth Mills
DATE OF TRIAL	4th July, 1923
LOCATION OF TRIAL	Stafford
PRESIDING JUDGE	Mister Justice Roche
PROSECUTION COUNSEL	F. Langley
DEFENCE COUNSEL	Mister Wood
NUMBER OF VICTIMS	1

VICTIMS DETAILS	
NAME	Catherine Hughes
AGE	80
DATE OF MURDER	Friday, 25th May, 1923
PLACE OF MURDER	Stafford Street, Eccleshall
METHOD OF KILLING	Cut throat
RELATIONSHIP TO KILLER	Mother

she must have held up her right arm because it was discovered that part of her right thumb had been hacked off.

Griffiths's defence was that he had been too drunk to form the intention to kill, but evidence was called to show that there had been many arguments between him and his mother and he had threatened her before.

His half-sister, Mary Annie Foster and her husband, George, who both lived with William and his mother, testified that there had been constant problems. Eventually the jury were convinced that Griffiths knew exactly what he was doing when he attacked his mother, and a guilty verdict was returned.

BY THE BEGINNING of 1920, Albert Burrows's life was one hell of a mess. A married man, he had met Hannah Calladine in 1918 and they had become lovers. Hannah already had a daughter, Elsie, but soon she found herself pregnant with Albert's child and a son, also named Albert, was born later that year.

Burrows now married Hannah, only to be promptly imprisoned for bigamy. When he came out of jail, Hannah moved in with him, since his real wife had left him and was claiming maintenance. His rent was soon in arrears and he had a bastardy order against him as well. He had to find a way to make things simpler all round.

On January 11th, 1920, Burrows took Hannah and his son onto the moors above Glossop, where he murdered them both, throwing their bodies down a disused mine shaft. Left at home with the five-year-old girl, he made a second trip the day after and Elsie's body was thrown down the same shaft to join her mother and brother.

With those encumbrances out of the way, Burrows contacted his real wife, told her that he had thrown Hannah and the children out and would henceforth be faithful to her. She took him back and for the next three years, Burrows lived with her and pretended that Hannah was still alive by writing frequent letters to her mother.

Had Albert Burrows committed no further offences, he might well have gotten away with three murders, but in 1923, that was all to

NAME	Albert Edward Burrows
AGE AT EXECUTION	62
DATE OF EXECUTION	Wednesday, 8th August, 1923
PLACE OF EXECUTION	Nottingham
HANGMAN	John Ellis
ASSISTANT	William Willis
DATE OF TRIAL	3rd July – 4th July, 1923
LOCATION OF TRIAL	Derby
PRESIDING JUDGE	Mister Justice Shearman
PROSECUTION COUNSEL	Sir Henry Maddocks M.P., Norman Birkett, Mister Loseby
DEFENCE COUNSEL	T. Norman Winning, Miss Geikie Cobb
NUMBER OF VICTIMS	4

VICTIMS DETAILS	
NAMES	Hannah Calladine; Albert Edward Calladine (Burrows)
AGE	28; 1
DATE OF MURDER	Sunday, January 11th, 1920
PLACE OF MURDER	Symmondley Moor, Glossop
METHOD OF KILLING	Probably battered
RELATIONSHIP TO KILLER	Bigamous wife; son
NAMES	Elsie Calladine (Large); Thomas Johnson Wood
AGES	5; 4
DATE OF MURDER	Monday, January 12th, 1920; Sunday, March 4th, 1923
PLACE OF MURDER	Symmondley Moor, Glossop
METHOD OF KILLING	Probably battered; strangled
RELATIONSHIP TO KILLER	None; none

change. On March 4th, 1923, a four-year-old boy, Thomas Wood, was reported as missing from home. Burrows had been seen with the boy and so naturally he was questioned by the police. Far from satisfied with his original explanations, the police continued with their investigation and eventually, Burrows took them to the mine shaft, where he had also disposed of Thomas. The boy was found, dead and sexually abused. Burrows was arrested and charged with the murder of Thomas Wood.

It was eight weeks more before police found the skeletons of Hannah Calladine and

The disused pit-shaft where Albert Edward Burrows disposed of four bodies.

her children and Burrows was now facing four charges of murder. There was little he could do to escape the noose. At his trial he did not go into the witness box and no defence witnesses were called.

The jury took a mere 13 minutes to return their verdict.

1923

JANE NAGI, WHOSE maiden name had been Brown, was the English widow of an Arab. In 1923, she had become engaged to a second Arab, Hassen Mohamed, and they were due to marry on Wednesday, March 14th. It was a date Jane never kept, as her fiancé shot her dead two days before the ceremony.

Jane worked at a restaurant at 107 East Holborn, South Shields, and on March 12th, she arrived for work at 3.00pm. Unfortunately, Jane was rather the worse for drink and so she was told to go home. She said she was looking for Hassen and, at about 4.00pm, he too turned up.

Almost immediately a quarrel broke out between the couple, during which Jane told Hassen that it was all over between them. At one stage, Jane swore at Hassen, clawed at his face and grabbed his throat. The row was so heated that the police were contacted and one Constable Walsh attended, cautioning both antagonists as to their future behaviour.

Hassen went into the kitchen whilst Jane stood in the doorway. Believing no doubt that it had simply been the drink talking, Hassen asked Jane if she would go out with him again. She refused, at which point Hassen stood and walked out of the restaurant.

Within three or four minutes, Hassen had returned. By now Jane was sitting on a sofa inside the kitchen and Hassen stood in the doorway, enjoying a cigarette. After spending a short time just looking at Jane, Hassen took out a revolver and shot her in her breast.

That, at least, was the story that other witnesses told. Hassen's tale was rather different. He claimed that he had first met Jane at some time between 3.00pm and 3.30pm and that they had arranged to meet up later at her parents' home. Some time after that, he heard that she was with another man at the restaurant and going over there, he found her sitting on Sam Ali's knee.

An argument followed and Hassen became involved in a fight with Ali. At one stage, Ali drew out a gun and threatened to shoot Hassen. They closed and the fight continued, during which the gun went off, the bullet striking Jane. The other people in the kitchen then overpowered him and between them

NAME	Hassen Mohamed
AGE AT EXECUTION	33
DATE OF EXECUTION	Wednesday, 8th August, 1923
PLACE OF EXECUTION	Durham
HANGMAN	Thomas Pierrepoint
ASSISTANT	Not known
DATE OF TRIAL	3rd July, 1923
LOCATION OF TRIAL	Durham
PRESIDING JUDGE	Lord Chief Justice, Lord Hewart
PROSECUTION COUNSEL	L.R. Lipsett
DEFENCE COUNSEL	A.P. Peaker
NUMBER OF VICTIMS	1

VICTIMS DETAILS	
NAME	Jane Nagi (Brown)
AGE	25
DATE OF MURDER	Monday, 12th March, 1923
PLACE OF MURDER	107 East Holborn, South Shields
METHOD OF KILLING	Shot
RELATIONSHIP TO KILLER	Girlfriend

they concocted a story, blaming him for the death of Jane.

In the end, the jury chose to believe the other witnesses and held that it had been Hassen's hand that held the gun and fired the fatal shot.

HELEN ELLIOTT GLANCED out of her window and saw the lorry stop. The driver went around the back as a young woman and a little girl climbed down. The driver pulled down a go-cart and a bundle, which he helped put onto the cart. Then Helen saw what looked like a human foot protrude from the bundle.

Helen told her sister what she had seen and together they left the house and began to follow the woman. She was seen pushing the bundle into the yard of 650 Duke Street. Helen saw two men and asked them for help.

Robert Foote went to the back of number 650 in time to see the woman scaling a wall into the next yard, whilst James Campbell saw the woman drop down into the yard of number 652. The men stopped her until the police arrived. Both heard her say that the bundle, wrapped in a red quilt, was a boy who her husband had killed. The bundle was opened and found to contain the body of 13-year-old John Johnston.

The woman was Susan Newell and the girl was Janet McLeod, her eight-year-old daughter from a previous marriage. They lived with Susan's second husband, John, at 2 Newlands Street, Coatbridge. After some investigation, both John and Susan were charged.

Mrs Young, the Newell's landlady, said she had heard Johnston going up to Susan's rooms at 7.00pm on June 20th. Mrs Young then heard Susan shout "Shut the door." Immediately there were three loud thumps.

The lorry driver, Thomas Dickson, said he had seen Susan pushing a cart, with the little girl sitting on top of the bundle. He offered them a lift and finally dropped them in Duke Street.

Janet McLeod said she had been playing when the newsboy called. When she went indoors she saw his body on the couch. Later her mother trussed him up into a bundle, which was placed on the cart. Janet had sat on top as they trudged towards Glasgow.

The postmortem was carried out by Professor Glaister, who gave four contributing causes of death. Johnston had been throttled, his windpipe compressed, he had been battered about the head and there were signs of burning, probably caused when he

NAME	Susan Newell
AGE AT EXECUTION	30
DATE OF EXECUTION	Wednesday, 10th October, 1923
PLACE OF EXECUTION	Glasgow, Duke Street
HANGMAN	John Ellis
ASSISTANT	William Willis
DATE OF TRIAL	18th September, 1923
LOCATION OF TRIAL	Glasgow
PRESIDING JUDGE	Lord Justice Alness
PROSECUTION COUNSEL	Lord Kinross, T.B. Simpson
DEFENCE COUNSEL	T.A. Gentles, M.G. Fisher
NUMBER OF VICTIMS	1

VICTIMS DETAILS	
NAME	John Johnston
AGE	13
DATE OF MURDER	Wednesday, 20th June, 1923
PLACE OF MURDER	2 Newlands Street, Coatbridge
METHOD OF KILLING	Battered/strangled
RELATIONSHIP TO KILLER	None

came into contact with the hearth fire whilst still alive.

John Newell was able to prove that he was not in Coatbridge at the time of the murder. He had been to his brother's funeral and had stayed over in Glasgow. The judge directed the jury to return a verdict of not guilty in his case.

Susan Newell was not as fortunate and after an absence of 37 minutes, the jury found her guilty. On October 10th she became the first woman executed in Glasgow since Helen Blackwood in 1853.

WILLIAM CREE LIVED at 47 Inglis Street, Dunfermline but often travelled into Edinburgh to catch a football match. One such occasion was on June 23rd.

At 9.15pm that same night, William Mitchell a waiter in a public house in Rose Street, saw Catherine Donoghue enter the bar with a man. They had a few drinks and left together at 10.00pm after the man had bought a gill of whisky and a bottle of Bass to take out. Later, Mitchell would identify the man as Cree.

Cree and Donoghue went to 40 Jamaica Street where she lived with Philip Murray. They were seen entering by Jessie McPhail who lived opposite. Then, at around 10.20pm, the sounds of a terrible fight came from number 40.

William McDonald, who lived in a different flat, heard wood breaking, followed by a man's voice crying "Oh don't!" There was the sound of breaking glass and a loud thud. Going outside, McDonald found Cree lying on the pavement covered with blood.

Catherine Laing lived above Murray and Donoghue. She heard the fight and went to her window in time to see a man coming through Murray's window. At first his hands, head and shoulders came through but them someone appeared to push him out. The frame gave way and he fell to the pavement. This was seen by another neighbour, Charles Cowan, who ran for the police.

Andrew Lamb was in a passageway below the house and when he heard breaking glass, went to see what was going on. He saw hands pushing Cree out of the window and he swore that those hands were Donoghue's.

Constable John McTaggart was in Howe Street when he heard about the incident. When he arrived he found Constable Thomson there and together they forced the door to Murray's flat and arrested Murray and Donoghue for assault. When, at 11.40pm, Cree died from his injuries, both were charged with murder. In the event, only Murray was to face a jury, Catherine Donoghue turning King's Evidence.

Murray said that he had not killed Cree. On the day in question he had gone out at 4.40pm, returned at 10.00pm, and fallen asleep on the

NAME	Philip Murray
AGE AT EXECUTION	31
DATE OF EXECUTION	Tuesday, 30th October, 1923
PLACE OF EXECUTION	Edinburgh, Calton
HANGMAN	John Ellis
ASSISTANT	Not known
DATE OF TRIAL	8th October – 9th October, 1923
LOCATION OF TRIAL	Edinburgh
PRESIDING JUDGE	Lord Justice Constable
PROSECUTION COUNSEL	Mister Fenton, Lord Kinross
DEFENCE COUNSEL	J. Anderson MacLaren, T.A.
NUMBER OF VICTIMS	1

VICTIMS DETAILS	
NAME	William Ronald Cree
AGE	30
DATE OF MURDER	Saturday, 23rd June, 1923
PLACE OF MURDER	40 Jamaica Street, Edinburgh
METHOD OF KILLING	Battered
RELATIONSHIP TO KILLER	None

bed. He was woken by voices and saw a man sitting by the fire. Murray asked him what he wanted and Cree replied that Donoghue had brought him. Murray asked him to leave and a fight broke out. At one stage Murray heard breaking glass and turning around, saw that the window was broken and Cree had vanished. The suggestion was that either Donoghue had pushed him out, or Cree had jumped in order to escape.

It took the jury 27 minutes to decide, by a majority verdict, that Murray was guilty of murder and he became the last man to be hanged at Calton prison.

FOR SOME DAYS, Mabel Edmunds had not been seen about the lodging house she ran and her guests were becoming concerned. They had asked Frederick Jesse, Mabel's nephew and a fellow lodger, if he knew what had happened to her, but his explanation that she had gone to Sheerness, did not seem convincing.

On July 23rd, a policeman found an envelope floating upon the river Thames and upon checking, it was discovered that this contained Mabel Edmunds's marriage certificate and a letter. Jesse was spoken to and again repeated the story about his aunt going to Sheerness.

Five days later, a handwritten note was pushed through the letterbox of Mabel's house. This curious note claimed to be from Mabel's estranged husband and intimated that she had been done away with and that her killer had drowned himself in the river. The note was taken to the police, who decided that it was time to search Mabel's house.

So it was that on July 30th, the police entered 156 York Road where, in an upstairs room, they found Mabel Edmunds. The body lay on the bed but the legs had been cut from it and lay on a table nearby. Jesse was questioned and eventually admitted responsibility.

Jesse's story was that he and his aunt had argued constantly over the fact that he owed her money. On July 21st, she nagged him about the fact that she had asked him to sell her piano for her and he had done nothing about it. He had gone to his room but she had followed him there and struck him, following this by throwing some caustic liquid into his eyes. They had struggled together and fallen onto the bed.

Eventually, Jesse's eyes cleared and to his horror he realised that his hands were around Mabel's throat and he had killed her. Frightened of what people would think, he decided to cut the body up but soon lost his nerve after removing the legs. He then came up with the idea of blaming her husband, so concocted the evidence by throwing papers into the Thames as if the man had drowned himself.

The jury took 35 minutes to dismiss this

NAME	Frederick William Maximilian Jesse
AGE AT EXECUTION	26
DATE OF EXECUTION	Thursday, 1st November, 1923
PLACE OF EXECUTION	Wandsworth
HANGMAN	John Ellis
ASSISTANT	Robert Baxter
DATE OF TRIAL	17th September – 18th September, 1923
LOCATION OF TRIAL	Old Bailey
PRESIDING JUDGE	Mister Justice Swift
PROSECUTION COUNSEL	Sir Richard D. Muir, G.D. Roberts
DEFENCE COUNSEL	G.L. Hardy, G.T. Abbott
NUMBER OF VICTIMS	1

VICTIMS DETAILS	
NAME	Mabel Jennings Edmunds
AGE	50
DATE OF MURDER	Saturday, 21st July, 1923
PLACE OF MURDER	156 York Road, Lambeth, London
METHOD OF KILLING	Strangled
RELATIONSHIP TO KILLER	Aunt

convoluted story and find Jesse guilty of murder.

JOHN EASTWOOD WAS the landlord of the Bay Horse Hotel at Sheffield and one of his barmen was John Joseph Clarke. Eastwood felt that Clarke was rather too friendly towards Mrs Eastwood and this caused so much friction between the couple that on June 30th, Eastwood left his wife and travelled to Blackpool with a married woman, Mildred Parramore.

Eastwood returned after almost a fortnight and immediately renewed the quarrel with his wife. As a result, he left once again and took lodgings with Arthur John Hilton, in Grove Street.

Things settled down for a short time but early on the morning of July 29th, Eastwood walked into Arthur Hilton's bedroom, carrying an axe and told Arthur and his wife that he was going to see Clarke and "knock him up". He then threw his door key onto a table, saying he wouldn't need it anymore, and left the house.

Some time later, Eastwood arrived at John Clarke's house in Lister Street and woke him and his wife, Eva, by throwing pebbles at his bedroom window. Seeing who it was, Clarke went downstairs and let Eastwood in. There followed the sounds of a struggle and when Eva Clarke went downstairs to investigate, she found her husband with a large wound in his head. Eastwood was on the point of leaving and later walked up to a policeman on duty, Constable Peach, explaining what he had done and adding: "I believe it is murder – in fact I am sure it is." In fact he was somewhat premature on that point. Clarke did not die from his wounds until the following day.

Found guilty of murder after the jury had deliberated for 30 minutes, Eastwood was asked if he had anything to say. He turned to face the judge and said: "I don't know sir, but whatever happened, I never meant it."

Eastwood's case set a number of firsts. It was Mister Justice Talbot's first death sentence and John Ellis's first execution as number one at Leeds prison. It was also a day short of 20 years since he had attended his first Leeds execution, that of Gallagher and Swann. It was also the occasion of two 'lasts', both Ellis and Seth Mills taking part in their last execution.

NAME	John William Eastwood
AGE AT EXECUTION	39
DATE OF EXECUTION	Friday, 28th December, 1923
PLACE OF EXECUTION	Leeds
HANGMAN	John Ellis
ASSISTANT	Seth Mills
DATE OF TRIAL	8th December, 1923
LOCATION OF TRIAL	Leeds
PRESIDING JUDGE	Mister Justice Talbot
PROSECUTION COUNSEL	W.J. Waugh, Walter Hedley
DEFENCE COUNSEL	F.J.O. Collington
NUMBER OF VICTIMS	1

VICTIMS DETAILS	
NAME	John Joseph Clarke (Died Monday, 30th July)
AGE	49
DATE OF MURDER	Sunday, 29th July, 1923
PLACE OF MURDER	Lister Road, Sheffield
METHOD OF KILLING	Battered
RELATIONSHIP TO KILLER	None

MATTHEW NUNN AND Minetta Kelly had been going out together since June 1923. They seemed to be very fond of each other and when, in September, she told him that she was pregnant by him, Nunn went to see her mother and formally asked permission to marry her.

Permission was given but there was a snag; Minetta wanted none of it. She told Nunn flatly that she did not want to marry him and whatever anger he felt at this rejection was made all the worse when he discovered that Joseph Hughes, another boyfriend of Minetta's, had found out about her condition, and had also asked her to marry him.

On September 11th, Minetta and Nunn went out together but at 2.00am the following morning, Nunn was alone when he stumbled up to the front door of a miner's house, with a badly gashed throat. Nunn could not speak, but scribbled a note saying that Minetta had done this to him, had now probably killed herself and would be found at Bushfields.

Minetta was indeed dead and in her lap, police found a razor. The latter belonged to Nunn's father. Nunn however, had an explanation for this, stating that Minetta had told him her father's own razor was being repaired and had asked if he could possibly borrow one. On the last night they spent together, Minetta had taken the razor from him, cut him and pushed him away and then expressed a desire to end her own life.

It was a plausible story, but Nunn had made two mistakes that were to cost him his own life. In the first place, whilst his own injuries might have been self-inflicted, Minetta's head was almost severed from her body and such wounds could not have been caused by her own hand. Secondly, probably believing that he would soon be dead, Nunn had left a note on the miner's table. Addressed to his mother it read: "This is the end. Think kindly of me. Tell Mrs Kelly I am sorry. This is the only way out. I can stand it no longer." Such a note obviously implied that it had been Nunn who had decided on this course of action, not Minetta Kelly.

Nevertheless, it still took the jury 50 minutes to reach their verdict. Nunn was guilty but with a recommendation to mercy. It

NAME	Matthew Frederick Atkinson Nunn
AGE AT EXECUTION	24
DATE OF EXECUTION	Wednesday, 2nd January, 1924
PLACE OF EXECUTION	Durham
HANGMAN	Thomas Pierrepoint
ASSISTANT	Not known
DATE OF TRIAL	14th November, 1923
LOCATION OF TRIAL	Durham
PRESIDING JUDGE	Mister Justice McCardie
PROSECUTION COUNSEL	G.F.L. Mortimer, R. Lipsett
DEFENCE COUNSEL	Mister Wilson
NUMBER OF VICTIMS	1

VICTIMS DETAILS	
NAME	Minetta Mary Kelly
AGE	20
DATE OF MURDER	Tuesday, 11th September, 1923
PLACE OF MURDER	Bushfields, Tantobie, Tanfield, County Durham
METHOD OF KILLING	Cut throat
RELATIONSHIP TO KILLER	Girlfriend

has been suggested that at the execution, the rope broke and Nunn fell into the pit, half-strangled. He had to wait almost half an hour before the apparatus was ready for him again.

ON JANUARY 4TH, 1924 police officers arrested a man in the Alexandra Park area of Manchester. This man, subsequently identified as Francis Wilson Booker, had been taken in for questioning on the subject of an assault committed on two small boys aged nine and 11. It was during that questioning that police deduced that there might be a link between Booker and another crime they were investigating.

Exactly four months earlier, on September 4th, 1923, Percy Sharpe had left home to visit the Labour Exchange in Queen Street, Manchester. He had never returned home. At just before 2.30pm that same afternoon, a railway worker named Etherington had heard screams coming from a wood close to the line on which he was working. Going to investigate, he had found Percy, almost naked, his shirt stained crimson with blood. The boy had been stabbed and was to die the following morning in hospital, but not before he had told his story.

Shortly after visiting the Labour Exchange, Percy had met a man in Oxford Road, and been offered a job. They had caught the bus together to Northenden and there, whilst taking a short cut through some woods, he had been attacked.

The boy had not been sexually molested, but police felt that was only because the attacker had been disturbed. There were no other clues and after some months the investigation stalled completely. Now the police had a man in custody who had attacked two other boys. Could there be a link?

When Booker's home was searched, a link was discovered. A box was found that contained Percy Sharpe's diary and Labour Exchange card. After digging over the allotment, police also found a pair of bloodstained braces and Sharpe's underwear. Booker was charged with murder.

At his trial, Booker claimed that he had found the items of clothing and other items in a parcel, on the road near Northenden on September 5th, the day after the murder. This story was countered by police evidence, which showed that officers had combed the entire area carefully for three full days and had found nothing at all.

NAME	Francis Wilson Booker
AGE AT EXECUTION	28
DATE OF EXECUTION	Tuesday, 8th April 1924
PLACE OF EXECUTION	Manchester
HANGMAN	William Willis
ASSISTANT	Robert Baxter
DATE OF TRIAL	26th February, 1924
LOCATION OF TRIAL	Manchester
PRESIDING JUDGE	Mister Justice Greer
PROSECUTION COUNSEL	B.S. Wingate-Saul
DEFENCE COUNSEL	Kenneth Burke
NUMBER OF VICTIMS	1

VICTIMS DETAILS	
NAME	Percy Sharpe (Died Wednesday, 5th September)
AGE	14
DATE OF MURDER	Tuesday, 4th September 1923
PLACE OF MURDER	Carr's Wood, Northenden, Cheshire
METHOD OF KILLING	Stabbed
RELATIONSHIP TO KILLER	None

Perhaps the strongest piece of circumstantial evidence against Booker, though, was his notebook. This listed a number of punishments that he would administer to children if they broke certain rules such as trespassing or riding a bicycle on the pathway.

Though he was found guilty of murder and sentenced to death, Booker had not been picked out of a line-up by Etherington or any other witness who had claimed to be in the woods at the time of the murder and he was in fact the fifth person arrested in connection with the murder of Percy Sharpe. Had he disposed of the clothing, he might have been the fifth to be released without charge.

AT 3.00PM ON Friday, March 7th, Nelson Leech called at the Ulster Bank in Queen Street, Belfast, to cash a cheque so that the wages at Purdy and Millard could be made up for the next day.

By 3.20pm, Leech, his assistant Alexander Briggs, Elizabeth Allen and a Mrs Fisher were in the office, sorting out the wage packets, when three masked men burst in. Immediately Leech made for the telephone box and a shot was fired over his head. This did nothing to discourage Leech, who continued into the box and grabbed the receiver. A second shot rang out and Leech fell to the floor, a bullet in his abdomen. The raiders fled empty-handed, followed by members of staff, who gave the alarm. Constable Francis Morteshead heard those cries and began to give chase.

Two of the men were faster than the officer and managed to make good their escape. The third man, who it transpired had an artificial leg, ran along Hammill Street, Galway Street, Durham Street and into Barrack Street, where he was cornered by Morteshead and told to surrender. The man aimed his gun at the constable and pulled the trigger. Fortunately for Morteshead the gun jammed and he was able to disarm the man, who turned out to be Michael Pratley.

That same evening, at 10.00pm, Nelson Leech died in the Royal Victoria Hospital, making the charge one of murder. Pratley, meanwhile, had admitted taking part in the hold-up but he denied being the man who had fired the fatal shot. He steadfastly refused to name the two men who had been with him.

Put on trial for murder, the prosecution admitted that Pratley was not necessarily the man who had actually killed Leech but held that if his death had occurred even accidentally during a robbery, then all those taking part were equally guilty of murder. That argument convinced the jury, who took less than an hour to return their guilty verdict.

This was not the first time that Pratley had been accused of murder. On May 22nd, 1922, three or four men had shot Councillor W.J. Twaddell in Garfield Street, Belfast. Two of those men had been arrested – Pratley and James Woods – but the Crown decided there

NAME	Michael Pratley
AGE AT EXECUTION	30
DATE OF EXECUTION	Thursday, 8th May, 1924
PLACE OF EXECUTION	Belfast
HANGMAN	William Willis
ASSISTANT	Robert Wilson
DATE OF TRIAL	10th April, 1924
LOCATION OF TRIAL	Belfast
PRESIDING JUDGE	Mister Justice Brown
PROSECUTION COUNSEL	Richard Best M.P.
DEFENCE COUNSEL	John H. Campbell
NUMBER OF VICTIMS	1

VICTIMS DETAILS

NAME	Nelson Leech
AGE	30
DATE OF MURDER	Friday, 7th March, 1924
PLACE OF MURDER	Purdy and Millard's, College Square North, Hamill Street, Belfast
METHOD OF KILLING	Shot
RELATIONSHIP TO KILLER	None

was not enough evidence against them and the case was not proceeded with.

A T THE END of 1923, Elizabeth Reaney had agreed to sell her house for £390. She had agreed to give vacant possession on February 23rd, 1924 and was to move to a new home in Buxton, Derbyshire. What she did not know was that the address she gave the removal men when she arranged her affairs, was a false one. Someone had duped Elizabeth in order to get his hands on her money. From the middle of February, Elizabeth began drawing cash from her account so that by February 20th, she must have held up to £530.

At about 10.10pm on February 22nd, the day before she was due to move house, Elizabeth was seen standing on her front doorstep. She was looking up and down the street as if waiting for someone. She was never seen alive again.

The following morning, the furniture van turned up, but instead of the expected trip to Buxton, the workmen found the body of Elizabeth Reaney. She had been battered to death.

A search of the house in Sunderland Road, revealed a quantity of banknotes, but not the amount Elizabeth had been known to draw from her account. There were also four letters, purporting to come from a Mr Goodson at an address in Leeds. The name and address were both false, but further investigations led to the name of William Wardell.

Wardell was an habitué of the Peel Hotel and it transpired that he had left there at 10.15pm on the night of the murder. He had left in the company of Leonard Heseltine but he said that he had parted company with Wardell at the end of Longside Lane. There was a fish and chip shop down there that Wardell was in the habit of visiting, but Elizabeth's house also lay in the same direction.

On February 27th, Wardell again visited the Peel Hotel and was told that the police were looking for him. Heseltine advised Wardell to go to the police station and clear his name. Reluctantly Wardell agreed but muttered prophetically that they would probably keep him there all night.

Wardell was interviewed at length and later

NAME	William Horsely Wardell
AGE AT EXECUTION	47
DATE OF EXECUTION	Wednesday, 18th June, 1924
PLACE OF EXECUTION	Leeds
HANGMAN	Thomas Pierrepoint
ASSISTANT	WILLIAM WILLIS
DATE OF TRIAL	8th May – 10th May, 1924
LOCATION OF TRIAL	Leeds
PRESIDING JUDGE	Mister Justice Avory
PROSECUTION COUNSEL	C.F. Lowenthal, C. Paley Scott, Frank Beverley
DEFENCE COUNSEL	C.J. Frankland
NUMBER OF VICTIMS	1

VICTIMS DETAILS	
NAME	Elizabeth Reaney
AGE	60
DATE OF MURDER	Friday, 22nd February, 1924
PLACE OF MURDER	23 Sunderland Road, Manningham, Bradford
METHOD OF KILLING	Battered
RELATIONSHIP TO KILLER	None

searched. The police found 13 banknotes that belonged to the same batch as those found at the murder scene. Later, comparisons of his handwriting showed that he had written the four letters found at Sunderland Road. The final piece of evidence was a notebook found on Wardell. On one page he had written Elizabeth Reaney's address and next to it was 'Goodson... Leeds.'

The evidence against Wardell was largely circumstantial. No bloodstains were ever found on any of his clothes and he did have an alternative explanation for the money found on his person. Unfortunately, the people he said he had obtained it from did not back up his story and this was enough for the jury.

CHARLES NORMAN BROOKER ran the branch of the Midland bank at Bordon Camp and travelled to it by bus with William Edward Hall, his opposite number at Lloyds.

On April 3rd, 1924, Brooker was surprised to see that Hall had not turned up for the bus. Hall went over to Lloyds but there was no reply to his knocking.

Nearby was a small post office. Brooker went across to see if the postmaster, Harry Payne, knew anything. Payne was just as puzzled and together they went back to the bank. A rear window was open and when Payne looked in, he saw Hall lying on the floor.

William Hall was dead. He had been shot in the head and throat and bank officials were able to say that the crime had taken place after closing time, which was 2.00pm, and that over £1,000, mainly in notes, had been stolen. Two soldiers from a nearby army camp then came forward with information. One, a signaller, had visited the bank and had been given a form to fill in. William Hall had told him to return with it later but when the signaller got back at 2.10pm, there was no reply. The killer may have been in the bank at that time.

The other soldier was Lance Corporal Goldenberg. He had gone to the bank to cash a cheque and had seen two men outside in a car. He was able to give the police excellent descriptions, and bragged that his evidence would lead to the conviction of the murderer.

A few days later, Goldenberg was seen by Sergeant Major Thomas Alliott. He was nervous and Alliott noticed that his pocket seemed to be stuffed with a packet. Alliott watched Goldenberg go into some latrines but when he left, the parcel was gone. Alliott investigated.

On one of the sills, Alliott found two clear footmarks. Alliott placed his feet in the prints and from his vantage point could clearly see in the roof beams a small package. It contained £500 in treasury notes.

Goldenberg was arrested the following day and more notes were found in his possession. In all, almost £1,000 was recovered. It was now that Goldenberg told the first of his two stories. He admitted that he had gone into the

NAME	Abraham (Jack) Goldenberg
AGE AT EXECUTION	22
DATE OF EXECUTION	Wednesday, 30th July, 1924
PLACE OF EXECUTION	Winchester
HANGMAN	Thomas Pierrepoint
ASSISTANT	William Willis
DATE OF TRIAL	19th June, 1924
LOCATION OF TRIAL	Winchester
PRESIDING JUDGE	Mister Justice Bailhache
PROSECUTION COUNSEL	Holman Gregory
DEFENCE COUNSEL	Mister Hancock
NUMBER OF VICTIMS	1

VICTIMS DETAILS	
NAME	William Edward Hall
AGE	28
DATE OF MURDER	Thursday, 3rd April, 1924
PLACE OF MURDER	Lloyds Bank, Bordon Camp, Bordon, Hampshire
METHOD OF KILLING	Shot
RELATIONSHIP TO KILLER	None

bank to cash a cheque at about 12.30pm and had returned just before 2.00pm. Once the doors had been closed, Goldenberg had drawn his gun and shot Hall, taking his keys and stealing the money.

The second story was that Goldenberg had had an accomplice, Meredith, who had been the one to go into the bank. Shots had been heard and when Meredith ran out, Goldenberg had gone to see what had happened. Finding William Hall dying from his wounds, Goldenberg had stolen money before escaping.

On one thing, Goldenberg had been correct. It was his evidence that helped to send the murderer to his punishment.

IN AUGUST 1923, Alfred Jones paid £1,350 for the Blue Anchor Hotel, in Byfleet, and installed himself as host. With him when he moved in was his wife, Mabel Theresa who had her own business venture, which failed soon afterwards, reducing her to bankruptcy. In order to escape her problems for a while, Mabel Jones decided to have a holiday in France. Alfred had a pub to run and chose to stay at home, so in January 1924, Mabel set out alone for the continent.

On January 9th, Mabel Jones arrived at Biarritz where she booked into the Victoria Hotel. It was here she met Jean Pierre Vacquier and an instant friendship developed between them. Although she spoke no French and he spoke no English, they purchased a dictionary and managed to converse by looking up words and phrases.

Mabel left the Victoria on January 15th but she was back on the 24th. It was about this time that she and Vacquier became lovers, for when she next moved on, Vacquier travelled with her as her husband.

In due course, Mabel returned to England, but Vacquier even followed her here and they met at the Hotel Russell in London on February 12th. The following day, Alfred Jones travelled to Margate, where he fell ill, necessitating an extended stay there. By the time he returned to the Blue Anchor on February 17th, Vacquier had been living there for three days.

The relationship between Mabel Jones and Vacquier became the talk of the hotel. Wherever she went he would follow like a lap dog. Moreover, he paid nothing for his upkeep and when Alfred Jones pointed this out to him, Vacquier stalled for time by saying that he was expecting a great deal of money for an invention he had just sold.

On March 1st, 1924, Vacquier kept up the pretence of being an inventor and dabbler in scientific matters when he visited a chemist in Southampton Row, London. There he asked for a number of chemicals, including two poisons, for experiments in wireless. After some deliberation, the assistant, Horace Bland, sold him what he had asked for, including enough strychnine to kill four people. Vacquier signed the poisons register

NAME	Jean Pierre Vacquier
AGE AT EXECUTION	45
DATE OF EXECUTION	Tuesday, 12th August, 1924
PLACE OF EXECUTION	Wandsworth
HANGMAN	Thomas Pierrepoint
ASSISTANT	William Willis, Thomas Phillips
DATE OF TRIAL	2nd July – 5th July 1924
LOCATION OF TRIAL	Guildford
PRESIDING JUDGE	Mister Justice Avory
PROSECUTION COUNSEL	Sir Patrick Hastings M.P., Edward Marshall-Hall, H.D. Roome, George Ansley
DEFENCE COUNSEL	Henry Curtis Bennett, A.B. Lucy
NUMBER OF VICTIMS	1

VICTIMS DETAILS	
NAME	Alfred George Poynter Jones
AGE	38
DATE OF MURDER	Saturday, 29th March, 1924
PLACE OF MURDER	Blue Anchor Hotel, Byfleet, Surrey
METHOD OF KILLING	Poisoned (by strychnine)
RELATIONSHIP TO KILLER	None

in the rather unfortunate name of 'Wanker' and returned to Byfleet. Bland would later identify Vacquier and Wanker as being one and the same.

One of the problems of being a pub landlord is that it is tempting occasionally to consume too much of one's own wares. Alfred Jones was a friendly host and would sometimes have a little too much too drink. When this happened, it was his custom to take a dose of bromo salts, which were kept in a jar behind the bar.

On Friday, March 28th, Alfred Jones supped deep from his own stock and the following morning, after breakfast, decided that a dose of salts was called for. As he drank down the solution of crystals, he suddenly exclaimed that they tasted very bitter indeed. His wife Mabel took a small taste and agreed that they were extremely bitter. Shortly afterwards, Alfred began to suffer from convulsions and at 12.15pm, he died in agony.

Before Alfred died, Mabel, no doubt suspicious of the salts, took the jar, which was then still half full of crystals, and hid it in a drawer in the kitchen. She was later to testify that she thought a doctor might want to test the salts to see if anything had been added or substituted. Unknown to her, Vacquier had followed her and must have seen where she hid them for when Mabel returned to the drawer after the death of her husband, the jar was missing. It was found back behind the bar, but now there were no crystals left. All that remained was a small residue of water from the rinsing out that had taken place. Nonetheless, the doctor would note that even this small quantity of water tasted exceedingly bitter. Further, Elizabeth Fisher, one of the staff in the hotel, would say that she saw Vacquier take the bottle from the drawer.

It was April 2nd before Mabel Jones formally accused Vacquier of poisoning her husband. After some argument, again with the aid of the dictionary and scribbled notes, Vacquier admitted to her that he had killed Alfred, so that they could be together. When, however, it became plain to Vacquier that an extra-marital affair was one thing to Mabel and murder was quite another, he packed his few belongings and left the Blue Anchor.

It was to be April 19th before Vacquier was traced and arrested. Sitting in the lounge of the Railway Hotel in Woking, he was taken into custody whilst listening to some French songs being played on the piano. Six days later, Alfred Jones's body was exhumed and tests showed that strychnine poisoning was indeed the cause of death. Vacquier was charged with murder.

Faced with the evidence against him, Vacquier tried to put the blame on anyone and everyone else. He suggested that he had seen Mabel Jones throwing away the contents of the salts jar. When that seemed to have no effect, he claimed the postman had killed Alfred because he was jealous of Vacquier and had tried to frame him. His final shot was that he had purchased the poisons and given a false name at the instigation of Mrs Jones's solicitor!

Not surprisingly perhaps, Vacquier was found guilty and sentenced to death.

AT 2.15PM ON Tuesday, June 10th, 1924, five-year-old Norman Pinchin was playing outside his home at 9 Crescent View, Salford. A friend, eight-year-old Eric Wilson, was with him and when they asked Norman's father, Harold Pinchin, if they could go to Peel Park, he readily gave his permission.

The two boys had not been in the park long when a man approached them and asked them to go with him. As a bribe, he offered Eric 4d to get two ice-cream wafers, but by the time Eric returned, Norman and the man had disappeared.

Eric's first thought was the ice-creams and, concerned that one might be wasted, he now proceeded to eat both of them. Soon, it came on to rain and Eric skipped off home. Meanwhile, Norman and the man were leaving the park and were seen by 14-year-old Norman Thomas.

Harry Barnes worked in a wood yard close by Windsor Bridge on the canal at Salford. It was now 3.45pm and Barnes was enjoying a break. He sat on a wall, looking out over the water as a young boy, hand in hand with a man, walked down the pathway and underneath the bridge. Ten minutes later, the pair reappeared but now the child, who was not wearing trousers, was held in the man's arms. Then, to Harry Barnes's horror, the man threw the child into the canal.

Barnes threw himself off the wall, dashed around to the canal path, passing the man on the way, and began searching for the little boy. Finding no signs, he then chased after the man and followed him through the Manchester streets.

As the man turned into The Crescent, Barnes saw two policemen on patrol. He ran across to them and told Constable Walter Smith and his colleague, James Lorinson, what he had seen. They apprehended the man, who identified himself as John Charles Horner, and took him back to the canal.

Again there was no sign of Norman Pinchin. The body was only found later when the canal was dragged. The boy's clothing matched that described by Barnes, and it was enough to incriminate Horner, who was put into an identification parade. Here he was picked out by both Eric Wilson and Norman Thomas.

NAME	John Charles Horner
AGE AT EXECUTION	23
DATE OF EXECUTION	Wednesday, 13th August, 1924
PLACE OF EXECUTION	Manchester
HANGMAN	William Willis
ASSISTANT	Not known
DATE OF TRIAL	17th July, 1924
LOCATION OF TRIAL	Manchester
PRESIDING JUDGE	Mister Justice Talbot
PROSECUTION COUNSEL	William Madden, Hugh Beazley
DEFENCE COUNSEL	Mister McKeever
NUMBER OF VICTIMS	1

VICTIMS DETAILS	
NAME	Norman Widdowson Pinchin
AGE	5
DATE OF MURDER	Tuesday, 10th June, 1924
PLACE OF MURDER	Near Windsor Bridge, on canal near Peel Park, Salford
METHOD OF KILLING	Shock
RELATIONSHIP TO KILLER	None

A medical examination showed that Norman Pinchin had not suffered death by drowning. He was already dead when he was thrown into the canal. Tests showed that he had been brutally raped and that this had caused him to die from shock.

Horner's defence was one of mistaken identity. He claimed that Barnes had got the wrong man and tried to discredit the evidence of the two child witnesses. The jury chose not to believe him.

HERBERT MAHON MARRIED on April 6th, 1910, but he was soon sent to prison for embezzlement and in 1916, received a five-year sentence when he battered a maid with a hammer during a robbery. Added to this, he was a notorious womaniser and had a string of affairs, yet still his wife, Jessie, stuck by him.

In 1923, Mahon met Emily Kaye and soon her name was added to his list of conquests. In March 1924, Emily went to Bournemouth to recover from influenza and was joined there by Mahon, who bought her a ring. The true reason for all this affection was that Mahon knew that Emily had over £400 in her bank account.

On April 5th, Emily told her family that she and Pat were emigrating to South Africa. She drew out all the money from her account, partly to help Mahon with the expense of setting up home on a new continent. The same day, Mahon rented a bungalow on the Crumbles, near Eastbourne, for the period April 11th to June 6th.

Emily travelled down to Eastbourne on Monday, April 7th and booked into the Kenilworth Court Hotel. She was expecting Mahon to join her on the afternoon of April 12th.

Mahon, though, was rather busy in London. On Thursday the 10th, he met Ethel Primrose Duncan and got her to agree to go out with him. She gave him her address and he said he would contact her.

Two days later, on the Saturday, Mahon travelled down to Eastbourne, met Emily and took her by taxi to the bungalow. He omitted to mention that earlier that afternoon he had called at a shop in Victoria Street and purchased a large knife and a meat saw. It was probably some time that day that Emily handed over to Mahon four £100 notes.

It is not known exactly when Emily Kaye died. She was certainly alive on April 13th, for she was seen by a butcher and also visited a neighbour to borrow some milk. She was also alive on the 14th. An employee of the Kenilworth Court said that Emily had called on either Monday or Tuesday, to pick up her mail. Subsequent events indicate that this was almost certainly the Monday and it is most

NAME	Patrick Herbert Mahon
AGE AT EXECUTION	34
DATE OF EXECUTION	Wednesday, 3rd September, 1924
PLACE OF EXECUTION	Wandsworth
HANGMAN	Thomas Pierrepoint
ASSISTANT	William Willis
DATE OF TRIAL	15th July – 19th July, 1924
LOCATION OF TRIAL	Lewes
PRESIDING JUDGE	Mister Justice Avory
PROSECUTION COUNSEL	Sir Henry Curtis Bennett, Cecil R. Havers, H.R. Howe
DEFENCE COUNSEL	James Dale Cassels M.P., Thomas Gates, C.R. Collingwood
NUMBER OF VICTIMS	1

VICTIMS DETAILS

NAME	Emily Beilby Kaye
AGE	38
DATE OF MURDER	circa Monday, 14th April, 1924
PLACE OF MURDER	Officer's House, Langney Bungalows, Westham, near the Crumbles, Eastbourne
METHOD OF KILLING	Battered (probably)
RELATIONSHIP TO KILLER	Girlfriend

likely that the same evening saw the death of Emily Kaye.

On Tuesday, April 15th, Ethel Duncan received a telegram from Mahon, asking him to met her the following day at Charing Cross. On the 16th, Mahon turned up with his wrist bandaged and told Ethel he had fallen off a bus. They had a meal and when Mahon invited Ethel away for the Easter weekend, she accepted. He arranged to meet her at Eastbourne station. The following day, Ethel received a telegraphic order for £4 to cover her expenses.

On Friday, April 18th, Ethel arrived at Eastbourne just before 2.00pm and Mahon took her to the bungalow. They stayed there for three nights whilst the body of Emily Kaye lay in a trunk. The same Friday, before Ethel's arrival, Mahon had started to dismember the corpse.

Ethel wanted to go shopping in Eastbourne on Saturday and she had no objections to Mahon, who was calling himself Waller, going to Plumpton races. On the way there he took the opportunity to send himself a telegram from Lewes Post Office. Purporting to come from a man named Lee, it asked 'Waller' to be back in London on Tuesday.

Mahon and Ethel travelled back to London together on Monday, April 21st, parting at around midnight. The following day, Mahon travelled back to Eastbourne and continued disposing of parts of Emily Kaye's body. Perhaps the most horrific part of the story involved the disposal of Emily's head. Mahon said that he placed it on the fire in the living room. As the flames licked around it, there was a sudden clap of thunder and Emily's eyes opened. He fled from the room in terror.

Jessie Mahon was used to her husband's philandering and she knew when something was going on. By the end of April, his behaviour had convinced her that yet another affair was taking place so Jessie searched some of Mahon's clothes and found a cloakroom ticket from Waterloo station. She took her suspicions to a friend, who happened to be an ex-policeman, and he went along to Waterloo, handed in the ticket and received a bag. Opening this he saw a knife and some bloodstained female clothing. Knowing that this indicated much more than a sexual fling, he put the bag back into storage and told the police, who decided to watch the station and wait for Mahon to pick the bag up himself.

At 6.30pm on May 2nd, Mahon called for his bag and was promptly arrested. Faced with the heavily bloodstained clothing he first attempted to claim that he had carried some dog's meat in the bag but when he saw that this story was getting him nowhere, he told a different tale altogether.

Mahon told the police about his affair with Emily Kaye and claimed that she had died on Tuesday, April 15th. According to Mahon, she had been with him when he sent the telegram to Ethel Duncan but that night they had argued over their relationship. He tried to walk away but she threw an axe at him. Luckily it missed and hit the door but she then leapt upon him and in the struggle they fell and Emily hit her head on a coal scuttle. She

was dead and he decided that he had to dispose of the body, as he knew his story would not be believed.

The reassembling of the body was a gruesome task, performed by the pathologist Sir Bernard Spilsbury. There were hundreds of pieces to put together and even then, without the head, it was impossible to say how Emily had met her death. She may have been strangled or possibly battered to death with the axe Mahon had claimed was thrown at him. Almost immediately, this part of his story was shown to be a lie. There was no trace of the impact of an axe on the door where Mahon had claimed it had struck.

The trial lasted five days and during it, four jurors had to be replaced due to illness. Found guilty, Mahon was executed on September 3rd, 1924 and even this was not without incident. As the trapdoors opened, Mahon leapt backwards. His back struck the edge of the trap, breaking his spine. Seconds later gravity carried him into the pit, the rope became taut and the spine was broken again, at the neck.

Spilsbury, who performed the postmortem, would describe Mahon as being "doubly hanged".

JOHN GRANT BRUCE, aged 16, was sitting on the back step of his next-door neighbour's house, cleaning a cycle lamp. Elizabeth Southgate watched him at work until suddenly her husband, Frederick, walked in through the garden gate.

John knew that Elizabeth and Frederick had recently separated and only five days before, Elizabeth had obtained a court order against her husband. It was plain that Frederick wanted to go inside and equally clear that Elizabeth wanted nothing to do with him. Thinking that it might be better if he was out of the way, John left the garden and went to his own back door. From there, he could see all that transpired between the Southgates.

After a few minutes, John saw Elizabeth running away from Frederick, who pursued her, drew a knife and plunged it into her back. Bravely, John ran forward and stopped Frederick continuing his attack upon his wife. As John tried to take care of Elizabeth, Frederick jumped upon his own cycle and rode away. Meanwhile, Elizabeth had died and John carried her body into his house.

The police were called and a full-scale search was launched for Frederick Southgate. But no trace of him could be found. In fact, Southgate had cycled to Colchester and at 9.15pm, was seen by James William Emms, the head night attendant at a mental hospital, wheeling his cycle into the grounds. Emms went out to talk to the stranger, who told him that he had lost his memory but thought he might have killed someone. Emms searched the man and found the court summons addressed to Frederick Southgate. With a name to go on, Emms then contacted the police, who were only too happy to take Southgate into custody.

Witnesses helped to piece together the story of Frederick and Elizabeth Southgate. The couple had married in 1921 and Elizabeth had brought some cash and property to the partnership, which she had promised to share with her new husband. Once they were married though, she had decided to keep the property for herself and things had never been the same between them ever since.

Walter Sage, who worked with Frederick,

NAME	Frederick Southgate
AGE AT EXECUTION	52
DATE OF EXECUTION	Thursday, 27th November, 1924
PLACE OF EXECUTION	Ipswich
HANGMAN	Not known
ASSISTANT	Not known
DATE OF TRIAL	6th November, 1924
LOCATION OF TRIAL	Chelmsford
PRESIDING JUDGE	Mister Justice Swift
PROSECUTION COUNSEL	Cecil Whiteley, Mister Ansley
DEFENCE COUNSEL	E.A. Digby
NUMBER OF VICTIMS	1

VICTIMS DETAILS

NAME	Elizabeth Southgate
AGE	circa 58
DATE OF MURDER	Saturday, 26th July, 1924
PLACE OF MURDER	John-de-Bois Cottages, John-de-Boise Hill, Ardleigh, Colchester
METHOD OF KILLING	Stabbed
RELATIONSHIP TO KILLER	Wife

said that the court summons had affected Frederick badly. He claimed that Elizabeth had deliberately made things look much worse than they were and on Friday, July 25th, Frederick had told Sage that he had no intention of paying Elizabeth any money but might "knock her on the head" if he saw her.

It seemed clear that Frederick was seeking to escape the noose by pleading insanity. His trip to the mental hospital and his apparent lack of memory were either genuine or a deliberate attempt to paint a picture of problems of sanity. In the event, the jury felt that Southgate was perfectly sane and therefore wholly responsible for his actions.

1924

ELIZABETH BOUSFIELD WAS the house-keeper to an 80-year-old gentleman named Thomas Senior and had worked for him for four years. Thomas shared his house with his nephew, George Barker, and William George Smith, another nephew, was a fairly regular visitor, living there when he was home from the sea. Also in the house were Elizabeth's three young children.

On August 13th, 1924, Thomas Senior, Elizabeth and William Smith all went to the cinema together. Later they returned to Arundel Street, where they had supper together.

At 7.40am the following morning, Olive Garrod was walking down Arundel Street when she saw three young children standing outside the door to number 86. All three children were crying and as Olive was about to ask them what the matter was, the door to number 86, opened and a man rushed out. Seconds later, Elizabeth Bousfield staggered out, her throat gushing blood. Olive screamed and that attracted the attention of Muriel Hunter, who lived opposite and who now rushed to help.

Just five minutes later, at 7.45am, Smith walked into the police station and told Constable Albert George Cordock that he had cut a woman's throat. Meanwhile, Thomas Senior who was very deaf and had heard nothing of what had occurred in his house, was being woken by police officers.

Smith claimed that he had been having a relationship with Elizabeth for almost two years and on the previous night, after he had settled down on the settee, he had heard Senior go into Elizabeth's bedroom and announce: "Come on Liz my old love. I'm going to fuck you." The following morning, he had spoken to Elizabeth about the matter and after a brief argument, she had rushed at him with a razor in her hand. They had struggled, and he had accidentally cut her throat.

Thomas Senior denied the claims of Smith and said he had never been intimate with his housekeeper. As a result, Smith was found guilty and condemned to death. Smith's story, though, was far from over.

At the same assizes, another case, somewhat similar to that of Smith, came up

NAME	William George Smith
AGE AT EXECUTION	26
DATE OF EXECUTION	Tuesday, 9th December, 1924
PLACE OF EXECUTION	Hull
HANGMAN	Thomas Pierrepoint
ASSISTANT	Robert Baxter
DATE OF TRIAL	19th November, 1924
LOCATION OF TRIAL	York
PRESIDING JUDGE	Mister Justice Talbot
PROSECUTION COUNSEL	C.S. Lowenthal, W.M. McFarlane
DEFENCE COUNSEL	R.F. Burnand
NUMBER OF VICTIMS	1

VICTIMS DETAILS	
NAME	Elizabeth Bousfield
AGE	29
DATE OF MURDER	Thursday, 14th August 1924
PLACE OF MURDER	86 Arundel Street, Hull
METHOD OF KILLING	Cut Throat
RELATIONSHIP TO KILLER	None/girlfriend

before the same judge and in this case, the jury returned a verdict of manslaughter, the guilty man receiving a sentence of 10 years. There was now a public outcry that two men should be treated in such different ways and a petition was organised for Smith. Once this was refused by the Home Secretary, there were calls for workmen to down tools, marches on Hull prison and even cries for the jail to be torn down.

On the morning of the execution, 2,000 people assembled outside the prison. The demonstrations were peaceful though and by 9.30am, half an hour after Smith had been hanged, most of them had already left the area.

CONSTABLE ALFRED CHEESEMAN was on duty in Market Place, Mansfield, at 1.40pm on June 28th, 1924, when Arthur Simms walked up to him and said that he wished to give himself up for murder: "It is my wife's sister. I done it this afternoon."

Back at the police station, Simms wrote out a note giving directions to the body of nine-year-old Rosa Armstrong. "Go straight up Alfreton Road to St. Mark's church. Turn down the ash road leading down the side of St. Mark's church. Turn on the first footpath to the left and she is under the hedge in the second field."

Rosa was the daughter of Maria and Edward Buttery, who lived at 78 Alfreton Road. Another of Maria's daughters was Ethel and she had married Arthur Simms, the man who was now confessing to murder.

At 12.15pm on June 27th, Rosa had arrived home from school for lunch, leaving one hour later, at 1.15pm. Later that afternoon, Maria had sent her stepdaughter to the school to collect some photographs and she had returned with the news that Rosa had not arrived back.

A search was organised and it was not long before John Pitt mentioned that he had seen Simms leaning against a wall at the school at around 1.00pm. Then Vera Randall, who kept the sweet shop on Alfreton Road, reported that a little girl fitting Rosa's description had been into her shop some time after 1.30pm, and had purchased a pennyworth of sweets. Maria knew that when she left home after having lunch, Rosa had no money.

There were other witnesses too. Marion Naylor had been haymaking at Fulwood Farm and had seen a man and a girl walking down the lane at the side of the church. James Marshall had also seen the couple.

By the early hours of Saturday morning, Maria Buttery felt that it was time she spoke to her son-in-law, Arthur Simms. She went around to his house at 13 Phoenix Street, Sutton, roused him from his bed and asked if he had seen Rosa. Simms's reply was: "No, God strike me dead if I have seen her." He added that he needed to use the toilet, vaulted over the gate and vanished into the night.

The search continued and Rosa's body was

NAME	Arthur Simms
AGE AT EXECUTION	25
DATE OF EXECUTION	Wednesday, 17th December, 1924
PLACE OF EXECUTION	Nottingham
HANGMAN	Thomas Pierrepoint
ASSISTANT	Robert Baxter
DATE OF TRIAL	29th October – 1st November, 1924
LOCATION OF TRIAL	Nottingham
PRESIDING JUDGE	Mister Commissioner Walker
PROSECUTION COUNSEL	Norman Birkett
DEFENCE COUNSEL	Mister Healey
NUMBER OF VICTIMS	1

VICTIMS DETAILS	
NAME	Rosa Armstrong
AGE	9
DATE OF MURDER	Friday, 27th June, 1924
PLACE OF MURDER	Field near Calladine Lane, Sutton-in-Ashfield
METHOD OF KILLING	Strangled
RELATIONSHIP TO KILLER	Sister-in-law

discovered one hour later. She had been strangled with one of her bootlaces and was still grasping the sweets she had bought.

There seemed to be no motive and Rosa had not been sexually assaulted. Simms's father, Joseph, said that Arthur had been behaving strangely ever since he had left the army. He frequently wanted to fight with people and on occasions had torn up his clothes and burnt them. The jury were not moved by this suggestion of mental instability, and Simms was found guilty.

1925

WILLIAM BIGNELL FIRST met Margaret Legg in 1917. She was married at the time but told William that she was single. They lived together for two weeks before he realised that she had given him venereal disease and went into hospital in order that he could effect a cure.

Although William now knew the truth about Margaret, they still kept in touch and in October, 1924, when she was living with her husband and child at Florence Street, Swindon, Margaret wrote to William asking him to come and live with her. She added that she would think of some excuse that would explain away his presence and so, on October 23rd, William moved in with Margaret. The following day, Margaret told a neighbour, Mrs Drury, that she loved William and intended running away with him.

On October 25th, the two lovers left Swindon and by nightfall had reached Tetbury, some 20 miles away. Here they spent an hour together in a public house, leaving there at 9.55pm.

By 10.30pm, William Bignell was back in the Market Place at Tetbury, but now he was alone. Seeing a policeman, William asked if he knew of any place where he might obtain lodgings for the night. Directions to two establishments were given but William failed to find a bed at either. Going back to the policeman, William talked for a time about where he was going to sleep and during the course of the conversation, Sergeant Merrett discovered that Bignell lived at Wootton-under-Edge and suggested that as this was within walking distance, he should go home.

William replied that he would not walk home for any man and the only solution was for the police to arrest him. Sergeant Merrett replied that he had no reason to arrest him, whereupon William confessed to the murder of Margaret Legg and described where the body would be found.

It took the jury at Bignell's trial 20 minutes to consider their verdict and on February 24th, the killer who confessed because he wanted a bed for the night, was executed at Shepton Mallet.

NAME	William Grover Bignell
AGE AT EXECUTION	32
DATE OF EXECUTION	Tuesday, 24th February, 1925
PLACE OF EXECUTION	Shepton Mallet
HANGMAN	Thomas Pierrepoint
ASSISTANT	Robert Baxter
DATE OF TRIAL	20th January, 1925
LOCATION OF TRIAL	Devizes
PRESIDING JUDGE	Mister Justice Roche
PROSECUTION COUNSEL	G.D. Roberts, E.A. Hawke
DEFENCE COUNSEL	Reginald Holt
NUMBER OF VICTIMS	1

VICTIMS DETAILS	
NAME	Margaret Legg
AGE	37
DATE OF MURDER	Saturday, 25th October, 1924
PLACE OF MURDER	Field near Tetbury, Long Newnton
METHOD OF KILLING	Cut throat
RELATIONSHIP TO KILLER	Girlfriend

WILLIAM BRESSINGTON was well known in the area where he lived – indeed, he was a figure of fun and ridicule. In addition to some rather strange personal habits, he often took to wearing women's make-up in public and dressing in female clothing, and yet this apparently ineffectual figure, confessed to the brutal murder of a young boy.

On the night of December 12th, 1924, Bressington called at the house of 12-year-old William Frederick Amos and told him that Elizabeth Morton, his 'Aunt Lizzie', wanted to see him. William said that he was looking after the children and couldn't leave them, whereupon Bressington said that eight-year-old Gilbert would do just as well.

Bressington returned home that night and confessed to his father that he had committed a murder. He took the disbelieving man back to the scene of the crime where Bressington senior discovered the sexually violated and strangled body of Gilbert Amos.

So furious was Mr Bressington at what his son had done, that a fight broke out between the two men – the elder Bressington had to be pulled from his son by Henry Shakespeare, who saw what was going on. Soon afterwards, Constable Hawkins arrived on the scene and having arrested William, heard him admit that he had killed the child by tying a tie around his neck.

At his trial at Bristol, Bressington pleaded guilty but the judge considered the matter and directed that a not guilty plea be entered instead. Bressington still admitted killing Gilbert but surprisingly perhaps, denied the sexual assault, claiming that he had procured the child for a man named James.

The defence had to be one of insanity. There was certainly a family history of madness. Charles Bressington, the accused's grandfather, had died in Keynsham Mental Infirmary. An uncle, named David, had been in Gloucester Asylum for the past 20 years and Francis, a cousin, had died in Fishponds Asylum.

Doctor Robert Phillips, who was a partner in a local asylum, testified that in his opinion, Bressington was a mental defective who had no appreciation of right and wrong. He went

NAME	William Francis Albert Bressington
AGE AT EXECUTION	21
DATE OF EXECUTION	Tuesday, 31st March, 1925
PLACE OF EXECUTION	Bristol
HANGMAN	Thomas Pierrepoint
ASSISTANT	Thomas Phillips
DATE OF TRIAL	16th February, 1925
LOCATION OF TRIAL	Bristol
PRESIDING JUDGE	Mister Justice Roche
PROSECUTION COUNSEL	S.H. Emmanuel, W.E.P. Done
DEFENCE COUNSEL	F.E. Wetherby, Mister Croom-Johnson
NUMBER OF VICTIMS	1

VICTIMS DETAILS	
NAME	Gilbert Caleb Amos
AGE	8
DATE OF MURDER	Friday, 12th December, 1924
PLACE OF MURDER	Cozen's Field, Staple Hill, Bristol
METHOD OF KILLING	Strangled
RELATIONSHIP TO KILLER	None

on to say that he would have no hesitation in certifying Bressington.

Even now, the evidence of Bressington's mental state had not come to an end. At the age of 15 he had tried to poison himself. In August 1919, he had joined the army but had soon been discharged, described as feeble minded. Yet, despite all this accumulation of evidence, which clearly showed that Bressington could not by any stretch of the imagination be described as sane, he was found guilty and condemned to death.

MARY PALFREY HAD been a widow since 1917 and over time had grown closer to her dead sister's husband, George Barton. Romance had blossomed and a date had been set for the wedding: February 5th, 1925.

The two lovers were in the habit of spending occasional weekends with Mary's brother, George Juby, in Wroxham, Norfolk. They stayed with George from Saturday, 17th January until Monday the 19th, when they returned to London. George thought they seemed to be in good spirits when they left Wroxham.

On the night of January 21st, there were other people sleeping in Mary's house at 12 Bartle Avenue. Mary's son, Edward Charles Palfrey was only 10 years of age and he had invited a friend over, 13-year-old Ivy Stevens, who lived at number 23. They went to bed at about 10.30pm.

The following morning both children went off to school and at that time, Mary Palfrey was in good health.

At 12.10pm, Edward Palfrey returned home for lunch and found his mother's body on the kitchen floor. She had been battered with a piece of iron pipe and her throat had been cut.

Elizabeth Carroll, a neighbour, had seen Mary in the garden at some time between 9.30am and 9.45am. Another neighbour, Alice Ratford, who lived at number 20, had seen George Barton leaving the house just before 10.00am. Since Barton had now vanished, tracing him became rather important.

On the 23rd January, Barton's son, Albert, received a postcard from his father. On this he asked for forgiveness for what he had done and added that he had only revenged his dead wife's name. He went on to say that he intended to flee abroad.

Barton did not go abroad, though. On January 24th, he gave himself up but said he had no knowledge of the crime. He had seen press reports that the police were looking for him, but insisted that he had had nothing to do with the murder.

Later, in a second statement, Barton admitted killing Mary but said he had done it out of jealousy. She had admitted to him that a sailor friend of hers was to visit after he had

NAME	George William Barton
AGE AT EXECUTION	59
DATE OF EXECUTION	Thursday, 2nd April, 1925
PLACE OF EXECUTION	Pentonville
HANGMAN	Robert Baxter
ASSISTANT	Robert Wilson
DATE OF TRIAL	26th February, 1925
LOCATION OF TRIAL	Old Bailey
PRESIDING JUDGE	Mister Justice Avory
PROSECUTION COUNSEL	Eustace Fulton
DEFENCE COUNSEL	Frederick Levy
NUMBER OF VICTIMS	1

VICTIMS DETAILS	
NAME	Mary May Palfrey
AGE	38
DATE OF MURDER	Thursday, 22nd January, 1925
PLACE OF MURDER	12 Bartle Avenue, East Ham, London
METHOD OF KILLING	Battered/cut throat
RELATIONSHIP TO KILLER	Sister-in-law/girlfriend

gone to work and the thought of that infuriated him. He took up the piece of iron and struck her on the head. Then, whilst Mary lay on the floor, George took his razor and cut her throat.

Found guilty and asked if he had anything to say, Barton replied that he was sorry he was not Ronald True, a killer who had been sentenced to death but subsequently adjudged to be insane, as then he would be sent to a convalescent home to dig up the garden. The judge then passed sentence of death whereupon Barton, snarled: "May you be hung tomorrow."

IN AUGUST, 1924, Margaret Anne Graham obtained a separation order from her husband, Henry. Margaret and her adopted two-year-old child then went to live with her mother, Mary Alice Burnett, whilst Henry found lodgings elsewhere and had to pay his estranged wife 15/- per week.

Sunday, December 21st, 1924, saw Margaret paying a visit to her sister, who was in the Royal Infirmary. With Margaret were her sister's husband, Robert Doleman, and her cousin, Matthew Swan. These three left the Infirmary at 3.15pm and began the walk back to Mary Burnett's house. They had not gone very far when Henry Graham came up behind them and Margaret stopped to talk to him whilst the two men walked on a little way and waited for her.

Henry Graham and his wife talked for some minutes. Then, suddenly, he struck out and hit Margaret in the face. She fell to the ground whereupon Henry took a knife out of his pocket, crouched down and stabbed her in the back, a number of times.

Robert Doleman ran back and tried to stop Henry, who threatened to stab him if he came any closer. Robert then ran off to get the police, whilst Henry tried to make good his escape, brandishing the knife at anyone who came near him.

By now a crowd of people had collected and as Henry Graham ran off, they began to follow, baying for his blood. John Robson, who lived in Drake Street, saw Henry run past his house. He still had the knife in his hand and seeing the crowd, Robson also joined in the chase. It was Robson who caught up with Henry and finally persuaded him to hand the knife over. Detective Thomas McManus arrived on the scene and took Graham back to the scene of the attack, where Police Constable John William Goode, who happened to live in the street, was tending to the victim's wounds. Such was the hostility of the crowd, though, that Henry had to be taken into protective custody and travelled in the ambulance with his wife.

Put on trial for his life and duly sentenced to death, Henry Graham thanked the jury, stating that he was quite satisfied as it was a case of a life for a life. An appeal was lodged

NAME	Henry Graham
AGE AT EXECUTION	42
DATE OF EXECUTION	Wednesday, 15th April, 1925
PLACE OF EXECUTION	Durham
HANGMAN	Thomas Pierrepoint
ASSISTANT	William Willis, Henry Pollard, Lionel Mann
DATE OF TRIAL	6th March, 1925
LOCATION OF TRIAL	Durham
PRESIDING JUDGE	Mister Justice Acton
PROSECUTION COUNSEL	H.S. Cautley, Ronald Ross
DEFENCE COUNSEL	Mister Wilson-Fox
NUMBER OF VICTIMS	1

VICTIMS DETAILS	
NAME	Margaret Ann Graham
AGE	30
DATE OF MURDER	Sunday, 21st December, 1924
PLACE OF MURDER	Outside 20 St Mark's Road, Sunderland
METHOD OF KILLING	Stabbed
RELATIONSHIP TO KILLER	Wife

in which it was suggested that Henry's unusual calmness after the attack, coupled with the fact that he had been blown up in the war which might have affected his mind, suggested insanity. The appeal was dismissed and on April 15th, Henry Graham was hanged at the same time as Thomas Shelton.

1925

THOMAS SHELTON AND Ruth Rodgers had known each other for six years and had been engaged to be married for the last four. Ruth worked as a confidential clerk at the offices of the City Floorcloth and Linoleum Company, of Pink Lane, Newcastle and her office manager there was one Walter Shiel. By December 1924, Thomas Shelton had begun to suspect that Shiel was more to Ruth than just her boss.

This jealousy led to arguments between Thomas and Ruth and he began to write her letters, which were not very pleasant to read. Ruth turned for advice to Shiel of all people and when he offered to escort her home if she was frightened, this only served to make the situation worse.

At 2.00pm on January 29th, 1925, Shelton called at the offices of John Clemo Trotter, an ex-policeman who now operated as a private investigator. Shelton gave his correct name, said he lived at 51 Southway, Sherriff Hill and wanted Trotter to check out whether his fiancée was seeing another man. He handed over some letters Ruth had written, gave a few personal details about her and then left, having made an appointment for the following day. It was an appointment Shelton would be unable to keep.

Ruth's married sister, Eleanor Holmes Hindhaugh Vest, had chosen January 29th to pay a visit to her mother's house, where Ruth also lived. At 7.10pm, Eleanor heard a loud knocking on the front door and when she opened it, found her sister curled up on the front doorstep, bleeding from a wound in her throat. Shelton was in the middle of the street and although his throat was also cut, he could still speak and shouted repeatedly: "Mrs Rodgers, I have done her in."

In fact there were two witnesses to the attack on Ruth Rodgers. Beatrice Ivy Scarth, who lived at number 18, was returning from the shops and saw Ruth talking to Shelton at her front door as she passed number 30. As Beatrice opened her own front door, she saw Ruth run into the centre of the road. Shelton followed her and caught her but Ruth managed to pull away and run back to number 30. Shelton followed, caught her again and attacked her.

NAME	Thomas Henry Shelton
AGE AT EXECUTION	25
DATE OF EXECUTION	Wednesday, 15th April, 1925
PLACE OF EXECUTION	Durham
HANGMAN	Thomas Pierrepoint
ASSISTANT	William Willis, Henry Pollard, Lionel Mann
DATE OF TRIAL	5th March, 1925
LOCATION OF TRIAL	Durham
PRESIDING JUDGE	Mister Justice Acton
PROSECUTION COUNSEL	G.F. Mortimer, Ronald Powell
DEFENCE COUNSEL	Archibald Wilson
NUMBER OF VICTIMS	1

VICTIMS DETAILS

NAME	Ruth Surtees Rodgers
AGE	25
DATE OF MURDER	Thursday, 29th January, 1925
PLACE OF MURDER	30 Abbey Street, Gateshead
METHOD OF KILLING	Cut throat
RELATIONSHIP TO KILLER	Girlfriend

Ruth Surtees Rodgers who was brutally mudered by Thomas Shelton.

Percy Makin Sale, who was lodging temporarily at number 34 was leaving that address, just seconds after the attack. As he closed the door he noticed a man lying down near number 30. Sale helped the man to his feet and asked him if he was all right but the reply was only a gurgle. The door to number 28, the house of Annie and John Carr then opened and Sale helped Shelton inside before going to fetch a doctor.

By the time the doctor arrived, Ruth Rodgers was already dead. Shelton's wound was fairly superficial and after treatment, he was well enough to be charged with murder. Reports of the crime appeared in the local newspapers next day and when these were read by John Trotter, he came forward and told police what Shelton had said to him.

Throughout the trial, Walter Shiel maintained that there had been nothing going on between him and Ruth, and that as a consequence, Shelton had no grounds for being jealous. For his part, Shelton had appeared very elated and exuberant after his arrest and this was used to try to paint a picture of insanity. How could a sane man who had killed his fiancée in such a fashion, seem so unperturbed and even happy afterwards?

The prosecution pointed out that there was no history of insanity in the family and that Shelton had threatened Ruth on more than one occasion. And this was the view that the jury sided with.

IN 1922, JOHN Thorne, unemployed and unable to get a job, borrowed £100 from his father, with whom he lived, and bought a field in Crowborough. Thorne had had enough of trying to find work. He had decided to set up his own business: a poultry farm.

Not having vast sums of money to play with, luxury accommodation was out of the question and for the next couple of years, Thorne's home was to be a wooden hut set amongst his chicken runs. Still, even though he lived in such poor circumstances, he could at least look forward to regular visits from his girlfriend, Elsie Cameron.

The only problem with Elsie was that she would keep talking about marriage. Thorne was quite happy to leave things as they were and had no intention of tying himself down to Elsie, or indeed any other girl for that matter. The situation changed, though, in November, 1924.

It was in that month that Elsie added a little extra weight to the discussions of marriage by informing Thorne that she was carrying his child. She now began to insist on marriage, leaving Thorne to simply decide on when the happy day would take place. Thorne, though, had even less reason to want to marry Elsie now. He had found himself another interest in the form of Elizabeth Ann Coldicott, a local girl with whom he was more than friendly.

On November 25th, Thorne wrote to Elsie and hinted that there was someone else. She wrote back demanding an explanation and after a couple of letters had been exchanged, visited Thorne at his poultry farm on the 30th. Somehow Thorne managed to stall her for the time being but Elsie said she would return.

The next visit took place on December 5th. Elsie set out from her home in Kensal Rise in time to get to Crowborough by the afternoon. Five days later, when Duncan Cameron, Elsie's father had heard nothing more from her, he sent a telegram to Thorne, asking if she had actually arrived. Thorne replied that she had not. Two days later, Elsie was reported as a missing person.

Thorne was extremely helpful when the police called to see him. No, he had not seen Elsie since her visit in November and he had

NAME	John Norman Holmes Thorne
AGE AT EXECUTION	24
DATE OF EXECUTION	Wednesday, 22nd April, 1925
PLACE OF EXECUTION	Wandsworth
HANGMAN	Thomas Pierrepoint
ASSISTANT	Robert Wilson
DATE OF TRIAL	11th March – 16th March, 1925
LOCATION OF TRIAL	Lewes
PRESIDING JUDGE	Mister Justice Finlay
PROSECUTION COUNSEL	Sir Henry Curtis Bennett, R.E. Negus
DEFENCE COUNSEL	James Dale Cassels, Mister Oakes, C.T. Abbott
NUMBER OF VICTIMS	1

VICTIMS DETAILS

NAME	Elsie Emily Cameron
AGE	26
DATE OF MURDER	Friday, 5th December, 1924
PLACE OF MURDER	Wesley Poultry Farm, Crowborough, East Sussex
METHOD OF KILLING	Battered
RELATIONSHIP TO KILLER	Girlfriend

no idea where she was now. He showed them around the farm and even posed for photographs for some gentlemen of the press who had also come down to investigate Elsie's disappearance. The police though, were far from satisfied with Thorne.

Two nurserymen who had been working in the fields had already told the police that they had seen a woman who fitted Elsie's description heading to the farm at about 5.30pm on December 5th. On January 14th, 1925, Thorne was taken into custody to answer further questions and whilst he was being interviewed, other officers took the opportunity to start digging up the farm.

The following day, January 15th, an attaché case was found that was identified as having belonged to Elsie Cameron. Faced with this piece of evidence, Thorne broke down and told the police where they could find Elsie's body. In fact, there were a number of different locations, for Thorne had cut her body up before burial.

Thorne's story was that he had been enjoying a cup of tea when Elsie came into his hut. She again reminded him that she was pregnant and again insisted on marriage. This time, though, she said she wasn't going to leave until he had named the day.

Tired of her nagging, Thorne had gone out for a walk and when he returned half an hour before midnight, was horrified to find that Elsie had thrown a rope over a beam in his hut and hanged herself. Fearful of what the police might think, Thorne dismembered and buried the body, but he claimed that this was his only crime. He was in no way responsible for Elsie's death.

Thorne did not, however, allow for the expertise of Bernard Spilsbury. The remains were examined and Spilsbury was able to say that the cause of death had been shock following a severe beating. There were no marks on either the throat, or indeed the beams in the hut, to show that a rope had been used. Spilsbury was also able to state that Elsie had not been pregnant when she died. However, there were disputes over this medical evidence. Spilsbury could not explain how Elsie's skull, which was abnormally thin, had not been shattered by a blow sufficiently strong enough to cause her death.

Found guilty, Thorne was executed at Wandsworth on April 22nd, 1925. It would have been Elsie Cameron's 27th birthday.

JAMES AND SARAH Sykes had been married for some 20 years and he was now working as an ice-cream salesman. Sarah believed she was a spiritualist medium and often gave readings for friends and neighbours. The two lived happily enough at Whit Lane in Pendleton at a house they shared with their lodger, Patrick Power, who had been with them since December, 1924.

By the middle of April, 1925, Power, who had agreed to pay rent of 14/- a week, was three weeks in arrears. He had also borrowed money from James so that his total indebtedness was now £5. This had not, however, caused any trouble between Power and his landlord and as far as James and Sarah Sykes knew, things were just the same as they had always been between them.

Saturday April 11th, saw James leaving for work as usual at 11.30am. By that time, Power had already been up and about for half an hour and when James went out, Power and Sarah were left alone together.

Sarah was not seen again until 2.45pm, when she visited a shop at the back of her house. Here she was served by Edith Margaret Rollins, who knew her well. Just 45 minutes later, Patrick Power walked into Pendleton police station where Constable Frederick Gibson was on duty.

"Are you on duty?" asked Power.

"Yes," replied the officer, "What do you want?"

"I wish to give myself up," continued Power, "I have killed my landlady."

Later, Power embellished his story somewhat: "I have hit my landlady on the head with a hammer. If she is not dead now she is near it and deserves it."

Sarah Ann Sykes had been the victim of a most brutal attack. She had suffered severe head injuries and had been stabbed 12 times in all, mostly about the head. She must have tried desperately to defend herself as the top of her right thumb had been severed as she held up her arm to ward off the knife.

All this came as a total shock to James Sykes when he returned home from work at 5.00pm, to find police officers waiting to tell him that his wife was in the mortuary. He

could suggest no reason for Power having attacked and killed Sarah.

On May 26th, Patrick Power faced the hangman, guilty of a murder apparently without motive.

NAME	Patrick Power
AGE AT EXECUTION	41
DATE OF EXECUTION	Tuesday, 26th May, 1925
PLACE OF EXECUTION	Manchester
HANGMAN	William Willis
ASSISTANT	Not known
DATE OF TRIAL	8th May, 1925
LOCATION OF TRIAL	Manchester
PRESIDING JUDGE	Mister Justice Findlay
PROSECUTION COUNSEL	Neville J. Laski
DEFENCE COUNSEL	Kenneth Burke
NUMBER OF VICTIMS	1

VICTIMS DETAILS	
NAME	Sarah Ann Sykes
AGE	46
DATE OF MURDER	Saturday, 11th April, 1925
PLACE OF MURDER	8 Whit Lane, Pendleton, Manchester
METHOD OF KILLING	Battered/stabbed
RELATIONSHIP TO KILLER	None

HUBERT DALTON AND Francis Ward had worked together for many years on a mineral railway line and were known to be close friends. Indeed, most Friday nights would see the two men meeting in the village pub to enjoy a few quiet drinks together, with other friends.

Although Francis was due to go on holiday, commencing Friday, October 3rd, 1924, he was still expected to turn up for his pint or two, but to the surprise of the customers who knew him so well, he failed to appear. His friend, Hubert was there, playing dominoes, but he made no comment about the non-appearance of Ward.

The following morning, Francis Ward's body was found, near a haystack which was next to Hubert Dalton's house. The motive appeared to be robbery. The linings of his pockets had been pulled out and his holiday money and two watches were missing. A bloodstained hammer was found nearby and inquiries revealed that it belonged to Hubert Dalton.

Further questioning revealed that Dalton had called at the house of a neighbour, late the previous night, and asked to borrow a candle. Medical tests showed that Ward had been battered to death but that his assailant had returned some hours later in order to cut his throat. Could it be that the candle had been used to light his way in the darkness?

A search of the area revealed that the two missing watches had been hidden in the haystack and in an outhouse, belonging to Dalton, a purse had been hidden. This was identified as belonging to the murdered man. It contained £12 in cash and Ward's railway ticket for his intended trip.

Hubert Dalton was found later that day, walking on the railway line where he had worked for so many years. He had a wound in his throat and was rushed to hospital after having collapsed.

Dalton claimed to have no memory of any attack on Ward, but did have some sort of recollection of throwing a hammer around. On the strength of that, and the stolen items found on his property, Dalton was charged with murder.

In effect, Hubert Dalton was tried twice.

NAME	Hubert Ernest Dalton
AGE AT EXECUTION	39
DATE OF EXECUTION	Wednesday, 10th June, 1925
PLACE OF EXECUTION	Hull
HANGMAN	Thomas Pierrepoint
ASSISTANT	Robert Baxter
DATE OF TRIAL	8th May, 1925
LOCATION OF TRIAL	Leeds
PRESIDING JUDGE	Mister Justice McCardie
PROSECUTION COUNSEL	G.F.L. Mortimer, J. Neal
DEFENCE COUNSEL	R.F. Burnand
NUMBER OF VICTIMS	1

VICTIMS DETAILS	
NAME	Francis Ward
AGE	68
DATE OF MURDER	Friday, 3rd October, 1924
PLACE OF MURDER	Ingleby Greenhow
METHOD OF KILLING	Battered/cut throat
RELATIONSHIP TO KILLER	None

The first jury, at York, were unable to agree whether he was sane or not. The second, at Leeds, had no such trouble and after hearing the evidence, took five minutes to decide that Dalton was both sane and guilty of murder.

DURING THE GREAT War many male preserves were opened up to women. One was the munitions industry and it was in such a factory that Edith Horrocks-Wilkinson first met James Winstanley. They embarked on a relationship, but it was one that soon fizzled out.

After the war, Edith became a barmaid in the Black Horse Hotel in Wigan. Here she met Harry Taylor and soon found herself pregnant. Harry offered to marry her but as soon as he had made the offer he withdrew it. The last thing he wanted was to be tied down to a wife and child.

In April 1920, Edith gave birth to a daughter, whom she also named Edith. Taylor paid his share of the child's upkeep and Edith returned to bar work.

In 1922 Harry announced that he was emigrating to America and that once he had made a life there, he would send for Edith. Harry sailed for the States, wrote regularly and continued to send money.

Not long after Harry had departed, Winstanley walked into the pub where Edith worked. The two hit it off again and in due course, they became lovers. When in 1923, the money from Harry suddenly dried up and the letters stopped, Edith and Winstanley grew closer still, but on more than one occasion, Edith displayed marks on her neck and body, which she explained away as over-exuberance on the part of her lover.

On Edith's birthday, in 1924, a letter arrived from America. Harry had included £10 for her fare to the States. After much soul-searching, Edith decided that she would join Harry, and ended the affair with James, but he fought hard for Edith and soon she was finding reasons to delay her departure. The affair started up again.

On May 7th, 1925, Edith arranged to meet Winstanley at the Bridgewater Arms near Gathurst. From there they went to a number of pubs before ending up at the Navigation Inn. They left at 9.00pm and were seen walking down the canal pathway.

That same night, Winstanley told his sister that he had murdered Edith. He then left the house and later, when the police called she told the officers what her brother had said.

NAME	James Winstanley
AGE AT EXECUTION	29
DATE OF EXECUTION	Wednesday, 5th August, 1925
PLACE OF EXECUTION	Liverpool
HANGMAN	William Willis
ASSISTANT	Robert Wilson
DATE OF TRIAL	18th June – 20th June, 1925
LOCATION OF TRIAL	Lancaster
PRESIDING JUDGE	Mister Justice Fraser
PROSECUTION COUNSEL	J.C. Jackson
DEFENCE COUNSEL	Mister Maxwell-Fyfe
NUMBER OF VICTIMS	1

VICTIMS DETAILS	
NAME	Edith Horrocks-Wilkinson
AGE	27
DATE OF MURDER	Thursday, 7th May, 1925
PLACE OF MURDER	Towpath of the Leeds/Liverpool canal, near the Navigation Inn, Shevington, near Wigan
METHOD OF KILLING	Strangled
RELATIONSHIP TO KILLER	Girlfriend

Winstanley was arrested at his brother's house and took the police to where the body was hidden in a thicket.

At his trial it was suggested that Winstanley had murdered Edith because she had made up her mind to go to America. The defence tried to say that the killing had been accidental. Winstanley had enjoyed inflicting pain during sex and had unwittingly carried this too far. The jury preferred the prosecution's version of events.

IN JANUARY 1925, James Makin married and he and his bride went to live at his uncle's house at 3 Cross Street, Newton Heath.

Joseph Howsley, Makin's uncle, arrived home from work at 5.50pm on May 4th, 1925. Just a few minutes later, his nephew's wife came in and after exchanging greetings, went upstairs to her bedroom.

A scream rang out and upon rushing upstairs to see what the matter was, Joseph Howsley was horrified to find the body of a woman, a complete stranger, in the room.

Witnesses helped to piece together the events of that afternoon. At around 3.30pm, Gertrude Jackson, who lived at number 42, was inside Hilda Collinge's shop at number 10, directly opposite Makin's house. She saw him enter the house, reappear, look around and then vanish back inside. Another minute passed and then a woman went up to the house and, without knocking, walked in.

Makin had gone into Manchester city centre. At 8.10pm he was seen near the Falstaff Hotel, in Market Place, by an old friend, Arthur Green. Makin invited Green for a drink and confessed that he was as good as under arrest as he had killed a woman in his wife's bedroom.

At first, Green thought these were the ramblings of someone who had consumed too much drink, but Makin went on to fill in the details. The woman was a prostitute and he had picked her up in Manchester and taken her back to his place. Having gone in first to make sure the coast was clear, they had then gone upstairs and had sex. Having finished, the woman asked for a bowl of water to clean herself with. This was probably down to the fact that she was actually menstruating at the time, but Makin got hold of a different idea and asked her if she had some disease she might have passed on to him.

Although he asked her three times, the woman did not reply and started to cry. That convinced Makin that he was correct and he picked up a bottle and struck her with it, rendering her unconscious. He then ran downstairs, collected a knife from the kitchen and drew it across her throat.

If this had not convinced Green, Makin's

NAME	James Makin
AGE AT EXECUTION	25
DATE OF EXECUTION	Tuesday, 11th August, 1925
PLACE OF EXECUTION	Manchester
HANGMAN	William Willis
ASSISTANT	Robert Baxter
DATE OF TRIAL	25th July, 1925
LOCATION OF TRIAL	Manchester
PRESIDING JUDGE	Mister Justice Wright
PROSECUTION COUNSEL	Cyril Atkinson M.P., Mister Goldie
DEFENCE COUNSEL	W. Gorman, Percy Butlin
NUMBER OF VICTIMS	1

VICTIMS DETAILS

NAME	Sarah Elizabeth Clutton
AGE	24
DATE OF MURDER	Monday, 4th May, 1925
PLACE OF MURDER	3 Cross Street, Newton Heath, Manchester
METHOD OF KILLING	Cut throat/battered
RELATIONSHIP TO KILLER	None

next actions certainly did. He took £9 out of his pocket and saying that he had no need for it any more, handed it over to his friend.

It was 9.45pm by the time James Makin got off the tram outside Newton Heath police station. He walked up to Superintendent Joseph Lansberry, identified himself and was taken into custody.

The final tragedy, perhaps, is that the crime was all for nothing. The postmortem report showed that Sarah Clutton was not suffering from any disease.

1925.

FRANCIS EDWARD RIX was the butler to Sir George Lloyd, the High Commissioner of Egypt, who lived at Charles Street, in Mayfair. It was part of the house routine that each morning, the maidservant would take Rix a cup of tea at 7.30am.

On the morning of Sunday, June 7th, the routine remained unchanged, but the tea was never consumed. As the maid knocked on the door and entered Rix's room, she saw that he was still in bed and covered with blood. A bloodstained hatchet lay on the floor of the bedroom and it was later determined that a small amount of money, a ring, a watch and a pair of boots were missing.

One of the first names to come to the attention of the police was Arthur Henry Bishop. Until recently, he had been employed at the house, as a hall-boy. After working there for some six months, Bishop had been dismissed by Rix in February and it was possible that with revenge in his mind, Bishop had murdered Rix.

Almost before the investigation had started, on June 8th, Bishop walked into a police station near Sittingbourne and gave himself up. He had in his hand a newspaper account of the murder and said that he had done it. When he was searched, some of Rix's belongings were found on his person and he readily talked of the details of the crime.

According to Bishop, the motive had indeed been robbery. He had already stolen some property from a Mrs Tennant of Cranbrook when he decided to return to his old employer's house to see what he could find there. At 1.30am on the Sunday, Bishop had gained entry through a basement window. Seeing a hatchet, he picked it up to use in the event of discovery, and crept slowly into the butler's bedroom. Thinking that Rix may well waken and attack him, Bishop pre-empted the situation by striking Rix on the head, then stealing what few things he could find. His only excuse was that he had been drinking solidly for three days before the attack.

Found guilty of wilful murder, Bishop was given no mercy on account of his youth. He was only 18 years old when he was executed.

NAME	Arthur Henry Bishop
AGE AT EXECUTION	18
DATE OF EXECUTION	Friday, 14th August, 1925
PLACE OF EXECUTION	Pentonville
HANGMAN	Robert Baxter
ASSISTANT	Henry Pollard, Edward Taylor, Robert Wilson
DATE OF TRIAL	16th July, 1925
LOCATION OF TRIAL	Old Bailey
PRESIDING JUDGE	Mister Justice Swift
PROSECUTION COUNSEL	Sir Travers Humphreys, Gerald Dodson
DEFENCE COUNSEL	Ernest Wetton
NUMBER OF VICTIMS	1

VICTIMS DETAILS	
NAME	Francis Edward Rix
AGE	26
DATE OF MURDER	Sunday, 7th June, 1925
PLACE OF MURDER	24 Charles Street, Mayfair, London
METHOD OF KILLING	Battered
RELATIONSHIP TO KILLER	None

SOMETIMES IT TAKES justice quite a while to catch up with a miscreant. In the case of William Cronin, it took 28 years.

Alice Garrett's husband had died early in 1924 and shortly afterwards, she began living with Cronin at 126 Old Street, Stepney. Their neighbour at number 128, Rose Blanks, often heard them quarrelling.

On the night of June 12th, just before midnight, William and Rose heard yet another argument from next door, but this time, Alice was heard to cry out "Murder!" William went to investigate. William returned ashen-faced, because Alice's head was hanging off.

Rose went next door to see for herself what had happened. As she entered the house, Cronin pushed past her and walked out into the street. William Blanks, meanwhile, had gone to fetch the police. Knowing what had happened, Alice cried out: "Stop him!" and Charles James Edmead, who was passing at the time, leapt upon Cronin and held him until the police arrived, even though Cronin pulled a razor on Edmead and managed to slash one of his fingers.

The story was a simple one. Cronin and Alice had lived together for about six months. They had first met when Cronin visited his sister, Emma Jane Sartain, who lived on the floor above Alice. According to Cronin, it was this same sister who told him that Alice had been seeing other men whilst he was at sea, and added that one of them was named Underwood. Emma would later deny this.

Cronin's defence was that someone else had killed Alice whilst they were asleep. The jury did not even leave the box before finding Cronin guilty. Cronin announced to the judge: "Thank you sir. I am very glad that you have sentenced an innocent man to death."

In fact this was the second time that Cronin had been on trial for his life at the Old Bailey. On July 23rd, 1897, an argument had broken out between a group of men and Henry Cuthbert, in Limehouse. The group accused Cuthbert of breaking a recent strike and at one stage, one of the accusers, Cronin, had rushed into Cuthbert's house at 16 Carr Street, and battered his 10-month-old daughter Eliza to death with a spade. Cronin was identified, arrested and charged with

NAME	William John Cronin
AGE AT EXECUTION	54
DATE OF EXECUTION	Friday, 14th August, 1925
PLACE OF EXECUTION	Pentonville
HANGMAN	Robert Baxter
ASSISTANT	Henry Pollard, Edward Taylor, Robert Wilson
DATE OF TRIAL	17th July, 1925
LOCATION OF TRIAL	Old Bailey
PRESIDING JUDGE	Mister Justice Swift
PROSECUTION COUNSEL	Perceval Clarke, G.D. Roberts
DEFENCE COUNSEL	W.A.L. Raeburn
NUMBER OF VICTIMS	1

VICTIMS DETAILS	
NAME	Alice Garnett
AGE	40
DATE OF MURDER	Friday, 12th June, 1925
PLACE OF MURDER	126 Old Street, Stepney, London
METHOD OF KILLING	Cut throat
RELATIONSHIP TO KILLER	Girlfriend

murder, appearing in court on September 14th, 1897.

Cronin said that he was with Mary Farrow at the time and claiming that he had never entered Cuthbert's house. Other witnesses, including Henry Corcoran, testified that in fact it was Henry Cuthbert who first attacked Cronin with the spade and suggestions were made that the baby might have been accidentally injured in the scuffle. All this was enough to have Cronin convicted of the reduced charge of manslaughter, for which he received seven years.

1925

A T FIRST GLANCE, it would seem that the lover affair between Alfred Bostock and Elizabeth Sherratt was like so many others. They both worked at the Parkgate Ironworks – Elizabeth in the offices and Alfred as a crane driver, and a friendship had developed into a passionate relationship. Unfortunately, also like so many other such affairs, one of the partners was already married.

Alfred had told Elizabeth that he was unhappy in his marriage and was going to ask his wife for a divorce. That was a lie and Alfred had no intention whatsoever of seeking a separation. He was quite happy to go on seeing Elizabeth in secret, and enjoying the brief times they could spend together.

For a time, Elizabeth saw the need for secrecy and even left the ironworks in order to keep the affair out of the public gaze. She took a job at the Parkgate Electra Picture Palace and naturally Bostock was a frequent visitor.

Fate has a habit of playing a part in such relationships and one day, Elizabeth told Arthur the happy news that she was expecting their child. Now there was no more need for secrecy and surely Alfred could use this as an excuse to make the final break that he had been putting off for so long. Alfred, though, had other ideas.

On May 3rd, 1925, Elizabeth's body was found in the river. She had been battered to death, her skull being fractured, and judging by the pools and splashes of blood on the towpath, had fought hard for her life. The police went back to Elizabeth's lodgings, made a thorough search for clues and discovered a large pile of intimate love letters from Bostock.

When spoken to by the police, Bostock admitted being Elizabeth's lover and even admitted being with her on the night of her death, but said they were only together for 10 minutes or so. He claimed that between 8.00pm and 10.00pm, he had been in the Forge and Rail Mill pub, but the alibi collapsed when other customers said they had not seen him that night.

The jury were out for 15 minutes and Alfred Bostock was found guilty. Asked if he had anything to say he replied: "I am innocent

NAME	Alfred David Bostock
AGE AT EXECUTION	25
DATE OF EXECUTION	Thursday, 3rd September, 1925
PLACE OF EXECUTION	Leeds
HANGMAN	Thomas Pierrepoint
ASSISTANT	Robert Wilson, Henry Pollard
DATE OF TRIAL	24th July – 25th July, 1925
LOCATION OF TRIAL	Leeds
PRESIDING JUDGE	Mister Justice Finlay
PROSECUTION COUNSEL	G.F.L. Mortimer
DEFENCE COUNSEL	G.H.B. Streatfeild
NUMBER OF VICTIMS	1

VICTIMS DETAILS	
NAME	Elizabeth M. Sherratt
AGE	24
DATE OF MURDER	Sunday, 3rd May, 1925
PLACE OF MURDER	River Don, near Roundwood Colliery, Rawmarsh, Rotherham
METHOD OF KILLING	Battered
RELATIONSHIP TO KILLER	Girlfriend

and if the dead girl's lips could only speak, they would tell you the same."

On September 3rd, 1925, Alfred Bostock was hanged alongside Wilfred Fowler.

IN EARLY 1925, the Fowlers and their gang were well known in the criminal fraternity around Sheffield and were a group to be feared and avoided at all costs. William Plommer, an ex-boxer, was not about to avoid anyone though, and he certainly knew no fear.

Plommer had already had a run-in with one of the Fowler henchmen and had battered him senseless and when, on April 26th, Plommer and another ex-boxer named Jack Clay ran into Wilfred Fowler and two more of his men, it was obvious that revenge was uppermost in their minds.

Fowler made his first move on Clay, believing him to be the easier target of the two. Plommer smiled and offered to watch the two henchmen whilst Clay took on Fowler, which he proceeded to do. The encounter ended with Fowler having to be carried away and threatening to get even with Plommer.

The next day, April 27th, Plommer was sitting in his front room at his home in Princess Street, when his son Thomas rushed in and told him that there was a group of men outside waiting to see him. Plommer was fully aware of who it was likely to be, but again he showed no fear and went out to face them.

There were nine members of the Fowler gang, including both the brothers and before Plommer could even make a move towards them, they were upon him with clubs, chains and knives. The police were called but it was too late for William Plommer. He staggered back to his home, fatally wounded and died in hospital later that day.

William Plommer had set an example to all the men of Sheffield. Given a hero's funeral in which thousands lined the streets, his bravery caused others to find their own courage and men came forward to give evidence against the criminals to the police. In total, 11 arrests were made.

The Fowlers, arrogant as ever, tried to suggest that Plommer had attacked them, and they had only acted in self-defence, but witnesses were called who testified to hearing Lawrence Fowler say to Plommer "You've done our kid and now we'll do for you." The trial lasted four days, four men being

NAMES	Wilfred Fowler; Lawrence Fowler
AGES AT EXECUTION	23; 25
DATES OF EXECUTION	Thursday, 3rd September, 1925; Friday, 4th September, 1925
PLACE OF EXECUTION	Leeds; Leeds
HANGMAN	Thomas Pierrepoint; Thomas Pierrepoint
ASSISTANT	Robert Wilson, Henry Pollard; Lionel Mann
DATE OF TRIAL	28th July – 31st July, 1925
LOCATION OF TRIAL	Leeds
PRESIDING JUDGE	Mister Justice Finlay
PROSECUTION COUNSEL	G.F.L. Mortimer
DEFENCE COUNSEL	G.H.B. Streatfeild
NUMBER OF VICTIMS	1

VICTIMS DETAILS	
NAME	William F. Plommer
AGE	33
DATE OF MURDER	Monday, April 27th, 1925
PLACE OF MURDER	Princess Street, Sheffield
METHOD OF KILLING	Battered/stabbed
RELATIONSHIP TO KILLERS	None; none

discharged on the third day at the direction of the judge.

The verdicts were all the police could have hoped for. Just two of the remaining seven, Frederick Goddard and Samuel Garvin, were found not guilty. Both Fowlers were found guilty of murder and sentenced to death. George Willis, Amos Stewart and Stanley Harker were all found guilty of manslaughter, the first two receiving 10-year sentences and Harker collecting seven.

Wilfred Fowler was the first to die on the gallows, joining Alfred Bostock on September 3rd. His brother Lawrence followed him the next day.

THERE WERE PERHAPS 100 people in the mob on Water Street in Glasgow and it was all over a quantity of jumpers and scarves.

Nathoo Mohammed was a street trader who lived in Clyde Street and he had refused to deal with a local gang. Now Mohammed, his wife Louie, and other Indians were at the house of Sundi Din and the mob, led by John McCormack, Robert Fletcher and John Keen, were outside, baying for blood.

Louie Mohammed advised her husband to leave the house, which he did, and she assumed that he had gone for the police. In fact, a 17-year-old youth, John Sterling had run to Canal Bridge where he found two constables and told them his story of a large mob in Water Street.

Whilst Sterling was still talking to the police, men were trying to break down the door to Sundi Din's house and at that point Noorh Mohammed, who was inside, rushed out with a broom to defend himself. A knife was plunged into his left breast. The stricken man was carried back upstairs but died later from his injuries.

The police arrested three men, – McCormack, Fletcher and Keen – and charged each of them with murder. All three appeared in court in early September, but it appeared that the strongest evidence was against John Keen.

Keen admitted that the knife belonged to him but claimed that someone else had taken it from his pocket and used it upon the dead man. This was largely negated when forensic evidence showed that blood had been found on Keen's clothing.

Richard Stephen had been on Water Street that night and he had seen Keen, the only man amongst the mob whom he knew personally, sporting a cut finger that he wrapped a handkerchief around. Stephen also saw Keen pass a knife to another man.

That man was Robert Purdon, who admitted that Keen had passed him the dagger after the stabbing. He in turn gave it to Joseph McCall, who hid it in an old building by the canal. Later Robert and his brother visited McCall and asked for the knife to be given back to them. McCall obliged and the two

NAME	John Keen
AGE AT EXECUTION	22
DATE OF EXECUTION	Thursday, 24th September, 1925
PLACE OF EXECUTION	Glasgow, Duke Street
HANGMAN	Thomas Pierrepoint
ASSISTANT	Not known
DATE OF TRIAL	1st September – 3rd September, 1925
LOCATION OF TRIAL	Glasgow
PRESIDING JUDGE	Lord Justice Ormindale
PROSECUTION COUNSEL	A. Maitland, L. Hill Watson
DEFENCE COUNSEL	William Mitchell, A.M.M. Williamson
NUMBER OF VICTIMS	1

VICTIMS DETAILS	
NAME	Noorh Mohammed
AGE	Not known
DATE OF MURDER	Saturday, 16th May, 1925
PLACE OF MURDER	56 Water Street, Port Dundas, Glasgow
METHOD OF KILLING	Stabbed
RELATIONSHIP TO KILLER	None

brothers then took it to the police station.

The jury took 35 minutes to arrive at their verdicts. McCormack, who had had the murder charge against him dropped on the final day of the trial, was found guilty of using intimidating behaviour and received a sentence of nine months. Fletcher was adjudged to be guilty of Culpable Homicide, which is the Scottish equivalent of manslaughter, and received seven years. Only Keen was found guilty of murder and sentenced to death.

IN MAY, 1925, Alice Mabel Whiteman obtained a separation order from her husband and, taking her children, moved in with her parents, William and Clara Squires.

The Squires were farm workers and on June 15th they were working in different fields at Town Farm, Swaffam. It was noon when Alice arrived at where her father was working and handed over his lunch. As he took a break, Alice pushed the pram containing her two children towards the field where her mother was working.

At 1.00pm, William Squires heard a scream and tore across the fields towards the sound. He found Alice, who had been badly battered and, looking up, was in time to see his son-in-law, Herbert Whiteman, running away from Clara, who fell to the ground in a crumpled heap.

It was 1.30pm by the time Whiteman was next seen, by his brother, Thomas William Whiteman. This was some one and a half miles from where the attack had taken place and Whiteman made no attempt to hide what he had done. "Kiss me goodbye," he said to his brother, "I have killed Mrs Squires and my wife."

Whiteman then walked to his mother's house, at Great Thorns. Hannah Whiteman allowed him to go inside the house. Whilst he was waiting for the police, Whiteman hid the murder weapon, a heavy spanner, in a pile of wood.

The police arrived and Whiteman was taken in. His initial story was that recently he had written his wife a letter, which she had not even bothered to reply to. That day he had gone to work as normal, but suddenly had come over all queer and walked to where he knew Clara Squires would be working. Seeing his wife nearby, he kissed his children and asked her again if she would return to him. "No, never!" she replied, whereupon he picked up a piece of iron and hit her twice.

Concerned for what he had done, Whiteman ran to his mother-in-law and asked her to come to her daughter's aid. Clara had made to hit him with the long fork she was using and he had hit out at her in self-defence. Only later did he admit to taking the spanner with him, telling officers where it could be found.

NAME	Herbert George Whiteman (Bloye)
AGE AT EXECUTION	27
DATE OF EXECUTION	Thursday, 12th November, 1925
PLACE OF EXECUTION	Norwich
HANGMAN	Robert Baxter
ASSISTANT	Edward Taylor
DATE OF TRIAL	19th October, 1925
LOCATION OF TRIAL	Norwich
PRESIDING JUDGE	Lord Chief Justice, Lord Hewart
PROSECUTION COUNSEL	Gerald Dodson
DEFENCE COUNSEL	A.S. Leighton
NUMBER OF VICTIMS	2

VICTIMS DETAILS	
NAME	Clara Squires (Died Wednesday, 17th June); Alice Mabel Squires (Died Monday, 3rd August)
AGE	52; not known
DATE OF MURDER	Monday, 15th June, 1925
PLACE OF MURDER	Field on Town Farm, Swaffham
METHOD OF KILLING	Battered; battered
RELATIONSHIP TO KILLER	Mother-in-law; wife

There should surely have been some concern over Whiteman's mental health. The prison medical reports said that he was of low intelligence and that whilst held in Norwich and Brixton prisons, he had a number of fits.

At the coroner's hearing on August 3rd, 1925, Whiteman had yet another fit, delaying the proceedings for some time. Yet despite all this he was found fit enough to stand trial and, having been found guilty of murder, was sentenced to death.

SAMUEL JOHNSON HAD been walking out with Beatrice Martin for two years and in that time he had been totally honest with her about his circumstances. Johnson was a married man, with three children, but he and his wife had now parted and there had been talk of a divorce so that he would be able to marry Beatrice.

Things were proceeding smoothly until May, 1925, when Beatrice told Johnson that she did not wish to get married. He suspected that there might be another man and eventually he discovered that this was indeed the case.

John Hunter was a sailor and he too was now seeing Beatrice. Johnson still turned up from time to time, but there were constant rows and eventually Johnson announced he would find Hunter and fight him. This state of affairs continued until the end of July, 1925.

Johnson called to see Beatrice on July 25th, when they argued because she did not want to go out with him. Johnson stormed out of her house in Wingfield Street and later that same night, Beatrice went out, to meet up with Hunter.

At midnight, Mary Alice Martin, Beatrice's mother, noticed Johnson standing by her front gate and told him to go away. When he didn't move, Mary called her husband, William, and he persuaded Johnson to leave.

The same scene was repeated the day after. Johnson called with a present for Beatrice, which she refused. He left the house, saying that it was the last present he would ever buy for anyone, and soon afterwards, Beatrice left to meet John Hunter.

It was 1.00am on July 27th and Beatrice had still not returned home. Mary Martin was on her way to bed when again she noticed Johnson near her front gate. When questioned, he told Mary that he was waiting for her daughter to come home. Mary said that it would do him little good and then retired for the night.

At around 2.00am, Beatrice arrived at the end of her street, where she parted from Hunter. As she walked to her gate, she noticed Johnson waiting for her and told him to go away.

Mary Martin was woken by the sound of

NAME	Samuel Johnson
AGE AT EXECUTION	29
DATE OF EXECUTION	Tuesday, 15th December, 1925
PLACE OF EXECUTION	Manchester
HANGMAN	William Willis
ASSISTANT	Thomas Phillips
DATE OF TRIAL	23rd November, 1925
LOCATION OF TRIAL	Manchester
PRESIDING JUDGE	Mister Justice Wright
PROSECUTION COUNSEL	None
DEFENCE COUNSEL	None
NUMBER OF VICTIMS	1

VICTIMS DETAILS	
NAME	Beatrice Philomena Martin
AGE	23
DATE OF MURDER	Monday, 27th July, 1925
PLACE OF MURDER	13 Wingfield Street, Stretford, Manchester
METHOD OF KILLING	Stabbed
RELATIONSHIP TO KILLER	Girlfriend

knocking at her front door. Running downstairs, she opened the door to find Beatrice and Johnson, both trying to gain admittance. Beatrice turned to Johnson and said: "You are not coming in here." Johnson drew out a knife and plunged it into Beatrice's back. Mary screamed, attracting the attention of John Hunter who ran back to see what had happened. As he arrived, Johnson walked off.

Johnson gave himself up to Constable Benjamin Whalley, in Chester Road, at 2.10am. They returned to the murder scene together and Johnson pointed out where he had thrown the knife.

With a witness to his attack, Johnson had no chance of escaping the ultimate penalty.

ADA TAYLOR WAS a married woman, but her husband had walked out on her in 1910, leaving her with her daughter, Jessie Kate Taylor. In due course, Jessie became a married woman and changed her name to Dutton and finally, around April 1924, Ada found a new man who moved in with her. His name was John Fisher.

John Fisher was not someone that could be termed a hard-working man. He had been out of regular employment for three years and did not seem too concerned with ending that state of affairs. He borrowed money on a regular basis from both Ada and Jessie and seldom, if ever, repaid it. This led to frequent arguments over money, but even this did not seem to move Fisher to action.

Yet another argument broke out on Sunday, October 25th, when Ada discovered that in order to obtain some money, Fisher had pawned a tablecloth that belonged to her. The row seemed to have died down though by 4.00pm, when Jessie went out.

Jessie returned at 9.55pm and was surprised to find the front door locked. Using her key, she went in and after looking in a couple of the rooms, found her mother lying in bed, apparently asleep, the bedclothes pulled up over her head. Receiving no reply to her questions, Jessie investigated further and discovered that her mother was covered in blood. Even before a police bulletin could be issued to tell officers to look out for Fisher, he had given himself up. At just about the same time the body of Ada Taylor was found by her daughter, two policemen boarded a tramcar. As Constable Charles Bent walked down the top deck, one of the passengers, Fisher, turned to him and said: "I have done a murder in Wright Street. I want to give myself up to you."

Back at the police station, Fisher admitted that he had killed Ada at around 5.30pm. Coldly he explained that at dinner time, he had sharpened all the knives, just as he usually did on a Sunday, but that all the time he was thinking of murder and kept back one of the knives.

That evening, he had sat in the kitchen reading, watching Jessie and waiting for an opportunity to kill her first before settling

NAME	John Fisher
AGE AT EXECUTION	58
DATE OF EXECUTION	Tuesday, 5th January, 1926
PLACE OF EXECUTION	Birmingham
HANGMAN	William Willis
ASSISTANT	Robert Wilson
DATE OF TRIAL	4th December, 1925
LOCATION OF TRIAL	Birmingham
PRESIDING JUDGE	Mister Justice Talbot
PROSECUTION COUNSEL	Mister Sanderson
DEFENCE COUNSEL	Douglas Jenkins
NUMBER OF VICTIMS	1

VICTIMS DETAILS	
NAME	Ada Taylor
AGE	56
DATE OF MURDER	Sunday, 25th October, 1925
PLACE OF MURDER	1 Back 27 Wright Street, Small Heath, Birmingham
METHOD OF KILLING	Cut throat/battered
RELATIONSHIP TO KILLER	Girlfriend

scores with her mother. Jessie had gone out though so, accepting failure in her case, he went upstairs to where Ada was having a nap and murdered her in her bed. He then went back downstairs, had a refreshing cup of tea before leaving at a 5.45pm and having a few pints in the local pubs.

John Fisher was executed for the murder of Ada Taylor. Jessie Dutton meanwhile must have wondered at just how close she came to being another victim.

I N APRIL 1920, Lorraine Lax married Elizabeth, but the relationship was not a happy one. Lorraine was rather too fond of both drink and gambling with the result that Elizabeth obtained not one, but two separation orders, the first in 1921 and the second in 1923. By 1925 though, they were back together yet again, living in lodgings at 51 Ripon Street, a house owned by Harry Bailey Antcliffe.

Alice Gardner, Elizabeth's sister, who was married to Henry Lycurgas Gardner, lived just a few doors away, at number 61 and at 6.45am on Monday, August 31st, they answered a knock at their front door. The visitor was Harry Antcliffe's wife, Clare, who asked Henry Gardner if he would come and attend to 'Lizzie'. Henry began to follow Clare back to her house when he spotted Lorraine Lax standing some 20 yards away. "It's no use," said Lax, "she's dead – I'm going to give myself up."

Elizabeth Lax was indeed dead, lying on her bed with her three children in the same room, unharmed. At Lax's own request, Antcliffe's son, Norman, accompanied him to the police station, where he told officers what he had done.

At his trial in Leeds, Lorraine Lax insisted that he had been provoked into killing Elizabeth. He claimed that as he had climbed out of bed on the morning in question, he had accidentally brushed against his wife's shoulder. He began dressing and whilst doing so, turned around and saw her advancing towards him with a razor in her hand. A struggle followed, during which he took the razor from her and killed her in the heat of the moment. He had sustained a slight wound in his own throat and Lax said that it had been caused by Elizabeth. Medical opinion, though, was that this had been self-inflicted and this, together with the amount of violence used on Elizabeth, led to a return of a guilty verdict.

NAME	Lorraine Lax
AGE AT EXECUTION	28
DATE OF EXECUTION	Thursday, 7th January, 1926
PLACE OF EXECUTION	Leeds
HANGMAN	Thomas Pierrepoint
ASSISTANT	William Willis
DATE OF TRIAL	1st December, 1925
LOCATION OF TRIAL	Leeds
PRESIDING JUDGE	Mister Justice Fraser
PROSECUTION COUNSEL	F. Beverley
DEFENCE COUNSEL	W.P. Donald
NUMBER OF VICTIMS	1

VICTIMS DETAILS

NAME	Elizabeth Lax
AGE	30
DATE OF MURDER	Monday, 31st August, 1925
PLACE OF MURDER	51 Ripon Street, Sheffield
METHOD OF KILLING	Cut throat
RELATIONSHIP TO KILLER	Wife

FLORENCE HARDWICK TURNED up for work at the Garibaldi Inn, at Worcester, on the morning of November 27th, 1925.

Getting no reply to her knocking, Florence opened the cellar door. There was an unmistakable smell of burning and upon further investigation, Florence found the dead bodies of Ernest and his wife, covered with paper that had been set alight. Both had been shot.

When the police arrived, they found one other body upstairs. Two-year-old Robert had been battered to death in his bed. His six-year-old sister Joan, however, was unharmed.

The motive for the crime was robbery, as someone had emptied the till. Later that same day, Constable William Devey was on duty in the city centre when he was approached by a probationary policeman, Herbert Burrows. Excitedly, Burrows asked Devey if he had heard about the murders of Ernest Laight and his wife.

Burrows told Devey that both had been shot during a robbery and that he, Burrows, had probably been one of the last people to see them alive. The previous night he had been in the Garibaldi. He did, after all, live opposite the pub at 92 Wylds Lane and it was his local.

The problem was that Burrows had told Devey he had heard about the shootings at 8.00am, whilst the police themselves were not aware that Ernest and Doris had been shot until 9.00am. Officers went around to Burrows's lodgings ,where a search revealed the stolen money and a revolver.

Faced with this evidence, Burrows confessed. He had been short of money so, staying on after the pub had closed, he had shot Ernest Laight in the cellar. Doris Laight had gone to see what the noise was and she too had been murdered. Robert had been battered to death because his crying might have alerted people.

Burrows pleaded not guilty, due to insanity. Evidence was called to show that he suffered from syphilis and it was held that this had affected his mind.

Found guilty, Burrows refused to enter an appeal. His only redeeming feature was the fact that before his execution, he had the

NAME	Herbert Burrows
AGE AT EXECUTION	23
DATE OF EXECUTION	Wednesday, 17th February, 1926
PLACE OF EXECUTION	Gloucester
HANGMAN	Thomas Pierrepoint
ASSISTANT	William Willis
DATE OF TRIAL	27th January 1926
LOCATION OF TRIAL	Worcester
PRESIDING JUDGE	Mister Justice Sankey
PROSECUTION COUNSEL	Geoffrey Lawrence
DEFENCE COUNSEL	A.F. Clements
NUMBER OF VICTIMS	3

VICTIMS DETAILS

NAME	Ernest George Elton Laight; Doris Sabrina Laight
AGE	31; 30
DATE OF MURDER	Friday, 27th November, 1925
PLACE OF MURDER	Garibaldi Inn, Wylds Lane, Gloucester
METHOD OF KILLING	Shot; shot
RELATIONSHIP TO KILLER	None; none

NAME	Robert Laight
AGE	2
DATE OF MURDER	Friday, 27th November, 1925
PLACE OF MURDER	Garibaldi Inn, Wylds Lane, Gloucester
METHOD OF KILLING	Battered
RELATIONSHIP TO KILLER	None

decency to write to Doris Laight's mother and confirm that rumours of an affair between them were unfounded.

1925

EDWARD RICHARDS WAS a salesman for Usher's Brewery. He was successful and occasionally, would carry large amounts of cash given in payment for new orders.

On December 23rd, 1925, Richards and a fellow worker, Samuel George Gray, visited Bath. They finally returned to Trowbridge at around midnight.

Richards lived in Victoria Avenue and shared his home with another brewery employee, Walter Stourton. On the evening of December 23rd, Walter had retired at 10.30pm, leaving the back door unlocked. Shortly after midnight, he was disturbed by something thrown at the window. When he looked out, he saw Richards in the garden, asking him to come down. At the same time, Walter heard a loud noise and as he ran downstairs, a motor bike started up and pulled away.

Edward Richards had been shot. Still alive, he managed to tell Walter that when he had arrived home, he had found two men inside the house. Upon challenging them, they had fired a gun at him. He died later in hospital.

Police inquiries led to the barracks of the Royal Horse Artillery, where two men had been on leave on the night of the crime. Ian Ronald Maxwell Stewart was due to report back to barracks at 10.45pm and John Lincoln at 11.45pm. Stewart was in camp, but left soon after and, taking his motor bike, drove to 41 Timball Street where Lincoln was staying. Both men then went back to barracks where Lincoln reported. Another soldier, named Hanton, saw Lincoln changing his clothes and going back out.

Further investigations revealed that Stewart had known Richards and was aware of his routine. Furthermore, Lincoln was seen earlier on December 23rd, taking a pistol and cartridges from the store. Both men were taken in for questioning and subsequently charged with murder.

Whilst in prison awaiting trial, John Lincoln wrote to his girlfriend In this letter he admitted firing the shots that had killed Richards, but claimed that Richards had fired first. The letter was given in evidence.

According to Lincoln, they had sneaked in through the back door, found some beer and

NAME	Ignatius Emanuel Napthali Trebich Lincoln (John Lincoln)
AGE AT EXECUTION	23
DATE OF EXECUTION	Tuesday, 2nd March, 1926
PLACE OF EXECUTION	Shepton Mallet
HANGMAN	Thomas Pierrepoint
ASSISTANT	Not known
DATE OF TRIAL	20th January – 21st January, 1926
LOCATION OF TRIAL	Devizes
PRESIDING JUDGE	Mister Justice Talbot
PROSECUTION COUNSEL	Rayner Goddard, W. Spencer
DEFENCE COUNSEL	F. Wiltshire, F.C. Williams, Mister Hemmerde
NUMBER OF VICTIMS	1

VICTIMS DETAILS
NAME	Edward Charles Ingram Richards
AGE	25
DATE OF MURDER	Thursday, 24th December, 1925
PLACE OF MURDER	Victoria Avenue, Trowbridge, Wiltshire
METHOD OF KILLING	Shot
RELATIONSHIP TO KILLER	None

brandy, and then heard the sound of Richards returning. Richards challenged the two intruders and fired his gun. Lincoln then fired through the doorway and must have hit Richards accidentally. He was, therefore, only guilty of manslaughter.

On the first day of the trial, the judge directed that there was not enough evidence to convict Stewart. The trial continued with Lincoln alone and after an absence of 15 minutes, the jury declared him guilty

SOMETIMES, JUSTICE MOVES exceedingly quickly. On February 8th, 1926, Harry Thompson murdered Rose Smith. Exactly 29 days later he was executed for that crime!

Rose Smith had been married twice. Divorced from her first husband, she had subsequently married Herbert Smith, a petty officer in the Royal Navy. In due course though, Rose allowed a third man into her life and Harry Thompson went to live with her and her three children, at 36 Cross Street.

At 10.00pm on February 8th, a loud scream was heard issuing from number 36. It disturbed the neighbours on both sides of the house. From number 38, Frederick George Garnett went out to investigate. He heard Harry's voice shout: "It's all over. It's done with", and then saw Harry pass by the front gate.

At number 34, Amelia Taunton also heard the scream and, seeing the children were in the backyard in a distressed state, took them home with her and put them to bed in her own house. She assumed there had been a row at number 36, so when she saw Frederick Garnett outside, called for him to go inside number 36 with her. They found Rose lying in the kitchen, her head almost severed from her body.

Garnett went to fetch the police, as it was quite obvious that Rose was beyond any help. Harry Thompson, meanwhile, had met up with a friend, George Edward Thomas Varney, whom he informed that he had, "Cut Rose's fucking head clean off." Varney naturally asked why, but Harry would only reply that he was going to the police station to give himself up.

George Varney walked with Harry until they encountered Constable Albert Thomas Best in the High Street. Harry handed Best a bloodstained razor with the words: "I have topped a bloody woman." On the way to the police station, Thompson showed no concern for what had happened to Rose, but sympathised with Varney, who had recently lost his mother.

Harry Thompson's behaviour at the station could hardly be described as rational. He kept laughing and seemed oblivious to the seriousness of what he had done. He made a

NAME	Henry (Harry) Thompson
AGE AT EXECUTION	36
DATE OF EXECUTION	Tuesday, 9th March, 1926
PLACE OF EXECUTION	Maidstone
HANGMAN	Thomas Pierrepoint
ASSISTANT	William Willis
DATE OF TRIAL	20th February, 1926
LOCATION OF TRIAL	Maidstone
PRESIDING JUDGE	Mister Justice Horridge
PROSECUTION COUNSEL	Mister Rentoul
DEFENCE COUNSEL	Mister Sharp
NUMBER OF VICTIMS	1

VICTIMS DETAILS	
NAME	Rose Smith
AGE	41
DATE OF MURDER	Monday, 8th February, 1926
PLACE OF MURDER	36 Cross Street, Chatham, Kent
METHOD OF KILLING	Cut throat
RELATIONSHIP TO KILLER	Girlfriend

full statement, again confessing his guilt, with the words: "I did it. I am guilty. I will just be as game to peg out myself."

In fact, this was a bad time for the town of Chatham. Three days after the attack on Rose Smith, Constable Francis Gregory cut the throats of his two children, Joyce aged four and two-year-old Audrey. Later the same day, he slashed his own throat and died from the injury.

GEORGE THOMAS AND his girlfriend, Marie Beddoe Thomas, had been seeing each other since December 1924. The relationship developed nicely until March 1925. On the 26th of that month, George visited Marie to complain about an insulting letter she had written to him. Marie refused to speak to him but her mother handed George a note Marie had written, saying simply that she was sorry.

The romance apparently being over, both George and Marie started seeing other people and both became unofficially engaged to their new paramours. However, the original feelings were still there and the couple started writing to each other and meeting up again.

As they did not wish to cause any scandal or hurt they people they were now seeing, these assignations were in secret. The two often used a young friend, Angelina Mary Francis, as a go-between.

For some reason, Marie wished to make George more protective towards her and told him that the new man in her life had been hitting her. The stories were untrue but they had the desired effect, and by the summer, George was telling Angelina that he and Marie intended to marry and get a position together.

The months drifted on and George's plans failed to materialise. By December, the pressure had begun to tell on him and he was growing more and more desperate to escape from this difficult situation. On December 4th, George bought himself a new knife, from a gentleman named David Sallis.

Two days later, as Marie and Harriett Maud Lewis were about to enter the chapel for evening service, George appeared and seemed to push Marie a couple of times. She fell to the floor and Harriett then realised that George had a knife in his hand. As she watched, he turned the blade upon himself and inflicted a serious wound in his chest.

There could be little doubt that George Thomas had intended to kill himself. He had already posted notes to this effect to Marie's mother, Angelina Francis, and an old family friend. George, however, recovered from his wounds and faced a charge of murder.

The jury considered their verdict for 50

NAME	George Thomas
AGE AT EXECUTION	26
DATE OF EXECUTION	Tuesday, 9th March, 1926
PLACE OF EXECUTION	Cardiff
HANGMAN	Robert Baxter
ASSISTANT	Thomas Phillips
DATE OF TRIAL	16th February, 1926
LOCATION OF TRIAL	Cardiff
PRESIDING JUDGE	Mister Justice Frazer
PROSECUTION COUNSEL	Artemus Jones, John Grace
DEFENCE COUNSEL	T.W. Langman
NUMBER OF VICTIMS	1

VICTIMS DETAILS	
NAME	Marie Beddoe Thomas
AGE	19
DATE OF MURDER	Sunday, 6th December, 1925
PLACE OF MURDER	Outside Zion Chapel, Wine Street, Pontlottyn, Rhymney Valley
METHOD OF KILLING	Stabbed
RELATIONSHIP TO KILLER	Girlfriend

minutes and at the end of that time, recommended George Thomas to mercy. He was however executed on the same day as Henry Thompson.

O N AUGUST 1ST, 1925, William Clark took a new wife, Frances, even though she was pregnant at the time with another man's child.

William knew full well who the father was. For three years, Frances had been seeing William Thorpe, but when she told him that she was with child, he refused to marry her. Luckily for Frances, she found a man who was willing to stand by her and it must have been with some relief that she changed her name from Godfrey to Clark.

After the wedding, the Clarks went to live with Frances's mother, Sarah Harriet Godfrey, at 9 Clarke Street, Bolton. They had been married just over three months when William Thorpe decided that although he did not want to marry Frances, he objected to the fact that someone else had.

On the morning of November 20th, William Clark rose for work at 5.00am and, after having his breakfast, left the house, locked the door and pushed the key under the door. One hour later, Sarah Godfrey heard a scream from her daughter-in-law's room. As Sarah dressed herself quickly, she heard the noise of footsteps on the stair. It was a tread she recognised easily.

When Sarah finally reached Frances, she found her lying on the bed with her throat gashed. Even though she was badly wounded, Frances managed to gasp one word: "Thorpe." It was not as if Sarah Godfrey required any confirmation of who the attacker had been. Thorpe only had one leg and as such, it was easy to determine that the footfalls had belonged to him.

Thorpe was picked up at his lodgings at 1 Crompton Fold, Bolton. He told the officers that after killing Frances he had tried to drown himself and produced a quantity of wet clothing to prove this. It transpired that since her marriage, Frances had been writing to Thorpe and it was plain that some of the feeling between them still survived.

It had all been too much for Thorpe, who couldn't stand the idea of the woman he had loved being with another man. With this in mind he had gone to her house, broken a window in the kitchen, entered her room and cut her throat.

NAME	William Henry Thorpe
AGE AT EXECUTION	45
DATE OF EXECUTION	Tuesday, 16th March, 1926
PLACE OF EXECUTION	Manchester
HANGMAN	William Willis
ASSISTANT	Not known
DATE OF TRIAL	24th February, 1926
LOCATION OF TRIAL	Manchester
PRESIDING JUDGE	Mister Justice Wright
PROSECUTION COUNSEL	Mister Laski
DEFENCE COUNSEL	Mister Gorman
NUMBER OF VICTIMS	1

VICTIMS DETAILS	
NAME	Frances Clark
AGE	39
DATE OF MURDER	Friday, 20th November, 1925
PLACE OF MURDER	9 Clarke Street, Bolton
METHOD OF KILLING	Cut throat
RELATIONSHIP TO KILLER	Ex-girlfriend

LOCK AH TAM was a successful Chinese businessman who had lived in Liverpool for some 30 years. Life was good until February 1918 when a group of Russian sailors decided to cause trouble in the Chinese Progress Club that Lock had founded. In the ensuing fight, Lock sustained a severe head wound and from that day onwards was subject to violent mood swings.

Although Lock never physically harmed his family, some of the rows, especially between him and his son, Lock Ling, were very tempestuous indeed. Fearful of the damage he might do to his beloved son, Lock Ah Tam sent Lock Ling to college in China.

The troubles were not confined just to Lock's new mood swings, however. In 1924 he suffered a severe business reversal that almost sent him to the bankruptcy courts. It served only to make a bad situation worse.

In November 1925, Lock's son returned from China. It was decided that a family party should be organised to celebrate and this took place on the night of December 1st, 1925. By all accounts, it was a great success. Then, in the early hours of the following morning, when all the guests had left, the mood swings returned.

Lock began to rage against his family until his son ran off to find a policeman. Whilst he was away, Lock Ah Tam finally snapped.

Constable Drysdale was on duty at Birkenhead Central Police Station. It had been a fairly quiet night when the telephone rang.

The caller was speaking in a foreign accent and it was very difficult to understand what he was getting at. Finally Drysdale was able to distinguish what had happened. Lock Ah Tam identified himself and asked the officer to send help: "Send you folks, please, I have killed my wife and children. "

In fact, Lock Ah Tam had shot three people. His wife and daughter, Cecilia, were already dead. Doris had also been shot and was to die soon from her wounds. Lock himself was calmly smoking a cigarette, waiting for the police to take him away.

The defence was one of insanity. However, it was pointed out that as soon as he had shot three members of his family, Lock had telephoned the police, which meant that he understood what he had done.

NAME	Lock Ah Tam
AGE AT EXECUTION	54
DATE OF EXECUTION	Tuesday, 23rd March, 1926
PLACE OF EXECUTION	Liverpool
HANGMAN	William Willis
ASSISTANT	Henry Pollard
DATE OF TRIAL	5th February – 6th February, 1926
LOCATION OF TRIAL	Chester
PRESIDING JUDGE	Mister Justice MacKinnon
PROSECUTION COUNSEL	Sir Ellis Griffith, Austin Jones
DEFENCE COUNSEL	Sir Edward Marshall Hall, John Grace M.P.
NUMBER OF VICTIMS	3

VICTIMS DETAILS

NAMES	Catherine Ah Tam; Doris Ah Tam (Died, Thursday, 21st January)
AGES	42; 19
DATE OF MURDER	Wednesday, 2nd December, 1925
PLACE OF MURDER	122 Prince Street, Birkenhead
METHOD OF KILLING	Shot; shot
RELATIONSHIP TO KILLER	Wife; daughter

NAME	Cecilia Ah Tam
AGE	17
DATE OF MURDER	Wednesday, 2nd December, 1925
PLACE OF MURDER	122 Prince Street, Birkenhead
METHOD OF KILLING	Shot
RELATIONSHIP TO KILLER	Daughter

A T 7.50AM ON January 1st, 1926, Mrs Walker left her home at 58 Arlington Road, Camden Town, to go to work. When she left, the only person remaining in the house was her daughter, Polly.

Less than half an hour later, Kathleen Lukey, who lived in rooms below the Walkers, heard a scream. Very soon afterwards, Kathleen heard the sounds of someone leaving the house, but did not see fit to report what she had heard.

Some hours later, at 1.00pm, Mrs Walker returned home. There being no sign of Polly, Mrs Walker went upstairs and there she found the body of her daughter, lying partly underneath her bed. Polly had been battered about the head. A bloodstained poker lay on the floor, as did a broken pair of heavy tongs. The killer had also strangled Polly, who had a stocking tied tightly around her throat.

Eugene de Vere, who lived nearby, had been paying attention to Polly for some time, though she had done little to encourage him. De Vere was insanely jealous and this had been made clear at a Christmas party held a few days before.

A young man named Alfred Leonard Miall had visited the Walkers and had offered to take Polly for a ride on his motorcycle. De Vere had made such a fuss that Polly had turned down Miall's offer. A later invitation to accompany Miall to a dance also met with objections and de Vere threatened to punch Miall if he persisted.

At a second party, held on New Year's Eve, Mrs Walker had told de Vere that if he kept on bothering Polly, she would be forced to send her away. That same night, de Vere lay awake in his room at 32 Delaney Street. At 7.00am, he was heard leaving by his landlady, Dorothy Wilkinson.

De Vere had a key to Polly's house. He let himself in and put the kettle on. A few moments later, Polly came downstairs in her night-dress and dressing gown. There was some argument and de Vere then ran after her and killed her in her bedroom.

On January 3rd, de Vere was arrested at a temperance hotel in Hitchin. He had walked most of the 32 miles and when arrested, admitted responsibility for Polly's death. De

NAME	Ewen Anderson Stitchell (Eugene de Vere)
AGE AT EXECUTION	25
DATE OF EXECUTION	Wednesday, 24th March, 1926
PLACE OF EXECUTION	Pentonville
HANGMAN	Robert Baxter
ASSISTANT	Thomas Phillips
DATE OF TRIAL	11th February – 12th February, 1926
LOCATION OF TRIAL	Old Bailey
PRESIDING JUDGE	Mister Justice Salter
PROSECUTION COUNSEL	Eustace Fulton, G.D. Roberts, Ronald Powell
DEFENCE COUNSEL	G.G. Raphael, M. Stevenson
NUMBER OF VICTIMS	1

VICTIMS DETAILS	
NAME	Polly Edith Walker
AGE	16
DATE OF MURDER	Friday, 1st January, 1926
PLACE OF MURDER	58 Arlington Road, Camden Town, London
METHOD OF KILLING	Strangled/battered
RELATIONSHIP TO KILLER	None

Vere, however, claimed provocation and showed a bite wound on his finger. At his trial it was pointed out that the small wound he had received, even if it had been inflicted by Polly, was hardly grounds for murder.

In his summing-up, the judge clarified the law on provocation. For the charge to be reduced to manslaughter, the amount of provocation had to be such that the average man would find it intolerable. The jury did not believe that Polly had provoked de Vere to this extent.

GEORGE SHARPLES HAD spent four years in a reformatory for breaking into a church at Crewe. Determined to make a fresh start, George moved down to Warwickshire, where he managed to get a job at Manor Farm.

Arthur Cecil Crabtree, who ran the farm, and his wife, Milly, were fully aware of George's past, and unfortunately Milly took it upon herself to tell everyone she met about it too.

George was very unhappy when it became general knowledge that he had been in a reformatory and decided that it might be better if he emigrated to Canada. He soon discovered that the Canadian authorities were refusing to take anyone with a criminal record. Reluctantly, George settled down to make the best of things.

George's only pleasure was his radio, which he spent long hours listening to. To begin with, George lived on the farm and his 10/- a week wage was enough to pay for his few simple pleasures. Then he was told he would have to find lodgings. He did receive a pay rise, taking his money to 27s 9d a week, but his lodgings now cost him £1, reducing his disposable income to less than 8/-. It now took him two full weeks to save 10/- to pay for a new licence for his beloved radio.

George thought about his troubles and came to believe that many of them had been caused by Milly Crabtree. She had told everyone about his past. The more George brooded, the more he determined that he wanted to kill her.

At 9.00am on January 13th, 1926, George went to work at the farm, and in the afternoon saw Milly pass by him. He saw her again later and on the third occasion, as she walked by, he took up a hammer and struck her on the head.

Dragging her into the front room, George struck Milly again and when she would not stop making a noise, wrapped some pyjamas around her head. Having determined that Milly was dead, George took a knife from a work bench and cut his throat, twice. Finding that he was still alive he then found a bottle marked 'poison', and drank it down, before laying down on a bed.

NAME	George Sharples
AGE AT EXECUTION	20
DATE OF EXECUTION	Tuesday, 13th April, 1926
PLACE OF EXECUTION	Birmingham
HANGMAN	William Willis
ASSISTANT	Robert Baxter
DATE OF TRIAL	9th March, 1926
LOCATION OF TRIAL	Birmingham
PRESIDING JUDGE	Mister Justice Shearman
PROSECUTION COUNSEL	J.G. Hunt, Leslie Marks
DEFENCE COUNSEL	T.R. Fitzwalker Butler
NUMBER OF VICTIMS	1

VICTIMS DETAILS	
NAME	Milly Illingworth Crabtree
AGE	25
DATE OF MURDER	Wednesday, 13th January, 1926
PLACE OF MURDER	Manor Farm, Ladbroke, Warwickshire
METHOD OF KILLING	Battered
RELATIONSHIP TO KILLER	None

It was Kathleen Agnes Crabtree, Milly's 10-year-old daughter, who found George. She had gone upstairs to tell her mother that the baby was crying. Milly Crabtree was already dead but George was rushed to the hospital, where he made a full recovery. Once he was well enough he was charged with murder and made a full statement confessing his guilt and detailing the reasons why he had done what he had.

On April 13th, George Sharples was executed for a brutal murder. But one wonders if things might just have been a little different had he really been given the second chance he so desperately craved.

LOUIE CALVERT EARNED her living as a prostitute and used many names in her trade. When she met Arthur Calvert early in 1925, she was using the name Louise Jackson and it was as Jackson that she was employed as his housekeeper, at 7 Railway Place, Leeds.

After six months Louie told Arthur she was pregnant. Although it was a lie, Arthur believed it and married her on August 5th, 1925. As the months went by, and there were no signs of the baby, Arthur grew suspicious. Louie then showed Arthur a letter from her sister in Dewsbury, inviting her to stay there. The letter was written by Louie herself.

On March 8th, 1926, Louie set off for Dewsbury, and on arrival sent Arthur a telegram. She then returned to Leeds, where she moved in with an old friend, Lily Waterhouse and put an advertisement in the Yorkshire Evening Post, offering a good home to a baby girl. A young mother answered and Louie agreed to adopt her baby.

Unfortunately, Lily had noticed that several items had vanished and believed that Louie had stolen them. On March 31st, she went to the police and took out a summons. At about 7.00pm, that night, a neighbour heard some strange noises coming from Lily's house. Soon afterwards Louie stepped out, carrying the baby and a large bag. She returned home to Arthur who was delighted with his new daughter.

At 5.00am on April 1st, Louie was seen by neighbours returning to Lily's house at Amberley Road. She left shortly afterwards carrying a large suitcase. When Arthur saw the case, Louie said that it held baby clothes from her sister.

On the same day, the summons that Lily had taken out, came up in court. When Lily did not appear, the police went to investigate. The officer received no answer to his knocking but gained access and found the body of Lily on the floor of one of the bedrooms.

A search revealed a letter to Louie Calvert. That evening, Detective Superintendent Pass visited the Calverts. Louie opened the door wearing Lily's headscarf and boots and when she told the story about the suitcase, Pass lifted it and said that it was much too heavy

NAME	Louie Calvert (Jackson)
AGE AT EXECUTION	33
DATE OF EXECUTION	Thursday, 24th June, 1926
PLACE OF EXECUTION	Manchester
HANGMAN	Thomas Pierrepoint
ASSISTANT	William Willis
DATE OF TRIAL	May, 1926
LOCATION OF TRIAL	Leeds
PRESIDING JUDGE	Mister Justice Wright
PROSECUTION COUNSEL	Mister Pashley
DEFENCE COUNSEL	E.G. Chappell
NUMBER OF VICTIMS	1 (probably 2)

VICTIMS DETAILS	
NAME	Lily Waterhouse
AGE	40
DATE OF MURDER	Wednesday, 31st March, 1926
PLACE OF MURDER	30 Amberley Road, Leeds
METHOD OF KILLING	Battered/strangled
RELATIONSHIP TO KILLER	None

for baby clothes. Upon opening it he discovered cutlery and crockery stolen from Lily Waterhouse. Louie was arrested.

Louie was tried and found guilty and when asked if she had anything to say, replied that she was pregnant. A doctor examined Louie, returning to court to say that it was a lie.

As the execution date approached, Louie made one last attempt to save her life, by admitting to another murder, that of John William Frobisher, in 1922. Frobisher's body had been found floating in a canal and had been identified by his housekeeper, Louisa Jackson, who was none other than Louie Calvert. However, this late confession failed to save her from the gallows.

IT IS THE DUTY of a jury to return a verdict in a criminal trial and where that verdict is guilty, they must be satisfied of that guilt, beyond a reasonable doubt. That last phrase is crucially important and sometimes, it is difficult to see that a jury has genuinely understood that fact. Such a case was that of the Dutchman Johannes Mommers.

At first, the case against Mommers looked to be a very strong one. He and Augusta Pionbini were nothing more than friends and on the evening of May 7th, 1926, had gone for a walk together after spending some time in a local pub.

At 10.00pm, Augusta's sister, Olive, heard a scream. Concerned, Olive woke her mother, who went downstairs to investigate. Walking into the kitchen she found Augusta with her throat cut. The young girl managed to gasp, "Oh Mummy, save me, save me", before she collapsed, dying 50 minutes later.

When Mommers was interviewed, he handed a razor over to the police. He said he had found Augusta with the razor in her hand, had taken it from her and put it into his pocket. He had then left and walked home. He had no idea that Augusta had already hurt herself, but if she was dead, he felt that it had to be a case of suicide. When Mommers's clothing was checked, bloodstains were discovered and he was charged with murder.

Augusta Pionbini was dead, but was it murder or suicide? The prosecution claimed that Mommers, a married man, was jealous of Augusta and killed her because she rejected him. The defence argument was that Augusta had wanted to go away with Mommers and when he refused, she cut her own throat. In such a case, reliance should therefore be placed on the medical evidence.

If Mommers had murdered Augusta, one might have expected to have found defence wounds on her hands or arms. Doctor Bronte, the pathologist, found no such wounds and testified that the direction and position of the wound was consistent with suicide. Admittedly, under cross-examination, he agreed that the wound was not inconsistent with a case of homicide, but at no stage did he say that the cut could not have been self-inflicted.

NAME	Johannes Josephus Cornelius Mommers
AGE AT EXECUTION	43
DATE OF EXECUTION	Tuesday, 27th July, 1926
PLACE OF EXECUTION	Pentonville
HANGMAN	Robert Baxter
ASSISTANT	William Willis
DATE OF TRIAL	16th June, 1926
LOCATION OF TRIAL	Chelmsford
PRESIDING JUDGE	Mister Justice Shearman
PROSECUTION COUNSEL	Sir Edward Marshall-Hall
DEFENCE COUNSEL	Mister Fior
NUMBER OF VICTIMS	1

VICTIMS DETAILS	
NAME	Augusta Violette Pionbini
AGE	22
DATE OF MURDER	Friday, 7th May, 1926
PLACE OF MURDER	Thundersley, Essex
METHOD OF KILLING	Cut throat
RELATIONSHIP TO KILLER	None

Doctor Hugh Ernest Griffiths also gave evidence. He was a Harley Street surgeon and a most eminent man in his field. He testified that Augusta's wounds were more consistent with suicide than murder. So, both experts seemed to indicate that Mommers could have been telling the truth.

This evidence surely should have put a seed of doubt in the minds of the jury, but they still returned a verdict of guilty. On July 27th, Johannes Mommers, possibly an innocent man, was executed at Pentonville.

WHEN JAMES SMITH tied the knot with Catherine, in January 1925, she had already been married once and brought two children to the new relationship. Unfortunately, largely due to James's terrible jealousy, there were problems from the beginning and by early 1926, Catherine had already left her new husband on three occasions, returning each time and trying, unsuccessfully to make a go of things.

In February 1926, James and Catherine parted for what was to be the last time and she returned, once again, to her parents' house at Silver Street, where her 16-year-old sister, Ellen Scott, also lived.

Catherine Smith's mother, also named Catherine Scott, owned another house at 23 Silver Street, and this was let out to number of families and individuals. Mrs Scott often checked on things as she was passing and when, on April 18th, she saw a number of men gambling there, including her son-in-law, James Smith, she wasted no time in calling the police.

Officers called, stopped the game and took a number of names for possible further action. James Smith was far from pleased and the following day, he and a few others, assembled outside number 6, and began shouting abuse and threats. Mrs Scott threatened to call the police again and the demonstration broke up, but not before James had threatened to take his revenge.

Ellen Scott left the house, on an errand, at 1.50pm on April 19th. When she left, her mother and sister were alone in the house but by the time she returned at 2.30pm, James Smith was also there, talking to his wife on the top landing of the house. Around 15 minutes later, Ellen and her mother heard a cry and went out to find Smith pulling his wife down the stairs. Catherine Smith was bleeding heavily from a wound in her breast. Without waiting to be told, Ellen Scott ran to fetch the police, returning soon afterwards with Constable Michael Hedley Smith.

James Smith had not gone very far. He had run outside and bumped into an old friend, Francis Patrick Simon to whom he had handed the bloodstained knife, asking him to go for the police. Simon did not need to do as

NAME	James Smith
AGE AT EXECUTION	23
DATE OF EXECUTION	Tuesday, 10th August, 1926
PLACE OF EXECUTION	Durham
HANGMAN	Thomas Pierrepoint
ASSISTANT	Thomas Philips
DATE OF TRIAL	2nd July, 1926
LOCATION OF TRIAL	Newcastle-upon-Tyne
PRESIDING JUDGE	Mister Justice Wright
PROSECUTION COUNSEL	Russell Vick
DEFENCE COUNSEL	Archibald Wilson
NUMBER OF VICTIMS	1

VICTIMS DETAILS	
NAME	Catherine Smith
AGE	26
DATE OF MURDER	Monday, 26th April, 1926
PLACE OF MURDER	6 Silver Street, Newcastle-upon-Tyne
METHOD OF KILLING	Stabbed
RELATIONSHIP TO KILLER	Wife

Smith had asked, for very soon, Constable Smith appeared and the knife was handed over to him.

James Smith tried to put forward a plea of insanity. At the magistrate's hearing he would only say: "I am not guilty, sir. I did not know what I was doing." At his trial, the jury felt that there was nothing in his plea and Smith was condemned to death.

ON THE EVENING of Sunday, June 6th, two gypsies walking across a field near Alton found, beneath a clump of bushes, the body of 14-year-old John Richard Thompson. John had been strangled with his own necktie and there were also wounds on his head that might have been deliberately inflicted, or perhaps caused when his body fell to the ground.

Thompson worked at Old Farm, for Captain Cookson and that gentleman confirmed that on the afternoon of Saturday, June 5th, he had paid the boy his wages, in the form of a 10/- note and two half crowns. Thompson had also been given a shilling to pay for some chicken meal that was needed at the farm and inquiries revealed that he had left the shop at around 5.00pm. Shortly afterwards, Thompson had been seen on the road that led to Basingstoke and at that time, he had been with a man.

It wasn't long before police felt sure that they had a name for the man seen with Thompson. On June 7th, Charles Edward Finden was taken in for questioning. Finden confessed that he had been in the area where the body was discovered but that he had fallen asleep in an area known as Flood Meadows. He had been there from around 2.30pm until 6.15pm.

A much more interesting story was told by Finden's wife. She told police officers that on June 5th, Finden had given her some money – a 10/- note and two half crowns. He told her that he had earned this money by doing some labouring work on the nearby tennis courts. When officers went to check this story, they discovered that Finden had never worked on the courts and this led them to charge him with the murder of John Thompson.

Finden tried his best to come up with a convincing story. He now claimed that the money had been unemployment benefit. Then he said he had been for a long walk and could name witnesses who had seen him along the way. The coincidence of the sum of money known to be in Thompson's possession and the one that Finden had given to his wife proved to be much too strong for the defence to break, however.

After an absence of 45 minutes, Charles

NAME	Charles Edward Finden
AGE AT EXECUTION	22
DATE OF EXECUTION	Thursday, 12th August, 1926
PLACE OF EXECUTION	Winchester
HANGMAN	Thomas Pierrepoint
ASSISTANT	Robert Baxter
DATE OF TRIAL	5th July – 6th July, 1926
LOCATION OF TRIAL	Winchester
PRESIDING JUDGE	Mister Justice Roche
PROSECUTION COUNSEL	Ernest Charles, T.J. O'Connor
DEFENCE COUNSEL	A.H. Armstrong
NUMBER OF VICTIMS	1

VICTIMS DETAILS	
NAME	John Richard Thompson
AGE	14
DATE OF MURDER	Saturday, 5th June, 1926
PLACE OF MURDER	Alton, Hampshire
METHOD OF KILLING	Battered/strangled
RELATIONSHIP TO KILLER	None

Edward Finden was found guilty and sentenced to death.

A SLAM KHAN ZARDAD had just completed his spell on watch, on board the China. The ship was preparing to sail later that day and Zardad and the young man he shared a cabin with, Khannar Jung Baz, had been together on the four-to-eight watch.

It was now 10.00am and Zardad lay on his bunk, relaxing. Baz had already been in his bed for the best part of an hour and was by now sound asleep. Zardad lay awake for an hour or so and was then surprised to see someone creeping into the cabin.

The figure was that of Hashankhan Samander and as Zardad watched, he crept into the cabin, left, returned and then left again. Then, when Samander returned for the third time, Zardad saw that he had a knife in his hand. Without further ceremony, Samander rushed to Baz's bed and stabbed him.

Baz woke immediately and cried out, only to receive two more wounds. The killer then crept back out of the cabin and, followed carefully by Zardad, made his way towards the second engineer's cabin. Here Zardad raised the alarm and Samander was taken into custody.

There had been bad blood between Baz and Samander almost from the first time they had met. Originally those two and Zardad had signed on the China at Bromley. From there they had been transferred to the S.S. Kalyan, before being moved back to the China. The first signs of trouble came on the Kalyan.

On May 9th, exactly two months before the murder, Baz had been fined two days' pay for attacking Samander with a pair of hair clippers, causing some deep wounds on his arms. The relationship between the two had not improved since that time.

At his trial, Samander made a futile attempt to put the blame onto someone else. He said that at about 9.30am on the morning of the murder, he had seen two men come on board the China. Shortly afterwards, he had gone ashore and when he returned at just before 11.00am, the two men were getting ready to leave. As Samander spoke to one of the men, the other said he needed to use the toilet and headed off towards the cabin where the terrible crime was committed. The next

NAME	Hashankhan Samander
AGE AT EXECUTION	36
DATE OF EXECUTION	Tuesday, 2nd November, 1926
PLACE OF EXECUTION	Pentonville
HANGMAN	Robert Baxter
ASSISTANT	Thomas Phillips
DATE OF TRIAL	14th September, 1926
LOCATION OF TRIAL	Old Bailey
PRESIDING JUDGE	Mister Justice Wright
PROSECUTION COUNSEL	Sir Travers Humphreys
DEFENCE COUNSEL	A.B. Lucy
NUMBER OF VICTIMS	1

VICTIMS DETAILS	
NAME	Khannar Jung Baz
AGE	23
DATE OF MURDER	Friday, 9th July, 1926
PLACE OF MURDER	On board the S.S. China, at Tilbury Docks, Essex
METHOD OF KILLING	Stabbed
RELATIONSHIP TO KILLER	None

thing he knew, he was being surrounded by other crewmen who said that he had just killed Khannar Baz. His defence therefore was that he knew nothing of the crime and he was not the assailant.

The jury preferred the story of Zardad the eye-witness, and Samander was found guilty of murder.

1926

JAMES LEAH HAD a drink problem and when he drank, he became quarrelsome. His family bore the brunt of his tantrums and one of his chief bones of contention seemed to be the attention that young men paid to his two daughters, Elsie and Louise.

On September 23rd, 1926, James had a major row with Elsie and her boyfriend, Frank Holland. So bad was this argument, that Elsie swore she would leave the house the following day. What James did not know at the time was that his other daughter, and his wife, had decided to go as well.

The next day, the three women left the house, but later Elsie and Louise returned to help tidy up and whilst they were there, Elsie was kind enough to prepare some food for her father. Afterwards, Elsie finished a little bit more packing and then left to find a taxi cab, leaving Louise alone with James, at Findlow Farm.

William Slater, a labourer, was enjoying his lunch break on Dickens Farm, some 300 yards from Findlow. It was just after noon when Slater saw a young girl, covered in blood, stagger to the back door of Dickens Farm, and enter the kitchen.

The foreman at Dickens Farm was William Leah, James's cousin. He was in the kitchen when Louise staggered in, bleeding badly from a wound in her throat. Louise's other sister, Margaret was also there and rushed to her sister's aid, but it was too late to save her.

James Leah was found soon afterwards, hiding in a fodder bin on the farm. He also had a wound in his throat but managed to gasp: "I did her in the kitchen. I then cut myself with the hay knife and then came in here to finish it with my knife. She is the best girl I have got and I couldn't bear her to go. My poor Louise."

James was duly convicted of murder but the jury did recommend him to mercy, understanding at least in part, the anguish he had suffered. The law took its course, though, and James Leah was hanged at Liverpool in November.

NAME	James Leah
AGE AT EXECUTION	60
DATE OF EXECUTION	Tuesday, 16th November, 1926
PLACE OF EXECUTION	Liverpool
HANGMAN	Thomas Pierrepoint
ASSISTANT	Lionel Mann
DATE OF TRIAL	27th October, 1926
LOCATION OF TRIAL	Chester
PRESIDING JUDGE	Mister Justice Fraser
PROSECUTION COUNSEL	Bertram Long
DEFENCE COUNSEL	Dallas Walters
NUMBER OF VICTIMS	1

VICTIMS DETAILS	
NAME	Louise Leah
AGE	20
DATE OF MURDER	Friday, 24th September, 1926
PLACE OF MURDER	Findlow Farm, Over Alderley
METHOD OF KILLING	Stabbed
RELATIONSHIP TO KILLER	Daughter

EVERY CLICHÉ HAS an element of truth and this was certainly the case with Charles Houghton. For once, the butler really did it!

Houghton had worked for the Woodhouse sisters for some 22 years, first as a footman and then as a butler. His work had always been satisfactory but then, in the summer of 1926, things began to change. Houghton took to drink, and his work began to suffer.

The sisters spoke to him on a number of occasions but nothing seemed to do the trick. Finally, on September 6th, 1926, Houghton was given 24 hours' notice, though he was also given a month's wages in lieu of compensation. Houghton protested that he needed more time. The sisters would not reconsider his dismissal, but he was eventually told that he could stay on until the end of the week. For the time being, that is where the matter was allowed to rest.

The following morning, Houghton made the ladies breakfast as usual and then, when he had cleared things away, he took a revolver and shot both Eleanor and Martha.

When the police arrived, they discovered that Houghton had locked himself into his room and could not be persuaded to come out. The door was forced and it was discovered that Houghton had cut his own throat. The wound was not life-threatening, however, and he recovered soon afterwards, in hospital.

Found guilty of murder, Houghton's original execution date was postponed when the authorities were notified that he wished to appeal against his sentence. The appeal was subsequently withdrawn and a new date set.

NAME	Charles Houghton
AGE AT EXECUTION	45
DATE OF EXECUTION	Friday, 3rd December, 1926
PLACE OF EXECUTION	Gloucester
HANGMAN	Thomas Pierrepoint
ASSISTANT	Not known
DATE OF TRIAL	5th November, 1926
LOCATION OF TRIAL	Hereford
PRESIDING JUDGE	Mister Justice Swift
PROSECUTION COUNSEL	Ronald Powell
DEFENCE COUNSEL	A.J. Long
NUMBER OF VICTIMS	2

VICTIMS DETAILS	
NAME	Eleanor Drinkwater Woodhouse; Martha Gordon Woodhouse
AGE	65; 57
DATE OF MURDER	Tuesday, 7th September, 1926
PLACE OF MURDER	Burghill Court, near Hereford
METHOD OF KILLING	Shot; shot
RELATIONSHIP TO KILLER	None; none

1926

WILLIAM JONES MARRIED Winifred on October 31st, 1925. Almost from the beginning it was not a happy match and William began ill-treating Winifred. By March 1926, Winifred was pregnant, but William's behaviour had not improved. She had had enough and went to see a solicitor.

It was March 8th when Winifred first saw Robert Wilkinson and made her complaint about William's treatment of her. He considered the matter and then, on March 26th, sent a solicitor's letter to William, demanding that he apologise, in writing, for his behaviour, or face the magistrates. William did send the required letter, but it did nothing to improve relations with his wife.

Winifred went to see Wilkinson again and on July 7th, he wrote a second letter to William. In this, Wilkinson pointed out that as Winifred was due to be confined soon, he had advised her to leave until after she had given birth. The letter went on to ask what William was prepared to do about maintenance for his wife and, when it was born, his child.

Three days later, on July 10th, William Jones, together with his mother, went to see Wilkinson at his offices. William said his wife was lying about his treatment of her and refused to make any offer of maintenance. The matter was left unresolved.

William was a member of the territorial army and that afternoon, he and others from his unit were to attend rifle practice on a local range. He attended the local drill hall and was issued with a rifle by the Quartermaster, Thomas Daniel Hart. William and others then began walking to the range.

Winifred was walking with a friend, Mary Ann Whitaker, in Corporation Street. They saw Jones but did not acknowledge him and though they were walking in the same direction, they stayed on opposite sides of the street. William cut through to Crib Lane, where he lived, and waited for Winifred to appear at the bottom of the street. When she did, a shot rang out and Winifred fell, to die soon afterwards.

William Jones claimed that the shooting was an accident. As he had been walking along, he explained, he had dropped his rifle and there must have been a round in the

NAME	William Cornelius Jones
AGE AT EXECUTION	22
DATE OF EXECUTION	Wednesday, 5th January, 1927
PLACE OF EXECUTION	Leeds
HANGMAN	Thomas Pierrepoint
ASSISTANT	Robert Baxter
DATE OF TRIAL	3rd December, 1926
LOCATION OF TRIAL	Leeds
PRESIDING JUDGE	Mister Justice MacCardie
PROSECUTION COUNSEL	C.F. Lowenthal, Reginald Ross
DEFENCE COUNSEL	R.F. Burnand
NUMBER OF VICTIMS	1

VICTIMS DETAILS	
NAME	Winifred Jones
AGE	18
DATE OF MURDER	Saturday, 10th July, 1926
PLACE OF MURDER	Crib Lane, Halifax
METHOD OF KILLING	Shot
RELATIONSHIP TO KILLER	Wife

breach, for it went off, much to his surprise. Unfortunately for him, a number of people gave evidence that led to a different interpretation.

To begin with, Thomas Hart said that all the rifles had been inspected before issue and none had rounds in the breach. Alice Mary Ward, a neighbour of Williams, testified that she had seen him put something into the breach of his rifle whilst he was waiting in Crib Street. Ada Greenwood, another neighbour, said she had seen William lift the rifle to his shoulder and take deliberate aim. All this was enough to demolish William's defence and convince the jury of his guilt.

1927

MADGE MAGGS DIDN'T like her first name and preferred to be called Daisy. A young and attractive girl, she lived with her brother and sister at 5 Grinstead Road, Deptford.

For some years, Daisy had been friendly with James Frederick Stratton, who lived with his grandmother at 7 Homerton Terrace, Morning Lane, Hackney. Things were fine until Christmas Day, 1926 when Daisy told him that the relationship was over.

Frederick wanted the friendship to continue and for a time, the two did meet up occasionally. They arranged to meet on Sunday, February 20th but to Frederick's dismay, Daisy did not turn up. He travelled to Deptford to discover what had happened to her and found her with another man.

The following day, Daisy was working at the International Exhibition at White City. Frederick knew about this and sent a message to her by means of an errand boy, Edmund Hean. When no reply came, a second message was sent with a delivery man, John Welch and this time Daisy replied and agreed to meet Frederick at Liverpool Street station at 7.30pm.

Frederick left his lodgings in time to meet Daisy and took with him a knife and an iron last, wrapped up in a piece of rag. The couple met and at one stage, Frederick went into the 'Mermaid' public house for a Guinness whilst she waited outside. When he came out, Frederick asked Daisy why she had stood him up on the previous evening and an argument developed. She denied that she was involved with another man, even when Frederick said he had seen them together.

They walked to Broad Street Station, where Frederick bought two return tickets to Hackney. Getting into a third-class carriage, nothing more was heard until the train stopped at signals close to Graham Street. A number of passengers then saw Frederick leap down from his carriage and walk along the line until he reached the engine. Here he shouted up to the fireman, Walter Edward Tidd, and told him that he had just murdered his ex-girlfriend, adding: " I hope she is dead, or it will mean ten years for me."

Daisy was indeed dead. After hitting her

NAME	James Frederick Stratton
AGE AT EXECUTION	26
DATE OF EXECUTION	Tuesday, 29th March, 1927
PLACE OF EXECUTION	Pentonville
HANGMAN	Robert Baxter
ASSISTANT	Lionel Mann
DATE OF TRIAL	8th March, 1927
LOCATION OF TRIAL	Old Bailey
PRESIDING JUDGE	Mister Justice Branson
PROSECUTION COUNSEL	Not known
DEFENCE COUNSEL	Not known
NUMBER OF VICTIMS	1

VICTIMS DETAILS	
NAME	Madge Dorothy Maggs (Daisy Dorothy Maggs)
AGE	25
DATE OF MURDER	Monday, 21st February, 1927
PLACE OF MURDER	In a railway carriage, near Graham Street, Hackney, London
METHOD OF KILLING	Stabbed/battered
RELATIONSHIP TO KILLER	Ex-girlfriend

with the last, Frederick had drawn the knife and stabbed her to death. The train was moved on and by coincidence, the body was first examined by a doctor at Dalston Junction, a location that had featured in the very first case in this book, that of Louisa Masset.

Frederick Stratton made no attempt to deny responsibility for Daisy's death. He readily confessed that he had been looking for an opportunity to 'do her in' since Christmas, and that this had been the first chance he had had.

Justice moved very swiftly and 36 days after the murder of Daisy Maggs, her killer died on the scaffold at Pentonville.

IN EFFECT, WILLIAM Knighton faced three trials before he eventually faced the hangman at Nottingham.

On the morning of Tuesday, February 8th, 1927, Knighton went into his mother's bedroom whilst she was asleep and cut her throat with a razor. There was no motive for the crime. The killer and his victim were on excellent terms and Knighton had done nothing to avoid justice. Later the same day he had given himself up to the police and admitted the killing, so that the only evidence against him was his own confession.

The defence had to be one of insanity. Evidence was called that Knighton was an epileptic but even so, he was found guilty and sentenced to death, on February 26th, 1927. The appeal was heard on March 21st, where it was further suggested that Knighton had committed the crime during an epileptic fit and that a special judgement of 'guilty but insane' should be returned. After due deliberation, the appeal was dismissed.

The entire matter was referred to the Home Secretary and when the defence supplied him with what appeared to be new evidence, the execution was cancelled and the matter sent back to the Court of Criminal Appeal.

Knighton's second appeal was heard on April 12th. The 'new' evidence was the testimony of Doris Ivy Knighton, William's sister. She testified that on the night of the murder she heard her mother coughing and moaning at approximately 1.00am. Her brother had come in shortly afterwards and asked what was the matter with their mother. Doris had then gone to check on Ada and found her dead. The suggestion was that Ada's husband had killed her and so William was totally innocent.

Doris's testimony was held to be totally spurious. William had, after all, confessed to the crime immediately after it had taken place and his father was not even called to refute the charge against him. Once again the appeal was dismissed and a new date set for the execution.

On April 27th, having lost two appeals, William Knighton was finally executed at Nottingham.

NAME	William Knighton
AGE AT EXECUTION	22
DATE OF EXECUTION	Wednesday, 27th April, 1927
PLACE OF EXECUTION	Nottingham
HANGMAN	Thomas Pierrepoint
ASSISTANT	Not known
DATE OF TRIAL	26th February, 1927
LOCATION OF TRIAL	Derby
PRESIDING JUDGE	Mister Justice Branson
PROSECUTION COUNSEL	Morris F. Healy
DEFENCE COUNSEL	Sir Henry Maddocks, T.R. Fitzwalter Butler
NUMBER OF VICTIMS	1

VICTIMS DETAILS	
NAME	Ada Knighton
AGE	55
DATE OF MURDER	Tuesday, 8th February, 1927
PLACE OF MURDER	1 Bethel Street, Ilkeston, Derbyshire
METHOD OF KILLING	Cut throat
RELATIONSHIP TO KILLER	Mother

OCCASIONALLY, THE ORDER in which things happen can assume a great deal of importance in a criminal investigation. Such a case led to the execution of two young men, Frederick Fuller and James Murphy.

James Staunton, a single man who lived alone, was the nightwatchman on a building site in Brancaster Lane, Purley. On the night of May 14th, 1927, a raid took place on that site and a large quantity of lead and brass was removed. More importantly, James Staunton had been battered and was discovered the following morning, very badly hurt.

Police inquiries at first concentrated on the theft of the lead and brass. It seemed obvious that whoever had stolen those metals had also attacked Staunton, in order to quieten him. Witnesses came forward who had spotted a grey Ford van, registration KX 871, in the vicinity, and this was traced to three men, Joseph Torch, James Cornelius Pearson and Hedley Albert McCormack. These three were picked up and charged on Thursday, May 19th, but it soon became clear that they had nothing to do with the death of James Staunton.

Inquiries now shifted to a young labourer who worked on the building site Staunton had been protecting, but who had not turned up for work on the Monday after the attack. Frederick Stephen Fuller was a married man and the father of six children; his wife was now pregnant once again. In due course he, and a friend of his, James Murphy, were traced to Doncaster and on May 23rd, they were both arrested at the Bridge Hotel in that town. They were brought back to London, and the story they told might well have saved their lives, had it been believed.

Fuller and Murphy both agreed that they had killed Staunton, but they denied murder. They said that they had gone to the site, and a fight had taken place between them and Staunton. Murphy had hit Staunton, who had fallen back and hit his head. Seeing that he was unconscious, the two men decided to rob him and, rifling his pockets, took the wages he had received the day before.

In court, it became plain that if Fuller and Murphy had gone to the site with the intention of robbing Staunton, and in the process of

NAMES	Frederick Stephen Fuller; James Murphy
AGES AT EXECUTION	35; 29
DATE OF EXECUTION	Wednesday, 3rd August, 1927
PLACE OF EXECUTION	Wandsworth
HANGMAN	Robert Baxter
ASSISTANT	Lionel Mann, Henry Pollard, Thomas Phillips
DATE OF TRIAL	5th July, 1927
LOCATION OF TRIAL	Guildford
PRESIDING JUDGE	Mister Justice Rowlatt
PROSECUTION COUNSEL	J.D. Cassels, Mister Moran
DEFENCE COUNSEL	C.R. Algar, S. Seuffert
NUMBER OF VICTIMS	1

VICTIMS DETAILS	
NAME	James Staunton (Died Tuesday, 17th May)
AGE	42
DATE OF MURDER	Saturday, 14th May, 1927
PLACE OF MURDER	Brancaster Lane, Sanderstead, London
METHOD OF KILLING	Battered
RELATIONSHIP TO KILLERS	None; none

doing so had assaulted him causing injuries that led to his death, then they were guilty of murder. However, if the robbery had followed what was a 'clean' fist fight, then Fuller and Murphy were guilty of manslaughter and their lives would be spared.

The jury faced a difficult decision, but after much deliberation, decided that the robbery came first and that therefore the two were guilty of murder. After the appeals had been heard and dismissed, the two men were hanged together at Wandsworth. In the meantime, Mrs Fuller had given birth to her seventh child.

1927

ON MAY 9TH, 1927, an unpleasant smell was noticed coming from a wicker trunk in the left-luggage department of Charing Cross Railway Station. Upon forcing open the trunk, the contents were revealed as five brown paper parcels. Inside each of those parcels was a separate portion of a female body.

The remains were sent to Sir Bernard Spilsbury, who was able to say that the cause of death had been asphyxia through strangulation, that the woman had been dead for about a week and that there were signs of bruising.

There was one other clue in the trunk, a pair of knickers in which was sewn the name P. Holt. When Mrs Holt was traced, she identified the underwear and, when given a description of the dead woman, was able to state that the body was that of Minnie Bonati.

Minnie was a prostitute and had last been seen alive on May 4th. Soon, two witnesses came forward. The first was Mr Ward, who identified the trunk as being one he had sold. The second witness was the taxi driver who had taken the trunk to Charing Cross. He had been hailed by a man standing in the doorway to offices at 86 Rochester Row.

At Rochester Row it was determined that one tenant, John Robinson, had not been seen for some days.

However, police did find a telegram addressed to Robinson at the Greyhound Hotel, in Hammersmith. This turned out to be Mrs Robinson, and she was most co-operative.

She told police that her husband met up with her occasionally. When the next meeting took place, John Robinson saw that she had a friend with her. The 'friend' identified himself as Chief Inspector George Cornish.

Robinson denied having anything to do with the death of Minnie Bonati, but a second search of the offices was organised and, in the folds of a wicker basket, police found a bloodstained match. It proved that violence had taken place and faced with this, Robinson made a statement, claiming that Minnie had propositioned him at Victoria Station. He agreed and took her back to the office where an argument broke out and they struggled.

NAME	John Robinson
AGE AT EXECUTION	36
DATE OF EXECUTION	Friday, 12th August, 1927
PLACE OF EXECUTION	Pentonville
HANGMAN	Robert Baxter
ASSISTANT	Robert Wilson
DATE OF TRIAL	11th July – 13th July, 1927
LOCATION OF TRIAL	Old Bailey
PRESIDING JUDGE	Mister Justice Swift
PROSECUTION COUNSEL	Percival Clarke
DEFENCE COUNSEL	Laurence Vine
NUMBER OF VICTIMS	1

VICTIMS DETAILS	
NAME	Minnie Alice Bonati
AGE	36
DATE OF MURDER	Wednesday, 4th May, 1927
PLACE OF MURDER	Office at 86 Rochester Row, London
METHOD OF KILLING	Strangled
RELATIONSHIP TO KILLER	None

Minnie fell and banged her head on a coal bucket. In a panic, Robinson fled the building.

The following morning Robinson discovered that Minnie still lay where she had fallen. He admitted buying the trunk and a knife to dismember her with, but he maintained that he had not killed her. Coincidentally, Robinson had purchased the knife from the same store Patrick Mahon had used in 1924!

At the trial, evidence was given to show that the injuries Minnie sustained could not have been caused by a fall against the coal bucket. Robinson's version of events collapsed and he was found guilty of murder.

ROBERT MOORE AND his wife Isabella had been married for some years and had two young children. Isabella also had a friend, Arthur Harnett, who paid regular visits to the house to see her.

In due course, Robert began to suspect that there might be more than pure friendship between Harnett and his wife and he forbade Harnett to call again. Isabella swore to Robert that there was nothing untoward going on and eventually Robert relented and gave permission for Harnett to call again as he wished. It was a decision he would come to regret.

On the afternoon of May 3rd, 1927, Robert Moore left for work at 1.00pm. Before he left, his wife told him she was going to visit the Y.M.C.A., that afternoon. When Robert returned at 10.30pm, he found the police, in the form of Constable Henry Sagar, waiting for him.

To begin with, Sagar would only say that he had received information that led him to believe that there might be something requiring his attention inside the house. They entered together and within a few minutes, they had discovered the body of Isabella, in the scullery.

In fact, the police already had the killer in custody. At some time before 10.00pm, Arthur Harnett had walked in to the Blue Bell Hotel where he had seen his friend, William Rogers. The two had a drink together and Harnett offered to sell Rogers his watch. When Rogers said he wasn't interested, Harnett gave him the watch for nothing and then also handed over the medals he had won in the war. He explained that he wouldn't need them any more, as he had killed a woman.

From there, Harnett walked to Market Street, where he found Constable Sagar. Approaching the officer, Harnett exclaimed: "Take me inside, Sagar. I have done something serious." Once inside the police station, Harnett went on to explain that he had cut a woman's throat in Westgate. He could give no motive for what he had done.

A motive is not necessary for a verdict of murder and despite a plea of insanity, Arthur Harnett was found guilty and executed.

NAME	Arthur Harnett
AGE AT EXECUTION	28
DATE OF EXECUTION	Friday, 2nd September, 1927
PLACE OF EXECUTION	Leeds
HANGMAN	Thomas Pierrepoint
ASSISTANT	Lionel Mann
DATE OF TRIAL	22nd July, 1927
LOCATION OF TRIAL	Leeds
PRESIDING JUDGE	Mister Justice Mackinnon
PROSECUTION COUNSEL	Anthony Hawke, C. Paley Scott
DEFENCE COUNSEL	Mister Wrangham
NUMBER OF VICTIMS	1

VICTIMS DETAILS	
NAME	Isabella Moore
AGE	33
DATE OF MURDER	Tuesday, 3rd May, 1927
PLACE OF MURDER	2 Westgate, Hemsworth
METHOD OF KILLING	Cut throat
RELATIONSHIP TO KILLER	None

1927

1927

JAMES LAWRIE GODDARD was walking down a footpath near Dam Wood at some time after 6.00pm on August 15th, 1927. Suddenly a man, William Robertson, appeared, covered in blood with a gaping wound in his throat.

Robertson could not speak but pointed repeatedly towards the woods. Goddard ran for a policeman and returned soon afterwards with Constable Charles McLoughlin. Robertson again pointed to the woods and, given a piece of paper, wrote: "I loved her only we could not live." Later he scribbled a second note: "She is in there. Save her, not me."

Rushed to hospital, Robertson wrote a third note, whilst he was being treated by Doctor Joseph Groghan. This one gave the name of Evelyn Mary Jennings, her address and the message that they had wanted to die together. Evelyn's body was found later, her throat cut so severely that she had almost been decapitated.

Robertson and Evelyn had been lovers but financial problems had led them to form a suicide pact. Once he had recovered, Robertson described how he and Evelyn had gone into the woods and she had lifted her throat to him so that he could kill her. After putting his coat over her body, to protect her from the flies he then cut his own throat.

The suicide pact was almost certainly true. Evelyn had, the day she died, sent a telegram and a letter to her brother, Thomas Atkinson Jennings. The letter read in part: "I am going out. Stiffy [Robertson's nickname] is going to do for me and himself as well. There is no luck anywhere for him, try as he will, and I cannot help anymore. We have had this alternative for weeks. Tried everything, so it must be done."

At his trial, it was suggested that financial problems and the fact that he had tried to kill himself showed Robertson was insane at the time of the crime. Nevertheless, even though the pact was probably real, he had still killed Evelyn and the jury held that he had known what he was doing. Robertson was therefore guilty of murder.

NAME	William Meynell Robertson
AGE AT EXECUTION	32
DATE OF EXECUTION	Tuesday, 6th December, 1927
PLACE OF EXECUTION	Liverpool
HANGMAN	Thomas Pierrepoint
ASSISTANT	Thomas Phillips
DATE OF TRIAL	28th October, 1927
LOCATION OF TRIAL	Liverpool
PRESIDING JUDGE	Mister Justice Acton
PROSECUTION COUNSEL	Fraser Harrison
DEFENCE COUNSEL	Maxwell Fyfe
NUMBER OF VICTIMS	1

VICTIMS DETAILS

NAME	Evelyn Mary Jennings
AGE	33
DATE OF MURDER	Monday, 15th August, 1927
PLACE OF MURDER	Dam Wood, Speke, near Liverpool
METHOD OF KILLING	Cut throat
RELATIONSHIP TO KILLER	Girlfriend

ELEANOR PILKINGTON HAD been walking out with Frederick Fielding for some four years, until, in the summer of 1927, Frederick had gone down to London as a probationary officer in the Metropolitan Police Force. Frederick successfully completed his three months' training, but then decided against a police career and returned to Rishton. One week later, Eleanor dropped her bombshell by calling off their engagement.

There was no other man involved in Eleanor's life, but Frederick found the whole situation very hard to accept. He took to drink, lost interest in life in general and finally lost both his job as an iron moulder, and his home. For this sad state of affairs, Frederick believed just one person was to blame: Eleanor Pilkington.

Saturday November 5th, 1927 saw Eleanor and her friend, Doris Walker, visiting Mercer Hall in Great Harwood, to attend a dance. After the ball was over, the two ladies caught a bus home and it was whilst walking the last few yards down the street that they saw Frederick Fielding approaching them.

Eleanor told Doris to ignore Frederick and moved to walk past him. Frederick barred the way and said he wanted to speak to 'Ellie' and, grabbing her arm, took her into a shop doorway. Eleanor simply could not be bothered with him and pushed past him, intending to finish her journey home. Frederick, though, was following and, as the two girls entered Spring Street where they both lived, he grabbed Eleanor around the shoulders, and taking a knife from his jacket, stabbed her twice.

Doris Walker managed to get her friend to her house, which was closer than Eleanor's, where she soon died from her injuries. A search was launched for Frederick but an hour later, he walked up to Constable Benjamin Greatorex, who was on his beat in Furthergate, Blackburn, and confessed to him that he had stabbed his girlfriend.

The trial opened at Manchester before Mister Justice Finlay and evidence was given that Fielding had threatened Eleanor just a week before the attack on her. Fielding had turned up at her house and when his knocking

NAME	Frederick Fielding
AGE AT EXECUTION	24
DATE OF EXECUTION	Tuesday, 3rd January, 1928
PLACE OF EXECUTION	Manchester
HANGMAN	Thomas Pierrepoint
ASSISTANT	Not known
DATE OF TRIAL	22nd November, 1927
LOCATION OF TRIAL	Manchester
PRESIDING JUDGE	Mister Justice Finlay
PROSECUTION COUNSEL	A. Leslie
DEFENCE COUNSEL	B. Ormerod
NUMBER OF VICTIMS	1

VICTIMS DETAILS	
NAME	Eleanor Pilkington
AGE	23
DATE OF MURDER	Saturday, 5th November, 1927
PLACE OF MURDER	Spring Street, Rishton, near Blackburn
METHOD OF KILLING	Stabbed
RELATIONSHIP TO KILLER	Girlfriend

had been ignored, had thrown stones through the windows and announced to Mr Fielding, Eleanor's father, that if he didn't fetch her, he would be without a daughter before the week was out.

Fielding tried to claim that he was so drunk that he had not known what he was doing. He had been to the Petre Arms and consumed at least eight pints of beer but despite this, the jury decided that Frederick Fielding was guilty of murder.

0928

BERTRAM KIRBY COULD not have been described as a stable individual. In 1915, at the height of hostilities, Kirby had been discharged from the army as being insane. Ten years later, in 1925, he had a serious operation, the result of which was that if anything he would now be more likely to suffer from mental trouble. On top of all that, by 1928, Kirby had once attempted suicide by taking laudanum, and was in severe financial difficulties.

Kirby had two sons, the youngest of which, eight-year-old Norman, lived at home with his parents. The other son, 25-year-old Harry, did not get on with his father and, because of family tensions, had moved in with Mrs Took, who lived nearby. Harry had been there for about three years.

On Monday, July 11th, 1927, the postman called at the Kirby house at 7.30am. At that time, Minnie Kirby was alive and well. She was also still in good health when Norman left for school at 8.30am. Shortly afterwards, Bertram visited Mrs Took and arranged for Norman to have his lunch with her. He explained that his wife had gone to London to see about a job and wouldn't be back until late that evening. Shortly afterwards, Kirby began to behave rather strangely.

Around 30 minutes after visiting Mrs Took, Kirby sold some clothing and that evening he visited the Wheatsheaf Inn, where he tried to sell his bungalow and cashed a cheque for £45. The following day, Minnie's body was discovered. She had been killed by a single blow from an axe and had apparently died whilst in the process of writing a letter. The unfinished note was found on Kirby when he was searched.

Kirby tried to suggest that there had been a suicide pact between him and Minnie, due to their severe financial problems. He had once worked on the railways but lately had been selling soft goods and hardware on a commission basis and had not been very successful. The prosecution, though, suggested that the letters found were written after the event in order to throw the police off the scent.

Despite the medical evidence, which clearly showed that Kirby had mental

NAME	Bertram Horace Kirby
AGE AT EXECUTION	47
DATE OF EXECUTION	Wednesday, 4th January, 1928
PLACE OF EXECUTION	Lincoln
HANGMAN	Thomas Pierrepoint
ASSISTANT	Henry Pollard
DATE OF TRIAL	1st November, 1927
LOCATION OF TRIAL	Lincoln
PRESIDING JUDGE	Mister Justice Swift
PROSECUTION COUNSEL	M. Healy
DEFENCE COUNSEL	W. Butler
NUMBER OF VICTIMS	1

VICTIMS DETAILS	
NAME	Minnie Eleanor Kirby
AGE	46
DATE OF MURDER	Monday, 11th July, 1927
PLACE OF MURDER	Louth
METHOD OF KILLING	Battered
RELATIONSHIP TO KILLER	Wife

problems, he was found guilty and sentenced to death. The original execution date was November 23rd, 1927 but this was cancelled when Kirby announced his intention to appeal. This was dismissed and, after having a few more precious weeks of life, Bertram Kirby was executed in the first week of January, 1928.

ON SEPTEMBER 13TH, 1927, Ada Elizabeth Dunn left her husband, John, after disagreements over financial matters. She returned to him on September 24th and later that same evening, was found dead in her home at Sacriston.

It was 12.50am when Arthur Holmes Trainer heard a shout of "Police!" Within seconds, Dunn had rushed up to him and explained that his wife had committed suicide. The police were called and in due course, the body of Ada Dunn was found near the back door of her house. She was dead and there were marks around her neck.

Dunn claimed that his wife had often spoken of suicide and in the early hours of the morning, he had discovered her hanging. He had cut her down and removed the noose but realising that he could not revive her, he ran for help. Unfortunately, it was too late to save her.

What seemed at first like quite a plausible story was soon shown to be nothing but a pack of lies. To begin with, no one else had heard Ada threaten suicide. Her own son, Richard, aged 11, reported that he had heard his parents arguing that night and this had been followed by some sort of choking sound. When he had called out to his father to ask what was happening, John Dunn had said everything was all right and that he and Ada were "only playing". This was confirmed by Richard's brother, nine-year-old Albert.

Police suspicions were first aroused by Dunn's behaviour after they had reached his house. Whilst the scene was still being examined, at around 1.30am, Dunn was busy cracking jokes with people who had come in to offer their assistance.

Forensic tests and careful measurements showed that the rope used to extinguish Ada's life had been too low down on her throat to be consistent with suicide and also, that had she attempted to hang herself, her feet would have reached the floor. The only explanation was that this was a case of murder, not suicide and Dunn was subsequently charged with killing his wife.

Dunn was most surprised to be discovered so rapidly and reacted badly to the charge. On the night of September 25th, he threw a

NAME	John Thomas Dunn
AGE AT EXECUTION	52
DATE OF EXECUTION	Friday, 6th January, 1928
PLACE OF EXECUTION	Durham
HANGMAN	Thomas Pierrepoint
ASSISTANT	Not known
DATE OF TRIAL	15th November, 1927
LOCATION OF TRIAL	Durham
PRESIDING JUDGE	Mister Justice Roche
PROSECUTION COUNSEL	C.F. Lowenthal, C. Paley Scott
DEFENCE COUNSEL	Archibald Wilson
NUMBER OF VICTIMS	1

VICTIMS DETAILS	
NAME	Ada Elizabeth Dunn
AGE	44
DATE OF MURDER	Saturday, 24th September, 1927
PLACE OF MURDER	2 Lumsdons Buildings, Sacriston, County Durham
METHOD OF KILLING	Strangled
RELATIONSHIP TO KILLER	Wife

tantrum in his cell, tore off all his clothing and was found naked the next morning. Whether this was pure anger or an attempt to demonstrate a degree of insanity and irrational behaviour was never made clear, but either way, it did nothing to save him from the gallows.

0928

CHARLES HICKS, A park-keeper at Richmond, was walking through the park on the morning of Wednesday, October 5th, 1927 when he noticed a bundle underneath bushes near the Robin Hood gate. Hicks walked over to examine the bundle and saw that it was the body of a young woman.

A search revealed a handbag, which contained a name and address: Constance Gertrude Oliver, of Falcon Grove, Battersea. Constance had fought hard for her life. There were extensive signs of a struggle near the bushes and her umbrella, broken into four pieces, was found close by. There were also signs that the murderer had tried to burn the body.

Her parents told the police that Constance had left home at 7.00pm on Sunday, October 2nd, to meet Sidney Bernard Goulter, the son of a retired police inspector, and he lived at 24 Bockhampton Road, Kingston-upon-Thames, with his parents. When police visited that address, Goulter's parents reported that he had not been seen since October 1st.

Goulter chose that same day, October 5th, to visit his parents again. They told Goulter about the police looking for him. He made no comment and left to catch a bus. The police had been waiting and he was arrested as he waited at the stop.

Goulter told the police that at the beginning of August, he had started work as an attendant on a coffee stall in Falcon Road, Battersea. Constance worked nearby and they had become friendly, arranging to meet, at Putney, on October 2nd.

The two caught a bus to the Robin Hood gate at Richmond. They took a walk and then sat down on a bench where Goulter suggested meeting again the following Monday. Constance explained that she had already agreed to go to the Lyceum with a girlfriend and two men. The thought of her going out with another man caused Goulter to lose his temper. He took Constance's umbrella from her and struck her with it. She fought back and hit him with her handbag whereupon he put his hands around her throat and throttled her into unconsciousness. Now he tore pieces from her underclothing and tied them around her neck in order to ensure that she remained

NAME	Sidney Bernard Goulter
AGE AT EXECUTION	25
DATE OF EXECUTION	Friday, 6th January, 1928
PLACE OF EXECUTION	Wandsworth
HANGMAN	Robert Baxter
ASSISTANT	Henry Pollard
DATE OF TRIAL	5th December, 1927
LOCATION OF TRIAL	Guildford
PRESIDING JUDGE	Mister Justice Horridge
PROSECUTION COUNSEL	James Dale Cassels M.P., Paul Bennett
DEFENCE COUNSEL	Laurence Vine, Richard Eagle
NUMBER OF VICTIMS	1

VICTIMS DETAILS	
NAME	Constance Gertrude Oliver
AGE	21
DATE OF MURDER	Sunday, 2nd October, 1927
PLACE OF MURDER	Richmond Park, London
METHOD OF KILLING	Battered/strangled
RELATIONSHIP TO KILLER	None

unconsciousness whilst he made his getaway. He lit a cigarette and did not see where he had thrown the match. It must have fallen onto her and partly burned her.

At his trial, Goulter maintained that the killing had been accidental. The defence suggested that the cloth had not been tied tightly around Constance's throat and that her neck might have swollen, tightening the cloth and strangling her. Sir Bernard Spilsbury disagreed and gave evidence that the cloth must have been tied tightly to begin with.

The jury took seven minutes to decide that the killing had been deliberate.

ON THURSDAY, OCTOBER 20th, 1927, George Edward Mottram returned home from work at the Tinsley Park Colliery at 10.45pm. The house was quiet and upon going into the kitchen, George discovered why. His wife, Mary Alice, lay dead on the kitchen floor, a piece of rope tied tightly around her neck.

The next day, October 21st, Samuel Case gave himself up. Case was well known to the Mottrams and Mary Alice had even been a bridesmaid at his wedding some three years before. He explained that they had been lovers and she had told him that she was pregnant by him.

When he went around to her house, on the morning of the 20th, Mary Alice had said that she would rather be dead than let her husband know. Then, as she bent forward to stir the fire, Case had taken his scarf and throttled her until she went black in the face. He had then taken a piece of clothes line and tied it around her throat before leaving the house.

It seemed to be an open-and-shut case and at the trial Samuel Case was indeed found guilty and sentenced to death. At the appeal though, a rather novel defence was put forward: someone else had confessed to the crime!

On November 17th, even before Case's trial took place, a convict at Manchester went to the Governor and confessed that he had murdered Mary. This man, William Walter Hartle, was a native of Liverpool and said that he and Case had walked from Liverpool to Sheffield, arriving there on the day of the murder.

Case had suggested that they break into a house and took Hartle to Ravenscar Road, where they entered the Mottram house. Soon after they had gained entry, Hartle heard a noise and hid in a cupboard. A woman came into the room. After some moments, Case entered and engaged the woman in conversation, after which Hartle burst out of the cupboard and, taking up a towel, strangled Mary Alice. He then went out into the garden and cut some rope from a clothes line, tying this around her throat and making sure she was dead.

NAME	Samuel Case
AGE AT EXECUTION	24
DATE OF EXECUTION	Saturday, 7th January, 1928
PLACE OF EXECUTION	Leeds
HANGMAN	Thomas Pierrepoint
ASSISTANT	Henry Pollard
DATE OF TRIAL	29th November, 1927
LOCATION OF TRIAL	Leeds
PRESIDING JUDGE	Mister Justice Roche
PROSECUTION COUNSEL	C. Paley Scott
DEFENCE COUNSEL	John Neal
NUMBER OF VICTIMS	1

VICTIMS DETAILS	
NAME	Mary Alice Mottram
AGE	24
DATE OF MURDER	Thursday, 20th October, 1927
PLACE OF MURDER	28 Ravenscar Road, Intake, Sheffield
METHOD OF KILLING	Strangled
RELATIONSHIP TO KILLER	Girlfriend

Much of what Hartle had said could not be squared with the evidence. He described getting the rope from the garden, but the clothes line had been stretched across the kitchen. He also described tying the knot at the back of Mary Alice's neck when, in fact, it had been tied at the front. There was also the fact that Hartle's description of the room did not agree with the layout. Finally he described Case as a slim, sandy-haired man, when in fact he was stocky and dark. It looked like Hartle, who had been arrested on October 29th for stealing cheques, had made up his story from newspaper reports. The appeal was dismissed.

AT 8.00AM ON October 15th, 1928, George Geddes was sailing his small boat on the river Clyde when he noticed a parcel on the bank. Recently the river level had been reduced by some 18 inches so that some repairs could be made to a bridge, and this was what had probably revealed the bundle. George steered his vessel to the bank and retrieved the parcel. Upon opening it he was horrified to find female body parts.

Other body parts were found later in other locations along the Clyde until finally a woman's head was discovered on October 17th. The finds led to a great deal of reporting in the local newspapers and it was these articles that brought two women into the police station.

Emily Meiklejohn lived in Thistle Street and she had walked into the station with a neighbour, Mrs McKay. Both women said that from the description of the body they believed that it might be Mrs McKay's mother-in-law, Agnes Arbuckle. Agnes lived at 213 Main Street and the neighbours there had noticed some odd behaviour over the last few weeks.

Mrs Arbuckle, a widow, lived alone and each Wednesday visited the post office to collect a 9/- pension due for a son who had been killed in the Great War. She had drawn that payment on September 28th and it had been paid out by Jean Fleming Forsyth, the cashier. However, Agnes had not attended the following Wednesday and none of her neighbours recalled seeing her after the 28th.

One of those neighbours, Agnes Torrance, told the police that on Friday the 30th, Mrs Arbuckle's son, James McKay, had told her that Mrs Arbuckle was on holiday in Rothesay. A couple of weeks later, though, on October 15th, James was back with his wife and some other people, moving furniture out of his mother's rooms.

Mrs Meiklejohn, who had gone to the police with Mrs McKay, told the officers investigating the murder that McKay had been selling all his furniture and was known to have some rather severe debts but, after his mother had vanished, he seemed to suddenly have money.

James McKay was arrested on suspicion and upon being searched, the police found a

NAME	James McKay
AGE AT EXECUTION	40
DATE OF EXECUTION	Tuesday, 24th January, 1928
PLACE OF EXECUTION	Glasgow, Duke Street
HANGMAN	Robert Baxter
ASSISTANT	Not known
DATE OF TRIAL	12th December, 1927
LOCATION OF TRIAL	Glasgow
PRESIDING JUDGE	Lord Justice Ormindale
PROSECUTION COUNSEL	James Hunter
DEFENCE COUNSEL	Mister McDonald
NUMBER OF VICTIMS	1

VICTIMS DETAILS

NAME	Agnes Arbuckle
AGE	Not known
DATE OF MURDER	circa Wednesday, 28th September, 1927
PLACE OF MURDER	213 Main Street, Glasgow
METHOD OF KILLING	Battered
RELATIONSHIP TO KILLER	Mother

sheet of paper bearing a number of attempts at his mother's signature. There was also a will, obviously forged, leaving all Agnes's property and money to him. After further questioning, James admitted that he had battered his mother to death with an axe, cut up her body and started to dump it. That grisly task was far from complete and at one stage James showed the officers further bundles of remains, hidden in a coal bunker in his mother's kitchen.

The only defence possible was insanity and when this failed, James McKay had the distinction of being the first Scottish murderer to appeal against his sentence. The sentence, however, was upheld.

DAI LEWIS OPERATED a small-time protection racket at Monmouth race track. He would rent out items such as chalk and boards to the bookies and insure them against 'accidents'. Unfortunately, there were other men offering the same service.

Another protection gang was led by the Rowlands brothers, John and Edward. They did not fail to notice when, on September 28th, 1927, Dai Lewis appeared on their patch. Lewis was aware that he was stepping on toes and had the foresight not to go home that night, booking instead into a hotel in St Mary Street.

On the 29th, Lewis was back at Monmouth track and then went back to the hotel in Cardiff. Going to the Blue Anchor pub, Lewis noted that there were a few of the Rowlands gang around and must have been relieved when they left. What he did not know was that they had just gone to a cafe across the road.

At closing time, Dai left the pub and was suddenly aware of being surrounded by a crowd of men. A fight followed and Lewis was stabbed in the throat. Still alive, he was rushed to hospital but refused to name his assailants.

Over the next few hours, there were two telephone calls to the hospital asking how Lewis was faring. Each time when the nurse asked the caller for his name, he rang off. The police monitored the line and when the caller rang for a third time, the call was traced to the Colonial Club, in Custom House Street, a known base for the Rowlands gang.

Five members of the gang were arrested: John Rowlands, Edward Rowlands, Daniel Driscoll, John Hughes and William Price. All were charged with attempted murder and when Lewis died, the questioning became more intense.

Finally, after days of pressure, John Rowlands made a statement. He claimed that it was Lewis who had drawn the knife and in the struggle, Rowlands must have accidentally stabbed him in the throat.

The police decided that they did not have enough evidence against John Hughes. The charges against him were dropped, but the other four were sent for trial on a charge of murder. That trial lasted for four days and

NAMES	Edward Rowlands; Daniel Driscoll
AGES AT EXECUTION	40; 34
DATE OF EXECUTION	Friday, 27th January, 1928
PLACE OF EXECUTION	Cardiff
HANGMAN	Robert Baxter
ASSISTANT	Thomas Phillips, Lionel Mann, Robert Wilson
DATE OF TRIAL	29th November – 2nd December, 1927
LOCATION OF TRIAL	Cardiff
PRESIDING JUDGE	Mister Justice Wright
PROSECUTION COUNSEL	Lord Hailsbury, T.W., Langman
DEFENCE COUNSEL	Lawrence Vine, Artemus Jones, Francis Powell, Trevor Hunter
NUMBER OF VICTIMS	1

VICTIMS DETAILS	
NAME	David (Dai) Lewis (Died Friday, 30th September)
AGE	Not known
DATE OF MURDER	Thursday, 29th September, 1927
PLACE OF MURDER	Outside Blue Anchor Pub, St Mary's Street, Cardiff
METHOD OF KILLING	Stabbed
RELATIONSHIP TO KILLERS	None; none

both Rowlands brothers and Driscoll were found guilty. Price was found not guilty.

A petition of 250,000 signatures was handed in, demanding a Home Office inquiry. Three doctors gave evidence claiming that Lewis had died from a heart attack and even a majority of the jury wrote to the Home Secretary asking for the death sentence not to be applied. Nevertheless, the appeal failed on January 11th, 1928.

John Rowlands never did face the hangman's noose. On the way to his appeal he had gone berserk in the prison van and was certified insane.

JAMES GILLON AND his sister Annie both worked at the home of Mr Geoffrey Holland at Lower Beeding. She was the housemaid and he was the under gardener and for the most part, they had a decent relationship with each other. James, though, was rather old-fashioned in his ways and thought that Annie was somewhat subservient to him.

On September 19th, 1927, Annie went off for the day to Brighton and when she returned, refused to get James's supper for him. She told him that if he wanted anything to eat, he had better prepare it for himself, and then promptly went off to bed.

James fared no better the following morning. Sitting in the servant's hall, he asked Annie if she was going to make his breakfast for him and when she again said, "No", James finally lost his temper.

The cook was busy in the kitchen when she heard the scream. Running into the servant's hall, she saw James holding Annie by the throat. She ran for help but by the time anyone could offer assistance, James Gillon had cut his sister's throat. He had also stabbed her in the back with such violence that one and a half inches of knife blade remained embedded in her spine.

Annie was rushed to hospital, where she

NAME	James Gillon
AGE AT EXECUTION	30
DATE OF EXECUTION	Tuesday, 31st January, 1928
PLACE OF EXECUTION	Wandsworth
HANGMAN	Robert Baxter
ASSISTANT	Thomas Phillips
DATE OF TRIAL	12th December, 1927
LOCATION OF TRIAL	Lewes
PRESIDING JUDGE	Mister Justice Horridge
PROSECUTION COUNSEL	John Flowers
DEFENCE COUNSEL	Thomas Gates
NUMBER OF VICTIMS	1

VICTIMS DETAILS	
NAME	Annie Gillon (Died Friday, 28th October)
AGE	28
DATE OF MURDER	Tuesday, 20th September, 1927
PLACE OF MURDER	Plummers Plain House, Lower Beeding, Sussex
METHOD OF KILLING	Cut throat/stabbed
RELATIONSHIP TO KILLER	Sister

The dying deposition of Annie Gillion, taken after she had been attacked by her brother.

was seen by Doctor Grenville Brend Tait, who, forgetting all pretence at a bedside manner, told Annie that she would probably soon be dead and asked if she would like to make a statement to the police. Annie agreed and told them how her brother had attacked her. James, who was present during this statement, then apologised to her for what he had done.

Annie Gillon held on to life for five weeks. The knife blade was never removed from her back as the surgeons held that it was much too dangerous to do so, and on October 28th, she finally died. James was now charged with murder.

At his trial, which took place at Lewes, Gillon tried to put forward a defence of insanity. Doctor F.R.P. Taylor of the Hellingly Mental Hospital testified that in his opinion, Gillon was a "high-grade mental defective". He went on to say that Gillon was suffering from degeneration of the brain, had an inferiority complex and at the time of the attack on his sister, was undoubtedly insane.

Despite this testimony, the jury returned their verdict in 15 minutes and James Gillon was sentenced to death.

CHARLES BROOMHEAD HAD enjoyed his night out with Olive Turner, the girl he loved. Having been to the cinema they now decided to have a quiet walk down the canal towpath, as so many other lovers did.

Charles and Olive had not gone very far when they were accosted by a stranger who announced that he was a policeman and was arresting them for trespass. Charles Broomhead respected authority and said that they would go with the man without offering any resistance. However, they had not gone very far when Charles began to grow suspicious.

As they walked, presumably towards the nearest police station, Charles noticed that there were other couples on the towpath. Not unreasonably, he demanded to know why they were not also being arrested and the police officer replied that he had two and that was enough for him. Whatever suspicions Charles held were certainly intensified when the policeman hinted that it may be possible to 'square' things with him. In other words, he was willing to let them go if they gave him money.

Convinced now that the policeman was nothing of the kind, Charles Broomhead reached into his pocket and brought out all he had, 4d. "Fourpence is no good to me," said the officer and now Charles had had enough.

Charles told the man that he was quite prepared to go with him, but Olive would not. He turned to his girlfriend and told her to run home. Without waiting to be told a second time, Olive began to run off, only to be followed by the stranger. Charles Broomhead followed and soon caught the stranger, who then turned suddenly and struck Charles, knocking him down and dazing him.

As Charles got to his feet he was just in time to see the man catch Olive and, throwing his arm around her waist, carry her off into the distance. Olive would not be seen again until her body was found in the canal the following morning. Her watch, which was still on her body, had stopped, pin-pointing the time she was thrown into the water at 11.41pm.

Police immediately appealed for witnesses and a number of people came forward. Doris

NAME	James Joseph Power
AGE AT EXECUTION	32
DATE OF EXECUTION	Tuesday, 31st January, 1928
PLACE OF EXECUTION	Birmingham
HANGMAN	Thomas Pierrepoint
ASSISTANT	Robert Wilson
DATE OF TRIAL	7th December – 9th December, 1927
LOCATION OF TRIAL	Birmingham
PRESIDING JUDGE	Mister Justice Swift
PROSECUTION COUNSEL	Sir Norman Birkett, W.E. Bousefield
DEFENCE COUNSEL	Sir Reginald Coventry, Mister Williams
NUMBER OF VICTIMS	1

VICTIMS DETAILS	
NAME	Olive Gordon Turner
AGE	18
DATE OF MURDER	Saturday, 2nd July, 1927
PLACE OF MURDER	Canal towpath at Winson Green, Birmingham
METHOD OF KILLING	Drowned
RELATIONSHIP TO KILLER	None

Emeny had also been to the cinema with her boyfriend, John Edgar Whillock, and they too were on the towpath at the time of the attack. They had seen the three people together and had been close to the woman when she was caught by the man she was trying to run away from. Whillock tried to interfere, but the man identified himself as a police officer and at that Whillock allowed him to go on his way. He swore he would know the man again.

Another important witness was John Godfree. He had seen the man standing on a bridge, watching couples pass by, and had seen him go up to Charles and Olive. The descriptions and information these people gave allowed police to decide that the man they wanted was James Power, who lived in Heath Green Road. He had been a policeman but had now left the force and he had come to their attention in the past for representing himself as still being a serving officer.

Taken in for questioning, Power was identified by Charles Broomhead, Doris Emeny, Edgar Whillock and John Godfree. Faced with these positive identifications,

Power replied that they were all mistaken and that he had not been anywhere near the canal on the day in question. That defence convinced no one, and Power was sentenced to death.

The appeal tried two different approaches. In the first place, they tried to discredit the testimony of the witnesses. Charles Broomhead, it was said, was interested in anyone being arrested. He had been the first suspect and the police had questioned him very closely indeed when he first reported the matter and his evidence seemed to improve in quality as time went on.

John Godfree admitted that he had only had a quick sideways glance at the man and both Doris Emery and Edgar Willock had described the man they had seen as wearing a white daisy in his buttonhole, whilst Power had been wearing a red rose.

It was also suggested that even if Power had carried off Olive, there was no proof that he was responsible for her death. He may well have robbed her but then she might have wandered off in the dark and fallen into the canal accidentally. The strength of this last point was reduced somewhat when evidence was given that there was no water in Olive's stomach, meaning that she was unconscious when she entered the water.

The appeal was dismissed and Power was executed at Birmingham, that prison being very close to the spot where Olive had died.

ALTHOUGH ARTHUR COLLINSON was the licensee of the New Inn, he also had a job in Glossop. His wife, Amy, took care of business at the pub.

On Friday, November 11th, 1927, when Arthur returned home, he could not gain entrance to the pub. A neighbour, Amos Dawson, had a key to one of the doors, so Arthur went and asked him for assistance. Upon entering the kitchen, they found Amy. Her throat had been cut and the carving knife used lay embedded in her neck. She had also been battered.

Amy had last been seen alive at 9.30am, when a local lad had delivered milk. After that time, no callers had gained admittance. The motive appeared to be robbery. Some £40 in notes was missing and the fact that the thief had known where to look led to the probability that he was local.

George Hayward had called at the inn on the day of the murder and had been seen by two people who knew him well: Arthur Lomas and Mrs Macbain. When Hayward was questioned, he admitted that he had called for some cigarettes but swore that Mrs Collinson was alive when he left.

As a matter of routine, Hayward was spoken to again on November 12th, but this time in front of his wife. When asked to confirm his story, his wife interrupted and said that he had told her he had been nowhere near the inn. Hayward's house was searched and this revealed that the waste pipe in the kitchen had recently been sawn off and a sum of over £32 was found hidden in the chimney breast.

Meanwhile, police had been checking out the murder scene and an alert constable spotted that one of the cistern covers in the toilet had been moved. One corner was broken and when the lid was lifted, a bloodstained piece of lead pipe was discovered. When this was checked against the pipe in Hayward's kitchen, an exact match was noted and Hayward was charged with murder.

At the trial, it was revealed that Hayward had financial problems. A commercial traveller, he had been dismissed from his job on October 11th for failing to account for money.

NAME	George Frederick Walter Hayward
AGE AT EXECUTION	32
DATE OF EXECUTION	Tuesday, 10th April, 1928
PLACE OF EXECUTION	Nottingham
HANGMAN	Thomas Pierrepoint
ASSISTANT	Henry Pollard
DATE OF TRIAL	20th February – 24th February, 1928
LOCATION OF TRIAL	Derby
PRESIDING JUDGE	Mister Justice Hawke
PROSECUTION COUNSEL	Sir Henry Maddocks, T. Norman Winning
DEFENCE COUNSEL	A.H. Davis
NUMBER OF VICTIMS	1

VICTIMS DETAILS	
NAME	Amy Collinson
AGE	36
DATE OF MURDER	Friday, 11th November, 1927
PLACE OF MURDER	The New Inn, Little Hayfield
METHOD OF KILLING	Cut throat/battered
RELATIONSHIP TO KILLER	None

Although considerably in debt, Hayward had given his wife £2 on the day of the murder and had also paid a £4 debt.

Witnesses reported that Hayward had caught a bus at a 10.45am, some 1,500 yards from the inn. Mrs Macbain said that she had seen Hayward at 10.23am. Since it would take him 12 minutes to get to the bus stop and since he spoke to Arthur Lomas for three minutes, that only gave him seven minutes to commit the murder.

After considering things carefully, the jury came to the conclusion that Hayward had enough time to commit the murder.

FREDERICK LOCK, THE father of four children, had lived with Florence Kitching ever since his wife had died. They had now been together for almost four years and although, like most couples, they had argued, there had been nothing to cause undue concern. In February though, things began to change.

On the 4th of February, Florence visited her aunt, Florence Nicholls, who lived at 19 Hardington Street, off the Edgware Road. Lock was with her and at one stage, picked up a knife and threatened Florence Kitching with it. Mrs Nicholls managed to take the knife from him, but then Lock struck Florence in the face. It was then that Florence wrote to her mother, Mrs O'Neill, who lived in Cornwall, and asked if she could go down there to stay.

As it happened, Florence's presence had been requested by her stepfather, who was seriously ill, and so Mrs O'Neill travelled up to London on February 8th, with the intention of taking Florence back with her.

Mrs O'Neill, her sister, Mrs Nicholls, Florence Kitching and Frederick Lock, all met up in London and visited the Lord Nelson pub. The two sisters went up to the bar to get themselves a drink and it was at that point that Frederick suggested that Florence should return home with him to see that the children's evening meal was prepared. Florence demurred and left the pub with Lock.

At a 1.45pm, Lock returned alone and announced to Mrs O'Neill that she was wanted at home, adding that she would be unable to take Florence to Cornwall now. When the ladies accompanied Lock to the house in Coopers Road, they found Florence lying on the kitchen floor with her throat cut. Lock bent down, kissed Florence and cried: "Oh my God, to think I had to do this."

Lock's defence was one of insanity. Doctor Reginald Hearn gave evidence that in his opinion, Lock did not know what he was doing at the time of the killing. He went on to say that Lock was in the early stages of dementia and would eventually become certifiable, if he lived.

After deliberating for 10 minutes, the jury

NAME	Frederick Lock
AGE AT EXECUTION	39
DATE OF EXECUTION	Thursday, 12th April, 1928
PLACE OF EXECUTION	Wandsworth
HANGMAN	Robert Baxter
ASSISTANT	Lionel Mann
DATE OF TRIAL	1st March, 1928
LOCATION OF TRIAL	Old Bailey
PRESIDING JUDGE	Mister Justice Humphreys
PROSECUTION COUNSEL	H.D. Roome, G.B. McClure
DEFENCE COUNSEL	G.P. Jordan
NUMBER OF VICTIMS	1

VICTIMS DETAILS	
NAME	Florence Alice Kitching
AGE	28
DATE OF MURDER	Wednesday, 8th February, 1928
PLACE OF MURDER	28 Coopers Road, Old Kent Road, London
METHOD OF KILLING	Cut throat
RELATIONSHIP TO KILLER	Girlfriend

returned their guilty verdict and Lock was sentenced to death. We will never know if Doctor Hearn's diagnosis was correct, for Lock did not live long enough for his mental problems to get any worse.

ONE OF THE most callous murders of the twentieth century took place in the early hours of the morning of September 27th, 1927.

Constable George Gutteridge had stopped a car and whilst apparently about to take down some details, had been shot twice in the head. Mortally wounded, the officer fell to the ground, only to have the killer walk up to him and shoot him twice more, once through each eye.

A car had been stolen from a doctor's house nearby and when this car was found abandoned in Brixton, the search for the killers moved to London. A list of criminals known to use firearms was drawn up.

In 1928, a stolen car was traced back to the garage of Frederick Guy Browne and arresting him for that theft, the officers took the opportunity to search his premises. A number of weapons were found, including two Webley revolvers. All the firearms were handed over to a weapons expert, who finally managed to establish that the newer of the two Webleys had been used to kill Gutteridge.

In the meantime, William Henry Kennedy, who had been working for Browne and living until recently in a back room at the garage, was arrested in Liverpool. He then gave a detailed statement in which he admitted being with Browne and stealing the doctor's car. He went on to say that they had been stopped by Gutteridge, who was shot by Browne as he asked questions. Browne then got out of the car and shot the officer through both eyes. By incriminating Browne, Kennedy was hoping to get off with a long prison sentence and escape the hangman's noose.

Though many writers have assumed that both men were guilty of this horrific murder, there is evidence that Browne was in fact innocent. According to Browne, the murder weapon had belonged to Kennedy, who had swapped it for another gun, some time in October 1927, after the murder had taken place. Browne had only recently moved house and claimed that on the night of the murder he was at home, with his wife. As might be expected, his wife did back up this story, but Browne's new landlady also made a statement agreeing that Browne was at home that evening. She was never called to give evidence.

NAMES	Frederick Guy Browne; William Henry Kennedy
AGES AT EXECUTION	47; 36
DATE OF EXECUTION	Thursday, 31st May, 1928
PLACES OF EXECUTION	Pentonville; Wandsworth
HANGMEN	Robert Baxter; Thomas Pierrepoint
ASSISTANTS	Henry Pollard; Robert Wilson
DATE OF TRIAL	23rd April – 27th April, 1928
LOCATION OF TRIAL	Old Bailey
PRESIDING JUDGE	Mister Justice Avory
PROSECUTION COUNSEL	Sir Boyd Merriman, H.D. Roome, Miss Enid Prosser
DEFENCE COUNSEL	E.F. Lever; Frank Powell
NUMBER OF VICTIMS	1

VICTIMS DETAILS	
NAME	George William Gutteridge
AGE	38
DATE OF MURDER	Tuesday, 27th September, 1927
PLACE OF MURDER	Near Howe Green, Essex
METHOD OF KILLING	Shot
RELATIONSHIP TO KILLERS	None; none

After receiving the sentence of death, Browne tried to commit suicide, went on hunger strike and smashed up his cell when his appeal was dismissed. This has been said to show that he was a difficult prisoner. It could just as easily have been put down as the actions of a frustrated man who knew he was innocent of a crime he was about to hang for.

1928

CLIFFORD WEBB WAS a man of habit. Every day he would call at his father's office and drive him home after work and Thursday, February 9th, 1928 was different only in the fact that Clifford also drove Frank Sweeny, a family friend, back to the flat in Pembridge Square.

Upon arrival, at about 6.30pm, the three walked up to Flat 3, where Alfred Webb was surprised to find that he could not gain entrance to his own flat. Someone inside had put the chain on the door and, through the broken glass panelling in the door, a figure could be seen moving about.

Alfred stayed where he was and asked Clifford and Frank Sweeny to fetch the police. From inside the flat a gruff voice commanded: "Put 'em up" as the two men ran off for help. They had not gone very far when they heard a shot ring out.

Clifford Webb turned back in time to see a man leave the flats and head off up the street. Rushing back upstairs, he found Alfred Webb lying unconscious, a bullet wound over his left eye. He died in hospital the following day.

A search of the area soon turned up the murder weapon, a Browning automatic. The gun had been thrown into a nearby garden, probably because a bullet had jammed in the breech, rendering it incapable of firing again.

Pictures of the Browning were published in the newspapers, along with the serial numbers and this led to its identification as a weapon stolen from Corporal James O'Brien of the R.A.F. It had been taken from him some years before, whilst he was at Tadcaster, and this, along with other evidence, led to the identification of Frederick Stewart, who lived at Portengrange Avenue, in Southend. Stewart was arrested at that address on February 23rd.

In due course, Stewart admitted that he had been the burglar but claimed that the shooting had been accidental. His story was that he had been hit in the face by Mr Webb. The action of being hit caused Stewart's hand to close and the reaction caused the gun to go off. He had not been aware that he had shot Mr Webb until he had read about it in the newspapers.

Stewart's story was shown to be unlikely.

NAME	Frederick Stewart
AGE AT EXECUTION	28
DATE OF EXECUTION	Wednesday, 6th June, 1928
PLACE OF EXECUTION	Pentonville
HANGMAN	Robert Baxter
ASSISTANT	Thomas Phillips
DATE OF TRIAL	18th April, 1928
LOCATION OF TRIAL	Old Bailey
PRESIDING JUDGE	Mister Justice Avory
PROSECUTION COUNSEL	Percival Clarke, G.D. Roberts, H.H. Elam
DEFENCE COUNSEL	E.F. Lever, L. Jellinek
NUMBER OF VICTIMS	1

VICTIMS DETAILS	
NAME	Alfred Charles Bertram Webb (Died Friday, 10th February)
AGE	46
DATE OF MURDER	Thursday, 9th February, 1928
PLACE OF MURDER	Flat 3, 20 Pembridge Square, Notting Hill, London
METHOD OF KILLING	Shot
RELATIONSHIP TO KILLER	None

Medical evidence said that the reaction to being hit in the face was more likely to be a loosening of the grip, rather than a tightening, but more telling was the absence of singeing around the wound. This indicated that the gun had been fired from some distance and negated the idea of a close encounter in which Stewart had been close enough for Webb to strike out at him.

That evidence was enough to send Frederick Stewart to the gallows.

WALTER BROOKS AND his wife, Beatrice, lived in Tithebarn Street, Preston and had taken in a lodger, Alfred Moore. The arrangement worked well enough, until Walter managed to convince himself that his wife was having an affair with Moore. Not being one to do things by halves, Walter Brookes decided to take matters into his own hands and bought himself a revolver.

On Wednesday, April 4th, Walter traced Beatrice and Alfred to a local pub, where he announced: "I shall not make trouble here." He waited until they left and followed them outside.

Constable True was walking down Avenham Road when he saw a flash and heard a woman scream. Rushing forward to assist, he promptly fell headlong over the body of Alfred Moore. True dragged himself to his feet and saw Beatrice Brooks staggering around on a nearby footpath whilst Walter ran off, having achieved what he set out to do.

Walter Brooks was arrested soon afterwards and denied all knowledge of the double murder. His defence was one of insanity and evidence was given that he had been involved in a bad car accident in 1924, since when his behaviour had been somewhat strange. Indeed, in 1925, at his wife's request, Walter had been detained in a mental hospital for three days.

None of this influenced the jury, who found Walter guilty of murder.

NAME	Walter Brooks
AGE AT EXECUTION	48
DATE OF EXECUTION	Thursday, 28th June, 1928
PLACE OF EXECUTION	Manchester
HANGMAN	Thomas Pierrepoint
ASSISTANT	Not known
DATE OF TRIAL	8th May, 1928
LOCATION OF TRIAL	Manchester
PRESIDING JUDGE	Mister Justice Charles
PROSECUTION COUNSEL	Mitchell Banks M.P., Mister Morris
DEFENCE COUNSEL	Mister Macbeth
NUMBER OF VICTIMS	2

VICTIMS DETAILS	
NAMES	Beatrice Brooks; Alfred Moore
AGES	48; 50
DATE OF MURDER	Wednesday, 4th April, 1928
PLACE OF MURDER	39 Avenham Road, Preston
METHOD OF KILLING	Shot; shot
RELATIONSHIP TO KILLER	Wife; none

1928

ALFRED ABSALOM HAD served in the army for two and a half years, leaving in 1923, and moving to Liverpool. He took a job in a mill, where he first met Mary Alice Reed. They began walking out together, and in due course became engaged.

It was in 1928 that Absalom started to become jealous of Mary and in turn, she began to cool towards him. In March of that year, Absalom started a new job, managing a fish and chip shop for his brother-in-law, and Mary visited him here in the evenings. As the nights grew lighter, though, she came less frequently and this only increased Absalom's feelings of jealousy.

William Cliffe was a neighbour of Mary's and had known her for 16 years. On May 4th, he repaired a puncture on Mary's bicycle and afterwards they went out for a ride. When Absalom visited at around 11.00pm and was told by Mary where she had been, he lost his temper and kicked the bicycle wheel so hard that it buckled.

Convinced that something was going on between Mary and Cliffe, Absalom decided it was time to act. At 4.00pm on May 11th, he purchased a new sheath knife from a shop in St John's Lane. Two hours later he was seen with Mary, in Sackville Street. No one actually saw a blow being struck, but Mary fell to the ground, bleeding from a wound in her throat. As Absalom ran off, he dropped the bloodstained knife.

Two men ran after the fleeing man and caught him at the end of the street. Asked why he had stabbed the girl, Absalom would only reply: "They drive you mad. She won't fool me anymore."

Mary Reed was still alive. Rushed to hospital she made a deposition saying that Absalom had asked her to go out with him. She had refused and he had drawn out the knife and stabbed her. She died six days later.

In his defence, Absalom told a story that was difficult to accept. He claimed that he had bought the knife to use in the fish and chip shop. He had it with him when he asked Mary out. When she turned him down, he took it out to frighten her. She turned to walk away and he put out a hand to stop her. Unfortunately, this was the hand holding the

NAME	Albert George Absalom
AGE AT EXECUTION	28
DATE OF EXECUTION	Wednesday, 25th July, 1928
PLACE OF EXECUTION	Liverpool
HANGMAN	Thomas Pierrepoint
ASSISTANT	Henry Pollard
DATE OF TRIAL	15th June, 1928
LOCATION OF TRIAL	Liverpool
PRESIDING JUDGE	Mister Justice Talbot
PROSECUTION COUNSEL	A.T. Crosthwaite
DEFENCE COUNSEL	Maxwell Fyfe
NUMBER OF VICTIMS	1

VICTIMS DETAILS	
NAME	Mary Alice Reed (Died Thursday, 17th May)
AGE	26
DATE OF MURDER	Friday, 11th May, 1928
PLACE OF MURDER	Sackville Street, Liverpool
METHOD OF KILLING	Stabbed/cut throat
RELATIONSHIP TO KILLER	Girlfriend

knife and he accidentally stabbed her. Asked why he had then run away, he replied that he became frightened when he saw the blood and realised what he had done.

That story was dismissed by the jury and Alfred George Absalom was sentenced to death. When he was executed at Liverpool, a large crowd of people gathered outside the prison and many of the women were seen to be in tears.

CHARLES HICKS ATTENDED chapel every Sunday morning. Things were no different on Sunday, February 19th, 1928, but after attending worship, Mr Hicks's young daughter pointed out that Mr Roadley's blinds were still down.

It crossed Hicks's mind that Roadley had been taken ill. Hicks listened at the window and could clearly hear heavy, laboured breathing. Hicks tried the door, found it unlocked, and discovered Roadley lying on his living-room floor, a large wound in the centre of his head. The doctor was called, but Richard Roadley was dead within two hours. The house had been ransacked and since local gossip had it that Roadley kept a good deal of cash in his cottage, it looked like a case of robbery and murder.

Over the next week or so, the police took four men in for questioning. All could account for their movements satisfactorily and all were released. It was then that William Maynard came to their attention.

Maynard lived in the area and had told police that he was at home at the time of the attack. His wife refused to confirm this story, so he was taken in for further questioning.

After some grilling, Maynard admitted taking part in a robbery at Roadley's house, but incriminated another man, Thomas Harris, as the killer. According to Maynard, he and Harris had gone to the cottage together and whilst Maynard was outside, Harris battered the old man with a hammer. He then told the officers where some of the stolen items could be found.

Luckily for Thomas Harris, he was able to prove that at the time of the attack on Richard Roadley, he was six miles away, at Jacobstow. After being detained for a full 24 hours, a much-relieved Harris was released and Maynard was charged with murder.

At his trial, Maynard's defence tried to suggest that Roadley had died as a result of a fall, which Doctor Holtby of Bude refuted, and also that Maynard had not made his statement to the police voluntarily. He claimed that four officers had been holding him and that he was forced to sign a statement, yet it was shown that the signature on that document was comparable

NAME	William John Maynard
AGE AT EXECUTION	36
DATE OF EXECUTION	Friday, 27th July, 1928
PLACE OF EXECUTION	Exeter
HANGMAN	Thomas Pierrepoint
ASSISTANT	Robert Wilson
DATE OF TRIAL	4th June – 5th June, 1928
LOCATION OF TRIAL	Bodmin
PRESIDING JUDGE	Mister Justice Swift
PROSECUTION COUNSEL	Rayner Goddard, A.H. Murphy
DEFENCE COUNSEL	W.T. Lawrance, Elliott Batt
NUMBER OF VICTIMS	1

VICTIMS DETAILS	
NAME	Richard Francis Roadley
AGE	84
DATE OF MURDER	Sunday, 19th February, 1928
PLACE OF MURDER	Titson, Marhamchurch, near Bude
METHOD OF KILLING	Battered
RELATIONSHIP TO KILLER	None

to others that Maynard agreed he had not signed under duress.

More telling was the testimony of John Marsh, who worked for Maynard. On February 18th he had asked Maynard for his wages and had been told that he was a little short at the moment. Yet, just two days later, Marsh had been paid in full and even been given extra money so that he could pay a bill that Maynard owed.

Found guilty and condemned to death, the original execution date of June 27th was postponed, pending an appeal. The appeal failed and exactly one month after the original date, William John Maynard kept his appointment with the hangman.

1928

THOMAS LEE WORKED as a boiler fireman at Lang's bakery and worked the night shift. In the early hours of March 22nd he was found by a colleague, sitting on a makeshift seat in the boiler room, his coat pulled up over his head. Lee had sustained a head injury. Rushed to the Royal Infirmary, he died without ever regaining consciousness.

The police immediately had a suspect, for on the night of March 21st, a man had accompanied Lee to his place of work. That man had been seen by Alexander Murdoch, another fireman at the bakery. When questioned, the man told Murdoch that he and Lee had been out drinking, and that he was going to supervise the boiler that night. Murdoch didn't care who did the work, as long as it was done, and asked no further questions.

The stranger had also been seen by James Gray and Joseph Martin, two other workers at Lang's. Both had been told that Lee had been drinking and that his shift would be taken care of whilst he "slept it off".

When the police visited Lee's house at 28 Cathedral Street and spoke to his wife, she also told then about the man who had been with her husband. They had come in together on the 21st but Thomas seemed anxious for the man to leave. For his part, the man seemed to be in a hurry to get to the bakehouse.

Meanwhile, the stranger, George Reynolds, had gone to a lodging house run by Mrs Gordon, in Tennant Street. He arrived at 1.15am on March 22nd and explained away his dirty hands and overalls by saying that he had been helping Lee in the bakehouse. After he had washed, Reynolds began to cry and said that he had done "… a very desperate action". He went on to admit that he had hit Lee with a firebar.

The next day, Mrs Tennant heard about Lee's death and took her story to the police. On Saturday March 24th, Detective Constable Alfred Rettie saw Reynolds in Ingram Street. When cautioned, Reynolds gave his name as John Smith, but he was taken to the police station, where Mrs Gordon identified him.

Two stories were told at Reynolds's trial. The prosecution held that this was a simple

NAME	George Reynolds
AGE AT EXECUTION	41
DATE OF EXECUTION	Friday, 3rd August, 1928
PLACE OF EXECUTION	Glasgow, Duke Street
HANGMAN	Robert Baxter
ASSISTANT	Not known
DATE OF TRIAL	25th June – 27th June, 1928
LOCATION OF TRIAL	Glasgow
PRESIDING JUDGE	Lord Justice Hunter
PROSECUTION COUNSEL	R.H. MacConnachie, J.R. Milligan
DEFENCE COUNSEL	Walter T. Watson, Ross MacLean
NUMBER OF VICTIMS	1

VICTIMS DETAILS	
NAME	Thomas Lee
AGE	Not known
DATE OF MURDER	Thursday, 22nd March, 1928
PLACE OF MURDER	Lang's Bread Co Ltd, 38 Wesleyan Street, Glasgow
METHOD OF KILLING	Battered
RELATIONSHIP TO KILLER	None

case of robbery that had ended in murder. For the defence, the story was that Lee had been asleep and when he woke he made a comment about Reynolds wanting to take his job. He then attacked Reynolds, who struck out to defend himself.

In the event, the jury chose to believe the prosecution's case and Reynolds was sentenced to death. He was due to hang on Wednesday, July 18th but this was cancelled when he announced his intention to appeal. That appeal was lost on July 16th.

THE MACAULEY FAMILY were well known around Armoy. They owned and farmed 300 acres of land and lived in a cottage at Mullaghduffbeg. The house was occupied by Andrew, his brother Leslie and two unmarried sisters, Margaret and Sarah.

On Thursday, May 24th, Andrew and Leslie were repairing some fencing, two of their labourers, William Smiley and Tommy McCaughan were ploughing a field and Kate Murdoch, a domestic servant, was behind the farmhouse, budding some potatoes.

At 12.50pm, Kate went into the house for lunch. Both Smiley and McCaughan were there and they too were given a meal. Ten minutes later, Sarah Macauley took some food to her brothers, staying with them until 1.25pm. At about the same time, Kate Murdoch took some cows to be watered. On they way back, she spotted Sarah and the two walked back to the farmhouse, after which Kate went back to her duties with the potatoes.

At 2.00pm, Kate Murdoch heard a shot. It sounded fairly close, but such sounds were common in the countryside and she thought no more about it. Ten minutes later she heard the sound of a horse, but could not place the direction the hoof-beats came from.

At 3.00pm, Kate went into the farmhouse and found the Macauley sisters lying on the kitchen floor in a pool of blood. Both had been shot in the head and the shotgun used lay on the floor. Kate dashed across the fields, found William Smiley and asked him to fetch the police. He climbed onto a horse and galloped away.

The motive for the crime soon became apparent. A cash box in an upstairs room had been emptied and this had contained at least £35. The killer had also taken £1 in silver and a gold watch and chain.

William Smiley soon fell under suspicion. At the police station, when informing Sergeant Connolly of the crime, he had said that the sisters had been murdered and the house raided, before anyone else knew of the missing items. Inquiries continued and, after the inquest, Smiley was arrested and charged with murder. When he was searched, three £10 notes were found in the toe of his right boot.

NAME	William Smiley (Smylie)
AGE AT EXECUTION	28
DATE OF EXECUTION	Wednesday, 8th August, 1928
PLACE OF EXECUTION	Belfast
HANGMAN	Thomas Pierrepoint
ASSISTANT	Robert Baxter
DATE OF TRIAL	10th July, 1928
LOCATION OF TRIAL	Belfast
PRESIDING JUDGE	Lord Chief Justice, Sir William Moore
PROSECUTION COUNSEL	A.B. Babington M.P., Mister Davidson, C.L. Sheil
DEFENCE COUNSEL	T.J. Campbell, William Boles
NUMBER OF VICTIMS	2

VICTIMS DETAILS	
NAMES	Margaret Macauley; Sarah Macauley
AGES	48; 43
DATE OF MURDER	Thursday, 24th May, 1928
PLACE OF MURDER	Mullaghduffbeg, near Armoy, County Antrim
METHOD OF KILLING	Shot; shot
RELATIONSHIP TO KILLER	None; none

In his defence, Smiley claimed that when the police and the Macauley brothers were at the farm, he had gone inside and seen what looked like a rolled-up £1 note lying under a dressing table. He had stolen it and only later found that it was three £10 notes. This story was disproved by Leslie Macauley who confirmed that once the police were on the scene, no one had been allowed inside the house.

The jury took 20 minutes to decide that Smiley was guilty. Once he received news that there was to be no reprieve, he made a full confession to the crime.

IN 1924, ABRAHAM Goldenberg was hanged for the murder of a bank clerk during a robbery. Norman Elliott would hang for almost exactly the same crime.

On February 16th, 1928, at 3.00pm, a heavy brass paperweight was hurtled through the window of the one-man branch of Lloyds Bank, at Ferryhill. People found the cashier, William Byland Abbey, badly wounded. Someone had robbed the bank of £200 after striking Abbey on the forehead and stabbing him in the neck. All Byland could say was that his assailant had been a tall man. He died from his injuries soon afterwards.

Gladys Turner was a bus conductor and on February 16th, at 3.50pm, a man she knew by sight, but not by name, had boarded her bus. She had seen the man earlier that same day, in Ferryhill, and now she jokingly reprimanded him for ignoring her on that occasion. To her surprise, he denied being in Ferryhill at all and this made her suspicious. Gladys knew that he was an attendant at the Durham County Asylum, in Sedgefield. This led the police to Norman Elliott.

Before February 16th, Elliott had had severe financial problems but on February 17th, he had paid almost £20, in cash, for some furniture and carpets. When taken in for questioning, Elliott was found to have over £145.

Elliott admitted his part in the robbery, but claimed that he had an accomplice and it was this man who had killed Abbey. According to his story, he had arranged to meet George Sinclair at the bank, around closing time. He found the bank door closed but it was opened almost immediately by a bloodstained Sinclair, who dragged him inside and thrust a quantity of money into his hands. This was how Elliott explained the bloodstains found on some of the notes, and on his clothing.

Elliott's story was, to say the least, rather weak. Whilst he had been seen in the area, no one had reported seeing a second, heavily bloodstained man. The prosecution held therefore that Sinclair did not exist, and that Elliott had acted alone.

Elliott's next ploy was to point out that he knew Abbey and that if he had been the attacker, surely Abbey would have named him

NAME	Norman Elliott
AGE AT EXECUTION	23
DATE OF EXECUTION	Friday, 10th August, 1928
PLACE OF EXECUTION	Durham
HANGMAN	Thomas Pierrepoint
ASSISTANT	Robert Wilson
DATE OF TRIAL	26th June – 27th June, 1928
LOCATION OF TRIAL	Durham
PRESIDING JUDGE	Mister Justice MacKinnon
PROSECUTION COUNSEL	G.F.L. Mortimer, G.H.B. Streatfeild
DEFENCE COUNSEL	A.R. Linsley
NUMBER OF VICTIMS	1

VICTIMS DETAILS	
NAME	William Byland Abbey
AGE	31
DATE OF MURDER	Thursday, 16th February, 1928
PLACE OF MURDER	Lloyds Bank, Ferryhill, Durham
METHOD OF KILLING	Battered/stabbed
RELATIONSHIP TO KILLER	None

instead of claiming that the man who had stabbed him was "a tall man". The prosecution countered this by pointing out that whilst it was true that both men lived in Spennymoor, there was no evidence that the two had ever met before February 16th. After an hour's deliberation, Elliott was found guilty and sentenced to death.

The links with the Goldenberg case of 1924 were complete. Both Goldenberg and Elliott had robbed branches of Lloyds Bank, occupied by lone cashiers. Both had claimed that the true miscreants were accomplices who did not exist, and both were hanged for their crimes.

ON JUNE 4TH, 1928, Isabella Wales celebrated her 20th birthday. The next day she was brutally murdered by her estranged husband.

Isabella, whose maiden name had been Hain, married Allen Wales on December 2nd, 1926. They lived together at various addresses but from the outset, Isabella's parents did not approve of their son-in-law and as a result, Isabella did not see her family for 11 weeks after the marriage. When she did start to visit again, she complained that Wales had started to beat her and sported bruises to prove her claims.

A son was born to Isabella on October 2nd, 1927, but this did nothing to improve her husband's treatment of her. Things came to a head on Saturday, June 2nd, 1928 when Isabella was out with her mother, Florence Hain and Wales met them by accident in Kirkgate. He began to shout and abuse Isabella so much that the family suggested that she should not go back with him to their house in Orchardfield Lane. Isabella agreed and spent that weekend at her cousin's home.

On Tuesday, June 5th, at 11.00am, Isabella and her cousin, Jessie Berry, called at Florence Hain's house in Pirniefield Place. They both said that they had met up with Wales, who had demanded that Isabella return home with him. She had refused. Later that day, Wales called at Pirniefield Place himself, with his mother, and again asked Isabella to return. When she still refused, Wales and his mother left.

It wasn't long before Wales was back. This time he was alone, and brandishing a knife. He dragged Isabella from the house and began hacking at her throat with the knife. This attack was witnessed not only by Isabella's family but by a number of neighbours including Robina Robertson who lived at number 15. She also heard Wales shout "You were asking for it and now you've got it."

It took the jury just under 40 minutes to find Wales guilty of murder, though surprisingly, this was by a majority verdict of 14 to one. The one dissenting voice may have been influenced by a report from Doctor W.M. McAlister and Dr Dodds Fairbairn who had examined Wales and determined that he had a

NAME	Allen Wales
AGE AT EXECUTION	22
DATE OF EXECUTION	Monday, 13th August, 1928
PLACE OF EXECUTION	Edinburgh, Saughton
HANGMAN	Robert Baxter
ASSISTANT	Henry Pollard
DATE OF TRIAL	23rd July, 1928
LOCATION OF TRIAL	Edinburgh
PRESIDING JUDGE	Lord Justice Anderson
PROSECUTION COUNSEL	A.M. MacRobert, R.H. Maconochie
DEFENCE COUNSEL	J.L. Wark, H. McKechnie
NUMBER OF VICTIMS	1

VICTIMS DETAILS	
NAME	Isabella Wales
AGE	20
DATE OF MURDER	Tuesday, 5th June, 1928
PLACE OF MURDER	17 Pirniefield Place, Leith
METHOD OF KILLING	Cut throat
RELATIONSHIP TO KILLER	Wife

mental age of 10 with a state of intelligence bordering on the feeble minded.

CHARLOTTE HARBER HAD been married for six years and had two children, both boys. Her husband, Sidney John Harber, worked at an ice-cream factory and it was here that he first met William Charles Benson. The two became friends and in February 1925, Benson moved in with the Harbers, as a lodger.

In August 1926, Sidney Harber discovered that his wife was having an affair with Benson and ordered him out of his house. As a result of Charlotte's pleading and promises that she would end the relationship, Benson was allowed back after an absence of just two days. It was a decision Sidney Harber would regret.

Despite Charlotte's promises, the affair with Benson started up again and, when Sidney found out in 1927, Benson was again ordered out of the house. This time he was not to return, but the involvement with Charlotte continued just as strongly as before.

In April 1928, Charlotte rented a room in Sutherland Place, Bayswater, using the name Mrs Benson. William stayed there and Charlotte took the opportunity of visiting each day. This continued for some months until Charlotte decided that the affair had to end and said she wished to go back to her husband.

On the night of September 5th, Charlotte stayed with Benson in a boarding house in Euston Road. It was to be the last night they spent together and no doubt she took the opportunity to explain to him that things were over between them.

The following day, September 6th, William Benson walked up to a policeman and said: "I want an ambulance. I have just killed my girl." He then took the officer to a field near Coulsdon Court golf course where the body of Charlotte lay. She had been stabbed in the breast and her unharmed baby lay close by, still in its perambulator.

Benson's defence was insanity. His mother gave evidence that some of her relatives had committed suicide but when pressed, had to admit that she had never entertained any doubts about her son's mental faculties, and the medical officer of Brixton prison, where Benson had been held, said he could find no signs of insanity in his prisoner.

After an absence of 15 minutes, the jury returned their guilty verdict and William Benson was sentenced to death.

NAME	William Charles Benson
AGE AT EXECUTION	25
DATE OF EXECUTION	Tuesday, 20th November, 1928
PLACE OF EXECUTION	Wandsworth
HANGMAN	Robert Baxter
ASSISTANT	Lionel Mann
DATE OF TRIAL	15th October, 1928
LOCATION OF TRIAL	Old Bailey
PRESIDING JUDGE	Mister Justice Finlay
PROSECUTION COUNSEL	Percival Clarke
DEFENCE COUNSEL	Laurence Vine
NUMBER OF VICTIMS	1

VICTIMS DETAILS	
NAME	Charlotte Alice Harber
AGE	26
DATE OF MURDER	Thursday, 6th September, 1928
PLACE OF MURDER	Near Coulsdon Court Golf Course, Surrey
METHOD OF KILLING	Stabbed
RELATIONSHIP TO KILLER	Girlfriend

FOR SOMEONE WHO appeared to have carefully planned the murder of his wife, Chung Yi Miao made some very elementary mistakes.

Chung met his future wife in New York, in October 1927. She was the daughter of a wealthy merchant from Macao and had gone to America to negotiate the sale of some rare jade objects. He was the son of a Chinese lawyer and had gone to America to complete his education. The couple began seeing each other and on May 12th, 1928, they were married in New York. An expensive honeymoon in America, England and Scotland was then booked.

June 1928 saw the newlyweds in the Lake District, one of the most beautiful parts of England, and on June 18th, Chung and his wife booked into the Borrowdale Gates Hotel at the southern end of Derwentwater.

The next day was sunny but not too warm so Chung pulled on a light brown overcoat before he and Wai set off for a pleasant walk through the countryside. They left at about 2.00pm. At 4.00pm, Chung returned alone and announced that his wife had gone alone into Keswick to buy some warmer clothes for herself.

Wai had not returned at dinner time and a fellow guest, Miss Crossley, spoke to Chung about her absence. Chung tried to dismiss her concerns but Miss Crossley was astute enough to realise that something was wrong.

At 10.00pm, Chung showed his first signs of any anxiety. He told a maid that his wife had still not returned and asked her what he should do. She, quite correctly, said that Chung should contact the police. Instead, he simply went to bed and did nothing.

Unbeknown to Chung though, his wife had already been found. Thomas Wilson, a local farmer, had been on his way to his local pub when he saw a woman lying down at a local beauty spot known as 'Cumma Catta'. He recognised the woman as Oriental and assumed therefore that she was the lady from the hotel but did not go near her in case he disturbed her. When he mentioned this in the pub, one of the people who overheard him was an off-duty policeman – Detective Constable Pendelbury. He suggested that they

NAME	Chung Yi Miao
AGE AT EXECUTION	28
DATE OF EXECUTION	Thursday, December 6th, 1928
PLACE OF EXECUTION	Manchester
HANGMAN	Thomas Pierrepoint
ASSISTANT	Not known
DATE OF TRIAL	22nd October – 23rd October, 1928
LOCATION OF TRIAL	Carlisle
PRESIDING JUDGE	Mister Justice Humphreys
PROSECUTION COUNSEL	J.E. Singleton, Mister Maxwell-Fyfe
DEFENCE COUNSEL	J.C. Jackson, W. Gorman
NUMBER OF VICTIMS	1

VICTIMS DETAILS	
NAME	Wai Sheung Sui
AGE	29
DATE OF MURDER	Tuesday, June 19th, 1928
PLACE OF MURDER	'Cumma Catta', Derwentwater, Lake District
METHOD OF KILLING	Strangled
RELATIONSHIP TO KILLER	Wife

should go and have a look and when they returned to the spot, they found the body of Wai Sheung Sui.

Wai was lying underneath an umbrella. The white cord that had been used to strangle her was still tied around her neck. Her skirt had been pulled up onto her breasts and her underwear had been removed, giving all the appearances of rape. Two rings were missing from her fingers, though she was still wearing an expensive, diamond-studded watch.

When Chung was roused from his bed, he made his first mistake. Told that his wife had been found he blurted out, "Had she knickers on?" He would later claim that his accent had caused the police to mishear and he had actually said necklace but even if we allow for that, he then immediately made his second mistake by saying, "It's terrible! My wife assaulted, robbed and murdered." At this stage, no one had mentioned the theft of the rings.

Slowly the evidence began to pile up. White cord was found in the hotel that was identical to that found around Wai's throat. Chung's brown overcoat was found to be stained with human blood and Wai had bled from the mouth. Finally, when Chung's room was carefully searched, two rolls of film were found. In case these might shed some clues, they were given to a local photographer to develop and as he unwrapped the second one, the two missing rings fell out. Chung was arrested and charged with his wife's murder.

At the trial in Carlisle a most interesting piece of paper was produced. It had been found amongst Chung's belongings and read: "Be sure to do it on the ship. Don't do it on the ship. Again consider on arrival in Europe." Chung admitted the words were in his handwriting but could not offer any explanation as to what they meant. The prosecution held that they were a sign of intent to commit murder and that therefore the crime was premeditated.

Chung's defence was that he had noticed two Orientals following him and his wife from the moment they had arrived in Scotland and again in the Lakes. Witnesses did come forward to say that they had seen two Chinese men in Keswick on the day of the murder but this was held to be coincidence and the weight of evidence against Chung led to the jury deciding he was guilty, after an absence of an hour.

Asked if he had anything to say, Chung began to make a speech attacking the way the judge had handled the case, but he was interrupted and sentenced to death. At the court of appeal, Chung conducted his own defence but it did little good; the appeal failed.

The one thing that remains unclear is the motive for Wai's murder. One school of thought is that she was killed for her money: Chung had married a wealthy woman and could not wait to get his hands on that wealth. Others believe that the motive was more traditionally Chinese. On May 25th, soon after she had been married, Wai had an operation because she had found it impossible to have intercourse. It has been suggested that this, together with other gynaecological concerns led Chung to believe that Wai would be unable to provide him with children and he saw murder as the quickest way out of his predicament.

TREVOR JOHN EDWARDS and Elsie Cook had been seeing each other for some months. Her parents Edgar and Annie Elizabeth were happy with the amorous entanglement. However, Mrs Cook was not quite as happy on June 2nd, 1928, when she discovered that Elsie was pregnant. A meeting took place at Elsie's house on June 6th and Edwards agreed that he would marry her. They discussed dates and finally, a July wedding was decided upon.

Edwards arranged to meet Elsie on the night of June 16th. Before 8.30pm, Edwards was calling in at the Brynffynnon Hotel in Llanwonno, where he ordered a pint of beer and a glass of cider. He explained to the licensee, Elizabeth Mary Morgan, that the cider was for his girlfriend, who was waiting outside. Elizabeth did see a young woman, standing near the pub gate.

Before he left the pub, Edwards bought a large flagon of cider and was seen walking off with his young lady. At around 8.30pm, they were seen near the village church by Percy John Down.

At 10.15am the following morning, David Griffiths was having a quiet sit down on the side of the mountain at Llanwonno. Suddenly he heard footsteps behind him and upon turning around, saw a man walking down the mountain. The man was covered in blood.

Some five minutes after this, William John James saw the same man. James was waiting for a friend when the man, Edwards, came up to him and asked for a match. James noticed the bloodstains and when he asked about them, Edwards explained that he had cut his throat. He went on to explain that he had killed his girlfriend on the mountain and gave details of where he body could be found.

Once the police had been called, Edwards repeated his story of murder. Elsie Cook was found just where Edwards had said she would be. The flagon lay broken nearby and Elsie's head had been almost severed from her body.

There could be no doubt that it was a case of premeditated murder. Edwards described how he had purchased the flagon with the express intention of battering Elsie to death with it. Once they got onto the mountain, he had struck out but she had merely been

NAME	Trevor John Edwards
AGE AT EXECUTION	21
DATE OF EXECUTION	Tuesday, 11th December, 1928
PLACE OF EXECUTION	Swansea
HANGMAN	Robert Baxter
ASSISTANT	Alfred Allen
DATE OF TRIAL	22nd November, 1928
LOCATION OF TRIAL	Cardiff
PRESIDING JUDGE	Mister Justice Branson
PROSECUTION COUNSEL	Godrey Parsons
DEFENCE COUNSEL	Morgan Evans
NUMBER OF VICTIMS	1

VICTIMS DETAILS	
NAME	Elsie Cook
AGE	21
DATE OF MURDER	Saturday, 16th June, 1928
PLACE OF MURDER	Hillside at Llanwonno
METHOD OF KILLING	Battered/cut throat
RELATIONSHIP TO KILLER	Girlfriend

stunned and had started fighting back. Finally he managed to overpower her and choked her before cutting her throat.

It only remained to discover the motive. Since the beginning of January Edwards had been seeing 16-year-old Annie Protheroe and had kept in touch with her once she had gone to work in Swinton, in August 1927. He had written to her to tell her that he had made Elsie pregnant and he felt this was a terrible mistake.

His own confession was more than enough to convict Edwards and he became the last man hanged in 1928.

MRS STIRR WAS a keen gardener. One day, scraping around near a hedge, she noticed something sticking out of a small mound of earth. On closer inspection, Mrs Stirr saw that this object was a human wrist.

The police discovered two bodies buried in the shallow grave: a man and a woman. The burials must have taken place that day, because the man had a head wound that was still bleeding slightly. The bodies were identified as Thomas Kirby and his wife Emily Frances.

The postmortem introduced fresh horrors into the murder. Whilst Thomas had been battered and his wife strangled, neither had been dead when they were placed in the earth. Soil was discovered deep in the windpipe of both victims. They had been buried alive.

It wasn't very long before police investigations revealed some interesting facts about one of Emily's grandsons, Charles Conlin. In the month prior to the murders, Conlin had earned £3-7s, yet on the morning the bodies were found, he bought himself a new motorcycle in Darlington, for which he paid £21-10s in cash, using the name Charles Murphy. The same night he went out with his girlfriend, Rose MacIntyre and showed her £20 in notes.

On Friday, September 21st, Conlin had watched his brother-in-law digging in the garden of his house in Centenary Crescent, where Conlin himself lodged. He had also seen where the spade was kept when it was put away. That night Conlin went out with a friend, whom he left at 9.40pm, but he did not return home until midnight. That same night, a car was stolen from near Centenary Crescent.

At 6.20am the following morning, another lodger, George Lumsden, saw Conlin walking across the fields at the back of the house. He was carrying a spade and was heading in the direction of the grave.

The police now believed they had their killer, their motive and their method. Conlin, desperately short of money, knew that Thomas Kirby sometimes carried substantial amounts of cash. Stealing a car, Conlin had driven the four miles to where they lived and

NAME	Charles William Conlin
AGE AT EXECUTION	22
DATE OF EXECUTION	Friday, 4th January, 1929
PLACE OF EXECUTION	Durham
HANGMAN	Thomas Pierrepoint
ASSISTANT	Not known
DATE OF TRIAL	15th November 1928
LOCATION OF TRIAL	Durham
PRESIDING JUDGE	Mister Justice Roche
PROSECUTION COUNSEL	C.F. Lowenthal, C. Paley Scott
DEFENCE COUNSEL	E.G. Sykes
NUMBER OF VICTIMS	2

VICTIMS DETAILS

NAMES	Thomas Kirby; Emily Frances Kirby
AGES	62; 64
DATE OF MURDER	Saturday, 22nd September, 1928
PLACE OF MURDER	Briar Garth, Norton
METHOD OF KILLING	Battered/buried alive; strangled/buried alive
RELATIONSHIP TO KILLER	Grandfather by marriage; grandmother

had spun them some story. The bed at the Kirby house had been slept in by one person, so one of them, probably Emily, was lured alone to her death, to be followed later by her husband. Conlin was arrested and when searched, was found to have in his possession a grey wallet subsequently identified as Thomas Kirby's.

Conlin did not bother to try to explain away the evidence built up against him, preferring instead to claim that he remembered nothing of the night in question. It did nothing to endear him to a jury who had no trouble in finding him guilty.

NATHAN MARKOVITCH RAN a butcher's shop at 17 Loddiges Road, Hackney, living above the establishment with his wife and their domestic servant, Annie Elizabeth Hatton, who had worked for them since February.

On Saturday, November 17th, 1928, Nathan took his wife to the theatre. They left home at around 8.00pm, and returned three hours later. Annie had been left behind, to look after the Markovitches' two young children, aged two years, and seven months.

As Nathan opened the door, he could hear the children crying. When he entered the kitchen he found why Annie had ignored her duties: she was lying, bound and gagged, on the kitchen floor, and was quite dead.

The police discovered that not only did Annie have a male friend, but that he had already exhibited violence towards her. Some six weeks before, Annie had returned home with her nose bleeding and had told Nathan and his wife that her boyfriend had hit her. Luckily, Annie had put a name to this man: John Dennis.

It took officers some time to determine that John Dennis was in fact Frank Hollington and he was arrested at his home, 65 Warner Place, Bethnal Green, on November 29th. He admitted that he had been involved with Annie and even confessed to killing her, but claimed that it was accidental.

Mrs Markovitch said that a few days before Annie's death she had heard her on the telephone, apologising to someone for failing to turn up as arranged. Hollington admitted that it had been he on the other end of the telephone. He had arranged to meet Annie at the Empress Picture Palace the Wednesday before she died but she had failed to turn up. When Hollington had gone looking for her, he had seen here in the company of another man.

On the night of Annie's death, Hollington had gone to visit her. They were in the kitchen – she ironing, he reading a newspaper – when he asked her again about standing him up. When she lied to him again, he lost control and hit her. Annie fell to the floor and Hollington hit her again before tying her up. He then stole a few small items to make it

NAME	Frank Hollington (John Dennis)
AGE AT EXECUTION	25
DATE OF EXECUTION	Wednesday, 20th February, 1929
PLACE OF EXECUTION	Pentonville
HANGMAN	Robert Baxter
ASSISTANT	Robert Wilson
DATE OF TRIAL	14th January, 1929
LOCATION OF TRIAL	Old Bailey
PRESIDING JUDGE	Mister Justice Humphreys
PROSECUTION COUNSEL	Eustace Fulton, G.D. Roberts
DEFENCE COUNSEL	Laurence Vine
NUMBER OF VICTIMS	1

VICTIMS DETAILS	
NAME	Annie Elizabeth Hatton
AGE	18
DATE OF MURDER	Saturday, 17th November, 1928
PLACE OF MURDER	17 Loddiges Road, Hackney, London
METHOD OF KILLING	Battered
RELATIONSHIP TO KILLER	Girlfriend

look like robbery. He claimed he had not known that Annie was dead until he read it in the newspapers.

One could not blame Hollington for trying to persuade the jury that he was guilty only of manslaughter, but he had made one error. If he had really thought that Annie was alive, why had he bothered to fake a robbery? Surely she would have woken in due course and told the Markovitches what had really happened. The jury thought much the same and found him guilty.

WILLIAM HOLMYARD RAN his own furniture business, even though he was now over 70 years of age. He ran the business from number 37 Tachbrook Street, Pimlico which was next door to where his son lived, at number 39.

On Friday, December 7th, 1928, old Mr Holmyard was discovered, badly battered, in the office at the back of his shop. Police inquiries soon led them to his grandson, also named William, who lived at number 39 with his parents.

At the police station, William John Holmyard made a statement confessing to the attack on his grandfather. He explained that he had until recently been a soldier, serving in India, and had been discharged on November 18th. Short of money he had borrowed £7 from his grandfather. Over the next few weeks, he had repaid some of this, but had then borrowed more until the debt became £17.

On the day of his grandfather's death, William walked into the office at the furniture shop and was greeted with questions about the money he owed. One thing led to another and an argument developed during which Holmyard picked up a pair of copper fire irons and struck his grandfather twice. Holmyard was charged with wounding.

On Monday, December 10th, William Holmyard died from his injuries and his grandson was now charged with murder. Holmyard changed his story and tried to say that he had been at Kennington on the afternoon of the murder and the statement he had made at the police station had not been a voluntary one. When this failed to convince, Holmyard claimed that the killing had been self-defence.

Holmyard was a slightly built man, whilst his grandfather had been well built and almost six feet tall. Holmyard now said that the argument had developed to such a stage that his grandfather had lifted a heavy chair above his head and was about to bring it crashing down when he struck out with the tongs in self-defence. None of this was believed and Holmyard was found guilty.

The appeal provided an interesting point of law. During the trial, the jury had been

NAME	William John Holmyard
AGE AT EXECUTION	24
DATE OF EXECUTION	Wednesday, 27th February, 1929
PLACE OF EXECUTION	Pentonville
HANGMAN	Robert Baxter
ASSISTANT	Lionel Mann
DATE OF TRIAL	15th January – 16th January, 1929
LOCATION OF TRIAL	Old Bailey
PRESIDING JUDGE	Mister Justice Humphreys
PROSECUTION COUNSEL	Percival Clarke, G.B. McClure
DEFENCE COUNSEL	Miss Venetia J.M. Stephenson, Doctor F. Hallis
NUMBER OF VICTIMS	1

VICTIMS DETAILS	
NAME	William Holmyard (Died Monday, 10th December)
AGE	circa 73
DATE OF MURDER	Friday, 7th December, 1928
PLACE OF MURDER	37 Tachbrook Street, Pimlico, London
METHOD OF KILLING	Battered
RELATIONSHIP TO KILLER	Grandfather

excluded at one stage whilst the legal representatives debated whether Holmyard's statements were admissible. It was said that whilst the jury were considering their verdict, a court bailiff had supplied them with newspapers that carried reports of the arguments whilst they had been out of court. The defence held that this invalidated the trial and at the very least, a retrial should be ordered. The appeal court judges did not agree.

O N SUNDAY, OCTOBER 28TH, 1928, at 11.00am, people passing down Northbrook Street in Liverpool, heard a woman crying for help.

Looking around to see where the shouts of: "Save me, save me" were coming from, they saw the door of number 110 thrown open and a young woman rush out, bleeding from a wound in her throat. She was followed almost immediately by a young man who, on seeing the crowd of witnesses, stood idly on the front doorstep and calmly asked if anyone had called the police.

The police were indeed called. The young woman, Mary Agnes Fontaine, was taken to hospital and the man, Joseph Reginald Clarke, was taken in for questioning. Inside the house, officers found that there had been a third player in this tragedy. In the sitting room of 110, Northbrook Street, they found the body of Mary Agnes's mother, Alice Fontaine. She had been strangled.

Joseph Clarke told his story readily. He had been seeing Mary Agnes for some time and had lodged with her and her mother since June 1st. They knew him as Reginald Kennedy and were also aware that he was unemployed.

On the day of the murder, Clarke had been in the sitting room with Mrs Fontaine when she began nagging him about getting a job, especially since he wasn't paying his way. After taking this for some time, Clarke put his hands around her throat and squeezed until Alice Fontaine stopped breathing. Clarke then walked into Mary Agnes's room and told her that he had just killed her mother and now intended killing her.

Unsurprisingly, Mary Agnes objected to being murdered and fought hard for her life. Clarke tried his best to strangle her but she managed to fight him off and screamed. Clarke snatched a piece of electrical flex and started to throttle Mary Agnes until he suddenly came to his senses and realised what he was doing to her. At that point, Clarke took a knife from his pocket and cut the flex. Rather than being grateful, Mary Agnes screamed again, and so Clarke cut her throat.

Mary Agnes now showed great courage and although bleeding badly, she managed to calm Clarke down. Then, seeing her

NAME	Joseph Reginald Victor Clarke (Reginald Kennedy)
AGE AT EXECUTION	21
DATE OF EXECUTION	Tuesday, 12th March, 1929
PLACE OF EXECUTION	Liverpool
HANGMAN	Thomas Pierrepoint
ASSISTANT	Henry Pollard
DATE OF TRIAL	4th February, 1929
LOCATION OF TRIAL	Liverpool
PRESIDING JUDGE	Mister Justice Finlay
PROSECUTION COUNSEL	J. Fraser Harrison
DEFENCE COUNSEL	Basil Neild
NUMBER OF VICTIMS	1

VICTIMS DETAILS

NAME	Alice Fontaine
AGE	55
DATE OF MURDER	Sunday, 28th October, 1928
PLACE OF MURDER	110 Northbrook Street, Princes Park, Liverpool
METHOD OF KILLING	Strangled
RELATIONSHIP TO KILLER	None

opportunity, she ran out into the street and managed to find someone to assist her.

When Clarke appeared in court, he pleaded guilty to the charge against him. Mister Justice Finlay made sure he understood the implications of that plea and when Clarke confirmed that he was fully aware of what it meant, he was sentenced to death. The entire proceedings had lasted five minutes.

WHILST IT IS true that in British courts, a defendant is innocent until proven guilty, that burden of proof shifts when a plea of insanity is lodged. It is not for the prosecution to prove that an individual is not insane, it for his defence to prove that he is. It was that difficulty which led George Cartledge to the gallows.

At 9.00am on January 2nd, 1929, Mrs Vickers was passing her neighbour's house when she saw Nellie Cartledge at the window, trying to attract her attention. Nellie shouted for Mrs Vickers to send for the police and an ambulance but by the time they arrived, Nellie was already dead from throat injuries. A bloodstained razor was found at the scene.

George Cartledge was also found inside the house. He appeared to be in a somewhat dazed condition and said he had no idea what had happened. Sergeant Dunbar and Constable James interviewed George at the scene of the crime and all he seemed to recall was that he might have hit his wife. It was later suggested that George only knew that much because his six-year-old daughter, Mary, had found her mother crying upstairs and had noticed blood on her father's hands.

It appeared that George had been receiving medical treatment for head pains. He had seen a doctor on December 3rd, saying that he also found it difficult to concentrate and was having difficulty sleeping. The doctor had last seen George on December 30th and thought at that time that he seemed to be much better.

In court, the defence was one of insanity. Doctor Shannon, the medical officer at Strangeways, reported that George was of below average mentality and had tried to commit suicide whilst in custody. Unfortunately for George, Doctor Shannon added that he could find no signs of actual insanity.

After being advised by the judge that the onus was on the defence to prove that George was insane, the jury retired to consider their verdict. They deliberated for two and three-quarter hours before deciding that this factor had not been proven and George was therefore guilty of murder. They did however add a recommendation to mercy.

George Cartledge appealed against his

NAME	George Henry Cartledge
AGE AT EXECUTION	27
DATE OF EXECUTION	Thursday, 4th April, 1929
PLACE OF EXECUTION	Manchester
HANGMAN	Thomas Pierrepoint
ASSISTANT	Not known
DATE OF TRIAL	26th February, 1929
LOCATION OF TRIAL	Manchester
PRESIDING JUDGE	Mister Justice Finlay
PROSECUTION COUNSEL	E.L. Fleming
DEFENCE COUNSEL	Mister Broadbent
NUMBER OF VICTIMS	1

VICTIMS DETAILS	
NAME	Ellen (Nellie) Cartledge
AGE	25
DATE OF MURDER	Wednesday, 2nd January, 1929
PLACE OF MURDER	2 Oak Street, Shaw, Oldham
METHOD OF KILLING	Cut throat
RELATIONSHIP TO KILLER	Wife

death sentence but this failed, the Lord Chief Justice adding that the recommendation of the jury was not a matter for him but rather for the Home Secretary to consider.

JAMES JOHNSON WAS well known to the police. A bookmaker, he had convictions for gambling offences, being drunk and disorderly, assault and theft, culminating in a prison sentence of 60 days, which he started on December 27th, 1928.

It was not long after Johnson had been released that he discovered that whilst he had been incarcerated, his wife had been entertaining another man, Billy Ridley. She denied any impropriety had taken place but two of her children, Nancy and Jenny, confirmed that something had been going on. This led to many arguments between James and Mary until, on May 9th, at 10.10pm, Mary made a complaint to Constable George Thomas Urwin.

Constable Urwin went back to Cannon Street with Mary and spoke to James about his behaviour. He in turn complained that she had hit him with a rolling pin and at one stage, Mary took a razor out of James's coat pocket and showed it to the policeman saying: "This is what he keeps for me." Those words would prove to be very prophetic.

On May 10th, the youngest child, three-year-old Irene Johnson, was taken to hospital.

The next day, May 11th, Mary left her mother at 11.15pm. At that time she and the children were all alive and well. Less than two hours later, at 1.00am on the morning of May 12th, Thomas Edward Held, who lodged on the same floor as the Johnsons, heard a thud, followed by a low moan. His father, William, also heard it and knowing the recent history of the Johnsons, was concerned enough to call for another neighbour, George Muckle.

Together the two men went to Johnson's door and knocked. Not only was there no reply, but a strong smell of gas told them that something was wrong. They forced open the door and having turned off the gas taps inside the house, went to fetch the police.

Mary Johnson was already dead, her throat cut. In another room, James lay on his bed, suffering badly from gas inhalation. His hands were heavily bloodstained. The three children in the house, Nancy aged 13, eight-year-old Jenny and five-year-old James, were all affected by gas, but luckily would later recover.

NAME	James Johnson
AGE AT EXECUTION	43
DATE OF EXECUTION	Wednesday, 7th August, 1929
PLACE OF EXECUTION	Durham
HANGMAN	Thomas Pierrepoint
ASSISTANT	Not known
DATE OF TRIAL	2nd July – 3rd July, 1929
LOCATION OF TRIAL	Newcastle
PRESIDING JUDGE	Mister Justice Finlay
PROSECUTION COUNSEL	Arthur Morley
DEFENCE COUNSEL	R.F. Burnand
NUMBER OF VICTIMS	1

VICTIMS DETAILS	
NAME	Mary Annie Johnson
AGE	Not known
DATE OF MURDER	Sunday, 12th May, 1929
PLACE OF MURDER	68 Cannon Street, Newcastle upon Tyne
METHOD OF KILLING	Cut throat
RELATIONSHIP TO KILLER	Wife

James Johnson was charged with the murder of his wife and the attempted murder of his three children. He tried to claim that it had been Mary who turned the gas on and then cut her own throat but his bloodstained hands and the fact that her wound was unlikely to be self-inflicted, were enough to convict him.

A RTHUR LESLIE RAVENEY, a soldier in the Royal Tank Corps, had served for over eight years without a blemish on his character when a minor offence saw him confined to barracks. During that sentence he found himself guarded by Leslie White.

On May 14th, Raveney left camp without permission and was reported as being absent without leave. He was picked up on the Great North Road, about five miles from Catterick and taken into custody pending the arrival of a military escort.

The military tender duly arrived, containing sergeants Brett and Prangnall, together with Private Leslie White. The two sergeants were in the front seat, leaving White to watch Raveney in the back. The vehicle set off for Catterick.

As the car passed Constable Burton and turned a bend, a loud report rang out. Thinking that he had a burst tyre, the driver, Prangnall, pulled over and Raveney took the opportunity to jump down from the vehicle and run off, leaving Leslie dead in the back.

A massive search was launched for Raveney. Shortly afterwards he was spotted, five miles away, near Finghall, by Constable Cartwright. The officer gave chase, first on foot and then on a horse commandeered from a group of gypsies, managing finally to drive Raveney into woods near Newton-le-Willows. Reinforcements were called up and in due course, Raveney was arrested in a quarry.

There was an immediate mystery to solve. Where had the murder weapon come from? Raveney had been searched at the police station and no gun had been found on him. The vehicle contained no weapons and the escort were not armed.

At Raveney's trial, the prosecution tried to suggest that Raveney had secreted the gun, possibly under an armpit. What was proved was that the gun used had been issued to Raveney on May 11th, but the accused man had a different explanation.

Raveney admitted that the gun was his, but claimed that he had lost it on May 12th. He suggested that White had stolen the weapon, probably to get him into trouble. Raveney decided that he would absent himself from camp so that if and when he was arrested, he

NAME	Arthur Leslie Raveney
AGE AT EXECUTION	24
DATE OF EXECUTION	Wednesday, 14th August, 1929
PLACE OF EXECUTION	Leeds
HANGMAN	Thomas Pierrepoint
ASSISTANT	Robert Wilson
DATE OF TRIAL	8th July, 1929
LOCATION OF TRIAL	York
PRESIDING JUDGE	Mister Justice MacKinnon
PROSECUTION COUNSEL	C.F. Lowenthal, C. Paley Scott
DEFENCE COUNSEL	A.R. Linsley
NUMBER OF VICTIMS	1

VICTIMS DETAILS	
NAME	Leslie Godfrey White
AGE	23
DATE OF MURDER	Tuesday, 14th May, 1929
PLACE OF MURDER	Constable Burton, near Wensleydale, North Yorkshire
METHOD OF KILLING	Shot
RELATIONSHIP TO KILLER	None

would be able to give formal evidence against White. He had had no intention of trying to escape and was quite content to be taken back to Catterick.

Once they had gone some distance, White had pulled out the revolver and threatened Raveney. He simply pushed the gun away and grabbed White's wrist. At that moment the vehicle took a bend and the gun went off accidentally. Whilst the story was feasible, it was devalued by the evidence of Private Walters, who reported that he had heard Raveney threaten White. As a result, the jury returned after an absence of 10 minutes and found Raveney guilty of murder.

JOHN MAGUIRE AND his wife, Ellen, had 10 children, whose ages ranged from 24 years, to 18 months. Eight of these children still lived at home with their parents and by September, 1929, Ellen was six months pregnant with child number 11.

With such a large household, each day was filled with activity. Things were much the same on September 5th, and by 7.00am, Ellen was already up and about, visiting the local market with her son, Edward Martin Maguire, whose 15th birthday was coming up on the 24th of the month. By 8.30am, Ellen was back home, enjoying a cup of tea with her 21-year-old daughter, Mary. Soon after this, Ellen had started her daily chores and was in the washhouse for much of the morning.

Lunch was a major organisational affair and at 12.15pm, Ellen and six of her children sat down to enjoy their midday meal but by 2.00pm, Ellen had been left alone with just two of her charges, Joseph, the youngest child, and three-year-old Lily. Up until this time, John Maguire had been out of the house.

At 1.00pm, John Maguire was calling into Hughes Brothers, a pawnbrokers at 116 Brownlow Hill, where he purchased a shiny new knife and a razor. He then returned home. At 2.30pm though, he was knocking on the door of Julia Kennedy who lived at 33a Newsham Street. As she opened the door to her neighbour, Maguire shouted: "Julia, come and see what I have done."

Julia and her husband, James Kennedy, known to his friends as Skinner, followed Maguire back to his house and found Ellen lying dead in the bedroom. As they gazed horror struck at the scene, Maguire turned on his heel, said he was going to give himself up and walked out of the house.

In fact, it was not until 7.30pm that Maguire finally walked into the police station, announced who he was to Sergeant William Smith, and gave himself up for the murder of his wife. His explanation was that she had been unfaithful to him and had as good as said that one of the children, Nellie, was not his.

Scientific evidence showed that Maguire had used both his new purchases on his wife. Ellen's wounds showed that she had first been stabbed in the back and then, whilst lying on

the floor, her throat had been hacked. Not surprisingly, considering all the evidence and his own statement to the police, the jury had no difficulty in finding him guilty.

NAME	John Maguire
AGE AT EXECUTION	43
DATE OF EXECUTION	Tuesday, 26th November, 1929
PLACE OF EXECUTION	Liverpool
HANGMAN	Thomas Pierrepoint
ASSISTANT	Thomas Phillips
DATE OF TRIAL	8th November, 1929
LOCATION OF TRIAL	Liverpool
PRESIDING JUDGE	Mister Justice Humphreys
PROSECUTION COUNSEL	P.M. Oliver M.P.
DEFENCE COUNSEL	Basil Neild
NUMBER OF VICTIMS	1

VICTIMS DETAILS	
NAME	Ellen Maguire
AGE	42
DATE OF MURDER	Thursday, 5th September, 1929
PLACE OF MURDER	39a Newsham Street, Scotland Road, Liverpool
METHOD OF KILLING	Cut throat/stabbed
RELATIONSHIP TO KILLER	Wife

IT IS SOMETIMES truly amazing at how stupid some murderers can be. One of the best examples must be Sidney Harry Fox.

Sidney was the fourth son of Rosaline Fox and undoubtedly her favourite. He discovered, quite early in life, that he could make money by using other people's cheque books. Never over bright at the planning of such crimes, Sidney would usually throw himself on the mercy of his victim and ask for one more chance, though occasionally he would have something of a greater hold over the person whose bank account he had just lightened. Sidney was an attractive young man and discovered that he was desired by certain other men. It was a simple matter to mix his homosexual tendencies with the business of stealing and such victims were highly unlikely to complain to the authorities.

Even so, there were enough people who would make complaints and Sidney Harry Fox saw the inside of a prison on more than one occasion. Each time he came out, his faithful mother was waiting to greet him. Indeed, not too honest herself, she and Sidney would often take a holiday in a nice hotel somewhere and leave without paying the bill.

In 1927, Rosaline Fox became friendly with a Mrs Morse and the two ladies decided to move into a flat together at Southsea in Hampshire. In due course they were joined by Sidney, who soon discovered that he could charm ladies as easily as he could charm men. Mrs Morse was quickly persuaded to take out a life insurance policy in Sidney's favour and not long afterwards was disturbed to find her room filling with gas. Not surprisingly, the relationship between her and Sidney cooled appreciably after that and soon Sidney and his mother were looking for lodgings elsewhere. Sidney helped himself to some of Mrs Morse's jewellery before he left and as a result, received a prison sentence of 15 months.

Sidney came out of prison in March 1929 and soon teamed up with his mother again.

It was on April 21st, 1929 that Rosaline Fox took out a will, leaving all her property to Sidney. Unfortunately, the property did not amount to much. Surely it would be better if there were an insurance policy, the proceeds of which would make the bequest more

NAME	Sidney Harry Fox
AGE AT EXECUTION	31
DATE OF EXECUTION	Tuesday, 8th April, 1930
PLACE OF EXECUTION	Maidstone
HANGMAN	Not known
ASSISTANT	Not known
DATE OF TRIAL	12th March, 1930
LOCATION OF TRIAL	Lewes
PRESIDING JUDGE	Mister Justice Rowlatt
PROSECUTION COUNSEL	Sir William A. Jowitt M.P., Sir Henry Curtis Bennett, Mister St. John Hutchinson, Gerald Thesiger
DEFENCE COUNSEL	J. D. Cassels, S.T.T. James, C. Pensotti
NUMBER OF VICTIMS	1

VICTIMS DETAILS	
NAME	Rosaline Fox
AGE	63
DATE OF MURDER	Wednesday, 23rd October, 1929
PLACE OF MURDER	Room 66, Metropole Hotel, Margate
METHOD OF KILLING	Strangled
RELATIONSHIP TO KILLER	Mother

worthwhile? So it was that very soon afterwards, Mrs Fox took out an insurance policy on her life.

The Foxs returned to their old lifestyle of staying in hotels and moving on without settling their bills. There were many hotels, mainly on the south coast, who suffered unpaid accounts because of them until, on October 16th, the pair arrived at the Metropole Hotel in Margate, Kent.

On Friday, October 18th, Sidney made a trip to Ramsgate and here spent the princely sum of 2/- on a short-term insurance policy on his mother's life. This entitled him to £1,000 in the event of his mother dying from accidental means. This policy, and the previous one that Rosaline herself had taken out, were both due to expire on Tuesday, October 22nd. It was on that day that Sidney demonstrated just how stupid he really could be.

Travelling to London, Sidney visited the offices of the insurance companies who held policies on his mother and arranged to have them extended until midnight of the 23rd. He then returned to Margate and the Metropole

499

Hotel. On the evening of the 23rd, Sidney took his mother to dinner and then escorted her back to her room.

It was 11.40pm, 20 minutes before the insurance policies expired, and Sidney Fox was rushing around the hotel corridors announcing that there was a fire. The hotel staff rushed to room 66 and managed to pull its occupant from the thick smoke that filled the room. It was too late, though. Rosaline Fox was dead. A doctor who was present declared that the cause of death was accidental suffocation.

The next day, Sidney obtained a death certificate and then visited a nearby solicitor, who advanced him £40 against the insurance policies. Then, as a final gesture, Sidney left the hotel, without bothering to pay his bill, though perhaps for once, this was understandable.

Sidney Fox was arrested in Norwich on November 3rd. The unpaid hotel bills gave the police enough to hold him on but the real investigation had been brought about by the insurance companies who were, not surprisingly, highly suspicious about the claim Sidney had made.

Rosaline Fox had been buried on October 29th, but her body was now exhumed and examined by the pathologist Sir Bernard Spilsbury. He determined that the cause of death was due to strangulation. Further investigation showed that the fire had been started deliberately, under the chair in which Mrs Fox had been sitting.

The final act of stupidity committed by Sidney Fox, came at his trial for the murder of his mother. He said that he had opened the communicating door to his mother's room and seen that it was on fire. He had then closed the door and ran downstairs for help. When questioned on this point, he said that he closed the door because he did not want the fire to spread into the rest of the hotel!

Found guilty of murder, Sidney Fox did not even bother to appeal against the verdict.

JAMES MCCANN WAS a rural postman whose delivery round was from Toomebridge to Crosskeys, a distance of some four to four and a half miles. Each day he would deliver mail to all the outlying houses and farms, but each Thursday, he had one other duty to perform. Friday was pensions day, so each Thursday, McCann would deliver the money to the Crosskeys Post Office.

On Thursday, May 16th, McCann left Toomebridge at 8.20am on his cycle. He should have arrived at Crosskeys at about 9.30am, but when he still not arrived by 10.00am, the post-mistress alerted the police. Fifteen minutes later, at 10.15am, McCann's body was found, in a field, 40 yards from the junction of Toome Road and Harris's Lane. He had been shot, at close range, in the throat and the pensions money, some £86, was missing.

One of the first jobs for the police was to trace and speak to all the owners of shotguns in the area. It was as a part of this investigation that District Inspector Lewis spoke to Samuel Cushnan who denied being anywhere near the murder spot on the day in question. Surprisingly, when Cushnan's gun was examined it was seen that the barrel was missing and Cushnan explained that it must have been stolen.

At the inquest on McCann, it was an easy matter to determine what time the postman had been killed. A number of labourers in the nearby fields, including Thomas Harris, had heard the shot at around 9.40am. Furthermore, the spot where McCann had died was not actually on his normal route but an almost empty bottle of poteen had been found nearby. It was the belief that McCann had been enticed to the field with a promise of alcohol and this in turn confirmed that it must have been by someone he knew and trusted.

Further enquiries led to witnesses who claimed they had seen Cushnan in the area, even though he had expressly said he was elsewhere, working on a potato field. When it was found that on the morning of the murder Cushnan had only turned up for work at 10.00am and that a piece of material found in a bramble bush near McCann's body matched

NAME	Samuel Cushnan (Cushnahan)
AGE AT EXECUTION	26
DATE OF EXECUTION	Tuesday, 8th April, 1930
PLACE OF EXECUTION	Belfast
HANGMAN	Thomas Pierrepoint
ASSISTANT	Robert Wilson
DATE OF TRIAL	5th March – 8th March, 1930
LOCATION OF TRIAL	Belfast
PRESIDING JUDGE	Lord Justice Moore
PROSECUTION COUNSEL	A.B. Babington M.P., J.C. Davison, C.L. Sheil
DEFENCE COUNSEL	William Lowry, J.H. Campbell
NUMBER OF VICTIMS	1

VICTIMS DETAILS

NAME	James McCann
AGE	24
DATE OF MURDER	Thursday, 16th May, 1929
PLACE OF MURDER	Toomebridge
METHOD OF KILLING	Shot
RELATIONSHIP TO KILLER	None

a jacket worn by Cushnan, the case against him seemed to be growing in strength. He was arrested and charged on May 29th.

Cushnan appeared before Mister Justice Wilson at Londonderry on December 3rd, 1929 but after four days, the jury were unable to agree on a verdict. Cushnan was sent for a second trial, at Belfast in March, and this time, after an absence of one hour, the jury announced that he was guilty.

1930

THE BRINGING TO justice of the killer of Vivian Messiter was an example of first-class police work and deduction.

Vivian Messiter had only come to England in September 1928 and took lodgings at 3 Carlton Road, Southampton. He took employment as a sales agent for the Wolf's Head Oil Company and rented a storeroom at 42 Grove Street, from which he would run the business. At the end of September he placed an advertisement in the local press for sub-agents to work for him and then, one month later, on October 30th, he vanished.

On November 1st, Messiter's landlord from Carlton Road, Mr Parrot, went around to the storeroom to see if he could find any trace of Mr Messiter. His guest had seemed such a pleasant, trustworthy gentleman and it seemed very strange that he should leave without telling anyone what his intentions were. All the storeroom doors were locked and there was no sign of Vivian Messiter.

In due course, the officers of the Wolf's Head company also became dismayed at not hearing from their new sales agent. At one stage the police were sent to check the storeroom but again, all the doors were locked and the premises were secure. Eventually the sales area could be neglected no longer and in the New Year, the company were forced to appoint a new agent, Mr Passmore.

On January 10th, Mr Passmore went to Grove Street to start work. He had to force the padlock, as Messiter had apparently taken the key away with him, but he gained entry and took a look around his new storeroom. It was then that the mystery of the disappearance of Vivian Messiter was solved. The body lay behind a pile of cases and had apparently been shot through the left eye.

The postmortem would later show that, in fact, Messiter had been battered to death. A heavy hammer had been brought down on his head three times, the last blow striking him in the left eye whilst he was lying on the floor. Such had been the force used, that the eye had been shoved into the skull, leaving a large hole that had all the appearance of a bullet wound.

One of the first clues discovered was a

NAME	William Henry Podmore
AGE AT EXECUTION	29
DATE OF EXECUTION	Tuesday, 22nd April, 1930
PLACE OF EXECUTION	Winchester
HANGMAN	Thomas Pierrepoint
ASSISTANT	Alfred Allen
DATE OF TRIAL	3rd March – 8th March, 1930
LOCATION OF TRIAL	Winchester
PRESIDING JUDGE	Lord Chief Justice, Lord Hewart
PROSECUTION COUNSEL	Sir Thomas Inskip, J.G. Trapnell
DEFENCE COUNSEL	H. du Parcq, T.R.C. Goff
NUMBER OF VICTIMS	1

VICTIMS DETAILS	
NAME	Vivian Messiter
AGE	57
DATE OF MURDER	Tuesday, 30th October, 1928
PLACE OF MURDER	42 Grove Street, Southampton
METHOD OF KILLING	Battered
RELATIONSHIP TO KILLER	None

receipt book from which two pages had been torn. The last receipt in the book was dated October 30th, though when the gentleman was traced and spoken to, he confirmed that the transaction actually took place on the 29th but was dated one day later, as the oil was due for delivery on that date. This implied that the 29th was the last day on which Messiter had done business, and fitted in with him being murdered on the 30th, the day he disappeared.

The next step was to consider what had been on the two missing pages. The second one had left an impression on the page below and this was seen to be another receipt, dated the 28th and signed with the initials W.F.T. Carbon sheets were found and these were shown to be covered with fictitious names. The deduction was that someone, possibly one of the sub-agents Mr Messiter had advertised for, had been placing fictitious orders in order to claim commission. If Messiter had found out about this, it might have been enough reason to kill him. It now became imperative to trace W.F.T.

The storeroom was searched with a fine tooth comb and two scraps of paper were found. On one of these was a note from Messiter to Mr W.F. Thomas and later, when Messiter's lodgings were searched, a letter was discovered. The letter was a reply to the advertisement Messiter had placed and bore the name William F. Thomas. Furthermore, it carried an address: 5 Cranberry Avenue, Southampton. When the address was checked, Thomas had already left and the forwarding address he had given turned out to be false.

The police were not to be beaten, though. The details they had on Thomas were circulated to other forces and some very interesting replies were received. Wiltshire police were looking for Thomas in connection with the theft of some wage packets on December 21st. After working for Messiter, Thomas had apparently gone to Salisbury and taken employment at a garage. Some wage packets had vanished and whilst the police were still making enquiries, Thomas too had disappeared. Thomas's lodgings were checked and here police discovered another scrap of paper, carrying the name Podmore and part of an address in Manchester.

The name Podmore was known to police in Manchester, where he was wanted for fraud. When descriptions were compared, police felt sure that Thomas and Podmore were one and the same.

The next breakthrough came from the police force in Stoke-on-Trent. They too had run into Podmore and they could supply more information. Podmore was known to spend time with a woman named Lily Hambleton. On January 17th, Lily was questioned at her home and told officers that she and Podmore had stayed at the Leicester Hotel in Vauxhall Bridge Road, in London. When this address was checked, the police finally caught up with William Henry Podmore.

It was important to build as strong as possible a case against Podmore. For too long he had stayed one step ahead of the law and this time the police determined to nail him. In order to hold him, Podmore was transferred to Manchester to face the fraud charges. Here he was sentenced to three months. Upon his release he was immediately re-arrested and transferred to Winchester, where he received a six months' sentence for theft. Meanwhile the police were putting their case together on a charge of murder.

Podmore had admitted being with Messiter on the day he had been murdered, but claimed he was alive and well when they parted. It was shown that Podmore had borrowed a heavy hammer from a friend in the motor trade and the murder weapon was identified as having been of the same type. The myriad of false names on the carbon paper were linked back to Podmore. Many were the names of people he had known in childhood, or the names of streets close to where he had lived. Finally, on his release from Winchester prison, Podmore was arrested and charged with murder.

The trial lasted five days and ended in a verdict of guilty. An appeal failed, as did a request to have the appeal sent to the House of Lords. On April 22nd, 1930, 18 months after the murder of Vivian Messiter, William Henry Podmore was hanged.

EDITH MAY PARKER had been off work ill but was now feeling much better. At 9.30am on Friday, April 11th, 1930, Edith, together with her younger sister, 15-year-old Eva Lillian Parker, left home for a walk on the Heath. Half an hour later, as they were walking down a narrow pathway, a man rushed out of some bushes, pushed past Eva and, without a word, plunged a knife into Edith's back.

Eva's screams for help brought another walker, Arthur Moyle, who tried to offer assistance and put his coat as a pillow under Edith's head, but it was to no avail. Edith died very soon afterwards. Of her assailant, there was no sign at all.

The first thoughts of the investigating officers were that a lunatic had escaped from the asylum nearby and carried out the crime, but this was soon shown to be wrong. The net spread wider. And then they remembered someone well known to them.

At 11.15pm on the same night that Edith Parker died, police called at the home of Albert Marjeram, in Albert Road, Belvedere, near Erith. In the not too distant past, Marjeram had come to their attention when he admitted committing a murder in a shop at Reading. That was shown to be a false confession but surely it was worth talking to him again.

Marjeram admitted being on the Heath at about the time of the murder, but at first denied any involvement in the matter. Then, after some consideration, he asked for a pencil and paper, and wrote out a detailed statement admitting his guilt.

Marjeram said that he had arrived on the Heath at about 9.00am. Soon afterwards he saw the two young girls together, ran up to them, and stabbed one of them. He said his intention had been to rob the women but he had been frightened off by the younger one screaming. He also said that he had no intention of killing anyone and thought he had only wounded her.

An attempt was made to show that Marjeram was insane. His mother testified that at the age of five, Albert had suffered from an abscess on his brain. Ever since he had behaved strangely. Once he had attacked

NAME	Albert Edward Marjeram
AGE AT EXECUTION	23
DATE OF EXECUTION	Wednesday, 11th June, 1930
PLACE OF EXECUTION	Wandsworth
HANGMAN	Thomas Pierrepoint
ASSISTANT	Henry Pollard
DATE OF TRIAL	22nd May, 1930
LOCATION OF TRIAL	Old Bailey
PRESIDING JUDGE	Mister Justice Humphreys
PROSECUTION COUNSEL	Eustace Fulton, G.B. McClure
DEFENCE COUNSEL	S.T. James
NUMBER OF VICTIMS	1

VICTIMS DETAILS	
NAME	Edith May Parker
AGE	23
DATE OF MURDER	Friday, 11th April, 1930
PLACE OF MURDER	Dartford Heath, Kent
METHOD OF KILLING	Stabbed
RELATIONSHIP TO KILLER	None

his mother and had tried to strangle his younger brother. He had also stuck a fork in a cat and in 1928, had tried to commit suicide by gassing himself.

None of this moved the jury, who returned a guilty verdict. The only mystery was the real motive behind the attack. Though Marjeram had claimed his intention was theft, it is probably more likely that the killing of Edith Parker was a sad attempt, by Marjeram, to attract attention to himself.

WILLIAM ANDREWS WORKED as a messenger for a company of drapers in Birmingham, and part of his duties included the taking of cash to the bank. On Monday, July 21st, 1930, Andrews was taking the sum of £908 for deposit when he was accosted by a thief who grabbed hold of him at the back of his neck with one hand, and struck him, very hard, on top of the head with the other.

There was only one witness to the attack, but Charles Henry Dowd also saw the assailant snatch the cash bag and then escape in a yellow car. This was, however, more than a case of robbery, for William Andrews had suffered a fractured skull and was to die from that injury.

Police soon knew the name of at least one of the men they were looking for. The yellow car had been hired one and a half hours before the robbery by one Herbert Charles Ridley. It was found abandoned soon afterwards, as was the empty cash bag. The search was now on for Ridley and his accomplice.

After some days, Ridley was arrested at Brighton, as was his partner in crime, Victor Edward Betts. Both men were put on trial for murder.

As far as Ridley was concerned, his defence was that he had only driven the car. It had been Betts who attacked Andrews, Betts who struck the blows and Betts who was responsible for his death. Before the robbery, Betts had told him that he was just going to push Andrews out of the way. Ridley claimed that had he known such violence was going to be used, he would have taken no part in the crime.

For his part, Betts said he had not used much violence at all. Evidence was given that Andrews had had an abnormally thin skull but this did nothing to condone the attack upon him. The prosecution claimed that since Andrews had died as a result of a robbery, Betts was guilty of murder, and since Ridley was party to the common design, he was equally guilty. The jury agreed and both men were sentenced to death.

Just days before the sentence was due to be carried out, the Home Secretary recommended a reprieve for Ridley, who was

NAME	Victor Edward Betts
AGE AT EXECUTION	21
DATE OF EXECUTION	Saturday, 3rd January, 1931
PLACE OF EXECUTION	Birmingham
HANGMAN	Thomas Pierrepoint
ASSISTANT	Alfred Allen
DATE OF TRIAL	4th December – 5th December, 1930
LOCATION OF TRIAL	Birmingham
PRESIDING JUDGE	Mister Commissioner Mitchell-Innes
PROSECUTION COUNSEL	Sir Henry Maddocks, M. Morris Healy
DEFENCE COUNSEL	Harold Eaden
NUMBER OF VICTIMS	1

1930

VICTIMS DETAILS	
NAME	William Thomas Andrews (Died Thursday, 24th July)
AGE	63
DATE OF MURDER	Monday, 21st July, 1930
PLACE OF MURDER	Corner of Victoria Road and Rifle Crescent, Aston, Birmingham
METHOD OF KILLING	Battered
RELATIONSHIP TO KILLER	None

sentenced to life imprisonment. There was to be no such mercy for the man who had struck the fatal blow.

1930

OLIVER PRESTON WAS a moneylender and Frederick Gill was one of his customers. Gill had borrowed a small amount of money but was now in such serious arrears with his payments that on July 18th, Preston was forced to get his solicitor to send a letter to Gill, demanding payment of the outstanding sum of £3-12s.

Gill had some rather serious financial problems. A driver by trade, he worked, on average, three days a week and earned an average of 27s-6d each week. His rent had been in arrears since April, he was being threatened with legal action by Preston and now his girlfriend was demanding a holiday he could not afford.

On July 20th, Gill tried to borrow yet more money when he visited a Bradford money lender and asked for a loan of £10. The money was not forthcoming and Gill seemingly had no way out of his predicament.

Four days later, on July 24th, Oliver Preston drew £80 from his bank, all in £1 notes. The very next day, Frederick Gill was seen leaving Preston's office, by a man named Stell. Gill told Stell that he had just been up to borrow another £10 and had been told to call back the following morning. Surprisingly though, Gill's finances seemed to improve from that night onwards.

On the evening of July 25th, Gill began to spend freely. He took his girlfriend out and spent around £15 and the day afterwards, July 26th, took her on holiday to Whitehaven. It was there, after the body of Preston had been discovered in his office, that Gill was arrested and charged with murder.

Gill denied killing Preston and claimed that the money he had spent of late came partly from savings and partly from a gambling win. When arrested, he still had £16 in cash upon his person, but even more importantly, his clothes and boots showed clear traces of human blood.

Frederick Gill had been seen in Preston's office on the day of the murder, had suddenly started spending money, and had bloodstained clothing. The evidence was circumstantial but it was enough for the jury to return a guilty verdict.

NAME	Frederick Gill
AGE AT EXECUTION	26
DATE OF EXECUTION	Wednesday, 4th February, 1931
PLACE OF EXECUTION	Leeds
HANGMAN	Thomas Pierrepoint
ASSISTANT	Robert Wilson
DATE OF TRIAL	10th December – 14th December, 1930
LOCATION OF TRIAL	Leeds
PRESIDING JUDGE	Mister Justice Talbot
PROSECUTION COUNSEL	C.F. Lowenthal, Arthur Henderson
DEFENCE COUNSEL	Ralph Cleworth
NUMBER OF VICTIMS	1

VICTIMS DETAILS	
NAME	Oliver Preston (Died Monday, 28th July)
AGE	Not known
DATE OF MURDER	Friday, 25th July, 1930
PLACE OF MURDER	Station Buildings, Keighley
METHOD OF KILLING	Battered
RELATIONSHIP TO KILLER	None

ALFRED ARTHUR ROUSE, a married man, had built up a harem of lovers all over the country. This had led to the birth of children and as a result, by 1931, Rouse was paying out half of his yearly salary in maintenance.

On June 7th, 1930, Agnes Keason was murdered at Epsom. The murderer was never caught and it was reading reports of this crime that planted an idea in Rouse's head. If he could disappear, then he could begin a new life. The trouble was, if he simply vanished, the police would search for him. No, if his idea were to succeed, people would have to think he was dead.

Rouse decided that he would find a man of the same age and build as himself, kill him and burn the body. And what better night than November 5th?

The first part of the plan worked well. The victim was left inside a blazing car on a lane near Hardingstone in Northampton-shire at 2.00am on November 6th. But then came disaster.

As Rouse walked down the lane, two men saw him clearly. Alfred Brown and William Bailey noticed the fire in the distance and asked Rouse if he knew what it was. He replied that it looked like a bonfire.

Rouse now knew that his plan had failed. The car would be identified as his, but the two men would come forward and identify him. Rouse decided instead to visit one of his many girlfriends, Ivy Jenkins, in Wales.

As Rouse expected, reports on the car appeared in the newspapers and once his name had also been published, he decided that it was time to return to London and face the music.

Rouse told the police that he had picked up a man near St Albans and upon reaching Northamptonshire, the engine had started to stall. Rouse realised they were low on petrol. Luckily he had a can in the car and he asked the man to fill the tank whilst he went to relieve himself. The man had asked for a cigarette and suddenly Rouse heard a dull explosion. The petrol had caught fire and Rouse could not save him.

There were, however, a couple of problems with this version of events. Firstly, why had

NAME	Alfred Arthur Rouse
AGE AT EXECUTION	36
DATE OF EXECUTION	Tuesday, 10th March, 1931
PLACE OF EXECUTION	Bedford
HANGMAN	Thomas Pierrepoint
ASSISTANT	Thomas Phillips
DATE OF TRIAL	26th January – 31st January, 1931
LOCATION OF TRIAL	Northampton
PRESIDING JUDGE	Mister Justice Talbot
PROSECUTION COUNSEL	Norman Birkett
DEFENCE COUNSEL	D.L. Finnemore
NUMBER OF VICTIMS	1

VICTIMS DETAILS	
NAME	Unknown Male
AGE	Not known
DATE OF MURDER	Thursday, November 6th, 1930
PLACE OF MURDER	Lane near Hardingstone, Northants
METHOD OF KILLING	Battered/burned
RELATIONSHIP TO KILLER	None

Rouse not asked Brown and Bailey for help and secondly, the police had found a mallet close by the car. A human hair was still adhering to this and it looked as though the victim had been battered before being burned. The dead man's skull could be of no assistance as his head had exploded due to the intense heat.

Found guilty, Rouse was executed on March 10th. He left a full confession to the murder, adding that he had picked the man up in a pub in Whetstone. The victim was a down-and-out. He remains an anonymous victim of a brutal crime.

1930

IN THE YEAR 1924, Henry Johnson married Sarah, but less than six years later, in January 1930, she left him and moved in with Francis Land at Waterhouse Place, in Rochdale.

For the best part of a year, Sarah and Francis lived together, but he often beat her and finally, on December 2nd, Sarah decided she had had enough. She turned up at the house of an old friend, Mrs Barlow and stayed with her for just one night, moving the next day to the home of another friend, Emily Whitehead.

Sarah stayed at Emily's house until December 6th, when they both moved to Emily's brother's house at 129 Oldham Road. That night, Sarah and Emily went for a drink at the Flying Horse pub. Land saw them and was waiting for them when they came out. Sarah announced that he had hit her once too often and that she was not going back to him. Land replied that he would murder her.

It was not until December 9th that Sarah and Emily saw Land again. This time he was much more amenable and Sarah said she would return to him if he got a job outside Rochdale. He agreed and they arranged to meet up again at 8.45pm on December 12th. That meeting took place as arranged. Sarah was still nervous and took Emily along but eventually she left them alone.

It was about 9.30pm when Land arrived, alone, at the Rochdale Social Club. He had a drink with a man named Chadwick, and they left together at 9.40pm, to go to the Grapes. Land appeared to be worried and when Chadwick asked him what the problem was, Land replied that he ought to be the most unnerved man in the room.

Meanwhile, Sarah had not returned home, so Emily went into town, where she ran into Land. She asked him what had happened to Sarah, and he replied that he had done her in. At that point Emily saw two men she knew and called them over. These two, Harry Wild and a friend named Haslam, questioned Land and he told them what he had done. They all set off towards Land's house, and when they met Police Inspector Banks in Toad Lane and informed him of the facts, he too accompanied them back to Waterhouse Place.

NAME	Francis Land
AGE AT EXECUTION	39
DATE OF EXECUTION	Thursday, 16th April, 1931
PLACE OF EXECUTION	Manchester
HANGMAN	Not known
ASSISTANT	Not known
DATE OF TRIAL	23rd February – 25th February, 1931
LOCATION OF TRIAL	Manchester
PRESIDING JUDGE	Mister Justice Charles
PROSECUTION COUNSEL	J.C. Jackson, P. Redmond Barry
DEFENCE COUNSEL	J.P. Ashworth
NUMBER OF VICTIMS	1

VICTIMS DETAILS	
NAME	Sarah Ellen Johnson
AGE	24
DATE OF MURDER	Friday, 12th December, 1930
PLACE OF MURDER	3 Waterhouse Place, Rochdale
METHOD OF KILLING	Cut throat
RELATIONSHIP TO KILLER	Girlfriend

The door was unlocked and there lay Sarah on the hearthrug, a gaping wound in her throat.

Although he had admitted to three people that he had murdered Sarah, Land pleaded not guilty at his trial, claiming that he had left his house at 5.00pm, and had not returned until 11.00pm, when he found the body. This was disproved by the evidence of Caroline Duggan, who testified that she had seen Sarah and Land together just after 9.00pm.

This was enough to find Francis Land guilty.

EVELYN VICTORIA HOLT lived with her aunt in McFarlane Road, Shepherd's Bush, and worked as a waitress in a Lyons Corner House in the West End. On Thursday, February 26th, 1931, Evelyn left for work at her usual time of 7.50am. Her aunt would never see her alive again.

A few weeks before Christmas, 1930, Evelyn had met Alexander Anastassiou, a native of Cyprus. He had just moved into the front room on the top floor of 65 Warren Street, his landlady being Lena Ballerini. Alexander and Evelyn started walking out together and soon became engaged.

There are many stories in this book of jealous men murdering their wives or girlfriends, but in this particular case, it was Evelyn who had the jealous streak. On the afternoon of February 26th, Evelyn had noticed Alexander talking to some girls and made her objections plain. Nevertheless, the couple still went out for a meal the same day, visited the pictures and had supper before returning to his room.

At 11.30pm that night, Lena Ballerini was in her lounge when she heard screams and a loud crash from upstairs. Running to investigate, Lena discovered that Alexander's door was locked. She demanded that he open up and after a few seconds the door creaked open. Lena saw a bundle on the floor, in a pool of blood. She went to fetch the police.

Constable James Murphy was the first officer on the scene. Alexander stood to one side and when Murphy entered, tried to pick up a razor. Murphy prevented Alexander from doing this, and took him down to the police station.

Anastassiou made a full statement of the events of that night. He explained that after getting back to his room, Evelyn had asked for a comb. He had handed one to her and she had seen that he kept his razor in the same drawer. They spoke about her jealousy and Anastassiou finally admitted that he had changed his mind, could no longer marry her, and was thinking of emigrating to America. Evelyn went into the drawer, took out Anastassiou's razor and threatened him with it.

Evelyn had added that she had friends

NAME	Alexander Anastassiou
AGE AT EXECUTION	23
DATE OF EXECUTION	Wednesday, 3rd June, 1931
PLACE OF EXECUTION	Pentonville
HANGMAN	Robert Baxter
ASSISTANT	Henry Pollard
DATE OF TRIAL	27th April, 1931
LOCATION OF TRIAL	Old Bailey
PRESIDING JUDGE	Mister Justice Swift
PROSECUTION COUNSEL	Eustace Fulton, L.A. Byrne
DEFENCE COUNSEL	S.T.T. James, M. Tenezopoulous
NUMBER OF VICTIMS	1

VICTIMS DETAILS	
NAME	Evelyn Victoria Holt
AGE	22
DATE OF MURDER	Thursday, 26th February, 1931
PLACE OF MURDER	65 Warren Street, Tottenham Court Road, London
METHOD OF KILLING	Cut throat
RELATIONSHIP TO KILLER	Girlfriend

who would get him for what he had done to her and at that point had attacked him with the razor. They struggled and finally he had managed to overpower her. Fearing for his life, he had cut her throat before he realised what he was doing. "It was her or me," he continued.

The decision for the jury was between murder and manslaughter. There were other wounds on Evelyn, mostly on her hands and arms, probably inflicted when she tried to defend herself. Anastassiou also had wounds but these were mainly marks inflicted by fingernails. After deliberating for 20 minutes, the jury announced that Anastassiou was guilty.

THOMAS DORNAN WAS a respected member of the community. A farmer, he had also been the sexton of the local Presbyterian church and had an unblemished character. All this was to change in late 1930.

In December of that year, Isabella Aitken gave birth to a child and claimed that the father was none other than Dornan. He admitted paternity and entered into an agreement to pay maintenance. Payments of 6/- per week were made but it wasn't long before Dornan was in arrears. He made what turned out to be the final contribution on March 26th, 1931, but even that only brought the payments up to January 1931. By May, Dornan was a full five months in arrears.

On May 22nd, Isabella and her elder sister, Margaret, were cutting peat from a bog. They were accompanied by Maude McCarthney and Ann Dickson. A man named John McBurney was working nearby. All five saw Dornan walk past at 2.30pm. He did not speak to anyone. Minutes later, Dornan was back and this time he was carrying a gun, though at first, Ann Dickson thought he was holding a stick.

As the people carried on working, Dornan raised the gun to his shoulder, took careful aim at Isabella and fired. The shot tore into her and as people scattered, Margaret went to her sister's aid. Dornan then turned the gun in Margaret's direction and fired into her.

Wounded, the two sisters huddled together and tried to limp away. Dornan went after them and continued firing into their bodies. When both women had fallen to the ground he stepped forward and continued firing into them until he knew that both were dead. Dornan then calmly walked off to his home, which was nearby. It was there that Dornan's wife Elizabeth, who had heard the shooting, asked him what he had done. "I shot the two Aitkens," Dornan replied.

Arrested and put on trial for his life, Dornan's defence was one of insanity, but Doctor M.J. Nolan, who had examined the prisoner, said that in his opinion, Dornan was perfectly sane at the time of the shooting and had known what he was doing. As a result, it took the jury only 32 minutes to return their guilty verdict.

NAME	Thomas Dornan
AGE AT EXECUTION	Not known
DATE OF EXECUTION	31st July, 1931
PLACE OF EXECUTION	Belfast
HANGMAN	Henry Pierrepoint
ASSISTANT	Robert Wilson
DATE OF TRIAL	8th July – 11th July, 1931
LOCATION OF TRIAL	Belfast
PRESIDING JUDGE	Lord Chief Justice, Sir William Moore
PROSECUTION COUNSEL	A.B. Babington M.P., J.C. Davison, C.L. Sheil
DEFENCE COUNSEL	William Lowry, James McSparran
NUMBER OF VICTIMS	2

VICTIMS DETAILS	
NAMES	Isabella Aitken; Margaret Aitken
AGES	20; 28
DATE OF MURDER	Friday, 22nd May, 1931
PLACE OF MURDER	Tuftarney Moss, Skerry East, near Newtowncrommelin
METHOD OF KILLING	Shot; shot
RELATIONSHIP TO KILLER	Ex-girlfriend; none

THE AREA WHERE Herbert William Ayres lived and died was a shanty town of huts and shacks, populated by the unemployed and homeless members of society. It was two of those members who cruelly battered him to death.

On June 1st, 1931, a body was discovered in a smouldering pile of rubbish. A gentleman named McGlade was cutting through the area on his way home from work, when he noticed a human hand protruding from the remains of a bonfire. When the mound was carefully scraped away by the police, a charred and unrecognisable body was discovered.

The remains were handed over to the redoubtable pathologist Sir Bernard Spilsbury, who determined that the victim had been dead for approximately three days. The cause of death was repeated blows to the head, at least one of which had left a deep, rectangular-shaped depression. There was but one form of identification on the body. By the strangest chance, the one unburnt portion, the hand, featured a tattoo of a heart pierced by a sword.

The population of the shanty town was questioned and the tattoo led one person to identify the dead man as Herbert William Ayres. It was noted that Ayres had vanished from his usual haunts a few days ago.

The crucial witness, though, was John Armstrong. He had just managed to find himself a job but until that fortunate occurrence he too had been one of those living in the area where the body was discovered. For some time he had been sleeping on the floor of a hut that belonged to two men known as 'Tiggy' and 'Moosh'.

One night he had been awakened by a noise outside and looking out, he saw his hosts battering Ayres, whom he knew as 'Pigsticker'. He later saw the prone figure of Pigsticker being carried towards the dump where it was found, but said nothing in case the two killers turned on him.

Tiggy and Moosh, identified as Oliver Newman and William Shelley, did not deny killing Ayres. In fact, they saw nothing wrong in what they had done. They explained that a few days before the murder, they had found Pigsticker stealing tea and sugar from their

NAMES	William Shelley (Moosh); Oliver Newman (Tiggy)
AGES AT EXECUTION	57; 61
DATE OF EXECUTION	Wednesday, 5th August, 1931
PLACE OF EXECUTION	Pentonville
HANGMAN	Robert Baxter
ASSISTANTS	Lionel Mann, Thomas Phillips, Robert Wilson
DATE OF TRIAL	24th June – 25th June, 1931
LOCATION OF TRIAL	Old Bailey
PRESIDING JUDGE	Mister Justice Swift
PROSECUTION COUNSEL	Eustace Fulton, G.B. McClure
DEFENCE COUNSEL	Francis Peregrine E.A. Jessel
NUMBER OF VICTIMS	1

VICTIMS DETAILS	
NAME	Herbert William Ayres (Pigsticker)
AGE	45
DATE OF MURDER	circa Friday, 29th May, 1931
PLACE OF MURDER	Scratchwood Sidings, Between Mill Hill and Elstree
METHOD OF KILLING	Battered
RELATIONSHIP TO KILLERS	None; none

hut and had given him a beating. When later some bread and bacon disappeared there seemed to be only one likely culprit, so this time they battered Pigsticker to death, using the flat back of an axe. When their hut was searched, the bloodstained axe was found beneath the floorboards. The back of the head fitted exactly into the depression in the skull of William Ayres.

The main prosecution witness at the trial was, of course, John Armstrong. His testimony sent the two callous killers to the scaffold.

WILLIAM JOHN CORBETT was a miner until he lost his job in November 1930. Not unnaturally, he subsequently became depressed, but this developed into something deeper and things began to prey on his mind so much that he had threatened to commit suicide.

On Tuesday, March 24th, 1931, Corbett's wife, Ethel, went to her local police station and reported that she felt her husband was behaving strangely. She pointed out that he had asked her for a razor, without telling her why he wanted it. She had to admit, though, that William had not actually threatened her so, under the circumstances, there was little the police could do.

The following day, an argument developed between Corbett and his wife, during which he struck her on the mouth with his fist. Seeing this attack upon her mother, Corbett's stepdaughter, Florence Matilda, went to her aid, only for Corbett to turn his attention towards her. Now it was time for Ethel Corbett to help her daughter out. She leapt upon Corbett, who managed to shake her off, take a razor from his pocket, and slash his wife's throat.

William Corbett now turned back to his stepdaughter and went for her with the same razor. She managed to catch hold of the handle, but it was plain that Corbett was the stronger of the two and would soon get the better of her. It was at this point that Ethel, despite her terrible wound, threw herself upon Corbett's back and managed to grapple him to the floor.

Corbett went on to cut his own throat but recovered in hospital and was put on trial for his wife's murder. He claimed to have no memory of what had taken place and this, together with the change that had come over him since he became unemployed, led to a defence of insanity. There was no demonstrable motive for the crime, either. But none of this helped Corbett.

NAME	William John Corbett
AGE AT EXECUTION	32
DATE OF EXECUTION	Wednesday, 12th August, 1931
PLACE OF EXECUTION	Cardiff
HANGMAN	Not known
ASSISTANT	Not known
DATE OF TRIAL	2nd July, 1931
LOCATION OF TRIAL	Swansea
PRESIDING JUDGE	Mister Commissioner Walker
PROSECUTION COUNSEL	Walter Samuel M.P., Ellis Lloyd M.P.
DEFENCE COUNSEL	Trevor Hunter, Matebele Davies
NUMBER OF VICTIMS	1

VICTIMS DETAILS	
NAME	Ethel Louisa Corbett
AGE	39
DATE OF MURDER	Wednesday, 25th March, 1931
PLACE OF MURDER	48 Caer Bragdy, off Lawrence Street, Caerphilly
METHOD OF KILLING	Cut throat
RELATIONSHIP TO KILLER	Wife

1931

HENRY DANIEL SEYMOUR was hanged despite the fact that no less than six witnesses swore they had seen the murder victim long after she was supposed to have been dead, and at a time that meant that Seymour could not possibly have been the killer.

Alice Louisa Kempson had arranged to go away to stay with a friend in London on Sunday August 2nd. When she had not turned up by Monday, the friend contacted Alice's brother, Albert Reynolds, who lived close to her, in Oxford. He went around to Alice's house and when he could get no answer to his knocking, climbed in through a window and found his sister battered and stabbed to death.

The first thing the police had to do was determine the time of death. There were breakfast things on the kitchen table, the bed had not been made, and Alice was still wearing hair curlers. A tradesman had tried to deliver some shoes Alice had purchased and he received no reply at 11.00am. All this led officers to believe that Alice had been murdered some time on the morning of Saturday, August 1st, probably around 10.00am.

Although an extensive police operation was launched and over 300 people were interviewed in just six days, inquiries were actually concentrating on just one name. Neighbours reported seeing a dark-haired man selling household items door to door, on the Saturday, and a business card had been found in Alice's front room. This gave the name Henry Seymour as a representative for Tellus Ltd, and gave an address in Oxford. It was soon discovered that Seymour had moved on from the address shown and further inquiries eventually led to an address in Preston Park, Brighton, where Seymour was eventually picked up, on August 15th.

Seymour denied any knowledge of the murder of Alice Kempson. He had been in Oxford on the night before the murder, but could explain his movements apart from a gap on the Saturday morning in question.

Seymour had booked into the Greyhound Hotel, Market Street, Aylesbury, on July 21st and had stayed there continually

NAME	Henry Daniel Seymour
AGE AT EXECUTION	39
DATE OF EXECUTION	Thursday, 10th December, 1931
PLACE OF EXECUTION	Oxford
HANGMAN	Not known
ASSISTANT	Not known
DATE OF TRIAL	20th October – 25th October, 1931
LOCATION OF TRIAL	Oxford
PRESIDING JUDGE	Mister Justice Swift
PROSECUTION COUNSEL	St John G. Micklethwait, Wilfred Price
DEFENCE COUNSEL	W.G. Earengey, E.R. Guest
NUMBER OF VICTIMS	1

VICTIMS DETAILS

NAME	Alice Louisa Kempson
AGE	58
DATE OF MURDER	Saturday, 1st August, 1931
PLACE OF MURDER	Boundary House, St Clements, Oxford
METHOD OF KILLING	Stabbed/battered
RELATIONSHIP TO KILLER	None

until July 31st, when he had travelled to Oxford. This part of his story was confirmed by the landlord of the Greyhound, Charles William Parkinson.

On Friday, July 31st, Seymour claimed he had missed his last bus back to Aylesbury and so had asked an old customer, Alice Mary Andrews, of Gypsy Lane, to put him up for the night. He arrived there at 10.30pm and left the following morning at 9.30am. Mrs Andrews was later to testify that Seymour had a hammer and a chisel in his possession, though he was to claim it was actually a hammer and a screwdriver.

At 11.03am on August 1st, Seymour caught a bus back to Aylesbury. The bus stop was some 22 minutes' walk from the murder scene, which meant that for Seymour to be the killer, Alice would have had to have been attacked at 10.30am at the latest. Seymour was identified as being a passenger on the bus and was back at the hotel in Aylesbury that evening.

Although the evidence against Seymour was circumstantial, he could well have been

513

the killer if the authorities had determined the right time of death. This, though, was not the case.

William Law testified that he had seen Alice in Pembroke Street, Oxford at 11.20am on August 1st. Sarah King, who knew Alice well, claimed that she had seen her enter a baker's shop in London Place, at 11.30am. This was confirmed by Evelyn Barrett, an assistant in the shop, who said that this was about the time that she served Alice.

Another shop assistant, John Woodward, who worked in a grocer's shop, said he served Alice at some time between noon and 1.00pm and Frederick Taylor, a painter, who had known Alice for 20 years, said he had seen her at about 12.30pm. Finally, Kate Barron, who had known Alice all her life, said she saw her near her home just before 3.00pm. Despite the evidence of these six witnesses, the jury, after an absence of 38 minutes, found Seymour guilty of murder.

One might have thought that the verdict would be overturned at the Court of Appeal, but here the witnesses were treated even more dismissively. It was held that all six had simply been mistaken about which day they had seen Alice!

On the strength of a business card and the fact that he had been in possession of a hammer on the morning of the murder, Henry Daniel Seymour took his last walk, to the scaffold, on December 10th, 1931.

LATE ON THE night of October 2nd, 1931, a man and a woman signed in to the Station Temperance Hotel at New Bridge Street, in Manchester, as Mr and Mrs Harry Stanley. Harry paid Walter Stead, the manager, 10/- and asked to be called at 8.00am the following morning.

In fact, Harry did not need his early-morning call, for at 8.00am, a maid, Mary Casey, saw him leaving. Of his wife, there was no sign and when she had still not appeared by noon, Mary Casey decided to enter the room anyway, so that she could clean it.

Mrs Stanley lay dead in the bed, a mottled brown tie knotted around her neck. The police were called and they soon identified 'Mrs Stanley' as Annie Riley of 25 Camp Street, Deansgate. At this stage they had no idea who her companion might have been.

The police did not have to wait very long for Mr Stanley to fall into their hands. Late on the night of Monday, October 5th, Solomon Stein walked into the police station, identified himself as Mr Stanley, and gave himself up as the killer of Annie Riley.

Stein explained that on October 2nd, he had gone to the Theatre Royal cinema, where he saw City Lights. He left at around 10.30pm and saw Annie at the corner of Market Street and Cross Street. She spoke to him, asking him where he was going. One thing led to another and eventually she said that she would spend the night with him, if he paid for a hotel room. He agreed and booked into the hotel on New Bridge Street.

At 6.00am, Stein woke and started to get dressed. Finding his tie in his hands he had it around Annie's neck before he knew what he was doing. At one stage during the act of strangling Annie, the tie broke and he then knotted both strips around Annie's throat. His only excuse for his actions was that he found he was missing 15/- and believed Annie might have stolen it.

After leaving the hotel he went home, telling his mother that he had stayed the night at a friend's house. After breakfast he went to work, but left after 10 minutes. He spent much of that Sunday walking around and at one stage found himself near Victoria Station. He saw a small crowd gathered at the hotel,

NAME Solomon Stein
AGE AT EXECUTION 21
DATE OF EXECUTION Tuesday, 15th December, 1931
PLACE OF EXECUTION Manchester
HANGMAN Thomas Pierrepoint
ASSISTANT Not known
DATE OF TRIAL 25th November, 1931
LOCATION OF TRIAL Manchester
PRESIDING JUDGE Mister Justice Finlay
PROSECUTION COUNSEL T. Eastham, Redmond Barry
DEFENCE COUNSEL Neville J. Laski, B.S. Wingate-Saul
NUMBER OF VICTIMS 1

VICTIMS DETAILS
NAME Annie Riley
AGE 28
DATE OF MURDER Saturday, 3rd October, 1931
PLACE OF MURDER Room 6, Station Temperance Hotel, New Bridge Street, Manchester
METHOD OF KILLING Strangled
RELATIONSHIP TO KILLER None

bought himself a paper and read about his crime. The following night, he gave himself up to the police.

Even now the drama was not over. At his trial, when asked how he pleaded, his counsel replied not guilty. Stein immediately shouted: "I say guilty." Mister Laski was given time to consult his client, but Stein refused to change his plea and after a few minutes, received the sentence of death.

ON THE MORNING of September 4th, 1931, James McCalmont was out collecting milk around Carrickfergus when his horse began to shy. There was something in the grass that was frightening the animal, and when James went to investigate he found the body of a man. Curiously, the man, was completely naked, except for a blue-and-white bathing cap, and he had been shot in the head.

The day before, another strange discovery had been made in Belfast. A pile of bloodstained clothing had been found outside a shop in Church Lane. The police correctly linked the clothing with the naked body and this led the investigation to concentrate on Belfast.

Publicity about these items led a maid, Rose McGoldrick to come forward. She told the police that she had been outside the railway station on Saturday, August 29th, when a man drew up in a car and started talking to her. They met the next day and during the subsequent trip out she saw a blue-and-white bathing cap in his coat pocket.

This evidence led to Ryan's Hotel at 2 Donegal Quay, Belfast, where Rose McGoldrick's friend had registered using the name Bernard Berman. He had a tall Turkish friend with him and this led to a name for the dead man: Achmet Musa.

Musa had been working for Bertram Mills's Circus in England as a servant to Zara Agha, who billed himself as the oldest man in the world, claiming to be 156! He was managed by Assim Redvan but there was a fourth man in the group, a friend of Musa's: Eddie Cullens. Furthermore, Cullens fitted the description of the man who had booked into Ryan's Hotel and who had taken Miss McGoldrick for a drive.

Cullens was arrested at Hyde Park Corner on September 20th and denied any involvement in Musa's death. There was, however, circumstantial evidence linking him with the crime.

Firstly, there was the testimony of David Nummie, who worked for the Belfast Steamship Company. His records showed a car, registration number VW 3265, arriving in the city, from Liverpool, on August 29th. The

NAME	Eddie Cullens
AGE AT EXECUTION	26
DATE OF EXECUTION	Wednesday, 13th January, 1932
PLACE OF EXECUTION	Belfast
HANGMAN	Thomas Pierrepoint
ASSISTANT	Not known
DATE OF TRIAL	8th December – 10th December, 1931
LOCATION OF TRIAL	Armagh
PRESIDING JUDGE	Lord Chief Justice, Sir William Moore
PROSECUTION COUNSEL	A.B. Babington M.P., J.C. Davison, William McWilliams
DEFENCE COUNSEL	William Lowry, B.J. Fox
NUMBER OF VICTIMS	1

VICTIMS DETAILS	
NAME	Achmet Musa
AGE	Not known
DATE OF MURDER	circa Wednesday, 2nd September, 1931
PLACE OF MURDER	Seskin, near Carrickfergus
METHOD OF KILLING	Shot
RELATIONSHIP TO KILLER	None

following Thursday, Cullens, using the name Berman, made the return trip.

Wallace Gibson was the circus manager and he testified that Musa and Cullens had left for Ireland together. When Cullens returned he was alone and said that Musa had stayed behind.

No motive for the murder could be suggested, but it took the jury 34 minutes to decide that Cullens was guilty. The original execution date was set for December 29th, 1931 but that was cancelled when Cullens announced his intention to appeal. When that failed, a new date was set and Cullens was hanged in January.

CONSTANCE INMAN WAS last seen alive by her friend and neighbour, 10-year-old Olga Roberts, on the evening of September 22nd, 1931. When, half an hour afterwards she was missed by her parents, a search of the area was organised but no trace of Constance could be found. She was reported missing that same night.

The following morning, Jane Birkett, the maid at 42 Park Range, saw what she at first thought was a doll in a garden on Dickenson Road. On closer inspection, this turned out to be the body of a child: Constance Inman.

Forensic tests showed that the girl had died from asphyxiation and marks upon her neck seemed to indicate that she had been strangled. She had not been killed where she was found and although her clothing was disarranged, it was not at first thought that she had been raped.

Police inquiries amongst Constance's friends revealed that Connie had spoken to them about a man she had met who had promised to give her some cigarette cards. A door-to-door set of interviews was now organised.

At number 97 Dickenson Road, officers encountered a lodger who gave his name as Price. He claimed he had been at the cinema on the night of the little girl's disappearance, but when his landlady, Mrs Broadhurst was spoken to, she gave information that suggested Price deserved a closer look.

Mrs Broadhurst made two interesting statements. The first was that her lodger had spoken about Constance's death and told her that he had bought a newspaper that gave the details of the event. Mrs Broadhurst found this difficult to accept because she knew that Price was illiterate. The second thing was that late on the night of Constance's disappearance, she and a fellow lodger had heard a noise that sounded like something being dragged along the hallway. They had not looked to see what was making the noise because they feared it might have been burglars.

Spoken to again, Price revealed that his real name was Rice and maintained that he had gone to the cinema on the night of September 22nd and had gone straight to bed

NAME	George Alfred Rice
AGE AT EXECUTION	32
DATE OF EXECUTION	Wednesday, 3rd February, 1932
PLACE OF EXECUTION	Manchester
HANGMAN	Thomas Pierrepoint
ASSISTANT	Not known
DATE OF TRIAL	14th December – 15th December, 1931
LOCATION OF TRIAL	Manchester
PRESIDING JUDGE	Mister Justice Finlay
PROSECUTION COUNSEL	J.C. Jackson M.P., Redmond Barry
DEFENCE COUNSEL	E.G. Hemmerde, T.H. Hinchcliffe
NUMBER OF VICTIMS	1

VICTIMS DETAILS	
NAME	Constance Inman
AGE	9
DATE OF MURDER	Tuesday, 22nd September, 1931
PLACE OF MURDER	97 Dickenson Road, Manchester
METHOD OF KILLING	Asphyxiated
RELATIONSHIP TO KILLER	None

when he returned home. He produced a cinema ticket stub, but this was for the wrong date. He was taken into the police station for further questioning.

On September 24th, Rice finally made a confession to knowing more about Constance's death. He had met her by arrangement at about 6.30pm and whilst cuddling her, she collapsed. He left her where she was and went to the pictures but when he returned, Constance had not moved. She was dead and thinking that he would be blamed, he decided to move the body. Late that night he had taken the body and gently placed her where she was finally found.

At Rice's trial, the medical opinion had shifted somewhat: now, Constance had 'probably' been raped. However, soon there were to be some very curious developments. In the first place, Rice had apparently produced a grammatically perfect statement. The defence tried to argue that this had been 'produced' by the police, but the latter would admit to nothing of the kind, insisting that it was all the work of

George Rice. The second interesting development was brought about due to the way poor Constance had actually died.

The prosecution maintained that the cuddling Rice referred to was his word for sexual intercourse and that he had strangled Constance whilst raping or attempting to rape her. However, Constance had been wearing a cheap bead necklace and it was just as likely that in holding her, Rice had tightened this against her throat accidentally and that Constance had died from vagal inhibition.

The fate of Rice pivoted on whether Constance had been raped or not. The judge directed that if he had raped her, or had intended to rape her, he was guilty of murder. If however the jury thought that he was guilty of merely an indecent assault upon Constance, they could return a verdict of manslaughter. After 40 minutes of deliberation the jury returned for clarification and having received it, announced that Rice was guilty of murder.

George Alfred Rice, had to be half carried to the scaffold on which he died. Whatever his intentions towards Constance, it is highly likely that her death was accidental and that Rice was not a murderer.

1932

O N NOVEMBER 30TH, 1931, William Goddard walked into the police station in his home town of Ipswich and confessed that he was responsible for the death of his skipper. He went on to explain how he had accidentally killed Charles William Lambert on board the barge Speranza.

According to Goddard, he had asked Lambert, on the previous Friday, if there was any mail for him. Lambert had answered that there were two letters for him, one of which was from his fiancée. Unfortunately, Lambert phrased things somewhat differently and used a most derogatory term about the woman Goddard was engaged to.

Goddard, having taken great exception to the words Lambert had used, lashed out and caught him with a punch on the jaw. Lambert fell backwards down the steps leading to his cabin and, concerned for his safety, Goddard went down to see if Lambert was all right. Lambert was indeed alive and well and held in one hand a rather heavy coal hammer. The two men came together and Goddard managed to wrestle the hammer from Lambert, and strike him with it, but only after sustaining an injury himself, to the back of the neck. Angry and frightened, Goddard then went for a walk and upon returning at 5.00pm, found that Lambert had not moved. He was dead, and in a panic, Goddard stole his watch and chain to make it look like a robbery.

The story was plausible enough, but Goddard had omitted one or two important details. To begin with, there was a rope knotted around Lambert's neck and medical evidence showed that he had been partly strangled. Goddard tried to explain this away by saying that his first thought had been to dispose of the body overboard. He had tied a rope around the neck in order to give himself a handhold but when he tried to pull the body up onto the deck, he found he could not manage the stairs, so placed the body on the bed instead.

There was also the matter of a disputed phrase. The police had testified that when he first came into the station in Ipswich, Goddard had admitted striking Lambert with the hammer but had then gone on to say that after Lambert had been hit, he was making

NAME	William Harold Goddard
AGE AT EXECUTION	25
DATE OF EXECUTION	Tuesday, 23rd February, 1932
PLACE OF EXECUTION	Pentonville
HANGMAN	Robert Baxter
ASSISTANT	Thomas Phillips
DATE OF TRIAL	19th January – 20th January, 1932
LOCATION OF TRIAL	Old Bailey
PRESIDING JUDGE	Mister Justice Finlay
PROSECUTION COUNSEL	Sir Percival Clarke, G.B. McClure
DEFENCE COUNSEL	Gerald Howard, Garth Moore
NUMBER OF VICTIMS	1

VICTIMS DETAILS	
NAME	Charles William Lambert
AGE	57
DATE OF MURDER	Friday, 27th November, 1931
PLACE OF MURDER	On board the barge Speranza, North Woolwich Causeway, London
METHOD OF KILLING	Battered/strangled
RELATIONSHIP TO KILLER	None

too much noise and so Goddard had to "finish him off". Goddard denied using this phrase, which did seem to indicate that the crime was not one of manslaughter, but a case of cold-blooded murder.

In the event, the jury preferred to believe the police version of Goddard's statement and a guilty verdict was returned.

THERE ARE MANY reasons for committing murder. Mabel Elizabeth Mathews was killed because of her bicycle lamp.

Late on the night of Saturday, December 19th, 1931, Mabel was discovered lying on the roadway not far from her home village of Burford. She died shortly afterwards.

A search of the area revealed Mabel's handbag. Her bicycle also lay close by, but the lamp was missing. The search spread ever wider and in due course, some one and a half miles away, towards Cheltenham, her shopping was found, as was a lamp – but not the one that had been on Mabel's bicycle. Close by the body, another find had been made. A man's mackintosh had been discarded and there was a quantity of sausage sandwiches in one pocket.

The trail of Mabel's property led police in the general direction her assailant had taken and officers were warned to be on the lookout. This led Constable Morgan to stop a cyclist at Abergavenny on December 20th. The man identified himself as George Pople but denied being anywhere near Burford the previous day. He explained that he was a soldier on leave and was now heading for home at Brecon.

Constable Morgan had noticed that Pople's shoes were very muddy. As a matter of routine, Pople was interviewed again, at his home, the following day and eventually confessed that he had been involved in the death of Mabel.

Pople explained that his month's leave had started on December 9th. He had taken his cycle and began touring the country, staying first at Bath, and then with relatives in London. He had left the capital on December 19th, intending to journey back to Brecon. On the way his lamp became defective and, as he was pushing the cycle down a country lane, he saw the lights of another bicycle coming towards him.

As the vehicle came level with him, Pople reached out to snatch the lamp, but fell into the cycle and knocked the rider off. She fell forward and struck a telegraph pole.

At the trial, it was shown that the relative Pople had stayed with in London had made him sausage sandwiches, and bloodstains

NAME	George Thomas Pople
AGE AT EXECUTION	22
DATE OF EXECUTION	Wednesday, 9th March, 1932
PLACE OF EXECUTION	Oxford
HANGMAN	Not known
ASSISTANT	Not known
DATE OF TRIAL	1st February – 2nd February, 1932
LOCATION OF TRIAL	Gloucester
PRESIDING JUDGE	Mister Justice Roche
PROSECUTION COUNSEL	Sir Reginald Coventry, G.K. Rose
DEFENCE COUNSEL	W.G. Earengey, E.R. Guest
NUMBER OF VICTIMS	1

VICTIMS DETAILS	
NAME	Mabel Elizabeth Mathews
AGE	56
DATE OF MURDER	Saturday, 19th December, 1931
PLACE OF MURDER	On the roadway between Burford and Cheltenham
METHOD OF KILLING	Battered
RELATIONSHIP TO KILLER	None

were found on his clothing. The crucial point, though, was the way in which Mabel received her injuries.

Pathologist Sir Bernard Spilsbury testified that it was impossible for Mabel to have been injured as Pople described. She had two wounds on the back of her head, 11 fractured ribs, a fractured jaw and massive internal bruising. These were more consistent with Mabel being knocked down, strangled and then being repeatedly struck with either a fist or a boot.

Pople's defence collapsed. As he received his death sentence, he stood to attention, tears streaming down his cheeks.

IN 1929, GEORGE Emanuel Michael, a coloured Danish subject from the West Indies, married a young lady named Theresa Mary Hempstock. Theresa had told George that she was a widow but, unfortunately for her as it turned out, this was a lie. Her husband was very much alive and the marriage to George Michael was a bigamous one.

For the best part of two years, the 'marriage' did well, until on December 12th, 1931, Theresa gave herself up to the police and told them that she had committed bigamy. The police released Theresa, but George could not forgive what he saw as a disgraceful insult. He left Theresa and moved into lodgings with a Mrs Morrison.

The events of that December day must have preyed heavily on George Michael's mind. Some time after Christmas, 1931, he had a quiet conversation with Mrs Morrison, in which he asked her what the penalty was for killing someone in this country. The thought of being hanged did not apparently frighten George, for he now set about paying Theresa back for what she had done to him.

It was 3.30pm on December 31st when George visited Theresa's house and made threats upon her life. To underline the fact that he was being serious, he then spent a few minutes smashing Theresa's windows, until the police were called and a young constable arrived. The police officer took George into the house, so that hopefully the peace could be restored. Theresa began to tell her story, whereupon George pushed past the police officer, drew out a knife and stabbed Theresa six times before plunging the knife into himself.

Theresa Hempstock was dead, but George Michael made a full recovery and was put on trial for murder. With a police officer as a witness to the crime, the verdict was the only one the jury really could return, the only surprise perhaps being that it still took them 50 minutes to reach it.

NAME	George Emanuel Michael
AGE AT EXECUTION	49
DATE OF EXECUTION	Wednesday, 27th April, 1932
PLACE OF EXECUTION	Hull
HANGMAN	Thomas Pierrepoint
ASSISTANT	Henry Pollard
DATE OF TRIAL	4th March, 1932
LOCATION OF TRIAL	Leeds
PRESIDING JUDGE	Mister Justice Humphreys
PROSECUTION COUNSEL	Arthur Morley
DEFENCE COUNSEL	J. Willoughby Jardine
NUMBER OF VICTIMS	1

VICTIMS DETAILS	
NAME	Theresa Mary Hempstock
AGE	47
DATE OF MURDER	Thursday, 31st December, 1931
PLACE OF MURDER	Upper Union Street, Hull
METHOD OF KILLING	Stabbed
RELATIONSHIP TO KILLER	Girlfriend

THOMAS RILEY WAS a native of Wigan, in Lancashire, but he had moved to Huddersfield where, at the end of July, 1931, he met Elizabeth Castle. They got on very well and Thomas subsequently moved in with her, at Lepton.

Minnie Fisher, Elizabeth's stepdaughter, lived next door to her and last saw Elizabeth alive at 5.00pm on December 16th. Some five hours later, Minnie heard someone wearing clogs enter Elizabeth's house. Since Thomas habitually wore clogs, she naturally assumed it was him.

The woman who delivered milk, Marian Copely Tolson, got no reply to her knocking on either the morning of the 17th or the 18th of December. This did not concern her too much, though. It may have been that Elizabeth had gone away for a few days.

It was not until December 19th, at 3.20pm, that Thomas Riley walked into Millgarth police station and there spoke to Sergeant Harry James. Thomas said that he wished to give himself up for murder and when he was not at first believed, shouted: "I'm fed up. I'm telling you the truth. We had a quarrel and I hit her on the head with a hammer." He then handed over a key and told the sergeant which house to go to.

Riley went on to explain that Elizabeth had come home on the evening of December 16th, carrying a jug of beer. They had a drink together but then an argument broke out and she called him an Irish bastard. He reached out, picked up a hammer and struck out with it, killing her in the process. At 10.00pm that night, he had gone to bed and the next day, after telling people that Elizabeth was visiting a sick friend, he travelled to Leeds, where he stayed overnight. On the 18th, Thomas went to Bradford, where he stayed at the Salvation Army Hostel, before going to Leeds on the 19th, and giving himself up.

Riley may have thought that he would escape the gallows on the strength of provocation, but his own confession was enough to convict him of murder. He was hanged at Leeds alongside John Henry Roberts.

NAME	Thomas Riley
AGE AT EXECUTION	36
DATE OF EXECUTION	Thursday, 28th April, 1932
PLACE OF EXECUTION	Leeds
HANGMAN	Thomas Pierrepoint
ASSISTANT	Alfred Allen, Thomas Phillips
DATE OF TRIAL	9th March, 1932
LOCATION OF TRIAL	Leeds
PRESIDING JUDGE	Mister Justice Humphreys
PROSECUTION COUNSEL	G.H.B. Streatfeild
DEFENCE COUNSEL	G. Raymond Hinchcliffe
NUMBER OF VICTIMS	1

VICTIMS DETAILS	
NAME	Elizabeth Castle
AGE	53
DATE OF MURDER	Wednesday, 16th December, 1931
PLACE OF MURDER	Kirk Vale, Lepton, near Huddersfield
METHOD OF KILLING	Battered
RELATIONSHIP TO KILLER	Girlfriend

1932

ALFRED GILL WAS a greengrocer who had a shop at 1260 Leeds Road, Bradford. He also had a mobile shop in which he sometimes had help, from John Henry Roberts.

At 9.00am on December 11th, Gill's wife, Louisa, saw him off to work. At the time Gill was carrying £50 in cash and would expect perhaps another £15 or £20 to be added to that, by the time he returned home.

There were various sightings of Gill during the day. Some time between 2.30pm and 3.00pm he was seen in the company of Roberts, by Josiah Knight. At 4.55pm, Gill was opening the gate to some piggeries he owned. He was seen here by William Betts.

By 8.00pm Gill had not returned home, and his wife set out to look for him. There was no sign of him at the shop so she returned home and gave her son, Alfred, his dinner. Then, after Alfred had finished, they both set out to look for him at the piggeries. Again there was no sign.

It was 12.45am the following morning when Alfred, together with his brother William, returned to the piggeries and found their father's body. He had been battered, his watch having stopped at 6.13. By 4.30am that same morning, police were calling on Roberts.

Roberts had financial problems. A court judgement for debt had been made against him in July 1931, and though ordered to pay just 2/- a week, he had made no payments. Checks revealed that some time around 6.30pm, Roberts had been in possession of one of Alfred Gill's horses. Roberts had a swollen left eye and claimed that this had been caused by a shaft of the cart hitting him. Further investigations showed that he had been in the Ring O' Bells pub with his girlfriend, Mary Ellen Eyres, at 8.00pm, whereupon he had left, returning an hour later having changed his clothes. When police examined his day clothes, they found extensive bloodstains.

Roberts was taken in and charged with murder. He was searched and a roll of banknotes found. This roll was held together with a band and witnesses swore that this was exactly how Alfred Gill kept his money.

Roberts's story was that he had killed Alfred after being provoked. At the piggeries,

NAME	John Henry Roberts
AGE AT EXECUTION	23
DATE OF EXECUTION	Thursday, 28th April, 1932
PLACE OF EXECUTION	Leeds
HANGMAN	Thomas Pierrepoint
ASSISTANT	Thomas Phillips, Alfred Allen
DATE OF TRIAL	11th March – 12th March, 1932
LOCATION OF TRIAL	Leeds
PRESIDING JUDGE	Mister Justice Humphreys
PROSECUTION COUNSEL	Walter Hedley, E.A. Hawke
DEFENCE COUNSEL	J. Willoughby Jardine
NUMBER OF VICTIMS	1

VICTIMS DETAILS	
NAME	Alfred Gill
AGE	55
DATE OF MURDER	Friday, 11th December, 1931
PLACE OF MURDER	Tyersal, Pudsey, near Bradford
METHOD OF KILLING	Battered
RELATIONSHIP TO KILLER	None

Roberts had upset some of the food Gill was giving to his pigs. Gill swore at Roberts, who struck out and hit Gill. In retaliation, Gill picked up a hammer and hit Roberts. A struggle followed and Gill fell to the ground whereupon Roberts took a heavy brick and battered him.

It was held, both at the trial and the appeal, that if Alfred Gill had indeed hit Roberts, the injuries found on him meant that he could only have sustained a glancing blow. As a result, he was found guilty and executed.

ANNETTE FRIEDSON WAS a frightened woman. On January 26th, 1932, she was so nervous that she even asked her brother, Samuel, to escort her to her place of work. Samuel saw her onto the tram that would take her to Fore Street, where Annette had worked as a typist for 12 years. Later that same morning, Annette was found on the stairway of the offices, her throat cut and a trail of blood leading down the stairs to the point where she had been attacked.

There was only one suspect: Maurice Freedman. Maurice was a married man, though he had omitted to mention this when he had first started walking out with Annette, in August 1930. When this fact came to light in October 1931, the family began to actively discourage Annette from seeing Freedman but, although the relationship did cool, the couple did go on seeing each other.

The fact of Freedman's marriage caused many disputes between him and Annette and they were often seen arguing. These arguments came to a head on Saturday, January 23rd, 1932 and to try to cool the situation, Annette agreed to meet Freedman the following day. She did not turn up. That was why she had been so frightened of going to work alone.

Freedman was arrested outside his lodgings in Oakfield Road, Clapton, on the evening of January 26th. He admitted the killing but said that it was not murder. He had gone to the offices and waited for Annette to arrive. This part of his testimony was backed up by witnesses, who saw a man they would later identify as Freedman waiting in the street opposite the offices where Annette worked. Both Ernest Carr and Arthur Samuel Barnaby saw Freedman rush across the road and accost a young woman. They put the time at approximately 9.15am.

Freedman and Annette argued at the foot of the staircase. They were seen here by a Mr Hilton who was there on business and he described the discussion between the two as heated. It was what happened next that would decide if Freedman was guilty of murder, or manslaughter.

According to Freedman, he asked Annette if they were to continue seeing each

NAME	Maurice Freedman
AGE AT EXECUTION	36
DATE OF EXECUTION	Wednesday, 4th May, 1932
PLACE OF EXECUTION	Pentonville
HANGMAN	Robert Baxter
ASSISTANT	Robert Wilson
DATE OF TRIAL	8th March – 9th March, 1932
LOCATION OF TRIAL	Old Bailey
PRESIDING JUDGE	Mister Justice Hawke
PROSECUTION COUNSEL	Sir Percival Clarke, L.A. Byrne
DEFENCE COUNSEL	Bernard Gillis, Gordon Bruce
NUMBER OF VICTIMS	1

VICTIMS DETAILS	
NAME	Annette Friedson
AGE	31
DATE OF MURDER	Tuesday, 26th January, 1932
PLACE OF MURDER	103 Fore Street, London
METHOD OF KILLING	Cut throat
RELATIONSHIP TO KILLER	Girlfriend

other and when she said no, he took a razor out of his pocket and held it to his own throat. He testified that he had no intention of harming either himself or Annette and wanted to simply frighten her. Instead, Annette reached out and grappled with him. In the struggle, the razor must have been accidentally drawn across Annette's throat, for the next thing he knew was that she had collapsed, bleeding badly.

The jury were not convinced. Surely if Freedman's story was true he would have gone for help. After deliberating for 30 minutes, they filed back into court and announced that Freedman was guilty.

TUESDAY, MARCH 22ND, 1932, was a normal school day for Naomi Farnworth. After having her morning lessons Annie, as she was known to her friends and family, had to travel to another school so that she could partake of her free dinner. She enjoyed a potato hash and was seen soon afterwards, at 12.30pm, in Mrs Brumfitt's fish and chip shop. She was with one of her friends, Doris Sharples.

By 6.30pm, Annie had not returned home and her parents began making enquiries. Whilst these searches were taking place, Charles Cowle approached Doris Sharples, asked if she had heard about the missing schoolgirl and added that she would be next.

When Annie could not be found, the police were called in. The next evening, Cowle and one of his friends, James Edward Foster, joined in the search between 5.30pm and 7.30pm. They spent the rest of the night together playing dominoes and still there was no trace of Annie.

On March 24th, at 9.45am, the police paid a visit to Cowle's house and told him that they had received information that Annie had run an errand for him on the day she disappeared. He then told the officers two slightly different stories.

In the first of these, Cowle admitted that he had sent Annie to Mrs Brumfitt's for fish and chips. She then returned to school and that was the last time he had seen her. The second story was much the same, but this time he said that Annie had spent 20 minutes in his house, enjoying some of his chips.

As a matter of routine, the police asked to look around the house. Upstairs they saw a large trunk. Cowle pointed at it, told them that Annie was inside and informed them that he had strangled her. Upon opening the trunk, it was seen that Cowle was telling the truth. Annie had been raped and strangled and a postmortem was to show not just potato hash in her stomach, but also chips, which had not been served at the school that day.

Cowle's defence was one of insanity and in this case at least it should surely have succeeded. He was a mental defective with a child's mentality and he explained how before the attack he had felt a funny feeling in his

NAME	Charles James Cowle
AGE AT EXECUTION	19
DATE OF EXECUTION	Wednesday, 18th May, 1932
PLACE OF EXECUTION	Manchester
HANGMAN	Thomas Pierrepoint
ASSISTANT	Not known
DATE OF TRIAL	26th April, 1932
LOCATION OF TRIAL	Manchester
PRESIDING JUDGE	Mister Justice Humphreys
PROSECUTION COUNSEL	Maxwell Fyfe
DEFENCE COUNSEL	T.M. Backhouse
NUMBER OF VICTIMS	1

VICTIMS DETAILS	
NAME	Naomi Annie Farnworth
AGE	6
DATE OF MURDER	Tuesday, 22nd March, 1932
PLACE OF MURDER	82 Kay Street, Darwen
METHOD OF KILLING	Strangled
RELATIONSHIP TO KILLER	None

head. Evidence was given that at the age of nine, Cowle had attacked a two-year-old boy, for which he was sent to a reform school and his father, Charles William Cowle, gave evidence that his son seemed to have no sense of pain.

Doctor Alexander Sturrock testified that in his opinion, Cowle had a split personality and would suffer from periods of violence and excitement alternating with dullness and negativism. The judge ruled that there could only be two possible verdicts, guilty or guilty whilst insane. The jury chose the former.

UNTIL JUNE, 1932, Gwendoline Warren lived with her husband, William, and her two children, a 12-year-old son, Ronald, and a baby daughter. This was not the picture of domestic happiness it might have seemed, though, for the baby was not William's and in that same month of June, Gwendoline went to live with her lover, Ernest Hutchinson. They rented a house together in Heywood Avenue, Maidenhead, using the name of Mr and Mrs Warren.

For a few months, everything seemed to be fine. On Saturday, September 10th, Ronald Warren went to stay with his aunt, Miss Fleet, at her home in East Burnham, Buckinghamshire. He only stayed one night and returned home on the Sunday. The next day, Monday, after having breakfast with his sister, Ronald returned to his aunt's, this time taking the baby with him. Ronald was due to return home on Wednesday, pick up his mother and the two of them would go back to Miss Fleet's for a few days.

When Ronald did get home on Wednesday, September 14th, Hutchinson would not let him in. Miss Fleet, concerned over this strange behaviour, accompanied Ronald back yet again, reaching Maidenhead that evening. Getting no reply to her constant knocking, Miss Fleet summoned assistance from a neighbour, Mr Hutton, who helped Ronald into the house where the body of Gwendoline was discovered, underneath a mattress piled high with cushions and bedding.

Of Hutchinson there was no sign, but a detailed description of him was published, leading to his arrest in Southend on September 15th. He had travelled there from London and was accompanied by a prostitute.

Hutchinson told the police a very strange story indeed. He admitted that he and Gwendoline had argued on the night of Saturday, September 10th. She had complained about him not having a job, but after some discussion they had made things up between them. That night, though, Gwendoline had gone to bed in the spare room.

The following morning, Hutchinson checked on Gwendoline and discovered that she had been suffocated. The front door was unlocked and from that he drew the

NAME	Ernest Hutchinson
AGE AT EXECUTION	43
DATE OF EXECUTION	Wednesday, 23rd November, 1932
PLACE OF EXECUTION	Oxford
HANGMAN	Not known
ASSISTANT	Not known
DATE OF TRIAL	14th October – 16th October, 1932
LOCATION OF TRIAL	Reading
PRESIDING JUDGE	Mister Justice MacKinnon
PROSECUTION COUNSEL	W.G. Earengey
DEFENCE COUNSEL	St John G. Micklethwait
NUMBER OF VICTIMS	1

VICTIMS DETAILS	
NAME	Gwendoline Annie Warren
AGE	37
DATE OF MURDER	circa Sunday, 11th September, 1932
PLACE OF MURDER	Heywood Avenue, Maidenhead
METHOD OF KILLING	Asphyxiated
RELATIONSHIP TO KILLER	Girlfriend

conclusion that someone had gained entry and killed Gwendoline. The person responsible was obviously her husband, William, since Hutchinson claimed he had written a number of threatening letters.

Hutchinson claimed that he had been too upset to report the matter to the authorities but had stayed in the house, with Gwendoline's body, for three days, lying to anyone who asked after her and telling them that she had gone to Birmingham. He sold some of her furniture in order to get some cash, finally leaving for London on September 14th.

It was at best a highly unlikely story and did nothing to convince the jury. They returned their verdict after deliberating for 70 minutes and as that verdict was announced, Ernest Hutchinson smiled broadly.

1933

JEREMIAH HANBURY HAD been having an affair with Jessie Payne for 10 weeks when she suddenly stopped him coming around to see her. Hanbury came to believe that she was seeing another man by the name of Bert Eardley and wasted no time in telling her husband, James Charles Payne, what she had been up to. For her part, Jessie told her husband, James, that she had had sex with Hanbury, but that he had raped her. Hanbury countered this by telling James that he had paid her for sex and Eardley was now probably doing the same.

It was a few minutes after 2.00pm on October 17th when Jessie's next-door neighbour, Edith Elizabeth Harris, saw Jessie in the yard, shaking out a tablecloth. Five minutes later, Hanbury appeared. He was covered in blood, was apparently suffering from a cut throat and announced: "Come on, I've done it now."

Ten minutes after that, at 2.15pm, Hanbury was seen walking towards the High Street by Louisa Phoebe Marsh. She could not forget the sight of the man, bleeding profusely from a wound in his throat and his strange mutterings: "Jerry said revenge. Jerry's had revenge."

A few minutes later, James Henry Round saw Hanbury, close by the church in High Street. Hanbury looked directly at him and calmly said: "I've done a murder." The next person Hanbury spoke to was Constable William Kirkham and having made the same admission, Hanbury was taken into custody, where he received medical attention.

The attack on Jessie Payne had been a frantic one. Hanbury had struck her twice with a hammer, rendering her unconscious. He had then knelt down and cut her throat, slashing a piece of flesh from his own right forefinger, which would later be found near Jessie's head.

At the trial, it was suggested that Hanbury was an unstable character and was insane at the time of the crime. Evidence was given that once before when crossed in love, Hanbury had tried to kill himself and there was a history of insanity in the family, but this did not sway the jury, who found him guilty as charged.

NAME	Jeremiah Hanbury
AGE AT EXECUTION	49
DATE OF EXECUTION	Thursday, 2nd February, 1933
PLACE OF EXECUTION	Birmingham
HANGMAN	Thomas Pierrepoint
ASSISTANT	Robert Wilson, Albert Pierrepoint
DATE OF TRIAL	8th December, 1932
LOCATION OF TRIAL	Birmingham
PRESIDING JUDGE	Mister Justice Humphreys
PROSECUTION COUNSEL	C.B. Marriott, Paul E. Sandlands
DEFENCE COUNSEL	John F. Bourke, G. Rogers
NUMBER OF VICTIMS	1

VICTIMS DETAILS	
NAME	Jessie Payne
AGE	39
DATE OF MURDER	Monday, 17th October, 1932
PLACE OF MURDER	11 The Leys, Brockmore, near Brierley Hill
METHOD OF KILLING	Battered/cut throat
RELATIONSHIP TO KILLER	Girlfriend

THE TWO BOYS were enjoying their game in the fields and woods around Derryane when suddenly one of them spied a woman, lying on the grass, apparently asleep. Not wanting to disturb her, the boys crept away and continued their game elsewhere.

The following day, August 3rd 1932, the two boys were back and discovered that the woman hadn't moved. They drew closer and only now saw that the woman's throat had been cut. They ran off to fetch the police.

The woman was identified as Minnie Reid, and she had been eight months pregnant. Investigations and medical reports showed that she had almost certainly died on the evening of July 27th.

It wasn't long before enquiries revealed that Minnie had been keeping company with Harold Courtney who lived in Church Street, Dungannon. There was, however, a complication since Courtney had become engaged to another girl, Louie Motum, on September 21st, 1932. Could it be that Minnie's child had been fathered by Courtney and he had killed her because of his new relationship?

Courtney was taken in for questioning and claimed that he had never had a relationship with Minnie, had not been in touch with her, was not the father of her child and had been in Armagh at the time Minnie had met her death. Most of those statements were shown to be false.

A letter from Minnie to Harold was found beneath his pillow, showing that they had arranged to meet on Tuesday the 26th. And, whilst it was true that Robert Stevenson confirmed that he had seen Courtney drive past him, in Armagh, at 8.30pm on July 27th, that gentleman was a relative by marriage and another witness, Richard McKinley, said that he had seen Stevenson on a bus in Newry at the time he was supposed to be waving to Courtney in Armagh. The implication was that Stevenson was lying.

Eventually Courtney was charged with murder and appeared at Downpatrick on December 10th. The five-day hearing ended with the jury being unable to agree on a verdict and Courtney was remanded to the next Armagh assizes.

NAME	Harold Courtney
AGE AT EXECUTION	28
DATE OF EXECUTION	Friday, 7th April, 1933
PLACE OF EXECUTION	Belfast
HANGMAN	Thomas Pierrepoint
ASSISTANT	Albert Pierrepoint
DATE OF TRIAL	15th March – 20th March, 1933
LOCATION OF TRIAL	Armagh
PRESIDING JUDGE	Lord Chief Justice, Sir William Moore
PROSECUTION COUNSEL	A.B. Babington M.P., J.D. Chambers, J.C. MacDermott
DEFENCE COUNSEL	William Lowry, B.J. Fox
NUMBER OF VICTIMS	1

VICTIMS DETAILS	
NAME	Minnie Reid
AGE	23
DATE OF MURDER	Wednesday, 27th July, 1932
PLACE OF MURDER	Field near Derryane
METHOD OF KILLING	Cut throat
RELATIONSHIP TO KILLER	Ex-girlfriend

A lot depended on the medical evidence. Professor John Young, who carried out the postmortem, had no doubt that this was a case of murder, but two other eminent medical practitioners, Professor Kirk and Doctor Whitlaw, both believed that it was more likely suicide. Neither could explain, however, why the murder weapon, found by Constable Brandon, was 14 feet away from the body in dense undergrowth, or why a glove had been forced into the wound in Minnie's neck.

After 75 minutes, the jury decided that Courtney was guilty, but added a strong recommendation to mercy.

ELIZABETH STANDLEY LIVED with her husband and two lodgers on the top floor of 13 Blackstock Road, Finsbury Park. At 8.00am on March 4th, 1933, Elizabeth was left alone when the last of the lodgers, Mr Cox, left for work. When he returned for lunch, just after noon, he discovered Elizabeth's body stuffed underneath her bed, a length of electric flex knotted around her throat.

Police found an immediate lead through the statement of Elizabeth Kerswell, who lived on the ground floor. She said that at around 9.30am, she had heard someone ringing Mrs Standley's bell. The door had been answered and Mrs Kerswell heard her neighbour say: "Are you coming up for a few minutes, Jack?"

It was fairly easy to determine who this Jack was. Elizabeth Standley had a nephew, Jack Puttnam, and it was known that he owed her money. In fact, Elizabeth had loaned him various sums, which now totalled £35, and she had been pressing Jack for repayment. Puttnam was interviewed the same day, but claimed that he had not seen his aunt for weeks. Officers knew that this was a lie, for Elizabeth had visited Puttnam the day before she had been killed, and so attention now focused on him.

Jack Puttnam was interviewed again on more than one occasion, finally being arrested on March 24th, after the police had found a bus conductor who recalled a man rushing for his bus on the day of the murder. The man had climbed on almost directly opposite Elizabeth's house and when faced with a line of men in an identity parade, the conductor, Louis Zachis, had no hesitation in picking out Jack Puttnam.

Puttnam made a full statement. He claimed he had gone to his aunt's home, where they had argued over the money he owed. Things had then become rather personal and Elizabeth had accused Jack of being involved with his brother's wife. She then pushed him and he hit out, striking her with his fist, stabbing her with a meat skewer and finally strangling her with flex from a radio.

Once in court, Puttnam withdrew his confession, claiming that he had only made his statement to keep his sister-in-law out of the matter. He claimed again that he was not at his aunt's house on the day of the murder, and that someone else must have committed the crime. Countering this was the testimony of Louis Zachis, and that was strong enough to convict Puttnam.

NAME	Jack Samuel Puttnam
AGE AT EXECUTION	31
DATE OF EXECUTION	Thursday, 8th June, 1933
PLACE OF EXECUTION	Pentonville
HANGMAN	Robert Baxter
ASSISTANT	Stanley cross
DATE OF TRIAL	1st May – 3rd May, 1933
LOCATION OF TRIAL	Old bailey
PRESIDING JUDGE	Mister Justice Hawke
PROSECUTION COUNSEL	Eustace Fulton, G.B. McClure, maxwell Turner
DEFENCE COUNSEL	Hector Hughes, S.T.T. james, A.T.N. Bellamy
NUMBER OF VICTIMS	1

VICTIMS DETAILS	
NAME	Elizabeth Mary Standley
AGE	44
DATE OF MURDER	Saturday, 4th March, 1933
PLACE OF MURDER	13 Blackstock Road, Finsbury Park, London
METHOD OF KILLING	Strangled/stabbed
RELATIONSHIP TO KILLER	Aunt

RICHARD HETHERINGTON DID not get on with his neighbour, Joseph Nixon. Nixon claimed that Hetherington owed him money, but Hetherington had counter-claimed that he was owed money for work he had done on Nixon's farm. By October 1932, Hetherington had made threats. As a result, the police had been called in and on October 2nd, Constable William Renwick had had a word with Hetherington about his behaviour.

On February 17th, 1933, Hetherington purchased a shotgun from Walter Henry Wilkinson, a gunsmith of Penrith. Two days later, Hetherington was with a neighbour, Ralph Powley, until midday. At that time he mentioned the problems he was having with Nixon and said that he would sort matters out and put him in the reservoir.

It was around 9.00am on February 20th when Thomas Parker smelled burning and saw smoke coming from the Nixons' bungalow. By the time he reached the house, it had all but burned down. Two bodies were found amongst the ashes. A subsequent examination showed that both had died from gunshot wounds.

Hetherington was spoken to on February 21st. He claimed that he didn't have a gun but once the Penrith gunsmith had been spoken to, a search of Hetherington's farm was organised and the stock was found in the barn. Later the barrel was found by Hetherington's mother, and handed over to the police.

Amongst the debris at Nixon's farm, a watch had been found that had stopped at 12.10. Hetherington could prove that he had visited George Albert and Margaret Wilson, and had not left until around 11.30pm. This meant that if the watch indicated the correct time of the murder, he could not be guilty. However, other evidence pointed to the crime having been committed earlier.

William Milner and Joseph Bowman had been in the area and reported hearing shots at 6.00pm. If the fire had been started then, it may well have been the flames that stopped the watch, much later than the time of the murder.

Perhaps the most damning piece of evidence was the testimony of Leonard

NAME	Richard Hetherington
AGE AT EXECUTION	36
DATE OF EXECUTION	Tuesday, 20th June, 1933
PLACE OF EXECUTION	Liverpool
HANGMAN	Thomas Pierrepoint
ASSISTANT	Albert Pierrepoint
DATE OF TRIAL	29th May – 31st May, 1933
LOCATION OF TRIAL	Appleby, Westmorland
PRESIDING JUDGE	Mister Justice MacNaghten
PROSECUTION COUNSEL	Sir Walter Greaves-Lord M.P., Maxwell Fyfe
DEFENCE COUNSEL	J.C. Jackson M.P., Glynn Blackledge
NUMBER OF VICTIMS	2

VICTIMS DETAILS	
NAMES	Joseph Nixon; Mary Ann Nixon
AGES	76; 75
DATE OF MURDER	Sunday, 19th February, 1933
PLACE OF MURDER	'East View', Newby
METHOD OF KILLING	Shot; shot
RELATIONSHIP TO KILLER	None; none

Wilson. When first interviewed by the police, Hetherington was asked if he knew about the fire and said that he had been told of it by Wilson when they met in Penrith High Street at around 1.00pm on February 20th. Wilson agreed that he had seen Hetherington at that time, but denied mentioning the fire.

The jury were out for three hours and 10 minutes before returning their verdict. Even before the trial, on May 3rd, Hetherington had tried to hang himself in his cell at Walton. On June 20th, the executioner made a more certain job of it.

1933

ALTHOUGH DOROTHY BREWER was only approaching her 13th birthday, she was a well-built girl and could easily have passed for 16 or 17 years of age. Since the age of seven she had lived with her grandparents and their son, her uncle, Frederick Morse, at Slough Green. In February, 1933, it was discovered that Dorothy was pregnant.

Her grandparents discovered this to be the case on February 21st. The following day they told Frederick and asked him if was the one responsible; he denied it vehemently. Within 24 hours, Dorothy was dead.

When Dorothy's body was found, snagged in an overhanging branch in a nearby river, foul play was immediately suspected and Morse was closely questioned. His first statement to the police claimed that on February 23rd, the day of Dorothy's death, he had gone to work at the West Hatch lime quarry as usual but had arranged to meet his niece later in the day some 200 yards away.

At the appointed time, Dorothy was waiting and together they walked to Curry Mallet. Here Morse visited the Bell Inn, where he had a couple of pints whilst Dorothy had a lemonade. Before they left, he purchased a half a pint of rum and then he and Dorothy took a walk towards the river. Morse had some rabbit traps to inspect so he left Dorothy in a shed, telling her to wait for him until he returned. When he did get back, she had gone and so he went to look for her by the river bank. At one stage he had fallen in, but he could find no trace of his niece.

The story was not very convincing and on March 1st, Morse was charged with murder. When the postmortem revealed that Dorothy had consumed a large quantity of rum before she died, Morse made a second statement in which he admitted a greater involvement.

According to this subsequent version, Morse and Dorothy had agreed to commit suicide. They had drunk the rum, no doubt as Dutch courage, and then jumped into the river, together. Almost immediately they both changed their minds and tried to get out. At one stage, Morse had managed to push Dorothy out onto the bank, but she had slipped back into the water. Finally, after much struggling, Morse had pulled

NAME	Frederick Morse
AGE AT EXECUTION	34
DATE OF EXECUTION	Tuesday, 25th July, 1933
PLACE OF EXECUTION	Bristol
HANGMAN	Thomas Pierrepoint
ASSISTANT	Not known
DATE OF TRIAL	7th June – 8th June, 1933
LOCATION OF TRIAL	Wells
PRESIDING JUDGE	Mister Justice Goddard
PROSECUTION COUNSEL	J.G. Trapnell, Ben Thomas
DEFENCE COUNSEL	J.D. Casswell, I.R. Dunne
NUMBER OF VICTIMS	1

VICTIMS DETAILS	
NAME	Doris (Dorothy) Winifred Brewer
AGE	12
DATE OF MURDER	Thursday, 23rd February, 1933
PLACE OF MURDER	River Rag, Curry Mallet, near Taunton
METHOD OF KILLING	Drowned
RELATIONSHIP TO KILLER	Niece

himself out but found that he was too weak to assist Dorothy.

Once the case came to trial, Morse reverted to his first statement, saying that he had only signed the second under police pressure. The jury were not persuaded.

VARNAVAS ANTORKA, A Cypriot, had come to England in 1928. At that time he did not speak a word of English, but through the years he taught himself the language and obtained employment as the silver washer at Bellometti's restaurant in Soho. Short tempered at the best of times, Antorka was no respecter of authority.

The head chef at Bellometti's was Boleslar Pankorski and he had absolute say over the work apportioned to the different employees. As Antorka's superior, he had no hesitation in giving instructions to the silver washer and these were not always taken without argument.

On Friday, May 12th, 1933, one of the cooks, Zacharias Panagi was in the larder when Pankorski came in and told Antorka to put some plates into the gas stove to warm. Antorka did not leap into immediate action and so to back up his instruction, Pankorski added that if he did not obey at once, Antorka would be dismissed. His exact words were: "You must do it. If you don't do it, you must finish now." Antorka was far from intimidated and said that if Pankorski didn't watch out, he would finish him first. Panagi did not hear the rest of the conversation, but it is probable that Pankorski did not stand for this gross insubordination and sacked Antorka on the spot, for 15 minutes later, at 1.00pm, a waiter, William Richard Summers, saw the chef and the silver washer in a corridor at the back of the restaurant. Pankorski was walking down a set of stairs and Antorka was waiting at the bottom. As the two met, Antorka grabbed Pankorski and screamed: "You gave me the sack, you bastard, you take me back or else I'll shoot you."

The next few minutes were lost in chaos. The two men began to struggle and suddenly a shot rang out. Two other waiters, Guiseppe Negrori and Antonio Antoniades, rushed forward to offer assistance and two other shots were fired. Pankorski fell dead and another employee, Mitchell Kikilaron, was wounded in the leg.

With so many witnesses, Antorka could not hope to deny that he was the killer. He had wasted no time in carrying out the threat overhead by Panagi. His landlady, Louisa

NAME	Varnavas Antorka
AGE AT EXECUTION	31
DATE OF EXECUTION	Thursday, 10th August, 1933
PLACE OF EXECUTION	Pentonville
HANGMAN	Robert Baxter
ASSISTANT	Henry Pollard
DATE OF TRIAL	27th June – 30th June, 1933
LOCATION OF TRIAL	Old Bailey
PRESIDING JUDGE	Mister Justice Humphreys
PROSECUTION COUNSEL	Eustace Fulton, G.B. McClure
DEFENCE COUNSEL	Mister Eastwood
NUMBER OF VICTIMS	1

VICTIMS DETAILS	
NAME	Boleslar Pankorski (Died Saturday, 13th May)
AGE	35
DATE OF MURDER	Friday, 12th May, 1933
PLACE OF MURDER	Bellometti Restaurant, 27 Soho Square, London
METHOD OF KILLING	Shot
RELATIONSHIP TO KILLER	None

Nutti, of 19 Arthur Street, gave evidence that shortly after midday, Antorka had rushed into the house and gone up to his room. After a very short time, he had run back outside. It seems that he had gone home for the gun and returned instantly to kill Pankorski.

The guilty verdict was little more than a formality and Varnavas Antorka faced the hangman at Pentonville on the 10th of August, 1933.

1933

ROBERT KIRBY HAD been seeing Grace Newing for some three months and she was now pregnant by him. Kirby was still welcome at her parents' house, though, and called there at 8.45pm on Thursday, July 6th, 1933.

As Kirby waited in the kitchen for Grace to return home from work, her young brother, 11-year-old George, amused himself by playing with a piece of cord. At 10.45pm, Grace's mother, Rosina May Newing, retired for the night. Grace would not finish work until 11.00pm and was only expected home at 11.30pm. By this time, Robert was alone, waiting.

In her bed, Rosina heard the sounds of a disturbance coming from downstairs. By the time she got downstairs, Robert had left and Grace lay dead on the floor, the cord her brother had been playing with knotted tightly around her throat.

Robert, meanwhile had walked to his mother's house, where he gently woke her and said: "I have done Gracie in." His brother, Charles William Kirby, who also lived at home, heard all this and said he was going to fetch the police. He would later encounter Constable Bird, whom he took to the scene of the crime in Stevens Road.

Robert meanwhile had gone to another brother's house, that of Francis Kirby in Westdown Road, Leyton. He arrived there at 6.20am and was arrested there 25 minutes later. His explanation for what had happened was: "The girl asked me to do it and I did her the favour!" In fact, this was not the first time Robert Kirby had known violence in his life. Some time before, his father had served a term of four years' imprisonment for attempting to murder his mother.

At Kirby's trial, his defence counsel wanted him to go into the witness box and tell his own story but Robert refused and after 15 minutes' deliberation, he was found guilty but with a recommendation to mercy.

NAME	Robert James Kirby
AGE AT EXECUTION	26
DATE OF EXECUTION	Wednesday, 11th October, 1933
PLACE OF EXECUTION	Pentonville
HANGMAN	Robert Baxter
ASSISTANT	Robert Wilson
DATE OF TRIAL	21st September, 1933
LOCATION OF TRIAL	Old Bailey
PRESIDING JUDGE	Mister Justice Swift
PROSECUTION COUNSEL	Eustace Fulton, E. Anthony Hawke
DEFENCE COUNSEL	Travers Peregrine
NUMBER OF VICTIMS	1

VICTIMS DETAILS	
NAME	Grace Ivy Newing
AGE	17
DATE OF MURDER	Friday, 7th July, 1933
PLACE OF MURDER	28 Stevens Road, Chadwell Heath, Essex
METHOD OF KILLING	Strangled
RELATIONSHIP TO KILLER	Girlfriend

ERNEST PARKER AND his twin brother, Sydney, ran the family fruiterer's business, but it seemed that their father, Thomas, and their sister, Lily, were always finding fault with Ernest.

On December 14th, 1932, Ernest was bound over for an assault on his father that had taken place on November 20th, and for a second attack, this time on Lily, on November 28th. There was further trouble on April 10th, 1933, when he again assaulted Lily. On April 13th, he struck Lily again. For this, Ernest received a prison sentence of two months' hard labour, being released on June 17th.

That same day, Ernest was again at the family home in Blooms Avenue and was again asked to stay away. Later he was heard talking to a friend, James Calvert, and threatened to kill both his father and sister.

The next time the police were called was on June 25th. At some time before 9.00am, Ernest had appeared in the back yard and been told to leave, by his father. The rear door was locked, but Ernest smashed a window, lifted the catch and entered the kitchen. Thomas Parker tried to eject his son but Ernest was getting the better of him when Lily intervened. For her trouble she was struck in the face and the police were called.

At 1.00pm, Ernest was back. He helped himself to lunch, after which the police called yet again and forced him to leave. Things then went quiet and at 3.00pm, Thomas Parker went out. When he returned after 4.00pm, he found Lily, badly injured, lying on her bed.

In fact, there had been a witness to the attack. Lily's 12-year-old daughter, Elsie May Parker, was in the house when she heard Ernest attacking her mother. Elsie saw the last few blows inflicted with an axe, before she managed to rush out into the street and find Constable Thomas Lindsay. As Lindsay returned with Elsie, Ernest gave himself up.

Lily was still alive, barely, and was rushed to Newcastle Royal Infirmary. At 8.30pm that evening, Ernest was asked if he would like to see her there and replied: "No, I hope the bugger will die. I only want the rope for the bugger and I will swing for her."

Lily died at 9.20pm and when charged with her murder, Ernest said: "Well, she

NAME	Ernest Wadge Parker (Scott)
AGE AT EXECUTION	25
DATE OF EXECUTION	Wednesday, 6th December, 1933
PLACE OF EXECUTION	Durham
HANGMAN	Thomas Pierrepoint
ASSISTANT	Not known
DATE OF TRIAL	14th November, 1933
LOCATION OF TRIAL	Durham
PRESIDING JUDGE	Mister Justice Humphreys
PROSECUTION COUNSEL	Mister Hedley, Mister Covingham
DEFENCE COUNSEL	J. Willoughby Jardine, Harvey Robson
NUMBER OF VICTIMS	1

VICTIMS DETAILS

NAME	Lily Parker (Scott)
AGE	36
DATE OF MURDER	Sunday, 25th June, 1933
PLACE OF MURDER	3 Blooms Avenue, Stanley, Co Durham
METHOD OF KILLING	Battered
RELATIONSHIP TO KILLER	Sister

asked for it and got it and my troubles are over, thank God."

Ernest Parker's only hope would be a defence of insanity. He had been an inmate of the Durham County Mental Hospital from August 24th, 1916, to February 17th, 1917, and his mother, Flora Emily Parker, had died in that same institution on June 4th, 1914, after being an inmate for almost two years. Nevertheless, he was found guilty of murder and executed at Durham.

1933

THE CASE OF William Burtoft was, to say the least, a most curious one.

The facts of the crime were simple enough. Some time after taking lunch on July 19th, 1933, Frances Levin counted the money in her purse and found that she had a total of 9/-. Shortly afterwards, at around 2.20pm, Frances's maidservant, Freda Phillips, saw her lying on the sofa in her living room. The maid busied herself for an hour or so before going upstairs to her bedroom, returning at 4.20pm.

Almost immediately she knew that something was wrong. There, on the hearthrug in front of the sofa, lay a bloodstained poker. Without waiting to see exactly what had happened, the maid ran for help, finding Samuel Woodcock, who was a chauffeur at a nearby house. Woodcock returned with the maid, and discovered that someone had battered Frances Levine about the head before running off with the contents of her purse. The unfortunate lady died later in hospital, making it into a case of murder.

Descriptions were given of a man seen loitering about Cheetham Hill Road and when, on July 27th, a man was picked up at Hyde, in Cheshire, it was seen that he matched the description and further inquiries were made.

According to evidence given by the police officers on the case, the man, William Burtoft, readily admitted his guilt and confessed to the murder of Frances Levine. Indeed, his statement began with the words: "I admit being the murderer of Mrs Levine, owing to drinking methylated spirit...." There were, however, a few unanswered questions regarding the degree to which the police had manufactured that statement.

The only evidence against Burtoft was his own confession and after a short time in custody, he withdrew it completely, saying it had been made under police duress. In court, the police explained that when questioned, Burtoft had made his statement during a period of half an hour, yet when this statement was examined in court, it was found to contain fractionally over 200 words. The explanation given was that Burtoft was speaking very slowly. At an average speed of

NAME	William Burtoft
AGE AT EXECUTION	47
DATE OF EXECUTION	Tuesday, 19th December, 1933
PLACE OF EXECUTION	Manchester
HANGMAN	Not known
ASSISTANT	Not known
DATE OF TRIAL	13th November – 14th November, 1933
LOCATION OF TRIAL	Manchester
PRESIDING JUDGE	Mister Justice Atkinson
PROSECUTION COUNSEL	Sir Walter Greaves-Lord M.P., E. Shackleton-Bailey
DEFENCE COUNSEL	B.S. Wingate-Saul
NUMBER OF VICTIMS	1

VICTIMS DETAILS	
NAME	Frances Levin
AGE	61
DATE OF MURDER	Wednesday, 19th July, 1933
PLACE OF MURDER	453 Cheetham Hill Road, Manchester
METHOD OF KILLING	Battered
RELATIONSHIP TO KILLER	None

seven words a minute, this was something of an understatement, but it was allowed to stand, and weighed very heavily against the accused man.

Found guilty and condemned to death, Burtoft was hanged at Strangeways prison, just around the corner from where Frances Levin had died. It was the first death sentence issued by Mister Justice Atkinson, who had only been appointed to the bench on May 15th, 1933.

AT ABOUT MIDNIGHT on Saturday, August 26th, 1933, Charles Fox and his wife, Gladys, retired for the night. They settled down into a sound sleep but at 1.40am, Gladys Fox was woken by the sound of breaking glass. Waking her husband, she told him that she thought there was someone downstairs, and Charles set out to investigate.

Gladys Fox followed her husband part way until she saw him reach the bottom of the stairs. At that point a shadowy figure rushed forward and began attacking Charles Fox. It was over in seconds. The mysterious assailant made good his escape whilst Charles Fox managed to stagger back upstairs, a knife embedded in his back. He was dead within minutes.

The police had quite a few clues to go on. The knife, which had in fact inflicted half a dozen wounds on Charles Fox, bore a most distinctive handle with coloured metal bands. It had been manufactured by J. Clarke and Sons, of Sheffield and subsequent inquiries revealed that only 19 had been produced. Outside, in the Fox's back yard, footprints were discovered and plaster casts taken. But perhaps more interestingly, it was revealed that a second burglary had taken place close by, that same morning.

Robert Newton ran a butcher's shop at 200 Bromford Lane. Some time after the murder of Charles Fox, someone had broken into the shop, used a needle and thread to repair their clothing, helped themselves to a wash and shave, eaten some pork and quenched their thirst by drinking milk from a bottle. There was also a second robbery that night. Someone had broken into a nearby lock-up garage and stolen Winifred Randle's car.

The milk bottle in Newton's shop bore a clear set of fingerprints and this led police to issue a description of the man they wanted to interview: Stanley Eric Hobday. A few days later, Hobday's photograph was also published.

Hobday, it seemed, had headed north, for in due course, the stolen car was found wrecked, in Cheshire, between Knutsford and Warrington. Then, at the end of August, the police got the breakthrough they had been waiting for.

NAME	Stanley Eric Hobday
AGE AT EXECUTION	21
DATE OF EXECUTION	Thursday, 28th December, 1933
PLACE OF EXECUTION	Birmingham
HANGMAN	Thomas Pierrepoint
ASSISTANT	Albert Pierrepoint
DATE OF TRIAL	14th November – 16th November, 1933
LOCATION OF TRIAL	Stafford
PRESIDING JUDGE	Mister Justice Talbot
PROSECUTION COUNSEL	W.G. Earengey, Ralph Thomas
DEFENCE COUNSEL	Sir Reginald Coventry, A.J. Long
NUMBER OF VICTIMS	1

VICTIMS DETAILS	
NAME	Charles William Fox
AGE	24
DATE OF MURDER	Sunday, 27th August, 1933
PLACE OF MURDER	8 Moor Street, West Bromwich
METHOD OF KILLING	Stabbed
RELATIONSHIP TO KILLER	None

Walter Barber worked at Townhead Farm, Rockcliffe, near Carlisle and he had been reading about the West Bromwich murder in the newspaper. He had also seen the photograph of Hobday and when, on August 30th, he saw a stranger who looked very much like that photograph, he told his employer, Mr Watt. He in turned telephoned the police and the stranger, who was indeed Hobday, was arrested soon afterwards.

Slowly the police built up their evidence. Hobday's fingerprints were found on the starting handle of the stolen car, showing that it was indeed he who had driven it northwards. Prints of his shoes were taken and compared with those found outside the Fox house and Hobday's whereabouts on the days preceding the murder were also checked out.

It transpired that he had been camping out in Warstone Fields, close to West Bromwich, until August 26th when he, and other campers were turned out. One of those other campers was 14-year-old Gilbert Pursell, who had pitched his tent next to Hobday's. In the few days they were together, Pursell saw the knife Hobday was using and identified it as the same one removed from Charles Fox's back.

Put on trial for murder, Hobday's defence was that although he had broken into Robert Newton's shop, he was not the man who had broken into Charles Fox's home. The defence asked the jury if it were possible that Hobday could have stabbed Fox, then travelled a few hundred yards to Newton's shop where after breaking in, he had washed, shaved, threaded a needle in order to repair a rip in his coat, helped himself to some food and drink and then driven off in a stolen car knowing full well that there would be police in the area by then.

Attempts were also made to discredit the footprint evidence by suggesting that the prints in the yard did not match Hobday's shoes exactly. But it was an uphill struggle and the distinctive knife weighed most heavily against Hobday.

Found guilty, there were two separate petitions for Hobday's reprieve, one of which based itself on his mental health. But neither moved the Home Secretary, who saw no reason to intervene.

IN 1932, ROY Gregory married the woman who had, a year before, already borne another man's child, a daughter whom she named Dorothy Margaret. By June of that year, Gregory's wife was pregnant again and in March 1933, she was taken into hospital awaiting the birth. Dorothy, by now two years old, was left in the care of her stepfather.

On March 9th, Gregory's sister called at the house and at 7.00pm, she put Dorothy to bed. An hour later she checked that Dorothy was still all right and saw that the child was sleeping peacefully. By 10.30pm, though, the cot was empty and the blankets were all smoothed down.

Gregory explained that he had decided to foster the child out, as he and his wife could not afford to keep Dorothy and the new baby. Dorothy had been taken away by some farming people and was being well looked after.

The situation continued for some months but Gregory's story had not been believed and eventually came to the attention of the police, who felt they had to investigate further. As a result of their inquiries, the cellar of Gregory's house was dug up and the body of Dorothy was discovered, on August 3rd, 1933.

Gregory could not deny any longer that he was responsible for Dorothy's death, but tried to claim that it had been an accident. In a moment of anger, when the child was crying, he had picked her up and thrown her onto a bed. Unfortunately, Dorothy had bounced up and struck the wall, causing her death. In a panic he had hidden the body and lied about the foster parents.

Medical evidence, though, did not support this latest lie. It was shown that Dorothy had been struck several severe blows, probably with a hammer. The prosecution therefore claimed that Gregory had simply decided to dispose of an unwanted child and was a cold-blooded murderer.

After deliberating for just over 40 minutes, the jury agreed with the prosecution and Gregory was sentenced to death.

NAME	Roy Gregory
AGE AT EXECUTION	28
DATE OF EXECUTION	Wednesday, 3rd January, 1934
PLACE OF EXECUTION	Hull
HANGMAN	Thomas Pierrepoint
ASSISTANT	Thomas Phillips
DATE OF TRIAL	20th November – 21st November, 1933
LOCATION OF TRIAL	York
PRESIDING JUDGE	Mister Justice Humphreys
PROSECUTION COUNSEL	Willoughby Jardine, H.R. Turton
DEFENCE COUNSEL	W. Hedley, Norman Black
NUMBER OF VICTIMS	1

VICTIMS DETAILS	
NAME	Dorothy Margaret Addinall
AGE	2
DATE OF MURDER	Thursday, 9th March, 1933
PLACE OF MURDER	40 Queen Street, Scarborough
METHOD OF KILLING	Battered
RELATIONSHIP TO KILLER	Step-daughter

1934

THERE WERE TWO sides to the character of Ernest Brown. One was the charming womaniser who was kind and gentle, but the other was that of a man with a foul temper and a reputation for violence.

The year 1933 saw Brown working as a groom for Frederick Morton. The job allowed Brown to satisfy two of his abiding passions – working with horses and the seduction of women – for within a few weeks, Brown had bedded Morton's wife, Dorothy Louise.

It is likely that Morton knew that his wife had slept with Brown, for when the two men argued and Brown quit his job, returning a few days later and asking to be reinstated, Morton did indeed take him back, but only as a sort of odd-job man. Brown was furious and his temper showed through in his work so much that the farm bailiff asked Morton to dismiss him. Morton refused. Perhaps he was enjoying the situation.

Farm business often took Frederick Morton away from home and this was the case on September 5th, 1933. On the same day, Brown was seen drinking heavily and was not seen to leave the Boot and Shoe Inn until 8.45pm. His intention, he declared, was to go to Saxton Grange and pick up one of Morton's cars in order to take a drive to Leeds.

When Brown arrived at the farm, Dorothy Morton did her best to stop him from stealing one of the cars. The relationship between the two had been over for some time and this only served to increase Brown's bitterness. Brown lashed out and hit Dorothy and as she ran inside the house, he followed her and took a shotgun from one of the rooms.

Over the next few hours, Brown was in and out of the house, terrorising Dorothy, her young daughter and the child's nurse, Anne Houseman. Shots were heard outside and finally, at 3.30am the next morning, a dull explosion was heard. Looking through the window, Dorothy saw that the garage was on fire and, having remained inactive long enough, she now snatched up her daughter and ran across the fields to raise the alarm, the telephone wires at Saxton Grange having been cut.

The police and the fire brigade arrived at the farm and when one of the cars was

NAME	Ernest Brown
AGE AT EXECUTION	35
DATE OF EXECUTION	Tuesday, 6th February, 1934
PLACE OF EXECUTION	Leeds
HANGMAN	Thomas Pierrepoint
ASSISTANT	Robert Wilson
DATE OF TRIAL	11th December – 14th December, 1933
LOCATION OF TRIAL	Leeds
PRESIDING JUDGE	Mister Justice Humphreys
PROSECUTION COUNSEL	C. Paley Scott, W.R. Lawrence
DEFENCE COUNSEL	G.H.B. Streatfeild, A.M. Hurwitz
NUMBER OF VICTIMS	1 (possibly 2)

VICTIMS DETAILS	
NAME	Frederick Ellison Morton
AGE	28
DATE OF MURDER	Tuesday, 5th September, 1933
PLACE OF MURDER	Saxton Grange Farm, Towton
METHOD OF KILLING	Shot/burned
RELATIONSHIP TO KILLER	None

dragged out into the cool night air, it was seen that there was a body inside. A postmortem would show that Frederick Morton had been shot and then his car set on fire.

Brown was arrested on September 7th and charged with murder. At the trial, scientific evidence was called to show that Morton had been killed at about 9.00pm. Blood was found on Brown's clothing and boots and on the shotgun he had taken from the farm. Brown's only line of defence was to claim that Morton must have been killed by another one of Dorothy's lovers and that he had nothing to do with Morton's death.

Found guilty after 20 minutes' deliberation and sentenced to death, a petition containing 10,000 signatures was subsequently sent to the Home Office, asking for mercy. The execution was postponed, but only whilst further inquiries were made into Brown's state of mind. Finally satisfied that Brown was sane, he was executed on February 6th, 1934.

One would think that at that point the story

of Ernest Brown should have ended. However, the condemned man said one last word, or perhaps one last group of words, whilst standing on the scaffold waiting for Pierrepoint to pull the lever, which added another twist to his case.

Thomas Pierrepoint could not be sure whether Brown said, "Ought to burn" or "Otterburn", but if it was the latter, then Brown might just have been confessing to another murder.

On Tuesday, January 6th, 1931, Evelyn Foster, who drove a taxi for her father's company, picked up a fare in Otterburn. The man asked to be taken to Ponteland but halfway there changed his mind and asked to go back to Otterburn. When Evelyn asked why, he struck out at her and then poured petrol over her and the taxi and set light to it. Evelyn died the following day, but not before she had been able to tell her story. At the time, the police believed that Evelyn had been hurt whilst setting fire to the cab for insurance purposes and the case was not fully investigated. When one recalls, though, that Otterburn is just a few miles from Saxton Grange Farm, that both cases involved a blazing car, and that final utterance from Brown, it is possible that Evelyn was telling the truth after all and that finally, her murderer paid the price for that terrible crime.

LOUIS HAMILTON AND Maud Bolton had known each other for several years and they married in July, 1933. Maud was already heavily pregnant and gave birth to a child a few weeks after the wedding.

At the beginning of their married life, the Hamiltons lived with Louis's sister, Beatrice Thackery, and her husband, but in November 1933, the couple moved in with Louis's parents, leaving the baby in Beatrice's care. This arrangement did not last long, and Louis's temper was a contributory factor in Maud's return to her mother's house, in December.

Louis demonstrated his temper again on December 23rd, when he went to see Maud and ended up kicking and assaulting her, not to mention hurling swear words at her and calling her names. The next day, Maud reported her husband's actions and he was served with a summons for assault. His only reply was that she had been asking for it.

Three days after his last attack, Louis again went to see his wife. Saying he had something to show her and threatening to kick the doors in if he was not given access to Maud, Louis was eventually persuaded that Maud was not at home and left to spend some time with his brother-in-law, with whom he discussed the summons he had received. He left that address at 3.30pm on December 26th.

In fact, Maud, her mother and her brother, were visiting the next-door neighbour, Mrs Thornton. At 4.00pm Maud went to leave. Waiting outside for her was Louis Hamilton.

Louis grabbed Maud and dragged her into her mother's house. He slammed the door shut and locked it behind him. In his hand, Louis held a knife and as Maud made to rise from a chair, Louis slashed her throat, causing her to collapse back.

Outside, a crowd waited to take charge of Louis, who was escorted to a nearby house to await the arrival of the police. Once Constable Savage arrived, Louis told him: "I quite realise what I have done."

A defence of epilepsy was put forward at the trial. Though no medical evidence could be found to suggest that Louis was a sufferer, Constable Savage remarked that he did appear to be dazed when he first took Louis into custody, and there was also the fact that Louis's father was an epileptic. The dazed appearance was put forward as a petit mal attack.

It was at best a weak defence and the jury rejected it, finding Louis guilty but with a recommendation to mercy.

NAME	Louis Hamilton
AGE AT EXECUTION	25
DATE OF EXECUTION	Friday, 6th April, 1934
PLACE OF EXECUTION	Leeds
HANGMAN	Thomas Pierrepoint
ASSISTANT	Alfred Allen
DATE OF TRIAL	15th March, 1934
LOCATION OF TRIAL	Leeds
PRESIDING JUDGE	Mister Commissioner Joy
PROSECUTION COUNSEL	Walter Hedley, H.B.H. Hylton-Foster
DEFENCE COUNSEL	J. Willoughby Jardine, Doctor E.C. Chappell
NUMBER OF VICTIMS	1

VICTIMS DETAILS	
NAME	Maud Hamilton
AGE	23
DATE OF MURDER	Tuesday, 26th December, 1933
PLACE OF MURDER	39 Jermyn Street, Stott Hill, Bradford
METHOD OF KILLING	Cut throat
RELATIONSHIP TO KILLER	Wife

B Y THE TIME Reginald Hinks had moved from London to Bath, in 1932, he had been dismissed from jobs, thrown out of the army and had a history of petty crime.

In 1933, it seemed as if Hinks was finally going to mend his ways. Taken on by Hoover as a salesman he soon met Constance Anne Jeffries, a divorced mother with a five-year-old daughter. Within months they were married and Hinks had moved into their home at 43 Milton Avenue. However, Hinks had discovered that Constance had a £2,000 inheritance and her father, James Pullen, who also lived with them, was a wealthy man.

Within a few months, Hinks had already embezzled the best part of £1,000 from the old man and moved to a new home, 'Wallasey', in Englishcombe Lane. Soon afterwards, Hinks dismissed the nurse who looked after James Pullen and tried to get rid of the old man by natural causes.

A series of bizarre incidents followed. Pullen was taken for walks and left in the busy city centre in the hope that he would be hit by traffic. On another occasion he was found wandering down a country lane, Hinks following him in his car. None of these were successful and so Hinks decided that more direct action was necessary.

On November 30th, 1933, the ambulance and police were called to Englishcombe Lane. Hinks had telephoned them to say that his father-in-law had been taking a bath and having popped downstairs to get clean towels, Hinks had found that Pullen had slipped down and was underneath the water. When officers arrived at the house, they found Pullen sitting up in the bath, looking quite hale and hearty.

The following day, the entire process was repeated. This time though, the emergency was a genuine one. James Pullen lay dead on the kitchen floor, an apparent case of suicide by gassing. At one stage Hinks even remarked that the doctor might find a bruise on the back of Pullen's head as Hinks might have caused him to bump his head when he pulled him out of the oven.

In addition to the bump on Pullen's head, however, there was also the consideration of how he had died. This frail and senile old man

NAME	Reginald Ivor Hinks
AGE AT EXECUTION	32
DATE OF EXECUTION	Thursday, 3rd May, 1934
PLACE OF EXECUTION	Bristol
HANGMAN	Thomas Pierrepoint
ASSISTANT	Not known
DATE OF TRIAL	5th March – 10th March, 1934
LOCATION OF TRIAL	Old Bailey
PRESIDING JUDGE	Mister Justice Branson
PROSECUTION COUNSEL	Mister Croom-Johnson
DEFENCE COUNSEL	Mister O'Connor
NUMBER OF VICTIMS	1

VICTIMS DETAILS	
NAME	James Pullen
AGE	85
DATE OF MURDER	Friday, 1st December, 1933
PLACE OF MURDER	'Wallasey', Englishcombe Lane, Bath
METHOD OF KILLING	Gassed
RELATIONSHIP TO KILLER	Father-in-law

had apparently had the sense to take an overcoat to place over the stove in order to keep the gas in and increase its effect. Hinks was arrested and charged with murder.

The last piece of evidence was the postmortem. It was shown conclusively that the bump had been inflicted before the gas had been inhaled. The jury had no problem in deciding that Hinks had struck Pullen, forced his head into the stove, put the coat over the top and switched on the gas.

1934

JOSEPH BEDFORD RAN the corner store at Clarence Street, Portslade and on the evening of November 13th, as Kathleen Russell left at 8.00pm, she noticed two men waiting outside.

At 9.50pm, a neighbour, Edward Myers noticed that there was still a light on in the shop and that some stock was still outside. Myers tried the door but it was locked. Thinking that the old man had been taken ill, Myers contacted the police.

Constable Peters shone his torch through the window and saw Bedford staggering around, his face covered in blood. The door was forced and Bedford, who by then had collapsed, was rushed to Shoreham Hospital. He died the following day.

Joseph Bedford was known to keep what little cash he had in two tins – one for the copper coins and one for silver and notes. Both tins had been emptied and amongst the few farthings scattered on the floor was an overcoat button. Behind the counter police also found a bowler hat. It was not Mr Bedford's size, so presumably had been lost by his attacker.

Inquiries gave the officers two names: Frederick Parker and Albert Probert. They were picked up in Worthing a few days after the murder; it transpired that on the day after the murder, Probert had had a new button sewn onto his overcoat.

After some intense questioning, Parker broke down and confessed to the robbery. He told the police that he and Probert had gone into the shop and, having locked the door behind them, he had produced an unloaded gun in order to frighten Bedford. Probert, though, had not waited to see the old man's reaction. Going behind the counter, he had struck Bedford and knocked him out. At this stage, Parker was not aware that Bedford had died from his injuries. For his part, Probert denied having taken any part in the crime. Nevertheless, both were charged with murder.

At the trial, Parker's defence was that as he had used no violence himself, he should only be guilty of manslaughter. Probert, faced with his partner's confession, now said that he had been involved and had hit Mr Bedford, but

that he must have hit his head as he fell backwards. Since he had not intended to kill, he too was only guilty of manslaughter.

The judge, Mister Justice Roche, intervened to explain the points of law to the jury. As far as Probert was concerned, if violence had been used that directly or even indirectly caused death, then it was murder. Turning to Parker's defence, the judge said that if robbery had been the intention and he had been a party to it, then he too was guilty of murder. After 35 minutes of deliberation, the guilty verdicts were returned.

NAMES	Albert Probert; Frederick William Parker
AGES AT EXECUTION	26; 21
DATE OF EXECUTION	Friday, 4th May, 1934
PLACE OF EXECUTION	Wandsworth
HANGMAN	Thomas Pierrepoint
ASSISTANTS	Stanley Cross, Albert Pierrepoint, Thomas Phillips
DATE OF TRIAL	14th March – 16th March, 1934
LOCATION OF TRIAL	Lewes
PRESIDING JUDGE	Mister Justice Roche
PROSECUTION COUNSEL	Henry Curtis-Bennett, R. Maxwell Turner
DEFENCE COUNSEL	John Flowers, J.D. Cassels, Thomas Gates, Alban Gordon
NUMBER OF VICTIMS	1

VICTIMS DETAILS	
NAME	Joseph Bedford (Died Tuesday, 14th November)
AGE	80
DATE OF MURDER	Monday, 13th November, 1933
PLACE OF MURDER	Clarence Street, Portslade, near Brighton
METHOD OF KILLING	Battered
RELATIONSHIP TO KILLERS	None; none

AT 8.30AM ON June 30th, 1934, Harry Tuffney walked into the police station in Marylebone Lane. He had a complaint to make.

Walking up to the duty officer, Tuffney moaned: "I've had my head over the gas ring since about four o'clock, but it's no use." Tuffney went on to explain that he had wanted to commit suicide because he had just murdered his girlfriend. Since there was a distinct aroma of gas issuing from Tuffney's clothing, the police felt that the other part of his statement also deserved closer examination and went to the address he had given.

Harry Tuffney lived in the back room on the second floor of 75 Star Street. He had been there for about seven weeks and had been introduced to the landlady, Elizabeth Warren, by the young lady who lived in the front bedroom on the same floor, Edith Longshaw. Harry and Edith had started going out together but things changed one day when he was repairing her handbag.

Inside the bag was a letter, signed by someone named Sidney, and this implied that he and Edith had been lovers. The couple did indeed know a Sidney, whose surname was Briggs, and he had just left his wife. According to Tuffney, this convinced him that Edith was about to finish with him and he determined that if he could not have her, no one else would.

On June 29th, Harry Tuffney paid 1s-3d for a new axe. That night he went to see Edith and argued with her about her wishing to separate from him. She tried to reassure him and as the night grew on, asked him to stay with her. Harry dutifully stayed in Edith's room until she had drifted off to sleep. Then he took the axe and, putting all his strength into the blow, brought it down once on Edith's head. The blade embedded itself in her head up to the wooden shaft and Edith died immediately.

The second part of Tuffney's plan was to take his own life. Placing a couple of cushions on the floor, close to the gas ring, he now lay down and waited to die. After some four hours, he gave up and walked down to the police station.

Tuffney's only hope of escaping the

NAME	Harry Tuffney
AGE AT EXECUTION	36
DATE OF EXECUTION	Tuesday, 9th October, 1934
PLACE OF EXECUTION	Pentonville
HANGMAN	Robert Baxter
ASSISTANT	Alfred Allen
DATE OF TRIAL	20th September, 1934
LOCATION OF TRIAL	Old Bailey
PRESIDING JUDGE	Mister Justice Atkinson
PROSECUTION COUNSEL	Eustace Fulton, E. Anthony Hawke
DEFENCE COUNSEL	Henry Curtis Bennett
NUMBER OF VICTIMS	1

VICTIMS DETAILS

NAME	Edith Kate Longshaw
AGE	38
DATE OF MURDER	Saturday, 30th June, 1934
PLACE OF MURDER	75 Star Street, Paddington, London
METHOD OF KILLING	Battered
RELATIONSHIP TO KILLER	Girlfriend

gallows was a plea of insanity. Evidence was called to show that there was a great deal of mental instability in his family. His mother had died in a mental hospital in 1928. One brother had been diagnosed as a congenital idiot and another had died in a home for mental defectives as a child. An aunt had also died in an asylum, but none of this helped Tuffney. Perhaps more telling was the fact that no trace of the letter from Sidney could be found, though of course, as Tuffney suggested, Edith could have destroyed it.

1934

DUDLEY HOARD WAS the manager of the Eastern Palace Cinema and with his wife, Maisie, lived on the premises. Monday August 6th, 1934 was a public holiday and so Dudley had been unable to bank the takings. As a result, there was now three days' money on the premises, a sum approaching £100.

On Tuesday, August 7th, the cleaners arrived at just after 8.00am. Surprised that the doors were locked, they had to wait until one of the keyholders turned up in order to gain entrance. Once inside, it was plain to see what had happened.

Dudley Hoard lay badly injured at the front of the balcony, his wife lay further along. Later that afternoon, Mr Hoard would die from his injuries, though Maisie would make a full recovery.

There were no signs of a forced entry, implying that possibly the assailant was someone known to Mr Hoard. Furthermore, Mrs Hoard was able to say that she and her husband had been roused by someone ringing the door bell. She heard her husband go downstairs and admit someone. And one of the employees was now missing.

John Stockwell was an attendant. Tuesday August 7th was his day off, but when he did not appear on the Wednesday, his description and photograph were published.

In fact, Stockwell had gone to Lowestoft, where he had taken lodgings with Mrs Alice Tripp. One day, Mrs Tripp was surprised to see her guest throw down a newspaper and announce that he was moving on to Yarmouth. When she picked up the paper, she saw Stockwell's photograph staring out at her. Mrs Tripp contacted the police, but Stockwell did not return.

The following day, Lowestoft police received a letter from Stockwell in which he admitted the attack on Hoard. He claimed he had not meant to kill and went on to say that he was going to drown himself. The same day a pile of clothes was found on the beach.

Stockwell, though, had moved on to Yarmouth where, using the name Smith, he booked into the Metropolitan Hotel. The manager became suspicious of his guest when he gave his home address as Luton, Hertfordshire, instead of Bedfordshire and

NAME	John Frederick Stockwell
AGE AT EXECUTION	19
DATE OF EXECUTION	Wednesday, 14th November, 1934
PLACE OF EXECUTION	Pentonville
HANGMAN	Robert Baxter
ASSISTANT	Robert Wilson
DATE OF TRIAL	22nd October, 1934
LOCATION OF TRIAL	Old Bailey
PRESIDING JUDGE	Mister Justice Goddard
PROSECUTION COUNSEL	G.B. McClure
DEFENCE COUNSEL	Frederick Levy
NUMBER OF VICTIMS	1

VICTIMS DETAILS	
NAME	Dudley Henry Hoard
AGE	40
DATE OF MURDER	Tuesday, 7th August, 1934
PLACE OF MURDER	Eastern Palace Cinema, Bow Road, East London
METHOD OF KILLING	Battered
RELATIONSHIP TO KILLER	None

when he also contacted the police, Stockwell was arrested.

John Stockwell outlined how, after the cinema had closed, he had returned and rung the bell. When Mr Hoard came down, Stockwell claimed that he had lost a 10/- note and asked if he could look for it. Having been granted admission, Stockwell took out an axe and battered Dudley Hoard. When Maisie appeared, he attacked her too.

When the trial opened, Stockwell at first entered a plea of not guilty. Almost before the proceedings had started, however, he passed a note to his counsel, changing that plea to guilty, whereupon he was sentenced to death.

AT THE OUTBREAK of the Great War, Ethel Lillie Brown, then aged 23, became pregnant. She refused to reveal the identity of the father and eventually, her parents decided to pass the child off as their own. So, Auriel Iris Tryphene Brown was born and brought up as Ethel's sister.

In the summer of 1918, Ethel married Arthur Major. They lived with Ethel's parents and in May 1920, a son, Lawrence, was born. It was 1929 before the Majors rented a bungalow of their own, in Kirkby on Bain. It was there that a neighbour told Arthur that Auriel was, in fact, Ethel's daughter. Arthur demanded to know who the father was. Ethel refused to reveal his identity and a rift developed between her and Arthur, who became something of a bully.

Ethel eventually moved back in with her parents temporarily. Even when she moved back in with Arthur, the situation remained far from ideal and then, in 1934, Ethel discovered that Arthur was receiving letters from another woman. She complained to her neighbours, the doctor, a solicitor and even the Chief Constable. Arthur in turn stated that he was no longer responsible for Ethel's debts.

On May 22nd, 1934, Arthur became ill with severe stomach pains. He grew steadily worse and died on May 24th. The cause of death was given as epilepsy and the funeral set for May 26th.

After Arthur's death, the coroner received an anonymous letter, signed 'Fairplay', asking him to look into the death. So, on the morning of the funeral, the police called at Ethel's home and took her in for questioning. A dog mentioned in the letter was exhumed and Arthur's body was examined. Both the dog and Arthur's body were found to contain strychnine.

Ethel's father had been a gamekeeper and kept some poisons in a chest at home. Ethel was now asked about these and she replied that she had no idea where he kept them, adding that she did not know that her husband had died of strychnine poisoning. This was highly significant, since no mention had been made of which poison had been used.

NAME	Ethel Lillie Major
AGE AT EXECUTION	42
DATE OF EXECUTION	Wednesday, 19th December, 1934
PLACE OF EXECUTION	Hull
HANGMAN	Thomas Pierrepoint
ASSISTANT	Albert Pierrepoint
DATE OF TRIAL	29th October – 1st November, 1934
LOCATION OF TRIAL	Lincoln
PRESIDING JUDGE	Mister Justice Charles
PROSECUTION COUNSEL	E. O'Sullivan, Paul Sandlands
DEFENCE COUNSEL	Norman Birkett, M.D. Van Oss, Mister Lewis
NUMBER OF VICTIMS	1

VICTIMS DETAILS	
NAME	Arthur Major
AGE	44
DATE OF MURDER	Thursday, 24th May, 1934
PLACE OF MURDER	No. 2 Council Houses, Kirkby on Bain, near Horncastle
METHOD OF KILLING	Poisoned (by strychnine)
RELATIONSHIP TO KILLER	Husband

A search of Ethel's parents' house revealed the chest. There were strychnine crystals present in it, but Mr Brown said the box had always been locked and the key had been lost years before. Unfortunately for Ethel, a key that fitted this lock was found in her handbag.

The defence at her subsequent trial rested on Arthur's cruelty to Ethel but the jury were out just over an hour before returning their guilty verdict. Ethel appealed on the grounds that the trial judge had been unfair in his summing-up, but this was dismissed.

Ethel Major was hanged at Hull in December. Her ghost is said to still haunt the prison.

WHEN FREDERICK RUSHWORTH met Lydia Binks in 1932, she was already separated from her husband. A simple girl with the mind of a child, Lydia began living with Frederick and in the summer of 1933, she found herself pregnant by him.

There was still a need to put food on the table and in January 1934, although she was seven months pregnant, Lydia took a job working on a holiday camp. She finally gave birth to a girl on March 1st and soon afterwards, the owner of the holiday camp said that he could not allow a baby to remain on the premises. Lydia told him that she would take care of the situation.

On March 25th, Lydia met Frederick at Wensley Bridge and told him that she thought it best if the child was placed with a nurse. The couple went for a walk in a woods nearby and would later tell different stories about what happened next. What is undisputed fact, is that the small child was no longer a problem and Lydia was able to continue working.

Months passed until the matter came to the attention of the local police. They determined to find out exactly who was taking care of the baby and questioned Lydia. She made no attempt to hide the truth and took officers to the wood where she had taken her walk with Rushworth. There she pointed out one particular spot and upon digging down, the body of the child was discovered. Tests would prove that she had been buried alive.

Both Lydia and Frederick were arrested. According to Lydia, Frederick had simply said that they could not afford a nurse and went on to suggest that they "put it away quietly". He had then dug the hole, taken the child, still in its basket, placed it in the hole and covered it with earth.

Frederick told a different story. The child had been quiet and unmoving and he thought Lydia had brought it to him because it was dead. All he had done was bury the child. He had not known she was still alive.

On the second day of the trial, both defendants were found guilty and sentenced to death. The original execution date of December 13th was changed once the appeal was announced and this was heard on

NAME	Frederick Rushworth
AGE AT EXECUTION	29
DATE OF EXECUTION	Tuesday, 1st January, 1935
PLACE OF EXECUTION	Leeds
HANGMAN	Thomas Pierrepoint
ASSISTANT	Sidney Cross
DATE OF TRIAL	20th November – 21st November, 1934
LOCATION OF TRIAL	York
PRESIDING JUDGE	Mister Justice Porter
PROSECUTION COUNSEL	C. Paley Scott, G.H.B. Streatfeild
DEFENCE COUNSEL	J Willoughby Jardine, Harvey Robson
NUMBER OF VICTIMS	1

VICTIMS DETAILS	
NAME	Unnamed child
AGE	24 days
DATE OF MURDER	Sunday, 25th March, 1934
PLACE OF MURDER	Leyburn, Middleham, North Yorkshire
METHOD OF KILLING	Buried alive
RELATIONSHIP TO KILLER	Daughter

December 17th. This failed and a new execution date of January 1st was set.

Lydia Binks was held in Durham, where she was due to face the hangman, but she received notice, on December 29th, that she had been reprieved since she wasn't the actual killer. There was no such mercy shown to Rushworth.

THE BODY OF Emily Yeomans was discovered in a wood on the morning of October 17th, 1934 and on the same day, the man who was eventually found guilty of murdering her, got married.

Emily was a waitress at a local cafe and lived with her uncle, Joseph Adams at 69 Garnet Place, off Dewsbury Road. On the evening of Tuesday, October 16th, she had left home to meet a man. Her uncle was unable to identify him, as were three boys who saw the couple walking towards the woods where her body would subsequently be discovered.

On the Tuesday afternoon, Blake met up with his future best man, Albert Schofield, and during the drinking session that followed, apparently told him all about a girl named Emily Yeomans. Blake bragged that he was meeting her later and at 7.40pm, Blake and Schofield split up and Blake was seen to walk off with a girl whom Schofield would later positively identify as Emily. Emily would be murdered some time between 8.00pm and 9.00pm that night and so Schofield's evidence was very damaging indeed.

On the day of the wedding itself, Schofield said that Blake further drew attention to himself by purchasing a copy of the Yorkshire Evening Post and showing him the article about the murder of Emily.

On the night of October 18th Blake got talking to a perfect stranger, John Jubb and told him that he had nowhere to sleep that night. Jubb invited Blake to stay the night with him and his family. The following morning, as a way of saying thank you for letting him stay, Blake gave Jubb a powder compact for his wife. The same compact would be identified later by three workmates of Emily's as belonging to her – the broken lid was very distinctive. However, other witnesses failed to agree that it was the one belonging to Emily and Blake's own wife claimed that it was hers.

In due course, Blake came to the attention of the police and was arrested on October 25th. The final apparent piece of evidence against him came when his clothing was examined and hairs were found that could possibly come from Emily Yeoman's pet cat.

Tried the following February, the jury took

NAME	David Maskill Blake
AGE AT EXECUTION	24
DATE OF EXECUTION	Thursday, 7th February, 1935
PLACE OF EXECUTION	Leeds
HANGMAN	Thomas Pierrepoint
ASSISTANT	Alfred Allen
DATE OF TRIAL	12th December – 15th December, 1934
LOCATION OF TRIAL	Leeds
PRESIDING JUDGE	Mister Justice Goddard
PROSECUTION COUNSEL	J. Willoughby Jardine, G.H.B. Streatfeild
DEFENCE COUNSEL	C. Paley Scott, H.B.H. Hylton-Foster
NUMBER OF VICTIMS	1

VICTIMS DETAILS	
NAME	Emily Yeomans
AGE	23
DATE OF MURDER	Tuesday, 16th October, 1934
PLACE OF MURDER	Middleton Woods, Near Leeds
METHOD OF KILLING	Strangled
RELATIONSHIP TO KILLER	None

75 minutes to decide that Blake had done enough to convince them that he was the murderer of Emily Yeomans. But the case does not end there.

At the time of the original police investigation, another man was arrested and subjected to police interrogation. Forensic evidence linked him to the dead girl, he had taken her out on more than one occasion, and he was identified by one of the boys who saw Emily meet the man on October 16th. During Blake's trial, this man was only identified as Man Number One. His name was Joseph Talbot.

1935

GEORGE HAMBLIN AND George Harvey were both inmates of the Westminster Poor Law Institution in Fulham Road. Hamblin was an unofficial bookmaker and used to make some extra money by taking small bets from the other occupants. One of those who regularly placed bets was George Harvey.

On the night of Thursday, October 25th, Harvey was out with a lady friend of his, a Mrs Barnes, and told her that he had lost a large amount of money on a horse. The following evening, George Hamblin was discovered battered to death in a storeroom at the Institute, a bloodstained hammer lying near his body.

Police investigations showed that one inmate had behaved somewhat suspiciously that same evening: George Frank Harvey. At 5.00pm, Harvey had asked for a pass, allowing him to stay out that night. It was noticed that when he handed in his workhouse clothing, a shirt was missing but before he could be questioned about the matter, he had already left.

Harvey stayed with Mrs Barnes for two days, at one stage taking her to the cinema. She would later give evidence that whilst at the cinema, Harvey had visited the toilet and in that same location, a shirt was found, along with a couple of ready reckoners and a cash pouch, all of which had belonged to the murdered man.

When Harvey returned to the Institute, he was arrested and charged with the murder of George Hamblin. He was searched and a total of £3-5s found in his possession. More crucial was the fact that he also held a postal order for 1s-6d and that was shown to have belonged to the dead man. Harvey claimed that he had known nothing of the murder until he read about it in the newspaper on October 27th. As for the money, he claimed to have earned that from the other inmates by selling tea at one or two pennies a cup. He went on to say that Hamblin had confided in him that he was being blackmailed. He showed Harvey a scribbled note with the mysterious message: "Yes, 13, Yes." but would not say what it meant.

Tried at the Old Bailey, it was proved that

NAME	Charles Malcolm Lake (George Frank Harvey)
AGE AT EXECUTION	37
DATE OF EXECUTION	Wednesday, 13th March, 1935
PLACE OF EXECUTION	Pentonville
HANGMAN	Robert Baxter
ASSISTANT	Henry Pollard
DATE OF TRIAL	21st January – 24th January, 1935
LOCATION OF TRIAL	Old Bailey
PRESIDING JUDGE	Mister Justice Atkinson
PROSECUTION COUNSEL	Eustace Fulton, L.A. Byrne
DEFENCE COUNSEL	F.J. Eastwood M.P.
NUMBER OF VICTIMS	1

VICTIMS DETAILS	
NAME	George Hamblin
AGE	Not known
DATE OF MURDER	Friday, 26th October, 1934
PLACE OF MURDER	Westminster Poor Law Institution, Fulham Road, Chelsea, London
METHOD OF KILLING	Battered
RELATIONSHIP TO KILLER	None

Harvey had been seen in the storeroom, with Hamblin, at 4.30pm. That, together with the evidence of the money, the shirt and the cash pouch, were enough to sentence Harvey to death.

At his trial, the prisoner had admitted that George Harvey was not his real name. He asked that his actual name not be revealed because his mother was very ill and knew nothing about the trouble he was in. Once the death sentence had been carried out though, the real name was revealed and George Harvey was shown to be Charles Malcolm Lake.

LEONARD BRIGSTOCK WAS a stoker petty officer on board H.M.S. Arethusa and on January 18th, 1935, he was reported for three minor breaches of discipline by Chief Petty Officer Hubert Deggan. As a result of that action, Brigstock was told to report to the master-at-arms who in turn said he would bring the matter to the attention of the captain.

On Saturday, January 19th, Brigstock went on leave and consumed several pints of beer in a local public house. Having brooded on his problems somewhat, he then went aboard H.M.S. Marshal Soult, where he found Deggan alone in the Petty Officer's mess. Deggan was alone and asleep, so Brigstock took his chance and slashed his throat. He then calmly went to another mess where he saw a fellow officer and handed him the razor he had used saying that he had just cut the chief petty officer's throat.

Brigstock's defence rested on a claim of insanity. His wife, Eileen Norah Brigstock, told of a weird dream her husband had related to her, in which he had defended her from the devil's mate. Evidence was also given that both Brigstock's brothers had displayed signs of mental instability. The fact that both were serving members of the Metropolitan Police said more about police selection methods than about Brigstock's mental state.

Found guilty and sentenced to death, further evidence was taken to the appeal hearing. The defence wished to call two new witnesses, one of whom had served with Brigstock in China. He would have testified that Brigstock had shown him a tattoo on his chest that he had said was an emblem of a secret society. The fresh evidence was not heard though, and the appeal was lost.

Even Brigstock's execution was not without incident. By this time, Mrs Van Der Elst had started her campaign to have the death sentence abolished and she organised a massive demonstration outside Wandsworth on the day Brigstock was hanged. In addition to loudspeaker vans playing 'Abide With Me' and masses of men with sandwich boards, there were even three aeroplanes circling over the prison with banners reading: "Stop the Death Sentence."

NAME	Leonard Albert Brigstock
AGE AT EXECUTION	33
DATE OF EXECUTION	Tuesday, 2nd April, 1935
PLACE OF EXECUTION	Wandsworth
HANGMAN	Robert Baxter
ASSISTANT	Robert Wilson
DATE OF TRIAL	19th February, 1935
LOCATION OF TRIAL	Maidstone
PRESIDING JUDGE	Lord Chief Justice, Lord Hewart
PROSECUTION COUNSEL	Frank Powell
DEFENCE COUNSEL	James Dale Cassels
NUMBER OF VICTIMS	1

VICTIMS DETAILS

NAME	Hubert Sidney Deggan
AGE	36
DATE OF MURDER	Saturday, 19th January, 1935
PLACE OF MURDER	On board H.M.S. Marshal Soult, Chatham, Kent
METHOD OF KILLING	Cut throat
RELATIONSHIP TO KILLER	None

1935

TWO BROTHERS WERE taking a stroll across the back of the East Brighton Golf Course, close to the famous Roedean School, when they heard a woman screaming.

Soon afterwards, two shots were heard and, going to investigate, the brothers saw a man run away from a concrete storage tank. Looking into the tank, the brothers saw the body of a young woman floating in the water.

The dead woman was soon identified as Edith Constance Drew-Bear, who worked as a cashier in a restaurant in Ship Street. She also lived in the same street, with her brother Harold Edwin Drew-Bear. He explained that he had last seen his sister at breakfast time that day and gave them the name of her boyfriend, Percy Charles Anderson, who lived in Lennox Street.

Anderson was interviewed that same evening and claimed that he did not know where his girlfriend was. Questioned further, Anderson went on to make a statement that gave a somewhat different story.

Anderson said he had met Edith that evening and they had gone for a walk up towards Roedean. Sitting down near the concrete tanks she had started to argue with him because another girl had smiled at him. He then felt a pain in his head and the next thing he remembered was being in the sea and having to swim for shore.

The latter part of the statement did seem to check out. A bus conductor was found who said that a man, whose clothes were dripping wet, had boarded his bus at Ovingdean. Victor Charles Parker, a newsagent, also gave evidence that Anderson had purchased cigarettes in his shop, at 7.30pm. At the time his clothes were soaking.

A postmortem examination of Edith's body revealed that although she had been shot, the bullets were of such a small calibre that they had served no purpose other than to render her unconscious. The actual cause of death was strangulation and a scarf, knotted tightly around her neck, was the murder weapon. The scarf was shown to belong to Anderson.

Anderson claimed that he had no knowledge of the murder. He had felt pains in his head and had no memory of anything until he came to his senses in the sea. He then

travelled home and changed his clothes. There was one point, though, that he could not explain. If his story was true, why had he had no thought for what might have happened to Edith? The jury did not feel that these were the actions of an innocent man.

The original execution date was March 28th, but the appeal caused that to be postponed. However, despite two petitions, containing in total over 100,000 signatures, the new date was set for April 16th.

NAME	Percy Charles Anderson
AGE AT EXECUTION	21
DATE OF EXECUTION	Tuesday, 16th April, 1935
PLACE OF EXECUTION	Wandsworth
HANGMAN	Thomas Pierrepoint
ASSISTANT	Alfred Allen
DATE OF TRIAL	7th March – 9th March, 1935
LOCATION OF TRIAL	Lewes
PRESIDING JUDGE	Lord Chief Justice, Lord Hewart
PROSECUTION COUNSEL	Sir Henry Curtis Bennett, Geoffrey Raphael
DEFENCE COUNSEL	Eric Neve
NUMBER OF VICTIMS	1

VICTIMS DETAILS	
NAME	Edith Constance Drew-Bear
AGE	21
DATE OF MURDER	Sunday, 25th November, 1934
PLACE OF MURDER	East Brighton Golf Course, Brighton
METHOD OF KILLING	Shot/strangled
RELATIONSHIP TO KILLER	Girlfriend

BAINBRIDGE, A PRIVATE in the Durham Light Infantry, was based at Blackdown Camp in Hampshire. Before joining the army he had worked as a clerk for a firm of solicitors. The managing clerk there was Edward Herdman and the two families were well known to each other.

On December 22nd, 1934, Bainbridge was granted leave. Over the next few days, he visited Herdman a number of times and said he wanted to make a will. So it was that at around 12.30pm on December 31st, Bainbridge again called on Herdman, discussed the will and asked him to formally draft it.

It was 6.15pm when Bainbridge called to see how things were progressing. Herdman's daughter was present and when she left at 7.50pm, Bainbridge left with her. It is certain that he returned to his home just down the street, for whilst his mother was talking to him, the clock struck eight. Bainbridge left soon afterwards and was next seen, at about 8.20pm, at a jeweller's, where he paid the last instalment on a ring for his fiancée, Helen Wright. He then caught a bus for Gateshead and a party.

Meanwhile, at 9.50pm, Edward Herdman's daughter returned home and finding the door locked, managed to gain entry through an open window. She found her father dead. A heavy poker lay near his body and a penknife lay on his chest. His wallet had been removed from his pocket but still had £40 inside it. Other money in the house had been stolen, though, and since Bainbridge had been one of the last people to see Herdman alive, he was traced to his party and taken in.

It was known that Bainbridge had been short of money before Christmas, and had already borrowed £18 from a moneylender. This same man had paid for a ring on the night of the murder and now had £5 more on his person. There was also a small bloodstain on his right cuff.

Bainbridge swore that he was innocent. He claimed that he had borrowed the money from a married woman but refused to give her name. What was a weak story became even weaker when J. McNally, a fellow soldier at Blackdown Camp, received an envelope postmarked Gateshead. Inside the

NAME	John Stephenson Bainbridge
AGE AT EXECUTION	24
DATE OF EXECUTION	Thursday, 9th May, 1935
PLACE OF EXECUTION	Durham
HANGMAN	Not known
ASSISTANT	Not known
DATE OF TRIAL	4th March – 8th March, 1935
LOCATION OF TRIAL	Durham
PRESIDING JUDGE	Mister Justice Goddard
PROSECUTION COUNSEL	C. Paley Scott, J. Charlesworth
DEFENCE COUNSEL	G. Russell Vick, J. Harvey Robson
NUMBER OF VICTIMS	1

VICTIMS DETAILS	
NAME	Edward Frederick Herdman
AGE	75
DATE OF MURDER	Monday, 31st December, 1934
PLACE OF MURDER	Salisbury Place, Bishop Auckland
METHOD OF KILLING	Battered/cut throat
RELATIONSHIP TO KILLER	None

envelope was £36 in cash, some of it bloodstained, and the writing appeared to be similar to Bainbridge's.

The trial lasted four days and at the end of it, Bainbridge was found guilty. His appeal was dismissed on April 15th but then, yet another development took place.

Bainbridge's mother received a letter from a woman who signed herself: "A Great Friend". She claimed that Bainbridge was innocent and that she was the woman who had lent him the money. It did not save Bainbridge from the rope, and her identity was a secret he took to his grave.

AMELIA NUTTALL HAD known John Bridge for most of her life, the two having grown up together. They had, by 1935, been going out together for seven years and in 1932 had become engaged. The wedding date had been set for June 8th, 1935. Then, in February of that year, Bridge changed and his behaviour towards his fiancée cooled appreciably.

It was, of course, a story of a romantic triangle and Bridge had fallen for a new love, Eileen Earl, with whom he worked. She was fully aware of the relationship between Bridge and Amelia and in April 1935, after some discussion on the matter, Bridge suggested to Eileen that he was thinking of breaking off his engagement.

At 5.00pm on April 14th, Bridge was with Eileen Earl. After parting, they met up again at 8.30pm and no doubt talked again of the problem caused by Amelia. Meanwhile, Amelia was at home and when her father, John, returned home at 10.15pm, he found the house in darkness. Turning on the light, he discovered Amelia lying dead on the kitchen floor. By that time, Bridge was back in the company of Eileen Earl.

John Bridge arrived home some time after 11.00pm, to be told that Millie had met with an accident. He immediately went, with his sister, to Amelia's home and from there was taken to the police station for questioning.

There was no sign of a forced entry at Amelia's house, which indicated that she had known her assailant, and allowed him in without argument. After some time, Bridge made a statement admitting that he had visited Amelia that evening and that he was responsible for her death.

Bridge's statement indicated that he had gone to see Amelia to break off their engagement. When told, she had become hysterical and had attacked him with a poker. Bridge fought with Amelia and took the poker from her. He claimed to have hit her before he knew what he was doing. Had he stopped at that point he might well have escaped with his life. What happened next though, sealed his fate.

Having struck Amelia, supposedly in self-defence, Bridge said that he then became

NAME	John Harris Bridge
AGE AT EXECUTION	25
DATE OF EXECUTION	Thursday, 30th May, 1935
PLACE OF EXECUTION	Manchester
HANGMAN	Not known
ASSISTANT	Not known
DATE OF TRIAL	3rd May, 1935
LOCATION OF TRIAL	Manchester
PRESIDING JUDGE	Mister Justice Hilbery
PROSECUTION COUNSEL	Maxwell Fyfe, Hartley Shawcross
DEFENCE COUNSEL	E.G. Hemmerde, Mister Hinchcliffe
NUMBER OF VICTIMS	1

VICTIMS DETAILS	
NAME	Amelia Nuttall
AGE	26
DATE OF MURDER	Sunday, 14th April, 1935
PLACE OF MURDER	52 Symons Street, Broughton, Salford
METHOD OF KILLING	Battered/cut throat
RELATIONSHIP TO KILLER	Girlfriend

frightened. Instead of seeking some assistance or even just running away, he then took a bread knife and cut Amelia's throat. There could be no justification for that action and as a result, Bridge was condemned to death.

On execution day, there were more protestations from Mrs Van Der Elst and her supporters, but such was public opinion over what Bridge had done that there were also some vociferous supporters of capital punishment to shout her down. One woman shouted: "If it was your girl, the boot would be on the other foot." Bridge, of course, was oblivious to all this as he took his last walk to the execution chamber.

GLADYS NOTT AND her husband, Henry William Nott, lived close by Arthur Henry Franklin and his brother on a smallholding in Hanham Woods. It was not long before something more than a friendship developed between Arthur and Gladys and in November 1933, Gladys took the big step of moving in with the Franklins.

Gladys had a small son, aged seven, and his father was determined that he should not move with his mother. He was, however, allowed to visit her at weekends and this state of affairs continued for almost 18 months.

By May 1935, Gladys had discovered that the grass had not, after all, been greener with the Franklins and determined to move back to her husband. The arrangements were made and Gladys packed her few belongings. At 10.00am on May 8th, she set out for the short journey from Arthur Franklin's home back to her husband. It was a journey she was never to complete.

No sooner had Gladys taken a few steps than a shot rang out and she fell to the ground, a bullet in her back. In a nearby field, Henry Nott heard his wife scream for help and dashed off to render what assistance he could. It was too late, though. Franklin had moved forward and whilst she lay on the ground, he had fired another bullet into her.

As Henry Nott arrived on the scene, Franklin lifted his single-barrelled shotgun and threatened that he would now kill him too. Instantly deducing that his life was in grave danger, Nott ran to his home nearby, in order to get his own gun, which he would use only in self-defence. Franklin followed, reloading his gun as he ran. As Nott reached his house, another shot rang out and Henry Nott was hit. Still Franklin came forward and when he was close to Nott, told him again that he would kill him. In fact, the only thing that saved Henry Nott's life was the fact that Franklin had run out of ammunition.

Franklin made no attempt to avoid the consequences of his actions. When two ladies, Mrs Dyer and Mrs Taylor, arrived on the scene, Franklin admitted that he had shot Gladys, and her husband. The police were called and he said the same to them.

Even at his trial, Franklin admitted

NAME	Arthur Henry Franklin
AGE AT EXECUTION	44
DATE OF EXECUTION	Tuesday, 25th June, 1935
PLACE OF EXECUTION	Gloucester
HANGMAN	Thomas Pierrepoint
ASSISTANT	Robert Wilson
DATE OF TRIAL	5th June, 1935
LOCATION OF TRIAL	Gloucester
PRESIDING JUDGE	Mister Justice Macnaghten
PROSECUTION COUNSEL	H.H. Maddox
DEFENCE COUNSEL	None
NUMBER OF VICTIMS	1

VICTIMS DETAILS	
NAME	Bessie Gladys Nott
AGE	28
DATE OF MURDER	Wednesday, May 8th, 1935
PLACE OF MURDER	Hanham Woods, Hanham Abbotts, near Bristol
METHOD OF KILLING	Shot
RELATIONSHIP TO KILLER	Girlfriend

responsibility, pleading guilty to the charge of murder.

WALTER WORTHINGTON WAS much older than the bride he married in November 1933. Whilst Sybil was only 28, Walter was 57 and already had three sons: 16-year-old David, Ronald who was 15 and six-year-old Bobby. Almost from the beginning, Walter was jealous of his young wife and felt that she might seek the company of someone closer to her own age.

On Saturday, March 9th, 1935, at around 6.30pm, David and Ronald were in the lounge of their home when their father came in carrying a shotgun. He broke open the gun, checked the breech, and placed it in a corner before sitting down. Soon afterwards Sybil entered the room, to get her coat. Walter asked her where she was going, but she failed to answer. He grabbed at the gun and shouting: "Stand Back!" fired at Sybil, who fell to the floor in a crumpled heap.

David Worthington ran out. Ronald asked his father why he had done the act, but Walter simply put on his coat, gave Ronald the key to the bureau, and left the house. Outside, Walter flagged down a passing lorry and asked the driver, Reginald Arthur Thompson, if he would give him a lift to the police station in St Ives. Thompson agreed but when he stopped at a shop, next door to the Crown Inn, along the way, Worthington jumped down and ran off. He arrived at the rectory soon after and told the rector, Alfred John Steed Steam, that he had shot his wife dead. Steam took Walter to the police station, arriving at 8.00pm.

Back at Worthington's house, Walter told Inspector Hodson that there was a letter for him in the bureau. Upon unlocking this, Hodson found a letter and a rim pessary. The letter was from the company which had manufactured it, stating that it was safe to continue using it. Worthington then explained that he was convinced his wife was having an affair. He had found the pessary missing when it should not have been and was sure that Sybil was using it with someone else. He then named her nephew, Lionel St John Churchill Wright, as her suspected lover.

Lionel Wright lived with his parents at the Crown Inn, Broughton, and they agreed that Sybil had been visiting them two or three times a week of late, and had even stayed for

NAME	Walter Osmond Worthington
AGE AT EXECUTION	57
DATE OF EXECUTION	Wednesday, 10th July, 1935
PLACE OF EXECUTION	Bedford
HANGMAN	Thomas Pierrepoint
ASSISTANT	Albert Pierrepoint
DATE OF TRIAL	20th May, 1935
LOCATION OF TRIAL	Huntingdon
PRESIDING JUDGE	Mister Justice Hawke
PROSECUTION COUNSEL	Roland Oliver, Geoffrey Howard
DEFENCE COUNSEL	John Flowers, W.B. Manley
NUMBER OF VICTIMS	1

VICTIMS DETAILS	
NAME	Sybil Emily Worthington
AGE	28
DATE OF MURDER	Saturday, 9th March, 1935
PLACE OF MURDER	The Meads, Broughton, Near St Ives, Huntingdon
METHOD OF KILLING	Shot
RELATIONSHIP TO KILLER	Wife

a full week in January. Lionel, though, denied that there had been anything improper between them.

Worthington could not deny that he was responsible for Sybil's death but claimed at his trial that it had been an accident. His story was that he picked up the gun to shoot himself but as he turned, the gun pointed in Sybil's direction and went off accidentally. That story was not believed.

THE YEAR 1935, saw the silver jubilee of King George and there were a number of celebrations throughout the country. In the small town of Langley Park, County Durham, one such celebration was the lighting of a large bonfire, on the night of May 6th.

On May 5th, Marjorie Graham and William Moore, were enjoying an ice-cream when they were joined by Amanda Sharp and George Hague. Amanda and George had been seeing each other since Christmas 1934, and George must have assumed that he would be accompanying Amanda to the bonfire. However, Amanda, who worked at the local hospital, told George that the matron had forbidden them to go.

Marjorie interrupted and said that this was not true. She was going with William and saw no reason why Amanda could not go with George. Amanda, though, remained firm.

On the night of May 6th, Amanda saw the lighting of the bonfire, but went with Hannah Close and other friends. She did see Hague briefly, when they returned home at around 8.30pm but he did not go into her house at 1 Garden Avenue.

There were a number of nurses walking up the driveway to work at the hospital that night. At 10.55pm, Elizabeth Ann Hall arrived and noticed George Hague standing on the right-hand side of the driveway, about halfway down.

Some 15 minutes later, at 11.10pm, Ellen Gallagher walked up the drive and saw a man step out of a clump of hedges. He startled her and apologised. She would later identify him as Hague.

It was 11.30pm by the time Amanda and another nurse, Mary Johnson, arrived. Hague jumped out of the bushes and announced that he wanted a word with Amanda. She agreed to talk to him and told Mary to go on without her. Mary walked on but turned back after a few steps.

To Mary Johnson's horror, both Amanda and George were lying on the ground, he on top of her. Mary ran back, pushed George off and helped Amanda to her feet. Only now did Mary see that Amanda's throat had been cut.

Amanda was assisted to the hospital and given medical attention, but died of her injuries within minutes. By the time the police arrived, there was no sign of Hague, but he was arrested at his home, Cross Fell House, 30 minutes after midnight.

At the trial, there was an attempt to claim that Hague had been insane. A cousin was a patient in the Durham County Mental Hospital. An aunt had died in a similar establishment in Yorkshire and his elder brother, John William Hague, had killed himself near Sheffield. Unfortunately for Hague, this defence failed.

NAME	George Hague
AGE AT EXECUTION	23
DATE OF EXECUTION	Tuesday, 16th July, 1935
PLACE OF EXECUTION	Durham
HANGMAN	Thomas Pierrepoint
ASSISTANT	Not known
DATE OF TRIAL	28th June – 29th June, 1935
LOCATION OF TRIAL	Durham
PRESIDING JUDGE	Mister Justice Du Parcq
PROSECUTION COUNSEL	J Willoughby Jardine
DEFENCE COUNSEL	J. Harvey Robson
NUMBER OF VICTIMS	1

VICTIMS DETAILS	
NAME	Amanda Sharp
AGE	20
DATE OF MURDER	Monday, 6th May, 1935
PLACE OF MURDER	Driveway to Langley Park Isolation Hospital, Langley Park, County Durham
METHOD OF KILLING	Cut throat
RELATIONSHIP TO KILLER	Girlfriend

1935

1935

RAYMOND HENRY BOUSQUET, a Canadian, was a boxer who fought under the professional name of Del Fontaine. Although Raymond was a married man, he did have his female admirers and one of these he met at the Locarno dance hall in Streatham. The girl introduced herself as Hilda Meek, saying she was 18 years old.

In fact, Hilda was only 16. A relationship started and continued for two years until Bousquet decided to returned to Winnipeg. There he was showered with letters from Hilda until eventually he decided to return. It was a bad decision, for soon he discovered that Hilda was being unfaithful to him.

On July 10th, 1935, Bousquet wrote a letter to Hilda in which he threatened to shoot her if she carried on with her affair. That evening, at 7.00pm, he met her in the Redcap pub at Camberwell, where he handed her the letter.

From the Redcap the couple moved on to the Cleve Hall Hotel at Denmark Hill before returning to the Redcap, where Hilda read Bousquet's letter. From the Redcap they went to The Surry, where Hilda left Bousquet, saying that she was going to fetch her mother.

After waiting for 20 minutes, Bousquet went to see what had happened to Hilda. The front door was locked, but Bousquet had a key and let himself in. Hilda's mother, Alice, was busily putting her make-up on. Meanwhile, Hilda was on the telephone, arranging to meet someone at 10.00pm.

In a rage, Bousquet grabbed the receiver and screamed that Hilda would not be there. Hilda calmly took the telephone back and said that she would be coming. A furious argument followed, which brought Alice into the room. Drawing out a gun, Bousquet began to fire indiscriminately. The women ran out into the street, to be followed by Bousquet, who shot them both.

Ignoring Alice, who would later recover, Bousquet now bent down and picked Hilda up in his arms, to take her back inside. The front door had closed behind him and Bousquet was forced to ask a woman to reach into his pocket, take out his key and open the door for him!

There were many witnesses to the scene in Aldred Road. William Henry McGuiness lived

NAME	Raymond Henry Bousquet
AGE AT EXECUTION	30
DATE OF EXECUTION	Tuesday, 29th October, 1935
PLACE OF EXECUTION	Wandsworth
HANGMAN	Robert Baxter
ASSISTANT	Thomas Phillips
DATE OF TRIAL	10th September – 16th September, 1935
LOCATION OF TRIAL	Old Bailey
PRESIDING JUDGE	Mister Justice Porter
PROSECUTION COUNSEL	Eustace Fulton, Christmas Humphreys
DEFENCE COUNSEL	David Hopkin
NUMBER OF VICTIMS	1

VICTIMS DETAILS	
NAME	Hilda Meek
AGE	19
DATE OF MURDER	Wednesday, 10th July, 1935
PLACE OF MURDER	Aldred Road, Kennington, London
METHOD OF KILLING	Shot
RELATIONSHIP TO KILLER	Girlfriend

in rooms above the Meeks and had seen everything from his front window. Cecil William Slade, who lived at number 62, had been outside on his bicycle and saw the whole thing. As for Bousquet himself, all he would say to the police was: "I have shot the girl I really care for. She has broken my heart and has ruined my life. I don't care if I die tonight."

Raymond Henry Bousquet was not to die that night. He finally joined Hilda on October 29th.

ON APRIL 20TH, 1935, Maxine Louise Gann met Allan James Grierson, at a club in Hammersmith. Maxine's mother, Louise, had a friend, Dorothy Maud Helen Riley, and she had arranged a holiday in Scotland. Dorothy wanted someone to look after her flat whilst she was away, and who better than the woman she had known since 1921, Louise Gann?

On June 1st, 1935, Louise moved into Dorothy's flat on the top floor of 19 Gloucester Road. That same day, Allan Grierson borrowed 30/- from Maxine Gann, telling her that he wanted to look for work. The next day, Maxine moved in at Gloucester Road.

On June 3rd, Maxine received a telephone call from Grierson, who told Maxine that he had nowhere to go. He was taken back to Dorothy Riley's flat and allowed to stay. Grierson repaid this kindness by stealing some of Dorothy's jewellery, pawning it in Oxford Street, and leaving the flat on June 7th.

The post of June 8th contained a short letter for Louise Gann. The note, from Grierson, said simply: "Forgive me, Allan." The letter also contained some pawn tickets, for the stolen items.

On June 10th, Grierson telephoned Maxine, apologised to her for what he had done and was allowed to return to the flat. As for the jewellery, Grierson swore he would redeem it. On June 13th Grierson said he had found himself a job, working in Great Portland Street. He would be starting the following Monday.

Monday June 17th saw the beginning of the supposed new job, but instead Grierson merely stole some more jewellery. Four days later, Grierson announced that his new job necessitated him driving a car to Torquay and asked if Maxine and her mother would like to accompany him. Maxine agreed but Louise declined.

The morning of June 22nd saw Maxine heading off to work after arranging to meet Grierson near Oxford Circus at 1.20pm. At the appointed time, Maxine appeared but there was no sign of Grierson. Thinking he might have let her mother know if there had been some sort of delay, Maxine then rang the flat, but there was no reply.

NAME	Allan James Grierson
AGE AT EXECUTION	27
DATE OF EXECUTION	Wednesday, 30th October, 1935
PLACE OF EXECUTION	Pentonville
HANGMAN	Robert Baxter
ASSISTANT	Henry Pollard
DATE OF TRIAL	10th September – 18th September, 1935
LOCATION OF TRIAL	Old Bailey
PRESIDING JUDGE	Mister Justice Porter
PROSECUTION COUNSEL	Eustace Fulton, L.A. Byrne
DEFENCE COUNSEL	W.F. Whithingstall
NUMBER OF VICTIMS	1

VICTIMS DETAILS

NAME	Louise Berthe Gann (Died Sunday, 23rd June)
AGE	circa 63
DATE OF MURDER	Saturday, 22nd June, 1935
PLACE OF MURDER	19 Gloucester Road, Regent's Park, London
METHOD OF KILLING	Battered
RELATIONSHIP TO KILLER	None

Maxine arrived back at the flat just before 2.00pm but found the door locked. Concerned that her mother might be ill, Maxine went to a nearby electricians, where she met Frederick Summers and told him of her concerns. Summers returned to the flat with Miss Gann and forced open the front door. The flat was in disarray and, once the bedroom door had also been forced, the battered body of Louise Gann was discovered. She had been hit repeatedly with an iron and died the following day.

Grierson's name and description were circulated and he was arrested on July 1st. Found guilty of murder, he paid the dread penalty for his crime at Pentonville.

ALTHOUGH SHE CALLED herself a nurse, Dorothy Waddingham's only nursing experience came when she was a maid at the infirmary at Burton-on-Trent. It was here that she met Thomas Willoughby Leech who, although he was much older than her, she married. They were together for eight years and she bore him three children: Edwin, Alan and Mary.

Once Thomas had died, from throat cancer, Dorothy became involved with her lodger, Ronald Joseph Sullivan, and together they opened a 'nursing' home at 32 Devon Drive, Nottingham. Dorothy was soon pregnant again and in due course gave birth to a son: Ronald.

The home must have been run with some degree of efficiency, for in January, 1935, Devon Drive received a visitor in the form of Miss Blagg from the County Nursing Association. She asked if Dorothy could take on two new residents, Louisa Baguley and her daughter Ada. Louisa was almost 90 but perhaps even more care needed to be given to 50-year-old Ada, who was crippled. Dorothy agreed to take them and they moved in on January 12th.

On February 26th, Dorothy's only other resident died and the loss of income caused Dorothy to start grumbling about the amount of time she had to spend on the Baguleys for what was relatively little financial reward. Still, there was one compensation. On May 4th, Ada Baguley made a new will leaving her money and the proceeds of her insurance policies, to Waddingham and Sullivan, in the event of her death. Eight days later, on May 12th, Louisa Baguley died.

A few months later, on September 11th, Ada Baguley also died, the cause of death being given as a cerebral haemorrhage. Dorothy hastily arranged a cremation but before this could be done, a postmortem was carried out. This revealed the presence of over three grains of morphine. Once this was brought to the attention of the police, the body of Louisa was exhumed and again the true cause of death was discovered to be morphine poisoning.

Both Dorothy Waddingham and Ronald Sullivan were sent for trial on a charge of

NAME	Dorothea Nancy Waddingham
AGE AT EXECUTION	36
DATE OF EXECUTION	Thursday, 16th April, 1936
PLACE OF EXECUTION	Birmingham
HANGMAN	Thomas Pierrepoint
ASSISTANT	Albert Pierrepoint
DATE OF TRIAL	24th February – 27th February, 1936
LOCATION OF TRIAL	Nottingham
PRESIDING JUDGE	Mister Justice Goddard
PROSECUTION COUNSEL	Norman Birkett
DEFENCE COUNSEL	J.F. Eales
NUMBER OF VICTIMS	2

VICTIMS DETAILS	
NAMES	Louisa Baguley; Ada Baguley
AGES	89; 50
DATES OF MURDERS	Sunday, 12th May, 1935; Wednesday, 11th September, 1935
PLACE OF MURDERS	32 Devon Drive, Nottingham
METHOD OF KILLING	Poisoned (by morphine)
RELATIONSHIP TO KILLER	None; none

murder but on the penultimate day, the judge directed that Sullivan be discharged as there was not enough evidence to convict him. The following day, 'nurse' Waddingham was sentenced to death.

ALTHOUGH DR BUCK Ruxton was not married to Isabella Van Ess, they lived as man and wife and she had adopted his surname and borne him three children. Ruxton had a foul temper and his insane jealousy meant that he was always accusing his wife of some indiscretion.

In 1935, Isabella wanted to see the Blackpool illuminations and so borrowed the family car and set off on the evening of September 14th. By arrangement she met her sisters who had travelled down from Edinburgh. It was not until 11.30pm that she began the return journey to Lancaster.

What actually happened was never accurately determined, but it seems likely that another row developed, grew more heated and ended with Ruxton throttling the life out of his wife. Mary Rogerson, the maid, must have seen this and so she too was strangled.

A doctor possesses certain skills and Ruxton now used these to butcher the bodies in his bathroom. All distinguishing features were removed and the body parts wrapped in newspaper, pillowcases and sheets. Ruxton then spread stories that his wife had gone on holiday with Mary.

A few days later, on the 19th of September, Ruxton was seen loading parcels into his car. Meanwhile, Mary's parents were disturbed that they had not heard from their daughter. Ruxton told them that Mary was pregnant and had gone away to get the matter sorted out. The story was not believed.

On September 29th, Susan Johnson who was touring Scotland, saw a bundle in the river Linn at Gardenholme, near Moffat. It was a human arm. The police found other bundles in the vicinity and soon established that they were dealing with two bodies. Furthermore, some of the parcels were wrapped in a newspaper that had been issued in Lancaster. The dates on those newspapers also helped to narrow down the dates on which they must have been dumped.

Over the next few days, Ruxton was interviewed. He was formally charged with the murder of Mary Rogerson on October 13th, and on November 5th, with that of his wife.

At the subsequent trial, it was shown that

NAME	Bukhtyar Rustomji Ratanji Hakim (Buck Ruxton)
AGE AT EXECUTION	36
DATE OF EXECUTION	Tuesday, 12th May, 1936
PLACE OF EXECUTION	Manchester
HANGMAN	Not known
ASSISTANT	Not known
DATE OF TRIAL	2nd March – 13th March, 1936
LOCATION OF TRIAL	Manchester
PRESIDING JUDGE	Mister Justice Singleton
PROSECUTION COUNSEL	J.C. Jackson, Maxwell Fyfe, Hartley Shawcross
DEFENCE COUNSEL	Norman Birkett, Philip Kershaw, Edward Slinger
NUMBER OF VICTIMS	2

VICTIMS DETAILS	
NAMES	Isabella Van Ess (Isabella Ruxton); Mary Rogerson
AGES	34; 20
DATE OF MURDER	Sunday, 15th September, 1935
PLACE OF MURDER	2 Dalton Square, Lancaster
METHOD OF KILLING	Strangled; strangled
RELATIONSHIP TO KILLER	Common-law wife; none

the distinguishing marks that had been deliberately excised from the bodies, matched what was known about the two missing women, and x-rays of the skulls were superimposed over photographs to show that the features matched. It was devastating testimony and on March 13th, the jury took just over an hour to return their verdict.

1933

FREDERICK FIELD WAS an aircraftman at Hendon aerodrome and on March 24th, 1936, he went absent without leave.

The previous day he had visited a lady friend, Florence Elizabeth McGregor of West Gardens, Tooting, and she was his first port of call on the 24th. This time, though, an argument developed and Field left, spending that night in a hut on an allotment at Wimbledon.

Field spent the next few nights sleeping rough until, on April 4th, after leaving a coffee stall, he encountered Beatrice Vilna Sutton. After explaining his circumstances, Beatrice agreed to put him up for the night and Field repaid her by strangling her. He left the flat just after 11.30pm that same night and was arrested as a deserter the following day.

On April 6th, Field was interviewed by Inspector Brown with regard to some missing cheques. It was at that meeting that Field confessed to murdering Beatrice, giving a detailed description of her flat and confirming that he had left pillows over her face. Field was charged with murder.

A strong case was built up. The coffee-stall owner, John Hennesey, had known Field for four years and he confirmed that he had left his stall at around 11.00pm on the night in question.

Two women were found and although their names were not revealed in open court, they confirmed that they had seen a man in a blue uniform, near Elmhurst mansions, Edgeley Road on the night of April 4th. What looked like a cast-iron case was much weakened, though, when Field withdrew his confession and came up with a totally different scenario.

According to this new story, Field had slept rough in a cupboard in Elmhurst Mansions for three nights. On the fourth night, April 4th, he heard the sounds of a quarrel and saw a man run out of the building. He went to investigate and found the body of Beatrice Sutton. Field went on to say that he wished to commit suicide so he took careful note of the layout of the apartment and how the body was positioned so that his subsequent confession would be credible. He had now given an alternative explanation for his presence in Beatrice's room, the sighting by the two unnamed women and his knowledge of the

NAME	Frederick Herbert Charles Field
AGE AT EXECUTION	32
DATE OF EXECUTION	Tuesday, 30th June, 1936
PLACE OF EXECUTION	Wandsworth
HANGMAN	Alfred Allen
ASSISTANT	Stanley Cross
DATE OF TRIAL	13th May, 1936
LOCATION OF TRIAL	Old Bailey
PRESIDING JUDGE	Mister Justice Charles
PROSECUTION COUNSEL	Eustace Fulton, L.A. Byrne
DEFENCE COUNSEL	Mister St. John Hutchinson, J.C. Leonard
NUMBER OF VICTIMS	1 (possibly 2)

VICTIMS DETAILS	
NAME	Beatrice Vilna Sutton
AGE	48
DATE OF MURDER	Saturday, 4th April, 1936
PLACE OF MURDER	Elmhurst Mansions, Clapham, London
METHOD OF KILLING	Strangled
RELATIONSHIP TO KILLER	None

crime. The jury had to decide which version was true.

In due course, Field was found guilty and sentenced to death. Only then was it revealed that he had behaved in a similar manner five years before.

Norah Upchurch had been found, strangled, in a deserted building in Shaftesbury Avenue on October 2nd, 1931. One of the men working on the building was Field and a year and a half later, he confessed to the crime. However, Field's account of the crime did not match the known facts and he was acquitted.

ELLEN WHITING WAS the wife of William and they had three children: 15-year-old William, Violet Ellen aged 13 and 10-year-old George. In October 1935, the Whitings were living at 219 Dover Road, Folkestone but unknown to William, Ellen was involved with another man, George Arthur Bryant.

At about this same time, Ellen's husband had to spend some time away from home. When he returned, on December 5th, it was to discover that his wife and family had moved on. William tried his best to trace them but it was not until some time later that he found her, living at London Road, Dover, with Bryant.

William was an understanding man. He did not cause a scene or make demands. He met Ellen a number of times and they soon came to be on friendly terms again. They last met up on May 16th, 1936, when they had a drink together and made arrangements to meet one week later, on May 23rd.

Two days before that, on May 21st, George Bryant was drinking in the Fountain Inn, on London Road. He arrived there at 2.10pm and left 15 minutes later, having bought a bottle of beer to take away. He had been served by Ellen Kingsworth, the wife of the licensee, Herbert, and she would remember the times precisely.

Bryant arrived home at 2.30pm, having been seen by his landlady, Marie Griggs. They had a brief conversation before Bryant went into his own rooms.

Violet Ellen Whiting and her youngest brother were in the house when Bryant came in. He seemed to be in a pleasant enough mood and gave Violet a shilling so that she could take George to the pictures. Bryant told Violet that he wanted to have a quiet chat with her mother and asked her not to come back before 6.00pm.

The next sighting of Ellen Whiting occurred at 3.20pm, when an insurance agent, Kenneth Robert Leighton Buckwell, called and spoke to her.

At 5.40pm, whilst Violet and George were still at the pictures, Bryant walked into the police station at Folkestone and announced that he wished to give himself up for causing the death of Mrs Whiting at around

NAME	George Arthur Bryant
AGE AT EXECUTION	38
DATE OF EXECUTION	Tuesday, 14th July, 1936
PLACE OF EXECUTION	Wandsworth
HANGMAN	Thomas Pierrepoint
ASSISTANT	Henry Pollard
DATE OF TRIAL	24th June, 1936
LOCATION OF TRIAL	Maidstone
PRESIDING JUDGE	Mister Justice Hilbery
PROSECUTION COUNSEL	R.E. Seaton
DEFENCE COUNSEL	None
NUMBER OF VICTIMS	1

VICTIMS DETAILS	
NAME	Ellen Margaret Mary Whiting
AGE	36
DATE OF MURDER	Thursday, 21st May, 1936
PLACE OF MURDER	301 London Road, Dover
METHOD OF KILLING	Battered/strangled
RELATIONSHIP TO KILLER	Girlfriend

4.30pm. By the time the two children arrived home at 6.15pm, the police were already waiting for them.

George Bryant made a full confession to the killing, saying that he had first hit Ellen with a bottle and then had strangled her. At his trial, he pleaded guilty. The judge directed that a plea of not guilty be entered but Bryant refused any legal representation and when the verdict was announced, agreed that it was the correct one. The most probable motive for all this was that Bryant believed Ellen was about to return to her husband.

THE EARLY 1920S were a time of trouble throughout Ireland and the British Army were present in force. Occasionally, local girls were known to fraternise with these soldiers and some even married them. One such girl was Charlotte McHugh. She decided that she would be better off living in England and the soldier she chose to take her there was Frederick Bryant. The couple were married in Wells, in Somerset, in 1922.

Times were difficult for Frederick and Charlotte. His job as a cowman, at a farm near Yeovil, didn't pay very much but luckily it did carry a tied cottage. Charlotte knew how to supplement the family income, though. Whilst Frederick was working, she would take men back to the cottage and entertain them for a few shillings. The local populace were scandalised but Frederick, who knew all about Charlotte's goings on, was an easygoing soul who didn't seem to understand the word 'jealousy'.

The year 1933 was to prove to be a fateful one for Charlotte. In that year, she first met Leonard Edward Parsons, who went under the name of Bill Moss. He had just split with his long-time lover, Priscilla Loveridge, and an instant attraction developed between him and Charlotte. Frederick too seemed to take a liking to Parsons and invited him to move in with him and Charlotte.

Once more scandal filled the neighbourhood. As soon as Frederick left for work, Parsons would climb into bed next to Charlotte and after a few weeks of this behaviour, Frederick was given the sack for allowing such things to go on under his roof.

There were always jobs for farm labourers, though, and Frederick soon found alternative employment at Coombe. Soon after he, Charlotte and their children moved to Coombe, the ubiquitous Parsons followed and the old arrangements continued.

Even the most patient of men has his limits and in due course, Frederick Bryant reached his. Parsons was ordered from the house, but in a demonstration of loyalty, Charlotte walked out too, taking a couple of the children with her. Two days later she returned and shortly afterwards, so did Parsons. Nothing, it seems, had changed after all.

NAME	Charlotte Bryant
AGE AT EXECUTION	33
DATE OF EXECUTION	Wednesday, 15th July, 1936
PLACE OF EXECUTION	Exeter
HANGMAN	Thomas Pierrepoint
ASSISTANT	Albert Pierrepoint
DATE OF TRIAL	27th May – 30th May, 1936
LOCATION OF TRIAL	Dorchester
PRESIDING JUDGE	Mister Justice MacKinnon
PROSECUTION COUNSEL	Sir Terence O'Connor
DEFENCE COUNSEL	J.D. Casswell
NUMBER OF VICTIMS	1

VICTIMS DETAILS	
NAME	Frederick Bryant
AGE	39
DATE OF MURDER	Sunday, 22nd December, 1935
PLACE OF MURDER	Coombe, Dorset
METHOD OF KILLING	Poisoned (by arsenic)
RELATIONSHIP TO KILLER	Husband

In 1935, Charlotte found herself pregnant again, but this time it was Parsons who was the father. At about the same time, Frederick Bryant started suffering from strange gastric attacks.

The first attack took place in May. Charlotte had gone out for the day with Parsons and when Frederick returned from work he found his dinner waiting for him, in the oven. After dining, Frederick became violently ill and a neighbour had to give him salt water to make him sick. The doctor diagnosed gastroenteritis and other attacks followed over the next few days.

Shortly after this, Parsons decided that he had had enough of these cosy domestic arrangements and left. At about the same time, Charlotte became friendly with Lucy Ostler, a widow with seven children. Charlotte even asked Frederick if Lucy and the children could move in with them but he, not surprisingly, said no.

On the night of December 21st, Lucy did spend the night with Charlotte because she had complained to Frederick that she felt nervous. That same night, Frederick was taken ill. He was rushed to hospital on December 22nd and died later that same day. The autopsy on his body revealed that the cause of death was arsenical poisoning.

It was now that Charlotte discovered that she was in reality alone in the world. A chemist was discovered in Yeovil who gave evidence that a woman had purchased arsenic weedkiller and signed the register with a cross. Since both Charlotte and Lucy were present on the night Frederick died, an identification parade was organised with both women present. The chemist failed to pick out either but the experience certainly frightened Lucy, who began to talk.

Lucy told the police that she had seen a green tin that Charlotte had said she must dispose of. The description of the tin matched that given by the chemist. Lucy went on to say that she had later seen Charlotte burning the tin and in due course, such a charred tin was discovered amongst ashes at the farm. The tin contained traces of arsenic. Charlotte Bryant was charged with murder.

The trial must have been a sad experience for Charlotte and not just because she was on trial for her life. Her friend Lucy, her lover Parsons and even two of her children, Ernest and Lily, gave evidence against her.

Doctor Gerald Roche Lynch, the senior analyst from the Home Office, gave evidence that the ashes where the tin was found contained 149 parts of arsenic per million and that this was an abnormally large amount. This figure would later prove to be significant.

Charlotte entered the witness box to fight for her life. She testified that on the night Frederick had died, she had gone to bed early and slept through until 7.00am the following morning. It was Lucy who had ministered to him. She went on to deny buying arsenic at any time and when asked about a coat, in one pocket in which traces of arsenic had been found, she said that the coat was not hers. She even put the coat on and the whole court saw that it was much too small for her.

The jury took an hour to return their guilty verdict. Asked if she had anything to say, she calmly and quietly said "I am not guilty." The judge was visibly moved as he passed the dread sentence of death by hanging.

The story of Charlotte Bryant was still not over, though. Mister Casswell, the defence barrister, received a letter from William Bone of the Imperial College of Science and Technology, refuting Doctor Lynch's findings over the amount of arsenic in the ashes at Coombe Farm. Bone pointed out that 140 parts per million was the normal amount of arsenic that he would expect to find and this destroyed part of the evidence against Charlotte.

The appeal was heard on June 29th, but the judges refused to hear William Bone's evidence. As a consequence, the appeal was dismissed and Charlotte was returned to prison to await her execution.

Her last days were spent in sadness. She refused to let her children visit her in case the experience upset them. She dictated a moving letter to the King, begging him to have pity on her and repeating that she was innocent. The King never saw the letter. It was intercepted and diverted to the Home Secretary.

Charlotte spent her last hours in prayer. Before she faced the hangman, she did admit to her solicitor that she had bought the weedkiller, but still maintained that she had not murdered Frederick.

The Home Office officials had one final cruelty to inflict on Charlotte Bryant. Fearful of demonstrations outside the prison, they brought her execution forward by one hour.

1936

ALICE WHYE WAS a married woman, but was living apart from her husband. In 1936, she was sharing a house with her mother at Cuthbert Road, Croydon, where she also took her two children. For almost a year now she had been seeing another man, Wallace Jenden, and he was a very jealous man.

In early April, 1936, there were signs that Jenden might cause trouble at some stage. When he encountered Alice's sister one day, he told her to tell Alice to: "... come here tonight or she will know about it. If I can't have her, no one else will."

Alice left home at 8.00pm on May 23rd. She was in the company of Jenden and the two were seen together in a public house, leaving there at a 9.45pm. Alice did not return home that night.

At 6.00am the following morning, Alice's mother, Mrs Miles, went to the hut where Jenden lived, to see if he knew where Alice was. The door was locked and there was no reply to her knocking. She returned a little later but met with no more success. Two hours later, at 8.00am, Alice's daughter, Eileen, also went to the allotment. This time Jenden was there but he claimed to have no knowledge of what had happened to Alice since they had parted the previous night.

That afternoon the police were contacted and Sergeant Scott went along to Jenden's hut. When Scott arrived, Jenden was lying on the pathway and appeared to have been drinking. Scott questioned him but again Jenden claimed not to know where Alice was. Not satisfied, Scott decided to hide close by and keep watch.

Scott had not been waiting very long when Jenden unlocked the door to his hut. Immediately Scott rushed into the hut and arrived just in time to stop Jenden from cutting his throat. The reason why was plain to see. There on the shed floor lay the body of Alice Whye. She had been stabbed and her throat had been cut.

At first Jenden admitted that he had killed Alice after an argument the previous night. Subsequently he withdrew this confession and claimed instead that he had found her body on the allotment and moved it into his hut.

NAME	Wallace Jenden
AGE AT EXECUTION	57
DATE OF EXECUTION	Wednesday, 5th August, 1936
PLACE OF EXECUTION	Wandsworth
HANGMAN	Thomas Pierrepoint
ASSISTANT	Robert Wilson
DATE OF TRIAL	3rd July, 1936
LOCATION OF TRIAL	Kingston upon Thames
PRESIDING JUDGE	Mister Justice Hilbery
PROSECUTION COUNSEL	John Flowers, Theodore Turner
DEFENCE COUNSEL	Stuart Horner
NUMBER OF VICTIMS	1

VICTIMS DETAILS	
NAME	Alice Whye
AGE	38
DATE OF MURDER	Saturday, 23rd May, 1936
PLACE OF MURDER	Stubbs Mead Allotments, Croydon
METHOD OF KILLING	Cut throat/stabbed
RELATIONSHIP TO KILLER	Girlfriend

The defence at Jenden's trial tried to claim that he had been so drunk that he was incapable of forming the intention to kill and could only be guilty of manslaughter. The jury, however, had the final say and they decided that Wallace Jenden was indeed guilty of murder.

THOMAS LINNEY WAS a retired bookmaker who still enjoyed a day's racing and that is just what he wanted on June 30th, 1936, when he went to Carlisle. Whilst he was away, someone battered his wife to death and stole cash kept in the house.

Harriet Linney had spent part of that Tuesday shopping in Sunderland but she was back home by 6.00pm because she was seen letting a tall, dark man into her house. Two hours later, a neighbour, Mrs Dunn, noticed that Harriet's back door had been open for some time so she went to see if there was anything wrong. She found Harriet's body in the kitchen. She had been battered to death and a broken beer bottle that lay nearby appeared to be the murder weapon.

Soon it was discovered that Harriet Linney's nephew, Christopher Jackson, had been seen getting on a bus at Sunderland. The bus was destined for Chester-le-Street, where Jackson had lodgings, and it was decided to interview him.

The police found that Jackson had severe financial problems. He was in arrears with his lodgings, had borrowed small sums of money and was being pressed for repayment. On the morning of June 30th, Jackson had told his landlady not to worry as he was going to Catterick to collect some money he was owed. When he returned that evening he paid £2 for his lodgings and cleared all his debts. On July 1st, Jackson was taken in for further questioning.

Whilst Jackson was busy helping police with their inquiries, his room was searched and a locked suitcase discovered. When this was forced open it was found to contain bloodstained clothing and a sum of over £9 in coins.

Faced with this evidence, Jackson made a statement admitting that he had killed his aunt. His said that he had gone to borrow money but she had said he was not worth helping and had called him names. He lost his temper, hit her with his fist and then picked up a bottle and smashed it over her head. Later he embellished this story somewhat by saying that Harriet had first attacked him with a flat iron. He claimed to have no intention of killing her.

NAME	Christopher Jackson
AGE AT EXECUTION	24
DATE OF EXECUTION	Wednesday, 16th December, 1936
PLACE OF EXECUTION	Durham
HANGMAN	Thomas Pierrepoint
ASSISTANT	Not known
DATE OF TRIAL	4th November, 1936
LOCATION OF TRIAL	Durham
PRESIDING JUDGE	Mister Justice Goddard
PROSECUTION COUNSEL	C. Paley Scott, H.R.B. Shepherd
DEFENCE COUNSEL	H.I.P. Hallet, J. Harvey Robson
NUMBER OF VICTIMS	1

VICTIMS DETAILS	
NAME	Harriet May Ferris Linney
AGE	62
DATE OF MURDER	Tuesday, 30th June, 1936
PLACE OF MURDER	1 Hetton Street, Sunderland
METHOD OF KILLING	Battered
RELATIONSHIP TO KILLER	Aunt

Medical evidence called at Jackson's trial showed that in fact Harriet had been struck four times on top of her head and twice more in the face. The jury believed that this was too much to accept as simple retaliation.

At Jackson's appeal, a request was made to call further evidence from a doctor in the prison where Jackson had been held on remand. Jackson wanted the doctor to testify that when admitted, he had shown evidence of bruising, which tended to support his story of being attacked with a flat iron. Nevertheless, the appeal was dismissed.

1937

RUTH CLARKSON LIVED alone and had not been seen by her neighbours since Friday, June 19th, 1936. Concerned for her safety, the police were contacted and an entry was forced on Monday, June 22nd. Ruth's body was discovered lying on the floor of her living room. She had been savagely battered to death and when police checked the rest of the house, they also discovered her pet dog, hanging from a bedpost.

Very soon, two valuable witnesses came forward and their information led to the arrest of Max Mayer Haslam, who was just four feet eight inches tall.

Thomas Barlow and John William Davieson were lodgers at the same location as Haslam and their combined information pointed to the fact that Haslam was the killer. Both men gave evidence that they had seen Haslam knocking on the door of Ruth Clarkson's house, on June 19th. They further reported that Haslam did not return to their lodgings that evening, and they did not see him again until 7.45am on June 20th. At that time, Haslam showed them both some jewellery and added that he had killed a dog that had attacked him.

Barlow went on to say that on June 22nd, Haslam had asked him if he would like to earn £200 by helping him to move a body. Haslam's intention was apparently to dump the body in a nearby swamp where it might never be found.

At the trial, Haslam's defence tried to paint a different picture of the events of June 19th. Haslam claimed that on June 6th, he had gone, with both Davieson and Barlow, to Ruth's house where they had lifted him over her back yard gate in an attempt to gain entrance. His suggestion therefore was that 10 days later, the other two had returned and killed Ruth Clarkson whilst stealing from her.

There were only two possible explanations for Davieson and Barlow knowing about the dog being killed at the same time as Ruth Clarkson. Either Haslam had indeed given them the information, or they were the guilty parties. The jury chose to believe the former scenario and Haslam was sentenced to death.

NAME	Max Mayer Haslam
AGE AT EXECUTION	23
DATE OF EXECUTION	Thursday, 4th February, 1937
PLACE OF EXECUTION	Manchester
HANGMAN	Not known
ASSISTANT	Not known
DATE OF TRIAL	8th December – 10th December, 1936
LOCATION OF TRIAL	Manchester
PRESIDING JUDGE	Mister Justice Lawrence
PROSECUTION COUNSEL	J.C. Jackson, Redmond Barry
DEFENCE COUNSEL	E.G. Hemmerde, J. Macawley
NUMBER OF VICTIMS	1

VICTIMS DETAILS	
NAME	Ruth Clarkson
AGE	74
DATE OF MURDER	circa Friday, 19th June, 1936
PLACE OF MURDER	Clayton Street, Nelson
METHOD OF KILLING	Battered
RELATIONSHIP TO KILLER	None

ANDREW BAGLEY, WHO also used the name John Smith, had lived with his married daughter, at various times, since June, 1933. The son-in-law, Mr Hart, had married for the second time, and had a daughter, Irene, aged 16. In addition to the three Harts, and Andrew Bagley himself, the house was also home to one of Andrew's sons, Ambrose, who was mentally retarded.

The sleeping arrangements at the Hart house were somewhat unusual. Mr and Mrs Hart had one bedroom which they shared with Ambrose. The other bedroom was occupied by Irene Hart and Bagley, who slept on a mattress on the floor. Although he was 46 years her senior, Bagley had more than a passing interest in Irene and viewed her as his 'girlfriend'.

On August 29th, 1936, Irene visited the cinema with a young male relative, Harold Hart, and a friend of his. When they returned, Bagley made a terrible scene, shouting that it was not right for a girl to go out with two men and anyway, she was his girl. The following day he apologised for his behaviour but two weeks later, much worse was to come.

At 6.30am on September 12th, Mr Hart went to work. A few hours later, at 9.00am, Irene ran an errand for her step-mother and when she returned, her step-mother left to do some shopping, leaving Irene with Bagley. Mrs Hart returned home at 11.00am and found Bagley in the kitchen. Irene was nowhere to be seen and Bagley said that he had given her a pound to buy a new dress for herself. Soon afterwards, he too left the house, saying that he was going to Sheffield.

When Irene did not return home, her parents became very concerned and decided to contact the police. However, whilst Mr Hart was actually at the police station, reporting the matter, his wife searched the house and found the body of Irene in a tin trunk. Irene had been strangled by means of a piece of clothes line and her mouth had been stuffed with newspaper. Some of her clothing had been forcibly removed.

All police forces received a detailed description of Bagley and he was finally picked up at Hucknall in Nottinghamshire on October 23rd. When arrested, Bagley tried to put the blame for Irene's death on a mysterious individual named Tom. According to him, Irene had gone out with Tom and returned to the house soon afterwards. Bagley did not know what happened between them but he saw Tom leave the house later and so he must be the killer.

The story of 'Tom' was held by the prosecution at Bagley's trial, to be one of pure fiction. The jury agreed.

NAME	Andrew Anderson Bagley (John Smith)
AGE AT EXECUTION	62
DATE OF EXECUTION	Wednesday, 10th February, 1937
PLACE OF EXECUTION	Leeds
HANGMAN	Thomas Pierrepoint
ASSISTANT	Robert Wilson
DATE OF TRIAL	30th November – 1st December, 1936
LOCATION OF TRIAL	Leeds
PRESIDING JUDGE	Mister Justice Goddard
PROSECUTION COUNSEL	J. Willoughby Jardine
DEFENCE COUNSEL	H.B.M. Hylton-Foster
NUMBER OF VICTIMS	1

VICTIMS DETAILS	
NAME	Irene Hart
AGE	16
DATE OF MURDER	Saturday, 12th September, 1936
PLACE OF MURDER	Hartington Road, Rotherham
METHOD OF KILLING	Strangled
RELATIONSHIP TO KILLER	None

BY THE END of April, 1937, Philip Davis's neighbours were becoming a little suspicious over his rather strange behaviour. To begin with, his wife and niece had not been seen for a few days. Wilhelmina had last been seen by a neighbour, Eliza Simpson, on April 20th, and Monica had been noticed by another neighbour, Gladys Mitchell, on April 21st. The very next day, April 22nd, Philip reported that his wife had left him and taken Monica with her. He repeated the same story the following day, with the added embellishment that Wilhelmina had also taken £15 of his savings.

On April 28th, Davis spoke to Mr William Andrew, who owned a garage next door and arranged to rent it. That same evening, Davis was seen moving barrowloads of soil and stones into the garage, and still there was no sign of Wilhelmina or her niece.

The story of his wife leaving him was repeated yet again on April 29th, when Davis wrote to his sister-in-law asking her to come and look after him. The net was closing, though, and gossip led to William Andrew visiting Davis on April 30th and asking for the garage key, so that he could inspect the premises. There, in an inspection pit, Andrew saw a pile of dirt and a rather unpleasant smell issuing from the same location told him that there was much more down there. He contacted the police, who discovered the two unclothed bodies.

Davis made no attempt to deny responsibility for his crimes. He confessed that he had battered Wilhelmina and Monica with a hammer but could offer no reason as to why he had done it.

At the subsequent trial, a defence of insanity was put forward. One would have thought that Davis would have had an excellent chance of success in this venture. At the age of 18, he had been certified insane and had been confined to an asylum. There was therefore a documented history of mental instability. Indeed, Doctor Blair of Camborne testified that Davis was insane and not responsible for his actions. The prosecution, though, paraded three doctors of their own, who all said that Davis was not insane and their combined evidence carried the day.

On July 27th, 1937, Philip Davis, a man

NAME	Philip Edward Percy Davis
AGE AT EXECUTION	30
DATE OF EXECUTION	Tuesday, 27th July, 1937
PLACE OF EXECUTION	Exeter
HANGMAN	Thomas Pierrepoint
ASSISTANT	Thomas Phillips
DATE OF TRIAL	15th June, 1937
LOCATION OF TRIAL	Bodmin
PRESIDING JUDGE	Mister Justice Lawrence
PROSECUTION COUNSEL	G.D. Roberts, L.B. Miller
DEFENCE COUNSEL	J. Lhind Pratt, Leslie Brooks
NUMBER OF VICTIMS	2

VICTIMS DETAILS	
NAMES	Wilhelmina Vermadell Davis; Monica Rowe
AGES	33; 15
DATE OF MURDER	circa Wednesday, 21st April, 1937
PLACE OF MURDER	Pendarven Street, Tuckingmill, near Camborne
METHOD OF KILLING	Battered/asphyxiated
RELATIONSHIP TO KILLER	Wife; niece

with a known history of insanity, was hanged for a crime without a motive.

FOR FIVE YEARS, Horace Brunt had been seeing Elsie Collier, the daughter of Hugo Collier and his wife, Kate Elizabeth. Brunt was a regular visitor at the farm the Colliers ran, even though Kate did not really approve of him.

On Friday, April 23rd, 1937, Hugo and Kate were building a fowl pen when Brunt arrived and offered his assistance. Kate gave him the brush off, said she didn't need his help and that he should go and see Elsie. The next day would be Kate Collier's last day alive.

Kate was seen outside her farm at noon on the Saturday, by a labourer, John Henry Baldwin. Some 30 minutes later, a lorry driver, Frederick Leslie Hallan, saw Brunt cycling towards that same farm. Not long afterwards, Hugo and Elsie returned to the farm to find Kate lying in the kitchen. She had been shot in the back of her neck and scientific tests would show that the gun had been held some distance from Kate when the trigger had been pulled. The murder weapon, a shotgun, had been replaced on the wall where it normally hung, though it had been put back the wrong way round. An empty cartridge was still inside the gun. The cartridge was of a different type to those normally used in the Collier home but when Horace Brunt's house, Rose Cottage, Upper Mayfield, was searched, the same type was found there.

At first Brunt denied any involvement in the shooting of Kate Collier, but eventually he made a statement saying that he had been to the farm and Kate had attacked him with a poker before taking down the gun and threatening him with it. They struggled briefly and Brunt seized the gun, which went off accidentally.

In the first place, a gunsmith from Chesterfield, Edgar Lester Urton, examined the shotgun and testified that it would be impossible for it to be fired by accident. Brunt had also apparently ignored the fact that had his story been true, it would have been impossible for Kate Collier to have been shot in the back of her neck, from a distance of some six to eight feet.

At his trial, which took place at Derby, Brunt claimed that he had been too upset at the time to get medical help for Kate and

NAME	Horace William Brunt
AGE AT EXECUTION	32
DATE OF EXECUTION	Thursday, 12th August, 1937
PLACE OF EXECUTION	Manchester
HANGMAN	Not known
ASSISTANT	Not known
DATE OF TRIAL	2nd July, 1937
LOCATION OF TRIAL	Derby
PRESIDING JUDGE	Mister Justice Singleton
PROSECUTION COUNSEL	Richard O'Sullivan, Graham R. Swanwick
DEFENCE COUNSEL	Maurice F. Healy, A.J. Flint
NUMBER OF VICTIMS	1

VICTIMS DETAILS	
NAME	Kate Elizabeth Collier
AGE	54
DATE OF MURDER	Saturday, 24th April, 1937
PLACE OF MURDER	Farm at Holland Road, Wood End, Bradley, near Ashbourne
METHOD OF KILLING	Shot
RELATIONSHIP TO KILLER	None

said that when he left he had not known whether she was alive or dead. He also admitted stealing £9 in cash from the farmhouse. This he claimed he had hidden in a tin that he buried nearby, but this money was never found.

The jury found his story of an accidental shooting too incredulous to accept and Horace Brunt was duly found guilty of murder. His appeal was lost on July 28th and he was hanged just over two weeks later.

The lonely farmhouse where Horace Brunt shot Kate Collier to death.

RUBY KEEN HAD many male admirers and seldom tied herself down to one. Unfortunately, one of her boyfriends, Leslie Stone, whom she first met in 1931, was not one to share her favours.

Soon after Stone met Ruby, he was posted to Hong Kong with the Royal Artillery. For some time they kept up a correspondence but soon the letters began to dry up. Ruby had become friendly with a local police officer and in due course she became engaged to him.

Leslie Stone was discharged from the army in December 1936 and was enjoying a drink in the Golden Bell on April 4th, when Ruby came in. He asked her out "for old time's sake", but Ruby was non-committal.

Exactly a week later, Stone was again in the Golden Bell, this time dressed in his best suit, a blue serge with shiny polished buttons. Ruby came in and they had a few drinks before moving on to first the Cross Keys and then the Stag Hotel. At around 10.00pm, they were seen leaving the pub and walking down The Firs, a local spot popular with lovers.

Half an hour later, another couple walked past Ruby and the man she was with, and thought he was a policeman. It must be remembered that in the dark, Stone's suit would look like a policeman's uniform.

The following morning, Ruby's body was discovered. She was almost naked and there were signs of a fierce struggle. That afternoon, Leslie Stone called at Constable McCarthy's house. He had heard of the murder and wished to clear himself. McCarthy was not at home so Stone went to the police station, where he said he had been with Ruby but had left her outside the Stag at 10.00pm. The officers knew that this was a lie. Two pub regulars who knew Ruby had followed them until they vanished down The Firs.

Meanwhile, forensic evidence was being built up. The killer had knelt by the body and there were two perfect imprints of his knees. Plaster casts were taken and it was shown that the weave imprint matched that on Stone's suit. Furthermore, although the suit had been cleaned, small grains of soil were found and these were of the same chemical

NAME	Leslie George Stone
AGE AT EXECUTION	24
DATE OF EXECUTION	Friday, 13th August, 1937
PLACE OF EXECUTION	Pentonville
HANGMAN	Thomas Pierrepoint
ASSISTANT	Alfred Allen
DATE OF TRIAL	28th June – 29th June, 1937
LOCATION OF TRIAL	Old Bailey
PRESIDING JUDGE	Lord Chief Justice, Lord Hewart
PROSECUTION COUNSEL	Richard O'Sullivan, Christmas Humphreys
DEFENCE COUNSEL	Maurice Healy
NUMBER OF VICTIMS	1

VICTIMS DETAILS	
NAME	Ruby Anne Keen
AGE	23
DATE OF MURDER	Sunday, 11th April, 1937
PLACE OF MURDER	Leighton Buzzard
METHOD OF KILLING	Strangled
RELATIONSHIP TO KILLER	Ex-girlfriend

type as the soil around the murder site. The final piece of evidence was a single fibre found stuck to the lining of Stone's jacket. It matched those on Ruby's slip.

At his trial, Stone first continued to deny any involvement in the murder. Then, on the second day, he changed his story and confessed that he had killed Ruby, but that it had been an accident. They had quarrelled, she had hit him and in the heat of the moment he had tightened her scarf, accidentally choking her.

The jury took less than half an hour to decide that Stone was still lying.

WEDNESDAY, MAY 12TH, 1937 was Coronation Day for King George VI and the nation enjoyed a public holiday. Many businesses were closed both that day and the next, due back on Friday, May 14th.

Stanley Herbert Wilton was a salesman for a furniture company of 22 Islington Green, London and early on the Friday, he received a visitor, bearing a letter. The note was, to say the least, direct: "Don't be frightened. There is a dead woman in number 22 and you can believe me, Stan. It is nothing to do with me, but you know what the police will say."

The note had been given to Hilton by Ethel Marshall, who was the girlfriend of Frederick George Murphy, the odd-job man at the warehouse. Hilton went to investigate and sure enough, there was a woman's body in the basement. She had been strangled and someone had hidden the body behind a tin trunk. The body was identified as Rosina Field.

A search was launched for Murphy but on May 15th, he walked into the police station at Poplar and said he wished to make a statement about the body in the warehouse.

Murphy claimed that he had gone into the warehouse on May 13th, in order to do some cleaning, and had discovered the body. He confessed to having moved Rosina but denied having anything to do with her death. He had told much the same story to Ethel Marshall, but inquiries showed that Murphy was apparently not telling the whole truth.

Morris Felberg, who knew Murphy, said that he had seen him going into the furniture store on Coronation Day. Murphy had a woman with him and though Felberg could not identify her, he could describe the distinctive blue coat she wore. Rosina Field had been wearing just such a coat.

Herbert Robert Fleming had known Murphy for 18 months and also knew Rosina, though he called her Rosie. He said that on Coronation Day, Rosie borrowed 2d from him so she could buy a cup of tea. Later, just after 8.00pm, he saw Rosie again and this time she was with Murphy. Two hours later he saw Murphy by himself.

The evidence of Fleming and Felberg linked Murphy with Rosina on the day she

NAME	Frederick George Murphy
AGE AT EXECUTION	53
DATE OF EXECUTION	Tuesday, 17th August, 1937
PLACE OF EXECUTION	Pentonville
HANGMAN	Alfred Allen
ASSISTANT	Thomas Phillips
DATE OF TRIAL	30th June – 2nd July, 1937
LOCATION OF TRIAL	Old Bailey
PRESIDING JUDGE	Lord Chief Justice, Lord Hewart
PROSECUTION COUNSEL	L.A. Byrne, Christmas Humphreys
DEFENCE COUNSEL	F. Ashe Lincoln, Michael Peacock
NUMBER OF VICTIMS	1

VICTIMS DETAILS	
NAME	Rosina Field
AGE	49
DATE OF MURDER	Wednesday, 12th May, 1937
PLACE OF MURDER	22 Islington Green, London
METHOD OF KILLING	Strangled
RELATIONSHIP TO KILLER	None

died and his admission that he had handled the body convinced the jury that he had also killed her. After a 45-minute deliberation, Murphy was found to be guilty but before he was sentenced to death, he made a long speech criticising the judge's summing-up.

In fact, this was the second occasion that Murphy had been on trial for his life. In 1929, Murphy had been accused of murdering Katherine Peck, but had been found not guilty. Katherine Peck had also had a nickname. By coincidence, that too was 'Rosie'.

LILIAN CHAMBERLAIN HAD been married for about a year and lived, with her husband, Ivan, in a one-roomed flat, opposite the hotel where she worked as a barmaid.

Lilian's husband worked in a restaurant car on the railway, and as such spent long periods away from home and was often away at night. On the afternoon of Wednesday, August 25th, Ivan left home for his latest trip and had been long gone when his wife returned home from the hotel at 10.45pm. When she did not turn up for work as expected the following day, a barman was sent across to see what the problem was. He found Lilian, wearing only her night-dress, lying dead. She had been badly beaten. but the cause of death was asphyxiation due to strangulation.

Someone else had not reported for work on that Thursday. John Thomas Rodgers was a barman and Wednesday had been his half-day. The coincidence of his absence was too much for the police to ignore and a full description of Rodgers was issued. Newspapers also carried reports and noted that Rodgers was wanted for questioning. These reports were seen by two men who knew Rodgers and when they saw him at Golder's Green station, one of them kept him talking whilst the other went for the police.

Rodgers told a most unlikely story. He claimed that he had used his half-day to spend some time at Ruislip and by the time he got back, the hotel was locked up for the night and he could not gain entrance. Knowing that Lilian and Ivan lived opposite, he knocked on their door with the intention of asking if they could put him up for the night. The door was open and upon entering, he found Lilian lying badly injured, but still alive. She managed to gasp out his name, and he held her, thus getting blood on his clothing.

His actions then were astounding to say the least. Rather than seeking assistance Rodgers found some of Ivan's clothes and changed into them. He then left the house, throwing his own shirt away on Southend Pier and disposing of his trousers in a woods near Northwood. When asked why he had not tried to fetch help, Rodgers replied: "With me it is self first, self last and self always." Despite this rather astonishing statement, it still took

NAME	John Thomas Rodgers
AGE AT EXECUTION	22
DATE OF EXECUTION	Thursday, 18th November, 1937
PLACE OF EXECUTION	Pentonville
HANGMAN	Thomas Pierrepoint
ASSISTANT	Henry Pollard
DATE OF TRIAL	18th October – 19th October, 1937
LOCATION OF TRIAL	Old Bailey
PRESIDING JUDGE	Mister Justice Charles
PROSECUTION COUNSEL	G.B. McClure, Christmas Humphreys, Cecil Campion
DEFENCE COUNSEL	Mister St. John Hutchinson, Derek Curtis Bennett
NUMBER OF VICTIMS	1

VICTIMS DETAILS	
NAME	Lilian Maud Chamberlain
AGE	25
DATE OF MURDER	Thursday, 26th August, 1937
PLACE OF MURDER	Green Lane, Northwood, Middlesex
METHOD OF KILLING	Battered/strangled
RELATIONSHIP TO KILLER	None

the jury two and a half hours of deliberation before they found Rodgers guilty of murder.

ERNEST JOHN MOSS had been a policeman at Brixham in Devon, but after his wife had left him, Moss became a taxi driver and moved to Exeter. It was here that he met Kitty Constance Bennett and soon the two became lovers. In due course, Ernest and Kitty took lodgings at Ilfracombe until finally they moved into a bungalow at Woolacombe, a pretty seaside town.

Not long after moving into the bungalow, Moss began to feel that he had made a mistake and that he no longer wished to live with Kitty. Rather than walk away or end the relationship in some other, simple manner, Moss decided that he would be best committing suicide, but soon found that he had not got the courage to carry out his plan. Moss was puzzling over what he should do when he saw Kitty bending down in front of him. Almost without thinking, Moss noticed a double-barrelled shotgun lying nearby and suddenly a solution to his problems presented itself.

Moss reached out, grabbed the gun and used it to batter Kitty to death. He then went to the police and admitted what he had done.

Tried at Exeter in November 1937, Moss insisted on pleading guilty to the charge. Mister Justice Hawke explained carefully to Moss the consequences of such an action and tried hard to get Moss to change his plea to one of not guilty. Moss would not be moved and after stating that he was fully aware of what the sentence would be, persisted in his plea of guilty. The judge had no alternative but to sentence Moss to death.

On December 7th, 1937, Ernest John Moss was hanged at Exeter. One cannot escape the thought that it might just have been his way of finally committing suicide.

NAME	Ernest John Moss
AGE AT EXECUTION	28
DATE OF EXECUTION	Tuesday, 7th December, 1937
PLACE OF EXECUTION	Exeter
HANGMAN	Thomas Pierrepoint
ASSISTANT	Albert Pierrepoint
DATE OF TRIAL	15th November, 1937
LOCATION OF TRIAL	Exeter
PRESIDING JUDGE	Mister Justice Hawke
PROSECUTION COUNSEL	G.D. Roberts, J.D. Casswell
DEFENCE COUNSEL	J.G. Trapnell, Henry Elam
NUMBER OF VICTIMS	1

VICTIMS DETAILS	
NAME	Kitty Constance Bennett
AGE	18
DATE OF MURDER	Saturday, 7th August, 1937
PLACE OF MURDER	Woolacombe, Devon
METHOD OF KILLING	Battered
RELATIONSHIP TO KILLER	Girlfriend

1937

IN 1934, AFTER he had left his wife, Frederick Nodder moved to Sheffield where he lodged for a time with Mr and Mrs Grimes of 9 Neil Road. In 1935, he moved to new lodgings with Mrs Grimes's sister, Mrs Tinsley, at 11 Thoresby Avenue, Newark. He only stayed there for three weeks and, despite some personal hygiene problems, proved to be very popular with Mrs Tinsley's children, who called him 'Uncle Fred'.

June 1936 saw Uncle Fred move into a house at East Retford. This was named 'Peacehaven' and was soon reduced to squalor by Nodder.

Mona, the 10-year-old daughter of Mrs Tinsley, did not come home from school on the evening of Tuesday, January 5th, 1937. The following day she was reported as a missing person and investigations soon revealed that she had been seen at the bus station in the company of her Uncle Fred. Nodder was interviewed at 'Peacehaven' and denied all knowledge of Mona but upon being faced with witnesses who had seen them together, finally told a story he hoped would convince the officers he had nothing to do with her disappearance.

According to Nodder, he had met Mona outside her school in Guildhall Street, Newark and she had asked him to take her to her aunt's house at Sheffield. He persuaded Mona to spend the night at his home and she slept in his bed whilst he occupied the settee downstairs. The next day he had taken her to Worksop and put her on the bus for Sheffield. He was arrested and charged with abduction.

At the trial, which took place before Mister Justice Swift at Birmingham, in March 1937, Nodder was found guilty and sentenced to seven years' imprisonment. When he was passing sentence, Mister Swift made a prophetic comment: "What you did with that little girl, what became of her, only you know. It may be that time will reveal the dreadful secret you carry in your breast."

The police believed that Mona had been abducted by Nodder, and subsequently murdered. Without her body though, the latter charge could not be pursued. Nodder began his prison sentence no doubt believing that he had escaped a more serious charge.

NAME	Frederick Nodder
AGE AT EXECUTION	44
DATE OF EXECUTION	Thursday, 30th December 1937
PLACE OF EXECUTION	Lincoln
HANGMAN	Not known
ASSISTANT	Not known
DATE OF TRIAL	22nd November – 23rd November, 1937
LOCATION OF TRIAL	Nottingham
PRESIDING JUDGE	Mister Justice Macnaghten
PROSECUTION COUNSEL	Norman Birkett, Richard Elwes
DEFENCE COUNSEL	Nigel Robinson, Maurice Healy
NUMBER OF VICTIMS	1

VICTIMS DETAILS	
NAME	Mona Lilian Tinsley
AGE	10
DATE OF MURDER	circa Wednesday, 6th January 1937
PLACE OF MURDER	'Peacehaven', Hayton, near East Retford
METHOD OF KILLING	Strangled
RELATIONSHIP TO KILLER	None

On June 6th, 1937, a group of people on the river Idle near Bawtry found the badly decomposed body of a young girl, floating in the water. Mona Tinsley had been found.

At the second trial, Nodder repeated his earlier story and claimed that Mona had obviously been lured off the Sheffield bus by someone else and murdered. He convinced no one and was sentenced to death. Mister Justice Swift, who had sentenced Nodder for abduction, did not live to see his prediction fulfilled though, having died in October 1937.

Hanged on December 30th, Nodder had the unique distinction of being tried twice, before two different judges and in two different cities.

IT IS PERHAPS true to say that one sentence hanged Walter Smith.

Smith was the mate on board the East Anglia, the captain of which was his best friend, Albert Edward Baker. In October 1937, the barge was docked at Felixstowe whilst a cargo of barley was unloaded. On the afternoon of October 22nd, Smith went ashore leaving the barge hatches open, and spent the rest of the day drinking himself into a stupor in various local public houses.

Many other sailors shouted to the East Anglia to draw attention to the fact that her hatches were open, but no reply was heard and no signs of movement were noticed. Eventually a couple of men ventured aboard, whereupon the body of Albert Baker was discovered. He had been shot three times. Once in the head and twice in the heart.

Smith was arrested and claimed to have no knowledge of the crime. At his trial, a defence of mania a potu was put forward. This Latin phrase means 'mania by drink' and its symptoms were an ungovernable fury, followed by complete amnesia of whatever had occurred. Basically, Smith was claiming that if he had killed Baker, he had no memory of doing so and had been unable to form an intention to kill. The crime would thus have been reduced to one of manslaughter.

Doctor Dickson of Norwich prison, had examined Smith and believed that he was genuinely suffering from amnesia, but unfortunately, Smith had made one simple mistake. When first spoken to by the police, and told that Baker was dead, Smith had allegedly replied: "You say the old man has been shot dead?" No one at that stage had mentioned that Baker had been shot. If Smith had no memory of the events on board the East Anglia how could he possibly know that Baker had been shot?

Found guilty and sentenced to death, further attempts were made to put forward a defence of insanity at Smith's appeal. When that too failed, he was hanged at Norwich in March, 1938.

NAME	Walter Smith
AGE AT EXECUTION	33
DATE OF EXECUTION	Tuesday, 8th March, 1938
PLACE OF EXECUTION	Norwich
HANGMAN	Thomas Pierrepoint
ASSISTANT	Not known
DATE OF TRIAL	20th January – 22nd January, 1938
LOCATION OF TRIAL	Ipswich
PRESIDING JUDGE	Mister Justice Singleton
PROSECUTION COUNSEL	Charles Doughty, Eric Neve
DEFENCE COUNSEL	Hugh Boileau, J. Grimmond
NUMBER OF VICTIMS	1

VICTIMS DETAILS	
NAME	Albert Edward Baker
AGE	28
DATE OF MURDER	Friday, 22nd October, 1937
PLACE OF MURDER	On board the barge East Anglia in Felixstowe Dock
METHOD OF KILLING	Shot
RELATIONSHIP TO KILLER	None

1938

ELIZA CALDWELL WAS Swiss by birth and had met her husband when he was interned during the Great War. They had fallen in love, married and by 1938 had a son and a daughter and were living in Rochdale, Lancashire.

Like so many others in this time of depression, Charles Caldwell was out of work. Financial matters were tight and as a result, there were constant arguments about cash between Charles and his wife, mainly centring around the fact that she did not give him enough beer money. After putting up with this for some considerable time, Eliza decided she had taken all she could, and left her husband.

Eliza had also, it seems, decided that the split was to be final and irrevocable, for on February 7th, she saw a solicitor and took out a summons against Charles for cruelty, desertion and a wilful neglect to maintain her. Over the next few days, Charles saw Eliza a number of times and tried to persuade her to come back to him, but she made it very plain that she was not interested in any form of reconciliation.

On Friday, February 11th, 1938, Eliza was talking to some friends of hers in Halifax Road, when Charles approached and once again asked her to come back to him. When again, Eliza said she wanted nothing to do with him, Charles drew out a knife and stabbed his wife. Bleeding badly, Eliza staggered into the nearest shop, a butchers, and collapsed onto the floor. She died soon afterwards from a wound close to her heart.

Charles Caldwell was arrested close by, in Whitehall Street, and charged with the murder of his wife. As the charges was read out to him, Charles remarked: "She is gone now. I don't want reprieving. I want the rope now."

At his trial, held at Manchester, Caldwell's defence was one of insanity. There was little chance of success and Caldwell was indeed found guilty, but not until the jury had returned to court and asked the learned judge if they had to be unanimous. The judge explained that they did and went on to further clarify the law relating to insanity. This point was referred to in Caldwell's appeal, when his

NAME	Charles James Caldwell
AGE AT EXECUTION	49
DATE OF EXECUTION	Wednesday, 20th April, 1938
PLACE OF EXECUTION	Manchester
HANGMAN	Not known
ASSISTANT	Not known
DATE OF TRIAL	14th March, 1938
LOCATION OF TRIAL	Manchester
PRESIDING JUDGE	Mister Justice Tucker
PROSECUTION COUNSEL	F.E. Pritchard, B.S. Wingate-Saul
DEFENCE COUNSEL	C.T.B. Leigh, W.H. Openshaw
NUMBER OF VICTIMS	1

VICTIMS DETAILS	
NAME	Eliza Augustina Caldwell
AGE	40
DATE OF MURDER	Friday, 11th February, 1938
PLACE OF MURDER	13 Halifax Road, Rochdale
METHOD OF KILLING	Stabbed
RELATIONSHIP TO KILLER	Wife

defence argued that the judge had led the jury, but the argument was dismissed and the sentence upheld.

THE STORY OF Robert William Hoolhouse is one of the darkest tragedies of this book and possibly one of the strongest arguments against capital punishment.

On Tuesday, January 18th, 1938, Margaret Dobson left her home at High Grange Farm, at 4.30pm. Her husband, Henry, expected Margaret to return at about 6.00pm but when she failed to appear, thought she might have stayed overnight at their daughter's home, in Newcastle.

The following day saw Henry up at dawn and by 8.00am, a number of his workers had arrived and the farm was a hive of activity. Having checked that everyone had enough work to do, Henry decided to walk into the village of Wolviston. It was by then 9.45am.

As Henry passed down the trackway that led to the main road, he saw something in one of his fields. Going to investigate, he was horrified to discover the body of his wife. Hardly believing his eyes, Henry walked around the body before setting off to the nearest police station.

Margaret Dobson had been brutally raped and then stabbed, and police believed they had a likely suspect in Robert Hoolhouse. The Hoolhouse family had worked for Mr Dobson five years before. An argument had cost Mr Hoolhouse and his son their jobs and the family their tied cottage. This perhaps was reason enough for someone to want to kill, and when it came to the attention of the authorities that Robert Hoolhouse was sporting some new scratches on his face, they decided to have a word with him.

At 1.15am on the morning of January 20th, Robert Hoolhouse was taken into custody and eventually charged with murder. In addition to the scratches on his face, bloodstains had been found on his clothing and his alibi did not check out.

Robert had claimed that on the day of the murder, January 18th, he had been at home at 6 Pickering Street, Haverton Hill, until about 12.30pm. He had then cycled to Wolviston, where he visited the home of a friend, William Husband, staying until 3.30pm. Cycling home via Cowpen, he arrived home at about 4.00pm. That evening, at 6.30pm, he caught the bus to Wolviston, where he again visited

NAME	Robert William Hoolhouse
AGE AT EXECUTION	21
DATE OF EXECUTION	Thursday, 26th May, 1938
PLACE OF EXECUTION	Durham
HANGMAN	Thomas Pierrepoint
ASSISTANT	Not known
DATE OF TRIAL	28th March – 30th March 1938
LOCATION OF TRIAL	Leeds
PRESIDING JUDGE	Mister Justice Wrottesley
PROSECUTION COUNSEL	C. Paley Scott, A.P. Peaker
DEFENCE COUNSEL	Arthur Morley, W.A. Macfarlane
NUMBER OF VICTIMS	1

VICTIMS DETAILS	
NAME	Margaret Jane Dobson
AGE	67
DATE OF MURDER	Tuesday, 18th January, 1938
PLACE OF MURDER	High Grange Farm, Wolviston, Co Durham
METHOD OF KILLING	Stabbed
RELATIONSHIP TO KILLER	None

William Husband and where he also saw John Lax and his sister, Dolly. He and Dolly caught a bus for Billingham, where they went to the pictures. At 11.00pm, Hoolhouse saw Dolly onto the bus for Wolviston after which he caught his own bus, for Haverton, arriving home at around 11.30pm.

On January 19th, Hoolhouse was again at home until 10.45am when he visited the Labour Exchange and signed on. From there he took a walk before returning home for lunch, after which he cycled to Wolviston again, falling off his bicycle on the way and sustaining scratches to his face. He stayed at William Husband's house until 2.15pm when he cycled home.

When police checked this extensive timetable, they found a discrepancy in the time that the Husbands and the Laxs said he had arrived later on January 18th. Hoolhouse made a second, brief statement in which he admitted that he must have got the times wrong and had left an hour later, arriving at Wolviston at 3.45pm instead of 2.45pm. For the police this was highly significant. Pathological examination of Margaret Dobson's stomach contents had put her time of death before 4.00pm and they now held that Hoolhouse had lied deliberately to hide the fact that he was killing Mrs Dobson at that time. Robert Hoolhouse was charged with murder.

Had Robert Hoolhouse had a half-decent barrister, he might well have escaped with his life. The evidence against him was flimsy to say the least. To begin with, Percy Swales had seen a man standing in the field, very close to where Margaret Dobson was finally discovered, at 5.30pm. This man was not Robert Hoolhouse and seemed to indicate that the true time of death was probably closer to 5.30pm, by which time Robert Hoolhouse was at home in Haverton Hill.

Next there was the evidence of the scratches on Robert's face. When Margaret Dobson was found, she still wore her heavy woollen gloves. The police had actually experimented with these gloves, trying to cause scratches on a volunteer's face. They did not succeed.

Hoolhouse had explained away the bloodstains on his clothing by saying that he had suffered from a boil that had burst. The forensic tests were made on a few spots of blood and no further tests were made that might have proved Hoolhouse's story.

Even more conclusive was the footprint evidence. Henry Dobson had walked around his wife's body and his footprints were plainly visible. However, beneath one of Mr Dobson's boot prints, was a different print. Plaster casts were taken of this and it was shown not to belong to Robert Hoolhouse. The defence barrister completely missed the significance of this vital clue. Since the print was beneath Henry Dobson's, it must have been there first and almost certainly belonged to the killer.

Finally there was the evidence of the semen stains, or more accurately the lack of them. Hoolhouse went to the police station in the same clothing he had worn on the day of the murder. This clothing was extensively tested and no trace of semen staining was found, yet Mrs Dobson had been raped and there was extensive semen stains on her body.

The jury were out for over four hours before returning their guilty verdict. Hoolhouse's parents were deeply shocked by the verdict. They were convinced that Robert was innocent and even had a taxi cab waiting outside the courthouse to take their son home.

Hoolhouse's appeal was lost on May 9th and despite a petition of 14,000 signatures, he was executed at Durham on May 26th, 1938, despite the fact that medical reports had shown that he had a mental age of less than 14.

Two important witnesses were never called at Robert's trial. Margaret Barker knew Robert well and had travelled by bus to Wolviston on January 18th. Robert was on the same bus, going to meet Dolly Lax so that he could take her to the cinema. Margaret spoke to Robert for part of the journey and gave a statement to the police that Robert had no scratches on his face at that time, when Margaret Dobson already lay dead.

Finally, Doris Teale, who lived next door to the Hoolhouses, said that she had seen Robert outside his house at about the time he was supposed to be murdering Margaret Dobson.

Robert Hoolhouse was just 21 years old when he died on the scaffold at Durham. Whatever else he may have been, it is highly unlikely that he was also a murderer.

JAN MOHAMED AND Aminul Hag were both members of the engine room crew of a ship and at first appeared to be very friendly towards each other. Then, on March 15th, all this changed. On that date, the two men had a violent argument, ending with Hag smashing an iron bar into Mohamed's face, causing him to lose several teeth. Soon afterwards, Hag was transferred to the S.S. Kabinga and it was hoped that everything would now be forgotten.

Mohamed, though, was not one to let things go so easily and he swore to have his revenge. On April 9th, he was spotted trying to board the Kabinga, and sent packing by the chief steward. Two days later though, Mohamed was to have a greater degree of success.

Monday, April 11th, saw Mohamed managing to get on board the Kabinga without being seen. He then waited in a passage for three hours, until Hag returned, and in the resulting argument, Hag was beaten to death with a heavy file.

On trial for his life, Mohamed tried to persuade the jury that he had acted in self-defence. According to his story, he had gone on board to talk to Hag but had immediately been attacked. Mohamed then picked up the first thing to hand and used it to defend himself. This just happened to be a file and it was shown that this weapon did belong to the S.S. Kabinga.

The prosecution, though, suggested that Mohamed had waited deliberately and battered Hag to death as soon as he saw him. They cited medical evidence that indicated the blow had been struck from behind, though under cross examination, their witness did agree that it was just possible that the fatal blow might have been struck from in front.

It was a simple decision for the jury. If Hag had been hit from behind, Mohamed was guilty of murder. If he had been struck from the front, it was a case of self-defence as Mohamed suggested. Taking into account the feud between the two men, the jury decided that Mohamed had deliberately killed Hag.

NAME	Jan Mohamed
AGE AT EXECUTION	30
DATE OF EXECUTION	Wednesday, 8th June, 1938
PLACE OF EXECUTION	Liverpool
HANGMAN	Not known
ASSISTANT	Not known
DATE OF TRIAL	27th April, 1938
LOCATION OF TRIAL	Manchester
PRESIDING JUDGE	Mister Justice Tucker
PROSECUTION COUNSEL	A.D. Gerrard
DEFENCE COUNSEL	R.S. Nicklin
NUMBER OF VICTIMS	1

VICTIMS DETAILS	
NAME	Aminul Hag
AGE	20
DATE OF MURDER	Monday, 11th April, 1938
PLACE OF MURDER	On board S.S. Kabinga, Gladstone Dock, Liverpool
METHOD OF KILLING	Battered
RELATIONSHIP TO KILLER	None

ALFRED RICHARDS HAD been described as an honest, hard-working father, devoted to his wife and three children, but all this changed at the beginning of February, 1938.

Alfred's wife, Kathleen, worked as an usherette in a cinema at Woolwich and here she became friendly with another employee, Grace Dolman. On the night of February 6th, the two ladies decided on a night out together, somewhat unadventurously to another cinema, but so much did they enjoy each other's company that it was rather late when Kathleen arrived home. Alfred was far from pleased.

The row was a violent one. Also living in the same house was Florence Reed, Kathleen's sister, Florence's husband Albert and their baby. Florence would later report that at one stage Alfred screamed that if he found Kathleen there the following day, he would kill her. Florence took Alfred at his word and the next day moved in with Mrs Dolman, the children being farmed out to various relatives.

Over the next few months, Kathleen went back to the house many times in order to see her sister and of course there was contact with Alfred, especially over the children. The last such occasion was on May 11th when Kathleen left a message for her husband saying that she wished to take the two youngest children on an outing on June 1st.

Alfred Richards usually left for work at 7.30am and before he left, he was in the habit of knocking on Albert Reed's door to make sure that he was awake. Nothing appeared to be different on the morning of May 30th. The tap on the door came and it was assumed that Alfred had gone to work.

It was 11.00am when Kathleen and Grace Dolman arrived to see Florence. They had been in the house just a few minutes when Kathleen went upstairs. A scream filled the house and when the women rushed out to see what the problem was, they saw Alfred Richards, his hands around Kathleen's throat, having already battered her into submission.

Grace Dolman ran to the house next door and telephoned the police but by the time they arrived, Alfred had already gone. At

NAME	Alfred Ernest Richards
AGE AT EXECUTION	38
DATE OF EXECUTION	Tuesday, 12th July, 1938
PLACE OF EXECUTION	Wandsworth
HANGMAN	Thomas Pierrepoint
ASSISTANT	Albert Pierrepoint
DATE OF TRIAL	25th June, 1938
LOCATION OF TRIAL	Maidstone
PRESIDING JUDGE	Mister Justice Humphreys
PROSECUTION COUNSEL	Geoffrey Lawrence
DEFENCE COUNSEL	Norman Parkes
NUMBER OF VICTIMS	1

VICTIMS DETAILS	
NAME	Kathleen Richards
AGE	37
DATE OF MURDER	Monday, 30th May, 1938
PLACE OF MURDER	270 Sutherland Avenue, Welling, Kent
METHOD OF KILLING	Battered
RELATIONSHIP TO KILLER	Wife

11.50am, he walked into Shooter's Hill police station and gave himself up for the murder of his wife.

There could only be one verdict and it took the jury 10 minutes to arrive at it, though they did add a strong recommendation to mercy.

IN JANUARY, 1937, Queenie Irene Ruffle gave birth to a son, whom she named Tony. Queenie lived with her parents at Dymchurch and was not in a position to take care of Tony. Neither was the father, William Graves and so the child was farmed out to foster parents who were paid 15/- a week. By agreement, Queenie and William were to pay 7s-6d a week each.

In October William began to fall into arrears with his payments. In fact, he only made three more payments after that date and it became important for him to reduce his contribution.

One solution was to find cheaper accommodation for the boy and, in March 1938, William said he had done so. He told Queenie's mother that he had found some friends at Canterbury who were willing to accept the child at a reduced rate. Mrs Raffle demanded a letter of confirmation and to meet the people concerned.

A few days later, William turned up again with a letter that purported to come from Charlie Green of Wincheap Road, Canterbury, confirming what William had already said. Mrs Ruffle agreed to take Tony to Ashford station at 6.00pm on Saturday, March 26th, where she would hand the child over to Charlie Green and his wife.

On the appointed day, Mrs Ruffle was on time but after waiting half an hour, only William Graves turned up, saying that the Greens had been delayed but he would take the child to Dover where he would meet them. Still Mrs Ruffle was wary and offered to accompany William to Dover. Only when he pointed out that she might not get back home that night did she finally give in and hand Tony over.

It was Monday, March 28th, before Mrs Ruffle saw a report in her local newspaper that a gentleman named Turner had found the strangled body of a male child under a hedge on the main Dover to Folkestone Road. Fearing the worse, she reported her suspicions to the police and later identified the body of Tony Ruffle. That same afternoon, William Graves was arrested.

At first, William denied any involvement in the death of his son but once a search of his

NAME	William James Graves
AGE AT EXECUTION	38
DATE OF EXECUTION	Tuesday, 19th July, 1938
PLACE OF EXECUTION	Wandsworth
HANGMAN	Thomas Pierrepoint
ASSISTANT	Thomas Phillips
DATE OF TRIAL	27th June, 1938
LOCATION OF TRIAL	Maidstone
PRESIDING JUDGE	Mister Justice Humphreys
PROSECUTION COUNSEL	F.J. Eastwood, G. Raphael
DEFENCE COUNSEL	John Flowers, R.J. Baxter
NUMBER OF VICTIMS	1

VICTIMS DETAILS	
NAME	Tony Ruffle
AGE	14 Months
DATE OF MURDER	Saturday, 26th March, 1938
PLACE OF MURDER	Dover
METHOD OF KILLING	Strangled
RELATIONSHIP TO KILLER	Son

premises had been made and blotting paper found on which was seen the Green letters in reverse, he made a full confession.

William Graves claimed that his original intention had been to take the child to Dover and abandon it. Along the way Tony began screaming and crying and finally, having endured this for some time, William decided instead to do away with him and strangled Tony with the coat he was wearing.

Found guilty after the jury had been out 10 minutes, William Graves, who had murdered his son to save 7s-6d a week, was executed at Wandsworth.

WILLIAM PARKER DID not deny that he had killed his wife, but if the jury had believed the rest of his story he might have escaped with a verdict of manslaughter.

At the end of April, 1938, Parker walked into a police station and told officers that he was responsible for the death of his wife, three days before. He went on to say that two other bodies lay in his house.

Jane Parker had been battered and the wounds she received would probably have led to her death. However, she had also had a piece of string knotted tightly around her throat. The two children had both been strangled and both had similar pieces of string knotted around their necks. It looked as if William had murdered his entire family.

William, though, claimed responsibility for just one of the deaths, that of his wife. His story was that he had found his wife with her hands around the throat of their two-month old son. He asked her what she was doing, to which she replied that it was too late. William went to investigate and discovered that Jane had murdered both their children by tying string around their necks.

Before he knew what was happening, Jane rushed at him with a poker. In an attempt to avoid her, he ran into the scullery, but she followed. William picked up the nearest object, a hammer, and battered Jane into unconsciousness. Then, remembering what she had done to the children, he took some string and tied it around her throat. He then left the house and wandered about for a few days until he decided to visit the police.

In fact, it was largely due to the testimony of one witness that Parker was not believed. Parker's sisters testified that some time after their brother's arrest, a neighbour, Mrs Hildreth King, had told them that Jane Parker had confided in her that she was very worried about money and had thought of killing herself and the children. When questioned, though, Hildreth denied any such conversation and it was now simply a case of whether the jury chose to believe William's story.

In the event, the story was not accepted and William was sentenced to death. On July 26th, the last member of the Parker family died, on the gallows.

NAME	William Parker
AGE AT EXECUTION	25
DATE OF EXECUTION	Tuesday, 26th July, 1938
PLACE OF EXECUTION	Durham
HANGMAN	Thomas Pierrepoint
ASSISTANT	Not known
DATE OF TRIAL	16th June – 17th June, 1938
LOCATION OF TRIAL	Newcastle upon Tyne
PRESIDING JUDGE	Mister Justice Atkinson
PROSECUTION COUNSEL	Russell Vick, Norman Harper
DEFENCE COUNSEL	G.H.B. Streatfeild, Clifford Cohen
NUMBER OF VICTIMS	1 (possibly 3)

VICTIMS DETAILS

NAME	Jane Ann Parker
AGE	24
DATE OF MURDER	Friday, 22nd April, 1938
PLACE OF MURDER	23 Edwin Street, Newcastle upon Tyne
METHOD OF KILLING	Battered/strangled
RELATIONSHIP TO KILLER	Wife

NAMES	Theresa Shirley Parker; Cecil Edward Parker
AGES	13 months; 2 months
DATE OF MURDER	Friday, 22nd April, 1938
PLACE OF MURDER	23 Edwin Street, Newcastle upon Tyne
METHOD OF KILLING	Strangled; strangled
RELATIONSHIP TO KILLER	Daughter; son

ROSE MURIEL ATKINS, a prostitute known as Irish Rose, had been brutally murdered. Her attacker had battered her about the head, stabbed her, left her lying in the road and, either accidentally or deliberately, driven off over her body.

To begin with, the investigations proceeded fairly slowly. The tyre tracks were identified as belonging to an Austin Seven or a Morris Minor and there was a witness who reported seeing Rose getting into a green van, but beyond that, nothing.

On Saturday, July 16th, the firm of G. Hart and Co, shoe repairers, reported one of their employees for theft. George Brain had apparently appropriated £32 of the company's money and had now vanished from his home at 18 St James Cottages, Richmond. What at first seemed to be a simple case of theft assumed much more importance when it was realised that Brain had been a driver for the company, had used a green van, and was a known customer of prostitutes.

As a matter of routine, the garage in Whitfield Place, where the van had been kept, was thoroughly searched. This soon revealed Rose's handbag, bearing a clear thumbprint that did not belong to Rose, and a bloodstained knife. A full-scale search was launched for Brain.

George Brain was to enjoy nine days' freedom. On July 25th, two police constables received a report that a man was living rough on the cliffs on the Isle of Sheppey. Going to check up, they found a dishevelled, unwashed man who seemed pleased to be arrested. He was none other than Brain.

When interviewed, Brain confessed to killing Rose, but claimed that he had not known what he was doing. He had picked Rose up at around 11.30pm on July 13th but when she asked for money, they got into an argument. Brain claimed that they struggled and Rose bit him on the finger. This drove him into a rage and he hit her, hard, with his fist. He then took up a starting handle, with which he continued the beating until he came to his senses and realised that he had killed her. He made no mention of the fact that he had also used a knife on Rose, or that he had driven over her after dumping her in the road.

NAME	George Brain
AGE AT EXECUTION	27
DATE OF EXECUTION	Tuesday, 1st November, 1938
PLACE OF EXECUTION	Wandsworth
HANGMAN	Thomas Pierrepoint
ASSISTANTS	Stanley Cross, Herbert Morris
DATE OF TRIAL	19th September – 20th September, 1938
LOCATION OF TRIAL	Old Bailey
PRESIDING JUDGE	Mister Justice Wrottesley
PROSECUTION COUNSEL	G.B. McClure, Christmas Humphreys
DEFENCE COUNSEL	Frederick Hallis
NUMBER OF VICTIMS	1

VICTIMS DETAILS	
NAME	Rose Muriel Atkins
AGE	30
DATE OF MURDER	circa Wednesday, 13th July, 1938
PLACE OF MURDER	Somerset Road, Wimbledon, London
METHOD OF KILLING	Battered/stabbed
RELATIONSHIP TO KILLER	None

As an extra safeguard, the fingerprint on the handbag was checked and this did indeed match the print of George Brain. His story of having no memory of the crime beyond the first blow did nothing to sway the jury who took 15 minutes to find Brain guilty.

JOHN DAYMOND HAD financial problems. On November 8th, 1938, he saw James Percival, the son of his former employer, and told him at the time that he only had a halfpenny to his name and had not eaten that day. By the very next morning, though, it seems that Daymond had thought of a way to solve his problems.

Percival's father, also named James, had employed Daymond during haymaking in the summer of that year. As a result, Daymond knew some of his habits, one of which was that he often carried large amounts of cash on his person.

At 6.30am on November 9th, Daymond was seen leaving the farm shed where he had been sleeping. Soon after this, James Percival junior saw his father lying on the ground in the engine shed. Going to investigate, James tried to lift his father and just caught a glimpse of John Daymond before a blow to the head rendered him unconscious. The noise of this attack was heard by Catherine Percival, who found her father and brother unconscious. She called a doctor and both men were rushed to hospital, where the elder Percival died the following day.

At 1.30pm on the day of the attack, John Daymond was found by police, hiding in a hayloft. Nearby was a bloodstained pick and Daymond admitted using this to attack the Percivals. All he had managed to take from the dead man's pockets before James Percival junior had disturbed him was a shilling, 18 pennies and four halfpennies, a total of 2s-8d.

Investigations revealed the extent of Daymond's financial problems. Until November 6th, he had been employed by William Foster, but had failed to turn up for work on November 7th. As a result of that he was dismissed the following day. Although he was owed no wages, he cried as he told Foster he had no money and out of kindness, Foster gave him a shilling. It was also discovered that Daymond owed almost £2 to George Smith and that another debt had been put in the hands of a firm of solicitors, Rigg and Strong.

Daymond's only defence was that he had not meant to kill James Irwin Percival, but medical evidence showed that five blows had been struck. The crime had been a simple case of murder in the furtherance of theft and the jury had no hesitation in convicting Daymond, though they did add a strong recommendation to mercy on account of his youth.

NAME	John Daymond
AGE AT EXECUTION	19
DATE OF EXECUTION	Wednesday, 8th February, 1939
PLACE OF EXECUTION	Durham
HANGMAN	Thomas Pierrepoint
ASSISTANT	Not known
DATE OF TRIAL	19th January, 1939
LOCATION OF TRIAL	Carlisle
PRESIDING JUDGE	Mister Justice Croom-Johnson
PROSECUTION COUNSEL	C.T.B. Leigh, W.H. Openshaw
DEFENCE COUNSEL	Selwyn Lloyd, N.B. Birrell
NUMBER OF VICTIMS	1

VICTIMS DETAILS

NAME	James Irwin Percival (Died Thursday, 10th November)
AGE	68
DATE OF MURDER	Wednesday, 9th November, 1938
PLACE OF MURDER	Aikhead, near Wigton
METHOD OF KILLING	Battered
RELATIONSHIP TO KILLER	None

KATHLEEN LAWRENCE, THE hotel chambermaid, was busying herself with her duties, when she came to room six. She knocked on the door but received no reply.

Kathleen went back downstairs to the manager, Richard Vaughan Jones, and told him that she could not gain access to room six. The manager took his master key and unlocked the door, whereupon the body of Peggy Pentecost, who preferred to use her second name, Irene, was discovered.

Investigations showed that Irene lived in Elm Grove, Brighton and that her supposed husband was Harry Armstrong, a manservant from Seaford. The couple had known each other for some time and had become engaged on December 31st. A full description of Harry Armstrong was circulated around the capital and he was picked up in Baker Street later that same afternoon.

The question of Harry Armstrong's guilt would be decided by a careful consideration of the time factor. Doctor Cedric Keith Simpson had put the time of death between 9.00pm and 11.30pm on the night of January 1st. Richard Jones, the hotel manager, testified that he had heard a door click shut at around 11.00pm and it was suggested that this was the sound of Armstrong leaving, after having murdered his fiancée. Armstrong, though, had an alibi for this time.

Armstrong claimed that he had left the hotel much earlier and at that time, Irene was alive and well. He had gone to a cafe in Westminster Bridge Road, where he met Rose Kirby, at a few minutes after 10.00pm. They left the cafe together at about 11.00pm and spent the night together in a hotel in Paddington. This story was confirmed in every respect by Rose.

Leaving aside any comment on Armstrong's morals, this timing meant that if he was the killer, he would have had to have murdered Irene by about 9.30pm. This was still possible within the time limits given by Doctor Simpson, but then who had closed the door at 11.00pm? More telling was a postcard found on Armstrong when he was arrested. Addressed to Irene's mother, it read: "This is the best way out. Love. Harry." Did this refer to the murder or the fact that he had had

NAME	Harry Armstrong
AGE AT EXECUTION	38
DATE OF EXECUTION	Tuesday, 21st March, 1939
PLACE OF EXECUTION	Wandsworth
HANGMAN	Thomas Phillips
ASSISTANT	Albert Pierrepoint
DATE OF TRIAL	1st March – 2nd March, 1939
LOCATION OF TRIAL	Old Bailey
PRESIDING JUDGE	Mister Justice Humphreys
PROSECUTION COUNSEL	L.I. Byrne
DEFENCE COUNSEL	J.F. Eastwood
NUMBER OF VICTIMS	1

VICTIMS DETAILS	
NAME	Peggy Irene Violet Pentecost
AGE	17
DATE OF MURDER	Sunday, 1st January, 1939
PLACE OF MURDER	Room 6, Hotel at 22 York Road, Lambeth, London
METHOD OF KILLING	Strangled
RELATIONSHIP TO KILLER	Girlfriend

second thoughts and did not intend going through with the marriage?

Found guilty and asked if he had anything to say before sentence of death was passed, Armstrong turned to the jury and said: "Ladies and gentlemen, I appreciate everything you have done. No doubt you have had a very difficult task. In spite of your verdict I am not guilty of the murder of Irene Pentecost."

Harry Armstrong decided not to appeal, preferring instead to rely on a petition for a reprieve on medical grounds. The plea did not succeed.

1939

DOCTOR DAY CAREFULLY examined the young man's hands. The man, who had given his name as Charles Jackson, claimed that he had hurt himself on a wood-cutting machine, but the doctor realised at once that he was looking at cuts that could only have been made by a knife or dagger. Furthermore, the same doctor had only recently finished looking at the body of another man, Ernest Percival Key, who had died on the way to hospital. Ernest Key had been murdered in his jeweller's shop and he too had been stabbed – some 30 times. Doctor Day told the police about Charles Jackson's wounds.

When he was interviewed it became clear that Charles Jackson was none other than William Thomas Butler, a man known to the police as a housebreaker. Had he graduated to jewel thief now? The more he talked, the more the police became convinced that he had.

The murderer had left behind a bowler hat in Ernest Key's shop and forensic examination of this had given police knowledge of the colour and length of the assailant's hair. Butler's was an exact match. On January 17th, 1939, the police felt that they had a strong enough case to charge Butler with murder.

The trial took place at the Old Bailey and started on February 15th. Butler now admitted going into the shop and to stealing some jewellery but claimed that he had stabbed Ernest Key in self-defence. Butler seemed to ignore the fact that Key was more than twice his age, and that he had stabbed him so many times in the face and neck. The jury felt that the story was ridiculous and returned a guilty verdict.

NAME	William Thomas Butler (Charles Jackson)
AGE AT EXECUTION	29
DATE OF EXECUTION	Wednesday, 29th March, 1939
PLACE OF EXECUTION	Wandsworth
HANGMAN	Thomas Pierrepoint
ASSISTANT	Thomas Phillips
DATE OF TRIAL	15th February – 16th February, 1939
LOCATION OF TRIAL	Old Bailey
PRESIDING JUDGE	Mister Justice Singleton
PROSECUTION COUNSEL	G.B. McClure
DEFENCE COUNSEL	David Maxwell Fyfe
NUMBER OF VICTIMS	1

VICTIMS DETAILS	
NAME	Ernest Percival Key
AGE	64
DATE OF MURDER	Saturday, 24th December, 1938
PLACE OF MURDER	74 Victoria Road, Surbiton
METHOD OF KILLING	Stabbed
RELATIONSHIP TO KILLER	None

STARTING IN SEPTEMBER, 1938, Ralph Smith began lodging with Beatrice Baxter at 63 Argyle Street, Swindon, in Wiltshire. They soon developed a deeper relationship but the trouble was that Smith wanted her to be faithful to him and Beatrice saw nothing wrong in friendships with other men.

These difficulties led Smith into sometimes turning violent. On January 10th, 1939, the police were called to Argyle Street at Beatrice's request. When they arrived, they found Beatrice bleeding from the mouth, demanding that they throw Smith out. The police managed to calm things down and when Smith said he had nowhere else to go, Beatrice relented somewhat and said he could stay one night, but had to leave the following morning. The next day, Smith did indeed leave the house.

There were no more developments until March 4th, when Smith thought that he should make some move to patch things up. As he approached Beatrice's house, he saw her leaving, and approached her, asking if she would take him back. Beatrice told him that she was going to meet someone else who was taking her to a dance and at that point, Smith drew out a razor and hacked the back of Beatrice's neck, causing a deep and vicious wound.

At 7.00pm that evening, Smith walked into Gorse Hill police station and gave himself up, saying that he had cut a woman's throat, but hoped that she wasn't dead. He was informed that Beatrice had passed away and that he would be charged with murder.

The defence was in two parts. In the first place, medical evidence was given that had the wound received medical attention and been plugged soon enough, Beatrice might well have survived. There was also the matter of Smith's claim that he had suffered a fractured skull in an accident at a steel works, 18 months previously, which may clearly have affected him mentally.

The police made a thorough attempt to trace details of this accident but none had been reported and it was put down as pure invention. It was also held that the fact that Beatrice might have been saved did not detract from what Smith had done and he

NAME	Ralph Smith
AGE AT EXECUTION	40
DATE OF EXECUTION	Wednesday, 7th June, 1939
PLACE OF EXECUTION	Gloucester
HANGMAN	Thomas Pierrepoint
ASSISTANT	Albert Pierrepoint
DATE OF TRIAL	3rd May, 1939
LOCATION OF TRIAL	Old Bailey
PRESIDING JUDGE	Mister Justice Atkinson
PROSECUTION COUNSEL	G.D. Roberts, Henry Irlam
DEFENCE COUNSEL	Bryant Irvine
NUMBER OF VICTIMS	1

VICTIMS DETAILS	
NAME	Beatrice Delia Baxter
AGE	53
DATE OF MURDER	Saturday, 4th March, 1939
PLACE OF MURDER	Back of Argyle Street, Swindon
METHOD OF KILLING	Cut throat
RELATIONSHIP TO KILLER	Ex-girlfriend

was directly responsible for her death. The verdict was one of wilful murder and in June 1939, Ralph Smith was the last man hanged at Gloucester.

LEONARD GEORGE HUCKER had once lodged with Mary Moncrieff and her daughter, Beatrice Maud Fullick and a relationship had developed between him and Beatrice.

It was never a very serious affair and it was not long before Leonard moved out. He had something of a temper, but somehow managed to claim that it was Mary who had the short fuse. Whatever the truth of the matter, there were a number of arguments between Leonard and his landlady and both no doubt thought it best when he made alternative living arrangements.

The relationship between Leonard and Beatrice cooled appreciably until, on August 11th, 1939, she sent him a letter card: "Dear Len, I shall not be seeing you again, as I have made further arrangements. Trix." Though Leonard wasn't to know it at the time, these further arrangements were a man named 'Reg' whom Beatrice had been seeing for some nine months.

On Tuesday, August 15th, Leonard bought a new scout's knife from Walter Cecil Silver. He then proceeded to sharpen the knife to a point in preparation for a visit the following day to Mary's house.

Beatrice left for work at 8.50am on August 16th, 1939 and at that time her mother was in good health. By 3.45pm, Leonard was striding into the police station on Harrow Road, where he told Constable John Reginald Bass that he had murdered a woman. He threw a cellar key onto the counter and when Constable John Moffat called at Victoria Villas, he found the body of Mary Moncrieff. She had been stabbed and the knife lay in her chest, embedded up to its hilt.

Though he admitted killing Mary, Leonard claimed that he had called around to talk and that Mary had started shouting at him because she thought Beatrice was pregnant and he was the father. During the course of the row, he lost his temper and stabbed Mary, whereupon she fell down the steps and into the cellar.

Beatrice Fullick said that this was a pack of lies. She had not discussed any pregnancy either with Leonard or her mother. This, plus the fact that Leonard had purchased the knife

NAME	Leonard George Hucker
AGE AT EXECUTION	30
DATE OF EXECUTION	Tuesday, 10th October, 1939
PLACE OF EXECUTION	Wandsworth
HANGMAN	Thomas Pierrepoint
ASSISTANT	Herbert Morris
DATE OF TRIAL	22nd September, 1939
LOCATION OF TRIAL	Old Bailey
PRESIDING JUDGE	Mister Justice Oliver
PROSECUTION COUNSEL	G.B. McClure
DEFENCE COUNSEL	Gerald Howard
NUMBER OF VICTIMS	1

VICTIMS DETAILS	
NAME	Mary Alice Maud Moncrieff (Fullick)
AGE	60
DATE OF MURDER	Wednesday, 16th August, 1939
PLACE OF MURDER	13 Victoria Villas, Willesden
METHOD OF KILLING	Stabbed
RELATIONSHIP TO KILLER	None

the day before and sharpened it to a point, indicated that the crime was premeditated and deliberate. That evidence was strong enough to condemn Leonard Hucker to death.

JOSEPH WILLIAM GOODWIN had first met Arthur Smith when both were soldiers serving in India. In March 1938, Goodwin returned to England and, in June 1939, the two friends met up again at Aldershot. They had a couple of nights out and then, on June 4th, Smith told Goodwin that he was having a few drinks with another friend, named Boon, and invited him to tag along.

The three men met up in Smith's tent on camp and started their session in the Red Lion at Thursley. From there they caught a bus into Hindhead where they went into a pub Smith knew well, the Royal Huts.

Smith was seen talking to a young woman and at closing time, they left together, arm in arm. Goodwin and Boon, after visiting the toilets, followed Smith outside. What exactly happened next depended upon which of the three soldiers stories was accepted, but whatever the details, the young woman, Mabel Maud Bundy, was battered and raped and left lying dead

The police produced witnesses who had seen Mabel with the three soldiers. One of these, Agnes Alice Dopson who had been out with her husband William, not only gave excellent descriptions but identified Stanley Boon at a parade, on July 5th. It was now just a matter of time before the other two were arrested and soon all three were charged with murder.

Forensic tests indicated that all three soldiers had been involved to one degree or another. Blood had been found on Boon's clothing, and semen on his trousers. Smith had blood on his tunic and around the fly region of his trousers and Goodwin had semen on his clothes and scratches on his shoes.

Smith did not tell much of a story. He had scratches on his face but could offer no explanation of how he had come by them. Boon had marks on his knuckles and came up with the story that he had been holding his hand over Mabel's mouth when Smith had hit her and caught his hand. He went on to admit that he attempted to have sex with the woman but Goodwin had pushed him out of the way and raped her himself.

Goodwin went into much more detail,

NAMES	Stanley Ernest Boon; Arthur John Smith
AGES AT EXECUTION	27; 26
DATES OF EXECUTION	Wednesday, 25th October, 1939; Thursday, 26th October, 1939
PLACE OF EXECUTION	Wandsworth; Wandsworth
HANGMAN	Thomas Pierrepoint; Thomas Pierrepoint
ASSISTANTS	Stanley Cross; Thomas Phillips
DATE OF TRIAL	12th September – 21st September, 1939
LOCATION OF TRIAL	Old Bailey
PRESIDING JUDGE	Mister Justice Oliver
PROSECUTION COUNSEL	G.B. McClure
DEFENCE COUNSEL	Not known; B. MacKenna
NUMBER OF VICTIMS	1

VICTIMS DETAILS	
NAME	Mabel Maud Bundy
AGE	44
DATE OF MURDER	Tuesday, July 4th, 1939
PLACE OF MURDER	Near Moorlands Hotel, Hindhead
METHOD OF KILLING	Battered
RELATIONSHIP TO KILLER	None; none

saying that Smith and Boon had attacked the girl. Smith had ripped at her clothing while Boon struck her before both took turns in raping her. Goodwin claimed that he had taken no part in the attack and in fact had tried to revive Mabel.

After much deliberation, the jury found Smith and Boon guilty of murder. Despite the stains on his clothing, Goodwin was found not guilty. Stanley Boon was executed on October 25th, 1939 and Arthur Smith followed him to the same scaffold one day later.

A T 2.30PM ON Friday, August 25th, 1939, Broadgate in Coventry was thronged with shoppers. Two minutes later, in a searing explosion of fire and noise, five people lay dead and another 50 had been injured.

The bomb had been placed in the carrier of a bicycle and left against the kerb outside a paint merchants, John Astley and Sons. When it detonated it took the lives of Elsie Ansell, who was preparing for her forthcoming wedding, Gwilym Rowland, who worked for Coventry Corporation, James Clay, who was over 80 years of age, John Corbett, a shop assistant aged 15 and a clerk named Rex Gentle. Three men were seen running away from the area and the crowd, incensed by what had happened, gave chase and would probably have lynched them save for the intervention of the police. As it happened, the men were in no way involved in the explosion, though this did give some idea of what public opinion was like at the time.

There had been other bomb attacks throughout the country of late, including one on an allotment at Coventry, on August 14th. All this activity had been placed at the door of the Irish Republican Army and a great deal of information had already been gathered by the security services. As a result, on the day following the Coventry bomb, five people were arrested at London and taken in for further questioning about the possession of explosives. They were: Daniel Jordan, John Evans, James O'Regan, Peter Barnes and Jack Gibson.

One of those men, Peter Barnes, had links with Coventry and further inquiries led to an address at 25 Clare Street. The house was searched and further explosives were found hidden in a hole dug beneath the stairs. As a result, the four occupants of that address were arrested and finally they, along with Peter Barnes, were placed on trial for murder.

The trial opened at Birmingham on December 11th, 1939. Facing the charges in addition to Peter Barnes, were James Richards, Joseph Hewitt, Mary Hewitt and Brigid O'Hara. The Hewitts were a married couple and Brigid O'Hara was the mother of Mary Hewitt. Richards was a lodger at their address.

NAMES	Peter Barnes; James Richards
AGES AT EXECUTION	32; 29
DATE OF EXECUTION	Wednesday, 7th February, 1940
PLACE OF EXECUTION	Birmingham
HANGMAN	Thomas Pierrepoint
ASSISTANTS	Thomas Phillips, Albert Pierrepoint, Stanley Cross
DATE OF TRIAL	11th December – 14th December, 1939
LOCATION OF TRIAL	Birmingham
PRESIDING JUDGE	Mister Justice Singleton
PROSECUTION COUNSEL	Richard O'Sullivan, Arthur Ward
DEFENCE COUNSEL	Albert Wood, Douglas Jenkins
NUMBER OF VICTIMS	5

VICTIMS DETAILS	
NAMES	Elsie Ansell; Gwilym Rowland
AGES	21; 50
DATE OF MURDER	Friday, 25th August, 1939
PLACE OF MURDER	Broadgate, Coventry
METHOD OF KILLING	Bombed; bombed
RELATIONSHIP TO KILLER	None; none
NAMES	John Corbett Arnott; James Clay
AGES	15; 81
DATE OF MURDER	Friday, 25th August, 1939
PLACE OF MURDER	Broadgate, Coventry
METHOD OF KILLING	Bombed; bombed
RELATIONSHIP TO KILLERS	None; none
NAME	Rex Gentle
AGE	30
DATE OF MURDER	Friday, 25th August, 1939
PLACE OF MURDER	Broadgate, Coventry
METHOD OF KILLING	Bombed
RELATIONSHIP TO KILLERS	None

As the trial continued, it became clear that the Hewitts and Mrs O'Hara had been nothing more than dupes and had no links with any terrorist organisation. For the other two defendants though, there was a good deal of evidence to link them with the Coventry bomb.

Barnes denied that he was a member of the I.R.A., and said he had not been involved in the explosion. However, a letter was read out that had been written by Barnes to a Jim Kelly in Ireland that seemed to bring this into question. It suggested that Barnes was travelling the country and certainly showed Irish sympathies. Moreover, it was dated August 24th, the day before the explosion that claimed five lives. There was also the fact that three packets of powder were found in Barnes's lodgings. These contained potassium chlorate, the main constituent of the Coventry bomb, and Barnes's explanation that he had purchased them from a woman in Oxford Street, believing they were shampoo, tooth powder and bath salts, seemed to be ludicrous in the extreme.

Richards was a different proposition. He fully admitted being a member of the I.R.A., and it appeared plain that it was he who had manufactured the bomb, in the sitting room of the Hewitts' house at 25 Clara Street.

After hearing all the evidence, the jury took 30 minutes to convict Barnes and Richards. The other three defendants were found not guilty and were released. The judge asked the two men if they had anything to say before sentence was passed.

Barnes claimed once again that he was innocent, but Richards made a short speech, thanking his defence team, claiming that he had taken part in the explosions as part of a just cause and ending with the words: "God Bless Ireland."

ELSIE MAY ELLINGTON lodged at 93 Inville Road, with Phyllis Rebecca Bridgen and Phyllis's eight-year-old son, Philip Thomas Bridgen. Elsie had been there for some 14 months and she had been visited there by her boyfriend, Ernest Edmund Hamerton.

The first occasion Hamerton visited Elsie at Inville Road was in July, 1939, when he had been allowed to stay the weekend, in a separate room. He returned again on January 8th, 1940, and stayed until the fateful day of January 16th.

On the night of January 15th, Hamerton asked Elsie to go to the pictures with him but she refused and so he went alone. Later, Elsie went out by herself and Phyllis, who was not feeling very well and so went to bed early, heard them coming in separately.

By the following morning, Phyllis was not feeling much better and so decided to stay in bed. She shouted to her son and asked him to give Elsie a call so that she might bring her up a cup of tea. It was 8.40am when Elsie brought the tea in before going downstairs, with Philip, to make him some cocoa.

Philip saw Elsie enter the scullery, to be followed by Hamerton, who slowly closed the door behind him. Some bumping noises were then heard, followed by a scream. Upstairs, Phyllis also heard that scream, but thought it came from outside. It was only when Philip ran upstairs and told her what he had witnessed that Phyllis began to become concerned.

Running downstairs, Phyllis saw Hamerton standing near the scullery door. She asked him what had been going on and he admitted that he had hit Elsie and was going for a doctor. He left the house and upon checking inside the scullery, Phyllis discovered the body of Elsie Ellington. She had been stabbed 24 times and the knife was still embedded in her heart.

In times of trouble, people tend to run to familiar ground and since Hamerton's roots were in Manchester, it seemed reasonable to assume that this is where he would make for. So it was that the London train was met by Constable John Reston Calder, who found Hamerton and arrested him. Hamerton was

NAME	Ernest Edmund Hamerton
AGE AT EXECUTION	25
DATE OF EXECUTION	Wednesday, 27th March, 1940
PLACE OF EXECUTION	Wandsworth
HANGMAN	Thomas Phillips
ASSISTANT	Alexander Riley
DATE OF TRIAL	8th February, 1940
LOCATION OF TRIAL	Old Bailey
PRESIDING JUDGE	Mister Justice Wrottesley
PROSECUTION COUNSEL	G.B. McClure, Gerald Howard
DEFENCE COUNSEL	F.B.J. Sharp
NUMBER OF VICTIMS	1

VICTIMS DETAILS	
NAME	Elsie May Ellington
AGE	28
DATE OF MURDER	Tuesday, 16th January, 1940
PLACE OF MURDER	93 Inville Road, Walworth, London
METHOD OF KILLING	Stabbed
RELATIONSHIP TO KILLER	Girlfriend

taken to Bootle Road police station where he was eventually given over to the custody of Detective Inspector Robert White from London, who took him back to the capital.

On that journey southwards, Hamerton made a full confession to the crime. He said that he had never been in trouble before but Elsie had promised to marry him and then changed her mind. He claimed that he had lost his temper and just stabbed her. His final words were: "It's no use, you can't pick up split milk. I'll have to pay for what I've done."

That last statement was indeed prophetic and that price was paid on March 27th.

1940

ANNE COOK HAD once been a professional dancer and now worked as a domestic servant at a hospital for officers, at 4 Percival Terrace, Brighton. One of her fellow workers was William Cowell, who was a night orderly, and a friendship developed between them.

On August 21st, 1939, Cowell asked another orderly to do a late shift for him as he was taking Anne to the circus, but at 9.55pm that night, Cowell returned alone and Anne was never seen again.

Police inquiries were begun and one of the first people they spoke to was Cowell. He agreed that he had arranged to meet Anne on Brighton seafront but claimed that when she turned up she told him she needed to borrow 15/- to pay for her train fare to London. She did not go to the circus with him and Cowell had no idea what had happened to her.

Further investigations turned up a witness who had seen Cowell coming out of a wood on the morning of August 22nd and it was in that same wood that Anne's body was discovered, on September 27th. She had been battered to death and the murder weapon appeared to be a broken wine bottle, which was found close by.

The day after Anne had been found, Cowell appeared voluntarily at the police station and repeated his earlier statement. At one stage he laughed and observed: "I hope you don't think I did it." It transpired that this was exactly what the police were thinking and after Cowell had been picked out of an identification parade as the man seen in the wood, he made a second statement in which he admitted killing Anne Cook.

According to this statement, he bought the bottle of wine and they met in the wood, where they quarrelled. He hit out with his fist and the blow rendered Anne unconscious. Then, whilst she lay on the ground, his mind went blank and he picked up a piece of wood and hit her with that, before smashing the bottle over her head. He returned to the wood the next day and covered the body with branches and brush and visited the scene each day for five days, to make sure everything was as he had left it.

In court, Cowell said that he had made the

NAME	William Charles Cowell
AGE AT EXECUTION	38
DATE OF EXECUTION	Wednesday, 24th April, 1940
PLACE OF EXECUTION	Wandsworth
HANGMAN	Thomas Pierrepoint
ASSISTANT	Stanley Cross
DATE OF TRIAL	6th March – 8th March, 1940
LOCATION OF TRIAL	Lewes
PRESIDING JUDGE	Mister Justice Humphreys
PROSECUTION COUNSEL	John Flowers, Gerald Thesiger
DEFENCE COUNSEL	Eric Neve, Alban Gordon
NUMBER OF VICTIMS	1

VICTIMS DETAILS	
NAME	Anne Farrow Cook
AGE	33
DATE OF MURDER	Monday, 21st August, 1939
PLACE OF MURDER	Wood near Hurstpierpoint, East Sussex
METHOD OF KILLING	Battered
RELATIONSHIP TO KILLER	None

second statement under force, a claim the police strenuously denied. It took the jury 40 minutes to dismiss that excuse.

JESSE SMITH WAS cycling home at 2.15am on February 29th, 1940 and, as he passed the Co-Operative store he noticed a light in the top window. Almost immediately the light was snapped out, but Smith thought he caught a glimpse of a face. It looked as if the place was being robbed, so Smith pedalled off to find the local constable, William Shiell.

In due course, Shiell, Smith and Constable William Stafford, returned to the store. Shiell shone his torch through the front window but saw nothing so the three moved to the back, where they found that bolts had been removed from the door. Leaving Smith and Stafford, Shiell returned to the front.

The sound of breaking glass filled the night air and Stafford and Smith ran around to the front to find that someone had crashed out through the large window and was now being chased by Constable Shiell. They were heading towards some waste ground at the back of Westley Road.

A shot rang out and as Smith and Stafford reached the open ground they found Shiell lying in the dirt, a bullet wound in his stomach. He managed to gasp out that there were two of them and that the one who was not armed had shouted to the other: "Let him have it."

Later, in the hospital, Shiell made a dying declaration giving a description of one of the men. Shiell said he looked very much like Fewsted, a footballer who played for Spennymoor, and had a ginger moustache. Shiell died at 4.30am on March 1st.

The police had a number of clues. A box of tools had been found near the cellar door of the shop. The getaway car used was found, partly burnt out. It had been stolen from Doctor John Downey Trail in Chester-le-Street on February 22nd and the tyres matched tracks found near where Shiell had been shot.

Vincent Ostler and William Appleby were both arrested in the early hours of March 4th. Appleby asked if he made a statement, would it be helping to hang Ostler? The police were non-committal and Appleby confessed that they had robbed the store but it had been Ostler who fired the fatal shot. Appleby denied shouting, "Let him have it."

Both men were found guilty and sentenced

NAMES	Vincent Ostler; William Appleby
AGES AT EXECUTION	24; 27
DATE OF EXECUTION	Thursday, 11th July, 1940
PLACE OF EXECUTION	Durham
HANGMAN	Thomas Pierrepoint
ASSISTANT	Not known
DATE OF TRIAL	6th May – 10th May, 1940
LOCATION OF TRIAL	Leeds
PRESIDING JUDGE	Mister Justice Hilbery
PROSECUTION COUNSEL	Russell Vick, Dennis Robson
DEFENCE COUNSEL	C. Paley Scott, J.S. Snowden; J. Willoughby Jardine, Willard Sexton
NUMBER OF VICTIMS	1

VICTIMS DETAILS	
NAME	William Ralph Shiell (Died Friday, 1st March)
AGE	28
DATE OF MURDER	Thursday, 29th February, 1940
PLACE OF MURDER	Back of Westley Road, Coxhoe, Co Durham
METHOD OF KILLING	Shot
RELATIONSHIP TO KILLERS	None; none

to death, though in the case of Appleby, the jury added a recommendation to mercy. However, the case has further significance when one considers what happened to Derek Bentley, in 1953.

Appleby claimed not to have shouted, "Let him have it", but the dying declaration of Constable Shiell said he had. It was held that although Ostler fired the shot, Appleby had encouraged him and was therefore equally guilty. The same words and claims were made for Derek Bentley.

1940

THE STORY OF Udham Singh, also known as Singh Azad, was almost a repeat of that of Madar Lal Dhingra in 1909.

On the afternoon of Wednesday, March 13th, 1940, a meeting took place at the Tudor Room of the Caxton Hall. The East India Association and the Royal Central Asian Society had organised a lecture on the state of affairs in Afghanistan, given by Brigadier General Sir Percy Sykes. On the platform with him, were a number of other distinguished guests.

After the lecture had finished, a number of speeches were made and at 4.30pm, the meeting broke up to a polite round of applause. People began to mingle into small groups and it was then that a well-built Asian walked down the central gangway, drew a revolver and fired six shots into the group of people on the platform.

Sir Louis Dane was hit in the arm and Lord Lanington was struck in the wrist. Lord Zetland had a very lucky escape, being hit twice in the chest but surviving. Not so lucky was Sir Michael O'Dwyer who had been hit twice – once in the heart and once in the kidney. He died immediately. The gunman was overpowered as he tried to run out of the building. He was later identified as Udham Singh, a Sikh extremist.

The murder may well have been a case of mistaken identity. Sir Michael had once served as Lieutenant Governor of the Punjab and during his spell of office, the Amritsar riots of 1919 had been put down with extreme brutality. The general responsible for this use of force was named O'Dyer and Singh may well have believed that the man he had killed was that general.

At his trial, Singh tried to claim that the shootings had been an accident! He claimed that it had been his intention to fire the gun at the ceiling, merely to frighten those in attendance. Six shots fired and six hits seemed to destroy much of this defence. The jury were out fractionally over an hour and a half before returning their verdict.

On July 31st, Udham Singh was executed at Pentonville, on the same scaffold that had seen the demise of Madar Lal Dhingra in 1909.

NAME	Udham Singh
AGE AT EXECUTION	37
DATE OF EXECUTION	Wednesday, 31st July, 1940
PLACE OF EXECUTION	Pentonville
HANGMAN	Stanley Cross
ASSISTANT	Albert Pierrepoint
DATE OF TRIAL	4th June – 5th June, 1940
LOCATION OF TRIAL	Old Bailey
PRESIDING JUDGE	Mister Justice Atkinson
PROSECUTION COUNSEL	G.B. McClure
DEFENCE COUNSEL	St. John Hutchinson
NUMBER OF VICTIMS	1

VICTIMS DETAILS	
NAME	Sir Michael O'Dwyer
AGE	75
DATE OF MURDER	Wednesday, 13th March, 1940
PLACE OF MURDER	Tudor Room, Caxton Hall, Westminster, London
METHOD OF KILLING	Shot
RELATIONSHIP TO KILLER	None

THERE WERE BETWEEN 30 and 40 people at the engagement party at 69 Ferry Road, Cardiff, on the night of February 3rd, 1940.

At 2.45am, Arthur Allen left with a group of friends. At the corner of Kent Street, they were joined by George Roberts, another party guest. Arthur said he had to get home and Roberts generously said he would look after him. The two walked off together, with Roberts having his arm around Arthur's shoulders.

Arthur wanted to telephone for a taxi but when they found a phone box, he realised he had no change. Roberts invited him back to his lodgings at number 54, saying that he would get some coppers for him. Once inside, he was also offered a cup of tea.

It was 4.30am when two men arrived at Grange Town police station. One of these men had been badly beaten and the other, who identified himself as a Mr Smith of Holmerdale Street, said he had stumbled over the injured man in Bradford Street. It was then that Marjorie Clifford walked in.

Marjorie was the sister of Nellie Scott, who owned 54 Kent Street. She too was a lodger at that address and told the police that she had gone to bed at 11.00pm, only to be woken in the early hours by the sound of a radio. Later still, she heard banging and what sounded like something being dragged about. Going down to investigate, she found bloodstains and had now come to report this. When she pointed out that Mr Smith was none other than George Roberts, he was held pending further inquiries.

Constable Arthur Jones returned with Marjorie Clifford and found not only bloodstains, but a wallet and clothing belonging to Arthur Allen. Back at the station, Roberts at first stuck to his story that he had found Allen in Bradford Street, but soon admitted that he had hit him with an iron bar.

Further evidence was found by Maurice Patrick Kemble, an auxiliary fireman on duty at the police station. At 7.00am, Roberts had asked him for a cigarette. Kemble handed over the packet but later found that there were five bloodstained one pound notes in the packet. It was a foolish attempt by Roberts to hide evidence.

NAME	George Edward Roberts
AGE AT EXECUTION	29
DATE OF EXECUTION	Thursday, 8th August, 1940
PLACE OF EXECUTION	Cardiff
HANGMAN	Not known
ASSISTANT	Not known
DATE OF TRIAL	16th July – 17th July, 1940
LOCATION OF TRIAL	Swansea
PRESIDING JUDGE	Mister Justice MacNaghten
PROSECUTION COUNSEL	Rowland Thomas, Godfrey Parsons
DEFENCE COUNSEL	O. Temple Morris M.P., H.H. Roskin
NUMBER OF VICTIMS	1

VICTIMS DETAILS	
NAME	Arthur John Allen (Died Tuesday, 9th April, 1940)
AGE	38
DATE OF MURDER	Sunday, 4th February, 1940
PLACE OF MURDER	54 Kent Street, Cardiff
METHOD OF KILLING	Battered
RELATIONSHIP TO KILLER	None

Allen made a statement, on March 26th, stating that he remembered sitting in the chair but then nothing until he woke to find his wounds being stitched. He died later and the charge became one of murder.

At his trial, Roberts attempted to suggest that he had stolen money from Allen, who had discovered the theft and attacked Roberts. He had taken up the bar in order to defend himself. This story was shown to be a lie by forensic evidence, which showed that Allen had been sitting down when he was attacked.

JOHN WRIGHT MARRIED his wife, Alice, in 1925 and by 1940, they had three children. It was those children, returning from school for lunch on May 22nd, who found Alice's battered body, lying on the kitchen floor.

Alice was still alive, though deeply unconscious. The children managed to get help from the neighbours and Alice was rushed to the Durham County Hospital, where she died later that same day. She never regained consciousness and gave no indication as to who had attacked her.

Before the doctors had even arrived though, Alice's husband, John Wright came home. He was told what had happened, by Mr Gibson, his next-door neighbour and rushed inside to see what help he could offer. At one stage he took off his coat and threw it over Alice's body, in order to keep her warm. This would have a good deal of significance later.

When the police investigation began, the house was carefully examined and in due course, a butcher's cleaver was discovered, which appeared to have traces of human blood upon it. John claimed that he had been using it to chop wood the previous night and had left it out. A routine test on the clothes worn by John was also made and spots of blood, of the same type as Alice's, were found on his shirt. Wright now recalled the incident with the coat and claimed that he must have picked up some blood when he leaned over his wife to cover her. It was noted however that the area of the shirt where the blood lay, would have been covered by the waistcoat he was wearing at the time.

When it was shown that John and Alice had argued the previous night, over an insurance policy payment, and that John had gone to the insurance company offices on the morning of the murder, to check that his wife's life policy was in place, the police felt they had enough to charge John with murder.

Throughout his trial, John Wright maintained that he was innocent of any crime. At one stage he admitted that during their marriage, his wife had had affairs with other men and the prosecution tried to suggest that this, coupled with the argument of the previous night and the matter of the insurance

NAME	John William Wright
AGE AT EXECUTION	41
DATE OF EXECUTION	Tuesday, 10th September, 1940
PLACE OF EXECUTION	Durham
HANGMAN	Thomas Pierrepoint
ASSISTANT	Not known
DATE OF TRIAL	25th July, 1940
LOCATION OF TRIAL	Leeds
PRESIDING JUDGE	Mister Justice Stable
PROSECUTION COUNSEL	C. Paley Scott, G.R. Hinchcliffe
DEFENCE COUNSEL	Willard Sexton
NUMBER OF VICTIMS	1

VICTIMS DETAILS	
NAME	Alice Wright
AGE	43
DATE OF MURDER	Wednesday, 22nd May, 1940
PLACE OF MURDER	Pixley Hills, Toronto, Bishop Auckland
METHOD OF KILLING	Battered
RELATIONSHIP TO KILLER	Wife

policy, had combined to turn John Wright into a murderer. It was a somewhat weak motive perhaps, but the bloodstain on Wright's shirt could not adequately be explained away and this it seems was enough to convince the jury.

DORIS GIRL WAS the wife of Gordon Edward Girl. They had married in 1931, had an eight-year-old daughter named Sybil and lived at 77 Hartfield Crescent with their lodger, Louise Bolton, who had been with them since the early part of June, 1940.

Some time in the April of that year, Doris had become friendly with Stanley Cole, a wood machinist. Soon, Cole began spending time at Hartfield Crescent and even began sleeping on the settee in the living room.

On August 22nd, 1940, at around 6.30pm, Louise Bolton returned home from work and found the house completely empty. Later, she walked down to the Crooked Billet pub where she knew Doris would probably be and was surprised to find Sybil outside. Louise spoke to Doris, who was inside the pub with Cole, and then took Sybil home. It was 10.00pm before Cole and Doris returned to the house.

Almost immediately, Cole smiled at Sybil and asked her why she had not waited for them adding: "Why let that bloody cow bring you home?" This was too much for Louise who said she was thinking of reporting the matter to the police and then went up to her room. Five minutes later, Cole came up to apologise.

It was 12.40am on August 23rd when Cole walked into Wimbledon police station. He was staggering and breathing heavily and announced that he had killed a woman at 77 Hartfield Crescent. He then began to sob like a child.

When police visited the house, they found the body of Doris Girl with the knife still embedded in her back. There had been just one blow but it had force behind it and Doris had died almost immediately.

Cole was interviewed but could offer no explanation for what he had done. He said that he and Doris had gone to the pub for a few drinks and a game of darts. After returning home, Louise and Sybil had gone to bed, leaving him alone with Doris. They had another few drinks and then at one stage, Doris bent forward and he had picked a knife up off the table and stabbed her. She had not provoked him. They had not argued. There was no reason for it.

At his trial, Cole refused to co-operate with

NAME	Stanley Edward Cole
AGE AT EXECUTION	23
DATE OF EXECUTION	Thursday, 31st October, 1940
PLACE OF EXECUTION	Wandsworth
HANGMAN	Thomas Pierrepoint
ASSISTANTS	Herbert Morris, Henry Kirk, Henry Critchell
DATE OF TRIAL	10th September – 12th September, 1940
LOCATION OF TRIAL	Old Bailey
PRESIDING JUDGE	Mister Justice Hallett
PROSECUTION COUNSEL	G.B. McClure, Christmas Humphreys
DEFENCE COUNSEL	Linton Thorpe, J.M. Buckland
NUMBER OF VICTIMS	1

VICTIMS DETAILS	
NAME	Doris Eugenia Girl
AGE	29
DATE OF MURDER	Friday, 23rd August, 1940
PLACE OF MURDER	77 Hartfield Crescent, Wimbledon, London
METHOD OF KILLING	Stabbed
RELATIONSHIP TO KILLER	None

his defence counsel and would not go into the witness box to explain his actions. The jury seemed to be just as baffled by the crime and after retiring for 35 minutes, returned to court to ask the judge for further guidance. In due course they returned a guilty verdict and Cole was condemned to death.

On the last day of October Cole, whose only previous brush with the law had been a single conviction for shopbreaking and stealing cigarettes in March, 1938, was hanged for what remains a totally unexplained murder.

WHEN, IN APRIL 1940, one of his employees refused to obey his orders, John Harrison had no hesitation in dismissing him. The man, William Cooper, swore that he would have his revenge.

Cooper knew that Harrison had two regular habits. One was the fact that every morning he fed his chickens in a hut in Seven Acre Field and the other was that he paid his workmen on Friday and would likely be carrying that cash on Friday, July 5th. Cooper took the opportunity of waiting in the hut for Harrison to arrive.

In fact, Cooper was seen entering the hut, at around 7.30am that Friday morning. Later, Lawrence Victor Ryecroft heard noises coming from the hut that he would describe as sounding like someone moving boxes around. When Harrison was found with his head battered in and a broken Tizer bottle scattered around the hut, Cooper was the prime suspect.

William Cooper was arrested and charged with robbery with violence. When Harrison died some days later in Peterborough Memorial Hospital, the charge was changed to one of murder and Cooper was heard to remark: "I didn't think it would turn out like this."

Cooper claimed that he had no idea why Harrison had dismissed him and on the day of the attack, had gone to the hut to ask him to explain. According to Cooper not only did Harrison refuse to tell him but started pushing him about and tried to strike him with a hammer. In retaliation and to protect himself, Cooper took the bottle out of his bag and struck out.

A more plausible story was put forward by the prosecution. Believing that Harrison would be carrying the men's wages and knowing that he went to the hut every day, he waited to ambush and rob him. John Henry Webb who was working nearby saw Harrison enter the hut at his usual time and also saw Cooper run out some minutes later and ride off on his bicycle.

Cooper was further incriminated by a cut on his finger, which he claimed to have received from his bicycle. Doctor Harkness, who examined the cut, said it was more

NAME	William Henry Cooper
AGE AT EXECUTION	24
DATE OF EXECUTION	Tuesday, 26th November, 1940
PLACE OF EXECUTION	Bedford
HANGMAN	Thomas Pierrepoint
ASSISTANT	Albert Pierrepoint
DATE OF TRIAL	17th October, 1940
LOCATION OF TRIAL	Cambridge
PRESIDING JUDGE	Mister Justice Singleton
PROSECUTION COUNSEL	John Flowers, E.G. Robey
DEFENCE COUNSEL	F.T. Alpe
NUMBER OF VICTIMS	1

VICTIMS DETAILS

NAME	John Joseph Harrison (Died Sunday, 21st July)
AGE	68
DATE OF MURDER	Friday, 5th July, 1940
PLACE OF MURDER	Hut on Seven Acre field, Thorney
METHOD OF KILLING	Battered
RELATIONSHIP TO KILLER	None

likely to have been caused by broken glass.

Cooper was found guilty after the jury had been out for 15 minutes, but the final irony was that for once, John Harrison had changed his habits and paid the men on the Thursday, the day before he was attacked. Instead of the £60 or £70 Cooper expected him to have, Harrison only carried three 10/- notes and a cheque.

THE SECOND WORLD War was to see a number of spies executed in London and the first three of these were arrested at the same time, very soon after setting foot on British soil.

Waldeburg was the only German, the other two being Dutch, Kieboom actually being born in Japan. They landed together with a wireless and a large amount of cash in one pound notes and were arrested almost immediately by troops with bayonets. Their instructions had been to pose as refugees from Europe, travel the country and pass out as much military information as possible. Fears of a German invasion were at their highest at this time and indeed, the three spies believed that they would soon be relieved by invading forces.

There was little chance of escape. The radio transmitter and its batteries had instructions and details printed in German, and the cover stories were soon exposed as weak. All three were sentenced to death, but Kieboom's execution was postponed pending an appeal.

Kieboom's story was that he had been forced to co-operate with the Germans because he feared reprisals against his family, who were back in occupied territory. In due course, Kieboom withdrew this appeal and was executed on the same gallows as the other two, exactly one week later.

NAMES	Jose Waldeburg; Carl Meier
AGES AT EXECUTION	25; 24
DATE OF EXECUTION	Tuesday, 10th December, 1940
PLACE OF EXECUTION	Pentonville
HANGMAN	Stanley Cross
ASSISTANTS	Albert Pierrepoint, Harry Kirk
DATE OF TRIAL	22nd November, 1940
LOCATION OF TRIAL	Old Bailey
PRESIDING JUDGE	Mister Justice Wrottesley
PROSECUTION COUNSEL	Sir William Jowitt
NUMBER OF VICTIMS	Hanged for spying

NAME	Charles Albert Van Dem Kieboom
AGE AT EXECUTION	26
DATE OF EXECUTION	Tuesday, 17th December, 1940
PLACE OF EXECUTION	Pentonville
HANGMAN	Stanley Cross
ASSISTANT	Herbert Morris
DATE OF TRIAL	22nd November, 1940
LOCATION OF TRIAL	Old Bailey
PRESIDING JUDGE	Mister Justice Wrottesley
PROSECUTION COUNSEL	Sir William Jowitt
NUMBER OF VICTIMS	Hanged for spying

1940

ACCORDING TO THE story he would later tell to the police, Edward Scoller had a happy marriage until July, 1939. It was then that things began to go wrong between him and his wife, Beatrice Barbara.

In that month, an argument took place over some furniture that Beatrice had sold to her relatives. The argument was so bad that Beatrice left Edward, though she did return to him after the weekend.

In the spring of 1940, there was another row over 10/- owed by her brother for the furniture she had sold. Once again Beatrice left her husband, this time staying away for a full week.

It was July 31st before the next quarrel, again over money and also over their son and his attempts to get work in Middlesborough. Beatrice walked out for the third time, leaving Edward alone in their home at St Paul's Road.

On August 12th, 1940, Beatrice went to visit some friends in Middlesborough. At the same time, Edward, between noon and 2.00pm, drank seven or eight pints of beer. He then went to work but, finding himself not fit to carry out his duties, left and headed for home. On the way, Edward stopped for another pint and a half, deciding then that he would find his wife and ask her to return to him.

When Edward found Beatrice she was talking to two friends, Mrs Bunney and Mrs Hethage. Edward and Beatrice walked off together but when he suggested she return to their home, Beatrice said she would only do so if he would get another house. Edward claimed that this was the last thing he remembered until he found his wife standing against him, her arms around his neck.

Edward tried to take Beatrice home but she soon fell to the ground. Thinking she had fainted, Edward tried to pick her up and carry her, but she was too heavy for him and he had to put her down. He then headed home, intending to get help.

In fact, Edward had stabbed Beatrice and though he would maintain that he had no knowledge of this, he nevertheless then tried to take his own life. When police forced an entry into his house, they found Edward hanging from a rope, which had embedded

NAME	Edward Scoller
AGE AT EXECUTION	42
DATE OF EXECUTION	Tuesday, 24th December, 1940
PLACE OF EXECUTION	Durham
HANGMAN	Thomas Pierrepoint
ASSISTANT	Not known
DATE OF TRIAL	6th November, 1940
LOCATION OF TRIAL	York
PRESIDING JUDGE	Mister Justice Cassels
PROSECUTION COUNSEL	Arthur Morley, Myles Archibald
DEFENCE COUNSEL	G.B. Sykes
NUMBER OF VICTIMS	1

VICTIMS DETAILS	
NAME	Beatrice Barbara Scoller
AGE	35
DATE OF MURDER	Monday, 12th August, 1940
PLACE OF MURDER	Near Milton Street, Middlesborough
METHOD OF KILLING	Stabbed
RELATIONSHIP TO KILLER	Wife

itself deeply into his neck. He had also slashed his wrists. Nevertheless, he eventually made a full recovery, though he did spend five weeks in hospital.

The trial lasted a total of seven and a half hours, 65 minutes of which were spent by the jury considering their verdict. They held that although Edward Scoller had consumed a good deal of alcohol, he was aware of his actions and was therefore guilty of wilful murder.

CLIFFORD HOLMES, A driver in the Royal Engineers, based at Gibraltar Barracks in Aldershot, had been a married man for some years but was now having some rather severe marital problems. His wife, Irene, had now said that she wanted a separation. Consequently, on October 5th, Clifford was given leave to return to Manchester and try to sort things out.

Clifford did not succeed in his attempts to patch up his marriage and on October 8th, appeared in court, where his wife was granted a separation order on the grounds of his persistent cruelty. It was now that Clifford Holmes made his first threat, within hearing of his wife's solicitor, Frank Ralph Johnson. Clifford shouted to his wife: "You won't get a penny out of me. I'll do you in first."

The next day, Clifford visited his wife at 450 Stockport Road, a house divided into rooms for lodgers. A neighbour, Mary Jane Butler, put Clifford's visit at 11.30am, but he returned again at 8.20pm that night and a scuffle took place between him and Irene. Worse was to come on October 10th.

On that day, Clifford had visited a number of pubs but although he had consumed a fair amount of alcohol, he was by all accounts still sober. It was 8.30pm when Florence Farrington, who also lived at 450 Stockport Road, heard a knock on the front door. Florence opened the door but immediately Clifford pushed past her and dashed upstairs to his wife's room, calling out for her to open the door to him. She refused and it was only now that Florence noticed that Clifford was carrying his rifle. Without further words, Clifford raised the gun and shot off the lock. As Florence ran for help, she heard another shot from inside Irene's room.

By the time the police arrived, Clifford Holmes had carried Irene downstairs and gently placed her on the settee in the kitchen. Irene had been shot but was still alive. For Clifford there was no turning back now. He drew out his bayonet and stabbed her three times. He was found kneeling beside Irene's body, crying bitterly.

Holmes said he had killed Irene because she had been unfaithful to him. His only regret seemed to be that he had not killed himself.

NAME	Clifford Holmes
AGE AT EXECUTION	24
DATE OF EXECUTION	Tuesday, 11th February, 1941
PLACE OF EXECUTION	Manchester
HANGMAN	Not known
ASSISTANT	Not known
DATE OF TRIAL	16th December – 17th December, 1940
LOCATION OF TRIAL	Manchester
PRESIDING JUDGE	Mister Justice Stable
PROSECUTION COUNSEL	Neville J. Laski, T.H. Hinchcliffe
DEFENCE COUNSEL	John Catterall Jolly, Percy Butlin
NUMBER OF VICTIMS	1

VICTIMS DETAILS	
NAME	Irene Holmes
AGE	23
DATE OF MURDER	Thursday, 10th October, 1940
PLACE OF MURDER	450 Stockport Road, Longsight, Manchester
METHOD OF KILLING	Shot/stabbed
RELATIONSHIP TO KILLER	Wife

He had managed to shoot himself in the arm, but the wound was not a serious one.

With his own confession and the evidence of Florence Farrington, there could be little doubt as to the outcome of the trial.

SEVENTEEN-YEAR-OLD William Elliott was minding his own business in Bertram Street, when he saw a man and a woman approaching him. The woman appeared to be distressed and trying to get away from the man, even asking Elliott if he would help her.

To his credit, Elliott did try to intervene. He asked the man, Henry Lyndo White, to leave the girl alone. White replied that the girl, Emily Wardle, would stay where she was until he had finished with her. Elliott walked away but as he did so, he looked back, in time to see White put his hand into his jacket pocket, take something out and then draw his hand across Emily's throat.

Rushing back, Elliott helped Emily to stagger to a shop at 47 Bertram Street. White watched this with interest, crossing to the other side of the road so that he could get a better view. He saw Elliott rush out of the shop, running to fetch the police, and calmly crossed over and entered the shop, where he sat on a table.

Ernest Unwin, the shopkeeper had tried to help Emily, but now told her attacker that she was dead. White seemed to be unperturbed, smiled and said that there was going to be another death. So saying, he cut his own throat and both wrists.

Rushed to hospital, White was given medical attention for three days before being charged with the murder of Emily Wardle. The motive, it seemed, had been nothing but jealousy. Although White himself was married, with four children, he had been separated from his wife, Annie, for some time and had been having an affair with Emily for seven years, though he had known her much longer. He believed that she had been seeing another man and whilst such two-timing behaviour was fine for him, he would not tolerate it in Emily.

Although the trial lasted two days, there could only be one result, especially with William Elliott's testimony. Henry White was hanged at Durham in March, 1941.

NAME	Henry Lyndo White
AGE AT EXECUTION	39
DATE OF EXECUTION	Thursday, 6th March, 1941
PLACE OF EXECUTION	Durham
HANGMAN	Thomas Pierrepoint
ASSISTANT	Not known
DATE OF TRIAL	14th February – 15th February, 1941
LOCATION OF TRIAL	Durham
PRESIDING JUDGE	Mister Justice Charles
PROSECUTION COUNSEL	Doctor J. Charlesworth
DEFENCE COUNSEL	J. Harvey Robson
NUMBER OF VICTIMS	1

VICTIMS DETAILS	
NAME	Emily Wardle
AGE	34
DATE OF MURDER	Sunday, 19th January, 1941
PLACE OF MURDER	Bertram Street, South Shields
METHOD OF KILLING	Cut throat
RELATIONSHIP TO KILLER	Girlfriend

JAMES JOSEPH HAGAN needed some cigarette papers and a copy of the evening newspaper, so at 6.45pm, he asked his 15-year-old daughter, Mary, if she wouldn't mind running to the shop for him. Mary left her house at 15 Brookside Avenue, Waterloo, soon afterwards. When she hadn't returned by 7.10pm, James became a little concerned.

In fact, it was not long afterwards that Mary was found, by Richard Browne and some of his friends, in a concrete blockhouse near Brook Vale Bridge. She had been raped and strangled. Her assailant had left clues and very soon police knew that they were probably looking for a soldier.

To begin with, a piece of bandage had been found by Mary's body, and this turned out to be an army field dressing. A witness, William Hindley, came forward, saying that he had seen a soldier standing by the bridge at around 5.45pm.

Thomas Henry Joseph Todd, aged 15, also came forward. He too had seen a soldier on the bridge on November 1st, the day before the murder. He could identify the figure, as he knew the family, and stated that the man was Samuel Morgan, a soldier in the First Battalion of the Irish Guards. Unfortunately, though, Morgan had gone absent without leave.

The breakthrough came on November 13th, when Constable William Halfacre saw a soldier loitering in a doorway on Streatham Hill, in London. Halfacre asked for identification and the soldier ran off. Eventually he was arrested at the corner of Telford Avenue.

Identified as Morgan, the soldier was sent to Liverpool, where he was interviewed about Mary Hagan. The dressing found near Mary's body was found to be an exact match for the dressing in Morgan's field kit and samples of soil from the blockhouse matched samples taken from his uniform.

Morgan at first tried to put forward a defence of alibi. He claimed that on the night of the murder he had been drinking in the Royal Hotel, at Seaforth. He had been seen there at around 7.40pm by his brother, Francis and a friend, James Shaw. Mary's death had been timed at around 7.30pm and it would

NAME	Samuel Morgan
AGE AT EXECUTION	28
DATE OF EXECUTION	Wednesday, 9th April, 1941
PLACE OF EXECUTION	Liverpool
HANGMAN	Thomas Pierrepoint
ASSISTANT	Herbert Morris
DATE OF TRIAL	10th February – 17th February, 1941
LOCATION OF TRIAL	Liverpool
PRESIDING JUDGE	Mister Justice Stable
PROSECUTION COUNSEL	E. Anthony Hawke
DEFENCE COUNSEL	Edward Wooll
NUMBER OF VICTIMS	1

VICTIMS DETAILS	
NAME	Mary Hagan
AGE	15
DATE OF MURDER	Saturday, 2nd November, 1940
PLACE OF MURDER	Waterloo, Liverpool
METHOD OF KILLING	Strangled
RELATIONSHIP TO KILLER	None

have been impossible for Morgan to have been the killer if this alibi stood. Later however, Morgan made a second statement in which he admitted meeting Mary on the bridge and taking her into the blockhouse.

Found guilty, an attempt was made at the appeal to suggest that his statement had not been voluntary and that if Mary's death had been caused as a result of an indecent assault, and not a rape, Morgan was entitled to a verdict of manslaughter. These technical arguments were dismissed and the sentence confirmed.

On April 9th, 1941, Morgan was hanged at Walton jail. It was nine days short of what would have been Mary Hagan's 16th birthday.

0940

GEORGE ARMSTRONG WAS a British-born subject, an engineer who had spent part of the period 1939 to 1940 serving at sea.

By early 1941, Armstrong was in the United States, then still neutral, where he approached one of the German consuls and offered his services as a spy for the Reich. His offer was accepted, but on returning to this country, so that he could carry out his duties, Armstrong was questioned and subsequently arrested and charged with spying.

Tried at the Old Bailey in May, Armstrong was found guilty and sentenced to death.

His appeal failed on June 23rd and the sentence was then confirmed.

On July 9th, Armstrong became the fourth man hanged as a spy during the Second World War, though he had in fact been the fifth to be sentenced to death. A woman, Dorothy Pamela O'Grady had been condemned but her sentence was subsequently quashed and she was given a term of 14 years in prison, on lesser charges.

NAME	George Johnson Armstrong
AGE AT EXECUTION	39
DATE OF EXECUTION	Wednesday, 9th July, 1941
PLACE OF EXECUTION	Wandsworth
HANGMAN	Thomas Pierrepoint
ASSISTANT	Stephen Wade
DATE OF TRIAL	8th May, 1941
LOCATION OF TRIAL	Old Bailey
PRESIDING JUDGE	Mister Justice Lewis
PROSECUTION COUNSEL	Not known
DEFENCE COUNSEL	Not known
NUMBER OF VICTIMS	Hanged for spying

MARGARET ANNIE GERRING was enjoying a pleasant stroll along Westgate in Morecambe, with her young man, John Pritchard Francis, when they heard a weak female voice from the other side of the road. Going to investigate, they found Elizabeth Smith standing against a concrete pillar. She was soaking wet, shivering with cold and very distressed. Margaret called for help to two airmen, William Thomas Linday and Frederick George Buckingham, and together the four of them carried Elizabeth to a nearby watchman's hut from where she was taken, by car, to the hospital.

Elizabeth was suffering from shock and at first, she seemed to respond to treatment. Unfortunately, she then suffered a relapse and died on December 2nd. An autopsy gave the causes of death as shock, inhalation bronchopneumonia and tuberculosis of part of one lung.

Police began their investigation by questioning Elizabeth's family. Her sister, Beatrice, said that Elizabeth had been seeing an aircraftman, David Williams, for some time. Their letters had been affectionate but Beatrice got the impression that Williams's feelings were much stronger than Elizabeth's.

Joyce Whitely lodged at the same address as Williams and she gave evidence that she had seen David and Elizabeth together at 4.30pm on November 30th. Joyce had then gone out for a short time, returning at 5.45pm when David and Elizabeth were leaving. At 8.45pm, David had returned alone, saying that he had argued with Elizabeth because she was seeing a soldier. Joyce also noticed that David's boots, socks, trousers and tunic cuffs were wet.

At the time Joyce was writing a letter and after a few minutes, David confessed to her that he had knocked Elizabeth out and held her head under the water, but added that she had been all right when he left her. Half an hour later, the police called and took David Williams into custody.

Once poor Elizabeth had died, Williams was charged with murder. In his statement he admitted that they had argued and that a slight struggle had taken place between them. At one point they had both fallen off a narrow

NAME	David Rodger Williams
AGE AT EXECUTION	33
DATE OF EXECUTION	Wednesday, 25th March, 1942
PLACE OF EXECUTION	Liverpool
HANGMAN	Not known
ASSISTANT	Not known
DATE OF TRIAL	4th February, 1942
LOCATION OF TRIAL	Liverpool
PRESIDING JUDGE	MISTER Justice Oliver
PROSECUTION COUNSEL	G.J. Lynsky, A.E. Baucher
DEFENCE COUNSEL	E. Rowson
NUMBER OF VICTIMS	1

VICTIMS DETAILS

NAME	Elizabeth Smith (Died Tuesday, 2nd December)
AGE	28
DATE OF MURDER	Sunday, 30th November, 1941
PLACE OF MURDER	Westgate, Morecambe
METHOD OF KILLING	Battered/asphyxiated
RELATIONSHIP TO KILLER	Girlfriend

bridge but he had managed to climb out of the water and had pulled Elizabeth out. He had then waited with her until she recovered before walking off in a kind of daze.

David's defence was therefore one of accidental death. James McFadzean, a pathologist, examined the clothing David Williams had been wearing and found that they showed signs of mud up to the knees of the trousers and up to the top of the arms on the jacket. This hardly fitted in with a fall into water but did seem to agree with a picture of him standing in the water, holding Elizabeth down.

It was enough for the jury to reject Williams's claims and find him guilty of murder.

IN OCTOBER, 1941, Muriel Golding broke off her engagement to Cyril Johnson. It was a decision that would lead to the deaths of two people.

The following month, Johnson, a soldier in the West Yorkshire Regiment, met up with Daisy Smail, who lived with her sister, Maggie, in Beaver Road, Ashford. Johnson told Daisy of his broken engagement and she extended a sympathetic ear. They became friendly and even went to a couple of dances together.

On February 5th, 1942, Johnson called on the Smails and arranged to take Daisy to a dance later that evening. Before that, Daisy had to go out with Maggie, and Johnson was allowed to remain alone in the house for a couple of hours. He amused himself by reading a murder mystery entitled A Question of Proof.

Daisy and Johnson went to the dance and he then saw her safely home. Johnson was supposed to report back to his unit that evening but told Daisy that he would risk leaving it until the morning as it was by now rather late. Daisy gave him permission to sleep on the sofa.

It was 6.00am on February 6th, when Daisy left to go to her work. When she returned later that day it was to find Maggie dead in bed. She had been battered around the head with a poker and a scarf was tied tightly around her neck. She was wearing nothing except a pyjama jacket.

If there were any doubts that Johnson had been the killer, these were dispelled the following day when his ex-fiancée, Muriel Golding, received a letter from Johnson. The letter mentioned that she would soon read about the murder and suggested to Muriel that it was in some way her fault. Johnson claimed that he had lived in hell since she had called off the engagement and since then he had hated all females. He went on to claim that Maggie had teased him, just like Muriel had, and this was why he had killed her.

Arrested and put on trial for murder, Johnson was found guilty and recommended to mercy on account of his youth. His original execution date was fixed for April 8th, but this was cancelled when Johnson gave notice of appeal. Subsequently, Johnson withdrew

NAME	Cyril Johnson
AGE AT EXECUTION	20
DATE OF EXECUTION	Wednesday, 15th April, 1942
PLACE OF EXECUTION	Wandsworth
HANGMAN	Thomas Pierrepoint
ASSISTANT	Henry Critchell
DATE OF TRIAL	19th March – 20th March, 1942
LOCATION OF TRIAL	Old Bailey
PRESIDING JUDGE	Mister Justice Croom-Johnson
PROSECUTION COUNSEL	Not known
DEFENCE COUNSEL	Hector Hughes
NUMBER OF VICTIMS	1

VICTIMS DETAILS	
NAME	Maggie Smail
AGE	29
DATE OF MURDER	Friday, 6th February, 1942
PLACE OF MURDER	Beaver Road, Ashford, Kent
METHOD OF KILLING	Battered/strangled
RELATIONSHIP TO KILLER	None

his appeal and a new date was set exactly one week later. Cyril Johnson had gained seven extra days of life.

FREDERICK AUSTIN, A married soldier from Colchester, had been stationed in Bristol and rather than have his wife, Lilian, living so far away from him, he found lodgings for her at a boarding house in Redlands.

After a brief leave, Austin was due back at his camp on January 31st. Early that evening though, the sound of a shot came from Austin's room and Frederick dashed downstairs to announce to his landlady that his rifle had gone off whilst he was cleaning it and he had accidentally shot his wife.

Lilian Austin was in fact already dead. Her body lay in front of the fireplace and it looked as if she had been sitting on a box that was positioned nearby and had been used as a sort of stool. Austin explained that his wife had been darning stockings at the time of the accident.

Doctor Webster, a Home Office expert, was called in to examine the room and Lilian's body to try to determine exactly what had happened. His investigations showed that the angle of entry of the bullet meant that the rifle that fired the shot had been held in the normal firing position at Austin's shoulder and the shooting could not therefore be accidental.

Faced with this evidence, Austin now admitted that three days before the shooting, Lilian had found a letter in his kit bag. This letter was from another woman and had led to an argument. At the time he had put a live round into his rifle in order to frighten her and had then forgotten all about it until he was cleaning the rifle and the shot was fired.

There was still the evidence of Doctor Webster to consider, though. If Austin had believed that the rifle was unloaded, having forgotten about the live round, why should he have deliberately aimed from the shoulder and pulled the trigger?

Nevertheless, the jury took two hours and 20 minutes to decide on Austin's guilt and even then recommended him to mercy on account of the apparent provocation he had suffered.

NAME	Frederick James Austin
AGE AT EXECUTION	28
DATE OF EXECUTION	Thursday, 30th April, 1942
PLACE OF EXECUTION	Bristol
HANGMAN	Not known
ASSISTANT	Not known
DATE OF TRIAL	3rd March, 1942
LOCATION OF TRIAL	Winchester
PRESIDING JUDGE	Lord Chief Justice, Lord Caldecote
PROSECUTION COUNSEL	G.D. Roberts, J. Scott Henderson
DEFENCE COUNSEL	J.G. Trapnell, W.J.M. Dennis
NUMBER OF VICTIMS	1

VICTIMS DETAILS	
NAME	Lilian Dorothy Pax Austin
AGE	22
DATE OF MURDER	Saturday, 31st January, 1942
PLACE OF MURDER	Montrose Avenue, Redlands, Bristol
METHOD OF KILLING	Shot
RELATIONSHIP TO KILLER	Wife

1942

WHEN TWO LITTLE girls, Doreen Hearne and Kathleen Trundell, did not return home from school on the afternoon of November 19th, 1941, a massive search was organised. Three days later, their bodies were found, some 40 yards apart, on either side of a pathway through Rough Wood, four miles away from their homes. Both girls had been rendered unconscious by strangulation, before being stabbed repeatedly in the throat and chest. They had not been sexually interfered with and the crime seemed to be completely without motive.

The police were fortunate in finding witnesses almost immediately. A group of children, also on their way home from school, said that they had seen the two girls climbing into an army lorry, which had then driven off towards High Wycombe. One witness, 13-year-old Norman George Page, added that the lorry had a poppy on the front and gave details of its identification numbers. The lorry was traced to an army camp at Haslemere Lodge, Yoxford, in Suffolk and investigations soon moved to that location.

An identification parade was organised and whilst four children failed to make an identification, one girl picked out a man whom she said looked like the driver of the lorry. This man was Harold Hill. When questioned further, Hill turned to a fellow soldier and said: "You saw me at twenty minutes past four."

The police read much into this statement. No one had mentioned that the girls had been seen climbing into the army lorry at around 4.15pm and so they believed that the only way Hill could have known that such a time was significant was if he was responsible for the crime. This completely misses two points.

In the first place, Hill could well have had an alibi involving another soldier who by coincidence he had seen at about 4.15pm or 4.20pm. Secondly, since schools tended to allow pupils to leave around 4.00pm, anyone should have known what time was the crucial one.

Be that as it may, the police dug further into Hill's movements. It was shown that his lorry speedometer had a discrepancy of 20 miles for which he could not account. There

NAME	Harold Hill
AGE AT EXECUTION	26
DATE OF EXECUTION	Friday, 1st May, 1942
PLACE OF EXECUTION	Oxford
HANGMAN	Not known
ASSISTANT	Not known
DATE OF TRIAL	2nd March – 5th March, 1942
LOCATION OF TRIAL	Old Bailey
PRESIDING JUDGE	Mister Justice Humphreys
PROSECUTION COUNSEL	P.E. Sandlands, Christmas Humphreys
DEFENCE COUNSEL	Richard O'Sullivan, S.L. Elborne
NUMBER OF VICTIMS	2

VICTIMS DETAILS	
NAMES	Doreen Joyce Hearne; Kathleen Trundell
AGES	8; 6
DATE OF MURDER	Wednesday, 19th November, 1941
PLACE OF MURDER	Rough Wood, Penn, Buckinghamshire
METHOD OF KILLING	Asphyxiated/stabbed
RELATIONSHIP TO KILLER	None; none

were bloodstains on a blouse and a pair of trousers found in his kit and he had no explanation for those. A khaki handkerchief had been found near one of the bodies and the laundry mark on this, RA 1019, was the same as marks found on items of Hill's clothing. Finally, one of his fingerprints was found on one of the children's gas masks and Hill had two previous convictions for assaults on young girls.

At his trial, Hill tried to put forward a defence of schizophrenia but the jury came to believe that the only thing he was suffering from was sadism.

JAMES RIGBY WAS enjoying a stroll through Victoria Park, in Southport, at around 10.00am on February 8th, 1942, when he came across the body of a young woman. Her clothing was badly torn and had been pulled down to just below her breasts, pinning her arms to her sides. Her dress was torn from top to bottom and the lower parts of her body had been exposed. Rigby ran off to tell the police what he had found.

The body was soon identified as that of Imeldred Osliff, an auxiliary nurse, who lived with her parents at 'Bowness', a house on Moss Lane, Churchtown. Her father, Frederick Osliff, soon gave police a name to work on. Imeldred had been seeing a young man named Douglas Edmondson and marriage had been discussed between them. Frederick and his wife had objected to the match, mainly because they were Roman Catholics and Edmondson wasn't, but the two had gone on seeing each other.

It soon became clear that Imeldred had probably died at some time after 9.00pm on the Saturday. A fellow nurse, Rose Evelyn Martin, said that she had taken a telephone call at 8.05pm on February 7th. Imeldred seemed rather annoyed when she took the call and left the hospital shortly afterwards, at 8.15pm.

The police were able to trace the movements of Edmondson. Joseph Dean was the manager of the Zetland Hotel and he said that Edmondson, whom he knew, had come into the hotel at 11.00am on February 7th. He stayed there until lunch time and returned again at 7.00pm, finally leaving at 9.00pm, announcing that he had an appointment to keep. A full-scale search was now launched for Douglas Edmondson.

For his part, Edmondson was doing his best to evade capture. He was known to be in Liverpool late on Sunday, February 8th, for he handed a suitcase in at the Y.M.C.A., and when it was opened this was found to contain a handbag and some letters, all of which were identified as belonging to Imeldred. The following day he was at Birmingham and it was here that he was finally arrested, at New Street Station. He immediately confessed to having killed Imeldred.

NAME	Douglas Edmondson
AGE AT EXECUTION	28
DATE OF EXECUTION	Wednesday, 24th June, 1942
PLACE OF EXECUTION	Liverpool
HANGMAN	Not known
ASSISTANT	Not known
DATE OF TRIAL	20th April, 1942
LOCATION OF TRIAL	Liverpool
PRESIDING JUDGE	Mister Justice Wrottesley
PROSECUTION COUNSEL	Neville J. Laski
DEFENCE COUNSEL	Edward Wooll
NUMBER OF VICTIMS	1

VICTIMS DETAILS	
NAME	Imeldred Maria Osliff
AGE	28
DATE OF MURDER	Saturday, 7th February, 1942
PLACE OF MURDER	Victoria Park, Southport, Lancashire
METHOD OF KILLING	Strangled
RELATIONSHIP TO KILLER	Girlfriend

Douglas Edmondson had already had a distinguished war by 1942. Having joined the navy in 1931, he was on board the Ark Royal when it suffered a 24-hour-long attack by enemy planes, and was also involved in the relief of troops from Dunkirk. Thereafter though, a change had come over Edmondson.

In June 1940 he had slashed his left wrist in a suicide attempt and his behaviour generally had become rather strange. For these reasons, an attempt was made to excuse his crime as one of insanity. That defence failed and, his appeal having been dismissed on June 8th, 1942, Edmondson was hanged at Liverpool.

1942

CONSIDERING THE CRIMES laid at his door, one would think that Gordon Cummins would have had almost as much publicity as his infamous ancestor, Jack the Ripper.

The original Ripper murdered some five women in the space of four months. Cummins murdered four women within a week. His crimes, though, were committed in the darkest days of the Second World War, when newsprint itself was restricted and his offences were not as widely reported as they should have been.

Married in 1936, Cummins was called up in 1941 and chose to join the R.A.F. After initial training he was billeted in St John's Wood, north London, early in 1942. In the February of that year, he went on a murder spree.

Cummins left St John's Wood on the night of Saturday, February 7th. After borrowing some money from his wife, he headed off to the bright lights of London. The following day, the body of Evelyn Hamilton was discovered in an air-raid shelter in Montagu Street. She had been strangled with her own scarf and the motive seemed to be robbery. Her handbag, containing around £80, was missing.

That same Sunday, Cummins met up with Evelyn Oatley, an attractive prostitute, who took him back to her flat in Wardour Street. Her body was discovered on February 10th. She had been strangled and savagely mutilated by means of a kitchen can-opener. Her killer had also cut her throat, after death.

His lust to kill temporarily satiated, Cummins did not attack again until Thursday, February 12th. On that day he strangled another prostitute, Margaret Lowe. She too was mutilated and this time Cummins used a knife and a razor.

The final victim was Doris Jouannet who was again strangled and mutilated in her flat at 187 Sussex Gardens, Paddington. Cummins had already collected a number of souvenirs from other victims and from Doris he took a fountain pen and a comb.

Although he had killed four women, Cummins still wanted more. On Friday he picked up another woman – Margaret Heywood, known as Greta. They had a drink and a bite to eat and then, whilst walking

NAME	Gordon Frederick Cummins
AGE AT EXECUTION	28
DATE OF EXECUTION	Thursday, 25th June, 1942
PLACE OF EXECUTION	Wandsworth
HANGMAN	Albert Pierrepoint
ASSISTANT	Harry Kirk
DATE OF TRIAL	27th April – 28th April, 1942
LOCATION OF TRIAL	Old Bailey
PRESIDING JUDGE	Mister Justice Asquith
PROSECUTION COUNSEL	G.B. McClure
DEFENCE COUNSEL	John Flowers
NUMBER OF VICTIMS	4 (possibly 6)

VICTIMS DETAILS	
NAMES	Evelyn Margaret Hamilton; Evelyn Oatley (Nita Ward)
AGES	40; 35
DATES OF MURDERS	Saturday, 7th February, 1942; Sunday, 8th February, 1942
PLACE OF MURDERS	Montagu Place, London; Wardour Street, London
METHOD OF KILLING	Strangled; strangled
RELATIONSHIP TO KILLER	None; none
NAMES	Margaret Florence Lowe; Doris Jouannet (Doris Robson)
AGES	43; 35
DATES OF MURDERS	Thursday, 12th February, 1942; Thursday, 12th February, 1942
PLACE OF MURDERS	Gosfield Street, London; 187 Sussex Gardens, London
METHOD OF KILLING	Strangled; strangled
RELATIONSHIP TO KILLER	None; none

down the Haymarket, Cummins began to pressurise her. She walked off but he caught up with her, dragged her into a doorway and began to throttle her. Greta passed out and would undoubtedly have become victim number five but for the intervention of a delivery boy, who went to see what was going on. Cummins fled the scene, leaving behind him his R.A.F. gas mask which had his name, rank and serial number on it.

Still determined to claim another victim, Cummins then picked up a prostitute who called herself Kathleen King, but whose real name was Mulcahy. She took him back to her flat at 29 Southwick Street. where he gave her £5 for sex. She began to undress. whereupon Cummins leapt upon her and tried to strangle her. More resourceful than the others, Kathleen kicked his shins and screamed loudly. This seemed to shock Cummins back to some kind of normality and after giving her another £5, he walked out, leaving behind his service belt.

Once the attacks had been reported and the gas mask and belt handed in, the police knew exactly who they were looking for. Traced to his billet, the police were dismayed to find that Cummins had an excellent alibi for three of the murders. The billet passbook showed clearly that Cummins had been checked in before midnight all that week. Further inquiries. though. led the officers to discover that men were in the habit of signing each other in and covering for colleagues who went back out after they had been checked. Indeed, another airman came forward to say that one night, he and Cummins had both left together, by means of a fire escape.

A search of Cummins's belongings was organised and here police found a cigarette case belonging to Margaret Lowe and another belonging to Evelyn Oatley. They also found Doris Jouannet's fountain pen, which even had her initials engraved upon it. Cummins's fingerprints were taken and these matched some that had been found in Margaret Lowe's flat and on the tin-opener he had used on Evelyn.

The trial lasted two days but the jury took only half an hour to return a guilty verdict on the one murder, that of Evelyn Oatley. In fact, two other murders had been attributed to Cummins: that of Maple Church in October 1941 and of a Mrs Humphries in Gloucester Crescent, shortly afterwards.

A LTHOUGH JOSE KEY and Alphonse Timmerman were hanged on the same day, for spying, their crimes were totally separate.

Key was a British subject who had been born in Gibraltar. And that is where he spied for the Axis powers, reporting the movements of land forces, Allied warships that passed through the port and air movements in and around the Rock. When he was arrested, he was found to be in possession of lists of ship and troop movements and was consequently sent back to England for trial.

Timmerman was Belgian and before the war had been a ship's steward. In this capacity he had visited many British ports and knew his way around them very well. He was sent to England in the autumn of 1941 and, posing as a refugee from war-torn Europe, was to concentrate on sending naval and military secrets back to Germany. When he was interviewed he was found to have crystals for making invisible ink and a large quantity of English and American money.

Both men were hanged on July 7th, just six days after Key's 34th birthday.

NAMES	Jose Estella Key; Alphonse Louis Eugene Timmerman
AGES AT EXECUTION	34; 28
DATE OF EXECUTION	Tuesday, 7th July, 1942
PLACE OF EXECUTION	Wandsworth
HANGMAN	Albert Pierrepoint
ASSISTANTS	Harry Kirk, Stephen Wade, Henry Critchell
DATE OF TRIAL	15th May – 18th May, 1942
LOCATION OF TRIAL	Old Bailey
PRESIDING JUDGE	Mister Justice Humphreys
PROSECUTION COUNSEL	Not known
DEFENCE COUNSEL	Not known
NUMBER OF VICTIMS	Hanged for spying

PAULINE BARKER HAD been married twice already when she became involved with a Greek man named Arthur Anderson, finally moving in with him, at 184 Belsize Road, London.

There were other people who rented rooms in that house, including Katherine Patricia Maher, and she would later say that Anderson did very little to help Pauline around the house. As a result of that there were many arguments between Pauline and Arthur and on some occasions he was known to hit her – he had once even threatened to shoot her.

Things grew so bad between Pauline and Arthur that on May 27th, 1942, Arthur packed his bags and moved back to his parents' house. Arthur's mother had also been married more than once and upon his arrival at her house, Arthur told his brother, Hector Demetrius Apergis, that the cause of the trouble was Lydia Barker, Pauline's mother. When she visited, the two women only seemed to have time for each other and he was excluded. In Arthur's opinion, the final straw had come when Pauline had gone to a party without him, and that was why he had moved out.

At around 1.00pm on May 31st, Arthur Anderson returned to Belsize Road and called out to Pauline. Katherine Maher heard Pauline reply that she was busy but nevertheless she went out to talk to Arthur for a few minutes. Pauline then returned to the house and after hanging around for a couple of minutes, Arthur walked off to the Princess of Wales public house, where both he and Pauline were well known.

Arthur was back in that same pub at 7.00pm and asked to speak to the landlord, Alfred Herbert Rice. Arthur announced to Mr Rice that he was going to commit a murder. Alfred Rice naturally enough thought that Arthur was joking and thought nothing more of it. Twenty minutes later though, Arthur returned, showed Rice a revolver and even removed a spent cartridge from the chamber. The gun was handed over, Arthur asking Rice to hide it and he would tell the police he had thrown it away. In fact, Alfred Rice later handed the murder weapon over to the police.

NAME	Arthur Anderson (Apergis)
AGE AT EXECUTION	52
DATE OF EXECUTION	Tuesday, 21st July, 1942
PLACE OF EXECUTION	Wandsworth
HANGMAN	Albert Pierrepoint
ASSISTANT	Herbert Morris
DATE OF TRIAL	23rd June, 1942
LOCATION OF TRIAL	Old Bailey
PRESIDING JUDGE	Not known
PROSECUTION COUNSEL	G.B. McClure, Christmas Humphreys
DEFENCE COUNSEL	Not known
NUMBER OF VICTIMS	1

VICTIMS DETAILS	
NAME	Pauline Barker
AGE	52
DATE OF MURDER	Sunday, 31st May, 1942
PLACE OF MURDER	184 Belsize Road, London
METHOD OF KILLING	Shot
RELATIONSHIP TO KILLER	Ex-girlfriend

Arthur had it seemed gone back to Belsize Road and asked yet another tenant there, Alan Philip Sedgwick, where Pauline was. Told she was in the kitchen, Arthur closed the door and went to that room. Three minutes later, a loud report rang out, followed by the sound of running footsteps and the front door being slammed. Alan Sedgwick found Pauline's body, lying on the kitchen floor.

Arthur Anderson was arrested by Inspector Harold Cripps at 7.45pm. He claimed to have no memory of the crime and denied telling Alfred Rice that he was going out to commit a murder. Those denials did nothing to save him from the hangman's rope.

1942

THERE WAS SOMETHING rather suspicious about the group of men walking down Kashmir Road and the men in the police car watching them decided to investigate. Sure enough, as soon as the car turned into Clonard Gardens, guns were drawn and shots were fired.

A running gun-battle followed, with the six gunmen finally running to the back of Cawnpore Street. There they rushed into the kitchen of number 53, to be followed quickly by Constable Patrick Murphy, his colleagues having gone around to the front of the house to block any escape.

Constable Murphy reached the middle of the kitchen before five bullets slammed into him and brought him down. It was by now 3.15pm and only moments later, the front door was burst down by other officers and, realising that there was no escape, the six gunmen lay down their arms and surrendered. All six were then charged with the murder of Constable Murphy.

An important witness at the trial was the firearms expert Robert Churchill. He testified that he had examined six weapons, 15 bullets, 24 cartridge cases and four misfired bullets. Of the five bullets recovered from the body of the dead constable, three had been fired from Exhibit Six, a Webley and two from Exhibit Two, a Luger. This, of course, proved that at least two of the accused had fired bullets into the victim and so were equally guilty of murder.

In the event, after a deliberation of more than two hours, the jury returned guilty verdicts against all six men: Joe Cahill, Henry Cordner, John Terence Oliver, William James Perry, Patrick Joseph Simpson, and Thomas Williams. An execution date of August 18th was set for all six men. This date was cancelled when the men announced their intention to appeal.

A petition for the reprieve of the condemned men was organised and by August 22nd, had attracted over 250,000 signatures. Five days later, on August 27th, the appeal was lost and all six death sentences were confirmed.

In the event, on August 30th, reprieves were announced for five of the six. All had

NAME	Thomas Joseph Williams
AGE AT EXECUTION	19
DATE OF EXECUTION	Wednesday, 2nd September, 1942
PLACE OF EXECUTION	Belfast
HANGMAN	Thomas Pierrepoint
ASSISTANT	Albert Pierrepoint
DATE OF TRIAL	28th July – 30th July, 1942
LOCATION OF TRIAL	Belfast
PRESIDING JUDGE	Lord Justice Murphy
PROSECUTION COUNSEL	J. McDermott, Edmond Warnock, C.L. Sheil
DEFENCE COUNSEL	Cecil Lavery, J. Agnew
NUMBER OF VICTIMS	1

VICTIMS DETAILS	
NAME	Patrick Murphy
AGE	38
DATE OF MURDER	Sunday, 5th April, 1942
PLACE OF MURDER	53 Cawnpore Street, Belfast
METHOD OF KILLING	Shot
RELATIONSHIP TO KILLER	None

their sentences commuted to life imprisonment with the exception of Patrick Simpson, the youngest man at 18 years, who had his sentence commuted to 15 years. No such mercy was shown to the sixth man, Thomas Williams, and he perished on the gallows at Belfast's Crumlin Road prison.

HAROLD MERRY WAS a married man with five children, whose ages ranged from one to 14 years. Nevertheless, in July 1941, he met and started paying attention to Joyce Dixon and they became lovers.

Merry told Joyce that he was a single man and the relationship developed to such a point that in January 1942, she took him to meet her mother, Kate Elizabeth Dixon. On March 20th, Merry approached Kate and asked for permission to become engaged to her daughter. Kate was pleased to accept and later gave permission for Merry to take Joyce down to London to buy the ring.

Joyce and Merry went to London and stayed at the Museum Hotel at 36 Bloomsbury Street. The manageress, Doris Vera Webster, would later give evidence that they booked in on March 21st, stayed until the 27th, and appeared to be very happy. It was whilst the lovers were in London that Kate discovered that Merry was married.

When Joyce returned on Friday, March 27th, her mother faced her with her news. Joyce saw Merry the following night and said she was very upset, but at the same time, she was not prepared to stop seeing Merry and made arrangements to meet him the next night.

On Saturday, March 29th, Joyce left home at 3.45pm. She never returned and the next morning, her brother, Victor Oliver Dixon, went out looking for her. Victor arrived at 205 Hewell Road, Redditch, where Merry lived with his wife, Florence. It was whilst Victor was talking to Florence that he heard a noise from upstairs and upon checking, found Merry with a cord twisted around his neck, trying to strangle himself. Victor removed the cord, accused Merry of doing something to his sister and was horrified to hear him then confess to killing her.

Merry told Victor where Joyce's body could be found. She was discovered by Constable Joseph Porter, floating in a pool in a field at Turves Green. Medical evidence would show that she had been strangled to the point of unconsciousness and then put into the water. The actual cause of death was drowning. Merry made a full confession but then, on April 2nd, he changed his mind.

NAME	Harold Oswald Merry
AGE AT EXECUTION	40
DATE OF EXECUTION	Thursday, 10th September, 1942
PLACE OF EXECUTION	Birmingham
HANGMAN	Thomas Pierrepoint
ASSISTANT	Henry Critchell
DATE OF TRIAL	17th July – 18th July, 1942
LOCATION OF TRIAL	Birmingham
PRESIDING JUDGE	Mister Justice Croom-Johnston
PROSECUTION COUNSEL	Paul F. Sandlands, A.P. Marshall
DEFENCE COUNSEL	John F. Bourke, G.T. Meredith
NUMBER OF VICTIMS	1

VICTIMS DETAILS	
NAME	Joyce Dixon
AGE	27
DATE OF MURDER	Saturday, 29th March, 1942
PLACE OF MURDER	Turves Green, Northfield, Birmingham
METHOD OF KILLING	Drowned/strangled
RELATIONSHIP TO KILLER	Girlfriend

Merry now claimed that they had decided on a suicide pact. He produced a note that he had written and that both he and Joyce had signed. He went on to say that they had gone to the field, where he had killed Joyce before trying to strangle himself. When he did not succeed, he tried to drown himself, but the water was not deep enough, so he returned home.

It was for the jury to decide if this was murder or manslaughter. Evidence was given that Joyce's signature on the suicide note was genuine but this did not save Harold Merry.

1942

SAMUEL DASHWOOD AND George Silverosa were two petty crooks who cared little for anyone or anything, apart from themselves.

Thursday, April 30th, 1942, saw the two men meet up in a cafe in Bethnal Green. Dashwood produced a .45 gun and announced to his friend that he was going to "do a job". Silverosa decided he would tag along.

Walking down Hackney Road, looking for a suitable target, Dashwood spotted a pawnbrokers. He suggested that this was a good place and Silverosa agreed. It was early closing day in the area, so they decided it might be better to wait until the shop was being shut up. They bided their time until around 1.00pm when Leonard Moules, who ran the shop, came out to put up the shutters.

Though Dashwood and Silverosa would argue which of them carried out the attack, Moules was followed into his shop and battered into unconsciousness. His safe was then ransacked and the two thieves made good their escape. Moules would never regain consciousness and died nine days later.

The police had two excellent clues. In the first place, a palm print had been left on the inside of the safe. Since the print did not match Leonard Moules's hands, it was reasonable to assume that it had been made by his attackers. In addition, a soldier came forward to say that he had been in a cafe in Bethnal Green on the morning of the murder when he had seen a man draw out a gun. The soldier gave good descriptions and said that the men referred to each other as George and Sam.

It was Dashwood who was arrested first. He put all the blame on Silverosa. In his turn, when Silverosa was picked up he blamed Dashwood for the attack. In fact, both men were very much implicated. The palm print turned out to be Silverosa's, but Moules's injuries were consistent with him being struck repeatedly with the gun and it was known that the weapon was Dashwood's.

The trial contained its own sensation when Dashwood dismissed his counsel on the penultimate day. He asked for fresh counsel and when this request was refused, said he would defend himself.

NAMES	Samuel Sydney Dashwood; George William Silverosa
AGES AT EXECUTION	23; 22
DATE OF EXECUTION	Thursday, 10th September, 1942
PLACE OF EXECUTION	Pentonville
HANGMAN	Albert Pierrepoint
ASSISTANTS	Herbert Morris, Steve Wade, Harry Kirk
DATE OF TRIAL	17th July – 21st July, 1942
LOCATION OF TRIAL	Old Bailey
PRESIDING JUDGE	Mister Justice Wrottesley
PROSECUTION COUNSEL	L.A. Byrne
DEFENCE COUNSEL	Serjeant Sullivan, Mister Fordham
NUMBER OF VICTIMS	1

VICTIMS DETAILS

NAME	Leonard Moules (Died Saturday, 9th May)
AGE	71
DATE OF MURDER	Thursday, 30th April, 1942
PLACE OF MURDER	Hackney Road, Shoreditch, London
METHOD OF KILLING	Battered
RELATIONSHIP TO KILLERS	None; none

At his appeal, Dashwood tried to suggest that because he had dismissed his counsel, he must have been insane at the time and should therefore have the verdict quashed. The judges rightly pointed out that this would set a precedent whereby in future any defendant could see how the trial was going and if he thought he might lose, dismiss his counsel towards the closing stages and later claim insanity.

On September 10th, the two men who had robbed and killed together were hanged together.

AT 8.20PM ON July 15th, 1942, 11-year-old Sheila Wilson went home for her supper. She should have been in for the night now, but as she was eating she told her mother, Edith, that she had been given 2d to run an errand afterwards.

Edith Wilson believed that one of the neighbours had asked Sheila to bring a newspaper and so gave her permission. So it was that at 8.33pm, Sheila ran off to complete her errand. She was never seen alive by her mother again.

Once it became clear that something had happened to Sheila, the police were called in. The description of Sheila's clothing – a green check dress – was to give the newspapers a 'hook', and they were to call the subsequent investigations the 'Girl in Green case'.

In fact, though she could not have known it, Edith Wilson had already visited the place where her daughter had been taken. Sheila's brother, Derek, reported that he had seen Sheila, earlier in the day, playing near number 19. Edith visited the house to ask Rose Ryder, who lived there, whether she or her children had seen anything of Sheila. They hadn't, and neither it seemed had Rose's lodger, Patrick William Kingston.

The police inquiries continued, but it was not until July 20th, that those investigations led them inexorably back to number 19, and the room occupied by Patrick Kingston. Sheila's body, a cord tied tightly around her neck, was found underneath the floorboards and the press headlines changed to stories of the 'Girl in Green murder'.

Kingston had disappeared and there seemed to be sightings of him all over the region. The day after Sheila had been found, a man fitting Kingston's description walked into Ilford police station and announced who he was, but by the time officers could attend, he had vanished again.

The press helped in the search. Kingston had been injured in a bomb blast in November 1940, and as a result he had a limp and a mutilated left hand. This description, along with his photograph, was published on July 22nd. Kingston was arrested later that same day and could only say that he had no idea why he had done it.

NAME	Patrick William Kingston
AGE AT EXECUTION	38
DATE OF EXECUTION	Tuesday, 6th October, 1942
PLACE OF EXECUTION	Wandsworth
HANGMAN	Albert Pierrepoint
ASSISTANT	Herbert Morris
DATE OF TRIAL	14th September, 1942
LOCATION OF TRIAL	Old Bailey
PRESIDING JUDGE	Mister Justice Hallett
PROSECUTION COUNSEL	Not known
DEFENCE COUNSEL	E.M. Hoy
NUMBER OF VICTIMS	1

VICTIMS DETAILS	
NAME	Sheila Margaret Wilson
AGE	11
DATE OF MURDER	Wednesday, 15th July, 1942
PLACE OF MURDER	19 Leahurst Road, Lewisham, London
METHOD OF KILLING	Strangled
RELATIONSHIP TO KILLER	None

At Kingston's trial, at the Old Bailey, he announced that he would rather plead guilty than have the case against him formally proved. As a result, he was sentenced to death, the entire proceedings lasting just five minutes.

Perhaps the greatest irony in this tragic case is that just two months before her death, Sheila Wilson had been in Dorset, where she had been evacuated for safety. In May 1942, she returned home, her parents believing that London was now safe enough.

1942

LIEUTENANT PATRICK LESLIE Rice had enjoyed his leave in Newcastle upon Tyne and now it was time to say goodbye to his wife of almost two months, Margaret.

Margaret was a corporal in the W.A.A.F., and although she had been born in Essex, where her parents still lived, she now lodged at Kenton. It was the early hours of Saturday, June 13th, 1942 when Margaret saw her husband off at Newcastle Central Station. She took no notice of the two young men enjoying a cup of coffee in the station buffet and set off to walk back to her billet.

It was 8.30am when a milkman named James Jones was making his deliveries along Claremont Road, Town Moor. As he passed near numbers 22 and 23, he saw something lying on the grass verge, behind a two-foot water pipe. Jones discovered that it was the body of Margaret Rice. Her clothing had been pulled up and her underclothing removed, leaving her naked from the neck down.

Amongst the items scattered around, officers discovered two pieces of the vulcanite handle of a revolver. It seemed logical to assume that Margaret had been battered with the handle of a gun, which had broken in the attack.

After some days, a young man named William Ambrose Collins made himself known to the police. Collins lived at 17 Framlington Place, Newcastle, very close to the murder scene. He admitted that he had been in the area at about the time of the murder and as such, thought it better to come forward. He gave a detailed explanation of his movements on the day Margaret died.

According to Collins, he had met a friend, Edward Bircham Morgan, at the Royal Oak pub, on the evening of Friday, June 12th. They ended up at Newcastle station at around 12.30am on Saturday morning, where they had a coffee together. Morgan then drove Collins to Park Terrace, close to Framlington Place, where the two men parted.

When Collins's story was checked with Morgan, he confirmed the times and the details, but he also told police that he had sold a Webley revolver to Collins, for the sum of 30/-, on the Friday night.

Collins's house was searched and

NAME	William Ambrose Collins
AGE AT EXECUTION	21
DATE OF EXECUTION	Wednesday, 28th October, 1942
PLACE OF EXECUTION	Durham
HANGMAN	Thomas Pierrepoint
ASSISTANT	Not known
DATE OF TRIAL	26th August – 27th August, 1942
LOCATION OF TRIAL	Newcastle
PRESIDING JUDGE	Mister Justice Cassels
PROSECUTION COUNSEL	C. Paley Scott, Doctor J. Charlesworth
DEFENCE COUNSEL	J. Harvey Robson
NUMBER OF VICTIMS	1

VICTIMS DETAILS	
NAME	Margaret Mary Rice
AGE	24
DATE OF MURDER	Saturday, 13th June, 1942
PLACE OF MURDER	Claremont Road, Town Moor, Newcastle
METHOD OF KILLING	Battered
RELATIONSHIP TO KILLER	None

underneath a bolster, the Webley was discovered. The handle was broken and one missing piece was found in a suitcase under the bed. Together with the other pieces the handle was now complete. Collins was charged with murder.

The trial lasted two days and Collins. a merchant navy apprentice, tried to put forward a defence that he was not responsible for his actions. He said that he had been in a cycle accident four years before and had sustained a head injury, which made him prone to mental instability. The jury took only 20 minutes to decide that this had no bearing on the case.

DUNCAN SCOTT-FORD, who was born in Plymouth in September, 1921, served as a merchant seaman on board a British vessel making regular trips between this country and Lisbon. As such, he proved a most attractive figure to German agents.

Approached in Lisbon, Scott-Ford heard the promises of untold financial rewards and agreed to work for Germany, supplying information on the British merchant navy in return for money. The deal was sealed with a payment of 1,800 Escudos, which at rates current in 1942, amounted to around £18.

Scott-Ford soon returned to Lisbon with information he had gathered and handed this over to his paymasters, who now sprang the trap they had so carefully constructed. There would be no more money and if Scott-Ford refused to carry on with his work, the Germans would let the British authorities know what he had been up to. And the penalty for spying was death.

Unable to extricate himself from this no-win situation, Scott-Ford continued to supply information about his ship and others in convoys. He gathered some of this knowledge by visiting bars in seaports and talking to other merchant seamen and service personnel. In due course these activities came to the attention of the British authorities and Scott-Ford was arrested. In his possession was found detailed information on ships, their movements, speeds and courses, and even the aircraft cover that would be provided.

There is little doubt that Scott-Ford could have been very dangerous to British and allied interests had his activities been allowed to continue longer than they did. As it turned out, his spying career was permanently curtailed on 3rd November, 1942.

NAME	Duncan Alexander Croall Scott-Ford
AGE AT EXECUTION	21
DATE OF EXECUTION	Tuesday, 3rd November, 1942
PLACE OF EXECUTION	Wandsworth
HANGMAN	Albert Pierrepoint
ASSISTANT	Harry Kirk
DATE OF TRIAL	16th October, 1942
LOCATION OF TRIAL	Old Bailey
PRESIDING JUDGE	Mister Justice Birkett
PROSECUTION COUNSEL	G B. McClure
DEFENCE COUNSEL	E. Anthony Hawke
NUMBER OF VICTIMS	Hanged for spying

1942

HERBERT BOUNDS WAS a hypochondriac. By the autumn of 1942, he had done no work for a year and had visited his doctor, Ansel Fry, a number of times, complaining about stomach pains. Bounds had convinced himself that he had some form of cancer but Doctor Fry, after having Bounds X-rayed, gave him a clean bill of health.

Herbert's concerns over his health caused problems at home as well. He had been married to Elizabeth since 1923 and they had had five children. Four of them, all boys, had died, leaving just a nine-year-old daughter and now mother, father and daughter all lived in one rented room at 113 Gloucester Road. Elizabeth had no time for her husband's malingering. Herbert thought her unfeeling and believed that her constant nagging only added to his illness. He felt that she had given him hell for 10 years. Indeed, he would later say that she had even struck him on occasion and had also said that she would poison him.

Things were no better on the morning of August 21st, 1942. Yet another argument broke out and Elizabeth grabbed a bread knife shouting: "I'll cut your throat, you bastard, if you don't soon get out and do something." According to Bounds, that was the final straw. Something inside him snapped and he seized a razor from the dressing table and lashed out in self-defence. Elizabeth's throat began to gush blood and her daughter ran screaming from the room. Bounds left the house, walked to the police box in Windmill Road, and gave himself up to Special Constable Harry Harding, saying: "Will you take me in charge? I have cut my wife's throat."

There had been other people in the house at the time. Elizabeth's three sisters were there. Rose Penfold and Trainette Penfold both lived there and her married sister, Louisa Bourne, had been visiting. None had actually seen the attack but all could fill in some details. Trainette reported that she heard a cry at 5.45am and had then seen Elizabeth's daughter run from their room.

Rose backed up that story and Louisa said she had given Elizabeth a towel to wrap around her wound. Elizabeth had then run from the house, in the direction of Doctor

NAME	Herbert Hiram Bounds
AGE AT EXECUTION	42
DATE OF EXECUTION	Friday, 6th November, 1942
PLACE OF EXECUTION	Wandsworth
HANGMAN	Thomas Pierrepoint
ASSISTANT	Henry Critchell
DATE OF TRIAL	16th September, 1942
LOCATION OF TRIAL	Old Bailey
PRESIDING JUDGE	Mister Justice Hallett
PROSECUTION COUNSEL	G.B. McClure
DEFENCE COUNSEL	Mister Figg
NUMBER OF VICTIMS	1

VICTIMS DETAILS	
NAME	Elizabeth Bounds
AGE	39
DATE OF MURDER	Friday, 21st August, 1942
PLACE OF MURDER	113 Gloucester Road, Croydon
METHOD OF KILLING	Cut throat
RELATIONSHIP TO KILLER	Wife

Fry's surgery, but had collapsed in Gloucester Road, close to the Two Brewers pub.

For his part, Bounds story that he had acted in self-defence seemed to be greatly weakened when it was discovered that the razor he had used belonged to Rose and had been taken from her cabinet. This implied that it had been a deliberate and planned attack, though Bounds tried to counter this by saying that he had intended committing suicide and had taken it for that reason.

It was, at best, a feeble story and failed to save Bounds from the gallows.

JOHANNES DRONKERS WAS born near Utrecht, in Holland, in April, 1896, and after serving as a seaman, he obtained employment in the Dutch General Post Office, just before the outbreak of war in 1939.

Dronkers was a supporter of Hitler and a member of the Dutch Nazi Party and had no hesitation in agreeing to serve Germany when he was approached. Dronkers then underwent training for many months before finally receiving his instructions. He was to travel to England and report on troop movements, paying special attention to American and Canadian troops in England. The information he gathered was to be sent to cover addresses in neutral countries and Dronkers had been taught how to manufacture invisible ink so his messages would pass unnoticed.

Dronkers left Holland on May 16th, 1942, in a small yacht and when picked up by a British trawler, tried to pass himself off as a Dutch refugee who had escaped from the Germans. As he set foot on the British vessel, Dronkers began singing and dancing for joy. The authorities, though, were far from satisfied with his answers and told him he would be detained whilst inquiries were made.

Dronkers did not keep up the pretence for long and soon admitted that he had been sent by the German Secret Service. After a trial at the Old Bailey, he became the 12th spy to be executed during the war.

NAME	Johannes Marinus Dronkers
AGE AT EXECUTION	46
DATE OF EXECUTION	Thursday, 31st December, 1942
PLACE OF EXECUTION	Wandsworth
HANGMAN	Albert Pierrepoint
ASSISTANT	Stephen Wade
DATE OF TRIAL	13th November – 17th November, 1942
LOCATION OF TRIAL	Old Bailey
PRESIDING JUDGE	Mister Justice Wrottesley
PROSECUTION COUNSEL	Not known
DEFENCE COUNSEL	Not known
NUMBER OF VICTIMS	Hanged for spying

1942

FRANCISCUS WINTER WAS a ship's steward who acting on the instructions of his German masters, obtained passage on a British ship, arriving in this country on July 31st, 1942. Posing as a refugee, Winter claimed that he had escaped from Belgium via France and Spain where he had been placed in a concentration camp for several weeks. Upon his release he had approached the British authorities saying that he wished to offer his services to the Allies and they obtained passage for him to Britain. The story, however, was not believed an on his arrival here, Winter was detained whilst further inquiries were made.

As a matter of routine, Winter was searched and over £100 worth of currency from Britain, America, France, Belgium and Spain was discovered. For the time being though, Winter stuck to his original story, claiming that he wanted to join the Free Belgian Force. Eventually he admitted he had been sent by the German Secret Service to report on the movements of convoys, and sending reports in invisible ink to safe addresses in neutral countries.

That was enough to convict Winter under the Treachery Act of 1940, and on January 26th, 1943, days after his 40th birthday, he became the 13th spy to be executed in the Second World War.

NAME	Franciscus Johannes Winter
AGE AT EXECUTION	40
DATE OF EXECUTION	Tuesday, 26th January, 1943
PLACE OF EXECUTION	Wandsworth
HANGMAN	Albert Pierrepoint
ASSISTANT	Henry Critchell
DATE OF TRIAL	4th December, 1942
LOCATION OF TRIAL	Old Bailey
PRESIDING JUDGE	Mister Justice Humphreys
PROSECUTION COUNSEL	Not known
DEFENCE COUNSEL	Not known
NUMBER OF VICTIMS	Hanged for spying

ON JULY 17TH, 1942, workmen demolishing a burnt-out church in Kennington Lane, London, lifted a large slab of stone. There, in a small cavity beneath, was a skeleton.

The skeleton still had the remains of a dried up womb, which showed two things: firstly that it was female, and secondly that the woman had only died in the last 12 to 18 months. Further examination, by Keith Simpson, showed that the body had been dismembered and buried in lime, and that she had died from strangulation.

An extrapolation of her height gave it as slightly in excess of five feet. A small amount of hair adhering to the skull gave the colour as brown, but greying and her age was put at somewhere between 40 and 50. The police examined their missing persons list and arrived at a likely candidate: Rachel Dobkin.

The hair colour matched and Rachel's age when she disappeared was 47. Even more interestingly, she had been the wife of Harry Dobkin, who had been the firewatcher on the church where the body had been found.

Rachel Dobkin had been reported missing by her sister who now provided police with a photograph. An X-ray of the skull, when superimposed on the picture, matched Rachel's features exactly. Rachel's dentist was traced and he identified the fillings in the remaining teeth. The body was that of Rachel Dobkin.

Harry and Rachel had married in September 1920, but so disastrous was the match that they separated after three days. Rachel, though, was pregnant and once her son had been born, she obtained a maintenance order against Harry. The payments were irregular and Harry was often chased for default, even serving some spells in prison.

On Good Friday, 1941, Rachel arranged to meet Harry in a cafe in Dalston, in order to collect some maintenance. She was never seen again, and was reported missing the following day. Surprisingly, a few days later, on the evening of April 14th, the church had burned down.

The trial took place at the Old Bailey, where counsel for the defence made an attempt to challenge the identification of the

NAME	Harry Dobkin
AGE AT EXECUTION	49
DATE OF EXECUTION	Wednesday, 27th January, 1943
PLACE OF EXECUTION	Wandsworth
HANGMAN	Albert Pierrepoint
ASSISTANT	Herbert Morris
DATE OF TRIAL	18th November – 23rd November, 1942
LOCATION OF TRIAL	Old Bailey
PRESIDING JUDGE	Not known
PROSECUTION COUNSEL	L.A. Byrne
DEFENCE COUNSEL	F.H. Lawton
NUMBER OF VICTIMS	1

VICTIMS DETAILS	
NAME	Rachel Dobkin
AGE	47
DATE OF MURDER	Friday, 11th April, 1941
PLACE OF MURDER	Probably Vauxhall Baptist Chapel, Kennington Lane, London
METHOD OF KILLING	Strangled
RELATIONSHIP TO KILLER	Wife

body. Keith Simpson had said that the woman had been around five feet tall. Mr Lawton then produced a missing-person notice, which described Rachel as around five feet three.

The description given had come from Rachel's sister, but upon being called to the stand, she said she that when giving details of her sister, she had said that they were about the same height and the man making the notes had just jotted down five feet three. The court waited with bated breath whilst the sister was measured. Her height was then given; just under five feet tall. It now took the jury only 20 minutes to return a guilty verdict.

1943

CATHERINE CARTWRIGHT Worrall lived at 2G Brig Street, with her 17-year-old son, John and their lodger, Ronald Roberts, who had been with them for some two years.

Roberts had some health problems that had kept him off his work as a firewatcher for Vickers Armstrong. His absences meant that Roberts had financial problems and some debts were becoming pressing but fortunately, on September 27th, Roberts won £8-8s on a football pool.

Nellie Pearson worked as a collector for the Midland Clothing Company and her duties involved calling on customers on a weekly basis. As far as Catherine Worrall was concerned, Nellie usually called at some time between 4.00pm and 4.30pm, each Monday.

October 5th was a Monday and Nellie started her rounds as usual. At 4.30pm, she visited Helen Robertshaw, who lived in Steamer Street, but when Catherine Worrall arrived home, she found that Nellie had not called at her home.

On that same day, Catherine had argued with Roberts and this had ended with her telling him to find alternative accommodation. Over the next few days, though, Roberts seemed to spend all his time cleaning and no doubt Catherine felt that this was an attempt to get into her good books. Catherine noticed that Roberts paid particular attention to her bedroom, which now smelled of fresh disinfectant.

Catherine's sister paid a visit on October 8th and told her that Nellie Pearson had gone missing. The very next day, the police called at 2G, Brig Street.

Catherine and Roberts were in the house and the officers asked to speak to Roberts alone. Asked to account for his movements on the Monday in question, Roberts said he had been to the cinema. The police countered this by saying that he had been seen in the area at about the time Nellie Pearson would have called at the house. Roberts now recalled that he had left the pictures early but still denied having seen Nellie.

Catherine returned and the police asked if she had any objections to them looking over the house. She gave her consent but collapsed in shock when Nellie's body was found in an

NAME	Ronald Roberts
AGE AT EXECUTION	28
DATE OF EXECUTION	Wednesday, 10th February, 1943
PLACE OF EXECUTION	Liverpool
HANGMAN	Thomas Pierrepoint
ASSISTANT	Harry Kirk
DATE OF TRIAL	9th December, 1942
LOCATION OF TRIAL	Manchester
PRESIDING JUDGE	Mister Justice Stable
PROSECUTION COUNSEL	C.J. Lynskey, A.E. Jalland
DEFENCE COUNSEL	Edward Wooll
NUMBER OF VICTIMS	1

VICTIMS DETAILS	
NAME	Nellie Pearson
AGE	37
DATE OF MURDER	Monday, 5th October, 1942
PLACE OF MURDER	2G Brig Street, Barrow-in-Furness
METHOD OF KILLING	Battered/stabbed
RELATIONSHIP TO KILLER	None

alcove in her bedroom, hidden behind some furniture. Catherine had slept next to a dead body for four nights!

Further investigations showed that Roberts had paid off all his debts from the time of Nellie's disappearance. When he again gave out the story of his win on the pools, checks were made and it was discovered that whilst he had made an entry, it had returned nothing.

Nellie had not just been robbed and murdered but had also been sexually assaulted. When she was found, her skirt had been rolled up onto her thighs and her knickers had been removed. The evidence against her killer was very strong and in February 1943, that killer was himself put to death.

PRIVATE DAVID COBB of the 827th Engineer Battalion had been on guard duty for some four hours, at Desborough Camp, Northamptonshire, when the officer of the day, Second Lieutenant Robert J Cobner, approached him.

Cobb had had enough and told Cobner that he was not willing to stay at his post any longer. He was immediately reprimanded for not holding his rifle properly and for failing to stand to attention when he was addressing an officer. Far from being chastised, Cobb replied that he was already confined to barracks and couldn't care less what the officer did. Cobner called for the sergeant of the guard.

The sergeant of the guard was actually a corporal named Mason and Cobner called for him to arrest Cobb. Corporal Mason took a step forward, whereupon Cobb lowered his rifle and, pointing it in Mason's direction, said he would not hand over his weapon until he was properly relieved from his post. Mason could see that Cobb wasn't bluffing and stopped in his tracks at which point Cobner moved forward to do the job himself. Cobb turned his rifle and shot the officer through the heart.

At his court martial, Cobb claimed that he had not known that Cobner was the officer of the day. This still did not excuse what he had done and, found guilty of murder, he was the first American soldier to die on the gallows at Shepton Mallet.

NAME	David Cobb
AGE AT EXECUTION	21
DATE OF EXECUTION	Friday, 12th March, 1943
PLACE OF EXECUTION	Shepton Mallet
HANGMAN	Not known
DATE OF TRIAL	6th January, 1943
LOCATION OF TRIAL	Cambridge
NUMBER OF VICTIMS	1

VICTIMS DETAILS	
NAME	Robert J. Cobner
AGE	Not known
DATE OF MURDER	Sunday, 27th December, 1942
PLACE OF MURDER	Desborough, Northamptonshire
METHOD OF KILLING	Shot
RELATIONSHIP TO KILLER	None

1943

1943

ROSE MARIA COOK lived at Rookery House, Abbeygate, in Colchester and was known to let out rooms. On the night of December 29th, 1942, at 10.00pm she answered the door to a man wearing a corporal's uniform who did not give his name, but asked to be put up for the night.

Rose agreed and allowed the soldier to use her son's room. He left the next day, just before 2.00pm but when Rose went to clean the room, she found that her guest had forced the locks on the wardrobe and stolen some clothes.

Meanwhile, the thief, William Turner, had changed into civilian clothes and moved to 48 North Hill, the house of Ida Ruth Walford. Here he identified himself as Corporal Swann and stayed until January 2nd, 1943. It was then that Ida found a case left in "Swann's" room had been broken into. She called the police and they arrived in time to arrest the occupant of the room.

Charged with stealing clothes from the house in Abbeygate, Turner was searched, and a quantity of money was found. When asked to explain this, Turner admitted that he had killed a woman at Audley Road.

According to Turner, he had been walking the streets, looking for some place to rob, when he came to 19 Audley Road. He knocked but there was no reply. Thinking there was no one at home, he opened the door with a wire but found an old woman bending over a chair in the kitchen. Turner rushed up behind her and put his arm around her neck, but she immediately went limp.

Turner carried the woman into another room and laid her down on the floor. He was then startled by a knock on the front door and when he answered it, found that it was a man asking for Ann Wade. Turner said she was out and going back discovered that she was not unconscious, but dead. He pushed the body under a bed before stealing some money and leaving.

It looked like an open-and-shut case, but then Turner changed his story. Now he said he had gone to the back door of the house and been invited in by Ann, for whom he did some work in the garden. It began to rain and Turner went back inside, where Ann made

NAME	William Henry Turner
AGE AT EXECUTION	19
DATE OF EXECUTION	Wednesday, 24th March, 1943
PLACE OF EXECUTION	Pentonville
HANGMAN	Thomas Pierrepoint
ASSISTANT	Henry Critchell
DATE OF TRIAL	4th February, 1943
LOCATION OF TRIAL	Chelmsford
PRESIDING JUDGE	Mister Justice Asquith
PROSECUTION COUNSEL	Gerald Howard
DEFENCE COUNSEL	Frank Phillips
NUMBER OF VICTIMS	1

VICTIMS DETAILS

NAME	Ann Elizabeth Wade
AGE	82
DATE OF MURDER	Saturday, 2nd January, 1943
PLACE OF MURDER	19 Audley Road, Colchester
METHOD OF KILLING	Strangled
RELATIONSHIP TO KILLER	None

him some tea. She turned her back on him and he put his arm around her neck. Basically, Turner was claiming that the killing had been an accident. Part at least of this story was verified by a neighbour, who had seen Turner working in Ann's garden.

Turner faced two trials. The first, also before Mister Justice Asquith, ended on February 2nd, when the jury failed to agree. The second jury had no such trouble.

IN AUGUST 1942, Dudley George Rayner, a Burmese, born in Rangoon and now a sergeant in the Pioneer Corps, married Josephine Colalucia, who was serving in the A.T.S. Dudley adored his young wife and when she was sent to join her unit in November 1942, and he temporarily lost touch with her, he was heartbroken.

Eventually of course, Dudley found out where his wife was and they managed to meet up at Guildford and renew their relationship. They then returned to their separate units and continued serving their adopted country. Finally, on February 6th, 1943, they obtained leave together and seemed to be very happy in each other's company at Anerley.

Dudley, though, had something on his mind. He was concerned over his wife's behaviour. After all, she was an attractive woman and they were spending so much time apart. Over the next couple of days, these doubts preyed on Dudley's mind. And then he snapped.

On the morning of February 8th, 1943, Dudley and Josephine had breakfast together. Afterwards, Dudley busied himself polishing Josephine's shoes for her and whilst he was performing this task, he noticed a hammer lying on the bedroom floor. Without warning, Dudley picked up the weapon and battered his wife to death.

Remanded at Penge, Rayner made no attempt to avoid the consequences of his actions. His only concern seemed to be his wife. At the first magistrate's hearing, Dudley's only request was that he be allowed to view his wife's body. He was told that this was a matter for the police, not the bench.

The trial took place at the Old Bailey and since Dudley insisted on pleading guilty, the entire proceedings were over with in nine minutes. Dudley chose not to appeal and there was no reprieve forthcoming. Finally, on the last day of March, Dudley George Rayner, who said he had killed his wife during a brainstorm, was executed.

NAME	Dudley George Rayner
AGE AT EXECUTION	26
DATE OF EXECUTION	Wednesday, 31st March, 1943
PLACE OF EXECUTION	Wandsworth
HANGMAN	Albert Pierrepoint
ASSISTANT	Stephen Wade
DATE OF TRIAL	12th March, 1943
LOCATION OF TRIAL	Old Bailey
PRESIDING JUDGE	Mister Justice Oliver
PROSECUTION COUNSEL	Not known
DEFENCE COUNSEL	A.L. Stevenson
NUMBER OF VICTIMS	1

VICTIMS DETAILS	
NAME	Josephine Rayner
AGE	19
DATE OF MURDER	Monday, 8th February, 1943
PLACE OF MURDER	Weighton Road, Anerley
METHOD OF KILLING	Battered
RELATIONSHIP TO KILLER	Wife

1943

WHEN ALBERT BATEMAN failed to return home, his wife went to the tobacconists he ran at Commercial Chambers, to see what had delayed him. The shop was locked, so Mrs Bateman went to the police who returned with her, arriving there at 8.30pm on Christmas Eve, 1942.

An entry was forced and there lay Albert's body. He had been battered to death and on the shop counter, someone had left a Webley revolver. The time of death would be put at around 6.00pm.

It seemed logical to assume that the revolver had been left behind by the killer. It was traced to Falmouth docks and here it was discovered that the man most likely to have access to it was Gordon Trenoweth.

Trenoweth was known to the police. A married man with five children, his wife had been in a mental institution since 1941, and Gordon had refused to pay money for her care. As a result, he had been in prison for default but was now living with his parents. It was there that he was arrested in the early hours of Christmas Day.

When Trenoweth was taken in, two packets of cigarettes were found on him, implying that he had recently visited a tobacconists. More telling was the fact that amongst the money found was a banknote that had been torn and repaired with a letterhead from Albert Bateman's shop.

There was yet more evidence to come. Fibres from one of Trenoweth's jackets were found on the revolver and traces of gun oil were discovered in his pockets. Bloodstains were also found, of the same type as the dead man.

Trenoweth denied being near Bateman's shop. He said he had purchased the cigarettes from Reginald Pearce's shop in the High Street, though neither Reginald nor his daughter could recall serving him.

Trenoweth claimed that he had gone to a coalyard, looking for work, arriving there at around 5.30pm. This was confirmed by Mr Osberg, who agreed that Trenoweth had given the correct time. Trenoweth's father, also named Gordon, confirmed that he was home at 5.40pm or just afterwards and Gordon's sister said he did not leave the

NAME	Gordon Horace Trenoweth
AGE AT EXECUTION	33
DATE OF EXECUTION	Tuesday, 6th April, 1943
PLACE OF EXECUTION	Exeter
HANGMAN	Thomas Pierrepoint
ASSISTANT	Herbert Morris
DATE OF TRIAL	11th February – 16th February, 1943
LOCATION OF TRIAL	Exeter
PRESIDING JUDGE	Mister Justice Tucker
PROSECUTION COUNSEL	J.D. Caswell
DEFENCE COUNSEL	J. Scott Henderson
NUMBER OF VICTIMS	1

VICTIMS DETAILS	
NAME	Albert James Bateman
AGE	61
DATE OF MURDER	Thursday, 24th December, 1942
PLACE OF MURDER	Commercial Chambers, Arnwenach Street, Falmouth
METHOD OF KILLING	Battered
RELATIONSHIP TO KILLER	None

house again until 6.30pm. If their testimony were believed then Gordon Trenoweth could not be the killer.

In the event, the jury chose to place more weight on the evidence of Dorothy Allen, whom Trenoweth had met in Truro, later that same night. She said that Gordon was spending money freely and this was confirmed by the barman at the Market Tavern, Frederick Griffiths. Where had this cash come from if not from Bateman's shop, and how had Trenoweth come to have in his possession a banknote that had certainly come from the dead man's shop?

Trenoweth was found guilty but with a strong recommendation to mercy. Nevertheless, on April 6th, 1943, he became the last man to be hanged at Exeter.

ON OCTOBER 7TH, 1942, a party of Marines on exercises on Hankley Common found a badly decomposed body. The pathological investigation fell to the hands of Professor Keith Simpson.

The clothing was female and careful inspection of the surrounding area revealed that the woman had probably been attacked elsewhere and dragged to the top of the hill, where she was found.

Simpson held that the woman had been stabbed in the head a number of times and had then been battered with a heavy weapon. The stab wounds were distinctive. In some wounds, particles of flesh had been pulled out, indicating that the knife must have had some sort of hooked point, like a parrot's beak.

The woman was identified as Joan Pearl Wolfe, a girl who had been living in a shelter built on the common by a French-Canadian Cree Indian named August Sangret, a soldier at the nearby Witley Camp.

A careful search of the common revealed Joan's identity card and a letter to Sangret telling him that she was pregnant. Sangret was interviewed at length and said he had last seen Joan in September. He confirmed that he had been her lover but knew nothing about her murder. Without the weapon itself, police felt unable to charge Sangret.

Many other soldiers at the camp were interviewed and finally one, Private Cowle, recalled that in August 1942 he had found a knife sticking in the bark of a tree close by the 'wigwam' where Joan had lived. He had taken the knife back to camp and handed it in to Corporal Harding. He too recalled the knife. It had been rather distinctive with its hooked point and he had passed it on to August Sangret. This linked Sangret to a knife that may have been the murder weapon, but without the knife itself, the police case was very weak.

On November 27th, 1942, Private Brown had been detailed to clean out a blocked drain close to the guardroom on Witley Camp. He removed all sorts of material but still there seemed to be something at the top of the drain. One final pull and Private Brown brought out a knife. It had a tip like a parrot's beak.

NAME	August Sangret
AGE AT EXECUTION	30
DATE OF EXECUTION	Thursday, 29th April, 1943
PLACE OF EXECUTION	Wandsworth
HANGMAN	Albert Pierrepoint
ASSISTANT	Henry Critchell
DATE OF TRIAL	24th February – 2nd March, 1943
LOCATION OF TRIAL	Kingston upon Thames
PRESIDING JUDGE	Mister Justice Macnaghten
PROSECUTION COUNSEL	Eric Neve, Geoffrey Lawrence
DEFENCE COUNSEL	Linton Thorpe, Laurence Vine
NUMBER OF VICTIMS	1

VICTIMS DETAILS	
NAME	Joan Pearl Wolfe
AGE	19
DATE OF MURDER	circa Sunday, 13th September, 1942
PLACE OF MURDER	Hankley Common, Godalming, Surrey
METHOD OF KILLING	Stabbed/battered
RELATIONSHIP TO KILLER	Girlfriend

Faced with the knife itself, Sangret admitted that it had belonged to Joan. By making that statement he had linked himself to the knife, which was shown to be the murder weapon. He was charged with murder.

At the trial, the defence tried to argue that the wounds inflicted on Joan might have been caused by some other weapon, but Simpson was adamant that only this particular knife could have inflicted the wounds. When the jury retired, they did so with two grisly exhibits: the knife and Joan Wolfe's skull.

After two hours, Sangret was found guilty, but with a strong recommendation to mercy.

1943

IT WAS NEW Year's Day, 1943 and Private Herald Smith had just been paid. With money in his pocket, Smith wanted a little rest and relaxation, and decided to absent himself from camp. He caught a train to London, where he met up with a fellow American, Private Harry English.

The two comrades took a hotel room together and spent the next week enjoying themselves, until the money ran out. There was nothing for it but to return to camp and face the music and on January 8th, 1943, Smith went back to Chiseldon.

Unfortunately for Smith, in the meantime his unit had moved on. He was now at a loss for what to do next, but at least he had somewhere to stay. The following day, January 9th, Smith went to the mess hall at lunch time. He enjoyed a meal there before walking to the squad room, where he found a loaded automatic pistol. Taking the gun, he walked back towards the mess hall but was stopped by Private Harry Jenkins.

The next few seconds were like a scene from High Noon. Jenkins moved towards his holster, Smith got to his gun first and drawing the automatic, shot Jenkins dead. A soldier came running out of a nearby barracks but Smith turned and fired over his head, forcing him to retreat.

Private Smith knew he was now in deep trouble, so he left the camp, caught a bus to Marlborough and from there, took a train to London. There, two days later, on January 11th, he was asked for his identity card by Police Constable James Watson, and taken into custody.

There could be little doubt as to the outcome and Smith made a full statement, confessing to the shooting. He was hanged in June.

NAME	Harold A. Smith
AGE AT EXECUTION	Not known
DATE OF EXECUTION	Friday, 25th June, 1943
PLACE OF EXECUTION	Shepton Mallet
HANGMAN	Not known
DATE OF TRIAL	12th March, 1943
LOCATION OF TRIAL	Bristol
NUMBER OF VICTIMS	1

VICTIMS DETAILS	
NAME	Harry Jenkins
AGE	Not known
DATE OF MURDER	Saturday, 9th January, 1943
PLACE OF MURDER	Chiseldon Camp, Swindon, Wiltshire
METHOD OF KILLING	Shot
RELATIONSHIP TO KILLER	None

A T 12.40PM ON January 31st, 1943, two members of the Home Guard, Leonard George Bailey and George Tilbury, were cycling from Halnaker when they noticed something lying in a field. Upon investigating they discovered the body of a W.A.A.F., Marguerite Burge. She was still alive, but died in the Royal West Sussex hospital later that day.

Initial investigations led to a number of witnesses. Leslie George Boxall lived in a lane near the scene and he reported that at 3.40pm on Saturday afternoon, he had seen a stationary army lorry and a W.A.A.F. leaning into its doorway.

Frank Goff, who lived next door to Leslie, confirmed this but added that he had seen the lorry pass soon afterwards and by now the W.A.A.F. was inside the cab. Another witness was Augusta Annie Norgate. She had passed a parked army lorry and seen a soldier in the field where Marguerite was later found. Later still, at around 4.15pm, Alfred Horner had passed the same parked lorry, but now the soldier was standing by the cab. Alfred particularly remembered this because the soldier had dashed around the back of the lorry as he approached.

It was not long before the name of Charles Raymond came to the fore. He was a French Canadian soldier and one of his compatriots, Arthur Patry, gave evidence that after church parade on the Sunday, Raymond had talked to him about whether the police could trace fingerprints when it had been raining. The tool box on Raymond's lorry was checked and a screwdriver was seen to be missing. Just such a weapon had been used on Marguerite and one found near the lorry did show a positive reaction for human blood.

When shown a photograph of the dead girl, Raymond said he had never seen her before and then tried to claim that the killer was Patry. Raymond said that he had seen Patry in the field with a girl and been told to clear off.

Patry showed that he had not left camp on the day of the murder. Raymond, however, was known to have been out in his lorry, making the case against him that much stronger.

There was however one final part to this

NAME	Charles Arthur Raymond
AGE AT EXECUTION	23
DATE OF EXECUTION	Saturday, 10th July, 1943
PLACE OF EXECUTION	Wandsworth
HANGMAN	Thomas Pierrepoint
ASSISTANT	Stephen Wade
DATE OF TRIAL	10th May – 14th May, 1943
LOCATION OF TRIAL	Old Bailey
PRESIDING JUDGE	Mister Justice Lawrence
PROSECUTION COUNSEL	Eric Neve, John C. Maude
DEFENCE COUNSEL	Thomas Carthew, Harold Brown
NUMBER OF VICTIMS	1

VICTIMS DETAILS	
NAME	Marguerite Beatrice Burge (Died, Sunday, 31st January)
AGE	22
DATE OF MURDER	Saturday, 30th January, 1943
PLACE OF MURDER	Field at Halnaker near Goodwood, West Sussex
METHOD OF KILLING	Stabbed
RELATIONSHIP TO KILLER	None

1943

story. On the Sunday morning, Raymond had invited Patry out for a drink with him and at one stage, as they passed the field where Marguerite was later found. Raymond said he had seen something and took Patry into the field. They found Marguerite still alive, but Patry became nervous and thought they might get into trouble so the matter was not reported. Perhaps Raymond was trying to provide evidence that Patry had indeed been in the field. If they had done something at that time, Marguerite would have had medical attention half an hour earlier and might well have lived.

1943

IT WAS EVERY mother's worst nightmare. Ada Clarke had sent her eight-year-old daughter, Vera, back to school after lunch on May 5th, 1943, but when Ada herself got in from work at 6.30pm, little Vera had still not returned home.

The first port of call was the school in Piggott Street, where it was discovered that Vera had left for home at the normal time. The police were called in and they soon found a number of witnesses.

Janet Blount, aged nine, said Vera had left school with her at 4.30pm. They parted soon afterwards but Vera had been seen again at 4.45pm, by another school friend, 10-year-old William Abbotts. William had seen Vera standing on the doorstep of 132a Bath Row. She had been talking to the man who lived there and William had seen him give Vera a piece of paper. She had then skipped off towards the greengrocers.

Police next checked at the greengrocers shop where the assistant, Winfred Rose Dooling reported serving a little girl fitting Vera's description with three pounds weight of potatoes. She put the time at 4.50pm.

The final witness was 13-year-old Dorothy Beatrice Binnion. She had also seen Vera on the doorstep of 132a Bath Row. The door had been open at the time.

Much of this was already known to the Clarke family by the time the police had been called in. Their own inquiries had found Dorothy Binnion and at one stage, Ada Clarke, her husband Charles, Dorothy and Vera's teacher, Reginald Milton London, had paid a visit to 132a, Bath Row, to see if any light could be shed on the matter.

The door was opened by William Quayle, who had lived in the house since May 1942. He denied all knowledge of Vera and said that no child was on his doorstep that night. Mr Clarke asked if they could come in and search the cellar. At first Quayle agreed without quibble, but then suddenly remembered that the door was locked. Mr and Mrs Clarke and the others then walked straight to the police station, not knowing that at the time of their visit, their daughter's body lay brutalised on Quayle's living-room carpet.

By the time Constable Cyril Smith returned

VICTIMS DETAILS	
NAME	Vera Clarke
AGE	8
DATE OF MURDER	Friday, 5th May, 1943
PLACE OF MURDER	132a Bath Row, Birmingham
METHOD OF KILLING	Strangled
RELATIONSHIP TO KILLER	None

NAME	William Quayle
AGE AT EXECUTION	52
DATE OF EXECUTION	Tuesday, 3rd August, 1943
PLACE OF EXECUTION	Birmingham
HANGMAN	Thomas Pierrepoint
ASSISTANT	Alexander Riley
DATE OF TRIAL	12th July, 1943
LOCATION OF TRIAL	Birmingham
PRESIDING JUDGE	Mister Justice Wrottesley
PROSECUTION COUNSEL	Arthur Ward, John F. Bourke
DEFENCE COUNSEL	Richard O'Sullivan, T.R. Whittingham
NUMBER OF VICTIMS	1

with the Clarkes to Bath Row, Quayle had gone out and there was no reply to their knocking. Constable Smith managed to gain entry through the cellar grating and emerged from the house carrying a child's coat. This was identified as Vera's. A later search of the premises also revealed a child's skipping rope identical to one Vera had been carrying when she disappeared.

In his first statement, made on May 6th, Quayle again denied knowing anything about Vera's whereabouts. He claimed to have been asleep in the chair at the times his door was supposed to be open and said he had no knowledge of how the coat and rope got into his home. Faced with the evidence of the eye witnesses, however, Quayle made a second statement that same night, in which he admitted killing Vera.

In this second statement, Quayle said that he had indeed sent Vera for some potatoes. She came into his house with the shopping and something seemed to snap inside him because he just rushed at her and strangled her. He left her body on the rug and went out to telephone his employers, Fisher and

Ludlow, where he was a works policeman, to get the night off work. Having done this, he visited a few pubs, returned home and fell asleep.

Waking at 4.00am, he had some tea before putting Vera's body into a hand cart and pushing her to a bombed-out house at 12 Spring Vale, Birmingham, where he dumped her under some rubble.

Even now Quayle could not tell the whole truth. When Vera was found, she was naked except for a pair of socks and one shoe and she had been brutally raped. Quayle still denied that he had anything to do with the sexual assault and could offer no explanation as to who might have been responsible for it.

Whilst held in prison awaiting trial, Quayle tried to kill himself by swallowing various objects, including an open safety pin. None of his attempts to avoid the hangman succeeded.

ELIZABETH CANFIELD WAS busily delivering milk on the morning of May 17th, 1943, when she called at number 9 Greenhill Park.

Receiving no reply to her knocking, Elizabeth realised that she could smell gas. Crouching down she noticed that the smell was stronger when she pushed open the letterbox, so she informed the first policeman she saw, Constable William Warner.

Warner went around the back of the house and through the kitchen window, saw the body of a woman lying on the floor. She was wearing blue pyjamas. Warner went to number 4, where there was a telephone, and from there contacted the police station for reinforcements and an ambulance. Then he and Nigel Stephen Arnold, the man who lived at number 4, returned to number 9, and broke in through the French windows. They turned off the grill on the stove and pulled the woman, Elsie Roe, into the hallway. It was too late, however: Elsie was already dead.

Nigel Arnold now told police that he had been wakened by screams at 6.50am. Looking out of his window he saw a woman, clad in blue pyjamas, being pulled about by a man he did not see clearly. The screaming stopped but, surprisingly, Arnold took no action. Later that morning, Arnold saw Gordon Roe leaving the house. He was carrying two suitcases.

The postmortem, carried out by Keith Simpson, showed that Elsie had been struck once from the front and possibly rendered unconscious. She then lay on the floor, face down, and five heavy blows were rained down upon her head. The cause of death, though, was carbon monoxide poisoning and the time of death was put at around 8.00am.

Roe, meanwhile, had travelled to Highcliffe in Hampshire, where he was being billeted with Emily Harriet Earley. It was here that he was interviewed at 10.00am and when his belongings were checked, bloodstained clothing was discovered. Since Roe could offer no satisfactory explanation, he was arrested and charged with his wife's murder.

Gerald Roe denied any involvement in Elsie's death. He said he had left the house at 8.45am that morning. When it became clear that this line of defence would not save Roe,

NAME	Gerald Elphinstone Roe
AGE AT EXECUTION	41
DATE OF EXECUTION	Tuesday, 3rd August, 1943
PLACE OF EXECUTION	Pentonville
HANGMAN	Albert Pierrepoint
ASSISTANT	Steve Wade
DATE OF TRIAL	18th June, 1943
LOCATION OF TRIAL	Not known
PRESIDING JUDGE	Mister Justice Humphreys
PROSECUTION COUNSEL	H.J. Hamblen
DEFENCE COUNSEL	G.D. Roberts, Frederick D. Levy
NUMBER OF VICTIMS	1

VICTIMS DETAILS	
NAME	Elsie Elphinstone Roe
AGE	43
DATE OF MURDER	Monday, 17th May, 1943
PLACE OF MURDER	9 Greenhill Park, Barnet Vale, Hertfordshire
METHOD OF KILLING	Gassed/battered
RELATIONSHIP TO KILLER	Wife

suggestions were made that there might be insanity in the family. His mother had been an in-patient at an asylum, but she had never been formally certified and whilst her behaviour had been described as 'peculiar' this hardly proved Roe's claims.

At Roe's appeal, it was suggested that the gas might have been turned on accidentally and as this was the actual cause of death, and as there was no proof that Gordon Roe had been the one to turn the grill on, the verdict was unsafe. The judges pointed out that the physical injuries played their own part in Elsie Roe's death and therefore it did not really matter who turned the gas on.

TREVOR ELVIN, A glass works engineer who lived in Grove Street, Barnsley, was in love with Violet Wakefield and they had discussed marriage. All seemed to be going well until Easter Saturday, when Violet dropped a bombshell and told Trevor that she wanted to call it all off.

There had to be a reason for this change of heart and slowly Elvin came to the conclusion that there had to be another man. Eventually he discovered a man he thought to be the guilty party: Robert Oakes.

On May 3rd, Elvin and Violet met up to discuss their problems. Things developed into an argument and Elvin made his suspicions clear when he complained of her association with 'Bob'. However, they agreed to meet up again the following day.

At 8.00am on May 4th, Elvin was seen with Violet, close to a fairground. He was later seen walking away from the area and by that time he was alone. Two hours later, at 10.00am, Violet was discovered, badly injured. She died in hospital later that same day.

Elvin, meanwhile, had vanished. Over the next few days he visited relatives at Otley and Blackpool before he was finally picked up and charged with Violet's murder.

The defence was one of insanity, based on the premise that Elvin's jealousy had affected his mind. A diary was produced in which Elvin had written that he was sure Violet was in love with Bob and this was said to show that the affair was preying on his mind. Robert Oakes, a lorry driver, and the cause of Elvin's jealousy, gave evidence that he had last seen Violet at half-past five on May 3rd, when he had given her a lift to Pontefract Road. He had no comment on Violet's break-up with Elvin.

In the event, the jury held that jealousy did not lead necessarily to insanity and Elvin had been fully aware of his actions. As a result, a guilty verdict was returned and Elvin was sentenced to death.

NAME	Trevor Elvin
AGE AT EXECUTION	21
DATE OF EXECUTION	Friday, 10th September, 1943
PLACE OF EXECUTION	Leeds
HANGMAN	Thomas Pierrepoint
ASSISTANT	Harry Kirk
DATE OF TRIAL	12th July, 1943
LOCATION OF TRIAL	Leeds
PRESIDING JUDGE	Mister Justice Tucker
PROSECUTION COUNSEL	Russell Vick, R. Cleworth
DEFENCE COUNSEL	G.H.B. Streatfeild, Myles Archibald
NUMBER OF VICTIMS	1

VICTIMS DETAILS

NAME	Violet Wakefield
AGE	20
DATE OF MURDER	Tuesday, 4th May, 1943
PLACE OF MURDER	Between Wellington Hotel and Wire Trellis Hotel, Barnsley
METHOD OF KILLING	Battered
RELATIONSHIP TO KILLER	Girlfriend

1943

1943

ANNETTE PEPPER WAS a married woman whose husband was a British prisoner of war, in Germany. Whilst he was away, though, Annette did not play the part of the patiently waiting wife – instead, she began to enjoy the company of other servicemen, including a Canadian soldier, Charles Eugene Gauthier. Unfortunately, Annette was also unfaithful to Gauthier and that was to lead directly to her death.

On March 15th, 1943, Gauthier called at Annette's house in Mile Oak Road, Portslade, but she refused him admittance and told him she intended spending the night with another Canadian soldier, Sergeant William Archibald Rendall. Gauthier left, only to return some time later with a Bren gun, which he had taken from a Home Guard store.

The first shot was fired through the closed front door and hit Rendall on the ankle. Realising that Gauthier meant business, Rendall hobbled away from the scene whilst Annette locked herself into a bedroom upstairs. Gauthier called for Annette to come down and talk to him. She shouted: "Give me your word of honour you won't shoot me." Gauthier gave his word and slowly Annette opened the door and began her descent of the stairs. Another shot rang out and Annette fell on the stairs. Gauthier then proceeded to fire three more bullets into her, ensuring that she was dead.

Charles Gauthier faced two trials for his life. The first trial took place in the ancient town of Lewes, before Mister Justice Humphreys but the jury twice failed to agree on a verdict and the case was moved to the Old Bailey, where it was heard in July, before Mister Justice Oliver.

At best, Gauthier's defence was weak. He claimed that he had not known what he was doing and even said that he had carried the Bren gun for some distance before he even realised he had it with him! The second jury had no trouble agreeing on their verdict and Gauthier was sentenced to death.

In fact, Gauthier was to spend a record 60 days in the condemned cell. After his appeal had failed, there was a request from the Canadian government to the House of Lords and a petition was also sent to the Home

NAME	Charles Eugene Gauthier
AGE AT EXECUTION	25
DATE OF EXECUTION	Friday, 24th September, 1943
PLACE OF EXECUTION	Wandsworth
HANGMAN	Albert Pierrepoint
ASSISTANT	Alex Riley
DATE OF TRIAL	25th July, 1943
LOCATION OF TRIAL	Old Bailey
PRESIDING JUDGE	Mister Justice Oliver
PROSECUTION COUNSEL	Sir Charles Doughty, H.J. Hannihan
DEFENCE COUNSEL	Eric Neve, B. Dutton Briant
NUMBER OF VICTIMS	1

VICTIMS DETAILS	
NAME	Annette Elizabeth Frederika Christina Pepper
AGE	30
DATE OF MURDER	Monday, 15th March, 1943
PLACE OF MURDER	'Hillcrest', 208 Mile Oak Road, Portslade, near Brighton
METHOD OF KILLING	Shot
RELATIONSHIP TO KILLER	Girlfriend

Secretary. All these efforts came to nothing and finally, on September 24th, Gauthier was executed.

Annette Pepper lying at the foot of the stairs after she had been shot.

THE PUBLIC HOUSE on Quill Lane, Putney, was a popular meeting place and on the night of July 13th, 1943, quite a crowd had gathered there. One of those customers was Terence Casey, a private in the Royal Army Medical Corps, who was staying with relatives in Fulham whilst he was on leave.

During the evening, Casey made advances towards the barmaid, Freda Gibbons, who told him not to be so silly as she was old enough to be his mother. Casey was persistent though, and said he would wait for her outside.

At around 9.30pm, Bridget Mitton, who lived locally and was known as 'the little Irish lady', came in for a bottle of stout. Soon afterwards, when Freda left to go home, she saw a soldier, Casey, waiting outside and hurried off before he could approach her. Freda also saw Bridget, talking to a friend and as Bridget said her goodbyes and walked off home, Freda noticed that the soldier followed her. It was now a few minutes after 11.00pm.

At 11.25pm, an air-raid warden, John Walton, heard strange noises coming from the garden of number 8 Gwendolen Street. This was the time of the black-out, so Walton shone his torch into the garden, where he saw a partly clothed woman and Casey. Walton shouted for the police and Casey was taken into custody. When cautioned he stated: "She cut up rough so I bashed her."

Police investigations showed that Bridget, after leaving the public house, had gone to visit a friend, Philip Tyrrell. She stayed with him for about 35 minutes and he was the man seen talking to her, by Freda Gibbons. Philip Tyrrell also noticed the soldier walk off in the same direction as Bridget.

Casey had, of course, been caught red-handed so his only hope of avoiding the death penalty was to show that he was not responsible for his actions. He claimed to have no memory from the time he left the public house to the time the police arrived and arrested him. Doctor Nelson Hill measured the electrical patterns from Casey's brain and said that he had found an abnormality which might suggest that drink and stress could mean that he would suffer from an aggressive form of epilepsy.

NAME	Terence Casey
AGE AT EXECUTION	22
DATE OF EXECUTION	Friday, 19th November, 1943
PLACE OF EXECUTION	Wandsworth
HANGMAN	Albert Pierrepoint
ASSISTANT	Henry Critchell
DATE OF TRIAL	22nd September – 24th September, 1943
LOCATION OF TRIAL	Old Bailey
PRESIDING JUDGE	Mister Justice Singleton
PROSECUTION COUNSEL	L.A. Byrne
DEFENCE COUNSEL	Joseph Yahunda
NUMBER OF VICTIMS	1

VICTIMS DETAILS	
NAME	Bridget Nora Mitton
AGE	45
DATE OF MURDER	Tuesday, 13th July, 1943
PLACE OF MURDER	8 Gwendolen Street, Putney, London
METHOD OF KILLING	Strangled
RELATIONSHIP TO KILLER	None

In the event, after retiring for 45 minutes, the jury found Casey guilty but added a recommendation to mercy.

1943

1943

MURIEL FAWDEN, A nurse, had gone to visit the cinema at Marlborough and at 7.45pm, as she left the theatre, she met up with a friend of hers, June Lay. Together, the two ladies walked back towards Savernake Hospital.

They had not gone very far when a coloured American soldier came up level with them and asked them where they were going. Muriel answered that they were heading for the hospital and it was not very far away. They then increased their pace and pulled slowly away from the stranger.

Some few minutes later, Muriel and June heard a firm shout: "Stand still, or I'll shoot." They turned to see the same soldier aiming his rifle at them. Frozen to the spot, they listened as he instructed them to get into some bushes at the side of the road.

Muriel stalled for time and said it was impossible to get through the fence at the point he had indicated, as there was barbed wire blocking the way. The soldier signalled for them to move back the way they had come and slowly the two women obeyed.

After walking a short distance, June saw her opportunity and shouted for Muriel to make a run for it. Shots rang out and June Lay fell dead in the roadway. Turning his attention now to Muriel, the serviceman fired bullets past her until she stopped. He then caught her up, dragged her into a nearby field where he spent some hours assaulting and raping her.

Luckily for Muriel, she was allowed to escape with her life and the next day, September 29th, having given her evidence to the police, the weapons of the entire American company were examined. It was soon determined that Lee Davis's rifle had been fired very recently and a test firing from this weapon showed that the patterns matched those on the bullets that had killed June Lay.

Faced with this evidence, Davis admitted the shooting but claimed he had aimed to fire over June's head. This did nothing to save him from the gallows but it seems that Davis could not believe that he would actually be executed. When the dreadful morning arrived and Davis was taken into the

NAME	Lee A. Davis
AGE AT EXECUTION	Not known
DATE OF EXECUTION	Tuesday, 14th December, 1943
PLACE OF EXECUTION	Shepton Mallet
HANGMAN	Albert Pierrepoint
DATE OF TRIAL	6th October, 1943
LOCATION OF TRIAL	Marlborough
NUMBER OF VICTIMS	1

VICTIMS DETAILS	
NAME	Cynthia June Lay
AGE	19
DATE OF MURDER	Tuesday, 28th September, 1943
PLACE OF MURDER	Near Savernake Hospital, London Hill, Marlborough
METHOD OF KILLING	Shot
RELATIONSHIP TO KILLER	None

execution chamber, he looked at the noose and cried: "Oh God, I'm going to die!"

GLADYS BREWER'S NEIGHBOURS were concerned. Although it was late morning, her black-out curtains had not been pulled back and there was no answer to their repeated knocking. When by 3.00pm that afternoon there was still no signs of Gladys and her young daughter, the police were called in.

Once an entry had been forced, the truth became all too evident. Gladys and two-year-old Shirley had been battered to death with a hammer. A note found on the arm of a chair, and addressed to Gladys's husband who was in the forces, read: "Dear Ernie. I am sorry to do this to you and please God forgive me, but I am afraid your wife is very immoral. We don't know you personally but we know your heart." The letter was unsigned.

It did not take police long to determine who they were looking for. Beneath Gladys's head someone had placed an R.A.F. tunic and other air force clothing was found in the house. Since Ernie Brewer was in the navy, it could not belong to him, so most likely had been brought by the killer. The letter was also written in the plural, implying that two people were involved. In due course it became clear that the police wanted to interview Charles Koopman and his wife, Gladys Patricia.

Koopman was an aircraftman from Hanwell who had married Patricia in 1941. He had been given a weekend leave because he was being posted to Bridlington, but had not reported for duty, having run off with his wife. Koopman had first met Gladys Brewer in 1938, and it transpired that he had met up with her again some 12 months previously, when he had introduced her to his wife.

The Koopmans were eventually arrested in Slough and both were initially charged with murder. Charles maintained from the start that his wife had not been involved and at the first magistrate's hearing, the charges against Gladys Koopman were dropped.

Koopman's statement revealed what had happened in the Brewer household. He admitted that he and his wife had arrived at the house on September 5th. On the 8th, they had gone out drinking and upon their return, he began teasing Gladys Brewer by turning down the gas when she was trying to read.

NAME	Charles William Koopman
AGE AT EXECUTION	23
DATE OF EXECUTION	Wednesday, 15th December, 1943
PLACE OF EXECUTION	Pentonville
HANGMAN	Thomas Pierrepoint
ASSISTANT	Stephen Wade
DATE OF TRIAL	26th October, 1943
LOCATION OF TRIAL	Old Bailey
PRESIDING JUDGE	Mister Justice Asquith
PROSECUTION COUNSEL	E. Anthony Hawke, H. Elam
DEFENCE COUNSEL	Linton Thorp, Sebag Shaw
NUMBER OF VICTIMS	2

VICTIMS DETAILS	
NAMES	Gladys Lavinia Brewer; Shirley Brewer
AGES	22; 2
DATE OF MURDER	Wednesday, 8th September, 1943
PLACE OF MURDER	1 Grove Flats, Grove Place, Ealing, London
METHOD OF KILLING	Battered; battered
RELATIONSHIP TO KILLER	None; none

She remonstrated with him and he picked up a hammer to frighten her. Before he knew what he had done, he had battered Gladys to death; his wife had stopped him at the end of the attack.

However, Gladys Koopman did not, it seems, interfere when Charles heard the baby crying, took it through to the bedroom and battered it to death with the same hammer. Koopman explained that he had killed Shirley because he didn't think she should be without her mother!

JOHN DORGAN AND his wife, Florence, had married in 1927 but had not always lived happily. By July, 1943, they were living in Madeira Place, Brighton, where they shared number 8a, with their lodger, Charles Fyfe.

From July 29th, John Dorgan began behaving rather strangely. It was on that day that Dorgan met George Windsor and Percy White on Brighton seafront. Whilst he was with them, Dorgan sold his overcoat to a stranger for £1 and later sold a clock to Laura Emily Hobbs, who worked at the Queen's Head Hotel, for 25/-.

The process of selling his belongings continued the following day. George Windsor met Dorgan at 6.00pm, in the Aquarium Inn, where Dorgan tried to sell Ernest Beasley a pair of earrings, for £7. Beasley was not interested but expressed more excitement when he was offered a radio for £9.

Dorgan, Beasley and Windsor went to the flat to see the radio before returning to the pub, where they met up with Percy White, who was then offered a wardrobe. Once more a trip to Madeira Place was made, and terms discussed. It was at this time that someone asked after Florence and was told that she had gone to Scotland.

Beasley had agreed to buy some of the furniture, together with the radio and, next morning, Thomas Bates, potman at the Queen's Head, lent Dorgan a barrow that he helped him load. It was whilst this was being loaded that Dorgan's daughter, Beatrice Primrose Blaker turned up.

Beatrice had called three times before on July 30th. At 10.00am she had seen her mother. Beatrice had called again at 7.00pm, and at 8.00pm, but there had been no reply. Somewhat concerned, she returned again at 9.20pm, with her husband, to find John showing people around the front room. She spoke to her father, who said Florence was out, but although Beatrice waited until 11.00pm, her mother did not return.

In fact, the last person to see Florence alive was the lodger, Charles Fyfe. He had left the house at 4.30pm when Florence was making tea, and did not return until 2.15pm on July 31st.

Immediately, Charles saw that things were

NAME	John Joseph Dorgan
AGE AT EXECUTION	47
DATE OF EXECUTION	Wednesday, 22nd December, 1943
PLACE OF EXECUTION	Wandsworth
HANGMAN	Thomas Pierrepoint
ASSISTANT	Henry Critchell
DATE OF TRIAL	2nd December
LOCATION OF TRIAL	Lewes
PRESIDING JUDGE	Mister Justice Charles
PROSECUTION COUNSEL	Mister Curtis Bennett
DEFENCE COUNSEL	Eric Neve
NUMBER OF VICTIMS	1

VICTIMS DETAILS	
NAME	Florence Elizabeth Agnes Dorgan
AGE	60
DATE OF MURDER	Friday, 30th July, 1943
PLACE OF MURDER	8a Madeira Place, Brighton
METHOD OF KILLING	Strangled
RELATIONSHIP TO KILLER	Wife

not as they usually were. The furniture had been moved and the wireless was missing. Somewhat confused, Fyfe went to his room to change. Taking off his shoes, he looked under the bed for his other pair and there found the body of Florence Dorgan.

John Dorgan was arrested that night at 7.30pm as he got out of a taxi at the Queen's Head public house. He readily admitted his guilt, stating: "I have done the old woman in. I have done it properly this time." The motive for this crime was that Florence had caught John selling some of her belongings and had objected.

GEORGE SAMUEL DIAS had consulted his wife, Doris, and she told him that he had to go to the police. Later that same night, August 18th, the police entered a bombed-out house at 4 Kitchen Street, and there found the body of Gwendoline Sweeney. She had been stabbed in the region of her vagina and had also been throttled. Acting on the information given by Dias, the police then called at the house of Catherine Williams and arrested her lodger, Thomas James.

Gwendoline Sweeney had last been seen alive on the night of August 17th when she had been in the company of two coloured men, later identified as Dias and James. They were seen in the Eagle public house by the barman, Lawrence Robinson, who said they came in around 7.45pm. Earlier, the same threesome had been seen in the King's Arms by the manager, George Hudson.

By 8.30pm, they were in the Bush Hotel on the corner of Blundell Street and St James's Street, where they were served by Jessie Wallace. A short time later, a police constable, John Millington, called in at an air-raid shelter and saw a woman in the company of a coloured man. He asked them to move on and saw them walk up Duke Street together where they were joined by another coloured man.

The final sighting of a coloured man took place at around 10.15pm, when John McKeown went out, looking for his granddaughter. He saw a man standing in the doorway of number 4 Kitchen Street, and they argued when McKeown asked him what he was up to. Shortly afterwards, McKeown was joined by his niece, Maria Russell, who had her torch knocked from her hand by the aggressive stranger. Maria ran for the police and soon encountered Constable Samuel Garrett who had a brief talk with the man.

That night, George Dias arrived home at 11.00pm. He did not see James again until late the next morning, when they went for a drink together. It was then that James confessed to him that he had killed the girl they were with the night before.

Dias thought his friend was joking and accompanied him back to the house where they had parted the previous night. Gwendoline was

NAME	Thomas James
AGE AT EXECUTION	26
DATE OF EXECUTION	Wednesday, 29th December, 1943
PLACE OF EXECUTION	Liverpool
HANGMAN	Not known
ASSISTANT	Not known
DATE OF TRIAL	4th November – 5th November, 1943
LOCATION OF TRIAL	Liverpool
PRESIDING JUDGE	Mister Justice Wrottesley
PROSECUTION COUNSEL	Glyn Blackledge
DEFENCE COUNSEL	Miss Rose Heilbron
NUMBER OF VICTIMS	1

VICTIMS DETAILS	
NAME	Gwendoline Sweeney
AGE	28
DATE OF MURDER	Tuesday, 17th August, 1943
PLACE OF MURDER	4 Kitchen Street, Liverpool
METHOD OF KILLING	Stabbed/strangled
RELATIONSHIP TO KILLER	None

lying in the rubble and was clearly dead. It was then that Dias went home to his wife and told her what he had seen and heard.

James denied any involvement in the murder of Gwendoline Sweeney, but made one fundamental mistake in his statement. He claimed that if he were to kill someone, he would kill with a knife: "Not me, I would not strangle anybody. I would knife them." Until this moment, the police had not mentioned the fact that Gwendoline had also been manually throttled.

That mistake was enough to send Thomas James to the gallows.

FOR SOME TIME, before 1943, Christos Georghiou and Savvas Demetriades had been partners in a cafe in Cardiff. They were close friends but all this changed when there was a disagreement over 30/-. Christos told Savvas that the partnership was dissolved. However, the tension between the two was, it seemed, finally ended when, in April 1943, Georghiou left Cardiff and moved down to London.

On October 24th though, Savvas also travelled down to London, on business. He first contacted a friend of his, Nicola Costas, who owned a cafe at 4 Goodge Place and Nicola agreed that Savvas could use his spare room.

At 11.00pm on October 24th, Nicola and Savvas went to another cafe, at 42 Dean Street. It was there that Savvas saw Georghiou. Later, when Nicola and Savvas were at another establishment at 91 Charlotte Street, Georghiou followed them there, but there was no conversation between them.

The next day, Savvas called on Christos Costa, who owned the cafe at Dean Street. The two men had a brief discussion before walking together down Dean Street. They turned into Old Compton Street. It was just after 3.00pm. Suddenly, a hand appeared on Savvas's shoulder. Costa and Savvas tried to turn and it was then that Costa saw a knife. He ran on and Savvas turned to face his attacker.

There were a number of witnesses who saw at least part of the attack. Alwyn Harry Percy Childs, who was nearby, saw the two men exchange blows. Savvas fell to the ground and whilst lying there, his assailant stepped forward and stabbed him in the chest.

Martha Zurrer, a Swiss tourist, was standing outside a cafe in Old Compton Street and saw a grey-suited man, with a knife in his hand, running away from the scene.

Savvas died at Charing Cross Hospital at 3.30pm. He had been stabbed three times, the fatal blow being one that had entered his chest near the right nipple and passed through his lung.

A search was launched for Christos Georghiou but he was missing from his lodgings at Conway Street. The police soon traced an old friend of his, Christina Douglas,

NAME	Christos Georghiou (Chris Trihas)
AGE AT EXECUTION	37
DATE OF EXECUTION	Wednesday, 2nd February, 1944
PLACE OF EXECUTION	Pentonville
HANGMAN	Albert Pierrepoint
ASSISTANT	Herbert Morris
DATE OF TRIAL	10th December, 1943
LOCATION OF TRIAL	Old Bailey
PRESIDING JUDGE	Not known
PROSECUTION COUNSEL	Walter Hedley
DEFENCE COUNSEL	Not known
NUMBER OF VICTIMS	1

VICTIMS DETAILS	
NAME	Savvas Demetriades
AGE	43
DATE OF MURDER	Monday, 25th October, 1943
PLACE OF MURDER	Old Compton Street, Soho, London
METHOD OF KILLING	Stabbed
RELATIONSHIP TO KILLER	None

who lived at 26 Marlborough Hill, Harrow. She had allowed Georghiou to stay in her spare room and it was there that he was arrested at 10.05am on the 26th.

Georghiou claimed to have no memory of the crime. He had been very drunk and all he could remember was having an argument with someone and being pushed.

It should be pointed out that although Georghiou was identified by Miss Zurrer, Alwyn Childs said that Georghiou was not the man he had seen attacking Savvas.

In the event, the jury felt they had enough evidence to convict and on February 2nd, 1944, Christos Georghiou became the first of four men that year to die on the gallows at Pentonville.

IN FEBRUARY, 1943, a Canadian soldier, Mervin McEwen, went absent from his unit. Moving to Halifax he began living in a disused army hut in Savile park and over the next few weeks was befriended by a retired postman, 82-year-old Mark Turner.

On the night of April 2nd, Turner invited McEwen and another friend named Crabtree, into his house. McEwen and Crabtree both left at 9.00pm and McEwen returned to his hut in the park.

Mister Hall lived next door to Turner and at 1.00am on the morning of April 3rd, he heard someone knocking on Turner's door. By 11.00am that same morning, there was no sign of Turner, who was normally up well before this time. Hall looked through Turner's window and, seeing the house in disarray, contacted the police.

Mark Turner had slept downstairs on a fold-up settee bed on the night of April 2nd, and this is where his body was found. He had been battered to death and fingerprints were found on a whisky bottle, a lemonade bottle and a pint pot. Also found was a soldier's battle dress and a cap badge of the Royal Canadian Corps, but of Mervin McEwen, the soldier who lived in the park, there was no sign.

In fact, McEwen had travelled to Manchester, where he met up with Annie Elizabeth Perfect. They grew close and began living as man and wife and for three months, McEwen, using the name James Acton, was safe.

On June 23rd, the police called at Annie's house, on a routine matter and questioned the man she was living with. Asked to identify himself he now claimed that his name was Mark Turney and produced an identity card. The alert policeman saw that the last letter in the surname, looked as if it had been altered from an 'r' and asked Mr Turney to sign his name as an added check. The signature was seen to read Mervin Turney.

It was too much for coincidence and in less than a minute, McEwen had unintentionally revealed the name of his victim and his own first name. Faced with this, McEwen admitted his real identity and was arrested.

McEwen admitted that he had gone back

NAME	Mervin Clare McEwen
AGE AT EXECUTION	35
DATE OF EXECUTION	Thursday, 3rd February, 1944
PLACE OF EXECUTION	Leeds
HANGMAN	Thomas Pierrepoint
ASSISTANT	Stephen Wade
DATE OF TRIAL	1st December – 2nd December, 1943
LOCATION OF TRIAL	Leeds
PRESIDING JUDGE	Mister Justice Stable
PROSECUTION COUNSEL	G.H.B. Streatfeild, Myles Archibald
DEFENCE COUNSEL	C. Paley Scott, J. McLusky
NUMBER OF VICTIMS	1

VICTIMS DETAILS	
NAME	Mark Turner
AGE	82
DATE OF MURDER	Saturday, 3rd April, 1943
PLACE OF MURDER	Moorfield Street, Halifax
METHOD OF KILLING	Battered
RELATIONSHIP TO KILLER	None

to Turner's house early on the morning of April 3rd. Gaining entry, he cooked himself some food and found a bottle of whisky. At one stage, McEwen dropped a plate, which woke Turner, and McEwen struck out, intending only to quieten him, not to kill. Once he realised Turner was dead, McEwen stole his identity card, altered the name to Turney, and caught the bus to Manchester.

The defence claimed that it was not a case of murder, as McEwen had drunk so much that he was incapable of forming the intention necessary to make the crime murder. It took the jury 40 minutes to reject that plea.

IN FEBRUARY, 1943, John Waters, who was based at Henley-on-Thames, met a local girl, Doris Staples, and they started walking out together. By July of that same year, Doris had decided that she didn't want to be tied down and had started cooling the relationship. Indeed, Waters even heard that she had been seeing other American servicemen, and decided to do something about it.

Doris worked at a drapers shop in Greys Road and on July 14th, repeated shots were heard from these premises. The civil and military police were called in and after a period of siege, a tear gas canister was thrown into the shop, and an entry forced.

The body of Doris Staples was discovered inside the drapers; she had sustained five bullet wounds. Her killer, Waters, was now in a toilet at the back of the shop, where he put the gun to his head and fired. Badly injured, he was rushed to hospital where slowly he recovered.

Found guilty of murder, Waters was hanged, despite a plea for clemency from his unit and local townspeople.

NAME	John H. Waters
AGE AT EXECUTION	39
DATE OF EXECUTION	Thursday, 10th February, 1944
PLACE OF EXECUTION	Shepton Mallet
HANGMAN	Not known
DATE OF TRIAL	29th November, 1943
LOCATION OF TRIAL	Watford
NUMBER OF VICTIMS	1

VICTIMS DETAILS	
NAME	Doris M. Staples
AGE	35
DATE OF MURDER	Wednesday, 14th July, 1943
PLACE OF MURDER	11a Greys Road, Henley-on-Thames
METHOD OF KILLING	Shot
RELATIONSHIP TO KILLER	Girlfriend

ONE OF THE problems encountered by an enemy agent is how to conceal his radio transmitter. The German authorities felt sure that they had solved this problem in the case of Oswald Job, by finding an alternative form of communication.

Job was the son of a German couple and had lived in Paris since 1911. Once France fell, Job was approached by the Germans and agreed to act as a spy. He was given extensive training and then told that his task would be to get to England and report back on morale and the damage caused by German bombing.

In 1943, Job was taken to the Spanish border by German agents and, having reached Lisbon, announced that he was a British subject who had escaped from German custody in France. He flew to England, landing here on November 1st, 1943.

Job was supplied with secret writing equipment hidden in the hollows of keys and told to write letters addressed to certain British people held in the St Denis internment camp. These letters would be intercepted by the Germans and the secret information decoded. The internees did not know how their names were being used.

The plan failed because the British authorities were not satisfied with Job's story and in due course he admitted being an agent for the Germans. At his trial though, Job claimed that he had fooled the Germans and only volunteered to spy for them so he could escape to England. This final attempt to escape the gallows failed.

NAME	Oswald John Job
AGE AT EXECUTION	58
DATE OF EXECUTION	Thursday, 16th March, 1944
PLACE OF EXECUTION	Pentonville
HANGMAN	Albert Pierrepoint
ASSISTANT	Harry Kirk
DATE OF TRIAL	24th January – 26th January, 1944
LOCATION OF TRIAL	Old Bailey
PRESIDING JUDGE	Mister Justice Stable
PROSECUTION COUNSEL	Not known
DEFENCE COUNSEL	Not known
NUMBER OF VICTIMS	Hanged for spying

1944

ON OCTOBER 3RD, 1931, Ernest Charles Digby married Violet Amy Gwendoline Thurley. On March 23rd, 1943, he bigamously married Olga Davy Hill, then aged 28.

Olga had already given birth to Digby's daughter, Doreen, who was born on May 18th, 1942. Two weeks afterwards, Digby had taken the child away, telling Olga that they could not afford to keep it and saying that he had found someone willing to adopt it. By the time the wedding took place, Olga was pregnant again.

Dawn Digby was born on October 21st, 1943. Within days, Digby was suggesting that they put this child out for adoption too. It was not until the middle of November that the decision was made. Dawn would also be adopted.

At 10.30am on November 15th, Digby, Olga and their daughter, walked towards the railway station. Digby was carrying the child and at one stage he fell behind. Olga waited for him and when he caught up, he was still carrying the heavy suitcase but there was no sign of Dawn. Olga asked no questions.

That evening, having returned to their lodgings in Milborne Port, Olga finally asked about Dawn. Digby said that everything was all right and later told their landlady, Edith Elizabeth Gibbs, that the child had been handed over to Olga's mother in London. Edith did not believe the story and reported the matter to the police. On November 21st, Olga was arrested by Inspector James Stephen Dunn.

The following day, Digby was arrested at his camp in Oxfordshire. It was then that witnesses came forward who said that Digby had been seen burying some rubbish. When the police excavated the area, they found the battered body of the child. The pathologist's report suggested that Dawn had been struck with the end of the heavy case her father had been carrying.

Digby made three statements, all equally incredulous. In the first, made on November 23rd, he admitted that he had abandoned his first child, and claimed to have no recollection of what had happened to the second! The next day he admitted that he had buried some rubbish, and in the third he finally admitted something to do with his daughter's death.

NAME	Ernest Charles Digby
AGE AT EXECUTION	34
DATE OF EXECUTION	Thursday, 16th March, 1944
PLACE OF EXECUTION	Bristol
HANGMAN	Not known
ASSISTANT	Not known
DATE OF TRIAL	25th January – 27th January, 1944
LOCATION OF TRIAL	Taunton
PRESIDING JUDGE	Mister Justice Singleton
PROSECUTION COUNSEL	F.S. Laskey
DEFENCE COUNSEL	F.A. Wilshire, O.C.M. Davis
NUMBER OF VICTIMS	1

VICTIMS DETAILS	
NAME	Dawn Digby
AGE	3 weeks
DATE OF MURDER	Monday, 15th November, 1943
PLACE OF MURDER	Woods near Milborne Port, Somerset
METHOD OF KILLING	Battered
RELATIONSHIP TO KILLER	Daughter

According to this statement, he had stumbled and fallen whilst carrying the baby and had then put her into the case. He then walked into a second woods, took Dawn out of the case and left her on the ground. Having returned from Yeovil, he went to check on his daughter and found she had rolled down a banking and was now dead. He put her back into the case and took her home with him before taking her up to camp and burying her.

Digby and Olga were both charged with murder. He was found guilty and sentenced to death, but Olga, perhaps surprisingly, received a not-guilty verdict.

ON DECEMBER 8TH, 1943, a taxicab was found abandoned in Haynes Green Lane, Marney. Inside was a bloodstained jacket, leading police officers to deduce that some kind of attack had taken place. In the pocket of that jacket, officers found a driving licence that gave the name of the cab driver as Henry Hailstone, who lived in Colchester. There now followed some brilliant police work which in due course led to the solution of a brutal murder.

The first clue was the fact that the cab had been parked on the wrong side of the road. This led the police to suggest that the assailant was someone used to driving on the opposite side of the road, possibly an American. A wide search of the area was organised and later that same day, a bloodstained mackintosh was found.

A name tag in this bore the name Captain J.J. Walker and in due course, this gentleman was traced. He informed the police that he had lost the coat on December 5th, when he had met a coloured American soldier who had stolen the coat, a bottle of whisky, and his Rolex watch. The thief, whoever he was, had left behind a gas mask and the name in this was J. Hill.

The body of Henry Hailstone was found in the grounds of Birch Rectory, on December 9th. Forensic examination showed that he had not been killed where he had been found and since he weighed over 11 stone, it was unlikely that one man could have carried his body to where it was found. This led detectives to assume that they were looking for at least two men.

The owner of the gas mask, Mr Hill, was now traced and he revealed that he had given his mask to another soldier, George Fowler. When Fowler himself was interviewed he at first claimed that he had lost the mask in Euston Square, but he was held on suspicion whilst his belongings were searched. This search turned up a pawn ticket, for a Rolex watch, in the name of Charlie Huntley. When Huntley was spoken to, he said that he had been given the watch by Private Leatherberry and when the watch was redeemed, Captain Walker identified it as his.

When Fowler was interviewed for a

NAME	J.C. Leatherberry
AGE AT EXECUTION	Not known
DATE OF EXECUTION	Thursday, 16th March, 1944
PLACE OF EXECUTION	Shepton Mallet
HANGMAN	Not known
DATE OF TRIAL	19th January, 1944
LOCATION OF TRIAL	Ipswich
NUMBER OF VICTIMS	1

VICTIMS DETAILS	
NAME	Henry (Harry) Claude Hailstone
AGE	28
DATE OF MURDER	Wednesday, 8th December, 1943
PLACE OF MURDER	Between Colchester and Marney
METHOD OF KILLING	Strangled/battered
RELATIONSHIP TO KILLER	None

second time, he admitted that he and Leatherberry had been involved in the killing of the taxi driver. The two men had taken the cab and it had been Leatherberry who strangled the driver, from behind.

Both men were found guilty but whereas Leatherberry was sentenced to death, Fowler received a life sentence as he had given evidence and had played only a minor part in the crime.

FLIGHT SERGEANT RONALD Murphy was simply carrying out part of his duties in inspecting the beds at the camp. With him was Corporal Archibald Taylor and when they reached the bed of aircraftman Sidney Delasalle, they found him in a most argumentative mood.

Delasalle began by complaining about the rations but his tone of voice and the way he addressed the flight sergeant did nothing to help his case. Murphy ended by commenting that the matter raised was none of Delasalle's business and if there was any further insolence, he would be taken to the station commander.

Instead of taking the warning to heart, Delasalle escalated matters by telling Murphy that he wanted to see him outside "with his coat off", meaning that he was inviting him to fight. That was too much for Murphy. Delasalle was put on a charge and as a result, ended up confined to camp for 14 days.

The next time the N.A.A.F.I. truck pulled up at the camp, an orderly queue of men formed, waiting for their tea. After a few minutes, Delasalle approached, carrying a rifle and shouted for the men to get out of his way. Once they had cleared he put the rifle to his shoulder and fired two shots into Murphy. In fact, four other men were injured – Capp, Hellier, Boast and Baxter – but they all recovered from their injuries.

Delasalle claimed that he resented the punishment he had received but bore no malice against Murphy in particular. He said he had no recollection of the crime until he realised he was being held down by some of the other men. Doctor Macadam testified that it was possible for Delasalle to have committed the crime in an automatic state and that he would possibly have no memory of the crime afterwards, but this was not enough to save his life.

Throughout the trial, Delasalle's wife, a Burmese girl, had listened to the evidence. Ronald Murphy's mother had also travelled up, from Brighton, but had remained outside the courtroom throughout. Once the verdict had been announced, it was Delasalle's wife who revealed it to Murphy's mother and the two women were then seen comforting one another. After all, they had both lost someone they loved.

NAME	Sidney James Delasalle
AGE AT EXECUTION	39
DATE OF EXECUTION	Thursday, 13th April, 1944
PLACE OF EXECUTION	Durham
HANGMAN	Albert Pierrepoint
ASSISTANT	Not known
DATE OF TRIAL	22nd March, 1944
LOCATION OF TRIAL	Leeds
PRESIDING JUDGE	Mister Justice Hallett
PROSECUTION COUNSEL	C. Paley Scott, R. Cleworth
DEFENCE COUNSEL	G.H.B. Streatfeild, W. Temple
NUMBER OF VICTIMS	1

VICTIMS DETAILS	
NAME	Ronald John Murphy
AGE	23
DATE OF MURDER	Friday, 4th February, 1944
PLACE OF MURDER	North Country Camp
METHOD OF KILLING	Shot
RELATIONSHIP TO KILLER	None

ON THE EVENING of March 6th, 1944, Private Wiley Harris and his friend, Private Robert Fils, were enjoying a night out in a bar in North Queen Street, Belfast, when Wiley was approached by a stranger, a man named Harry Coogan.

Coogan asked Wiley if he wanted a woman and when he heard the positive reply, pointed to a young woman, Eileen Megaw. A price of £1 was agreed and Coogan took Wiley and Megaw to an air-raid shelter at the top of Earl Street.

The money was handed over to Eileen, in coins, and then she and Wiley went into the shelter. Coogan remained outside, saying he would keep watch. The two potential lovers had only just begun their preliminaries when Coogan shouted that the police were coming. Wiley and Megaw rushed outside but there was no sign of the police. Not unnaturally, Wiley wished to return to the shelter, but Eileen now seemed reluctant to continue with their activities.

Wiley demanded his money back but Coogan told Eileen to keep it. At that point, Eileen decided to run for it, still holding on to Wiley's money. However, as she ran, the coins began to fall from her and Wiley began to pick them up. As he did so, Coogan struck him in the face. Immediately, Wiley drew his knife and in the ensuing fight, stabbed Coogan 17 times.

Under the circumstances of the attack, Wiley tried to convince the court martial that he had acted in self-defence. Had he stabbed Coogan once or perhaps twice, he might well have escaped with his life, but 17 wounds were just too many to accept.

NAME Wiley Harris
AGE AT EXECUTION Not known
DATE OF EXECUTION Friday, 26th May, 1944
PLACE OF EXECUTION Shepton Mallet
HANGMAN Not known
DATE OF TRIAL Not known
LOCATION OF TRIAL Not known
NUMBER OF VICTIMS 1

VICTIMS DETAILS
NAME Harry Coogan
AGE Not known
DATE OF MURDER Monday, 6th March, 1944
PLACE OF MURDER Earl Street, Belfast
METHOD OF KILLING Stabbed
RELATIONSHIP TO KILLER None

1944

BY THE TIME Alex Miranda returned to his camp at Broomhill, he was already much the worse for drink, having been found urinating in the street at Honiton by Special Sergeant William Durbin and Police Constable North. They arrested Miranda and arranged for transport back to Broomhill.

Back at the camp, Miranda's behaviour did not improve. He was argumentative and threw insults at Sergeant Thomas Evison, who was actually asleep at the time. A few minutes later a shot rang out and Miranda announced to the rest of the hut: "Your worries are over now, boys. I have shot the sergeant."

For Miranda though, the trouble was just beginning. Tried before a court martial, he was found guilty of murder and sentenced to death by shooting. The sentence was carried out at Shepton Mallet on May 30th, 1944, by a 10-man firing squad. Miranda was the seventh American to be executed at the prison, but the first to be killed in such a manner.

NAME	Alex F. Miranda
AGE AT EXECUTION	20
DATE OF EXECUTION	Tuesday, 30th May, 1944
PLACE OF EXECUTION	Shepton Mallet
HANGMAN	Shot
DATE OF TRIAL	20th March, 1944
LOCATION OF TRIAL	Not known
NUMBER OF VICTIMS	1

VICTIMS DETAILS	
NAME	Thomas Evison
AGE	Not known
DATE OF MURDER	Sunday, 5th March, 1944
PLACE OF MURDER	Broomhill Camp, Devon
METHOD OF KILLING	Shot
RELATIONSHIP TO KILLER	None

O N FEBRUARY 15TH, 1944, Arthur Belcher paid a visit to his allotment off Sherard Road, Eltham, and was horrified to find there the body of a young woman, a scarf knotted tightly around her neck. Police inquiries soon turned up the identity discs of Iris Miriam Deeley, a leading aircraftwoman in the W.A.A.F.

Iris had a pass from Kidbrooke camp and had arranged to meet up her fiancé, William Quill. At around 8.30pm on the Sunday night, Iris and William had gone to Charing Cross station so that she could catch the train back to Kidbrooke, but by the time they arrived, the train had already left and Iris decided to wait for the 11.25pm to Lewisham, from where she would walk back to the base.

Iris was indeed seen later at Lewisham High Street, where she met up with a soldier who then walked on with her, towards the spot where her body was subsequently discovered. The police now knew they were looking for a serviceman.

The breakthrough came on February 22nd, at another station, St Pancras. An army sergeant was busy kissing a W.A.A.F. goodbye when an alert railway policeman noticed that he was wearing medal ribbons he was not entitled to. The sergeant was taken in for further questioning.

Searched at the police station, he was found to be in possession of some clothing coupons in the name of W. Quill, which immediately linked him to the murder of Iris Miriam Deeley.

The army sergeant was a deserter by the name of Ernest Kemp and at first he denied any knowledge of the murder. He agreed that he had been in Lewisham and was the young man seen talking to Iris, but insisted that he had left her near the railway arch.

There was, however, one more piece of evidence that linked Kemp to the murder. Close by the body, some size-11 footprints had been found. When Kemp's shoes were checked, these were also found to be size 11.

Faced with this evidence, Kemp finally admitted that he had killed Iris. He said he had touched her breasts and when she had objected, he had pushed her to the ground and started undressing her. In the process of

NAME	Ernest James Harman Kemp
AGE AT EXECUTION	21
DATE OF EXECUTION	Tuesday, 6th June, 1944
PLACE OF EXECUTION	Wandsworth
HANGMAN	Albert Pierrepoint
ASSISTANT	Herbert Morris
DATE OF TRIAL	18th April, 1944
LOCATION OF TRIAL	Old Bailey
PRESIDING JUDGE	Mister Justice Cassels
PROSECUTION COUNSEL	F.H. Lawton
DEFENCE COUNSEL	L.A. Byrne
NUMBER OF VICTIMS	1

VICTIMS DETAILS	
NAME	Iris Miriam Deeley
AGE	21
DATE OF MURDER	Monday, 14th February, 1944
PLACE OF MURDER	Sherard Road, Eltham, London
METHOD OF KILLING	Strangled
RELATIONSHIP TO KILLER	None

this attack, Kemp grasped Iris's scarf and twisted it around her neck. The more she struggled, the more he pulled until eventually she stopped. At that point, Kemp left the murder scene, without raping Iris.

At his trial, Kemp pleaded guilty to manslaughter but not guilty to murder. After hearing the evidence, the jury took 15 minutes to decide that Kemp was a murderer, though they did recommend him to mercy.

On June 6th, D-Day, whilst many of his comrades were fighting on the beaches of Normandy, Ernest James Harman Kemp, kept a appointment with Albert Pierrepoint in the execution chamber at Wandsworth.

PIERRE NEUKERMANS HAD served in the Belgian army, being invalided out in 1938, at the age of 22. In 1940, he tried to escape to France but when this proved to be impossible, he returned to Brussels. Eventually he was approached by the German authorities and agreed to act as a spy.

In 1943, Neukermans was put across the border between France and Spain with a cover story that he had escaped from enemy territory. From Spain he travelled to Lisbon, and from there to London, arriving there on July 16th.

Upon being questioned, Neukermans said he had tried to escape twice. The first time he had been assisted by two Belgians, Louis and Georges, but when this attempt failed, he had managed to escape alone.

At first, the story was believed and he was put to work as a clerk in the offices of the Belgian government in England. From here he sent information to Germany about the location of Belgian troops in England.

After a few months, Neukermans was again questioned and this time, his cover story was proved false. He admitted that the Louis he had referred to was Louis Debray and Georges was Georges Hollevoet. Both were agents of the German Secret Service.

His guilt proved he was sentenced to death and executed almost one year after he had first landed in England.

NAME	Pierre Richard Charles Neukermans
AGE AT EXECUTION	28
DATE OF EXECUTION	Friday, 23rd June, 1944
PLACE OF EXECUTION	Pentonville
HANGMAN	Albert Pierrepoint
ASSISTANT	Alex Riley
DATE OF TRIAL	28th April – 1st May, 1944
LOCATION OF TRIAL	Old Bailey
PRESIDING JUDGE	Mister Justice Macnaghten
PROSECUTION COUNSEL	Not known
DEFENCE COUNSEL	Not known
NUMBER OF VICTIMS	Hanged for spying

V AN HOVE WAS a native of Antwerp who in 1940, tried to escape to France. Finding the border closed, he returned to Antwerp, where he earned a living as a waiter.

In an effort to earn a little extra money, Van Hove dabbled in the black market and this brought him to the attention of the police. Knowing that he might find himself in serious trouble, he contacted an acquaintance who worked for the German Secret Service, and offered his assistance.

Van Hove was moved to a German airfield in northern France where he spied on his fellow workmates, reporting any resistance activities or support until, in 1942, he said he wished to operate outside German-held territory. His offer was accepted and he was told to leave via Switzerland, escape to England and report back on Allied plans for the invasion of Europe.

The Swiss escape failed and Van Hove returned to Belgium. Here he signed on a German ship bound for Sweden, where he deserted and contacted the Belgian authorities in exile, saying he was anxious to get to England and fight for the Allied forces.

Van Hove arrived in England on February 11th, 1943 but his story was not accepted and under interrogation he admitted that he was an agent.

NAME	Joseph Jan Van Hove
AGE AT EXECUTION	27
DATE OF EXECUTION	Wednesday, 12th July, 1944
PLACE OF EXECUTION	Pentonville
HANGMAN	Albert Pierrepoint
ASSISTANT	Stephen Wade
DATE OF TRIAL	23rd May – 24th May, 1944
LOCATION OF TRIAL	Old Bailey
PRESIDING JUDGE	Mister Justice Hallett
PROSECUTION COUNSEL	Not known
DEFENCE COUNSEL	Not known
NUMBER OF VICTIMS	Hanged for spying

GLADYS MAY APPLETON and her boyfriend, George Leslie Barker, were happy together and their future looked bright. All that was to be taken away by one man.

Gladys and George last saw each other on the night of March 19th, 1944. She spent part of that evening at his home at 11 Knowsley Road, leaving there at 10.45pm to walk home to 101 Bishop Road, where Gladys lived with her father. The following morning, at 7.45am, her raped and strangled body was found by Betsy Barnes, a postwoman delivering mail to The Elms, on Cowley Hill Lane.

Inquiries revealed that a young Scots soldier had been seen in the area the previous night. Jeannie Galvin had arrived at her home at 10 Gamble Avenue, at around 10.45pm. She had been accosted by the soldier who at first was just friendly, but as she reached home, he said he was determined to kiss her goodnight and she became afraid. She had the presence of mind not to panic and told him to leave her alone.

When the gardens around Jeannie's house were examined, two sets of footprints were found. One of these was Jeannie's but the other was not. Casts were taken and moves made to trace the soldier.

The nearest army camp was at Rainford and it transpired that two soldiers had been absent without leave on the night in question. These two, John Hunter Sanderson, and John Gordon Davidson, were interviewed.

Sanderson admitted that he and Davidson had left the camp around 6.00pm and had visited a pub called the Bottle and Glass. After a few drinks, they moved on to St Helens, arriving there after 8.00pm. By 8.20pm, they were in the Rifle Corps Hotel where they got talking to two other soldiers, Lance Corporal Green and Private Henry. They stayed together until 10.00pm when two girls appeared and he and Davidson went off with them.

Both men had their eyes on the same girl, but it appeared to be Sanderson who was having most success. Eventually, Davidson took the hint and left his friend with the girl. Sanderson finished his statement by saying that he had not seen Davidson again until 6.30am the next morning.

NAME	John Gordon Davidson
AGE AT EXECUTION	19
DATE OF EXECUTION	Wednesday, 12th July, 1944
PLACE OF EXECUTION	Liverpool
HANGMAN	Not known
ASSISTANT	Not known
DATE OF TRIAL	8th May, 1944
LOCATION OF TRIAL	Manchester
PRESIDING JUDGE	Mister Justice Hilbery
PROSECUTION COUNSEL	Neville Laski, F.J. Sandbach
DEFENCE COUNSEL	Kenneth Burke
NUMBER OF VICTIMS	1

VICTIMS DETAILS	
NAME	Gladys May Appleton
AGE	27
DATE OF MURDER	Sunday, 19th March, 1944
PLACE OF MURDER	Grounds of The Elms, Cowley Hill Lane, St Helens
METHOD OF KILLING	Strangled
RELATIONSHIP TO KILLER	None

When Davidson's shoes were compared with the casts taken from Gamble Avenue, they were found to match. Davidson also fitted the description given by Jeannie Galvin and it became clear that he was the Scot seen in the area. At first he denied all knowledge of the crime but later admitted that he had killed Gladys.

At his trial, Davidson tried to put forward a plea of insanity but there was no evidence of mental instability in his background. At his appeal, he claimed that he was so drunk at the time of the attack that he did not know what he was doing. The court refused to interfere with the original verdict.

BURNETT ESTILL, THE third officer on board the Pacific Shipper went to turn off a light in one of the cabins on the night of April 8th, 1944, when he noticed a rather unpleasant smell coming from the chief radio officer's cabin. Estill tried the door, but it was locked, so he returned to his own quarters.

At 11.00pm that same night, Estill was in a cabin below when he noticed a small pool of blood on the floor. Looking up he saw that the pool was being formed by a small trickle, dripping down from the roof. He alerted others on board and the door to the radio officer's cabin was unlocked. There they found the battered body of James William Percey.

Police investigations soon pieced together what seemed to have happened. Percey, a native of Montreal in Canada, had recently drawn some £87 from the Mercantile Marine Office in Liverpool. This money had been compensation for property Percey had lost when he had been torpedoed and some of the notes were from a batch, numbered consecutively from A 88 E 514001 to 514500. These notes were now missing, so the motive for the crime appeared to be robbery.

It was also fairly easy to determine who had committed that robbery. James Galbraith, a merchant navy chief steward who lived in Moss Road, Stretford, had been seen coming on board the Pacific Shipper, with Percey, on August 6th. The day before, Galbraith had borrowed 10/- from a friend and had said he was short of money and yet, on the afternoon Percey was last seen alive, Galbraith had purchased a new coat for £7. More tellingly, this and other purchases traced to Galbraith were paid for with notes from the batch quoted. Eventually, 40 such notes were traced to Galbraith, who was finally picked up on Tuesday, April 11th.

Galbraith admitted he had been with Percey. They had gone on board Percey's ship to drink beer and had stayed together for an hour and a half. Galbraith even admitted stealing the money from Percey, but claimed that when he left him, he was still alive and well.

On the third and final day of Galbraith's trial, the jury retired to decide on their

NAME	James Galbraith
AGE AT EXECUTION	26
DATE OF EXECUTION	Wednesday, 26th July, 1944
PLACE OF EXECUTION	Manchester
HANGMAN	Not known
ASSISTANT	Not known
DATE OF TRIAL	9th May – 11th May, 1944
LOCATION OF TRIAL	Manchester
PRESIDING JUDGE	Mister Justice Hilbery
PROSECUTION COUNSEL	Neville J. Laski, F.J.V. Sandbach
DEFENCE COUNSEL	Edward Wooll, Percy Butlin
NUMBER OF VICTIMS	1

VICTIMS DETAILS	
NAME	James William Percey
AGE	48
DATE OF MURDER	Thursday, 6th April, 1944
PLACE OF MURDER	On board the Pacific Shipper, at Salford Docks, Manchester
METHOD OF KILLING	Battered
RELATIONSHIP TO KILLER	None

verdict. They felt they had heard enough evidence to suggest that the man who robbed Percey was the same man who had killed him, and Galbraith was found guilty of murder.

NORA EMILY PAYNE was a clerk employed by the Petroleum Board, and had been associating with William Cowle since 1941, although he was a married man, living apart from his wife.

After lunch on May 18th, 1944, Nora left her home at 7 Lytton Road, Leicester, at her usual time of 1.40pm, in order to make her way back to work. It was a journey she would never complete. Twenty minutes later, at 2.00pm, a Mrs Kimberley heard a scream coming from a passageway that ran close by her home in Springfield Road.

Mrs Kimberley turned, in time to see a man walk out of the passageway, look around, walk back, return again and run off. Within seconds, Nora Payne also appeared from the passageway, holding her hand to her neck in an attempt to staunch the flow of blood from a severe stab wound. Nora was rushed to Leicester Royal Infirmary, where she died later the same day.

By the time Nora passed away, her assailant was already in custody. Five minutes after the attack, William Cowle had walked up to a policeman on duty and said: "I have just stabbed someone. It was a girl. I did it in a fit of temper." Cowle was cautioned and taken into custody, later to be charged with murder.

The motive was plain enough. In a suitcase in Cowle's hotel room in Belmont Street, was found a number of letters from Nora, the latest of which broke off their association. Cowle had gone to speak to her and when it became clear that Nora would not change her mind, he had drawn out a dagger and stabbed her.

The trial was originally set for Leicester assizes, but was postponed and moved to Nottingham. Found guilty, Cowle was sentenced to death, after which he thanked the judge before being taken to the cells below the court.

On August 8th, Cowle was hanged at Leicester together with William Meffen, both having been sentenced by the same judge. It was the first double hanging at that prison for 41 years.

NAME	William Alfred Cowle
AGE AT EXECUTION	31
DATE OF EXECUTION	Tuesday, 8th August, 1944
PLACE OF EXECUTION	Leicester
HANGMAN	Albert Pierrepoint
ASSISTANT	Not known
DATE OF TRIAL	26th June, 1944
LOCATION OF TRIAL	Nottingham
PRESIDING JUDGE	Mister Justice Singleton
PROSECUTION COUNSEL	W.K. Carter
DEFENCE COUNSEL	Arthur Ward, L.C. Graham-Dixon
NUMBER OF VICTIMS	1

VICTIMS DETAILS	
NAME	Nora Emily Payne
AGE	32
DATE OF MURDER	Thursday, 18th May, 1944
PLACE OF MURDER	Springfield Road, Leicester
METHOD OF KILLING	Stabbed
RELATIONSHIP TO KILLER	Ex-girlfriend

G EORGE MEFFEN LOVED all his family, but that love was rather possessive and when a young man began to pay attention to one of his children, Meffen felt he had to take action.

Meffen, his married daughter, Lily Calladine and his stepdaughter, Winifred Stanley, all worked for Derby Cables Limited, as did George Birks, who took a shine to Winifred. Meffen made it plain that he did not approve, but Winifred was a grown woman and would make her own decisions. She started seeing George on a regular basis and Meffen took things badly, on one occasion saying to Lily that if Winifred continued with her behaviour, he would give her a good thrashing.

Things came to a head on the night of February 22nd. Once again Winifred spent some time with George, but this time she did not return home. That night, Meffen sat at home, crying uncontrollably.

It was not until two days later that Meffen managed to confront George Birks and demanded confirmation that he had spent the night with Winifred. George denied it, but Meffen was far from satisfied. It was to be another five days before he finally snapped.

At 6.45am on February 29th, the family were getting themselves ready for work. Winifred was in the bathroom and no one took particular notice when Meffen followed her into the room. Seconds later a terrible scream rang out from the bathroom. The door was locked but eventually Lily, her mother, and her sister, Elaine Bishop, managed to gain access, only to find Meffen, a razor in his hand and Winifred lying on the floor, a gaping wound in her throat.

Lily tried to take the razor from her father but he would have none of it. He did not hurt any other member of the family but was heard to shout: "No, I've done it and now I'll hang" before he calmly went to his room, changed his clothes and left the house.

George Meffen did not run far. He found the nearest policeman and gave himself up. In his pocket was found a note, in his handwriting, apparently penned the night before. In this he begged forgiveness for what he had to do, one sentence reading: "I don't

know when I shall do it but it is bound to come." This clearly implied that the crime was premeditated.

Meffen claimed later that he had no memory of either the attack on Winifred, or of writing the note. This attempt to put forward a defence based on temporary insanity failed and the jury took slightly over half an hour to find Meffen guilty as charged.

NAME William Frederick George Meffen
AGE AT EXECUTION 52
DATE OF EXECUTION Tuesday, 8th August, 1944
PLACE OF EXECUTION Leicester
HANGMAN Albert Pierrepoint
ASSISTANT Not known
DATE OF TRIAL 19th June, 1944
LOCATION OF TRIAL Derby
PRESIDING JUDGE Mister Justice Singleton
PROSECUTION COUNSEL Walter Kelly Carter
DEFENCE COUNSEL T. Norman Winning, G.A. Myers-Ward
NUMBER OF VICTIMS 1

VICTIMS DETAILS
NAME Winfred Ellen Stanley
AGE 38
DATE OF MURDER Tuesday, 29th February, 1944
PLACE OF MURDER 453 Nottingham Road, Chaddesden
METHOD OF KILLING Cut throat
RELATIONSHIP TO KILLER Stepdaughter

1944

ON THE EVENING of Sunday, March 4th, 1944, Dorothy Holmes left a dance at Bishop's Cleeve, in Gloucestershire. Dorothy had been with her boyfriend, an American serviceman named Edward Hefferman, and the two had not gone very far when they realised they were being followed by two other soldiers.

At about midnight, as Hefferman stood at the end of Brookside Lane, the two soldiers moved forward, one of them striking him in the face, with a bottle. Hefferman ran for assistance but whilst he was gone, the two men dragged Dorothy into a nearby field, where they both raped her.

Dorothy survived her ordeal and the following day, investigators found footprints in the field where she had been attacked. Plaster casts of these prints were taken and a comparison made with the shoes of all personnel at the nearby camp. This led to the arrest of two men, Eliga Brinson and Willie Smith. Both were found guilty and sentenced to death.

NAMES	Eliga Brinson; Willie Smith
AGES AT EXECUTION	Not known
DATE OF EXECUTION	Friday, 11th August, 1944
PLACE OF EXECUTION	Shepton Mallet
HANGMAN	Not known
DATE OF TRIAL	28th April – 29th April, 1944
LOCATION OF TRIAL	Cheltenham
NUMBER OF VICTIMS	Hanged for rape

BEATRICE MAUD REYNOLDS lived at Gunnislake in Cornwall, where she was an active helper in her local branch of the British Legion. She had been in the Legion Hall on the evening of Wednesday, July 26th, 1944 and left at around 10.40pm. Walking home, she was suddenly aware that an American soldier had appeared at her side.

Trying her best to extricate herself from his unwanted conversation, Beatrice stopped to talk to a friend of hers, Jean Elizabeth Blight, who was standing near her front gate. The soldier walked on and no doubt Beatrice thought she had shaken him off at last. After a few moments though, the soldier reappeared and asked Jean Blight for a goodnight kiss. Beatrice took the opportunity to walk on again.

She had not gone very far when the soldier again appeared at her side. This time, though, he did not settle for conversation and dragged her over a hedge and into a nearby field. There he struck her, stole her watch and raped her.

The next day, July 27th, the entire camp at Whitchurch Down, near Tavistock, the nearest American base, was put on parade and examined by Jean Blight. She had no hesitation in picking out Madison Thomas and tests showed blood on his trousers belonging to the same group as that of Beatrice Reynolds. More importantly, it was a different group to Thomas's own, and therefore he could not claim that he had cut himself, or suffered an accident and that the blood was his.

Tried at Plymouth, Thomas was sentenced to death and became the third rapist to die on the scaffold at Shepton Mallet.

NAME	Madison Thomas
AGE AT EXECUTION	Not known
DATE OF EXECUTION	Thursday, 12th October, 1944
PLACE OF EXECUTION	Shepton Mallet
HANGMAN	Not known
DATE OF TRIAL	21st August, 1944
LOCATION OF TRIAL	Plymouth
NUMBER OF VICTIMS	Hanged for rape

1944

1944

ON SATURDAY, JUNE 17th, 1944, a session of rather heavy drinking took place in the recreational hall at the Drill Hall Camp, in Westbury. Even here, though, there were limits as to what time drinks were sold and so, when Benjamin Pyegate came in late and was told that he would not be served, he was not in the best of tempers.

Back in the billet, an argument broke out between four men: Pyegate, James Alexander, Roy Easley and C.A. Dempsey. During the fracas that followed, Pyegate made threats against Alexander and kicked him in the groin. Not surprisingly, Alexander doubled up with pain and bent forward. As he did so, Pyegate drew out a knife and plunged it into Alexander's neck, killing him instantly.

The court martial at Tidworth lasted just one day and Pyegate was sentenced to die by shooting. On November 30th, he became the second and last American to be executed by firing squad at Shepton Mallet prison.

Note: Some sources suggest that there was one more execution of an American soldier, that of Thomas Bell, who was supposedly hanged on January 31st, 1944, for rape. In fact, Bell's sentence was commuted to life imprisonment. The author is in receipt of a letter from the Department of the Army in Falls Church, Virginia, confirming this.

NAME	Benjamin Pyegate
AGE AT EXECUTION	Not known
DATE OF EXECUTION	Tuesday, 28th November, 1944
PLACE OF EXECUTION	Shepton Mallet
HANGMAN	Shot
DATE OF TRIAL	15th July, 1944
LOCATION OF TRIAL	Tidworth, Wiltshire
NUMBER OF VICTIMS	1

VICTIMS DETAILS	
NAME	James E. Alexander
AGE	Not known
DATE OF MURDER	Saturday, 17th June, 1944
PLACE OF MURDER	Drill Hall Camp, West End Road, Westbury
METHOD OF KILLING	Stabbed
RELATIONSHIP TO KILLER	None

ON THE NIGHT of August 22nd, 1944, Mr Green left the Smiths Arms public house, in Ashford, at closing time. As he left, two American servicemen followed him out and walked towards a field. By the most extraordinary coincidence, those same two servicemen would, just a few minutes later, encounter Mr Green's daughter Betty, whom they would rape and kill.

When Betty Green did not return home that night, she was reported missing, and her body was discovered at 7.15am the following morning, just a few hundred yards from where her father had seen the Americans. He took his evidence to the police and later picked out both men at an identity parade.

Hair and fibre samples were taken from both Ernest Lee Clark and Augustine M. Guerra and found to match other samples taken from Betty Green's body. Faced with this evidence, both men now confessed to the attack.

Clark admitted that he had approached Betty and asked her to go for a walk with him. When she had refused, he had picked her up bodily and carried her into a field. When she started to scream, Guerra put his hand over her mouth to quieten her and then both men took their turn in raping her. They both maintained that they had not realised Betty was dead when they left her.

Both men were found guilty, sentenced to death and executed together.

NAMES	Ernest Lee Clark; Augustine M. Guerra
AGES AT EXECUTION	Not known
DATE OF EXECUTION	Monday, 8th January, 1945
PLACE OF EXECUTION	Shepton Mallet
HANGMAN	Not known
DATE OF TRIAL	22nd September, 1944
LOCATION OF TRIAL	Ashford, Kent
NUMBER OF VICTIMS	1

1945

VICTIMS DETAILS	
NAME	Elizabeth (Betty) Green
AGE	15
DATE OF MURDER	Tuesday, 22nd August, 1944
PLACE OF MURDER	Ashford, Kent
METHOD OF KILLING	Strangled
RELATIONSHIP TO KILLERS	None; none

DOROTHY HILLMAN WAS heavily pregnant and living with her husband's parents at Palmer's Cross Cottages. At 6.20pm on September 7th, 1944, she told them that she would take the dog for a walk and call in at the Leathern Bottle pub for some tobacco and cigarettes.

When Dorothy did not return, a search was organised and soon she was found by the side of the road, 370 yards north of the pub. She had been stabbed 11 times and would die in the Warren Road Hospital, Guildford, on September 22nd. Before that she would give birth to a stillborn child.

A schoolboy had seen Dorothy talking to a coloured soldier, who had a woman's bicycle with him. Later that same night, such a soldier was found, on the road to Hascombe.

Horace Beresford Gordon, a Jamaican, was serving in the Royal Canadian Ordnance Corps, and had been in England since October 1941. At first he denied any knowledge of the attack. He stated that he had borrowed the bicycle from a friend, Mrs Manning, who lived in Horsham, had left his camp, at Prior's Wood, Farncombe, at 5.50pm and was cycling back to Horsham when he was picked up.

The evidence against Gordon built up quickly. First, blood and mud had been found on his uniform. When this blood was tested, it proved to be Group B, the same as Dorothy's. Further, chewing gum wrappers had been found at the scene of the crime and when Gordon was searched, other sticks of gum with the same wrappers were discovered.

Gordon now told a second story. He said that he was cycling when a girl, covered in blood, stopped him. She said she had been attacked so he rode off to tell the police at Cranleigh but must have taken the wrong road and was picked up instead near Hascombe.

At this time, Dorothy was still alive and made a dying deposition, identifying Gordon as her attacker. She went on to say that he had tried to interfere with her and when she resisted, had produced a knife. Gordon now changed his story yet again.

In this third version of events, Gordon had started talking to Dorothy and had given her

NAME	Horace Beresford Gordon
AGE AT EXECUTION	28
DATE OF EXECUTION	Tuesday, 9th January, 1945
PLACE OF EXECUTION	Wandsworth
HANGMAN	Albert Pierrepoint
ASSISTANT	Stephen Wade
DATE OF TRIAL	30th November – 1st December, 1944
LOCATION OF TRIAL	Kingston upon Thames
PRESIDING JUDGE	Mister Justice Humphreys
PROSECUTION COUNSEL	Linton Thorpe, G. Pollock
DEFENCE COUNSEL	J.P. Eddy, Laurence Vine
NUMBER OF VICTIMS	1

VICTIMS DETAILS	
NAME	Dorothy May Hillman (Died Friday, 22nd September)
AGE	18
DATE OF MURDER	Thursday, 7th September, 1944
PLACE OF MURDER	On the Bramley/Horsham road
METHOD OF KILLING	Stabbed
RELATIONSHIP TO KILLER	None

some gum and chocolate. He had taken off his pack and when he put it back on, the straps became twisted so he asked Dorothy to straighten them but she must have misunderstood as she accused him of trying to interfere with her, called him names and slapped his face. His knife fell out of his pocket and as he retrieved it, Dorothy moved and her neck came down upon the blade.

This final version of the event did still not explain how Dorothy 'accidentally' sustained 11 wounds. It was not surprising that the jury returned a guilty verdict.

AMELIA KNOWLES RAN a small second-hand shop in Tarrant Street, Arundel. She was an eccentric lady and her neighbours often heard her shouting and arguing at non-existent intruders. So, unsurprisingly, when she faced a real threat and shouted for help, she was ignored.

It was 11.00am on September 18th, when a neighbour noticed that the milk had not been taken in from the doorstep of number 20. There was no reply to knocks on the front door, so the police were called. An entry was forced and Amelia was found, battered to death.

Initial inquiries revealed that the neighbours had heard screams at some time between midnight and 1.00am. Amelia had been heard shouting: "Get out of here you beast. Murder! Help!" It was safe to assume that this pin-pointed the time of the attack.

Further witnesses came forward, including Mrs Dorothy Louisa Darvell who lived at number 24. On September 18th, she had seen a man in R.A.F. uniform standing on the doorstep of number 20. Since it was by then 11.15pm, Dorothy felt that he was up to no good and demanded to know what he was after. He said he owed Mrs Knowles some money and wanted to pay her. At such a late hour, this seemed to be rather unlikely. so Dorothy Darvell told him to be on his way. As he turned to leave, another uniformed figure across the road shouted: "Is that you Paddy?" and the two men went off together.

The police now sought to trace an airman whose nickname was 'Paddy'. Investigations led to Leading Aircraftman Andrew Brown. It was also discovered that Brown had suddenly started spending rather freely of late, and had shown his girlfriend a roll of banknotes on the afternoon of the 18th, explaining that his family in Belfast had sent him some money.

It was September 26th, by the time Brown was formally interviewed and he soon admitted that he had killed Amelia Knowles. He said that he had been passing her house, on the way back to his lodgings in Arundel, when he had heard some strange noises from inside. Brown knocked on the door, which was opened by Amelia. He then forced his way in, whereupon Amelia flew at him and a

NAME	Andrew Brown
AGE AT EXECUTION	26
DATE OF EXECUTION	Tuesday, 30th January, 1945
PLACE OF EXECUTION	Wandsworth
HANGMAN	Albert Pierrepoint
ASSISTANT	Stephen Wade
DATE OF TRIAL	7th December, 1944
LOCATION OF TRIAL	Lewes
PRESIDING JUDGE	Mister Justice Humphreys
PROSECUTION COUNSEL	Cecil R. Havers, R.H. Blundell
DEFENCE COUNSEL	Eric Neve, Harold Brown
NUMBER OF VICTIMS	1

VICTIMS DETAILS

NAME	Amelia Elizabeth Ann Knowles
AGE	69
DATE OF MURDER	Monday, 18th September, 1944
PLACE OF MURDER	20 Tarrant Street, Arundel, West Sussex
METHOD OF KILLING	Battered
RELATIONSHIP TO KILLER	None

struggle took place, in the course of which he accidentally killed her.

At his trial, at Lewes, in reply to the question asking him how he wished to plead, Brown replied: "Not guilty of murder, sir – guilty of manslaughter." Unfortunately for Brown, medical evidence was called to show that Amelia's injuries were consistent with her being kneeled on whilst lying on the floor. This hardly fitted the scenario painted by Brown and as such, it took the jury only 11 minutes to convict him.

1945

HILDA GRANGE LIVED at 3 Back Lane, Clayton Heights, and her house adjoined the yard at the back of the Nags Head pub, run by Jane Coulton. On the morning of September 21st, 1944, Hilda noticed that there was a broken window at the back of the pub and also that a glass panel in the back door had been smashed. Hilda called in the police.

Constable Frank Thorpe found the rear door unlocked and entered the premises, shouting for Jane. He finally found her lying in bed, a stocking tied tightly around her neck. She had been struck, probably with a fist, before she had been strangled. Tests would show that the killer had bled in the room, possibly after having cut his hand on some of the broken glass – Jane was Group B, but there were traces of Group A blood at the scene of the crime too.

The motive appeared to be robbery. Money was missing from the pub, as was some of Jane's jewellery. Descriptions of the missing items were now circulated.

Arthur Thompson, a soldier, had visited the Nags Head a number of times with a comrade, Thomas Thomson. Arthur had mentioned to him that he was short of money and intended breaking in somewhere to get some. Then, in the small hours of September 21st, Thompson had visited the Westwood Hospital where some of his friends were, and paid them money he owed. Even more tellingly, Thompson had now gone absent without leave.

Thompson had headed for Lancashire. At 1.00pm on September 21st, he was in the Barrack Tavern in Burnley, where he told the licensee, George Ormerod, that he was a discharged soldier. The next day, he appeared at a jeweller's shop in Market Street, Lancaster, where a ring was exchanged for a gold watch. The ring had belonged to Jane Coulton. On the 23rd, Thompson, sold the watch for £4-10s, to a jeweller in Heysham. The next day, Thompson walked into the Globe Hotel at Overton. The licensee, George Slater, became suspicious when Thompson tried to sell yet another ring. The police were called and Thompson was arrested.

Thompson had identification papers in the name of R.N. Reid and was taken in

NAME	Arthur Thompson
AGE AT EXECUTION	34
DATE OF EXECUTION	Wednesday, 31st January, 1945
PLACE OF EXECUTION	Leeds
HANGMAN	Thomas Pierrepoint
ASSISTANT	Herbert Harris
DATE OF TRIAL	6th December – 8th December, 1944
LOCATION OF TRIAL	Leeds
PRESIDING JUDGE	Mister Justice Oliver
PROSECUTION COUNSEL	G.H.B. Streatfeild, Myles Archibald
DEFENCE COUNSEL	J. Stanley Snowden, Eric Greenwood
NUMBER OF VICTIMS	1

VICTIMS DETAILS	
NAME	Jane Coulton
AGE	69
DATE OF MURDER	Thursday, 21st September, 1944
PLACE OF MURDER	Nags Head Inn, Clayton Heights, Bradford
METHOD OF KILLING	Battered/strangled
RELATIONSHIP TO KILLER	None

whilst these were checked out. On the way to the police station, he asked if the car could be stopped so that he could urinate, but permission was denied and the journey completed.

Sergeant Sidney Wood had driven the police car and neither he, nor any other officer used it again that day. Later, Wood noticed that one of the mats had been moved. Lifting it, he found a small parcel and when this was opened, it revealed jewellery that had belonged to Jane Coulton.

Finally, it was noticed that Thompson's hands had small cuts on them and after tests his blood was revealed to be Group A. That evidence was enough to convict and hang him.

BY OCTOBER 3RD, 1944, Karl Hulten had already been absent without leave, from the American army for six weeks. On that same day 'Ricky', as he liked to call himself, was introduced to attractive, 18-year-old Elizabeth Maud Jones, who liked to call herself 'Georgina'.

Len Bexley, a mutual friend of both Hulten and Jones, made the introductions at a London cafe. Hulten was captivated by Jones and asked her out, even though he already had a steady girlfriend, Joyce Cook. Jones agreed to meet him that same night.

Elizabeth Jones waited outside the cinema, but when Hulten did not show, she finally gave up and started for her home at 311 King Street, Hammersmith. Suddenly a ten-wheel American truck pulled up and there in the driving seat was the grinning face of Karl Hulten. The two new friends went for a drive towards Reading and whilst they were travelling, Hulten told her that he had been a gangster back in Chicago and that they were now driving around in a stolen truck. The lifestyle he told her about seemed to excite Jones, and she did nothing to discourage him in his romancing.

Over the next few days, the couple met a number of times and had some adventures together. On Wednesday October 4th they robbed a girl, again near Reading and on October 5th, an abortive robbery attempt on a taxi cab revealed that Hulten was in possession of a gun. That same day they also robbed a young girl near Windsor.

Hulten spent much of October 6th with his first girlfriend, Joyce Cook, but that night he was again in Jones's company and again the idea of robbing a taxi occurred to them. In the early hours of October 7th, Jones flagged down a cab and asked the driver, George Heath, to drive them out to Chiswick.

Upon arrival at their destination, as Heath turned around to collect his fare, Hulten drew his pistol and shot him once. Hulten would later say that the gun went off accidentally as his sleeve caught on the door handle, but whatever the truth of the matter, Hulten now told Heath to move across to the passenger seat, unless he wanted more of the same. Heath did as he was told and Hulten climbed

NAME	Karl Gustav Hulten
AGE AT EXECUTION	22
DATE OF EXECUTION	Thursday, 8th March, 1945
PLACE OF EXECUTION	Pentonville
HANGMAN	Albert Pierrepoint
ASSISTANT	Henry Critchell
DATE OF TRIAL	16th January, 1945
LOCATION OF TRIAL	Old Bailey
PRESIDING JUDGE	Mister Justice Charles
PROSECUTION COUNSEL	L.A. Byrne
DEFENCE COUNSEL	John Maud
NUMBER OF VICTIMS	1

VICTIMS DETAILS	
NAME	George Edward Heath
AGE	34
DATE OF MURDER	Saturday, 7th October, 1944
PLACE OF MURDER	In taxi cab, Chiswick, London
METHOD OF KILLING	Shot
RELATIONSHIP TO KILLER	None

into the driving seat and headed off towards Staines. Somewhere on that journey, George Heath died from the effect of the wound he had suffered. His body was left in a ditch near Staines whilst Hulten and Jones headed back for London in the stolen cab.

Heath's body was discovered at around 9.00am on October 7th. His driving licence, identity card and other documents had been found an hour earlier and now a description of the stolen cab was circulated. For two days, Hulten and Jones used the cab without incident but just after 8.00pm on October 9th, Constable Walters saw the vehicle parked at Hammersmith, and contacted his superiors. Joined by two other officers, Walters and his colleagues watched and waited.

It was 9.00pm before Hulten climbed into the cab and started the engine. Stopped immediately, he was searched and found to be armed. He gave his name as Second Lieutenant Richard Allen of the American army and claimed he had found the cab abandoned near Newbury. It was the early hours of the next morning before Hulten's real name was determined and he was charged with murder.

Two days after his arrest, Hulten offered to tell officers about his partner, Elizabeth Jones, and she was picked up for questioning on October 11th. After making a statement, she was allowed home, the police not connecting her with the murder at this stage. Later that day, Elizabeth Jones was unwise enough to talk about the killing to Henry Kimberley, a War Reserve policeman, who passed what she had said on to the police. She was interviewed again, made a full confession to her involvement but said that she had only acted out of fear of Hulten. To counter her claims, Hulten then made a fresh statement of his own saying that Jones had encouraged him in what he had done and that she had taken a much more active part than she had indicated. Both were charged with murder and the American authorities waived their rights so that Hulten could be tried in a British court.

After a trial lasting six days, both Hulten and Jones were found guilty and sentenced to death. Jones was reprieved two days before she was due to be hanged and would eventually be released from prison in January 1954. For Hulten, there was no reprieve.

THE BODY OF W.A.A.F. Winifred Evans lay face down in the ditch. She had been battered and raped but the cause of death had been asphyxiation. In the course of the attack on her, Winifred's face had been forced down into the mud and she had suffocated.

Piecing together Winifred's movements of the previous night, the police discovered that she had been to a dance with a fellow W.A.A.F., Corporal Margaret Johns. When Corporal Johns was interviewed, she said that they had returned to camp just before midnight and had parted at about 12.05am. Winifred headed off for duty at the signal office whilst Margaret visited the women's toilets. Here, Margaret was surprised to find an airman in full R.A.F. uniform. He was very drunk indeed.

Margaret demanded to know what he was doing. He managed say that he was lost and asked if he was in Number One camp. She told him in no uncertain terms that he wasn't, took him outside and pointed him in the right direction. It was the same direction that Winifred had walked, just a few minutes before.

The police concentrated their efforts on camp Number One and discovered that an aircraftman had been seen coming in some time after 1.00am and that early that morning he had been assiduously cleaning his uniform.

The airman, Arthur Heys, was interviewed. He admitted the incident with Corporal Johns, but denied any involvement in the attack on Winifred Evans. The police were far from convinced. Why had it taken Heys the best part of an hour to go from the women's toilets in the W.A.A.F. camp, to his own billet?

His uniform was taken for examination. The test results, at first, appeared to be conclusive. Although the uniform had been cleaned, microscopic examination revealed the presence of brick dust, and the ditch where Winifred had been found contained brick rubble. There were also four hairs on his tunic that matched samples taken from Winifred's body. Wishing to eliminate all possible errors, the forensic team even visited Heys's wife in Colne, Lancashire and took hair samples from her. Her hair was also an exact match for the samples taken from his tunic.

NAME	Arthur Heys
AGE AT EXECUTION	37
DATE OF EXECUTION	Tuesday, 13th March, 1945
PLACE OF EXECUTION	Norwich
HANGMAN	Not known
ASSISTANT	Not known
DATE OF TRIAL	22nd January – 24th January, 1945
LOCATION OF TRIAL	Bury St Edmunds
PRESIDING JUDGE	Mister Justice MacNaghten
PROSECUTION COUNSEL	John Flowers
DEFENCE COUNSEL	F.T. Alpe, M.P. Solomon
NUMBER OF VICTIMS	1

VICTIMS DETAILS	
NAME	Winifred Mary Evans
AGE	27
DATE OF MURDER	Thursday, 9th November, 1944
PLACE OF MURDER	Ditch at Ellough, near Beccles, Suffolk
METHOD OF KILLING	Asphyxiated
RELATIONSHIP TO KILLER	None

Nevertheless, the police felt they had enough and charged Heys with murder.

Before the trial even started, Heys made a fatal mistake. His commanding officer received an anonymous letter that purported to be from the real killer and stated that an innocent man was in jail. It gave details that only the killer could know, but it also included a reference to Heys, the 'innocent' man, as having been drunk and lost. Apart from the police, only two people knew of the drunken encounter with Corporal Johns: Margaret Johns herself and Arthur Heys.

In writing that letter, Heys had gone a long way to placing the noose around his own neck.

ON SUNDAY, DECEMBER 3RD, 1944, Joyce Brown, who was nine months pregnant at the time, left her home at 12 Bonfire Close, Chard, in Somerset.

It was about 8.00pm and Joyce had not gone far when she became aware that she was being followed. Turning around, she saw that there were two coloured American soldiers behind her. Before she could take any action, the two men had caught up with her, grabbed her and dragged her along the road to a gate leading to Bonfire Orchard. Joyce was forced into the orchard at knifepoint, where she was raped by both men.

The following day, the clothing of all the servicemen at the nearby camp was checked and it was discovered that Robert L. Pearson and Parson Jones both had wet and muddy trousers. When interviewed, both men admitted having sex with Joyce but claimed it was with her consent. The fact that Joyce was heavily pregnant and the bruises she displayed showed that this defence was both cruel and untruthful and both men were subsequently sentenced to death.

On March 17th, 1945, Pearson and Jones were involved in the second double execution at Shepton Mallet within three months.

NAMES	Robert L. Pearson; Parson Jones
AGES AT EXECUTION	Not known
DATE OF EXECUTION	Saturday, 17th March, 1945
PLACE OF EXECUTION	Shepton Mallet
HANGMAN	Not known
DATE OF TRIAL	16th December, 1944
LOCATION OF TRIAL	Chard, Somerset
NUMBER OF VICTIMS	Hanged for rape

WILLIAM HARRISON WAS based with the American forces in Northern Ireland, where he soon became friendly with the Wylie family of Killycolpy, in County Tyrone.

The Wylie family had been very kind to Harrison and on September 25th, 1944, he said that he wished to repay them by buying them a present. He asked if he could take their daughter, seven-and-a-half-year-old Patricia, along for the walk, and her parents readily agreed. On the journey to the shops, Harrison took the child into a nearby field where he sexually assaulted her before strangling her.

The brutal crime could only have one result and on April 7th, 1945, Harrison was executed at Shepton Mallet.

NAME	William Harrison
AGE AT EXECUTION	Not known
DATE OF EXECUTION	Saturday, 7th April, 1945
PLACE OF EXECUTION	Shepton Mallet
HANGMAN	Not known
DATE OF TRIAL	18th November, 1944
LOCATION OF TRIAL	Not known
NUMBER OF VICTIMS	1

VICTIMS DETAILS	
NAME	Patricia Wylie
AGE	7
DATE OF MURDER	Monday, 25th September, 1944
PLACE OF MURDER	Killycolpy, Co Tyrone
METHOD OF KILLING	Strangled
RELATIONSHIP TO KILLER	None

1945

SIR ERIC TEICHMAN and his wife had just finished having lunch on December 3rd, 1944, when they heard what sounded like shots coming from the woods near their home. Concerned about trespassers, Sir Eric decided to investigate and set out, unarmed, for the woods. When Sir Eric did not return, a search was organised and at midnight, his body was discovered; he had been shot through the head.

Nearby was an American airfield and this was immediately sealed. The bullet extracted from the body was identified as one from a .38 carbine and all those in the airfield were checked. Whilst this was going on, an airman came forward and said that he had seen George Smith and Leonard S. Wojtacha leaving the camp, with their carbines, on the day of the shooting. The two men were now questioned very closely.

In due course, Wojtacha made a full statement saying that he and Smith had gone out to do some hunting. After firing at various targets, including a cow, Wojtacha noticed a man come up behind them. Sir Eric demanded their names and at that, Smith turned, levelled his gun at the intruder, and shot him in the head. On December 7th, Smith was charged with murder and made a full confession.

The court martial opened on January 8th, 1945 and immediately Smith withdrew the statement he had made, saying that it had been obtained under duress. Nevertheless, on the fifth day, he was found guilty and sentenced to death.

Moves were made to save Smith's life and even Sir Eric's widow pleaded for his life to be spared. The authorities were not to be moved and Smith was executed on V.E. Day.

NAME	George E. Smith
AGE AT EXECUTION	Not known
DATE OF EXECUTION	Tuesday, 8th May, 1945
PLACE OF EXECUTION	Shepton Mallet
HANGMAN	Not known
DATE OF TRIAL	8th January – 13th January, 1945
LOCATION OF TRIAL	Attlebridge, Norfolk
NUMBER OF VICTIMS	1

VICTIMS DETAILS	
NAME	Eric Teichman
AGE	61
DATE OF MURDER	Sunday, 3rd December, 1944
PLACE OF MURDER	Woods near Honingham Hall, Attlebridge, Norfolk
METHOD OF KILLING	Shot
RELATIONSHIP TO KILLER	None

AT 3.15AM ON Sunday, August 6th, 1944, Agnes Cope, 75 years of age, lay asleep in her bedroom at 15 Sandy Lane, Rugeley, Staffordshire, when she was awoken by the sounds of someone on her staircase. Shortly afterwards, the figure of a man appeared in the bedroom doorway. Thinking that she was about to become the victim of a robbery, Agnes announced that she had no money but the man made it clear that he was looking for something else. He left after raping her and later that same morning, Agnes told her story to the police.

Nearby was a prisoner-of-war camp and a quick check revealed that only one man had been out the previous night. Aniceto Martinez, a guard at the camp, was questioned and admitted that he had raped Agnes. Fibre samples from his clothing matched some taken from Agnes's bedroom and Martinez was put on trial for his life.

Found guilty, Martinez became the last American to be executed at Shepton Mallet and the last man hanged for rape in the United Kingdom.

NAME	Aniceto Martinez
AGE AT EXECUTION	Not known
DATE OF EXECUTION	Friday, 15th June, 1945
PLACE OF EXECUTION	Shepton Mallet
HANGMAN	Not known
DATE OF TRIAL	21st February, 1945
LOCATION OF TRIAL	Lichfield
NUMBER OF VICTIMS	Hanged for rape

THERE COULD BE no doubt that Howard John Grossley, a Canadian soldier, killed his lover, Lily Griffiths. But was it a case of murder?

Grossley was a married man but his wife was back in Canada. In 1941, serving in Britain, he met Lily and soon they began living together as man and wife – she even gave birth to a son in 1943. Although they were happy enough together, the time would come when Grossley had to return to his own country and by 1945, this had begun to prey on his mind. Grossley finally decided that things might be easier for Lily if he simply killed himself and this is exactly what he chose to do.

As Grossley and Lily walked down a country lane near New Road in Porthcawl, Grossley told Lily of his decision and, producing a gun, made to carry out the deed there and then. A struggle followed and finally it was Lily who fell to the ground, mortally wounded.

Grossley explained to the police that his intention had been to kill himself and that Lily had been hit accidentally when she tried to prevent him. Lily, who had been rushed to hospital, made a deathbed statement agreeing with all that Grossley had said and confirming that she had struggled with him. Despite that, Howard Grossley was charged with wilful murder.

At the trial, the defence claimed that there was no evidence of any intention to commit murder and the charge should be, at worst, one of manslaughter. The prosecution, however, maintained that the pulling back of the breech on the gun and the squeezing of the trigger had been deliberate enough acts and also claimed that at the moment Lily had been shot, the gun had been levelled at her, as if it had been deliberately aimed.

Even though the victim had also stated that this was no murder, the jury found Grossley guilty and after losing his appeal, Grossley was hanged.

NAME	Howard Joseph Grossley
AGE AT EXECUTION	37
DATE OF EXECUTION	Wednesday, 5th September, 1945
PLACE OF EXECUTION	Cardiff
HANGMAN	Not known
ASSISTANT	Not known
DATE OF TRIAL	11th July – 12th July, 1945
LOCATION OF TRIAL	Swansea
PRESIDING JUDGE	Mister Justice Singleton
PROSECUTION COUNSEL	Ralph Sutton
DEFENCE COUNSEL	H. Glyn-Jones
NUMBER OF VICTIMS	1

VICTIMS DETAILS	
NAME	Lily Griffiths (Died Friday, March 16th)
AGE	29
DATE OF MURDER	Monday, 12th March, 1945
PLACE OF MURDER	Lane near New Road, Porthcawl
METHOD OF KILLING	Shot
RELATIONSHIP TO KILLER	Girlfriend

DENNIS WILSON, A railway fireman, was returning home from work at around 1.00am on April 29th. As he walked down Beeston Road, he noticed a man running away from Doctor Dewar's house.

Some 20 minutes later, another night worker, Joseph Edward Charles Freshwater also passed the doctor's house and noticed what looked like a sack close to the car in the driveway.

It was not until 8.10am that a third worker, William Ernest Whitaker, noticed that the sacking in Doctor Dewar's driveway was in fact the body of a man. Whitaker called in the police.

Doctor Dewar was quite dead, his head having been battered, most probably by means of an axe. The time of death was put at around 1.00am, just about the time Dennis Wilson had seen a man running away from the area.

The first thing the police discovered was a possible motive for the murder. Doctor Dewar, it seemed, had a weakness for women and had enjoyed more than one affair in his time. Discrete inquiries were made but appeared to be leading nowhere and the investigation ground to a halt, until one of those women, Laura Walker, came forward, in late May.

NAME	Thomas Eric Richardson
AGE AT EXECUTION	27
DATE OF EXECUTION	Friday, 7th September, 1945
PLACE OF EXECUTION	Leeds
HANGMAN	Thomas Pierrepoint
ASSISTANT	Herbert Harris
DATE OF TRIAL	16th July – 18th July, 1945
LOCATION OF TRIAL	Leeds
PRESIDING JUDGE	Mister Justice Hallett
PROSECUTION COUNSEL	G.H.B. Streatfeild, Myles Archibald
DEFENCE COUNSEL	C.B. Fenwick, Rudolph Lyons
NUMBER OF VICTIMS	1

VICTIMS DETAILS	
NAME	David Walker Dewar
AGE	41
DATE OF MURDER	Sunday, 29th April, 1945
PLACE OF MURDER	Driveway of 176 Beeston Road, Leeds
METHOD OF KILLING	Battered
RELATIONSHIP TO KILLER	None

The body of Doctor Dewar lying in his driveway.

Laura Walker was a married woman but her husband was in the forces and abroad at the time. She had known Dewar before her marriage and he had been their family doctor since 1931. Since her marriage, her friendship with Dewar had been renewed and they had started seeing each other regularly.

Thomas Eric Richardson was a good friend of Laura's husband and in due course, he also became a close friend of Laura's. She told him of her relationship with Doctor Dewar and Richardson expressed his disapproval.

Laura had seen Richardson at around 7.00pm on the night of April 28th and had mentioned that she was seeing Dewar later, adding that she would not be home until after midnight. Richardson tried to persuade her not to go but she was quite determined to keep the appointment.

Dewar and Laura went out that evening and at 12.45am, he dropped her off at her home. About 35 minutes later, Richardson called and stayed with Laura until around 5.00am.

None of this would have raised Laura

Walker's suspicions, but some weeks later, Richardson confessed that it was he who had murdered Dewar. On May 21st, Richardson was arrested and questioned about the killing, which he admitted after he had been allowed to see Laura.

Put on trial for murder, Richardson was found guilty, but with a strong recommendation to mercy. That recommendation did not save his life.

ONE OF THE duties of a prisoner of war is to try his best to escape. It was just such a planned escape that led to the deaths of six men.

Comrie Camp held many German prisoners and it was to here that a number of German prisoners were moved after an abortive escape from a camp in Devizes. Someone, it seems, had given them away and who more likely than a man who was not even a National Socialist. The finger of suspicion was pointed at Feldwebel Wolfgang Rosterg, who had been captured in Normandy. His 'comrades' decided that Rosterg would have to face a court martial.

On the morning of December 23rd, Rosterg was dragged from his bed in Number 4 hut and badly beaten. Then, a rope placed around his neck, he was dragged to the latrines nearby where the rope was thrown over a pipe and Rosterg was hanged. He was almost certainly dead already, as being pulled along by the neck had strangled him. The men who had killed him hoped that the British guards would believe it to be a case of suicide, but the extensive beating made that impossible.

The investigation soon revealed a number of German P.O.W.s who were willing to talk and eventually eight men were placed on trial for murder. In addition to the five named above, also standing in the dock at the prisoner of war 'cage' in Kensington Palace Gardens, were Rolf Herzig, Herbert Wunderlich and Hans Klein. Many witnesses were called, but all names were kept secret in case there should be reprisals either against them, or against their families back in Germany.

For the most part, the accused men readily admitted their part in the killing of Rosterg, but failed to see why they were on trial for it. Had he not been a traitor to them and Germany? Had he not deserved to die?

On the third day of the trial, it was directed that Hans Klein be acquitted as there was not sufficient evidence against him. The other seven men endured a trial lasting almost two weeks, at the end of which, Wunderlich was also acquitted. The other men had to wait for verification of the sentences passed upon them.

NAMES	Joachim Palme-Goltz; Josep Mertins; Heintz Brueling
AGES AT EXECUTION	20; 21; 22
DATE OF EXECUTION	Saturday, 6th October, 1945
PLACE OF EXECUTION	Pentonville
HANGMAN	Albert Pierrepoint
ASSISTANTS	Steve Wade, Harry Allen
DATE OF TRIAL	2nd July – 12th July, 1945
LOCATION OF TRIAL	Kensington, London
PRESIDING JUDGE	Military court martial
PROSECUTION COUNSEL	Major R.A.L. Hillard
DEFENCE COUNSEL	Major R. Evans
NUMBER OF VICTIMS	1

NAMES	Erich Koenig; Kurt Zuchlsdorff
AGES AT EXECUTION	20; 20
DATE OF EXECUTION	Saturday, 6th October, 1945
PLACE OF EXECUTION	Pentonville
HANGMAN	Albert Pierrepoint
ASSISTANTS	Steve Wade, Harry Allen
DATE OF TRIAL	2nd July – 12th July, 1945
LOCATION OF TRIAL	Kensington, London
PRESIDING JUDGE	Military court martial
PROSECUTION COUNSEL	Major R.A.L. Hillard
DEFENCE COUNSEL	Captain R. Willis
NUMBER OF VICTIMS	1

VICTIMS DETAILS	
NAME	Sergeant Major Wolfgang Rosterg
AGE	35
DATE OF MURDER	Saturday, 23rd December, 1944
PLACE OF MURDER	Comrie Prison Camp, Perthshire
METHOD OF KILLING	Battered/strangled
RELATIONSHIP TO KILLERS	None to any of accused

In due course it was announced that Rolf Herzig was to be sentenced to life imprisonment, whilst the other five received sentences of death.

693

AT 5.30PM ON July 11th, 1945, neighbours in Denecroft Crescent heard screams coming from Vera Guest's house. A few minutes later they noticed a man, in some sort of uniform, walking down the garden and into the road. The neighbours went to see if everything was all right but, getting no answer, forced an entry at the back of the house. The strangled body of Vera Guest was discovered inside.

The police did not have to look far for their suspect. Vera's boyfriend was a lorry driver, a married man named Ronald Mauri, and a search was launched to trace him. Hardly before that search had got under way, Mauri wrote an astonishing letter, to his employer in Nottingham, claiming to have killed Vera and adding that he intended to kill six more people before he committed suicide. Two of these intended victims were neighbours of Vera, three more lived in London and the last one lived in Nottingham. The letter went on to say that Mauri was armed with a gun and that he wouldn't hesitate to kill any policeman who got too close.

Another letter was sent to Vera's parents, Frank and Nora Guest. Mauri claimed that Vera had asked him to kill her. He again repeated the threat to kill six more people but now blamed the police, whom he claimed had framed him for a robbery, in Nottingham.

On July 15th, in a terrible storm, Mauri was spotted in a car in Monmouthshire. Police were alerted and, taking Mauri's threats seriously, the officers were issued with firearms. The car was subsequently found abandoned but Mauri was seen running into a small wood. The police followed, called on Mauri to stop and when he didn't, fired at him. Mauri was hit in the head but the wound was not serious and he was taken to Monmouth Hospital.

When interviewed, Mauri told a complex story. He claimed that the police had framed him for a cigarette robbery in Nottingham. Faced with this he had told Vera that he wanted to kill himself. She said she did not want to live without him and asked him to kill her first.

Mauri replied that she was too young to die but Vera had insisted and had thrown herself

NAME	Ronald Bertram Mauri
AGE AT EXECUTION	32
DATE OF EXECUTION	Wednesday, 31st October, 1945
PLACE OF EXECUTION	Wandsworth
HANGMAN	Albert Pierrepoint
ASSISTANT	Harry Kirk
DATE OF TRIAL	20th September, 1945
LOCATION OF TRIAL	Old Bailey
PRESIDING JUDGE	Mister Justice Tucker
PROSECUTION COUNSEL	L.A. Byrne
DEFENCE COUNSEL	Henry Curtis Bennett
NUMBER OF VICTIMS	1

VICTIMS DETAILS	
NAME	Vera Guest
AGE	18
DATE OF MURDER	Wednesday, 11th July, 1945
PLACE OF MURDER	Denecroft Crescent, Hillingdon, Middlesex
METHOD OF KILLING	Strangled
RELATIONSHIP TO KILLER	Girlfriend

onto a gas stove, injuring her head and knocking herself out. Mauri had then tied a scarf around her neck, strangled her and sat down to write the his letters.

At his trial, the letters and his own statement to the police weighed heavily against Mauri and he was sentenced to death.

IN DECEMBER 1944, at a prison camp in Scotland, a German prisoner was murdered because his fellow internees believed he had given away an escape plan. For that crime, five men were to be hanged. The murder of Gerhardt Rettig was a similar sort of crime and this time, two men faced the noose.

Gerhardt Rettig was not a National Socialist and rumour in the camp had it that he was an informer to the British. An escape tunnel had been dug and it wouldn't be long now before some of the camp inmates made good their escapes. So, when a search was made, by the guards, on March 24th and the tunnel easily discovered, the Germans came to believe that they just might have known exactly where to look and that someone had tipped them off.

Talking amongst themselves, it was soon revealed that Rettig had been seen, at around 4.00pm, passing a piece of paper through the barbed wire, to one of the British guards. The German leader, or Lagerfuhrer, was informed and he told Rettig and a close friend of his who was also not a National Socialist, that for their own safety they should pack their kit and he would arrange for them to be shipped to another camp.

Both men began packing but were interrupted at 5.30pm by roll call. Having attended this, they returned to their hut to finish their preparations for a move. At one stage Rettig had to leave the hut, only to return a few minutes later, pursued by a baying crowd of 20 or more fellow prisoners.

The crowd chased Rettig, catching him and beating him with their fists. Rettig's close friend noticed that the ringleaders seemed to be Kuehne and Schmittendorf, along with two other men, Heinz Ditzler and Juergen Kersting. After enduring a severe beating, Rettig was pushed outside where an even larger crowd had assembled. There were now up to 100 men shouting: "Beat him to death" and "Hang him." The beating began all over again and Schmittendorf was seen to kick Rettig in the head.

Finally it was all over and the broken body of Gerhardt Rettig was rushed to hospital, where he died at 8.15pm that same night. The

NAMES	Armin Kuehne; Emil Schmittendorf
AGES AT EXECUTION	21; 31
DATE OF EXECUTION	Friday, 16th November, 1945
PLACE OF EXECUTION	Pentonville
HANGMAN	Albert Pierrepoint
ASSISTANT	Alex Riley
DATE OF TRIAL	7th August – 13th August, 1945
LOCATION OF TRIAL	Kensington, London
PRESIDING JUDGE	Military court martial
PROSECUTION COUNSEL	Major R.A.L. Hillard
DEFENCE COUNSEL	Lieutenant A.C. Brands
NUMBER OF VICTIMS	1

VICTIMS DETAILS	
NAME	Gerhardt Rettig
AGE	25
DATE OF MURDER	Saturday, 24th March, 1945
PLACE OF MURDER	Prison camp near Sheffield
METHOD OF KILLING	Battered
RELATIONSHIP TO KILLERS	None; none

four ringleaders were arrested and taken to London to be put on trial in Kensington Palace Gardens.

All four men denied any involvement in the attack. Once again the witnesses were not named for fear of reprisals and after a trial lasting almost a week, Ditzler and Kersting were acquitted, Kuehne and Schmittendorf being sentenced to death. They were executed together, some six weeks after their five comrades, on the same gallows and with the same executioner officiating.

JOHN AMERY WAS the son of Cabinet Minister Leo Amery and the elder brother of Julian Amery. Whilst his family may have displayed a distinguished record, John was an arrogant and worthless individual with a much overdeveloped sense of his own importance.

By the time he was 24, in 1936, Amery had been declared bankrupt. At about the same time he was a gun runner during the Spanish Civil War, rather predictably choosing to support the fascist Franco.

In 1942, Amery travelled to Berlin and offered his services to the German government. He was feted by the National Socialists and made propaganda speeches in Norway, France, Belgium, Yugoslavia and Italy. He also made radio broadcasts and travelled prisoner-of-war camps trying to persuade interned British soldiers and civilians to join a force to fight for the Germans, on the Russian front. This 'force' was named the Legion of Saint George and later renamed the British Free Corps. It had about as much success as anything else Amery ever turned his hand to.

Amery was arrested in Italy on Saturday, July 7th, 1945 and flown from Milan to England under a military escort. As soon as he landed he was arrested and charged with treason.

The first trial date was September 12th but this was postponed. It had been suggested that Amery had become a naturalised Spanish citizen during his gun-running escapades and as such, owed no allegiance to the British Crown. His brother Julian was given special permission to fly to Spain and collect any evidence he could find. The second date of October 17th was postponed because Julian had not yet returned.

When Amery finally stood before Mister Justice Humphreys at the Old Bailey, he pleaded guilty and the entire proceedings lasted a mere eight minutes before sentence of death was passed.

NAME	John Amery
AGE AT EXECUTION	33
DATE OF EXECUTION	Wednesday, 19th December, 1945
PLACE OF EXECUTION	Wandsworth
HANGMAN	Albert Pierrepoint
ASSISTANT	Henry Critchell
DATE OF TRIAL	28th November, 1945
LOCATION OF TRIAL	Old Bailey
PRESIDING JUDGE	Mister Justice Humphreys
PROSECUTION COUNSEL	Sir Hartley Shawcross
DEFENCE COUNSEL	G.O. Slade
NUMBER OF VICTIMS	Hanged for treason

AUGUST 16TH, 1945, was a time for celebrations at the Heavy Anti-Aircraft Battery at Thorpe Bay, in Essex. After all, it was the occasion of the Allied victory over Japan. Unfortunately, when people have too much to drink, tempers run short, and the men at Thorpe Bay were no exception to that rule.

The trouble began when James McNicol saw his girlfriend, Jean Neale, dancing with some men from the R.A.F. During the evening, the arguments grew and soon there was trouble between McNicol and two of his fellow sergeants from the battery – Donald Kirkaldie and Leonard William Cox.

The festivities ended and the servicemen made for their billets. Kirkaldie, Cox and two others slept in one particular Nissen hut and at 3.00am on the morning of August 17th, Cox was woken by someone trying the locked door.

As he shook the sleep from his eyes, Cox heard the sound of glass breaking and suddenly the hut was bathed in light. Cox looked towards the door and saw that a hand was being withdrawn through a broken pane of glass, having switched on the light. A few seconds passed and then a rifle barrel appeared through the same pane.

A shot was fired and Cox was wounded. A second shot rang out and Kirkaldie, hit in the throat, died immediately. The culprit was James McNicol and he was arrested later that same day.

McNicol claimed that the killing was accidental. He said he had fired blindly to frighten Cox and Kirkaldie but admitted that he had intended to wound Cox. He went on to say that Cox had threatened to kill him and this was his way of retaliating.

Jean Neale gave evidence, saying that she had only been out with McNicol four times. The night before the shooting, McNicol had asked her to go to an empty hut for what he termed a 'flirtation' and when she refused, he lost his temper. Realising that their relationship could not progress much further, Jean told McNicol that she was finished with him and the prosecution held that this was the final straw and McNicol had gone to the hut intending to kill.

NAME	James McNicol
AGE AT EXECUTION	30
DATE OF EXECUTION	Friday, 21st December, 1945
PLACE OF EXECUTION	Pentonville
HANGMAN	Albert Pierrepoint
ASSISTANT	Herbert Morris, Stephen Wade
DATE OF TRIAL	13th November, 1945
LOCATION OF TRIAL	Chelmsford
PRESIDING JUDGE	Mister Justice Lewis
PROSECUTION COUNSEL	Cecil Havers
DEFENCE COUNSEL	Tristram Beresford
NUMBER OF VICTIMS	1

VICTIMS DETAILS	
NAME	Donald Alfred Richard Kirkaldie
AGE	28
DATE OF MURDER	Friday, 17th August, 1945
PLACE OF MURDER	Thorpe Bay, Essex
METHOD OF KILLING	Shot
RELATIONSHIP TO KILLER	None

When Leonard Cox spoke, he admitted that he had threatened McNicol but denied that he had said he would kill him. The two men had been friendly enough up until August 16th and when they had argued on that night, Cox had said that if it wasn't for the fact that he risked losing his stripes, he would "do something" to McNicol.

None of this was held to be an excuse for what McNicol had done and his admission that he had intended to shoot Cox meant that he was held to be guilty of murder. His appeal was heard on the same day as John Riley Young's and both were dismissed. They were hanged together at Pentonville.

WHEN 17-YEAR-OLD Eva Rosemary Lucas returned home on the evening of June 6th, 1945, she discovered to her horror that both her parents, Frederick and Cissie, had been brutally battered to death.

The motive was obviously one of robbery. Frederick Lucas ran a jeweller's shop in London and various items had been stolen from the house. The assailant had apparently been in something of a hurry, as a gold ring, dropped in haste, had been left on the doormat.

The police had quite a few clues to go on. The next-door neighbour, Mrs Stephens, reported that a young man had called at 'Cranham', just after 10.00am on the morning of the murder. He had knocked on the door, received no reply and then gone next door to tell Mrs Stephens that he had had an appointment with Mr Lucas at 8.30am, but his car had broken down. He asked Mrs Stephens to let her neighbours know that he had called, and said his name was Mr James.

In addition to the description of this caller, there were two other clues. Rubber heel prints were found on the floor and a trouser fly button was found in the murder room. When Mr Lucas's trousers were checked, none was seen to have a missing button, meaning that it almost certainly came from his assailant.

Meanwhile, Mrs Wheeler, who lived in Morley Road, Barking, was having trouble with her brother, John Riley Young. Young had called on his sister in the afternoon of June 7th and asked if he could stay there. That same day, he paid £500, all in £5 notes, into a business bank account in the name of Moore and Young, at Barclays Bank in High Street South, East Ham.

Some time that afternoon, Young slashed his wrists, but the wounds were not very deep and after being bandaged, he required no further attention. The following day, though, saw further developments along these lines. Young went upstairs at noon and soon afterwards his sister smelled gas. Upon checking on her brother she found that he had torn a gas pipe from the wall and placed it into his mouth. Young was rushed to hospital and arrested there on June 9th. As the police

NAME	John Riley Young
AGE AT EXECUTION	40
DATE OF EXECUTION	Friday, 21st December, 1945
PLACE OF EXECUTION	Pentonville
HANGMAN	Albert Pierrepoint
ASSISTANT	Herbert Morris, Stephen Wade
DATE OF TRIAL	9th November, 1945
LOCATION OF TRIAL	Chelmsford
PRESIDING JUDGE	Mister Justice Lewis
PROSECUTION COUNSEL	John Flowers, Gerald Howard
DEFENCE COUNSEL	J.P. Eddy, Mister Simmonds
NUMBER OF VICTIMS	2

VICTIMS DETAILS

NAMES	Frederick Benjamin Lucas; Cissie Clara Lucas
AGES	52; 50
DATE OF MURDER	Wednesday, 6th June, 1945
PLACE OF MURDER	'Cranham', Undercliffe Gardens, Leigh-on-Sea
METHOD OF KILLING	Battered; battered
RELATIONSHIP TO KILLER	None; none

walked into the ward, Young announced: "I have been expecting you. It was me and I want to get it off my chest."

Young made a full confession to the murder of Mr and Mrs Lucas, saying that he was at a loss to know how it had happened.

ON SEPTEMBER 13TH, 1945, Captain John Ritchie of the Canadian Army, travelled to London and stayed at the Y.M.C.A. Officer's Club. The following evening, Ritchie dined with some friends at the Criterion restaurant. He left there at 10.00pm, with a fellow Canadian, Lieutenant James Alexander Findlay. Less than two hours later, Captain Ritchie had been brutally battered to death.

It was 11.45pm when Police Sergeant John Dimsey and Constable Charles Pearce were walking down Bouchier Street. They passed two soldiers walking in the opposite direction and seconds later, found the body of Captain Ritchie, his head in a pool of blood. The two policemen turned and saw the soldiers make a run for it. They gave chase, but the two men split up. Dimsey managed to capture one of the soldiers, who turned out to be Robert Blaine. They returned to where Ritchie lay and Blaine then said that the other soldier had been the one who had hit him.

Back at the police station, Blaine went into further detail. He claimed that the other soldier was known to him by the name of Jack Connolly. Blaine had known Connolly for three or four weeks and they drank together, sometimes at the Duke of York, and sometimes at the Alfred's Head.

On the night of the murder, they had left the pub at about 11.00pm and went to visit a cafe. On the way there, they passed a pile of bricks. Connolly picked one up, gave it to Blaine and asked him to keep hold of it for him. Blaine assumed they would use it later to assist with a break-in, so he concealed it inside his tunic. Later, as they walked down Bouchier Street, Connolly asked for the brick back and then used it to batter Ritchie to death.

Bloodstains were found on Blaine's clothing and when he was searched, police found £5 in cash, together with Ritchie's bank book and cheque book. Blaine admitted that he had rifled Ritchie's pockets but still maintained that it had been Connolly who struck the fatal blows.

The trial lasted four days and Blaine, who had a long record of theft, dating from 1938, was found guilty and sentenced to death. His appeal was dismissed on December 13th and

NAME	Reginald Douglas Johnson (Robert Blaine)
AGE AT EXECUTION	24
DATE OF EXECUTION	Saturday, 29th December, 1945
PLACE OF EXECUTION	Wandsworth
HANGMAN	Albert Pierrepoint
ASSISTANT	Harry Kirk
DATE OF TRIAL	13th November – 16th November, 1945
LOCATION OF TRIAL	Old Bailey
PRESIDING JUDGE	Mister Justice Humphreys
PROSECUTION COUNSEL	L.A. Byrne, Gerald Howard
DEFENCE COUNSEL	Not known
NUMBER OF VICTIMS	1

VICTIMS DETAILS	
NAME	John Alexander Ritchie
AGE	Not known
DATE OF MURDER	Friday, 14th September, 1945
PLACE OF MURDER	Bourchier Street, Soho, London
METHOD OF KILLING	Battered
RELATIONSHIP TO KILLER	None

he was executed 16 days later. No trace of Jack Connolly was found and so one of the killers of Captain Ritchie did manage to escape the hangman's noose.

WILLIAM JOYCE, WHO became infamous as Lord Haw Haw in the war years, was accused of treason and, in effect, found guilty because he had a British passport.

In March 1933, Joyce joined the British Fascist movement and four months later, on July 4th, he applied for a British passport, giving his place of birth as Galway in Ireland, which made him a British subject. Four years later, Sir Oswald Mosley dismissed Joyce from the organisation in which he had risen to be director of propaganda. Joyce now formed his own movement, the National Socialist League, which would be disbanded shortly before the outbreak of war with Germany.

In July 1938, Joyce applied for a one year's renewal of his passport and did the same one year later, in July, 1939. By this time of course, the signs of war were there for all to see and Joyce did not wait for the declaration to occur. On August 25th, 1939, Joyce left Britain for Germany. His movements are not known with any degree of precision until he was next heard of, in Germany, on September 18th. By then, a state of war existed between Britain and Germany.

Joyce's war career is well documented. As the war was drawing to a close, Joyce fled Hamburg and made for the border with Denmark. He was captured there by British troops on May 28th, being shot in the thigh when it was thought he was about to draw a gun and resist arrest. The problems arose because Joyce had lied about his place of birth. He was actually born in Brooklyn and was therefore an American citizen. Joyce even suggested that in September 1940, he had acquired German citizenship, thus complicating the matter even further. He argued that as he owed no allegiance to the Crown, he could not be guilty of treason.

At his trial, the British passport played a prominent part. At the time of his flight to Germany, Joyce undoubtedly carried a passport from this country and it was argued that he, even as an alien, owed allegiance to the King. He was found guilty and sentenced to death.

Joyce's appeal began on October 30th and lasted until November 1st, the dismissal being announced on November 7th. He was granted

NAME	William Joyce
AGE AT EXECUTION	39
DATE OF EXECUTION	Thursday, 3rd January, 1946
PLACE OF EXECUTION	Wandsworth
HANGMAN	Albert Pierrepoint
ASSISTANT	Alex Riley
DATE OF TRIAL	17th September – 19th September, 1945
LOCATION OF TRIAL	Old Bailey
PRESIDING JUDGE	Mister Justice Tucker
PROSECUTION COUNSEL	Sir Hartley Shawcross, L.A. Byrne, Gerald Howard
DEFENCE COUNSEL	G.O. Slade, Derek Curtis-Bennett, J. Burge
NUMBER OF VICTIMS	Hanged for treason

leave to appeal to the House of Lords and their decision was given on December 19th. By a majority of four to one, they decided against him. Lord Porter's being the one dissenting voice.

THEODORE SCHURCH REMAINS a figure shrouded in mystery, greatly overshadowed by another traitor, William Joyce, who was hanged the day before him.

Born in London of Swiss parents, Schurch was a supporter of Nazi ideology and joined the British Union of Fascists in 1934. Two years later he joined the army, and became a private in the R.A.S.C., stationed at Woolwich.

Captured by the Italians in the North African theatre he readily offered his services to them and was enrolled as a spy. Mixing with the other prisoners of war, he would report back to his masters on any items of information that might be of use to them and seven of the ten charges he faced at his trial referred to this period in his life.

At the trial, one of the people who gave evidence was Lieutenant Archibald Hart who had been landed secretly on Sicily to report on the beaches there prior to an Allied landing. He was captured and sent to Rome and found that one of his fellow prisoners, whom he knew as Captain Richards, brought him tea regularly and constantly seemed to be asking questions. Other prisoners warned him not to trust Captain Richards, so no information was revealed. And Richards, it turned out, was none other than Theodore Schurch.

In 1944, Schurch was repeating his previous services for the Germans in southern France, northern Italy and even Switzerland and other charges related to this time. He also faced a single charge of desertion with intent to join the enemy.

Found guilty, the sentence was death and once this sentence had been confirmed, Schurch was executed, to remain ever since hidden in the shadows cast by Lord Haw Haw. Yet Schurch has his own place in history as the last man executed for treason in this country.

NAME	Theodore William John Schurch
AGE AT EXECUTION	27
DATE OF EXECUTION	Friday, 4th January, 1946
PLACE OF EXECUTION	Pentonville
HANGMAN	Albert Pierrepoint
ASSISTANT	Alex Riley
DATE OF TRIAL	17th September, 1945
LOCATION OF TRIAL	Old Bailey
PRESIDING JUDGE	Military Court Martial
PROSECUTION COUNSEL	Major R.A.L. Hilliard
DEFENCE COUNSEL	Not known
NUMBER OF VICTIMS	Hanged for treason

WILLIAM BATTY HAD known Nellie Gray, of 45 Prince Street, for some three years and had convinced himself that she was the woman for him. Unfortunately, Nellie was a married woman whose husband, Samuel, was in the army.

By August 1945, Samuel Gray was serving in Burma, but on the 9th of that month, he sent a telegram to Nellie to say that he would be home on leave the following day. Batty came to hear of this and vowed that he would speak to Samuel and if he would not let Nellie go, he would shoot him.

Samuel arrived home on August 10th. The next night, at around 11.00pm, there was a knock on the front door of number 45. Nellie answered the door and, seeing that it was Batty, closed it on him. Some 10 minutes later, Batty was still outside, sitting on the wall of number 20, opposite the Gray house. He was seen by Alice Spilsbury and he asked her to knock at the door and tell Mrs Gray that someone wanted to see her. Alice was frightened and ran off up the street. Seconds later she heard the sound of a shot. Though no one had been injured, Batty it seems had been testing the Luger he had in his possession.

On August 14th, Batty wrote to Nellie, asking her to go away with him. Not only did

NAME	William Batty
AGE AT EXECUTION	27
DATE OF EXECUTION	Tuesday, 8th January, 1946
PLACE OF EXECUTION	Leeds
HANGMAN	Thomas Pierrepoint
ASSISTANT	Harry Allen
DATE OF TRIAL	29th November – 30th November, 1945
LOCATION OF TRIAL	Leeds
PRESIDING JUDGE	Mister Justice Lynskey
PROSECUTION COUNSEL	G.H.B. Streatfeild
DEFENCE COUNSEL	C.B. Fenwick
NUMBER OF VICTIMS	1

VICTIMS DETAILS	
NAME	Samuel Hammond Gray
AGE	33
DATE OF MURDER	Tuesday, 14th August, 1945
PLACE OF MURDER	45 Prince Street, Dudley Hill, Bradford
METHOD OF KILLING	Shot
RELATIONSHIP TO KILLER	None

she refuse but she showed her husband the letter, telling him that nothing had been going on with Batty. So it was that when another knock came to the door, after 10.30pm, it was Samuel who answered it. It was Batty, and he asked to speak to Nellie. Samuel demanded to know who he was and Batty replied: "I am nobody." He then raised his hand and fired a single shot into Samuel's body.

There were a number of witnesses to the shooting. Margaret Ripley, the Grays' next-door neighbour, was in Nellie's house at the time and recognised Batty's voice at the door. James Arthur Sefton and his wife, Elsie May, saw Batty running away from the scene. Margaret Ripley ran for help, but it was too late for Samuel.

Batty knew it was only a matter of time before he was captured, so he ran to Ireton Street, where his mother lived. He knew that she would probably be at the house of her friend, Florence Heavysides, at number 33, but

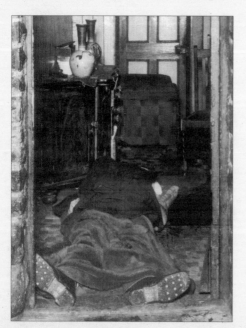

Samuel Gray lying dead in his own doorway. A coat has been thrown over the body out of respect.

was told that she had gone home early. When Batty got to his mother's house at number 65, he found the police waiting for him.

At the trial, one witness, Albert Edward Leeming said that he had been playing dominoes with Batty in the Cross Keys Hotel, until 10.00pm on the 14th. He testified that Batty appeared to be quite normal, thus greatly reducing any hopes of a defence based on insanity.

MICHAL NIESCIOR WAS a chef at the Royal Crescent Convalescent Home, in Brighton and it was in that seaside town that he first met Jessie Eileen Elphick, at a dance. They became friendly and in 1945, Niescior moved in with her at her house at 69 Abinger Road, Portslade.

Jessie was a married lady and her husband, Charles, had joined up in July 1939. It was not until 1942, that Charles was sent to serve overseas and this served to cool even further what relationship existed between them. At first Charles sent money regularly but even this stopped in 1944, and Jessie must have felt that she was entitled to build a new life for herself.

On August 10th, 1945, Charles Elphick returned home unexpectedly. He was somewhat surprised to discover his wife naked in the bath and a strange man in his bed. Charles put his foot down and insisted that Niescior had to go. To this ultimatum, Jessie Elphick replied: "If he goes, so do I." That evening all three spent a rather uneasy night under the same roof.

Jessie was true to her word and the very next day, she and Niescior moved into rooms in Gardner Street, Portslade. It was not long, though, before they argued and Jessie moved back in with Charles. Soon afterwards they went on holiday to Hastings, from where Jessie sent letters to Niescior. The relationship between them was still, it seems, very much alive.

Charles Elphick and his wife went to bed at 11.20pm on October 22nd. They had not been there long when they heard a constant pounding on the front door. Charles saw that his caller was Michal Niescior and he appeared to be armed with a carving knife. Taking a hammer for protection, Charles and Jessie went downstairs. As soon as the door was opened, Niescior leapt forward and stabbed Charles, who was rushed to hospital, where he died at 9.00am the following day. When charged with the murder, Niescior shouted: "Let them take me from here and shoot me right away."

In his defence, Niescior claimed that he had gone to Elphick's house to return a bicycle and saw that Charles was armed with

NAME	Michal Niescior
AGE AT EXECUTION	29
DATE OF EXECUTION	Thursday, 31st January, 1946
PLACE OF EXECUTION	Wandsworth
HANGMAN	Albert Pierrepoint
ASSISTANT	Stephen Wade
DATE OF TRIAL	10th December – 11th December, 1945
LOCATION OF TRIAL	Lewes
PRESIDING JUDGE	Mister Justice Wrottesley
PROSECUTION COUNSEL	Tristram Beresford, Granville Sharpe
DEFENCE COUNSEL	Eric Neve, Harold Brown
NUMBER OF VICTIMS	1

VICTIMS DETAILS

NAME	Charles Elphick (Died Tuesday, 23rd October)
AGE	42
DATE OF MURDER	Monday, 22nd October, 1945
PLACE OF MURDER	Outside 69 Abinger Road, Portslade, near Brighton
METHOD OF KILLING	Stabbed
RELATIONSHIP TO KILLER	None

what looked like a small axe. They struggled and Niescior managed to take the weapon from Elphick and strike him with it before taking the knife out of his pocket and stabbing him in self-defence.

It was a difficult case for the jury, who took 65 minutes to decide that Niescior had gone with the intention of deliberately killing Charles Elphick and was therefore guilty of murder. However, they felt that he had been sorely provoked and so included a strong recommendation to mercy. It did not save Michal Niescior's life.

THERE HAD BEEN some trouble, a street fight. Mrs Brady was talking to her friend at the corner of Carrick Street and Argyle Street about those terrible gangs, when she saw a tram stop.

A few people alighted and amongst them were Mrs Brady's son, John, her daughter Mary and Mary's husband, William Butler. Mrs Brady approached them and mentioned the trouble and added that another of her sons, Thomas, had not yet come home. Seeing that his mother was concerned, John Brady said that he would go and find Thomas. It was then around 10.40pm on October 20th, 1945.

Other people had seen that tram arrive, one of them being John Patrick Smyth who had been to the cinema with his girlfriend. They were walking home and noticed, on the corner of Douglas Street and Argyle Street, a gang of eight youths. Those youths knew that Smyth belonged to a gang called the Dougie Boys and since they were in a different gang, the Iona Boys, Smyth was considered fair game.

One of the gang produced a bayonet and with a shout of "Where is the Dougie Boys" advanced towards Smyth. Smyth ran, just as the tram arrived. He noticed along the way that two of the gang chasing him were John Lyon and John Alexander Rennie.

Joseph Brady, another of Mrs Brady's sons, was also a member of the Iona Boys but he wasn't with the group on the corner that night. He too saw the tram and his brother John alighting. The next thing he knew there was shouting from Washington Street and upon going to investigate he found John lying on the pavement with stab wounds to his face.

Eventually four men were charged with murder: John Lyon, John Alexander Rennie, Hugh Crosbie and his brother, Alexander Crosbie. Those four were picked out by a number of witnesses, including Thomas Kerr who had also seen the attack but curiously, many of those witnesses admitted that they had made their identifications only because they new the defendants by sight and had 'heard' on the grapevine that they had been there.

Despite this fragile evidence, only Hugh Crosbie succeeded in obtaining a verdict of

NAME	John Lyon
AGE AT EXECUTION	21
DATE OF EXECUTION	Friday, 8th February, 1946
PLACE OF EXECUTION	Glasgow, Barlinnie
HANGMAN	Albert Pierrepoint
ASSISTANT	Not known
DATE OF TRIAL	11th December – 15th December, 1945
LOCATION OF TRIAL	Glasgow
PRESIDING JUDGE	Lord Justice Mackay
PROSECUTION COUNSEL	Sinclair Shaw
DEFENCE COUNSEL	Robert McInnes
NUMBER OF VICTIMS	1

VICTIMS DETAILS

NAME	John Brady
AGE	19
DATE OF MURDER	Saturday, 20th October, 1945
PLACE OF MURDER	Washington Street, Glasgow
METHOD OF KILLING	Stabbed
RELATIONSHIP TO KILLER	None

Not Proven, though he was sentenced to three years for disorderly conduct and assault. The other three prisoners were all sentenced to death and their executions were originally set for January 5th, 1946.

The appeals were heard on January 16th when it was announced that one of the witnesses who claimed to have seen the prisoners had since been charged with perjury. Furthermore, a new witness, John Moore, had come forward to say that he had seen Rennie on a tram at the time of the crime. As a result, the sentence on Rennie was quashed, though the other death sentences remained.

On February 5th, Alexander Crosbie was reprieved, leaving John Lyon to face the noose alone.

CHARLES EDWARD PRESCOTT, a royal marine who lived in Biglands, Wigton, had for some time been walking out with 18-year-old Isabelle Young, known to her friends as Belle. In due course though, the friendship cooled; matters had not been helped by Prescott seeing Belle with another man, at a dance on October 17th, and threatening to shoot her. On October 26th, 1945, Belle announced that she did not want the relationship to continue, though she did say she wished to remain friends, and told Prescott that he could write to her if he wished.

Prescott took this rejection rather badly and four days later, on October 30th, he struck out at Belle, drew a dagger and threatened to injure her. Showing remarkable presence of mind, Belle managed to get the weapon off Prescott and threw it over a fence.

On the night of November 19th, 1945, Belle's sister, Sarah Jean, was showing some family photographs to Belle, their brother George, and two of the farmhands. Suddenly a shot rang out and Sarah fell to the floor, dead. The bullet had passed through one of the farm windows.

One hour later, Prescott walked into a reading room at Waverton and announced that he had shot Belle Young. There were a number of witnesses to this statement, including John Geoffrey Waugh, Lawrence Ismay, Thomas Warton, Allan Little and John William Strong. It was Ismay who telephoned for the police and when Sergeant Laydon arrived, Prescott ejected a cartridge from his rifle and was found to have another 24 rounds of ammunition on him.

During his wait in the reading room, Prescott also stated that he hoped he had hit the right person, as there had been quite a crowd in the farmhouse and he had fired from more than 100 yards away.

At his trial, Prescott denied that he had said anything whilst in the reading room and despite the testimony of the five witnesses, persisted in claiming that he had not fired deliberately. He had gone to the farm to see Belle and had tried to attract her attention by walking backwards and forwards near the windows. Whilst doing this, he had left his

NAME	Charles Edward Prescott
AGE AT EXECUTION	23
DATE OF EXECUTION	Tuesday, 5th March, 1946
PLACE OF EXECUTION	Durham
HANGMAN	Thomas Pierrepoint
ASSISTANT	Not known
DATE OF TRIAL	15th January – 17th January, 1946
LOCATION OF TRIAL	Carlisle
PRESIDING JUDGE	Mister Justice Lynskey
PROSECUTION COUNSEL	W. Gorman, Selwyn Lloyd M.P.
DEFENCE COUNSEL	Denis Gerrard, R.S. Nicklin
NUMBER OF VICTIMS	1

VICTIMS DETAILS	
NAME	Sarah Jean Young
AGE	19
DATE OF MURDER	Monday, 19th November, 1945
PLACE OF MURDER	Crummock Bank Farm, near Waverton, Wigton
METHOD OF KILLING	Shot
RELATIONSHIP TO KILLER	None

rifle resting against a fence and at one stage had heard a noise, which turned out to be a horse. This noise startled him, he swung round and the gun went off accidentally. Prescott further denied that he had told an officer that on November 7th, he had waited behind a hedge for 48 hours, in order to "do his girl in".

The story told by Prescott was unlikely to say the least and the jury had no trouble in rejecting it.

JOAN CLEGG, THE 20-year-old unmarried daughter of Arthur Clegg, found herself pregnant in 1945. Her mother had a nervous condition, so Joan managed to keep her condition secret from her but Joan told Arthur that the father was a man named Bob, although it has been suggested that the father was none other than Arthur himself. Whatever the truth of that, Arthur told Joan that no one would find out about the baby and that he was taking steps to have the child adopted once it was born.

On October 19th, Joan gave birth to a girl, whom she named Jill. Ten days later, the mother left the hospital, but the baby remained behind for the time being. The staff at the hospital were fully aware that the child was up for adoption and indeed they had found some friends of a hospital social worker who were interested in taking Jill. Unfortunately, these plans fell through and on October 30th, Arthur Clegg took the child from the care of the nurses at 4.45pm. When he arrived home, though, he was alone.

Clegg told Joan that some friends were looking after the child but a few days later, on November 6th, Jill's body was washed up on the banks of the River Thames. The sad bundle still had a wristband attached that read "baby Clegg".

Interviewed by the police, Clegg claimed that he had taken the child to an adoption agency but before actually entering the premises, he met a woman on the steps. She identified herself as Mrs Clarke and told him she had just lost her own baby and was looking to adopt. Clegg handed over Jill and that was the last time he saw the child. Clegg may have revealed more of the truth when the police first approached him and said they wished to talk to him about his granddaughter's death. "Ah well," he exclaimed, "I have been expecting this."

The mysterious Mrs Clarke was never traced, which was perhaps not surprising, and Clegg's story was dismissed by the jury. On the day he was hanged, his victim would have been exactly five months old.

NAME	Arthur Clegg
AGE AT EXECUTION	42
DATE OF EXECUTION	Tuesday, 19th March, 1946
PLACE OF EXECUTION	Wandsworth
HANGMAN	Albert Pierrepoint
ASSISTANT	Herbert Morris
DATE OF TRIAL	7th February – 8th February, 1946
LOCATION OF TRIAL	Old Bailey
PRESIDING JUDGE	Mister Justice Croom-Johnson
PROSECUTION COUNSEL	E. Anthony Hawke
DEFENCE COUNSEL	Melford Stevenson
NUMBER OF VICTIMS	1

VICTIMS DETAILS	
NAME	Jill Clegg
AGE	11 days
DATE OF MURDER	Tuesday, October 30th, 1945
PLACE OF MURDER	Somewhere in London
METHOD OF KILLING	Drowned
RELATIONSHIP TO KILLER	Granddaughter

HANNAH BURNS WAS a married woman, separated from her husband, but allowed Arthur Charles, a coloured seaman, to move into her home at 14 Albermarle Street, South Shields. However, whilst Charles was at sea in November 1944, Hannah also began seeing John Duplessis, another seaman.

On November 26th, 1944, Charles returned home to find Duplessis there and an argument followed. Constable Charles Welsh saw Duplessis off the premises and advised Charles to take action through the magistrate's court. There, for the time being, the matter rested.

In due course, though, Charles and Hannah drifted apart until, in the summer of 1945, he moved out and took lodgings in Dean Street. Very soon afterwards, Duplessis moved in with Hannah.

Charles and Duplessis both still needed work and in September 1945, they signed on the same ship, at Glasgow. The work lasted until November 28th, when both were paid off and returned to South Shields.

The following night, November 29th, Duplessis and Hannah met up at the Locomotive Inn. Charles was also there and at one stage Hannah handed over a letter that had arrived at his old address. Eventually, Hannah and Duplessis returned to Albermarle Street. Duplessis went to bed whilst Hannah carried out a few last-minute chores.

At one stage, Hannah went to her back door to empty a bowl of water and was shocked to see Charles there, a revolver in his hand. He pushed past her and walked to where Duplessis lay in bed.

Charles challenged Duplessis to fight but the latter, seeing the revolver, declined. Charles persisted until finally Duplessis said: "Shoot if you are going to shoot." At that, Charles smiled and exclaimed: "I have been waiting for this." He then fired all six shots.

Five of those shots struck home. Hannah had run off to fetch the police as soon as she heard the first shot, so she did not see Charles leave, return after a few moments and again level the gun at Duplessis, asking him if he wanted any more. Despite the bullet wounds, it would be a further five weeks before John

NAME	Arthur Charles
AGE AT EXECUTION	34
DATE OF EXECUTION	Tuesday, 26th March, 1946
PLACE OF EXECUTION	Durham
HANGMAN	Stephen Wade
ASSISTANT	Not known
DATE OF TRIAL	14th February, 1946
LOCATION OF TRIAL	Durham
PRESIDING JUDGE	Mister Justice Oliver
PROSECUTION COUNSEL	Doctor J. Charlesworth
DEFENCE COUNSEL	William Temple
NUMBER OF VICTIMS	1

VICTIMS DETAILS	
NAME	John Duplessis (Died, Monday, 31st December)
AGE	35
DATE OF MURDER	Thursday, 29th November, 1945
PLACE OF MURDER	14 Albermarle Street, South Shields
METHOD OF KILLING	Shot
RELATIONSHIP TO KILLER	None

Duplessis would die, from septicaemia.

Arthur Charles was arrested at his lodgings in Dean Street. He claimed that he had never owned a revolver and that he had been nowhere near Albermarle Street. When Duplessis made a deposition from his hospital bed, and the assailant was also identified by Hannah Burns, he persisted in saying that it was a case of mistaken identity.

A month before the trial, a seven-year-old boy, playing near some railway arches, found a rusty revolver that still contained six empty cartridge cases. The weapon was identified by Hannah as the one Charles had been carrying, but still Charles claimed he had not been to her house that night.

After a deliberation of two hours, the jury returned their guilty verdict. Charles's appeal was dismissed on March 11th, and just over two weeks later, he was hanged.

THE BODY OF Reuben Martirosoff, known as Russian Robert, lay in the back of his car. He had been shot through the head, and a .32 cartridge case and a bullet from a Walther automatic pistol were found on the front seat. There were also fingerprints at the scene of the crime that did not belong to Reuben.

Over the next couple of days, police investigations led them to the names of two Polish soldiers, Marion Grondkowski and Henryk Malinowski, who lived together in a flat at Ilford. The flat was raided and the murder weapon was found.

Also living at the flat, on a temporary basis, was Josef Novakhalcz. He said he had spent some time with the two Poles on the night of October 31st and that Malinowski had told him of his intention to fool Reuben into going out for a drink with the two of them, only for them to shoot and rob him.

As for the two accused, they were now busy blaming each other for the crime. Grondkowski claimed that he did not own a gun, even though one of his suits was found to include a special revolver pocket. His story was that all three men had gone to a club near Marble Arch and were drinking whisky.

Soon after midnight, they all got into Reuben's car, with Malinowski in the back seat. Suddenly there was a loud bang. Grondkowski ran from the car but his partner told him to come back, adding that he had already killed one and was quite happy to kill another.

Grondkowski's story was rather different. He claimed that he and Reuben had been good friends and he knew of many places where Reuben, a black-market dealer, hid his money, and he could have taken some of this without killing him. He did, however, admit that he and Grondkowski had taken £160 from the body.

At the beginning of the trial, an attempt was made to have them tried separately, but this failed. Further drama followed when one of the jurymen asked to be excused as he stated he was against capital punishment. His request was granted and he was replaced.

The trial lasted three days, after which both were hanged at Wandsworth but even now there was more controversy.

NAMES	Marion Grondkowski; Henryk Malinowski
AGES AT EXECUTION	32; 24
DATE OF EXECUTION	Tuesday, 2nd April, 1946
PLACE OF EXECUTION	Wandsworth
HANGMAN	Albert Pierrepoint
ASSISTANTS	Harry Kirk, Alex Riley
DATE OF TRIAL	11th February – 13th February, 1946
LOCATION OF TRIAL	Old Bailey
PRESIDING JUDGE	Mister Justice Croom-Johnson
PROSECUTION COUNSEL	E. Anthony Hawke
DEFENCE COUNSEL	Melford Stevenson, S. Lewis Langdon; J.D. Caswell, Victor Durand
NUMBER OF VICTIMS	1 (possibly 2)

VICTIMS DETAILS	
NAME	Reuben Martirosoff
AGE	39
DATE OF MURDER	Thursday, 1st November, 1945
PLACE OF MURDER	Chepstow Place, Notting Hill, London
METHOD OF KILLING	Shot
RELATIONSHIP TO KILLERS	None; none

Grondkowski was executed at 9.00am and in the interval of one hour before Malinowski faced the same fate at 10.00am, a man climbed onto the prison roof and began tearing off slates. Warders were forced to climb onto the roof and seize him.

One question remains. The spot where Reuben's car was discovered was less than a mile away from the location where weeks before, the body of Frank Everitt was found, in his taxi cab. He too had been robbed and shot in the head. Had he been the first victim of the two Poles?

1945

ON THE NIGHT of November 23rd, four men went out drinking. Joseph, Edward and John Gordon had met up with Duncan Reevie, their brother-in-law, at around 5.00pm. They had stayed in one pub until 7.30pm when they moved on to a second. They were there until around 9.00pm, and then split up.

Joseph Gordon was the first to leave, for by the time Edward went to his sister's house, Joseph was already there. The two brothers were not there for long when Reevie came in and announced, "You had better go out, your brother John is in the stair, bleeding to death."

Going down the stairwell, they found John suffering from a deep wound to his throat. John was rushed to the Royal Infirmary where he was found to be dead.

Reevie told the police that in the second pub he had met up with a friend, John Keatings. Along with John Gordon, they had left only to find Daniel Bonnar outside, determined to fight. Keating took off his coat whilst Reevie stepped forward. Seeing that his challenge was about to be met, Bonnar made a run for it. Reevie and Keating gave chase, during which they noticed that Bonnar had a hatchet in his hand.

Keating bade his friends goodnight and Reevie and John Gordon began to walk home. It was then that two men leapt on them: Bonnar and Patrick Carraher. While Bonnar fought with Reevie, Carraher went for Gordon. It was over in seconds and as the two assailants ran off, Gordon slumped to the pavement, bleeding badly. Reevie tried to carry him home but could only make it part way up the stairwell.

When the police interviewed Bonnar he said that he had spent that evening with one of his friends, Thomas Watt, and they had been the ones challenged to fight. He and Watt ran off and met up with Carraher. Together the three of them went looking for their tormentors. Bonnar admitted that he had attacked Reevie but he had not seen what Carraher did to Gordon.

The police charged Carraher, Bonnar and Watt but in due course the charges against the latter two were dropped. Much was made of the fact that the murder weapon, a chisel, had

NAME	Patrick Carraher
AGE AT EXECUTION	39
DATE OF EXECUTION	Saturday, 6th April, 1946
PLACE OF EXECUTION	Glasgow, Barlinnie
HANGMAN	Not known
ASSISTANT	Not known
DATE OF TRIAL	28th February – 2nd March, 1946
LOCATION OF TRIAL	Glasgow
PRESIDING JUDGE	Lord Justice Russell
PROSECUTION COUNSEL	Douglas Johnston, K.W.B. Middleton
DEFENCE COUNSEL	J.R. Philip, H.V. Ford
NUMBER OF VICTIMS	1

VICTIMS DETAILS	
NAME	John Gordon
AGE	39
DATE OF MURDER	Friday, 23rd November, 1945
PLACE OF MURDER	Taylor Street, Townhead, Glasgow
METHOD OF KILLING	Stabbed
RELATIONSHIP TO KILLER	None

a blade of two inches whilst the wound was four inches deep. Medical evidence was given that such a blade, driven with force into the soft tissues, could cause a deeper wound. Carraher was found guilty, his original execution date being set for March 23rd, but an unsuccessful appeal put that back.

This was the second time that Carraher had faced a trial for murder. In August 1938 he had stabbed 23-year-old James Sydney Emden Shaw on the corner of Ballater Street and Thistle Street, Glasgow. Tried before Lord Justice Pitman on September 12th, 1938, he was found guilty of culpable homicide and sentenced to three years.

IRENE WINN WAS a 21-year-old married woman whose husband was a soldier, serving overseas. Harold Berry was also married, and had four children. Despite these facts, the two still went away together for a two-day holiday to London, starting on January 5th, 1946. They travelled first class, stayed in a good hotel and Harold spent money freely, even offering at one stage to replace £20 that Irene lost when her purse was stolen by a pickpocket.

On the same day that the couple travelled down to London, a 15-year-old messenger boy, Frederick Walter Theabold, found the body of a moneylender's manager, Bernard Philipps, in a desolate spot between Winsford and Northwich. Philipps had been stabbed and the murder weapon, a commando knife, lay underneath the body.

Investigations showed that Philipps had last been seen alive at his office at the Refuge Lending Society, at 11.00am on January 3rd. A man had called, seeking a loan, giving his name as George Wood. Wood claimed that he lived at Moss Side poultry farm at Tarporley and wished to borrow money against the farm. Philipps set out with Wood to inspect the farm, taking with him the £50 in cash that Wood wished to borrow. The cash was held in a brown leather briefcase.

It seemed that the killer knew the locale very well, and eventually the free-spending Harold Berry came to the attention of the police. He was a local man who worked at a bacon factory earning £5 per week. How could such a man afford a first-class trip to London?

Berry's house was searched and a bloodstained coat was found. A leather wallet was also discovered, containing over £22 in cash. Further investigations showed that on January 4th, Berry had purchased a new suit, costing five guineas, from William Ernest Dodd, showing that he had come into money at the time Philipps was killed. Finally, Philipps's wallet and cigarette lighter were found in Berry's possession.

Berry claimed that he had never been to the offices of the Refuge Lending Society and had never met Philipps. He explained the wallet and lighter by claiming that a sailor

NAME	Harold Berry
AGE AT EXECUTION	30
DATE OF EXECUTION	Tuesday, 9th April, 1946
PLACE OF EXECUTION	Manchester
HANGMAN	Not known
ASSISTANT	Not known
DATE OF TRIAL	11th February – 14th February, 1946
LOCATION OF TRIAL	Chester
PRESIDING JUDGE	Mister Justice Stable
PROSECUTION COUNSEL	H. Glyn Jones, Arthian Davies
DEFENCE COUNSEL	Edmund Davies, J.P. Elsten
NUMBER OF VICTIMS	1

VICTIMS DETAILS	
NAME	Bernard Philipps
AGE	37
DATE OF MURDER	Thursday, 3rd January, 1946
PLACE OF MURDER	Near Moulton Hill Farm, Winsford
METHOD OF KILLING	Stabbed
RELATIONSHIP TO KILLER	None

named William Greenwood had given them to him, along with £5 in cash, in part repayment of a £20 loan. He also said that the rest of the money had come from a 40-1 winning horse a few months previously, though he couldn't remember the horse's name.

The final piece of evidence linking Berry with the crime came from his wife, Jessie. She testified that she had seen a commando knife in a scabbard. Her son, Allan, had been playing with it and she had told her husband to get rid of it in case he hurt himself. That, together with the rest of the evidence, was enough to send Harold Berry to the gallows.

1945

ON MONDAY, NOVEMBER 26Th, 1945, a young man, brandishing a gun, walked into the shop owned by Henry Dutton and demanded that he hand over the money in the till. When Dutton did not immediately comply with this order, two shots were fired into his stomach.

Dutton staggered outside the shop, into Great Jackson Street, where he collapsed. Rushed to hospital, he died from his wounds four days later, but not before giving a description of his assailant. The attacker was said to be about 25 years old, 5 feet 7 inches tall, clean shaven and wearing a trilby hat.

The day after the shooting, whilst Henry Dutton was still fighting for his life, accounts of the attack appeared in the local newspapers. At the Salvation Army hostel, Martin Patrick Coffey saw one of those reports and laughingly announced to two witnesses, John Irvine and William Phelan, that he had "done the job". The police were informed and Coffey was questioned the same day. He was asked to explain his movements and when his answers were not satisfactory, he was held in custody whilst further inquiries were made.

Whilst it was true that Coffey fitted the description of the attacker, there was initially no other evidence to connect him with the crime. No stolen property was found and no bloodstains were found on his clothing. However, when a search of the hostel was made, the murder weapon was discovered on top of a cupboard. Its location, though, linked the weapon with John Irvine, who admitted he had taken the gun from Coffey as he wanted it as a souvenir of the war.

When the gun was found, Coffey made a statement admitting that he was responsible for the shooting. Once Henry Dutton had died, the charge became one of murder and Martin

NAME	Martin Patrick Coffey
AGE AT EXECUTION	24
DATE OF EXECUTION	Wednesday, 24th April, 1946
PLACE OF EXECUTION	Manchester
HANGMAN	Not known
ASSISTANT	Not known
DATE OF TRIAL	12th March, 1946
LOCATION OF TRIAL	Manchester
PRESIDING JUDGE	Mister Justice Morris
PROSECUTION COUNSEL	F.E. Pritchard
DEFENCE COUNSEL	Kenneth Burke
NUMBER OF VICTIMS	1

VICTIMS DETAILS

NAME	Henry Dutton (Died Friday, 30th November)
AGE	72
DATE OF MURDER	Monday, 26th November, 1945
PLACE OF MURDER	57 Great Jackson Street, Manchester
METHOD OF KILLING	Shot
RELATIONSHIP TO KILLER	None

Coffey was now on trial for his life.

The defence tried to suggest that Coffey was a romancer and had simply made up the story to impress people. The jury were not convinced and Coffey was found guilty.

The dilapidated shop on Great Jackson Street where Henry Dutton was killed.

O N THE EVENING of Saturday, November 17th, 1945, Leonard Holmes's parents paid him a visit at the bungalow he shared with his wife, Peggy, and their six children. The next evening, all the four adults visited the Carpenter's Arms for a drink and it was noted that Leonard and Peggy seemed to be happy with each other. Things were rather different on the Monday, though. On that day Leonard travelled to Huddersfield and told a friend, May Shaw, that Peggy had left him.

In fact, May Shaw had been warned to expect this by a telegram, sent by Leonard on the 17th. She had first met Leonard in 1943, when he was a soldier stationed at Huddersfield and their friendship developed to the point where Leonard asked her if she would live with him if Peggy ever left. May said that she would and the telegram, which read: "See you Sunday or Monday for sure. Be prepared. OK. All fixed. Len" seemed to suggest that at last things had been sorted out.

Leonard stayed with May until Tuesday evening and then said he had to head for home. It was a journey he never completed, for the police were watching for him and he was arrested at Retford station. The charge was murder.

Whilst Leonard was away on the Monday, his brother had called and, receiving no reply, felt that there might be something wrong. He forced an entry and found Peggy's body. When Leonard was faced with this knowledge, he replied: "There is only one answer to the charge. I admit it."

Leonard claimed that he believed his wife might have been unfaithful. Whilst they had been in the pub with his parents, he thought he caught her winking at two airmen and when they got home, he faced her with this and an argument broke out. In anger he picked up a coal hammer and struck her. She was still alive but Leonard felt she was beyond help, so he strangled her. He looked at his watch, which put the time of Peggy's death at 2.04am.

Leonard then washed himself and burned his bloodstained clothes. He waited for the children to get up, gave them breakfast and took them to school after having instructed them to go to their grandmother's house that evening.

NAME	Leonard Holmes
AGE AT EXECUTION	32
DATE OF EXECUTION	Tuesday, 28th May, 1946
PLACE OF EXECUTION	Lincoln
HANGMAN	Not known
ASSISTANT	Not known
DATE OF TRIAL	28th February, 1946
LOCATION OF TRIAL	Nottingham
PRESIDING JUDGE	Mister Justice Charles
PROSECUTION COUNSEL	Arthur Ward, Rodger Winn
DEFENCE COUNSEL	P.E. Sandlands, Mrs E.K. Lane
NUMBER OF VICTIMS	1

VICTIMS DETAILS	
NAME	Peggy Agnes Holmes
AGE	29
DATE OF MURDER	Monday, 19th November, 1945
PLACE OF MURDER	Central Avenue, Walesby
METHOD OF KILLING	Battered/strangled
RELATIONSHIP TO KILLER	Wife

Leonard also had an explanation for the highly incriminating telegram that he had sent before the attack on his wife and which implied premeditation on his part. He said that he had seen a packed suitcase and was convinced that Peggy was about to leave him. He simply took the opportunity to contact May and suggest that things might be about to work out for them.

In his summing-up, Mister Justice Charles suggested that manslaughter was not applicable in this case and the jury might think that it was a very cold-blooded murder. They agreed.

1946

ELLA STAUNTON WAS a former beauty queen and dancer, who had been separated from her husband, Thomas, for more than seven years. Living at 113 Ullet Road, Liverpool, she now ran a ladies hairdressers, known as Bobby's, at 7 Tempest Hey.

On May 20th, 1946, it was noticed that the shop was not locked and secured at the usual time and so, at around 5.00pm, two plain-clothes police officers entered the premises to investigate. There they found Ella's body. She had been stabbed about the head and face and strangled with a length of flex.

Police attention fell upon Ella's boyfriend, Thomas Hendren, a baker by trade, who had been missing from his home at 9 Roe Street, Birkenhead, since May 10th. A full-scale search was launched for the missing man.

Two days after the murder, on May 22nd, a railway porter who needed to answer a call of nature was entering the toilets on the station when he dropped his bunch of keys. Bending down to pick them up, he noticed something jammed behind a waste pipe. These items turned out to be Hendren's identity card and other documents. Hendren himself was picked up the following day and charged with murder.

At his trial, Hendren's defence was one of insanity. His brother, William James Hendren, explained that Thomas had had some terrible war experiences in Singapore. He had been engaged but this had been broken off in 1945 and it had affected him badly. At the time he had even attempted suicide by gassing. It was also said that Hendren had a terrible temper and flared up easily.

The insanity defence was greatly weakened when evidence was given that after the murder, Hendren had bought a mackintosh to put over the clothes he was wearing. This implied that he was fully aware of what he had done and was sensible enough to try to avoid capture.

After due consideration, the jury concluded that Hendren had been sane at the time of the attack on Ella and was therefore guilty of murder.

NAME	Thomas Hendren
AGE AT EXECUTION	31
DATE OF EXECUTION	Wednesday, 17th July, 1946
PLACE OF EXECUTION	Liverpool
HANGMAN	Not known
ASSISTANT	Not known
DATE OF TRIAL	27th June, 1946
LOCATION OF TRIAL	Liverpool
PRESIDING JUDGE	Mister Justice Oliver
PROSECUTION COUNSEL	H.I. Nelson, Robertson Crichton
DEFENCE COUNSEL	Basil E. Neild, Leslie Rigg
NUMBER OF VICTIMS	1

VICTIMS DETAILS

NAME	Ella Valentine Staunton
AGE	41
DATE OF MURDER	Monday, 20th May, 1946
PLACE OF MURDER	7 Tempest Hey, Liverpool
METHOD OF KILLING	Stabbed/strangled
RELATIONSHIP TO KILLER	Girlfriend

WALTER CLAYTON, A married man, lived at 63 Balmoral Road, Morecambe. A soldier, most of his service had been spent in Burma but in April, 1946, he was on leave from India. It was on the 5th of that month, on a casual visit to the Ship Hotel, that he first met an ex-W.A.A.F., Joyce Jacques.

The two new friends got on so well that Clayton found himself invited back to Joyce's lodgings at 48 Christie Avenue. They spent the night together and over the next few days, Clayton was a constant visitor. On April 12th, the lovers had an argument when it seemed that she was about to jilt Clayton, but the matter blew over and they remained friends.

Clayton and Joyce spent that day travelling around various public houses, but at 5.00pm they were back at Joyce's lodgings, where Clayton ominously asked her landlady, Doris Walker, if she had a dagger she could let him have. She said she could not help him and later, Joyce and Clayton were out together again.

At 6.15pm, they were seen in the Battery Hotel, where they were served by Evelyn Shepherd. She would later report that after leaving together, Clayton returned alone at around 9.00pm, leaving after a single drink.

It was some time around 10.00pm when Clayton appeared on the Central Pier and asked a steward, Joseph Bradley, if he had seen his wife. Mrs Clayton was dancing with Bradley's daughter and Bradley pointed them out. Clayton then asked his wife to go for a walk with him and, once alone, told her that he had just strangled Joyce.

Clayton was arrested at his home at 2.30am on the morning of Saturday, April 13th. His trial was originally set for Lancaster assizes but the defence not being ready, the case was put back to Manchester. Clayton insisted on pleading guilty and the entire proceedings were over in three minutes.

Joyce, it seems, had foretold her own death. Amongst her belongings, back at her lodgings, police found a diary. One entry read: "I know that one day you will murder me, because your passion is the better of you." The entire affair between them had lasted exactly one week.

NAME	Walter Clayton
AGE AT EXECUTION	22
DATE OF EXECUTION	Wednesday, 7th August, 1946
PLACE OF EXECUTION	Liverpool
HANGMAN	Albert Pierrepoint
ASSISTANT	Stephen Wade
DATE OF TRIAL	16th July, 1946
LOCATION OF TRIAL	Manchester
PRESIDING JUDGE	Mister Justice Stable
PROSECUTION COUNSEL	Patrick Cussen
DEFENCE COUNSEL	Basil E. Neild, Miss Rose Heilbron
NUMBER OF VICTIMS	1

VICTIMS DETAILS	
NAME	Joyce Jacques
AGE	23
DATE OF MURDER	Friday, 12th April, 1946
PLACE OF MURDER	Foreshore at Morecambe, Lancashire
METHOD OF KILLING	Strangled
RELATIONSHIP TO KILLER	Girlfriend

JAMES DEEKAN AND his wife had enjoyed their trip to the cinema and now, as they walked up Edinburgh Road at 8.25pm, they were looking forward to getting home to number 524. It was then that James saw a light on upstairs. He was sure that all the lights had been off when they left. There was only one explanation: they had burglars.

Leaving his wife outside, James dashed to a neighbour's house. Luckily, that neighbour, James Straiton, was a retired detective sergeant, so he would know what to do.

Collecting a truncheon, James Straiton accompanied his neighbour in through the back of the house. Almost immediately they saw two youths at the top of the stairs and called out for them to surrender. One of the youths drew a gun but showing no fear, Straiton rushed forward and caught him a blow on the head. The two men grappled for a few seconds and shots were fired. Soon James Straiton fell to the floor, fatally wounded with a bullet in his stomach and the two burglars took the chance to make good their escape.

James Deekan was able to supply a good description of the two burglars. Two other witnesses, John Johnson and William Allison, a bus driver and conductor had been standing next to their bus at a nearby terminus when the shots rang out. Seeing two men rush out of Edinburgh Road they followed in their bus, but lost them when they ran up Piershill Street which was too narrow for the bus. Johnson and Allison were also able to supply descriptions.

For a time, the police investigation got nowhere, but then it was decided to try a different tack. Although the killing of James Stainton was an opportune crime, the two men seemed to be accomplished burglars. It was decided then to link the crime to a spate of such burglaries and in one of those, at Golfhill Drive, a piece of broken glass had revealed a partial thumbprint. Painstaking work now linked that print to 19-year-old John Caldwell, who lived in Fielden Street.

Arrested on suspicion on April 1st, Caldwell was readily identified by James Deekan. This in turn led to the arrest of his partner in crime, a 15-year-old youth who

NAME	John Caldwell
AGE AT EXECUTION	20
DATE OF EXECUTION	Saturday, 10th August, 1946
PLACE OF EXECUTION	Glasgow, Barlinnie
HANGMAN	Albert Pierrepoint
ASSISTANT	Not known
DATE OF TRIAL	25th June – 26th June, 1946
LOCATION OF TRIAL	Glasgow
PRESIDING JUDGE	Lord Justice Stevenson
PROSECUTION COUNSEL	Douglas Johnston, J.B.W. Christie
DEFENCE COUNSEL	J.F. Gordon Thomson, R. Levitt
NUMBER OF VICTIMS	1

VICTIMS DETAILS	
NAME	James Straiton
AGE	61
DATE OF MURDER	Tuesday, 26th March, 1946
PLACE OF MURDER	524 Edinburgh Road, Glasgow
METHOD OF KILLING	Shot
RELATIONSHIP TO KILLER	None

could not be named for legal reasons. Only Caldwell was charged with murder and he faced his trial in June.

Found guilty and sentenced to death the original execution date was cancelled when Caldwell appealed. That appeal was lost on July 23rd and before the death sentence was carried out, John Caldwell 'celebrated' his 20th birthday.

HERBERT CHAPMAN ARRIVED at John Whatman's house at 9.00am on Sunday, March 3rd and found that Whatman had been brutally murdered. The lonely house had been ransacked and John Whatman's body lay in the yard, covered with an old coat. He had been shot twice. Once in the shoulder and once in the head.

The motive was obvious. The house was in disarray and the safe had been broken open and emptied of cash. A heavy gold watch was also missing. The local police decided to call in the services of Scotland Yard.

It was a relatively simple matter to pin-point the time of death. Whatman had last been seen alive by a neighbour at 5.30pm on Saturday the 2nd. It was also discovered that he had told one of his friends that he was expecting some company on Saturday evening. It became urgent to trace that 'company' and find out if he knew anything about the crime.

Diligent police work identified Whatman's caller as Sydney John Smith, who was traced to his lodgings at 51 High Street, Markyate, Hertfordshire, where he was picked up on March 7th. After questioning, he admitted that he had killed Whatman but claimed that it was self-defence.

Smith claimed that he had gone to Whatman's house to sell him a revolver. Whatman not only refused to purchase the gun, but drew out his own gun and threatened Smith with it. A struggle followed in which Whatman managed to knock the wind out of Smith, even though he was almost 50 years older. As Smith gasped on the floor he saw Whatman raising his gun but Smith was quick enough to fire first.

The story was at best unlikely, and the prosecution painted a much more believable picture, which involved Smith striking Whatman before shooting him twice and ransacking the house. The jury preferred that version and on September 6th, 1946, Smith was hanged alongside David Baillie Mason.

NAME	Sydney John Smith
AGE AT EXECUTION	24
DATE OF EXECUTION	Friday, 6th September, 1946
PLACE OF EXECUTION	Wandsworth
HANGMAN	Albert Pierrepoint
ASSISTANT	Henry Critchell, Harry Allen
DATE OF TRIAL	18th July, 1946
LOCATION OF TRIAL	Lewes
PRESIDING JUDGE	Mister Justice Singleton
PROSECUTION COUNSEL	Anthony H. Marlowe, T. Southall
DEFENCE COUNSEL	Aiken Watson, B. Dutton Briant
NUMBER OF VICTIMS	1

VICTIMS DETAILS	
NAME	John Whatman
AGE	72
DATE OF MURDER	Saturday, 2nd March, 1946
PLACE OF MURDER	'The Choice', Blackpath Lane, Hollington, Hastings
METHOD OF KILLING	Shot/battered
RELATIONSHIP TO KILLER	None

1946

DOROTHY MASON WORKED as a domestic servant at a nursery. It was her habit to take her son, David John, in with her and, when she did some extra work as a hairdresser, in the evenings, her husband, David, would pick up the boy on his way home from work.

On May 28th, 1946, Dorothy left the nursery at 3.00pm. This was one of the evenings her son was left behind for David to pick up. Unfortunately, Dorothy had forgotten to mention this and the child was still at the nursery at 7.00pm. Later that night, Dorothy Mason returned home. At 10.30pm, the woman who lived in the flat upstairs, Miss Reader, heard a bumping noise and a woman's cry.

At around 4.00am the following morning, David Mason was at Doctor Taylor's, in Wallington, asking him to visit his wife as she had had collapsed. Doctor Taylor attended and found that Dorothy was dead. As he was leaving, Mason asked the doctor if he would also take a look at his son. The doctor returned and found the child dead in his cot. The police were called in. A postmortem on both bodies revealed that Dorothy had been strangled and the boy had died from asphyxiation.

Mason initially told the police that he and Dorothy had constant rows and on the night in question, after one such argument, he had bent over his wife whilst she was lying on the bed. He then suffered some kind of black out and when he woke, he was still bending over Dorothy but she was now dead. It was only with his next story that Mason might have been approaching the truth.

According to this version, Dorothy had returned home to be told that the child was in bed but not asleep. She retorted: "I will make the little brat sleep" and then went up to his bedroom. Soon afterwards, Mason went upstairs to find his wife smothering her son.

Mason demanded to know why she had killed their son. Dorothy then attacked him. In the struggle that followed, Mason tried to push Dorothy away and at one stage put his hands around her throat. Only when it was all over did he find that he had killed her. He had not told the truth originally because he

NAME	David Baillie Mason
AGE AT EXECUTION	39
DATE OF EXECUTION	Friday, 6th September, 1946
PLACE OF EXECUTION	Wandsworth
HANGMAN	Albert Pierrepoint
ASSISTANT	Harry Allen, Henry Critchell
DATE OF TRIAL	22nd July – 25th July, 1946
LOCATION OF TRIAL	Old Bailey
PRESIDING JUDGE	Mister Justice Cassels
PROSECUTION COUNSEL	E. Anthony Hawke
DEFENCE COUNSEL	Russell Vick
NUMBER OF VICTIMS	1 (possibly 2)

VICTIMS DETAILS	
NAME	Dorothy Louisa Mildred Mason
AGE	36
DATE OF MURDER	Tuesday, 28th May, 1946
PLACE OF MURDER	12a Haslemere Close, Wallington
METHOD OF KILLING	Strangled
RELATIONSHIP TO KILLER	Wife

wanted to protect his wife's memory.

At Mason's trial, one of the people who gave evidence was William Richard Frederick Rogers, Dorothy's brother. He said that Mason had been devoted to his son, whereas Dorothy had always treated him with indifference. Rogers went on to say that he believed his sister was capable of doing what Mason had described.

Had David Mason told his story in the first place he might well have escaped with a verdict of manslaughter. As it was, the jury took 40 minutes to decide that the crime was deliberate.

NEVILLE GEORGE CLEVELLY Heath already had quite a reputation before he became a double murderer. By the end of 1945, he had been court-martialled three times, received a three-year borstal sentence for stealing, and fined for wearing medals and a uniform he was not entitled to. This was the kind of man who met Margery Gardner in May, 1946.

Margery was a pleasure-loving lady who had somewhat unusual sexual proclivities. She liked flagellation and bondage and since Heath was a sadist, it seemed as if the two might have been made for each other.

On May 1st, 1946, the couple booked in to the Pembridge Court Hotel, in London and had their first attempt at satisfying each other's tastes. So carried away did Heath become that Miss Gardner's screams attracted the interest of the hotel detective and it may well be that his intervention was all that prevented the first murder taking place on that date. It was nothing new to Heath. He had already had a similar experience with a different lady at the Strand Hotel in March. Neither woman made an official complaint.

It was in June 1946 that Neville Heath's life became rather more tangled. On the 15th of the month, Heath went to a W.R.N.S. dance in Chelsea and it was here that he met 19-year-old Yvonne Symonds. They got on well from the start and after talking to her for some time, Heath took Yvonne to the Panama club in South Kensington. From there they moved on to the Overseas Club where Yvonne was staying, and she agreed to spend the next day in the company of the charming and very handsome man who had shown her such a good time.

The date on June 16th must have gone very well indeed, for Heath ended up proposing to Yvonne. She not only accepted but agreed to spend the night with him at the Pembridge Court Hotel. Luckily for her, nothing untoward happened and on the following day, Yvonne returned to her parents' home in Worthing, Sussex.

Three days later, on June 20th, Heath again met up with Margery Gardner. She too was taken to the Panama Club in Cromwell Place, from where they left together, just after

NAME	Neville George Clevelly Heath
AGE AT EXECUTION	28
DATE OF EXECUTION	Wednesday, 16th October, 1946
PLACE OF EXECUTION	Pentonville
HANGMAN	Albert Pierrepoint
ASSISTANT	Harry Kirk
DATE OF TRIAL	24th September – 26th September, 1946
LOCATION OF TRIAL	Old Bailey
PRESIDING JUDGE	Mister Justice Morris
PROSECUTION COUNSEL	E. Anthony Hawke, Henry Elam
DEFENCE COUNSEL	J.D. Casswell, E.A. Jessel, Mister Asher
NUMBER OF VICTIMS	2

VICTIMS DETAILS	
NAMES	Margery Aimee Brownell Gardner; Doreen Marshall
AGES	32; 21
DATES OF MURDERS	Friday, 21st June, 1946; Thursday, 4th July, 1946
PLACE OF MURDER	Room 4, Pembridge Court Hotel, Notting Hill Gate, London; Branksome Chine, Bournemouth
METHOD OF KILLING	Asphyxiated; cut throat
RELATIONSHIP TO KILLER	Girlfriend; none

midnight. Taking a taxi, Heath and Margery were taken to the Pembridge Hotel, where they occupied room 4. None of the other guests would later report hearing any noise in the night.

On June 21st, Alice Wyatt was busy cleaning out the rooms of the hotel. Reaching room 4, she knocked and when there was no reply, walked in, the door being unlocked. Both beds had apparently been slept in and something was still occupying one of the beds. On closer inspection, Mrs Wyatt found that it was the body of Margery Gardner. Margery, covered with the bedclothes, lay naked on her back, her right arm underneath her. Her ankles were tied together with a handkerchief and there were marks on her wrists that showed that her hands had been tied too, though no ligature was found. Her face and chin were bruised, signifying that she had been struck. There were also 17 scourge marks on her body, which appeared to have been made with a whip that had left a curious diamond-weave pattern on her flesh.

The catalogue of injuries was still far from complete. Both breasts had been bitten, one so severely that the nipple was almost off and something rough had been inserted into her vagina and revolved, causing much bleeding. What was worse, was that examinations would show that all these terrible injuries had been inflicted before death, which had been caused by suffocation, possibly from a gag or from having her face forced into a pillow in order to stifle her screams.

Heath was nowhere to be seen. The same day that the body of Margery was discovered, he had telephoned his fiancée, Yvonne Symonds, in Worthing and arranged to go down to meet her. He arrived in Sussex that afternoon and booked in to the Ocean Hotel.

Yvonne met Heath on the morning of June 22nd. It was Heath who brought up the subject of the murder in London that featured in the morning paper. Somewhat enigmatically he said he would tell her something about it later. They then went off together to meet Yvonne's parents, who were charmed by the dashing Heath. They all went to a local golf club together and that evening, Heath treated Yvonne to dinner at the Blue Peter Club in Angmering.

It was whilst they were enjoying their meal that Yvonne reminded Heath that he had promised to tell her something about the London killing. He informed her that it had taken place in the very hotel room they had shared together on June 16th, and that he had actually seen the body. He explained that he had met the unfortunate victim the day before she was murdered. She was with a man and they had nowhere to go, so Heath kindly gave her his room keys and said she could entertain her friend there. Heath then took Yvonne home before returning to the Ocean Hotel.

On the next day, Yvonne's parents read more about the London murder and were dismayed to find that the police were looking for Neville Heath. Yvonne rang Heath at his hotel and asked him to explain the police's interest in him. Heath tried to put her mind at rest, telling her that the police must merely want some more information and that he was going back to London immediately to talk to them. Heath did leave Worthing that afternoon, but not to go to London. He merely moved down the coast to Bournemouth, where he booked in to the Tollard Royal Hotel, using the name Group Captain Rupert Brook.

Before he left Worthing, though, Heath did contact Scotland Yard. He wrote a letter to Chief Inspector Barratt, repeating to him the story he had told to Yvonne, but adding that he had returned to the room at 2.00am and found the body himself. He added that the man Margery had been with was named Jack, but that that was all he could let them know.

On June 27th, Heath attended at dance at the Pavilion, in Bournemouth. Here he met a girl named Peggy and a few days later, on July 3rd, whilst he was sitting on a bench on the promenade, Heath again saw Peggy. This time she was with a friend, Doreen Marshall. The three fell into conversation and when Peggy left, Doreen stayed on, talking freely to the handsome group captain.

Doreen had been ill and was down in Bournemouth from her home in Pinner, for recuperation. She told Heath that she was staying at the Norfolk Hotel and readily accepted when he invited her to the Tollard for afternoon tea. She also accepted when Heath invited her to dinner later on and met him again that evening at 8.15pm. The couple dined until after 10.00pm when they moved to the hotel's writing room. Here they continued to talk until around 11.30pm when they were seen to leave together and sit on a seat near the hotel.

On July 5th, the manager of the Norfolk Hotel, growing concerned over Miss Marshall, who had not been seen for two days, telephoned Mister Relf, the manager of the Tollard Royal. He mentioned that Miss Marshall had said she was dining with a friend there and asked him to see if this friend had any further information on her whereabouts.

It was July 6th before Mister Relf had a chance to talk to Group Captain Brooks and ask him about his dinner guest. Heath denied that the woman he had dined with was Doreen Marshall and even agreed to talk to the police when Relf suggested it.

When Heath did telephone the police station he was told that the officer in charge of investigating Miss Marshall's disappearance was out. Heath said he would call back, which he did at 3.30pm. He spoke to D.C. Souter, who asked if Heath would go in to the police station and take a look at a photograph of the missing girl in order to give a proper identification. Heath agreed to pop in at 5.30pm.

When he arrived at Bournemouth police station, Doreen's father and sister were already there, having travelled down from Pinner. Heath consoled them, looked at the photograph and confirmed that it was indeed the lady he had dined with. He then began to give Souter an outline of his movements on the night the girl had vanished.

Souter was a good policeman and as Heath was talking, Souter was struck by the resemblance he bore to the description circulated by Scotland Yard of a man they wanted to interview over the death of Margery Gardner. Souter informed his superiors of his suspicions before asking Group Captain Brook if he was in reality Neville Heath. Heath denied it but was detained until he could be interviewed by Detective Inspector George Gates.

When D.I. Gates finally spoke to the group captain, Heath asked if he could just return quickly to his hotel and fetch his jacket. Gates, highly suspicious over this request, went himself to the hotel and brought back the jacket, which was then searched. A cloakroom ticket was discovered and when it was redeemed by the police, Gates found himself with a suitcase that had been left at Bournemouth station. Upon opening it, he found items of clothing labelled 'Heath', a bloodstained scarf and a riding switch with a diamond-weave pattern. He knew then that he had the right man in custody.

Heath was taken back to London on July 7th, and charged with the murder of Margery Gardner on July 8th. On that same evening, the body of Doreen Marshall was discovered in bushes at Bournemouth.

Doreen Marshall's body was naked except for one shoe, her clothes having been thrown over the body in order to conceal it. She had been struck several times on the head and her throat had been cut. Her body was very badly mutilated. One nipple had been bitten off and there were jagged cuts from her vagina up to her chest. Something rough, possibly a tree branch, had been pushed into her vagina and her anus.

At Heath's trial, the defence was one of insanity. Medical evidence was called, which showed that although he was a sexual degenerate, a pervert and a sadist, he was nevertheless sane and therefore responsible for his actions. Sentenced to death, Heath paid for his crimes on October 26th, 1946. His last request was for a double whisky!

THE STORY OF Arthur Robert Boyce was unique in that it is the only case in this book that involved, albeit indirectly, a European monarch.

Boyce was a painter by trade, working on the Palace Pier at Brighton. It was in this south-coast resort that he first met Elizabeth McLindon and the two soon became lovers, even though he was already married.

In late May, 1946, Elizabeth gained employment as housekeeper at 45 Chester Square, Belgravia. The house belonged to the King of Greece, but he was seldom there and for the most part, Elizabeth lived in the house alone. Taking advantage of this opportunity, Elizabeth asked Boyce to move in with her, which he did on June 1st.

June 8th was the anniversary of V.E. Day and it was also the last day Elizabeth McLindon was seen alive. At some stage during the day, a neighbour in Chester Square saw Elizabeth slam the door of number 45, and walk hurriedly to the opposite corner of the Square, before vanishing from sight. Very shortly afterwards, Boyce was seen to walk into the Square, pass 45 and walk off in the same direction as Elizabeth. It was reported that Boyce looked angry.

The following day, June 9th, the King of Greece paid a visit to the house. There was no sign of his housekeeper, but a door to a downstairs room was locked. At this stage, no further investigation was launched and the King left Chester Square the same day.

On June 12th, the King's private secretary, Sophocles Papanikoladu, called at the house. Again there was no sign of the housekeeper but there was a letter for her behind the door. Whilst the secretary was at the house, the telephone rang and the caller, who gave the name Boyce, asked to speak to the housekeeper. When Sophocles said he had no idea where she was, Boyce said he was very anxious about her.

The letter Sophocles had found was also from Boyce and was in much the same vein as his telephone call. It was followed the next day by another letter, again from Boyce, begging Elizabeth to contact him. Elizabeth had been missing long enough, and there was still the mystery of the locked room

NAME	Arthur Robert Boyce
AGE AT EXECUTION	45
DATE OF EXECUTION	Friday, 1st November, 1946
PLACE OF EXECUTION	Pentonville
HANGMAN	Albert Pierrepoint
ASSISTANT	Henry Critchell
DATE OF TRIAL	16th September – 19th September, 1946
LOCATION OF TRIAL	Old Bailey
PRESIDING JUDGE	Mister Justice Morris
PROSECUTION COUNSEL	E. Anthony Hawke, Henry Elam
DEFENCE COUNSEL	Derek Curtis-Bennett, R.E. Seaton
NUMBER OF VICTIMS	1

VICTIMS DETAILS	
NAME	Elizabeth McLindon
AGE	41
DATE OF MURDER	Saturday, 8th June, 1946
PLACE OF MURDER	45 Chester Square, Belgravia, London
METHOD OF KILLING	Shot
RELATIONSHIP TO KILLER	Girlfriend

downstairs. The police were called, an entry forced and the body of Elizabeth was found. She was sitting in a chair and had been shot through the back of the head.

The most obvious suspect appeared to be Boyce and he was interviewed in Brighton. He admitted that he had seen Elizabeth on June 8th. They had gone out together to watch a V.E.-Day parade and returned to Chester Square where they made love. That afternoon, whilst they were still in bed, the doorbell rang and Elizabeth answered it, returning after a minute or so to tell Boyce that the King was due to call that night.

She suggested that Boyce return to his home at Elder Street, Brighton and come back the following day. Boyce claimed that he never saw Elizabeth again.

When it came to the question of a weapon, Boyce also admitted that he had possessed a Colt .45 which, at Elizabeth's request, he had thrown into the sea from the Palace Pier. Elizabeth had been shot with a .32 and this too was once in Boyce's possession.

Boyce claimed that a man named Rowland

had offered him a .32 for £9. He thought this was too high a price and had intended sending the gun back to Rowland, but Elizabeth said she was frightened of being at Chester Square by herself, so he gave it to her, for her protection.

Letters were found in Elizabeth's belongings suggesting that marriage had been discussed between them. The police felt that this was at odds with Boyce's claim that she was fully aware that he was a married man, and was held to be a possible motive. Eventually, Boyce was charged with murder.

The circumstantial evidence did seem to point to Boyce. He had lived with Elizabeth, had provided the murder weapon, was with her on the day she died and appeared to have a motive. It was true that Elizabeth had had a number of lovers, but there was no evidence that anyone else had been in the house at Chester Square.

Boyce was tried, found guilty and sentenced to death, but there was an interesting postscript to the case. On July 3rd, a man named Arthur Clegg was arrested and Elizabeth's name and address was found on him when he was searched. On August 30th, this same Clegg was being held at Maidstone Court where a note, written in block capitals, was found beneath the cells. The note read: "The man Clegg is mixed up in a case of murder. He say's [Sic] they can't touch him now as they have a man called Boyce in Brixton Prison."

It was held that Clegg had written the note himself, though no reasonable explanation was put forward as to why he should have and he was never held to be a serious suspect in the McLindon case.

A T THE AGE of 19, Frank Josiah Freiyer joined the R.A.F., as a volunteer. Later, he served with the 8th Army and was involved in the conflict at El Alamein. This was the man who in October 1946, stood accused of a crime described by his defence counsel as a "murder without a motive".

For some weeks, Freiyer had been seeing 19-year-old Joyce Brierley and she was totally devoted to him. Unfortunately, it seems that Freiyer had simply grown tired of the relationship and Joyce was fully aware of this fact.

On September 2nd, Joyce wrote a letter to Freiyer saying that if he wanted to finish with her, he could. She was giving him a way out of the involvement if wanted it, but he did not take advantage of the opportunity. Later that same month, Joyce went to Canvey Island with Freiyer and his mother and when she returned, on Saturday, September 14th, her father, John Brierley, noticed that she seemed to be subdued and depressed.

Joyce wrote a second letter to Freiyer, saying that her own mother had suggested she might be throwing herself at him. Once more she gave Freiyer a way out if he wanted it and ended by suggesting they see how things go over the next couple of weeks, implying that if he wanted it then, they could finish the relationship.

It was 10.36pm on September 20th when Freiyer walked into Woolwich police station and said he wished to give himself up for killing a woman in the park. He went on to make a full statement in which he said that he and Joyce had gone to the park at 9.30pm and had taken a seat in a shelter close to the bandstand.

They talked for a while until, at 10.15pm, they decided to make their way to their respective homes: he to 2 Liffler Road and she to 99 Brewery Road. They began kissing each other goodnight and as they did so, he put his hands around her throat and began to squeeze. Joyce struggled and even managed to bite Freiyer's nose, but he was too strong for her and continued the pressure on her neck until she was dead.

In fact, there had been two witnesses to the actual murder. Jack Norton Hazeldine and

NAME	Frank Josiah Freiyer
AGE AT EXECUTION	26
DATE OF EXECUTION	Wednesday, 13th November, 1946
PLACE OF EXECUTION	Wandsworth
HANGMAN	Albert Pierrepoint
ASSISTANT	Harry Kirk
DATE OF TRIAL	25th October, 1946
LOCATION OF TRIAL	Old Bailey
PRESIDING JUDGE	Mister Justice Stable
PROSECUTION COUNSEL	Mister Crump
DEFENCE COUNSEL	J.P. Eddy
NUMBER OF VICTIMS	1

VICTIMS DETAILS	
NAME	Joyce Brierley
AGE	19
DATE OF MURDER	Friday, 20th September, 1946
PLACE OF MURDER	Shelter in Maryon Park, Charlton, London
METHOD OF KILLING	Strangled
RELATIONSHIP TO KILLER	Girlfriend

his own girlfriend, Miss Beecroft, had wanted to spend some time in the shelter. As they approached, they saw Freiyer with his hands around Joyce's throat, but thinking they were a courting couple getting somewhat amorous, Hazeldine and his girlfriend averted their eyes and went on their way.

No one could understand why Freiyer had murdered Joyce, the girl who loved him so much. She had given him the opportunity to leave her but he had chosen this method instead to end their liaison. Found guilty of a motiveless murder, he was executed at Wandsworth in November.

JUNE 30TH, 1946, was a happy day for Catherine Cooper. Not only was it her 18th birthday, but it was also the date of her engagement to her boyfriend, Arthur Rushton. Unfortunately, Arthur had neglected to mention that he already had a wife.

Not long afterwards, Rushton's mother found out what had happened and told Catherine's parents that her son was already married. Catherine's parents handled the matter well and after telling Catherine the truth, left the decision over what happened to her. She decided to continue seeing Arthur, but those meetings were now much less frequent.

On September 2nd, Arthur called at Catherine's house to ask her to return the presents he had given her. Catherine's mother saw her return a watch and some other small trinkets and the couple were seen talking together in a passage opposite the house by her father and 14-year-old Flora Potter, a neighbour.

As Flora watched from her window, she saw Arthur strike Catherine in the chest, followed soon afterwards by a second blow. Rushton ran off whilst Catherine staggered towards her front door. Bravely, Flora chased after Rushton, but lost him at Brook Street. She did see him shoving a knife into his coat pocket.

Catherine was rushed to the hospital having been stabbed in the heart. She was dead on arrival. Very soon afterwards, Rushton was found in the grounds of the same hospital and admitted that he had taken poison.

In fact, Rushton had drunk disinfectant. After he made a full recovery, he was charged with murder. In his statement to the police, he said: "I could not marry her, so I made sure nobody else could. I know it is murder. I will finish with a noose round my neck."

According to Rushton, Catherine had known he was married and he had told her he was going to get a divorce. It was true that he had served divorce papers on his wife, Josephine, but he did not have the money to proceed. On the day of the stabbing, he had told Catherine that he was going to rejoin the army. They both broke down at the

NAME	Arthur Rushton
AGE AT EXECUTION	31
DATE OF EXECUTION	Tuesday, 19th November, 1946
PLACE OF EXECUTION	Liverpool
HANGMAN	Not known
ASSISTANT	Not known
DATE OF TRIAL	31st October – 1st November, 1946
LOCATION OF TRIAL	Chester
PRESIDING JUDGE	Mister Justice Lynskey
PROSECUTION COUNSEL	H. Glyn Jones, G. Lind Smith
DEFENCE COUNSEL	Matabele Davis, Jones Roberts
NUMBER OF VICTIMS	1

VICTIMS DETAILS	
NAME	Catherine Cooper
AGE	18
DATE OF MURDER	Monday, 2nd September, 1946
PLACE OF MURDER	Price Street, Birkenhead
METHOD OF KILLING	Stabbed
RELATIONSHIP TO KILLER	Girlfriend

knowledge that they would see so much less of each other. The next thing he remembered was that he was running through the streets and an ambulance was at Catherine's house. He ran after the ambulance to the hospital and once inside the grounds, he drank some disinfectant he had in a bottle in his pocket.

There were a couple of hold-ups at the trial. To begin with, one of the women jurors had to be re-sworn as she had neglected to removed her gloves when she took the oath. The prosecution also had problems, when they couldn't find an ordnance survey map of the murder scene. But despite these hitches, Rushton was found guilty and sentenced to death.

1943

MONA VANDERSTAY HAD led an interesting life. A former weightlifter, jujitsu expert and variety artist she was also the mother of five children and now lived in Camden Road, Holloway with her husband, Robert.

On the night of Saturday, July 20th, Mona had been into town to visit a cinema, and caught a bus home some time between 10.00pm and 11.00pm. It was a journey she would never complete – the following morning her strangled body was discovered in the churchyard close to her home. There was no signs of a struggle but her assailant had searched through her handbag and removed any items he felt might be useful. He had, however, missed or ignored a purse containing £12 in cash.

In due course, a sailor serving on H.M.S. Victory at Portsmouth, was arrested on a charge of stealing clothing. His name was John Mathieson and when a search of his belongs was made, it revealed a chequebook in the name of Robert Vanderstay.

Other items taken from Mona were also found and Mathieson's clothing was found to show bloodstains that were Group B, the same as Mona's. Mathieson was now questioned about the murder.

Mathieson claimed to have no recollection of the actual attack. He said that he had been drinking on the Saturday night in question and recalled meeting Mona on a bus. He also had a hazy recollection of going into some 'gardens' and hitting out after Mona had hit him – implying that he was not responsible for his actions at the time of the attack. However, what counted heavily against him was the fact that he had carefully sorted through her possessions afterwards, selecting the ones that he wanted and discarding the rest.

At the trial, it was intimated that Mathieson had attacked Mona whilst suffering from a form of sleepwalking and was therefore not guilty of murder. The psychiatrist, Doctor A.S. Paterson suggested instead that Mathieson should be found guilty but insane. In the event, that defence did not work and the jury decided that Mathieson had been fully aware of what he was doing.

NAME	John Mathieson
AGE AT EXECUTION	23
DATE OF EXECUTION	Tuesday, 10th December, 1946
PLACE OF EXECUTION	Pentonville
HANGMAN	Albert Pierrepoint
ASSISTANT	Harry Allen
DATE OF TRIAL	19th October – 23rd October, 1946
LOCATION OF TRIAL	Old Bailey
PRESIDING JUDGE	Mister Justice Stable
PROSECUTION COUNSEL	E. Anthony Hawke
DEFENCE COUNSEL	John C. Maude
NUMBER OF VICTIMS	1

VICTIMS DETAILS	
NAME	Mona Victoria Vanderstay
AGE	46
DATE OF MURDER	Saturday, 20th July, 1946
PLACE OF MURDER	St Luke's Churchyard, Holloway, London
METHOD OF KILLING	Strangled
RELATIONSHIP TO KILLER	None

ELIZABETH BERRISFORD WAS separated from her husband and lived at 6, Cromwell Street, with her 12-year-old daughter. Elizabeth also had son, Harry, who was in the army.

There was another occupant of the house. Irene Dunning had known Elizabeth for some years and now lodged with her. In July 1945, Irene's lover, Stanley Sheminant, was also allowed to move in.

Sheminant, it seems, had financial problems. In April 1946, a bicycle belonging to Harry Berrisford disappeared and it seemed most likely that Sheminant had stolen it, though nothing could be proved at the time.

On May 17th, 1946, Harry came home on leave and visited his mother at her place of work. He left there at 2.30pm, but when Elizabeth got home, Harry, it appeared, had already left. Irene Dunning said she had made him some eggs and bread before he went.

Elizabeth never heard from Harry again and her suspicions grew that something must have happened to him. When, on June 27th, she saw Sheminant wearing a pair of khaki trousers that were Harry's, Elizabeth demanded that he take them off as they did not belong to him.

The front room downstairs was rented by Sheminant and Irene and kept constantly locked. It was not until July 8th that Elizabeth managed to gain access and whilst in there, noticed that the lino near the fire had been moved. The following day she took her suspicions to the authorities. The police visited but left without finding out anything new.

On July 19th, Elizabeth again gained access to the front room. This time she noticed a rather disagreeable smell and when she lifted the linoleum and a loose floorboard, she saw part of a decomposing human leg. Later, the police recovered the body of Harry Berrisford.

A search of Sheminant's belongings revealed some pawn tickets. Since Harry had gone missing, Sheminant had been systematically pawning his belongings at a brokers in Hope Street, Stoke-on-Trent.

Irene said that on May 17th, Harry Berrisford had come into the house at 2.15pm

NAME	Stanley Sheminant
AGE AT EXECUTION	28
DATE OF EXECUTION	Friday, 3rd January, 1947
PLACE OF EXECUTION	Liverpool
HANGMAN	Not known
ASSISTANT	Not known
DATE OF TRIAL	26th November – 29th November, 1946
LOCATION OF TRIAL	Stafford
PRESIDING JUDGE	Mister Justice Hilbery
PROSECUTION COUNSEL	Mister Sharp, Mister Richardson
DEFENCE COUNSEL	A.E. Longland
NUMBER OF VICTIMS	1

VICTIMS DETAILS	
NAME	Harry Berrisford
AGE	20
DATE OF MURDER	Friday, 17th May, 1946
PLACE OF MURDER	6 Cromwell Street, Hanley, Stoke-on-Trent
METHOD OF KILLING	Battered
RELATIONSHIP TO KILLER	None

and she had cooked him some eggs, bread and butter. Half an hour later, she left on an errand, leaving Sheminant alone with Harry. When she returned, there was no sign of Harry and Sheminant was replacing some linoleum in front of the fireplace. That night, Sheminant confessed to her that he had battered Harry to death and buried him under the floorboards in the front room. He threatened to kill her if she breathed a word of this to anyone and, fearful for her life, she had remained silent ever since.

That evidence helped to put a noose around Stanley Sheminant's neck.

HARRY PHILPOTT WAS passing the disused Topcliffe Pit at 3.30pm on September 21st, 1946, when he spotted a pool of blood. Finding a trail, he followed it and found a penknife. A little further along, he discovered a gun. He continued to follow the trail, only to discover, in a nearby ditch, the body of Doctor Neil MacLeod. MacLeod had been shot three times, once in the neck, once in the chest and once in the face.

Doctor John Owen Schofield, who examined the body, found it to be still warm, and put the time of death between 2.15pm and 3.15pm that afternoon. It became an urgent matter to piece together the dead man's movements.

Kathleen Townsend was Doctor MacLeod's receptionist and she told the police that MacLeod had left the surgery at 25 Park Square, just before 2.00pm. Another doctor, Rhoda Hicks Bulter Adamson, saw MacLeod going to his car. They chatted for 10 minutes or so before Rhoda walked away. She then saw a young man, in battledress, run towards MacLeod's car and climb in. One other witness was able to possibly narrow down the time of death. William Alcock Smith, a farm labourer, said that he heard a shot some time after 2.30pm.

One of the most pressing matters was to trace MacLeod's car, a Ford V8, registration number BDN 114. Details of this were circulated and it was seen, at a 11.45pm, parked in Pudsey. Police Sergeant Metcalfe then arrested the man who had climbed out of it, a soldier named Albert Sabin. Asked how he had come by Doctor MacLeod's car, Sabin promptly replied that he had killed him.

Sabin claimed that he knew MacLeod and on September 21st, he had gone to the surgery with the intention of having some money off MacLeod. Sabin had taken a gun with him and claimed that he only recalled firing once, but he stole some money from MacLeod before dragging his body to the ditch and driving off in the car.

Later, Sabin made an additional statement in which he claimed that MacLeod had once tried to sexually interfere with him but had apologised as soon as he had objected. On the day of MacLeod's death, the doctor had

NAME	Albert Sabin
AGE AT EXECUTION	21
DATE OF EXECUTION	Thursday, 30th January, 1947
PLACE OF EXECUTION	Leeds
HANGMAN	Stephen Wade
ASSISTANT	Harry Kirk
DATE OF TRIAL	5th December – 6th December, 1946
LOCATION OF TRIAL	Leeds
PRESIDING JUDGE	Mister Justice Henn-Collins
PROSECUTION COUNSEL	C.B. Fenwick, G.W. Wrangham
DEFENCE COUNSEL	C. Paley-Scott, A.M. Hurwitz
NUMBER OF VICTIMS	1

VICTIMS DETAILS	
NAME	Neil MacLeod
AGE	52
DATE OF MURDER	Saturday, 21st September, 1946
PLACE OF MURDER	Topcliffe Pit Lane, Morley, Leeds
METHOD OF KILLING	Shot
RELATIONSHIP TO KILLER	None

promised him a lift to the camp but turned off down the pit road, claiming that he had a call to make. Once they were out of sight, MacLeod had again tried to interfere with him and as Sabin climbed out of the car, MacLeod tried to pull him back in and the gun went off accidentally. Tests showed that there were semen stains on MacLeod's clothing, but this could equally well have been a natural reaction at the point of death.

The evidence pointed to a deliberate murder, committed for gain, and Sabin of Oldbury, Birmingham, was sentenced to death.

WALTER GRAHAM ROWLAND may have been in the unique position of being reprieved for a murder he did commit and hanged for one he did not!

On October 20th, 1946, a woman's body was discovered on a bomb site close to the junction of Cumberland Street and Deansgate in Manchester. The woman had been battered to death and the bloodstained hammer used to kill her lay close by. An identity card gave the woman's name as Olive Balchin, a known prostitute.

Police investigations brought forward a number of witnesses. Norman Mercer, the landlord of the Dog and Partridge on Deansgate was walking his dog at around midnight when he saw a man and woman arguing close to where the body was subsequently discovered. He gave a detailed description of the man.

Edward MacDonald told police that he had sold a hammer that might have been the murder weapon, on the 19th of the month. The description he gave of the purchaser was very close to that given by Mercer. Finally, Elizabeth Copley, a waitress, said she had seen two women with a man, in her cafe. The younger woman she identified as Olive Balchin and the man was described as carrying a long parcel, which might have been the hammer.

Checks on Olive's clients revealed the name of Walter Rowland. He was already known to the police and was picked up on October 26th.

Rowland admitted knowing Olive and even gave the police a possible motive. He gave the officers a card that showed he was being treated for venereal disease and he believed he might have picked this up from Olive. In fact, the postmortem showed that Olive had not suffered from V.D., but nevertheless, this could have been a reason to kill.

The case against Rowland seemed to be rather weak, especially since he had an excellent alibi. At 7.30pm on the night of the murder, Rowland had visited his mother, Mrs Agnes Hall, at her home at 65 Bridge Street, New Mills. He had remained there until 9.20pm when he went to catch a bus to Stockport.

NAME	Walter Graham Rowland
AGE AT EXECUTION	39
DATE OF EXECUTION	Thursday, 27th February, 1947
PLACE OF EXECUTION	Manchester
HANGMAN	Albert Pierrepoint
ASSISTANT	Not known
DATE OF TRIAL	12th December – 16th December, 1946
LOCATION OF TRIAL	Manchester
PRESIDING JUDGE	Mister Justice Sellers
PROSECUTION COUNSEL	Basil Neild, B.S. Wingate-Saul
DEFENCE COUNSEL	Kenneth Burke, H. Openshaw
NUMBER OF VICTIMS	1

VICTIMS DETAILS	
NAME	Olive Balchin
AGE	40
DATE OF MURDER	Sunday, 20th October, 1946
PLACE OF MURDER	Bomb site, Cumberland Street, Manchester
METHOD OF KILLING	Battered
RELATIONSHIP TO KILLER	None

Rowland then claimed that he was in The Wellington public house until late. Here he had an excellent witness to back up his story: Police Sergeant Jones. Rowland could not remember the exact times he was in the pub but recalled that at one stage he saw two policemen walk from one bar to the other. Sergeant Jones testified that he and a constable had been in the pub at 10.30pm. This was independent confirmation of Rowland's story thus far.

From the pub, Rowland caught a bus to Ardwick where he went to a fish and chip shop before going to a lodging house at 81 Brunswick Street where he signed the register at about 11.00pm. The landlord of the lodging house agreed with Rowland's timing and produced the register as evidence. At the time of the murder therefore, Rowland was in bed in Ardwick, miles from the murder site. Despite all this evidence, the jury still returned a guilty verdict and Rowland was sentenced to death.

The story, though, was far from over. On January 22nd, 1947, the governor of Walton jail received a note from one of his prisoners. David Ware was in jail for theft from a Salvation Army hostel and he now confessed to the murder of Olive Balchin. Two days later he made a detailed confession to the police in which he claimed to have killed Olive shortly after 9.00pm. An inquiry was ordered by the Home Secretary.

Astoundingly, the inquiry came to the conclusion that Ware had been wrong about the time of the murder and had pieced together his confession from newspaper reports. The time of the murder was held to be around 11.15pm and another lodging-house register showed that Ware was in bed by that time. As for the register that had been produced to show that Rowland was also in bed at the supposed time of the murder, the inquiry held that this had been falsified and the lodging-house keeper was lying. Thus were the facts made to fit in the case of Walter Rowland.

When, shortly afterwards, Ware withdrew his confession, the authorities held that they had been right all along and Rowland was hanged on February 27th. There are, however, two interesting postscripts to this case.

Walter Rowland had once before been convicted of murder. In 1934 he had murdered his own daughter and been sentenced to death. He was later reprieved and released from prison.

On July 10th, 1951, David John Ware tried to batter a woman to death in Bristol. He had bought himself a new hammer with which to commit the crime. Tried on November 16th, he was found guilty but insane and committed to Broadmoor where he hanged himself in his cell on April 1st, 1954. The case of Walter Rowland was not reopened.

DAGMAR PETRZYWALKSKI, KNOWN as Miss Peters, lived in a hut at Kingsdown and it was a lorry driver who found her strangled body hidden behind some bushes. Initial police inquiries led nowhere until they discovered that a string bag Miss Peters had been carrying was missing.

Perhaps the motive for the crime had been robbery and it seemed logical to assume that if the bag could be traced, the murderer may be discovered. So it was that a duplicate bag was knitted and pictures of it were published in the local press. These were seen by a schoolboy, Peter Graham Nash.

Peter came forward and said that he had found the string bag in Clare Park Lake, and given it to Kate Heasey. Peter showed detectives exactly where he had found the bag and a series of experiments then followed in which bags were dropped into the stream that fed the lake, at various points. These exhaustive tests showed that if the bag had been dumped into the stream above some nearby cider mills, it would not have reached the lake. This indicated that the person who disposed of it might have called at the mills on the day of the murder.

Only two people had called on the day in question and one was rapidly eliminated. The other one, Sidney Sinclair, proved to be a different matter. Sinclair, whose real name was Harold Hagger, a Londoner, had 16 previous convictions for larceny, shopbreaking and assault, and seemed a likely candidate for the attacker of Miss Peters.

Interviewed for the first time on November 9th, Hagger, who lived at 25 Little Abingdon, Cambridge, denied any knowledge of the crime. Exactly two weeks later though, on November 23rd, Hagger asked to see Chief Inspector Fabian. Hagger said that something had been preying on his conscience and he had been unable to sleep. He then admitted to killing Miss Peters, but claimed that it had been accidental.

Hagger claimed that he had picked Miss Peters up, in his lorry, when she had asked him for a lift. Along the way she asked him to pull over to the side of the road and asked him if he had any money. As they were talking

NAME	Harold Hagger (Sydney Sinclair)
AGE AT EXECUTION	45
DATE OF EXECUTION	Tuesday, 18th March, 1947
PLACE OF EXECUTION	Wandsworth
HANGMAN	Albert Pierrepoint
ASSISTANT	Henry Critchell
DATE OF TRIAL	27th February – 28th February, 1947
LOCATION OF TRIAL	Maidstone
PRESIDING JUDGE	Mister Justice Byrne
PROSECUTION COUNSEL	Derek Curtis Bennett
DEFENCE COUNSEL	Melford Stevenson, W. Scrivens
NUMBER OF VICTIMS	1

VICTIMS DETAILS	
NAME	Dagmar Petrzywalkski (Miss Peters)
AGE	48
DATE OF MURDER	Thursday, 31st October, 1946
PLACE OF MURDER	Wrotham Hill, Kent
METHOD OF KILLING	Strangled
RELATIONSHIP TO KILLER	None

Hagger noticed that Miss Peters was trying to steal his wallet and in the struggle that followed, he hit her and pulled tight a scarf around her neck. Only when she stopped fighting did he realise that she was dead.

It must be remembered that Miss Peters could do nothing to defend herself against Hagger's claims that she had been trying to rob him. Whatever the truth of those claims, the jury chose to believe that Hagger had deliberately killed Miss Peters and he was executed at Wandsworth, in March.

1947

FREDERICK REYNOLDS, A bookmaker, had been having a relationship with Beatrice Greenberg for 18 years, even though they were both married to other partners.

The couple had a ritual. He would approach her house whistling one of Bing Crosby's tunes and she would rush to the window, knowing it was him. Then, if her husband, Sidney, was out of the way, Reynolds would be admitted to her flat.

The night of December 17th, 1946, was like so many others. Once the public houses had closed, Reynolds approached the house, whistling his tune, but there was no sign of life at Beatrice's window. Thinking that she might have just popped out briefly, Reynolds took a short walk and then returned. This time when he signalled, Beatrice appeared at the window and Reynolds went up to the flat.

According to Reynolds's later evidence, he recalled seeing Beatrice and she told him to go back downstairs as Sidney would be home at any minute. With that, she gave out a terrific scream and pushed him to one side. Reynolds remembered seeing a flash and then nothing. In fact, he had taken a gun from his pocket and shot Beatrice dead.

Interviewed by the police, Reynolds said he had no recollection of putting the gun in his coat pocket, but he added: "Now I know it was my hand that took her life, I am ready to die to be with her."

There was a small moment of drama at Reynolds's trial. Giving evidence, he claimed that his own wife had known about the affair between himself and Beatrice as they had worked together for a short time in 1938, and Beatrice had mentioned it to her. At that point, Sidney Greenberg shouted: "That is a damned lie sir!"

Whatever the truth of that claim, there could be no doubt that it had been Reynolds's hand that had fired the shot and the fact that he was drunk at the time was no excuse for what he had done.

NAME	Frederick William Reynolds
AGE AT EXECUTION	39
DATE OF EXECUTION	Wednesday, 26th March, 1947
PLACE OF EXECUTION	Pentonville
HANGMAN	Albert Pierrepoint
ASSISTANT	Harry Kirk
DATE OF TRIAL	7th February, 1947
LOCATION OF TRIAL	Old Bailey
PRESIDING JUDGE	Not known
PROSECUTION COUNSEL	E. Anthony Hawke
DEFENCE COUNSEL	Eric Cuddon
NUMBER OF VICTIMS	1

VICTIMS DETAILS	
NAME	Beatrice Greenberg
AGE	40
DATE OF MURDER	Tuesday, 17th December, 1946
PLACE OF MURDER	Avenell Road, Highbury, London
METHOD OF KILLING	Shot
RELATIONSHIP TO KILLER	Girlfriend

IN EARLY 1947, Margaret Williams left her husband, David, and moved to Merton where she lodged with Mrs Lynch, at 16 Parkleigh Road. She applied for and was granted maintenance and although David tried to get her to return to him, Margaret seemed immovable.

On the morning of February 6th, Margaret left her lodgings to go to work. Outside the house she was met by her husband and words were exchanged between them. Then, suddenly, David produced a hammer and struck Margaret on the back of the head. She fell to the ground, whereupon David crouched down and began frantically banging her head on the road. Finally satisfied, David Williams covered Margaret with his coat. She was rushed to hospital but her injuries were so grave that she died soon after admittance.

David Williams claimed that he and Margaret had been meeting in secret almost from the time they had parted. Once they had made love in a secluded part of Regent's Park and on another occasion they had cuddled each other in a cinema. David claimed that his wife asked him not to let on to Mrs Lynch that they were meeting and things had been fine until he overheard a conversation that implied Margaret was double-crossing him. It was then he decided to kill her.

On the morning of the attack, David had risen at 5.00am and caught a train to South Wimbledon. He had then waited for Margaret to leave and after asking her to return to him, which she refused to do, he had battered her.

The defence was one of insanity. A lodger at David's home, gave evidence that Williams had been depressed and had tried to gas himself on Sunday, February 2nd. Evidence was also called which showed that David had been discharged from the army, suffering from neurasthenia and his father revealed that David's uncle and a cousin were deranged and that another cousin had committed suicide. David himself had threatened suicide when he was 13 years old, but all this was countered by Doctor Hugh Grierson, who had examined David and testified that he was sane.

Found guilty of murder, Williams was asked if he had anything to say. He answered:

NAME	David John Williams
AGE AT EXECUTION	26
DATE OF EXECUTION	Tuesday, 15th April, 1947
PLACE OF EXECUTION	Wandsworth
HANGMAN	Albert Pierrepoint
ASSISTANT	Harry Kirk
DATE OF TRIAL	7th March, 1947
LOCATION OF TRIAL	Kingston upon Thames
PRESIDING JUDGE	Mister Justice Byrne
PROSECUTION COUNSEL	Gilbert Beyfus, F. Milton
DEFENCE COUNSEL	J.P. Eddy, C.E.B. Roberts
NUMBER OF VICTIMS	1

VICTIMS DETAILS	
NAME	Margaret Williams
AGE	26
DATE OF MURDER	Thursday, 6th February, 1947
PLACE OF MURDER	Parkleigh Road, Merton
METHOD OF KILLING	Battered
RELATIONSHIP TO KILLER	Wife

"I would like to say I am very sorry for what I did to my beloved wife Margaret, whom I have always loved." He was then condemned to death.

ERIC BRIGGS HAD met his wife, Gertrude, some time in 1932. She already had two daughters, Irene and Barbara Dugdale and they lived with the Eric and Gertrude. Eric, though, was engaged in an affair with his stepdaughter, Irene, and was the father of her three children. Gertrude did not discover the truth until early in 1947.

Gertrude worked as a plate washer at the Queen's Hotel and left for work each evening at 6.00pm, not getting home until the small hours. She went out as normal on February 9th, 1947.

The police woke the household by hammering on the door at 4.45am on February 10th. Eric was informed that his wife had been murdered in Fenton Street. James Patrick Sweeney had been walking home, 30 minutes after midnight, when he came across Gertrude lying amongst the snow. She had been stabbed more than 40 times, mainly around the neck and face, and had died on the way to hospital. It was then that the police noticed that Eric had blood on his hands.

When asked to explain, Briggs confessed that he had been having sex with his stepdaughter. He claimed that they had gone to bed together at around 11.30pm and he had got blood on his hands from fondling her whilst she was having her period. Irene agreed that they had made love, and that she was menstruating, but denied that he had touched her in such a way for him to have blood on his hands.

In fact, another man had already confessed to the murder. Dennis Wood was under arrest for an attack on Elizabeth Donoghue when he claimed that he had also attacked a woman in Leeds. The police held that the confession was spurious and he had gained much of his information from newspapers. Eventually, Wood was sentenced to be detained at His Majesty's pleasure, but the fact remains that some of his statement shows a rather detailed knowledge of the murder of Gertrude Briggs.

Eric himself at first denied all knowledge of the stabbing of Gertrude. But whilst he was held in Leeds prison, a fellow inmate, John Christopher O'Connor, said that Briggs had confessed to him that he had murdered his wife.

NAME	Eric Charles Briggs
AGE AT EXECUTION	40
DATE OF EXECUTION	Friday, 20th June, 1947
PLACE OF EXECUTION	Leeds
HANGMAN	Stephen Wade
ASSISTANT	Harry Kirk
DATE OF TRIAL	8th May – 13th May, 1947
LOCATION OF TRIAL	Leeds
PRESIDING JUDGE	Mister Justice Pritchard
PROSECUTION COUNSEL	G.H.B. Streatfeild, Norman Black
DEFENCE COUNSEL	H.B.H. Hylton Foster, A.M. Hurwitz
NUMBER OF VICTIMS	1

VICTIMS DETAILS	
NAME	Gertrude Briggs
AGE	49
DATE OF MURDER	Monday, 10th February, 1947
PLACE OF MURDER	Opposite 86 Fenton Street, Leeds
METHOD OF KILLING	Stabbed
RELATIONSHIP TO KILLER	Wife

For his own part, Briggs had already confessed to being involved in his wife's death, but had claimed it was an accident. He had waited for his wife in Fenton Street and they had argued yet again over what he was doing with Irene. Suddenly he grabbed hold of her, everything went black and before he realised what was happening, she lay on the ground, bleeding from wounds in her throat.

In the event, after a five-day trial, Briggs was found guilty of murder and in June, this most unsavoury of characters was executed.

THE WOMAN LAY on her back inside the ruined building, her scarf knotted tightly around her throat and forensic tests showed that she had had sex shortly before she had died. It did not take the police long to identify her. Edith Simmonite was a known prostitute and it was a simple matter to trace her movements on the night of March 7th, 1947.

Winnie Bentley was a barmaid at the Sun Inn and she said that Edith had been drinking in the company of two men: William Smedley and Matthew Frayne. Both of these men lived in the same hostel in West Bar and when interviewed, both admitted being with Edith on the night she died.

Smedley claimed that they had said goodnight to her at the foot of the hostel steps. Unfortunately for Smedley, Frayne did not support this story. He claimed that when he went upstairs, Smedley was still talking to Edith at the corner of the street.

Charlotte Harriet Johnson, who made up the beds at the hostel, said that on the night of March 7th, Smedley's bed had not been slept in. The man who had the next cubicle, Charles Dawn, added that he had heard no noise from Smedley that night.

It was now that Smedley made his first statement to the police. He claimed that there was a mysterious Irishman involved in Edith's death. He admitted that he had not gone upstairs with Frayne, but as he said goodnight to Edith, the Irishman came up, spoke to her and then went off with her. The day afterwards, Smedley saw the Irishman again and he admitted that he had killed Edith, and said he was going off to Rhyl.

The police did their best to trace this Irishman. At one stage, Smedley was even taken to Rhyl to try to pick out the man. Then, on May 9th, Smedley sent a telegram to his sister: "Come Saturday morning. Urgent. Brother in terrible trouble." When Smedley's sister, Doris Butler, appeared in answer to this summons, Smedley admitted to her that he had killed Edith because she would not leave him alone. Just a few days later, on May 13th, Smedley was arrested and charged.

Smedley's second statement painted a rather different picture of the events of March 7th. He now admitted that he had gone with

NAME	William Smedley
AGE AT EXECUTION	38
DATE OF EXECUTION	Thursday, 14th August, 1947
PLACE OF EXECUTION	Leeds
HANGMAN	Steve Wade
ASSISTANT	Harry Kirk
DATE OF TRIAL	21st July – 22nd July, 1947
LOCATION OF TRIAL	Leeds
PRESIDING JUDGE	Mister Justice Pritchard
PROSECUTION COUNSEL	G. Raymond Hinchcliffe
DEFENCE COUNSEL	Alistair Sharp
NUMBER OF VICTIMS	1

VICTIMS DETAILS	
NAME	Edith Simmonite
AGE	27
DATE OF MURDER	Friday, 7th March, 1947
PLACE OF MURDER	Derelict building, Bridge Street, Sheffield
METHOD OF KILLING	Strangled
RELATIONSHIP TO KILLER	None

Edith and had sex with her. Only afterwards did she mention that she had venereal disease, at which point he grasped her scarf and strangled her.

Another factor might have been that Smedley had had some money stolen and believed that Edith was the thief. Smedley may have killed Edith because she infected him, but there is also the possibility that he had allowed this theft to prey on his mind and finally decided to do something about it.

Whatever the truth of the motive, Smedley was duly found guilty of murder.

IN FEBRUARY, 1947, Percy Baker and his wife, Alice, were at the shop of Mr Slack, a general dealer. Whilst Percy and Alice were in the shop, a young man, John Edward Gartside, came in and was introduced to them.

Towards the end of May, 1947, Percy and Alice vanished. They did not turn up for a visit to their friend Leonard Doughty on May 22nd, Doughty made some enquiries and found that not only had they not been seen, but they had sold most of their furniture to a dealer in Oldham.

Having investigated further, Doughty and other friends contacted the police, who visited the Manchester Street, Oldham office of Gold Lea and Company. Here they were shown various documents purporting to have been signed by Percy Baker. These were forgeries and in due course, the police came to talk to John Edward Gartside.

Gartside was a dealer in second-hand furniture and had a shop in Dobcross. When interviewed, he admitted selling the furniture and also purchasing Baker's car, but claimed that this had been a business transaction. He had met Percy by accident a number of times and in due course, Baker had told him that he and his wife were thinking of parting. When this became a reality, Gartside called at the farm on May 20th and purchased the furnishings for £250. Gartside claimed he had last seen Mr Baker on May 23rd. Before he had left, Percy had also sold his car, for the sum of £200.

Officers made a thorough search of the farm building and found extensive signs of blood. Someone, it appeared, had met with violence at the farm.

On May 29th, Gartside made his second statement. Now he added that he had left a couple of guns with Percy, for repair. On the night of May 20th, when Gartside had gone to discuss buying the furniture, an argument had broken out between Percy and Alice, which had ended with Percy picking up the rifle and shooting Alice. In a state of panic, Gartside tried to seize the revolver, which went off accidentally, wounding Percy.

Seeing Baker squirming in agony, Gartside now picked up the rifle and fired two shots into him, in order to put him out of his pain.

NAME	John Edward Gartside
AGE AT EXECUTION	24
DATE OF EXECUTION	Thursday, 21st August, 1947
PLACE OF EXECUTION	Leeds
HANGMAN	Steve Wade
ASSISTANT	Henry Critchell
DATE OF TRIAL	28th July – 29th July, 1947
LOCATION OF TRIAL	Leeds
PRESIDING JUDGE	Mister Justice Pritchard
PROSECUTION COUNSEL	G.H.B. Streatfeild, J. Stanley Snowden
DEFENCE COUNSEL	G. Raymond Hinchcliffe, A. Brian Boyle
NUMBER OF VICTIMS	2

VICTIMS DETAILS	
NAMES	Percy Baker; Alice Baker
AGES	44; 42
DATE OF MURDER	Tuesday, 20th May, 1947
PLACE OF MURDER	Manor House Farm, Dobcross, Saddleworth
METHOD OF KILLING	Shot; shot
RELATIONSHIP TO KILLER	None; none

That night, Gartside buried the bodies in a nearby field and came up with the idea of selling the furniture to make it look as if the couple had gone away.

There were, however, two major problems with Gartside's statements. In the first place, witnesses were called who swore that the Bakers had been a devoted couple. There was also the forensic evidence which showed that the bullet in Alice's head had been fired from a distance of no more than three inches.

That was enough to convince the jury that Gartside was guilty of murder.

AT 2.00PM ON April 28th, 1947, three robbers ran into Jay's Jewellers at 73/75 Charlotte Street. The staff put up a brave resistance. Ernest Stock, the director slammed the safe shut, and was clubbed for his trouble. Bertram Keates, the assistant manager, set off the alarm and was shot at. The upshot was that the three felons fled empty-handed.

The getaway car was going nowhere – a lorry had blocked it in – so the three ran off on foot. At this point Alec de Antiquis, steered his motor-cycle in front of one of the robbers and blocked his path. His reward was a bullet in the head, from which he was later to die, and the three men escaped. Shortly afterwards, a man on his way to an appointment passed the scene of the murder. He was Albert Pierrepoint and he was to meet up, briefly, with two of the robbers in the future.

Two days later a taxi driver came forward to say he had seen two men in an obvious hurry, rush into an office block at 191 Tottenham Court Road, after the shooting. The building was searched and in an empty office, police found a raincoat. Whoever had left the raincoat had carefully snipped out all the labels. What he had not known was that there was another label inside the lining. The coat was traced to a manufacturers in Leeds and they traced it to one of their outlets in Deptford High Street.

During this time, rationing was still in force and to avoid fraud, purchasers of clothing had to give a name and address for the shopkeeper's records. The coat had been sold on December 30th, 1946, to a gentleman in Bermondsey. When he was interviewed he reported that his wife had lent the raincoat to her brother, Charles Jenkins.

It was now a simple matter to trace Jenkins. He was not picked out of a line-up by over 20 witnesses but nevertheless, after much questioning and further investigation, the other two men were identified and so Christopher James Geraghty and Terence John Peter Rolt, were arrested. All three were charged with murder.

In the meantime, two guns used in the raid had been found in the mudflats of the Thames. Ballistics proved that one had been

NAMES	Christopher James Geraghty; Charles Henry Jenkins
AGES AT EXECUTION	23; 21
DATE OF EXECUTION	Friday, 19th September, 1947
PLACE OF EXECUTION	Pentonville
HANGMAN	Albert Pierrepoint
ASSISTANTS	Henry Critchell, Harry Allen
DATE OF TRIAL	21st July – 28th July, 1947
LOCATION OF TRIAL	Old Bailey
PRESIDING JUDGE	Mister Justice Hallett
PROSECUTION COUNSEL	E. Anthony Hawke, Henry Elam
DEFENCE COUNSEL	Russell Vick; Paul Wrighton
NUMBER OF VICTIMS	1

VICTIMS DETAILS	
NAME	Alec de Antiquis
AGE	35
DATE OF MURDER	Monday, 28th April, 1947
PLACE OF MURDER	Charlotte Street, London
METHOD OF KILLING	Shot
RELATIONSHIP TO KILLERS	None; none

the murder weapon and the other had fired the shot at Bertram Keates.

The trial lasted a full week and all three men were found guilty, though it had been Geraghty who had fired the fatal shot. Because Holt was only 17 he was sentenced to be detained during His Majesty's pleasure. The other two were sentenced to death.

After the appeals had failed, Jenkins and Geraghty stood together on the scaffold at Pentonville, where they were hanged by the man who had briefly passed the scene of their crime.

1947

DURING THE DAY, the George Inn at Middlezoy was not usually a very busy establishment but nevertheless, there were regular callers and when, at 11.10am on September 13th, 1947, no reply came to some insistent knocking, the police were called in.

Constable Coombes forced an entry and found that the licensee, Emily Bowers, was dead. Furthermore, there were signs that a struggle had taken place and that this could well be a case of murder.

It might be thought that the motive for this attack would have been robbery, but nothing had been taken and medical examination of Emily's body showed that she had died from an oedema of the lung, caused by exhaustion. Apparently she had fought her attacker so hard that she had simply died from the efforts. The search for the attacker began.

In the same village, there was a Polish resettlement camp and it was discovered that one of the men from there, a staff sergeant named Eugeniusz Jurkiewicz, had not only been in the pub the night before the attack, but had been rather friendly towards Emily. He was interviewed and soon admitted the part he had played in her death.

Jurkiewicz, speaking through an interpreter, said that he had been to the pub many times, including the night of September 12th. Emily danced with him and kissed him afterwards and it was the memory of this that made him return, after midnight, break a window and gain access to Emily's bedroom. He denied trying to rape Emily, but admitted gripping her throat tightly at one stage, to stop her crying out.

As the trial opened at Bristol assizes and Jurkiewicz was asked how he pleaded, he replied guilty. His defence counsel immediately intervened and submitted that the correct plea was not guilty but after a trial lasting two days, the jury found that the prosecution had proved its case to their satisfaction and Jurkiewicz was sentenced to death.

NAME	Eugeniusz Jurkiewicz
AGE AT EXECUTION	34
DATE OF EXECUTION	Tuesday, 30th December, 1947
PLACE OF EXECUTION	Bristol
HANGMAN	Not known
ASSISTANT	Not known
DATE OF TRIAL	25th November – 26th November, 1947
LOCATION OF TRIAL	Bristol
PRESIDING JUDGE	Lord Chief Justice, Lord Goddard
PROSECUTION COUNSEL	Stuart Bates, W. Esling
DEFENCE COUNSEL	E.E.S. Montague, Humphrey Edmunds
NUMBER OF VICTIMS	1

VICTIMS DETAILS	
NAME	Emily Bowers
AGE	76
DATE OF MURDER	Saturday, 13th September, 1947
PLACE OF MURDER	George Inn, Middlezoy, near Bridgewater
METHOD OF KILLING	Exhaustion
RELATIONSHIP TO KILLER	None

AT 6.05AM, ON October 10th, 1947, Stella Kathleen Mitchell called for her workmate, Joyce Parkin. She was surprised that there was no reply, but continued on her way to work.

Over six hours later, at 12.45pm, Doris Corcoran, who lived next door to the Parkins, saw that their back door was partly open. Through that door she saw the body of Maurice Parkins and she immediately called the police.

Constable Douglas Reuben Porter was the first officer on the scene. Maurice Parkin lay on the scullery floor. His trousers had been partially pulled down and his genital area had been badly mutilated. In the living room lay his sister, Joyce, and his mother Alison. Both were naked and both had their legs spread wide apart. All three were dead.

The medical examination would reveal fresh horrors. Maurice's missing genitals were found in his mother's mouth and a cigarette stump had been forced into her vagina. Joyce also had a cigarette stump in her throat and all three had been manually strangled. There were no signs of a forced entry, leading police to believe that the victims had known their attacker.

Inquiries led to the name of George Henry Whelpton, who although married, had been seeing Alison for the last few months. He was employed as a driver for the Blue Line Bus Company and the police rang their offices and asked if Whelpton was on duty. Told that he wasn't, the offices were told that they should inform the police if he turned up. When Whelpton did appear, asking for his pay packet, he was kept talking whilst the police were called.

When interviewed, Whelpton admitted the killings, saying that he and Alison had argued and he killed her. According to his statement, he had gone to Alison's house and had had supper. Joyce and Maurice had then gone to bed, leaving him alone with Alison. She broached the subject of money and in the argument that followed, she made to attack him, whereupon he reached out and throttled her. Having killed Alison, Whelpton then made to leave but Maurice appeared in the kitchen and he too made a lunge for George.

NAME	George Henry Whelpton
AGE AT EXECUTION	31
DATE OF EXECUTION	Wednesday, 7th January, 1948
PLACE OF EXECUTION	Leeds
HANGMAN	Steve Wade
ASSISTANT	Harry Kirk
DATE OF TRIAL	17th December, 1947
LOCATION OF TRIAL	Leeds
PRESIDING JUDGE	Mister Justice Morris
PROSECUTION COUNSEL	H. Malone, J.R. Cumming-Bruce
DEFENCE COUNSEL	Ralph Cleworth, Ernest Ould
NUMBER OF VICTIMS	3

VICTIMS DETAILS

NAMES	Alison Gertrude Parkin; Joyce Parkin
AGES	48; 23
DATE OF MURDER	Thursday, 9th October, 1947
PLACE OF MURDER	4 Wainwright Road, Doncaster
METHOD OF KILLING	Strangled; strangled
RELATIONSHIP TO KILLER	Girlfriend; none

NAME	Maurice Parkin
AGE	15
DATE OF MURDER	Thursday, 9th October, 1947
PLACE OF MURDER	4 Wainwright Road, Doncaster
METHOD OF KILLING	Strangled
RELATIONSHIP TO KILLER	None

Whelpton remembered hitting him and Maurice collapsing onto the floor when Joyce appeared in the living room and she too was struck. He claimed to have no memory of killing either Joyce or Maurice and could not recall inflicting the mutilations.

The prosecution painted a more reasonable picture. Whelpton later admitted having sex with Joyce and it was suggested that Alison had caught them, causing him to kill both of them. Later he killed Maurice to silence him. That version of events was accepted by the jury and Whelpton was convicted.

1948

AT AROUND 6.30PM on the evening of October 11th, 1947, a gentleman named Phillips enjoyed a quiet drink in the Butcher's Arms at Wattstown. As he left the pub, having finished his drink, Phillips ran into Evan Evans, a neighbour of his, and was invited to return for a game of cards. The two men went back into the Butcher's Arms and at one stage Phillips saw Evans approached by another customer, 76-year-old Rachel Allen. Although Phillips couldn't hear what was actually said, he did hear Evans quite rudely tell Rachel to go away.

Evans left the pub at 10.00pm and 15 minutes later, Rachel Allen was heard shouting at someone in the street outside her home. She was heard to cry: "If you don't go from here I'll report you to the police." Just over an hour later, at 11.20pm, Rachel's battered body was found near her front door.

Scotland Yard were called in and it was not long before the altercation with Evans, inside the public house, came to their attention and Evans was interviewed at his home by Chief Inspector Capstick and Sergeant Stoneham. They searched his home and found, hidden in the sofa, a bloodstained brown suit. Evans now admitted that it was he who had killed Rachel.

Evans claimed that as he had passed Rachel's house, she had called him a filthy pig, so he punched her in the face. She fell into her yard and he then hit her again whilst she was on the ground. Still not satisfied that he had done enough, Evans then picked Rachel up so that he could punch her again and ended by kicking her repeatedly, including a number of times in her face.

At Evans's trial, Mr Justice Byrne, in his 45-minute summing-up, described the killing of Rachel Allen as a callous and filthy murder.

NAME	Evan Hadyn Evans
AGE AT EXECUTION	22
DATE OF EXECUTION	Tuesday, 3rd February, 1948
PLACE OF EXECUTION	Cardiff
HANGMAN	Not known
ASSISTANT	Not known
DATE OF TRIAL	15th December, 1947
LOCATION OF TRIAL	Cardiff
PRESIDING JUDGE	Mister Justice Byrne
PROSECUTION COUNSEL	Arthian Davies, Elwyn Jones
DEFENCE COUNSEL	Hubert Llewellyn Williams, Morgan Owen
NUMBER OF VICTIMS	1

VICTIMS DETAILS	
NAME	Rachel Allen
AGE	76
DATE OF MURDER	Saturday, 11th October, 1947
PLACE OF MURDER	Wattstown, near Pontypridd
METHOD OF KILLING	Battered
RELATIONSHIP TO KILLER	None

ARCHIBALD MCINTYRE LEFT home for work at 8.00am on September 26th, 1947. As he did so he noticed what he thought was a man's head, hiding in the bracken to the left of the cottage – but surely that couldn't be? There had been a heavy dew that morning and there were no footprints showing that a man was hiding there. Archibald thought it was his imagination playing a trick on him and carried on to work.

At 5.15pm, Archibald was back home and it was clear that there was something wrong. His terrier dog was barking furiously, there were letters and the newspaper still on the mat and all the doors were locked. At that moment a neighbour, Mr McKercher arrived and together they forced an entry to the cottage. There, on Archibald's own bed they found his mother, Catherine, covered by a mattress and bedding. When these were removed the two men saw to their horror that Catherine was dead.

The motive for the murder appeared to be one of robbery. Peter McIntyre, Archibald's father and Catherine's husband, confirmed that two registered envelopes were missing from the house. Both had contained cash, to a total value of £85-17s-3d, and in addition, some clothing coupons had been taken, along with a gold watch.

The police began by searching the area around the cottage and soon found parts of a shotgun in the undergrowth close by. This was identified as one that had been stolen from Tulloch Farm in Oldmeldrum on September 18th. Isabella Clubb, who owned that farm, had reported that the gun had vanished at the same time as a Polish private who had been working there. It was that information which led to descriptions of the missing private, Stanislaw Myskza.

It wasn't until October 2nd that two alert constables spotted a man fitting Myskza's description on a disused R.A.F. site three miles from Peterhead. They gave chase and cornered their man who, when asked for his name, readily admitted that he was indeed the man they were looking for.

Put on trial for murder, Myskza claimed that he had been insane at the time of the murder. Two medical witnesses, Doctor Jan

NAME	Stanislaw Myskza
AGE AT EXECUTION	23
DATE OF EXECUTION	Friday, 6th February, 1948
PLACE OF EXECUTION	Perth
HANGMAN	Albert Pierrepoint
ASSISTANT	Not known
DATE OF TRIAL	6th January – 10th January, 1948
LOCATION OF TRIAL	Perth
PRESIDING JUDGE	Lord Justice Sorn
PROSECUTION COUNSEL	H.R. Leslie, H.S. Wilson
DEFENCE COUNSEL	F.C. Watt
NUMBER OF VICTIMS	1

VICTIMS DETAILS

NAME	Catherine McIntyre
AGE	47
DATE OF MURDER	Friday, 26th September, 1947
PLACE OF MURDER	Tower Cottage, Bolfracks Hill, Kenmore, near Aberfeldy
METHOD OF KILLING	Battered
RELATIONSHIP TO KILLER	None

Leyberg and Doctor Charles David Bruce were then called to give their opinions and both said that Myskza was undoubtedly sane. A third doctor, Angus McNiven, also stated that the prisoner was sane, but was of below average intelligence and emotionally unstable.

After a deliberation of 20 minutes, the jury returned a guilty verdict and on February 6th, 1948, Myskza became the first man to be executed at Perth since 1909.

1948

AT 9.30PM ON November 14th, 1947, Florence Wright heard screams and a groan coming from next door. Knowing that the premises were occupied by Percy Bushby, a crippled watchmaker who lived alone with his cat, Toby, Florence went to investigate and, as she reached her front door, she saw a young man leaving Percy's house. Florence went inside number 11 where she found Percy's body. He had been strangled and an empty wallet lay on the table.

The investigation led to Walter John Cross, who was picked up the following day. He admitted that he and another man, Walter Leslie Bull, had been to Percy's shop some three weeks before in order to sell some items. They had also been back on Wednesday, November 12th, when Bull had sold some items for 12s-6d, but Cross initially maintained that he had not been near the shop on the night that Percy died.

Questioned further, Cross finally admitted that he and Bull had planned to rob the old man, but at the end, he had done so alone. He explained that Bull had noticed Percy had a wallet full of money and he had suggested that they return to the shop, where he would hold on to the old man whilst Cross took his wallet. On the night in question, Bull had failed to turn up, so Cross had gone on alone. He had earlier been given a key by Bull, whom Cross said had fitted the new lock to Percy's door.

Cross said that as he entered the shop he saw Percy coming towards him. The old man shouted and then collapsed onto the floor. Cross claimed that he had never touched Percy, apart from taking his wallet and that if he had been strangled, someone else must have entered later and committed the crime.

Much of this story centred on the involvement of Walter Bull. He was interviewed and said that he had only known Cross for five or six weeks. He agreed that they had visited the shop together, but insisted that it had been Cross who spotted the money in Percy's wallet and Cross who had suggested robbery. Bull was approached with the idea of committing the crime together but told Cross that he wasn't interested.

There was one other victim in the murder of Percy Bushby. A home could not be found

NAME	Walter John Cross
AGE AT EXECUTION	21
DATE OF EXECUTION	Thursday, 19th February, 1948
PLACE OF EXECUTION	Pentonville
HANGMAN	Albert Pierrepoint
ASSISTANT	Harry Allen
DATE OF TRIAL	14th January – 16th January, 1948
LOCATION OF TRIAL	Old Bailey
PRESIDING JUDGE	Mister Justice Cassels
PROSECUTION COUNSEL	E. Anthony Hawke
DEFENCE COUNSEL	Richard O'Sullivan
NUMBER OF VICTIMS	1

VICTIMS DETAILS	
NAME	Percy Bushby
AGE	55
DATE OF MURDER	Friday, 14th November, 1947
PLACE OF MURDER	11 King Edward Road, Barking, London
METHOD OF KILLING	Strangled
RELATIONSHIP TO KILLER	None

for Toby, his feline companion of 15 years and the unfortunate animal had to be put to sleep.

FLORENCE BENTLEY LIVED at 5 Henrietta Square, Yarmouth but worked as a chambermaid at a local guest house at 1 Camperdown. Her employer there was Miriam Ann Prior, a married woman, whose brother, Stanley Joseph Clarke, had been walking out with Florence for some time.

Stanley Clarke was committed to this relationship and went so far as to ask Florence to marry him. When she refused, Stanley, in front of witnesses, swore that he would murder her. It was a threat that was to become reality all too soon.

On June 16th, Florence was working as usual when Stanley called on her at the guest house. They were seen together in the kitchen by Miriam who would later testify that Florence looked to be rather frightened. Florence finally went upstairs to carry out her appointed tasks, only to be followed a few minutes later by Stanley.

A terrible scream filled the air and when Miriam dashed out of the kitchen, she was in time to see Florence dashing down the stairs, pursued by Stanley, who had a knife in his hand. Florence collapsed and as Miriam attended to her, Stanley calmly walked out into the street.

Miriam had sustained three wounds. One was to the back of her head, but the two more serious ones had pierced both her lungs. Stanley, meanwhile, had walked to a telephone box at Burgh castle, from where he contacted the police, told them what had happened and said he would wait for them until they arrived.

Charged with murder, Stanley Clarke seemed determined to follow Florence just as soon as he could. At the magistrate's court, Doctor Tann was giving evidence of his finding of the body when the prosecutor, Mr Grace, picked up the murder weapon, a butcher's knife. Clarke shook his head, dove past Constable Davey who was guarding the box, and threw himself head-first down the concrete steps leading to the dock.

When the case came to trial in the higher court at Norwich, Clarke pleaded guilty and the entire proceedings were over in four minutes. There was no appeal and no reprieve. Two weeks before the appointed

NAME	Stanley Joseph Clarke
AGE AT EXECUTION	34
DATE OF EXECUTION	Thursday, 18th November, 1948
PLACE OF EXECUTION	Norwich
HANGMAN	Not known
ASSISTANT	Not known
DATE OF TRIAL	20th October, 1948
LOCATION OF TRIAL	Norwich
PRESIDING JUDGE	Mister Justice Cassels
PROSECUTION COUNSEL	E. Grace
DEFENCE COUNSEL	F.T. Alpe
NUMBER OF VICTIMS	1

VICTIMS DETAILS	
NAME	Florence May Bentley
AGE	32
DATE OF MURDER	Wednesday, 16th June, 1948
PLACE OF MURDER	1 Camperdown, Great Yarmouth
METHOD OF KILLING	Stabbed
RELATIONSHIP TO KILLER	Girlfriend

date, Stanley was confirmed by the Bishop of Norwich and on November 18th, he became the first man to be executed since the controversy over the 'no hanging' clause in the Criminal Justice Bill, which had been passed in April and suspended capital punishment for five years, subsequently reversed by the House of Lords. The very next day, he was followed by the second.

1948

STAFF NURSE GWENDOLINE Humphreys had done her rounds just after midnight and everything had been correct in ward CH3, the children's ward. There were only six youngsters in the ward and all seem to have settled down for the night.

At 1.20am, nurse Humphreys felt a draught and returning to ward CH3 saw that the doors to the porch were open. It was always happening. Maintenance still hadn't fixed that faulty catch.

Unfortunately, it wasn't the wind that had caused the doors to open. Upon closer inspection, nurse Humphreys saw that cot number four was empty. It should have contained June Devaney, not quite four years old, who was recuperating from a mild dose of pneumonia and was due to go home later that day. Furthermore, the sides of the cot were still up, meaning that the child had to have been lifted out by someone. A track of footprints on the waxed floor seemed to underline this fact, as did a large Winchester bottle found under the missing child's cot.

An immediate search was organised but no trace of June could be found. The police were called in at 1.45am and they soon organised their own search, not just of the hospital, but also of the extensive grounds. It was not until 3.17am that the body of June Anne Devaney was found, close to the boundary wall. She lay face down on the grass, her nightdress pulled up. Her left buttock had been bitten and massive head injuries indicted that she had been held by the feet or ankles and swung against the wall. Later examinations would show that the child had also been raped.

Mister Looms, the Chief Constable, wasted no time in calling in Scotland Yard and by 4.00am that same morning, Detective Chief Inspector Jack Capstick had been assigned to the case. He was in Blackburn later that same day.

Ward CH3 had already been fingerprinted, as had the Winchester bottle found under the child's cot. Once staff prints had been eliminated, one set of unidentified prints remained on the bottle and Capstick reasoned that they must belong to June's killer. He had the fingerprint records checked, but drew a

NAME	Peter Griffiths
AGE AT EXECUTION	22
DATE OF EXECUTION	Friday, 19th November, 1948
PLACE OF EXECUTION	Liverpool
HANGMAN	Albert Pierrepoint
ASSISTANT	Not known
DATE OF TRIAL	15th October – 18th October, 1948
LOCATION OF TRIAL	Lancaster
PRESIDING JUDGE	Mister Justice Oliver
PROSECUTION COUNSEL	W. Gorman, D.J. Brabin
DEFENCE COUNSEL	Basil Neild, J. di Vi Nahum
NUMBER OF VICTIMS	1

VICTIMS DETAILS	
NAME	June Anne Devaney
AGE	3
DATE OF MURDER	Sunday, 16th May, 1948
PLACE OF MURDER	Grounds of Queen's Park Hospital, Blackburn
METHOD OF KILLING	Battered
RELATIONSHIP TO KILLER	None

blank. The killer, whoever he was, did not have a criminal record.

It was then that Capstick took what was a very controversial decision. He decided to ask for the fingerprints of every male over the age of 16, who had been in Blackburn on the 14th/15th of May. It was an enormous task but once he had explained to the people of that town, and promised that all prints would be destroyed afterwards, the populace co-operated readily. Using the electoral roll, 20 officers under Inspector William Barton, took two months to take over 46,000 sets of prints. None matched those found on the bottle.

Just when it seemed that the entire operation would be a total disaster, Capstick remembered that not everyone might be registered on the electoral roll. In 1948, some goods were still rationed and when the registration numbers on ration cards were checked against the electoral roll, it was noticed that about 200 names had been missed. These were people who had just returned from the army and so were not yet registered to vote. Once again the fingerprint department swung into action, tracking down these 200 men.

On August 12th, 1948, set number 46,253 was found to match the prints on the Winchester bottle. These prints belonged to Peter Griffiths, an ex-guardsman who lived at 31 Birley Street, Blackburn. The next day, as Griffiths was leaving his house on his way to work, he was arrested and taken in for questioning.

At first, Griffiths denied all knowledge of the crime. Capstick noticed, however, that he was wringing his hands together during questioning, a possible sign of inner turmoil. Gently he said, "Don't you think you'd feel better if you told me what happened that night?" After sitting in silence for a few moments, Griffiths began to tell his story.

On the night of Saturday, 15th May, Griffiths had left home at 6.00pm. He went first of all to the Dun House Hotel, where he consumed five pints of bitter. From there, he moved on to Yate's Wine Lodge, where he added two pints of Guinness and a couple of double rums. Returning to the Dun House, he topped this up with another six pints, not leaving until closing time.

As he was walking down Jubilee Street, he saw a man sitting in his car and asked him for a light. They got talking and the man offered him a lift part way home, dropping him off outside the hospital. Griffiths remembered being outside the gates, which he must have climbed over as he next recalled finding himself in the hospital grounds.

Walking to the outside of the children's ward, Griffiths then took off his shoes and went in through the unlocked porch doors. He heard a noise and thought the nurse might be coming so he went back outside and waited. When he saw that the coast was clear he went back into the children's ward.

He recalled picking up the Winchester bottle, which he later put down on the floor. He then looked in to all the cots in turn until once again he thought he heard someone coming. He turned and half fell against a cot, waking the occupant, June Anne Devaney. She started to cry and he picked her up and took her outside. Once she was on the grass she started to cry again so he picked her up

and swung her against the wall. He then returned to the porch, put on his shoes and went home, arriving there at about 2.00am. The following day, when his parents asked him what time he had arrived home, he had told them that it was just after midnight.

At his trial, Griffiths pleaded not guilty. The police, though, had more evidence in order to prove their case. In addition to the fingerprints and his confession, fibres from one of Griffiths's suit were found to match some found on June's nightdress and fibres from his socks matched scrapings taken from the footprints on the ward floor. Finally, bloodstains found on his jacket were Group A, the same group as June's.

The jury were out for just 23 minutes before returning a guilty verdict. The tall young ex-guardsman was hanged at Walton on November 19th, 1948. A couple of weeks before, on November 3rd, the police had kept their word and destroyed almost 47,000 sets of fingerprints.

1948

ON MONDAY, JUNE 1st, 1948, a milkman noticed that the milk had not been taken in at 'Wynford' a large, rambling house in Raypark Avenue, Maidenhead. He knew that an elderly and somewhat eccentric lady, Minnie Lee, lived alone in the house, so he contacted the police.

The police broke into the house, taking with them Mrs Lee's solicitor, Kenneth Ruffe Thomas. There seemed to be no sign of Mrs Lee but when Kenneth Thomas, more out of instinct than anything else, opened a large metal trunk, the body of Mrs Lee was discovered.

Minnie Lee had been badly beaten about the head but the real cause of death was asphyxiation. Her assailant had also tied her hands behind her back, and gagged her. The house had been ransacked and amongst all the dust in the unkempt rooms, police found a cardboard box that bore the clear impression of a finger.

The print was only a partial one, but records showed that it belonged to a known criminal, George Russell, who had previous convictions for housebreaking. Russell was eventually picked up in St Albans and when faced with the fingerprint evidence, admitted that he had visited the house and asked about a job as a gardener. At first, though, he denied being involved in the death of Mrs Lee.

It was then that Russell made a statement which condemned him. He turned to the officer in charge of the interrogation and said: "… Did I murder this poor woman for something she was supposed to have, and had not?" There were local rumours that Mrs Lee was a wealthy woman. This was not, in fact, the case, but how could Russell have known that, unless he had searched the house for valuables that did not exist?

That statement, together with the fingerprint evidence was enough to convict Russell of murder.

NAME	George Russell
AGE AT EXECUTION	45
DATE OF EXECUTION	Thursday, 2nd December, 1948
PLACE OF EXECUTION	Oxford
HANGMAN	Not known
ASSISTANT	Not known
DATE OF TRIAL	15th October – 16th October, 1948
LOCATION OF TRIAL	Reading
PRESIDING JUDGE	Mister Justice Hallett
PROSECUTION COUNSEL	A.J. Long
DEFENCE COUNSEL	Eric Sachs
NUMBER OF VICTIMS	1

VICTIMS DETAILS	
NAME	Minnie Freeman Lee
AGE	94
DATE OF MURDER	circa Saturday, 29th May, 1948
PLACE OF MURDER	'Wynford', Raypark Avenue, Maidenhead
METHOD OF KILLING	Battered/asphyxiated
RELATIONSHIP TO KILLER	None

JOHN ANTHONY PARRY was on the afternoon shift on June 8th, 1948, and so he left home to arrive at work by 2.00pm. He finished at 10.00pm, arrived home at around 10.25pm, and was surprised to find that his wife was not there.

Although she had not left him a note, John assumed that Sillvinea had gone to the pictures, but when she didn't return he went for a walk around the village, to see if there were any parties going on that she might have gone to. Still there was no sign and after a night of worrying, John reported his wife missing, at 10.00am the next morning.

Constable Daniel Plummer had been on duty nearby and made a note of what John Parry had to say. Just 45 minutes later, an ashen-faced Parry was back. He had found his wife, dead, under the bed in the spare room.

Sillvinea Parry had been brutally put to death and now, when an examination of the house was made, two bloody footprints were found in the toilet. The killer had stepped into a pool of the woman's blood and then walked into the bathroom, leaving his mark behind him. Bloody palmprints were also found and police knew that it would be a simple matter to prove their case against the killer, once he was arrested.

It was now that John Parry told the police about a family friend, Clifford Godfrey Wills. At 2.30pm that afternoon, officers paid a visit to Wills's house at 3 Cromwell Place. They found Wills, in bed, wearing a white shirt that was heavily bloodstained. He claimed that he had been involved in a fight with a man named George Logan the previous night. Wills was taken in for questioning and when Logan was interviewed he said that there had been no such argument, let alone a fight, though he had seen Wills in the pub.

Wills then made a number of statements. In the first, he denied any knowledge of Sillvinea's murder and said he had not even seen her since the previous Tuesday. A second statement referred again to the fight with Logan and a third saw an admission of a three-year affair with the dead woman. Wills now claimed that she had been seeing someone else and so he had decided to kill himself. Still he denied any involvement in the murder.

NAME	Clifford Godfrey Wills
AGE AT EXECUTION	31
DATE OF EXECUTION	Thursday, 9th December, 1948
PLACE OF EXECUTION	Cardiff
HANGMAN	Stephen Wade
ASSISTANT	Not known
DATE OF TRIAL	8th November – 9th November, 1948
LOCATION OF TRIAL	Newport
PRESIDING JUDGE	Mister Justice Hallett
PROSECUTION COUNSEL	Cartwright Sharp, Paul Layton
DEFENCE COUNSEL	A.J. Long, Mister Underwood
NUMBER OF VICTIMS	1

VICTIMS DETAILS	
NAME	Sillvinea May Parry
AGE	32
DATE OF MURDER	Thursday, 8th June, 1948
PLACE OF MURDER	11 Wayfield Crescent, Pontnewydd
METHOD OF KILLING	Battered/stabbed/strangled
RELATIONSHIP TO KILLER	Girlfriend

Forensic tests showed that the footprints in blood matched a pair of shoes belonging to Wills and the palmprints also matched with impressions taken from his hands. As if further incrimination were required, at one stage Wills remarked to a policeman sitting nearby: "What's it like to be sat next to a killer?"

All this evidence was more than enough to convince a jury that Sillvinea Parry had died at the hands of her self-confessed lover, Clifford Wills.

1948

EMILY HAINSWORTH LIVED at 6 Law Lane, and as her next-door neighbour, Ernest Westwood was getting on in years, she used to call in at regular intervals and tidy up the house. Emily saw Ernest at 9.30pm on September 24th, 1948 and said she would call in again the following day. When she arrived at 11.15am on the Friday, she found Ernest in his bed, still alive but badly injured, and the house apparently robbed.

On that same morning, Edna Green, who lived at 54 New Street, just around the corner from Law Lane, came downstairs to find a letter on her mat. Opening it, she read: "I have been to your place but I see you was not up. I will be back on Monday or Tuesday." The letter was from Arthur Osborne, a young man who had called a number of times before.

It soon became clear that Osborne was a man the police needed to talk to. To begin with, Edna reported that he had spoken about the dead man on September 23rd, two days before the attack. Osborne had asked if Ernest lived alone and remarked that he – Westwood – wouldn't be badly off. Moreover, Osborne had been seen loitering near the rear of Westwood's house at around 9.15pm, on September 24th.

Reports of the crime were published and eventually, on September 26th, a full story, naming Osborne as the man police wanted to interview, was published in the News of the World.

Osborne had gone down to the Chichester area of West Sussex. He had a fiancée down here, Dorothy Emily Ellen Ball, whom he had arranged to marry on September 25th, the day of the murder. All the arrangements had been made, the church booked and a honeymoon arranged but when Osborne sent his fiancée a telegram saying that he might be late, she cancelled all the bookings. Osborne did finally arrive and apologised, then booked into his lodgings at 35 Lewes Road, the home of Jane Santon.

It was Jane Santon's husband who showed Osborne the newspaper report and Osborne immediately promised to return north and explain that it was all a mistake. He boarded a train but the police were informed of his

NAME	Arthur George Osborne
AGE AT EXECUTION	28
DATE OF EXECUTION	Thursday, 30th December, 1948
PLACE OF EXECUTION	Leeds
HANGMAN	Stephen Wade
ASSISTANT	Harry Allen
DATE OF TRIAL	30th November – 1st December, 1948
LOCATION OF TRIAL	Leeds
PRESIDING JUDGE	Mister Justice Slade
PROSECUTION COUNSEL	G. Raymond Hincncliffe
DEFENCE COUNSEL	H.R.B. Shepherd, Ralph Cleworth
NUMBER OF VICTIMS	1

VICTIMS DETAILS	
NAME	Ernest Hargreaves Westwood
AGE	70
DATE OF MURDER	Saturday, 25th September, 1948
PLACE OF MURDER	'Craggan', Law Lane, Southowram
METHOD OF KILLING	Stabbed
RELATIONSHIP TO KILLER	None

movements anyway and Osborne was picked up at Sutton.

Osborne's prints were taken and found to match some of those found on the window where Ernest Westwood's killer had gained access. Osborne now made a full statement saying that he had gone to steal from Westwood and had forced open the window with a large, heavy screwdriver. He had found some money and had then gone upstairs to see if he could find anything else. He had heard a voice in the dark and something was thrown at him. He had then lashed out and must have killed Westwood accidentally.

Found guilty of murder, Osborne was executed at Leeds on December 30th, 1948. It was his 28th birthday.

O N AUGUST 29TH, 1948, the body of Nancy Chadwick was discovered outside the house of Margaret Allen, in Rawtenstall, Lancashire. Nancy had been brutally battered about the head. As the police began door-to-door inquiries in the area, they noticed that they were being followed by Margaret Allen.

Margaret was a lesbian who preferred to dress in men's clothing, and demanded to be called 'Bill'. The 20th of 21 children, she had spent the war years as a bus conductress but, after her mother died in 1943, Margaret had lost interest in her appearance, began smoking heavily and ate badly.

Police officers called on Margaret as part of their routine procedure on September 1st, and noticed straight away that there were bloodstains splashed up the wall just inside her front door. When this was pointed out to Margaret, she confessed that she had killed Nancy. Apparently the old woman had annoyed her and Margaret had smashed her over the head with a hammer, in order to quieten her. She added that she was in: "… one of my funny moods".

Put on trial for murder, and appearing in the dock dressed in a man's suit, Margaret's defence was one of insanity but her confession and statements to police weighed heavily against her and she was convicted. The entire proceedings lasted only five hours, the jury deliberating for 10 minutes.

On January 12th, 1949, Margaret Allen became the first woman to die on the gallows since Charlotte Bryant in 1936.

NAME	Margaret Allen
AGE AT EXECUTION	42
DATE OF EXECUTION	Wednesday, 12th January, 1949
PLACE OF EXECUTION	Manchester
HANGMAN	Albert Pierrepoint
ASSISTANT	Not known
DATE OF TRIAL	8th December, 1948
LOCATION OF TRIAL	Manchester
PRESIDING JUDGE	Mister Justice Sellers
PROSECUTION COUNSEL	A. Denis Gerrard
DEFENCE COUNSEL	Not known
NUMBER OF VICTIMS	1

VICTIMS DETAILS	
NAME	Nancy Ellen Chadwick
AGE	68
DATE OF MURDER	Saturday, 28th August, 1948
PLACE OF MURDER	Bacup Road, Rawtenstall
METHOD OF KILLING	Battered
RELATIONSHIP TO KILLER	None

1949

GEORGE SEMINI, A fit, powerfully built Maltese boxer, had enjoyed a pleasant night out with his girlfriend, Marjorie Sheila Seabridge, and was now walking the young lady home. As the couple passed the Talbot Hotel, they noticed three men standing outside. Ignoring them, Semini and his girl walked past whereupon one of the men made what Semini thought was a derogatory comment about Marjorie: "Blimey, she's a big 'un."

Semini, showing no fear, walked up to the three men and struck Frederick Robert Woodyatt, the one who had made the remark. It was a powerful punch and Woodyatt crashed to the ground. It was at that point that another of the group, Joseph Gibbons chose to interfere, telling his compatriot to get up and fight.

It was obvious to all that this was just what Semini wanted and, being a boxer, he might well have caused some serious injury. Two gentlemen passing by realised this and restrained Semini by grabbing hold of an arm each. They were no match for him, though, and he threw them off and drew out a knife shouting: "I'll get the two of them."

The fight that followed was over very quickly and at the end, Joseph Gibbons lay dying on the pavement, a knife wound to his chest. Woodyatt was also injured in the shoulder and a third man, Charles Stanley, had been stabbed in the knee. Semini ran off but was later arrested at the Miner's Hostel where he was staying. At first he denied even being near the Talbot Hotel but faced with the eye witnesses, Semini was arrested and charged with murder.

The defence was, to say the least, unique in the twentieth century. It would have been difficult to claim self-defence. True, Semini was outnumbered and the men had insulted his girl, but by his own admission he had struck the first blow and he had escalated matters from a fist fight to one involving the use of a knife. Instead, the defence counsel claimed that it was a matter of 'chance medley'.

Basically, chance medley referred to the killing of a person whilst involved in a sudden affray. Whilst it might well be held that such

NAME	George Semini
AGE AT EXECUTION	24
DATE OF EXECUTION	Thursday, 27th January, 1949
PLACE OF EXECUTION	Liverpool
HANGMAN	Not known
ASSISTANT	Not known
DATE OF TRIAL	30th November, 1948
LOCATION OF TRIAL	Stafford
PRESIDING JUDGE	Mister Justice Hallett
PROSECUTION COUNSEL	Eric Sachs, Norman Carr
DEFENCE COUNSEL	Cartwright Sharp, E. Brian Gibbens
NUMBER OF VICTIMS	1

VICTIMS DETAILS	
NAME	Joseph Gibbons
AGE	22
DATE OF MURDER	Sunday, 10th October, 1948
PLACE OF MURDER	Outside Talbot Dance Hall, Newcastle-under-Lyme
METHOD OF KILLING	Stabbed
RELATIONSHIP TO KILLER	None

circumstances did indeed apply in Semini's case, it was said that chance medley could no longer apply in modern society. The law was applicable in the days when men were accustomed to carrying swords for their own defence, and when duelling was common and accepted, but it had no place in England in the 1940s. Semini was found guilty of murder.

The execution was originally set for January 12th, 1949, but this was postponed on the orders of the Home Secretary as the reasons for dismissal of the appeal had not been published. Once this was done, a new date was set and Semini was hanged at the end of January.

O N THE NIGHT of November 19th, 1948, some time after 11.00pm, one of the inmates of the Sherwood Borstal Institution, Kenneth Strickson, went to Christopher Morrow, one of the guards and said: "Will you go to the chapel – I have killed the matron."

Upon investigation, Morrow found the body of Irene May Phillips, lying in the vestry of the chapel. Irene had been battered about the head and although still alive when found, died later in hospital. She had not been sexually assaulted.

Irene Phillips was one of two matrons and had been at the institute since 1947. She was popular with the inmates and Strickson, it seemed, had thought that there might be more than a professional relationship between them.

On November 18th, the day before the attack, Strickson had spoken to another inmate, Enoch Roberts. Strickson intimated that he had made a comment to Irene about her breasts and she had taken it in good part, remarking that it was a good job she was broad-minded.

The next morning, at 7.30am, Strickson had again spoken to Roberts and suggested he was going to visit the matron later in the chapel, to see what he could get out of her. When Roberts asked Strickson what he would do if she screamed out, Strickson replied that he would cosh her if she did.

It appeared that this is exactly what had happened. Strickson had made some sort of advance towards Irene. She had rebuked him and had received 16 blows to her head as a result. The attack had taken place some time before 11.00am – a man named Bradshaw had called on Irene at that time, and received no reply.

At the trial, an attempt was made to show that there was a history of insanity in Strickson's family. It was stated that his father had been an inmate of an asylum and had died after swallowing a fork. None of this saved Strickson from his fate. Found guilty of murder, he was hanged at Lincoln on March 22nd.

NAME	Kenneth Strickson
AGE AT EXECUTION	21
DATE OF EXECUTION	Tuesday, 22nd March, 1949
PLACE OF EXECUTION	Lincoln
HANGMAN	Not known
ASSISTANT	Not known
DATE OF TRIAL	2nd March, 1949
LOCATION OF TRIAL	Nottingham
PRESIDING JUDGE	Mister Justice Lynskey
PROSECUTION COUNSEL	Arthur Ward
DEFENCE COUNSEL	R.T. Paget M.P.
NUMBER OF VICTIMS	1

VICTIMS DETAILS

NAME	Irene May Phillips
AGE	46
DATE OF MURDER	Friday, 19th November, 1948
PLACE OF MURDER	Sherwood Borstal Institution, Nottingham
METHOD OF KILLING	Battered
RELATIONSHIP TO KILLER	None

1949

1949

ON THE MORNING of November 22nd, 1948, the body of Joan Marney was found in Sutton Park, Birmingham. Lying beneath a small holly tree, which gave the crime its press epithet of the 'Holly Bush Murder', Joan had been strangled and a corner of her plastic mackintosh had been forced into her mouth, no doubt to stifle her cries.

Joan, who lived at 75 Sidcup Road, Kingstanding, had spent the previous night at the Odeon cinema at Perry Barr and it was assumed that she might have met her killer here, or on her way home. However, before the police investigation could even get into full swing, James Farrell, then 18 years old, walked in to Steelhouse Lane police station and gave himself up as an absentee from the armed forces.

Almost immediately it was noted that he fitted the description of a man seen with Joan the previous night and when questioned on the matter, he readily admitted that he had killed the young girl.

Farrell said that he had indeed met Joan at the cinema. They got talking and she told him that she was 17 years old. Joan did look older than her years and Farrell had no reason to doubt what she had told him. Eventually he invited her to go for a walk in Sutton park and she agreed, providing she was home by 9.30pm.

Once inside the bushes in the park, Farrell had grown somewhat amorous and whilst Joan protested that she wanted to go home, Farrell pushed her onto the ground and attempted to make love to her. Joan struggled, cried out and said she would report Farrell to the police once she got home. It was perhaps that one sentence which sealed her fate.

Putting his hand on her throat, Farrell now deliberately kept on kissing Joan so that she could not draw breath, or scream out. Then, as Joan struggled, Farrell tightened his grip until he was squeezing her throat with all his strength. Eventually the struggles ceased and Farrell knew that Joan was dead.

The defence at Farrell's trial was one of insanity and it seemed that there was indeed evidence that there might be something wrong mentally with the defendant. The day before the murder, November 20th, Farrell's

NAME	James Farrell
AGE AT EXECUTION	19
DATE OF EXECUTION	Tuesday, 29th March, 1949
PLACE OF EXECUTION	Birmingham
HANGMAN	Albert Pierrepoint
ASSISTANT	Harry Kirk
DATE OF TRIAL	10th March, 1949
LOCATION OF TRIAL	Birmingham
PRESIDING JUDGE	Mister Justice Lynskey
PROSECUTION COUNSEL	Paul Sandlands, C. Shawcross
DEFENCE COUNSEL	R.C. Vaughan, Geoffrey Lane
NUMBER OF VICTIMS	1

VICTIMS DETAILS	
NAME	Joan Mary Marney
AGE	14
DATE OF MURDER	Sunday, 21st November, 1948
PLACE OF MURDER	Banner Gate entrance, Sutton Park, Birmingham
METHOD OF KILLING	Strangled
RELATIONSHIP TO KILLER	None

father, Nathaniel, had found James semi-conscious in front of the gas stove at their home. In addition, it was stated that his mother had been in the Lodge Road Asylum for the past three and a half years.

Despite this, the jury held that Farrell was sane and fully aware of his actions. They returned a verdict of guilty and James Farrell was sentenced to death. He 'celebrated' his 19th birthday in the condemned cell, awaiting execution, the sentence being carried out on March 29th, with Syd Dernley observing the proceedings as part of his training as an assistant executioner.

HARRY SAUL MICHAELSON was hurt, but had no idea how he had sustained his injuries. Staggering about outside his home at 75 Furzecroft, a basement flat, he managed to attract the attention of the night porter, who called for medical assistance.

Michaelson had a deep wound on his forehead and this, together with other head injuries, led to him having to undergo brain surgery later that same day. It did him no good. The following day, Harry Michaelson died.

The police made a detailed examination of Michaelson's flat and found no sign of a forced entry. They were, however, able to determine what weapon had been used on the unfortunate man. A tubular metal chair showed obvious signs of blood and amongst the stains, the investigating officers found a palm print and fingerprints. It was then a simple matter to trace their owner, Harry Lewis, a known thief.

Lewis was picked up on January 18th, 1949 and charged with murder. His story was that he had been wandering the streets, with no money to his name. Seeing a window open in the basement flat, he climbed in to see if there was anything worth stealing. He noticed the sleeping form of a man in the bed and tried his best not to disturb him, but after finding a wallet and moving down the hallway towards the rest of the flat, Lewis was dismayed to hear a voice demanding who he was.

Returning to the bedroom, Lewis picked up the first available weapon, which just happened to be the tubular chair, and struck the man twice in the head. Lewis had then left by the same window he had come in through.

At the subsequent trial at the Old Bailey, Lewis's defence counsel attempted to suggest that Harry Michaelson had died not as a result of the attack on him, but as a result of the brain surgery. Even had such a case been demonstrable, it would have been unlikely to succeed as, of course, it could have been argued that it had been Lewis's assault that had caused the surgery to become necessary. However, such debate was not needed, as Doctor Donald Teare gave evidence that Mr Michaelson would have died, with or without the operation, as a result of the injuries he had sustained.

NAME	Harry Lewis
AGE AT EXECUTION	21
DATE OF EXECUTION	Thursday, 21st April, 1949
PLACE OF EXECUTION	Pentonville
HANGMAN	Albert Pierrepoint
ASSISTANT	Harry Allen
DATE OF TRIAL	7 March, 1949
LOCATION OF TRIAL	Old Bailey
PRESIDING JUDGE	Lord Chief Justice, Lord Goddard
PROSECUTION COUNSEL	E. Anthony Hawke
DEFENCE COUNSEL	Not known
NUMBER OF VICTIMS	1

VICTIMS DETAILS	
NAME	Harry Saul Michaelson (Died Monday, 27th December)
AGE	50
DATE OF MURDER	Sunday, 26th December, 1948
PLACE OF MURDER	75 Furzecroft, George Street, Marylebone, London
METHOD OF KILLING	Battered
RELATIONSHIP TO KILLER	None

Found guilty, but with a recommendation for mercy, Harry Lewis was sentenced to death. The recommendation did not move the Home Secretary to interfere and on April 21st, 1949, the sentence was carried out.

DENNIS NEVILLE HAD not had a lucky life. In August 1941, though he was only 14, he lied about his age and joined the army. The truth was soon discovered and after a couple of weeks, he was dismissed from the service. In July 1943, he joined up again, only to be captured in France six days after D-Day. Neville remained a prisoner until May, 1945 but before this, his elder brother had been killed in action, in Burma. Still fate had not finished with Dennis Neville.

In June 1945, his father was murdered and Dennis had to cope with the fact that the man who was the chief suspect was acquitted. His father's death affected Dennis profoundly and he admitted that he harboured thoughts of revenge. What is certain is that Dennis changed after the loss of his father, and was no longer the happy young man he had once been.

When the body of Marian Poskitt was discovered on the morning of February 20th, it soon became clear that she had spent at least part of the previous evening in the company of Dennis Neville, a man she had known for some eight years or so. Dennis was picked up at his brother Joseph's house at 19 Hulme Street, Batley, and taken in to the police station.

Dennis readily confessed his part in Marian's death. He explained that he had gone out at 7.45pm on February 19th, and met Marian's parents in the West Town Inn, on Huddersfield Road. They had told him that Marian was with friends in the Clarence Hotel and in due course, Dennis went there and had a drink with her.

At a few minutes after 9.00pm, he left the Clarence, had a drink in the Stag and Pheasant, and then went into Dewsbury where he had yet another drink in the Crown and Cushion, before going to the Galleon Ballroom. It was here, at 10.20pm, that he saw Marian again. She nodded and they exchanged greetings and later, at 11.30pm, she asked him to see her home.

Neville explained that they walked as far as St Matthew's playing fields, where they sat down on the grass. They talked together for a time and then Dennis suddenly sank his fingers into Marian's throat, throttling her into

NAME	Dennis Neville
AGE AT EXECUTION	22
DATE OF EXECUTION	Thursday, 2nd June, 1949
PLACE OF EXECUTION	Leeds
HANGMAN	Stephen Wade
ASSISTANT	Harry Allen
DATE OF TRIAL	12th May, 1949
LOCATION OF TRIAL	Leeds
PRESIDING JUDGE	Mister Justice Finnemore
PROSECUTION COUNSEL	H.B.H. Hylton-Foster
DEFENCE COUNSEL	Ralph Cleworth
NUMBER OF VICTIMS	1

VICTIMS DETAILS	
NAME	Marian Poskitt
AGE	21
DATE OF MURDER	Sunday, 20th February, 1949
PLACE OF MURDER	St Matthew's playing field, Dewsbury
METHOD OF KILLING	Strangled
RELATIONSHIP TO KILLER	None

unconsciousness. He left her at around 1.00am and either could not or would not explain why he had attacked her.

His own confession was enough to convict Dennis Neville of murder and he was executed at Leeds on June 2nd. It was yet another tragedy for his family to bear.

O N THE AFTERNOON of April 1st, 1949, Bernard Cooper was picked up by the police, in Islington, for being drunk. Taken into the station, he was soon released on bail and told to report the following morning. Cooper never did report as, though the police did not know it at the time, he had earlier strangled his wife and shoved her body underneath their bed.

Mary Cooper's body was found at 8.00pm that evening by her 14-year-old daughter, Sheila, and a full-scale search was launched for Bernard. He would not be picked up until April 6th, when a school caretaker at the Girl's County School in Maidstone Road, Ashford, Kent, found Cooper on the premises at 7.10am and contacted the police. Cooper made a statement to the police, running to several thousand words, and the story he told was a most sordid one.

Some time earlier, 14-year-old Sheila had had a legal abortion, the authorities believing that she had been raped. Cooper now confessed that he had committed incest with her and that he was the father of the child. Mary had been told the truth and had forgiven him but at 3.15am on April 1st, she had again brought the subject up and reproached him for what he had done.

As the discussion continued, Mary had become hysterical and he had lost control. First he slapped her face and when this did not have the desired effect, Cooper took a stocking from the end of the bed, tied it around his wife's throat and strangled her. He went on to claim that he had called Sheila into the bedroom and told her what he had done, asking her to run away with him but she had refused.

In fact, the jury chose to believe Sheila's version of events. She said that when she and the other two children got up on April 1st, her father said that Mary had had a bad night but was now asleep and should not be disturbed. He then left the house and it was not until the evening that Sheila checked on her mother.

Found guilty after a deliberation of 11 minutes, Bernard Cooper, a thoroughly unsavoury character, was hanged on June 21st.

NAME	Bernard Alfred Peter Cooper
AGE AT EXECUTION	40
DATE OF EXECUTION	Tuesday, 21st June, 1949
PLACE OF EXECUTION	Pentonville
HANGMAN	Albert Pierrepoint
ASSISTANT	Harry Kirk
DATE OF TRIAL	18th May, 1949
LOCATION OF TRIAL	Old Bailey
PRESIDING JUDGE	Not known
PROSECUTION COUNSEL	E. Anthony Hawke
DEFENCE COUNSEL	Malcolm Morris
NUMBER OF VICTIMS	1

VICTIMS DETAILS	
NAME	Mary Elizabeth Cooper
AGE	38
DATE OF MURDER	Friday, 1st April, 1949
PLACE OF MURDER	Davisville Road, Shepherd's Bush, London
METHOD OF KILLING	Strangled
RELATIONSHIP TO KILLER	Wife

IT WAS PERHAPS no surprise that Doreen Messenger's parents did not approve of her relationship with Sydney Chamberlain. He was, after all, twice her age.

There were arguments at her home in Meadow Way, Heavitree, Exeter but the couple still arranged to meet on Friday, February 18th, after Doreen had finished work.

According to Chamberlain's later statement, the lovers drove to Teignmouth with the intention of going to the pictures together but Doreen had changed her mind so they drove up to Haldon Moor and parked the car in what they called their "special place".

The couple talked about the difficulties they were having and as Chamberlain kissed Doreen, she started to cry and said that she would rather be dead than leave him. They remained on the moor until it was almost dawn, at which stage Doreen said she would get a good hiding when she did get home, and didn't really want to go. At that, Chamberlain put his hands around Doreen's throat and began to squeeze.

After some moments, Doreen's body began to shudder. Chamberlain stopped the pressure on her throat and asked Doreen if she was all right. She did not reply, but leaned forward and kissed him, whereupon he resumed his activity until Doreen fell unconscious.

Chamberlain noticed that she was still breathing, so now he took off his belt and continued strangling Doreen with that. When she was finally dead, Chamberlain removed the body from the car, laid her down on the moor, stripped her naked and had sex with the body.

The only defence possible was one of insanity. Chamberlain's sister, Florence Annie Coxenham testified how when she was eight years old, her brother had stabbed her under the left eye with some scissors. As a result, she was blind in that eye.

Doctor Sandifer described how Chamberlain had been smiling as he told the story of how he had had sex with Doreen's body and the doctor determined that in his opinion, Chamberlain was a psychopath with a mental age of 11. As a result of all this, Mister Elam asked for a verdict of guilty but insane.

NAME	Sydney Archibald Frederick Chamberlain
AGE AT EXECUTION	31
DATE OF EXECUTION	Thursday, 28th July, 1949
PLACE OF EXECUTION	Winchester
HANGMAN	Albert Pierrepoint
ASSISTANT	Harry Allen
DATE OF TRIAL	16th June – 17th June, 1949
LOCATION OF TRIAL	Winchester
PRESIDING JUDGE	Mister Justice Jones
PROSECUTION COUNSEL	J. D. Casswell, A.S. Trapnell
DEFENCE COUNSEL	Henry Elam, R. Ormrod
NUMBER OF VICTIMS	1

VICTIMS DETAILS	
NAME	Doreen Primrose Messenger
AGE	15
DATE OF MURDER	Saturday, 19th February, 1949
PLACE OF MURDER	Haldon Moor
METHOD OF KILLING	Strangled
RELATIONSHIP TO KILLER	Girlfriend

The trial lasted two days and at the end, the jury took 30 minutes to decide that Chamberlain was guilty but sane. As a result, the penalty was death.

SUNDAY, JUNE 5TH, 1949, had been a most pleasant evening all round. Rex Harvey Jones and his brothers had been enjoying a drinking session at a club in Neath and Beatrice Watts, known as Peggy, and some of her friends had been to a dance in Morriston. By chance, the two groups met up at the bus stop at Victoria Gardens in Neath and that chance occurrence was to lead to the deaths of two people.

The bus was crowded and a number of people were standing. Beatrice found herself a seat but gave it up to Rex and then sat on his lap. Eventually they reached their stop and as other people walked off in one direction, Rex said he would see Beatrice home. They were last seen heading off together down a dark and lonely country road.

At 1.15am on June 6th, the telephone rang in the local police station and was answered by Constable Michael. Rex said he was in a telephone box at Abercregan and asked Michael to come down there by car. The reason he gave was to the point: "I have killed a girl. I have killed Peggy Watts."

In fact, Michael travelled by bicycle to the telephone box, where he found Rex Jones waiting for him. Jones directed Michael to the body of Beatrice Watts, but could offer no explanation for killing her. He explained that they had gone into the plantation and made love. Then, after they had finished, he had placed his hands around her throat and throttled the life out of her. He had no idea why he had done this terrible thing.

His own confession meant that the guilty verdict was a mere formality but the jury did add a strong recommendation to mercy. On August 4th, Jones, and Robert Mackintosh, who had been sentenced the day after Jones, were executed together at Swansea. They were the first hangings there since 1928.

NAME	Rex Harvey Jones
AGE AT EXECUTION	21
DATE OF EXECUTION	Thursday, 4th August, 1949
PLACE OF EXECUTION	Swansea
HANGMAN	Albert Pierrepoint
ASSISTANT	Not known
DATE OF TRIAL	12th July, 1949
LOCATION OF TRIAL	Swansea
PRESIDING JUDGE	Mister Justice Croom-Johnson
PROSECUTION COUNSEL	H. Edmund Davies, Gerwyn Thomas
DEFENCE COUNSEL	Arthian Davies, Dyfan Roberts
NUMBER OF VICTIMS	1

VICTIMS DETAILS

NAME	Beatrice May Watts
AGE	20
DATE OF MURDER	Sunday, 5th June, 1949
PLACE OF MURDER	Forestry Plantation, Nantybar, Cymmer
METHOD OF KILLING	Strangled
RELATIONSHIP TO KILLER	None

IT WAS JUST before 7.00pm on June 3rd, 1949, when Margaret Mary Beechey asked her 16-year-old daughter, Beryl, to run an errand for her. Giving her 10/-, she asked Beryl to take the money to Mrs Mackintosh. The two families were quite close friends and indeed, at one stage, had even lived in the same house.

At 7.30pm, a Mrs Richards saw Beryl getting off the bus outside the Municipal Buildings and saw her walking down towards Vivian Terrace, which led to Vivian Square. The young girl was not seen alive again but at 6.00am the following morning, her body was discovered on a railway embankment, some 60 yards from the Mackintosh house. She had been raped and strangled.

The first port of call for the police was Mrs Mackintosh's and amongst the people they spoke to was her son, Robert. He worked at the Port Talbot steelworks and claimed that he had arrived home at around 6.00pm. He admitted that Beryl had called whilst he was busy cleaning the house and that she left after giving him the 10/-, which he handed over to his mother when she got home at 8.30pm.

The house was examined as a matter of routine and bloodstains were found in the kitchen and under the bed in Robert's room. Tests on Beryl's clothing also showed that she had at some stage been in contact with the side wall of the staircase in Mackintosh's house. Confronted with this evidence, Robert changed his story.

Robert Mackintosh now said that he had invited Beryl into the house and something suddenly came over him. He remembered nothing then until he woke to find himself in bed and Beryl's body lying half under it. Hurriedly he carried the girl downstairs, put a coat over her and carried her to the railway line where he dropped her over a low wall. He then cleaned the house, before his mother arrived.

That cleaning had not been thorough enough to remove all traces of Robert Mackintosh's crime and he was sentenced to death after a one-day trial.

NAME	Robert Thomas Mackintosh
AGE AT EXECUTION	21
DATE OF EXECUTION	Thursday, 4th August, 1949
PLACE OF EXECUTION	Swansea
HANGMAN	Albert Pierrepoint
ASSISTANT	Not known
DATE OF TRIAL	13th July, 1949
LOCATION OF TRIAL	Swansea
PRESIDING JUDGE	Mister Justice Croom-Johnson
PROSECUTION COUNSEL	H. Vincent Lloyd-Jones, Campbell Prosser
DEFENCE COUNSEL	H. Glyn Jones, Alun T. Davies
NUMBER OF VICTIMS	1

VICTIMS DETAILS	
NAME	Beryl Beechey
AGE	16
DATE OF MURDER	Friday, 3rd June, 1949
PLACE OF MURDER	Vivien Square, Aberavon
METHOD OF KILLING	Strangled
RELATIONSHIP TO KILLER	None

IT IS SAID that children commonly rebel against their parents' values. Perhaps there is no better example of this than John George Haigh.

Haigh's parents were Plymouth Brethren and brought up their son in a strict religious background. They did not, however, succeed in inculcating their beliefs into him.

When he was 25, Haigh got a 15-month prison sentence for taking deposits on cars that didn't exist, and in November 1937, he received four years for a share fraud. A third sentence of 21 months followed in 1941, for stealing.

Haigh had married on July 6th, 1934 but his wife left him whilst he was serving his first prison sentence. Between those first two sentences, Haigh, who had a genuinely inventive mind, worked as a repairman for William Donald McSwann, who ran a number of amusement arcades. The McSwann family would become Haigh's first victims.

In the summer of 1944, freed from his third prison sentence, Haigh happened to bump into William Donald McSwann again. Haigh told McSwann that he had rented a basement store at 79 Gloucester Road, where he made pin-ball machines. He was working on one now. Perhaps McSwann would like to have a look? McSwann agreed and accompanied Haigh to the store.

There was another reason for McSwann to be interested in his old friend and employee. The war in Europe was still raging and McSwann wished to avoid being called up. Haigh intimated that he could help him out there. So it was that both men visited the store in September, 1944, after meeting at The Goat public house, in Kensington High Street.

Once McSwann was in the basement, Haigh took a cosh and battered the young man to death. His body was then stripped of valuables and tipped into a 40-gallon tank, which was then topped up with acid.

Haigh had experimented with the effects of acid on flesh whilst in prison. He had put the bodies of mice into the corrosive liquid and timed how long it took for the body to dissolve. He thought it would be the perfect way of removing all trace of a murder and with this first attempt, it certainly seemed to

NAME	John George Haigh
AGE AT EXECUTION	40
DATE OF EXECUTION	Wednesday, 10th August, 1949
PLACE OF EXECUTION	Wandsworth
HANGMAN	Albert Pierrepoint
ASSISTANT	Harry Kirk
DATE OF TRIAL	18th July – 19th July, 1949
LOCATION OF TRIAL	Lewes
PRESIDING JUDGE	Mister Justice Humphreys
PROSECUTION COUNSEL	Sir Hartley Shawcross, Gerald Haywood, Eric Neve
DEFENCE COUNSEL	Sir David Maxwell Fyfe, G.R.F. Morris, David Neve
NUMBER OF VICTIMS	6 (possibly 9)

VICTIMS' DETAILS

NAMES	William Donald McSwann; William McSwann
AGES	Not known
DATE OF MURDER	Saturday, 9th September, 1944; July, 1945
PLACE OF MURDER	79 Gloucester Road, London, SW7
METHOD OF KILLING	Battered; battered
RELATIONSHIP TO KILLER	None; none

NAMES	Amy McSwann; Archibald Henderson
AGES	Not known; 52
DATE OF MURDER	July, 1945; Monday 16th February, 1948
PLACE OF MURDER	79 Gloucester Road, London, SW7; Leopold Road, Crawley
METHOD OF KILLING	Battered; shot
RELATIONSHIP TO KILLER	None; none

NAMES	Rosalie Henderson; Olive Henrietta Helen Olivia Robarts Durand-Deacon
AGES	41; 69
DATES OF MURDERS	Monday 16th February, 1948; Friday, 18th February, 1949
PLACE OF MURDER	Leopold Road, Crawley; Leopold Road, Crawley
METHOD OF KILLING	Shot; shot
RELATIONSHIP TO KILLER	None; none

do the trick. In due course, the body of William Donald McSwann, or more correctly the sludge that was all that remained of it, was poured down a manhole in the basement where he had been murdered.

Haigh's next task was to keep McSwann's

parents happy. One of his many talents was forgery and he now produced a number of letters, ostensibly from their son, which were posted to the McSwanns outlining that he had gone into hiding to avoid his call-up. If anything, the McSwanns were grateful that Haigh had been able to help!

Less than a year later, the McSwanns were both murdered by Haigh. They were lured separately to the basement store in Gloucester Road, where each was bludgeoned to death and their bodies dissolved in acid. Haigh then used his forgery skills to obtain the title to the property the McSwanns owned. He also sold their furniture and some shares. Having made over £4,000, he felt it was time for him to move on.

In 1945, Haigh ran into another old friend, Edward Jones, the Managing Director of Hurstlea Products, an engineering firm. They had first met in 1935 and Jones was well aware of Haigh's inventive mind. He offered Haigh a job that was unsalaried and largely titular, as a salesman for the London area. Haigh accepted, if only because there was a storeroom at Giles Yard, Off Leopold Road, Crawley, that Jones said Haigh could use.

Doctor Archibald Henderson was a successful man, a man of property and position. He and his attractive wife, Rose, lived in a large house at Dawes Road in Fulham. This had been converted to flats and Doctor Henderson wished to sell them. One of the prospective buyers who saw the properties advertised was John Haigh.

Haigh viewed the flats and even put in an offer. The Hendersons found Haigh charming and even kept in touch when Haigh's offer did not turn into anything more substantial. Thus, when the Hendersons said they were going down to Brighton for a few days, Haigh knew of their plans and booked into the same hotel, the Metropole.

On February 16th, 1948, Doctor Henderson and his wife vanished. What had happened was that Haigh had lured Archibald Henderson to his storeroom at Crawley, where he had shot him with his own gun, taken earlier from his home in Fulham. Returning to Brighton, Haigh told Amy Henderson that her husband had been taken

ill, but he would drive her up to see him. Once in the storeroom, she too was shot. Both bodies were then dissolved in acid.

The motive for all Haigh's murders was pure gain. This was to be his most successful killing ever. Again using his talent for forgery, he managed to convince the Henderson's family and servants that they had gone to South Africa. He then appropriated their property and sold it.

It was not until 1949 that Doctor Henderson's brother became concerned. In that year he asked the B.B.C., to appeal for his brother to return home as their mother was seriously ill. Haigh had been so convincing, that even now Doctor Henderson's brother believed that if anything had happened to the missing couple, it had happened in South Africa!

For two years now, Haigh had been living as a permanent guest at the Onslow Court Hotel, South Kensington. He was well known to the other guests, and often passed the time of day with some of the elderly ladies who stayed there. By 1949 though, Haigh knew he was in financial trouble again. His bank account was overdrawn and his hotel bill was in arrears. He had to do something to generate more income. It was then that Mrs Durand-Deacon fell into his clutches.

Olive Durand-Deacon was a wealthy and astute businesswoman. One day she was examining some artificial fingernails a guest had given her when Haigh, whom she knew quite well, came over to talk to her. She seemed fascinated by the fingernails and Haigh, never being one to miss a chance, said that he had a factory in Crawley where he could make such things quite cheaply. He asked if she would like to accompany him there to look at the facilities and she readily agreed.

On February 14th, 1949, Haigh went to see his old friend Edward Jones and asked him for a loan of £50, to be repaid in five days. Returning to his hotel, Haigh used most of this money to settle his account with the Onslow Court. With this pressure off, he could now concentrate on realising his latest asset, Olive Durand-Deacon.

On February 18th, Haigh drove Olive down

to Crawley. There, whilst she was examining some paper that Haigh said could be used in the manufacture of false fingernails, Haigh drew out his revolver and shot her through the back of the head. Stripped of all valuables, including jewellery and a fur coat, Olive Durand-Deacon was consigned to a drum of acid and left to dissolve slowly into sludge.

The next day however, Haigh encountered a problem. Mrs Constance Lane, another guest at the hotel and a friend of Mrs Durand-Deacon, expressed concern over her missing friend. She said she wished to go to the police and, knowing he would be unable to dissuade her, Haigh said he would go with her.

At Chelsea police station, Haigh told his story. Yes, he had arranged to take Mrs Durand-Deacon to visit his factory in Crawley but he had waited at the agreed rendezvous and she had not appeared. He had gone on to Crawley by himself but he had not seen the missing woman since. For the time being at least, the police seemed to be satisfied, but unbeknown to Haigh, Detective Inspector Shelley Symes, acting on a hunch, had decided to look up Haigh's criminal record. It made very interesting reading.

Over the next couple of days, Haigh returned to Crawley and topped up the acid in the drum. It was three days later that the police visited the Onslow Court and asked to speak to John George Haigh.

On February 26th, 1949, the police forced an entry in the Leopold Road storeroom. They found a .38 Webley revolver, carboys of acid, rubber gloves, a stirrup-pump, bloodstains on the wall and a receipt for the cleaning of a fur coat, which turned out to belong to Olive Durand-Deacon. Later checks showed that some of the missing woman's jewellery had been sold. They began to question Haigh very closely indeed.

For some time, Haigh would tell them nothing. Then, suddenly he said, "Tell me frankly, what are the chances of anybody being released from Broadmoor?" He paused and then added, "Mrs Durand-Deacon doesn't exist. I've destroyed her with acid. How can you prove murder if there is no body?" He then went on to relate a fantastic story of not one murder, but nine!

He told the police how he had murdered Mrs Durand-Deacon, the Hendersons and the McSwanns, adding three more for extra effect. Haigh claimed that he had also murdered a woman and a young man at Gloucester Road and a woman named Mary at Crawley. The police did not place much credence on these three killings, believing that Haigh just added those to increase his total. The most startling confession though, was that John Haigh was a vampire!

Haigh claimed that ever since he had been a child he had been fascinated by blood. He had had recurring nightmares involving a forest of crucifixes and chalices of blood. He had deliberately injured himself so that he could taste his own blood and, most macabre of all, when he had killed each of his victims, he had made an incision in their throats, taken a small glassful of blood and drunk it. It now became plain that the questions about Broadmoor had a purpose. Haigh was trying to say that he was insane.

Meanwhile, back at Crawley, the police were examining the sludge that covered the yard outside the storeroom. Haigh had been wrong when he said that no trace of Olive Durand-Deacon remained, for 18 fragments of bone were found, which were identified as human and other items turned up unscathed, including a pair of dentures that were found to have been made for Mrs Durand-Deacon.

The newspapers had a field day with the stories but one, the *Daily Mirror*, overstepped the mark and in its edition of March 4th, 1949, described Haigh as a vampire who drank his victims' blood, before the verdict had been reached. The paper was fined £10,000 and its editor, Silvester Bolam, was jailed for three months.

The defence failed and it took the jury 17 minutes to find that Haigh was guilty of murder. He was hanged on August 10th, by Albert Pierrepoint who used a calf-leather wrist strap, which he reserved for special occasions!

1949

1949

LUCY WILSON HAD been living apart from her husband for some time and since 1945, had been living with the new man in her life, William John Davies, at 34 Terminus Place, Eastbourne.

At some time during the first week of March, 1949, Lucy accused Davies of having an affair with another woman. He denied this but she would not be swayed from her opinion. Things grew worse between them until on March 5th, he said he had had enough and ordered her to leave his house. Lucy did as she was told.

The next day, March 6th, Davies had a change of heart and went to Campbell's Restaurant, also on Terminus Place, where Lucy worked as a counter hand, to ask her to return to him. She wanted none of this and told him she was quite content to leave things as they were. On the 7th, Davies saw her leave the restaurant with another man and now became convinced that he might well have lost Lucy for ever.

Jean Copeland was a cook at Campbell's and she saw Davies come back into the restaurant on the morning of March 8th. At first, there seemed to be no problem but then Jean saw Davies follow Lucy upstairs. Almost immediately there came a terrible scream and when Jean rushed to the foot of the stairs, she saw Davies struggling with Lucy. He had a knife in his hand and Lucy had her hand to her face. Lucy fell and Davies shouted: "What have I done to you, Luce?"

In fact, Davies had stabbed Lucy a number of times, the fatal wound being one through the left eye, which penetrated the brain. It would take Lucy some days to die. Davies was first charged with attempted murder, a charge which became one of wilful murder on March 23rd.

Davies said that he had gone to see Lucy to ask her one more time to withdraw her accusations against him. She had refused whereupon he attacked her with the knife. Davies explained: "I lost my head and picked up the knife and struck her." He claimed he had only intended to frighten Lucy and had no intention of killing her.

Davies went on to say that he had no memory of the actual attack and only 'came to' when he saw her lying on the floor.

Jealousy was no excuse for the taking of a life and despite his explanations, Davies was found guilty of murder at his Lewes trial, and sentenced to death.

NAME	William John Davies
AGE AT EXECUTION	30
DATE OF EXECUTION	Tuesday, 16th August, 1949
PLACE OF EXECUTION	Wandsworth
HANGMAN	Albert Pierrepoint
ASSISTANT	Harry Kirk
DATE OF TRIAL	14th July, 1949
LOCATION OF TRIAL	Lewes
PRESIDING JUDGE	Mister Justice Humphreys
PROSECUTION COUNSEL	Theodore Turner, Geoffrey Lawrence
DEFENCE COUNSEL	John Flowers, C.J.T. Pensotti
NUMBER OF VICTIMS	1

VICTIMS DETAILS	
NAME	Lucy Wilson (Died Wednesday, 23rd March)
AGE	37
DATE OF MURDER	Tuesday, 8th March, 1949
PLACE OF MURDER	Campbell's Restaurant, 186 Terminus Place, Eastbourne
METHOD OF KILLING	Stabbed
RELATIONSHIP TO KILLER	Girlfriend

FOR ALMOST FIVE years, the murder of a young girl in a German wood remained unsolved. Then, out of the blue, a written confession caught up with the man who had written it and the miscreant was finally brought to justice.

Germany in July, 1945, was a shattered country, occupied by foreign troops, including members of the B.L.A., or British Liberation Army. It was in that same month that the body of Waltraut Lehman was found near Rotenburg. She had been shot and the flowers she had been picking, lay near her body. Troops from the B.L.A., stationed in the area, were questioned, but no light could be thrown on the murder and the crime remained unsolved.

On November 18th, 1948, an ex-member of that B.L.A. handed a sealed envelope to a friend named Nichol. In time, this envelope found its way to the hands of Major Harvey, who opened it and read the short, handwritten note inside.

"To the Police. I was in the B.L.A., in July 1945, in a company of the Pioneer Corps. It was a day in July that I killed a woman. The military police were seeing all the men but before they saw me I was on the road to England." The note was signed William Jones.

When Jones, now a farmer, was interviewed, he readily confessed to the murder of Waltraut Lehman. He explained that he had met her in the woods a few times before the fateful day but on this occasion he offered her some cigarettes. She said something to him in German, which he took to be some sort of curse, and before he knew what was happening, he had squeezed the trigger of his rifle and shot her dead.

At Jones's trial, his mother, Maude, who had travelled down from Doncaster, told how at the age of seven, William had been kicked in the head by a horse. Ever since that time he had displayed a rather short temper, which seemed to be especially bad at the time of the new moon. She also explained that her son had not even gone to school until he was 13, and still had trouble reading and writing.

None of this saved Jones from his own

NAME	William Claude Hodson Jones
AGE AT EXECUTION	31
DATE OF EXECUTION	Wednesday, 28th September, 1949
PLACE OF EXECUTION	Pentonville
HANGMAN	Albert Pierrepoint
ASSISTANT	Harry Allen
DATE OF TRIAL	8th September, 1949
LOCATION OF TRIAL	Old Bailey
PRESIDING JUDGE	Not known
PROSECUTION COUNSEL	E. Anthony Hawke
DEFENCE COUNSEL	Not known
NUMBER OF VICTIMS	1

VICTIMS DETAILS	
NAME	Waltraut Lehman
AGE	24
DATE OF MURDER	July, 1945
PLACE OF MURDER	Woods at Rotenburg, Germany
METHOD OF KILLING	Shot
RELATIONSHIP TO KILLER	None

fate and he was executed in September. However, had he never written that brief note, there is no doubt that he would have escaped the noose.

JOHN WILSON MET Lucy Nightingale for the first time in the King's Head at Easington, on Friday, August 12th, 1949. The following night, he killed her.

Having enjoyed each other's company on Friday, John and Lucy arranged to meet the next day. After enjoying one drink in the Liberalty, they caught a bus to Murton and here went on a tour of the local hostelries. Having been into the British Legion, the Traveller's Rest, the Colliery Inn and then the Victoria Inn, known locally as the High House, they caught a bus back to Cold Healedon and from there, decided to walk the rest of the way home.

John Wilson had been seen in Lucy's company by a number of witnesses. Ann Lamb, the barmaid at the Traveller's Rest said that they had had one drink before leaving. Wilson's own brother, Henry, saw them together in the Victoria Inn and later saw them at the fairground next to Murton Colliery. Leslie O'Connor had been in the bus queue in Cold Healedon and saw Wilson walking across the fields with Lucy. All of this was merely extra evidence for the police, for their best witness was Wilson himself.

In the early hours of Sunday morning, Wilson called at his sister Jane's house, where he told them that he had killed Lucy. They did not take him seriously, so Wilson walked on to his father's house at 17 St Andrews Terrace. Here he repeated his claims to his father and his brother, Harry Wilson. Finally he was believed and the police were called.

When the officers arrived, the first thing Wilson did was hand over Lucy's watch and ring, which he had taken from the body. He explained that as he and Lucy had been walking across the fields, she had started talking about money and had demanded 10/- for sex. He had flown into a rage, attacked Lucy, tore her clothing and raped her. Then, seeing that she was dead, he covered the body with more than a dozen sheaves of corn before walking to the Pemberton Arms, where he knocked on the door, was allowed in by the landlord and given two glasses of rum. From here he walked to his sister's house and confessed his guilt.

John Wilson's own statement confirmed

NAME	John Wilson
AGE AT EXECUTION	26
DATE OF EXECUTION	Tuesday, 13th December, 1949
PLACE OF EXECUTION	Durham
HANGMAN	Not known
ASSISTANT	Not known
DATE OF TRIAL	2nd November, 1949
LOCATION OF TRIAL	Durham
PRESIDING JUDGE	Mister Justice Oliver
PROSECUTION COUNSEL	C.B. Fenwick, C. Cohen
DEFENCE COUNSEL	H.B.H. Hylton Foster, J.T. Hanlon
NUMBER OF VICTIMS	1

VICTIMS DETAILS	
NAME	Lucy Nightingale
AGE	25
DATE OF MURDER	Saturday, 13th August, 1949
PLACE OF MURDER	Cornfield at Cold Healedon, County Durham
METHOD OF KILLING	Strangled
RELATIONSHIP TO KILLER	None

that guilt and he was hanged at the same time as Benjamin Roberts.

BENJAMIN ROBERTS WAS very fond of Lilian Vickers, but unfortunately, she much preferred the company of another man, Alan Neal. Those circumstances would lead to her death and Roberts's execution.

On August 14th, 1949, Alan and Lilian had tea with Roberts at his house. It was whilst they were there that Roberts showed Alan a gun he was cleaning.

Lilian left some time after 4.30pm, to be followed an hour later by Alan. He returned at 6.30pm when he and Benjamin went out to the Eden Arms at Rushfield. They met up with Lilian at 11.00pm at the post office and all three returned to Benjamin's house. Also present were Benjamin's parents, his sister and her husband.

After spending some time there, Alan and Lilian left together and enjoyed a brief interlude in the street outside, kissing each other goodnight. It was then that they saw Benjamin leave the house and go to the allotments nearby. Curious, they decided to follow.

Before they had walked very far, Benjamin reappeared with his gun, which he pointed at them, announcing that it was loaded. A shot was fired and Lilian fell to the ground. Alan Neal ran off – as a second shot was fired – only to encounter Benjamin's father, John William Roberts, who had heard the shots and gone to investigate. He and Alan returned to the allotments, where they found Benjamin lying on top of Lilian, having shot himself in the head.

Benjamin Roberts recovered from his head wound but as Lilian was dead, he now faced a charge of murder. His story was that he had fired the gun without having any intention of shooting anyone but as soon as he had seen Lilian fall, he had turned the gun upon himself. This did nothing to condone what Benjamin had done and he was still found guilty of murder.

NAME	Benjamin Roberts
AGE AT EXECUTION	23
DATE OF EXECUTION	Tuesday, 13th December, 1949
PLACE OF EXECUTION	Durham
HANGMAN	Not known
ASSISTANT	Not known
DATE OF TRIAL	31st October – 1st November, 1949
LOCATION OF TRIAL	Durham
PRESIDING JUDGE	Mister Justice Oliver
PROSECUTION COUNSEL	C.B. Fenwick, N.S. Harper
DEFENCE COUNSEL	Ralph Cleworth, W. Temple
NUMBER OF VICTIMS	1

VICTIMS DETAILS	
NAME	Lilian Vickers
AGE	21
DATE OF MURDER	Monday, 15th August, 1949
PLACE OF MURDER	Behind a shed on allotments, Chilton
METHOD OF KILLING	Shot
RELATIONSHIP TO KILLER	None

IN 1941, MABEL Violet Rose met Ernest Soper Couzins, who was in the army at the time, and an affair started between them, even though both were married. For a time Couzins even moved in with Mabel but once her husband returned from the forces, Couzins moved back in with his wife and children at 22 Glenside Avenue, a few doors away from where Mabel lived.

Around this time, Mabel's daughter lent Couzins £50, for which she received an I.O.U., and in the winter of 1947, he got a job stoking the boilers at the same place where Mabel worked, agreeing to give his 7s-6d wages to her daughter in order to repay the debt.

In 1948, Mabel's husband stopped her seeing Couzins altogether and she spent some time off work ill. Couzins now left his job, which was taken over by Mabel's son-in-law, Victor Desmond Elias. At about the same time, Mabel and Victor began pressing Couzins to repay the money he owed.

On August 3rd, Victor left for work at 6.55am and at 7.20am, Mabel turned up to clean the offices. As she arrived, she saw that the door was ajar and found Couzins there. He announced that he had locked Victor in a cupboard downstairs and produced a revolver with which he claimed to have finished him off.

As Mabel ran downstairs, she saw Couzins put the gun to his head and heard the clicks as the hammer fell on empty chambers. Minutes later, Mabel found Victor's body, lying on the boiler room floor. The police were called and Sergeant Thomas Dryson found Couzins, still in the manager's office, having now wounded himself in the throat.

In addition to being shot, Victor had had other injuries inflicted upon his body after death. He had been stabbed a number of times and had also had his throat cut. Once he had recovered, Couzins claimed that he had gone to the offices to persuade Victor to give him his old job back and had taken out the gun to threaten him. Victor had merely laughed and before Couzins knew what was happening, the gun had gone off. He said he had no recollection of anything that occurred after that and so could not remember inflicting the other injuries.

NAME	Ernest Soper Couzins
AGE AT EXECUTION	49
DATE OF EXECUTION	Friday, 30th December, 1949
PLACE OF EXECUTION	Wandsworth
HANGMAN	Albert Pierrepoint
ASSISTANT	Harry Allen
DATE OF TRIAL	19th November, 1949
LOCATION OF TRIAL	Maidstone
PRESIDING JUDGE	Mister Justice Croom-Johnson
PROSECUTION COUNSEL	Aiken Watson, R.H.L. Royle
DEFENCE COUNSEL	Derek Curtis-Bennett, Malcolm Morris
NUMBER OF VICTIMS	1

VICTIMS DETAILS	
NAME	Victor Desmond Elias
AGE	30
DATE OF MURDER	Wednesday, 3rd August, 1949
PLACE OF MURDER	34 St George's Place, Canterbury
METHOD OF KILLING	Shot
RELATIONSHIP TO KILLER	None

At his trial, Couzins stated that he had repaid £25 of the £50 he had originally borrowed and had wanted the rest of the debt cancelled as he estimated he had spent much more than the remaining £25 on Mabel, but she and Victor refused. Couzins went on to say that his head seemed to swell up and go bang and it was suggested by the defence that this was a symptom of emotional tension and acute anxiety.

Found guilty, Couzins was executed at Wandsworth, the last man to die on the gallows in the 1940s.

O N OCTOBER 6TH, 1949, Daniel Raven and his wife Marie had their first child, a son. Marie Raven had been confined in a nursing home in Muswell Hill and on October 10th, Daniel visited her there, along with Marie's father and mother – Leopold and Esther Goodman. Marie's parents left just after 9.00pm, to be followed later by Daniel himself. Around 90 minutes later, Daniel's telephone rang. It was the police asking him to call round at his parents-in-law's house.

At 9.50pm that night, Frederick Fraiman, Marie's brother-in-law, together with his family, had called at the Goodman home to ask how Marie and the baby were. Frederick was surprised to find there was no reply. He managed to find an open window and climbed into the house. Almost the first thing he noticed was the battered bodies of Leopold and Esther.

It was obvious that the motive for the double murder had not been robbery. There was a great deal of cash in the house, none of which had been touched.

When Raven arrived at the Goodman house, he seemed to be genuinely upset. The police, though, noticed that his clothing appeared to be particularly pristine. Taken in for further questioning, he was asked to hand over his house keys, which he did.

The police entered Raven's house in Edgwarebury Lane just before midnight. Immediately they noticed a strong smell of burning and found the remains of a suit burning in the stove. They retrieved what little was left and examinations later would reveal the presence of bloodstains of the same rare group as that belonging to the Goodmans.

The police scenario was that after leaving the nursing home, Raven had driven to the Goodman house and battered them to death with the base of a television aerial. He then drove home, where he tried to scrub the blood off his clothes. Failing to do so, he decided to burn them, changing into a fresh shirt and suit when the police telephoned. The motive for the murder could not be determined.

Raven's first defence was that he had called on the Goodmans after leaving the nursing home, but had left them alive and well. He had then visited a cousin's house,

NAME	Daniel Raven
AGE AT EXECUTION	23
DATE OF EXECUTION	Friday, 6th January, 1950
PLACE OF EXECUTION	Pentonville
HANGMAN	Albert Pierrepoint
ASSISTANT	Harry Kirk
DATE OF TRIAL	22nd November – 24th November, 1949
LOCATION OF TRIAL	Old Bailey
PRESIDING JUDGE	Mister Justice Cassels
PROSECUTION COUNSEL	E. Anthony Hawke
DEFENCE COUNSEL	John Maude
NUMBER OF VICTIMS	2

VICTIMS DETAILS

NAMES	Leopold Goodman; Esther Goodman
AGES	49; 47
DATE OF MURDER	Monday, 10th October, 1949
PLACE OF MURDER	Ashcombe Gardens, Edgware
METHOD OF KILLING	Battered; battered
RELATIONSHIP TO KILLER	Father-in-law; mother-in-law

before returning to the Goodmans. Getting no reply this time, he had done what Frederick Fraiman had, and climbed through the window. The blood on his clothing was from his examination of the bodies. When the police had telephoned he had panicked and decided to burn his clothes. The defence did not convince the jury and Raven was found guilty.

The appeal tried a different approach: the defence suggested that Raven had been insane. He had been discharged from the R.A.F. after being in a plane crash and ever since had suffered from blackouts and a form of epilepsy. This too did nothing to alter the verdict and the sentence was upheld.

AT SOME TIME after 8.30pm, on November 5th, 1949, James Frank Rivett was seen with his young girlfriend, Christine Cuddon. The time they spent together must have been fairly brief, because by 10.00pm, James was back at his father's house, in Denmark Road. He did not stay long though, pausing only to pick up a shotgun and some cartridges.

By 11.20pm, James was at the house of a friend, where he announced that he had killed Christine. After talking for a short time, James was persuaded to go to the police station, where he made a full confession to strangling Christine, though he would not say why he had done so.

The police drove to the cycle shed at the Sir John Leman School on the outskirts of the town. There, sure enough, they found the body of Christine Cuddon. Forensic tests would show that Christine had engaged in sexual intercourse shortly before her death.

Rivett appeared to show no emotion over what he had done. Put into a cell for the night, he immediately dropped off to sleep. The following day he made a more complete statement, in which he said that he had killed Christine because her father had told her he wished her to stop seeing Rivett. He explained that after killing Christine he had thought of killing himself, which was why he had taken the gun out with him. His courage had failed him though, and he could not go through with it.

What might have seemed to be a straightforward case turned out to be nothing of the kind. Rivett's defence was one of insanity but before the trial itself could take place, a jury had to be sworn to decide on his sanity and whether he was fit to plead. This hearing took place at Ipswich on January 20th, 1950, and despite two doctors giving evidence in which they stated that Rivett was not sane, the jury decided that he was.

The trial was due to begin on January 27th, at Norwich but at the start of the proceedings, the defence applied for the insanity issue to be re-tried, which it then was. Once again a jury decided that Rivett was fit to plead. The third jury were then empanelled and the trial proper began.

NAME	James Frank Rivett
AGE AT EXECUTION	21
DATE OF EXECUTION	Wednesday, 8th March, 1950
PLACE OF EXECUTION	Norwich
HANGMAN	Not known
ASSISTANT	Not known
DATE OF TRIAL	27th January, 1950
LOCATION OF TRIAL	Norwich
PRESIDING JUDGE	Mister Justice Stable
PROSECUTION COUNSEL	Granville Sharp, Robert Hales
DEFENCE COUNSEL	Sir Charles Doughty, F.T. Alpe
NUMBER OF VICTIMS	1

VICTIMS DETAILS	
NAME	Christine Ruth Cuddon
AGE	17
DATE OF MURDER	Saturday, 5th November, 1949
PLACE OF MURDER	Cycle shed at Sir John Leman School, Beccles
METHOD OF KILLING	Strangled
RELATIONSHIP TO KILLER	Girlfriend

Immediately Rivett pleaded guilty but at the judge's direction, a plea of not guilty was entered and the evidence was heard. It was claimed that Rivett was suffering from schizophrenia and was therefore not responsible for his actions, but after hearing his confession, the jury decided that Rivett was guilty as charged.

On March 8th, 1950, James Frank Rivett whose sanity had been decided by two juries, and his guilt by a third, was executed at Norwich.

THE YOUNG MAN who walked into the police station in Merthyr Tydfil looked frightened and unsure of himself. It was little wonder. He was about to confess to killing his wife.

The date was November 20th, 1949 and the young man was Timothy John Evans, aged 25. Although a local man, he had lived in London for some time, with his 19-year-old wife Beryl and their young baby daughter, Geraldine.

Evans told the police that his wife had recently become pregnant again. As it was, his wages as a van-driver hardly enabled the family to survive, and they knew that they could ill afford another mouth to feed. Beryl had immediately suggested an abortion, which Evans had not agreed with, but it seemed she was adamant that she would not have this child.

One day whilst returning from a trip he stopped off at a transport cafe and spoke to a man who gave him a bottle of liquid, which he said would terminate the pregnancy. Upon returning home, his wife had found this bottle in his jacket pocket and asked him what it was for. Reluctantly he had told her and she had determined to end her pregnancy the very next day.

On the following day, November 8th, Evans had returned home to find his wife dead. The abortion had obviously gone wrong and he was now left with a body on his hands. In the early hours of November 9th, he had gone downstairs from his top-floor flat, with his wife's body, and put her down a drain outside his home at 10 Rillington Place. He had then quit his job, sold all his furniture, left London and gone to his aunt's house in Wales, where he had been for the past two weeks or so.

The Welsh police telephoned their colleagues in London, who immediately visited Rillington Place and found the manhole cover outside the house, just as Evans as said it would be. An officer heaved at the cover, expecting to find a woman's body, but found instead that he could not budge the heavy metal disc. It eventually took four officers to lift the cover that the frail Evans claimed to have lifted by himself. There was nothing down the manhole. The diligent officers did establish, though, that

NAME	Timothy John Evans
AGE AT EXECUTION	25
DATE OF EXECUTION	Thursday, 9th March, 1950
PLACE OF EXECUTION	Pentonville
HANGMAN	Albert Pierrepoint
ASSISTANT	Syd Dearnley
DATE OF TRIAL	11th January – 13th January, 1950
LOCATION OF TRIAL	Old Bailey
PRESIDING JUDGE	Mister Justice Lewis
PROSECUTION COUNSEL	Christmas Humphreys, Henry Elam
DEFENCE COUNSEL	Malcolm Morris
NUMBER OF VICTIMS	2 (possibly)

VICTIMS DETAILS

NAMES	Beryl Susanna Evans; Geraldine Evans
AGES	19; 14 months
DATES OF MURDERS	Tuesday, 8th November, 1949; Thursday, 10th November, 1949
PLACE OF MURDER	10 Rillington Place, Notting Hill, London
METHOD OF KILLING	Strangled; strangled
RELATIONSHIPS TO KILLER	Wife; daughter

Beryl and Geraldine Evans were indeed missing from home.

When the Welsh police told Evans that no trace of his wife had been found, he made a second statement in which a different story unfolded. He maintained that it was true that his wife was pregnant and she had wanted an abortion, but now there was no mysterious bottle of liquid bought from a man in a transport cafe. In this statement, Evans said that he had received help from a man who lived in the ground floor flat at Rillington Place, one John Reginald Halliday Christie.

This revised story held that Christie had offered to help arrange an abortion. Evans had returned home from work on the day the operation was due to take place, and found his wife dead, lying on their bed, covered by an eiderdown. She had been bleeding from the mouth and nose and from between her legs. Christie told him that the operation had gone wrong and that they must conceal the body or they would both go to prison.

Christie left Evans alone in the kitchen to think and returned shortly afterwards to inform Evans that his wife's body had been put in the vacant first-floor flat. Christie said he would dispose of the body down the drain in the middle of the night and Evans believed that this is what he had done. Furthermore, Christie had said that he knew a couple in East Acton who would look after Geraldine.

Once again the police returned to Rillington Place, whilst Evans was taken down to London for further questioning. By the time he arrived at Scotland Yard, police had found the bodies of his wife and child.

Both Beryl and Geraldine had been discovered wrapped in a green tablecloth, hidden behind some wood in a wash-house in the back garden of 10 Rillington Place. Both had been strangled by some kind of ligature and in Geraldine's case, a tie had been used that was still knotted so tightly around her neck that it had to be cut off.

Evans now made a third statement in which he stated that it was he who was responsible for the two deaths. He claimed that Beryl had incurred too many debts and that they had argued over money. He had strangled her with a piece of rope and then taken her body to the empty first-floor flat, on the evening of the 8th of November. On Thursday the 10th, he came home from work and strangled Geraldine with his tie, then hid both bodies in the washhouse. Evans was charged with the murder of Geraldine Evans.

It was customary in Britain to proceed against an individual with one murder only, no matter how many they might have committed. Had the police pursued Evans with the murder of his wife, it is possible that he might have escaped with a plea of manslaughter. No such plea could be attached to the murder of a small baby and it was for this reason that Evans was charged with the murder of his daughter. It was a decision that was to have far-reaching effects years later.

At Evans's trial he retracted his confession and again blamed Christie for the murders of his wife and child. Christie denied all knowledge of the crime when questioned in the witness box and came across as a very believable witness. Evans was found guilty and executed in March, 1950. There, for three years, the matter rested. Evans had been found guilty of murder and paid the due penalty for his crime. And then, all hell broke loose at 10 Rillington Place.

The story of John Reginald Halliday Christie is mentioned elsewhere in this book. Here, suffice it to say that Christie was found guilty of murdering at least seven women, one of whom was Beryl Evans. Although he denied murdering Geraldine, the crime for which Evans had hanged, Christie's guilt did throw doubt on Evans's conviction and an inquiry was called.

The Brabin inquiry did not, as many people think, state that Evans was an innocent man. It determined that Evans had probably killed his wife, but that Christie had killed Geraldine. Since Evans had been charged with and convicted of the murder of Geraldine, he was in fact innocent of that crime and therefore should not have been hanged. As a result, he was granted a pardon, the first one granted in the twentieth century.

ON SATURDAY MARCH 19th, 1949, the Cameo Cinema was playing to an almost full house and the takings at the cashier's desk had been excellent.

Mrs Jackman took the money along to the manager's office where Mr Thomas and his assistant, Mr Catterall would sort it into denominations and get it ready for banking. As Mrs Jackman returned to her post, she heard six shots coming from the office. Bravely, both she and Patrick Griffin, the doorman, went to investigate and were in time to see a masked man make his getaway down the back stairs. Checking in the office, Mrs Jackman was shocked to find Leonard Thomas dead and John Catterall badly wounded. He would die soon afterwards, making the crime a double murder.

Many police interviews were conducted and many informers were leaned upon, but it seemed that no one knew anything about the murder. Slowly the investigation grew to a halt.

Then, in September 1949, the police received an anonymous letter from an informant who wanted to do a deal. In return for protection, he said he would name the men who had committed the robbery at the Cameo Cinema. If the officers were interested they were told to place an advertisement in the Liverpool Echo. The police were only to eager to co-operate and the advertisement was placed as directed. On September 29th, James Philip Northam saw the reply to his letter and telephoned the police to arrange a meeting.

When that meeting took place, Northam told the police that he had overheard two men planning the robbery. George Kelly and Charles Connolly, two men known to the police, were duly arrested, questioned, and charged with the murders. It soon transpired that Connolly had only been the look-out and it had been Kelly who had done the shooting, but when the case opened in January 1950 at Liverpool, both men faced the same charges.

The defence was led by Miss Rose Heilbron who would later go on to become the first female High Court judge. After 13 days of evidence, though, the jury could not agree and the judge, Mister Justice Oliver was forced to order a retrial.

NAME	George Kelly
AGE AT EXECUTION	27
DATE OF EXECUTION	Tuesday, 28th March, 1950
PLACE OF EXECUTION	Liverpool
HANGMAN	Albert Pierrepoint
ASSISTANT	Syd Dernley
DATE OF TRIAL	2nd February – 8th February, 1950
LOCATION OF TRIAL	Liverpool
PRESIDING JUDGE	Mister Justice Cassels
PROSECUTION COUNSEL	W. Gorman
DEFENCE COUNSEL	Miss Rose Heilbron
NUMBER OF VICTIMS	2

VICTIMS DETAILS	
NAMES	Leonard Thomas; John Bernard Catterall
AGES	44; 25
DATE OF MURDER	Saturday, 19th March, 1949
PLACE OF MURDER	Cameo Cinema, Webster Road, Wavertree, Liverpool
METHOD OF KILLING	Shot; shot
RELATIONSHIP TO KILLER	None; none

The second trial took place the following month and this time, the two men were to be tried separately. This time, the jury did agree and Kelly was sentenced to death. Connolly made his appearance on February 13th and as no evidence was offered on the murder charge, the judge directed that he be found not guilty. He was not so fortunate when it came to the robbery charges, receiving a 10-year sentence.

IT WAS 4.00AM on December 31st, 1949, when Piotr Maksimowski walked into Beaconsfield police station, showed that he had slashed his own wrists and claimed that he had done the same to a woman, Dilys Campbell, in a wood at Bowerwood. Officers went to the scene and soon found Dilys's body. Her wrists and throat had been cut and close by lay a handbag, a pair of gloves and a safety razor blade.

Maksimowski claimed that he and Dilys had arranged a suicide pact and explained why it had come about. He had been seeing Dilys for five months and had been under the impression that she was a widow and there was no bar to their relationship. However, he had now discovered that she was in fact married, to Peter Campbell, of Shackleton Road, Slough, who was very much alive. She was also the mother of two children.

On the night of the murder, Maksimowski and Dilys had been out drinking and had then made their way to the woods. A discussion about the situation followed and eventually Dilys said that if they had to continue to live like this, they would be better off dead. Maksimowski then took out his razor and cut Dilys's wrists. She looked up into his eyes and said, "Finish me, Pete", whereupon he cut her throat, covered her with a blanket and then slashed his own wrists.

Maksimowski's defence counsel tried to suggest that he had been insane at the time of the crime and Doctor Kipping, the police surgeon, did give evidence in which he suggested that the accused man was obsessed with death. He was nevertheless found guilty. When the judge, Mister Croom-Johnson asked if he had anything to say before the sentence was pronounced, Maksimowski asked if he could be shot, instead of being hanged. The judge, quite rightly, said that he did not have the power to make any ruling on that, and gave the death sentence in the usual form.

There was no appeal and so exactly three weeks after the trial had ended, Piotr Maksimowski faced Albert Pierrepoint at Birmingham. Finally the suicide pact was complete.

NAME Piotr Maksimowski

AGE AT EXECUTION 33

DATE OF EXECUTION Wednesday, 29th March, 1950

PLACE OF EXECUTION Birmingham

HANGMAN Albert Pierrepoint

ASSISTANT Syd Dernley

DATE OF TRIAL 8th March, 1950

LOCATION OF TRIAL Warwick

PRESIDING JUDGE Mister Justice Croom-Johnson

PROSECUTION COUNSEL Mister Fearnley-Whittingstall

DEFENCE COUNSEL K. Berry

NUMBER OF VICTIMS 1

VICTIMS DETAILS

NAME Dilys Doreen Campbell

AGE 30

DATE OF MURDER Saturday, 31st December, 1949

PLACE OF MURDER Wood at Bowerwood, Beaconsfield

METHOD OF KILLING Cut throat/wrists

RELATIONSHIP TO KILLER Girlfriend

1950

1950

AT 10.00AM ON November 16th, 1949, two men burst into a jeweller's shop in Leeds and demanded that the proprietor hand over all the money he had on the premises.

Abraham Levine was not about to let these thugs rob him, so instead of doing as they had asked, he grabbed one of them and fought with him. The other thief, seeing his companion in trouble, clubbed Levine to the floor with his gun butt. Levine tenaciously held on to the other man until two shots rang out. Both would-be thieves then fled, empty-handed, scattering the crowds in the street outside by firing their guns into the air. Abraham Levine died from his wounds the following day.

On November 17th, one of the bullets taken from Levine's body was examined and traced to a batch taken during a robbery at a gunsmith's shop a few days previously. Further investigations led to two men being arrested at Southport, on November 18th.

Walter Sharpe, aged 20 and Gordon Lannen, just 17, were interviewed separately and it soon became clear that it had been Sharpe who had fired the fatal shot. Sharpe, though he admitted that he had shot Levine, claimed that it had been an accident. The gun had gone off whilst they were struggling and he had no intention of killing the man. Both men were charged with murder.

The trial took place in Leeds in March before Mister Justice Streatfeild. Once again Sharpe told his story of an accidental shooting, but the law held that if violence had been used in the furtherance of a crime then the charge was murder and not manslaughter. Both men were found guilty after a deliberation of less than 20 minutes, and Lannen, being too young for the death penalty, was sentenced to be detained during His Majesty's pleasure.

For Sharpe there was no such escape. He was hanged at Leeds on March 30th.

NAME	Walter Sharpe
AGE AT EXECUTION	20
DATE OF EXECUTION	Thursday, 30th March, 1950
PLACE OF EXECUTION	Leeds
HANGMAN	Steve Wade
ASSISTANT	Harry Allen
DATE OF TRIAL	9th March – 10th March, 1950
LOCATION OF TRIAL	Leeds
PRESIDING JUDGE	Mister Justice Streatfeild
PROSECUTION COUNSEL	Godfrey Russell Vick, Carl Aarvold
DEFENCE COUNSEL	G. Raymond Hinchcliffe
NUMBER OF VICTIMS	1

VICTIMS DETAILS	
NAME	Abraham Harry Levine (Died Thursday, 17th November)
AGE	49
DATE OF MURDER	Wednesday, 16th November, 1949
PLACE OF MURDER	132 Albion Street, Leeds
METHOD OF KILLING	Battered/shot
RELATIONSHIP TO KILLER	None

AT 10.45AM ON October 10th, 1949, William Henry Llewellyn left his home to keep an appointment with one of his tenant farmers, Albert Edward Jenkins, who was negotiating to purchase his 28-acre holding, known as Lower Furzehill Farm. No one else saw William that day and when he did not arrive home for dinner, a search was launched. The following morning, his battered body was discovered, wrapped in a tarpaulin and buried in a shallow grave.

When interviewed by the police, Jenkins agreed that he had sent William a letter asking him to call. He added that by the time William arrived, at around 11.00am, Jenkins's wife and children had already left for Pembroke fair, so there were no witnesses to the business the two men discussed.

According to Jenkins, William agreed terms and Jenkins paid him £1,000 for the farm. He gave William this money in cash and also added another £50 for rent he still owed. He ended by saying that they had parted amicably after William had signed a receipt for the money.

Further investigations suggested that this story was somewhat unlikely. John Edward Ronald Penny had sold Jenkins a tractor on hire purchase and Jenkins was in arrears with his payments. In addition, Jenkins's bank account was more than £136 overdrawn on the day he claimed to have paid William Llewellyn over £1,000 in cash.

More evidence came from Mr Codd, who was an expert on artificial insemination and who had an appointment with Jenkins on the morning of October 10th. Codd was on time but saw Jenkins drive past him, on his tractor. Mr Codd noticed that on the back of the tractor was a bundle, wrapped in a tarpaulin.

As if this were not enough, Jenkins's clothing was bloodstained. Police Sergeant Thomas took soil samples from around the front door of the farm and found these to be heavily contaminated with blood and even contained pieces of human bone. Jenkins was charged with murder.

Jenkins tried his best to implicate two men whom he said had called at his farm between noon and 1.00pm on the day of the murder, asking for a jug of tea. His suggestion was that

NAME	Albert Edward Jenkins
AGE AT EXECUTION	38
DATE OF EXECUTION	Wednesday, 19th April, 1950
PLACE OF EXECUTION	Swansea
HANGMAN	Not known
ASSISTANT	Not known
DATE OF TRIAL	27th February – 2nd March, 1950
LOCATION OF TRIAL	Haverfordwest
PRESIDING JUDGE	Mister Justice Byrne
PROSECUTION COUNSEL	Arthian Davies, Roderic Bowen M.P.
DEFENCE COUNSEL	H. Vincent Lloyd-Jones, Rowe Harding
NUMBER OF VICTIMS	1

VICTIMS DETAILS	
NAME	William Henry Llewellyn
AGE	52
DATE OF MURDER	Monday, 10th October, 1949
PLACE OF MURDER	Lower Furzehill Farm, Rosemarket
METHOD OF KILLING	Battered
RELATIONSHIP TO KILLER	None

they had killed William for the money he was carrying. But the evidence continued to mount up against him.

Frederick William Mathias testified that he had seen Jenkins in the claypit where the body was discovered. Jenkins was carrying a long-handled shovel at the time and that afternoon, Jenkins had been seen riding the bicycle William had used to travel to his farm.

The circumstantial evidence against Jenkins was damning and after an absence of 105 minutes, the jury returned a verdict of guilty. On April 19th, at Swansea, Jenkins earned his little place in history by becoming the first Pembrokeshire man to be executed since 1825.

IF IT HADN'T INVOLVED the murder of a brave citizen, the story of Redel and Gower would have passed for high comedy.

In 1950, these two young men, both Polish, were unemployed and desperate for money. One day, as they sat on the top deck of a bus, they passed a small branch of Lloyds Bank. The only staff on the premises were a single cashier and a rather elderly security guard. It looked to be an easy target.

The robbery was set for Monday, March 13th, 1950. The night before, Redel and Gower went out on a heavy drinking session. The original plan had involved them stealing a motorbike as a getaway vehicle, but on Monday they were still the worse for drink and had to abandon the idea. The two master thieves had to travel to the robbery by bus!

Redel and Gower entered the bank. Redel pulled out a revolver and threatened the cashier, Ronald Wall, and the guard, John Bullock, as Gower leapt over the counter and grabbed what he thought was a pile of cash. Unfortunately, he had managed to liberate just £28 and a large quantity of bank paying-in slips. Thinking that they had achieved what they had come for, the two thieves ran out into the street, neglecting to tie up the two staff members, who promptly followed them and raised the alarm.

Having travelled to the robbery by bus, Gower and Redel had no option but to try to escape the same way. They leapt onto a passing bus but were immediately forced off when John Bullock ran alongside shouting; "Stop, there are bandits on your bus!"

The two bungling robbers were now chased by members of the public. One of those public-spirited citizens was Bob Taylor, a keep-fit fanatic and judo expert. He soon caught up to Redel and began to grapple with him. A shot rang out and Bob Taylor fell to the ground, a bullet in his head.

Redel and Gower were picked up within an hour of the robbery and subsequently found guilty of murder. There was no doubt that Redel and actually fired the shot, and attempts were made to save Gower. His verdict carried a strong recommendation for mercy but it was held that he was engaged in

NAMES	Roman Redel; Zbigniew Gower
AGES AT EXECUTION	23; 23
DATE OF EXECUTION	Friday, 7th July, 1950
PLACE OF EXECUTION	Winchester
HANGMAN	Albert Pierrepoint
ASSISTANTS	Harry Kirk, Harry Allen, Syd Dernley
DATE OF TRIAL	22nd May – 23rd May, 1950
LOCATION OF TRIAL	Salisbury
PRESIDING JUDGE	Mister Justice Oliver
PROSECUTION COUNSEL	G.D. Roberts, Cyril Williams
DEFENCE COUNSEL	Ewen Montague, G. Hope Scott; C.F. Ingle, G.G. MacDonald
NUMBER OF VICTIMS	1

VICTIMS DETAILS	
NAME	Robert Taylor
AGE	30
DATE OF MURDER	Monday, 13th March, 1950
PLACE OF MURDER	North View, Bristol
METHOD OF KILLING	Shot
RELATIONSHIP TO KILLERS	None; none

a common purpose with Redel and therefore was equally as guilty of murder.

Redel and Gower were hanged together at Winchester in July 1950. As one of the assistants, Syd Dernley, moved to strap Redel's feet, he fumbled the job and allowed the strap to fall. In a firm voice, Redel told Dernley to do his job properly. Dernley succeeded at his second attempt, and moments later the defiant Pole was dead.

FOR SIX WEEKS or so, George Brown had lived with Mary Longhurst at 26 King Street, North Shields. That association had come to an end around March 3rd, 1950, when George had moved to 52 Princes Street. George and Mary still saw each other, even though she told him that she might go to live with another man and had started seeing Frank Dougal Bouchier.

On March 9th, Mary and George were seen arguing in the street but that particular difference must have ended amicably, for George spent that night at Mary's house and was seen leaving early the following morning. However, the arguments were soon started anew and later that day, Mary went to the police station and made a complaint against George. As a result, George was interviewed by officers and told to stay away from Mary's house.

It was 10.50pm on March 10th when a neighbour, Benjamin Hedley, heard heavy footsteps on the stairs of the house where Mary rented rooms. These were followed by shouts, screams and the sound of the footsteps returning. The neighbour contacted the police and when they attended, they found the body of Mary Longhurst on her bed. She had been strangled and the cord used to kill her had also been tied around the foot of her bed, holding her head firmly. Her terrified young daughter was still huddled in the bed where her mother's body lay.

It was natural that George Brown would be picked up and interviewed. He claimed that he had not been anywhere near Mary's home that night. He had visited a local pub, gone for a long walk and then returned home. However, that alibi could not be confirmed and after deliberating for 30 minutes, the jury at Brown's trial decided that he was guilty of murder.

NAME	George Finlay Brown
AGE AT EXECUTION	23
DATE OF EXECUTION	Tuesday, 11th July, 1950
PLACE OF EXECUTION	Durham
HANGMAN	Albert Pierrepoint
ASSISTANT	Not known
DATE OF TRIAL	30th May – 31st May, 1950
LOCATION OF TRIAL	Newcastle
PRESIDING JUDGE	Mister Justice Morris
PROSECUTION COUNSEL	E.G. Robey, F.B.H. Hylton-Foster
DEFENCE COUNSEL	H.R.B. Shepherd
NUMBER OF VICTIMS	1

VICTIMS DETAILS

NAME	Mary Victoria Longhurst
AGE	23
DATE OF MURDER	Friday, 10th March, 1950
PLACE OF MURDER	26 King Street, North Shields
METHOD OF KILLING	Strangled
RELATIONSHIP TO KILLER	Girlfriend

1950

1950

A CHANCE ENCOUNTER at a cinema led to the deaths of two people.

Lily Palmer, a mental defective who had been waiting three years for a place in an institution, noticed the young man who was shown into the seat next to hers and when she saw him again a short time later, they recognised each other and fell into conversation. After some discussion the man, Ronald Atwell, invited Lily to go for a drink and she agreed. They went into the Horse and Jockey pub where they were seen by a farmer, Mister Davey, laughing and joking together. The same farmer saw them leave together at a few minutes after 9.30pm.

By coincidence, it was Mister Davey who, 12 hours later, was to find the battered and bloody body of Lily Palmer. Davey was walking towards some of his outbuildings when he noticed some items of clothing fluttering in a hedge. Going over to investigate, he found the almost naked body lying in the field. It was just two hours later that Ronald Atwell was arrested at his place of employment. He made a full confession to the killing.

At his trial in Wells, Atwell made a half-hearted attempt to shift some of the blame for his crime onto the dead girl. After they had had a few drinks, they went for a walk together and Lily confessed that she had slept with a man just a few hours beforehand. Atwell claimed that he did little more than kiss her, whereupon Lily took off her clothes and lay down ready for sex. Atwell looked at her, thought of another man being with her so recently and was filled with disgust.

Unable to make love to her, Atwell began to walk away whereupon Lily insulted him and swore at him. He lost his temper and battered her to death. He stated: "I lost my temper and struck her with my fist, either on the mouth or nose. I think I went on hitting her and then put my hands around her throat. The next thing I remember is just kicking her. I came to my senses and realised what I had done."

The jury took just six minutes to return their verdict of guilty.

NAME	Ronald Douglas Atwell
AGE AT EXECUTION	24
DATE OF EXECUTION	Thursday, July 13th, 1950
PLACE OF EXECUTION	Bristol
HANGMAN	Albert Pierrepoint
ASSISTANT	Syd Dernley
DATE OF TRIAL	31st May – 1st June, 1950
LOCATION OF TRIAL	Wells
PRESIDING JUDGE	Mister Justice Oliver
PROSECUTION COUNSEL	Ewen Montague, J.N. Hutchieson
DEFENCE COUNSEL	Cyril Harvey, G.A. Forrest
NUMBER OF VICTIMS	1

VICTIMS DETAILS	
NAME	Lily Irene Palmer
AGE	26
DATE OF MURDER	Saturday, 15th April, 1950
PLACE OF MURDER	Wembdon Fields, Bridgwater, Somerset
METHOD OF KILLING	Battered
RELATIONSHIP TO KILLER	None

IN 1944, FRANCIS Henry Wilson and his wife, Gladys, lived in Shildon. It was at that time that Gladys first met John Walker, who was in the army. Gladys did not have a happy marriage and it was perhaps natural that she should seek solace in the company of Walker. Soon afterwards, the Wilsons moved to Station Road in Brompton and when, in 1947, Walker was demobbed, he went there to lodge with them.

In due course, the domestic arrangements at Station Road, altered. So it was that by 1950, Francis Wilson was sleeping in the small back bedroom of the house, whilst Gladys and John Walker, shared the larger front bedroom. Francis was still occasionally violent towards his wife but now Walker was in a position to offer her protection and comfort, even though he was just five feet tall.

It was Gladys's custom to give her husband 10/- each week for him to spend on himself. On April 29th though, for some reason, she only gave Francis 5/-. And this made him very angry indeed.

Gladys went to the pictures at 8.00pm that same evening, leaving Francis and John Walker alone in the house at Station Road. According to his later statement, Walker then had a conversation with Francis in which the latter referred to the fact that his money was 5/- short and added: "When I get her on her own, I will knock the living daylights out of her."

Gladys returned at 11.00pm. Walker was still up but there was no sign of Francis. This in itself was not unusual. Man and wife did not sleep together, and he often retired before she did.

At 6.30am the following morning, John Walker woke Gladys with a cup of tea and told her that he would have to go away as her husband was lying dead in the kitchen. He then admitted that he had killed Francis when he had threatened to attack Gladys. Some 15 minutes later, Walker left the house and was last seen cycling towards Darlington.

The body of Francis Henry Wilson lay in the small scullery at the back of the kitchen. He had been struck six times with an axe, which lay close by his body. A search was

NAME	John Walker
AGE AT EXECUTION	48
DATE OF EXECUTION	Thursday, 13th July, 1950
PLACE OF EXECUTION	Durham
HANGMAN	Steve Wade
ASSISTANT	Not known
DATE OF TRIAL	22nd June, 1950
LOCATION OF TRIAL	York
PRESIDING JUDGE	Mister Justice Croom-Johnson
PROSECUTION COUNSEL	H.R.B. Shepherd, John M. McLuskey
DEFENCE COUNSEL	Harvey Robson
NUMBER OF VICTIMS	1

VICTIMS DETAILS	
NAME	Francis Henry Wilson
AGE	45
DATE OF MURDER	Saturday, 29th April, 1950
PLACE OF MURDER	Station Road, Brompton, near Northallerton
METHOD OF KILLING	Battered
RELATIONSHIP TO KILLER	None

now launched for Walker, and he was picked up later the same day, in Bishop Auckland.

John Walker never denied being the killer of Francis Wilson, claiming that he had struck out only to protect Gladys from her husband's violence. The story was undoubtedly true, but it did nothing to save him from the hangman's rope.

THE DISCOVERY OF the bodies of two children in a pushchair on wasteland at Bognor Regis led police to the address of their parents, in Grange Close, New Malden. Here they found a third body, that of Doris Maude Price. Her husband, Albert, was missing and a full-scale search was organised for him.

Albert Price had in fact returned to London, where he was picked up on June 13th. He readily admitted that he had killed his wife and children. Price explained that he had had severe financial problems, which had started when he had incurred gambling debts in May, 1948. Ever since then things had grown worse and worse until eventually, things got so bad that he decided the only way out was to kill his wife, his family and himself.

On June 3rd, whilst Doris was asleep in their prefabricated home, he had taken an axe and battered her to death. The next day he had dressed both the children and taken them to Bognor Regis on the Sussex coast. It was there, on the Monday that he had given them sleeping pills mixed in with their food and once they were unconscious, had suffocated them. His intention then had been to return to London and kill himself, but at this late stage his nerve had failed him.

Price's only hope lay in a verdict of guilty but insane. Mr Du Cann argued eloquently on his behalf but in the event, the best he obtained was guilty but with a strong recommendation to mercy. An appeal failed and permission was refused for Price to appeal to the House of Lords. The final hope passed when it was announced, on August 15th, that the Home Secretary saw no grounds on which he could recommend a reprieve. Albert Price was executed the following day.

NAME	Albert Price
AGE AT EXECUTION	32
DATE OF EXECUTION	Wednesday, 16th August, 1950
PLACE OF EXECUTION	Wandsworth
HANGMAN	Albert Pierrepoint
ASSISTANT	Harry Allen
DATE OF TRIAL	12th July, 1950
LOCATION OF TRIAL	Old Bailey
PRESIDING JUDGE	Mister Justice Parker
PROSECUTION COUNSEL	Christmas Humphreys
DEFENCE COUNSEL	C.G.L. Du Cann, Alan Garfitt
NUMBER OF VICTIMS	3

VICTIMS DETAILS

NAME	Doris Maude Price
AGE	26
DATE OF MURDER	Saturday, 3rd June, 1950
PLACE OF MURDER	20 Grange Close, New Malden
METHOD OF KILLING	Battered
RELATIONSHIP TO KILLER	Wife

NAMES	Jennifer Valerie Price; Maureen Ann Price
AGES	3; 18 months
DATE OF MURDER	Monday, 5th June, 1950
PLACE OF MURDER	Wasteland at Fish Lane, Bognor Regis
METHOD OF KILLING	Asphyxiated; asphyxiated
RELATIONSHIP TO KILLER	Daughter; daughter

PATRICK CLARK WAS enjoying a quiet drink in the pub at 12–14 Orkney Street on July 7th, when four men walked in and one demanded to know what he was looking at. Whatever answer Patrick gave wasn't what the men were looking for and he was punched in the eye and a broken glass drawn across his face. Though Patrick didn't know who had just attacked him, one of his friends, Michael McKibbens knew that two of his assailants were brothers – Paul Christopher Harris and Claude Milford Harris.

The other two men with the Harris brothers were Walter Drennan and Francis Millar. Drennan had something in particular on his mind, though. His sister, Margaret Murray, who was married to another Francis, was having some trouble with her husband. He had fractured her arm with a beer bottle on June 30th and now Drennan determined that it was time to sort him out.

The four men walked to Margaret's house at 151 Neptune Street to find Murray with Richard Boyle and Martin Dunleavy. Immediately it was clear that Drennan was looking for trouble with Murray but fortunately Boyle managed to manhandle Drennan out of the house before any fighting could start. Once outside a bottle, wielded almost certainly by Drennan, rendered Boyle semi-conscious.

There were witnesses to what happened next. Janet Hogg was looking out of her window at 82 Kintra Street when she saw men struggling at the back of Neptune Street. One man was on the floor and the others were kicking him. Janet saw the injured man climb to his feet and stagger off.

That staggering man, Martin Dunleavy, was next seen by John Auld who lived at 171 Neptune Street. Just before this he had seen four men, all with bottles in their pockets, go into number 151.

Dunleavy had a deep, jagged wound in his neck, caused by broken glass, and though he was taken to hospital, he died the same day. Witnesses were spoken to and all four of the assailants were arrested and charged with murder.

Before the case came to court, the charges against 28-year-old Francis Millar were

NAME	Paul Christopher Harris
AGE AT EXECUTION	28
DATE OF EXECUTION	Monday, 30th October, 1950
PLACE OF EXECUTION	Glasgow, Barlinnie
HANGMAN	Albert Pierrepoint
ASSISTANT	Not known
DATE OF TRIAL	6th September – 9th September, 1950
LOCATION OF TRIAL	Glasgow
PRESIDING JUDGE	Lord Justice Thomson
PROSECUTION COUNSEL	Harold Leslie
DEFENCE COUNSEL	J.R. Philip
NUMBER OF VICTIMS	1

VICTIMS DETAILS	
NAME	Martin Dunleavy
AGE	38
DATE OF MURDER	Friday, 7th July, 1950
PLACE OF MURDER	151 Neptune Street, Glasgow
METHOD OF KILLING	Stabbed
RELATIONSHIP TO KILLER	None

dropped. The remaining three were sent for trial and after a four-day hearing, Drennan was found not guilty whilst the Harris brothers were sentenced to death.

The original execution date was set for September 30th but cancelled when an appeal was entered. That appeal was heard over two days, October 11th and 12th, after which both death sentences were confirmed. Only now did Paul Harris admit that he alone had struck the fatal blow. As a result, the execution of Claude Milford Harris was cancelled 36 hours before it was due to take place and temporarily put back until November 6th.

Paul Harris was hanged on October 30th and before his brother's sentence could be carried out on the 6th, the confession Paul had made resulted in Claude's reprieve.

1950

PATRICK TURNAGE WAS a man who feared jail more than he feared the hangman's noose.

Turnage had been born in India but now lived in South Africa. A merchant seaman, his ship, the S.S. Absalom, docked at Billingham Reach on the River Tees on July 22nd, 1950. Later that same day, Turnage caught a bus into town and discreetly asked the conductor if he knew where he could obtain the company of a certain type of lady. The conductor suggested he try the Victoria Hotel in Joseph Street.

Although Julia Beesley was 78 years old, she still plied her trade as a prostitute and, after visiting a number of pubs in the town, on the look-out for possible clients, Julia finally arrived at the Victoria Hotel, where she met Turnage. He too had had little success thus far and by now he had consumed quite a lot of alcohol and was rather the worse for wear. The two got into conversation and Turnage eventually suggested that they go back to his ship where they could have a few more drinks before discussing further business transactions. Turnage and Julia took a taxi back to his ship and as he paid the fare, Turnage remarked to the driver that he needn't wait, the woman would be staying all night.

It is standard practice to place one member of the crew on watch duty whilst ships are in dock and the watchman on the Absalom saw the taxi pull away. He watched as the couple moved towards the ship and then saw them stop. Raised voices were heard, though he couldn't distinguish what was said. Finally, the woman stormed off in the direction the taxi had just gone. Turnage watched her for a moment, then he went after her.

One hour after this episode, Turnage was walking back onto the Absalom. He was alone. The watchman asked him if he had caught up with the woman and Turnage said he hadn't. This didn't seem to be the whole truth though, for Turnage was carrying a woman's handbag.

Robert Beesley grew concerned when his mother failed to return home and at 11.00am the following morning, he reported

NAME	Patrick Turnage
AGE AT EXECUTION	31
DATE OF EXECUTION	Tuesday, 14th November, 1950
PLACE OF EXECUTION	Durham
HANGMAN	Steve Wade
ASSISTANT	Syd Dearnley
DATE OF TRIAL	26th October, 1950
LOCATION OF TRIAL	Durham
PRESIDING JUDGE	Mister Justice Hallett
PROSECUTION COUNSEL	Not known
DEFENCE COUNSEL	Herbert Shepherd
NUMBER OF VICTIMS	1

VICTIMS DETAILS	
NAME	Julia Beesley
AGE	78
DATE OF MURDER	Saturday, 22nd July, 1950
PLACE OF MURDER	Northborough Road, Stockton-on-Tees
METHOD OF KILLING	Strangled
RELATIONSHIP TO KILLER	None

her missing to the police. Her body was found at 2.00pm that afternoon by John Walker, a chargehand navvy. Walker had been cycling home when something caught his eye in a ditch. It was the strangled body of Julia Beesley.

Julia had been seen in the company of a seaman and found close to the docks. Once the watchman and taxi driver had been interviewed, the police knew that Patrick Turnage was the man they were looking for. He was arrested at 5.30pm on the same day the body had been found.

Turnage made no attempt to deny that he had been with Julia and handed over her handbag to the police. He emphatically denied murdering her, though. His story was that they had argued over sex and when he followed her and caught up with her, they had argued again and he had pushed her into the ditch. He had not deliberately strangled her and indeed, the postmortem suggested that death could have been caused by the simple act of tightening the clothing around Julia's neck. It looked extremely unlikely that a murder charge could be made to stick, but nevertheless, Turnage was charged.

On October 26th, 1950, two days before the case was due to come to court, Turnage asked to see Detective Chief Inspector Rowell, who had investigated the case. When the meeting took place, at Durham prison, Turnage informed Rowell that he wished to plead guilty to the charge of murder. He was advised to see his legal representative and discuss the matter with him.

At a second meeting, Turnage again stated that he wished to plead guilty to murder. He said that he had known what he was doing and that he had also known that Julia was dead when he left her.

When the case came to court, Turnage did plead guilty. The judge informed Turnage that he would still call the Chief Inspector to give evidence over what had occurred in the previous 48 hours. There was no other evidence and, the plea having now been accepted, Turnage was sentenced to death. The entire proceedings had taken seven minutes.

Patrick Turnage had deliberately chosen to die. He told prison officers that he simply could not face up to 15 years in prison and so had pleaded guilty to murder in order to avoid that fate. On the morning of the execution, the cell door swung open and for a moment there was a flicker of fear and apprehension on Patrick Turnage's face. Then he smiled and stood to face the men who would end his time in jail.

1950

NORMAN GOLDTHORPE HAD a reputation of being a man with a foul temper. He had also known a degree of success with the women in his life, but just lately this appeared to have deserted him. His wife had gone off with a soldier and his mistress, Marguerite Myers had gone back to her husband in Yorkshire.

A night of heavy drinking and brooding on his situation had put Goldthorpe into one of his foulest moods yet and it was then that he decided to go looking for an elderly prostitute he knew – Emma Howe.

Goldthorpe's first port of call was The Great Eastern, a pub that Emma was known to frequent. He was told that she had been in that evening, but had now gone home to Owles Court. Goldthorpe went to the Court but knocked on the wrong door. The neighbour knew Emma and directed Goldthorpe to the correct address. That evening, after having sex with Emma, Goldthorpe strangled her. He left in the early hours of the morning, closing the door quietly, unaware that another neighbour had seen him.

Almost as soon as the body had been found, the police knew who they were looking for. Goldthorpe had been seen arriving and leaving and was arrested very shortly afterwards, in the same pub, The Great Eastern.

The trial took place before Mister Justice Hilbery. Goldthorpe's defence was one of insanity and after hearing the evidence, the jury retired. They sent out a request for tea, whereupon the judge had them brought back into court and gave them a severe dressing down, telling them that there were no facilities for providing refreshments. Whether the lack of tea had any influence is not known, but the jury took only eight minutes to return a guilty verdict.

The execution of Goldthorpe was a story in itself. Syd Dernley, the assistant hangman, took a book of ribald verses along to the prison and the night before the execution, he, the chief hangman Kirk and a prison guard were exchanging stories and laughing loudly. It was only when someone knocked on the floor that they realised they were above the

NAME	Norman Goldthorpe
AGE AT EXECUTION	40
DATE OF EXECUTION	Friday, 24th November, 1950
PLACE OF EXECUTION	Norwich
HANGMAN	Harry Kirk
ASSISTANT	Syd Dernley
DATE OF TRIAL	11th October, 1950
LOCATION OF TRIAL	Norwich
PRESIDING JUDGE	Mister Justice Hilbery
PROSECUTION COUNSEL	Gerald Howard, A.G. Friend
DEFENCE COUNSEL	F.T. Alpe
NUMBER OF VICTIMS	1

VICTIMS DETAILS	
NAME	Emma Howe
AGE	66
DATE OF MURDER	Friday, 11th August, 1950
PLACE OF MURDER	2 Owles Court, Row 52, Yarmouth
METHOD OF KILLING	Strangled
RELATIONSHIP TO KILLER	None

condemned cell! Goldthorpe seems not to have been too disturbed though, as they later heard him singing.

This hanging was the one and only time that Harry Kirk was the chief hangman. After the drop was operated, Goldthorpe was heard gurgling in the pit. The terrible sounds lasted between 30 seconds to minute, though when the doctor examined Goldthorpe, no heartbeat could be detected.

After the body was taken down it was discovered that the noose was not tight about the neck as it should have been. The hood had caught in the eyelet of the noose and prevented it from tightening. It was to be Harry Kirk's first and last mistake. He was never called on to officiate at a hanging again.

ELIZA WOOD LIVED in Knott Street, Oldham and for some 18 months, had been involved with James Henry Corbitt, who had once lodged with her mother, but who was now living in Portland Street, Manchester.

On the night of August 19th, Corbitt and Eliza booked a room at the Prince of Wales Hotel. They went up at 11.30pm and at a few minutes after midnight, the licensee, Alfred Egan, heard a loud bump from the room they shared. Egan went to see what the problem was and Corbitt shouted from behind the door that everything was all right, he had simply fallen out of bed.

Corbitt left the hotel early next morning and some time afterwards, a cleaner opened the door to tidy the room and discovered the naked and strangled body of Eliza Wood, with the word 'whore' inked onto her forehead. Corbitt was arrested on August 21st.

When interviewed, Corbitt said that he did not know why he had killed Eliza. He claimed that she had started shouting at him and he grabbed her by the throat. After that he tied a bootlace around her neck to finish her off.

A diary found in Corbitt's possession showed that his relationship with Eliza had been a difficult one. An entry for March 11th said that he had had a date with her at 8.30pm, but she had failed to turn up. By April 29th, Eliza was again confessing undying love but they argued on July 22nd and there were hints that Corbitt was contemplating killing her.

An entry for July 23rd showed that the contemplation had become concrete. The

NAME	James Henry Corbitt
AGE AT EXECUTION	37
DATE OF EXECUTION	Tuesday, 28th November, 1950
PLACE OF EXECUTION	Manchester
HANGMAN	Albert Pierrepoint
ASSISTANT	Not known
DATE OF TRIAL	6th November, 1950
LOCATION OF TRIAL	Liverpool
PRESIDING JUDGE	Mister Justice Lynskey
PROSECUTION COUNSEL	Edward Wooll
DEFENCE COUNSEL	E. Rowson
NUMBER OF VICTIMS	1

VICTIMS DETAILS

NAME	Eliza Wood
AGE	36
DATE OF MURDER	Sunday, 20th August, 1950
PLACE OF MURDER	Room 7, Prince of Wales Hotel, Stamford Street, Ashton-under-Lyne
METHOD OF KILLING	Strangled
RELATIONSHIP TO KILLER	Girlfriend

entry for that date showed that Corbitt had decided to kill Eliza and was merely trying to decide how to do it. Just a few weeks later, those thoughts would be put into practice and Eliza would meet her death at his hands.

At the trial, it became clear that Corbitt had tried to give Eliza up, believing that she was involved with another man, named Tommy. He had said he would give her another chance if she gave Tommy up, but she had not changed and he had decided to kill her. He was found guilty and sentenced to death.

Corbitt died at the hands of Albert Pierrepoint, a man known to him. From a popular song at the time, they had nicknamed each other 'Tish' and 'Tosh'. On the morning of the execution, the two men stood briefly in the condemned cell and exchanged greetings before Pierrepoint ended the life of a man he had called a friend.

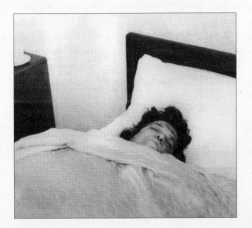

The body of Eliza Wood lying in bed in the Prince of Wales Hotel. The word 'whore' is written on her forehead.

FREDERICK GEORGE WORTH came home for lunch on September 20th, and at that time his mother, Ethel, was alive and well. She was also still alive at 2.00pm when Mr Clark passed her house and saw her standing at her window. When Frederick returned home at 5.30pm, though, he was surprised not to be greeted by his mother as he entered. Then he discovered why. Ethel Worth was slumped in a chair by her sitting-room fire, her face covered by a woollen garment. She had first been battered with some blunt instrument and then strangled.

One of the first people the police spoke to in the course of their investigations was Edward Woodfield. His sister and brother lived next door to Ethel and Edward had been seen in Hughenden Road on the morning of the murder. At first, Edward claimed that he had visited the Labour Exchange that morning, but when told that he had been seen, he broke down and confessed to the murder.

Edward explained that he had thought he might be able to get some money from Ethel. That July she had lent him £2 and the week before, she had been generous enough to supply him with another £1. Before he visited Ethel he picked up a lemonade bottle and when she answered the door, said that he had come to repay what he owed her. Once inside he had battered her with the bottle. She had fallen into her chair and begged him not to hurt her, whereupon an impulse to strangle her came over him. After Ethel was dead, Edward stole some money, a watch and a pair of field glasses, which he buried near his own back door.

At the trial, the prosecution called medical evidence showing that more than one blow had been struck and suggested that a frenzied attack had taken place. The defence called witnesses who confirmed that Edward was a mild-mannered man who never lost his temper and since he had by his own admission killed Ethel Worth, he must therefore have been insane at the time. As confirmation of this, it was shown that Edward had suffered from a blood clot on his brain in 1947.

The jury took almost three hours to finally decide that Edward Woodfield was guilty of

NAME	Edward Isaac Woodfield
AGE AT EXECUTION	49
DATE OF EXECUTION	Thursday, 14th December, 1950
PLACE OF EXECUTION	Bristol
HANGMAN	Not known
ASSISTANT	Not known
DATE OF TRIAL	22nd November – 23rd November, 1950
LOCATION OF TRIAL	Bristol
PRESIDING JUDGE	Mister Justice Devlin
PROSECUTION COUNSEL	John Maude, C.M. Lavington
DEFENCE COUNSEL	J.D. Casswell, Kenneth Bain
NUMBER OF VICTIMS	1

VICTIMS DETAILS	
NAME	Ethel Merinda Worth
AGE	65
DATE OF MURDER	Wednesday, 20th September, 1950
PLACE OF MURDER	1 Hughenden Road, Horfield, Bristol
METHOD OF KILLING	Battered/strangled
RELATIONSHIP TO KILLER	None

murder, placing great store on the suggestion that since he had tried to hide the evidence he was fully aware of what he was doing and that the crime had therefore been premeditated.

IN THE EARLY hours of July 29th, 1950, two telephone calls to the police reported a woman's body lying in the road. Those reports brought Constable William Kevan, to investigate.

The body lay in Prospecthill Road and it seemed obvious that she had been the victim of a hit and run, but Constable Kevan was suspicious. There was no broken glass and the skidmark pattern seemed to have been made by vehicles travelling in the opposite direction. When the subsequent postmortem proved that the woman's legs had not been broken, the police knew they were looking at a case of murder.

Reports on the victim caused Mrs Johnston to come forward. A friend of hers had asked her to look after her young baby but had not returned home. This led to an identification for the victim. She was Catherine McCluskey who lived at 239 Nicholson Street and had two children, John Anthony and Patrick Joseph.

Mrs Johnston also mentioned to the investigating officers that Catherine had been involved with one of their colleagues, who was the father of one of her children. Though Mrs Johnston didn't know the officer's full name, she was able to supply a surname: Robertson.

Investigations led to the identification of James Ronald Robertson, a married man. On the night of the murder he had been on the beat with Constable Dugald Moffat who confirmed that at 11.15pm Robertson absented himself and did not return until 1.10am.

Further investigations showed that Robertson drove an Austin saloon car, registration DYS 570, and examinations showed damage to the underside of this vehicle. Bloodstains and human hair were found adhering to the body of the car and the exhaust pipe was damaged. Furthermore, it was shown that the car was stolen and bore false number plates.

Robertson was charged not only with murder but with stealing a car from James Burns Cameron, on May 31st, and with stealing car registration books from a garage at 147 Cumberland Street, owned by

NAME	James Ronald Robertson
AGE AT EXECUTION	33
DATE OF EXECUTION	Saturday, 16th December, 1950
PLACE OF EXECUTION	Glasgow, Barlinnie
HANGMAN	Albert Pierrepoint
ASSISTANT	Not known
DATE OF TRIAL	6th November – 13th November, 1950
LOCATION OF TRIAL	Glasgow
PRESIDING JUDGE	Lord Justice Keith
PROSECUTION COUNSEL	Harold Leslie
DEFENCE COUNSEL	John Cameron
NUMBER OF VICTIMS	1

VICTIMS DETAILS	
NAME	Catherine McCluskey
AGE	40
DATE OF MURDER	Friday, 28th July, 1950
PLACE OF MURDER	Prospecthill Road, Glasgow
METHOD OF KILLING	Battered
RELATIONSHIP TO KILLER	Girlfriend

Alexander Mitchell. The prosecution case was that Robertson had rendered Catherine unconscious by striking her, and then running over her, twice, with the car.

Robertson denied all the charges. He claimed that he had found the car abandoned on some waste ground and on a different day had found the log books in a Gorbals backyard. As for Catherine McCluskey, he admitted he had seen her on the night she died but said that they had argued and that he had abandoned her in Prospecthill Road. Driving on, he changed his mind and reversed to pick her up again. He hit something and found to his horror that he had accidentally reversed into Catherine. Therefore he had killed her, but it was an accident.

The jury took 65 minutes to decide that Robertson was lying and his execution was set for December 4th. This was cancelled when Robertson appealed but once that was lost, on November 28th, a new date was set.

1950

ON JULY 9TH, 1950, the body of Ruth Massey was found on some wasteland on Springfield Road, Leeds. Her throat had been cut and an immediate murder investigation was launched.

Police soon discovered that Ruth had been seen in the Brougham Arms Hotel at around 10.00pm the previous night, and that she had been in the company of a man named Nicholas Persoulious Crosby. In due course he was picked up for questioning, whereupon he claimed to have no knowledge of anything that had happened after he left the hotel. His cousin, Gladys Crosby, told a different story, though. She told police that Nicholas had given her a full account of the events of the previous night, including the killing of Ruth Massey.

Charged with murder, Crosby now told a slightly different story. He admitted that he had been drinking with Ruth, but said that there had also been another man present, who was tall and wore a grey suit. After leaving the Birmingham Arms, the three of them walked to the murder spot where Crosby walked off, leaving the man alone with Ruth.

Crosby further stated that after a few seconds, he heard a scream and upon going back to Ruth, found her with her throat cut. He then walked the other man home! On the strength of this, the defence attempted to suggest that Crosby was shielding someone else – this mysterious grey-suited man. At one stage, the defence counsel, Mr Shepherd, asked Crosby if he had killed Ruth, to which he replied: "To be sure sir I don't know if I did. If I did, I don't remember." The jury were not convinced and returned a guilty verdict.

Under normal circumstances, Crosby would have been executed at Leeds, but that prison was undergoing structural alterations at the time. He was therefore transferred to Manchester, where the sentence was carried out on December 19th, 1950.

NAME Nicholas Persoulious Crosby
AGE AT EXECUTION 22
DATE OF EXECUTION Tuesday, 19th December, 1950
PLACE OF EXECUTION Manchester
HANGMAN Albert Pierrepoint
ASSISTANT Syd Dernley
DATE OF TRIAL 27th November – 29th November, 1950
LOCATION OF TRIAL Leeds
PRESIDING JUDGE Mister Justice Finnemore
PROSECUTION COUNSEL H.B.H. Hylton Foster M.P., Alastair Sharp
DEFENCE COUNSEL H.R.B. Shepherd, Henry C. Scott
NUMBER OF VICTIMS 1

VICTIMS DETAILS

NAME Ruth Massey
AGE 19
DATE OF MURDER Saturday, 8th July, 1950
PLACE OF MURDER Springfield Road, Leeds
METHOD OF KILLING Cut throat
RELATIONSHIP TO KILLER None

WHEN JOHN EDGE returned home from work at 5.30pm on September 6th, 1950, he was surprised to find the door of the public house locked. Eventually he gained entry through a side door and found his mother dead in a chair. Jewellery was missing, as was a total of around £85 in cash.

On September 7th, police officers visited the Apley Industrial Hostel and searched the rooms. In the room belonging to Frank Griffin, they found a bloodstained shirt and a canvas bag with a large number of coins in it. Griffin made a statement saying that this was money he had saved and that the shirt did not belong to him.

It was soon discovered that Griffin had recently lost his job and had been borrowing money. It was also shown that on the night of the murder, he had redeemed a debt, offering William Henry Perry 5/- interest for his trouble, but before more evidence could be obtained Griffin left his lodgings, claiming that he was going to Birmingham. In fact, Griffin travelled to Ironbridge, where he booked into the Tontine Hotel, giving the name Jenkins.

On Sunday, September 10th the hotel landlord became suspicious of his new guest, and telephoned the police. Mister 'Jenkins' was asked if he had ever been to the Queen's Head Inn. At that, Griffin put his head into his hands and sobbed: "It was not worth it. I did not get much. She fell down." He then went on to describe how he had hit Jane with a pint mug before stealing what money he could find. Later he would withdraw part of that statement and say that he had not hit Jane at all.

Griffin made a statement in which he claimed that he had gone into the pub at 2.30pm. After having two pints and ordering a third, Jane had asked him if he would prefer a cup of tea instead. Griffin agreed and followed Jane through to the back but on his way, he saw the money in the till and helped himself. Jane caught Griffin in the act of stealing whereupon he pushed her out of the way. She fell back, catching her head on the corner of a crate and when he tried to lift her, fell a second time.

It was true that hairs matching Jane's were

NAME	Frank Griffin
AGE AT EXECUTION	40
DATE OF EXECUTION	Thursday, 4th January, 1951
PLACE OF EXECUTION	Shrewsbury
HANGMAN	Not known
ASSISTANT	Not known
DATE OF TRIAL	20th November – 22nd November, 1950
LOCATION OF TRIAL	Shrewsbury
PRESIDING JUDGE	Mister Justice Cassels
PROSECUTION COUNSEL	John Foster, W. Field Hunt
DEFENCE COUNSEL	A.J. Long, G.K. Mynett
NUMBER OF VICTIMS	1

VICTIMS DETAILS	
NAME	Jane Edge
AGE	74
DATE OF MURDER	Wednesday, 6th September, 1950
PLACE OF MURDER	Queen's Head Inn, Ketley, Shropshire
METHOD OF KILLING	Battered
RELATIONSHIP TO KILLER	None

found on the corner of a crate of bottles and Professor Webster gave evidence that Jane's injuries would have been unlikely to cause death in a normal healthy person.

The jury were out for almost two hours before returning and asking for clarification between murder and manslaughter. After receiving this from Mister Justice Cassels, they took a further 30 minutes before deciding that Griffin was guilty of murder. After losing his appeal on December 19th, Frank Griffin became the first man since 1923 to be hanged at Shrewsbury.

NENAD KOVACEVIC AND Radomir Djorovic were both Yugoslavian, and had been on opposite sides in the Second World War. Whilst Nenad had fought with the Resistance and had suffered from the loss of his father, two brothers and three sisters, Radomir had been a supporter of the Nazis. Both had come to England after the war and worked at the Star Paper Mill, in Blackburn.

On Sunday, October 8th, 1950, they had been invited for dinner to the house of Ankiea Mileusnic and her sister, two more Yugoslavians, at Edenfield. As they took a short cut along the railway line it came on to rain and they took shelter in a worker's hut close to Ewood Bridge.

Early the following morning, a gang of workers checked inside that hut and found a battered body with all forms of identification removed. The foreman, William Crook, telephoned the police and their investigations soon revealed that a Yugoslav named Djorovic had failed to turn up for a dinner appointment.

Further checking revealed that he had been in the company of Kovacevic, who had gone missing from his lodgings in Caton Street. It transpired that Nenad had asked about coach times to London and been told that he could not catch one direct from Blackburn, but would have to go to Blackpool first. In due course, it was discovered that he had boarded the Blackpool to London coach and this was intercepted at Cannock.

Nenad at first denied any involvement in the death of Radomir but when he was searched, property from the dead man was found and Nenad then admitted his part in the crime. According to Nenad, the two men had sheltered from the rain and talk had moved to the war. Nenad had been upset by the memories of the family he had lost and Radomir mocked this, finally challenging him to fight. During the struggle that followed, Nenad had reached out, seized an axe and battered Radomir to death.

At the trial, the prosecution tried to suggest that the crime had been premeditated, since Nenad had stolen Radomir's coat and property including a watch, a wallet and some cash. The defence

NAME	Nenad Kovacevic
AGE AT EXECUTION	29
DATE OF EXECUTION	Friday, 26th January, 1951
PLACE OF EXECUTION	Manchester
HANGMAN	Albert Pierrepoint
ASSISTANT	Harry Allen
DATE OF TRIAL	7th December, 1950
LOCATION OF TRIAL	Manchester
PRESIDING JUDGE	Mister Justice Jones
PROSECUTION COUNSEL	H.I. Nelson
DEFENCE COUNSEL	Kenneth Burke
NUMBER OF VICTIMS	1

VICTIMS DETAILS	
NAME	Radomir Djorovic
AGE	26
DATE OF MURDER	Sunday, 8th November, 1950
PLACE OF MURDER	Workman's hut on railway, Ewood Bridge, near Ramsbottom
METHOD OF KILLING	Battered
RELATIONSHIP TO KILLER	None

suggested that Nenad had taken the coat just to protect himself from the rain and the other items had been in the pockets. Nenad had been sorely provoked and should be only guilty of manslaughter.

The jury took 85 minutes to decide that Nenad was guilty of murder. An appeal failed, as did one from the exiled King of Yugoslavia, King Peter, who asked for clemency for his countryman. None of this moved the authorities and Nenad was executed on January 26th. He fought all the way to the gallows.

ALTHOUGH WILLIAM WATKINS was a married man, he had been associating for five years with a woman named Florence May White and they already had a child which was, by 1951, three years old. Florence was now pregnant with their second child and she eventually gave birth to a healthy baby boy.

In the early hours of January 21st, William took the baby in order to give him a bath. Not long afterwards he returned to Florence and informed her that as he was washing the child, he had slipped, fallen into the water and died. William did not, however, report the matter to the police.

When the matter did finally come to the attention of the police, they called at Watkins's rooms and found the child's body, head down in a pillow case. Watkins had no satisfactory answers to any of the questions he was asked. He could not explain how, if the matter had been an accident, the child had come to be in a pillowcase. Neither could he explain why he had told friends and neighbours, who knew of Florence's condition, that a doctor and a midwife had been called to the birth when both those statements were untrue and finally, Watkins could not explain why he had apparently taken no steps to revive the baby when it 'fell' into the water.

William Watkins was extremely deaf and at his trial, the charge had to be repeated to him by a warder standing in the dock. After hearing the evidence, the jury retired for two and a half hours before finding Watkins guilty.

NAME	William Arthur Watkins
AGE AT EXECUTION	49
DATE OF EXECUTION	Tuesday, 3rd April, 1951
PLACE OF EXECUTION	Birmingham
HANGMAN	Albert Pierrepoint
ASSISTANT	Harry Allen
DATE OF TRIAL	15th March – 16th March, 1951
LOCATION OF TRIAL	Birmingham
PRESIDING JUDGE	Mister Justice Finnemore
PROSECUTION COUNSEL	R.T. Paget
DEFENCE COUNSEL	Not known
NUMBER OF VICTIMS	1

VICTIMS DETAILS	
NAME	Unnamed male child
AGE	Newborn
DATE OF MURDER	Sunday, 21st January, 1951
PLACE OF MURDER	6 Back 69 Clifton Road, Balsall Heath, Birmingham
METHOD OF KILLING	Drowned
RELATIONSHIP TO KILLER	Son

1950

FREDERICK GOSLING, KNOWN as Old Gossy, lived over his shop at Clay Corner and rumour had it that he had money hidden on the premises. What was certain was that every time he needed to change a note he would pop into the back of the shop, reappearing with the correct money.

On January 11th, 1951, police were called to Old Gossy's shop. The old man had been attacked by two men who left when a group of schoolgirls came in. Gossy could not give much of a description and the police marked it down as a robbery attempt.

At 9.00am the next morning, the police were called back to Gossy's shop, by the milkman. This time Gossy lay on his bed, bound and gagged. A bruise over one eye showed that he had also been hit. Gossy had been smothered to death and some £60 had been taken.

A tip-off revealed that the Brown brothers were involved in the robbery. The first to be picked up was 27-year-old Frederick Brown who spoke readily of the events of the 11th but denied being involved in the murder on the 12th. He did give officers enough information for them to pick up his brother Joseph and Edward Charles Smith, a friend. All three men were held on charges of assault, but subsequently the charge against Edward Smith and Joseph Brown was changed to one of murder.

Frederick Brown's story was that all three of them had gone to the shop, with the intention of robbing it, on January 11th. Frederick had stayed in the car whilst the other two men went inside the shop. Their plan was that they would buy something and give Gossy a note. When he went into the back to get change, one of them would lock the door whilst the other followed Gossy and found the money. However, Frederick stated, in their haste they forgot to lock the shop door. When the bunch of schoolgirls came in, they ran.

Frederick continued by saying that the next day he had seen his brother and Smith. They told him that they had gone back to the shop and got away with the money but they had had to tie the old man up. An identification parade was organised, but 12

NAMES	Joseph Brown; Edward Charles Smith
AGES AT EXECUTION	33; 33
DATE OF EXECUTION	Wednesday, 25th April, 1951
PLACE OF EXECUTION	Wandsworth
HANGMAN	Albert Pierrepoint
ASSISTANTS	Harry Allen, Syd Dernley
DATE OF TRIAL	1st March – 5th March, 1951
LOCATION OF TRIAL	Kingston, Surrey
PRESIDING JUDGE	Mister Justice Parker
PROSECUTION COUNSEL	Gerald Howard M.P., J.S. Bass
DEFENCE COUNSEL	A. Marlowe M.P., H.J. Hamblen; Derek Curtis Bennett, James Burge
NUMBER OF VICTIMS	1

VICTIMS DETAILS	
NAME	Frederick Gosling
AGE	79
DATE OF MURDER	Friday, 12th January, 1951
PLACE OF MURDER	Clay Corner, Chertsey
METHOD OF KILLING	Asphyxiated
RELATIONSHIP TO KILLERS	None; none

people who were around on the day of the murder, failed to pick out either of the accused. Despite this, Edward Smith and Joseph Brown were both found guilty and sentenced to death.

Smith showed no fear of the gallows. On the morning of his execution, his hands were pinioned behind his back and one of the assistant hangmen, Syd Dearnley took hold of his arm to lead him to the execution chamber. Smith pulled away from him and said, "Leave me alone – I'll walk on my own."

ALICE ROBERTS WAS a widow, living in the quiet seaside resort of Worthing, just up the coast from Brighton, in Sussex. Living with her was her lodger, James Virrels, a labourer, and in due course, something more substantial sprang up between them and marriage was spoken about.

On Monday, January 29th, 1951, Virrels went to work as usual but returned home at 11.45am. Soon after he had entered the house, neighbours heard a loud scream, but presumed that this was one of the children playing and took no action.

Soon afterwards, Virrels was seen leaving Kingsland Road. He walked to a nearby pub and, shaking somewhat, ordered a double rum for himself. After finishing his drink, Virrels carried on to the house of his brother, at 9 Downlands Avenue. When he arrived, Virrels was still very pale and rather nervous. It was then that he announced to his sister-in-law: "I have committed murder. I have done her in."

Virrels went on to explain that when he had returned home for lunch, Alice and he had argued and she had come for him with a dagger in her hand. In the struggle that followed, Virrels managed to get the knife away from Kate, and then used it on her. Still not satisfied with his work, he had then taken an axe and bludgeoned her to death with it. When the police surgeon examined the body, he found no fewer that 40 separate stab wounds and Virrels was charged with murder.

Virrels's defence was that he had acted in self defence but the level of violence used made this argument a very weak one, and the jury had no difficulty in deciding that this was a case of murder.

NAME	James Virrels
AGE AT EXECUTION	56
DATE OF EXECUTION	Thursday, 26th April, 1951
PLACE OF EXECUTION	Wandsworth
HANGMAN	Albert Pierrepoint
ASSISTANT	Syd Dernley
DATE OF TRIAL	12th March – 13th March, 1951
LOCATION OF TRIAL	Lewes
PRESIDING JUDGE	Mister Justice Parker
PROSECUTION COUNSEL	Anthony Marlowe, Malcolm Morris
DEFENCE COUNSEL	Derek Curtis Bennett, Stanley Rees
NUMBER OF VICTIMS	1

VICTIMS DETAILS

NAME	Alice Kate Roberts
AGE	40
DATE OF MURDER	Monday, 29th January, 1951
PLACE OF MURDER	56 Kingsland Road, Broadwater, Worthing
METHOD OF KILLING	Stabbed/battered
RELATIONSHIP TO KILLER	None/girlfriend

TEN-YEAR-OLD ALAN Blackley was a helpful boy and was in the habit of calling on 50-year-old Alice Morgan after school, to see if she wanted him to run any errands for her. He paid such a visit at 4.30pm on Friday, February 2nd, 1951, but saw Alice on her settee, covered by a blanket. Thinking she was asleep, Alan left quietly without disturbing her.

Alice's next visitor was Thomas Brougham, a postman, who called three times on the Saturday to deliver a registered parcel. His third call was just after noon and, told by a neighbour that Alice was in, Brougham tried the door, found it unlocked and walked gingerly inside. Alice was still on the settee but Thomas Brougham tried to rouse her and found to his horror that she was dead. A silk stocking was tied around her neck, and there were facial injuries.

The man responsible for Alice's death was soon traced and spoken to by the police at 11.30pm on February 3rd. James Inglis lived in Great Passage Street, Hull, and had known Alice for two weeks. He came to the attention of the police when he attacked his landlady, Amy Gray. She required eight stitches in a face wound and when interviewed, Inglis mentioned that he had killed a woman in Cambridge Street.

Inglis and Alice had been seen together, in two public houses, on the night of February 1st, and had been reported as leaving together at some time between 7.00pm and 8.00pm. Alice had been complaining of a pain in her shoulder. Inglis, though, was back at the pub at about 9.10pm saying Alice was not well and he had put her to bed. He admitted to the police, however, that in the intervening period, he had argued with Alice and had struck out at her. Inglis went on to say that the next thing he knew was that Alice was dead, so he covered her with a coat and left. Ever since he had been unable to sleep and had constantly seen Alice's "bloody face".

Once again the defence was one of insanity. Inglis's maternal grandmother had died in a mental hospital so there was a history of insanity in the family, and in 1945, Inglis had been discharged from the army, having diagnosed as suffering from a

psychopathic personality and spending three months in Banstead hospital as a result.

After a two-day trial, the conclusion that the jury reached was that Inglis was not insane and was therefore guilty of murder.

NAME	James Inglis
AGE AT EXECUTION	29
DATE OF EXECUTION	Tuesday, 8th May, 1951
PLACE OF EXECUTION	Manchester
HANGMAN	Not known
ASSISTANT	Not known
DATE OF TRIAL	19th April – 20th April, 1951
LOCATION OF TRIAL	Leeds
PRESIDING JUDGE	Mister Justice Ormerod
PROSECUTION COUNSEL	H.R.B. Shepherd
DEFENCE COUNSEL	Raymond Hinchcliffe
NUMBER OF VICTIMS	1

VICTIMS DETAILS	
NAME	Alice Morgan
AGE	50
DATE OF MURDER	Thursday, 1st February, 1951
PLACE OF MURDER	Eton Terrace, Cambridge Street, Hull
METHOD OF KILLING	Battered/strangled
RELATIONSHIP TO KILLER	None

EIGHT-YEAR-OLD Irene Shaughnessy must have thought her father's memory was failing. No sooner had she returned from one errand than he sent her on another. Starting with the purchase of a stamp, little Irene was sent out a total of four times to make separate purchases. What she could not know was that her father, William, was taking the opportunity to clear up the mess he had made when he had murdered his wife, and to hide the body in a cupboard.

That night, William took his son, Ronald, and his daughter Joyce, out to several public houses in order to celebrate a visit from his brother. The following day, William strangled Joyce and, leaving her body on a bed, took the rest of his family off to London whilst he decided what to do.

In all, William had six children. His eldest daughter, Zena Knight, was a married woman, and Joyce of course was now dead, but now William was in the capital with Ronald, Shirley, Billy and Irene. The next day, 16-year-old Ronald was allowed to return home. It was he who found his sister's body and contacted the police and they soon discovered Marie's corpse, still hidden in the cupboard underneath the stairs.

Although Ronald assisted the police in their inquiries, telling them what had happened after the family had left the house, it was not until December 23rd that William was seen in Gatcombe Avenue, and arrested. He denied any involvement in the death of either his wife or daughter.

As is the custom, at his trial, Shaughnessy faced only one charge, that of the murder of his wife. He claimed that he had returned home and found her dead and had hidden the body and sent Irene out a number of times, so that she would not be distressed at the sight. After a trial lasting four days, the jury took one hour and 40 minutes, which included a break for lunch, to decide that it had been William's hand that had been responsible for Marie's death. The murder of Joyce Shaughnessy was allowed to remain on file.

NAME William Edward Shaughnessy
AGE AT EXECUTION 48
DATE OF EXECUTION Wednesday, 9th May, 1951
PLACE OF EXECUTION Winchester
HANGMAN Not known
ASSISTANT Not known
DATE OF TRIAL 9th March – 13th March, 1951
LOCATION OF TRIAL Winchester
PRESIDING JUDGE Mister Justice Byrne
PROSECUTION COUNSEL J. Scott Henderson, Robert Hughes
DEFENCE COUNSEL E.E.S. Montagu, Norman Broderick
NUMBER OF VICTIMS 2

VICTIMS DETAILS

NAMES Marie Alexine Shaughnessy; Joyce Shaughnessy
AGES 46; 20
DATE OF MURDER Monday, 18th December, 1950; Tuesday, 19th December, 1950
PLACE OF MURDER 319 Arundel Street, Portsmouth
METHOD OF KILLING Battered/strangled; strangled
RELATIONSHIP TO KILLER Wife; daughter

WALTER WYLD, AN ex-Rugby League player, had an arrangement with his neighbour, Mrs Ruby. If he ever failed to appear by lunchtime, she was to check that he was all right. So, when Walter failed to show himself on January 28th, Mrs Ruby looked through his kitchen window. Walter's body lay on the floor. He had been battered about the head and stabbed, most probably by means of a bayonet.

It was thought that the motive for the crime was robbery, although apparently nothing had been taken and police officers found a hidden cache of money, containing £73 in notes.

A witness was soon found who reported that he had seen a man outside Walter's house, early on the Sunday morning. The description fitted someone known to Walter Wyld: John Dand.

Wyld had once lent Dand's wife £3, and although this had been repaid, Dand had subsequently borrowed it again and Walter was now pressing him for repayment as his rent was due and he needed the money back. Further investigations showed that Dand had spent part of the night of January 27th, in the company of Sergeant James McIrvine of the Royal Signals. Based at Fulwood, McIrvine and Dand had served together in the Western Desert campaign and Dand had turned up at the sergeant's mess in the afternoon. The two men went into York for a few drinks, parting at 9.30pm when McIrvine met some other friends. That would have given him plenty of time to get to Wyld's house and commit the crime.

When Dand was picked up he denied any involvement in the crime, but once his clothing had been examined and bloodstains found, he admitted that he had killed Wyld, accidentally, during a row about money. Later still, Dand withdrew this confession and denied that he had ever been at Wyld's house.

At the trial, the defence tried to back up Dand's denial by claiming that he could not possibly have committed the crime. Although Wyld was a much older man, he had been an athlete and was a powerfully built man. It was suggested that Dand was not big enough to be physically capable of

NAME	John Dand
AGE AT EXECUTION	32
DATE OF EXECUTION	Tuesday, 12th June, 1951
PLACE OF EXECUTION	Manchester
HANGMAN	Not known
ASSISTANT	Not known
DATE OF TRIAL	23rd April – 26th April, 1951
LOCATION OF TRIAL	Leeds
PRESIDING JUDGE	Mister Justice Gorman
PROSECUTION COUNSEL	Mister Hylton-Foster, Alistair Sharp
DEFENCE COUNSEL	H.R.B. Shepherd, Geoffrey Veale
NUMBER OF VICTIMS	1

VICTIMS DETAILS	
NAME	Walter Wyld
AGE	72
DATE OF MURDER	Saturday, 27th January, 1951
PLACE OF MURDER	199 Huntingdon Road, York
METHOD OF KILLING	Battered/stabbed
RELATIONSHIP TO KILLER	None

the crime and that the true perpetrator must have been a much larger man. The jury were not convinced and after a four-day trial, found Dand guilty as charged. At the time, the execution shed at Leeds was undergoing refurbishment, so Dand was transferred across to Lancashire and the sentence of death was carried out at Manchester.

THE MURDER OF Mona Mather was senseless and without motive. Her killer took her life simply because he wished to.

The two miners leaving Wharton Hall Colliery early on the morning of April 9th, were not sure at first what the bundle was in the field near their pit. Only on closer inspection did they see that it was the body of a young woman, her scarf tied tightly around her neck.

Investigations showed that on the previous night, Mona had been drinking at the George and Dragon pub. She had been with her brother and his wife, but Mona had left, alone, at 10.20pm. As she went out, a man wearing a grey coat followed Mona outside. This was the last time she was seen alive. The police were keen to find the man who had followed her out and was seen at a nearby Wakes fairground shortly afterwards. In due course a possible name for the suspect was given to police, who went to 3 John Street, Tyldesley, to speak to Jack Wright.

Wright made a full statement and confessed to the murder in a matter-of-fact manner. At one part of his statement he said: "I have always had it at the back of my mind to do a job like this." He went on to explain how the crime had been carried out.

Wright said that he had first met Mona the previous September. He had seen her again in the pub, that evening, followed her outside and asked her if she would like to go to the fair with him. After a few minutes there, he said he would walk her home and on the way he felt an impulse to kill her. They stopped close to the point where Mona's body was found and Wright throttled her into unconsciousness with his bare hands. Then, fearful that he might be seen if he stayed where he was, he lifted Mona into a nearby field and finished her off with her own scarf. He then went home, had some supper and went to bed where he slept soundly, satisfied with what he had done.

Interviewed by Charles Vaillant, a consultant psychologist, Wright remained as cold and detached as ever, at one stage remarking: "You may think I am stupid, but I believe some evil spirit has taken control of my body and the only thing for me is

NAME	Jack Wright
AGE AT EXECUTION	31
DATE OF EXECUTION	Tuesday, 3rd July, 1951
PLACE OF EXECUTION	Manchester
HANGMAN	Not known
ASSISTANT	Not known
DATE OF TRIAL	11th June – 12th June, 1951
LOCATION OF TRIAL	Liverpool
PRESIDING JUDGE	Mister Justice Oliver
PROSECUTION COUNSEL	H.I. Nelson, J.M. Davies
DEFENCE COUNSEL	J. Robertson Crichton, Leslie Rigg
NUMBER OF VICTIMS	1

VICTIMS DETAILS

NAME	Mona Mather
AGE	28
DATE OF MURDER	Sunday, 8th April, 1951
PLACE OF MURDER	Wharton Fold, Little Hulton, near Bolton
METHOD OF KILLING	Strangled
RELATIONSHIP TO KILLER	None

death. I am not one for suicide." Doctor Vaillant would later testify that Wright was of very poor intelligence and was an aggressive psychopath. He was not mad though, and so faced a trial for his life. That trial lasted two days. His own chilling description of the crime meant that there could only be one verdict.

On July 3rd, the psychopath who had wanted to die was finally granted his wish.

ELLEN LUDKIN HAD been seeing Alfred Reynolds for two and a half years. Though her parents did not approve of the association, they put their daughter's happiness first and when she announced, in October 1950, that she was pregnant, they agreed to the marriage if Alfred would find himself a job and provide a home for Ellen.

Alfred found himself a job but when he lost this, in January 1951, Ellen's parents said that the wedding could now not go ahead. Reynolds was most upset.

It was late on February 7th, when Reynolds turned up at Ellen's house asking if he could speak to her. Mr Ludkin was already in bed and called down from his window and told Reynolds to go away. Reynolds left, but returned at 2.00pm the next day.

Now Reynolds was invited into the house and spent some 20 minutes talking to Ellen. The couple then went for a walk. Gladys Ludkin, Ellen's mother, watched Reynolds stray into a nearby field, pick up a 12-bore shotgun and heard her daughter shout: "Alfie." It was the last word she ever spoke. A shot rang out and Ellen Ludkin fell dead.

Gladys ran for help but both she and Mr Mayer, the man who came to her aid, were held at bay by Reynolds. After a few minutes of this stand-off, Reynolds ran off to his parents' house and told them what he had done. Later he returned to the scene of the crime and gave himself up.

Reynolds explained that he had told Ellen he felt it better if they parted. She begged him not to leave her, told him that she loved him and said she would kill herself. Eventually they decided to kill themselves. He had taken the gun and shot her but had failed to kill himself.

There was no doubt that Reynolds was responsible for Ellen's death, but should he have hanged for it? His father, also named Arthur George Reynolds, testified that his son suffered from terrible nightmares and head pains and had threatened suicide in the past. The existence of the nightmares was confirmed by the medical evidence given by Doctor Cartledge. Further evidence was given that Reynolds was almost a mental defective and only had a mental age of 11 or 12.

NAME	Alfred George Reynolds
AGE AT EXECUTION	25
DATE OF EXECUTION	Thursday, 19th July, 1951
PLACE OF EXECUTION	Norwich
HANGMAN	Not known
ASSISTANT	Not known
DATE OF TRIAL	4th June, 1951
LOCATION OF TRIAL	Norwich
PRESIDING JUDGE	Mister Justice Parker
PROSECUTION COUNSEL	Gerald Howard, Garth Moore
DEFENCE COUNSEL	Montague Berryman, Tudor Evans
NUMBER OF VICTIMS	1

VICTIMS DETAILS	
NAME	Ellen May Ludkin
AGE	19
DATE OF MURDER	Thursday, 8th February, 1951
PLACE OF MURDER	Park Farm Cottages, Dereham, Norfolk
METHOD OF KILLING	Shot
RELATIONSHIP TO KILLER	Girlfriend

Even in prison, Reynolds showed signs that indicated that he was not thinking straight. He seemed to be obsessed with Ellen and wrote to her father, asking for photographs of her and of her grave. He simply could not understand why there was never any reply.

On July 19th, Alfred Reynolds was hanged alongside Dennis Moore. It was the first double execution at Norwich this century and the last time the gallows was ever used at that particular establishment.

D ENNIS MOORE FIRST met Eileen Cullen in June 1950. They soon became a devoted couple and, once they discovered she was pregnant, agreed to marry and plans were made for the big day, which had been set for February 17th, 1951. Two weeks before the wedding, on February 3rd, Dennis, Eileen and Eileen's sister, Evelyn, went out to select the wedding dress. Whilst they were out they visited Dennis's father, Albert, at his fruit and veg stall in the market.

That evening, Eileen visited her doctor, accompanied by Dennis, and they discussed the progress of the pregnancy. Afterwards, the two lovers walked off together, to a meadow in Oak Lane, where there was a cowshed. Inside that cowshed, Dennis asked Eileen for sex. She had always found this aspect of their relationship unpleasant, and had often refused Dennis in the past. Those feelings, coupled with her present condition, led Eileen to refuse Dennis once again – whereupon he strangled her.

When the police found Eileen's body, there was a card next to it and written upon it, in lipstick, was the message: "I love her. Goodbye." Eileen, however, had not simply been strangled. After death her throat had been cut; a large bread knife lay nearby.

During the trial, the knife became crucially important. The prosecution attempted to suggest that Dennis had taken it from the fruit stall when he had visited it that afternoon. This would have meant that the crime was premeditated. The defence, however, maintained that Dennis had returned home, collected the knife and returned to inflict the throat injuries. Victor Sewell, Dennis's brother-in-law, testified that the knife had not come from the stall and Albert Moore gave evidence that the knife had been at their home that evening. This was backed up by Bessie Moore, Dennis's mother, who said she had used it to prepare some food and had put it away at 7.30pm.

Evidence was also given that Dennis Moore had a temper and often went into a kind of blackout. A previous girlfriend, Irene Grace Hambling, told how after an argument, Dennis had tried to strangle her. The attempt had not been a serious one and Dennis had

NAME	Dennis Albert Reginald Moore
AGE AT EXECUTION	22
DATE OF EXECUTION	Thursday, 19th July, 1951
PLACE OF EXECUTION	Norwich
HANGMAN	Not known
ASSISTANT	Not known
DATE OF TRIAL	31st May – 1st June, 1951
LOCATION OF TRIAL	Norwich
PRESIDING JUDGE	Mister Justice Parker
PROSECUTION COUNSEL	John Flowers, Edward Clark
DEFENCE COUNSEL	F.T. Alpe, Michael Havers
NUMBER OF VICTIMS	1

VICTIMS DETAILS	
NAME	Eileen Emily Rose Cullen
AGE	21
DATE OF MURDER	Saturday, 3rd February, 1951
PLACE OF MURDER	Oak Lane, Norwich
METHOD OF KILLING	Strangled/cut throat
RELATIONSHIP TO KILLER	Girlfriend

had no memory of it afterwards when she mentioned it to him.

Robert Rickers, who had done his National Service with Dennis, said that once Dennis had been play-fighting with another soldier. After some time, Dennis had become excited and grabbed the soldier's throat. Had they not pulled him off he might well have killed him and yet he had shown no inclination to kill beforehand.

Despite all this testimony, which indicated that the crime was committed on the spur of the moment and that the perpetrator might well have suffered some kind of blackout, Dennis Moore was found guilty and sentenced to hang.

0950

THE CALL CAME through to the police station at 2.50am on May 22nd and was answered by Constable James Little: there was a madman running around somewhere near Holme Avenue. All patrol officers were notified.

At 4.00am, further reports put the location of the man at Irish Street and there were suggestions that he might be carrying a shotgun. Cars were sent out to check and it was one such car, driven by Sergeant William Gibson, which turned from High Street into Bank Street. There, standing against a wall, his hands behind his back, was a young man. Gibson stopped the car and asked the man what he was doing.

Without speaking the man drew his hands from behind his back to reveal that he was carrying a shotgun. The first barrel was fired through the side window of the car, shattering the glass and killing Sergeant Gibson outright.

There were two other police officers in the patrol car. Constable Andrew Hope was sitting in the front passenger seat and when he saw his colleague shot, he made to assist him. Another shot rang out and Hope was hit in both arms. So bad was the wound that both his arms were broken and it was with some difficulty that he finally managed to get out of the vehicle.

The assailant was opening the gun, ready to reload when the third officer, Constable Robert Campbell leapt from the car and threw himself upon the gunman. A struggle followed, but Campbell pinned him. He cried out for some handcuffs and had to take those belonging to Constable Hope. That officer was so badly injured that he couldn't even hand his own cuffs over. Hope had to kneel on the floor near Campbell so that he could get them himself from Hope's pocket.

Back at the police station, the gunman was identified as Robert Dobie Smith and investigations showed that the original telephone call had been made by Andrew Smith, his brother. Robert had been upset by the recent death of a friend, Allan Service, and by the fact that his love for a much younger girl, 19-year-old Joan Gillespie, had not been returned. As a result he had forced Andrew to write a long letter explaining his actions, then make a telephone call to the police. Part of that long letter made his intentions perfectly clear: "When I get out of this door tonight I will shoot the first policeman I see...."

Put on trial, the defence's argument was that Robert had been insane at the time of the shooting. That defence was largely negated by the testimony of Doctor Arthur Joseph Gordon Hunter, who described Smith as perfectly sane.

Smith was originally due to hang on August 17th, but that was postponed when he entered an appeal. This was lost on August 28th, and the new date of September 15th was then set.

NAME	Robert Dobie Smith
AGE AT EXECUTION	30
DATE OF EXECUTION	13th September, 1951
PLACE OF EXECUTION	Edinburgh, Saughton
HANGMAN	Not known
ASSISTANT	Not known
DATE OF TRIAL	24th July – 27th July, 1951
LOCATION OF TRIAL	Dumfries
PRESIDING JUDGE	Lord Justice Mackay
PROSECUTION COUNSEL	Harold R. Leslie, W. McIlwraith
DEFENCE COUNSEL	John Cameron, J.R. Fiddes
NUMBER OF VICTIMS	1

VICTIMS DETAILS	
NAME	William Gibson
AGE	Not known
DATE OF MURDER	22nd May, 1951
PLACE OF MURDER	Bank Street, Dumfries
METHOD OF KILLING	Shot
RELATIONSHIP TO KILLER	None

O N SATURDAY, AUGUST 11th, 1951, John O'Connor gave himself up to the police and admitted that he had killed his landlady, Eugenie le Maire. He then went on to make a detailed statement describing exactly what had happened.

O'Connor said that on the night of August 10th, he had visited several London pubs and had finally arrived home, rather late, by taxi. His 82-year-old landlady, Eugenie welcomed him back and began making him some tea. Without warning. O'Connor then seized Eugenie by the throat and attempted to strangle her. Although she did not die, Eugenie did lose consciousness, whereupon O'Connor then raped her before going up to his room. Some time later, having thought about what he had done, O'Connor went back downstairs, took up a bread knife and stabbed Eugenie in the heart and lungs.

In court, it was explained that in this case, there were three possible verdicts: guilty, not guilty and guilty but insane. Since by his own admission, O'Connor was responsible for Eugenie's death, it seemed to be narrowed down to two possibilities, but O'Connor now removed the last of those alternatives.

Mr Hemming, O'Connor's defence counsel, wished to introduce evidence on the sanity of his client but O'Connor expressly forbade it. As a result, O'Connor did not go into the witness box and no evidence was called for the defence. This being the case, it took the jury no more than 10 minutes to return the only verdict left open to them and O'Connor was sentenced to death. In fact, O'Connor had faced two juries, the first having decided that he was fit to plead.

There was no appeal and 22 days after receiving his sentence, John O'Connor was executed for what was a motiveless and senseless murder.

NAME	John O'Connor
AGE AT EXECUTION	29
DATE OF EXECUTION	Wednesday, 24th October, 1951
PLACE OF EXECUTION	Pentonville
HANGMAN	Albert Pierrepoint
ASSISTANT	Harry Allen
DATE OF TRIAL	2nd October, 1951
LOCATION OF TRIAL	Old Bailey
PRESIDING JUDGE	Mister Justice Barry
PROSECUTION COUNSEL	Christmas Humphreys
DEFENCE COUNSEL	W. Hemming
NUMBER OF VICTIMS	1

VICTIMS DETAILS

NAME	Eugenie le Maire
AGE	82
DATE OF MURDER	Saturday, 11th August, 1951
PLACE OF MURDER	15 Perham Road, West Kensington, London
METHOD OF KILLING	Strangled/stabbed
RELATIONSHIP TO KILLER	None

AT AROUND NOON on August 9th, 1951, the body of Mabel Tattershaw was discovered in a derelict orchard at Sherwood Vale, in Nottingham. The man who first found the body, Herbert Leonard Mills, had telephoned the News of the World and they in turn had contacted the police.

The story that Mills told was so incredulous that it immediately attracted attention to himself. Mills claimed that he had gone to the orchard on August 8th, in order to read poetry. He had found the body, sat down and read a poem before deciding what to do. He had thought of contacting the police directly but felt that they might suspect him, so, after thinking things over, he telephoned the newspaper and spoke to a reporter, William Brown Blackley.

Mills made his first mistake when he told Blackley that it was clear that the woman had been strangled. In fact, this was not clear until the postmortem. Mabel Tattershaw had been badly beaten about the head and anyone finding the body might be expected to believe that this was the cause of death. Surely only her killer would know that she had been strangled.

Over the next few days, both William Blackley and the chief crime reporter, Norman Rae, cosseted Mills and got him to write a story on what it was like to find a body. For this, Mills was paid a total of £80 and it became clear that in effect, his so-called fictitious story was a confession to the murder. Mills was arrested and charged.

Even in death Mabel Tattershaw remained a victim. At the hearing at the Magistrate's Court, she was described by the prosecution as a "woman of small significance". Mills had by now made a full confession to the crime, stating at one point that: "the strangling itself was easily accomplished."

Mills had met Mabel at a cinema and they had gone together to the orchard, where he had killed her. He had long dreamt of committing the perfect murder and saw this as a chance to try out his theories. For a such a motive was the life of Mabel Tattershaw taken.

At his trial, Mills tried to withdraw all he had said thus far. He now claimed that he had

NAME	Herbert Leonard Mills
AGE AT EXECUTION	19
DATE OF EXECUTION	Tuesday, 11th December, 1951
PLACE OF EXECUTION	Lincoln
HANGMAN	Albert Pierrepoint
ASSISTANT	Not known
DATE OF TRIAL	19th November – 22nd November, 1951
LOCATION OF TRIAL	Nottingham
PRESIDING JUDGE	Mister Justice Byrne
PROSECUTION COUNSEL	R.C. Vaughan
DEFENCE COUNSEL	Richard Elwes
NUMBER OF VICTIMS	1

VICTIMS DETAILS	
NAME	Mabel Tattershaw
AGE	48
DATE OF MURDER	Friday, 3rd August, 1951
PLACE OF MURDER	Sherwood Vale, Nottingham
METHOD OF KILLING	Battered/strangled
RELATIONSHIP TO KILLER	None

not murdered Mabel but had, as he first claimed, simply found the body. His reason for confessing was that he believed that if he were accused of murder, put on trial for his life and then acquitted, his story would be worth so much more to the press. The jury, though, had much too much sense to accept the words of this totally worthless liar and Mills was convicted and sentenced to death.

AT 5.45PM ON August 1st, 1951, Shiela Attwood went out to play with her friends, close to her home in Caversham Road, Birmingham. When she did not return home that night, her parents and neighbours organised a search but no trace of the child could be found.

The police continued the search well into the night but it was not until 11.25am on August 2nd, that Shiela's body was found by Mrs Ada Ford and her daughter. The child lay behind a privet edge that separated 32 Caversham Road from land belonging to Birmingham Corporation. A string lay knotted about her neck and a postmortem would show that she had been strangled manually as well as by means of the ligature. She had also been sexually assaulted.

As a matter of routine, all the residents of Caversham Road were interviewed. The occupant of number 34, Horace Carter, was interviewed at his place of work. At first he denied any knowledge of the killing and remarked that his conscience was clear. Carter was offered a lift home by the police, so that the questioning could continue, and on the way, suddenly said that he had not meant to hurt the child. Later, at the police station, Carter gave a full written account of what had happened. He claimed to have offered Shiela some sweets and then asked her to go upstairs with him. At the time he had no evil intentions towards her. But then he went on to relate how he had attacked her and killed her.

The only defence could be one of insanity. Carter was described at his trial as having a psychopathic personality with little regard for his own fate, or the death of others. The jury, which included three women, took 15 minutes to decide that Carter knew full well what he was doing and was therefore guilty of murder.

Horace Carter managed to see in the New Year. He was hanged on the first day of 1952.

NAME	Horace Carter
AGE AT EXECUTION	31
DATE OF EXECUTION	Tuesday, 1st January, 1952
PLACE OF EXECUTION	Birmingham
HANGMAN	Albert Pierrepoint
ASSISTANT	Syd Dernley
DATE OF TRIAL	12th December, 1951
LOCATION OF TRIAL	Birmingham
PRESIDING JUDGE	Mister Justice Cassels
PROSECUTION COUNSEL	Walker Carter
DEFENCE COUNSEL	Richard Elwes
NUMBER OF VICTIMS	1

VICTIMS DETAILS

NAME	Shiela Ethel Attwood
AGE	11
DATE OF MURDER	Wednesday, 1st August, 1951
PLACE OF MURDER	34 Caversham Road, Birmingham
METHOD OF KILLING	Strangled
RELATIONSHIP TO KILLER	None

1952

ON AUGUST 12TH, 1951, the body of George Camp was discovered on the building site in Wythenshawe where he acted as the nightwatchman. His injuries were appalling. George had been brutally beaten, his ribs and jaw had been fractured and the fatal blow had occurred when a plank weighing 48lbs had been dropped onto his body. The police investigation rapidly got nowhere.

On October 8th, Alan Bradley, one of the inmates of Strangeways jail in Manchester made an application to see the governor. At that interview, Bradley, who had been free at the time of the murder of George Camp, said that he wanted to tell the authorities what he knew of the crime. He then made a statement implicating two men by name. Four days later, on October 12th, Bradley again asked to see the police and this time he told a different version of the events of August 12th.

Bradley said he had known Camp, a homosexual, for some years and various indecent acts had taken place between them over that time period. On August 12th, Camp had taken Bradley drinking, buying him a total of 10 pints and then expecting sexual favours in return. Finding the act distasteful, Bradley tried to get away and hit out at Camp. He claimed that there had been no intention to kill.

In fact, Bradley had a dual defence. Firstly it was suggested that Camps had died by accident. Since it had been the blow from the plank that had proved fatal, it was pointed out that this may have fallen on him accidentally and since Bradley would not then have administered the fatal blow, he could not be guilty of murder. The second aspect of the defence was that Bradley had suffered severe provocation and that if it was held that he had killed Camp, the charge should be reduced to manslaughter.

Alan Bradley faced two trials, both at Manchester. The first, which took place before Mister Justice Lynskey ended when the judge ordered a retrial. At one stage, Bradley picking up the court bible and throwing it at the judge. One week later, at the second trial, a guilty verdict was returned and Bradley was sentenced to death.

NAME	Alfred Bradley
AGE AT EXECUTION	24
DATE OF EXECUTION	Tuesday, 15th January, 1952
PLACE OF EXECUTION	Manchester
HANGMAN	Not known
ASSISTANT	Not known
DATE OF TRIAL	6th December – 7th December, 1951
LOCATION OF TRIAL	Manchester
PRESIDING JUDGE	Mister Justice Stable
PROSECUTION COUNSEL	A.D. Gerrard
DEFENCE COUNSEL	Kenneth Burke
NUMBER OF VICTIMS	1

VICTIMS DETAILS	
NAME	George Camp
AGE	58
DATE OF MURDER	Sunday, 12th August, 1951
PLACE OF MURDER	Crossacres Estate building site, Wythenshawe, Manchester
METHOD OF KILLING	Battered
RELATIONSHIP TO KILLER	None

THERE WASN'T A great deal of money to be made from poultry farming, so Alfred Moore took to supplementing his income with crime. In addition to running the remote farm at Kirkheaton, Moore would commit burglaries and take anything that could help out his finances

Moore's name had come to the attention of the police and so on the night of Saturday July 14th, 1951, it was decided to stake out the farm in the hope that Moore would return with the proceeds of his latest robbery and be caught red-handed. For some hours, the officers settled down to wait.

At 2.00am on Sunday morning, five shots rang out and in the chaos that followed it was discovered that two police officers had been hit. Detective Inspector Duncan Fraser was already dead but his colleague, Police Constable Arthur Jagger, was still hanging on to life. The young officer was rushed to hospital.

Back at the farmhouse, the remaining officers determined that Moore was now back inside. The place was surrounded and in due course, Moore was arrested for murder.

Moore claimed that he had in fact been home since midnight. As a farmer he did own a weapon but only a shotgun. He did not own a revolver and it was such a weapon that had been used to fire the fatal shots. A search of the farmhouse was organised and though a shotgun was found, together with burglar's tools, stolen property and a pair of wet boots, no revolver was found, even when an army mine-detector was used.

The police, though, did have an eye witness in the shape of the wounded Arthur Jagger. An identity parade was organised at the officer's sick bed and he managed to pick out Alfred Moore. The next day a special magistrate's court was convened at the hospital and Jagger gave evidence even though he was badly hurt. The next day, Constable Jagger died.

Alfred Moore was tried for murder at Leeds and the dying testimony of Arthur Jagger proved conclusive. Moore was hanged in February 1952, but the murder weapon has never been found.

NAME	Alfred Moore
AGE AT EXECUTION	36
DATE OF EXECUTION	Wednesday, 6th February, 1952
PLACE OF EXECUTION	Leeds
HANGMAN	Steve Wade
ASSISTANT	Harry Allen
DATE OF TRIAL	10th December – 13th December, 1951
LOCATION OF TRIAL	Leeds
PRESIDING JUDGE	Mister Justice Pearson
PROSECUTION COUNSEL	G. Raymond Hinchcliffe, F. Norman Black
DEFENCE COUNSEL	H.B.H. Hylton-Foster, C.R. Dean
NUMBER OF VICTIMS	2

VICTIMS DETAILS

NAMES	Duncan A. Fraser; Arthur Jagger (Died Monday, 16th July, 1951)
AGES	46; 44
DATE OF MURDER	Sunday, 15th July, 1951
PLACE OF MURDER	Whinney Close Farm, Kirkheaton, Huddersfield
METHOD OF KILLING	Shot; shot
RELATIONSHIP TO KILLER	None; none

1952

IT WAS QUITE a shock for Sarah Owen. At 9.45pm on Saturday, December 8th, 1951, Sarah was on her way to visit her married daughter, Audrey Grogan, when she saw, sprawled on the ground, the body of a woman, a bloodstained stone lying close by. Even more terrible, the body appeared to be that of her daughter. With her heart pounding, Sarah crouched down and gently lifted the head. The body was not that of Audrey Grogan, but of a woman who lived near by – Eileen Harris.

Eileen was a married woman with three young children: Susan, Jennifer and Vernon. They lived with Eileen's parents at 31 Queen's Avenue, whilst her husband, Herbert Roy Harris, lived at 77 Queen's Avenue with his own parents. This arrangement was a temporary one whilst the couple waited for a council house.

Investigations showed that Eileen had left home at around 5.15pm on the Saturday, to go to the Plaza picture house. Here she had been seen at 5.30pm, by Emily George who stated that Eileen had been looking for Herbert. He apparently had not turned up. Police looked for him at his parents' house; he was not there, but they did find a bloodstained mackintosh, scarf and gloves.

At 8.30am on December 9th, Harris booked into the Regent Palace Hotel in London. Later that same day, the receptionist, Christine Daphne Forrester, recognised the name from press reports and informed the police. Harris was arrested and taken back to Mold.

When charged with murder, Harris replied that it had not been intentional. He went on to explain that he and his wife had been forced to leave their last home because of their constant fighting. Deciding that a council house was the best way out of their difficulties, they had chosen to have a third child, hoping that this would speed up the rehousing process for them.

On the day of Eileen's death, at 5.30pm, Herbert called at her home to find that she had already left for the cinema. This upset Herbert who tried to catch Eileen up. When he failed to do this, he went for a drink in the Ship before finally going directly to the Plaza where he met up with Eileen.

NAME	Herbert Roy Harris
AGE AT EXECUTION	23
DATE OF EXECUTION	Tuesday, 26th February, 1952
PLACE OF EXECUTION	Manchester
HANGMAN	Not known
ASSISTANT	Not known
DATE OF TRIAL	5th February, 1952
LOCATION OF TRIAL	Monmouth
PRESIDING JUDGE	Mister Justice Oliver
PROSECUTION COUNSEL	H. Vincent Jones, Bertram Richards
DEFENCE COUNSEL	H. Glyn-Jones, W.L. Mars-Jones
NUMBER OF VICTIMS	1

VICTIMS DETAILS

NAME	Eileen Harris
AGE	22
DATE OF MURDER	Saturday, 8th December, 1951
PLACE OF MURDER	Huntley Bridge, Flint
METHOD OF KILLING	Battered
RELATIONSHIP TO KILLER	Wife

Angry at being kept waiting, an argument broke out and the couple ended up by hitting each other. Herbert saw a large stone on the ground, picked it up and struck out, catching Eileen on the head. He then panicked, went home, washed his coat and left for London. He claimed that he had not known that Eileen was dead until he read it in the newspaper.

Found guilty of murder, Herbert Roy Harris was hanged on February 26th, 1952. Within 12 weeks, three children, the youngest not yet six months old, had lost both parents.

FOR MORE THAN five years, Evelyn McDonald had been living with a Bengali seaman named Montez Ullah. However, on one of Ullah's absences at sea, Evelyn moved in with Ullah's cousin, Tahir Ali.

Tahir was also a seaman and when he went on his next voyage, he naturally assumed that on his return Evelyn would be waiting for him. However, when his ship did finally dock, Ali found to his dismay that Evelyn and Ullah were living at Adelaide Street, South Shields. Also living in the same house was a friend of Evelyn's, Mary Lucas.

In early November, there was an argument between Tahir and Evelyn. Mary Lucas had to separate the couple, whereupon Takir said that he would finish Evelyn and if Mary got in the way, he would finish her too. Things then quietened down for a couple of weeks, until November 20th.

On that evening, Evelyn and Mary went to a pub at 7.30pm. They were joined later by Tahir and Evelyn's mother, the latter leaving at around 10.00pm. Evelyn, Mary and Tahir left together and Tahir told Evelyn that he wanted her to come home with him. When she refused, a struggle followed during which Tahir took out a flick knife, pressed the button that controlled the blade and stabbed Evelyn three times. Two of those wounds entered Evelyn's back, puncturing her lungs, the third, to her chest, cut the pulmonary artery.

At the police station, Tahir seemed unruffled by his predicament, telling officers: "Well, I am here, do what you like." He went on to say that he had spent something between £500 and £600 on Evelyn and considered she had made a fool of him.

Found guilty of murder and condemned to death, the local Moslem population tried to save the life of Tahir Ali by contacting the prime minister of Pakistan and asking him to intervene. It had no effect and Ali was hanged in March.

NAME	Tahir Ali
AGE AT EXECUTION	39
DATE OF EXECUTION	Friday, 21st March, 1952
PLACE OF EXECUTION	Durham
HANGMAN	Not known
ASSISTANT	Not known
DATE OF TRIAL	31st January – 1st February, 1952
LOCATION OF TRIAL	Durham
PRESIDING JUDGE	Mister Justice Hallett
PROSECUTION COUNSEL	H.R.B. Shepherd. Gordon Smith
DEFENCE COUNSEL	G.S. Waller, W. Johnson
NUMBER OF VICTIMS	1

VICTIMS DETAILS	
NAME	Evelyn McDonald
AGE	25
DATE OF MURDER	Tuesday, 20th November, 1951
PLACE OF MURDER	Adelaide Street, South Shields
METHOD OF KILLING	Stabbed
RELATIONSHIP TO KILLER	Girlfriend

1952

THE ENCYCLOPAEDIA OF EXECUTIONS

MARY MALONE WAS talking to her friend, Elizabeth Malcolm and standing close by was Mary's husband, Martin. Suddenly, the sound of a disturbance echoed across the dance hall floor and Martin saw that his friend, William Mullen Loudon was in trouble with a gang of youths. Martin Malone ran across to help and was rewarded for his trouble by being stabbed. He died from his injuries.

It wasn't long before the man who had wielded the knife was identified as James Smith and he was arrested on November 17th. He appeared in court in February, pleaded guilty to assaulting Loudon but denied murdering Malone. The stabbing was, he claimed, self-defence.

There were a number of witnesses to the crime, possibly the most important being William Loudon himself. He testified that he was talking to a young lady named Elizabeth Clark when someone tapped him on the shoulder. This was followed by a pain in his side and only later did he discover that he had been stabbed. This was backed up by Elizabeth herself.

Annie Mackay Keenan said she saw Smith get up from a chair in order to dance with a young lady. Suddenly Smith told the girl to "Wait a minute" and then walked over to Loudon, put his left hand on his shoulder and struck him with his right hand.

The motive for this appeared to be some trouble that had taken place at the dance entrance hall earlier. Robert Hume said he had seen a fight at the entrance and four men had been ejected. Later they pushed their way back in and, after the attack upon Loudon and Malone, it had been Hume who held on to Smith until his friends demanded he be released.

In his defence, Smith claimed that the trouble had been caused by Loudon and Malone. They had fought with one of his friends and hurt him quite badly. Turning to the stabbing of Loudon, Smith claimed that this had been and act of self-defence prompted by Loudon producing his own knife. Then, when Malone came over, also carrying a knife, they struggled and the next thing he knew, Malone was on the floor, bleeding.

NAME	James Smith
AGE AT EXECUTION	21
DATE OF EXECUTION	Saturday, 12th April, 1952
PLACE OF EXECUTION	Glasgow, Barlinnie
HANGMAN	Albert Pierrepoint
ASSISTANT	Steve Wade
DATE OF TRIAL	26th February – 27th February, 1952
LOCATION OF TRIAL	Glasgow
PRESIDING JUDGE	Lord Justice Cooper
PROSECUTION COUNSEL	Doctor D.M. Campbell, F. Walker
DEFENCE COUNSEL	Francis Duffy, F.C. Watt
NUMBER OF VICTIMS	1

VICTIMS DETAILS	
NAME	Martin Joseph Malone
AGE	34
DATE OF MURDER	Friday, 16th November, 1951
PLACE OF MURDER	Ancient Order of Hibernian's Hall, Royston Road, Glasgow
METHOD OF KILLING	Stabbed
RELATIONSHIP TO KILLER	None

On the second day of the trial, the prosecution admitted that a second knife had been found on the dance floor but also volunteered the astounding statement that it had not been tested by forensics for blood!

Found guilty and sentenced to death, Smith's appeal was heard over four days from March 19th until March 22nd. Much was made of the second weapon, which might have suggested that Smith was telling the truth after all. The three appeal court judged ruled, however, that the second dagger was not germane to the case.

ALICE RIMMER LIVED alone in the Wavertree area of Liverpool and local gossip had it that she had money hidden inside her house. That gossip reached the ears of someone who chose to see if the stories were true.

On the day of her murder, Alice had been out and came home quite late. As she let herself into the house, she was confronted by burglars who were already inside.

In an attempt to find out where any money might be hidden, the burglars savagely beat Alice Rimmer, inflicting more than a dozen injuries upon her head. It took her some considerable time to die.

The following evening her son called to visit and, getting no reply, he crouched down and peered through the letterbox. There on the floor lay the body of his mother, lying in a pool of blood. Close by lay a bunch of flowers she had bought for herself the previous evening.

Police investigations soon led to two Manchester-based youths, Edward Devlin and Alfred Burns. They said they were not involved in the death of Alice Rimmer and as an alibi gave the name of a third man, who said they were all robbing a factory in Manchester at the time of the attack. Nevertheless, the police still charged Devlin and Burns with murder.

Throughout the trial both men behaved badly, criticising the judge and the jury. The case went to appeal and was even referred to the Home Secretary of the day, Sir David Maxwell Fyfe. The Home Secretary appointed Albert Gerrard QC to look into the case but on April 25th, 1952, his report confirmed that Devlin and Burns were guilty of murder.

Although it was known that the two youths were no angels, public opinion believed that there had been a miscarriage of justice. If the alibi were true then Devlin and Burns could not have been in Liverpool killing Alice Rimmer whilst they were breaking into a factory in Manchester. A petition was organised and a massive campaign orchestrated to secure a reprieve. It was all to no avail.

On the following Sunday, April 27th, newspapers reported that both men had made

NAMES	Edward Devlin; Alfred Burns
AGES AT EXECUTION	22; 21
DATE OF EXECUTION	Friday, 25th April, 1952
PLACE OF EXECUTION	Liverpool
HANGMAN	Albert Pierrepoint
ASSISTANTS	Syd Dernley, Robert Leslie Stewart, Harry Smith
DATE OF TRIAL	12th February – 27th February, 1952
LOCATION OF TRIAL	Liverpool
PRESIDING JUDGE	Mister Justice Finnemore
PROSECUTION COUNSEL	Basil Neild
DEFENCE COUNSEL	Rose Heilbron; Noel B. Goldie
NUMBER OF VICTIMS	1

VICTIMS DETAILS	
NAME	Alice Rimmer
AGE	54
DATE OF MURDER	Sunday, 19th August, 1951
PLACE OF MURDER	Cranborne Road, Liverpool
METHOD OF KILLING	Battered
RELATIONSHIP TO KILLERS	None; none

a full confession in the condemned cells before the execution. Whatever the truth of that, Syd Dernley, one of the assistant hangman would later write in his memoirs that neither man made any utterances whilst on the gallows.

1952

JOAN MARION THOMAS was a young widow, living in Dunraven Place, Bridgend. For a short time she had been associating with Ajit Singh, a Sikh of Elder House, Bridgend. Her family objected to that association but Singh had a way to deal with that criticism. He would kill Joan Thomas.

Joan's sister had spent some time in hospital and Joan went to visit her, along with Mildred Valerie Williams, a friend. As they stood at the bus stop, Singh approached them and asked Joan what her plans were for that evening. Joan told him to mind his own business and ignored him until the bus turned up. However, Singh climbed onto the same vehicle and all three travelled off towards the hospital.

Singh knew where Joan's sister was and so when the bus arrived outside Cefn Hirgoed, he got off first and waited for the two ladies to follow him. Once again Singh approached Joan and more words were exchanged. Mildred Williams walked on a little way but suddenly she heard Joan scream: "He's got a gun!"

Turning, Mildred saw that Singh had opened his coat to show Joan that he was armed with a German self-loading pistol. Joan began to run towards the hospital but Singh ran after her, firing as he went. Joan was hit twice in the back and Singh managed to catch up with her whereupon he fired once more, this bullet penetrating Joan's heart. He then crouched down and cradled her in his arms, telling astounded witnesses, "She very sick."

In fact, two people had been shot that afternoon. One of the wild shots Singh had sprayed at Joan had missed her and wounded a passer-by by the name of Beryl Gore in the ear. Soon afterwards. Sergeant Geoffrey Robinson came upon the scene and demanded to know what had happened. Singh, still nursing Joan, looked up and announced: "I shoot her."

The trial lasted two days and at the end of it, Singh was found guilty. The foreman of the jury was visibly moved as he announced the verdict and had difficulty in finishing his words. The jury added the strongest possible recommendation to mercy, but it failed to save the life of Ajit Singh.

NAME	Ajit Singh
AGE AT EXECUTION	27
DATE OF EXECUTION	Wednesday, 7th May, 1952
PLACE OF EXECUTION	Cardiff
HANGMAN	Not known
ASSISTANT	Not known
DATE OF TRIAL	19th March – 20th March, 1952
LOCATION OF TRIAL	Cardiff
PRESIDING JUDGE	Mister Justice Byrne
PROSECUTION COUNSEL	H. Edmund Davies, Eifion Evans
DEFENCE COUNSEL	Vincent Lloyd-Jones, T.E.R. Rhys-Roberts
NUMBER OF VICTIMS	1

VICTIMS DETAILS

NAME	Joan Marion Thomas
AGE	26
DATE OF MURDER	Sunday, 30th December, 1951
PLACE OF MURDER	Outside Cefn Hirgoed Isolation Hospital, Bridgend
METHOD OF KILLING	Shot
RELATIONSHIP TO KILLER	Girlfriend

IT WAS LATE on Friday, January 4th, 1952, when the occupants of Oakley Square in London heard shouting and screaming. Looking through their windows, a number of people saw a coloured man leaving number 10, and half-run, half-walk down the street.

Seconds later, others found Joseph Aaku inside his rooms. He had been slashed across the face and had several stab wounds in the back of his neck, one of which had almost severed his spinal cord. He was admitted to the National Temperance Hospital, where he died that same night, at 11.17pm.

The police knew that the assailant had also been wounded. Aaku had Group A blood but there were also signs of Group O blood at the crime scene. The motive too appeared to be plain. A large quantity of hemp was found in Aaku's rooms and it was assumed that there had been some sort of disagreement over drugs, though Aaku's gold watch had been taken.

It was on January 8th, that Backary Manneh, a fellow worker of Aaku's at Euston Station, was first spoken to. As Manneh was outlining his movements, it was noticed that his right hand was cut and badly swollen. Manneh explained that he had been mugged, in Tottenham Court Road, on the evening of January 5th. For the time being, the story was accepted.

The condition of Manneh's hand did not improve and he sought medical attention on January 9th. The following day he was admitted to St George's in the East Hospital and here he was interviewed again, on January 12th, when he repeated his story of the mugging.

At about the same time the police discovered that Manneh might have been somewhat economical with the truth. To begin with, an acquaintance of Manneh's, Denba Jadama, told officers that he had seen Manneh on January 9th. He had a heavily bandaged hand and specifically asked Jadama not to mention this to the police. Did Manneh have something to hide?

Soon afterwards, Simon Litwin was spoken to. On January 7th, he had bought a gold watch from Manneh for the sum of £2. Litwin had taken the watch to a jeweller for

NAME	Backary Manneh
AGE AT EXECUTION	25
DATE OF EXECUTION	Tuesday, 27th May, 1952
PLACE OF EXECUTION	Pentonville
HANGMAN	Albert Pierrepoint
ASSISTANT	Harry Smith
DATE OF TRIAL	25th March – 27th March, 1952
LOCATION OF TRIAL	Old Bailey
PRESIDING JUDGE	Mister Justice Gorman
PROSECUTION COUNSEL	J.F. Claxton
DEFENCE COUNSEL	J. Sarsh
NUMBER OF VICTIMS	1

VICTIMS DETAILS	
NAME	Joseph Aaku
AGE	28
DATE OF MURDER	Friday, 4th January, 1952
PLACE OF MURDER	10 Oakley Square, London
METHOD OF KILLING	Stabbed
RELATIONSHIP TO KILLER	None

repair and once the back had been removed, traces of blood were found. The watch was identified as belonging to Aaku. On January 14th, the police again visited Manneh in hospital and arrested him.

The trial lasted three days and at the end of it, Manneh was found guilty. Mister Justice Gorman donned the black cap in order to pronounce the sentence of death, whereupon a spectator from the public gallery leapt to his feet and shouted: "Take the black cap off and abide by the law of God. Thou shalt not kill." He was escorted from the courtroom.

IN 1939, AFTER a whirlwind romance lasting only one week, Jeannie Todd married Patrick Deveney. They were very happy to begin with and within a year, Jeannie had given birth to their first child. Then things began to change and by 1942, the once mild Patrick had been discharged from the army as having a psychopathic personality.

Four more children were born to the union but by 1952, the relationship between Patrick and Jeannie had become strained and their were now constant arguments between them. By February 23rd of that year, Jeannie was telling her brother, George Todd, that she intended leaving Patrick and on that same day, George's wife, Agnes Todd, witnessed the latest row between them.

Agnes had been at Jeannie's house when Patrick came in having had a few drinks. Jeannie reminded him that he owed her 1s-5d for some cigarettes and a newspaper but he countered this by demanding 2s-6d for scrubbing the floor. An argument began during which Patrick threw a bag at his wife, hitting her in the face. It ended with Jeannie running down the stairs being chased by Patrick who was throwing milk bottles at her. Fortunately, they all missed.

At 6.30pm on February 26th, Patrick Deveney walked into Greenock police station and confessed to having killed his wife. When officers were sent to the family home they found Jeannie's body lying under a pile of bedclothes. A bloodstained hammer lay nearby.

Put on trial for murder, Deveney's defence was that he did not know what he was doing at the time and should therefore be found guilty of culpable homicide, the Scottish equivalent of manslaughter. Since that defence rested on Deveney's state of mind, he was examined by Doctor Thomas Roger who testified that whilst Deveney was sane, he did tend towards psychopathic behaviour. He was not insane, though, and as such, his defence failed and he was found guilty of murder after the jury had deliberated for 40 minutes.

Deveney did not appeal against his sentence and was hanged at Barlinnie 23 days later.

NAME	Patrick Gallagher Deveney
AGE AT EXECUTION	42
DATE OF EXECUTION	Thursday, 29th May, 1952
PLACE OF EXECUTION	Glasgow, Barlinnie
HANGMAN	Albert Pierrepoint
ASSISTANT	Steve Wade
DATE OF TRIAL	6th May, 1952
LOCATION OF TRIAL	Glasgow
PRESIDING JUDGE	Lord Justice Keith
PROSECUTION COUNSEL	D.M. Campbell
DEFENCE COUNSEL	Hector McKechnie
NUMBER OF VICTIMS	1

VICTIMS DETAILS

NAME	Jeannie Deveney
AGE	37
DATE OF MURDER	Tuesday, 26th February, 1952
PLACE OF MURDER	115 Blackburn Street, Glasgow
METHOD OF KILLING	Battered/stabbed
RELATIONSHIP TO KILLER	Wife

HARRY HUXLEY HAD known Ada Royce since 1945. She was married to Charles Henry Royce and had three children, George, June and Anthony but by his own admission, Huxley was the father of the youngest of these, Tony, and paid money to Ada for the child's upkeep.

Throughout their relationship, Ada had remained at home with her husband, living at 21 Dee Park, Holt. It was a difficult situation but Ada's attempt to simplify it by telling Harry that she didn't want to see him again did not have the desired effect. On Christmas Day, 1951, Huxley borrowed a gun and two cartridges from Albert Lowe, telling him that he wished to a shoot a pheasant.

Saturday, December 29th, saw Ada enjoying a quiet drink, with her sister-in-law, Ellen Mary Royce, in the Geddington Arms pub. In the same hostelry, drinking separately, was Huxley and seeing him there, the two women decided to try a different pub, the Golden Lion. Soon afterwards though, Ada received a message there, from Huxley, asking her to meet him. She refused.

In due course, Ada and Ellen began walking home together but they had not gone very far when Huxley appeared and tried to engage Ada in conversation. As the group walked slowly on, Ellen saw William Bithell, Ada's brother, and went to have a chat with him, leaving Ada and Huxley together. Moments later a shot rang out and Ellen turned to see Ada falling to the ground.

William Bithell ran forward to offer aid to his sister and as he did so, Huxley turned the gun upon himself and fired a second shot, striking himself in the chest. As it happened, Huxley would recover from his wound, being released from hospital on February 11th, 1952, and it has been suggested that it was the metal buckle on Huxley's braces that partially deflected the shot and saved his life.

Facing a charge of murder, Huxley tried to claim that the shooting had been accidental. He said he was merely waving the gun about in order to frighten Ada, when the weapon went off and killed her. Seeing what he had done, he then decided to take his own life.

Whilst it was true that tests showed that the weapon was highly unstable and that the

NAME	Harry Huxley
AGE AT EXECUTION	43
DATE OF EXECUTION	Tuesday, 8th July, 1952
PLACE OF EXECUTION	Shrewsbury
HANGMAN	Not known
ASSISTANT	Not known
DATE OF TRIAL	19th May – 20th May, 1952
LOCATION OF TRIAL	Ruthin
PRESIDING JUDGE	Mister Justice Croom-Johnson
PROSECUTION COUNSEL	A.H. Edmund Davies, W.L. Mars-Jones
DEFENCE COUNSEL	Miss Rose Heilbron, Bertrand Richards
NUMBER OF VICTIMS	1

VICTIMS DETAILS	
NAME	Ada Royce
AGE	32
DATE OF MURDER	Saturday, 29th December, 1951
PLACE OF MURDER	Castle Street, Holt
METHOD OF KILLING	Shot
RELATIONSHIP TO KILLER	Girlfriend

right-hand hammer could go off without being touched, this scenario was greatly weakened by a note, found on Huxley and addressed to his mother. In this he apologised to her and said that this was the only way out, suggesting that the crime was premeditated. In his defence, Huxley said that the note was written because he was going to go away and was not an indication that he planned to injure Ada Royce.

In the event, the jury decided that Huxley was guilty but did add a recommendation to mercy.

1952

THOMAS EAMES MARRIED shortly before the Second World War broke out. Joining the forces in 1940, Eames's marriage broke up soon afterwards and in 1947, he met Muriel Bent. They fell in love and Eames married Muriel bigamously. For that offence he served two days' imprisonment but on his release, they continued to live together and in due course, Muriel gave birth to Eames's child.

The relationship between Eames and Muriel was never a perfect one and there were many arguments between them. Eventually Muriel decided she had had enough and left the house in Northumberland Terrace. She had after all, found herself another man.

Eames saw Muriel twice with her new man, the last occasion being on February 26th when he approached them and asked Muriel if she would call around to the old house the following day, in order to collect a letter. Muriel agreed.

The following morning, Thomas Eames took a table knife to his place of work, borrowed a file from a workmate named Thomas Bell, and spent 30 minutes sharpening the weapon into a two-edged dagger. He then returned home and waited for Muriel to call.

When Muriel arrived, Eames asked her if she intended to marry this other man of hers. She said she did and then moved to kiss Eames goodbye. As she did so, he took out the newly sharpened knife and stabbed Muriel twice, in the back. He then told his brother-in-law, Ronald William Greep what he had done and asked him to accompany him to the police station, where Eames gave himself up.

Though Eames could not read or write, he dictated his statement to Detective Superintendent McConnach, saying that he had killed Muriel out of jealousy. Charged with the murder, he appeared at Exeter assizes in June.

An attempt was made to show that Eames had been temporarily insane at the time of the killing, due to the effects of worry, stress and not eating. Ronald Greep gave evidence, saying that he had seen Eames most nights and had seen the deterioration in him. He

NAME	Thomas Eames
AGE AT EXECUTION	31
DATE OF EXECUTION	Tuesday, 15th July, 1952
PLACE OF EXECUTION	Bristol
HANGMAN	Not known
ASSISTANT	Not known
DATE OF TRIAL	23rd June, 1952
LOCATION OF TRIAL	Exeter
PRESIDING JUDGE	Mister Justice Lynskey
PROSECUTION COUNSEL	Ewan Montagu, J.F.E. Stephenson
DEFENCE COUNSEL	N.F. Fox Andrews, H.S. Ruttle
NUMBER OF VICTIMS	1

VICTIMS DETAILS	
NAME	Muriel Elsie Bent
AGE	26
DATE OF MURDER	Wednesday, 27th February, 1952
PLACE OF MURDER	3 Northumberland Terrace, West Hoe, Plymouth
METHOD OF KILLING	Stabbed
RELATIONSHIP TO KILLER	Girlfriend

appeared to be getting more and more worked up with each passing day and had told Ronald that he couldn't eat or sleep and had severe stomach pains. He had called around at 8.30pm on the evening that Muriel died and suddenly seemed to be his old self again. Then he had explained what he had done.

Mister Justice Lynskey was fair in his summing-up, pointing out that Eames could have been temporarily insane at the time of the killing, but the jury were convinced Eames had known what he was doing and found him guilty, though they did add a recommendation to mercy.

JOHANNA HALLAHAN HAD worked at the Elgin Court Hotel for five weeks. A beautiful and popular girl, she was engaged to Charles Patrick Hughes, who lived in Cavendish Road, Croydon.

Johanna last saw Charles at 3.15pm on April 21st, 1952, and they arranged to meet up later, when Johanna came off duty. She never kept that appointment.

Tuesday, April 22nd, was Johanna's day off, so no one was surprised when she did not appear that day. It was also the day off for another member of staff, a porter named Frank Burgess.

Wednesday was a different matter and when neither Johanna nor Burgess attended for work, the proprietor, Mr Peel, investigated.

Getting no reply to his knocking on Johanna's door, Mr Peel went around the back and looked through her window. Seeing a pair of women's legs, he took his pass keys and unlocked the door. Johanna had been strangled and the gas meter in her room forced open. Further, the meter in Burgess's room had also been forced.

The police found a letter in Burgess's room, which appeared to be a confession to the crime. Burgess had been on probation earlier in the year for an attack on a taxi driver and the letter was addressed to his probation officer, Frank Arthur Hepworth. Burgess apologised for letting Mr Hepworth down and said he did not know why he had killed Joan. The letter went on to admit that it took her a long time to die and included the chilling line: "I found it was in quite a fit of laughter that I killed her."

At 2.00am on the 23rd, before Johanna's body was discovered, Burgess had taken a taxi to Waterloo Bridge. Here he met a soldier, Private Raymond Baxter, and the two men fell into conversation. At one stage Burgess asked Baxter for a pen and paper and wrote: "Burgess, 2, Elgin Court Hotel, Elgin Road, East Croydon. 22. J Hallahan." Burgess told Baxter to watch for those names, adding: "It's serious. I could hang for it."

It was not long before the police closed on Burgess. He freely admitted that he was responsible for Johanna's death, though he could give no motive for the crime. He went

NAME	Frank Burgess
AGE AT EXECUTION	21
DATE OF EXECUTION	Tuesday, 22nd July, 1952
PLACE OF EXECUTION	Wandsworth
HANGMAN	Albert Pierrepoint
ASSISTANT	Syd Dernley
DATE OF TRIAL	30th June, 1952
LOCATION OF TRIAL	Kingston upon Thames
PRESIDING JUDGE	Mister Justice Streatfeild
PROSECUTION COUNSEL	Roy Wilson
DEFENCE COUNSEL	F.H. Cassels
NUMBER OF VICTIMS	1

VICTIMS DETAILS	
NAME	Johanna Hallahan
AGE	22
DATE OF MURDER	Monday, 21st April, 1952
PLACE OF MURDER	Elgin Court Hotel, Elgin Road, East Croydon
METHOD OF KILLING	Strangled
RELATIONSHIP TO KILLER	None

on to say that on the evening he killed her, Johanna was getting ready to go out. He asked her to lend him some money. She gave him a £1 note and some loose change and then he killed her.

The trial was but a formality. On July 22nd, the motiveless killer was hanged at Wandsworth.

ETHEL ELIZA MEADOWS knew that Oliver Butler was a married man but he had told her that he was getting a divorce and she had no reason to disbelieve him. Besides, Oliver and her daughter, Rose, appeared to be so much in love. For these reasons, Ethel allowed Butler to move into her house.

Just before noon on May 19th, 1952, Oliver and Rose set out for a walk towards Wroxton. The next sighting of Oliver was at 3.30pm when he called at a railway signal box and asked to use the telephone to call the police. He explained that he had strangled Rose. The signalman, Arthur Edward Phipps would later report that Oliver seemed to be rather distressed and by the time Countable Robinson reached the box, Oliver was crying.

Butler's story was that the crime had been accidental. Rose, he claimed, was somewhat insecure and had convinced herself that one day Butler would return to his wife. As a result, she saw no reason to stay faithful to him and suggested that she should go out with other men. After all, she was an attractive woman, popular with the local men.

At this point, Butler had placed his hands around Rose's throat, with the intention of frightening her. His move did not have the desired effect, for Rose merely laughed and dared him to continue. He then lost his temper and must have squeezed too hard, because she had collapsed and died. Butler put this down to the fact that Rose had a weak heart, which was the first her family had ever heard of this particular affliction.

In later statements, Butler embellished his story somewhat. Rose, it appeared, had once been told by a fortune teller that she would be murdered and had told him she would rather he did it than someone else. He also claimed that upon reaching the spot where she died, he and Rose had first made love and she had remarked that it was a good place for a murder.

Butler's evidence did not convince the jury, who found him guilty of murder. After losing his appeal on July 18th, Butler became the last man to be executed at Oxford.

NAME	Oliver George Butler
AGE AT EXECUTION	24
DATE OF EXECUTION	Tuesday, 12th August, 1952
PLACE OF EXECUTION	Oxford
HANGMAN	Not known
ASSISTANT	Not known
DATE OF TRIAL	4th July, 1952
LOCATION OF TRIAL	Stafford
PRESIDING JUDGE	Mister Justice Hallett
PROSECUTION COUNSEL	E. Ryder Richardson
DEFENCE COUNSEL	G.G. Baker
NUMBER OF VICTIMS	1

VICTIMS DETAILS	
NAME	Rose Margaret Meadows
AGE	21
DATE OF MURDER	Monday, 19th May, 1952
PLACE OF MURDER	Field near Horley, Banbury
METHOD OF KILLING	Strangled
RELATIONSHIP TO KILLER	Girlfriend

AT A FEW minutes after 8.00pm on March 6th, 1952, the shop bell rang at 203–204 Bute Street, Cardiff. In living accommodation at the back of the shop, was the proprietor, Lily Volpert, her mother, her sister – Mrs Miara – and her niece. Lily left the others and went to serve her customer.

At 8.20pm, a neighbour, William Archbold, also visited Lily's shop, in order to make a purchase. When no one came to serve him, William stamped his feet to attract someone's attention, but then, as he half-turned towards the right, he saw the reason he had not been attended to. Lily's body lay on the shop floor, her throat gashed. William ran for the police.

Information flowed rapidly into the hands of the investigating officers. A man named Harold Cover came forward to say that he had seen a coloured man, Mahmood Mattan, standing in the porchway of the shop at 8.15pm. This put the Somali at the scene of the crime at about the time the murder was committed.

A sum approaching £120 had been taken from the shop. The police discovered another witness, Mary Gray, who ran a second-hand clothing shop in Bridge Street. She knew Mattan, who had been a customer of hers before, and reported that just before 9.00pm on the night of the murder, Mattan had visited her shop. He was out of breath when he arrived and seemed to have a large wad of money. This particularly attracted her notice, since Mattan was unemployed at the time.

Mattan lived at a lodging house in Davis Street, run by Ernest Leonard Harrison, and even Mr Harrison gave evidence against Mattan. In the days immediately following the murder, Mattan had talked freely to him about the matter and described how a single assailant could have inflicted the injuries by pulling the victim's head back by the hair. Scientific tests had already showed the police that this was the method used in the case of Lily Volpert.

The final piece of evidence came when Mattan's clothing was taken and examined. Eighty-seven minute spots of human blood were found on a right shoe, whilst a further 18 were found on the left.

Charged with murder, Mattan's defence

NAME	Mahmood Hussein Mattan
AGE AT EXECUTION	28
DATE OF EXECUTION	Wednesday, 3rd September, 1952
PLACE OF EXECUTION	Cardiff
HANGMAN	Not known
ASSISTANT	Not known
DATE OF TRIAL	22nd July – 24th July, 1952
LOCATION OF TRIAL	Swansea
PRESIDING JUDGE	Mister Justice Ormerod
PROSECUTION COUNSEL	H. Edmund Davies, Alun T. Davies, Bryan Rees
DEFENCE COUNSEL	T.E.R. Rhys-Roberts, Peter Hopkin Morgan
NUMBER OF VICTIMS	1

VICTIMS DETAILS	
NAME	Lily Volpert
AGE	41
DATE OF MURDER	Thursday, 6th March, 1952
PLACE OF MURDER	203–204 Bute Street, Cardiff
METHOD OF KILLING	Cut throat
RELATIONSHIP TO KILLER	None

was to deny everything. He had not been in Lily's shop since 1949. He did not show Mary Gray a large quantity of money and had not discussed the murder with his landlord describing how it could have been committed. After listening to all the evidence, the jury considered their verdict for one hour and 35 minutes. Found guilty, Mattan was executed at Cardiff in September.

Only much later did it become plain that Mattan was not guilty of the crime which had claimed his life. Mrs Gray had allegedly asked another witness to back up her story and Harold Cover was himself discredited as a witness when it was found that he had described the man he had seen as having a gold tooth. Mattan had no such distinguishing feature, but Tehar Gass, another suspect at the time, had.

Furthermore, Mattan's estranged wife had testified that she had seen her husband at about the time Mrs Volpert was being murdered. Finally, as if further evidence were needed, there was the matter of an illegal identification parade conducted by the police, the results of which were never released to the defence. Joyce Sullivan, a 12-year-old, had also seen a coloured man outside Lily Volpert's shop. She was taken to the police station and there one man only, Mattan, was brought out for her to identify. Joyce swore that he was not the man she had seen.

All of this led to Mattan's conviction being quashed on February 4th, 1998. The State had taken a mere 46 years to acknowledge that it had hanged an innocent man.

THE TAXI DRIVER, Mister Gillespie, picked up the young couple from Uxbridge station and was told to drive to Chalfont Road, Maple Cross, near Rickmansworth. It was a journey that the young lady, Maureen Cox, would never complete, for on the way her companion, John Godar, stabbed her 23 times in her left temple and cheek, 28 times in her chest and eight times in her throat.

Gillespie stopped the taxi when he heard Maureen scream for help. The scream was followed by a frenzied knocking on the door of the taxi. When he opened the door the body of Maureen, which was slumped on the floor, covered in blood, nearly fell out. Godar commented, "I think I've hurt her. He then asked Gillespie to take him to Uxbridge police station where he gave himself up.

When interviewed by Chief Inspector Richardson and Inspector Gladwell, Godar said: "I would sooner let it go. I just want to go where she is, and as quickly as possible, and no messing about." He then admitted that the motive for this vicious crime had been simple jealousy.

Godar and Maureen had been going out together for 10 months but by the time of her death, Maureen had begun to have her doubts about the relationship. Only recently she had discovered that Godar had been married and divorced and had a child. This had caused her to rethink the situation and in the taxi cab on the way to her home, she had also talked to Godar about a date she intended to have, with another man, on the following Sunday. This was all too much for Godar who drew out a knife and attacked Maureen in a frenzy.

Godar's sanity had to be considered carefully. Doctor Rossiter Lewis gave evidence that in his opinion, Godar was suffering from mental problems which caused him to have an outburst of temporary insanity lasting less than a minute, during which he killed Maureen. This was countered by the testimony of Doctor Matheson of Brixton prison who said that he could find no evidence of insanity.

It was, of course, the duty of the defence to prove conclusively that Godar had been insane at the time of the crime and this they failed to do. The jury made their decision in 40 minutes and made no recommendation to mercy.

NAME	John Howard Godar
AGE AT EXECUTION	31
DATE OF EXECUTION	Friday, 5th September, 1952
PLACE OF EXECUTION	Pentonville
HANGMAN	Albert Pierrepoint
ASSISTANT	Robert Leslie Stewart
DATE OF TRIAL	7th July – 8th July, 1952
LOCATION OF TRIAL	Old Bailey
PRESIDING JUDGE	Mister Justice Barry
PROSECUTION COUNSEL	Christmas Humphreys, K.S. Lewis
DEFENCE COUNSEL	B. Wigoder
NUMBER OF VICTIMS	1

VICTIMS DETAILS	
NAME	Maureen Jones Cox
AGE	20
DATE OF MURDER	Friday, 6th June, 1952
PLACE OF MURDER	In a taxi cab, Uxbridge, London
METHOD OF KILLING	Stabbed
RELATIONSHIP TO KILLER	Girlfriend

1952

KRYSTYNA SKARBEK, A native of Poland, had served the Allies well during the Second World War, and had been rewarded with the George Medal, an O.B.E., and the Croix de Guerre.

When hostilities broke out, she had been living in East Africa and immediately offered to help Britain. She was sent to Hungary where she helped to establish a resistance and lines of communications. For her pains, she was arrested twice by the Gestapo but managed to get away.

Leaving Hungary, Krystyna also served in Turkey and, after undergoing parachute training, was dropped into France, where she worked with the Resistance. Finally, she served in Italy and, after the war, moved to England, took out British citizenship and changed her name to Christine Granville.

Christine lived in peaceful retirement until June 15th, 1952. On that day she was in the foyer of the Shelbourne Hotel when a man rushed forward and stabbed her in the chest. The knife was embedded in Christine's flesh up to the hilt and penetrated her heart. She died immediately and her assailant was arrested.

Dennis Muldowney, the killer, claimed that he had attacked Christine through jealousy. He said that they had been lovers but he had found out that she was seeing another man. He had seen them together in April and had decided that he would kill Christine and then take his own life.

Muldowney did not see Christine again until June 15th, when he saw her going into the hotel. He followed her, stopped her and asked her to return some letters he had written to her. She replied that she had burned them; added that she wanted nothing more to do with him and finished by saying that she was leaving for the Continent. It was then that he drew out the knife and killed her.

At Muldowney's trial, he refused all offers of legal assistance and representation and insisted on pleading guilty. The evidence was still heard though, and at one stage, Christine's friends and relatives, represented by Mister Roger Frisby, were able to say that there was no truth in what Muldowney had said about a relationship between himself

NAME	Dennis George Muldowney
AGE AT EXECUTION	41
DATE OF EXECUTION	Tuesday, 30th September, 1952
PLACE OF EXECUTION	Pentonville
HANGMAN	Albert Pierrepoint
ASSISTANT	Harry Smith
DATE OF TRIAL	10th September – 11th September, 1952
LOCATION OF TRIAL	Old Bailey
PRESIDING JUDGE	Mister Justice Donovan
PROSECUTION COUNSEL	Christmas Humphreys
DEFENCE COUNSEL	None
NUMBER OF VICTIMS	1

VICTIMS DETAILS	
NAME	Countess Krystyna Skarbek (Christine Granville)
AGE	37
DATE OF MURDER	Sunday, 15th June, 1952
PLACE OF MURDER	Foyer of the Shelbourne Hotel, 1 Lexham Gardens, Kensington, London
METHOD OF KILLING	Stabbed
RELATIONSHIP TO KILLER	None

and Christine. It was all a figment of his imagination.

The verdict was a foregone conclusion. Muldowney did not appeal or petition for a reprieve and was hanged at the same time as wife-murderer Raymond Cull.

RAYMOND CULL AND his wife, Jean, were constantly arguing over money and his jealousy and eventually this proved too much for Jean. She left the marital home at Thorne Close, Northolt and returned to her father's house in Shadwell Drive.

Raymond tried to get Jean to return to him. He wrote her several love letters, but she was not to be moved. On June 29th, she wrote him a final letter, making her position absolutely plain: "I don't want you anymore. Please understand, I just don't want to see you anymore."

At midnight that same day, Jean's father was woken from his sleep by a terrible scream coming from her bedroom. He ran to offer assistance and discovered Jean lying on the floor with Cull standing over her, a 17-inch bayonet in his hand. Cull then proceeded to chase the dead girl's father from his own house before escaping to his sister's home, where he announced: "I think I have stabbed Jeannie." The police were called and Cull handed over the bayonet saying: "I did it guv, with this bayonet. She has been two-timing me."

Cull told the police that he had been out drinking that evening and had consumed 17 pints of beer. Making up his mind that he had to speak to Jean, Cull had taken the bayonet with him just to frighten her father if he should try to bar him from the house. Cull found that all the doors were locked by the time he arrived at Shadwell Drive but climbed in through a window and took off his shoes so he would not disturb anyone. Cull recalled going to his wife's room and waking her whereupon she grabbed for the bayonet and in the struggle that followed, she fell over, accidentally collapsing onto the blade.

The postmortem was carried out by Doctor Donald Teare who showed that the only way the fatal wound could have been inflicted would be for the bayonet to have been swung so that it struck with some degree of force. This implied that the killing was not accidental and, as a result, Cull was found guilty of murder, though the jury did add a recommendation to mercy.

NAME Raymond John Cull

AGE AT EXECUTION 25

DATE OF EXECUTION Tuesday, 30th September, 1952

PLACE OF EXECUTION Pentonville

HANGMAN Albert Pierrepoint

ASSISTANT Harry Smith, Robert Leslie Stewart

DATE OF TRIAL 11th September – 12th September, 1952

LOCATION OF TRIAL Old Bailey

PRESIDING JUDGE Mister Justice Donovan

PROSECUTION COUNSEL Christmas Humphreys

DEFENCE COUNSEL John Maude

NUMBER OF VICTIMS 1

VICTIMS DETAILS

NAME Jean Frances Cull

AGE 17

DATE OF MURDER Sunday, 29th June, 1952

PLACE OF MURDER Shadwell Drive, Northolt, Middlesex

METHOD OF KILLING Stabbed

RELATIONSHIP TO KILLER Wife

1952

PETER JOHNSON AND Charles Mead, both street traders in London, would describe each other as being the best of friends. Even friends have disagreements though, and when these two argued, on June 28th, the argument developed into a fight during which Johnson picked up a 16-lb lump of concrete, which he used to batter Mead to death.

Johnson did not deny killing Mead, but claimed that it had been in self-defence. It had been Mead who had first wielded the weapon, he told police. Johnson had merely taken it from him and used it against Mead in defence of his own life. If that story were accepted, then Johnson was guilty only of manslaughter.

The trial took place at the Old Bailey and Johnson pleaded not guilty. On the first day of the trial, Johnson became somewhat agitated at one point and after struggling with the warders guarding him in the box, he had to be taken down to the cells below the court. There was further drama to come on day two.

Johnson had claimed that at one point in the struggle with Mead, he had held the concrete block in his hand and at the same time, had managed to remove his jacket. Asked to demonstrate this to the jury, Johnson found that he was unable to duplicate the movement. Once again Johnson became agitated and Mister Humphreys took his chance to press Johnson on an earlier statement to the police in which he claimed he had deliberately struck Mead with the block whilst he lay on the ground. Johnson announced that he wished to change his plea.

As a result of all these events, the jury of 10 men and two women took only 30 minutes to decide that the killing had been deliberate. Passing sentence, Mister Justice Donovan pointed out that Johnson had a long record of violence. Johnson merely shrugged his shoulders and smiled.

NAME	Peter Cyril Johnson
AGE AT EXECUTION	24
DATE OF EXECUTION	Thursday, 9th October, 1952
PLACE OF EXECUTION	Pentonville
HANGMAN	Albert Pierrepoint
ASSISTANT	Harry Allen
DATE OF TRIAL	17th September – 18th September, 1952
LOCATION OF TRIAL	Old Bailey
PRESIDING JUDGE	Mister Justice Donovan
PROSECUTION COUNSEL	Christmas Humphreys
DEFENCE COUNSEL	Not known
NUMBER OF VICTIMS	1

VICTIMS DETAILS

NAME	Charles Mead
AGE	24
DATE OF MURDER	Saturday, 28th June, 1952
PLACE OF MURDER	Bethnal Green Gardens, London
METHOD OF KILLING	Battered
RELATIONSHIP TO KILLER	None

DONALD SIMON MARRIED his wife in 1943. Soon afterwards they emigrated to Canada, but Eunice became homesick and in 1947, the couple returned to England.

The following year, Donald began drinking heavily and this, amongst other reasons, caused Eunice to leave him, in November, 1951. By 1952, Eunice was living at 20 Seymour Road, with her mother, Isabel, whilst Donald was staying in Northampton Avenue, Slough. More importantly perhaps, a friendship had developed between Eunice and another man.

Victor Brades had originally been a dancing partner of Eunice's. Donald had objected to their seeing each other but once he and Eunice had split, the association became more frequent and Victor started taking Eunice to theatres, public houses and other places of entertainment.

On the evening of June 21st, Victor and Eunice had been enjoying a drink at the King's Arms in Windsor with his cousin, James Howard and James's wife. Once the group had broken up, Victor walked Eunice home.

It was 11.40pm when Norman Broad heard shots and the sound of a woman screaming. Rushing to Seymour Road, he saw two bodies lying in the street. Near one of them, the woman, crouched the form of Donald Simon. He was gazing down at his wife's body crying: "What have I done?"

Victor Brades was already dead, having been shot four times. Eunice had received two wounds and was to die in hospital the following day. Donald Simon readily confessed to killing both of them.

There could be no doubt that the crime had been one of premeditation. Earlier that evening, Simon had called at Eunice's mother's house and asked if his wife was still seeing Brades. He then waited for them to arrive home, shooting them as soon as they appeared.

With his own confession and the evidence of Norman Broad, there could only be one verdict. Sentenced to death on the one indictment, that of the murder of his wife, Simon was hanged at Shrewsbury, the second man to be executed there that year.

NAME	Donald Neil Simon
AGE AT EXECUTION	32
DATE OF EXECUTION	Thursday, 23rd October, 1952
PLACE OF EXECUTION	Shrewsbury
HANGMAN	Not known
ASSISTANT	Not known
DATE OF TRIAL	29th July, 1952
LOCATION OF TRIAL	Birmingham
PRESIDING JUDGE	Mister Justice Jones
PROSECUTION COUNSEL	C.N. Shawcross
DEFENCE COUNSEL	Richard O'Sullivan
NUMBER OF VICTIMS	2

VICTIMS DETAILS

NAMES	Eunice Marjorie Joyce Simon (Died Sunday, 22nd June, 1952); Victor Brades
AGES	28; 27
DATE OF MURDER	Saturday, 21st June, 1952
PLACE OF MURDER	Seymour Road, Off Church Street, Chalvey, near Slough
METHOD OF KILLING	Shot; shot
RELATIONSHIP TO KILLER	Wife; none

1952

IN 1947, ERIC Norcliffe, an ex-R.A.F. gunner, married Kathleen. The couple could not set up their own home together for some time, due to the post-war housing shortage, and it was not until April 1952, that they managed to move to Hammerwater Drive, Warsop.

Most families have routines and the Norcliffe family was no different. Eric was in the habit of rising early each morning, waking the children, and then taking his wife a cup of tea. This apparently cosy domesticity was repeated as usual on June 25th, 1952, but the veneer was about to crack.

When Kathleen herself came downstairs and asked Eric why he had not made the breakfast, an argument broke out and Eric told her that this was her job, not his. Soon afterwards, when Kathleen told Eric she was going out shopping, a second argument took place, but Kathleen still left and bought what she needed for the day.

Upon her return, Kathleen found that Eric had not made the dinner. A third row now took place. Finally Kathleen decided to cook the meal herself but asked Eric to cut up the cabbage.

The knife Eric took to perform this task was not sharp enough so he used his own sheath knife to chop up the vegetable. Once more Kathleen found fault, telling Eric that he was not cutting the cabbage properly and calling him a bastard into the bargain. That was the final straw for Eric. He stabbed Kathleen 12 times, leaving her dead on the kitchen floor.

Eric freely admitted to the police that he had stabbed Kathleen because she had called him a bastard. His only hope to avoid the hangman was to try to show that he had not known what he was doing at the time.

Doctor Woddis, called by the defence, suggested that Eric had suffered from melancholia for 12 months. A common aspect of this condition was temporary amnesia and so Eric might not have been aware of his actions at the time of the crime. Eric's father, Archibald Norcliffe, testified that his son spent long periods with his head held in his hands, sighing heavily and an old friend, Henry Dennett, told how Eric had changed recently and was

NAME	Eric Norcliffe
AGE AT EXECUTION	30
DATE OF EXECUTION	Friday, 12th December, 1952
PLACE OF EXECUTION	Lincoln
HANGMAN	Not known
ASSISTANT	Not known
DATE OF TRIAL	20th November, 1952
LOCATION OF TRIAL	Nottingham
PRESIDING JUDGE	Mister Justice Hallett
PROSECUTION COUNSEL	Richard O'Sullivan, Anthony Cripps
DEFENCE COUNSEL	W.A. Fearnley-Whittingstall, P.D. Cotes-Preedy
NUMBER OF VICTIMS	1

VICTIMS DETAILS	
NAME	Kathleen Vera Norcliffe
AGE	23
DATE OF MURDER	Wednesday, 25th June, 1952
PLACE OF MURDER	59 Hammerwater Drive, Warsop
METHOD OF KILLING	Stabbed
RELATIONSHIP TO KILLER	Wife

now very different from his old friendly self.

The jury were not convinced that Eric Norcliffe had been unaware of his actions and found him guilty as charged.

THE ATMOSPHERE IN the flat in Melville House must have been difficult, to say the least. There were two camps, each made up of feuding family members, sharing the same address and hardly speaking to each other.

On one side was John Kenneth Livesey and his wife. On the other was Harry Small, his wife Stephanie, and their 13-year-old daughter, Patricia. Harry and Stephanie were Livesey's in-laws, and the two groups hated each other with a passion.

On July 15th, Stephanie argued with her daughter, Livesey's wife, and was seen pulling the girl's hair and dragging her about the house. Livesey intervened and struck Harry at which point he was told to leave the house. Livesey ignored the request.

Eleven days later, on July 26th, Harry and Patricia were at a neighbour's house, watching television which was still a rarity at the time. John Livesey had been left alone with his mother-in-law.

Undoubtedly there followed yet another row but finally John snapped. The emotion of the past swelled up inside him and he ended up stabbing Stephanie in the back, 24 times. He then abandoned his wife and fled the house.

It was only a matter of time before Livesey was picked up and charged with murder. He, of course, related the stories of the long history of nagging and ill-will between the two family groups and claimed that although he had been sorely provoked, he had not killed his mother-in-law.

At the trial, the prosecution made much of the fact that Livesey had run away, but that was hardly proof of murder. If, as he claimed, he had simply found the body, Livesey must have known that the family history would make him a prime suspect and surely that was reason enough for his flight. The jury, though, eventually returned a guilty verdict and Livesey was sentenced to death, still protesting that he was innocent.

The appeal was dismissed on December 1st, with Livesey's own counsel saying that he saw no way he could possibly support it. Even now, John Livesey maintained that it was not his hand that had taken the life of Stephanie Small.

NAME	John Kenneth Livesey
AGE AT EXECUTION	23
DATE OF EXECUTION	Wednesday, 17th December, 1952
PLACE OF EXECUTION	Wandsworth
HANGMAN	Albert Pierrepoint
ASSISTANT	Syd Dernley
DATE OF TRIAL	24th October, 1952
LOCATION OF TRIAL	Old Bailey
PRESIDING JUDGE	Mister Justice Hilbery
PROSECUTION COUNSEL	Christmas Humphreys
DEFENCE COUNSEL	Derek Curtis-Bennett
NUMBER OF VICTIMS	1

VICTIMS DETAILS	
NAME	Stephanie Marie Small
AGE	49
DATE OF MURDER	Saturday, 26th July, 1952
PLACE OF MURDER	Melville House, Blackheath Hill, Blackheath, London
METHOD OF KILLING	Stabbed
RELATIONSHIP TO KILLER	Mother-in-law

Executed at Wandsworth, Livesey could not even escape drama in death. After his body had been left on the rope for the statutory hour, he was taken down by the executioner and his assistant. Syd Dernley, thinking that the atmosphere was rather serious, even for such an event, remarked as he removed Livesey's clothing that he had a magnificent set of "vital parts". This crass, infantile and unfeeling comment found its way to the ears of the authorities. Dernley was to take part in just one more execution, for which he had already been commissioned.

THE BODY OF Alice Wiltshaw was discovered by her husband when he returned home on July 16th, 1952. She was lying in a pool of blood in the kitchen of her house and her death had been a most cruel one.

The trail of blood led police to the conclusion that Alice had been attacked in the kitchen. The poor woman had tried to escape down a corridor and her assailant had followed her, hitting as he went. All kinds of weapons had been used in the attack: a large log, vases, ornaments and finally a three-foot long poker, all of which were found heavily bloodstained. Alice had finally made her way back to the kitchen and as she lay on the floor, dying, the callous killer had stabbed her through the head with the poker, repeatedly shoving it up through her chin, into her skull. The killer had left behind a footprint and a pair of bloodstained gloves. Over £3,000 worth of jewellery was found to be missing.

There was no sign of a break-in and the crime had taken place when the servants were all off duty. This suggested that the killer was someone Alice Wiltshaw knew and someone who knew the household routine. Both suggested that an ex-employee would be the right kind of candidate. The prime suspect appeared to be Leslie Green who had been dismissed just a few weeks previously for disobedience.

Further inquires led to witnesses describing a man, who fitted Green's description, eating in the bar of the Station Hotel in Stafford and leaving at 3.30pm. The same man was back in the hotel three hours later and this fitted in with the approximate time of Alice Wiltshaw's murder.

A few days later, Green was traced and when his girlfriend was interviewed she showed them some rings Green had given her. These had been taken from the dead woman's fingers and linked Green to the crime. The final piece of evidence was a tear in the thumb of the left-hand glove found at the scene of the crime. The tear matched exactly with the mark of a healed cut on Green's thumb, showing that the gloves had belonged to him. Green was found guilty of murder and hanged at Winson Green prison on December 23rd,

NAME	Leslie Green
AGE AT EXECUTION	29
DATE OF EXECUTION	Tuesday, 23rd December, 1952
PLACE OF EXECUTION	Birmingham
HANGMAN	Albert Pierrepoint
ASSISTANT	Syd Dernley
DATE OF TRIAL	3rd December – 5th December, 1952
LOCATION OF TRIAL	Stafford
PRESIDING JUDGE	Mister Justice Stable
PROSECUTION COUNSEL	E. Ryder Richardson, J.F. Bourke
DEFENCE COUNSEL	G.G. Baker, G.T. Meredith
NUMBER OF VICTIMS	1

VICTIMS DETAILS	
NAME	Alice Wiltshaw
AGE	62
DATE OF MURDER	Wednesday, 16th July, 1952
PLACE OF MURDER	Barlaston, Staffordshire
METHOD OF KILLING	Battered/stabbed
RELATIONSHIP TO KILLER	None

1952. Most of the jewellery Green had taken has never been recovered.

HERBERT APPLEBY HAD been in the army for two years and had spent most of his service days in the Middle East. When home on leave, he lived with his mother, father and elder brother at 96 Laing Street, Grangetown and was happily involved with a young lady named Lilian Robbins, known to her friends as Dolly.

Saturday, September 20th, 1952, started out as a happy day for the Appleby family. Herbert was a groomsman at the wedding of a friend and Dolly had accompanied him to the festivities. It was at the reception afterwards that Herbert saw Dolly on a couch with John David Thomas, the groom's stepbrother.

Immediately Herbert managed to convince himself that Thomas was trying to steal Dolly from him. Picking up a kitchen knife, Appleby moved forward and stabbed Thomas dead. He then got into a taxi, driven by William Henry Flower, and asked him to drive to the police station. On the way there, Appleby told Flower what he had done and added: "He is dead. I shall hang."

At the police station, Appleby was seen by Sergeant Ellis to whom he said: "I have stabbed a man and killed him and that is that." He was then charged with the murder of John David Thomas.

Insanity was again the defence. Appleby was examined by Doctor Cuthbert who would testify that he believed that Appleby was suffering from clouded consciousness at the time of the attack and would not have known what he was doing. This state might have only lasted for a few seconds, to be followed by a period of lucidness.

Evidence was also given that instruments used to deliver Appleby when he was born, had caused a squint and may also have caused brain damage. He was moody and had been known to sleepwalk. Appleby had threatened suicide on more than one occasion and had even attempted it in 1950. Finally, there was evidence of epilepsy in the family.

To counter this, the prosecution called Doctor Pickering, the medical officer at Durham prison. He gave the opinion that Appleby was perfectly sane and that the

NAME	Herbert Appleby
AGE AT EXECUTION	21
DATE OF EXECUTION	Wednesday, 24th December, 1952
PLACE OF EXECUTION	Durham
HANGMAN	Not known
ASSISTANT	Not known
DATE OF TRIAL	4th December – 5th December, 1952
LOCATION OF TRIAL	Leeds
PRESIDING JUDGE	Mister Justice Cassels
PROSECUTION COUNSEL	H.R.B. Shepherd, John M. McLusky
DEFENCE COUNSEL	G.R. Hinchcliffe, T.R. Nevin
NUMBER OF VICTIMS	1

VICTIMS DETAILS	
NAME	John David Thomas
AGE	29
DATE OF MURDER	Saturday, 20th September, 1952
PLACE OF MURDER	18 Lee Road, Grangetown, near Middlesborough
METHOD OF KILLING	Stabbed
RELATIONSHIP TO KILLER	None

killing of Thomas was due to nothing more than temper aggravated by the consumption of alcohol.

In the event, the prosecution opinion carried the day and after a two-day trial, Herbert Appleby was found guilty and sentenced to death. He was hanged on Christmas Eve.

GEOFFREY DEAN, A married man with a five-year-old daughter, worked in the ticket office at Ash Vale station. Then one day in August, 1952, he attended to a customer who asked about the times of boat trains from Victoria to Dover. In the course of that conversation, Dean discovered that he was talking to a fellow rail employee, John James Alcott.

The following morning, just before 7.00am, Alcott returned and was kindly invited into the staff room by Dean. Shortly afterwards, another employee, a porter named Wright, went into that same staff room where he saw Alcott cleaning his fingernails with a large sheath knife.

At 8.45pm on August 22nd, Corporal Vincent went to Ash Vale ticket office and found that the wooden partition was closed. Vincent could hear noises from inside the office but no one came to attend to him. A few minutes later, a junior porter named Bull, saw lights go on in the booking office but still there was no one to attend to the customers. Thinking that Mr Dean might have been taken ill, Bull pulled himself up to the top of the locked door and looked into the office through a small window. Though he could not see any too clearly, he did see a pair of feet and a great deal of blood.

An entry was forced. The safe was open and bags of cash lay strewn about the floor. It would later be deduced that just over £168 was missing. More serious was the fact that Geoffrey Dean had been brutally stabbed to death. There were 20 wounds on his body.

Meanwhile, John Alcott had travelled to Aldershot where, at 10.20pm, he took lodgings in Victoria Road with a Mrs Dagger and signed in as J.J. Alcott. It was only a matter of time before he was traced there by the police and he then made a full confession to the crime, telling officers that he had hidden the knife up a chimney at his lodging house. The knife was found exactly where Alcott said it was.

In addition to the confession and the murder weapon, Alcott had also left a fingerprint at the scene of the crime and was identified as the visitor seen in the staff room, talking to Dean. The guilty verdict was a mere

NAME	John James Alcott
AGE AT EXECUTION	22
DATE OF EXECUTION	Friday, 2nd January, 1953
PLACE OF EXECUTION	Wandsworth
HANGMAN	Albert Pierrepoint
ASSISTANT	Harry Smith
DATE OF TRIAL	19th November, 1952
LOCATION OF TRIAL	Kingston upon Thames
PRESIDING JUDGE	Mister Justice Finnemore
PROSECUTION COUNSEL	John Flowers
DEFENCE COUNSEL	C.G.L. Du Cann
NUMBER OF VICTIMS	1

VICTIMS DETAILS	
NAME	Geoffrey Charles 'Dixie' Dean
AGE	27
DATE OF MURDER	Friday, 22nd August, 1952
PLACE OF MURDER	Ash Vale station, near Aldershot
METHOD OF KILLING	Stabbed
RELATIONSHIP TO KILLER	None

formality, though an attempt was made to say that Alcott had been insane at the time.

Alcott's appeal was dismissed on December 17th, and his execution date was now fixed. Once before, John Alcott had been in this position. In 1949, whilst in the Grenadier Guards, Alcott had been sentenced to death by a court-martial for the murder of a nightwatchman at Montabaur, in Germany. On that occasion the sentence had not been confirmed and he had escaped death, on a technicality. This time he was not so fortunate.

THOMAS ALEXANDER OWNED Huntlygate Farm which lay along the Lanark to Carstairs road and one of his tenants was somewhat unusual. Michael Connolly lived in a hut 420 yards south of the road, in one of Alexander's fields. He was a quiet enough and the only complaint he had ever made was that occasionally, some of the cows came a little close to his home. Thomas solved the problem by placing some barbed wire around the hut.

Michael was retired and as such, entitled to a state pension. This he collected, from Lanark, each Friday, and things were no different on Friday, August 15th, 1952. Indeed, after collecting his money, Michael was seen heading back to his hut by Thomas Alexander himself.

On August 22nd, however, Michael Connolly failed to collect his pension. Two days later, on August 24th, Thomas Alexander went to the hut to check that everything was all right. He found Connolly's battered body lying on his bed. There was shattered glass lying about and footsteps leading away from the hut.

An examination of the body by Professor Andrew Allinson showed that death was due to a fracture of the skull, lacerations of the brain and internal haemorrhage. There was a good deal of blood and it seemed likely that the killer would have stains on his clothing. The attack would have taken place on or about Sunday, August 17th.

Investigations brought forward a number of witnesses. James Jarvie was a part-time barman at the Clyde Valley Hotel at Kirkfieldbank and on August 17th he had seen a man he knew to be George Shaw spending a good deal of money. He had a rolled up bundle of £1 notes in his hand and didn't seem to care how many he spent. His companion, George Dunn, was also flush with cash. This was confirmed by Thomas Miller, one of the customers, who said that Shaw had bought him lots to drink.

The police soon picked up Shaw and Dunn and their clothing was examined. Professor Allinson found bloodstains on Shaw's clothing that were the same group as that of the dead man. Other stains were found on

NAME	George Francis Shaw
AGE AT EXECUTION	25
DATE OF EXECUTION	Monday, 26th January, 1953
PLACE OF EXECUTION	Glasgow, Barlinnie
HANGMAN	Not known
ASSISTANT	Not known
DATE OF TRIAL	2nd December – 9th December, 1952
LOCATION OF TRIAL	Glasgow
PRESIDING JUDGE	Lord Justice Carmont
PROSECUTION COUNSEL	Norman E. Sloan
DEFENCE COUNSEL	Hector McKechnie
NUMBER OF VICTIMS	1

VICTIMS DETAILS	
NAME	Michael Connolly (Conly)
AGE	78
DATE OF MURDER	Sunday, 17th August, 1952
PLACE OF MURDER	Huntlygate Farm, Lanark to Carstairs Road, Lanark
METHOD OF KILLING	Battered
RELATIONSHIP TO KILLER	None

Dunn's khaki battledress. That, plus the testimony of other witnesses such as Kathleen Wallace who had seen them close to the hut at 3.15pm on August 17th, was enough to charge them both.

At the trial, the jury were out for one hour and 40 minutes before finding Shaw guilty of murder and Dunn, who had a mental age of eight, guilty of culpable homicide. Dunn was sent to a mental institution whilst Shaw had his execution date set for December 30th, 1952.

That execution was postponed when Shaw entered an appeal. The appeal was dismissed on January 5th, 1953.

BY THE TIME he reached adulthood, Derek Bentley had already had his fair share of misfortune. One of a set of twins, his brother died within two hours of his birth, and Derek himself was not expected to survive for long.

Derek did survive though, his next difficulty coming at the age of four when he fell from a lorry he was playing on. Landing on his head, Derek had to be rushed to hospital where it was diagnosed that the fall had brought on an epileptic seizure. His parents were told that he would never be the same again.

At the age of seven, a bomb fell on the air-raid shelter Derek and his family were occupying and Derek had to be dug free. A similar occurrence came at the age of 11, when one of Hitler's flying bombs demolished the family house in Blackfriars.

By 1948, the Bentley family were living at 1 Fairview Road and Derek's father, William, had set up a workshop in a shed in the back garden, where Derek could amuse himself pottering about with the televisions and radios he loved to take apart, but it was also in 1948, that Derek came to the attention of the law for the first time.

In March, Derek was charged with attempted shop-breaking and theft. He was bound over for two years. Later that same year he left school but within two weeks was in trouble again for taking some tools that had been left on a bomb site. This time Derek was sent to approved school in Bristol and it was here that he would be educationally assessed as having an IQ in the mid-60s and a reading age of about four and a half.

Bentley was released in July 1950. He returned home a quieter, more introverted youth than ever and, ashamed of being a Borstal boy, didn't even go out for over a year. Slowly his family brought him out of his shell until eventually he found employment as a furniture mover with a company called Albert Hutchins. Unfortunately this was not to last for long. In March 1952, Derek strained his back and had to give the job up.

Before this, at Christmas 1951, Derek had been introduced to Christopher Craig. Craig was three years younger than Derek and had

NAME	Derek William Bentley
AGE AT EXECUTION	19
DATE OF EXECUTION	Wednesday, 28th January, 1953
PLACE OF EXECUTION	Wandsworth
HANGMAN	Albert Pierrepoint
ASSISTANT	Harry Allen
DATE OF TRIAL	9th December – 11th December, 1952
LOCATION OF TRIAL	Old Bailey
PRESIDING JUDGE	Lord Chief Justice, Lord Goddard
PROSECUTION COUNSEL	Christmas Humphreys, John Stuart Bass
DEFENCE COUNSEL	Frank Cassels
NUMBER OF VICTIMS	1

VICTIMS DETAILS	
NAME	Sydney Miles
AGE	42
DATE OF MURDER	Sunday, 2nd November, 1952
PLACE OF MURDER	Roof of Barlow and Parkers, Tamworth Road, Croydon
METHOD OF KILLING	Shot
RELATIONSHIP TO KILLER	None

attended the same school at one stage. It is possible that Derek already knew Craig from school but it was only at this time that the two started seeing each other regularly.

Christopher Craig was born on May 19th, 1936, the youngest of nine children. He came from a secure family background, the only problem being Christopher's eldest brother – Niven. Niven made his living by crime and Christopher greatly admired his tough-guy image. So much so that when Niven Craig was sentenced to 12 years' imprisonment for an armed robbery, Christopher Craig took it very badly indeed.

Derek Bentley's parents did not approve of Christopher Craig and actively discouraged the friendship between them. Nevertheless, the two did meet regularly, along with two other friends: Norman Parsley and Frank Farzey. All William Bentley's fears were to become realised on the night of November 2nd, 1952.

On that Sunday evening, Derek was watching television at home when Craig called for him. The door was answered by

Derek's mother Lillian, who told Craig that Derek was not in. Shortly afterwards, Norman and Frank called and Derek was allowed to go out with them. What Derek's parents could not know was that Christopher Craig was waiting for him at the end of the street.

After some talk, Parsley and Farzey left the other two, who caught a bus to Croydon. They walked down Tamworth Road until Craig stopped outside a warehouse and looked in through a window. On impulse Craig suggested they break in and soon he and Bentley were climbing over the large iron gates that led to the interior of the yard.

Across the road from the warehouse, John and Edith Ware were just putting their young daughter to bed when she excitedly pointed out that two men were climbing over the gates of Barlow and Parker's warehouse. John Ware correctly deduced that the two youths were up to no good, rushed to a nearby telephone box and telephoned the police. Meanwhile Craig, followed immediately by Bentley, had climbed a drainpipe that took them to the roof of the warehouse.

What happened next on that roof has been subject to constant interpretation ever since. The bare facts of the case are that the police arrived, an officer, Detective Constable Frederick Fairfax, was shot after arresting Bentley and later, a second officer, Constable Sydney Miles was shot dead.

According to the police version, Fairfax arrived on the scene with a number of other officers. He climbed the gates and the drainpipe and saw the two youths on the roof. He identified himself as a police officer and arrested Derek Bentley. Bentley then pulled away and shouted "Let him have it Chris", whereupon Craig fired at Fairfax, wounding him in the shoulder.

Two other officers, Constable Norman Harrison and Constable James Christie McDonald heard Bentley shout those words and all three waited on the rooftop for armed officers to arrive, Fairfax still holding on to Derek Bentley. Shortly afterwards the door of a stairhead burst open and Constable Miles rushed out to be shot in the head by Craig. Craig continued to fire at the officers until Derek Bentley was taken downstairs by

the three officers who had now been joined by a fourth: Constable Robert Jaggs. Fairfax then returned with a firearm and as all the police officers rushed at Craig, who had by now run out of ammunition, the killer jumped over the edge of the roof, landing on a greenhouse in the next-door garden and badly injuring himself.

However, another story has been told about the events of that night. Constable Claude Pain was also present on that roof. In fact, he was the second officer to arrive, reaching the roof just before Fairfax was shot. He did not hear Derek Bentley shout anything to Craig, but he was not called to give evidence. It should also be remembered that both Bentley and Craig denied that any such shout was ever made.

The trial opened on December 9th, 1952, in front of the Lord Chief Justice, Rayner Goddard. Throughout the trial he interrupted constantly, usually to underline a point made by the prosecution. His most telling display of bias occurred in his summing-up, when he picked up a knuckle-duster, with a metal spike on one end, which had been found in Derek Bentley's possession.

Goddard put the knuckle-duster on and, describing it as a fearsome weapon, slammed it into the woodwork of the bench. Bentley had claimed that this was given to him by Craig on the night of the shooting. Derek had not wanted anything to do with it, but Craig had simply put it into his pocket. It should be noted that this weapon was found in Bentley's right-hand pocket when he was searched by Fairfax. Derek Bentley was left-handed.

There was no doubt that Christopher Craig was guilty of murder. Derek Bentley claimed that he had not known that Craig had a gun until he actually started to use it. He also denied that he had uttered the words "Let him have it Chris." Had those words been uttered, then they may well have been open to two interpretations – either hand the weapon over, or fire. Had the words been said, then surely Derek Bentley would have testified that he meant 'hand the weapon over'. The fact remains that he denied ever saying them.

The matter becomes even more curious when one recalls that on July 11th, 1940, two

1953

men named Ostler and Appleby were hanged for the murder of a policeman. These two had broken into a warehouse and been interrupted by a policeman whereupon Appleby had said to Ostler "Let him have it, he is all alone." Although Ostler did the shooting, Appleby was also hanged as he had been held to have incited Ostler to fire. It bears a striking similarity to the case of Craig and Bentley.

After an absence of 75 minutes, the jury returned guilty verdicts on both young men, recommending Bentley to mercy. Craig was ordered to be detained during Her Majesty's pleasure and would eventually serve 10 and a half years in jail. Derek Bentley was sentenced to death.

Over the next few weeks, strenuous efforts were made to secure a reprieve but it was all to no avail. Derek Bentley was hanged on January 28th, 1953. Four of the policemen involved received awards for their gallantry. Fairfax received the George Cross, Harrison and McDonald received the George Medal and Jaggs was awarded the British Empire Medal. There was still no mention of Constable Pain.

There were constant attempts ever since to have Derek Bentley granted a posthumous pardon, due in no small part to the efforts of Derek's sister Iris who campaigned for him ever since his execution, first with Derek's parents and then, after their deaths, alone. Finally, in 1998, after disgraceful delays from the State, that pardon was granted.

THE GIFFARDS WERE a very successful family. Charles Giffard was the senior partner in a firm of solicitors, clerk to the local Justices and the Under Sheriff of Cornwall. His wife, Elizabeth, was vice-chairman of the St Austell Conservative Association and president of the Conservative Women's Association. Their son, though, was a complete failure.

Miles had been to Rugby school, from where he had been asked to leave but applied himself well to sports at Blundell's, his next school, and managed to play cricket for Cornwall. He served in the Royal Navy for three years, then dabbled in law and estate agency, neither of which he took seriously. He lived largely off an allowance from his father.

In late 1952, Miles met Gabrielle Vallance, and a relationship developed between the two. Unfortunately, Charles Giffard did not approve of Gabrielle and on his instructions, Miles was forced to abandon her. On November 4th, he wrote to Gabrielle and told her that he saw no solution short of killing his father.

At 5.30pm on November 7th, Miles telephoned Gabrielle and told her that he would probably be coming to London for the weekend. He said he would ring back to confirm the details. At 7.30pm, Miles's parents returned home and the slaughter began.

Charles Giffard was putting away the car when Miles came into the garage and battered him over the head with an iron pipe. Miles then went into the house and found his mother in the kitchen. She too was attacked with the pipe. Her skull was crushed and an arm broken. Miles now rang Gabrielle to confirm that he would be able to borrow his father's car and would be coming to London.

Going to the garage to take the car out, Miles was rather disconcerted to find that his father was still alive. Checking on his mother, he found that she was slowly regaining consciousness too. Still alive, he put his mother into a wheelbarrow, rolled her down to the edge of the cliff and tipped her over. He repeated the process with his father and then drove off to London.

Both bodies were found the following morning and when Miles was traced and

NAME	Miles William Giffard
AGE AT EXECUTION	27
DATE OF EXECUTION	Tuesday, 24th February, 1953
PLACE OF EXECUTION	Bristol
HANGMAN	Not known
ASSISTANT	Not known
DATE OF TRIAL	4th February – 6th February, 1953
LOCATION OF TRIAL	Bodmin
PRESIDING JUDGE	Mister Justice Oliver
PROSECUTION COUNSEL	John Scott Henderson
DEFENCE COUNSEL	John Maude
NUMBER OF VICTIMS	2

VICTIMS DETAILS	
NAMES	Charles Giffard; Elizabeth Giffard
AGES	53; 56
DATE OF MURDER	Friday, 7th November, 1952
PLACE OF MURDER	St Austell, Cornwall
METHOD OF KILLING	Battered; battered
RELATIONSHIP TO KILLER	Father; mother

arrested, it was found that he had sold some of his mother's jewellery in London, using his own name, and still had some bloodstained clothing on the back seat of the car. Miles had already confessed his crime to Gabrielle.

Miles's defence was one of insanity. He had been seen by a psychiatrist as a young boy and mental deterioration had been demonstrated. There was also that fact that he had been very repressed by an over-strict father, but none of this swayed the jury who were out for just over half an hour before returning their verdict of guilty.

1953

GEORGE WALKER RAN the strangest of shops at Warbreck Moor, in Liverpool. Filled to the brim with all sorts of esoteric and wondrous goods, the door was always locked. Potential customers were forced to knock in order to gain admittance, and wait for old George to let them in.

On the night of January 14th, George's two dogs kept the entire neighbourhood awake with their incessant barking. One neighbour went to check if George was all right but when she received no reply, she assumed that he might have gone away. Finally though, on January 15th, Marion Owen telephoned the police.

When the police forced their way in, they found George lying dead at the foot of his stairs. This was no tragic accident though. George had been battered to death. The murder weapon, an axe, was found, as were some bloody footprints which showed that the assailant had worn shoes with crepe soles.

The dead man's sister, Mary Walker, recalled a thin, pale man who had called to repair some clocks. The same description was given by two schoolboys who had called at the shop on January 13th – the door had been opened by a pale man, with a large nose. The descriptions were published in the local newspapers.

On January 19th, Iris Tucker read those descriptions and became convinced that they fitted her boyfriend, John Todd. She took her suspicions to her father who, not being overly enamoured of Todd anyway, informed the police. Todd was picked up that afternoon at his home in Roxburgh Street and a bloodstained mackintosh found amongst his possessions.

In fact, the police had already spoken to John Todd. He had replied to an earlier appeal for anyone who had had business at the shop to come forward for elimination purposes. Todd had reported on January 16th, made his statement and been allowed to leave.

Todd admitted that he had been at the shop early on the day of the murder. He had repaired some clocks and then, as he was leaving, the old man had stumbled and fallen against him. Sustaining a bloody nose, Walker had somehow rubbed the blood along his

NAME	John Todd
AGE AT EXECUTION	20
DATE OF EXECUTION	Tuesday, 19th May, 1953
PLACE OF EXECUTION	Liverpool
HANGMAN	Albert Pierrepoint
ASSISTANT	John Broadbent
DATE OF TRIAL	8th April – 9th April, 1953
LOCATION OF TRIAL	Liverpool
PRESIDING JUDGE	Mister Justice Cassels
PROSECUTION COUNSEL	Edward Wooll
DEFENCE COUNSEL	Miss Rose Heilbron
NUMBER OF VICTIMS	1

VICTIMS DETAILS	
NAME	George Walker
AGE	82
DATE OF MURDER	Wednesday, 14th January, 1953
PLACE OF MURDER	98 Warbreck Moor, Aintree, Liverpool
METHOD OF KILLING	Battered
RELATIONSHIP TO KILLER	None

coat. George Walker had been alive when he left the shop and so someone else must have gained access later in the day and killed him.

The story was highly unlikely, especially as no mention of this had been made when Todd had made his first statement. There was also the fact that Iris Tucker testified that Todd had always worn a raincoat but that on the Saturday after the murder, she had seen him in an overcoat and Todd had told her that he had lost his other coat. The jury had little trouble in rejecting the defence out of hand.

1953

BY THE OUTBREAK of war in 1939, Christie had been dismissed from a number of jobs and had served prison sentences for petty theft and assault. A special constable in the War Reserve Police, Christie would patrol the streets at night, making sure that the blackout regulations were being properly observed.

In August 1943, Christie met Ruth Fuerst, who worked in a munitions factory in Mayfair. She told him she was frightened of the bombing and as Ethel, Christie's wife was away from home, he saw an opportunity to invite the rather nervous Ruth back to his ground-floor flat at 10 Rillington Place.

After meeting two or three times, according to Christie's later statements to the police, Ruth offered herself to Christie, who made love to her and whilst doing so, strangled her. Hiding her body temporarily under the floorboards in his front room he later dug a grave in the back garden and buried the body late at night.

The next victim was Muriel Eady, who worked in the canteen at Ultra Radio in Acton where Christie began working in late 1943. A regular visitor to Rillington Place, usually with her boyfriend, in October 1944, Muriel made the mistake of visiting Christie by herself.

The unfortunate Muriel had a bad cold but Christie said he knew something that could clear her head. Bubbling household gas through a solution of Friar's Balsam, Muriel was rendered unconscious and then died the same way that Ruth Fuerst had and was buried in the same location, the back garden.

During the war, Ruth Fuerst's skull came to the surface but the cold-blooded Christie simply threw it into a bombed house at 133 St Mark's Road, where it was assumed to belong to an unknown victim of the blitz.

For a number of years Christie did not kill again. It is possible that he had found himself a new sexual partner who satisfied his peculiar desires but the opportunity to kill again came in 1949. The year before, Timothy Evans, his wife Beryl and baby daughter Geraldine, had moved in to the top floor of 10 Rillington Place. Their relationship had always been tempestuous and when in late

NAME John Reginald Halliday Christie

AGE AT EXECUTION 55

DATE OF EXECUTION Wednesday, 15th July, 1953

PLACE OF EXECUTION Pentonville

HANGMAN Albert Pierrepoint

ASSISTANT Harry Smith

DATE OF TRIAL 22nd June – 25th June, 1953

LOCATION OF TRIAL Old Bailey

PRESIDING JUDGE Mister Justice Finnemore

PROSECUTION COUNSEL Sir Lionel Heald

DEFENCE COUNSEL Derek Curtis Bennett

NUMBER OF VICTIMS 7 (possibly as many as 12)

VICTIMS DETAILS

NAMES Ruth Fuerst; Muriel Eady

AGES 21; 31

DATE OF MURDER August, 1943; October, 1944

PLACE OF MURDER 10 Rillington Place, Notting Hill, London

METHOD OF KILLING Strangled; strangled

RELATIONSHIP TO KILLER None; none

NAME Beryl Evans

AGE 19

DATE OF MURDER Tuesday, 8th November, 1949

PLACE OF MURDER 10 Rillington Place, Notting Hill, London

METHOD OF KILLING Strangled

RELATIONSHIP TO KILLER None

NAMES Ethel Christie; Kathleen Maloney

AGES Not known; 26

DATE OF MURDER circa Sunday, 14th December, 1952; January, 1953

PLACE OF MURDER 10 Rillington Place, Notting Hill, London

METHOD OF KILLING Strangled; strangled

RELATIONSHIP TO KILLER Wife; none

NAMES Rita Nelson; Hectorina MacLennan

AGES 25; 25

DATE OF MURDER January, 1953; circa Friday, 6th March, 1953

PLACE OF MURDER 10 Rillington Place, Notting Hill, London

METHOD OF KILLING Strangled; strangled

RELATIONSHIP TO KILLER None; none

1949, Beryl became pregnant and said she wanted an abortion, the arguments began anew. It is possible that this gave Christie his chance. Whatever else transpired, in November 1949, both Beryl and the baby were murdered and Timothy Evans eventually paid the price for that crime, being hanged at Pentonville on March 9th, 1950. Although he had originally confessed to the crime, he had subsequently claimed that Christie had killed both Beryl and Geraldine.

At his own trial, Christie would admit to being the killer of Beryl Evans but always denied murdering young Geraldine. Whatever the truth of the matter, and this is still hotly debated to the present day, Timothy Evans was eventually to receive a full pardon. For a couple of years, Christie again settled down to what passed for a normal life for him. Then, in late 1952, the floodgates suddenly burst open.

Ethel Christie was last seen alive on December 12th, 1952. When she died is not known with precision, but it is certain that she was murdered and her body hidden under the floorboards in the front room, around that date. The reason for this act is not accurately known but it was the catalyst for Christie to go on a murder spree. There were now no restraints.

In January 1953, Christie sold most of his furniture, keeping just a mattress, a table and two chairs, one of which was a deckchair. The following month he picked up Hectorina MacLennan, took her home with him and strangled her after introducing her to his trick with the Friar's Balsam and the household gas. He put her body in an alcove in the kitchen.

The same month, this was repeated with Kathleen Maloney and Rita Nelson. Both were strangled, intercourse taking place at the time of death, and both bodies joining Hectorina's in the alcove. With four bodies hidden in his rooms, Christie decided it was time to move on.

On March 13th, Christie sublet his rooms to a Mr and Mrs Reilly, taking three months rent in advance. One week later he took his dog to the vet and had it destroyed. Some time before this he had papered over the kitchen

alcove containing the bodies of the three murdered women. Having tied up all these loose ends, Christie simply walked out of Rillington Place, never to return.

When the Reillys moved into number 10, they noticed a rather unpleasant smell in the kitchen but they were not to have time to investigate. The very next day they were visited by the landlord, Charles Brown, who pointed out that Christie had no right to sublet and threw the Reillys out. He had his own tenants in mind, but first he would have to clean the place up a little.

On March 24th, Beresford Brown, the man who lodged upstairs, was clearing up the rooms so recently vacated by Christie. Knocking on part of the kitchen wall, he noticed that it sounded hollow. He ripped off a loose piece of wallpaper, looked into the darkness and was horrified to see the naked back of a woman.

The police carefully removed the three bodies. Each had been strangled with a ligature, each had been gassed, but not fatally and each had had intercourse at about the time of their deaths. The house was searched and it wasn't long before a fourth body was found, under the floorboards. Ethel Christie had also been strangled with a ligature, but there was no sign of gassing or intercourse.

The papers of March 25th were full of reports on the macabre discoveries in Rillington Place. Christie undoubtedly saw those reports and left Rowton House, where he had been staying. He began to wander aimlessly around the streets of London, sleeping rough.

The discoveries were still not complete though, and the two bodies in the back garden were soon unearthed. A total of six women had been found in Rillington Place and the police were now rather interested in tracing John Reginald Halliday Christie.

On March 31st, Police Constable Tom Ledger was walking along the embankment, south of the river, near Putney Bridge. He noticed a shabby, unshaven man, leaning on the embankment, looking down at the river. The man gave his name as John Waddington and said he lived at Westbourne Grove. The police officer was not satisfied and asked the man to remove his hat. The bald dome was unmistakable. Christie had been found.

Arrested and taken to Putney police station, Christie readily made statements admitting his guilt. He later admitted murdering Beryl Evans, commenting coldly "the more the merrier", though it may well be that this particular confession was false. It seemed that he hoped to avoid the hangman's noose with a plea of insanity and felt that the more murders he admitted to, the better chance he would have of escaping with his life.

Both Beryl and Geraldine had been strangled with a ligature – Christie's method of murder – though no carbon monoxide gas was found in the bodies. It is true that Donald Teare, who did the original postmortem examination, did not in fact check for carbon monoxide, as he had no knowledge of that such methods had been already used in Rillington Place, but all eminent authorities at the time agreed that the signs of such poisoning would have been so pronounced that such an expert could not have missed them. It seems probable then that carbon monoxide was not used in the murder of Beryl Evans.

Christie's usual method, adopted in every case except that of his wife, was to get his victim to inhale carbon monoxide gas from the household supply until she became unconscious. He would then strangle them, whilst engaging in intercourse. If he had killed Beryl, especially if we believe the abortion story that Evans told at the time, then it is more likely than not that he would have employed such a method.

There was also evidence that Beryl had been beaten before she was murdered. This was certainly not Christie's style. It must be remembered that Christie only confessed to killing Beryl after he had been in custody for some time and was trying to add to his tally of murders in order to increase the chances of success for a plea of insanity.

The trial began at the Old Bailey on June 22nd, 1953 and as expected the defence was guilty, but insane. It took the jury 85 minutes to dismiss that plea and return a verdict of guilty of murder.

One of the items of evidence found by the police was a tobacco tin containing neatly arranged tufts of pubic hair. Christie claimed that these trophies came from Beryl Evans and the three victims walled up in his kitchen alcove. Subsequent tests showed that this could not have been the case. One of the trophies may possibly have belonged to his wife but the other three remained unidentified.

It may be that these 'trophies' were obtained by innocent methods but it is equally possible that Christie may have taken them from one, or perhaps four other victims.

1953

1953

EACH EVENING, BEFORE he and his wife retired for the night, George Laughton was in the habit of putting a wooden shutter up at his scullery window, to afford some extra security. Things were no different on the night of March 9th, 1953, but when George rose the following morning, he found that someone had removed that shutter. George also noticed that the bedroom window of the house next door was open.

George and his wife went to work, but on Mrs Laughton's return home at 3.00pm, she discovered the naked body of her neighbour, Flora Jane Gilligan, lying beneath her bedroom window. It appeared that Flora had fallen and sustained injuries that had proved fatal, but medical examination showed that Flora had also been raped and an attempt had been made to strangle her. The police were looking at a case of murder.

A number of fingerprints were found at the scene of the crime, both on a window frame and on a brandy bottle. It was decided to take sets of prints from various groups, including the soldiers at nearby Strensall. It was then that a matching set was discovered and Philip Henry, a soldier in the King's Own Yorkshire Light Infantry, was arrested for murder.

Henry denied even knowing Diamond Street and claimed that he had caught the last bus to camp, from the railway station. Inquiries showed that no one else on that bus could recall seeing Henry and Private Harry Clegram, who slept in the bed next to Henry's, reported that Henry was not in the barrack room at 11.45pm.

Henry's uniform was checked for forensic evidence and on March 16th, a splinter of pinewood was found embedded in the fibres. It was of similar material as the window frame from which Flora had been pushed.

At Henry's trial, the jury retired to consider their verdict. After an hour's deliberation, they returned and asked to visit the scene of the crime. Although Mister Justice Jones claimed never to have heard of such a thing before, he ordered that a bus be laid on for the jury and they returned to court after an absence of some 30 minutes. Then, after a further two hours consideration, they returned their verdict of guilty.

NAME	Philip Henry
AGE AT EXECUTION	25
DATE OF EXECUTION	Thursday, 30th July, 1953
PLACE OF EXECUTION	Leeds
HANGMAN	Albert Pierrepoint
ASSISTANT	Royston Rickard
DATE OF TRIAL	16th June – 18th June, 1953
LOCATION OF TRIAL	York
PRESIDING JUDGE	Mister Justice Jones
PROSECUTION COUNSEL	G. Raymond Hinchcliffe, R. Withers Payne
DEFENCE COUNSEL	Geoffrey Veale, R. Rawden-Smith
NUMBER OF VICTIMS	1

VICTIMS DETAILS	
NAME	Flora Jane Gilligan
AGE	76
DATE OF MURDER	Tuesday, 10th March, 1953
PLACE OF MURDER	80 Diamond Street, York
METHOD OF KILLING	Strangled/battered
RELATIONSHIP TO KILLER	None

Philip Henry was executed at Leeds on July 30th. It was the only occasion that Albert Pierrepoint would ever officiate at that particular prison.

BY THE TIME Louisa Merrifield married Alfred in 1950, she had already lost two previous husbands. Joseph Ellison, with whom she had four children, died in 1949 and a second husband had died only 10 weeks after she had married him. Louisa had also served a jail sentence for ration book fraud and had her children taken into care.

Sarah Ricketts had herself lost two husbands. Sarah was now 79 and although she could look after herself she wanted someone who would take care of her nice bungalow in Devonshire Road. Sarah took on Louisa and 71-year-old Alfred. They started work on March 12th, 1953.

On March 31st, Sarah Ricketts made a new will leaving the bungalow to Louisa. When Alfred raised objections to the omission of his name, it was agreed that he and Louisa would get half each. Even before the new will, Louisa had told people that she had come into an inheritance. On March 25th she told an ex-lodger that an old woman had died and left her a bungalow.

The most telling comment was probably made on April 12th when Louisa mentioned to a friend that she had to go home to lay out an elderly woman who had died. When further questions were asked, Louisa replied; "She's not dead yet, but she soon will be."

On April 13th, Sarah Ricketts complained to her milkman that she was not getting enough to eat and the Merrifields seemed to be taking all her money. On Tuesday, April 14th, Sarah died.

One of the women Louisa had spoken to about the bungalow thought it highly suspicious that she had been told about Sarah's death well before it had happened, and communicated those suspicions to the police. A postmortem was carried out and this revealed the presence of phosphorus in the form of Rodine, a rat poison.

The police searched the bungalow to try to find the tin of poison. When this failed, they dug over the gardens but still came up with nothing. Louisa seemed oblivious to all this fuss, offering to make the officers tea and asking the Salvation Army band who were outside, to play 'Abide with Me'. Eventually, even without the tin as evidence, Louisa was

NAME	Louisa May Merrifield
AGE AT EXECUTION	46
DATE OF EXECUTION	Friday, 18th September, 1953
PLACE OF EXECUTION	Manchester
HANGMAN	Albert Pierrepoint
ASSISTANT	Not known
DATE OF TRIAL	20th July – 31st July, 1953
LOCATION OF TRIAL	Manchester
PRESIDING JUDGE	Mister Justice Glyn-Jones
PROSECUTION COUNSEL	Sir Lionel Heald
DEFENCE COUNSEL	J. Di V. Nahum
NUMBER OF VICTIMS	1

VICTIMS DETAILS	
NAME	Sarah Ricketts
AGE	79
DATE OF MURDER	Tuesday, 14th April, 1953
PLACE OF MURDER	339 Devonshire Road, Blackpool
METHOD OF KILLING	Poisoned (by phosphorus)
RELATIONSHIP TO KILLER	None

arrested and charged with murder. Two weeks later, Alfred was also charged.

Eventually Louisa was found guilty of murder. The jury failed to agree as far as Alfred was concerned and he was released, to die nine years later. There is however an interesting post script to this case.

At the trial, Professor J.N. Webster said he did not agree that Sarah had died from phosphorus poisoning. He agreed that Rodine had been administered but it was not the cause of death. He believed that Sarah had died from necrosis of the liver. If that was correct, then Louisa Merrifield should only have been charged with attempted murder.

1953

ARTHUR EDWARD POLSUE, a lodger at 22 College Street, Swindon, heard screaming and cries of "Murder!" just before midnight on Coronation Day, June 2nd, 1953. Going to investigate, he found his landlord, Arthur Bayley Court, lying in the corridor, covered in blood. Arthur ran next door for help, telephoned the police and returned to number 22, with Mr and Mrs Messenger, who lived next door and had also heard the commotion.

Arthur helped Mr Court to his bed. Although injured he would recover from his wounds. His wife, Beatrice was not as fortunate. She lay dead in a chair and nearby sat John Owen Greenway, another lodger, his hands heavily bloodstained.

The police arrived soon afterwards, to find Greenway now in the kitchen. He was crying and saying: "Don't let me see her. What have I done? Is she dead?" The story he later told, was a full admission to the murder of Beatrice Court.

Greenway explained that he had lodged with the Courts for some time and had become very close to Christopher Percy, with whom he shared a double bed. On May 29th, Percy had returned to Wales, the native land of both he and Greenway. Percy left his friend a note saying that he had gone because the food was so bad and suggesting that if he wanted to get in touch, Greenway should telephone his sister.

On May 30th, Greenway did indeed telephone Percy's sister but could not find out where his dear friend had gone. He rang again on June 1st, and yet again on June 2nd. Still having no luck, and bitterly disappointed, he returned to his lodgings at some time after 11.30pm, called Beatrice down and showed her the note, saying that she was responsible for his friend leaving.

Beatrice claimed that it wasn't her fault Percy had gone. An argument developed and at its height, Greenway seized a hatchet and battered Beatrice to death. The noise caused Arthur Court to come down and he too was then attacked.

At his trial, Greenway pleaded guilty to murder and was sentenced to death. He did not appeal and was executed 18 days later.

NAME	John Owen Greenway
AGE AT EXECUTION	27
DATE OF EXECUTION	Tuesday, 20th October, 1953
PLACE OF EXECUTION	Bristol
HANGMAN	Albert Pierrepoint
ASSISTANT	Harry Allen
DATE OF TRIAL	2nd October, 1953
LOCATION OF TRIAL	Devizes
PRESIDING JUDGE	Mister Justice Parker
PROSECUTION COUNSEL	P.F.Y. Radcliffe
DEFENCE COUNSEL	A.C. Munro Kerr
NUMBER OF VICTIMS	1

VICTIMS DETAILS	
NAME	Beatrice Ann Court
AGE	68
DATE OF MURDER	Tuesday, 2nd June, 1953
PLACE OF MURDER	22 College Street, Swindon
METHOD OF KILLING	Battered
RELATIONSHIP TO KILLER	None

THE THREE YOUNG boys were enjoying their game in the woods near Cork Lane, Blaby. Suddenly they came across a sight which put all thoughts of play from their minds. There, in a small thicket, lay the body of 12-year-old Janet Warner, a silk stocking and a school tie, knotted tightly around her neck.

Janet had lived at 141 Leicester Road, Glenhills. Her father, Walter, reported that she had just gone out to take her little dog for a walk and since Janet had not been sexually assaulted, it appeared that the crime was completely without motive.

In due course, police officers were led to an address in Uppingham Road, Leicester, where Joseph Christopher Reynolds lived. Described by his landlady as the perfect lodger – quiet, clean and tidy – Reynolds had gone missing but, once his description had been circulated, he was finally picked up in Belvior Street, Leicester, early on the morning of May 25th. He made a full statement confessing to the crime.

Reynolds's story was a cold and cruel one. He described how he had been feeling, for 10 days or so, that he wanted to kill someone. His original plan was to murder a man who each day walked along the canal at Aylestone, but on the day in question, May 22nd, the man did not appear. Discouraged, Reynolds was just about to give up and go home, when Janet Warner appeared with her dog.

Reynolds got talking to the young girl and suggested that they go rabbitting in the woods. She agreed but once inside the woods, he grabbed her, punched her and forced her to the ground.

Janet fought hard for her life but Reynolds was too strong and finally managed to strangle her. At one stage, Reynolds told police officers; "The little girl was very brave in the face of death. I hope when my time comes I will be half as brave."

At his trial, Reynolds insisted on pleading guilty, adding; "I deserve the extreme punishment for my crime." Mister Justice Pilcher agreed, and sentenced Reynolds to death. The entire proceedings had taken four minutes.

NAME Joseph Christopher Reynolds

AGE AT EXECUTION 31

DATE OF EXECUTION Tuesday, 17th November, 1953

PLACE OF EXECUTION Leicester

HANGMAN Albert Pierrepoint

ASSISTANT Robert Leslie Stewart

DATE OF TRIAL 26th October, 1953

LOCATION OF TRIAL Leicester

PRESIDING JUDGE Mister Justice Pilcher

PROSECUTION COUNSEL None

DEFENCE COUNSEL R.C. Vaughan

NUMBER OF VICTIMS 1

1953

VICTIMS DETAILS

NAME Janet Mary Warner

AGE 12

DATE OF MURDER Friday, 22nd May, 1953

PLACE OF MURDER Bluebanks Spinney, Cork Lane, Blaby

METHOD OF KILLING Strangled

RELATIONSHIP TO KILLER None

1953

O N SEPTEMBER 14TH, 1953, Mister Karol Wagner left his home at Halifax and travelled to see some friends in Blackpool. His wife, Irene, stayed behind, along with their lodgers, one whom was a Polish railway worker named Stanislaw Juras.

Two days later, on September 16th, Mrs Fisher was walking past the Wagner house when she heard a woman scream, twice. It was now a few minutes after 10.00pm and less than half an hour later, at 10.30pm, another lodger in the house detected a strong smell of gas. Going to investigate, the lodger found that someone had disconnected the gas tap in the cellar. He fixed the problem and went to report the matter to Irene.

Failing to find Irene, the lodger, now accompanied by another resident, tried Juras's door. The door was locked but they could tell that there was someone inside. The two men went outside and saw Juras at his window but he refused to come down or open the door for them.

An hour later, a neighbour, Mrs Marsland, saw Juras leaving the house through his window. Slowly he lowered himself to the street before slipping off into the darkness.

Juras's door was still locked when Karol Wagner returned home. There still being no sign of his wife, Karol contacted the police who forced open the locked door and found Irene inside. She was quite dead, having been strangled and later medical reports would suggest that she had been killed in a frenzied attack.

It was not long before Juras was arrested and charged with the murder of his landlady. Juras freely admitted killing Irene but denied that there was any intent. He claimed that he and Irene were in love but this was countered by Karol Wagner who said that although he felt that Juras was attracted to his wife, she had hated and feared him. Mister Herbert, who led for the defence quite rightly asked what Irene was doing in Juras's room if she felt that way about him but no satisfactory answer could be given.

After an absence of 10 minutes, the jury found Juras guilty of murder. Asked if he had anything to say before sentence was passed, Juras replied: "I want to be executed today."

NAME	Stanislaw Juras
AGE AT EXECUTION	43
DATE OF EXECUTION	Thursday, 17th December, 1953
PLACE OF EXECUTION	Manchester
HANGMAN	Not known
ASSISTANT	Not known
DATE OF TRIAL	25th November – 26th November, 1953
LOCATION OF TRIAL	Leeds
PRESIDING JUDGE	Mister Justice Stable
PROSECUTION COUNSEL	J.F. Drabble, J.S. Snowden
DEFENCE COUNSEL	J.B. Herbert, A. Sharp
NUMBER OF VICTIMS	1

VICTIMS DETAILS	
NAME	Irene Wagner
AGE	29
DATE OF MURDER	Wednesday, 16th September, 1953
PLACE OF MURDER	Trinity Place, Halifax
METHOD OF KILLING	Strangled
RELATIONSHIP TO KILLER	None

His wish was not granted and he had to wait until December 17th.

ON JULY 14TH, 1953, Herman and Charlotte Schreiber married and Charlotte moved into their home at Boundaries Road, Balham. Once they had settled in, Charlotte's daughter, Miriam Gray, came to join them, there were also three lodgers, one of whom was John Francis Wilkinson.

At 8.00pm on August 14th, Miriam was put to bed on a divan in the kitchen. Later the rest of the household retired and all remained quiet until 1.00am the following morning when Herman Schreiber was woken by a loud bang.

Two hours later, Charlotte was woken by the sound of breaking glass and at 5.45am, the front door was slammed. None of these occurrences disturbed the Schreibers enough for them to get up and investigate and it was not until 6.30am that they finally rose.

To Charlotte and Herman's surprise, they found the downstairs full of smoke and upon checking further, found a small fire had been lit on the kitchen floor. The blaze was extinguished but poor Miriam was found to be dead. However, when Doctor Philip Chandler examined the child, he was able to say that the cause had not been the fire or the smoke. Miriam had been dead for some hours. Later tests would show that she had been struck three times on the head with a blunt instrument, and there had been some attempt at sexual intercourse.

Wilkinson was the only person missing from the house. As a result of a very accurate description being circulated, Wilkinson was arrested at Hinchley Wood at 1.35am on August 16th. He was heard to say: "I'm glad you picked me up."

Wilkinson readily described what had happened on the fatal evening. He said that he had gone down to the cellar and taken a bottle of vermouth and a bottle of beer. These he consumed in his room and then he broke a chair and taking one of the legs, wrapped it in a piece of blanket, went downstairs. Finding Miriam he struck her with the chair leg and then squeezed her throat. He then took off her pyjama bottoms, tried to have sex with her and when he couldn't manage it, put the pyjamas back on her body. He then packed

NAME	John Francis Wilkinson
AGE AT EXECUTION	24
DATE OF EXECUTION	Friday, 18th December, 1953
PLACE OF EXECUTION	Wandsworth
HANGMAN	Stephen Wade
ASSISTANT	Royston Rickard
DATE OF TRIAL	2nd November – 3rd November, 1953
LOCATION OF TRIAL	Old Bailey
PRESIDING JUDGE	Mister Justice Hilbery
PROSECUTION COUNSEL	Christmas Humphreys
DEFENCE COUNSEL	Gilbert Rowntree
NUMBER OF VICTIMS	1

VICTIMS DETAILS	
NAME	Miriam Susan Gray
AGE	5
DATE OF MURDER	Saturday, 15th August, 1953
PLACE OF MURDER	Boundaries Road, Balham, London
METHOD OF KILLING	Battered
RELATIONSHIP TO KILLER	None

some food tins into a suitcase before setting fire to two towels on the kitchen floor and leaving the house.

At the trial, evidence was given that Wilkinson was one of 10 children, four of whom had already died from fits. Other relatives had spent time in various asylums and he too had been advised to seek treatment in a mental sanatorium. Doctor Desmond Curran agreed that Wilkinson was abnormal with a psychotic personality but added that he was sane. As a result, it took the jury 45 minutes to find Wilkinson guilty as charged.

1953

O N MAY 31ST, 1953, two young girls, Barbara Songhurst and Christine Reed, were seen on the Thames towpath, cycling towards home. It was between 11.00pm and 11.30pm but neither girl was ever to reach her destination.

The following day, June 1st, Barbara's body was found in the river near Richmond. She had been badly battered about the head, stabbed in the back and raped. Five days after that, on June 6th, Christine's body was discovered, also at Richmond. She had been stabbed 10 times.

At the end of that same month, police detained a man, Alfred Charles Whiteway, in connection with an assault on two women in Surrey, one of whom had been raped. There were three immediate factors which linked Whiteway with the two murders on the towpath. One was that rape had been a factor in that crime, the second was that Whiteway lived in the area, and the third was that Whiteway travelled around on a cycle and both of the dead girls had been attacked on a cycle path. Whiteway was taken in for questioning on the two murders.

At first he denied all knowledge of the crimes. A married man, Whiteway was separated from his wife. He lived with his parents at Teddington whilst she lived at Kingston but he claimed to be with her at the time the girls were murdered. Then, when a police officer was cleaning out the patrol car that had brought in Whiteway, an axe was found hidden under one of the seats. Forensic tests showed that this axe had been used to inflict the head injuries on the two girls.

Further tests showed that one of Whiteway's shoes had traces of human blood on it and when faced with this evidence, Whiteway finally confessed to the murders. He said that on the night of the murder, he had only seen one girl at first. Thinking that she was a likely victim for his next rape, he hit her over the head and she fell. Only then did he notice the second girl who was down by the lock and screaming. He ran over quickly and battered her into unconsciousness. It was at that moment that he realised that he had seen the other girl before and that she knew him and would be able to identify them. His only

NAME	Alfred Charles Whiteway
AGE AT EXECUTION	22
DATE OF EXECUTION	Tuesday, December 22nd, 1953
PLACE OF EXECUTION	Wandsworth
HANGMAN	Albert Pierrepoint
ASSISTANT	John Broadbent
DATE OF TRIAL	26th October – 30th October, 1953
LOCATION OF TRIAL	Old Bailey
PRESIDING JUDGE	Mister Justice Hilbery
PROSECUTION COUNSEL	Christmas Humphreys
DEFENCE COUNSEL	Peter Rawlinson
NUMBER OF VICTIMS	2

VICTIMS DETAILS	
NAMES	Barbara Songhurst; Christine Reed
AGES	16; 18
DATE OF MURDER	Sunday, May 31st, 1953
PLACE OF MURDER	Thames Towpath, Teddington, London
METHOD OF KILLING	Battered/stabbed; battered/stabbed
RELATIONSHIP TO KILLER	None; none

way to avoid capture, was to kill them both.

At his subsequent trial at the Old Bailey, Whiteway pleaded not guilty and claimed that he had never confessed to anything. It was suggested that the police had manufactured the confession in order to frame Whiteway but it still took the jury less than an hour to state that they believed him to be guilty.

GEORGE JAMES NEWLAND had been in the army and during his service, had been stationed at a camp close to Orsett, near Grays, in Essex. The young soldier befriended an elderly couple who lived in a nearby bungalow, Henry John Tandy and his wife, Honor Grace. Newland showed them a great deal of kindness, often taking them cigarettes and tea as presents.

Having done his military service, Newland became a metal caster and returned to his home at Cogan Avenue, Walthamstow, in London. It was there, in May, 1953, that Newland decided that he needed a new suit and, desperate for money, hatched a cruel and terrible plan.

On the morning of May 30th, Newland bought himself some apples and oranges but then, before leaving home, he placed his father's claw hammer in the same bag. He then travelled to Orsett and appeared at the Tandys' bungalow.

As Newland looked in the front window, the Tandys saw him and, pleased that he had decided to visit, beckoned him inside with the greeting; "Come in Ginger…." Newland went inside and for a while, the three of them talked as old friends. It was then that Newland drew the hammer from his bag and battered Honor Tandy without mercy.

Once Honor had been battered unconscious, Newland then turned his attention towards Henry Tandy, who received similar treatment. As a result of this brutal attack, Henry Tandy was to lose his life and Honor would spend a good deal of time in hospital before she recovered. For his efforts, Newland escaped with just £8-5s.

It was the next day before Newland was interviewed by the police and after being cautioned, admitted responsibility saying that he was sorry for what he had done. Later, he was to claim that he had been thinking of a way to get some money when he had seen a violent film and been given the idea of a robbery.

Newland was tried on November 13th and found guilty of murder. His appeal having failed on December 7th, he was executed two days before Christmas.

NAME	George James Newland
AGE AT EXECUTION	21
DATE OF EXECUTION	Wednesday, 23rd December, 1953
PLACE OF EXECUTION	Pentonville
HANGMAN	Albert Pierrepoint
ASSISTANT	Harry Allen
DATE OF TRIAL	13th November, 1953
LOCATION OF TRIAL	Chelmsford
PRESIDING JUDGE	Mister Justice Streatfeild
PROSECUTION COUNSEL	R.L.D. Thomas
DEFENCE COUNSEL	Anthony Marlowe
NUMBER OF VICTIMS	1

VICTIMS DETAILS	
NAME	Henry John Tandy
AGE	65
DATE OF MURDER	Saturday, 30th May, 1953
PLACE OF MURDER	Grosvenor Road, Orsett, Essex
METHOD OF KILLING	Battered
RELATIONSHIP TO KILLER	None

1953

ROBERT MOORE AND his partner, Thomas William Bramley, were car dealers and both knew Edward Watson, another car dealer, from the various auctions they all attended.

On April 23rd, 1953, Watson sold Moore a car that had a defective chassis. The car cost £55 and Moore had to spend a further £6 on repairs, taking the cost to £61.

When Moore sold it back to Watson for £52, he had lost £9 on the deal and felt that he had been cheated. He began to plot his revenge.

Moore next met Watson at an auction in Leeds, on Saturday, May 30th and seeing that Watson had a large number of pound notes on him, Moore decided on his course of action and told Watson that he knew of a car he might be interested in. They arranged to meet the following day when Moore would take Watson to see the car, in Harrogate.

On May 31st, Moore purchased a Winchester .22 rifle and a silencer, from William Metcalfe who noticed that there was a spade in the boot of Moore's car. Anita Watson became concerned when her husband did not return from his meeting with Moore and went to look for him. Moore said he had not kept their appointment but Mrs Watson was far from satisfied and on June 2nd, contacted the police. Moore repeated his story to Detective Sergeant Wilby and when the matter of the rifle and spade were mentioned, Moore laughed and said: "You don't think I've shot and buried him do you?"

In fact, this was exactly what Moore had done and when he was found, shortly afterwards, having tried to gas himself, Moore was questioned again whereupon he admitted the shooting and took the police to where he had buried the body.

Edward Watson had been shot five times at close range. Moore now tried to suggest that he had used the gun merely to threaten and frighten Watson who had grabbed the barrel. As the two men struggled, the gun had gone off a number of times but the killing had been accidental.

Whilst it was true that Watson's wounds were consistent with such a view, they were also consistent with Moore's earlier claims that he had shot Watson from two or three

NAME	Robert William Moore
AGE AT EXECUTION	26
DATE OF EXECUTION	Tuesday, 5th January, 1954
PLACE OF EXECUTION	Leeds
HANGMAN	Stephen Wade
ASSISTANT	Harry Smith
DATE OF TRIAL	23rd November – 25th November, 1953
LOCATION OF TRIAL	Leeds
PRESIDING JUDGE	Mister Justice Stable
PROSECUTION COUNSEL	G. Raymond Hinchcliffe, B. Gillis
DEFENCE COUNSEL	Rudolph Lyons, E.J. Parris
NUMBER OF VICTIMS	1

VICTIMS DETAILS	
NAME	Edward Watson
AGE	27
DATE OF MURDER	Sunday, 31st May, 1953
PLACE OF MURDER	Plantation at Fewston
METHOD OF KILLING	Shot
RELATIONSHIP TO KILLER	None

feet. There was also the matter of the spade. Why had Moore had this with him before he met Watson unless the burial of the body had been premeditated?

The 'accidental' version of events was mentioned for the first time during Moore's trial and the jury, after hearing the rest of the evidence, decided that it was nothing more than an attempt to avoid the hangman's noose. Moore was found guilty and executed at Leeds.

FOR SIX MONTHS, DORIS Douglas had lived with Czelslaw Kowalewski, a Polish miner, but the problem was that she only lived with him for part of each week. The rest of the time she acted as housekeeper to 60-year-old James McGough and his 16-year-old son, Anthony. For much of that time, Kowalewski was unaware of this and once he did find out, they argued about the matter.

On the night of Friday, October 5th, 1953, Kowalewski and Doris were out drinking with another man, when a further argument broke out. Kowalewski stormed out and when later, their drinking companion was found, badly beaten, the description he gave of his assailant fitted the Pole.

Doris made her way home alone but was joined in Briggate by Kowalewski. It was now very late and there must have been further argument between them for at 11.45pm, a gentleman named Ernest Wakefield heard a woman screaming. Ernest looked from his window and saw Doris on the ground. Kowalewski was leaning over her and beating her. Eventually Doris escaped, ran to a telephone box and after making a call to the police, was escorted home by Constable John Shaw.

Once Doris was home, Shaw went back to his duties. Neither he nor Doris could have known how determined Kowalewski was to sort this matter out, for shortly after 12.30am, he knocked on the front door.

Seeing who the caller was, James McGough slammed the door in Kowalewski's face. The household retired for the night but Kowalewski was not to be outdone. Smashing two panes of glass in the door, he gained entry and found Doris, who was by now ready for bed.

Kowalewski struck and kicked Doris a number of times but the wound that proved fatal was a stab to the head with a knife of the type used by boy scouts. The assailant then ran off into the night.

Kowalewski's description was published, as was a photograph of him. This enabled a shopkeeper, Pat Howieson, to recognise the killer when he went into her father's shop on Lawrence Avenue on October 7th. The police were called but by the time they arrived,

NAME	Czelslaw Kowalewski
AGE AT EXECUTION	32
DATE OF EXECUTION	Friday, 8th January, 1954
PLACE OF EXECUTION	Manchester
HANGMAN	Not known
ASSISTANT	Not known
DATE OF TRIAL	13th December – 17th December, 1953
LOCATION OF TRIAL	Leeds
PRESIDING JUDGE	Mister Justice Stable
PROSECUTION COUNSEL	Rudolph Lyons, J. McLusky
DEFENCE COUNSEL	H.R.B. Shepherd, E.J. Parris
NUMBER OF VICTIMS	1

VICTIMS DETAILS

NAME	Doris Douglas
AGE	29
DATE OF MURDER	Tuesday, 6th October, 1953
PLACE OF MURDER	77 Moynihan House, Quarry Hill Flats, Leeds
METHOD OF KILLING	Battered/stabbed
RELATIONSHIP TO KILLER	Girlfriend

Kowalewski had again disappeared. However, when he returned to the same shop on October 9th, Kowalewski was finally arrested.

Kowalewski's clothing was found to be heavily bloodstained, the murder weapon was found on him, as was a series of postcards on which he had written a diary describing how he had committed the crime.

Kowalewski could not deny killing Doris but claimed that he was too drunk at the time to form the intention to kill. He claimed that he had no memory of the crime and that he should be guilty only of manslaughter. The jury of 10 men and two women considered their verdict for only 15 minutes before disagreeing.

BETTY SMITH HAD enjoyed herself at the school social and by 8.30pm, was heading home. She stayed there only briefly, telling her mother that she wished to visit a neighbour, Desmond Hooper and his family.

Hooper had a seven-year-old son, Keith, and Betty spent an hour playing dominoes with him. When the time came for Keith to go to bed, Betty prepared to leave and Keith heard his father saying goodbye to her at around 10.40pm. Soon after this, Hooper went out, leaving a note for his wife, in which he said he was going out to get some pigeons.

Meanwhile, back at Betty's home, her mother, Dorothy Smith had fallen asleep. When she woke it was late and since Betty was still not home, Mrs Smith went to Hooper's house to see where she was.

Whilst Mrs Smith was at Hooper's home, Desmond came back in. It was then about 1.45am and Mrs Smith thought that Hooper appeared odd, wearing no tie, his trousers wet and muddy and he was perspiring heavily. Hooper agreed to telephone the police, but apparently asked that no one said what time he had come in.

A widespread search was launched and eventually, on July 24th, Detective Superintendent Evans found a jacket near the top of an air shaft on a canal, some two miles from Betty's home. The shaft was checked and 40 feet down, in a few feet of water, Betty's body was discovered.

A number of points led the police towards Desmond Hooper. In the first place, his own brother, Bernard, identified the jacket as one he had sold to Desmond, in 1951. A further identification was made by a tailor, George Herbert Lee, who had made a repair on it.

There was also the fact that there was no one to confirm Hooper's story about the pigeons. He claimed to have gone to the farm of Richard Edward Harris but that gentleman did not see him.

Hooper tried to suggest that someone else was responsible for the death of Betty Smith, saying that 17-year-old Clive Albert Lloyd had a grudge against Betty because she had hit his sister, Maureen. He went on to say that he had heard Lloyd say he was going to do something to Betty in order to get revenge and added

NAME	Desmond Donald Hooper
AGE AT EXECUTION	27
DATE OF EXECUTION	Tuesday, 26th January, 1954
PLACE OF EXECUTION	Shrewsbury
HANGMAN	Albert Pierrepoint
ASSISTANT	Robert Leslie Stewart
DATE OF TRIAL	23rd November – 27th November, 1953
LOCATION OF TRIAL	Shrewsbury
PRESIDING JUDGE	Mister Justice Cassels
PROSECUTION COUNSEL	E. Ryder Richardson, Paul Wrightson
DEFENCE COUNSEL	G.G. Baker, Peter Northcote
NUMBER OF VICTIMS	1

VICTIMS DETAILS	
NAME	Betty Selina Smith
AGE	12
DATE OF MURDER	Tuesday, 21st July, 1953
PLACE OF MURDER	Shropshire Union Canal, near Shrewsbury
METHOD OF KILLING	Strangled/drowned
RELATIONSHIP TO KILLER	None

that Lloyd had once told him that the shaft would be a good place to hide a body. Lloyd denied this and said that he had been at home since 9.30pm on the night Betty was killed, though he did admit that he had once borrowed a jacket from Hooper similar to the one found.

The trial lasted two days and the jury decided that Desmond Hooper was guilty of murder even though the evidence against him was purely circumstantial. He went to the gallows maintaining his innocence.

WILLIAM LUBINA, A Polish miner, had first met Charlotte Ball and her husband, in 1948. By 1953, he had been lodging with them for some time and in due course, fell in love with Charlotte.

On June 25th, 1953, Lubina had his knife sharpened at the colliery where he worked. Later that same day, Mr Ball, who was disabled, went out for a short time leaving his wife with Lubina and another man named Varty. As Ball returned, he heard Charlotte screaming and both he and Varty saw Lubina apparently striking Charlotte.

As the two men rushed forward to help save Charlotte from this attack, Lubina ran into another room where he began beating his head against a mirror. Meanwhile, Varty and Charlotte's husband discovered that she had been stabbed in the chest six times, and was already dead.

Lubina was taken into custody where it was found that he had seven cuts to his right temple and three stab wounds in his own chest. Nevertheless, after receiving medical treatment, he was adjudged to be well enough to face a charge of murder.

A search of the house in Springfield Street revealed a letter from Lubina to Charlotte, written in German and confessing his undying love. Amongst Lubina's belongings were found five photographs of Charlotte and he had no hesitation in confirming to the police that he was in love with the woman he had killed.

He went on to explain that they had argued two weeks beforehand and she had hit him at that time. On the night of Charlotte's death, they had argued again and she had punched and kicked him, causing him to lose his balance and fall to the floor. He reached out and grabbed for something on the table and it was only when he was hitting Charlotte that he realised he had picked up a knife. When arrested, Lubina would only say: "I kill her. I want no defence."

Lubina denied that the crime was premeditated but his story did not fit the facts in that he had sharpened his knife on the day of the attack. It was enough to send him to the gallows.

NAME	William Lubina
AGE AT EXECUTION	42
DATE OF EXECUTION	Wednesday, 27th January, 1954
PLACE OF EXECUTION	Leeds
HANGMAN	Stephen Wade
ASSISTANT	Harry Allen
DATE OF TRIAL	27th November, 1953
LOCATION OF TRIAL	Leeds
PRESIDING JUDGE	Mister Justice Stable
PROSECUTION COUNSEL	H.B.H. Hylton-Foster, G.N. Black
DEFENCE COUNSEL	J.B. Herbert, C. Forester-Paton
NUMBER OF VICTIMS	1

VICTIMS DETAILS	
NAME	Charlotte Ball
AGE	39
DATE OF MURDER	Thursday, 25th June, 1953
PLACE OF MURDER	Springfield Street, Barnsley
METHOD OF KILLING	Stabbed
RELATIONSHIP TO KILLER	None

1954

FOR THREE YEARS, James Doohan had been involved with Yvonne Maureen Deighton. He had suggested marriage but when she turned him down on February 8th, 1954, he managed to convince himself that the cause of that refusal was Yvonne's stepfather, Herbert Ketley, and plotted his revenge.

On the morning of February 9th, Doohan borrowed a gun from a friend, giving the excuse that he wanted to go shooting on the moors. That same evening, Doohan visited Ketley at his home and the two men were seen walking off together. Later still, Doohan walked into Queensborough police station and admitted that he had shot a man.

Doohan's statement was an emotionless confession describing how he had aimed the gun at the nape of Ketley's neck and that after firing, he had checked for a pulse and heartbeat to make sure that the man he hated was dead.

At the trial, it became clear that Doohan had been mistaken about Ketley. Yvonne said that her stepfather had never said he disliked Doohan and the only reason she had refused Doohan's offer of marriage was simply that she did not think her feelings were strong enough.

The defence was one of insanity. Doctor Gordon Ambrose had examined Doohan when he was in the army and described him as schizophrenic and showing evidence of a split personality. Doohan himself said he had heard voices telling him to kill Ketley but the medical officer of Canterbury prison where Doohan had been held said he could find no evidence of insanity.

Found guilty and asked if he had anything to say, Doohan replied that he and Yvonne were in it together. The statement was ignored and sentence of death was then passed. Doohan clasped his hands, raised them above his head and shouted "Cheers" before being taken down to the cells.

NAME	James Reginald Doohan
AGE AT EXECUTION	24
DATE OF EXECUTION	Wednesday, 14th April, 1954
PLACE OF EXECUTION	Wandsworth
HANGMAN	Albert Pierrepoint
ASSISTANT	Harry Allen
DATE OF TRIAL	22nd March – 23rd March, 1954
LOCATION OF TRIAL	Maidstone
PRESIDING JUDGE	Mister Justice Sellars
PROSECUTION COUNSEL	Tristram Beresford
DEFENCE COUNSEL	S. Cope Morgan
NUMBER OF VICTIMS	1

VICTIMS DETAILS

NAME	Herbert Victor Ketley
AGE	40
DATE OF MURDER	Tuesday, 9th February, 1954
PLACE OF MURDER	Rushenden Marshes
METHOD OF KILLING	Shot
RELATIONSHIP TO KILLER	None

ALBERT GEORGE HALL started his new job as caretaker at the Park Congregational Church on Monday, 10th August, 1953. Two days later, Mary Hackett, vanished from her home, almost directly opposite the church.

The crypt of the church was searched early on. Hall was most co-operative and even provided the police with tea and biscuits whilst they moved furniture about and looked for the child. They found nothing.

Twelve days after Mary had gone missing, the Chief Constable made a public appeal, asking for the key holders of empty properties to come forward so that their premises could be searched. In the meantime, as a matter of routine, the crypt of the church had been checked out for a second time.

On August 28th, Scotland Yard were called in to assist. The following day, Saturday, August 29th, Detective Superintendent John Ball and Detective Sergeant Dennis Hawkins arrived in Halifax.

One of the first moves Ball and Hawkins carried out was to organise a third search of the church crypt. Once again Albert Hall was more than helpful and once again he provided tea and biscuits.

Whilst that third search was taking place, Superintendent Hall noticed that in a corner, on top of a pile of furniture, were two opened cans of paint. Hall asked about these and mentioned to Albert Hall that it might be a good idea to put the lids back on as the tins would soon dry up. Hall, affable as ever, said he had lost the lids. Over the next few days, the two tins of paint preyed on Superintendent Hall's mind. The only solution that came to mind was that the smell of paint might be used to mask something else.

On September 21st, the police returned to the crypt for a fourth time. This time they were equipped with heavy digging tools and the smile vanished from Hall's face. It wasn't long before they found the body of little Mary Hackett, her skull fractured by repeated heavy blows.

The police knew that they had no hard evidence against Hall, so a round the clock surveillance was put on him. He was followed to Scalebor Park Hospital, an asylum, and

NAME	Albert George Hall
AGE AT EXECUTION	48
DATE OF EXECUTION	Thursday, 22nd April, 1954
PLACE OF EXECUTION	Leeds
HANGMAN	Steve Wade
ASSISTANT	Harry Smith
DATE OF TRIAL	12th March, 1954
LOCATION OF TRIAL	Leeds
PRESIDING JUDGE	Mister Justice Pearson
PROSECUTION COUNSEL	H.B.H. Hylton-Foster
DEFENCE COUNSEL	Rudolph Lyons
NUMBER OF VICTIMS	1

VICTIMS DETAILS	
NAME	Mary Hackett
AGE	6
DATE OF MURDER	Wednesday, 12th August, 1953
PLACE OF MURDER	Probably the Park Congregational Church, Lister Lane, Halifax
METHOD OF KILLING	Battered
RELATIONSHIP TO KILLER	None

once he had left, his doctor, Doctor Valentine, was interviewed. He explained that Hall had once been a patient there and had come to see him to ask his advice about the fact that he might be suspected of being involved in Mary's death. The details he gave of the girl's injuries could only have been known by the person who killed her and as a result of that, Hall was finally arrested and charged.

After hearing all the evidence, the jury were out for almost six and a half hours before finding Hall guilty. Hall's execution was fixed for March 31st, but postponed when he gave notice of appeal.

LESLEY NISBET AND Margaret Curran were friends who loved to play together. On Friday December 11th the two girls spent a good deal of the afternoon in each other's company playing around the flats in Greenside Row.

At 5.00pm, Jane Archman Nisbet, Lesley's mother, found that she could see neither of the girls. By 5.30pm, Jane was in the local public house, finding her common-law husband, John Murray Sinclair, to tell him that Lesley and Margaret were missing. So distressed was Jane by now that a neighbour, John Lynch, who was drinking with Jane's husband, offered to buy her a drink as a pick-me-up.

A thorough search revealed nothing and neither family, friends, neighbours nor the police could find any trace of the two friends. That is until 11.30pm, when Elizabeth McKail mentioned to her mother that the outside lavatory appeared to be locked.

Mrs McKail gave her daughter a knife to prise open the door. Elizabeth returned to the lavatory and finally managed to force the door open. Only now did she see that there were two bodies inside the toilet. The missing girls had been found, murdered.

Detective Constable Thomas Gow was placed in charge of guarding the toilets whilst his colleagues visited the houses in the district. At one stage a drunken John Lynch appeared and loudly announced that if he could find the man who had done this terrible deed he would strangle him personally.

Doctor Fiddes made an examination of both bodies and determined that both had been either strangled or suffocated. Furthermore, the youngest girl had a woman's stocking and a piece of floral material still tied around her neck and one of the girls had a safety pin missing from her clothing.

It was during the police examination of John Lynch's house that he suddenly cried out "Take me, I did it." Later, when the police spoke to his live-in lover, Annie Hall, they discovered that she had left two stockings hanging over the fireplace when she went to work but upon her return, only one remained. Further, the piece of floral material found around Margaret's throat matched an apron

NAME	John Lynch
AGE AT EXECUTION	45
DATE OF EXECUTION	Friday, 23rd April, 1954
PLACE OF EXECUTION	Edinburgh, Saughton
HANGMAN	Not known
ASSISTANT	Not known
DATE OF TRIAL	23rd March – 26th March, 1954
LOCATION OF TRIAL	Edinburgh
PRESIDING JUDGE	Lord Justice Thomson
PROSECUTION COUNSEL	W.R. Milligan, V.D.B. Skae
DEFENCE COUNSEL	W.I.R. Fraser, A. Stewart
NUMBER OF VICTIMS	2

VICTIMS DETAILS

NAMES	Lesley Jean Nisbet (Sinclair); Margaret Curran (Johnson)
AGES	4; 3
DATE OF MURDER	Friday, 11th December, 1953
PLACE OF MURDER	5 Marshall's Court, Greenside Row, Edinburgh
METHOD OF KILLING	Asphyxiated; asphyxiated
RELATIONSHIP TO KILLER	None; none

she owned. As if more evidence was needed, the safety-pin missing from one child was found in the ashes of the fire in Lynch's home at 5 Marshall's Court.

Put on trial for murder, Lynch claimed that he had never called out that he had done the murders but had shouted something about the police trying to pin the crime upon him. Found guilty, his original execution date was set for April 15th but cancelled when he announced his intention to appeal.

That appeal was dismissed on April 6th and the execution rescheduled.

JOHN HARRIES AND his wife, Phoebe went to Chapel at 7.00pm on October 16th, 1953. At about 8.30pm, a friend, Robert Morris called. He did not stay more than 10 minutes but whilst he was there, John Harries's adopted nephew, Thomas Harries paid a visit and was still there at 8.40pm, when Robert Morris left.

The following morning, Robert Harries called at a nearby farm and asked 15-year-old Brian Richard Powell if he could help him out on his uncle's farm. Harries explained that his uncle and aunt had gone away on holiday and left him in charge. Powell was happy to oblige.

Over the next few weeks, Harries repeated his story about his aunt and uncle going away and claimed to have received a letter from them in London. People had grown suspicious, though, and they brought the matter to the attention of the police. Harries was interviewed but there was little the police could do.

Before John Harries had vanished, he had given Thomas a cheque for £9. At the time, Thomas Harries had severe financial problems and by the time the cheque was credited to Thomas's account, the amount had been altered to £909. Since John Harries only had a balance of £123 at the time, the cheque was returned unpaid.

The police now believed that they had their motive. Thomas had thought that his uncle had a much greater balance in his bank account, had seen a way to clear his debts. There was still no clue as to the location of John and Phoebe, though, and it was decided to try a little subterfuge.

On the night of November 15th, police officers tied thin green strands of string around every exit from the farm. Then, making as much noise as possible, they waited until they saw a light snap on in the house. The following morning they saw that one of the strings was broken and now, the search concentrated on the field the entrance led to. It wasn't long before some of the kale in the field was seen to be disturbed and when the police dug down, the battered bodies of John and Phoebe Harries were discovered.

Thomas Harries still claimed that he had

NAME	Thomas Ronald Lewis Harries
AGE AT EXECUTION	25
DATE OF EXECUTION	Wednesday, 28th April, 1954
PLACE OF EXECUTION	Swansea
HANGMAN	Albert Pierrepoint
ASSISTANT	Not known
DATE OF TRIAL	8th March – 16th March, 1954
LOCATION OF TRIAL	Carmarthen
PRESIDING JUDGE	Mister Justice Havers
PROSECUTION COUNSEL	H. Edmund Davies, W.L. Mars-Jones, Ronald Waterhouse
DEFENCE COUNSEL	H. Vincent Lloyd-Jones, Frank Davies
NUMBER OF VICTIMS	2

VICTIMS DETAILS	
NAMES	John Harries; Phoebe Harries
AGES	63; 54
DATE OF MURDER	Friday, 16th October, 1953
PLACE OF MURDER	Probably Cadno Farm, Llanginning, Carmarthenshire
METHOD OF KILLING	Battered; battered
RELATIONSHIP TO KILLER	'Uncle'; 'Aunt'

nothing to do with the murders. He had left them alive on the night of October 16th, returning the following morning to take them to Carmarthen station from where they caught the train to London.

Harries's story was flimsy to say the least and coupled with the matter of the altered cheque, was enough to convict him of double murder.

GEORGE SMART DIED simply because he was in the wrong place at the wrong time. Smart was one of two porters at the Aban Court Hotel, and on Monday, March 9th, 1954, he started a week on the night shift, as it was his turn on the week-long rota.

It had just gone midnight when Smart opened the door to a woman resident. He was seen just once more that night when the hall porter exchanged pleasantries with him at 1.00am. The next time anyone encountered George Smart was at 7.45am when the head waiter found his bound and gagged body in the serving quarters.

The motive appeared to be one of robbery. Some £2 in cash was missing, along with a large quantity of cigarettes. Police determined that the thief had gained entrance through the coal cellar, presumably had been disturbed by Smart and had battered him before tying him up. Although he had been badly injured, the actual cause of death was asphyxiation caused by the gagging of Smart's mouth.

On the same day as George Smart's body was discovered, Ian Arthur Grant, who worked at Olympia, told a fellow employee named Chapman that he and Kenneth Gilbert had "done a man in". He went on to explain that they had stored the cigarettes in the left luggage office at Victoria Station and asked Chapman to pick them up for him. Chapman took the ticket and said he would do this favour for Grant, but instead, Chapman went straight to the police.

Grant and Gilbert were soon picked up and charged with murder. Investigations showed that Gilbert had actually worked at the Aban Court for three months in 1953, so knew his way around the place.

At the trial, both men pleaded not guilty to murder, though they fully admitted their part in George Smart's death. Grant said that he had seen Smart with his arm raised, about to hit him with a torch he was holding, so Grant hit him once in the stomach. It was Gilbert who then struck Smart, very hard and who hit him again and again once Smart had been tied up.

Gilbert admitted that he had hit Smart but claimed he had only struck him twice before gagging him. Gilbert said he had not hit Smart

NAMES	Kenneth Gilbert; Ian Arthur Grant
AGES AT EXECUTION	22; 24
DATE OF EXECUTION	Thursday, 17th June, 1954
PLACE OF EXECUTION	Pentonville
HANGMAN	Albert Pierrepoint
ASSISTANT	Royston Rickard, J Grant, Harry Smith
DATE OF TRIAL	10th May, 1954
LOCATION OF TRIAL	Old Bailey
PRESIDING JUDGE	Mister Justice Glyn-Jones
PROSECUTION COUNSEL	Christmas Humphreys, Mervyn Griffiths-Jones
DEFENCE COUNSEL	John Hazan; Petre Crowder
NUMBER OF VICTIMS	1

VICTIMS DETAILS	
NAME	George Smart
AGE	55
DATE OF MURDER	Tuesday, 9th March, 1954
PLACE OF MURDER	Aban Court Hotel, Harrington Gardens, Kensington, London
METHOD OF KILLING	Battered/asphyxiated
RELATIONSHIP TO KILLERS	None; none

after the man had been tied up. The jury held both men equally responsible and both were sentenced to death.

At the appeal, the defence did its best to suggest that since neither man had gone to the hotel with the intention of killing Smart, the crime should be one of manslaughter. It was pointed out though that since they had gone on a robbery prepared to use violence to overcome any resistance, they were guilty as charged and the appeal was lost.

MARIE BRADSHAW LIVED with her husband, George Edward Bradshaw, in Alfred Street, Bury, but she was also involved with another man, Milton Taylor, who lived in the same street.

Eventually, Marie and Milton ran way together and made a new home, in Crewe. George tried to get his wife to return, but she told him that the only way she would come home to him, would be in a box.

The very next day after making this statement, Marie and Milton were in Nantwich where they decided to spend the night sleeping in a small hut. It was in that same hut that Marie's words proved to be prophetic and she met her death at the hands of Taylor.

Taylor gave himself up to the police and confessed that he had strangled Marie with his tie. The reason he gave for this action, was that she would not let him sleep! Apparently Marie had gone on and on at him, and finally he had had enough and killed her.

Taylor was an ex-Borstal boy but at his trial, an attempt was made to show that he had not been responsible for his actions. Doctor Isaac Frost, a psychiatrist, testified that Milton was a moron who had no idea of the difference between right and wrong. Milton, though, seemed determined to hang and Doctor Frost had to admit that Milton had told him that he had strangled someone because he just felt like it. Milton went on to say that he had got satisfaction from the act and felt better after he had done it. He even said that he thought anybody should strangle anybody if they felt like it!

Despite the obvious signs that Milton Taylor's sanity was not all that it should be, he was found guilty and sentenced to hang. That sentence was carried out at Liverpool in June.

NAME	Milton Taylor
AGE AT EXECUTION	23
DATE OF EXECUTION	Tuesday, 22nd June, 1954
PLACE OF EXECUTION	Liverpool
HANGMAN	Not known
ASSISTANT	Not known
DATE OF TRIAL	3rd June, 1954
LOCATION OF TRIAL	Chester
PRESIDING JUDGE	Mister Justice Byrne
PROSECUTION COUNSEL	Elwyn Jones
DEFENCE COUNSEL	Edmund Davies
NUMBER OF VICTIMS	1

VICTIMS DETAILS	
NAME	Marie Bradshaw
AGE	25
DATE OF MURDER	Sunday, 21st February, 1954
PLACE OF MURDER	Nantwich, Cheshire
METHOD OF KILLING	Strangled
RELATIONSHIP TO KILLER	Girlfriend

1954

THERE WERE THREE people living at 57 Tron Square, Edinburgh. The head of the house was Elizabeth McGarry and with her lived two children from a previous marriage, 16-year-old Jean Elisabeth and George.

In fact, the family background was slightly more complex. Elizabeth had previously been married to George Alexander Robertson. However, since Mr McGarry had left the scene, George had moved back in and then been forced out again because of his violence. Indeed, so frightened were they of George Alexander that ever since he had left, Elizabeth had been in the habit of bolting the door each night, putting a chair behind the door and a poker nearby.

On the evening of February 27th, 1954, several friends visited 57 Tron Square. It had been a good night but as they retired, Elizabeth forgot to put the chair back behind the door.

Jean Elizabeth Robertson was asleep but something woke her in the early hours of Sunday morning. It was the sound of her father whispering. Jean walked out onto the lobby in time to see her father sticking a knife in his son's head. George Alexander then turned his attentions to Jean and began attacking her.

The events that followed were confusing to Jean. She recalled her brother sitting on a chair and asking her to fetch the doctor but then her father came back and carried her mother upstairs over his shoulder. George managed to get out of the house and ran to Catherine Hay's, a neighbour who lived at number 42, but his father followed him and attacked him again. The Hays saw George Alexander stab his son at least three more times before carrying the boy's lifeless body back to number 57.

Mr and Mrs Hay ran to the police station and told Detective Sergeant Walter Middlemist what they had witnessed. The officer immediately dashed to 57 Tron Square and found Robertson with his head inside the gas oven. The other three members of the family had all been bound and gagged and stabbed repeatedly. Only Jean would recover from her wounds.

Robertson wished to plead guilty to

NAME	George Alexander Robertson
AGE AT EXECUTION	40
DATE OF EXECUTION	Wednesday, 23rd June, 1954
PLACE OF EXECUTION	Edinburgh, Saughton
HANGMAN	Not known
ASSISTANT	Not known
DATE OF TRIAL	1st June – 2nd June, 1954
LOCATION OF TRIAL	Edinburgh
PRESIDING JUDGE	Lord Justice Thomson
PROSECUTION COUNSEL	W.R. Milligan, William Grant
DEFENCE COUNSEL	N.A. Sloan, R.D. Ireland
NUMBER OF VICTIMS	2

VICTIMS DETAILS	
NAMES	Elizabeth Robertson; George Alexander Robertson
AGES	Not known
DATE OF MURDER	Sunday, 28th February, 1954
PLACE OF MURDER	57 Tron Square, Edinburgh; 42 Tron Square, Edinburgh
METHOD OF KILLING	Stabbed; stabbed
RELATIONSHIP TO KILLER	Ex-wife; son

murder but the courts would not allow it and a plea of not guilty was entered. The defence tried to say that George was insane at the time and so not responsible for his actions. Medical opinion differed with Doctor Reginald Baillie saying that Robertson was perfectly sane whilst Doctor William Blyth gave the opinion that the defendant was suffering from diminished responsibility.

The jury took one hour to decide that Robertson was guilty. Asked if he had anything to say he replied that the proceedings had been a waste of time. He did not enter an appeal and was executed exactly three weeks after his trial had ended.

WILLIAM HEPPER, A painter of flowers and portraits, lived in Chelsea but had a studio in Hove. His daughter had a friend, Margaret Spevick, who in early 1954 had fallen from a wall and broken her arm. Hepper suggested that Margaret be allowed to accompany him back to Hove where she could recuperate whilst he painted her portrait. After some thought, her mother finally agreed and on February 3rd, 1954, Hepper and the child travelled down to the south coast.

A couple of postcards were sent back to London and it seemed that Margaret was having a good time. The arrangement was that on February 7th, Mrs Spevick would travel down to Brighton and be met at the station by Hepper and her daughter. Mrs Spevick made the trip, but there was no one to meet her.

Mrs Spevick had unfortunately not taken the address of the studio with her and so had no alternative but to return to London to pick up the address and to see if by mistake, Hepper and Margaret had returned home.

The painter and his model had not returned to London, and, finding the address of the studio in Hove, Mrs Spevick returned to the south coast. On arrival at the studio in Hove, she was somewhat dismayed to find that there was no reply to her knocking. She approached the caretaker, who let her in with his pass key.

The studio was nothing more than a dingy one-roomed flatlet and Mrs Spevick found that its only occupant was her daughter who lay on the bed, naked, raped and strangled. Her unfinished portrait lay on an easel to one side of the bed. A massive hunt was launched for William Hepper.

Unbeknown to the police, Hepper had fled to his native Spain. From here he wrote to a number of friends and relatives asking for money. One of those relatives, an uncle, had seen the reports of the crime in Hove and felt it his duty to report the whereabouts of Hepper to the police. So it was that Hepper was discovered, arrested and finally extradited to Britain.

The trial started in July and Hepper's defence was that he had no memory of what had taken place in the flat in Hove. He had left

NAME	William Sanchez de Pina Hepper
AGE AT EXECUTION	62
DATE OF EXECUTION	Wednesday, 11th August, 1954
PLACE OF EXECUTION	Wandsworth
HANGMAN	Albert Pierrepoint
ASSISTANT	Royston Rickard
DATE OF TRIAL	19th July – 22nd July, 1954
LOCATION OF TRIAL	Lewes
PRESIDING JUDGE	Mister Justice Jones
PROSECUTION COUNSEL	R.F. Levy, R. Maxwell Turner
DEFENCE COUNSEL	Derek Curtis Bennett, John McManus
NUMBER OF VICTIMS	1

VICTIMS DETAILS	
NAME	Margaret Rose Louise Spevick
AGE	11
DATE OF MURDER	Thursday, 4th February, 1954
PLACE OF MURDER	Room 14, 112 Western Road, Hove, near Brighton
METHOD OF KILLING	Strangled
RELATIONSHIP TO KILLER	None

Margaret alive, giving her the return train fare to London, whilst he travelled to Spain to see a dying brother. He claimed that he seemed to remember a dream where he argued and fought with his ex-wife but stated flatly that he had not murdered Margaret. He also refuted the idea that he had raped her by saying that he had suffered from sexual impotence for some time.

The jury were not convinced.

IN DECEMBER 1947, Kenneth Mulligan married Doreen and the following year she gave birth to a daughter, Linda.

Around November, 1952, Doreen met Harold Fowler and within three weeks, they had become lovers. In due course, Kenneth Mulligan found out about this affair and after a number of arguments, Doreen left Kenneth, in November, 1953. Soon afterwards, she gave birth to a son.

At first, Doreen lived alone but soon afterwards moved in with her sister, at Henry Road. On May 8th, 1954, Doreen's sister moved out and Harold Fowler moved in.

Kenneth Mulligan still loved his wife and had not given up hopes of getting her to return to him. With this in mind, Kenneth wrote a moving and warm letter to Doreen, begging her to return to him. Doreen received this note on May 18th and that evening, Kenneth received a visit from Fowler who told him in no uncertain terms that his wife would not be returning to him. The following night, Kenneth decided to pay Doreen a personal visit.

Kenneth arrived at Henry Road at 8.00pm only to be told by John McLellan, who was baby-sitting, that Doreen had gone to the cinema with Fowler. Kenneth told McLellan that he would wait and at 9.00pm, the couple returned.

It seemed that Kenneth Mulligan had finally accepted that he had lost Doreen for he asked only for his marriage certificate, possibly so he could seek a divorce, and also a photograph of Linda. As he was leaving, Kenneth called Doreen a fool and pushed her out of the way, causing her to strike her head against a wall. At this, a struggle between Kenneth and Fowler broke out, at the end of which, Kenneth Mulligan collapsed, having been stabbed in the stomach.

When interviewed by the police, Fowler claimed that the stabbing had been accidental. The knife had been on the table and he had picked it up because he was afraid Mulligan might use it on him and Doreen. During the argument, Mulligan had rushed at Fowler and must have run onto the knife. However, the knife had penetrated two layers of clothing and had gone seven inches into

NAME	Harold Fowler
AGE AT EXECUTION	21
DATE OF EXECUTION	Thursday, 12th August, 1954
PLACE OF EXECUTION	Lincoln
HANGMAN	Not known
ASSISTANT	Not known
DATE OF TRIAL	24th June – 25th June, 1954
LOCATION OF TRIAL	Nottingham
PRESIDING JUDGE	Mister Justice Sellers
PROSECUTION COUNSEL	W.A. Fearnley-Whittingstall
DEFENCE COUNSEL	P.D. Cotes-Preedy
NUMBER OF VICTIMS	1

VICTIMS DETAILS

NAME	Kenneth Joseph George Mulligan
AGE	28
DATE OF MURDER	Wednesday, 19th May, 1954
PLACE OF MURDER	25 Henry Road, West Bridgford
METHOD OF KILLING	Stabbed
RELATIONSHIP TO KILLER	None

Mulligan's body, indicating that considerable force had been used. Further, the knife's sheath was found underneath the settee, suggesting that it had been unsheathed deliberately after being picked up.

The jury took 70 minutes to decide that Fowler's story was a lie and that he had deliberately killed Kenneth Mulligan. The appeal was dismissed on July 28th and on August 11th, it was announced that there would be no reprieve. Fowler was executed the following day.

IN 1952, RUPERT Geoffrey Wells met Nellie Officer and at Christmas, 1953, he moved into her house at Elton Road, Kingston upon Thames. Wells, though, had a drink problem and this gave Nellie some concerns.

On the night of Saturday, May 8th, Nellie was working as usual at the Old Crown Hotel. During the evening she got talking to one of the customers who, by coincidence, also bore the name Wells.

Nellie told Sidney George Wells that she was nervous and he offered to accompany her home that evening. Sidney did indeed go home with Nellie and after searching the house from top to bottom for her, to make sure that there was no one else on the premises, he settled down for the night in the sitting room, in case Rupert returned home drunk.

The following morning, Sidney left the house at 9.10am. Just five minutes later, Mary Theresa Tuffen, the neighbour at number 7, heard screams coming from Nellie's house.

Mary went to investigate and saw a man, wearing a brown coat, creeping about the house. Soon afterwards she saw Nellie's lodger, Rupert Wells, going into the house and so took no further action.

Rupert Wells was next seen at 12.20pm when he walked into the Borough Arms on Park Road and announced to the landlord, Henry McDermott: "I have murdered Nellie." Earlier that day he had been into another pub where he had consumed three double gins and three bottles of beer. Here he had intimated that he was in some kind of trouble, but would not go into greater detail.

After listening to Rupert's story, Henry McDermott telephoned the police. Police Constable Low arrived soon afterwards and he, McDermott and Wells all went to Nellie's house together. Nellie was sitting in an armchair. She had been strangled.

Wells's defence was really in two parts. In the first place he contended that he had drunk so much the night before that he did not know what he was doing, but coupled with this was the fact that he had been taking Phenergan. Phenergan was a hypnotic sedative and one of the side-effects of this, albeit it a very rare one, was disorientation.

NAME	Rupert Geoffrey Wells
AGE AT EXECUTION	53
DATE OF EXECUTION	Wednesday, 1st September, 1954
PLACE OF EXECUTION	Wandsworth
HANGMAN	Albert Pierrepoint
ASSISTANT	Robert Leslie Stewart
DATE OF TRIAL	26th July – 28th July, 1954
LOCATION OF TRIAL	Lewes
PRESIDING JUDGE	Mister Justice Jones
PROSECUTION COUNSEL	Derek Curtis-Bennett
DEFENCE COUNSEL	Hamilton Barnes
NUMBER OF VICTIMS	1

VICTIMS DETAILS	
NAME	Nellie Officer
AGE	46
DATE OF MURDER	Sunday, 9th May, 1954
PLACE OF MURDER	5 Elton Road, Kingston upon Thames
METHOD OF KILLING	Strangled
RELATIONSHIP TO KILLER	Girlfriend

At one point in his statement, Wells said: "I was blind drunk and didn't know what I was doing. It's all blank. I don't remember how Mrs Officer met her death."

At first, the trial was set for the Kingston assizes but had to be postponed because a defence witness was abroad. As a result of that, it took place at Lewes some three weeks later. It lasted three days and at the end of that time, Wells was found guilty as charged after the jury had considered their verdict for 51 minutes.

1954

EDWARD REID AND Arthur White shared a room in a lodging house run by Mrs Fairweather. For some reason, Reid was in something of a temper on the evening of April 3rd, 1954, and argued with White whilst they were having dinner. That night, both men went out drinking, Reid returning at 10.40pm and White some time later.

Albert Clough, another lodger, had also been out and when he returned, he stumbled over a bundle in the back yard of the lodging house. This turned out to be the body of Arthur White, lying in a pool of blood.

The police were called and Constable Priestly was the first officer on the scene. He surmised that White had fallen from his bedroom window on the top floor and went up to investigate the matter further. Here he found Reid, half undressed and rather tipsy but upon examining the room, Priestly found blood inside as well as outside. There were also signs of a struggle inside the room and blood on Reid's face. The inference was that Reid had battered White and then thrown his body from the window to make it look like an accident.

Taken in for questioning, Reid denied any knowledge of an attack on White but it was noted that his right hand was swollen. Reid claimed that he had done this at work, claimed he had gone straight to bed when he got home and had not even seen White, let alone attacked him. The police felt that there was enough evidence to charge Reid with murder, to which Reid replied: "I had nowt to do with that."

At his trial, Reid tried to explain the blood on his face by saying that he had cut himself shaving before he had gone out on the night of April 3rd. To counter this, the prosecution called Mrs Fairweather and her daughter, Mrs Manton, both of whom had seen Reid return home and denied that there had been any blood on him at that time.

The jury deliberated for 75 minutes before finding Reid guilty of murder.

NAME	Edward Lindsay Reid
AGE AT EXECUTION	24
DATE OF EXECUTION	Wednesday, 1st September, 1954
PLACE OF EXECUTION	Leeds
HANGMAN	Stephen Wade
ASSISTANT	Harry Smith
DATE OF TRIAL	5th July – 6th July, 1954
LOCATION OF TRIAL	Leeds
PRESIDING JUDGE	Mister Justice Donovan
PROSECUTION COUNSEL	T. Basil Herbert, Felix Denny
DEFENCE COUNSEL	H.R.B. Shepherd, T.R. Nevin
NUMBER OF VICTIMS	1

VICTIMS DETAILS	
NAME	Arthur White
AGE	40
DATE OF MURDER	Saturday, 3rd April, 1954
PLACE OF MURDER	17 Claremont, Great Horton Road, Bradford
METHOD OF KILLING	Battered
RELATIONSHIP TO KILLER	None

BY THE TIME Styllou Christofi came to England to join her son, Stavros, and his German born wife Hella, in July 1953, she already knew what it was like to be tried for murder. Back in Cyprus, at the age of 25, Styllou had been put on trial for killing her mother-in-law by ramming a burning torch down her throat. She had been found not guilty!

Stavros was a waiter at the Cafe de Paris in London's West End, and his wife worked in a fashion shop. They had three children and a happy married life together. Styllou, though, was a woman of the old school and made her feelings plain. Speaking little English she constantly found fault with Hella and the way she chose to bring up her children. Hella put up with this for some time but finally her patience snapped and she gave Stavros an ultimatum.

Hella had arranged to take the children on a holiday to her family in Germany and she demanded that upon her return, Stavros would have shipped his mother back to Cyprus. Stavros spoke to his mother about this and Styllou decided to herself that if someone had to go, it would be Hella.

On July 29th, 1954, after Stavros had left for work and the children were safely in bed, Styllou picked up the heavy ash-plate from the fireplace and struck Hella over the head. She then took a scarf and strangled the life out of the helpless woman before dragging her body into the garden.

At around midnight, a neighbour, John Young noticed the glow of flames in the Christofi's back yard and went to investigate. Seeing what looked like a tailor's dummy on fire, Mr Young took no further action when he saw Styllou come out and stoke up the flames.

At 1.00am the following morning, Mr Burstoff and his wife were on their way home from their restaurant. Running into the street and hurling herself in front of the car, Styllou shouted: "Please come. Fire burning. Children sleeping."

Mr Burstoff rushed to help but soon discovered that the fire was in fact a human body. Styllou had tried to burn the corpse by covering it with paraffin-soaked newspaper.

Styllou claimed that she had been woken

NAME	Styllou Pantopiou Christofi
AGE AT EXECUTION	53
DATE OF EXECUTION	Wednesday, 15th December, 1954
PLACE OF EXECUTION	Holloway
HANGMAN	Albert Pierrepoint
ASSISTANT	Not known
DATE OF TRIAL	28th October, 1954
LOCATION OF TRIAL	Old Bailey
PRESIDING JUDGE	Not known
PROSECUTION COUNSEL	Christmas Humphreys
DEFENCE COUNSEL	Not known
NUMBER OF VICTIMS	1

VICTIMS DETAILS	
NAME	Hella Christofi
AGE	36
DATE OF MURDER	Thursday, 29th July, 1954
PLACE OF MURDER	11 South Hill Park, Hampstead, London
METHOD OF KILLING	Battered/strangled
RELATIONSHIP TO KILLER	Daughter-in-law

from her sleep by the smell of smoke and upon investigating had found Hella's body in the yard. Later, though, Hella's wedding ring was found in Styllou's room, wrapped in a piece of newspaper.

Styllou Christofi was tried and found guilty of murder. Being a member of the Greek Orthodox church, Styllou asked that a cross from that church be placed where she could see it in the execution cell. The request was granted and the cross was nailed to the wall in front of the drop. It remained there until the cell was dismantled in 1967.

Only one more condemned woman would ever see that cross.

The house at 62 Cannon Street, Hanley, should have been a happy one. Annie Shenton, the woman who occupied the house along with her son, six-year-old Dennis, was about to be married to her lodger, William Arthur Salt. The date had been set and the ceremony was to take place on Saturday, December 18th. Unfortunately, before that happy event could take place, Annie's son was dead and her fiancé was in custody having admitted to his murder.

On December 16th, Dennis went to classes as normal, at St John's School, Birch Terrace. About an hour afterwards, William Salt also appeared at the school and claimed that he wished to take the boy to see his grandmother. Salt was well known at the school and had taken the boy out on other occasions. There was no reason for the teacher or the headmistress to feel that anything would be different this time and so Dennis was allowed to leave with Salt.

At 12.30pm, Annie also called at the school and discovered that her son had been taken away. She too had no concerns but certainly had at 6.00pm when Salt returned home alone. Salt told Annie that the boy was with his sister at Runcorn and when Annie suggested they go over there by train and pick Dennis up, Salt readily agreed. On the way to the station though, Salt slipped away and her suspicions raised, Annie called in the police.

William Salt spent that night at the house of friends of his, Mr and Mrs Morris and was picked up in a nearby public house the following day. When interviewed, Salt readily admitted that Dennis was dead. Furthermore, he took the police to the canal where they found the drowned body of the boy. Salt's comment at the time was: "He got on my nerves. We were walking along the towpath hand in hand. The urge came over me and I swung him into the water."

An attempt was made to show that Salt was insane. He had suffered two head injuries in road accidents. The first of these had occurred in 1935, the second taking place in 1953, and he had also been in a colliery accident in 1937. Ever since, Salt had complained of headaches and had been afraid of going out in the dark. However, much of

NAME	William Arthur Salt
AGE AT EXECUTION	43
DATE OF EXECUTION	Tuesday, 29th March, 1955
PLACE OF EXECUTION	Liverpool
HANGMAN	Not known
ASSISTANT	Not known
DATE OF TRIAL	8th March – 9th March, 1955
LOCATION OF TRIAL	Stafford
PRESIDING JUDGE	Mister Justice Devlin
PROSECUTION COUNSEL	E. Ryder Richardson
DEFENCE COUNSEL	G.G. Baker
NUMBER OF VICTIMS	1

VICTIMS DETAILS	
NAME	Dennis John Shenton
AGE	6
DATE OF MURDER	Thursday, 16th December, 1954
PLACE OF MURDER	Canal at Trentham
METHOD OF KILLING	Drowned
RELATIONSHIP TO KILLER	None

this was countered by the prosecution, who showed that Salt was already married and knew he would be committing bigamy if and when he married Annie. They suggested that this, preying on his mind just two days before the ceremony, had led to the deliberate murder of Dennis Shenton.

It was the prosecution case that carried more weight with the jury and after considering their verdict for 75 minutes, Salt was found guilty and sentenced to death.

O N THE MORNING of February 10th, 1955, the almost naked body of Rose Elizabeth Fairhurst was discovered on a bomb site at the junction of Loman Street and Great Suffolk Street, in London. Her clothing had been ripped off with great force, she had been badly beaten, strangled and there was evidence of semen staining on her right thigh.

When investigations began into Rose's movements of the previous night, it was discovered that she had spent some time in the Alfred's Head pub, where she had been drinking with Ruby Johnstone. Ruby said that Rose had been approached by Sydney Joseph Clarke who had offered her 10/- for a 'quickie'. They had left together at 9.30pm. Clarke had also been seen by Linda Dancey who left the Swan pub in Blackfriars Road at around 10.30pm. By then he was alone and had also tried to proposition her saying: "Come on girl, I've got a few bob."

Clarke was traced to a hostel named Rowton House. When interviewed there he claimed that he had been in Bristol on the night of the murder. The night porter there, Brindley Thomas Pedrick, confirmed that Clarke had arrived at Rowton House just before midnight on the night of February 9th, and had told him that he had just arrived from Bristol. Further investigations showed that Ruby and Linda had been telling the truth. Another lodging house manager, George Henry Harding, of Bruce House, gave evidence that Clarke had been staying there until the night of the murder.

At first, Clarke denied any involvement in the crime, but blood tests showed that Clarke was a group AB secretor. This was the same blood group as the semen found on Rose's body and covered only about two per cent of the population. Faced with this evidence, Clarke made a second statement admitting his part in the death of Rose Fairhurst.

Clarke said that he had been drinking heavily. Seeing Rose he approached her for sex and offered her 10/-. They walked to the bomb site and found an old mattress. Clarke wanted Rose to lie on the mattress but she refused. After some argument he persuaded her to get onto the mattress but once he had laid down with her, he "went mad" and

NAME	Sydney Joseph Clarke
AGE AT EXECUTION	33
DATE OF EXECUTION	Thursday, 14th April, 1955
PLACE OF EXECUTION	Wandsworth
HANGMAN	Albert Pierrepoint
ASSISTANT	Robert Leslie Stewart
DATE OF TRIAL	23rd March, 1955
LOCATION OF TRIAL	Old Bailey
PRESIDING JUDGE	Not known
PROSECUTION COUNSEL	Christmas Humphreys
DEFENCE COUNSEL	Geoffrey D. Roberts
NUMBER OF VICTIMS	1

VICTIMS DETAILS	
NAME	Rose Elizabeth Fairhurst
AGE	circa 45
DATE OF MURDER	Wednesday, 9th February, 1955
PLACE OF MURDER	Loman Street, Southwark, London
METHOD OF KILLING	Strangled/battered
RELATIONSHIP TO KILLER	None

attacked her. He claimed to remember nothing else until he found himself in a cafe under Waterloo Bridge. He went back to his lodgings, packed his belongings into a suitcase which he left at King's Cross station before booking in at Rowton House.

At the trial, the defence asked for a verdict of guilty but insane. It was pointed out that his paternal grandfather had died in a mental hospital in 1899, though Doctor J.C.M. Matheson testified that Clarke was a sadist, but was not insane. There could therefore only be one verdict and Clarke was found guilty.

WINSTON SHAW MARRIED in 1937, but only lived with his wife for a few months. In 1951, he met Jean Tate and they began living together. She bore him two children but the relationship was not all that it should have been. Jean left Winston in 1954, but in September of that year, he persuaded her to return and they took lodgings together in Cunliffe Terrace, Manningham Lane, Bradford.

Even this reconciliation was not all that it appeared. Winston had arranged for his wife to take care of the two children, leaving him and Jean alone, but in effect, Jean was held prisoner for some months. It was not until officers from the N.S.P.C.C. visited that the truth came out and Jean was removed. In due course she was moved to a safe address in a flat at Knaresborough hospital.

Eventually, Winston managed to trace Jean and on the afternoon of December 3rd, 1954, he visited her, taking a powder compact as a present for Jean and a teddy bear for the eldest child. By chance, the police were at the flat at the time and after Jean told Winston that she did not want his gifts, or him, the officers escorted Winston from the flat, at Jean's request.

Later that same day, Winston Shaw took lodgings close to Jean's flat and bought himself a shiny new axe, from a shop around the corner. At 8.00pm, Winston left his new lodgings, returning at 9.45pm. At 11.30pm the police called and he was taken in for questioning about the murder of Jean Tate.

Winston admitted that he had gone back to Jean's flat with the intention of making up their differences. As he arrived, Winston heard a man's voice from inside and as he entered, the man demanded to know who he was and then took up a chair to attack him with. Winston just happened to have the axe he had purchased and lashed out blindly with it to defend himself. He suggested it was possible that he might have struck Jean accidentally in the confusion and when it was pointed out that she had been struck five times with the axe, merely claimed that they had all been accidental blows.

Jean had also been stabbed 25 times. Winston denied having anything to do with

NAME	Winston Shaw
AGE AT EXECUTION	39
DATE OF EXECUTION	Wednesday, 4th May, 1955
PLACE OF EXECUTION	Leeds
HANGMAN	Stephen Wade
ASSISTANT	Harry Smith
DATE OF TRIAL	15th March – 17th March, 1955
LOCATION OF TRIAL	Leeds
PRESIDING JUDGE	Mister Justice Pearce
PROSECUTION COUNSEL	Godfrey Russell Vick, Henry C. Scott
DEFENCE COUNSEL	G.S. Waller, Vivian Hurwitz
NUMBER OF VICTIMS	1

VICTIMS DETAILS	
NAME	Jean Tate
AGE	24
DATE OF MURDER	Friday, 3rd December, 1954
PLACE OF MURDER	Flat 1, Knaresborough Hospital
METHOD OF KILLING	Battered/stabbed
RELATIONSHIP TO KILLER	Ex-girlfriend

this, even though the knife that had been used was found in the bathroom at his lodgings. He could also offer no reasonable explanation as to why, if his story were true, he had not summoned help for a woman he professed to love.

Throughout his three-day trial, Winston stuck to his story that his striking of Jean with the axe had been unintentional, that he had not stabbed her and that he had acted in self-defence when he had been attacked by a strange man. The jury were not convinced.

O N THE MORNING of December 16th, 1954, a broken window was discovered at The Hollies, the home of Mary Ann Dodsley. The police were called in. They entered the house and found Mary upstairs beneath a pile of bedclothes. Someone had tried to rape her and in the process of the attack, had strangled her.

Two Scotland Yard detectives were called in: Superintendent John Ball and Sergeant Mesher. They soon discovered an excellent palm print on the glass of the broken window. The intruder had, it seemed, flexed his hand backwards to avoid leaving fingerprints, but the detectives knew that the palm print was just as individual and the impression was lifted. They also discovered a footprint inside the house, though this was less identifiable.

As a matter of routine, Mansfield police, who were in charge of the investigation, took 68 palm prints of local residents. These, together with the print from the glass, were examined by Superintendent Maurice Ray of the fingerprint department. He found one print that had no less than 16 points of similarity with the one from the cottage. Since only six were necessary for a positive identification, this was more than sufficient and the owner of the print, James Robinson, was arrested for murder.

A lot rested on the actual time of Mary Dodsley's death. The prosecution produced a pathologist who maintained that the time could not be narrowed down beyond a band from 11.00pm on the night of December 15th, to 1.00am on the 16th. However, a different pathologist, working for the defence, claimed that he could narrow it down to some time between 9.00pm and 10.00pm. Since Robinson could show that he was drinking in a local public house until just after 10.00pm, that would of course clear him of any involvement in the crime.

There was much argument over the precision given by the defence pathologist but much of that was reduced in importance when it was pointed out that Robinson's palm print had been found at the scene of the crime. He had claimed that he had not been near the house but could offer no explanation for how his palm print came to be on the glass

NAME	James Robinson
AGE AT EXECUTION	27
DATE OF EXECUTION	Tuesday, 24th May, 1955
PLACE OF EXECUTION	Lincoln
HANGMAN	Not known
ASSISTANT	Not known
DATE OF TRIAL	25th March – 29th March, 1955
LOCATION OF TRIAL	Birmingham
PRESIDING JUDGE	Mister Justice Jones
PROSECUTION COUNSEL	R.C. Vaughan, J.M. Griffiths-Jones
DEFENCE COUNSEL	J.C. Bickford Smith
NUMBER OF VICTIMS	1

VICTIMS DETAILS	
NAME	Mary Ann Dodsley
AGE	83
DATE OF MURDER	Wednesday, 15th December, 1954
PLACE OF MURDER	The Hollies, Skegby, Nottinghamshire
METHOD OF KILLING	Strangled
RELATIONSHIP TO KILLER	None

of the window at The Hollies. That was enough to convict Robinson, the only time that a palm print, not backed up by other evidence, had convicted a man of murder.

The appeal was heard on May 9th, when again much was made of the time differences between the two pathologist's reports, but without success. To the end, Robinson maintained his innocence. One of his last letters, from the condemned cell, was to his mother and in that he repeated that he was not responsible for this crime.

BY 1955, DOROTHY Dearlove had been separated from her husband for the best part of two years. A child had been born just before Dorothy parted from her husband and now mother and child lived with Dorothy's sister, Margaret Boothroyd and their mother, Mary Catherine, at 18 Clarence Road, Seacombe.

When Dorothy first moved into Clarence Road, Mary Catherine Boothroyd had one lodger already. Richard Gowler had lived with the Boothroyds since 1951 and seemed to be a model tenant, but the arrival of Dorothy was to change all that.

The couple grew close and eventually became lovers. On Boxing Day 1954, Mary found out what had been going on under her roof, and invited Gowler to leave as soon as possible. Mary did relent shortly afterwards, but everyone knew that the situation could never return to what it had been and Gowler finally left in early February, 1955. Unfortunately, the occupants of Clarence Road had not seen the last of Richard Gowler. He called many times after his departure and often made threats against all three women in the house. The police had to be called out several times but no further action was ever taken against him.

On the night of March 11th, Dorothy Dearlove lay asleep in her bed when she felt something on her throat. Waking, she realised that someone was in her bedroom. She screamed very loudly and almost immediately realised that the intruder was Richard Gowler.

Although Dorothy could not know it, Gowler was armed with a vicious, 20-inch long marline spike and with this he now proceeded to stab Dorothy. She continued to scream and in due course, Gowler ran out of the room, into the hallway, where he met Mary Boothroyd. The final upshot, as Gowler left the house, was that Dorothy was badly injured and her mother lay dead. Dorothy's sister, Margaret, rang the police.

When he was arrested, Gowler admitted that he had broken into Mary Boothroyd's house. He maintained that his intention was to try to talk to Dorothy. He had already made two or three appointments with her, which she had failed to keep, and he saw this as the

NAME	Richard Gowler
AGE AT EXECUTION	43
DATE OF EXECUTION	Tuesday, 21st June, 1955
PLACE OF EXECUTION	Liverpool
HANGMAN	Not known
ASSISTANT	Not known
DATE OF TRIAL	2nd June, 1955
LOCATION OF TRIAL	Chester
PRESIDING JUDGE	Mister Justice Sellers
PROSECUTION COUNSEL	Edmund Davies
DEFENCE COUNSEL	Emlyn Hooson
NUMBER OF VICTIMS	1

VICTIMS DETAILS	
NAME	Mary Catherine Boothroyd
AGE	53
DATE OF MURDER	Friday, 11th March, 1955
PLACE OF MURDER	18 Clarence Road, Seacombe
METHOD OF KILLING	Stabbed
RELATIONSHIP TO KILLER	None

only chance to discuss matters with her. He had taken the marline spike with him in case he had needed to force a window or door and had no intention of hurting anyone. He said that he deeply regretted killing Mary, of whom he had been very fond.

This latter statement was taken up by Gowler's defence. They suggested that as Gowler had no wilful intention and no malice aforethought, he could be guilty only of manslaughter. After 45 minutes' deliberation, the jury made it clear that they felt the crime was murder, and Gowler was sentenced to death.

Despite a petition of 65,000 signatures, presented to the Home Secretary on June 17th, Richard Gowler failed to avoid his fate and was hanged just four days later.

VIOLET MAY ROBERTS last saw her daughter, Mary, at around 3.30pm on Tuesday, May 10th, 1955. That was when Mary left her home at 25 Roxby Road, Winterton, to catch the 3.40pm bus to Scunthorpe where she intended going to a club.

Although she was unmarried, Mary already had a son who would be two years of age in October, and was pregnant again. Mary enjoyed herself at the club and left some time before midnight. Outside she fell into conversation with a man with a bicycle. By coincidence, he had the same surname as her, although they were not related.

In the early hours of the morning of May 11th, the police received a telephone call from Spencer Avenue, Scunthorpe. The caller identified himself as Kenneth Roberts, a married man with two children. He explained that he had met a girl outside a club and within the hour, had strangled her with her own chiffon scarf. He had then cycled home, told his wife what he had done and then contacted the police. Later, Roberts took officers to a woodyard in Winterton Road, where Georgina's body was discovered.

Roberts explained that he believed Georgina was dead when he tied the scarf around her neck and at the time of his attack on her, he had just "gone crazy". Despite his own description of what he had done, Roberts pleaded not guilty at his trial, which took place at Nottingham. He called no evidence in his defence and was soon found guilty.

There was no appeal and no reprieve and finally, just 20 days after the trial, Roberts was hanged for the murder of his namesake.

NAME	Kenneth Roberts
AGE AT EXECUTION	24
DATE OF EXECUTION	Tuesday, 12th July, 1955
PLACE OF EXECUTION	Lincoln
HANGMAN	Steve Wade
ASSISTANT	Robert Leslie Stewart
DATE OF TRIAL	21st June – 22nd June, 1955
LOCATION OF TRIAL	Nottingham
PRESIDING JUDGE	Mister Justice Finnemore
PROSECUTION COUNSEL	C.N. Shawcross
DEFENCE COUNSEL	E. Daly Lewis
NUMBER OF VICTIMS	1

VICTIMS DETAILS	
NAME	Mary Georgina Roberts
AGE	18
DATE OF MURDER	Wednesday, 11th May, 1955
PLACE OF MURDER	Woodyard off Winterton Road, Scunthorpe
METHOD OF KILLING	Strangled
RELATIONSHIP TO KILLER	None

RUTH ELLIS WAS born Ruth Neilson in 1926 in Rhyl, North Wales, though this was only the name she was registered under. Her real name was actually Ruth Hornby but her father, a musician, changed his name for professional reasons. By the time she met David Blakely in the early 1950s, Ruth had had two children and a failed marriage.

Ruth moved to London in 1941 and not long afterwards was involved in an affair with a Canadian serviceman named Clare. Finding herself pregnant at the end of 1943, she was dismayed to find out that Clare was in fact married and had three children back in Canada. Her son was born on September 15th, 1944 and, being christened Andria Clare, would be known as Andy throughout his life.

Ruth's introduction to the seedy world of London nightclubs came when she saw an advertisement offering £1 per hour for nude models, at a camera club. Ruth signed herself up and it was there she met Morrie Conley, who owned a number of clubs, one of which was the Court Club at 58 Duke Street. Conley offered Ruth a job as a hostess at the Court at £5 per week, plus commission on sales.

In the Spring of 1950, Ruth met the man who was to give her the surname that would go down in history. George Ellis, a dentist, had just obtained a divorce from his first wife. He became infatuated with Ruth, they soon became engaged and married on November 8th, 1950. The relationship was a disaster from the start and after many arguments they finally split in 1951. At the time, Ruth was pregnant with her second child, a girl, who was born in the October of that year and was named Georgina. She would later be taken north by her father, for adoption. Having shaken off the shackles of marriage, Ruth returned to Conley's clubs.

The year 1953 saw the first meeting between Ruth Ellis and David Blakely. It was not an auspicious occasion. David behaved boorishly and insulted some of Ruth's fellow hostesses. She left him in no doubt that she was annoyed.

In October, Ruth was invited to become manageress of another of Conley's clubs, The Little Club at 37 Brompton Road, Knightsbridge. There was a flat over the club

NAME	Ruth Ellis
AGE AT EXECUTION	28
DATE OF EXECUTION	Wednesday, 13th July, 1955
PLACE OF EXECUTION	Holloway
HANGMAN	Albert Pierrepoint
ASSISTANT	Not known
DATE OF TRIAL	20th June – 21st June, 1955
LOCATION OF TRIAL	Old Bailey
PRESIDING JUDGE	Mister Justice Havers
PROSECUTION COUNSEL	Christmas Humphreys, Mervyn Griffith-Jones, Miss Jean Southworth
DEFENCE COUNSEL	Melford Stevenson, Sebag Shaw, Peter Rawlinson
NUMBER OF VICTIMS	1

VICTIMS DETAILS	
NAME	David Moffat Drummond Blakely
AGE	25
DATE OF MURDER	Sunday, 10th April, 1955
PLACE OF MURDER	Outside the Magdala Tavern, South Hill Park, London
METHOD OF KILLING	Shot
RELATIONSHIP TO KILLER	Boyfriend

and Ruth suddenly found herself much better off. Ensconced in her new home and job, one of her first customers was David Blakely.

On this occasion though, David showed the other side of his character. He was charming and witty and they felt an instant attraction between them. Within a week they had become lovers.

Another one of the many men Ruth had met at the Little Club, was Desmond Cussen, an ex-bomber pilot, who developed an instant dislike of Blakely. He would also play a major part in Ruth Ellis's life.

David Blakely liked fast cars. With a friend and business partner, Anthony Findlater, he was in the process of designing and building a new racing car, which they had named the Emperor. This rather expensive interest proved to be a great drain on his finances and so he was constantly short of money. This did not help in his relationship with Ruth.

The fact that David seemed to be ashamed of Ruth, also did little to help matters between them. One weekend when he drove Ruth to

Penn in Buckinghamshire, where his parents lived, David went in to the local pub and upon finding that his mother was there, refused to take Ruth in and brought her out a drink which she was forced to consume in the car.

In June 1954, David went as a co-driver to Le Mans, for the famous 24-hour race. When he did not return at the time he had promised, Ruth got her revenge by taking Desmond Cussen as her lover. David was furious but it did not have the effect Ruth thought it would. Far from ending the affair with David, it served, if anything, to intensify it.

The October of that year saw Ruth dismissed from her job at the Little Club, due to falling levels of takings. Now she was not only out of a job but had also lost the flat that went with it. She moved in to Cussen's flat in Goodwood Court, Devonshire Street and David was once more in a furious rage.

Ruth stayed in Cussen's flat until the following February. She had been seeing David continuously for some time already, but now they both decided that the time had come to find a place together. They rented a bedsitter at 44 Egerton Gardens, in the names of Mr and Mrs Ellis.

On April 2nd, David's car, the Emperor, blew up in a race. For some reason he chose to blame Ruth for this, telling her that she was a jinx. It had not helped matters that a few days before, Ruth had discovered that she was again pregnant. The argument turned into a full-scale row, during which David struck Ruth in the stomach. She lost the baby and was ill until April 5th.

For some time Ruth had been jealous of the friendship David shared with his partner, Anthony Findlater, and his wife, Carole. Ruth knew that some years before David had had an affair with Carole Findlater and she was never totally convinced that it was all over between the two of them. Then, over the Easter weekend, things hit an all-time low.

Friday the 8th of April saw David drinking with the Findlaters in their favourite public house, the Magdala Tavern on South Hill Park. David told them that he was supposed to be calling for Ruth that evening but couldn't face doing so. He said he wanted the relationship to end but couldn't seem to get away from her.

Carole Findlater suggested that David spent the weekend with them at their flat at 29 Tanza Road. David readily agreed.

At 9.30pm that evening, Ruth rang the Findlaters and asked if David was with them. Anthony, who picked up the telephone, said that he wasn't. Ruth didn't believe him and so rang Desmond Cussen and asked him to drive her to Tanza Road.

Cussen duly obliged and upon her arrival, Ruth saw David's station wagon outside the flat, confirming that he was probably inside. She rang the doorbell, but there was no answer. Going to a local telephone box, she rang the flat again but the receiver was put down as soon as she spoke. Furious, Ruth took Cussen's torch from his car, walked over to David's station wagon and smashed in the rear window. The police were called and Ruth was advised to go home. This she did, but not until 2.00am.

On Saturday morning, Ruth again telephoned Tanza Road and again the receiver was put down when she spoke. The faithful Desmond drove her back to the flat and Ruth hid in a doorway just down the road, spying on the Findlaters' flat. That evening she saw a party at the flat and at 10.00pm, finally saw David emerge, an attractive woman on his arm.

By Sunday, April 10th, Ruth had spent a great deal of time brooding over David. It was some time on that day that she finally decided to kill him.

Carole Findlater had run out of cigarettes and also needed some more drink. David and a friend of his, Chris Gunnell, had offered to drive down to the Magdala and pick some up. Whilst they were there they enjoyed a quiet drink together, finally leaving at about 9.30pm.

Chris Gunnell walked to the front passenger seat whilst David fumbled for his car keys. A blonde woman stepped forward and shouted "David...." She was ignored. Ruth reached into her handbag and took out a .38 Smith and Wesson revolver. Once again she called his name. This time David spun round, saw the gun and ran around the back of his car. Ruth fired twice at his fleeing form.

In all, Ruth shot David Blakely four times.

She fired six times in all, one bullet missing completely, the other ricocheting off a wall and hitting a passer-by, Mrs Gladys Yule, in her thumb. The gun clicked again and again, the chambers empty. It was to be Ruth's one regret. She had intended to save the last bullet for herself.

People poured out of the Magdala and Ruth asked someone to call the police. She need not have bothered. The man she spoke to was an off-duty policeman, Alan Thompson, and it was he who arrested her.

Ruth Ellis's trial was held at the Old Bailey. It is said that one question sealed her fate. Christmas Humphreys, leading for the prosecution asked Ruth, "Mrs Ellis, when you fired the revolver at close range into the body of David Blakely, what did you intend to do?" Ruth simply replied: "It is obvious when I shot him I intended to kill him." The jury were out for 14 minutes before returning their verdict of guilty of murder.

Ruth refused to appeal against her sentence and wrote a letter of apology to David's mother. Basically, Ruth believed that she ought to die in order to repay the debt. It is said that she walked bravely to her death after taking a small tot of brandy to fortify her. So brave was she that even the executioner, Albert Pierrepoint, wrote to Ruth's mother after the execution, remarking on how courageous she had been.

There still remained the mystery of where Ruth had got the gun she used on David Blakely. Whilst in prison she told her parents and one of her solicitors that Desmond Cussen had given her the gun, cleaned it for her and shown her how to use it. Furthermore, it was he who drove her to Tanza Road on the night of the murder. Seeing that the station wagon was not outside, Ruth had walked down to the Magdala to see if David was there.

Cussen denied being involved in any way and, interviewed many years later in Australia, he confessed that he thought Ruth would be reprieved. Ruth's son Andy, who tragically took his own life years later, confirmed Ruth's story at least in part. He said he had seen Cussen showing her how to use the weapon.

We may never know the truth. What is true is that Ruth Ellis became the last woman to hang in England, renewing the public clamour for the ending of the death penalty.

DONALD LAINTON WAS discovered, in his snow-covered car, in a road leading to Birchen Bower Farm, on the night of February 25th, 1955. He had been stabbed four times, one of the wounds having penetrated his eye, passing into his brain. He was still alive when found, but died in hospital early the following day.

Police inquiries concentrated on the belief that Lainton, a commercial traveller, had picked up a hitch-hiker who had subsequently killed him. Witnesses came forward who said they had seen a man trying to free the car from the deep snow and though he was too far away for them to give a detailed description, the times fitted with the fact that someone had telephoned a taxi firm from a call box some two miles away from the scene of the attack. Other witnesses described a man they had seen with Lainton in the Coach and Horses pub at Pasturefields, near Hixon.

In due course, Frederick Arthur Cross was arrested in Warwickshire. Cross had been living in a hut on a disused R.A.F. station at Hixon, and made no attempt to deny his guilt. In fact, he seemed eager to pay the price for his crime, claiming that he wanted no legal aid or defence.

The trial took place on July 5th. Cross was very deaf and all the details had to be repeated to him. Once again he insisted that he was guilty and refused any defence. He said he had killed Lainton because his wife had left him and he wished to die himself. He had purchased rat poison with which to take his own life but after his courage failed him, he needed to find another way to end it all. Then he met Donald Lainton and knew that if he killed him, he would be hanged for it. The judge, Mr Justice Gorman, had no alternative but to sentence Cross to death.

There was no appeal and the Home Secretary of the day decided that there would be no reprieve. Frederick Arthur Cross was hanged at Birmingham on July 26th, exactly three weeks after the trial. It was Albert Pierrepoint's last execution at Birmingham.

NAME	Frederick Arthur Cross
AGE AT EXECUTION	33
DATE OF EXECUTION	Tuesday, 26th July, 1955
PLACE OF EXECUTION	Birmingham
HANGMAN	Albert Pierrepoint
ASSISTANT	Harry Allen
DATE OF TRIAL	5th July, 1955
LOCATION OF TRIAL	Stafford
PRESIDING JUDGE	Mister Justice Gorman
PROSECUTION COUNSEL	None
DEFENCE COUNSEL	None
NUMBER OF VICTIMS	1

VICTIMS DETAILS

NAME	Donald Haywood Lainton (Died Saturday, 26th February)
AGE	28
DATE OF MURDER	Friday, 25th February, 1955
PLACE OF MURDER	Driveway of Birchen Bower Farm, Willslock, near Uttoxeter
METHOD OF KILLING	Stabbed
RELATIONSHIP TO KILLER	None

WILLIAM HARMER WAS one of five children, a well-mannered boy who was happy to help out his parents whenever he could. So, when his father asked him to go out and call in his younger brother, he did not hesitate.

It was 9.00pm on Friday, 27th August, 1954 when William left his house in Vere Street, Wigan, and made his way towards the banks of the Leeds and Liverpool canal, where his brother would most likely be found.

At some time around 9.20pm, Joseph Kelly, aged 20, was also out looking for a child, his six-year-old daughter, Barbara. As he walked across a piece of wasteland known locally as 'The Sands', he came across the body of William Harmer.

At first Kelly thought the boy had merely fallen and hurt his foot but when he saw the blood he called across 71-year-old Joseph Mawdesley who was passing by. The boy managed to gasp out where he lived and together Kelly and Mawdesley carried the child home to his parents. Neither man realised how badly hurt Harmer was, though, and when he died on the way to the hospital, the police had to make a special appeal for the pair of good Samaritans to come forward and be eliminated from their inquiries.

William Harmer had been stabbed 11 times in total, the fatal wound being one to the throat. The weapon used was a small penknife and this led police to link the attack with one that had taken place earlier that same night.

Seven-year-old William Mitchell had also been playing near the canal when a man had grabbed him and plunged a penknife into his chest. Luckily for William, his screams attracted the attention of two men, who chased his assailant away. Together they gave a description of the man concerned. The most striking feature was that the man had very blond, almost white hair.

The police launched a massive inquiry, but it rapidly ran out of steam. At the end of October, Scotland Yard were called in and two detectives arrived from London. They repeated much of the previous work, interviewed witnesses again and made fresh

NAME	Norman William Green
AGE AT EXECUTION	25
DATE OF EXECUTION	Wednesday, 27th July, 1955
PLACE OF EXECUTION	Liverpool
HANGMAN	Albert Pierrepoint
ASSISTANT	Not known
DATE OF TRIAL	30th June – 5th July, 1955
LOCATION OF TRIAL	Manchester
PRESIDING JUDGE	Mister Justice Oliver
PROSECUTION COUNSEL	Daniel Brabin, F.J. Nance
DEFENCE COUNSEL	J.D. Robertson Crichton, Edward Steele
NUMBER OF VICTIMS	2

VICTIMS DETAILS

NAMES	William Harmer; Norman Yates
AGES	11; 10
DATE OF MURDER	Friday, 27th August, 1954; Monday, 11th April, 1955
PLACES OF MURDERS	Field off Miry Lane, Wigan; Back Hope Street, Ince, near Wigan
METHOD OF KILLING	Stabbed; stabbed
RELATIONSHIP TO KILLER	None; none

appeals for help from the public, but they too got nowhere.

The 11th of April, 1955 was Bank Holiday Monday and all the shops were shut. At 9.00pm at a house in Heywood Street, Lower Ince, a region to the east of the town, Mrs Yates had just run out of sugar. She too had a helpful son, 10-year-old Norman and she asked him if he would run to his aunt's house, which was just a few streets away, to see if she had any to spare. Norman went without hesitation.

The sounds of Norman's screams attracted a number of people, but they were too late to save his life. He had been stabbed four times, with a penknife, and died that night in Wigan Infirmary. Once again a man had been seen running away from the murder scene, and once again he was described as having almost white hair.

One of the men who fitted that description was Norman William Green, a corn miller who worked close to his home at 102 Hallgate, near the centre of town. Officers who called to ask Green a few questions about his movements recently did not find his answers satisfactory and he was taken to the police station for further questioning. He denied being anywhere near Ince on the night of Norman Yates's death.

A number of the witnesses who had come forward were men drinking in the Railway Hotel, close to the scene of Yates's murder. They had revealed that one of their fellow drinkers, a man with white hair, had left the pub just before the child had been attacked. The police told Green that they were quite willing to bring those witnesses in to identify him, at which point he changed his story for the first time and admitted being in the Railway. However, he still denied being involved in the murder.

Whilst Green was being held, his house was visited and various items of his clothing were taken away for examination. When some of these were found to exhibit positive reactions for blood of the same type as Norman Yates's, Green changed his story for a second time. He now admitted killing both Yates and Harmer. He even took detectives to his place of work and there, in a sack of corn on the top floor, he pointed out where they would find the murder weapon.

Green's defence was one of insanity and at one stage it appeared as if it may succeed. After an absence of four hours, the jury came back into court and asked Mister Justice Oliver to clarify the law on insanity. After a further 20 minutes though, they reached a unanimous verdict: Green was guilty of murder.

There was no appeal. Green's defence instead relied on an application direct to the Home Secretary, asking for a reprieve. It was not forthcoming and Green was hanged.

One unsolved mystery remains about the case, however. Just five weeks before the death of William Harmer, which Green admitted to causing, another child had died in Wigan. Six-year old William Schofield had been playing on fields near his home in Lisbon Street, Higher Ince, on June 19th, 1954. He had been found bleeding from stab wounds and died from those injuries. The police believed that he had fallen victim to an over-exuberant game of 'Cowboys and Indians' and made no further inquiries. However, William Schofield had been stabbed with a small penknife and in view of what was to happen later, one cannot help but wonder if he was not Norman Green's first victim.

1955

AT 8.40AM ON May 31st, 1955, Corbett Roberts, a native of Jamaica, walked into the headquarters of Birmingham C.I.D., and announced: "I have done my wife in."

Later that morning, officers attending at 113 Frederick Road, Aston, found the battered body of Doris Roberts, lying by her bed. Her killer had used two hammers on her.

Roberts explained that there had been some money taken within the family group and he had been the person accused of stealing it. His wife, far from supporting him, had believed that he was the thief.

On the morning in question, there was a small quantity of money on the breakfast table, which Roberts intended to use for his weekly living and travelling expenses. As he reached out to take it, Doris had snatched it and when he demanded that she give it to him, had replied: "You will have to kill me for that money." In the argument that followed, Roberts took a hammer and battered Doris repeatedly. When the shaft broke, he paused to get a second hammer and continued with the beating. Then, when he was quite sure that Doris was dead, Roberts walked to the police station and gave himself up.

Corbett Roberts was determined to put his head into the hangman's noose. Although he said he had never intended to kill Doris and had done so in a moment of passion, he refused legal aid saying: "I am not interested because I am guilty." Held on remand and asked if he any objections he replied: "I entirely leave myself in your hands. I entitle you to take my life."

At his trial, Roberts seemed more concerned with his property than his life. He stated that he wanted none of his money to be given to his children and wished it to go to an old people's institution instead.

NAME	Corbett Montague Roberts
AGE AT EXECUTION	46
DATE OF EXECUTION	Tuesday, 2nd August, 1955
PLACE OF EXECUTION	Birmingham
HANGMAN	Stephen Wade
ASSISTANT	Harry Allen
DATE OF TRIAL	22nd July, 1955
LOCATION OF TRIAL	Birmingham
PRESIDING JUDGE	Mister Justice Gorman
PROSECUTION COUNSEL	Richard O'Sullivan
DEFENCE COUNSEL	R.K. Brown, A.P. Marshall
NUMBER OF VICTIMS	1

VICTIMS DETAILS	
NAME	Doris Acquilla Roberts
AGE	41
DATE OF MURDER	Tuesday, 31st May, 1955
PLACE OF MURDER	113 Frederick Road, Aston, Birmingham
METHOD OF KILLING	Battered
RELATIONSHIP TO KILLER	Wife

AT 4.00PM ON June 8th, 1955, Evelyn Higgins left the Frederick Bird School, in Coventry. After visiting a hairdresser's shop, which she left at around 5.00pm, she made for home at 26 Lowther Street. It was a journey she would never complete.

Once Evelyn had been reported missing, two 14-year-old girls came forward and said that a man driving a black car had tried to pick them up, just a few minutes before the last known sighting of Evelyn Higgins. They described the driver as having light brown hair that was going grey, but in many ways the description of the car matched that given by a man cycling in Shaw Lane. The car was said to be a Standard 9, two-door saloon, dated 1937 or 1938. The rear number plate was on the extreme off-side instead of being in the centre and had been hand-painted in a rather amateurish manner. Finally, the car had a Union Jack motif on the bonnet.

On June 11th, 1955, Ernest Harding was discovered attempting to commit suicide by leading a hose from the exhaust of the very car the police were looking for. When he recovered, he told a number of different stories that related to Evelyn's death.

In the first, he claimed he had been to the pictures at the time Evelyn had been picked up. In due course, he admitted that Evelyn had been in his car but he insisted that he had no memory of anything that had happened until he saw her dead body. He had a spade in the car, so in a panic he drove to some woods near Coleshill and buried her. On June 12th, Evelyn's body was found where Harding had said it was. She was eight inches down and had been stabbed in the throat, though there were also signs of attempted suffocation. Before she died, Evelyn had been sexually assaulted.

Harding changed his story again. He now remembered trying to have sex with Evelyn and admitted putting his hand over her mouth. He still claimed to have no memory of anything else.

The only defence could be one of insanity. Harding was a married man and his wife, Martha, testified that since an accident in 1952, he had had blackouts after which he would have no memory of what he had

NAME	Ernest Charles Harding
AGE AT EXECUTION	42
DATE OF EXECUTION	Tuesday, 9th August, 1955
PLACE OF EXECUTION	Birmingham
HANGMAN	Stephen Wade
ASSISTANT	Robert Leslie Stewart
DATE OF TRIAL	21st July, 1955
LOCATION OF TRIAL	Birmingham
PRESIDING JUDGE	Mister Justice Lynskey
PROSECUTION COUNSEL	R.C. Vaughan
DEFENCE COUNSEL	Claude Duveen
NUMBER OF VICTIMS	1

VICTIMS DETAILS	
NAME	Evelyn Patricia Higgins
AGE	10
DATE OF MURDER	Wednesday, 8th June, 1955
PLACE OF MURDER	Probably Coleshill, near Coventry
METHOD OF KILLING	Stabbed
RELATIONSHIP TO KILLER	None

done. She went on to say that on the night of Evelyn's abduction, Ernest had returned home at 7.15pm and had appeared to be quite normal.

As far as the medical evidence was concerned, a psychiatrist, Doctor Arthur Hale, said that Harding knew what he was doing during the assault but possibly not during the killing. This was refuted by Doctor Percy Coats, the prison medical officer who said that Harding was perfectly sane.

That doubt was enough for the jury to decide that Harding had been fully aware of what he had been doing and was guilty of murder.

WHEN ALEC WILKINSON married Maureen Farrell in 1954, he was very much in love with her and yet, no matter what he tried to do, his mother-in-law found ways to belittle his achievements. Nothing he could ever do was good enough.

When they had first married, the Wilkinsons had lived with Alec's parents, but the pressure from Clara Farrell soon led to Maureen returning home to her. Alec tried everything he knew to get Maureen to come back, but it was all to no avail.

On Saturday, April 30th, Alec spent the entire day drinking and at closing time, as he sat hunched over a cup of coffee in a late-night cafe, he brooded on his position. Finally he decided that he had to make one last attempt to get Maureen to return to him.

When Alec's taxi arrived outside Clara Farrell's house, Alec could plainly see the woman he hated through her lounge window. He assumed that she would be waiting up for Maureen, who had probably spent the night out with some friends. Sure enough, a few minutes later, Maureen arrived home in the company of a couple of girlfriends. Alec watched Maureen go into the house, took a deep breath and walked up to the front door.

His knock was answered by Clara Farrell who immediately launched into a tirade of abuse and tried to push him away. That was it. Alec had reached his breaking point. One punch knocked Clara Farrell to the floor. Leaping onto her, Alec began battering Clara's head into the floor again and again and when Maureen tried to intervene, another punch rendered her unconscious. Alec then took a knife from the kitchen and stabbed Clara to death. His hatred still not satiated, Alec then piled furniture over the body and set it alight.

All this racket had been heard by the next-door neighbour, Mr Butler, who went to investigate. As he entered the house by the front door and started to put out the flames, Alec left through the back. Shortly afterwards he gave himself up to the police.

Alec Wilkinson never showed any regret over what he had done. Asked at his trial whether he was sorry for what he had done to his mother-in-law, Alec shook his head and replied: "No sir, I'm not."

NAME	Alec Wilkinson
AGE AT EXECUTION	22
DATE OF EXECUTION	Friday, 12th August, 1955
PLACE OF EXECUTION	Leeds
HANGMAN	Steve Wade
ASSISTANT	Robert Leslie Stewart
DATE OF TRIAL	20th June – 29th June, 1955
LOCATION OF TRIAL	Sheffield
PRESIDING JUDGE	Lord Chief Justice, Lord Goddard
PROSECUTION COUNSEL	Sir Geoffrey Russell Vick
DEFENCE COUNSEL	John Parris
NUMBER OF VICTIMS	1

VICTIMS DETAILS

NAME	Clara Farrell
AGE	50
DATE OF MURDER	Sunday, 1st May, 1955
PLACE OF MURDER	Bradbury Balk Lane, Wombwell
METHOD OF KILLING	Stabbed
RELATIONSHIP TO KILLER	Mother-in-law

The defence tried to reduce the charge to manslaughter by pointing out that Alec had been severely provoked, but he was still found guilty and sentenced to death. Despite a petition for his reprieve containing over 35,000 signatures, Alec Wilkinson was hanged at Armley jail in August.

There were no executions at all in the United
Kingdom in 1956.

1957

THE CRIME COMMITTED by John Wilson Vickers was nothing out of the ordinary. It became extraordinary because of the debate over capital punishment.

Vickers was a petty thief who targeted the grocery shop run by Jane Duckett. The shop looked to be an easy target. Miss Duckett lived alone and was rather deaf, so Vickers thought it would be a simple matter to break in, steal any money and make good his escape. So it was that at 2.00am on Monday, April 15th, 1957, Vickers gained entry into the shop in Tait Street.

Unfortunately, Miss Duckett heard the disturbance he made. Dressed only in her night-dress, she began to descend the steps to see what the noise was. Vickers hid behind the steps, hoping Miss Duckett would not see him, but she turned and ran at him with her arms raised. Vickers struck out, hit her a number of times and left her lying on the floor whilst he searched the house.

Vickers was soon captured and scratches on his face seemed to support his story of Miss Duckett attacking him. None of this excused his actions, though, and Vickers faced a charge of capital murder.

There had been no executions since August 1955. Parliament had brought in the Homicide Act, which became law on March 21st, 1957, and which maintained that certain classes of murder would be punishable by death. Section 5 covered the killing of a person whilst in the furtherance of theft.

Vickers was indeed found guilty, and sentenced to death, but his case had raised a difficult point of law. The new act seemed to indicate that if there was no malice aforethought, the accused could not be guilty of murder. The appeal court of three judges thought this point of law so crucial that they adjourned the appeal to a panel of five judges.

When the appeal was heard, it was held that where the accused had inflicted grievous bodily harm in the furtherance of another offence, such as rape or robbery, and that violence and to death, the person was guilty of capital murder. As a result of this decision, the sentence on Vickers was upheld.

The defence sought to appeal to the House of Lords, but the Attorney General, Sir

NAME	John Wilson Vickers
AGE AT EXECUTION	22
DATE OF EXECUTION	Tuesday, 23rd July, 1957
PLACE OF EXECUTION	Durham
HANGMAN	Not known
ASSISTANT	Not known
DATE OF TRIAL	23rd May, 1957
LOCATION OF TRIAL	Carlisle
PRESIDING JUDGE	Mister Justice Hinchcliffe
PROSECUTION COUNSEL	Jack di V. Nahum, D.P. Bailey
DEFENCE COUNSEL	D.J. Brabin, C. Morris Jones
NUMBER OF VICTIMS	1

VICTIMS DETAILS	
NAME	Jane Duckett
AGE	72
DATE OF MURDER	Monday, 15th April, 1957
PLACE OF MURDER	Tait Street, Carlisle
METHOD OF KILLING	Battered
RELATIONSHIP TO KILLER	None

Reginald Manningham-Butler, refused permission. For this, a motion of censure against him was placed in the House of Commons. Sir Reginald refused to change his mind.

In fact, although Vickers was the first man to suffer death by hanging under the new Homicide Act, he was not the first to be sentenced to death. That distinction must go to Ronald Patrick Dunbar of Newcastle upon Tyne. He was sentenced on May 16th, but the sentence was commuted to one of life imprisonment.

DAVID ALAN KEASEY ran a gent's outfitters shop and was killed over a sweater.

Dennis Howard was fascinated by guns. He collected them and, by May 1957, had acquired quite an armoury, together with the necessary ammunition. On Friday, May 17th, 1957, Howard took one of those guns, a Mauser automatic, with him when he visited David Keasey's shop.

Howard asked David to show him a particular sweater he wanted and when the young man did so, Howard drew out his gun and threatened David with it. David Keasey was not one to simply submit meekly though, and he grabbed the gun and struggled with the potential thief.

At one stage, David Keasey was somehow turned around so that he had his back to Howard, but still the two grappled for possession of the weapon. It was then that the gun went off accidentally and David fell, a bullet in his back.

When Howard was arrested and charged with murder his statement contained a phrase in which he admitted that he had cocked the gun before he went into the shop. That phrase was to prove very telling indeed.

Howard had gone into the shop to steal and therefore, under Section 5 of the Homicide Act, the charge was one of capital murder. Found guilty, he was sentenced to death. At his appeal hearing, attempts were again made to show that he had had no intention to kill and therefore the offence was not murder.

It was now that Howard's earlier statement came back to haunt him. The judges held that since he had cocked the gun before entering the shop, he was obviously prepared to use it. Under those circumstances, there was no possibility of the crime being reduced to manslaughter and the verdict had to stand.

In December 1957, Howard became only the second man to die on the scaffold since the law had been changed. By coincidence, both executed men had been sentenced by the same judge.

NAME	Dennis Howard
AGE AT EXECUTION	24
DATE OF EXECUTION	Wednesday, 4th December, 1957
PLACE OF EXECUTION	Birmingham
HANGMAN	Harry Allen
ASSISTANT	Royston Rickard
DATE OF TRIAL	17th October – 18th October, 1957
LOCATION OF TRIAL	Worcester
PRESIDING JUDGE	Mister Justice Hinchcliffe
PROSECUTION COUNSEL	G.G. Baker, Patrick Medd
DEFENCE COUNSEL	R.G. Micklethwait, Stephen Brown
NUMBER OF VICTIMS	1

VICTIMS DETAILS	
NAME	David Alan Keasey
AGE	21
DATE OF MURDER	Friday, 17th May, 1957
PLACE OF MURDER	21 Wolverhampton Street, Dudley, Birmingham
METHOD OF KILLING	Shot
RELATIONSHIP TO KILLER	None

1957

VIVIAN FREDERICK TEED had been in trouble since the age of 13. One of nine children, he had become known for acts of vandalism and theft and things did not improve once he had joined the R.A.F. Teed had gone absent without leave, attacked a man for which he was given a sentence of three years and upon his release, received a further sentence, this time of two years, for another assault. This was the man who, on November 15th, 1957, decided that he would rob the post office in Fforesfach. Teed thought there would be no one at home but to be on the safe side, knocked on the door to check.

To Teed's surprise, the door was opened by the proprietor, William Williams, known locally as Will Bankie. Teed pushed Williams back into the post office, struck him with a hammer and, leaving the man in a pool of blood, took his keys and searched the premises. He found nothing worth stealing.

Williams's body was found the following day when Margaret John could not gain entry to the post office and looked through the letterbox. The police forced an entry and found the murder weapon and footprints left in the old man's blood.

Ronald Thomas Franklin Williams had known Teed for several months and he reported that in October, Teed had told him that he had 'weighed up' a job at the post office. Furthermore, he had seen Teed on November 15th and Teed confessed that he had done the job and hit the old man, but had left empty handed as he couldn't find the safe keys. Teed was arrested on November 18th.

At first, Teed denied all knowledge of the crime, though eventually he admitted that he had been responsible. Although he had not actually stolen anything, he had entered the post office with the intention of stealing. His crime was therefore committed in the furtherance of theft and the charge was a capital one.

At Teed's trial, the defence tried to suggest that he was suffering from an abnormality of the mind. Doctor Jones said that in his opinion, Teed had a psychopathic personality with aggressive tendencies but Doctor Fenton, who saw Teed in prison, countered

that by stating that he believed Teed was perfectly normal.

The jury were out for four and a half hours and twice disagreed on their verdict. Returning to court, the judge informed them that there were four possible verdicts: guilty in pursuance of theft, guilty of non-capital murder, guilty of manslaughter, or not guilty. Finally they decided that Teed was guilty of the capital offence.

Teed's appeal was dismissed on April 21st. On May 3rd, the Home Secretary announced that he could find no grounds for a reprieve and two days later, Teed became only the third man to be hanged since the 1957 Homicide Act had been passed.

NAME Vivian Frederick Teed
AGE AT EXECUTION 24
DATE OF EXECUTION Tuesday, 6th May, 1958
PLACE OF EXECUTION Swansea
HANGMAN Not known
ASSISTANT Not known
DATE OF TRIAL 17th March – 18th March, 1958
LOCATION OF TRIAL Cardiff
PRESIDING JUDGE Mister Justice Salmon
PROSECUTION COUNSEL W.L. Mars-Jones, E.P. Wallis-Jones
DEFENCE COUNSEL F. Elwyn Jones M.P., Dyfan Roberts
NUMBER OF VICTIMS 1

VICTIMS DETAILS
NAME William Williams
AGE 73
DATE OF MURDER Friday, 15th November, 1957
PLACE OF MURDER 870 Carmarthen Road, Fforesfach, Swansea
METHOD OF KILLING Battered
RELATIONSHIP TO KILLER None

ON SEPTEMBER 17TH, 1956, three members of the Watt family were murdered in their home. Ten days later William Watt, the husband of one of the victims, Marion, was arrested and charged despite the fact that he insisted he was 80 miles away at the time. He was remanded, to Barlinnie.

A few days after this, on October 2nd, Peter Manuel was sentenced to 18 months for a break-in at a colliery. He too was sent to Barlinnie and immediately it became clear that the Watt murders fascinated him. He wrote to William Watt's solicitor, saying that he knew William was innocent. Fortunately for William Watt, there was no evidence to connect him to the murders and the charges were dropped.

On November 30th, 1957, Manuel was released and was soon contacting both William Watt and his solicitor. Meetings were arranged and at one stage, when he was alone with Watt, Manuel proved that he knew much more about the murders than he had thus far admitted. He gave a detailed layout of the bungalow where the crimes took place, and described how they were committed. His story was that there had been a botched raid by a convict named Charles Tallis and two accomplices. William Watt was no fool. Before long, he knew that Manuel was the real killer. But he had no proof.

On January 1st, 1958, a very similar crime took place when three members of the Smart family were also murdered. The investigation again threw up the name of Peter Manuel and, on January 14th, his home was raided. Articles stolen in a burglary were recovered and Manuel was arrested. The police made it very clear that they were also linking him with the Smart murders and in due course, Manuel made a confession to eight murders.

Manuel claimed that his first murder was that of 17-year-old Annie Kneilands, whose battered body had been found near the fifth tee of the East Kilbride Golf Course at Capelrig on Monday, January 2nd, 1956. Next he claimed the murders of the Watt family and the Smarts and also admitted to murdering Isabelle Cooke, who had been missing since

NAME Peter Thomas Anthony Manuel
AGE AT EXECUTION 32
DATE OF EXECUTION Friday, 11th July, 1958
PLACE OF EXECUTION Glasgow, Barlinnie
HANGMAN Harry Allen
ASSISTANT Not known
DATE OF TRIAL 12th May – 29th May, 1958
LOCATION OF TRIAL Glasgow
PRESIDING JUDGE Lord Justice Cameron
PROSECUTION COUNSEL M.G. Gillies, R.I. Sutherland
DEFENCE COUNSEL Harald R. Leslie, W.R. Grieve, A.M. Morison
NUMBER OF VICTIMS 7 (probably 11)

VICTIMS' DETAILS

NAMES Marion Hunter McDonald Watt; Vivienne Isabella Reid Watt
AGES Not known; 16
DATE OF MURDER Monday, 17th September, 1956
PLACE OF MURDER 5 Fennsbank Avenue, High Burnside, Rutherglen
METHOD OF KILLING Shot; shot
RELATIONSHIP TO KILLER None; none

NAME Margaret Hunter Brown
AGE Not known
DATE OF MURDER Monday, 17th September, 1956
PLACE OF MURDER 5 Fennsbank Avenue, High Burnside, Rutherglen
METHOD OF KILLING Shot
RELATIONSHIP TO KILLER None

NAME Isabelle Wallace Cooke
AGE 17
DATE OF MURDER Saturday, 28th December, 1957
PLACE OF MURDER Footpath near Mount Vernon Avenue, Mount Vernon
METHOD OF KILLING Strangled
RELATIONSHIP TO KILLER None

NAMES Peter James Smart; Doris Smart; Michael Smart
AGES Not known; not known; 10
DATE OF MURDER Wednesday, 1st January, 1958
PLACE OF MURDER 38 Sheepburn Road, Uddingston
METHOD OF KILLING Shot; shot; shot
RELATIONSHIP TO KILLER None; none; none

1958

late December. Manuel took the police to the field where he had buried Isabelle.

At his trial, Manuel withdrew his confession, claiming that he had been forced into making it. On the ninth day of the trial he dismissed his counsel and began conducting his own defence, with some skill. On the final day, the judge directed the jury to formally acquit Manuel of the murder of Annie Kneilands as there was no evidence, other than his own confession. The jury had more than enough evidence on the other charges and Manuel was found guilty of seven murders.

The original execution date was set for June 19th, but that was postponed after an appeal was entered. That was heard over two days, June 24th and 25th, and dismissed. Only then did Manuel admit to three other murders, all committed in England, and one as early as 1954.

THE MAN WALKED into the cafe in Coventry and announced to the proprietor: "I am in trouble. I have killed a man." The police were called and the man, identified as Matthew Kavanagh, told them how he had killed a fellow lodger at his home in Hillmorton Road, Rugby.

According to Kavanagh, Isaiah Dixon had returned to the lodging house much the worse for drink and Kavanagh thought he might well take advantage of this and try to steal some cash from him. Feigning interest in Dixon's well-being, Kavanagh assisted Dixon to his room where he strangled him with his own tie. Kavanagh was arrested and charged with capital murder.

At the trial, Kavanagh's defence counsel claimed that Dixon's death might well have been accidental. It was true that Kavanagh had stolen money, but the killing could be put down to vagal inhibition, a muscle reflex that meant Kavanagh was not responsible for his actions. The jury were out for 40 minutes considering their verdict and they decided that Kavanagh was responsible. Since the crime had been committed in the furtherance of theft, the sentence was death by hanging.

In fact, this was the second time Matthew Kavanagh had been involved in a death. In June 1957, he had made a telephone call to the police and admitted that he had something to do with the death of a woman named Evelyn Ulla.

Her body was found close to the Wheatsheaf Hotel in Sheldon and Kavanagh said that he had known her for some time. They had been to the pictures and visited a few public houses then, as they walked homewards, she complained of the cold. He took hold of Evelyn's scarf to pull it tighter and before he knew what was happening, she had collapsed, dead, at his feet.

On that occasion, Kavanagh was charged with murder but this was reduced to one of manslaughter at the magistrate's court. Once he came to trial at Birmingham assizes, the proceedings were stopped by the judge, Mister Justice Lynskey, who directed that Kavanagh be acquitted as there was not enough evidence to proceed. It was suggested

NAME	Matthew Kavanagh
AGE AT EXECUTION	32
DATE OF EXECUTION	Tuesday, 12th August, 1958
PLACE OF EXECUTION	Birmingham
HANGMAN	Harry Allen
ASSISTANT	Thomas Cunliffe
DATE OF TRIAL	2nd July – 3rd July, 1958
LOCATION OF TRIAL	Warwick
PRESIDING JUDGE	Mister Justice Streatfeild
PROSECUTION COUNSEL	R.K. Brownal, Colin Coley
DEFENCE COUNSEL	J.A. Grieves, P.J. Cox
NUMBER OF VICTIMS	1

VICTIMS DETAILS	
NAME	Isaiah Dixon
AGE	60
DATE OF MURDER	Saturday, 12th April, 1958
PLACE OF MURDER	Hillmorton Road, Rugby
METHOD OF KILLING	Strangled
RELATIONSHIP TO KILLER	None

that Evelyn may well have died as a result of vagal inhibition!

On that occasion, Kavanagh had walked away a free man, moving to Rugby soon afterwards. He was not as fortunate in 1958.

BY 1958, A distinction had been made between murder and capital murder. If a murderer killed in the furtherance of theft for instance, he was held to be guilty of a capital offence and would face the hangman. This distinction became crucial in the case of Frank Stokes.

On April 14th, 1958, Linda Ash was brutally battered to death with a hammer. Neighbours gave a description of a man who had asked directions to her house and this fitted with that given by Mrs Sybil Tate who lodged with the victim and had left this young man talking to Violet at her front door. It was also Mrs Tate who found the unconscious form of Violet Ash and called the police.

On April 25th, Frank Stokes walked into Cannon Row police station, in London and told the officer on the desk that he had murdered a woman. He then confessed to being the killer of Violet Ash. He explained that he had answered her advertisement for a gardener and had asked for 4/- an hour. She had given him a hammer and told him that he could have the job but she would only pay him 3s-6d. He then lost his temper and started hitting her. He claimed that he had taken nothing from the house, apart from the key he used to lock the door. As he had stolen nothing, the crime was not a capital offence.

When he had been taken into custody, Stokes was searched and on him was found a cheap wallet. This was possibly the same as one Violet Ash had in her possession and if it could be shown that this had been stolen, the crime would now be a capital one.

At his trial, Stokes pleaded guilty to murder but not guilty to capital murder. During the course of that trial, Stokes admitted that he had also answered an advertisement for a gardener at Ewell in Surrey and this was where he had stolen the wallet from. This of course suggested that theft had also been his intention at the house in Newcastle and greatly weakened Stokes's case.

After a three-day trial, Stokes was found guilty of the capital offence and sentenced to death. After losing his appeal, he was hanged at Durham in September. There are, however, questions remaining about the case.

NAME	Frank Stokes
AGE AT EXECUTION	44
DATE OF EXECUTION	Wednesday, 3rd September, 1958
PLACE OF EXECUTION	Durham
HANGMAN	Not known
ASSISTANT	Not known
DATE OF TRIAL	21st July – 23rd July, 1958
LOCATION OF TRIAL	Leeds
PRESIDING JUDGE	Mister Justice Edmund Davies
PROSECUTION COUNSEL	Bernard Gillis, Rawdon Smith
DEFENCE COUNSEL	G.S. Waller, W. Steer
NUMBER OF VICTIMS	1

VICTIMS DETAILS

NAME	Linda Violet Ash (Died Tuesday, 15th April)
AGE	75
DATE OF MURDER	Monday, 14th April, 1958
PLACE OF MURDER	41 Marlborough Avenue, Gosforth, Newcastle upon Tyne
METHOD OF KILLING	Battered
RELATIONSHIP TO KILLER	None

If Stokes had indeed stolen the wallet from Violet Ash, why had he not destroyed it or thrown it away in the 11 days before his arrest, and if it had come from an earlier robbery in Surrey, then the prosecution had not proved that this was a capital case and Frank Stokes should not have hanged.

PRIVATE BRIAN CHANDLER of the R.A.M.C., absented himself on June 8th, 1958, and travelled to Darlington. It was there that he met up with Marian Munro and Pauline Blair.

The night of June 9th saw Chandler spending the night with both girls, and another soldier, in a caravan near Darlington. The following day, the other soldier returned to his unit whilst Chandler and the girls discussed how they could get some money together.

Chandler suggested committing a robbery and when Marian told him of Martha Dodd, an old woman she had once worked for, Chandler decided that she would be the ideal target.

On June 10th, Marian, Pauline and Chandler visited Martha to see if there was anything worth stealing. Marian used the excuse of looking for work to explain their presence and Martha told her that she might have some the next day. All Chandler managed to purloin was a bicycle, but he failed to find a buyer for it and so reverted to the plan of robbing Martha. Marian expressed her concern that the old woman would recognise her. Callously, Chandler remarked that he would have to kill her in that case.

On June 11th Marian and Chandler separated for a few hours. At 3.30pm Chandler met her, a friend of hers called Evelyn Pigg and a man named Harrison, outside the Royal cinema. Chandler was smoking a cigarette and when Marian asked him where he had got the money to pay for them, Chandler replied that he had killed a woman. Harrison and Evelyn noticed that Chandler had blood on his trousers.

Martha Dodds's body was not found until 10.00pm that night. She had been battered to death, with at least 19 separate wounds being inflicted. That night, Chandler and Marian slept at the house of a Mr and Mrs Hill. The following morning, Mr Hill told Chandler that the police were looking for him and accompanied Chandler to the station.

At first Chandler said he knew nothing about the crime but then he changed his mind and said he wished to get it off his chest. He confessed to killing Martha but

NAME	Brian Chandler
AGE AT EXECUTION	20
DATE OF EXECUTION	Wednesday, 17th December, 1958
PLACE OF EXECUTION	Durham
HANGMAN	Not known
ASSISTANT	Not known
DATE OF TRIAL	27th October – 29th October, 1958
LOCATION OF TRIAL	Durham
PRESIDING JUDGE	Mister Justice Ashworth
PROSECUTION COUNSEL	Rudolph Lyons
DEFENCE COUNSEL	Stanley Price
NUMBER OF VICTIMS	1

VICTIMS DETAILS	
NAME	Martha Annie Dodd
AGE	83
DATE OF MURDER	Wednesday, 11th June, 1958
PLACE OF MURDER	4a Victoria Road, Darlington
METHOD OF KILLING	Battered
RELATIONSHIP TO KILLER	None

said he had not intended to do so. He had gone to offer her his services as a gardener. She had given him a bucket, which happened to have a hammer inside, and then offered him 3/- an hour. He had refused to accept that, whereupon Martha lost her temper, seized the hammer and attacked him with it. He maintained that he had only hit out to protect himself.

Once the case came to trial, Chandler changed his story. Now he suggested that he had found Martha dead when he arrived and that it had been Marian Munro whom he saw standing over the body.

The jury took one an a half hours to decide that this story too was so many lies and that Chandler had killed alone and deliberately, in the pursuance of theft.

AT 9.00PM ON September 30th, 1958, Richard Turner, the manager of the Co-Operative store at Lepton, went to lock up the safe.

By 11.10pm he had still not returned home and his wife, becoming rather concerned, asked Mr Howe to go to the shop with her, to see if anything was amiss. When they arrived at the shop, they found the doors locked, but all the lights on. They then contacted the assistant manager who brought his keys, opened the doors and found that there had been an intruder. A carton was filled with cigarettes and children's clothing and nearby they found the body of Richard Turner.

Earlier that day, Ernest Raymond Jones had been in Huddersfield and told a dealer there that he had 30,000 cigarettes to dispose of. Jones told a friend that he was going to do a job and this would be the proceeds. Later, after the incident at Lepton, Jones said he had been forced to hit someone, but only once. In due course, this came to the notice of the police and Jones was arrested for murder.

Jones told the police that he had first broken into the store in 1957, and thought it was about time he went back. He got inside and made up the carton of clothing and cigarettes and then, upon going into the offices, was surprised to find the safe open. At first, Jones thought that another burglar had beaten him to the prize, but then he heard noises and saw the lights click on downstairs. Jones hid, hoping that Richard Turner would walk past him, but when he stopped at the top of the stairs, Jones hit him, once, on the head and then made good his escape. He maintained that he had carried no weapon and that he had only intended to render Turner unconscious, but the blow had fractured his skull and the crime was one of capital murder.

Found guilty and sentenced to death, Jones's appeal, heard on January 26th, 1959, raised an interesting point as to whether the crime was indeed one committed in the furtherance of theft.

Jones maintained that at the time of the attack on Turner, he had already stolen money from the safe, and prepared his carton of clothing and cigarettes. The theft was

NAME	Ernest Raymond Jones
AGE AT EXECUTION	39
DATE OF EXECUTION	Tuesday, 10th February, 1959
PLACE OF EXECUTION	Leeds
HANGMAN	Harry Allen
ASSISTANT	Harry Smith
DATE OF TRIAL	10th December, 1958
LOCATION OF TRIAL	Leeds
PRESIDING JUDGE	Mister Justice Hinchcliffe
PROSECUTION COUNSEL	Geoffrey Veale, R.W. Payne
DEFENCE COUNSEL	Bernard Gillis, A.M. Hurwitz
NUMBER OF VICTIMS	1

VICTIMS DETAILS	
NAME	Richard Turner
AGE	Not Known
DATE OF MURDER	Tuesday, 30th September, 1958
PLACE OF MURDER	Co-Operative store, Lepton, Near Huddersfield
METHOD OF KILLING	Battered
RELATIONSHIP TO KILLER	None

therefore complete and as the blow killing Turner was inflicted afterwards, it was not committed to further the theft and was therefore not a capital offence.

The appeal court judges quoted an earlier case in which it was held; "If a burglar is interrupted and if he murders in order to get away, it is still murder done in the course of theft." The appeal was dismissed and Jones was duly hanged.

As THE REST of the country was waiting to see in the new year of 1959, 60 year-old Norah Summerfield was being battered to death in her bungalow at Harlington Road, Hillingdon. It would be the afternoon of January 2nd before Norah's body was discovered and a murder hunt started.

One of the miscreants had been talking. Joseph Chrimes had talked of his plans to break into the bungalow to Michael Ulrich. These two later met Ronald Hedley Charles Pritchard near the bungalow, but Ulrich went home and was not involved in the robbery. The following day, even before Norah had been found, Chrimes spoke to Ulrich's brother, John, and confessed that he had 'done the old lady in.'

Chrimes and Pritchard were both arrested in early morning police swoops on January 6th. Each eventually admitted that they were responsible for stealing a clock, a cigarette case, some spoons and other items, but each blamed the other for the murder.

According to Chrimes, it had been Pritchard who battered Norah to death, but Pritchard said that after they had entered the bungalow, Norah appeared and Chrimes began to hit her with a tyre lever. Pritchard had tried to intervene but Chrimes just pushed him out of the way and carried on battering Norah. Both men were charged with capital murder.

At the trial, both men pleaded guilty to breaking and entering. It was then that the prosecution said that they would offer no evidence against 18 year-old Pritchard on the charge of murder. He then gave evidence against Chrimes.

After the jury had been considering their verdict for an hour, they returned into court and asked the judge to explain why no evidence had been offered against Pritchard on the charge of murder. Mister Justice Donovan explained that this was not consistent with the prosecution's case which held that Chrimes's hand had struck the fatal blow. The only way Pritchard could have been guilty was if he had been actively urging Chrimes on and this was not suggested.

Eventually the verdict was reached. Chrimes was sentenced to death for capital

murder whilst Pritchard was sent to borstal for his part in the robbery. Chrimes's appeal was dismissed on April 10th, and he was executed on April 28th.

NAME	Joseph Chrimes
AGE AT EXECUTION	30
DATE OF EXECUTION	Tuesday, 28th April, 1959
PLACE OF EXECUTION	Pentonville
HANGMAN	Harry Allen
ASSISTANT	Royston Rickard
DATE OF TRIAL	3rd March – 4th March, 1959
LOCATION OF TRIAL	Old Bailey
PRESIDING JUDGE	Mister Justice Donovan
PROSECUTION COUNSEL	Christmas Humphreys, E.J.P. Cussen
DEFENCE COUNSEL	Tristram Beresford, John Rogers
NUMBER OF VICTIMS	1

VICTIMS DETAILS	
NAME	Norah Summerfield
AGE	60
DATE OF MURDER	Wednesday, 31st December, 1958
PLACE OF MURDER	Harlington Road, Hillingdon
METHOD OF KILLING	Battered
RELATIONSHIP TO KILLER	None

SUNDAY, DECEMBER 14TH, 1958 was Ronald Marwood's wedding anniversary and he decided to go out for a few drinks. His wife preferred to stay at her home in Huntingdon Street, Islington, and spend the night watching television.

Marwood met up with a group of his friends, including Mick Bloom and eventually they ended up at Gray's Dance Hall on Seven Sisters Road in Holloway. By the time the trouble broke out with a rival group of youths, Ronald Marwood had consumed about 10 pints of beer and was probably not thinking too clearly.

There were a few separate scuffles and someone pulled out a small axe which they swung at Marwood's head. Marwood fell down and when he pulled himself to his feet, made to walk away, holding a handkerchief to his head to staunch a small wound. It was then that he noticed Mick Bloom being spoken to by a policeman. Marwood believed his friend was being picked out for special treatment and objected to this so went up to interfere.

The policeman, Constable Raymond Summers, gently pushed Marwood to one side and told him to go away. Marwood would later claim that at the time he had his hands in his pockets and the policeman punched him but whatever the truth of that, Marwood retaliated and struck back. Summers fell to the pavement and Marwood ran off.

At 5.00am the following morning, Marwood was one of the men police interviewed. Constable Summers had been stabbed and this was now a case of capital murder. The police did not have enough evidence to charge anyone at this early stage and Marwood was released, a very frightened man indeed.

It was not until 8.00pm on January 22nd, 1959, that Marwood walked back into the police station and admitted that he was the man who had stabbed Summers. At 11.00pm, he was charged with murder.

Throughout his trial, Marwood maintained that he had not even been aware of the knife in his hand and that he had no intention of hurting the policeman, let alone killing him. He was nevertheless found guilty and sentenced to death.

NAME	Ronald Henry Marwood
AGE AT EXECUTION	25
DATE OF EXECUTION	Friday, 8th May, 1959
PLACE OF EXECUTION	Pentonville
HANGMAN	Harry Allen
ASSISTANT	Harry Robinson
DATE OF TRIAL	19th March, 1959
LOCATION OF TRIAL	Old Bailey
PRESIDING JUDGE	Mister Justice Gorman
PROSECUTION COUNSEL	Christmas Humphreys, E.J.P. Cussen
DEFENCE COUNSEL	Neil Lawson, M. Levene
NUMBER OF VICTIMS	1

VICTIMS DETAILS

NAME	Raymond Henry Summers
AGE	23
DATE OF MURDER	Sunday, 14th December, 1958
PLACE OF MURDER	Seven Sisters Road, Holloway, London
METHOD OF KILLING	Stabbed
RELATIONSHIP TO KILLER	None

Moves were made to obtain a reprieve. One hundred and fifty Members of Parliament, mostly Labour, signed an appeal for Marwood and there was also a public petition for mercy. A last minute appeal to the Attorney General for fiat to appeal to the House of Lords was rejected on the rather unfeeling grounds that it was out of time. The appeal should have been made within seven days and the authorities were not to be moved simply because a man's life was at stake.

The day before the execution, a demonstration took place inside Pentonville jail and on May 8th, a crowd of nearly 1,000 people assembled outside the prison gates. None of these efforts saved Marwood.

CHARLES FREDERICK BARRETT, a Boer War veteran, lived on the ground floor and first floor of 11 Belmont Road, Southampton. Other rooms were rented by Mr Finn, and for a time there were two other people living there, the housekeeper, Mrs Tatum and her husband, Michael George Tatum.

From January 10th, 1959, Michael Tatum moved out of Belmont Road and went to live at 36 Cambridge Road. His wife though stayed behind and continued to minister to Charles Barrett.

Mr Finn worked nights. On the night of January 15th, he left the house at 7.00pm, and returned the following morning at 7.30am. Noticing that doors were open that should be closed, Mr Finn investigated and discovered the unconscious Mr Barrett. The weapon used to attack him was a knobkerrie, an African weapon which had been given to Charles by the writer H. Rider Haggard. Charles Barrett died later that same day.

There were two important factors which led the police to Michael Tatum. First, the assailant had not forced an entry and it was known that Tatum had a key. Secondly, the person who had battered Charles Barrett had wielded the knobkerrie with his left hand and Tatum was known to be left handed.

Taken in for questioning, Tatum at first claimed that he had spent the night of the attack drinking in various pubs and had met up with a man named Derek who had given him £7. Later, Tatum changed his story and claimed that he had gone to the house to see his wife.

Tatum had been accompanied by a friend, Terence Richard Thatcher but once they were inside the house, the two men thought of robbery. Tatum admitted he had stolen a wallet but it had been Thatcher who took the knobkerrie from the wall and used it to batter Barrett.

Tatum could give few details of Terence Thatcher but a gentleman of that name was traced. He had no connection with Tatum, and was able to prove that he had been nowhere near Southampton on the night of the attack. Tatum claimed that this Terry Thatcher was not the one he knew.

NAME	Michael George Tatum
AGE AT EXECUTION	24
DATE OF EXECUTION	Thursday, 14th May, 1959
PLACE OF EXECUTION	Winchester
HANGMAN	Robert Leslie Stewart
ASSISTANT	Thomas Cunliffe
DATE OF TRIAL	19th March – 23rd March, 1959
LOCATION OF TRIAL	Winchester
PRESIDING JUDGE	Mister Justice Cassels
PROSECUTION COUNSEL	Norman Skelhorn, Jeremy Hutchinson
DEFENCE COUNSEL	E.S. Fay, Patrick Back
NUMBER OF VICTIMS	1

VICTIMS DETAILS	
NAME	Charles Frederick Barrett (Died Friday, 16th January)
AGE	85
DATE OF MURDER	Thursday, 15th January, 1959
PLACE OF MURDER	11 Belmont Road, Portswood, Southampton
METHOD OF KILLING	Battered
RELATIONSHIP TO KILLER	None

The trial opened at Winchester on March 19th. Attempts were made to throw doubts on whether Tatum was responsible for his actions. It was said that he lived in a fantasy world. He had invented stories of sporting achievements and claimed he had won trophies for various events and had once told friends that his wife had died. They had even organised a collection for a wreath, until they discovered that she was very much alive and well!

On the fourth day, Tatum was found guilty and sentenced to death as the crime was a capital one. The appeal was dismissed on April 27th.

BERNARD HUGH WALDEN was an assistant lecturer in physics at Rotherham Technical College and he had grown rather fond of a clerk who worked at the same college, Joyce Moran. For her part, Joyce was much more interested in an ex-student named Neil Saxton and this particular triangle was to lead to the deaths of all three people.

It was 7.30pm on April 7th, 1959, and lectures were in full swing throughout the college. Bernard Walden was walking down one of the corridors when he saw Joyce talking to Neil. There was no argument, no scene, but Walden simply strode on to his locker, took out a revolver and returned to where they young couple were talking.

The first shot struck Neil Saxton and he fell dead, in the entrance hall. Walden then turned his attention to Joyce who he shot six times. The last three bullets were fired into her back as she lay on the floor. Walden then left the College, got into his car and drove off.

The car was subsequently found abandoned in Leeds but Walden himself was not arrested until May 1st, when he was picked up in Reading. Put on trial for the double murder, Walden pleaded diminished responsibility. Doctor James Valentine, a consultant psychiatrist, said that Walden was suffering from chronic paranoiac development and was grossly abnormal, but other medical experts, including Doctor Frazier, disagreed and implied that this was a simple case of jealousy and unrequited love. For his own part, Walden did not help his case when he announced during his trial that since he was a cripple, he had the right to carry a gun to put him on equal terms and that he had a right to kill!

Walden's first execution date was July 23rd, but this was postponed when his appeal was announced. Once that failed, a new date of August 14th was set. This time there was no delay and on that date, the third person in this tragic triangle was hanged.

NAME	Bernard Hugh Walden
AGE AT EXECUTION	33
DATE OF EXECUTION	Friday, 14th August, 1959
PLACE OF EXECUTION	Leeds
HANGMAN	Harry Allen
ASSISTANT	Thomas Cunliffe
DATE OF TRIAL	30th June – 1st July, 1959
LOCATION OF TRIAL	Sheffield
PRESIDING JUDGE	Mister Justice Paull
PROSECUTION COUNSEL	G.S. Waller, J.B. Willis
DEFENCE COUNSEL	H.C. Scott, J.F.S. Cobb
NUMBER OF VICTIMS	2

VICTIMS DETAILS	
NAME	Joyce Moran; Neil Saxton
AGE	21; 20
DATE OF MURDER	Tuesday, 7th April, 1959
PLACE OF MURDER	Rotherham Technical College
METHOD OF KILLING	Shot; Shot
RELATIONSHIP TO KILLER	None; None

WHEN JOHN PERREE vanished, the detective who investigated was ideally placed. After all, Constable Vibert's sister had been John Perree's landlady.

Constable Vibert began by tracing the missing man's movements. He determined that Perree had been in the Tenby Inn, with a friend named Francis Hutchet. The two had left together not long before closing time. When Hutchet was routinely questioned he informed Vibert that after leaving the Tenby he had driven Perree to another pub, the Hare and Hounds at St Brelade but he had simply dropped Perree there and had not gone inside himself. Curiously, when the landlord of the Hare and Hounds, John George Gallichan, was interviewed he said that Hutchet had been inside with Perree. Constable Vibert continued his investigation but seemed to come up against a brick wall.

Alan and Ann Heath were brother and sister enjoying a holiday and on Saturday April 4th were playing amongst the sand dunes at Mont a la Brune, St Brelade. Enjoying their game, Alan saw something protruding from the sand and upon closer inspection found that it was a man's shoe. He told his mother, Georgette, what he had discovered and she in turn told a passer-by, Paul Godefroy, who informed the police. Perree's body had been found and someone had shot him in the face at close range.

That same evening Constable Vibert visited Hutchet at his home, 65 Le Geyt Flats on Springfield Road, St Saviour. The answers he received were far from satisfactory and at 5.00am on the Sunday, Hutchet was charged with murder.

At his subsequent trial it became clear that the motive for the crime had been theft. On his visits to the two public houses on the night he had vanished, Perree had been spending freely and no money had been found on the body. However, pieces of rope had been found buried in the dune along with Perree and these matched other pieces found in Hutchet's room.

There was much debate over the admissibility of one particular piece of evidence. Whilst Hutchet had been in prison awaiting trial, a letter had been smuggled out,

NAME	Francis Joseph Hutchet
AGE AT EXECUTION	31
DATE OF EXECUTION	Friday, 9th October, 1959
PLACE OF EXECUTION	St Helier, Jersey
HANGMAN	Harry Allen
ASSISTANT	Two assistants, not named
DATE OF TRIAL	7th September – 10th September, 1959
LOCATION OF TRIAL	St Helier
PRESIDING JUDGE	Bailiff C.S. Harrison and three jurats
PROSECUTION COUNSEL	R.H. Le Masurier
DEFENCE COUNSEL	J.C.K.H. Valpy
NUMBER OF VICTIMS	1

VICTIMS DETAILS	
NAME	John Perree
AGE	45
DATE OF MURDER	Monday, 30th March, 1959
PLACE OF MURDER	St Brelade, Jersey
METHOD OF KILLING	Shot
RELATIONSHIP TO KILLER	None

on prison paper, and given to Mrs Grace Kemp. In part, the letter asked her to copy out the letter in her own hand and post it to the police station anonymously. It purported to be a confession to the murder signed by two men, Jim and Tom. Fortunately for the police, Mrs Kemp had handed the letter over to them and it seemed to confirm that Hutchet was trying to fake a confession from two unknown males.

After various legal arguments the letter was ruled admissible and counted heavily against Hutchet. The jury of 24 took 85 minutes to return a unanimous verdict that Hutchet was guilty of murder.

THE TRIAL OF Guenther Podola was unique. Whilst others had claimed to have no memory of the events on a particular day, Podola claimed that as a direct result of his arrest, he had no memory of the crime he was alleged to have committed.

Podola had been born in Germany and after the war had emigrated to Canada. Living a life of crime, he was deported in 1958 and eventually came to London, in May, 1959. He survived on the proceeds of burglaries and, not a particularly successful thief, he was soon well known to the police.

On July 13th, 1959, Podola was arrested on suspicion of burglary. He had broken into a house and then telephoned the woman who lived there and threatened to blackmail her. The two arresting officers were both Detective Sergeants; Raymond William Purdy and John Sandford. Podola broke free from them and after a chase was cornered in a block of flats at Onslow Square.

Rearrested and told to stand in a corner, the two policemen were momentarily distracted and Podola took the opportunity to draw out a gun and shoot Purdy. Whilst John Sandford ministered to his colleague, Podola again escaped.

The next clue came on July 15th when Purdy's widow contacted the police. Her husband's belongings had been returned but an address book was not his. It belonged to Podola and it appeared that Purdy had taken it when he had arrested him. The names were checked and this led police to the Claremont House Hotel at 95 Queen's Gate, Kensington.

The occupant of room 15 was identified as Podola. On July 16th, officers assembled outside and upon a signal being given, the door was broken down. Unfortunately, Podola was right behind the door and when it was smashed down, and he received a nasty crack on the head. Taken to hospital, it was July 20th before Podola was fit enough to be charged. He claimed to have no knowledge of what the police were talking about.

The initial trial began on September 10th, but this was just to decide if Podola's loss of memory was genuine. Some doctors said Podola could not possibly be faking, others said he obviously was. It was not until

NAME	Guenther Fritz Erwin Podola
AGE AT EXECUTION	30
DATE OF EXECUTION	Thursday, 5th November, 1959
PLACE OF EXECUTION	Wandsworth
HANGMAN	Harry Allen
ASSISTANT	Royston Rickard
DATE OF TRIAL	24th September – 25th September, 1959
LOCATION OF TRIAL	Old Bailey
PRESIDING JUDGE	Mister Justice H.E. Davies
PROSECUTION COUNSEL	Maxwell Turner
DEFENCE COUNSEL	Frederick Lawton
NUMBER OF VICTIMS	1

VICTIMS DETAILS	
NAME	Raymond William Purdy
AGE	40
DATE OF MURDER	Monday, 13th July, 1959
PLACE OF MURDER	105 Onslow Square, London
METHOD OF KILLING	Shot
RELATIONSHIP TO KILLER	None

September 23rd that the jury decided that Podola was faking. A new jury was then sworn in the following day and the trial for murder started.

Asked how he wished to plead, Podola persisted in his claim that he had no memory, could give no explanation of the killing and could offer no defence. It took the jury an hour and a half to reach their verdict. The appeal also failed, it being held that just because a man had no memory of events it did not excuse him from them.

On November 5th, 1959, Guenther Podola became the last man to hang for the murder of a policeman.

1960

LILY PARRY STILL ran her shop in Summers Street, Nottingham, even though she was by now 73 years of age. Lily lived with Judith Reddish, a young girl who helped her out at the shop and on the night of April 22nd, 1960, Judith went to bed at 10.00pm after making sure that the doors were securely locked.

Judith was up at 6.50am the following morning and immediately noticed blood oozing from beneath Lily's bedroom door. The old woman had been battered to death, and her handbag, which she habitually took to bed with her, was missing. The police were called and a murder investigation began.

Inquiries soon gave police the name of John Louis Constantine. He lived in Waterloo Promenade with his 19-year-old wife, Valerie, but he also had a room that backed on to Lily Parry's shop. He had been seeing another woman, June Ann Tomlinson and when she was spoken to, she told police that she had left Constantine at 10.20pm on the night of the murder, yet his wife reported that he had only arrived home at 1.20am.

Constantine was now interviewed at length and admitted killing Lily, saying that he had broken into the shop and she had heard him. In his panic, he had hit out at her two or three times with the crowbar he was carrying but he had not meant to kill her.

Five days later though, Constantine changed his story, claiming that he had had an accomplice named Brian Walker and it had been him who had killed Lily. Constantine explained that Walker was not the man's real name but it had been him who went upstairs, him that encountered the old woman, and him that battered her to death. Later he revealed that Walker's real name was Patrick Joseph Colothan.

Colothan was a workmate of Constantine's and admitted that the two of them had discussed the possibility of committing a £6,000 payroll robbery. On the night of April 22nd though, he was outside Nottingham, drinking with some friends until around quarter past midnight. This alibi was checked and found to stand up.

Constantine was charged alone with the murder of Lily Parry.

NAME	John Louis Constantine
AGE AT EXECUTION	23
DATE OF EXECUTION	Thursday, 1st September, 1960
PLACE OF EXECUTION	Lincoln
HANGMAN	Not known
ASSISTANT	Not known
DATE OF TRIAL	18th July – 22nd July, 1960
LOCATION OF TRIAL	Birmingham
PRESIDING JUDGE	Mister Justice Ashworth
PROSECUTION COUNSEL	J.A. Grieves
DEFENCE COUNSEL	Not known
NUMBER OF VICTIMS	1

VICTIMS DETAILS

NAME	Lily Parry
AGE	73
DATE OF MURDER	Friday, 22nd April, 1960
PLACE OF MURDER	Summers Street, Nottingham
METHOD OF KILLING	Battered
RELATIONSHIP TO KILLER	None

The trial, in July 1960, lasted five days and at the end, Constantine was sentenced to death by hanging. The appeal was dismissed on August 15th and Constantine was executed at Lincoln.

O N FEBRUARY 2ND, 1957, Thomas Guyan married his new bride, Margaret May. A son, Charles, was born in September 1958, and a second, Keith, in February, 1961. There were, however, problems even this early in the marriage, because the father of the second child was not Thomas.

The marital problems came to a head in 1962 when Margaret May Guyan consulted a solicitor about a divorce. Then, in December of that same year she went to work at John R. Stephen Fish Curers and there met a new admirer, Henry Burnett.

By May 1963, Margaret had moved out of Jackson Terrace and into the Burnett home. Five days later, on May 21st, Keith and Burnett moved to 40 Shene Terrace.

However, Henry Burnett believed that Margaret might leave him, so he took to locking her in the house when he went out. Unsurprisingly, therefore, when Margaret bumped into her husband by accident, on May 31st, she readily agreed to go back to him.

Margaret Guyan arrived at 40 Shene Terrace at 4.00pm, to collect her son Keith. Her grandmother, Georgina Cattanagh, went with her. As soon as Margaret announced her intentions Burnett cried out, "Margaret, Margaret, you are not going to leave me." He then drew out a knife and put it to Margaret's throat, closing the door behind him.

Mrs Cattanagh banged on the door and demanded Margaret's release. Minutes later Burnett threw open the door and ran off down the street. Margaret was shaken but unhurt. The two women made their way back to Jackson Terrace.

But that was not the end of the matter. Henry Burnett had gone to his sister-in-law's house at 22 Danestone Terrace, Bridge of Don, collected his brother's shotgun, and headed for Jackson Terrace.

Hearing Mrs Cattanagh scream, "You can't come in here", Thomas Guyan jumped to his feet. As he opened the kitchen door he was met by Burnett. A shot rang out and Guyan fell, having been shot in the face. Burnett then dragged Margaret out, his right arm around her waist and the gun in his left hand.

Burnett dragged Margaret as far as a garage – James G. Mutch (Motors) Limited of

NAME	Henry John Burnett
AGE AT EXECUTION	21
DATE OF EXECUTION	Thursday, 15th August, 1963
PLACE OF EXECUTION	Aberdeen
HANGMAN	Harry Allen
ASSISTANT	Not known
DATE OF TRIAL	23rd July – 25th July, 1963
LOCATION OF TRIAL	Aberdeen
PRESIDING JUDGE	Lord Justice Wheatley
PROSECUTION COUNSEL	W.R. Grieve
DEFENCE COUNSEL	R.R. Taylor
NUMBER OF VICTIMS	1

VICTIMS DETAILS	
NAME	Thomas Guyan
AGE	27
DATE OF MURDER	31st May, 1963
PLACE OF MURDER	14 Jackson Terrace, Aberdeen
METHOD OF KILLING	Shot
RELATIONSHIP TO KILLER	None

Seaforth Road – where he stole a car belonging to John Innes Irvine. The police began following the car, which was driving towards Peterhead. Burnett realised that there was nowhere to run and pulled the car over. He offered no resistance as he was arrested by Constable James G. Reaper and Constable Mitchell.

Burnett's defence was that at the time of the crime he was insane or alternatively, that this was a case of diminished responsibility. Both defences failed after the jury had considered the evidence for 25 minutes. Sentenced to death, both Burnett's own family and that of the victim petitioned for his reprieve.

There was, however, no appeal and on July 15th, Burnett became the first man to be executed in Aberdeen since John Booth on October 21st, 1857, and the last man ever to be hanged in Scotland.

1963

WILLIAM ROWE WAS a recluse who lived alone at Nanjarrow Farm, in Cornwall. The farm was full of dirt and grime, but local gossip had it that the old man was sitting on a hidden fortune. One of the men who had heard those stories was Russell Pascoe, who had once done some odd jobs for Rowe.

By August 1963, Pascoe was living with a friend of his, Dennis Whitty, and three young girls. This fivesome occupied an old caravan near Truro and when Pascoe told Whitty about the treasures that might be hidden at Nanjarrow, the two made their minds up to take them.

On the night of August 14th, Pascoe and Whitty left the caravan on Pascoe's motorbike, telling the girls that they were going out on a job. They drove straight to Nanjarrow Farm, arriving there at about 11.00pm.

The murder of William Rowe was brutal. Having been beaten with an iron bar and a starting handle, he was also stabbed a number of times, including once in the throat. The house was then ransacked before Pascoe and Whitty returned to the caravan, bearing their booty of just £4. The girls would later report that although Pascoe looked nervous, Whitty was smiling.

The police found that not only were they dealing with cold-blooded killers, but also totally incompetent thieves. A police search of the premises turned up hidden caches of money and valuables worth well over £3,000.

Roadblocks were set up around the area and it was this action that gave the police a breakthrough. On August 16th, Pascoe rode through Constantine on his motorbike and was stopped as a matter of routine. Not only was he recognised by the police, but his answers did not satisfy them. He was taken in and eventually admitted his part in the crime. His evidence led to Whitty being arrested and both men were then charged with murder.

Pascoe's story was that he had only tapped Rowe with a small iron bar, to render him unconscious. He claimed that it had been Whitty who battered the old man after that, and Whitty who had used the knife. In his turn, Whitty claimed that he had stabbed Rowe, but only because he was terrified of Pascoe and had done as he was told. The jury

NAMES	Russell Pascoe; Dennis John Whitty
AGES AT EXECUTION	24; 22
DATE OF EXECUTION	Tuesday, 17th December, 1963
PLACES OF EXECUTION	Bristol; Winchester
HANGMEN	Harry Allen; Robert Leslie Stewart
ASSISTANT	Not known; H.F. Robinson
DATE OF TRIAL	29th October – 2nd November, 1963
LOCATION OF TRIAL	Bodmin
PRESIDING JUDGE	Mister Justice Thesiger
PROSECUTION COUNSEL	Norman Brodrick
DEFENCE COUNSEL	James P. Comyn; Norman Skelhorn
NUMBER OF VICTIMS	1

VICTIMS DETAILS	
NAME	William Garfield Rowe
AGE	64
DATE OF MURDER	Wednesday, 14th August, 1963
PLACE OF MURDER	Nanjarrow Farm, Constantine, near Falmouth
METHOD OF KILLING	Battered/stabbed
RELATIONSHIP TO KILLERS	None; none

believed that both men had played an active part in the crime.

In a sense, August 14th was the second time that William Rowe had 'died'. A deserter from the First World War, he had been hidden by his family until an amnesty for deserters was declared by the Queen at the start of her reign. At that, Rowe came out of hiding, having been assumed dead for almost 40 years.

JOSEPH FAWCETT GLANCED at his watch. It was 3.00am on April 7th, 1964 and the noise from next door had woken him. There were a couple of loud thuds followed by a scream. He went to investigate.

Both the front and back doors of number 28 King's Avenue, were locked. At this point a second neighbour, Walter Lister, who had also heard the racket, came to investigate too. There was no reply from number 28 and the two neighbours decided to call the police.

When the police did arrive, the spare key Joseph held was handed over by Mrs Fawcett. Sergeant James Park, together with Joseph, ventured into the quiet house at about 3.30am. At the foot of the stairs lay the battered and stabbed body of John Alan West.

A search of the premises produced a raincoat. It was the wrong size for Mister West, so it was a reasonable to assume that it belonged to his attacker. The job of the investigating officers was made much easier when they found, in one of the raincoat pockets, a medallion inscribed "G.O. Evans, July, 1961." They also discovered a piece of paper with the name Norma O'Brien and a Liverpool address on it.

When Norma O'Brien was interviewed, she told the officers that G.O. Evans was Gwynne Owen Evans, whose real name was John Robson Welby, and who was also known as Ginger. She also provided the officers with his address. Once in custody, Ginger Evans gave the police the name Peter Anthony Allen, and when Allen was picked up, he had John West's watch in his pocket.

The story that the two men told was simple enough. Evans had once worked with West at the Lakeland Laundry. Short of money, Evans had decided to visit West and try to borrow some. Allen had gone with him, even taking his wife and children along for the ride. An argument had followed and West had been struck with a cosh and then stabbed in the heart. The only disagreement between Allen and Evans was that each said the other was the one who had killed West.

At the trial at Manchester, both men were found guilty of murder and sentenced to death. Allen and Evans took their places on the scaffold at Liverpool and Manchester

NAMES	Peter Anthony Allen; Gwynne Owen Evans (John Robson Welby)
AGES AT EXECUTION	21; 24
DATE OF EXECUTION	Thursday, 13th August, 1964
PLACES OF EXECUTION	Liverpool; Manchester
HANGMEN	Robert Leslie Stuart; Harry Allen
ASSISTANTS	Not known; not known
DATE OF TRIAL	July 1st – July 7th, 1964
LOCATION OF TRIAL	Manchester
PRESIDING JUDGE	Mister Justice Ashworth
PROSECUTION COUNSEL	J.D. Cantley, J. Bamber
DEFENCE COUNSEL	S.G. Nance, J. Naylor; G.W. Guthrie Jones, Morris Jones
NUMBER OF VICTIMS	1

VICTIMS DETAILS	
NAME	John Alan West
AGE	53
DATE OF MURDER	Tuesday, 7th April, 1964
PLACE OF MURDER	28 King's Avenue, Seaton, Workington
METHOD OF KILLING	Battered/stabbed
RELATIONSHIP TO KILLERS	None; none

respectively on the 13th of August, 1964. Though they could not know it, they were to go down in history as the last two men hanged in the United Kingdom.

Other men were sentenced to death but reprieved. On November 9th, 1965, capital punishment was suspended for five years. On December 16th, 1969 that decision was confirmed and though moves have been made to restore hanging, it thus far remains a thing of the past.

DIARY

January

1ST

1907 – Execution of John Davis
1916 – Execution of Lee Kun
1917 – Murder of William Watterton
1923 – Murder of Bernard Quinn
1926 – Murder of Polly Edith Walker
1935 – Execution of Frederick Rushworth
1939 – Murder of Peggy Irene Violet Pentecost
1952 – Execution of Horace Carter
1958 – Murder of Peter James Smart, Doris Smart and Michael Smart

2ND

1905 – Arthur Devereux dismissed from his job
1922 – Katharine Mary Armstrong's body exhumed
1922 – Maud Atkin's body found
1924 – Execution of Matthew Frederick Atkinson Nunn
1929 – Murder of Ellen Cartledge
1943 – Murder of Ann Elizabeth Wade
1953 – Execution of John James Alcott
1956 – Murder of Annie Kneilands
1959 – Norah Summerfield's body found

3RD

1922 – Arrest of Percy James Atkin
1923 – Execution of George Frederick Edisbury
1926 – Arrest of Ewen Anderson Stitchell
1928 – Execution of Frederick Fielding
1931 – Execution of Victor Edward Betts
1934 – Execution of Roy Gregory
1946 – Execution of William Joyce
1946 – Murder of Bernard Philipps
1947 – Execution of Stanley Sheminant

4TH

1924 – Arrest of Francis Wilson Booker
1928 – Execution of Bertram Horace Kirby
1929 – Execution of Charles William Conlin
1946 – Execution of Theodore William John Schurch
1951 – Execution of Frank Griffin
1952 – Murder of Joseph Aaku

5TH

1904 – Execution of Joseph Moran
1923 – Execution of Lee Doon
1923 – Trial of William Rooney starts
1926 – Execution of John Fisher
1927 – Execution of William Cornelius Jones
1946 – Bernard Philipps's body found
1946 – Original execution date for John Lyon, John Alexander Rennie and Alexander Crosbie
1953 – George Francis Shaw loses his appeal
1954 – Execution of Robert William Moore

6TH

1909 – Execution of John Esmond Murphy

1920 – Execution of Lewis Massey
1920 – Execution of Hyman Perdovitch
1920 – Execution of David Caplan
1928 – Execution of John Thomas Dunn
1928 – Execution of Sidney Bernard Goulter
1931 – Evelyn Foster attacked
1937 – Probable date of murder of Mona Lilian Tinsley
1943 – Trial of David Cobb
1948 – Trial of Stanislaw Myskza starts
1950 – Execution of Daniel Raven
1959 – Arrest of Joseph Chrimes
1961 – Second cancelled execution date of Wasyl Gnypiuk

7TH

1907 – Trial of Thomas Connan starts
1913 – Execution of Albert Rumens
1919 – Execution of Benjamin Hindle Benson
1921 – Execution of George Edwin Freeman Quinton Lever
1922 – Murder of Mary Williamson
1926 – Execution of Lorraine Lax
1928 – Execution of Samuel Case
1931 – Evelyn Foster dies
1948 – Execution of George Henry Whelpton

8TH

1919 – Execution of George Cardwell and Percy Barrett
1923 – Trial of William Rooney ends
1945 – Execution of Ernest Lee Clark and Augustine M Guerra
1945 – Trial of George E. Smith starts
1946 – Execution of William Batty
1954 – Execution of Czelslaw Kowalewski

9TH

1900 – Execution of Louisa Josephine Jemima Masset
1901 – George Joseph Smith sentenced to two years for receiving
1907 – Trial of Thomas Connan ends
1923 – Execution of Edith Jessie Thompson and Frederick Edward Bywaters
1924 – Mabel Jones meets Jean Pierre Vacquier
1943 – Murder of Harry Jenkins
1945 – Execution of Horace Beresford Gordon

10TH

1910 – Murder of Annie Covell
1918 – Trial of Arthur Stamrowsky
1929 – Vivian Messiter's body found
1948 – Trial of Stanislaw Myskza ends

11TH

1901 – Execution of William Woods
1920 – Murders of Hannah Calladine and Albert Edward Calladine
1921 – Herbert Rowse Armstrong buys a quarter of a pound of Arsenic
1928 – Edward Rowlands and Daniel Driscoll lose their appeals
1943 – Arrest of Harold A. Smith
1950 – Trial of Timothy John Evans starts

12TH

1920 – Murder of Elsie Calladine
1935 – Louisa Baguley and Ada Baguley move in
  with Dorothea Waddingham
1949 – Execution of Margaret Allen
1949 – Original execution date set for
  George Semini
1951 – Murder of Frederick Gosling

13TH

1911 – Trial of George Newton
1917 – Murder of Henry Lynch
1918 – Clemence Verelst attacked
1921 – Trial of George Arthur Bailey starts
1926 – Murder of Milly Illingworth Crabtree
1932 – Execution of Eddie Cullens
1945 – Trial of George E Smith ends
1950 – Trial of Timothy John Evans ends

14TH

1918 – Trial of Joseph Jones starts
1922 – Murder of Margaret Evans
1929 – Trial of Frank Hollington
1948 – Trial of Walter John Cross starts
1952 – Arrest of Backary Manneh
1953 – Murder of George Walker
1958 – Arrest of Peter Thomas Anthony Manuel

15TH

1903 – Trial of Amelia Sach and Annie
  Walters starts
1912 – Arrest of Margaret Ann Seddon
1918 – Clemence Verelst dies
1918 – Trial of Verney Hasser starts
1918 – Trial of Joseph Jones ends
1925 – Elsie Emily Cameron's body found
1929 – Trial of William John Holmyard starts
1946 – Trial of Charles Edward Prescott starts
1952 – Execution of Alfred Bradley
1953 – George Walker's body found
1959 – Charles Frederick Barrett attacked

16TH

1903 – Trial of Amelia Sach and Annie
  Walters ends
1918 – Trial of Verney Hasser ends
1918 – Trial of Louis Voisin starts
1919 – Trial of Joseph Rose
1920 – Murder of Annie Maria Wilson
1929 – Trial of William John Holmyard ends
1940 – Murder of Elsie May Ellington
1945 – Trial of Karl Gustav Hulten
1946 – Death sentence on John Alexander
  Rennie quashed
1948 – Trial of Walter John Cross ends
1959 – Charles Frederick Barrett dies

17TH

1901 – Murder of William Pearson
1921 – Trial of George Arthur Bailey ends
1946 – Trial of Charles Edward Prescott ends

18TH

1918 – Trial of Louis Voisin ends
1928 – Norman Elliott marries Elizabeth
1938 – Murder of Margaret Jane Dobson
1949 – Arrest of Harry Lewis
1961 – Trial of Jack Day starts

19TH

1922 – Herbert Rowse Armstrong charged
  with murder
1932 – Trial of William Harold Goddard starts
1935 – Murder of Hubert Sidney Deggan
1938 – Margaret Jane Dobson's body found
1939 – Trial of John Daymond
1941 – Murder of Emily Wardle
1944 – Trial of J.C. Leatherberry
1953 – Arrest of John Todd

20TH

1925 – Trial of William Grover Bignell
1926 – Trial of John Lincoln starts
1932 – Trial of William Harold Goddard ends
1938 – Arrest of Robert William Hoolhouse
1938 – Trial of Walter Smith starts
1950 – A jury decides that James Frank
  Rivett is sane
1961 – Trial of Jack Day ends

21ST

1926 – Trial of John Lincoln ends
1926 – Doris Ah Tam dies
1935 – Trial of Charles Malcolm Lake starts
1951 – Murder of an unnamed male child by
  William Arthur Watkins

22ND

1921 – Katharine Mary Armstrong leaves hospital
1925 – Murder of Mary May Palfrey
1938 – Trial of Walter Smith ends
1945 – Trial of Arthur Heys starts
1947 – David Ware confesses to the murder of
  Olive Balchin
1959 – Arrest of Ronald Henry Marwood
1962 – Trial of James Hanratty starts

23RD

Nothing known

24TH

1911 – Murder of Ann Harris
1920 – Murder of Edith Annie Swainston
1925 – Arrest of George William Barton
1928 – Execution of James McKay
1935 – Trial of Charles Malcolm Lake ends
1944 – Trial of Oswald John Job starts
1945 – Trial of Arthur Heys ends

25TH

1902 – Murder of Charlotte Cheeseman
1911 – Ann Harris's body found
1944 – Trial of Ernest Charles Digby starts

26TH

1902 – Charlotte Cheeseman's body found
1905 – Murder of Elizabeth Jane Rickus
1910 – Trial of William Murphy
1931 – Trial of Alfred Arthur Rouse starts
1932 – Murder of Annette Friedson
1943 – Execution of Franciscus Johannes Winter
1944 – Trial of Oswald John Job ends
1951 – Execution of Nenad Kovacevic
1953 – Execution of George Francis Shaw
1954 – Execution of Desmond Donald Hooper
1959 – Ernest Raymond Jones loses his appeal

27TH

1913 – Ada Louise James attacked
1926 – Trial of Herbert Burrows
1928 – Execution of Edward Rowlands and
       Daniel Driscoll
1941 – Murder of Albert Edward Farley
1943 – Execution of Harry Dobkin
1944 – Trial of Ernest Charles Digby ends
1949 – Execution of George Semini
1950 – Trial of James Frank Rivett
1951 – Murder of Walter Wyld
1954 – Execution of William Lubina
1961 – Execution of Wasyl Gnypiuk

28TH

1901 – Trial of Samson Silas Samson starts
1905 – Murder of Beatrice Devereux, Laurence
       Devereux and Evelyn Devereux
1907 – Rhoda Willis starts work for David Evans
1911 – Arrest of William Henry Palmer
1913 – Ada Louise James dies
1913 – Arrest of Edward Henry Palmer
1942 – Trial of Harold Dorian Trevor starts
1951 – Walter Wyld's body found
1953 – Execution of Derek William Bentley
1961 – Murder of Pearl Gamble

29TH

1901 – Trial of Samson Silas Samson ends
1903 – Trial of William Hughes
1904 – Murder of Mary Elizabeth Gilbert
1913 – Execution of George Mackay
1913 – Execution of Edward Hopwood
1925 – Murder of Ruth Surtees Rodgers
1942 – Trial of Harold Dorian Trevor ends
1951 – Murder of Alice Kate Roberts

30TH

1922 – Trial of William Harkness starts
1942 – Execution of Arthur Peach
1943 – Marguerite Beatrice Burge attacked
1945 – Execution of Andrew Brown
1947 – Execution of Albert Sabin

31ST

1905 – Murder of Albert Matthews
1911 – Execution of George Newton
1922 – Trial of William Harkness ends
1928 – Execution of James Joseph Power
1928 – Execution of James Gillon
1931 – Trial of Alfred Arthur Rouse ends

1942 – Murder of Lilian Dorothy Pax Austin
1943 – Marguerite Beatrice Burge dies
1945 – Execution of Arthur Thompson
1946 – Execution of Michal Niescior
1952 – Trial of Tahir Ali starts

February

1ST

1908 – Murder of Amelia Bell Wood
1909 – Trial of Jeremiah O'Connor
1910 – Probable date of murder of Cora Turner
       (Mrs Crippen)
1915 – Arrest of George Joseph Smith
1922 – Trial of Edward Ernest Black starts
1932 – Trial of George Thomas Pople starts
1951 – Murder of Alice Morgan
1952 – Trial of Tahir Ali ends

2ND

1914 – Trial of George Ball starts
1920 – Trial of William Wright
1922 – Trial of Edward Ernest Black ends
1932 – Trial of George Thomas Pople ends
1933 – Execution of Jeremiah Hanbury
1943 – First trial of William Henry Turner ends
       with jury undecided
1944 – Execution of Christos Georghiou
1950 – Trial of George Kelly starts
1951 – Alice Morgan's body found

3RD

1903 – Execution of Amelia Sach and
       Annie Walters
1913 – Trial of George Cunliffe
1914 – Trial of James Honeyands
1920 – Murder of Henry Senior
1932 – Execution of George Alfred Rice
1944 – Execution of Mervin Clare McEwen
1948 – Execution of Evan Hadyn Evans
1951 – Arrest of James Inglis
1951 – Murder of Eileen Emily Rose Cullen

4TH

1904 – Murder of Martha Eliza Simpson
1910 – Trial of Joseph Wren
1913 – Execution of Eric James Sedgewick
1921 – Execution of Jack Alfred Field and William
       Thomas Gray
1929 – Trial of Joseph Reginald Victor Clarke
1931 – Execution of Frederick Gill
1937 – Execution of Max Mayer Haslam
1940 – Arthur John Allen attacked
1942 – Trial of David Rodger Williams
1943 – Second trial of William Henry Turner
1944 – Murder of Ronald John Murphy
1953 – Trial of Miles William Giffard starts
1954 – Murder of Margaret Rose Louise Spevick
1998 – Murder conviction of Mahmood Hussein
       Mattan quashed

5TH

1906 – Trial of John Griffiths starts
1910 – Annie Finn marries Thomas Henderson

1911 – Murder of Sarah Chilvers
1914 – Trial of George Ball ends
1926 – Trial of Lock Ah Tam starts
1946 – Alexander Crosbie reprieved
1952 – Trial of Herbert Roy Harris

6TH

1902 – George Woolfe arrested
1906 – Trial of John Griffiths ends
1908 – Trial of Joseph Hume starts
1920 – Murder of Sarah Jane Howard
1923 – Murder of Alice May Cheshire
1926 – Trial of Lock Ah Tam ends
1934 – Execution of Ernest Brown
1942 – Murder of Maggie Smail
1947 – Murder of Margaret Williams
1948 – Execution of Stanislaw Myszka
1952 – Execution of Alfred Moore
1953 – Trial of Miles William Giffard ends
1961 – First trial of Samuel McLaughlin starts

7TH

1905 – Arthur Devereux moves the trunk
containing the bodies of his family into storage.
1908 – Trial of Joseph Hume ends
1912 – Trial of Myer Abramovitch starts
1919 – Arthur Goslett bigamously marries Daisy
Ellen Holt
1920 – Sarah Jane Howard's body found
1922 – Trial of William Sullivan starts
1935 – Execution of David Maskill Blake
1940 – Execution of Peter Barnes and
James Richards
1942 – Murder of Imeldred Maria Osliff
1942 – Murder of Evelyn Margaret Hamilton
1946 – Trial of Arthur Clegg starts
1947 – Trial of Frederick Reynolds
1954 – Margaret Rose Louise Spevick's body found
1961 – Original execution date for Jack Day

8TH

1912 – Trial of Myer Abramovitch ends
1922 – Trial of William Sullivan ends
1923 – Execution of William Rooney
1926 – Murder of Rose Smith
1927 – Murder of Ada Knighton
1928 – Murder of Florence Alice Kitching
1939 – Execution of John Daymond
1940 – Trial of Ernest Edmund Hamerton
1942 – Imeldred Maria Osliff's body found
1942 – Murder of Evelyn Oatley
1942 – Evelyn Margaret Hamilton's body found
1943 – Murder of Josephine Rayner
1946 – Execution of John Lyon
1946 – Trial of Arthur Clegg ends
1950 – Trial of George Kelly ends
1951 – Murder of Ellen May Ludkin

9TH

1917 – Trial of Leo George O'Donnell starts
1928 – Alfred Charles Bertram Webb attacked
1942 – Arrest of Douglas Edmondson
1954 – Murder of Herbert Victor Ketley
1955 – Murder of Rose Elizabeth Fairhurst
1961 – Execution of George Riley

10TH

1905 – Trial of Edward Harrison
1909 – Trial of Thomas Mead
1917 – Trial of Leo George O'Donnell ends
1928 – Alfred Charles Bertram Webb dies
1937 – Execution of Andrew Anderson Bagley
1941 – Trial of Samuel Morgan starts
1942 – Evelyn Oatley's body found
1943 – Execution of Ronald Roberts
1944 – Execution of John H. Waters
1947 – Murder of Gertrude Briggs
1955 – Rose Elizabeth Fairhurst's body found
1959 – Execution of Ernest Raymond Jones

11TH

1910 – Trial of George Henry Perry
1926 – Trial of Ewen Anderson Stitchell starts
1938 – Murder of Eliza Augustina Caldwell
1941 – Execution of Clifford Holmes
1943 – Trial of Gordon Horace Trenoweth starts
1943 – Joseph Jan Van Hove arrives in England
1946 – Trial of Marion Grondkowski and Henryk
Malinowski starts
1946 – Trial of Harold Berry starts
1952 – Harry Huxley is released from hospital
1961 – First trial of Samuel McLaughlin ends
with jury undecided
1961 – Arrest of Robert Andrew McGladdery

12TH

1903 – Trial of Edgar Owen starts
1909 – Trial of Ernest Hutchinson
1918 – Execution of Arthur Stamrowsky
1921 – Murder of Doris Appleton
1926 – Trial of Ewen Anderson Stitchell ends
1942 – Murder of Margaret Florence Lowe
1942 – Murder of Doris Jouannet
1952 – Trial of Edward Devlin and Alfred Burns
starts

13TH

1901 – Murder of Elizabeth Taylor
1903 – Trial of Edgar Owen ends
1942 – Attack upon Margaret Heywood –
she survives
1942 – Attack upon Kathleen King – she survives
1946 – Trial of Marion Grondkowski and
Henryk Malinowski ends

14TH

1920 – Murder of Ivy Woolfenden
1941 – Trial of Henry Lyndo White starts
1944 – Murder of Iris Miriam Deeley
1946 – Trial of Arthur Charles
1946 – Trial of Harold Berry ends

15TH

1901 – Murder of Victor Baileff
1904 – Trial of Sidney George Smith
1910 – Execution of William Murphy
1917 – Trial of Thomas Clinton
1917 – Murder of Lily Tindale
1939 – Trial of William Thomas Butler starts
1941 – Trial of Henry Lyndo White ends

1944 – Iris Miriam Deeley's body found

16TH

1900 – Trial of Ada Chard-Williams starts
1909 – Murder of Michael Swinton Brown
1920 – Murder of Ida Prescott
1922 – Trial of Percy James Atkin starts
1923 – Trial of William Francis Albert Bressington
1926 – Trial of George Thomas
1928 – Murder of William Byland Abbey
1939 – Trial of William Thomas Butler ends
1943 – Trial of Gordon Horace Trenoweth ends
1948 – Murder of Archibald Henderson and
    Rosalie Henderson

17TH

1900 – Trial of Ada Chard-Williams ends
1903 – Execution of William Hughes
1903 – Murder of Harry Short
1922 – Trial of Percy James Atkin ends
1926 – Execution of Herbert Burrows
1941 – Trial of Samuel Morgan ends
1962 – Trial of James Hanratty ends

18TH

1914 – Trial of Josiah Davies
1916 – Trial of Frederick Holmes
1916 – Trial of Reginald Haslam
1922 – Helen Harkness reprieved
1949 – Murder of Olive Durand-Deacon

19TH

1901 – Execution of Samson Silas Salmon
1907 – Execution of Thomas Connan
1913 – Trial of Edward Henry Palmer
1919 – Execution of Joseph Rose
1919 – Murder of Elizabeth Gaskin
1928 – Murder of Richard Francis Roadley
1933 – Murder of Joseph Nixon and Mary
    Ann Nixon
1935 – Trial of Leonard Albert Brigstock
1948 – Execution of Walter John Cross
1949 – Murder of Doreen Primrose Messenger

20TH

1903 – Trial of Samuel Henry Smith
1908 – Murder of Mary Jane Dodds
1909 – Cecilia Harris attacked
1926 – Trial of Henry Thompson
1928 – Arrest of Norman Elliott
1928 – Funeral of William Byland Abbey
1928 – Trial of George Frederick Walter Hayward
    starts
1929 – Execution of Frank Hollington
1933 – Bodies of Joseph Nixon and
    Mary Ann Nixon found
1949 – Murder of Marian Poskitt

21ST

1901 – John Harrison marries Alice Wright
1908 – Murder of James MacCraw
1909 – Arrest of John Edmunds
1918 – Execution of Joseph Jones
1919 – Arrest of Henry Thomas Gaskin

1922 – Execution of William Harkness
1927 – Murder of Madge Dorothy Maggs
1945 – Trial of Aniceto Martinez
1954 – Murder of Marie Bradshaw

22ND

1910 – Execution of Joseph Wren
1921 – Murder of Katharine Mary Armstrong
1923 – Trial of George Perry
1924 – Murder of Elizabeth Reaney
1944 – Arrest of Ernest James Harman Kemp

23RD

1908 – Funeral of Mary Jane Dodds
1909 – Execution of Jeremiah O'Connor
1909 – Thomas Mead's appeal dismissed
1910 – Trial of Thomas Clements starts
1919 – Elizabeth Gaskin's body found
1920 – Trial of Frederick Rothwell Holt starts
1923 – Trial of Daniel Cassidy
1924 – Elizabeth Reaney's body found
1928 – Arrest of Frederick Stewart
1931 – Trial of Francis Land starts
1932 – Execution of William Harold Goddard
1933 – Murder of Doris Winifred Brewer

24TH

1900 – Henry Smith attacked
1910 – Trial of Thomas Clements ends
1921 – Trial of Frederick Quarmby starts
1925 – Execution of William Grover Bignell
1926 – Trial of William Henry Thorpe
1928 – Trial of George Frederick Walter
    Hayward ends
1936 – Trial of Dorothea Nancy Waddingham starts
1943 – Trial of August Sangret starts
1953 – Execution of Miles William Giffard
1961 – Murder of Eli Myers

25TH

1901 – Trial of Herbert John Bennett starts
1902 – Trial of Harold Amos Apted starts
1913 – Execution of George Cunliffe
1915 – Arrest of Carl Frederick Muller
1921 – Trial of Frederick Quarmby ends
1921 – Funeral of Katherine Mary Armstrong
1931 – Trial of Francis Land ends
1955 – Donald Haywood Lainton attacked

26TH

1902 – Trial of Harold Amos Apted ends
1904 – Murder of Mary Pike
1914 – Execution of George Ball
1914 – Elizabeth Alice Spooner attacked
1918 – Original execution date of Louis Voisin
1924 – Trial of Francis Wilson Booker
1925 – Trial of George William Barton
1927 – Trial of William Knighton
1929 – Trial of George Henry Cartledge
1931 – Murder of Evelyn Victoria Holt
1949 – Arrest of John George Haigh
1952 – Murder of Jeannie Deveney
1952 – Trial of James Smith starts
1952 – Execution of Herbert Roy Harris

1955 – Donald Haywood Lainton dies

27TH

1902 – Trial of Richard Wigley
1906 – Execution of John Griffiths
1914 – Elizabeth Alice Spooner dies
1920 – Trial of Frederick Rothwell Holt ends
1924 – Arrest of William Horsely Wardell
1929 – Execution of William John Holmyard
1936 – Trial of Dorothea Nancy Waddingham ends
1947 – Trial of Harold Hagger starts
1947 – Execution of Walter Graham Rowland
1950 – Trial of Albert Edward Jenkins starts
1952 – Trial of Edward Devlin and Alfred Burns ends
1952 – Trial of James Smith ends
1952 – Murder of Muriel Elsie Bent

28TH

1905 – Execution of Edward Harrison
1908 – Trial of Robert Lawman
1912 – Trial of John Williams
1917 – Murder of Julia Ann Johnson
1923 – Trial of Frederick Wood starts
1946 – Trial of Patrick Carraher starts
1946 – Trial of Leonard Holmes
1947 – Trial of Harold Hagger ends
1954 – Murder of Elizabeth Robertson and George Alexander Robertson and attack upon Jean Elisabeth Robertson

29TH

1940 – William Ralph Shiell attacked
1944 – Murder of Winifred Ellen Stanley

March

1ST

1910 – Execution of George Henry Perry
1922 – Trial of James Hutton Williamson
1923 – Trial of Bernard Pomroy
1924 – Jean Pierre Vacquier purchases strychnine
1928 – Trial of Frederick Lock
1933 – Arrest of Frederick Morse
1934 – Child born to Lydia Binks and Frederick Rushworth
1939 – Trial of Harry Armstrong starts
1940 – William Ralph Shiell dies
1951 – Trial of Joseph Brown and Edward Charles Smith starts

2ND

1901 – Trial of George Henry Parker
1901 – Trial of Herbert John Bennett ends
1907 – Murder of Fanny Adelaide Moore
1908 – Trial of Joseph William Noble starts
1909 – Execution of Ernest Hutchinson
1918 – Execution of Louis Marie Joseph Voisin
1921 – Execution of George Arthur Bailey
1923 – Trial of Frederick Wood ends
1926 – Execution of John Lincoln
1936 – Trial of Buck Ruxton starts
1939 – Trial of Harry Armstrong ends
1942 – Trial of Harold Hill starts

1943 – Trial of August Sangret ends
1946 – Trial of Patrick Carraher ends
1946 – Murder of John Whatman
1949 – Trial of Kenneth Strickson
1950 – Trial of Albert Edward Jenkins ends

3RD

1903 – Execution of Edgar Owen
1904 – Start of first trial of Joseph Fee
1906 – Jane Gamble attacked
1908 – Trial of Joseph William Noble ends
1923 – Execution of Daniel Cassidy
1930 – Trial of William Henry Podmore starts
1942 – Trial of Frederick James Austin
1946 – John Whatman's body found
1959 – Trial of Joseph Chrimes starts
1961 – Murder of Elsie May Batten

4TH

1905 – Murder of Catherine Balhard
1906 – Jane Gamble dies
1910 – Murder of Alfred Doggett
1912 – Trial of Frederick Henry Seddon starts
1920 – Trial of William Hall
1923 – Murder of Thomas Johnson Wood
1932 – Trial of George Emanuel Michael
1933 – Murder of Elizabeth Mary Standley
1935 – Trial of John Stephenson Bainbridge starts
1939 – Murder of Beatrice Delia Baxter
1940 – Arrest of Vincent Ostler and William Appleby
1944 – Dorothy Holmes is raped
1959 – Trial of Joseph Chrimes ends

5TH

1904 – End of first trial of Joseph Fee
1908 – Execution of Joseph Hume
1909 – Trial of Joseph Edwin Jones
1914 – Trial of Robert Upton
1917 – Trial of William James Robinson starts
1918 – Execution of Verney Hasser
1922 – Trial of Edmund Hugh Tonbridge
1925 – Trial of Thomas Henry Shelton
1930 – Second trial of Samuel Cushnan starts
1934 – Trial of Reginald Ivor Hinks starts
1942 – Trial of Harold Hill ends
1944 – Arrest of Eliga Brinson and Willie Smith
1944 – Murder of Thomas Evison
1946 – Execution of Charles Edward Prescott
1951 – Trial of Joseph Brown and Edward Charles Smith ends

6TH

1900 – Execution of Ada Chard-Williams
1902 – Trial of Arthur Richardson
1902 – Murder of Margaret Pamphilon
1905 – Arrest of Alfred Bridgeman
1912 – Execution of Myer Abramovitch
1914 – Trial of Edgar Lewis George Bindon
1917 – Trial of Alec Bakerlis
1922 – Trial of Frederick Alexander Keeling starts
1925 – Trial of Thomas Henry Shelton
1940 – Trial of William Charles Cowell starts
1941 – Execution of Henry Lyndo White
1944 – Murder of Harry Coogan

1945 – Elizabeth Maud Jones is reprieved
1952 – Murder of Lily Volpert
1953 – Probable date of murder of
Hectorina MacLennan
1961 – Jack Day loses his appeal

7TH

1907 – Trial of Joseph Jones
1917 – Trial of William James Robinson ends
1922 – Trial of Frederick Alexander Keeling ends
1924 – Murder of Nelson Leech
1935 – Trial of Percy Charles Anderson starts
1946 – Arrest of Sydney John Smith
1947 – Trial of David John Williams
1947 – Murder of Edith Simmonite
1949 – Trial of Harry Lewis

8TH

1904 – Trial of James Henry Clarkson
1916 – Execution of Frederick Holmes
1917 – Murder of Alexander Imlach
1927 – Trial of James Frederick Stratton
1930 – Trial of William Henry Podmore ends
1930 – Second trial of Samuel Cushnan ends
1932 – Trial of Maurice Freedman starts
1935 – Trial of John Stephenson Bainbridge ends
1938 – Execution of Walter Smith
1940 – Trial of William Charles Cowell ends
1945 – Execution of Karl Gustav Hulten
1949 – Lucy Wilson attacked
1950 – Execution of James Frank Rivett
1950 – Trial of Piotr Maksimowski
1954 – Trial of Thomas Ronald Lewis Harries starts
1955 – Trial of William Arthur Salt starts

9TH

1904 – Execution of Sidney George Smith
1905 – Trial of John Hutchinson
1917 – Trial of John William Thompson
1920 – Trial of Miles McHugh
1926 – Execution of Henry Thompson
1926 – Execution of George Thomas
1926 – Trial of George Sharples
1932 – Trial of Maurice Freedman ends
1932 – Trial of Thomas Riley
1932 – Execution of George Thomas Pople
1933 – Murder of Dorothy Margaret Addinall
1935 – Trial of Percy Charles Anderson ends
1935 – Murder of Sybil Emily Worthington
1950 – Execution of Timothy John Evans
1950 – Trial of Walter Sharpe starts
1951 – Trial of William Edward Shaughnessy starts
1954 – Murder of George Smart
1955 – Trial of William Arthur Salt ends

10TH

1903 – Execution of Samuel Henry Smith
1911 – Murder of Mary Seymour
1913 – Trial of Walter William Sykes
1914 – Execution of Josiah Davies
1920 – Execution of William Wright
1931 – Execution of Alfred Arthur Rouse
1934 – Trial of Reginald Ivor Hinks ends
1949 – Trial of James Farrell
1950 – Trial of Walter Sharpe ends

1950 – Murder of Mary Victoria Longhurst
1953 – Murder of Flora Jane Gilligan

11TH

1903 – Start of Joseph Moran's first trial
1907 – Trial of Edwin James Moore
1909 – Trial of Walter Elliott
1911 – Mary Seymour's body found
1925 – Trial of John Norman Holmes Thorne starts
1932 – Trial of John Henry Roberts starts
1942 – Execution of Harold Dorian Trevor
1946 – Arthur Charles loses his appeal
1955 – Murder of Mary Catherine Boothroyd

12TH

1903 – End of Joseph Moran's first trial
1904 – Trial of Henry Jones
1909 – Execution of Thomas Mead
1909 – Trial of See Lee
1909 – Murder of Annie Thompson
1914 – Execution of James Honeyands
1923 – Murder of Jane Nagi
1929 – Execution of Joseph Reginald Victor Clarke
1930 – Trial of Sidney Harry Fox
1932 – Trial of John Henry Roberts ends
1943 – Trial of Dudley George Rayner
1943 – Trial of Harold A. Smith
1943 – Execution of David Cobb
1945 – Lily Griffiths attacked
1946 – Trial of Martin Patrick Coffey
1951 – Trial of James Virrels starts
1954 – Trial of Albert George Hall

13TH

1916 – Reginald Haslam loses his appeal
1935 – Execution of Charles Malcolm Lake
1940 – Murder of Michael O'Dwyer
1945 – Execution of Arthur Heys
1950 – Murder of Robert Taylor
1951 – Trial of James Virrels ends
1951 – Trial of William Edward Shaughnessy ends
1953 – John Reginald Halliday Christie sublets
his rooms

14TH

1912 – Trial of Frederick Henry Seddon ends
1923 – Murder of Wilhelmina Nicholson
1934 – Trial of Albert Probert and Frederick
William Parker starts
1938 – Trial of Charles James Caldwell

15TH

1901 – Trial of Joseph Arthur Shufflebotham
1904 – Murder of Alice Foster
1909 – Inquest on Annie Thompson opens
1920 – Trial of Thomas Caler starts
1922 – Alice White attacked
1933 – Second trial of Harold Courtney starts
1934 – Trial of Louis Hamilton
1938 – Aminul Hag argues with Jan Mohamed
1943 – Murder of Annette Elizabeth Frederika
Christina Pepper
1951 – Trial of William Arthur Watkins starts
1955 – Trial of Winston Shaw starts

16TH

1903 – Trial of George Chapman starts
1909 – Murder of William Sproull
1920 – Original execution date of Frederick Rothwell Holt
1920 – Trial of Thomas Caler ends
1925 – Trial of John Norman Holmes Thorne ends
1926 – Execution of William Henry Thorpe
1934 – Trial of Albert Probert and Frederick William Parker ends
1944 – Execution of Oswald John Job
1944 – Execution of Ernest Charles Digby
1944 – Execution of J.C. Leatherberry
1945 – Lily Griffiths dies
1951 – Trial of William Arthur Watkins ends
1954 – Trial of Thomas Ronald Lewis Harries ends

17TH

1904 – Trial of Charles Samuel Dyer
1945 – Execution of Robert L Pearson and Parson Jones
1955 – Trial of Winston Shaw ends
1958 – Trial of Vivian Frederick Teed starts

18TH

1902 – Execution of Harold Amos Apted
1902 – Execution of Richard Wigley
1903 – Arrest of Samuel Dougal
1907 – Murder of Lucy Wilson
1908 – Murder of William Berryman and Jean Berryman
1910 – Murder of John Innes Nisbet
1918 – Trial of Louis Van De Kerkhove
1920 – Trial of Thomas Hargreaves Wilson
1947 – Execution of Harold Hagger
1958 – Trial of Vivian Frederick Teed ends

19TH

1901 – Execution of George Henry Parker
1903 – Trial of George Chapman ends
1912 – Execution of John Williams
1913 – Execution of Edward Henry Palmer
1917 – Trial of Robert Gadsby
1942 – Trial of Cyril Johnson starts
1944 – Murder of Gladys May Appleton
1946 – Execution of Arthur Clegg
1949 – Murder of Leonard Thomas and John Bernard Catterall
1952 – Trial of Ajit Singh starts
1959 – Trial of Ronald Henry Marwood
1959 – Trial of Michael George Tatum starts

20TH

1900 – Henry Smith dies
1904 – John Go Hing attacked
1908 – Funeral of William and Jean Berryman
1908 – Arrest of John Berryman
1916 – Trial of Ludovico Zender starts
1933 – Second trial of Harold Courtney ends
1942 – Trial of Cyril Johnson ends
1944 – Trial of Alex F. Miranda
1944 – Gladys May Appleton's body found
1952 – Trial of Ajit Singh ends
1961 – Trial of Victor John Terry starts

21ST

1901 – Execution of Herbert John Bennett
1910 – Arrest of John Alexander Dickman
1917 – Execution of Thomas Clinton
1920 – Murder of Alice Pearson
1922 – Execution of James Hutton Williamson
1927 – William Knighton loses his first appeal
1939 – Execution of Harry Armstrong
1952 – Execution of Tahir Ali

22ND

1916 – Trial of Ludovico Zender ends
1920 – Alice Pearson's body found
1928 – Murder of Thomas Lee
1932 – Murder of Naomi Annie Farnworth
1944 – Trial of Sidney James Delasalle
1949 – Execution of Kenneth Strickson
1952 – James Smith loses his appeal
1954 – Trial of James Reginald Doohan starts

23RD

1904 – John Go Hing dies
1905 – Mary Elizabeth Hancocks attacked
1906 – Trial of Harold Walters
1913 – Murder of Julian Biros
1915 – George Joseph Smith charged with three murders
1920 – Execution of William Hall
1922 – Execution of William Sullivan
1926 – Execution of Lock Ah Tam
1943 – Ernest Charles Digby bigamously marries Olga Davy Hill
1946 – Original execution date for Patrick Carraher
1949 – Lucy Wilson dies
1954 – Trial of James Reginald Doohan ends
1954 – Trial of John Lynch starts
1955 – Trial of Sydney Joseph Clarke
1959 – Trial of Michael George Tatum ends

24TH

1903 – Trial of William George Hudson
1908 – Execution of Joseph William Noble
1908 – Execution of Robert Lawman
1909 – Arrest of Alexander Edmundstone
1910 – Execution of Thomas Clements
1914 – Execution of Robert Upton
1922 – Execution of Edward Ernest Black
1926 – Execution of Ewen Anderson Stitchell
1928 – Arrest of George Reynolds
1932 – Naomi Annie Farnworth's body found
1932 – Arrest of Charles James Cowle
1933 – Arrest of Jack Samuel Puttnam
1935 – Original execution date for Percy Charles Anderson
1936 – Frederick Herbert Charles Field goes absent without leave
1943 – Execution of William Henry Turner
1945 – Murder of Gerhardt Rettig
1953 – The first three bodies are found at 10 Rillington Place, London

25TH

1902 – Execution of Arthur Richardson

1911 – Murder of Elizabeth Anne Kempster
1914 – Execution of Edgar Lewis George Bindon
1931 – Murder of Ethel Louisa Corbett
1934 – Murder of the unnamed Rushworth child
1942 – Execution of David Rodger Williams
1952 – Trial of Backary Manneh starts
1955 – Trial of James Robinson starts

26TH

1905 – Mary Elizabeth Hancocks dies
1907 – Execution of Joseph Jones
1909 – Joseph Edwin Jones loses appeal
1910 – Murder of Thomas William Henderson
1938 – Murder of Tony Ruffle
1946 – Execution of Arthur Charles
1946 – Murder of James Straiton
1947 – Execution of Frederick Reynolds
1954 – Trial of John Lynch ends

27TH

1905 – Murder of Thomas Farrow. Ann Farrow
        attacked
1917 – Execution of John William Thompson
1920 – Murder of Ada Ellor
1940 – Execution of Ernest Edmund Hamerton
1952 – Trial of Backary Manneh ends

28TH

1904 – Dennis Lowthian attacked
1910 – Murder of John Healey
1923 – Execution of George Perry
1938 – Arrest of William James Graves
1938 – Trial of Robert William Hoolhouse starts
1950 – Execution of George Kelly
1961 – Trial of Victor John Terry ends

29TH

1904 – Execution of James Henry Clarkson
1904 – Execution of Henry Jones
1905 – Execution of John Hutchinson
1916 – Execution of Reginald Haslam
1917 – Execution of Leo George O'Donnell
1924 – Murder of Alfred George Poynter Jones
1927 – Execution of James Frederick Stratton
1939 – Execution of William Thomas Butler
1941 – Murder of Jane Turner
1942 – Murder of Joyce Green
1949 – Execution of James Farrell
1950 – Execution of Piotr Maksimowski
1955 – Trial of James Robinson ends
1955 – Execution of William Arthur Salt
1961 – Execution of Jack Day

30TH

1909 – Execution of Edmund Walter Elliott
1909 – Execution of See Lee
1909 – Murder of Hester Harriet Richards
1920 – Miles McHugh loses his appeal
1938 – Trial of Robert William Hoolhouse ends
1942 – Joyce Green's body found
1950 – Execution of Walter Sharpe
1959 – Murder of John Perree

31ST

1905 – Ann Farrow dies
1909 – Trial of William Joseph Foy
1913 – Murder of Winifred Mary Mitchell
1925 – Execution of William Francis
        Albert Bressington
1926 – Murder of Lily Waterhouse
1943 – Execution of Dudley George Rayner
1953 – Arrest of John Reginald Halliday Christie
1953 – Sarah Ricketts makes a will leaving her
        property to Louisa May Merrifield
1954 – Original execution date for
        Albert George Hall

April
1ST

1913 – Lilian Wharton attacked
1926 – Lily Waterhouse's body found
1946 – Arrest of John Caldwell
1949 – Murder of Mary Elizabeth Cooper
1954 – David John Ware commits suicide in prison

2ND

1901 – Execution of Joseph Arthur Shufflebotham
1907 – Execution of James Moore
1925 – Execution of George William Barton
1935 – Execution of Leonard Albert Brigstock
1946 – Execution of Marion Grondkowski and
        Henryk Malinowski

3RD

1905 – Arrest of Alfred Stratton
1922 – Trial of Herbert Rowse Armstrong starts
1924 – Murder of William Edward Hall
1943 – Murder of Mark Turner
1951 – Execution of William Arthur Watkins
1954 – Murder of Arthur White

4TH

1902 – Murder of Elizabeth Marsland
1905 – Arrest of Albert Stratton
1914 – Percy Evelyn Clifford and Maud Clifford go
        to Brighton
1928 – Murder of Beatrice Brooks and
        Alfred Moore
1929 – Execution of George Henry Cartledge
1936 – Murder of Beatrice Vilna Sutton
1959 – John Perree's body found
1959 – Arrest of Francis Joseph Hutchet
1962 – Execution of James Hanratty

5TH

1901 – Murder of Frederick William Acland
        Hamilton
1905 – Execution of Charles Samuel Dyer
1905 – Trial of Alfred Bridgeman
1923 – Execution of Bernard Pomroy
1936 – Arrest of Frederick Herbert Charles Field
1942 – Murder of Patrick Murphy
1946 – Walter Clayton meets Joyce Jacques

6TH

1910 – Patrick Herbert Mahon marries Jessie
1913 – Elizabeth Ellen Hearne attacked
1934 – Execution of Louis Hamilton
1943 – Execution of Gordon Horace Trenoweth
1944 – Murder of James William Percey
1946 – Execution of Patrick Carraher
1949 – Arrest of Bernard Alfred Peter Cooper
1954 – John Lynch loses his appeal
1960 – Murder of John Cremin

7TH

1903 – Execution of George Chapman
1913 – Elizabeth Ellen Hearne dies
1914 – Murder of Maud Clifford
1922 – Execution of Percy James Atkin
1924 – Emily Beilby Kaye goes to Eastbourne
1933 – Execution of Harold Courtney
1945 – Execution of William Harrison
1959 – Murder of Joyce Moran and Neil Saxton
1964 – Murder of John Alan West

8TH

1913 – Lilian Wharton dies
1924 – Execution of Francis Wilson Booker
1930 – Execution of Sidney Harry Fox
1930 – Execution of Samuel Cushnan
1942 – Original execution date set for
  Cyril Johnson
1944 – James William Percey's body found
1951 – Murder of Mona Mather
1953 – Trial of John Todd starts

9TH

1912 – William Wallace Galbraith marries
  Mary May Kirby
1918 – Execution of Louis Van De Kerkhove
1921 – Murder of Olive Jackson
1940 – Arthur John Allen dies
1941 – Execution of Samuel Morgan
1946 – Execution of Harold Berry
1951 – Mona Mather's body found
1953 – Trial of John Todd ends

10TH

1902 – Murder of Sophia Jane Hepworth
1906 – Execution of Harold Walters
1913 – Murder of Alice Catlow More
1917 – Execution of Alec Bakerlis
1921 – Arrest of Thomas Wilson
1923 – Execution of Frederick Wood
1924 – Trial of Michael Pratley
1928 – Execution of George Frederick
  Walter Hayward
1955 – Murder of David Moffat Drummond Blakely
1959 – Joseph Chrimes loses his appeal

11TH

1902 – Trial of Charles Robert Earl starts
1916 – Execution of Ludovico Hurwitz y Zender
1922 – Execution of Frederick Alexander Keeling
1925 – Murder of Sarah Ann Sykes
1930 – Murder of Edith May Parker
1937 – Murder of Ruby Ann Keen

1938 – Murder of Aminul Haq
1941 – Murder of Rachel Dobkin
1933 – Arrest of James Galbraith
1955 – Murder of Norman Yates

12TH

1902 – Sophia Jane Hepworth's body found
1927 – William Knighton loses his second appeal
1928 – Execution of Frederick Lock
1937 – Ruby Anne Keen's body found
1946 – Murder of Joyce Jacques
1952 – Execution of James Smith
1958 – Murder of Isiah Dixon

13TH

1905 – Bodies of Beatrice, Laurence and
  Evelyn Devereux found
1909 – Execution of Joseph Edwin Jones
1920 – Execution of Frederick Rothwell Holt
1922 – Trial of Herbert Rowse Armstrong ends
1926 – Execution of George Sharples
1944 – Execution of Sidney James Delasalle
1946 – Arrest of Walter Clayton

14TH

1902 – Trial of Charles Robert Earl ends
1902 – Trial of George Woolfe starts
1920 – Execution of Thomas Caler
1924 – Probable date of murder of
  Emily Beilby Kaye
1935 – Murder of Amelia Nuttall
1953 – Murder of Sarah Ricketts
1954 – Execution of James Reginald Doohan
1955 – Execution of Sydney Joseph Clarke
1958 – Linda Violet Ash is attacked

15TH

1913 – Murders of Andrew Barton, George
  Bertram Mussell and
  Sarah Ellen Grice
1925 – Execution of Henry Graham
1925 – Execution of Thomas Henry Shelton
1935 – John Stephenson Bainbridge
  loses his appeal
1942 – Execution of Cyril Johnson
1947 – Execution of David John Williams
1950 – Murder of Lily Irene Palmer
1954 – Original execution date for John Lynch
1957 – Murder of Jane Duckett
1958 – Linda Violet Ash dies

16TH

1902 – Trial of George Woolfe ends
1903 – Murder of John Flanagan
1910 – Arrest of Thomas Craig
1917 – Murders of Margaret Alderson Hodgson
  and Margaret Hodgson
1920 – Execution of Miles McHugh
1922 – Murder of Alice Gertrude Pountney
1931 – Execution of Francis Land
1935 – Execution of Percy Charles Anderson
1936 – Execution of Dorothea Nancy Waddingham

17TH

1909 – Arrest of Walter Davis
1917 – Execution of William James Robinson

18TH

1912 – Execution of Frederick Henry Seddon
1917 – Execution of Robert Gadsby
1922 – Execution of Edmund Hugh Tonbridge
1928 – Trial of Frederick Stewart
1944 – Trial of Ernest James Harman Kemp

19TH

1911 – Trial of Thomas Seymour
1924 – Arrest of Jean Pierre Vacquier
1950 – Execution of Albert Edward Jenkins
1951 – Trial of James Inglis starts

20TH

1907 – Murder of Richard Beck and Elizabeth Beck
1916 – Arrest of Roger David Casement
1935 – Maxine Louise Gann meets
       Allan James Grierson
1942 – Trial of Douglas Edmondson
1951 – Trial of James Inglis ends

21ST

1920 – Trial of William Waddington
1937 – Murder of Wilhelmina Vernadell Davis
       and Monica Rowe
1949 – Execution of Harry Lewis
1952 – Murder of Johanna Hallahan
1958 – Vivian Frederick Teed loses his appeal

22ND

1909 – Trial of Morris and Marks Reuben starts
1914 – Trial of Joseph Spooner
1920 – Trial of Herbert Edward Rawson Salisbury
1925 – Execution of John Norman Holmes Thorne
1930 – Execution of William Henry Podmore
1938 – Probable date of murders of Jane Ann
       Parker, Theresa Shirley Parker and
       Cecil Edward Parker
1954 – Execution of Albert George Hall
1960 – Murder of Lily Parry

23RD

1903 – Probable date of murder of Caroline Tuffen
1904 – Murder of Agnes Allen
1908 – Trial of John Ramsbottom
1909 – Trial of Morris and Marks Reuben ends
1913 – Execution of Walter William Sykes
1928 – Trial of Frederick Guy Browne and
       William Henry Kennedy starts
1951 – Trial of John Dand starts
1952 – Johanna Hallahan's body found
1954 – Execution of John Lynch

24TH

1917 – Trial of Thomas McGuiness starts
1937 – Murder of Kate Elizabeth Collier
1940 – Execution of William Charles Cowell
1946 – Execution of Martin Patrick Coffey
1961 – Trial of Zsiga Pankotia starts
1961 – Second trial of Samuel McLaughlin starts

25TH

1914 – Murder of Ada Stone
1917 – Trial of Thomas McGuiness ends
1922 – Murder of Ellen Thompson
1938 – Arrest of William Parker
1951 – Execution of Joseph Brown and
       Edward Charles Smith
1952 – Execution of Edward Devlin and
       Alfred Burns
1958 – Arrest of Frank Stokes

26TH

1905 – Execution of Alfred Bridgeman
1926 – Murder of Catherine Smith
1932 – Trial of Charles James Cowle
1951 – Trial of John Dand ends
1951 – Execution of James Virrels
1961 – Trial of Zsiga Pankotia ends

27TH

1899 – Samuel Douglas and Camille Holland
       move in to Moat House Farm
1903 – Camille Cecile Holland's body found
1905 – Ellen Maria Goodspeed attacked
1925 – Murder of William Plommer
1927 – Execution of William Knighton
1928 – Trial of Frederick Guy Browne and
       William Henry Kennedy ends
1931 – Trial of Alexander Anastassiou
1932 – Execution of George Emanuel Michael
1938 – Trial of Jan Mohamed
1942 – Trial of Gorden Frederick Cummins starts
1959 – Michael George Tatum loses his appeal

28TH

1911 – Trial of Michael Collins
1919 – Murders of Alice Cornish senior, Alice
       Cornish junior and Marie Cornish
1919 – Walter Cornish attacked
1922 – Trial of Henry Jacoby
1932 – Execution of Thomas Riley
1932 – Execution of John Henry Roberts
1942 – Trial of Gordon Frederick Cummins ends
1944 – Trial of Pierre Richard Charles Neukermans
       starts
1944 – Trial of Eliga Brinson and Willie Smith
       starts
1947 – Murder of Alec de Antiquis
1954 – Execution of Thomas Ronald Lewis Harries
1959 – Execution of Joseph Chrimes

29TH

1896 – Henry Starr found not guilty of the murder
       of Eleanor Coulthard
1902 – Execution of Charles Robert Earl
1910 – Trial of Thomas William Jesshope
1914 – Murder of Frances Priscilla Hunter
1943 – Execution of August Sangret
1944 – Trial of Eliga Brinson and Willie Smith ends
1945 – Murder of David Walker Dewar
1950 – Murder of Francis Henry Wilson
1961 – Second trial of Samuel McLaughlin ends

30TH

1919 – Walter Cornish dies
1937 – Bodies of Wilhelmina Vernadell Davis and Monica Rowe found
1938 – Execution of Charles James Caldwell
1942 – Execution of Frederick James Austin
1942 – Attack upon Leonard Moules

May

1ST

1920 – Murder of Evelyn Goslett
1933 – Trial of Jack Samuel Puttnam starts
1941 – Murder of Harry Distleman
1942 – Execution of Harold Hill
1944 – Trial of Pierre Richard Charles Neukermans ends
1955 – Murder of Clara Farrell
1959 – Arrest of Bernard Hugh Walden

2ND

1902 – Trial of Thomas Marsland
1909 – Murder of Emily Barnes Trewarthen Tredrea
1913 – Winifred Mary Mitchell's body found
1919 – Arrest of Henry Perry
1920 – Evelyn Goslett's body found
1921 – Trial of Thomas Wilson
1924 – Arrest of Patrick Herbert Mahon

3RD

1900 – Trial of Henry Grove
1923 – Murder of Nellie Pearce
1925 – Murder of Elizabeth Sherratt
1927 – Murder of Isabella Moore
1933 – Trial of Jack Samuel Puttnam ends
1933 – Richard Hetherington attempts suicide
1934 – Execution of Reginald Ivor Hinks
1935 – Trial of John Harris Bridge
1939 – Trial of Ralph Smith

4TH

1900 – Thomas Mellor and his family evicted from their home
1920 – Trial of Albert Fraser and James Rollins starts
1925 – Murder of Sarah Elizabeth Clutton
1927 – Murder of Minnie Alice Bonati
1932 – Execution of Maurice Freedman
1934 – Execution of Albert Probert and Frederick William Parker
1943 – Murder of Violet Wakefield
1955 – Execution of Winston Shaw
1962 – Murder of Sarah Isabella Cross

5TH

1905 – Trial of Alfred and Albert Stratton starts
1909 – Cecilia Harris dies
1920 – Trial of Albert Fraser and James Rollins ends
1943 – Murder of Vera Clarke

6TH

1902 – Execution of George Woolfe
1905 – Trial of Alfred and Albert Stratton ends
1919 – Four members of the Cornish family buried
1920 – Execution of Thomas Hargreaves Wilson
1921 – Execution of Frederick Quarmby
1935 – Murder of Amanda Sharp
1940 – Trial of Vincent Ostler and William Appleby starts
1952 – Trial of Patrick Gallagher Deveney
1958 – Execution of Vivian Frederick Teed

7TH

1903 – Caroline Tuffen's body found
1905 – Ellen Maria Goodspeed dies
1907 – Rhoda Willis abandons a child in Cardiff; the child later dies from exposure
1925 – Murder of Edith Horrocks-Wilkinson
1926 – Murder of Augusta Violette Pionbini
1935 – Arrest of George Hague
1952 – Execution of Ajit Singh

8TH

1909 – Execution of William Joseph Foy
1919 – Murder of Ellen Crossland
1924 – Execution of Michael Pratley
1924 – Trial of William Horsley Wardell starts
1925 – Trial of Hubert Ernest Dalton
1925 – Trial of Patrick Power
1928 – Trial of Walter Brooks
1935 – Murder of Bessie Gladys Nott
1941 – Trial of George Johnson Armstrong
1944 – Trial of John Gordon Davidson
1945 – Execution of George E. Smith
1947 – Trial of Eric Charles Briggs starts
1951 – Execution of James Inglis
1959 – Execution of Ronald Henry Marwood

9TH

1899 – Samuel Dougal takes on Florence Havis as a servant girl
1904 – Trial of William Kirwan
1911 – Execution of Thomas Seymour
1926 – Khannar Jung Baz attacks Hashankhan Samander
1927 – Minnie Alice Bonati's body found
1935 – Execution of John Stephenson Bainbridge
1938 – Robert William Hoolhouse loses his appeal
1942 – Leonard Moules dies
1944 – Trial of James Galbraith starts
1951 – Execution of William Edward Shaughnessy
1954 – Murder of Nellie Officer
1955 – James Robinson loses his appeal

10TH

1902 – Murder of Hannah Middleton
1904 – Trial of Ping Lun
1904 – Murder of Jane Hirst
1924 – Trial of William Horsely Wardell ends
1940 – Trial of Vincent Ostler and William Appleby ends
1943 – Trial of Charles Arthur Raymond starts
1952 – Trial of Kenneth Gilbert and Ian Arthur Grant

11TH

1900 – Murder of Ada Beecroft and Annie Beecroft
1902 – Hannah Middleton's body found
1920 – Execution of Herbert Edward Rawson Salisbury
1920 – Execution of William Waddington
1928 – Mary Alice Reed attacked
1944 – Trial of James Galbraith ends
1955 – Murder of Mary Georgina Roberts

12TH

1900 – Bodies of Ada and Annie Beecroft found in canal
1903 – Execution of William George Hudson
1903 – Trial of Gustav Rau and Willem Schmidt starts
1908 – Execution of John Ramsbottom
1909 – Murder of Emily Ramsbottom
1922 – Trial of Hiram Thompson
1928 – Chung Yi Miao marries Wai Sheung Sui
1929 – Murder of Mary Annie Johnson
1933 – Attack upon Boleslar Pankorski
1935 – Murder of Louisa Baguley
1936 – Execution of Buck Ruxton
1937 – Murder of Rosina Field
1949 – Trial of Dennis Neville
1958 – Trial of Peter Thomas Anthony Manuel starts
1961 – Murder of Hubert Roderick Twells Buxton and Alice Buxton
1961 – Trial of Edwin Albert Arthur Bush starts

13TH

1900 – Edith Margaret Poole attacked
1906 – Murder of Elizabeth Baldwin
1909 – Emily Ramsbottom's body found
1920 – Trial of William Thomas Aldred
1933 – Boleslar Pankorski dies
1936 – Trial of Frederick Herbert Charles Field
1947 – Trial of Eric Charles Briggs ends
1947 – Arrest of William Smedley
1961 – Bodies of Hubert Roderick Twells Buxton and Alice Buxton found
1961 – Trial of Edwin Albert Arthur Bush ends

14TH

1903 – Trial of Gustav Rau and Willem Schmidt ends
1914 – Execution of Joseph Spooner
1927 – James Staunton attacked
1929 – Murder of Leslie Godfrey White
1941 – Arrest of Karel Richard Richter
1943 – Trial of Charles Arthur Raymond ends
1959 – Execution of Michael George Tatum

15TH

1907 – The child abandoned by Rhoda Willis on the 7th dies
1909 – Mark Shawcross writes to the police confessing to murder
1913 – Murder of Ann Elizabeth Ryder
1937 – Arrest of Frederick George Murphy
1942 – Trial of Jose Estella Key and Alphonse Louis Eugene Timmerman starts

16TH

1910 – Murder of Elizabeth Ely
1912 – Alice Beetham ends her relationship with Arthur Birkett
1915 – Murder of Nora Barrett
1917 – Execution of Thomas McGuiness
1925 – Murder of Noorh Mohammed
1929 – Murder of James McCann
1942 – Johannes Marinus Dronkers leaves for England
1948 – Murder of June Anne Devaney

17TH

1910 – Elizabeth Ely's body found
1915 – Arrest of Frank Steele
1922 – Murder of George Stanley Grimshaw
1927 – James Staunton dies
1928 – Mary Alice Reed dies
1943 – Murder of Elsie Elphinstone Roe
1946 – Murder of Harry Berrisford
1957 – Murder of David Alan Keasey
1961 – Original execution date for Samuel McLaughlin

18TH

1904 – Murder of Dennis Lowthian
1932 – Execution of Charles James Cowle
1941 – Murder of Margaret Ellen Knight
1942 – Trial of Jose Estella Key and Alphonse Louis Eugene Timmerman ends
1944 – Murder of Nora Emily Payne
1949 – Trial of Bernard Alfred Peter Cooper

19TH

1899 – Murder of Camille Cecile Holland
1952 – Murder of Rose Margaret Meadows
1952 – Trial of Harry Huxley starts
1953 – Execution of John Todd
1954 – Murder of Kenneth Joseph George Mulligan

20TH

1902 – Execution of Thomas Marsland
1909 – Execution of Morris and Marks Reuben
1909 – Arrest of Mark Shawcross
1912 – Murder of Alice Beetham
1916 – Murder of Florence Beatrice Butler
1922 – William James Yeldham marries Elsie Florence
1935 – Trial of Walter Osmond Worthington
1941 – Probable date of murder of Phyllis Elizabeth Crocker and Eileen Alice Crocker.
1946 – Murder of Ella Valentine Staunton
1947 – Murder of Percy Baker and Alice Baker
1952 – Trial of Harry Huxley ends

21ST

1923 – Trial of John Henry Savage
1936 – Murder of Ellen Margaret Mary Whiting
1945 – Arrest of Thomas Eric Richardson

22ND

1900 – Execution of Henry Grove
1900 – Edith Margaret Poole dies
1903 – Murder of Maud Garrett

1930 – Trial of Albert Edward Marjeram
1931 – Murder of Isabella Aitken and Margaret Aitken
1934 – Arthur Major falls ill
1940 – Murder of Alice Wright
1950 – Trial of Roman Redel and Zbigniew Gower starts
1951 – Murder of William Gibson and attack upon Andrew Hope
1953 – Murder of Janet Mary Warner

23RD

1903 – Arrest of Bernard White
1905 – Execution of Alfred and Albert Stratton
1927 – Arrest of Frederick Stephen Fuller and James Murphy
1936 – Murder of Alice Whye
1944 – Trial of Joseph Jan Van Hove starts
1946 – Arrest of Thomas Hendren
1950 – Trial of Roman Redel and Zbigniew Gower ends
1957 – Trial of John Wilson Vickers

24TH

1910 – Murders of Jane Ellen Coulson and Thomas Coulson
1911 – Execution of Michael Collins
1921 – Execution of Thomas Wilson
1928 – Murder of Margaret Macauley and Sarah Macauley
1934 – Murder of Arthur Major
1944 – Trial of Joseph Jan Van Hove ends
1955 – Execution of James Robinson

25TH

1903 – Murder of William Ariel Wilkinson
1908 – Murder of Ellen Ann Ballington
1910 – Execution of Thomas William Jesshope
1923 – Murder of Catherine Hughes
1953 – Arrest of John Christopher Reynolds
1961 – Execution of Victor John Terry

26TH

1903 – Murder of Sarah Ann Pachett
1920 – Execution of Albert James Fraser and James Rollins
1925 – Execution of Patrick Power
1938 – Execution of Robert William Hoolhouse
1944 – Execution of Wiley Harris

27TH

1919 – Trial of Henry Perry
1936 – Trial of Charlotte Bryant starts
1952 – Execution of Backary Manneh

28TH

1910 – Trial of James Henry Hancock
1914 – Trial of Walter James White
1920 – Trial of Frederick William Storey starts
1945 – Arrest of William Joyce
1946 – Execution of Leonard Holmes
1946 – Murder of Dorothy Louisa Mildred Mason

29TH

1903 – Sarah Ann Patchett's body found
1915 – Arrest of Willem Johannes Roos
1920 – Trial of Frederick William Storey ends
1929 – Arrest of Samuel Cushnan
1931 – Probable date of murder of Herbert William Ayres
1933 – Trial of Richard Hetherington starts
1946 – Dorothy Louisa Mildred Mason's body found
1948 – Probable date of murder of Minnie Freeman Lee
1952 – Execution of Patrick Gallagher Deveney
1958 – Trial of Peter Thomas Anthony Manuel ends

30TH

1922 – Execution of Hiram Thompson
1922 – Murder of Margaret Fullerton
1935 – Execution of John Harris Bridge
1936 – Trial of Charlotte Bryant ends
1938 – Murder of Kathleen Richards
1944 – Execution of Alex F. Miranda
1950 – Trial of George Finlay Brown starts
1953 – Murder of Henry John Tandy

31ST

1904 – Execution of William Kirwan
1904 – Execution of Ping Lun
1905 – Trial of Alfred John Heal
1922 – Execution of Herbert Rowse Armstrong
1923 – Trial of Rowland Duck
1928 – Execution of Frederick Guy Browne and William Henry Kennedy
1933 – Trial of Richard Hetherington ends
1942 – Murder of Pauline Barker
1950 – Trial of George Finlay Brown ends
1950 – Trial of Ronald Douglas Atwell starts
1951 – Trial of Dennis Albert Reginald Moore starts
1953 – Murder of Edward Watson
1953 – Arrest of George James Newland
1953 – Murder of Barbara Songhurst and Christine Reed
1955 – Murder of Doris Acquilla Roberts
1963 – Murder of Thomas Guyan

June

1ST

1903 – Murder of Maud Luen
1911 – Trial of Arthur Garrod
1915 – Arrest of Haicke Janssen
1931 – Herbert William Ayres's body found
1946 – Arthur Robert Boyce moves in with Elizabeth McLindon
1948 – Minnie Freeman Lee's body found
1950 – Trial of Ronald Douglas Atwell ends
1951 – Trial of Dennis Albert Reginald Moore ends
1953 – Barbara Songhurst's body found
1954 – Trial of George Alexander Robertson starts

2ND

1903 – Execution of Gustav Rau and Willem Schmidt
1913 – Trial of Henry Longden
1915 – Trial of Carl Frederick Muller starts
1941 – Trial of David Miller Jennings starts
1949 – Execution of Dennis Neville
1953 – Murder of Beatrice Ann Court
1954 – Trial of George Alexander Robertson ends
1955 – Trial of Richard Gowler
1962 – Murder of Thomas Arthur Bates

3RD

1913 – Trial of William Walter Burton starts
1914 – Murder of Henry Pugsley
1922 – Margaret Fullerton's body found
1931 – Execution of Alexander Anastassiou
1941 – Trial of David Miller Jennings ends
1949 – Murder of Beryl Beechey
1950 – Murder of Doris Maude Price
1954 – Trial of Milton Taylor

4TH

1907 – Murder of the otherwise unnamed Treasure child
1913 – Trial of William Walter Burton ends
1915 – Trial of Carl Frederick Muller ends
1915 – Arrest of George T Breeckow
1928 – Trial of William John Maynard starts
1940 – Trial of Udham Singh starts
1949 – Beryl Beechey's body found
1951 – Trial of Alfred George Reynolds

5TH

1913 – Bodies of William Higgins and John Higgins found
1915 – Murder of Nellie Marriott
1915 – Arrest of Fernando Buschman
1926 – Murder of John Richard Thompson
1928 – Trial of William John Maynard ends
1928 – Murder of Isabella Wales
1935 – Trial of Arthur Henry Franklin
1940 – Trial of Udham Singh ends
1949 – Murder of Beatrice May Watts
1950 – Murder of Jennifer Valerie Price and Maureen Ann Price
1961 – Zsiga Pankotia loses his appeal

6TH

1903 – Murder of William Swann
1926 – John Richard Thompson's body found
1928 – Execution of Frederick Stewart
1937 – Mona Lilian Tinsley's body found
1944 – Execution of Ernest James Harman Kemp
1945 – Murder of Frederick Benjamin Lucas and Cissie Clara Lucas
1949 – Beatrice May Watts's body found
1952 – Murder of Maureen Jones Cox
1953 – Christine Reed's body found

7TH

1901 – John Joyce charged with assault
1908 – Murder of Jane Wallace
1909 – Trial of John Edmunds

1913 – Trial of Thomas Fletcher
1922 – Execution of Henry Julius Jacoby
1925 – Murder of Francis Edward Rix
1926 – Arrest of Charles Edward Finden
1933 – Trial of Frederick Morse starts
1939 – Execution of Ralph Smith

8TH

1900 – Probable date of murder of Mary Ann Blewitt
1909 – Trial of Alexander Edmundstone starts
1925 – Arrest of Arthur Henry Bishop
1933 – Trial of Frederick Morse ends
1933 – Execution of Jack Samuel Puttnam
1938 – Execution of Jan Mohamed
1942 – Douglas Edmondson loses his appeal
1946 – Murder of Elizabeth McLindon
1948 – Murder of Sillvinea May Parry
1955 – Murder of Evelyn Patricia Higgins

9TH

1908 – Murder of Gertrude Siddle
1909 – Trial of Alexander Edmundstone ends
1910 – The missing money bag in the Innes murder case found down a pit shaft
1945 – Arrest of John Riley Young
1948 – Sillvinea May Parry's body found
1948 – Arrest of Clifford Godfrey Wills

10TH

1901 – Murder of John Nugent
1924 – Murder of Norman Widdowson Pinchin
1925 – Execution of Hubert Ernest Dalton

11TH

1904 – George Breeze moves in with the Chisholm family
1909 – Trial of Walter Davis
1911 – Murder of Alice Emily Brewster
1919 – Murder of Minnie Foster
1923 – Execution of John Henry Savage
1930 – Execution of Albert Edward Marjeram
1941 – William Anderson attacked
1951 – Trial of Jack Wright starts
1955 – Arrest of Ernest Charles Harding
1958 – Murder of Martha Annie Dodd

12TH

1911 – Trial of William Henry Palmer starts
1914 – Arthur Goslett marries Evelyn Mear
1925 – Murder of Alice Garnett
1941 – Trial of Karl Theodore Drucke and Werner Henrich Walti starts
1951 – Trial of Jack Wright ends
1951 – Execution of John Dand
1955 – Evelyn Patricia Higgins's body found

13TH

1911 – Trial of William Henry Palmer ends
1941 – Arrest of Edward Walter Anderson
1941 – Trial of Karl Theodore Drucke and Werner Henrich Walti ends
1942 – Murder of Margaret Mary Rice
1946 – Elizabeth McLindon's body found

1950 – Arrest of Albert Price

14TH

1910 – Execution of James Henry Hancock

15TH

1910 – Trial of Frederick Foreman
1925 – Clara Squires and Alice Mabel Squires attacked
1928 – Trial of Albert George Absalom
1937 – Trial of Philip Edward Percy Davis
1945 – Execution of Aniceto Martinez
1952 – Murder of Krystyna Skarbek

16TH

1914 – Execution of Walter James White
1920 – Execution of Frederick William Storey
1926 – Trial of Johannes Josephus Cornelius Mommers
1928 – Murder of Elsie Cook
1938 – Trial of William Parker starts
1948 – Murder of Florence May Bentley
1949 – Trial of Sydney Archibald Frederick Chamberlain starts
1953 – Trial of Philip Henry starts

17TH

1900 – Body of Mary Ann Blewitt found
1901 – Trial of Valeri Giovanni
1905 – Murder of Hadjou Idder
1925 – Clara Squires dies
1933 – Ernest Wadge Parker released from prison
1938 – Trial of William Parker ends
1944 – Murder of James E. Alexander
1949 – Trial of Sydney Archibald Frederick Chamberlain ends
1954 – Execution of Kenneth Gilbert and Ian Arthur Grant

18TH

1924 – Execution of William Horsely Wardell
1925 – Trial of James Winstanley starts
1943 – Trial of Gerald Elphistone Roe
1953 – Trial of Philip Henry ends

19TH

1903 – Trial of Charles Howell
1916 – Murder of Alice Clara Gregory
1924 – Trial of Abraham Goldenberg
1928 – Murder of Wai Sheung Sui
1936 – Probable date of murder of Ruth Clarkson
1941 – William Anderson dies
1944 – Trial of William Frederick George Meffen
1958 – Original execution date for Peter Thomas Anthony Manuel

20TH

1905 – Execution of Alfred John Heal
1911 – Execution of Arthur Garrod
1923 – Murder of John Johnston
1925 – Trial of James Winstanley ends
1933 – Execution of Richard Hetherington
1947 – Execution of Eric Charles Briggs
1955 – Trial of Ruth Ellis starts

1955 – Trial of Alec Wilkinson starts

21ST

1917 – Henry Arthur Hollyer attacked
1920 – Trial of Arthur Andrew Clement Goslett starts
1946 – Murder of Margery Aimee Brownell Gardner
1949 – Execution of Bernard Alfred Peter Cooper
1952 – Murder of Victor Brades and attack upon Eunice Marjorie Joyce Simon
1955 – Trial of Ruth Ellis ends
1955 – Trial of Kenneth Roberts starts
1955 – Execution of Richard Gowler

22ND

1900 – Murder of Catherine Amelia Irwin
1903 – Trial of Samuel Herbert Dougal starts
1904 – Trial of Samuel Rowledge
1915 – Trial of George Joseph Smith starts
1920 – Execution of William Thomas Aldred
1920 – Trial of Arthur Andrew Clement Goslett ends
1922 – Murder of Henry Wilson
1935 – Louise Berthe Gann attacked
1936 – Ruth Clarkson's body found
1950 – Trial of John Walker
1952 – Eunice Marjorie Joyce Simon dies
1952 – Trial of Frank Burgess
1953 – Trial of John Reginald Halliday Christie starts
1954 – Execution of Milton Taylor
1955 – Trial of Kenneth Roberts ends

23RD

1903 – Trial of Samuel Herbert Dougal ends
1904 – Trial of John Sullivan
1908 – Trial of Edward Johnstone
1913 – Murder of Matilda Penny
1915 – Execution of Carl Frederick Muller
1919 – Murder of Zee Ming Wu
1923 – Murder of William Ronald Cree
1935 – Louise Berthe Gann dies
1941 – George Johnson Armstrong loses his appeal
1942 – Trial of Arthur Anderson
1943 – Arrest of Mervin Clare McEwen
1944 – Execution of Pierre Richard Charles Neukermans
1952 – Trial of Thomas Eames
1954 – Execution of George Alexander Robertson

24TH

1909 – Walter Davis loses his appeal
1909 – Trial of William Hampton
1913 – Execution of William Walter Burton
1926 – Execution of Louie Calvert
1931 – Trial of William Shelley and Oliver Newman starts
1936 – Trial of George Arthur Bryant
1942 – Execution of Douglas Edmondson
1954 – Trial of Harold Fowler starts

25TH

1902 – Trial of Samuel Middleton
1902 – Murder of Nancy Price

929

1907 – Trial of William Edward Slack
1910 – Trial of Thomas Craig
1917 – Henry Arthur Hollyer dies
1919 – Trial of Thomas Foster
1928 – Trial of George Reynolds starts
1931 – Trial of William Shelley and Oliver Newman ends
1933 – Murder of Lily Parker
1935 – Execution of Arthur Henry Franklin
1938 – Trial of Alfred Ernest Richards
1942 – Execution of Gordon Frederick Cummins
1943 – Execution of Harold A. Smith
1946 – Trial of John Caldwell starts
1952 – Murder of Kathleen Vera Norcliffe
1953 – Murder of Charlotte Ball
1953 – Trial of John Reginald Halliday Christie ends
1954 – Trial of Harold Fowler ends
1958 – Peter Thomas Anthony Manuel loses his appeal
1960 – Allan Edward John Jee attacked

26TH

1902 – Nancy Price's body found. John Bedford arrested
1902 – Murder of Elizabeth Dyson
1916 – Trial of Roger David Casement starts
1928 – Trial of Norman Elliott starts
1944 – Trial of William Alfred Cowle
1946 – Trial of John Caldwell ends

27TH

1900 – Trial of Alfred Highfield
1901 – Murder of Amy Eugenie Russell
1919 – Zee Ming Wu's body found
1924 – Murder of Rosa Armstrong
1928 – Trial of Norman Elliott ends
1928 – Trial of George Reynolds ends
1928 – Original execution date of William John Maynard
1933 – Trial of Varnavas Antorka starts
1938 – Trial of William James Graves
1946 – Trial of Thomas Hendren
1960 – Allan Edward John Jee dies

28TH

1902 – Miriam Jane Tye attacked
1913 – Probable date of murders of Nellie Kathleen Robertson, Frederick Ernest Robertson and Beatrice Maud Robertson
1924 – Arrest of Arthur Simms
1928 – Execution of Walter Brooks
1935 – Trial of George Hague starts
1937 – Trial of Leslie George Stone starts
1952 – Murder of Charles Mead

29TH

1903 – Trial of Thomas Porter and Thomas Preston starts
1907 – Murder of Lilian Jane Charlton
1916 – Trial of Roger David Casement ends
1935 – Trial of George Hague ends
1936 – Charlotte Bryant loses her appeal
1937 – Trial of Leslie George Stone ends

1952 – Murder of Jean Frances Cull
1955 – Trial of Alec Wilkinson ends
1961 – Execution of Zsiga Pankotia

30TH

1902 – Miriam Jane Tye dies
1903 – Trial of Thomas Porter and Thomas Preston ends
1914 – Murder of Harriett Ann Whybrow
1933 – Trial of Varnavas Antorka ends
1934 – Murder of Edith Kate Longshaw
1936 – Execution of Frederick Herbert Charles Field
1936 – Murder of Harriett May Ferris Linney
1937 – Trial of Frederick George Murphy starts
1941 – Bodies of Phyllis Elizabeth Crocker and Eileen Alice Crocker found
1946 – Arthur Rushton becomes engaged to Catherine Cooper
1959 – Trial of Bernard Hugh Walden starts
1955 – Trial of Norman William Green starts

July

1ST

1908 – Trial of Matthew James Dodds
1909 – Murder of William Hutt Curzon-Wylie and Doctor Cawas Lalcaca
1915 – Trial of George Joseph Smith ends
1935 – Arrest of Allan James Grierson
1959 – Trial of Bernard Hugh Walden ends
1964 – Trial of Peter Anthony Allen and Gwynne Owen Evans starts

2ND

1902 – Trial of William Churcher
1904 – Murder of Susan Humphries
1913 – Trial of John Vickers Amos starts
1915 – Arrest of Ludovico Zender
1924 – Trial of Jean Pierre Vacquier starts
1926 – Trial of James Smith
1927 – Murder of Olive Gordon Turner
1929 – Trial of James Johnson starts
1931 – Trial of William John Corbett
1937 – Trial of Horace William Brunt
1937 – Trial of Frederick George Murphy ends
1945 – Trial of Joachim Palme-Goltz, Josep Mertins, Heintz Brueling, Erich Koenig and Kurt Zuchlsdorff starts
1958 – Trial of Matthew Kavanagh starts

3RD

1900 – Arrest of Charles Oliver Blewitt
1905 – Murder of Rebecca Tattersall
1909 – Execution of John Edmunds
1913 – Trial of John Vickers Amos ends
1915 – Murder of Alice Anderson
1919 – Trial of John Crossland
1922 – Trial of Thomas Henry Allaway starts
1923 – Trial of Hassen Mohamed
1923 – Trial of Albert Edward Burrows starts
1927 – Olive Gordon Turner's body found
1929 – Trial of James Johnson ends
1936 – Trial of Wallace Jenden

1951 – Execution of Jack Wright
1958 – Trial of Matthew Kavanagh ends

4TH

1909 – Thomas Craig writes a threatening letter to Annie Finn
1910 – Trial of John Alexander Dickman starts
1919 – Trial of Henry Thomas Gaskin
1923 – Execution of Rowland Duck
1923 – Trial of William Griffiths
1923 – Trial of Albert Edward Burrows ends
1939 – Murder of Mabel Maud Bundy
1941 – Trial of Antonio Mancini
1946 – Murder of Doreen Marshall
1952 – Trial of Oliver George Butler

5TH

1904 – Trial of Thomas Gunning
1904 – Second trial of Joseph Fee starts
1912 – Trial of Arthur Birkett
1913 – Trial of James Ryder
1915 – Murder of Harriett Reeve
1924 – Trial of Jean Pierre Vacquier ends
1926 – Trial of Charles Edward Finden starts
1927 – Trial of Frederick Stephen Fuller and James Murphy
1940 – John Joseph Harrison attacked
1954 – Trial of Edward Lindsay Reid starts
1955 – Trial of Frederick Arthur Cross
1955 – Trial of Norman William Green ends

6TH

1900 – Murder of Pauline Lacey
1903 – Trial of Leonard Pachett
1904 – Murder of Margaret Jane Chisholm
1909 – Trial of Mark Shawcross
1910 – Trial of John Alexander Dickman ends
1915 – Trial of Robert Rosenthal
1915 – Trial of Frank Steele
1920 – Trial of James Ellor starts
1926 – Trial of Charles Edward Finden ends
1934 – John George Haigh marries
1946 – Arrest of Neville George Clevelly Heath
1954 – Trial of Edward Lindsay Reid ends
1961 – Execution of Edwin Albert Arthur Bush

7TH

1901 – Murder of Louisa Claydon
1903 – Execution of Charles Howell
1907 – James and Ada Ellor marry
1908 – Trial of Frederick Ballington
1909 – Murder of Cissie Archer
1914 – Trial of Herbert Brooker
1922 – Trial of Elijah Pountney
1922 – Trial of Thomas Henry Allaway ends
1933 – Murder of Grace Ivy Newing
1942 – Execution of Jose Estella Key and Alphonse Louis Eugene Timmerman
1945 – Arrest of John Amery
1950 – Execution of Roman Redel and Zbigniew Gower
1950 – Murder of Martin Dunleavy
1952 – Trial of John Howard Godar starts
1964 – Trial of Peter Anthony Allen and Gwynne

Owen Evans ends

8TH

1904 – Second trial of Joseph Fee ends
1910 – Chief Inspector Walter Dew visits Hawley Harvey Crippen at Hilldrop Crescent, London
1913 – Execution of Henry Longden
1914 – Trial of Percy Evelyn Clifford
1916 – Catherine Sullivan attacked
1920 – Trial of James Ellor ends
1929 – Trial of Arthur Leslie Raveney
1931 – Trial of Thomas Dornan starts
1941 – Trial of John Smith
1946 – Neville George Clevelly Heath charged with murder
1946 – Doreen Marshall's body found
1950 – Murder of Ruth Massey
1952 – Execution of Harry Huxley
1952 – Trial of John Howard Godar ends

9TH

1901 – Execution of Valeri Giovanni
1903 – Start of second trial of Joseph Moran
1906 – Murder of Eliza Marsh
1909 – Execution of Walter Davis
1910 – Hawley Harvey Crippen and Ethel Le Neve flee London
1913 – Execution of Thomas Fletcher
1916 – Catherine Sullivan dies
1926 – Murder of Khannar Jung Baz
1941 – Execution of George Johnson Armstrong
1950 – Ruth Massey's body found

10TH

1900 – John William Kew attacked
1909 – Murders of Matilda Lambert, John Lambert, Annie Lambert and Samuel Lambert
1914 – Murder of James Warren
1919 – Execution of Henry Perry
1926 – Murder of Winifred Jones
1928 – Trial of William Smiley
1935 – Execution of Walter Osmond Worthington
1935 – Murder of Hilda Meek
1943 – Execution of Charles Arthur Raymond
1951 – David Ware attempts murder near Bristol

11TH

1900 – John William Kew dies
1902 – Trial of John Bedford
1903 – Murder of Jane Haywood
1917 – Trial of William Thomas Hodgson starts
1918 – Murder of Ruth Elizabeth Moore
1927 – Murder of Minnie Eleanor Kirby
1927 – Trial of John Robinson starts
1931 – Trial of Thomas Dornan ends
1940 – Execution of Vincent Ostler and William Appleby
1941 – Trial of Edward Walker Anderson starts
1945 – Trial of Howard John Grossley starts
1945 – Murder of Vera Guest
1950 – Execution of George Finlay Brown
1958 – Execution of Peter Thomas Anthony Manuel

12TH

1901 – Trial of Charles Richard Thomas Watkins
1904 – Execution of John Sullivan
1910 – Execution of Thomas Craig
1915 – Trial of William Allen Butler
1927 – Minnie Eleanor Kirby's body found
1938 – Execution of Alfred Ernest Richards
1941 – Trial of Edward Walker Anderson ends
1943 – Trial of William Quayle
1943 – Trial of Trevor Elvin
1944 – Execution of Joseph Jan Van Hove
1944 – Execution of John Gordon Davidson
1945 – Trial of Joachim Palme-Goltz,
    Josep Mertins, Heintz Brueling,
    Erich Koenig and Kurt Zuchlsdorff ends.
1945 – Trial of Howard John Grossley ends
1949 – Trial of Rex Harvey Jones
1950 – Trial of Albert Price
1955 – Execution of Kenneth Roberts

13TH

1904 – Execution of Samuel Rowledge
1905 – Trial of Ferat Mohamed Ben Ali
1905 – Patrick Durkin attacked
1912 – Murder of Beatrice Constance Annie Mundy
1917 – Trial of William James Hodgson ends
1927 – Trial of John Robinson ends
1938 – Probable date of murder of Rose Muriel Atkins
1943 – Murder of Bridget Nora Mitton
1949 – Trial of Robert Thomas Mackintosh
1950 – Execution of Ronald Douglas Atwell
1950 – Execution of John Walker
1955 – Execution of Ruth Ellis
1959 – Murder of Raymond William Purdy

14TH

1903 – Execution of Samuel Herbert Dougal
1908 – Trial of Thomas Siddle
1910 – Execution of Frederick Foreman
1913 – Trial of Frank Greening
1936 – Execution of George Arthur Bryant
1941 – Murder of Nellie Thorpe
1943 – Murder of Doris M Staples
1949 – Trial of William John Davies

15TH

1902 – Execution of Samuel Middleton
1910 – Murder of Isabella Wilson
1911 – Charles Coleman released from prison
1911 – Murder of Rose Anna Gurney
1915 – Execution of Robert Rosenthal
1924 – Trial of Patrick Herbert Mahon starts
1936 – Execution of Charlotte Bryant
1942 – Murder of Shiela Margaret Wilson
1944 – Trial of Benjamin Pyegate
1945 – Arrest of Ronald Bertram Mauri
1951 – Murder of Duncan A. Fraser and
    attack upon Arthur Jagger
1952 – Execution of Thomas Eames
1953 – Execution of John Reginald Halliday
    Christie

16TH

1904 – Trial of George Breeze
1907 – Execution of William Edward Slack

1907 – Trial of Charles Paterson
1907 – Murder of Unity Annie Butler
1909 – Execution of Alexander Edmundstone
1911 – Edward Hill marries Mary Jane
1912 – Murder of Minnie Morris
1915 – Trial of Haicke Janssen and Willem Roos
    starts
1925 – Trial of Arthur Henry Bishop
1928 – George Reynolds loses his appeal
1935 – Execution of George Hague
1940 – Trial of George Edward Roberts starts
1943 – Pierre Richard Charles Neukermans arrives
    in London
1945 – Trial of Thomas Eric Richardson starts
1946 – Trial of Walter Clayton
1951 – Arthur Jagger dies
1952 – Murder of Alice Wiltshaw
1959 – Arrest of Guenther Fritz Erwin Podola

17TH

1900 – Execution of Alfred Highfield
1906 – Trial of Edward Glynn
1915 – Trial of Haicke Janssen and Willem Roos
    ends
1922 – Trial of William James Yeldham starts
1924 – Trial of John Charles Horner
1925 – Trial of William John Cronin
1940 – Trial of George Edward Roberts ends
1942 – Trial of Harold Oswald Merry starts
1942 – Rachel Dobkin's body found
1942 – Trial of Samuel Sydney Dashwood and
    George William Silverosa starts
1946 – Execution of Thomas Hendren
1960 – Murder of Louise Surgey
1961 – Trial of Henryk Niemasz starts

18TH

1906 – Murder of Pierre Le Guen
1911 – Murder of Rosetta Tarkenter
1913 – Trial of Hugh McLaren
1922 – Trial of Joseph O'Sullivan and
    Reginald Dunne
1928 – George Reynolds's original execution date
1942 – Trial of Harold Oswald Merry ends
1945 – Trial of Thomas Eric Richardson ends
1946 – Trial of Sydney John Smith
1949 – Trial of John George Haigh starts
1952 – Oliver George Butler loses his appeal
1960 – Trial of John Louis Constantine starts

19TH

1905 – Patrick Durkin dies
1906 – Pierre Le Guen's body found
1911 – Execution of William Henry Palmer
1915 – Trial of Walter Marriott
1922 – Trial of William James Yeldham ends
1924 – Trial of Patrick Herbert Mahon ends
1933 – Murder of Frances Levin
1938 – Execution of William James Graves
1946 – Harry Berrisford's body found
1949 – Trial of John George Haigh ends
1951 – Execution of Alfred George Reynolds
1951 – Execution of Dennis Albert Reginald Moore
1954 – Trial of William Sanchez de Pina Hepper
    starts

1960 – Arrest of Norman Harris and
Francis Forsyth

20TH

1905 – Trial of William Alfred Hancocks
1908 – Trial of John Berryman starts
1909 – Execution of William Hampton
1915 – Trial of George Marshall
1942 – Shiela Margaret Wilson's body found
1946 – John Caldwell loses his appeal
1946 – Murder of Mona Victoria Vanderstay
1953 – Trial of Louisa May Merrifield starts
1961 – Trial of Henryk Niemasz ends

21ST

1903 – Execution of Thomas Porter and
Thomas Preston
1906 – Trial of Thomas Acomb Mouncer
1909 – Trial of Julius Wammer
1910 – Trial of John Raper Coulson
1912 – Murder of Rosabella Smith
1923 – Murder of Mabel Jennings Edmunds
1930 – Attack upon William Thomas Andrews
1940 – John Joseph Harrison dies
1941 – Trial of Eli Richards starts
1942 – Arrest of Patrick William Kingston
1942 – Trial of Samuel Sydney Dashwood and
George William Silverosa ends
1942 – Execution of Arthur Anderson
1946 – Mona Victoria Vanderstay's body found
1947 – Trial of Christopher James Geraghty and
Charles Henry Jenkins starts
1947 – Trial of William Smedley starts
1953 – Murder of Betty Selina Smith
1955 – Trial of Ernest Charles Harding
1958 – Trial of Frank Stokes starts
1960 – Louise Surgey's body found

22ND

1902 – Execution of William Churcher
1902 – Trial of William Lane
1903 – Trial of William Joseph Tuffen
1905 – Murder of Alice Clover
1907 – Trial of Richard Clifford Brinkley starts
1908 – Trial of John Berryman ends
1909 – Trial of Richard Justin
1911 – Murder of Mary Elizabeth Speller
1913 – Execution of John Vickers Amos
1916 – Trial of Daniel Sullivan
1919 – Execution of John Crossland
1922 – Trial of Simon McGeown
1927 – Trial of Arthur Harnett
1941 – Trial of Eli Richards ends
1946 – Trial of David Baillie Mason starts
1947 – Trial of William Smedley ends
1950 – Murder of Julia Beesley
1952 – Execution of Frank Burgess
1952 – Trial of Mahmood Hussein Mattan starts
1954 – Trial of William Sanchez de Pina Hepper
ends
1955 – Trial of Corbett Montague Roberts

23RD

1897 – Murder of Eliza Cuthbert

1901 – Trial of Ernest Walter Wickham
1907 – Trial of Rhoda Willis starts
1909 – Trial of Madar Lal Dhingra
1910 – Mary Jenkin attacked
1912 – Execution of Arthur Birkett
1928 – Trial of Allen Wales
1950 – Julia Beesley's body found
1950 – Arrest of Patrick Turnage
1957 – Execution of John Wilson Vickers
1958 – Trial of Frank Stokes ends
1959 – Original execution date for
Bernard Hugh Walden
1963 – Trial of Henry John Burnett starts

24TH

1902 – Trial of George William Hibbs
1907 – Trial of Rhoda Willis ends
1910 – Mary Jenkin dies
1923 – Execution of William Griffiths
1925 – Trial of Alfred David Bostock starts
1930 – William Thomas Andrews dies
1941 – Execution of David Miller Jennings
1951 – Trial of Robert Dobie Smith starts
1952 – Trial of Mahmood Hussein Mattan ends
1953 – Betty Selina Smith's body found

25TH

1907 – Trial of Richard Clifford Brinkley ends
1911 – Murder of Mary Jane Hill
1919 – Djang Djing Sung tries to kill
Kuo Doung Dsou
1921 – Trial of Lester Augustus Hamilton
1925 – Trial of James Makin
1925 – Trial of Alfred David Bostock ends
1928 – Execution of Albert George Absalom
1930 – Oliver Preston attacked
1933 – Execution of Frederick Morse
1938 – Arrest of George Brain
1940 – Trial of John William Wright
1943 – Trial of Charles Eugene Gauthier
1946 – Trial of David Baillie Mason ends
1961 – Execution of Samuel McLaughlin
1963 – Trial of Henry John Burnett ends

26TH

1904 – Execution of Thomas Gunning
1905 – Trial of Arthur Devereux starts
1911 – Murder of Margaret Phillips
1912 – Murder of Rose Philp
1913 – Murder of Daniel Wright Bardsley
1915 – Murder of James Crawford
1924 – Murder of Elizabeth Southgate
1938 – Execution of William Parker
1944 – Execution of James Galbraith
1944 – Beatrice Maud Reynolds is raped
1952 – Murder of Stephanie Marie Small
1954 – Trial of Rupert Geoffrey Wells starts
1955 – Execution of Frederick Arthur Cross

27TH

1900 – Trial of William James Irwin
1900 – Trial of Charles Benjamin Backhouse
1901 – Murder of Alice Ann Wright
1914 – Percy Evelyn Clifford loses his appeal

1920 – Execution of Arthur Andrew
Clement Goslett
1925 – Murder of Beatrice Philomena Martin
1926 – Execution of Johannes Josephus
Cornelius Mommers
1928 – Execution of William John Maynard
1932 – Murder of Minnie Reid
1933 – Arrest of William Burtoft
1937 – Execution of Philip Edward Percy Davis
1944 – Arrest of Madison Thomas
1951 – Trial of Robert Dobie Smith ends
1955 – Execution of Norman William Green

28TH

1900 – Trial of Thomas Mellor
1903 – Execution of Leonard Pachett
1908 – Execution of Frederick Ballington
1913 – Murder of Martha Jane Beeby
1914 – Execution of Herbert Brooker
1919 – Murder of Lucy Nightingale
1925 – Trial of Wilfred Fowler and
Lawrence Fowler starts
1930 – Oliver Preston dies
1937 – Horace William Brunt loses his appeal
1942 – Trial of Thomas Joseph Williams starts
1947 – Trial of Christopher James Geraghty and
Charles Henry Jenkins ends
1947 – Trial of John Edward Gartside starts
1949 – Execution of Sydney Archibald Frederick
Chamberlain
1950 – Murder of Catherine McCluskey
1954 – Harold Fowler loses his appeal
1954 – Trial of Rupert Geoffrey Wells ends

29TH

1904 – Trial of John Thomas Kay
1904 – Trial of Samuel Holden
1904 – Murder of John Dalby
1905 – Trial of Arthur Devereux ends
1905 – Trial of Thomas George Tattersall
1919 – Lucy Nightingale's body found
1922 – Murder of Winifred Drinkwater
1923 – John Joseph Clarke attacked
1947 – Trial of John Edward Gartside ends
1950 – Catherine McCluskey's body found
1952 – Trial of Donald Neil Simon
1954 – Murder of Hella Christofi

30TH

1900 – First trial of Charles Oliver Blewitt
1901 – Execution of Charles Richard
Thomas Watkins
1902 – Execution of John Bedford
1908 – George Joseph Smith marries Edith Pegler
1915 – Execution of Haicke Janssen and
Willem Roos
1922 – Arrest of George Frederick Edisbury
1923 – Mabel Jennings Edmunds's body found
1923 – John Joseph Clarke dies
1924 – Execution of Abraham Goldenberg
1942 – Trial of Thomas Joseph Williams ends
1943 – Murder of Florence Elizabeth Agnes Dorgan
1953 – Execution of Philip Henry

31ST

1901 – Trial of John Joyce
1908 – Murder of Thomas Wilkinson
1910 – Murder of Mary Thompson
1910 – Hawley Harvey Crippen and
Ethel Le Neve arrested
1919 – Execution of Thomas Foster
1921 – Murder of Thomas O'Connor
1925 – Trial of Wilfred Fowler and
Lawrence Fowler ends
1931 – Execution of Thomas Dornan
1940 – Execution of Udham Singh
1941 – Execution of Edward Walker Anderson
1943 – Florence Elizabeth Agnes Dorgan's
body found
1943 – Arrest of John Joseph Dorgan
1953 – Trial of Louisa May Merrifield ends

August
1ST

1902 – Samuel Dougal divorces his wife,
Sarah White
1905 – Execution of Ferat Mohamed Ben Ali
1908 – Arrest of John William Ellwood
1910 – Mary Thompson's body found
1910 – Arrest of Henry Thompson
1919 – Murder of Mary Doyle
1925 – William Clark marries Frances
1931 – Murder of Alice Louisa Kempson
1951 – Murder of Shiela Ethel Attwood

2ND

1900 – Trial of William Augustus Lacey
1904 – Execution of George Breeze
1919 – Arrest of James Adams
1951 – Shiela Ethel Attwood's body found
1955 – Execution of Corbett Montague Roberts

3RD

1909 – Execution of Mark Shawcross
1916 – Execution of Roger David Casement
1925 – Alice Mabel Squires dies
1927 – Execution of Frederick Stephen Fuller and
James Murphy
1928 – Execution of George Reynolds
1931 – Alice Louisa Kempson's body found
1932 – Minnie Reid's body found
1943 – Execution of William Quayle
1943 – Execution of Gerald Elphinstone Roe
1949 – Murder of Victor Desmond Elias
1951 – Murder of Mabel Tattershaw

4TH

1903 – Arrest of John Gallagher
1908 – Execution of Thomas Siddle
1920 – Herbert Rowse Armstrong buys three tins
of arsenic
1941 – Trial of Josef Jakobs starts
1949 – Execution of Rex Harvey Jones
1949 – Execution of Robert Thomas Mackintosh

5TH

1905 – Murder of Mary Fallon

1908 – Execution of Matthew James Dodds
1925 – Execution of James Winstanley
1925 – Arthur Calvert marries Louie
1931 – Execution of William Shelley and
Oliver Newman
1936 – Execution of Wallace Jenden
1941 – Execution of Josef Jakobs ends

6TH

1900 – Second trial of Charles Oliver Blewitt starts
1941 – Execution of Karl Theodore Drucke and
Werner Henrich Walti
1944 – Agnes Cope is raped

7TH

1892 – Samuel Dougal marries his third wife,
Sarah White.
1900 – Second trial of Charles Oliver Blewitt ends
1906 – Murder of Catherine Hartigan
1906 – Execution of Edward Glynn
1907 – Execution of Charles Paterson
1929 – Execution of James Johnson
1934 – Murder of Dudley Henry Hoard
1937 – Murder of Kitty Constance Bennett
1945 – Trial of Armin Kuehne and Emil
Schmittendorf starts
1946 – Execution of Walter Clayton

8TH

1903 – Murder of Eliza Range
1919 – Execution of Henry Thomas Gaskin
1923 – Execution of Albert Edward Burrows
1923 – Execution of Hassen Mohamed
1928 – Execution of William Smiley
1940 – Execution of George Edward Roberts
1944 – Execution of William Alfred Cowle
1944 – Execution of William Frederick
George Meffen

9TH

1903 – Arrest of Charles Wood Whittaker
1905 – Execution of William Alfred Hancocks
1906 – Execution of Thomas Acomb Mouncer
1910 – Execution of John Raper Coulson
1910 – Execution of John Alexander Dickman
1916 – Murder of Caroline McGhee
1919 – Murder of Elizabeth Ann Quinn
1951 – Mabel Tattershaw's body found
1955 – Execution of Ernest Charles Harding

10TH

1909 – Execution of Julius Wammer
1915 – Execution of Walter Marriott
1915 – Arrest of Irving Guy Ries
1922 – Execution of Joseph O'Sullivan and
Reginald Dunne
1926 – Execution of James Smith
1928 – Execution of Norman Elliott
1933 – Execution of Varnavas Antorka
1945 – Samuel Hammond Gray returns
home to Bradford
1945 – Charles Elphick returns home to Portslade
1946 – Execution of John Caldwell
1949 – Execution of John George Haigh

11TH

1903 – Execution of William Joseph Tuffen
1905 – Murder of Mary Jane Welsh
1909 – Murder of Elizabeth Ann Patrick
1914 – Execution of Percy Evelyn Clifford
1915 – Execution of Frank Steele
1917 – Murder of Elizabeth Cox
1919 – Murder of Rebecca Jane Quinn
1920 – Execution of James Ellor
1922 – Execution of Elijah Pountney
1925 – Execution of James Makin
1944 – Execution of Eliga Brinson and Willie Smith
1950 – Murder of Emma Howe
1951 – Murder of Eugenie Le Maire
1954 – Execution of William Sanchez
de Pina Hepper

12TH

1902 – Execution of William Lane
1902 – Esther Elizabeth Bedford attacked
1924 – Execution of Jean Pierre Vacquier
1926 – Execution of Charles Edward Finden
1927 – Execution of John Robinson
1931 – Execution of William John Corbett
1937 – Execution of Horace William Brunt
1940 – Murder of Beatrice Barbara Scoller
1949 – Lucy Nightingale meets John Wilson
1951 – Murder of George Camp
1952 – Execution of Oliver George Butler
1953 – Probable date of murder of Mary Hackett
1954 – Execution of Harold Fowler
1955 – Execution of Alec Wilkinson
1958 – Execution of Matthew Kavanagh

13TH

1901 – Execution of Ernest Walter Wickham
1902 – Execution of George William Hibbs
1907 – Execution of Richard Clifford Brinkley
1913 – Execution of Frank Greening
1913 – Execution of James Ryder
1915 – Execution of George Joseph Smith
1924 – Execution of John Charles Horner
1928 – Execution of Allen Wales
1937 – Execution of Leslie George Stone
1945 – Trial of Armin Kuehne and Emil
Schmittendorf ends
1948 – Arrest of Peter Griffiths
1949 – Murder of Lucy Nightingale
1964 – Execution of Peter Anthony Allen and
Gwynne Owen Evans

14TH

1900 – Execution of William James Irwin
1900 – Frederick Lawder Backhouse reprieved
1907 – Execution of Rhoda Willis, on her birthday
1912 – Murder of Mary May Galbraith
1913 – Execution of Hugh McLaren
1924 – Murder of Elizabeth Bousfield
1925 – Execution of Arthur Henry Bishop
1925 – Execution of William John Cronin
1929 – Execution of Arthur Leslie Raveney
1941 – Execution of Josef Jakobs
1945 – Murder of Samuel Hammond Gray
1947 – Execution of William Smedley

1959 – Execution of Bernard Hugh Walden
1963 – Murder of William Garfield Rowe

15TH

1902 – Esther Elizabeth Bedford dies
1905 – Execution of Arthur Devereux
1905 – Execution of Thomas George Tattersall
1919 – Murder of Soloman Franks
1927 – Murder of Evelyn Mary Jennings
1931 – Arrest of Henry Daniel Seymour
1949 – Murder of Lilian Vickers
1953 – Murder of Miriam Susan Gray
1960 – John Louis Constantine loses his appeal
1963 – Execution of Henry John Burnett

16TH

1900 – Execution of Charles Benjamin Backhouse
1900 – Execution of Thomas Mellor
1902 – Murder of Mary Ina Stewart
1904 – Execution of John Thomas Kay
1904 – Execution of Samuel Holden
1916 – Execution of William Allen Butler
1917 – Execution of William Thomas Hodgson
1918 – Rhoda Walker attacked
1921 – Execution of Lester Augustus Hamilton
1939 – Murder of Mary Alice Maud Moncrieff
1949 – Execution of William John Davies
1950 – Execution of Albert Price
1953 – Arrest of John Francis Wilkinson
1963 – Arrest of Russell Pascoe

17TH

1908 – Murder of Annie Dorothy Lawrence
1909 – Execution of Madar Lal Dhingra
1915 – Execution of George Marshall
1918 – Rhoda Walker dies
1922 – Execution of Simon McGeown
1937 – Execution of Frederick George Murphy
1943 – Murder of Gwendoline Sweeney
1945 – Murder of Donald Alfred Richard Kirkaldie
1951 – Original execution date for
Robert Dobie Smith
1952 – Murder of Michael Connolly

18TH

1902 – Body of Mary Ina Stewart found
1942 – Original execution date for Joe Cahill,
Henry Cordner, John Terence Oliver,
William James Perry, Patrick Joseph S
Simpson and Thomas Williams.
1943 – Gwendoline Sweeney's body found
1943 – Arrest of Thomas James

19TH

1908 – Execution of Edward Johnstone
1909 – Execution of Richard Justin
1911 – Murder of Harriett Ann Eckhardt
1912 – Murder of Emily Violet Hubbard
1920 – Murder of Irene Violet Munro
1922 – Execution of Thomas Henry Allaway
1951 – Murder of Alice Rimmer

20TH

1901 – Execution of John Joyce
1908 – Execution of John Berryman

1915 – Trial of Ernest Melin starts
1915 – Trial of Augusto Roggen
1920 – Irene Violet Munro's body found
1950 – Murder of Eliza Wood
1951 – Alice Rimmer's body found

21ST

1900 – Execution of William Augustus Lacey
1900 – Joseph Holden attacks his grandson,
George Eldred
1915 – Trial of Ernest Melin ends
1939 – Murder of Anne Farrow Cook
1942 – Murder of Elizabeth Bounds
1944 – Trial of Madison Thomas
1947 – Execution of John Edward Gartside
1950 – Arrest of James Henry Corbitt

22ND

1914 – Murder of Sarah Ann Eayres
1920 – Katharine Mary Armstrong
admitted to hospital
1944 – Murder of Elizabeth Green
1952 – Murder of Geoffrey Charles Dean

23RD

1906 – Murder of Albert Watson and
Emma Watson
1940 – Murder of Doris Eugenia Girl
1944 – Elizabeth Green's body found
1960 – Murder of Keith Godfrey Arthur
1961 – Murder of Michael Gregsten and attack
upon Valerie Storey

24TH

1902 – Murder of Eliza Chetwynd senior,
Eliza Chetwynd junior and the unnamed
Chetwynd child
1952 – Michael Connolly's body found

25TH

1900 – Murder of Ada Gubb Burrett
1939 – Murder of Elsie Ansell, Gwilym Rowland,
John Corbett Arnott, James Clay and
Rex Gentle
1939 – William Joyce leaves Britain for Germany
1960 – Keith Godfrey Arthur's body found

26TH

1908 – Murder of Thomas Tompkins
1910 – George Joseph Smith marries Bessie Mundy
1937 – Murder of Lilian Maud Chamberlain
1942 – Trial of William Ambrose Collins starts

27TH

1900 – Murder of Sarah Willett
1918 – Murder of Annie Mayne
1933 – Murder of Charles William Fox
1942 – Joe Cahill, Henry Cordner, John Terence
Oliver, William James Perry, Patrick Joseph
Simpson and Thomas Williams lose their
appeals
1942 – Trial of William Ambrose Collins ends
1954 – Murder of William Harmer

28TH

1900 – Execution of Charles Oliver Blewitt
1902 – Murder of Henry Groves
1909 – Murder of Florence Lily Freeman
1911 – Murder of Elizabeth Loake
1914 – Murder of Louisa Frembd
1948 – Murder of Nancy Ellen Chadwick
1951 – Robert Dobie Smith loses his appeal

29TH

1948 – Nancy Ellen Chadwick's body found

30TH

1933 – Arrest of Stanley Eric Hobday
1942 – Reprieves announced for Joe Cahill,
Henry Cordner John Terence Oliver,
William James Perry, and Patrick
Joseph Simpson.

31ST

1925 – Murder of Elizabeth Lax

September

1ST

1911 – Eliza Mary Barrow falls ill
1925 – Trial of John Keen starts
1948 – Arrest of Margaret Allen
1954 – Execution of Rupert Geoffrey Wells
1954 – Execution of Edward Lindsay Reid
1960 – Execution of John Louis Constantine

2ND

1911 – Murder of Caroline Fletcher
1927 – Execution of Arthur Harnett
1931 – Murder of Achmet Musa
1942 – Execution of Thomas Joseph Williams
1946 – Murder of Catherine Cooper

3RD

1901 – Murder of Hermann Francis Jung
1924 – Execution of Patrick Herbert Mahon
1925 – Trial of John Keen ends
1925 – Execution of Alfred David Bostock
1925 – Execution of Wilfred Fowler
1952 – Execution of Mahmood Hussein Mattan
1958 – Execution of Frank Stokes

4TH

1923 – Percy Sharpe attacked
1925 – Execution of Lawrence Fowler
1931 – Achmet Musa's body found
1941 – Execution of John Smith

5TH

1900 – Murder of John Dawes
1920 – Arrest of Jack Alfred Field and
William Thomas Gray
1922 – Murder of Frances Florence Pacey
1923 – Percy Sharpe dies
1929 – Murder of Ellen Maguire
1933 – Murder of Frederick Ellison Morton
1945 – Execution of Howard Joseph Grossley

1952 – Execution of John Howard Godar

6TH

1903 – Murder of Ellen Newman
1910 – Murder of Louisa Ann Rawcliffe
1911 – Trial of Francisco Carlos Godhino starts
1912 – Murder of Mabel Ann Maryan
1916 – Execution of Daniel Sullivan
1926 – Charles Houghton dismissed from his job
1928 – Murder of Charlotte Alice Harber
1933 – Frederick Ellison Morton's body found
1946 – Execution of Sydney John Smith
1946 – Execution of David Baillie Mason
1950 – Trial of Paul Christopher Harris starts
1950 – Murder of Jane Edge

7TH

1910 – Louisa Ann Rawcliffe's body found
1911 – Trial of Francisco Carlos Godhino ends
1922 – Murder of Rosilla Patience Barton
1926 – Murder of Eleanor Drinkwater Woodhouse
and Martha Gordon Drinkwater
1944 – Dorothy May Hillman attacked
1945 – Execution of Thomas Eric Richardson
1950 – Arrest of Frank Griffin
1959 – Trial of Francis Joseph Hutchet starts
1961 – Mrs Dalal attacked

8TH

1900 – Murder of Isabella Bowes
1943 – Murder of Gladys Lavinia Brewer and
Shirley Brewer
1949 – Trial of William Claude Hodson Jones
1961 – Execution of Henryk Niemasz

9TH

1911 – Lucy Kennedy attacked
1915 – Murder of Charlotte Kent
1922 – Murder of Sing Lee
1944 – Murder of William Donald McSwann
1950 – Trial of Paul Christopher Harris ends

10TH

1902 – Murder of Margaret Annie Andrews
1903 – Alice Woodman moves in with
Sidney George Smith
1906 – Murder of Sophia Lovell
1907 – Murder of Rachel Hannah Stills
1913 – Trial of Patrick Higgins starts
1915 – Execution of Ernest Waldemar Melin
1935 – Trial of Raymond Henry Bousquet starts
1935 – Trial of Allan James Grierson starts
1940 – Execution of John William Wright
1940 – Trial of Stanley Edward Cole starts
1942 – Execution of Harold Oswald Merry
1942 – Execution of Samuel Sydney Dashwood
and George William Silverosa
1943 – Execution of Trevor Elvin
1952 – Trial of Dennis George Muldowney starts
1959 – Trial of Francis Joseph Hutchet ends

11TH

1902 – Trial of John MacDonald
1902 – Isabella Walton attacked

1902 – Murder of Nora Walton and Mrs Young
1904 – Trial of John Emlyn Jones
1911 – Trial of Edward Hill starts
1911 – Lucy Kennedy dies
1913 – Trial of Patrick Higgins ends
1920 – Murder of Lydia Westwood
1923 – Murder of Minetta Mary Kelly
1932 – Probable date of murder of
Gwendoline Annie Warren
1935 – Murder of Ada Baguley
1952 – Trial of Dennis George Muldowney ends
1952 – Trial of Raymond John Cull starts

12TH

1905 – Murder of Martha Smith
1911 – Trial of Edward Hill ends
1912 – Trial of Sargent Philp
1912 – Murder of Clara Elizabeth Carter
1936 – Murder of Irene Hart
1938 – Patrick Carraher awarded three years
for culpable homicide
1939 – Trial of Stanley Ernest Boon and
Arthur John Smith starts
1940 – Trial of Stanley Edward Cole ends
1952 – Trial of Raymond John Cull ends

13TH

1900 – Trial of John Charles Parr
1902 – Murder of Sarah Jane Leggett
1927 – Ada Elizabeth Dunn leaves her husband,
John Thomas Dunn
1942 – Probable date of murder of
Joan Pearl Wolfe
1947 – Murder of Emily Bowers
1951 – Execution of Robert Dobie Smith

14TH

1897 – William John Cronin found guilty of the
manslaughter of Eliza Cuthbert
1900 – Trial of William Burrett
1911 – Murder of Eliza Mary Barrow
1915 – Trial of George T. Breeckow starts
1926 – Trial of Hashankhan Samander
1932 – Gwendoline Annie Warren's body found
1942 – Trial of Patrick William Kingston
1945 – Murder of John Alexander Ritchie

15TH

1900 – Using the surname 'Hood', Mary Jane
Bennett goes to Great Yarmouth
1932 – Arrest of Ernest Hutchinson
1935 – Murder of Isabella Van Ess and
Mary Rogerson
1941 – Trial of Lionel Rupert Nathan Watson starts

16TH

1911 – Funeral of Eliza Mary Barrow
1935 – Trial of Raymond Henry Bousquet ends
1942 – Trial of Herbert Hiram Bounds
1946 – Trial of Arthur Robert Boyce starts
1953 – Murder of Irene Wagner

17TH

1901 – Murder of Maggie Ann Lieutand

1915 – Execution of Augusto Alfredo Roggen
1919 – Trial of Frank George Warren starts
1923 – Trial of Frederick William Maximilian
Jesse starts
1945 – Trial of Theodore William John Schurch
1945 – Trial of William Joyce starts
1952 – Trial of Peter Cyril Johnson starts
1956 – Murder of Marion Hunter McDonald Watt,
Vivienne Isabella Reid Watt and
Margaret Hunter Brown

18TH

1902 – Isabella Walton dies
1903 – Murder of Esther Swinford
1919 – Trial of Frank George Warren ends
1923 – Trial of Frederick William Maximilian Jesse
ends
1923 – Trial of Susan Newell
1935 – Trial of Allan James Grierson ends
1941 – Trial of Lionel Rupert Nathan Watson ends
1944 – Murder of Amelia Elizabeth Ann Knowles
1952 – Trial of Peter Cyril Johnson ends
1953 – Execution of Louisa May Merrifield

19TH

1915 – Murder of Frances Johnson
1941 – Execution of Eli Richards
1945 – Trial of William Joyce ends
1946 – Trial of Arthur Robert Boyce ends
1947 – Execution of Christopher James Geraghty
and Charles Henry Jenkins

20TH

1901 – Murder of John Ferguson
1903 – Murder of Annie Marshall
1915 – Trial of George T. Breeckow ends
1921 – Poisoned chocolates are delivered to
Oswald Martin
1927 – Annie Gillon attacked
1931 – Arrest of Eddie Cullens
1934 – Trial of Harry Tuffney
1945 – Trial of Ronald Bertram Mauri
1946 – Murder of Joyce Brierley
1950 – Murder of Ethel Merinda Worth
1952 – Murder of John David Thomas
1960 – Trial of Norman James Harris and
Francis Forsyth starts

21ST

1915 – Arrest of John James Thornley
1933 – Trial of Robert James Kirby
1939 – Trial of Stanley Ernest Boon and
Arthur John Smith ends
1941 – Murder of Kitty Lyon
1944 – Murder of Jane Coulton
1947 – Murder of Neil MacLeod
1953 – Mary Hackett's body found

22ND

1900 – Murder of Mary Jane Bennett
1903 – Annie Marshall's body found
1928 – Murder of Thomas Kirby and
Emily Frances Kirby
1931 – Murder of Constance Inman

1939 – Trial of Leonard George Hucker
1941 – Arrest of Arthur Peach
1943 – Trial of Terence Casey starts
1944 – Dorothy May Hillman dies
1944 – Trial of Ernest Lee Clark and
Augustine M. Guerra
1961 – Arrest of Peter Louis Alphon

23RD

1899 – Probable date of murder of
Selina Ellen Jones
1900 – Mary Jane Bennett's body found
1902 – Murder of Emily Chambers and
Mary Oakley
1920 – Murder of Dorothy May Saunders
1920 – Murder of Fanny Zetoun
1922 – Murder of Ivy Dora Prentice
1922 – Frederick Edward Bywaters returns
to England
1928 – Bodies of Thomas Kirby and Emily Frances
Kirby found
1931 – Constance Inman's body found

24TH

1903 – Murder of Martha Jane Hardwick
1907 – Probable date of murder of John
Barclay Smith
1925 – Execution of John Keen
1926 – Murder of Louise Leah
1927 – Murder of Ada Elizabeth Dunn
1943 – Trial of Terence Casey ends
1943 – Execution of Charles Eugene Gauthier
1944 – Arrest of Arthur Thompson
1946 – Trial of Neville George Clevelly Heath starts
1959 – Trial of Guenther Fritz Erwin Podola starts

25TH

1905 – Mary Allen attacked
1920 – Murder of Harriett Lever
1944 – Murder of Patricia Wylie
1948 – Murder of Ernest Hargreaves Westwood
1959 – Trial of Guenther Fritz Erwin Podola ends

26TH

1900 – Murder of Bridget McGivern
1944 – Arrest of Andrew Brown
1946 – Trial of Neville George Clevelly Heath ends
1947 – Murder of Catherine McIntyre
1948 – Arrest of Arthur George Osborne
1960 – Trial of Norman James Harris and
Francis Forsyth ends

27TH

1899 – Body of Selina Ellen Jones found in
the river Thames
1905 – Mary Allen dies
1927 – Murder of George William Gutteridge
1939 – Anne Farrow Cook's body found

28TH

1905 – Murder of Francis Walter Evans
1911 – Murder of Edith Griffiths
1912 – Murder of Florence Alice Bernadette Silles
1927 – Probable date of murder of Agnes Arbuckle

1943 – Murder of Cynthia June Lay
1943 – Muriel Fawden attacked
1949 – Execution of William Claude Hodson Jones

29TH

1907 – Body of John Barclay Smith found
1915 – Trial of Fernando Buschman starts
1920 – Murder of Kate Lilian Bailey
1927 – David Lewis attacked
1935 – Body parts found near Moffat,
Scotland – these are of
Isabella Van Ess and Mary Rogerson

30TH

1901 – Murder of Anna McKenna
1902 – Execution of John MacDonald
1915 – Trial of Fernando Buschman ends
1927 – David Lewis dies
1950 – Original execution date for Paul
Christopher Harris and Claude
Milford Harris
1952 – Execution of Dennis George Muldowney
1952 – Execution of Raymond John Cull
1958 – Murder of Richard Turner

October

1ST

1901 – Patrick McKenna charged with murder
1907 – John Ramsbottom marries Charlotte
1912 – Execution of Sargent Philp

2ND

1900 – Execution of John Charles Parr
1912 – Arrest of William Charles Adolphus Beal
1913 – Execution of Patrick Higgins
1914 – Arrest of Carl Hans Lody
1920 – Body of Kate Lilian Bailey found
1927 – Murder of Constance Gertrude Oliver
1931 – Murder of Norah Upchurch
1947 – Arrest of Stanislaw Myskza
1951 – Trial of John O'Connor
1953 – Trial of John Owen Greenway
1956 – Peter Thomas Anthony Manuel gets 18
months for robbery

3RD

1900 – Execution of William Burrett
1924 – Murder of Francis Ward
1931 – Murder of Annie Riley
1931 – Ernest Charles Digby marries Violet Amy
Gwendoline Thurley
1944 – Karl Gustav Hulten meets Elizabeth
Maud Jones

4TH

1902 – Murder of Hannah Shea
1905 – Murder of Annie Yarnold
1915 – Trial of Irving Guy Ries starts
1922 – Murder of Percy Thompson
1924 – Francis Ward's body found

5TH

1915 – Trial of Irving Guy Ries ends
1927 – Constance Gertrude Oliver's body found
1927 – Arrest of Sidney Bernard Goulter
1931 – Arrest of Solomon Stein
1942 – Murder of Nellie Pearson

6TH

1903 – Murder of Esther Atkins
1942 – Execution of Patrick William Kingston
1943 – Trial of Lee A. Davis
1945 – Execution of Joachim Palme-Goltz,
    Josep Mertins, Heintz Brueling, Erich
    Koenig and Kurt Zuchlsdorff
1953 – Murder of Doris Douglas

7TH

1903 – Esther Atkins's body found
1916 – Catherine Convery attacked
1919 – Execution of Frank George Warren
1942 – Joan Pearl Wolfe's body found
1944 – Murder of George Edward Heath

8TH

1903 – Arrest of William Brown
1907 – Murder of Catherine Gear
1920 – Murder of Mary Riley
1923 – Trial of Philip Murray starts
1960 – Murder of Adeline Mary Smith

9TH

1912 – Murder of Arthur Walls
1923 – Trial of Philip Murray ends
1934 – Execution of Harry Tuffney
1942 – Nellie Pearson's body found
1944 – Arrest of Karl Gustav Hulten
1947 – Murder of Alison Gertrude Parkin,
    Joyce Parkin
    and Maurice Parkin
1952 – Execution of Peter Cyril Johnson
1953 – Arrest of Czelslaw Kowalewski
1959 – Execution of Francis Joseph Hutchet
1961 – Trial of Robert Andrew McGladdery starts

10TH

1908 – Murder of Margaret Bouldry
1923 – Execution of Susan Newell
1939 – Execution of Leonard George Hucker
1940 – Murder of Irene Holmes
1947 – Bodies of Alison Gertrude Parkin,
    Joyce Parkin and Maurice Parkin found
1947 – Arrest of George Henry Whelpton
1948 – Murder of Joseph Gibbons
1949 – Murder of William Henry Llewellyn
1949 – Murder of Leopold Goodman and
    Esther Goodman
1962 – Trial of Oswald Augustus Grey starts

11TH

1908 – Murder of Susan Wilson
1933 – Execution of Robert James Kirby
1944 – Arrest of Elizabeth Maud Jones
1947 – Murder of Rachel Allen
1949 – William Henry Llewellyn's body found

1949 – Arrest of Daniel Raven
1950 – Trial of Norman Goldthorpe
1961 – Arrest of James Hanratty

12TH

1904 – Murder of Matilda Emily Farmer
1908 – Murder of Elizabeth Warburton
1944 – Execution of Madison Thomas
1950 – Paul Christopher Harris and Claude Milford
    Harris lose their appeals
1951 – Alan Bradley is charged with murder
1962 – Trial of Oswald Augustus Grey ends

13TH

1899 – Louisa Masset writes to Helen Gentle
    asking for the return of her son
1916 – Catherine Convery dies
1935 – Buck Ruxton charged with the murder
    of Mary Rogerson

14TH

1907 – Trial of William Austin
1910 – Trial of William Broome starts
1919 – Murder of Herman Caplan and
    Maurice Caplan
1919 – Freda Caplan attacked
1932 – Trial of Ernest Hutchinson starts
1941 – Murder of Theodora Jessie Greenhill

15TH

1910 – Trial of William Broome ends
1913 – Trial of Frederick Seekings
1914 – Trial of Charles Frembd
1919 – Freda Caplan dies
1927 – Agnes Arbuckle's body found
1928 – Trial of William Charles Benson
1948 – Trial of Peter Griffiths starts
1948 – Trial of George Russell starts
1962 – Trial of James Smith starts

16TH

1903 – Arrest of Thomas Cowdrey
1904 – Arrest of Joseph Potter and Charles Wade
1911 – Trial of Frederick Henry Thomas
1915 – Murder of Clara Thomas
1932 – Trial of Ernest Hutchinson ends
1934 – Murder of Emily Yeomans
1942 – Trial of Duncan Alexander
    Croall Scott-Ford
1946 – Execution of Neville George Clevelly Heath
1948 – Trial of George Russell ends
1953 – Murder of John Harries and Phoebe Harries
1961 – Trial of Robert Andrew McGladdery ends

17TH

1911 – Execution of Francisco Carlos Godhino
1911 – Execution of Edward Hill
1932 – Murder of Jessie Payne
1934 – Emily Yeomans's body found
1934 – David Maskill Blake marries
1940 – Trial of William Henry Cooper
1957 – Trial of Dennis Howard starts

18TH

1902 – Murder of Emily Coates
1902 – Murder of Jane Elizabeth Allen
1910 – Trial of Hawley Harvey Crippen starts
1913 – Amelia Bradfield attacked
1929 – Sidney Harry Fox insures his mother, Rosaline Fox
1937 – Trial of John Thomas Rodgers starts
1941 – Arrest of Harold Dorian Trevor
1948 – Trial of Peter Griffiths ends
1957 – Trial of Dennis Howard ends
1960 – Murder of Nellie McLaughlin
1962 – Trial of James Smith ends

19TH

1905 – Trial of George William Butler
1912 – Trial of Robert Galloway
1915 – Execution of Fernando Buschman
1915 – Trial of William Benjamin Reeve
1925 – Trial of Herbert George Whiteman
1937 – Trial of John Thomas Rodgers ends
1945 – Jill Clegg born
1946 – Trial of John Mathieson starts

20TH

1914 – Trial of Henry Quartley
1914 – Trial of John Francis Eayres
1927 – Murder of Mary Alice Mottram
1931 – Trial of Henry Daniel Seymour starts
1945 – Murder of John Brady
1946 – Murder of Olive Balchin
1948 – Trial of Stanley Joseph Clarke
1953 – Execution of John Owen Greenway
1960 – Arrest of Samuel McLaughlin

21ST

1903 – Trial of Charles Jeremiah Slowe
1913 – Murder of Annie Cotterill
1919 – Trial of James Adams
1921 – Annie Black falls ill
1927 – Arrest of Samuel Case
1941 – Trial of Karel Richard Richter starts
1943 – Dawn Digby born

22ND

1902 – Trial of Patrick Leggett
1902 – Murder of Maud Eliza Marsh
1910 – Trial of Hawley Harvey Crippen ends
1913 – Trial of Frederick Albert Robertson starts
1913 – Arrest of George Frederick Law
1919 – Trial of Djang Djing Sung
1928 – Trial of Chung Yi Miao starts
1934 – Trial of John Frederick Stockwell
1937 – Murder of Albert Edward Baker
1945 – Charles Elphick attacked

23RD

1902 – Trial of Henry Williams
1908 – Trial of James Phipps
1914 – Trial of Arnold Warren
1928 – Trial of Chung Yi Miao ends
1929 – Murder of Rosaline Fox
1936 – Arrest of Andrew Anderson Bagley
1945 – Charles Elphick dies

1946 – Trial of John Mathieson ends
1952 – Execution of Donald Neil Simon

24TH

1905 – Trial of Pasha Liffey
1907 – Arrest of Joseph Hume
1913 – Trial of Frederick Albert Robertson ends
1941 – Trial of Karel Richard Richter ends
1951 – Execution of John O'Connor
1952 – Trial of John Kenneth Livesey

25TH

1906 – Trial of Frederick Reynolds
1910 – Trial of Ethel Le Neve – found not guilty
1911 – Probable date of murder of William Higgins and John Higgins
1920 – Murder of Jane Darwell
1924 – Murder of Margaret Legg
1925 – Murder of Ada Taylor
1931 – Trial of Henry Daniel Seymour ends
1934 – Arrest of David Maskill Blake
1939 – Execution of Stanley Ernest Boon
1943 – Murder of Savvas Demetriades
1946 – Trial of Frank Josiah Freiyer

26TH

1915 – Execution of George T. Breeckow
1921 – Murder of Margaret Thomas
1921 – Oswald Martin poisoned
1934 – Murder of George Hamblin
1939 – Execution of Arthur John Smith
1943 – Arrest of Christos Georghiou
1943 – Trial of Charles William Koopman
1945 – Isabelle Young ends her relationship with Charles Edward Prescott
1946 – Arrest of Walter Graham Rowland
1950 – Trial of Patrick Turnage
1953 – Trial of Alfred Charles Whiteway starts
1953 – Trial of Joseph Christopher Reynolds

27TH

1899 – Murder of Manfred Louis Masset
1900 – Margaret Morrison attacked
1908 – Trial of James Nicholls
1910 – Trial of Thomas Rawcliffe
1913 – Amelia Bradfield dies
1915 – Execution of Irving Guy Ries
1915 – Trial of John James Thornley
1926 – Trial of James Leah
1958 – Trial of Brian Chandler starts

28TH

1900 – Arrest of James Joseph Bergin
1901 – Trial of Marcel Fougeron starts
1903 – Trial of Edward Richard Palmer
1910 – Murder of Andrew Simon
1912 – Trial of Gilbert Oswald Smith
1918 – Murder of Sarah Rose and Isabella Rose
1919 – Murder of Annie Coulbeck
1927 – Trial of William Meynell Robertson
1927 – Annie Gillon dies
1928 – Murder of Alice Fontaine
1942 – Execution of William Ambrose Collins

1950 – Execution of Claude Milford Harris
is postponed
1954 – Trial of Styllou Pantopiou Christofi

29TH

1900 – Margaret Morrison dies
1901 – Trial of Marcel Fougeron ends
1915 – Trial of Young Hill
1921 – Edward Ernest Black purchases
two ounces of arsenic
1924 – Trial of Arthur Simms starts
1929 – Funeral of Rosaline Fox
1934 – Trial of Ethel Lillie Major starts
1935 – Execution of Raymond Henry Bousquet
1941 – Murder of Christina Rose Dicksee
1941 – Trial of Thomas William Thorpe
1958 – Trial of Brian Chandler ends
1962 – Oswald Augustus Grey loses his appeal
1963 – Trial of Russell Pascoe and Dennis John
Whitty starts

30TH

1922 – Trial of George Robinson
1923 – Execution of Philip Murray
1935 – Execution of Allan James Grierson
1945 – William Joyce's appeal hearing starts
1945 – Murder of Jill Clegg
1950 – Execution of Paul Christopher Harris
1953 – Trial of Alfred Charles Whiteway ends
1962 – Original execution date for Oswald
Augustus Grey

31ST

1899 – Arrest of Louisa Masset
1917 – Murder of Emilienne Gerard
1920 – Murder of George Henry Shenton
1921 – Murder of Elizabeth Benjamin
1922 – Trial of Frank Fowler
1925 – William Jones marries Winifred
1940 – Execution of Stanley Edward Cole
1941 – Execution of Antonio Mancini
1945 – Execution of Ronald Bertram Mauri
1946 – Trial of Arthur Rushton starts
1947 – Murder of Dagmar Petrzywalski
1949 – Trial of Benjamin Roberts starts

November

1ST

1907 – Trial of William Duddles
1907 – Murder of John Patterson
1921 – Elizabeth Benjamin's body found
1923 – Execution of Frederick William
Maximilian Jesse
1924 – Trial of Arthur Simms ends
1927 – Trial of Bertram Horace Kirby
1928 – Probable date of murder of Vivian Messiter
1934 – Trial of Ethel Lillie Major ends
1938 – Execution of George Brain
1943 – Oswald John Job lands in England
1945 – William Joyce's appeal hearing
ends in failure
1945 – Murder of Reuben Martirosoff
1946 – Execution of Arthur Robert Boyce

1946 – Trial of Arthur Rushton ends
1949 – Trial of Benjamin Roberts ends

2ND

1898 – Arthur Devereux marries Beatrice
1917 – Emilienne Gerard's body found
1918 – Murder of Mary Ellen Rooney
1919 – Trial of David Caplan
1922 – Murder of Lily Johnston
1926 – Execution of Hashankhan Samander
1940 – Murder of Mary Hagan
1949 – Trial of John Wilson
1952 – Murder of Sydney Miles
1953 – Trial of John Francis Wilkinson starts
1963 – Trial of Russell Pascoe and
Dennis John Whitty ends

3RD

1916 – Trial of Frederick Brooks
1922 – Arrest of William Rooney
1929 – Arrest of Sidney Harry Fox
1942 – Execution of Duncan Alexander Croall
Scott-Ford
1953 – Trial of John Francis Wilkinson ends

4TH

1910 – Trial of Henry Thompson
1913 – Execution of Frederick Seekings
1913 – Murder of Martha Hodgkins
1913 – George Joseph Smith marries
Alice Burnham
1914 – Execution of Charles Frembd
1919 – Margaret Hird attacked
1936 – Trial of Christopher Jackson
1943 – Trial of Thomas James starts

5TH

1907 – Execution of William Austin
1912 – Execution of Robert Galloway
1915 – Trial of Albert Meyer starts
1919 – Trial of Ernest Bernard Scott
1919 – Margaret Hird dies
1926 – Trial of Charles Houghton
1927 – Murder of Eleanor Pilkington
1935 – Buck Ruxton charged with the murder of
Isabella Van Ess
1943 – Trial of Thomas James ends
1949 – Murder of Christine Ruth Cuddon
1959 –Execution of Guenther Fritz
Erwin Podola
1960 – Anthony Joseph Miller is charged
with murder
1962 – James Smith loses his appeal

6TH

1902 – William Hughes released from prison
1906 – Trial of Edward Hartigan
1914 – Execution of Carl Hans Lody
1915 – Trial of Albert Meyer ends
1915 – Murder of Alice Kaye
1917 – Arrest of Louis Voisin
1919 – Trial of Ambrose Quinn
1919 – Murder of Mary Ann Dixon
1924 – Trial of Frederick Southgate

1930 – Murder of an unknown male by Alfred Arthur Rouse
1940 – Trial of Edward Scoller
1942 – Execution of Herbert Hiram Bounds
1945 – Jill Clegg's body found
1950 – Trial of James Henry Corbitt
1950 – Trial of James Ronald Robertson starts

7TH

1905 – Execution of George William Butler
1908 – Frederick Schlitte attacked
1952 – Murder of Charles Giffard and Elizabeth Giffard

8TH

1910 – Original execution date set for Hawley Harvey Crippen
1911 – Trial of Michael Fagan
1912 – Murder of Kate Butler
1913 – Trial of Augustus John Penny
1917 – Trial of Thomas Cox
1917 – Oliver Gilbert Imlay attacked
1921 – Edward Ernest Black leaves his home
1929 – Trial of John Maguire
1948 – Trial of Clifford Godfrey Wills starts
1949 – Murder of Beryl Susanna Evans
1950 – Murder of Radomir Djorovic

9TH

1908 – Frederick Schlitte dies
1913 – Murder of Maud Mulholland
1920 – Trial of Cyril Victor Tennyson Saunders
1938 – James Irwin Percival attacked
1944 – Murder of Winifred Mary Evans
1945 – Trial of John Riley Young
1948 – Trial of Clifford Godfrey Wills ends
1950 – Radomir Djorovic's body found

10TH

1902 – Murder of Jane Hannah Hughes
1903 – Execution of Charles Jeremiah Slowe
1908 – Trial of John William Ellwood starts
1909 – Trial of Abel Atherton starts
1911 – Trial of Henry Phillips
1914 – Execution of John Francis Eayres
1914 – Execution of Henry Quartley
1938 – James Irwin Percival dies
1949 – Murder of Geraldine Evans
1960 – Execution of Norman James Harris and Francis Forsyth
1960 – Murder of John Henry Pull

11TH

1902 – Execution of Henry Williams
1908 – Trial of John William Ellwood ends
1908 – Joseph Edwin Jones fined 20/- for assault
1909 – Trial of Abel Atherton ends
1909 – Murders of Charles Thomas and Mary Thomas
1911 – Trial of Joseph Fletcher
1912 – Trial of William Charles Adolphus Beal
1917 – Oliver Gilbert Imlay dies
1919 – Execution of James Adams
1921 – Murder of Annie Black

1927 – Murder of Amy Collinson

12TH

1902 – Execution of Patrick Leggett
1903 – Trial of Bernard White starts
1904 – Murder of Samuel Barker
1908 – Execution of James Phipps
1908 – Murder of Charlotte Jones
1909 – Trial of Samuel Atherley
1909 – Bodies of Charles Thomas and Mary Thomas found
1914 – Execution of Arnold Warren
1917 – Trial of William Cananagh
1917 – Edward Tighe attacked
1925 – Execution of Herbert George Whiteman
1941 – Execution of Lionel Rupert Nathan Watson

13TH

1900 – Trial of Joseph Holden
1901 – Trial of Patrick McKenna
1903 – Trial of Bernard White ends
1903 – Trial of Charles Wood Whittaker
1906 – Execution of Frederick Reynolds
1908 – James Nicholls loses his appeal
1920 – Trial of James Riley
1933 – Trial of William Burtoft starts
1933 – Joseph Bedford attacked
1940 – Arrest of Samuel Morgan
1942 – Trial of Johannes Marinus Dronkers starts
1945 – Trial of James McNichol
1945 – Trial of Reginald Douglas Johnson starts
1946 – Execution of Frank Josiah Freiyer
1950 – Trial of James Ronald Robertson ends
1953 – Trial of George James Newland
1960 – Arrest of Victor John Terry

14TH

1902 – Trial of Henry McWiggins starts
1902 – Trial of William Chambers
1905 – Execution of Pasha Liffey
1906 – Trial of Richard Buckham
1921 – Percy James Atkin bigamously marries Margaret Milton
1923 – Trial of Matthew Frederick Atkinson Nunn
1933 – Trial of William Burtoft ends
1933 – Trial of Ernest Wadge Parker
1933 – Trial of Stanley Eric Hobday starts
1933 – Joseph Bedford dies
1934 – Execution of John Frederick Stockwell
1941 – Trial of John Ernest Smith
1947 – Murder of Percy Bushby
1950 – Execution of Patrick Turnage
1960 – Trial of Anthony Joseph Miller starts

15TH

1901 – Trial of John Miller and John Robert Miller
1902 – Trial of Henry McWiggins ends
1910 – Execution of Thomas Rawcliffe
1911 – Execution of Frederick Henry Thomas
1911 – Eliza Mary Barrow's body exhumed
1912 – Murders of Amy Collinson and Frances Alice Nicholson
1916 – Trial of Joseph Deans
1927 – Trial of John Thomas Dunn

1928 – Trial of Charles William Conlin
1937 – Trial of Ernest John Moss
1943 – Murder of Dawn Digby
1947 – Arrest of Walter John Cross
1957 – Murder of William Williams

16TH

1905 – Trial of Henry Perkins
1915 – Execution of William Benjamin Reeve
1921 – Trial of Edward O'Connor
1926 – Execution of James Leah
1933 – Trial of Stanley Eric Hobday ends
1945 – Execution of Armin Kuehne and
    Emil Schmittendorf
1945 – Trial of Reginald Douglas Johnson ends
1949 – Abraham Harry Levine is attacked
1951 – David Ware is sent to Broadmoor
1951 – Murder of Martin Joseph Malone
1957 – William Williams's body found

17TH

1901 – Murder weapon found in the William
    Woods case
1903 – Execution of Edward Richard Palmer
1906 – Murder of Jane Harrison
1908 – Murder of Clara Jane Hannaford
1915 – Trial of Lee Kun
1917 – Edward Tighe dies
1921 – Arrest of William Sullivan
1922 – Trial of William Rider
1927 – William Walter Hartle falsely confesses to
    murder of Mary Alice Mottram
1928 – Murder of Annie Elizabeth Hatton
1942 – Trial of Johannes Marinus Dronkers ends
1949 – Abraham Harry Levine dies
1951 – Arrest of James Smith
1953 – Execution of Joseph Christopher Reynolds
1960 – Trial of Anthony Joseph Miller ends
1960 – Trial of Wasyl Gnypiuk starts

18TH

1902 – Probable date of the murder of the
    infant Galley
1902 – Murder of Lucy Margaret Lingard
1904 – Trial of Joseph Potter and Charles
    Wade starts
1905 – Trial of William Yarnold
1910 – Trial of Noah Woolf
1920 – Trial of Marks Goodmacher
1937 – Execution of John Thomas Rodgers
1942 – Trial of Harry Dobkin starts
1944 – Trial of William Harrison
1948 – Execution of Stanley Joseph Clarke
1949 – Arrest of Walter Sharpe and
    Gordon Lannen
1957 – Arrest of Vivian Frederick Teed
1960 – Trial of Wasyl Gnypiuk ends

19TH

1901 – Execution of Marcel Fougeron
1902 – Trial of Thomas Fairclough Barrow
1909 – Trial of John Freeman
1920 – Trial of Samuel Westwood
1924 – Trial of William George Smith

1941 – Murder of Doreen Joyce Hearne and
    Kathleen Trundell
1943 – Execution of Terence Casey
1945 – Murder of Sarah Jean Young
1945 – Murder of Peggy Agnes Holmes
1946 – Execution of Arthur Rushton
1948 – Execution of Peter Griffiths
1948 – Murder of Irene May Phillips
1949 – Trial of Ernest Soper Couzins
1951 – Trial of Herbert Leonard Mills starts
1952 – Trial of John James Alcott

20TH

1901 – Arthur Richardson released from prison
1902 – Murder of Rose Ann McCann
1907 – Execution of William Duddles
1908 – Trial of William Bouldry
1911 – Trial of George Loake
1912 – Trial of William Wallace Galbraith
1920 – Trial of Charles Colclough
1925 – Murder of Frances Clark
1928 – Execution of William Charles Benson
1933 – Trial of Roy Gregory starts
1934 – Trial of Frederick Rushworth starts
1945 – Arrest of Leonard Holmes
1949 – Arrest of Timothy John Evans
1950 – Trial of Frank Griffin starts
1951 – Murder of Evelyn McDonald
1952 – Trial of Eric Norcliffe
1962 – Execution of Oswald Augustus Grey

21ST

1901 – Trial of Alexander Claydon
1903 – Trial of James Duffy
1903 – Arrest of Joseph Moran
1904 – Trial of Joseph Potter and
    Charles Wade ends
1907 – Trial of George Stills
1911 – Trial of Walter Martyn
1911 – Trial of Charles Coleman
1914 – Trial of George Anderson
1921 – Arrest of Edward Ernest Black
1921 – Murder of Maud Atkin
1933 – Trial of Roy Gregory ends
1934 – Trial of Frederick Rushworth ends
1943 – Arrest of Olga Davy Hill
1948 – Murder of Joan Mary Marney

22ND

1902 – Trial of Jeremiah Callaghan
1902 – Elizabeth Taylor's body exhumed
1910 – Execution of Henry Thompson
1911 – Trial of John Edward Tarkenter
1927 – Trial of Frederick Fielding
1928 – Trial of Trevor John Edwards
1940 – Trial of Jose Waldeburg, Carl Meier and
    Charles Albert Van Dem Kieboom
1941 – Bodies of Doreen Joyce Hearne and
    Kathleen Trundell found
1943 – Arrest of Ernest Charles Digby
1948 – Joan Mary Marney's body found
1949 – Trial of Daniel Raven starts
1950 – Trial of Edward Isaac Woodfield starts
1950 – Trial of Frank Griffin ends
1951 – Trial of Herbert Leonard Mills ends

23RD

1901 – Trial of John George Thompson
1901 – Thomas Marsland marries Elizabeth
1910 – Execution of Hawley Harvey Crippen
1917 – Arrest of Edward Sharp
1925 – Trial of Samuel Johnson
1927 – Bertram Horace Kirby's original
     execution date
1932 – Execution of Ernest Hutchinson
1942 – Trial of Harry Dobkin ends
1945 – Murder of John Gordon
1946 – Arrest of Harold Hagger
1950 – Trial of Edward Isaac Woodfield ends
1953 – Trial of Desmond Donald Hooper starts
1953 – Trial of Robert William Moore starts

24TH

1900 – Trial of John Bowes
1902 – Trial of Samuel Walton
1903 – Trial of William Brown and
     Thomas Cowdrey starts
1903 – Murder of Mary Hannah Starr
1910 – Execution of William Broome
1910 – Trial of Henry Ison
1912 – Murder of Annie Wentworth Davis
1913 – Trial of Edward Ernest Kelly
1915 – Trial of John William McCartney
1921 – Murder of Emily Agnes Dewberry
1941 – Trial of Arthur Peach starts
1949 – Trial of Daniel Raven ends
1950 – Execution of Norman Goldthorpe

25TH

1918 – Trial of William Rooney
1931 – Trial of Solomon Stein
1934 – Murder of Edith Constance Drew-Bear
1947 – Trial of Eugeniusz Jurkiewicz starts
1953 – Trial of Stanislaw Juras starts
1953 – Trial of Robert William Moore ends

26TH

1902 – Trial of Thomas Nicholson
1902 – Trial of William Brown
1908 – Trial of Harry Taylor Parker
1912 – Execution of Gilbert Oswald Smith
1913 – Execution of Augustus John Penny
1916 – Murder of Alfred Williams
1919 – Execution of Ernest Bernard Scott
1919 – Execution of Ambrose Quinn
1929 – Execution of John Maguire
1940 – Execution of William Henry Cooper
1941 – Trial of Arthur Peach ends
1945 – Henry Dutton attacked
1946 – Trial of Stanley Sheminant starts
1947 – Trial of Eugeniusz Jurkiewicz ends
1953 – Trial of Stanislaw Juras ends

27TH

1903 – Trial of William Brown and
     Thomas Cowdrey ends
1906 – Execution of Edward Hartigan
1912 – Trial of Alfred John Lawrence
1913 – Execution of Frederick Albert Robertson
1915 – Execution of Albert Meyer

1917 – Murder of Joseph Harold Durkin
1922 – Trial of George Frederick Edisbury
1924 – Execution of Frederick Southgate
1925 – Murder of Ernest George Elton Laight,
     Doris Sabrina Laight and Robert Laight
1931 – Murder of Charles William Lambert
1942 – The murder weapon found in the
     August Sangret case
1945 – Arrest of Martin Patrick Coffey
1950 – Trial of Nicholas Persoulious starts
1953 – Trial of Desmond Donald Hooper ends
1953 – Trial of William Lubina

28TH

1901 – Murder of Sarah Hebden
1903 – Trial of William Haywood
1904 – Trial of Eric Lange
1908 – Murder of Clara Howell
1911 – Trial of George William Parker
1916 – Trial of James Howarth Hargreaves
1944 – Execution of Benjamin Pyegate
1945 – Trial of John Amery
1950 – Execution of James Henry Corbitt
1950 – James Ronald Robertson loses his appeal
1962 – Execution of James Smith

29TH

1908 – Clara Howell's body found
1915 – Trial of Harry Thompson
1920 – Trial of George Edwin Freeman
     Quinton Lever
1927 – Trial of Samuel Case
1927 – Trial of Edward Rowlands and
     Daniel Driscoll starts
1928 – Arrest of Frank Hollington
1943 – Trial of John H. Waters
1945 – John Duplessis attacked
1945 – Trial of William Batty starts
1946 – Trial of Stanley Sheminant ends
1950 – Trial of Nicholas Persoulious ends

30TH

1901 – Murder of Mary Ellen Bowen
1918 – Trial of John William Walsh
1920 – Execution of James Riley
1920 – Execution of Cyril Victor Tennyson
     Saunders
1931 – Arrest of William Harold Goddard
1936 – Trial of Andrew Anderson Bagley starts
1941 – Elizabeth Smith attacked
1944 – Trial of Horace Beresford Gordon starts
1945 – Henry Dutton dies
1945 – Trial of William Batty ends
1948 – Trial of George Semini
1948 – Trial of Arthur George Osborne starts
1957 – Peter Thomas Anthony Manuel is
     released from prison

December

1ST

1902 – Murders of John William Darby,
     Beatrice Darby and Ethel Darby
1903 – Execution of Bernard White

THE ENCYCLOPAEDIA OF EXECUTIONS

1903 – Trial of Charles William Ashton
1904 – Trial of Edmund Hall
1905 – Trial of Samuel Curtis
1906 – Murder of Edmund Clarke
1915 – Execution of John James Thornley
1915 – Execution of Young Hill
1925 – Trial of Lorraine Lax
1933 – Murder of James Pullen
1936 – Trial of Andrew Anderson Bagley ends
1943 – Trial of Mervin Clare McEwen starts
1944 – Trial of Horace Beresford Gordon ends
1948 – Trial of Arthur George Osborne ends
1952 – John Kenneth Livesey loses his appeal

2ND

1901 – Trial of John Harrison
1902 – Execution of Henry McWiggins
1902 – Trial of William James Bolton
1903 – Execution of Charles Wood Whittaker
1903 – Third trial of Joseph Moran starts
1908 – Execution of James Nicholls
1913 – Trial of George Frederick Law
1918 – Trial of Benjamin Hindle Benson
1922 – Trial of Lee Doon
1925 – Murder of Catherine Ah Tam and
       Cecilia Ah Tam
1925 – Doris Ah Tam attacked
1927 – Trial of Edward Rowlands and
       Daniel Driscoll ends
1930 – Sarah Ellen Johnson leaves Francis Land
1941 – Elizabeth Smith dies
1943 – Trial of John Joseph Dorgan
1943 – Trial of Mervin Clare McEwen ends
1948 – Execution of George Russell
1952 – Trial of George Francis Shaw starts

3RD

1901 – Execution of Patrick McKenna
1903 – Third trial of Joseph Moran ends
1908 – Execution of John William Ellwood
1917 – William Cavanagh loses his appeal
1918 – Trial of George Cardwell and Percy Barrett
1919 – Execution of Djang Djing Sung
1919 – Trial of Lewis Massey
1920 – Murder of Christine Ann Alexandra Smith
1926 – Execution of Charles Houghton
1926 – Trial of William Cornelius Jones
1929 – Trial of Samuel Cushnan starts
1941 – Execution of John Ernest Smith
1944 – Joyce Brown is raped
1944 – Murder of Eric Teichman
1952 – Trial of Leslie Green starts
1954 – Murder of Jean Tate

4TH

1900 – Execution of Joseph Holden
1900 – Trial of James Joseph Bergin
1902 – Execution of William Chambers
1906 – Execution of Richard Buckham
1908 – Yun Yap attacked
1911 – Arrest of Frederick Henry Seddon
1925 – Trial of John Fisher
1930 – Trial of Victor Edward Betts starts
1942 – Trial of Franciscus Johannes Winter

1950 – Original execution date for James
       Ronald Robertson
1952 – Trial of Herbert Appleby starts
1957 – Execution of Dennis Howard

5TH

1899 – Ada Chard-Williams writes to the police
       denying murder
1905 – Execution of William Yarnold
1905 – Trial of John Silk
1906 – Trial of Walter Marsh
1908 – Arrest of See Lee
1919 – Trial of Hyman Perdovitch
1924 – Murder of Elsie Emily Cameron
1927 – Trial of Sidney Bernard Goulter
1930 – Trial of Victor Edward Betts ends
1946 – Trial of Albert Sabin starts
1952 – Trial of Herbert Appleby ends
1952 – Trial of Leslie Green ends

6TH

1905 – Execution of Henry Perkins
1911 – Execution of Michael Fagan
1922 – Trial of Edith Jessie Thompson and
       Frederick Edward Bywaters starts
1925 – Murder of Marie Beddoe Thomas
1927 – Execution of William Meynell Robertson
1928 – Execution of Chung Yi Miao
1933 – Execution of Ernest Wadge Parker
1944 – Trial of Arthur Thompson starts
1946 – Trial of Albert Sabin ends
1951 – Trial of Alfred Bradley starts

7TH

1901 – Execution of John Miller and
       John Robert Miller
1903 – Trial of Henry Bertram Starr
1905 – Trial of George Smith
1908 – Yun Yap dies
1909 – Execution of John Freeman
1915 – Original execution date for Lee Kun
1927 – Trial of James Joseph Power starts
1928 – William Holmyard attacked
1929 – Trial of Samuel Cushnan ends
1937 – Execution of Ernest John Moss
1944 – Trial of Andrew Brown
1944 – George E. Smith charged with murder
1950 – Trial of Nenad Kovacevic
1951 – Trial of Alfred Bradley ends
1953 – George James Newland loses his appeal
1960 – Original execution date for Wasyl Gnypiuk
1960 – Original execution date for Anthony Joseph
       Miller and the day he loses his appeal
1960 – Trial of George Riley starts

8TH

1902 – Trial of George Place
1902 – Probable date of murder of Alexander
       MacLeod, Julius Herrson and Patrick Durran
1903 – Execution of James Duffy
1904 – Third trial of Joseph Fee starts
1904 – Trial of Arthur Jeffries
1905 – Trial of Frederick William Edge
1908 – Execution of William Bouldry

946

1909 – Execution of Abel Atherton
1915 – Murder of Sarah Woodall
1923 – Trial of John William Eastwood
1931 – Trial of Eddie Cullens starts
1932 – Trial of Jeremiah Hanbury
1936 – Trial of Max Mayer Haslam starts
1943 – Murder of Henry Claude Hailstone
1944 – Trial of Arthur Thompson ends
1948 – Trial of Margaret Allen
1951 – Murder of Eileen Harris
1957 – Murder of Sidney Dunn

9TH

1900 – Trial of William Woods
1902 – Execution of Thomas Fairclough Barrow
1902 – Isabella Mary Spinks's body exhumed
1903 – Trial of John Gallagher and Emily Swann
1912 – Trial of Edward Hopwood starts
1915 – Sarah Woodall's body found
1915 – Arrest of Frederick Holmes
1920 – Trial of Edwin Sowerby
1921 – Arrest of Frederick Alexander Keeling
1924 – Execution of William George Smith
1927 – Trial of James Joseph Power ends
1942 – Trial of Ronald Roberts
1943 – Henry Claude Hailstone's body found
1948 – Execution of Clifford Godfrey Wills
1951 – Arrest of Herbert Roy Harris
1952 – Trial of George Francis Shaw ends
1952 – Trial of Derek William Bentley starts

10TH

1901 – Execution of John George Thompson
1904 – Third trial of Joseph Fee ends
1906 – Trial of John Davis
1911 – Murder of Hilda Mary Josephine Williams
1912 – Execution of William Charles Adolphus Beal
1913 – Murder of Christina Catherine Bradfield
1928 – William Holmyard dies
1930 – Trial of Frederick Gill starts
1931 – Trial of Eddie Cullens ends
1931 – Execution of Henry Daniel Seymour
1932 – First trial of Harold Courtney starts
1936 – Trial of Max Mayer Haslam ends
1940 – Execution of Jose Waldeburg and Carl Meier
1941 – Execution of Karel Richard Richter
1943 – Trial of Christos Georghiou
1945 – Trial of Michal Niescior starts
1946 – Execution of John Mathieson
1951 – Trial of Alfred Moore starts
1958 – Trial of Ernest Raymond Jones

11TH

1900 – Question in Parliament about Joseph Holden's sanity
1908 – Trial of Patrick Collins
1912 – Trial of Edward Hopwood ends
1913 – Christina Catherine Bradfield's body found
1917 – Arrest of Arthur Stamrowsky
1922 – Trial of Edith Jessie Thompson and Frederick Edward Bywaters ends
1928 – Execution of Trevor John Edwards
1931 – Murder of Alfred Gill

1933 – Trial of Ernest Brown starts
1939 – Trial of Peter Barnes and James Richards starts
1945 – Trial of Michal Niescior ends
1945 – Trial of John Lyon starts
1951 – Execution of Herbert Leonard Mills
1952 – Trial of Derek William Bentley ends
1953 – Murder of Lesley Jean Nisbet and Margaret Curran

12TH

1900 – Execution of John Bowes
1901 – Original execution date for Alexander Claydon
1902 – Execution of Jeremiah Callaghan
1911 – Execution of Walter Martyn
1911 – Execution of John Edward Tarkenter
1912 – Trial of George Mackay starts
1913 – Arrest of Samuel Eltoft
1913 – Murder of Alice Burnham
1916 – Execution of Frederick Brooks
1924 – Murder of Gilbert Caleb Amos
1927 – Trial of James McKay
1927 – Trial of James Gillon
1930 – Murder of Sarah Ellen Johnson
1931 – Alfred Gill's body found
1934 – Trial of David Maskill Blake starts
1946 – Trial of Walter Graham Rowland starts
1951 – Trial of Horace Carter
1952 – Execution of Eric Norcliffe
1960 – Trial of George Riley ends

13TH

1899 – Trial of Louisa Masset starts
1901 – Execution of Alexander Claydon
1904 – Execution of Joseph Potter and Charles Wade
1907 – Execution of George Stills
1920 – Trial of Jack Alfred Field and William Thomas Gray starts
1922 – Execution of George Robinson
1922 – Execution of Frank Fowler
1934 – Frederick Rushworth's original execution date
1945 – Reginald Douglas Johnson loses his appeal
1949 – Execution of John Wilson
1949 – Execution of Benjamin Roberts
1951 – Trial of Alfred Moore ends
1953 – Trial of Czelslaw Kowalewski starts

14TH

1902 – Probable date of murder of Fred Abrahamson and Alexander Shaw
1903 – Murder of Alice Woodman
1908 – Trial of John Esmond Murphy starts
1908 – Murder of Mary Donnelly
1909 – Execution of Samuel Atherley
1911 – Execution of Henry Phillips
1912 – Trial of George Mackay ends
1919 – Murders of Gladys May Ibrahim and Aysha Emily Ibrahim
1930 – Trial of Frederick Gill ends
1931 – Trial of George Alfred Rice starts
1933 – Trial of Ernest Brown ends

947

1939 – Trial of Peter Barnes and James Richards ends
1943 – Execution of Lee A. Davis
1950 – Execution of Edward Isaac Woodfield
1952 – Probable date of murder of Ethel Christie
1958 – Murder of Raymond Henry Summers

15TH

1900 – Murder of Lucy Smith
1903 – Execution of William Haywood
1908 – Execution of Harry Taylor Parker
1908 – Trial of John Esmond Murphy ends
1911 – Execution of Joseph Fletcher
1919 – Bodies of Gladys May Ibrahim and Aysha Emily Ibrahim found
1925 – Execution of Samuel Johnson
1931 – Trial of George Alfred Rice ends
1931 – Execution of Solomon Stein
1932 – First trial of Harold Courtney ends
1934 – Trial of David Maskill Blake ends
1943 – Execution of Charles William Koopman
1945 – Trial of John Lyon ends
1947 – Trial of Evan Hadyn Evans
1954 – Execution of Styllou Pantopiou Christofi
1954 – Murder of Mary Ann Dodsley

16TH

1902 – Execution of Thomas Nicholson
1902 – Execution of Samuel Walton
1902 – Execution of William Brown
1903 – John Flanaghan's body found
1912 – Trial of Albert Rumens
1913 – Edward Hilton reprieved
1931 – Murder of Elizabeth Castle
1936 – Execution of Christopher Jackson
1940 – Trial of Clifford Holmes starts
1944 – Trial of Robert L. Pearson and Parson Jones
1946 – Trial of Walter Graham Rowland ends
1950 – Execution of James Ronald Robertson
1954 – Mary Ann Dodsley's body found
1954 – Murder of Dennis John Shenton

17TH

1902 – Probable date of murder of Gustav Johansen
1913 – Execution of Ernest Edward Kelly
1914 – George Joseph Smith marries Margaret Elizabeth Lofty
1918 – Execution of John William Walsh
1918 – Execution of William Rooney
1920 – Trial of Jack Alfred Field and William Thomas Gray ends
1924 – Execution of Arthur Simms
1934 – Frederick Rushworth loses his appeal
1940 – Execution of Charles Albert Van Dem Kieboom
1940 – Trial of Clifford Holmes ends
1946 – Murder of Beatrice Greenberg
1947 – Trial of George Henry Whelpton
1952 – John James Alcott loses his appeal
1952 – Execution of John Kenneth Livesey
1953 – Trial of Czeslaw Kowalewski ends
1953 – Execution of Stanislaw Juras
1958 – Execution of Brian Chandler

1963 – Execution of Russell Pascoe and Dennis John Whitty

18TH

1899 – Trial of Louisa Masset ends
1912 – Execution of Alfred John Lawrence
1914 – Murder of Margaret Elizabeth Lofty
1917 – Execution of William Cavanagh
1922 – Murder of Margaret Gilchrist White
1950 – Murder of Marie Alexine Shaugnessy
1953 – Execution of John Francis Wilkinson

19TH

1902 – Probable date of murder of Alexander Bravo
1905 – Murder of Catherine Garrity
1911 – Execution of George William Parker
1916 – Execution of James Howarth Hargreaves
1917 – Execution of Thomas Cox
1922 – Execution of William Rider
1931 – Murder of Mabel Elizabeth Mathews
1931 – Arrest of Thomas Riley
1933 – Execution of William Burtoft
1934 – Execution of Ethel Lillie Major
1945 – Execution of John Amery
1945 – House of Lords rejects William Joyce's appeal
1950 – Execution of Nicholas Persoulious Crosby
1950 – Murder of Joyce Shaughnessy
1950 – Frank Griffin loses his appeal

20TH

1904 – Execution of Edmund Hall
1905 – Execution of Samuel Curtis
1905 – Catherine Garrity's body found
1912 – Execution of William Wallace Galbraith
1913 – Arrest of George Ball
1916 – Execution of Joseph Deans
1961 – Execution of Robert Andrew McGladdery

21ST

1904 – Execution of Eric Lange
1910 – Execution of Noah Woolf
1911 – Execution of Charles Coleman
1913 – Murder of Charles Gribben
1914 – Funeral of Margaret Elizabeth Lofty
1921 – Murder of Irene May Wilkins
1924 – Murder of Margaret Ann Graham
1931 – Arrest of George Thomas Pople
1945 – Execution of James McNicol
1945 – Execution of John Riley Young

22ND

1903 – Execution of Charles William Ashton
1904 – Execution of Joseph Fee
1915 – Execution of Harry Thompson
1921 – Execution of Edward O'Connor
1921 – Irene May Wilkins's body found
1935 – Murder of Frederick Bryant
1943 – Execution of John Joseph Dorgan
1953 – Execution of Alfred Charles Whiteway
1960 – Execution of Anthony Joseph Miller

23RD

1902 – Execution of William James Bolton
1902 – John Garland attacked by Edgar Owen
1905 – Murder of Sarah Ann McConnell
1914 – Execution of George Anderson
1915 – Murder of Isabella Holmes Conway
1919 – Murder of Kathleen Harriett Elsie Breaks
1922 – Arrest of Frederick Wood
1941 – Execution of Thomas William Thorpe
1944 – Murder of Wolfgang Rosterg
1950 – Arrest of William Shaughnessy
1952 – Execution of Leslie Green
1953 – Execution of George James Newland

24TH

1901 – Execution of John Harrison
1908 – Murder of Hannah Maria Whiteley
1908 – Murder of Mary Ann Rees
1910 – Murder of Ada Roker
1919 – Kathleen Harriett Elsie Breaks's body found
1925 – Murder of Edward Charles Ingram Richards
1938 – Murder of Ernest Percival Key
1940 – Execution of Edward Scoller
1942 – Murder of Albert James Bateman
1952 – Execution of Herbert Appleby

25TH

1897 – Murder of Isabella Mary Spink
1909 – Murder of Gwen Ellen Jones
1916 – Winifred Ellen Fortt attacked
1942 – Arrest of Gordon Horace Trenoweth

26TH

1922 – Murder of Emma Perry
1933 – Murder of Maud Hamilton
1948 – Harry Saul Michaelson is attacked

27TH

1900 – Execution of James Joseph Bergin
1903 – Murder of Elizabeth Mary Lynas
1905 – Execution of Frederick William Edge
1906 – Execution of Walter Marsh
1911 – Murders of Solomon Milstein and
Annie Milstein
1928 – James Johnson is sent to prison for 60 days
1942 – Murder of Robert J. Cobner
1948 – Harry Saul Michaelson dies

28TH

1899 – Joseph Shufflebotham marries Elizabeth
1900 – Murder of Elizabeth Shufflebotham
1902 – Gustav Rau and Willem Schmidt picked
up by S.S. Brunswick
1905 – Execution of George Smith
1909 – Murder of John Collins
1911 – Execution of George Loake
1911 – Bodies of Solomon Milstein and
Annie Milstein found
1911 – Arrest of Myer Abramovitch
1916 – Winifred Ellen Fortt dies
1923 – Execution of John William Eastwood
1933 – Execution of Stanley Eric Hobday
1957 – Murder of Isabelle Wallace Cooke

29TH

1903 – Execution of John Gallagher and
Emily Swann
1903 – Execution of Henry Bertram Starr
1904 – Execution of Arthur Jeffries
1905 – Execution of John Silk
1910 – Execution of Henry Ison
1912 – Arrest of Walter William Sykes
1915 – Execution of John William McCartney
1931 – Original execution date for Eddie Cullens
1934 – Lydia Binks reprieved
1943 – Execution of Thomas James
1945 – Execution of Reginald Douglas Johnson
1951 – Murder of Ada Royce

30TH

1902 – Execution of George Place
1908 – Execution of Patrick Collins
1920 – Execution of Marks Goodmacher
1920 – Execution of Edwin Sowerby
1920 – Execution of Samuel Westwood
1937 – Execution of Frederick Nodder
1947 – Execution of Eugeniusz Jurkiewicz
1948 – Execution of Arthur George Osborne
1949 – Execution of Ernest Soper Couzins
1951 – Murder of Joan Marion Thomas
1952 – Original date set for execution of
George Francis Shaw

31ST

1901 – Murder of Frances Eliza O'Rourke
1913 – Execution of George Frederick Law
1920 – Execution of Charles Colclough
1921 – Arrest of Herbert Rowse Armstrong
1930 – Herbert Charles Ridley reprieved
1931 – Murder of Theresa Mary Hempstock
1935 – Murder of Edward Frederick Herdman
1942 – Execution of Johannes Marinus Dronkers
1945 – John Duplessis dies
1949 – Murder of Dilys Doreen Campbell
1958 – Murder of Norah Summerfield

PRISONS

Aberdeen (1)

Henry Burnett	15th August, 1963

Armagh (1)

Joseph Fee	22nd December, 1904

Bedford (7)

William Chambers	4th December, 1902
William Benjamin Reeve	16th November, 1915
Alfred Arthur Rouse	10th March, 1931
Walter Osmond Worthington	10th July, 1935
William Henry Cooper	26th November, 1940
Jack Day	29th March, 1961
James Hanratty	4th April, 1962

Belfast (12)

William Woods	11th January, 1901
Richard Justin	19th August, 1909
Simon McGeown	17th August, 1922
Michael Pratley	8th May, 1924
William Smiley	8th August, 1928
Samuel Cushnan	8th April, 1930
Thomas Dornan	31st July, 1931
Eddie Cullens	13th January, 1932
Harold Courtney	7th April, 1933
Thomas Williams	2nd September, 1942
Samuel McLaughlin	25th July, 1961
Robert McGladdery	10th December, 1961

Birmingham (35)

John Joyce	20th August, 1901
Charles Samuel Dyer	5th April, 1904
Samuel Holden	17th August, 1904
Frank Greening	13th August, 1913
William Allen Butler	16th August, 1916
Louis Van De Kerkhove	9th July, 1918
Henry Thomas Gaskin	8th August, 1919
Samuel Westwood	30th December, 1920
Edward O'Connor	22nd December, 1921
Elijah Pountney	11th August, 1922
William Rider	19th December, 1922
John Fusher	5th January,1926
George Sharples	13th April, 1926
James Joseph Power	31st January, 1928
Victor Edward Betts	3rd January, 1931
Jeremiah Hanbury	2nd February, 1933
Stanley Eric Hobday	29th December,1933
Dorothea Nancy Waddingham	16th April,1936
Peter Barnes	7th February, 1940
James Richards	7th February, 1940
Eli Richards	19th September, 1941
Arthur Peach	30th January, 1942
Harold Oswald Merry	4th September, 1942
William Quayle	3rd August, 1943
James Farrell	29th March, 1949
Piotr Maksimowski	29th March, 1950
William Arthur Watkins	3rd April, 1951
Horace Carter	1st January, 1952
Leslie Green	23rd December, 1952
Frederick Arthur Cross	26th July, 1955
Corbett Montague Roberts	2nd August, 1955
Ernest Charles Harding	9th September, 1955
Dennis Howard	4th December, 1957
Matthew Kavanagh	12th August, 1958
Oswald Augustus Grey	20th November, 1962

Bodmin (2)

Valeri Giovanni	9th July, 1901
William Hampton	20th July, 1909

Bristol (13)

Edward Henry Palmer	19th March, 1913
William Francis Albert Bressington	31st March, 1925
Frederick Morse	25th July, 1933
Reginald Ivor Hinks	3rd May, 1934
Frederick James Austin	30th April, 1942
Ernest Charles Digby	16th March, 1944
Eugeniusz Jurkiewicz	30th December, 1947
Ronald Douglas Atwell	13th July, 1950
Edward Isaac Woodfield	14th December, 1950
Thomas Eames	15th July, 1952
Miles William Giffard	24th February, 1953
John Owen Greenway	20th October, 1953
Russell Pascoe	17th December, 1963

Cambridge (2)

James Henry Hancock	14th June, 1910
Frederick Seekings	4th November, 1913

Cardiff (20)

William Lacey	21st August, 1900
Eric Lange (Eugene Lorenz)	20th December, 1904
Rhoda Willis (Leslie James)	14th August, 1907
George Still	13th December, 1907
Patrick (Noah Percy) Collins	30th December, 1908
Hugh McLaren	14th August, 1913
Edgar Lewis Bindon	25th March, 1914
Alec Bakerlis	10th April, 1917
Thomas Caler	14th April, 1920
Lester Hamilton	16th August, 1921
George Thomas	9th March, 1926
Edward Rowlands	27th January, 1928
Daniel Driscoll	27th January, 1928
William John Corbett	3rd September, 1952

George Edward Roberts	5th August 1940
Howard John Grossley	5th September 1945
Hadyn Evan Evans	3rd February 1948
Clifford Godfrey Wills	9th December 1948
Ajit Singh	7th May 1952
Mahmood Hussein Mattan	3rd September 1952

Carnarvon (1)

William Murphy	15th February, 1910

Chelmsford (9)

William Burrett	8th October, 1900
Charles Howell	7th July, 1903
Samuel Herbert Dougal	8th July, 1903
Bernard White	1st December, 1903
Richard Buckham	5th December, 1906
Frederick Foreman	14th July, 1910
George Newton	31st January, 1911
William Charles Adolphus Beal	10th December, 1912
Charles Frembd	4th November, 1914

Derby (4)

John Bedford	30th July, 1902
John Silk	29th December, 1905
Walter Marsh	27th December, 1906
William Edward Slack	16th July, 1907

Devizes (1)

Edward Richard Palmer	17th November, 1903

Dorchester (2)

William Walter Burton	24th June, 1913
David Miller Jennings	24th June, 1941

Durham (55)

John Bowes	12th December, 1900
John George Thompson	10th December, 1901
Samuel Walton	16th December, 1902
Thomas Nicholson	16th December, 1902
James Duffy	8th December, 1903
George Breeze	2nd August, 1904
Joseph William Noble	24th March, 1908
Robert Lawman	24th March, 1908
Matthew James Dodds	5th August, 1908
Jeremiah O'Connor	23rd February, 1909
Abel Atherton	8th December, 1909
Thomas Craig	12th July, 1910
Robert Upton	24th March, 1914
Frank Steele	11th August, 1915
Joseph Deans	20th December, 1916
William Hall	28th March, 1920
James Riley	30th November, 1920
James Hutton Williamson	21st March, 1922
Daniel Cassidy	3rd April, 1923
Hassen Mohamed	8th August, 1923
Matthew Frederick	

Atkinson Nunn	2nd January, 1924
Henry Graham	15th April, 1925
Thomas Henry Shelton	15th April, 1925
James Smith	10th August, 1926
John Thomas Dunn	6th January,1928
Norman Elliott	10th August, 1928
Charles William Conlin	4th January, 1929
James Johnson	7th August, 1929
Ernest Wadge Parker	6th December, 1933
John Stephenson Bainbridge	9th May,1935
George Hague	16th July, 1935
Christopher Jackson	16th December, 1936
Robert William Hoolhouse	26th May, 1938
William Parker	26th July, 1938
John Daymond	8th February, 1939
Vincent Ostler	11th July, 1940
William Appleby	11th July, 1940
John William Wright	10th September, 1940
Edward Scoller	24th December, 1940
Henry Lyndo White	6th March, 1941
Edward Walker Anderson	31st July, 1941
William Ambrose Collins	28th October, 1942
Sidney James Delasalle	13th April, 1944
Charles Edward Prescott	5th March, 1946
Arthur Charles	26th March, 1946
John Wilson	13th December, 1949
Benjamin Roberts	13th December, 1949
George Finlay Brown	11th July, 1950
John Walker	13th July, 1950
Patrick George Turnage	14th November, 1950
Tahir Ali	21st March, 1952
Herbert Appleby	24th December, 1952
John Wilson Vickers	23rd July, 1957
Frank Stokes	3rd September, 1958
Brian Chandler	17th December, 1958

Edinburgh, Calton (3)

Patrick Higgins	2nd October, 1913
John Henry Savage	11th June, 1923
Philip Murray	30th October, 1923

Edinburgh, Saughton (4)

Allen Wales	13th August, 1928
Robert Dobie Smith	15th September, 1951
John Lynch	23rd April, 1954
George Alexander Robertson	23rd June, 1954

Exeter (11)

Edmund Walter Elliott	30th March, 1909
George Cunliffe	25th February, 1913
James Honeyands	2nd March, 1914
Frederick Brooks	12th December, 1916
Cyril Victor Tennyson Saunders	30th November, 1920
Edward Ernest Black	24th March, 1922
William John Maynard	27th July, 1928

Charlotte Bryant	15th July, 1936
Philip Edward Percy Davis	27th July, 1937
Ernest John Moss	7th December, 1937
Gordon Horace Trenoweth	6th April, 1943

Glasgow, Duke Street (12)

Patrick Leggett	12th November, 1902
Thomas Gunning	26th July, 1904
Pasha Liffey	14th November, 1905
Thomas McGuiness	16th May, 1917
James Adams	26th May, 1920
James Rollins	26th May, 1920
William Harkness	21st February, 1922
Susan Newell	10th October, 1923
John Keen	24th September, 1925
James McKay	24th January, 1928
George Reynolds	3rd August, 1928

Glasgow, Barlinnie (10)

John Lyon	8th February, 1946
Patrick Carraher	6th April, 1946
John Caldwell	10th August, 1946
Christopher Harris	30th October, 1950
James Ronald Robertson	16th December, 1950
James Smith	12th April, 1952
Patrick Gallagher Deveney	29th May, 1952
George Shaw	26th January, 1953
Peter Manuel	11th July, 1958
Anthony Miller	22nd December, 1960

Gloucester (7)

Sidney George Smith	9th March, 1904
Gilbert Oswald Smith	26th November, 1912
Herbert Rouse Armstrong	31st May, 1922
Herbert Burrows	17th February, 1926
Charles Houghton	3rd December, 1926
Arthur Henry Franklin	25th June, 1935
Ralph Smith	7th June, 1939

Hereford (1)

William Haywood	15th December, 1903

Hull (10)

Arthur Richardson	25th March, 1902
William James Bolton	23rd December, 1902
Charles William Ashton	22nd December, 1903
Thomas Siddle	4th August, 1908
John Freeman	7th December, 1909
William George Smith	9th December, 1924
Hubert Ernest Dalton	10th June, 1925
George Emanuel Michael	27th April, 1932
Roy Gregory	3rd January, 1934
Ethel Lillie Major	19th December, 1934

Inverness (1)

Joseph Hume	5th March, 1908

Ipswich (3)

Arthur Garrod	20th June, 1911
Frederick William Storey	15th June, 1920
Frederick Southgate	27th November, 1924

Knutsford (4)

William Alfred Hancocks	9th August, 1905
Edward Hartigan	27th November, 1906
James Phipps	12th November, 1908
John Williams	19th March, 1912

Lancaster (1)

Thomas Rawcliffe	15th November, 1910

Leeds (68)

Charles Backhouse	16th August, 1900
Thomas Mellor	16th August, 1900
Charles Oliver Blewitt	28th August, 1900
John Gallagher	29th December, 1903
Emily Swann	29th December, 1903
James Henry Clarkson	29th March, 1904
John Thomas Kay	17th August, 1904
Edmund Hall	20th December, 1904
Arthur Jeffries	29th December, 1904
Thomas George Tattersall	15th August, 1905
George Smith	28th December, 1905
John William Ellwood	3rd December, 1908
Thomas Mead	12th March, 1909
John Raper Coulson	9th August, 1910
Henry Ison	29th December, 1910
John William Thompson	27th March, 1917
Robert Gadsby	18th April, 1917
John William Walsh	17th December, 1918
Benjamin Hindle Benson	7th January, 1919
George Cardwell	8th January, 1919
Percy Barrett	8th January, 1919
Louis Massey	6th January, 1920
Miles McHugh	16th April, 1920
Thomas Hargreaves Wilson	6th May, 1920
Edwin Sowerby	30th December, 1920
Lee Doon	5th January, 1923
John William Eastwood	28th December, 1923
William Horsley Wardell	18th June, 1924
Alfred Davis Bostock	3rd September, 1925
Wilfred Fowler	3rd September, 1925
Lawrence Fowler	4th September, 1925
Lorraine Lax	7th January, 1926
William Cornelius Jones	5th January, 1927
Arthur Harnett	2nd September, 1927
Samuel Case	7th January, 1928
Arthur Leslie Raveny	14th August, 1929
Frederick Gill	4th February, 1931
John Henry Roberts	28th April, 1932
Thomas Riley	28th April, 1932
Ernest Brown	6th February, 1934
Louis Hamilton	6th April, 1934
Frederick Rushworth	1st January, 1935

David Maskill Blake	7th February, 1935
Andrew Anderson Bagley	10th February, 1937
Trevor Elvin	10th September, 1943
Mervin Clare McEwen	3rd February, 1944
Arthur Thompson	31st January, 1945
Thomas Eric Richardson	7th September, 1945
William Batty	8th January, 1946
Albert Sabin	30th January, 1947
Eric Briggs	20th June, 1947
William Smedley	14th August, 1947
John Edward Gartside	21st August, 1947
George Henry Whelpton	7th January, 1948
Arthur George Osborne	30th December, 1948
Dennis Neville	2nd June, 1949
Walter Sharpe	30th March, 1950
Alfred Moore	6th February, 1952
Philip Henry	30th July, 1953
Robert William Moore	5th January, 1954
William Lubina	27th January, 1954
Albert George Hall	22nd April, 1954
Edward Lindsay Reid	1st September, 1954
Winston Shaw	4th May, 1955
Alec Wilkinson	12th August, 1955
Ernest Raymond Jones	10th February, 1959
Bernard Hugh Walden	14th August, 1959
Zsiga Pankotia	29th June, 1961

Leicester (8)

Thomas Porter	21st July, 1903
Thomas Preston	21st July, 1903
William Henry Palmer	19th July, 1911
Arnold Warren	12th November, 1914
Thomas William Thorpe	23rd December, 1941
William Alfred Cowle	8th August, 1944
William Frederick George Meffen	8th August, 1944
Joseph Christopher Reynolds	17th November, 1953

Lewes (4)

Albert Rumens	7th January, 1913
George Mackay	29th January, 1913
Herbert Brooker	28th July, 1914
Percy Evelyn Clifford	11th August, 1914

Lincoln (17)

Samuel Henry Smith	10th March, 1903
Leonard Patchett	28th July, 1903
William Duddles	20th November, 1907
William Wright	10th March, 1920
George Robinson	13th December, 1922
Frank Fowler	13th December, 1922
Bertram Horace Kirby	4th January, 1928
Frederick Nodder	30th December, 1937
Leonard Holmes	28th May, 1946
Kenneth Strickson	22nd March, 1949
Herbert Leonard Mills	11th December, 1951
Eric Norcliffe	12th December, 1952

Harold Fowler	12th August, 1954
James Robinson	24th May, 1955
Kenneth Roberts	12th July, 1955
John Louis Constantine	1st September, 1960
Wasyl Gnypiuk	27th January, 1961

Liverpool (54)

James Joseph Bergin	27th December, 1900
John Harrison	24th December, 1901
Thomas Marsland	20th May, 1902
Gustav Rau	2nd June, 1903
Willem Schmidt	2nd June, 1903
Henry Starr	29th December, 1903
William Kirwan	31st May, 1904
Ping Lun	31st May, 1904
Charles Paterson	7th August, 1907
See Lee	30th March, 1909
Henry Thompson	22nd November, 1910
Thomas Seymour	9th May, 1911
Michael Fagan	6th December, 1911
Joseph Fletcher	15th December, 1911
George Ball (Sumner)	26th February, 1914
Joseph Spooner	14th May, 1914
John James Thornley	1st December, 1915
Young Hill	1st December, 1915
William Thomas Hodgson	16th August, 1917
John Crossland	22nd July, 1919
Herbert Edward Rawson Salisbury	11th May, 1920
William Waddington	11th May, 1920
James Ellor	11th August, 1920
Frederick Wood	10th April, 1923
James Winstanley	5th August, 1925
Lock Ah Tam	23rd March, 1926
James Leah	16th November, 1926
William Meynell Robertson	6th December, 1927
Albert George Absalom	25th July, 1928
Joseph Reginald Clarke	12th March, 1929
John Maguire	26th November, 1929
Richard Hetherington	26th June, 1933
Jan Mohamed	8th June, 1938
Samuel Morgan	9th April, 1941
David Rodger Williams	25th March, 1942
Douglas Edmondson	24th June, 1942
Ronald Roberts	10th February, 1943
Thomas James	29th December, 1943
John Gordon Davidson	12th July, 1944
Thomas Hendren	17th July, 1946
Walter Clayton	7th August, 1946
Arthur Rushton	19th November, 1946
Stanley Sheminant	3rd January, 1947
Peter Griffiths	19th November, 1948
George Semini	27th January, 1949
George Kelly	28th March, 1950
Edward Francis Devlin	25th April, 1952
Alfred Burns	25th April, 1952
John Todd	19th May, 1953

Milton Taylor	22nd June, 1954
William Arthur Salt	29th March, 1955
Richard Gowler	21st June, 1955
Norman William Green	27th July, 1955
Peter Anthony Allen	13th August, 1964

London, Holloway (5)

Amelia Sach	3rd February, 1903
Annie Walters	3rd February, 1903
Edith Jessie Thompson	9th January, 1923
Styllou Christofi	16th December, 1954
Ruth Ellis	13th July, 1955

London, Newgate (9)

Louisa Josephine Jemima Masset	9th January, 1900
Ada Chard-Williams	8th March, 1900
Henry Grove	22nd May, 1900
Alfred Highfield	17th July, 1900
William James Irwin	14th August, 1900
John Parr	2nd October, 1900
Samson Silas Salmon	19th February, 1901
Marcel Fougeron	19th November, 1901
George Woolfe	6th May, 1902

London, Pentonville (120)

John Macdonald	30th September, 1902
Henry Williams	11th November, 1902
Thomas Fairclough Barrow	9th December, 1902
Charles Jeremiah Slowe	10th November, 1903
John Sullivan	12th July, 1904
Joseph Conrad	13th December, 1904
Charles Wade	13th December, 1904
Alfred Bridgeman	26th April, 1905
Arthur Devereux	15th August, 1905
George William Butler,	7th November, 1905
John Esmond Murphy	6th January, 1909
Morris Reuben	20th May, 1909
Marks Reuben	20th May, 1909
Madar Dal Dhingra	17th August, 1909
George Henry Perry	1st March, 1910
Hawley Harvey Crippen	23rd November, 1910
Noah Woolf	21st December, 1910
Michael Collins	24th May, 1911
Francisco Charles Godhino	17th October, 1911
Edward Hill	17th October, 1911
Myer Abramovitch	6th March, 1912
Frederick Henry Seddon	18th April, 1912
Edward Hopwood	29th January, 1913
Henry Longden	28th July, 1913
Frederick Albert Robertson	27th November, 1913
Lee Kun	1st January, 1916
Roger Casement	3rd August, 1916
William James Robinson	17th April, 1917
Louis Marie Joseph Voisin	2nd March, 1918
Henry Perry (Beckett)	10th July, 1919

Thomas Foster	31st July, 1919
Frank George Warren	7th October, 1919
Arthur A.C. Goslett (Godrey)	27th July, 1920
Mark Goodmacher	30th December, 1920
Frederick Alexander Keeling	11th April, 1922
Edmund Hugh Tonbridge	18th April, 1922
Henry Julius Jacoby	7th June, 1922
William James Yeldham	5th September, 1922
Frederick Edward Bywaters	9th January, 1923
Bernard Pomroy	5th April, 1923
Rowland Duck	4th July, 1923
George William Barton	2nd April, 1925
William John Cronin	14th August, 1925
Arthur Henry Bishop	14th August, 1925
Eugene De Vere	24th March, 1926
Johannes Josephus Cornelius Mommers	27th July, 1926
Hashankhan Samander	2nd November, 1926
James Frederick Stratton	29th March, 1927
John Robinson	12th August, 1927
Frederick Guy Browne	31st May, 1928
Frederick Stewart	6th June, 1928
Frank Hollington	20th February, 1929
William John Holmyard	27th February, 1929
Alexander Anastassiou	3rd June, 1931
William Shelley	5th August, 1931
Oliver Newman	5th August, 1931
William Harold Goddard	23rd February, 1932
Maurice Freedman	4th May, 1932
Jack Samuel Puttnam	8th June, 1933
Varnavas Loizi Antorka	10th August, 1933
Robert James Kirby	11th October, 1933
Harry Tuffney	9th October, 1934
John Frederick Stockwell	14th November, 1934
Charles Lake	13th March, 1935
Allan James Grierson	30th October, 1935
Leslie George Stone	13th August, 1937
Frederick George Murphy	17th August, 1937
John Thomas Rogers	18th November, 1937
Udham Singh	31st July, 1940
Jose Waldeburg	10th December, 1940
Carl Meier	10th December, 1940
Charles Albert Van Dem Kieboom	17th December, 1940
Antonio Mancini	31st October, 1941
Lionel Rupert Nathan Watson	12th November, 1941
Samuel Dashwood	10th September, 1942
George Silverosa	10th September, 1942
William Henry Turner	24th March, 1943
Gerald Elphistone Roe	3rd August, 1943
Charles William Koopman	15th December, 1943
Christos Georghiou	2nd February, 1944
Oswald John Job	16th March, 1944
Pierre Richard Charles Neukerman	23rd June, 1944
Joseph Jan Van Hove	12th July, 1944

Karl Gustav Hulten	8th March, 1945
Erich Keonig	6th October, 1945
Joachim Palme-Goltz	6th October, 1945
Kurt Zeuhlsdorf	6th October, 1945
Heintz Brueling	6th October, 1945
Josep Mertins	6th October, 1945
Armin Kuelne	16th November, 1945
Emil Schmittendorf	16th November, 1945
James McNicol	21st December, 1945
John Riley Young	21st December, 1945
Theodore William John Schurch	4th January, 1946
Neville George Clevelly Heath	16th October, 1946
Arthur Robert Boyce	1st November, 1946
John Mathieson	10th December, 1946
Frederick William Reynolds	26th March, 1947
Christopher James Gerachty	19th September, 1947
Charles Henry Jenkins	19th September, 1947
Walter John Cross	19th February, 1948
Harry Lewis	21st April, 1949
Bernard Alfred Peter Copper	21st June, 1949
William Claude Hodson Jones	28th September, 1949
Daniel Raven	6th January, 1950
Timothy John Evans	9th March, 1950
John O'Connor	24th October, 1951
Backary Manneh	27th May, 1952
John Howard Godar	7th September, 1952
Dennis George Muldowney	30th September, 1952
Raymond John Cull	30th September, 1952
Peter Cyril Johnson	9th October, 1952
John Reginald Halliday Christie	15th July, 1953
George James Newland	23rd December, 1953
Ian Arthur Grant	17th June, 1954
Kenneth Gilbert	17th June, 1954
Joseph Chrimes	28th April, 1959
Ronald Henry Marwood	8th May, 1959
Norman James Harris	10th November, 1960
Edwin Albert Arthur Bush	6th July, 1961

London, The Tower (12)

Carl Hans Lody	6th November, 1914
Carl Frederick Muller	23rd June, 1915
Willem Johannes Roos	30th July, 1915
Haicke Marinus Petrius Janssen	30th July, 1915
Ernest Waldemar Melin	10th September, 1915
Augusto Alfredo Roggen	17th September, 1915
Fernando Buschman	19th October, 1915
George T. Breeckow	26th October, 1915
Irving Guy Ries	27th October, 1915
Albert Meyer	27th November, 1915
Ludovico Hurwitz Y Zender	11th April, 1916
Josef Jakobs	15th August, 1941

London, Wandsworth (117)

George Henry Parker	19th March, 1901
Ernest Walter Wickham	18th August, 1901
Charles Robert Earl	29th April, 1902
George William Hibbs	13th December, 1902
William Brown	16th December, 1902
Edgar Owen (Edwards)	3rd March, 1903
George Chapman	7th April, 1903
William Joseph Tuffen	11th August, 1903
Edward Harrison	28th February, 1905
Alfred Stratton	23rd May, 1905
Albert Ernest Stratton	23rd May, 1905
Alfred John Heal	20th June, 1905
Frederick Reynolds	13th November, 1906
Richard Brinkley	13th August, 1907
Julius Wammer	10th August, 1909
Thomas William Jesshope	25th May, 1910
Frederick Henry Thomas	15th November, 1911
Sargent Philp	1st October, 1912
Robert Rosenthal	15th July, 1915
George Marshall	17th August, 1915
Athur Harold Victor De Stamir	12th February, 1918
Joseph Jones	21st February, 1918
Jack Alfred Field	4th February, 1921
William Thomas Gray	4th February, 1921
Joseph O'Sullivan	10th August, 1922
Reginald Dunne	10th August, 1922
Frederick William Maximilian Jesse	1st November, 1923
Jean Pierre Vacquier	12th August, 1924
Patrick Herbert Mahon	3rd September, 1924
John Norman Holmes Thorne	22nd April, 1925
James Murphy	3rd August, 1927
Frederick Stephen Fuller	3rd August, 1927
Sidney Bernard Goulter	6th January, 1928
James Gillon	31st January, 1928
Frederick Lock	12th April, 1928
William Henry Kennedy	31st May, 1928
William Charles Benson	20th November, 1928
Albert Edward Marjeram	11th June, 1930
Albert Probert	4th May, 1934
Frederick William Parker	4th May, 1934
Leonard Albert Brigstock	2nd April, 1935
Percy Charles Anderson	16th April, 1935
Raymond Henry Bousquet	29th October, 1935
Frederick Herbert Charles Field	30th June, 1936
George Arthur Bryant	14th July, 1936
Wallace Jenden	5th August, 1936
Alfred Ernest Richards	12th July, 1938
William James Graves	19th July, 1938
George Brain	1st November, 1938
Harry Armstrong	21st March, 1939
William Thomas Butler	29th March, 1939
Leonard George Hucker	10th October, 1939
Stanley Ernest Boon	25th October, 1939

Arthur John Smith	26th October, 1939
Ernest Edmund Hammerton	27th March, 1940
William Charles Cowell	24th April, 1940
Stanley Edward Cole	31st October, 1940
George Johnson Armstrong	9th July, 1941
Karle Theodore Drucke	6th August, 1941
Werner Henrich Walti	6th August, 1941
John Ernest Smith	3rd December, 1941
Karel Richard Richter	10th December, 1941
Harold Dorian Trevor	11th March, 1942
Cyril Johnson	15th April, 1942
Gordon Frederick Cummins	25th June, 1942
Jose Estella Key	7th July, 1942
Alphones L.E. Timmerman	7th July, 1942
Arthur Anderson	21st July, 1942
Patrick William Kingston	6th October, 1942
Duncan Alexander Croall Scott-Ford	3rd November, 1942
Herbert Hiram Bounds	6th November, 1942
Johannes Maximum Marinus Dronkers	31st December, 1942
Franciscus Johannes Winter	26th January, 1943
Harry Dobkin	27th January, 1943
Dudley George Rayner	31st March, 1943
August,Sangret	29th April, 1943
Charles Arthur Raymond	10th July, 1943
Charles Eugene Gauthier	24th September, 1943
Terence Casey	19th November, 1943
John Joseph Dorgan	22nd December, 1943
Ernest James Harman Kemp	6th June, 1944
Horace Beresford Gordon	9th January, 1945
Andrew Brown	30th January, 1945
Ronald Bertram Mauri	31st October, 1945
John Amery	19th December, 1945
Robert Blaine	29th December, 1945
William Joyce	3rd January, 1946
Michal Niescior	31st January, 1946
Arthur Clegg	19th March, 1946
Marion Grondkowski	2nd April, 1946
Henryk Malinowski	2nd April, 1946
Sydney John Smith	6th September, 1946
David Baillie Mason	6th September, 1946
Frank Joseph Freiyer	13th November, 1946
Harold Hagger	18th March, 1947
David John Williams	15th April, 1947
John George Haigh	10th August, 1949
William John Davies	16th August, 1949
Ernest Soper Couzins	30th December, 1949
Albert Price	16th August, 1950
Joseph Brown	25th April, 1951
Edward Charles Smith	25th April, 1951
James Virrels	26th April, 1951
Frank Burgess	22nd July, 1952
John Kenneth Livesey	17th December, 1952
John James Alcott	2nd January, 1953
Derek William Bentley	28th January, 1953

John Francis Wilkinson	18th December, 1953
Alfred Charles Whiteway	22nd December, 1953
James Reginald Doohan	14th April, 1954
William Sanchez De Pina Hepper	11th August, 1954
Rupert Geoffrey Wells	1st September, 1954
Sydney Joseph Clarke	14th April, 1955
Guenther Fritz Erwin Podola	5th November, 1959
Francis Forsyth	10th November, 1960
Victor John Terry	25th May, 1961
Henryk Niemasz	8th September, 1961

Londonderry (3)

Joseph Moran	5th January, 1904
John Berryman	20th August, 1908
William Rooney	8th February, 1923

Maidstone (11)

Charles Thomas Richard Watkins	30th July, 1901
Harold Amos Apted	18th March, 1902
Ferat Mohamed Ben Ali	1st August, 1905
Samuel Curtis	20th December, 1905
William Bouldry	8th December, 1908
George William Parker	19th December, 1911
Alfred John Lawrence	18th December, 1912
George Joseph Smith	13th August, 1915
George Edward Francis Quinton Lever	7th January, 1921
Harold Thompson	9th March, 1926
Sidney Harry Fox	8th April, 1930

Manchester (71)

Joseph Holden	4th December, 1900
Patrick McKenna	3rd December, 1901
Henry McWiggins	2nd December, 1902
William George Hudson	12th May, 1903
Charles Whittaker	2nd December, 1903
John Griffiths	27th February, 1906
John Ramsbottom	12th May, 1908
Frederick Ballington	28th July, 1908
Mark Shawcross	3rd August, 1909
Joseph Wren	22nd February, 1910
Walter Martyn	12th December, 1911
John Edward Tarkenter	12th December, 1911
Arthur Birkett	23rd July, 1912
James Ryder	13th August, 1913
Ernest Kelly	17th December, 1913
Frederick Holmes	8th March, 1916
Reginald Haslam	29th March, 1916
James Howarth Hargreaves	19th December, 1916
Thomas Clinton	21st March, 1917
William Rooney	17th December, 1918
Hyman Perdovitch	6th January, 1920
David Caplan	6th January, 1920
Frederick Rothwell Holt	13th April, 1920
William Thomas Aldred	22nd June, 1920
Charles Colclough	31st December, 1920

Frederick Quarmby	5th May, 1921
Thomas Wilson	24th May, 1921
Hiram Thompson	30th May, 1922
George Frederick Edisbury	3rd January, 1923
George Perry	28th March, 1923
Francis Wilson Booker	8th April, 1924
John Charles Horner	13th August, 1924
Patrick Power	26th May, 1925
James Makin	11th August, 1925
Samuel Johnson	15th December, 1925
William Thorpe	16th March, 1926
Louie Calvert	24th June, 1926
Frederick Fielding	3rd January, 1928
Walter Brooks	28th June, 1928
Chung Yi Miao	6th December, 1928
George Cartledge	4th April, 1929
Francis Land	16th April, 1931
Solomon Stein	15th December, 1931
George Alfred Rice	3rd February, 1932
Charles James Cowle	18th May, 1932
William Burtoft	19th December, 1933
John Harris Bridge	30th May, 1935
Buck Ruxton	12th May, 1936
Max Mayer Haslam	5th February, 1937
Horace William Brunt	12th August, 1937
Charles James Caldwell	20th April, 1938
Clifford Holmes	11th February, 1941
John Smith	4th September, 1941
James Galbraith	26th July, 1944
Harold Berry	9th April, 1946
Martin Patrick Coffey	24th April, 1946
Walter Graham Rowland	27th February, 1947
Margaret Allen	12th January, 1949
James Henry Corbitt	28th November, 1950
Nicholas Persoulious Crosby	19th December, 1950
Nenad Kovacevic	26th January, 1951
James Inglis	8th May, 1951
John Dand	12th June, 1951
Jack Wright	3rd July, 1951
Alfred Bradley	15th January, 1952
Herbert Roy Harris	26th February, 1952
Louisa May,Merrifield	18th September, 1953
Stanislaw Juras	17th December, 1953
Czelslaw Kowalewski	8th January, 1954
James Smith	28th November, 1962
Gwynne Owen Evans	13th August, 1964

Newcastle (8)

John Miller	7th December, 1901
John Robert Miller	7th December, 1901
Henry Perkins	6th December, 1905
John Alexander Dickman	9th August, 1910
John Vickers Amos	22nd July, 1913
William Cavanagh	18th December, 1917
Ambrose Quinn	26th November, 1919
Ernest Bernard Scott	26th November, 1919

Northampton (3)

Alexander Claydon	13th December, 1901
Samuel Rowledge	13th July, 1904
John Eayres	10th November, 1914

Norwich (11)

Herbert John Bennett	21st March, 1901
James Nichols	2nd November, 1908
Robert Galloway	5th November, 1912
Herbert George Bloye	12th November, 1925
Walter Smith	8th March, 1938
Arthur Heys	13th March, 1945
Stanley Joseph Clarke	18th November, 1948
James Frank Rivett	8th March, 1950
Norman Goldthorpe	24th November, 1950
Alfred George Reynolds	19th July, 1951
Dennis Albert Reginald Moore	19th July, 1951

Nottingham (8)

John Hutchinson	29th March, 1905
Edward Glynn	7th August, 1906
Samuel Atherley	14th December, 1909
Percy James Atkins	7th April, 1922
Albert Edward Burrows	6th August, 1923
Arthur Simms	17th December, 1924
William Knighton	27th April, 1927
George Frederick Walter Hayward	10th April, 1928

Oxford (8)

Joseph Rose	19th February, 1919
George Arthur Bailey	2nd March, 1921
Henry Daniel Seymour	10th December, 1931
George Thomas Pople	9th March, 1932
Ernest Hutchinson	23rd November, 1932
Harold Hill	1st May, 1942
George Russell	2nd December, 1948
Oliver George Butler	12th August, 1952

Perth (3)

Edward Johnstone	19th August, 1908
Alexander Edmundstone	6th July, 1909
Stanislaw Miszka	6th February, 1948

Reading (3)

William George Thomas Charles Austin	5th November, 1907
William Broome	24th November, 1910
Eric James Sedgwick	4th February, 1913

Ruthin (1)

William Hughes	17th February, 1903

Shepton Mallet (22)

Henry Quartley	10th November, 1914
Verney Hasser	5th March, 1918
William Grover Bignell	24th February, 1925

John Lincoln	2nd March, 1926
David Cobb	12th March, 1943
Harold A. Smith	25th June, 1943
Lee A. Davis	14th December, 1943
John H. Waters	10th February, 1944
J.C. Leatherberry	16th March, 1944
Wiley Harris	26th May, 1944
Alex F. Miranda	30th May, 1944
Eliga Brinson	11th August, 1944
Willie Smith	11th August, 1944
Madison Thomas	12th October, 1944
Benjamin Pyegate	28th November, 1944
Ernest Lee Clark	8th January, 1945
Augustine M. Guerra	8th January, 1945
Robert L. Pearson	17th March, 1945
Parson Jones	17th March, 1945
William Harrison	7th April, 1945
George E. Smith	8th May, 1945
Anicet Martinez	15th June, 1945

Shrewsbury (8)

Richard Wigley	18th March, 1902
Thomas Cox	19th December, 1917
William Griffiths	24th July, 1923
Frank Griffin	4th January, 1951
Harry Huxley	8th July, 1952
Donald Neil Simon	23rd October, 1952
Desmond Donald Hooper	26th January, 1954
George Riley	9th February, 1961

St Albans (2)

Charles Coleman	21st December, 1911
George Anderson	23rd December, 1914

St Helier (2)

Thomas Connan	19th February, 1907
Francis Joseph Hutchet	9th October, 1959

Stafford (8)

James Arthur Shufflebotham	2nd April, 1901
William Lane	12th August, 1902
Henry Jones	29th March, 1904
William Frederick Edge	27th December, 1905
Joseph Jones	26th March, 1907
Joseph Edward Jones	14th April, 1909
George Loake	28th December, 1911
Josiah Davies	10th March, 1914

Swansea (9)

William Joseph Foy	8th May, 1909
Henry Phillips	14th December, 1911
Daniel Sullivan	6th September, 1916
Trevor John Edwards	11th December, 1928
Rex Harvey Jones	4th August, 1949
Robert Thomas Mackintosh	4th August, 1949
Albert Edward Jenkins	19th April, 1950
Thomas Ronald Lewis Harries	28th April, 1954

Vivian Frederick Teed	6th May, 1958

Usk (4)

Jeremiah Callaghan	12th December, 1902
John Edmunds	3rd July, 1909
Thomas Clements	24th March, 1910
William Sullivan	23rd March, 1922

Wakefield (10)

Harry Walters	10th April, 1906
Thomas Acomb Mouncer	9th August, 1906
Ernest Hutchinson	2nd March, 1909
Walter Davies	9th July, 1909
William Wallace Galbraith	20th December, 1912
Walter William Sykes	23rd April, 1913
George Frederick Law	31st December, 1913
Walter Marriott	10th August, 1915
Harry Thompson	22nd December, 1915
John William McCartney	29th December, 1915

Warwick (4)

George Place	30th December, 1902
John Davis	1st January, 1907
Edwin James Moore	3rd April, 1907
Henry Taylor Parker	15th December, 1908

Winchester (16)

William Churcher	22nd July, 1902
William Brown	16th December, 1903
Thomas Cowdrey	16th December, 1903
Augustus John Penny	26th November, 1913
Walter James White	16th June, 1914
Leo George O'Donnell	29th March, 1917
Thomas Henry Allaway	19th August, 1922
Abraham Goldenberg	30th July, 1924
Charles Edward Finden	12th August, 1926
William Henry Podmore	22nd April, 1930
Sydney Archibald Frederick Chamerlain	28th July, 1949
Roman Redel	7th July, 1950
Zbigniew Gower	7th July, 1950
William Edward Shaughnessy	9th May, 1951
Michael George Tatum	14th May, 1959
Dennis John Whitty	17th December, 1963

Worcester (4)

Samuel Middleton	15th July, 1902
William Yarnold	5th December, 1905
Thomas Fletcher	9th July, 1913
Djang Djin Sung	3rd December, 1919